The Family, Law and Society
Cases and Materials

The Family, Law and Society Cases and Materials

Fifth edition

Dame Brenda Hale DBE, MA (Cantab)

Lord Justice of Appeal;
Visiting Professor of Law, King's College, London

Judge David Pearl MA, LLM, PhD (Cantab)

Circuit Judge, President, Care Standards Tribunal;
Honorary Professor, University of East Anglia;
Bencher of Gray's Inn;
Life Fellow, Fitzwilliam College, Cambridge

Elizabeth J Cooke MA (Oxon), LLM (Reading)

Solicitor; Director, Centre for Property Law and Reader in Law,
University of Reading

Philip D Bates LLB, MA (Sheffield)

Lecturer in Law, King's College, London

Butterworths
LexisNexis™

Members of the LexisNexis Group worldwide

United Kingdom	Butterworths Tolley, a Division of Reed Elsevier (UK) Ltd, Halsbury House, 35 Chancery Lane, LONDON, WC2A 1EL, and 4 Hill Street, EDINBURGH EH2 3JZ
Argentina	Abeledo Perrot, Jurisprudencia Argentina and Depalma, BUENOS AIRES
Australia	Butterworths, a Division of Reed International Books Australia Pty Ltd, CHATSWOOD, New South Wales
Austria	ARD Betriebsdienst and Verlag Orac, VIENNA
Canada	Butterworths Canada Ltd, MARKHAM, Ontario
Chile	Publitecsa and Conosur Ltda, SANTIAGO DE CHILE
Czech Republic	Orac sro, PRAGUE
France	Editions du Juris-Classeur SA, PARIS
Hong Kong	Butterworths Asia (Hong Kong), HONG KONG
Hungary	Hvg Orac, BUDAPEST
India	Butterworths India, NEW DELHI
Ireland	Butterworths (Ireland) Ltd, DUBLIN
Italy	Giuffré, MILAN
Malaysia	Malayan Law Journal Sdn Bhd, KUALA LUMPUR
New Zealand	NexisLexis Butterworths, WELLINGTON
Poland	Wydawnictwa Prawnicze PWN, WARSAW
Singapore	Butterworths Asia, SINGAPORE
South Africa	Butterworths Publishers (Pty) Ltd, DURBAN
Switzerland	Stämpfli Verlag AG, BERNE
USA	LexisNexis, DAYTON, Ohio

A CIP Catalogue record for this book is available from the British Library.

ISBN 0 406 98587 1

Typeset by Doyle & Co, Colchester
Printed and bound in Great Britain by The Bath Press, Bath

Visit Butterworths LexisNexis *direct* at www.butterworths.com

Preface

The point of this book is to introduce students of family law to all sorts of materials that they will not find in a conventional law library but which will breathe life into the dry bones of the statutes and case law. Serious students at any level need to know about the social and economic trends which shape contemporary family life, about the research which explores how family life and family law work, about the policy debates which have led to the present state of our law, and about how it might develop in future.

There have been three particularly important developments since the fourth edition in 1996. First and foremost is the Human Rights Act 1998, which has a bearing on all areas of family law but particularly the law relating to children. We have incorporated it into the discussion throughout the book rather than treating it as a separate subject. Second is the increasing recognition in the law of the significance of domestic violence, and the harm that it can do to children even if they themselves have not been attacked. Third is the long awaited Adoption and Children Bill which we hope will hit the statute book later this year: all our references are to the Bill as it left the House of Commons on 21 May 2002 although there will obviously be later changes. The Bill confirms how right we were in the fourth edition to treat married and unmarried couples together rather than relegating cohabitation to a separate chapter.

When we first wrote this book in 1982, we were both experienced University law teachers. Since then, we have both become judges. We may know more about how family law works in practice but we know less about what law students need to know. We were therefore delighted to welcome two new authors, Lizzie Cooke, and Phil Bates, to join us in preparing the fourth edition.

All four of us have played a part in this fifth edition, but we would like to say a particular thank you to Lizzie Cooke, who has done the lion's share of the work, some of it in difficult circumstances, and deserves the lion's share of the credit for what has been achieved. She does not, however, deserve the lion's share of the blame for its errors and omissions, because we have all taken equal responsibility for trying to get things right. We have tried to be up to date with developments up to the end of May 2002.

26 July 2002

Brenda Hale
David Pearl

v

Contents

Table of statutes

References in bold type indicate where the section of an Act is set out in part or in full.

Table of cases

Pages on which cases are principally treated are indicated by the use of **bold** figures.

C

D

E

H

N

X

Chapter 1

The family and the law

1.1 Definitions of 'household' and 'family'

1.2 Approaches to the history of the family

1.3 The law's response to the family

1.4 The human rights perspective

In this chapter we ask, first, 'what is a family?' The answer is complex and colourful, within our multi-ethnic and culturally diverse society. We then take a brief look back at the history of the family and how it has developed; this historical perspective is an aid to our understanding of the way we live today. Having built up a picture of the family, we look at the way the law responds to the family. That, of course, is the theme of this book; here we consider how far legal recognition of the family corresponds to the sociological reality we have surveyed. At this point we introduce the Human Rights Act 1998, and some of the provisions of the European Convention on Human Rights; the provisions of that convention are going to flavour much of what we say throughout the book.

1.1 Definitions of 'household' and 'family'

Most people understand that the word *family* refers to a group of persons related to each other by blood and/or marriage. The introduction of an additional word, such as 'immediate', suggests that the members of the family probably live together within a single household, and (although to a variable extent) pool their resources for the common well-being of the unit. However, many important questions are immediately raised by this series of assumptions. Is it necessary for the members of the family to be related in the manner described? Is it a prerequisite that there be a single household? Why should members pool resources?

The family's structure will vary from group to group. Most are based on monogamous marriages, although there are still some cultures which tolerate polygamous marriages. In the England of the early twenty-first century, we must not assume that the answer to the question 'What is a family?' is necessarily going to produce a simple and straightforward response. In the context of a traditional Indian family, or a Chinese family, the familial group may be much larger than a simple household; there may be a pooling of certain resources only; financial obligations may be extended to a wider kinship group than the familial nexus.

The following extract comes from the Judicial Studies Board's *Handbook on Ethnic Minority Issues* (1995):

3. COMPOSITION OF FAMILIES

There are a number of common stereotypes about the composition of ethnic minority families in Britain, the accuracy of which it is important to ascertain. These include that ethnic minority families are larger in size than those of the indigenous majority; that South Asian families take the form of 'extended families'; and that Afro-Caribbean families consist typically of a single mother bringing up children on her own.

Despite the fact that these images may have some basis in reality, as rigid stereotypes they can be misleading and dangerous. They over-generalise certain tendencies, and conceal the existence of considerable diversity in family composition among Britain's minority ethnic communities. They also do nothing to help with understanding why there may be differences in family patterns between ethnic groups.

3.1 Family Size

By 'family size' is normally meant 'size of household'. Statistics for the size of households do in fact show some quite substantial differences between ethnic groups. For example, both Indian and Pakistani/Bangladeshi households – averaging 3.8 and 4.8 persons respectively – tend to be considerably larger than households classified as 'white', which average at 2.5. Households classified as 'West Indian' on the other hand are on average almost identical in size to white households with an average of 2.6 (Labour Force Survey).

It is important to bear in mind that when overall averages differ in this way, they tend to highlight – and thus perhaps exaggerate – the differences. Not only do averages of this kind conceal substantial variation within each group, but they conceal also a great deal of overlap in the distribution of family size between the groups. Thus 60% of Pakistani/Bangladeshi families, and 84% of Indian families, are of between 1 and 5 persons in size, the range that accounts for almost all of the white families.

On the other hand, the fact that 41% of Pakistani/Bangladeshi households include 6 persons or more, as compared with 2% in the white group, is clearly a very substantial difference. Further statistical breakdown shows that part of this difference can be attributed to the larger numbers of children in such households. The other part is explained by the much more frequent presence of more than two adults than in 'white' homes.

To some extent these differences may be explained by cultural factors, which include marriage and child-bearing practices, and the greater strength of obligations to elderly parents and other kin. The differences, however, should not be presumed to be due to cultural factors alone. Economic circumstances are also important, as are the age profiles of minority ethnic communities, which tend (especially within the Bangladeshi community) to be relatively youthful due to their immigration being more recent.

3.2 Extended families

One of the cultural factors which explains the larger size of South Asian households in Britain is undoubtedly the greater significance of what is often referred to as the 'extended family'. This term, however, may refer to various features and can sometimes be misleading, and it is important to clarify the respects in which this applies to South Asian communities.

In the white British context, the 'extended family' usually means one of two things: a household which consists of three generations (i.e. including grandparents/grandchildren), or a wider network of relatives who are felt to belong to one another and cooperate in certain ways. Generally speaking, the former is usually viewed as a temporary arrangement when it occurs: a married child is waiting to be able to obtain a home of its own, or a widowed grandparent is taken in so that he or she does not have to live alone. The latter is most often observed and referred to at temporary gatherings such as weddings or funerals, though in some circles (e.g. established working-class or rural communities, or among Travellers) this network may be of much greater significance in people's social and economic lives.

In all these examples, however, it remains the case that the primary unit is seen as the 'nuclear family', and the 'extension' is relative to this nucleus which is in control of its own affairs. In the white British context, therefore, the 'extended family' is precisely what the word implies: an extension of a nuclear unit of parents and children which is assumed to be the appropriate and basic core.

At first sight, there may appear to be no difficulty about applying this term also to families from the Indian sub-continent, and to those from other parts of the world. For example, the term may be presumed to apply to their tendency to form larger households, due to the presence of a wider range of relatives than that of parent and child alone. Likewise, it may be applied to the commonly observed tendency for such families to maintain a greater degree of social contact than the white British, and to use family ties commonly as the basis for business partnerships as well.

Care needs to be taken, however, over whether this term (and the thinking behind it) captures the distinctive character of these cultural patterns, and whether it is in danger of misleading us as to why these patterns occur. The important point to appreciate, here, is that not all family systems operate on the same principles as the white British one, and that misunderstanding can arise by assuming this is so.

Unlike the white British family system, most Asian and African systems traditionally have not operated on the basis that there is a 'nuclear unit' of parents and children that should be autonomous and sovereign. Their view, on the contrary, has tended to be that the interests of individual parents and children should be seen as subordinate to the wider group of kin as a whole. The membership of this group is most commonly defined in terms of shared patrilineal descent (i.e. in the male line), although matrilineal descent is used in some areas, notably in parts of West Africa. This larger group will act corporately in dealing with a wide range of affairs – certainly most economic and property matters, and often marriage and domestic affairs as well.

In family systems of the above kind, the 'nuclear family' as a biologically related group is usually given some degree of recognition, and in most cases would co-reside. However, it would be a mistake to view the group as a whole as 'made up' of such units in terms of how it organises its affairs: such families are not 'extended' in the British sense, but function traditionally as enduring corporate units of persons related through the male (or in some cases female) line.

On the Indian sub-continent, this family pattern has generally been known as the 'joint-family' system. The term 'joint-family' refers to the common situation that, following the death of the father as head of the family, the sons jointly inherit and manage the family property, forming a single corporate kinship group together with their wives and children. In China, those sharing descent in the male line would similarly own and manage property corporately, the ethos of solidarity among patrilineal kin being especially strong due to belief in the spiritual powers of dead ancestors over the living.

Family systems of this kind are probably far older and certainly have been far more extensive across the world than the fragmented 'nuclear' British/European forms. Early urban civilisations were built upon them – but they tend to break down in the face of the more aggressive kinds of urbanisation and change in the modern era. For migrants, however, they often continue to provide a framework within which life can be organised, even if this may need to be modified and adapted to circumstances for which such traditional family patterns were not devised. Features such as corporate family enterprises, and 'arranged marriages', should therefore be expected to be maintained to some degree within migrant communities (perhaps even for several generations), and they need to be understood in terms of their original context and not solely as departures from their host country's norms.

If the term 'extended family' is used to refer to Asian and African families, therefore, it is important that the distinctive character of such family traditions is appreciated. This does not imply that such traditions will be always maintained: some people may not wish to do so anyway, whilst others in attempting to do so may find practical problems in their way. The effects of migration and of immigration controls can be very divisive for such families, and the small size of housing units in Britain also constrains the establishment of traditional corporate family groups.

Nonetheless, the higher degree of family cooperation (especially among the migrant generation) often found among Asian and African as compared with the white British population is witness to the strength of such cultural traditions. For example, a married son with his wife and children may readily continue to live under the same roof as his father, even in a relatively small home, as it is not traditionally the norm to move away on marriage as among white British families. On the other hand, some South Asian households recorded in the statistics as 'nuclear-family households' will be socially autonomous units as the term implies; but many may, despite their spatial separation, be extremely closely linked with other households in the traditional way. Localised settlement, and activities such as weekend visiting and use of the telephone, are examples of ways in which the physical obstacles to family unity can be overcome.

The current version of this handbook, Judicial Studies Board's Equal Treatment Bench Book (1999), can be found at www.jsboard.co.uk.

Mary Chamberlain, in 'Brothers and sisters, uncles and aunts: a lateral perspective on Caribbean Families' (chapter 9 in Elizabeth B. Silva and Carol Smart (eds.), *The new family?* (1999), has collected some case-studies, which powerfully illustrate the way the extended West Indian family works. Here is one family's experience:

Arianne was born in Trinidad in 1931, the eldest of five children as well as 'quite a lot of half-sisters', who originated in the first marriages of both her parents. Arianne's grandmother came from Venezuela, trading goods in Trinidad until eventually settling there. Arianne's father was born in Trinidad, of (African) Venezuelan parents, although her family was ethnically diverse, 'pure, pure [Amer] Indian....we grow with them. On the father's side, we have Chinese ... we have Assyrian ... we're all kind of people in our family... oh, it was ... colourful.'

Her mother, though born in Venezuela, was brought up in Trinidad (while *her* mother was travelling) by her elder siblings, in particular 'the eldest ... [who] used to see after the smaller ones. So my mother stay here and she went to school here in Trinidad'. The parenting role of siblings in this family continued across the generations. Arianne grew up with her seven siblings, including two from her mother's first marriage, and a cousin, 'like sisters'. Her father died when Arianne was 15, and when she was 18 her mother; her aunt who was also her godmother, assumed the role of parent looking after Arianne, her brothers and sisters and by this time another nephew. The family was surrounded by aunts and uncles and, as with Maude's experience, the metaphor of family extended throughout the neighbourhood, from material support ('anything we give ... this is for Mr Joe, this is for this body, this is [for those] less fortunate ... there's so much in this giving ... they have something, they will send something to give') to control.

> 'You hardly could have misbehaved really long ago, you know, because ... family, and the neighbours... want to know what going on. Why you here? Who you know, what you know. If they see you talking to anybody that they know, well, let us say, a loose person, somebody whom, you know, bad to the parents... they would call you and tell you "Listen, you must not keep that person's company, because they would lead you astray".'

Moral and practical guidance in sexual matters was assumed to be the province of older women in the neighbourhood, 'I always have older people friend ..., my mother hadn't any course to tell us anything, but she used to tell us ... everything. ... What to do, what not to do, what we mustn't do, what to expect'. Arianne became pregnant when she was 20 and gave birth to her only child, Clarissa, in 1951. She did not marry Clarissa's father and although he supported Clarissa when he could, Arianne had to work to keep them both, moving from the country to a suburb of Port-of-Spain in order to do so. Arianne's siblings remained in Rio Claw. Although Arianne was not the oldest in the family (her half-siblings preceded her) she was the eldest girl and was 'always . . . responsible for everybody ... everyone turned to her ... If they had problems ... anything at all, it's "Auntie Ad would sort it out"'.

As a child Clarissa spent her holidays with her grandparents, who owned a cocoa plantation, and her aunts and uncles where 'all the children would be growing up together'. Her grandfather played the quatro in a Parang (traditional folk) band and 'we would go round with him as well, to all the houses ... he liked all his grandchildren'. Clarissa describes her father as a 'lady's man'. It was not until she was in her teens that Clarissa discovered that she had eight other brothers and sisters and 'last year, I found I had another one'.

Clarissa was her mother's only child although, in addition to her siblings through her father, Clarissa also had a number of step-siblings, the children of the man with whom her mother eventually lived during Clarissa's adolescence. Prior to that, however, Arianne shared a household with another family in Lavantille, replicating here her 'siblings' left behind. It was there that Clarissa spent her formative years as a singleton child.

> '... we grew up together... we were never alone. We were either with Aunty Iris, as I call her, or Mum was there, and Mum would have the two girls, or Auntie Iris would be looking after us. ... They're in America at the moment. They're all married with their families in America ... [we are] like sisters ... we had people like Aunt Iris and friends who had their own families and who were ... sort of like sisters ... they were that close. ... It was like having aunties, really ... you felt as part of the family. ... I was always treated like one of the family. ... I really had a lot of influences from the families. And basically, you know, had a lot of family life.'

Arianne's 'way of life' incorporated not only the creation of substitute families, but within that replicated the role of elder sister: 'my mother ... was always being called upon to do something for everyone, and so I've had loads of aunts and uncles, by virtue of being friends of hers. ... there have always been people around'.

Clarissa came to England to train as a nurse, and had a child by a Barbadian 'who turned out just like my father, really'. She did not marry him and, like her mother, found herself having to work and bring up a child alone, removed (like her mother) from broader family networks. It may have been that earlier childhood experience of co-parenting which inspired her own choice of childrearing pattern. Clarissa re-created a communal home, first with her aunt whom she describes as a:

> 'respectful aunt, not family aunt. She is someone I met when I first came over, one of my friends ... because we're Trinidadians together, we all sort of cottoned on ... so at the time when I got pregnant I stayed with her.'

And then with her daughter's childminder which was:

> 'extremely convenient. I didn't have to go anywhere, to take [my daughter] anywhere, I just leave and go to work and come back. And that seemed to work out well enough. ... [She] *was*, to *be honest, like another mother*. She really loved [my daughter]. [She] was the life and soul of her ... she loved children.'

Such a pattern may be seen as a variant of 'child shifting'..., although in the case of both Arianne and her mother, they remained present in the household. It may also be seen as an example of co-mothering, common in Latin America and now emerging as a recognized pattern in some Latin American regions, and African American communities in the USA. Three generations had migrated, Arianne's mother from Venezuela, Arianne from the country to the city, and Clarissa from Trinidad to England, and all adopted strategies which incorporated collaterals — blood or 'respectful' — in a coparenting role. 'I was', as Clarissa says, 'quite happy to bring [my daughter] up the way I was brought up'.

It is important to be clear about the difference in meaning between household and family.

A *household* according to Stone, writing about the family in England from 1500-1800, consists of persons 'living under one roof'. In *The Family, Sex and Marriage in England 1500-1800* (1977), he says:

The core of any household is clearly the family, namely members related by blood or marriage, usually the conjugal pair and their unmarried children, but sometimes including grandparents, the married children, or occasionally kin relatives. But most households also included non-kin inmates, sojourners, boarders or lodgers, occupying rooms vacated by children or kin, as well as indentured apprentices and resident servants, employed either for domestic work about the house or as an additional resident labour force for the fields or the shop.

Laslett and Wall, in their seminal work *Household and Family in Past Time*, published in 1972, define the two words 'household' and 'family' in the context of the historical demographic data which they collect and analyse:

It must be strongly stressed that in this vocabulary the word *family* does not denote a complete coresident domestic group, though it may appear as an abbreviated title. The word *household* particularly indicates the fact of shared location, kinship and activity. Hence all solitaries have to be taken to be households, for they are living with themselves, and this is the case when they have servants with them, since servants are taken as household members. ...

The expression *simple family* is used to cover what is variously described as the *nuclear family*, the *elementary family* or (not very logically, since spouses are not physiologically connected) the *biological family*. It consists of a married couple, or a married couple with offspring, or of a widowed person with offspring. The concept is of the conjugal link as the structural principle. ... For a simple family to appear then, it is necessary for at least two individuals connected by that link or arising from that link to be coresident: *conjugal family unit* (CFU) is a preciser term employed to describe all possible groups so structured.

No solitary can form a conjugal family unit and for such a group to subsist it is necessary for at least two immediate partners (spouses and/or offspring) to be present. More remotely connected persons, whose existence implies more than one conjugal link, do not constitute a conjugal family unit if they reside together with no one else except servants. Nor do brothers and sisters. Hence a widow with a child forms a conjugal family unit, but a widow with a grandchild does not, nor does an aunt with a nephew. Whenever a conjugal family unit is found on its own, it is always taken to be a household, just as solitaries are, and such a coresident domestic group is called a *simple family household*. ...

An *extended family household* [or stem family] consists of a conjugal family unit with the addition of one or more relatives other than offspring, the whole group living together on its own or with servants. It is thus identical with the simple family household except for the additional item or items.

Multiple family households comprise all forms of domestic group which include two or more conjugal family units connected by kinship or by marriage. The disposition of a secondary unit, that is of a constituent unit which does not contain the head of the whole household, is said to be UP if its conjugal link involves a generation earlier than that of the head, as for example when his father and mother live with him. Such a secondary unit can include offspring of the head's parents other than the head himself, that is his resident unmarried brothers or sisters, and the presence of such persons keeps this secondary unit in being if one or other of the head's parents dies. A secondary unit is disposed DOWN if, for example, a head's married son lives with him along with his wife and perhaps offspring, with similar implications about siblings and widowhood. ...

If conjugal family units within households of the multiple kind are all disposed laterally, as when married brothers and/or sisters live together, the overall arrangement is the one often referred to as the 'fraternal joint family' by social anthropologists.

Questions

(i)   Is your family a simple family household, an extended family household or a multiple family household?

(ii) What about your grandparents' family?

It is necessary to consider another introductory matter, namely the difference between *familial experience* and *familial ideology*. There may be a correspondence between experience and ideology; however, it has been argued by Laslett and Wall that although the nuclear monogamous family has a claim to universality, it has never possessed a normative and ideological force:

There must be few behavioural institutions of which it can be said that ideology and experience are entirely congruent. No one would question that the English society of our day is correctly described as monogamous, because monogamous behaviour is nearly universal amongst a people whose belief in monogamy as a value is very widespread, and whose conduct is consistent with monogamy as the norm. It could be called the marital institution under which the English live, for no other distinct practice-with-belief exists alongside it as an alternative. Yet divorce is now quite frequent, scepticism about single spouse unions often encountered, and sexual intercourse outside marriage a commonplace. Indeed we know that children have been begotten illegitimately in appreciable numbers in England during the whole period for which figures can be recovered. ...

Departure from the monogamous ideal of behaviour, amongst English people nowadays, and perhaps amongst their ancestors, has been particularly conspicuous within the elite, and rejection of the beliefs associated with monogamy especially common with the intellectuals, the makers of opinions and of norms. Monogamy as an institution, then, has been underwritten by a general correspondence of ideology and experience, but is consistent with an appreciable degree of disharmony between the two. We do not find ourselves enquiring how much they could diverge before a practice ceased to be *the* institution, and became one amongst others, *an* institution. We do not easily contemplate a situation where plural institutions, or highly variable behaviour, exist in one society at one time in such matters as sexual behaviour and marriage.

Yet if we turn to the question of how far any of the forms of the coresident domestic group, ... could be called *the* institution, or *an* institution, of the societies where examples of them are found, this issue becomes inescapable. Glancing again at England as it is today, it seems safe enough to claim that the nuclear family, the simple family household, is *the* familial institution, and that again because experience of it, belief in it, willingness to obey its norms, are in fact all congruent with each other. The nuclear family, of course, complements the English institution of monogamy in a particular way. But it has, and has had for hundreds of years as far as we can yet see, a markedly better claim to universality in behaviour and experience than monogamous marriage with exclusively marital sexual intercourse. Yet the nuclear family never seems to have possessed the normative force, certainly not the ideological potential of monogamy, in England or indeed in Western culture.

The hiatus, therefore, between familial experience and familial ideology is of a somewhat different character than that which divides the two in the matter of monogamy. The intellectuals and opinion makers who deal in the ideology of our world, have a tendency to deplore the circumstance that the complex family household is not sufficiently established as a norm in our society. Extended and even multiple households exist amongst us, but not in anything like enough numbers to ensure that the widowed and the elderly unmarried have a family to live in, or our children the emotional advantage of the presence of the extended kin in the households where they grow up.

Bear this last sentence in mind when you consider the issues raised in Chapter 4.

Laslett and Wall's definition of monogamy may be contrasted with the following extract from Engels, *Origins of the Family, Private Property and the State* (1884):

Sex love in the relation of husband and wife is and can become the rule only among the oppressed classes, that is, at the present day, among the proletariat, no matter whether this relationship is officially sanctioned or not. But all the foundations of classical monogamy are removed. Here there is a complete absence of all property, for the safeguarding and inheritance of which monogamy and male domination were established. Therefore, there is no stimulus whatever here to assert male domination. ...

Moreover, since large-scale industry has transferred the woman from the house to the labour market and the factory, and makes her, often enough, the bread winner of the family, the last remnants of male domination in the proletarian home have lost all foundation – except, perhaps, for some of that brutality towards women which became firmly rooted with the establishment of monogamy. Thus, the proletarian family is no longer monogamian in the strict sense, even in cases of the most passionate love and strictest faithfulness of the two parties, and despite all spiritual and worldly benedictions which may have been received. ...

Questions

(i)   Polygamy is permitted in some cultures; for example, in classical Islamic law a man is permitted four wives; the husband inherits a large slice of his wife's property, but she does have rights of ownership while she is alive and can inherit a share of the estate of her deceased father. Do you think that polygamy has anything to do with: (a) control of property; and (b) male domination?

(ii)   Do you think that a male worker has a vested interest in the domination of his wife and children?

(iii) Section 8(3) of the Immigration Act 1971 states that the provisions introduced under the Act for immigration control shall not apply to any person so long as he is a member of a mission, or 'a person who is a member of the family and forms part of the household of such a member'. Are the following exempt from control:

    (a)   the distant cousin of a Pakistani diplomat who has been looked after by this diplomat and his wife after the death of the parents;

    (b)   the fourth wife of a Yemeni diplomat who has been provided with separate accommodation by her husband in Yemen in accordance with Islamic law; and

    (c)   the young brother of an Indian diplomat who has equal rights with the diplomat in the joint property they have both inherited from their father?

The changed nature of the monogamous partnership is highlighted by Jane Lewis, in 'Family Policy in the post-War period' (chapter 4 in Sanford Katz, John Eekelaar and Mavis Maclean (eds.), *Cross Currents* (2000)):

In the European context, it has long been thought that family policy is something that the continental European countries (especially France) had and Britain did not. Not until the 1990s did government, first Conservative and then Labour, attempt to formulate a family policy. However ... the absence of an explicit family policy does not mean that governments do not have one. This chapter begins with the assumptions underlying policies and seeks to show how the story of the development of family policy in Britain has been the movement away from a relatively firm and coherent set of (implicit) assumptions about what the family looks like and how it works. Only with the dawning realization as to the profound and rapid change in family patterns over the past twenty-five years and especially over the last decade has government put the family on the policy agenda.

Not surprisingly, historically government has assumed the existence of a two-parent family, in which the husband and father's primary task is to earn and maintain and that of the wife and mother to care. This rendered the woman dependent on a male breadwinner, and women gained entitlements in respect of modern welfare policies chiefly as wives rather than as mothers. Indeed the early feminist literature on the post-war welfare state emphasized the extent to which social policies represented 'the state organisation of domestic life'. Certainly, the assumptions about female dependency were the same ones that made it possible for the vote to be confined to male 'heads of families' throughout the nineteenth century and part of the twentieth.

However, the social reality is more complicated. Women's position in the modern welfare state is more complex than that of men, and has also undergone more change. Broadly speaking, the proportion in the labour market of women with children has increased dramatically, but the amount of unpaid domestic work (housework and caring work for young and old) carried out by men has changed very little. The mix of work (although not necessarily the kind of work) performed by women has changed much more than the mix of work performed by men. The sources of income for women have therefore also changed. During the twentieth century there was a major shift away from dependence on individual male relatives (especially husbands), and towards increased dependence on the labour market for married women and for single women without children, and dependence on the state for lone women with children. In the case of the latter, modern social welfare policies have permitted the transformation of traditional family forms and the formation of autonomous households by lone mothers, while at the same time attempting to enforce assumptions about men's obligation to maintain. Thus state policies have in practice often been Janus-faced in this respect.

The nature of the relationship between the increase in women's employment, the development of state benefit programmes, and the increasing autonomy of women is a highly fraught subject. The position of the family as a mediating institution between the individual and the state has undergone huge change. The fundamental dilemma for government at the end of the twentieth century has become how far it can or should treat adult family members as independent individuals. In face of the increasing proportion of adult women in the workforce, should it completely abandon any notion of dependency inherent in the male breadwinner model? In face of changing family forms, with less marriage, later marriage, more cohabitation, and more lone motherhood, should it abandon the attempt to regulate family life via the law of husband and wife? If so, does this not mean that new measures are needed to secure the position of children? Family policy in the form of public *and* private law has never been entirely coherent in its treatment of family members at the level of either principles or practice. The trend in terms of the social reality has been towards greater 'individualization', although this does not mean that women have become fully individualized. In the closing years of the twentieth century the problem for government has become how far to recognize the changing social reality, the problem being that in taking steps to recognize it, the law may also promote it.

We shall be returning to this theme in Chapter 3. Before we look more generally at the law's response to the family, let us pause and look back at the way the family has developed, and the different ways in which scholars have described its development.

1.2   Approaches to the history of the family

In *Approaches to the History of the Western Family* (1980), Anderson distinguishes three approaches to family history: the demographic approach, the sentiments approach, and the household economic approach. These three schools of thought emphasise different aspects of the available source material. The extracts in this section have been selected to provide illustrations of the debate upon which family historians remain engaged.

1.2.1 The demographic approach

Peter Laslett and his co-workers at the Cambridge ESRC group for the History of Population and Social Structure are the major writers who adhere to this approach.

A particular matter which must be of considerable interest for the policymakers of the present time is the historical evidence relating to the size of households, and whether this information has a bearing on the size, type and function of the family. It is to this question that the Laslett team has directed its gaze. Laslett suggests that the 'mean household size' (including servants in England) 'has remained more or less constant at about 4.75 from the sixteenth century right through the industrialisation period until the end of the nineteenth century when a steady decline set in to a figure of about three in contemporary censuses'. The work of the Group is based on 100 English communities at dates between 1574 and 1821. 70% of households are classed as two-generational and 24% as one generational. Only 6% contain relatives of three different generations and less than 1% of four generations. The major conclusion is that a nuclear familial form 'may have been one of the enduring and fundamental characteristics of the Western family system'. Indeed, Alan MacFarlane in *Origins of English Individualism* (1978) has argued that the nuclear family as a behavioural fact has existed in England since 1200.

However, other research has tended to suggest that this view is a gross exaggeration and overgeneralisation. In Southern and Eastern Europe, households were of a more complex type (see Berkner, 1977). Indeed even in relation to England, Laslett's conclusions have been doubted, as Anderson explains in *Approaches to the History of the Western Family (1500-1914)* (1980):

If we imagine a household where land is transferred to a son on his marriage and the son subsequently has children of his own, then, if this occurs before his father's death, a three-generation family will appear in a census listing. A few years later, when the father has died, only a widow, married child and grandchildren will be left and the evidence for a stem household becomes ambiguous. On the widow's death, a nuclear household will result and the census listing will reveal no evidence of any extension at all. Nevertheless – and this is the crucial point – while no stem-family *household* is present, a stem-family *organisation* remains since, in due course, the same process will be repeated by the next generation. Indeed, even where no stem-family system is in operation the availability of data on ages frequently shows a marked life-cycle effect in household data which is not apparent in aggregate data.

What is at issue is the life cycle of the family: first, newly-married couple; second, nuclear family with children; third, extended family; and fourth, back again to nuclear family. Static listings of households conceal this pattern.

The conclusions of Laslett and other members of the group are also criticised by Edward Shorter, in *The Making of the Modern Family* (1975):

In earlier writings on the history of the family, sociologists acquired the bad habit of assuming that families before the Industrial Revolution were organized in clans or were at least highly 'extended'. Because any historian with even a passing familiarity with Europe's social history would realize at once the inaccuracy of that assumption, a revisionist reaction developed in the 1960s: the nuclear family was 'unearthed' time and again in history, to the accompaniment of loud shouts of discovery. As often happens to revisionists, these writers fell over backwards attempting to overturn the conventional wisdom; instead of merely correcting the sociologists' fantasies about clans and sprawling patriarchies, they tended to proclaim that at most times and places it was the conjugal family – mother, father, children, and servants – that had prevailed. The revisionists thus proceeded to create a little fantasy of their own; the nuclear family as a historical constant.

Now, many kinless families did exist; indeed, they often represented a majority of all households. But to get a sense of the typical experience of the average person, we must ask what kind of household a child would most likely have been socialized in: extended (stem), or nuclear? And there is a good chance that in better-off households as opposed to poorer ones, and in east Europe as opposed to west Europe, the average child was raised in a dwelling that contained many relatives besides his mother and father. ...

Conjugal groups *minus* kin also turned up frequently enough in rural Europe. There were, for example, the pastoral regions of the Netherlands, where the grandparents seldom lived with the farmer and his wife. In Norwegian villages relatives co-resided with propertied peasants only about a fifth of the time, and the percentage was even lower among the cottagers. Across much of Lower Austria and in at least two well-documented villages in Salzburg province, three-generation households were unusual. ...

Yet we must still consider the possibility that in such communities many households might, at some point in time, have contained several generations, but that death snatched away the grandparents before the census-taker arrived. Thus in the census they appeared as single-family units, whereas they might actually have been, for a period of years, stem families.

However, in many other areas of western and central Europe, the stem family was commonplace and the kinless family an anomaly. Frédéric Le Play, the nineteenth-century French sociologist, coined the term *famille souche* to denote families that passed on a given farm undivided from one generation to the next over long periods of time.

1.2.2 The economic approach

A question often asked is why a detailed knowledge of household composition should necessarily tell us much about familial behaviour. Indeed, there are many who see household composition as a by-product of more fundamental economic processes. There is a group of writers who seek to interpret the historical data relating both to households and to families in the context of the economic realities of the period and of the region. The major question is based around the value of the household as a means of production. Anderson summarises these writings for us, in the context of the family economy of the Western peasant, in *Approaches to the History of the Western Family (1500-1914)* (1980):

This approach has taken as its central concept the often unconscious 'strategies' employed by family members to maintain a customary standard of living, both for themselves in the present and, under certain circumstances, for themselves and their descendants in the future. The types of strategies available are constrained in a number of ways: by the family's resource-generating potential (particularly its age/sex composition); by the mode of production in which the family is involved; by the income-generating relationships which are implied by that mode; by law and custom regarding property acquisition (including inheritance); by the possibilities of access to alternative resource-generating activities (including wage-labour or domestic manufacturing) or resource-providing rights (including, for example, both customary rights to pasture animals on common land and social welfare provision); by the intervention of powerful groups external to the family (landlords, employers and others with power in the local community); by customs limiting the range of resource-generating options which individuals see as practically available at a point in time (for example, ideas over what is appropriate work for women).

For the Western peasant or yeoman farmer, the principal scarce resource was land, so family strategies were constrained by the conditions under which land could be obtained and by the labour inputs required to work it. The literature on continental Europe, on Ireland, and on some areas of England even in the early nineteenth century, portrays the dominant peasant/ yeoman pattern as one where the family's subsistence needs could be met only through the continual application of the labour of all its members to productive tasks in agriculture or, to a greater or lesser extent, in certain craft or other domestically organised productive activities. Almost all production was intended either for family use or for local and known markets.

One of the central problems of the peasant family, from this perspective, was the need to ensure that enough labour was available to meet current and future needs while yet not having too many mouths to feed for the resource-generating capacity of the means of production. On the one hand it was necessary to avoid childless marriages, which gave no security for old age (hence perhaps norms encouraging premarital intercourse to ensure marriage only to fertile girls). On the other hand too many children threatened current subsistence. This problem could, however, in some places be solved by one or more strategic responses. For example: one could acquire more productive resources as children grew ..., one could expand non-agricultural activities and devote more effort to domestic craft production (but this was not always available) ..., one could restrict family size by marriage to older women ..., by some form of contraception (found in seventeenth-century England, eighteenth- and early-nineteenth-century Sweden and many other places) ... or by some other strategy such as prolonging breast feeding. Finally, as in England, Scandinavia and elsewhere, poor households could regulate their numbers by sending 'surplus' children into service at an early age.

1.2.3 The sentiments approach

There is another group of writers which is not prepared either to see household composition as a by-product of fundamental economic processes, or to deduce the historical development of the Western family from demographic sources. Shorter (1975) and Stone (1977, 1990) in particular have emphasised what has been termed 'the tale of sentiments'. Anderson illustrates the difference in the approach between Laslett, and the work of Shorter and Stone: 'The demographic approach started from a particular set of documents, by which their questions and conclusions have been constrained. The sentiments writers began with a set of questions about the ideas associated with family behaviour and were then faced with the problem of finding suitable source material to throw light on such ideas.'

The following extract is taken from Stone's chapter on family characteristics, in *The Family, Sex and Marriage in England 1500-1800* (1977):

In the sixteenth century, relations between spouses in rich families were often fairly remote. Living in big houses, each with his or her own bedroom and servants, husband and wife were primarily members of a functioning social universe of a large household and were rarely in private together. ... Their marriage was usually arranged rather than consensual, in essence the outcome of an economic deal or a political alliance between two families. The transaction was sealed by the wedding and by the physical union of two individuals, while the emotional ties were left to develop at a later date. If they did not take place, and if the husband could find sexual alternatives through casual liaisons, the emotional outlet through marriage was largely non-existent for either husband or wife.

In any case, the expectations of felicity from marriage were pragmatically low, and there were many reasons why disappointment was minimal. The first is that the pair did not need to see very much of one another, either in elite circles, where they could go their own way, or among the plebs, where leisure activities were segregated, with the men resorting to the ale-house, and the women to each other's houses. ...

The second reason why such a system was so readily accepted was the high adult mortality rates, which severely reduced the companionship element in marriage and increased its purely reproductive and nurturance functions. There was a less than fifty-fifty chance that the husband and wife would both remain alive more than a year or two after the departure from the home of the last child, so that friendship was hardly necessary. William Stout's comment on a marriage in 1699 could stand as an epitaph for many sixteenth- and seventeenth-century couples: 'they lived very disagreeably but had many children.'

Nor was the position very different amongst the lower classes in pre-nineteenth century France:

Eighteenth-century middle-class observers of social relations among the labouring classes, peasants and urban *petite bourgeoisie* in France could find no trace of affection in the marital relationship. Their observations may be biased by class and background, but if they are at all accurate, they must reflect a permanent feature of the traditional European society. All over France, 'If the horse and the wife fall sick at the same time, the ... peasant rushes to the blacksmith to care for the animal, and leaves the task of healing his wife to nature.' If necessary, the wife could be replaced very cheaply, while the family economy depended on the health of the animal. This peasant pragmatism was confirmed by traditional proverbs, such as 'rich is the man whose wife is dead and horse alive.' The same lack of marital sentiment was evident in the towns. '*L'amitié*, that delicious sentiment, is scarcely known. There are in these little towns only marriages of convenience; nobody appreciates that true happiness consists in making others happy, who always reward us in kind.'

This bleak portrait is modified in a number of ways by Stone himself:

This rather pessimistic view of a society with little love and generally low and widely diffused affect needs to be modified if it is accurately to reflect the truth. Romantic love and sexual intrigue were certainly the subject of much poetry of the sixteenth and early seventeenth centuries, and of many of Shakespeare's plays. It was also a reality which existed in one very restricted social group: the one in which it had always existed since the twelfth century, that is the households of the prince and the great nobles. Here, and here alone, well-born young persons of both sexes were thrown together away from parental supervision and in a situation of considerable freedom as they performed their duties as courtiers, ladies and gentlemen in waiting, tutors and governesses to the children. They also had a great deal of leisure, and in the enclosed hot-house atmosphere of these great houses, love intrigues flourished as nowhere else.

The second modification of the pessimistic general description of affective relations concerns a far wider group, including many who were subjected to the loveless arranged marriage, which was normal among the propertied classes. It is clear from correspondence and wills that in a considerable number of cases, some degree of affection, or at least a good working partnership, developed after the marriage. In practice, as anthropologists have everywhere discovered, the arranged marriage works far less badly than those educated in a romantic culture would suppose, partly because the expectations of happiness from it are not set unrealistically high, and partly because it is a fact that sentiment can fairly easily adapt to social command. In any case, love is rarely blind, in the sense that it tends to be channelled along socially acceptable lines, towards persons of the other sex of similar background. This greatly increases the probability that an arranged marriage, provided it is not undertaken purely for mercenary considerations and that there is not too great a discrepancy in age, physical attractiveness or temperament, may well work out not too badly. This is especially the case where leisure is segregated, so that the pair are not thrown together too much, and where both have a multitude of outside interests and companions to divert them. In a 'low affect' society, a 'low affect' marriage is often perfectly satisfactory.

The final modification to be made to the bleak affective picture is that, owing to the high adult death rate and the late age of marriage, by no means all marriages among persons of property in the sixteenth century were arranged by the parents, since many of them were dead: marriages by choice certainly occurred, although freedom of choice was far more difficult to achieve for women other than widows.

Similar considerations are the basis of Shorter's work. Here he describes the change to 'domesticity', in *The Making of the Modern Family* (1975):

The 'companionate' marriage is customarily seen as the hallmark of contemporary family life, the husband and wife being friends rather than superordinate and subordinate, sharing tasks and affection. Perhaps that is correct. But the emotional cement of the modern family binds more than the husband and wife; it fixes the children, as well, into this sentimental unit. The notion of companionship doesn't necessarily say anything about the relationship between the couple and their children. Also, 'companionship' implies incorrectly that some form of intense romantic attachment continues to unite the couple. Both ideas are incomplete, and for that reason I prefer the expression 'domesticity' in demarcating the modern family from the traditional.

Domesticity, or the family's awareness of itself as a precious emotional unit that must be protected with privacy and isolation from outside intrusion, was the third spearhead of the great onrush of sentiment in modern times. Romantic love detached the couple from communal sexual supervision and turned them towards affection. Maternal love created a sentimental nest within which the modern family would ensconce itself, and it removed many women from involvement with community life. Domesticity, beyond that, sealed off the family as a whole from its traditional interaction with the surrounding world. The members of the family came to feel far more solidarity with one another than they did with their various age and sex peer groups.

Stone's thesis has been commented on critically by other historians. For example, Keith Wrightson in *English Society 1580-1680* (1982) writes:

Stone's powerful arguments and adventurous hypotheses constitute the most ambitious attempt yet undertaken to interpret the development of the English family over time. Nevertheless they are seriously open to question in both their characterization of family life in later sixteenth and seventeenth century England and in their account of change within this period. Although he is undoubtedly aware of the major distinctions which may have existed between social groups in England, Stone has devoted insufficient care to the exploration of the experience of the mass of the population. As a result his interpretation has been elaborated on the basis of the historical experience of the aristocracy, upper gentry and urban plutocracy with which he is primarily concerned and retains at its heart the tacit assumption that analytical categories derived from their experience can somehow be extended to encapsulate phases in the history of the English family. This is a mistaken assumption. For whatever their historical prominence, the familial behaviour of the English elite was very far from representative of that of their countrymen. Nor can shifts in their behaviour be asserted to have been significant advances in familial development when set in the full context of the already established and persisting characteristics of the family life of their social inferiors.

In a later extract, Wrightson continues:

Of marital relations in late sixteenth- and seventeenth-century England, much remains obscure. The weight of the evidence reviewed here, however, suggests that, despite the inevitable counter-examples and the individual and social variation which is to be expected, there is little reason to follow Professor Stone in regarding the rise of the companionate marriage as a new phenomenon for the later seventeenth and eighteenth centuries. It seems to have been already well established. It is true that the best of our evidence is derived from the diaries of deeply religious people, puritans who had especial cause to follow the advice of moral teachers on the subject of mutuality. Yet such supplementary evidence as can be gathered does not suggest that they were unusual in their marital relations, while the teachings of the moralists themselves were neither new, nor distinctively Puritan. They represented for the most part the mainstream of opinion on the best practice in marriage. In the present state of our knowledge it would seem unwise to make too sharp a dichotomy between the 'patriarchal' and the 'companionate' marriage, and to erect these qualities into a typology of successive stages of family development. It may well be that these are less evolutionary stages of familial progress, than the poles of an enduring continuum in marital relations in a society which accepted both the primacy of male authority and the ideal of marriage as a practical and emotional partnership. Most people established their roles within marriage somewhere between the two, with the emphasis, for the most part, on the latter.

Given these wide differences of perspective, it is appropriate to pause and to ask what relevance is there for a lawyer in the first decade of the twenty-first century to have answers to the questions raised by the historians. It is to this matter that we now turn.

1.2.4 The relevance of the history of the family

Anderson asks the question whether family history can 'justify itself', in *Sociology of the Family* (now 1980):

... It can do so above all by drawing out the implications of these changes for the kind of family life which is possible today and, above all, by demonstrating that old moralities and old behaviours cannot meet new situations and that, accordingly, present problems require new and not obsolete solutions.

Perhaps the most significant, and certainly analytically the most difficult of these changes have been in the family's relation to production. The peasant household was the focus of production with head and spouse organizing production using the household's own labour and exploiting and co-ordinating the contribution of all household members. Each class of individual had a clearly prescribed role and each member was dependent on the activities of all the others. In this situation there is a high degree of role interdependence both between spouses and between generations. ... Not merely was production a joint activity but almost all consumption was either shared or was undertaken in some way or other on behalf of the household.

By contrast, under our kind of capitalist system of production, work for the mass of the population becomes directed by others who select and reward labour on an individualistic basis. One or more household members leaves the domestic arena and each is remunerated by outsiders on a basis which normally takes no account of his or her family situation. The wage received is the personal property of the individual, is dependent on the individual's own level of activity and achievement, and is paid to the individual in private leaving him or her to negotiate with the rest of the family over how and to what extent the money is to be distributed in order to satisfy their wants.

The contrast between the jointness of income generation in the peasant family and its individualistic basis under capitalism was, to a considerable extent, concealed under early capitalist production by the continued participation of all except the youngest family members in income-generating activities. Even after legislation had removed children from full time factory employment there remained within local communities significant opportunities for children to add to family resources through cash or goods in kind obtained in return for odd jobs done outside school hours. In addition, the substantial levels of labour input required to process food and other materials for domestic consumption, together with the significant amount of domestic productive activity for both home production and for the market, allowed those who remained in the domestic arena to contribute significantly to family resource generation processes. Thus, in as far as the husband earned income outside the home on behalf of the family, the children (and particularly the male children) sought odd jobs on behalf of the family, and the wife (aided by the female children) produced domestically on behalf of the family, all resources being pooled together, the role interdependence remained and there was little analytical difference between this situation and the peasant system where the husband and male children worked in the outfield producing in part marketable products to pay the rent, while wife and female children worked in the infield and the home on the production and reproduction of labour power. Of course, because wages were the private property of the individual there was no guarantee that wages were in fact pooled – as the harrowing descriptions of the wives of nineteenth-century factory workers trying to extract their husbands from public houses on pay day testify. ...

Models which assume that family-based decision making took place over how necessary income should be generated and over who should work in which sectors of production, have a clear empirical fit with data from most nineteenth- and early twentieth-century working-class communities.

However, developments of the last fifty years have moved most families significantly away from this position. Children have become almost totally dependent. They leave the home daily for education which is oriented far more to their individual futures than to their current family roles and subsequently enter the labour force to receive pay much of which is again retained for their own use even in the very few years that now typically remain between starting work and marriage. In this way children have almost totally ceased to be part of an interdependent resource-generating system. Similarly, in as far as both spouses enter the labour force and each receives a private reward for labour (and particularly as in many dual career families where outside workers come in to perform most of the domestic work, which anyway can now if desired require a much smaller labour input), the work of the spouses can no longer so easily be seen as a co-operative productive activity or even as involving a complementary division of labour where each performs different but interrelated tasks on behalf of the family unit. ... The ties between family members thus become based not on an interdependence rooted in co-operative productive activity essential for survival, but on personal interdependence oriented towards the joint attainment of essentially intrinsic 'projects' of highly diverse kinds.

However, these aspirations are much more susceptible to change over time than are the basic survival objectives of pre-industrial European societies, and their interpersonal basis is much more fragile. ... Thus it is not surprising that wherever we see communities moving from family groups based on property and co-operative production, so we also see a decline in parental involvement in mate selection and, usually, a fall in the age of marriage and a rise in marital instability.

These changes are further facilitated by the parallel changes in the roles of children in the family, which involve both a drastic reduction in the power of parents over their children and in their 'interests' in their children's future welfare. ...

Viewed in a historical perspective, therefore, there is in the contemporary capitalist world a marked lack of structural support for familial bonds. In addition, demographic changes have increased the emphasis on intrinsic functions of marriage through the reduction in the period of the family life cycle which is devoted to the bearing and rearing of small children. Marriage at a younger age and an increase in life expectancy among adults have combined roughly to double the average duration of marriages unbroken by social dissolution; the median duration of such marriages is rapidly approaching fifty years. At the same time, the fall in family size and the concentration of childbirth into the earlier years of marriage has led for the first time to a situation where the majority of the life span of marriages does not involve the bearing of and caring for, small children; far from being a brief interval in old age, the 'empty nest' situation, with all its attendant problems of role reallocation, is fast coming to comprise a majority of the marital cycle. Increased leisure has only come to extend still further the time and the energy available for interpersonal relationships between spouses and thus, by inference at least, to make more problematical a lack of success in them. ...

Equally importantly, the other main prop to traditional family morality – close community supervision – has also been undermined and, indeed, in a comparative perspective, family behaviour has become the most private and personal of all areas of behaviour, almost totally free from external supervision and control.

Anderson concludes his review:

The study of the history of the Western family shows quite clearly that we cannot go back to a strict conformity to the family morality that we have inherited from the past without also – which is clearly impossible – reverting to the economic and social relations of the past. We are not peasants any more and thus cannot sustain a peasant morality. We have to develop new institutions and new behaviours to cope with new situations.

One aspect of family forms which is often overlooked when discussing the history of the family is the fact that the UK has a history of population migration, and immigration has necessarily brought with it a number of family forms different from traditional patterns. Adrian Wilson summarises this trend for us in *Family* (1985):

Such families put a much greater emphasis on the demands and duties of kinship. Asian families are a clear example of this. Family members feel that they have obligations both to their kin in Britain and also to the rest of their family, who are still resident in the home village. Many Indian families in Britain continue to provide financial support for their relatives in India.

The family structure of many ethnic groups tends to be both hierarchical and patriarchal. Ballard (1982) argues that the basic pattern of the south Asian family consists of a man, his sons and grandsons, together with their wives and unmarried daughters. This family has been transferred into a British setting. The man is clearly the head of the household, controlling the family finances, and negotiating the major family decisions. R. Oakley (1982) suggests that a similar pattern is true for Greek Cypriot families living in London. The Cypriot husband is an authoritarian figure, the source of family discipline. It is the husband who handles all the external dealings of the family with the wider society. Conjugal roles are essentially segregated, although complementary to each other.

The male-dominated nature of family life creates a very different experience for women within the ethnic minorities. In the early years of immigration, many women found themselves cut off from outside society. Social and language barriers kept them trapped in the domestic setting. Some Asian families created a state of purdah for their womenfolk, setting them apart from society at large. Oakley contrasts the social isolation of Cypriot women in England with the physical openness and outdoor character of life in Cyprus.

The reason for the attempt by ethnic minorities to control the lives of women lies in the need to maintain family honour. It is important that family members do not bring shame on the family name. Every member should be seen to behave properly. Inevitably, life in a British environment has thrown up major challenges to this traditional view of family life.

Serious problems have been created with the second generation, the immigrants' children, who were born and have been brought up in the United Kingdom. School teaches these children to want more independence. The socializing influence of the family stresses loyalty and obedience. It must also be remembered that many of the first-generation immigrants grew up in societies where there was no such thing as adolescence or youth culture, so conflict is inevitable when their children act like British teenagers. However, ethnic minority families have proved to be more flexible than was at first expected. An example of this flexibility can be seen in the way that the traditional arranged marriage is being modified to allow young people some say in the process.

West Indian families in Britain present a further distinct family pattern that reflects their culture of origin. The colonial system that was based on slavery weakened the bonds between men and women. The lack of a stable employment system left the man unable to support a family by his own efforts. The mother-child relationship became the central structure of the family.

Driver (1982) and Barrow (1982) use studies of family structures in the West Indies to suggest three models of family life. The first type is the conventional nuclear family household. Such a family form was most typical of the respectable and more affluent section of the community. The second type was a common-law household, where a man and a woman lived together with their children, but without a formal marriage. Third, there was the female-dominated household, where women had to care for their children and provide an income, without the presence of a man. Studies conducted in the West Indies suggested that each type accounted for about a third of all households in the West Indies.

Driver suggests that these family forms have been transplanted into the British West Indian community. He suggests that there are two types of black family structure in Britain. There is the nuclear family, where both partners share the full range of domestic roles. But there is also the mother-centered family. Driver says this is again associated with the lack of stable employment for men. The black mother is left to bring up the children, run the home, and provide an income. She must do this in England without the range of support that she could have obtained from female relatives in the West Indies. This kind of family might even be growing in Britain, providing a clear contrast to both Asian and traditional English family patterns.

It is hard to predict how ethnic minority families will develop with the third and subsequent generations. The size of minority families is dropping rapidly. Young couples seem to be more sceptical about the need to maintain such a wide family network. But the young Asians, Chinese, and Cypriots are well aware of their different cultural heritages. For many of these young people, their family life will be a compromise between the two cultures they inhabit.

Question

Does a possibly false view of family history in this country prevent us from accepting that families fall today and have always fallen into different types?

1.3   The law's response to the family

The challenge for the law is to respond to the wide range of family patterns we see in society today. It has been very difficult for legal systems to develop the necessary breadth of vision. Elizabeth Silva and Carol Smart, in 'The "New" Practices and Policies of Family Life' (chapter 1 of their edited volume, *The new family?* (1999)), describe the contrast between family statistics and the expectations of the law-makers:

The Stability of Political Rhetoric
In the last decade, both in the UK and in the USA, there has been a growing public concern over what is happening to the family. This concern has been fuelled by conservative politicians and commentators who have seen changes in family life as bringing social disorder in their wake...While there is a widespread consensus that society is undergoing a process of rapid and radical change, political rhetoric tends to claim that the family is an institution which must not change. The family is still supposed to stand outside and above economic restructuring, market forces and financial, legal, technological and political change, as a pillar of supposed stability. This political mantra on the family is not peculiar to Conservative governments but has also become a theme of New Labour in Britain. In his first major Conference speech after winning the General Election in 1997, the Prime Minister Tony Blair stated:

> We cannot say we want a strong and secure society when we ignore its very foundations: family life. This is not about preaching to individuals about their private lives. It is addressing a huge social problem. Attitudes have changed. The world has changed, but I am a modern man leading a modern country and this is a modern crisis. Nearly 100,000 teenage

pregnancies every year; elderly parents with whom families cannot cope; children growing up without role models they can respect and learn from; more and deeper poverty; more crime; more truancy; more neglect of educational opportunities, and above all more unhappiness. Every area of this government's policy will be scrutinized to see how it affects family Life. Every policy examined, every initiative tested, every avenue explored to see how we strengthen our families. (*The Guardian*, 1.10.97)

Strong families are, of course, seen as conjugal, heterosexual parents with an employed male breadwinner. Lone mothers and gay couples do not, by definition, constitute strong families in this rhetoric. On the contrary, they are part of the problem and part of the process of destabilizing the necessary fortitude of the proper family.

Blair's speech is typical of the political approach which acknowledges social change, while striving to hold fast to a model of family life which is associated with a particular cultural and economic moment in British history. Yet his emphasis on lone motherhood, absent fathers and a cycle of deprivation is clearly more a rhetorical device than a good reflection of typical family patterns. This point is important, because although family practices are changing, particularly over the life course, the amount of change within and across families is often exaggerated in popular rhetoric to achieve a specific political goal. We might, for example, be forgiven for imagining that the conjugal nuclear family was on the point of extinction. Yet in 1996 73 per cent of households were composed of heterosexual couples (with just under 90 per cent of these being married), 50 per cent of these households had children, and 40 per cent had dependent children (i.e., under 16 years). Only 9 per cent of households with dependent children were headed by lone parents (Office for National Statistics, 1997).

Notwithstanding the fact that family life may not have changed that dramatically, the political rhetoric sees this change as the slippery slope. Moreover, this alarmist device is potentially supported by changes in behaviour which may, in time, become trends which do signify major changes. Thus statistical indicators show that, although most people still marry and have children at some point in their lives, the average age at marriage has increased, and people have fewer children and become parents later in life. Women are now better educated, have greater control of their fertility, and may be becoming less enamoured of the triple burden of paid work, housework and childcare. The number of families living solely on a man's wage has dropped significantly in the late 1990s, with fewer people thinking that a wife's job is solely to look after the home and the family ... As Blair suggests in his speech, it may be changes in attitudes, rather than in household composition, that are seen as so alarming and destabilizing. Ultimately, statistical trends are contradictory. We might say that there is both continuity and diversity in family life at the end of the twentieth century. This means that although there is a numerical dominance in the form of two-parent families, this organization no longer defines so exclusively what it is like to live in a family, or what a family *is*. We live in a context where the normative European model of the conjugal couple living in a nuclear household is losing force. It is this ideological slippage that the political rhetoric seems to address just as much as actual shifts in family practices. Indeed, ... government policies on families are contradictory in their implementation. The meaning of a family, the significance of marriage and the importance of genetic parenthood, for example, may all be treated differently in different areas of policy. Thus the Children Act prioritizes parenthood over marriage, but immigration law gives priority to legal marriage; laws regulating assisted reproduction repudiate the possibility of gay and lesbian parenthood, while adoption policy will allow for gay or lesbian (or single-parent) adoption. Yet at the rhetorical level there is little tolerance for this kind of diversity and although policies are contradictory, the lack of political commitment to diversity means that newer family practices cannot assume, or rely on, policy support. What support there may be, happens almost by accident. It is therefore, part of our argument that policy formulation needs to be more open to diversity, rather than, as Blair would have it, focusing on 'strengthening' the family which inevitably means prioritizing the conjugal heterosexual couple and their children.

Europe, it seems, is no more enlightened than Britain in this respect, as Clare McGlynn explains in 'The Europeanisation of family law' (2001):

The concept of 'family' in European Community law

[A serious] concern with the emerging EU family law is with the potential ideological foundations of any potential family laws and their subsequent interpretation by the Court of Justice. This concern arises from an analysis of how the Court of Justice has thus far developed a concept of 'family' in Community law. I have argued elsewhere that the Court of Justice has developed a concept of the 'model European family' against which all individuals and family form are judged. This 'model European family' is a reproduction of the traditional 'nuclear' family: that of the heterosexual married union, in which the husband is head of the family and principal breadwinner and the wife is the primary childcarer. It is also a conceptualisation of family which reinforces the notion of children as dependants. This conceptualisation, though mythic and imaginary, as it bears little relation to the realities of family life in the EU, is none the less a powerful concept in Community law. The 'model European family' excludes some families from Community law rights, privileges specific relationships and perpetuates discrimination against both women and men.

The construction of this concept of 'family' stems from the court's jurisprudence in the area of free movement of persons and sex equality law. In the free movement area, the court in *Netherlands v Reed* held that a 'spouse', for the purpose of the grant of free movement 'family rights', is to be delimited to married persons, and does not therefore include cohabitants, either heterosexual or homosexual. A Community law 'family', therefore, entails heterosexual partnerships which are accorded the status of 'family' only via marriage. Equally, whereas marriage bequeaths the status of 'family', divorce appears to take it away. Furthermore, the court's limited interpretation of the concept of 'worker', on which many free movement rights are based, effectively excludes all informal/unpaid care work. This significantly limits the rights of many women to exercise free movement and where they do so, will render them dependent on a male 'worker'. The jurisprudence in this field has led Isabella Moebius and Erika Szyszczak to argue persuasively that the free movement rules are based on a 'male breadwinner family model' which 'reproduces and reinforces traditional patterns of gender relations and dependency within the family'.

This articulation of the concept of 'family' in the area of free movement of persons has been entrenched in recent judgments relating to the rights of gays and lesbians under the Community's sex equality laws. In *Grant v South West Trains Ltd* [1998] 1 FLR 839 the court refused to extend the scope of the Equal Treatment Directive to cover discrimination on the grounds of sexual orientation. In doing so, the court justified its refusal to extend the law on the basis that there is a lack of consensus among member states about whether 'stable relationships between persons of the same sex may be regarded as equivalent to stable relationships between persons of the opposite sex'. It continued that member states held this position 'for the purpose of protecting the family'. Apparently, therefore, same-sex partnerships do not constitute a 'family', nor are they deemed worthy of the protection of Community law. The Court of First Instance relied on this expression of the limits of Community law when faced with the argument that same-sex partners, registered as a partnership under national laws granting them similar rights to those of married partners, should be treated as 'spouses'. It held that *'Community* notions of marriage and partnership exclusively address a relationship founded on civil marriage in the traditional sense of the term'. It is arguable that Community law is seeking to uphold the institution of marriage by according it a privileged status, thereby reproducing patterns of inequality in the member states. Individuals and partnerships that do not conform to this normative family model, even those whose relationship may closely approximate the 'male breadwinner' model of 'coupledom', such as in *Netherlands v Reed* and *Grant,* fall outside the remit of Community law.

Nevertheless, the law is moving on. There have been two major developments since the last edition of this book. First, the decision of the House of Lords in *Fitzpatrick v Sterling Housing Association Ltd* [2001] 1 AC 27, [1999] 4 All ER 705, [1999] 3 WLR 1113, [2000] 1 FLR 271 has overtaken much of the earlier case law in this jurisdiction; second, the incorporation into domestic law of the European Convention on Human Rights has given a new emphasis to our law and has awakened new possibilities.

First, then, let us look at *Fitzpatrick*. The case stands at the end of a long line of cases in which the courts have had to decide whether or not two individuals have lived together 'as man and wife' or whether or not a given individual is a member of another's family, for the purpose of succession to tenancies under various statutory regimes. The results of the earlier cases were not generous; in *Harrogate Borough Council v Simpson* [1986] 2 FLR 91, [1986] Fam Law 359, the Court of Appeal held that a woman who lived in council accommodation with another woman, a secure tenant, and who shared a 'committed, monogamous, homosexual relationship' with her, was not a 'member of the tenant's family' within the meaning of s. 113(1), (2) of the Housing Act 1985, and accordingly was not entitled to succeed to the tenancy on the death of the tenant (s. 87 of the 1985 Act).

Against that background came Mr Fitzpatrick's application to take over the tenancy of his partner, Mr Thompson. Waite LJ, in the Court of Appeal ([1998] Ch 304, [1998] 2 WLR 225, [1997] 4 All ER 991, [1998] 1 FLR 43, [1998] 1 FCR 417, 30 HLR 576) summarises the facts:

The short but difficult question raised by this appeal is whether the surviving partner in a stable and permanent homosexual relationship can claim succession rights under the Rent Acts in respect of premises of which the deceased partner was a protected tenant. The facts are not in dispute. Mr John Thompson became the statutory tenant of a flat, No 75 Ravenscourt Road, London W6 (the flat), in 1972. The appellant, Mr Fitzpatrick, moved in to live with him there in 1976, and the two of them maintained from then onwards a close, loving and faithful homosexual relationship. Early in 1986 Mr Thompson suffered, as a result of a fall, head injuries which required surgery and then a stroke which left him a tetraplegic. From the summer of that year Mr Fitzpatrick nursed him at home, and dedicated himself to providing, with love and devotion, the constant care which he required. In 1994 Mr Thompson died.

The landlords are a charity providing families and individuals with accommodation at affordable rents. It is common ground that they do not qualify as a housing action trust within the terms of the Housing Act 1985 (as now amended), and that they accordingly fall to be treated as private landlords subject to the Rent Acts. Mr Fitzpatrick applied to take over the tenancy of the flat (which comprises four rooms plus kitchen and bathroom) but the landlords, though willing to rehouse him in smaller accommodation in another of their properties, were not prepared to agree.

Mr Fitzpatrick applied to the West London County Court for a determination that he was entitled to succeed to the tenancy of the flat. His application was given a careful and sympathetic hearing in the Central London Trials Centre by Judge Colin Smith QC, who on 19 April 1996 dismissed it with obvious reluctance, holding that he was constrained by law to treat him as being outside the statutory definitions of a person entitled to succeed on the death of a statutory tenant. From that decision Mr Fitzpatrick now appeals to this court.

The Rent Act 1977 provided that Mr Fitzpatrick could succeed to the tenancy if he was, in relation to the tenant, (a) a spouse, (b) someone living with him or her as wife or husband, (c) a member of his or her family residing with him or her in the dwelling house at the time of and for a period of two years before his death. The Court of Appeal, by a majority, decided that Mr Fitzpatrick fell within none of these three categories. Waite LJ discussed the relevant cases and explained:

If endurance, stability, interdependence and devotion were the sole hallmarks of family membership, there could be no doubt about this case at all. Mr Fitzpatrick and Mr Thompson lived together for a longer period than many marriages endure these days. They were devoted and faithful, giving each other mutual help and support in a life which shared many of the highest qualities to be found in heterosexual attachments, married or unmarried. To adopt an interpretation of the statute that allowed all sexual partners, whether of the same or opposite sex, to enjoy the privilege of succession to tenancies protected by the Rent Acts would, moreover, be consistent not only with social justice but also with the respect accorded by modern society to those of the same sex who undertake a permanent commitment to a shared life.

The survey which I have undertaken in this judgment shows, however, that the law in England regarding succession to statutory tenancies is firmly rooted in the concept of the family as an entity bound together by ties of kinship (including adoptive status) or marriage. The only relaxation, first by court decision and then by statute, has been a willingness to treat heterosexual cohabitants as if they were husband and wife. That was a restrictive extension, offensive to social justice and tolerance because it excludes lesbians and gays. It is out of tune with modern acceptance of the need to avoid any discrimination on the ground of sexual orientation. In that respect I wholly agree with the comments of Ward LJ. The question is: how is it to be put right?

Discrimination is not, unfortunately, the only arbitrary feature in this area of the law. Endemic within its system is a high risk of harsh or anomalous results – excluding from rights of succession many deserving instances of common households in which the survivor would have a strong moral case to succeed to the tenancy. Friends of long standing (widowers or spinsters for example) who share accommodation in old age without any sexual element in their relationship, but who often give and receive much the same kind of devoted care as we have admired in this case, are (and always have been) excluded. If succession rights are to be extended to couples of the same sex in a sexually based relationship, would it be right to continue to exclude friends? If friends are to be included, how is the stability and permanence of their household to be defined?

These questions have to be judged in the light of a further policy consideration – fairness to home-owners. Every enlargement of the class of potential successors to rent controlled tenancies involves a deeper invasion of rights of house-owners to possession of their own property. That there is a need to reconcile these competing social priorities is something on which it would be easy to find a broad consensus. The difficulty arises when it comes to finding ways and means. At that point opinions are bound to vary, and a political judgment may in the end become necessary. That is what makes the process of reconciliation a task better suited to the legislative function of Parliament than to the interpretative role of the courts.

The law of succession to Rent Act protected tenancies is, in short, arbitrary and discriminatory. No one today would attempt to defend the favour it accords, outside the marriage tie, to heterosexual relationships over same-sex households. Few would support the potential for unfairness involved in a law which gives automatic succession rights to wives (however faithless) and children (however feckless) and at the same time denies any hope of succession to friends, however devoted their loyalty to the joint household. The judge was nevertheless right, in my view, to resist the temptation to change a bad law by giving it a new linguistic twist. He correctly acknowledged that such changes could only be made by Parliament.

They are changes which will certainly need to be made, if Parliament is to fulfil its function of reflecting the spirit of our times – in particular the spirit which recognises the value of all abiding relationships, the heterosexual, the lesbian, the gay – or even those which are not sexually based at all. As the law now stands, however, I feel bound, notwithstanding the respect and sympathy to which Mr Fitzpatrick is entitled, to dismiss the appeal.

Ward LJ dissented. He discussed the courts' approach in earlier cases, and then went on to take a wider view:

I agree with Waite and Roch LJJ that we should not permit sociological evidence to be given to assist in finding the current ordinary meaning of the words we have to construe. That may come as some surprise to our brothers and sisters in Canada where very interesting developments are occurring, aided by the kind of expert evidence we have rejected. These developments have been made possible by the use of the Canadian Charter of Rights and Freedoms and the Canadian Human Rights Act 1985. We were referred to *A-G of Canada v Mossop* (1993) 100 DLR (4th) 658, where the issue was whether an individual in a long term homosexual relationship was properly denied bereavement leave payable to the members of a deceased employee's 'immediate family', which included a 'common law spouse' defined to mean a person of the opposite sex. The question was whether this was a prohibited discrimination on the grounds of 'family status'. The majority defined 'family' narrowly in terms of the traditional family being one composed of a married man and woman and their children. The minority (at 714) were prepared to take a broader view, because 'not all variables are present in any given family and there is no one variable that is present in all families'. In the view of the minority (at 705), a family might be 'two or more persons who share resources, share responsibility for decisions, share values and goals, and have commitments to one another over time'.

I have discovered that challenges along these lines have continued. In *Egan v Canada (A-G of Quebec, intervener)* (1995) 124 DLR (4th) 609 the issue was whether the younger partner of a homosexual couple should be treated as the elder's 'spouse' for the purposes of old age pension. Section 15 of the Charter prohibits discrimination based on 'race, national or ethnic origin, colour, religion, sex, age or mental or physical disability'. The court was unanimous in finding that sexual orientation was a ground of discrimination. La Forest J (at 619) said:

'. . . I have no difficulty accepting the appellants' contention that whether or not sexual orientation is based on biological or physiological factors, which may be a matter of some controversy, it is a deeply personal characteristic that is either unchangeable or changeable only at unacceptable personal costs, and so falls within the ambit of s. 15 protection as being analogous to the enumerated grounds.'

The court was divided as to whether this was in fact discrimination or not. In the judgment of four members of the court, per Cory J (at 677):

'. . . looking at the Act from the perspective of the appellants, it can be seen that the legislation denies homosexual couples equal benefit of the law. The Act does this not on the basis of merit or need, but solely on the basis of sexual orientation. The definition of "spouse" as someone of the opposite sex reinforces the stereotype that homosexuals cannot and do not form lasting, caring, mutually supportive relationships with economic interdependence in the same manner as heterosexual couples. The appellants' relationship vividly demonstrates the error of that approach.'

That might have been written with this appeal in mind.

This has been carried even further by the Ontario Court of Appeal in *M v H* (1996) 132 DLR (4th) 538, upholding the decision. That involved a claim made after the breakdown of a lesbian relationship in which one party claimed against the other interim and permanent support under the Family Law Act 1990, which defined 'spouse' to include a man and a woman who were not married to each other and had lived together in a 'conjugal relationship'. That definition was held to discriminate against those who lived together in a same-sex relationship and to escape censure, a 'man and a woman' who have cohabited together in a conjugal relationship should be read as 'two persons' who have cohabited together.

So far as the European Convention for the Protection of Human Rights and Fundamental Freedoms ... is concerned, the respondent in *Harrogate BC v Simpson* (1984) 17 HLR 205, having failed to get leave to appeal to the House of Lords, went to the European Commission of Human Rights. They held:

'As regards family life, the Commission recalls that it has already found that, despite the modern evolution of attitudes towards homosexuality, a stable homosexual relationship between two men does not fall within the scope of the right to respect for family life ensured by Article 8 of the Convention.'

As regards private life, the Commission accepted that the applicant's relationship did constitute a matter affecting their private life but, as the applicant then lived alone, there was no current interference. Even if there was a breach of her right to respect for her home, such interference was in accordance with the law and was necessary for the protection of the contractual rights of the landlord to have the property back at the end of the tenancy. The commissioner accepted that the treatment accorded to the applicant was different from the treatment she would have received if the partners had been of different sexes and accepted, it would seem, that sexual orientation was a sufficient ground of discrimination but the commission considered that the family (to which the relationship of a heterosexual unmarried couple living together as husband and wife can be assimilated) merited special protection in society and was therefore justified.

So far as I can check, the decisions upon which the court there relied were *X v UK* (1983) 32 D & R 220 and *Kerkhoven v Netherlands* App No 15666/89. I know of no later consideration of the position of gay and lesbian partners.

As I draft this judgment, I hear that *Grant v South-West Trains* begins its hearing before the Court of Justice of the European Communities to decide whether the applicant, a female employee, has been discriminated against on the grounds of sex in breach of the Equal Pay Act 1970, art 119 of the EC Treaty and/or the Council Directive (EEC) 76/207 on the implementation of the principle of equal treatment for men and women as regards access to employment, vocational training and promotion, and working conditions (the equal treatment directive). Her contract entitled her to certain travel concessions for:

'(a) the employee's spouse (ie legally married husband or wife) and (b) One common law opposite sex spouse, but in this case the applicant must make a statutory declaration that a meaningful relationship (ie living together) has existed for a period of two years or over.'

The applicant was refused the concession for her same-sex partner. The industrial tribunal referred the matter to the European Court to decide whether this discrimination based on sexual orientation is unlawful. Time will tell...

I note the resolution of the European Parliament on equal rights for homosexuals and lesbians in the European Community of 8 February 1994 (OJ C 61 28.2.94 p 40) to sweep away any unequal treatment based on sexual orientation. I note too how a number of European countries have begun moves in that direction by permitting same-sex couples to enter into agreements regulating their property and inheritance rights just as non-married heterosexual couples can do. This is allowed in Denmark, Norway, Sweden, Greenland, Iceland, Hungary and Holland. In the Australian Capital Territory, the Domestic Act 1994 has gone so far as to define 'domestic relationship' as—

'A personal relationship (other than a legal marriage) between two adults in which one provides personal or financial commitment and support of a domestic nature for the material benefit of the other, and includes de facto marriage.'

Denmark and Holland are debating gay marriage. The Supreme Court of Hawaii has ruled it unconstitutional to deny homosexuals the right to marry and the United States government has appealed that ruling to the Supreme Court. On the other hand, the New Zealand court has denied a claim by lesbians to be permitted to marry.

Interesting though these developments may be, they are no more than straws in the wind. Of much greater direct significance is the decision of the New York Court of Appeals in *Braschi v Stahl Associates Co* (1989) 544 NYS 2d 784. For those in the majority, it was fundamental that in construing the words of a statute 'the legislative intent is the great and the controlling principle'. They held (at 787):

> 'To accomplish its goals, the Legislature recognized that not only would rents have to be controlled, but that evictions would have to be regulated and controlled as well . . . The manifest intent of this section is to restrict the landowner's ability to evict a narrow class of occupants other than the tenant of record.'

They reached their conclusions (at 788-789) that:

> '. . . we conclude that the term family . . . should not be rigidly restricted to those people who have formalised their relationship by obtaining, for instance, a marriage certificate or an adoption order. The intended protection against sudden eviction should not rest on fictitious legal distinctions or genetic history, but instead should find its foundation in the reality of family life. In the context of eviction, a more realistic, and certainly equally valid, view of a family includes two adult lifetime partners whose relationship is long term and characterised by an emotional and financial commitment and interdependence . . . This definition of "family" is consistent with both of the competing purposes of the rent-control laws: the protection of individuals from sudden dislocation and the gradual transition to a free market system. Family members, whether or not related by blood or law, who have always treated the apartment as their family home will be protected against the hardship of eviction following the death of the named tenant, thereby furthering the Legislature's goals of preventing dislocation and preserving family units which might otherwise be broken apart upon conviction. This approach will foster the transition from rent control to rent stabilisation by drawing a distinction between those individuals who are, in fact, genuine family members, and those who are mere room mates.'

The minority did not appear to take great issue with that view of the purpose of the Act, but in their judgment (at 793):

> 'The State concerns underlying this provision include the orderly and just succession of property interests (which includes protecting a deceased's spouse and family from loss of their longtime home) and the professed State objective that there be a gradual transition from government regulation to a normal market of free bargaining between landlord and tenant.'

In the conclusion of the minority (at 793), however:

> 'Those objectives require a weighing of the interests of certain individuals living with the tenant of record at his or her death and the interests of the landlord in regaining possession of its property and re-renting it under the less onerous rent-stabilization laws. The interests are properly balanced if the regulation's exception is applied by using objectively verifiable relationships based on blood, marriage and adoption, as the State has historically done in estate succession laws, family court acts and similar legislation . . . Such an interpretation promotes certainty and consistency in the law and obviates the need for drawn out hearings and litigation focusing on such intangibles as the strength and duration of the relationship and the extent of the emotional and financial interdependency.'

These were powerful arguments both ways.

MY APPROACH TO THE QUESTION OF CONSTRUCTION

(1) I begin with the purpose of the 1977 Act, which is essentially to give tenants fair rents and a status of irremovability. ...

As Lord Greene MR had said earlier in *Cumming v Danson* [1942] 2 All ER 653 at 654, the Acts were 'for the protection of tenants and not Acts for the penalising of landlords'. The teleological interpretation supports the conclusion that there is no justification for limiting the class of persons entitled to the benefit of the 1977 Act on the basis that the interference with the landlord's right to possession should be curtailed because the Act has a penal effect: on the contrary, the broad purpose of the Act is to preserve the family home for tenants and their successors. Consequently, those who occupy the property as their home should wherever it is possible – but of course not beyond that – be given protection against eviction.

(2) As I have already explained, the words of this Act must be given their contemporary meaning. Professor Ronald Dworkin expressed the point well in *Law's Empire* (1986) p 348, when he said:

'[The judge] interprets not just the statute's text but its life, the process that begins before it becomes law and extends far beyond that moment . . . [the judge's] interpretation changes as the story develops.'

Since families are dynamic, the statutory interpretation must equally reflect the motive forces, physical or moral, affecting behaviour and change in domestic organisation. On reading Professor Zimmermann's article, 'Statutes and the Common Law: A Continental Perspective' [1997] CLJ 315 at 323, I realise, with some apprehension (but with some pleasure at the recollection of it), how close I am to a return to Celsus *The Digest of Justinian* D 1, 3, 17, whose rule of interpretation was 'Scire leges non hoc est verba earum tenere, sed vim ac potestatem': to know the laws is not a matter of sticking to their words, but of grasping their force and tendency.

(3) Since the inception of the Rent Acts in or before 1920, the home of members of the tenant's family has been preserved for them. As the decided cases show, the meaning of family has been progressively extended. The movement has been away from the confines of relationships by blood and by marriage to the reality of family life, and from de jure to de facto relationships ... The trend in the cases, as I see them, is to shift the focus, or the emphasis, from structure and components to function and appearance – what a family does rather than what it is, or putting it another way, a family is what a family does. I see this as a functionalist approach to construction as opposed to a formalist approach. Thus, whether the *Carega Properties* test is satisfied, ie whether there is 'at least a broadly recognisable de facto familial nexus', or a conjugal nexus, depends on how closely the alternative family or couple resemble the traditional family or husband and wife in function if not in precise form.

(4) We do not have (or should I say we do not yet have?) the equivalent of the Canadian Charter of Rights and Freedoms which enables the judges to strike down offensive discriminatory legislation. I must, therefore, be faithful to Parliament's sovereign will. Nevertheless, I am entitled to presume that Parliament always intends to conform to the rule of law as a constitutional principle and accordingly to respect the constitutional rights of the individual to enjoy equality under the law ... If, therefore, there is doubt about the ordinary meaning of the words of the statute, I would strain to place upon them that construction which produces a dignified result consistent with the purpose of the Act.

(5) To exclude same-sex couples from the protection the 1977 Act proclaims the inevitable message that society judges their relationship to be less worthy of respect, concern and consideration than the relationship between members of the opposite sex. The fundamental human dignity of the homosexual couple is severely and palpably affected by the impugned distinction. The distinction is drawn on grounds relating to their personal characteristics, their sexual orientation. If the law is as my Lords state it to be, then it discriminates against a not insignificant proportion of the population who will justly complain that they have been denied their constitutional right to equal treatment under the law.

(6) There being no remedy to cure such injustice, my approach will, therefore, be to say that if I find the statute ambiguous, or even if I were left in doubt as to its meaning, then I should err on the side of preventing that discrimination.

WAS THE APPELLANT LIVING WITH THE ORIGINAL TENANT AS HIS WIFE OR HUSBAND?

(1) 'As' means 'in the manner of' and suggests how the couple functioned, not what they were. I agree with the test of Woolf J in *Crake v Supplementary Benefits Commission, Butterworth v Supplementary Benefits Commission* [1982] 1 All ER 498 at 502 which, so far as I can tell, was not referred to this court in *Harrogate BC v Simpson* (1984) 17 HLR 205. There being no dispute but that the appellant and the deceased were living together, it is 'necessary to go on and ascertain in so far as this is possible, the manner in which and why they (were) living together in the same household'. If asked, 'Why?', would not both they and also the heterosexual couple equally well reply, 'Because we love each other and are committed to devote comfort and support to each other'? I can readily envisage that the immediate response to the question, 'How do you two live together?' may well be, 'As a gay couple'. But when the next question is asked, 'In what manner do you, a gay couple, live together?' would their answer be any different from that given by the heterosexual couple save only in the one respect that in their case their sexual relations are homosexual, not heterosexual? No distinction can sensibly be drawn between the two couples in terms of love, nurturing, fidelity, durability, emotional and economic interdependence – to name but some and no means all of the hallmarks of a relationship between a husband and his wife.

(2) With regard to the only distinguishing feature, sexual activity, that is a function of the relationship of a husband and his wife, a man and his mistress and it is a function of homosexual lovers. That the activity takes place between members of different sexes or of the same sex is a

matter of form not function. Since the test I would apply is functionalistic, the formalistic difference can be ignored.

(3) It was Parliament's will in 1996 that public sector homosexual partners enjoyed protection from eviction, albeit only by use of guidelines issued to the local authority. Given that the broad intention of the 1977 Act is to protect against the loss of one's home, then conferring protection by extending para 2(2) to include the homosexual partnership is to provide the private sector tenants with security comparable to their public sector counterparts. Since the Glenda Jackson amendment was withdrawn in order not to exclude the homosexual couple but to extend protection to others, I consider I am more likely to reflect Parliament's will by finding for the appellant than by finding against him.

(4) I would say there is no essential difference between a homosexual and a heterosexual couple and accordingly I would find that the appellant had lived with the deceased tenant as his husband or wife.

WAS THE APPELLANT A MEMBER OF THE ORIGINAL TENANT'S FAMILY?

(1) The Oxford English Dictionary (compact edn, 1979) defines family as:

'1. The servants of a house or establishment; the household; 2. The body of persons who live in one house or under one head, including parents, children, servants etc.; 3. The group of persons consisting of the parents and their children whether actually living together or not; in wider sense, the unity formed by those who are nearly connected by blood or affinity . . .'

Mr Chapman contends for the third meaning. This is the 'traditional' family. The moment one uses the adjective to qualify the noun, the clearer it is that the meaning is wide.

(2) Hoggett (Hale J), Pearl (Judge Pearl), Cooke and Bates state in their work *The Family, Law and Society* (4th edn, 1996) p 1:

'In the England of the 1990s, we must not assume that the answer to the question "What is a family?" is necessarily going to produce a simple and straight forward response . . .'

Should one not, therefore, also question the validity of a heterosexual stereotype for the family?

(3) The test has to be whether the relationship of the appellant to the deceased was one where there is at least a broadly recognisable de facto familial nexus. I would not define that familial nexus in terms of its structures or components: I would rather focus on familial functions. The question is more what a family does rather than what a family is. A family unit is a social organisation which functions through its linking its members closely together. The functions may be procreative, sexual, sociable, economic, emotional. The list is not exhaustive. Not all families function in the same way. Save for the ability to procreate, these functions were present in the relationship between the deceased and the appellant.

(4) Whilst there clearly is no right of self-determination it cannot be immaterial to have regard to the view the parties have of their own relationship. If the officious commuter on the Clapham omnibus had paid a visit to the deceased's household, asked all the relevant questions about their relationship and asked the deceased finally, 'What is Mr Fitzpatrick to you? Is he one of the family?', it seems to me to be inconceivable that the deceased would not have testily suppressed him by replying, 'Of course he is'. I doubt whether the ordinary man would be surprised by the answer as he apparently would have been hearing Ms Simpson. I am quite certain that he would not treat the answer as an abuse of the English language. Indeed, I am satisfied that the ordinary man is liberated enough to accept in 1997, or even in 1994, looking broadly at the appellant's life and comparing it with the other rich patterns of family life he knows, that the bond between the appellant and the deceased was de facto familial.

(5) I would therefore conclude that if, which is my preferred view, they were not living as a husband and his wife would live, then at least they were living as members of a family.

CONCLUSIONS

… In my judgment, our society has shown itself to be tolerant enough to free itself from the burdens of stereotype and prejudice in all their subtle and ugly manifestations. The common man may be vaguely disapproving of the homosexual relationship which is not for him but, having shrugged his shoulders, he would recognise that the relationship was to all intents and purposes a marriage between those partners. They lived a life akin to that of any husband and wife. They were so bound together that they constituted a family.

I would, for my part, answer both questions posed at the beginning of this judgment in the affirmative.

I have not reached this decision lightly. In truth, it has caused me a great deal of anxiety. I have worried that I have gone too far. If it is a matter for Parliament, and not for me, I hope Parliament will consider it soon. I have endeavoured to reflect public opinion as I see it but I am very conscious that public opinion on this topic is a continuum and it is not easy to see where the line is to be drawn. As Bingham MR said in *R v Ministry of Defence, ex p Smith* [1996] 1 All ER 257 at 263, [1996] QB 517 at 554: 'A belief which represented unquestioned orthodoxy in year X may have become questionable by year Y and unsustainable by year Z.'

I have come to a clear conclusion that *Harrogate BC v Simpson* was decided in year X; Waite and Roch LJJ, for reasons with which I could well have agreed, believe us to be in year Y whereas I have been persuaded that the discrimination would be thought by the broad mass of the people to be so unsustainable that this must by now be year Z. To conclude otherwise would be to stand like King Canute, ordering the tide to recede when the tide in favour of equality rolls relentlessly forward and shows no sign of ebbing. If I am to be criticised – and of course I will be – then I prefer to be criticised, on an issue like this, for being ahead of the times, rather than behind the times. My hope, to reflect the intent of this judgment, is that I am in step with the times. For my part, I would have allowed this appeal.

Mr Fitzpatrick's claim was eventually successful. The House of Lords ([2001] 1 AC 27, [1999] 4 All ER 705, [1999] 3 WLR 1113, [2000] 1 FCR 21, [2000] Fam Law 14) agreed with the Court of Appeal majority that the couple were not living as husband and wife, but followed the lead of Ward LJ in holding, by a majority, that Mr Fitzpatrick was a member of the tenant's family. Lord Slynn of Hadley, having discussed the facts and the legal background, came to the conclusion that Mr Fitzpatrick could not fall within the category 'spouse' or 'living with the tenant as husband or wife', because those categories required partners of different sexes. Was he a member of the tenant's family?

Given, on the basis of these earlier decisions that the word [family] is to be applied flexibly, and does not cover only legally binding relationships, it is necessary to ask what are its characteristics in this legislation and, to answer that question, to ask further what was Parliament's purpose. It seems to me that the intention in 1920 was that not just the legal wife but also the other members of the family unit occupying the property on the death of the tenant with him should qualify for the succession. The former did not need to prove a qualifying period; as a member of the tenant's family a two-year residence had to be shown. If more than one person qualified, then, if no agreement could be reached between them, the court decided who should succeed.

The hallmarks of the relationship were essentially that there should be a degree of mutual inter-dependence, of the sharing of lives, of caring and love, of commitment and support. In respect of legal relationships these are presumed, though evidently they are not always present, as the family law and criminal courts know only too well. In de facto relationships these are capable, if proved, of creating membership of the tenant's family. If, as I consider, this was the purpose of the legislation, the question is then who in 1994 or today (I draw no distinction between them) are capable in law of being members of the tenant's family. It is not who would have been so considered in 1920. In considering this question it is necessary to have regard to changes in attitude...

In *Barclays Bank plc v O'Brien* [1993] 4 All ER 417 at 431, [1994] 1 AC 180 at 198 Lord Browne-Wilkinson (with whom other members of the House agreed) said that in relation to the equity arising from undue influence in a loan transaction:

'But in my judgment the same principles are applicable to all other cases where there is an emotional relationship between cohabitees. The "tenderness" shown by the law to married women is not based on the marriage ceremony but reflects the underlying risk of one cohabitee exploiting the emotional involvement and trust of the other. Now that unmarried cohabitation, whether heterosexual or homosexual, is widespread in our society, the law should recognise this.'

In particular, if the 1988 amendment had not been made ('as his or her wife or husband') I would have no hesitation in holding today when, it appears, one-third of younger people live together unmarried, that where there is a stable, loving and caring relationship which is not intended to be merely temporary and where the couple live together broadly as they would if they were married, that each can be a member of the other's family for the purpose of the 1977 Act.

If, as I think, in the light of all the authorities this is the proper interpretation of the 1920 Act I hold that as a matter of law a same-sex partner of a deceased tenant can establish the necessary familial link. They are capable of being, in Russell LJ's words in *Ross v Collins*, 'a broadly recognisable de facto familial nexus' (see [1964] 1 All ER 861 at 866, [1964] 1 WLR 425 at 432). It is then a question of fact as to whether he or she does establish the necessary link.

It is accordingly not necessary to consider the alternative question as to whether by 1999 the meaning of the word in the 1920 Act needs to be updated. I prefer to say that it is not the meaning which has changed but that those who are capable of falling within the words have changed.

We have been referred to a number of authorities in other jurisdictions. I wish to mention only two. Your Lordships' attention has been drawn to *Braschi v Stahl Associates Co* (1989) 544 NYS 2d 784. There the issue was as to the meaning of the New York City Rent and Eviction Regulations which provided that a landlord might not dispossess 'either the surviving spouse of the deceased tenant or some other member of the deceased's tenant's family who has been living with the tenant.' The majority of the New York Court of Appeals held (at 788-789):

> 'The intended protection against sudden eviction should not rest on fictitious legal distinctions or genetic history, but instead should find its foundation in the reality of family life. In the context of eviction, a more realistic, and certainly equally valid, view of a family includes two adult lifetime partners whose relationship is long term and characterized by an emotional and financial commitment and interdependence.'

In law therefore a same-sex partner of the deceased tenant was, it was held, able to qualify if he could produce the necessary evidence.

The second case to which I refer is *El-Al Israeli Airlines Ltd v Danilowitz* Case 712/94 (1994) vol 1 National Journal of Sexual Orientation Law 304. That was a case involving the provision of airline tickets for a married spouse and an unmarried cohabitant of a different sex. It was not provided to same-sex partners. Vice-Chief Justice Barak said:

> 'The benefit is thus provided to a lasting living-together partnership which displays a strongly tied up social relationship. It is therefore obvious, in my view, that to take this benefit away from homosexual spouses constitutes a discriminatory violation of the equality principle. The differentiating reason standing behind this decision has to do with sexual orientation. But this latter fact was both immaterial and unfair . . . Does a homosexual cohabitation differ from a heterosexual one, as far as partnership, unity and a social-cell relationship are concerned?'

I refer to these judgments in order to show the attitudes being adopted in other jurisdictions, and there are other examples. On the other hand, the Convention for the Protection of Human Rights and Fundamental Freedoms refers to family and family life in arts 8 and 12, and the Court of Human Rights has not so far accepted claims by same-sex partners to family rights. Leaving aside the fact that these cases are still in an early stage of development of the law and that attitudes may change as to what is acceptable throughout Europe, I do not consider that these decisions impinge on the decision which your Lordships have to take on a specific statutory provision

It seems to be suggested that the result which I have so far indicated would be cataclysmic. In relation to this Act it is plainly not so. The onus on one person claiming that he or she was a member of the same-sex original tenant's family will involve that person establishing rather than merely asserting the necessary indicia of the relationship. A transient superficial relationship will not do even if it is intimate. Mere cohabitation by friends as a matter of convenience will not do. There is, in any event, a minimum residence qualification; the succession is limited to that of the of the original tenant. Far from being cataclysmic it is, as both the county court judge and the Court of Appeal appear to recognise, and as I consider, in accordance with contemporary notions of social justice. In other statutes, in other contexts, the same meaning may or may not be the right one. If a narrower meaning is required, so be it. It seems also to be suggested that such a result in this statute undermines the traditional (whether religious or social) concept of marriage and the family. It does nothing of the sort. It merely recognises that, for the purposes of this Act, two people of the same sex can be regarded as having established membership of a family, one of the most significant of human relationships which both gives benefits and imposes obligations.

It is plain on the findings of the county court judge that in this case, on the view of the law which I have accepted, on the facts the appellant succeeds as a member of Mr Thompson's family living with him at his death.

On that ground I would allow the appeal.

Questions

(i) If Mr Fitzpatrick's partner had died in 1960, what would have been the result of the application to succeed to the tenancy? Would Mr Fitzpatrick have even bothered to apply?
(ii) Suppose Mr Fitzpatrick and Mr Thompson's relationship had been an unhappy one; or suppose it had not been monogamous; or suppose Mr Fitzpatrick had not given up his job to look after his partner; would Mr Fitzpatrick's appeal have succeeded?
(iii) Could you now give a legal definition of the family?

1.4   The human rights perspective

Following the implementation of the Human Rights Act 1998, most of the European Convention on Human Rights is incorporated into our domestic law. Of this long document, perhaps the articles most frequently in the minds of family lawyers are Arts. 8 and 12:

Article 8
1. Everyone has the right to respect for his private and family life, his home and his correspondence.
2. There shall be no interference by a public authority with the exercise of this right except such as is in accordance with the law and is necessary in a democratic society in the interests of national security, public safety or the economic well-being of the country, for the prevention of disorder or crime, for the protection of health or morals, or for the protection of the rights and freedoms of others.

This article was considered by the European Court of Human Rights in *Keegan v Ireland* (1994) 18 EHRR 342:

Keegan v Ireland (family life: adoption)
(1994) 18 EHRR 342, European Court of Human Rights

The applicant met his girlfriend in May 1986, and they began living together in February 1987. In February 1988, it was confirmed that she was pregnant. The conception was the result of a deliberate decision, and the couple had planned to marry. Shortly afterwards, however, the relationship broke down and they ceased to cohabit. After the child was born, she was placed for adoption by the mother without the applicant's knowledge or consent. The relevant provisions of the Adoption Act 1952 permitted the adoption of a child born outside marriage without the consent of the natural father. The applicant applied to the Circuit Court, under the Guardianship of Infants Act 1964, to be appointed as the child's guardian, which would have enabled him to challenge the proposed adoption. He was appointed guardian and awarded custody of the child. The decision of the Circuit Court was upheld by the High Court, but on appeal by way of case stated the Supreme Court ruled that the wishes of the natural father should not be considered if the prospective adopters could achieve a quality of welfare which was to an important degree better. The case was remitted to the High Court. On the rehearing a consultant psychiatrist gave evidence that if the placement with the prospective adopters was disturbed after a period of over a year, the child was likely to suffer trauma and to have difficulty in forming relationships of trust.

The High Court therefore declined to appoint the applicant as guardian. An adoption order was subsequently made.

Judgment of the court:

A. Applicability of Article 8

42. The Government maintained that the sporadic and unstable relationship between the applicant and the mother had come to an end before the birth of the child and did not have the minimal levels of seriousness, depth and commitment to cross the threshold into family life within the meaning of Article 8. Moreover, there was no period during the life of the child in which a recognised family life involving her had been in existence. In their view neither a mere blood link nor a sincere and heartfelt desire for family life were enough to create it.

43. For both the applicant and the Commission, on the other hand, his links with the child were sufficient to establish family life. They stressed that his daughter was the fruit of a planned decision taken in the context of a loving relationship.

44. The Court recalls that the notion of the 'family' in this provision is not confined solely to marriage-based relationships and may encompass other *de facto* 'family' ties where the parties are living together outside of marriage. A child born out of such a relationship is *ipso iure* part of that 'family' unit from the moment of his birth and by the very fact of it. There thus exists between the child and his parents a bond amounting to family life even if at the time of his or her birth the parents are no longer cohabiting or if their relationship has then ended.

45. In the present case, the relationship between the applicant and the child's mother lasted for two years during one of which they cohabited. Moreover, the conception of their child was the result of a deliberate decision and they had also planned to get married. Their relationship at this time had thus the hallmark of family life for the purposes of Article 8. The fact that it subsequently broke down does not alter this conclusion any more than it would for a couple who were lawfully married and in a similar situation. It follows that from the moment of the child's birth there existed between the applicant and his daughter a bond amounting to family life.

...

50. According to the principles set out by the Court in its caselaw, where the existence of a family tie with a child has been established, the State must act in a manner calculated to enable that tie to be developed and legal safeguards must be created that render possible as from the moment of birth the child's integration in his family (see, mutatis mutandis, the *Marckx v Belgium* judgment of 13 June 1979, Series A no. 31, p. 15, para. 31...). In this context reference may be made to the principle laid down in Article 7 of the United Nations Convention on the Rights of the Child of 20 November 1989 that a child has, as far as possible, the right to be cared for by his or her parents. It is, moreover, appropriate to recall that the mutual enjoyment by parent and child of each other's company constitutes a fundamental element of family life even when the relationship between the parents has broken down.

51. In the present case the obligations inherent in Article 8 are closely intertwined, bearing in mind the State's involvement in the adoption process. The fact that Irish law permitted the secret placement of the child for adoption without the applicant's knowledge or consent, leading to the bonding of the child with the proposed adopters and to the subsequent making of an adoption order, amounted to an interference with his right to respect for family life. Such interference is permissible only if the conditions set out in paragraph 2 of Article 8 are satisfied.

Held unanimously:

(i) that it was unnecessary to examine the Government's preliminary objection concerning the applicant's standing to complain on behalf of his daughter;

(ii) that the remainder of the Government's preliminary objections should be dismissed;

(iii) that Article 8 applied in the instant case and had been violated;

(iv) that Article 6(1) had been violated;

(v) that it was unnecessary to examine the applicant's complaint under Article 14;

(vi) that Ireland was to pay, within three months, IR£12,000 in respect of non-pecuniary and pecuniary damage, and in respect of costs and expenses, the sums resulting from the calculation to be made in accordance with paragraph 71 of the judgment.

Another decision on the unmarried family was and *Kroon v Netherlands* (1994) 19 EHRR 263. Not surprisingly, the case law of the European Court of Human Rights has continued to explore and develop the meaning of 'family life'. It is has done so by looking at particular relationships (grandparents/grandchildren: *Price v UK* (1988) 55 DR 1988; siblings: *Moustaquim v Belgium* (1991) 13 EHRR 802), and their nature in individual cases; for example, not all unmarried fathers will have family life with their children. In *K and T v Finland* [2001] 2 FLR 707, one of the many issues considered was the lawfulness of the removal of a newborn baby from her mother into emergency care, immediately after her birth; it was held that mother and baby had a family life, and that in this case their right had been interfered with:

[168] ... the taking of a new-born baby into public care at the moment of its birth is an extremely harsh measure. There must be extraordinarily compelling reasons before a baby can be physically removed from the care of its mother, against her will, immediately after birth as a consequence of a procedure in which neither she nor her partner has been involved. The shock and disarray felt by even a perfectly healthy mother are easy to imagine. The court is not satisfied that such reasons have been shown to exist in the present case in relation to the child J.

K and J were both in hospital care at the time. The authorities had known about the forthcoming birth for months in advance and were well aware of K's mental problems, so that the situation was not an emergency in the sense of being unforeseen. The Government has not suggested that other possible ways of protecting the new-born baby J from the risk of physical harm from the mother were even considered. It is not for the court to take the place of the Finnish child welfare authorities and to speculate as to the best child care measures in the particular case. But when such a drastic measure for the mother, depriving her absolutely of her new-born child immediately on birth, was contemplated, it was incumbent on the competent national authorities to examine whether some less intrusive interference into family life, at such a critical point in the lives of the parents and child, was not possible.

The reasons relied on by the national authorities were relevant but, in the court's view, not sufficient to justify the serious intervention in the family life of the applicants. Even having regard to the national authorities' margin of appreciation, the Court considers that the making of the emergency care order in respect of J and the methods used in implementing that decision were disproportionate in their effects on the applicants' potential for enjoying a family life with their new-born child as from her birth. This being so, whilst there may have been a 'necessity' to take some precautionary measures to protect the child J, the interference in the applicants' family life entailed in the emergency care order made in respect of J cannot be regarded as having been 'necessary' in a democratic society.

Questions

(i) Is the view of 'family life' developed by the European Court of Human Rights in *Keegan v Ireland* (1994) 18 EHRR 342, *Kroon v Netherlands* (1994) 19 EHRR 263 and *K and T v Finland* [2001] 2 FLR 707 different from your own understanding of what is meant by 'family life' and, if so, how does it differ?

(ii) To what extent is the understanding of the House of Lords different from that of the European Court? (See p. 26 above.)

As is clear from the above extract from *K and T v Finland*, the court (and of course the courts in this country) must consider not only whether or not there is family life but also whether or not it has been interfered with contrary to Art. 8 (2).

X,Y and Z v UK
[1997] 2 FLR 892, European Court of Human Rights

The application here was for a decision on whether or not the refusal to register X as the father of Z amounted to a violation of Art. 8. The facts are summarised by the court as follows:

(12) The applicants are British citizens, resident in Manchester, England. The first applicant, 'X', was born in 1955 and works as a college lecturer. X is a female-to-male transsexual and will be referred to throughout this judgment using the male personal pronouns 'he', 'him' and 'his'. Since 1979 he has lived in a permanent and stable union with the second applicant, 'Y', a woman born in 1959. The third applicant, 'Z', was born in 1992 to the second applicant as a result of artificial insemination by donor ('AID'). Y has subsequently given birth to a second child by the same method.

(13) X was born with a female body. However, from the age of 4 he felt himself to be a sexual misfit and was drawn to 'masculine' roles of behaviour. This discrepancy caused him to suffer suicidal depression during adolescence. In 1975 he started to take hormone treatment and to live and work as a man. In 1979 he began living with Y and later that year he underwent gender reassignment surgery, having been accepted for treatment after counselling and psychological testing.

(14) In 1990 X and Y applied through their general practitioner ('GP') for AID. ... In November 1991 the hospital ethics committee agreed to provide treatment as requested by the applicants. They asked X to acknowledge himself to be the father of the child within the meaning of the Human Fertility and Embryology Act 1990.

(16) On 30 January 1992 Y was impregnated through AID treatment with sperm from an anonymous donor. X was present throughout the process. Z was born on 13 October 1992...

(18) ... following Z's birth, X and Y attempted to register the child in their joint names as mother and father. However, X was not permitted to be registered as the child's father and that part of the register was left blank. Z was given X's surname in the register.

(19) In November 1995 X's existing job contract came to an end and he applied for approximately 30 posts. The only job offer which he received was from a university in Botswana. The conditions of service included accommodation and free education for the dependents of the employee. However, X decided not to accept the job when he was informed by a Botswanan official that only spouses and biological or adopted children would qualify as 'dependents'. He subsequently obtained another job in Manchester where he continues to work.

The court had to consider whether or not the applicants shared a family life; and, if so, whether or not the registration rules amounted to a failure to respect their family life:

The existence of 'family life'

(33) The applicants submitted that they had shared a 'family life' within the meaning of Art 8 since Z's birth. They emphasised that, according to the jurisprudence of the Commission and the Court, social reality, rather than formal legal status, was decisive. Thus, it was important to note that X had irrevocably changed many of his physical characteristics and provided financial and emotional support to Y and Z. To all appearances, the applicants lived as a traditional family.

(34) The Government did not accept that the concept of 'family life' applied to the relationships between X and Y or X and Z. They reasoned that X and Y had to be treated as two women living together, because X was still regarded as female under domestic law and a complete change of sex was not medically possible. Case-law of the Commission indicated that a 'family' could not be based on two unrelated persons of the same sex, including a lesbian couple... Nor could X be said to enjoy 'family life' with Z since he was not related to the child by blood, marriage or adoption.

At the hearing before the Court, Counsel for the Government accepted that if X and Y applied for and were granted a joint residence order in respect of Z, it would be difficult to maintain that there was no 'family life' for the purposes of Art 8.

(35) The Commission considered that the relationship between X and Y could not be equated with that of a lesbian couple, since X was living in society as a man, having undergone gender reassignment surgery. Aside from the fact that X was registered at birth as a woman and was therefore under a legal incapacity to marry Y or be registered as Z's father, the applicant's situation was indistinguishable from the traditional notion of 'family life'.

(36) The Court recalls that the notion of 'family life' in Art 8 is not confined solely to families based on marriage and may encompass other de facto relationships (see *Marckx v Belgium* (1979) 2 EHRR 330, § 31, *Keegan v Ireland* (1994) 18 EHRR 342, para (44) and *Kroon and Others v the Netherlands* (1994) 19 EHRR 263, § 30). When deciding whether a relationship can be said to amount to 'family life', a number of factors may be relevant, including whether the couple live together, the length of their relationship and whether they

have demonstrated their commitment to each other by having children together or by any other means (see, for example, the above-mentioned *Kroon and Others* judgment, loc cit).

(37) In the present case, the Court notes that X is a transsexual who has undergone gender reassignment surgery. He has lived with Y, to all appearances as her male partner, since 1979. The couple applied jointly for, and were granted, treatment by AID to allow Y to have a child. X was involved throughout that process and has acted as Z's 'father' in every respect since the birth... In these circumstances, the Court considers that de facto family ties link the three applicants.

It follows that Art 8 is applicable.

B. Compliance with Art 8

...

1. The arguments as to the applicable general principles

(38) The applicants pointed out that the Court had recognised in *The Rees Case* [1987] 2 FLR 111, para 47, that the need for appropriate legal measures affecting transsexuals should be kept under review having regard in particular to scientific and societal developments. They maintained that there had been significant development since that decision: in particular, the European Parliament and the Parliamentary Assembly of the Council of Europe had called for comprehensive recognition of transsexual identity ...; the European Court of Justice had decided that the dismissal of a transsexual for a reason related to gender reassignment amounted to discrimination contrary to Community Directive 76/207 (*P v S and Another (Sex Discrimination)* [1996] 2 FLR 347); and scientific research had been published which suggested that transsexuality was not merely a psychological disorder, but had a physiological basis in the structure of the brain ...These developments made it appropriate for the Court to re-examine the principles underlying its decisions in the above-mentioned *Rees Case* and *Cossey v UK* [1991] 2 FLR 492, insofar as they had an impact on the present problem. The Court should now hold that the notion of respect for family and/or private life required States to recognise the present sexual identity of post-operative transsexuals for legal purposes, including parental rights.

However, they also emphasised that the issue in their case was very different from that in *Rees* and *Cossey*, since X was not seeking to amend his own birth certificate but rather to be named in Z's birth certificate as her father. They submitted that the margin of appreciation afforded to the respondent State should be narrower in such a case and the need for positive action to ensure respect much stronger, having regard to the interests of the child in having her social father recognised as such by law.

(39) The Government contended that Contracting States enjoyed a wide margin of appreciation in relation to the complex issues raised by transsexuality, in view of the lack of a uniform approach to the problem and the transitional state of the law. They denied that there had been any significant change in the scientific or legal position with regard to transsexuals: despite recent research, there still remained uncertainty as to the essential nature of the condition

...

Like the applicants, they stressed that the present case was not merely concerned with transsexuality. Since it also raised difficult and novel questions relating to the treatment of children born by AID, the State should enjoy a very broad margin of appreciation.

(40) The Commission referred to a clear trend within the Contracting States towards the legal recognition of gender reassignment. It took the view that, in the case of a transsexual who had undergone reassignment surgery in the Contracting State and who lived there as part of a family relationship, there had to be a presumption in favour of legal recognition of that relationship, the denial of which required special justification.

2. The Court's general approach

(41) The Court reiterates that, although the essential object of Art 8 is to protect the individual against arbitrary interferences by the public authorities, there may in addition be positive obligations inherent in an effective respect for private or family life. The boundaries between the State's positive and negative obligations under this provision do not always lend themselves to precise definition; none the less, the applicable principles are similar. In both contexts, regard must be had to the fair balance that has to be struck between the competing interests of the individual and of the community a whole, and in both cases the State enjoys a certain margin of appreciation ...

(42) The present case is distinguishable from the previous cases concerning transsexuals which have been brought before the Court ..., because here the applicants' complaint is not that the domestic law makes no provision for the recognition of the transsexual's change of identity, but rather that it is not possible for such a person to be registered as the father of a child; indeed,

it is for this reason that the Court is examining this case in relation to family, rather than private, life.

(43) It is true that the Court has held in the past that where the existence of a family tie with a child has been established, the State must act in a manner calculated to enable that tie to be developed and legal safeguards must be established that render possible, from the moment of birth or as soon as practicable thereafter, the child's integration in his ... However, hitherto in this context it has been called upon to consider only family ties existing between biological parents and their offspring. The present case raises different issues, since Z was conceived by AID and is not related, in the biological sense, to X, who is a transsexual.

(44) The Court observes that there is no common European standard with regard to the granting of parental rights to transsexuals. In addition, it has not been established before the Court that there exists any generally shared approach amongst the High Contracting Parties with regard to the manner in which the social relationship between a child conceived by AID and the person who performs the role of father should be reflected in law ... Since the issues in the case, therefore, touch on areas where there is little common ground amongst the Member States of the Council of Europe and, generally speaking, the law appears to be in a transitional stage, the respondent State must be afforded a wide margin of appreciation ...

3. Whether a fair balance was struck in the instant case

(47) First, the Court observes that the community as a whole has an interest in maintaining a coherent system of family law which places the best interests of the child at the forefront. In this respect, the Court notes that, whilst it has not been suggested that the amendment to the law sought by the applicants would be harmful to the interests of Z or of children conceived by AID in general, it is not clear that it would necessarily be to the advantage of such children.

In these circumstances, the Court considers that the State may justifiably be cautious in changing the law, since it is possible that the amendment sought might have undesirable or unforeseen ramifications for children in Z's position. Furthermore, such an amendment might have implications in other areas of family law. For example, the law might be open to criticism on the ground of inconsistency if a female-to-male transsexual were granted the possibility of becoming a 'father' in law while still being treated for other legal purposes as female and capable of contracting marriage to a man.

(48) Against these general interests, the Court must weigh the disadvantages suffered by the applicants as a result of the refusal to recognise X in law as Z's 'father'.

The applicants identify a number of legal consequences flowing from this lack of recognition ... For example, they point to the fact that if X were to die intestate, Z would have no automatic right of inheritance. The Court notes, however, that the problem could be solved in practice if X were to make a will. No evidence has been adduced to show that X is the beneficiary of any transmissible tenancies of the type referred to; similarly, since Z is a British citizen by birth and can trace connection through her mother in immigration and nationality matters, she will not be disadvantaged in this respect by the lack of a legal relationship with X.

The Court considers, therefore, that these legal consequences would be unlikely to cause undue hardship given the facts of the present case.

(49) In addition, the applicants claimed that Z might suffer various social or developmental difficulties. Thus, it was argued that she would be caused distress on those occasions when it was necessary to produce her birth certificate.

In relation to the absence of X's name on the birth certificate, the Court notes, first, that unless X and Y choose to make such information public, neither the child nor any third party will know that this absence is a consequence of the fact that X was born female. It follows that the applicants are in a similar position to any other family where, for whatever reason, the person who performs the role of the child's 'father' is not registered as such. The Court does not find it established that any particular stigma still attaches to children or families in such circumstances.

Secondly, the Court recalls that in the UK a birth certificate is not in common use for administrative or identification purposes and that there are few occasions when it is necessary to produce a full length certificate.

(50) The applicants were also concerned, more generally, that Z's sense of personal identity and security within her family would be affected by the lack of legal recognition of X as father.

In this respect, the Court notes that X is not prevented in any way from acting as Z's father in the social sense. Thus, for example, he lives with her, providing emotional and financial support to her and Y, and he is free to describe himself to her and others as her 'father' and to give her his surname ... Furthermore, together with Y, he could apply for a joint residence order in respect of Z, which would automatically confer on them full parental responsibility for her in English law...

(51) It is impossible to predict the extent to which the absence of a legal connection between X and Z will affect the latter's development. As previously mentioned, at the present time there is uncertainty with regard to how the interests of children in Z's position can best be protected ... and the Court should not adopt or impose any single viewpoint.

(52) In conclusion, given that transsexuality raises complex scientific, legal, moral and social issues, in respect of which there is no generally shared approach among the Contracting States, the Court is of the opinion that Art 8 cannot, in this context, be taken to imply an obligation for the respondent State formally to recognise as the father of a child a person who is not the biological father. That being so, the fact that the law of the UK does not allow special legal recognition of the relationship between X and Z does not amount to a failure to respect family life within the meaning of that provision.

It follows that there has been no violation of Art 8 of the Convention.

Questions

(i)   Do you think that X should have been registered as Z's father?
(ii) Do you think Z has a right to know about her biological parentage? Or about X's gender reassignment?
(iii) Do you think X and Y should be able to get married? (Come back to this when you have read Chapter 2.)

Article 12 concerns marriage and family formation:

Article 12
Men and women of marriageable age have the right to marry and to found a family, according to the national laws governing the exercise of this right.

Clearly, being married is not the same as being a family; but marriage, and cohabitation, are important components of family life, and it is to them that we turn in the next chapter.

Bibliography

1.1   Definitions of 'household' and 'family'

We quoted from:
M. Chamberlain 'Brothers and sisters, uncles and aunts: a lateral perspective on Caribbean Families' in E.B. Silva and C. Smart (eds.), *The new family?* (1999) London, Sage, pp. 135–138.

F. Engels, *Origins of the Family, Private Property and the State* (1884) New York, Lawrence and Wishart, p. 244.

Judicial Studies Board, *Handbook on Ethnic Minority Issues* (1994, now 1995) chapter 6, paras 3.1–3.2.

P. Laslett and R. Wall, *Household and Family in Past Time* (1972) Cambridge, Cambridge University Press, pp. 28–30, 63, 64.

J. Lewis, 'Family Policy in the post-War period' S. Katz, J. Eekelaar and M. Maclean (eds.), *Cross Currents* (2000) Oxford, Oxford University Press.

L. Stone, *The Family, Sex, and Marriage in England 1500-1800* (1977) London, Weidenfeld and Nicholson, pp. 26-27, 102-104.

Additional reading
R. Ballard, 'South Asian Families' in R.N. Rapoport, M. Fogarty and R. Rapoport (eds.), *Families in Britain* (1982) London, Routledge.

J. Barrow, 'West Indian Families: An Insider's Perspective' in R.N. Rapoport,
M. Fogarty and R. Rapoport (eds.), *Families in Britain* (1982) London,
Routledge.

G. Driver 'West Indian Families: An Anthropological Perspective' in
R.N. Rapoport, M. Fogarty and R. Rapoport (eds.), *Families in Britain* (1982)
London, Routledge.

Judicial Studies Board's Equal Treatment Bench Book (1999): www.jsboard.co.uk/
etad/index.htm.

R. Oakley, 'Cypriot Families' in R.N. Rapoport, M. Fogarty and
R. Rapoport (eds.), *Families in Britain* (1982) London, Routledge.

S. Poulter, *English Law and Ethnic Minority Customs* (1986) London,
Butterworths.

1.2   Approaches to the history of the family

We quoted from:

M. Anderson, *Approaches to the History of the Western Family (1500-1914)*
(1980) London and Basingstoke, Macmillan, pp. 40, 51, 69.

M. Anderson (ed.), *Sociology of the Family* (1980) Harmondsworth, Penguin
Books, p. 81.

E. Shorter, *The Making of the Modern Family* (1975) New York, Basic Books;
(1977) London, Fontana, p. 38

L. Stone, *The Family, Sex, and Marriage in England 1500-1800* (1977) London,
Weidenfeld and Nicholson, pp. 26–27, 102–104.

K. Wrightson, *English Society 1580-1680* (1982) London, Routledge, an
imprint of Taylor & Francis Books Ltd, pp. 71, 103, 104.

A. Wilson, *Family* (1985) London and New York, Tavistock Publications,
pp. 78–81.

Additional reading

A. MacFarlane, *Origins of English Individualism: the Family, Property and
Social Transition* (1978) Oxford, Blackwell.

L.K. Berkner, 'Peasant Household Organization and Demographic Change
in Lower Saxony (1689-1766)' in R.D. Lee (ed.), *Population Patterns in
the Past* (1977) New York and London, Academic Press.

L. Fox Harding, *Family, State and Social Policy*, (1996) Basingstoke, Macmillan.

L. Stone, *Road to Divorce; England 1530-1987* (1990) Oxford, Oxford
University Press.

1.3   The law's response to the family

We quoted from:

E.B. Silva and C. Smart, 'The "New" Practices and Policies of Family Life'
in E.B. Silva and C. Smart (eds.), *The new family?* (1999) London, Sage
Publications Ltd, pp. 2–4.

A. McGlynn, 'The Europeanisation of family law' [2001] Child and Family
Law Quarterly 35.

Additional reading

M.A. Glendon, *State, Law and Family* (1977) Amsterdam, North Holland.

K. Boele-Woelki, 'The Road Towards a European Family Law' vol 1.1
Electronic Journal of Comparative Law (November 1997): www.ejcl.org/
11/art11-1.html.

S. Cretney and F.M.B. Reynolds, 'The limits of the judicial function' [2000] 116 Law Quarterly Review 181.

J. Dewar, 'The normal chaos of family law' [1988] 61 Modern Law Review 467.

A.L. James and M.P.M. Richards, 'Sociological perspectives, family policy, family law and children: Adult thinking and sociological tinkering' (1999) 21(1) Journal of Social Welfare and Family Law 23–29.

N. Wikeley, '*Fitzpatrick v Sterling Housing Association Ltd*: Same-sex partnerships and succession to Rent Act tenancies' [1998] Child and Family Law Quarterly 191.

1.4   The human rights perspective

Additional reading

C. Archbold, 'Family Law-Making and Human Rights in the United Kingdom' Mavis Maclean (ed.), *Making Law for Families* (2000) Oxford, Hart Publishing.

G. Douglas, *An introduction to Family Law* (2001) Oxford, Oxford University Press, pp. 41–57.

D. Feldman, 'The Developing Scope of Article 8 of the European Convention on Human Rights' (1995) 1 European Human Rights Law Review 265.

C. Lind, 'Perception of sex in the legal determination of fatherhood' [1997] Child and Family Law Quarterly 401.

H. Swindells, M. Kushner, A. Neaves, R. Skilbeck, *Family Law and the Human Rights Act 1998* (1998) Bristol, Jordans/Family Law.

Chapter 2

The legal structure of marriage and cohabitation

In this chapter we look at the way the law responds to marriage and to cohabitation; both, of course, are family relationships, and the question for the law to decide is how similar or different the two forms should be. We look first at the factual and legal background – at the patterns of marriage and cohabitation today, and the law's treatment of these different forms of partnership. Then we look for a definition of marriage. We also look at void and voidable marriage to discover the law's response to what it regards as improper or incomplete 'marriages'. In part 4 we move on to an examination of the options for the future legal development of cohabitation, looking in particular at the registered partnership in some other jurisdictions. Among those options are some based upon contract, and so finally we look at cohabitation contracts and their continuing relevance, and at the possible uses of contract within marriage.

2.1   The factual background

Early editions of this book had separate chapters on the legal structure of marriage and on the issue of cohabitation. However, we now treat cohabitation and marriage in a single chapter, echoing as it does the reality of how most people now run their lives.

'Cohabitation' is defined in *Social Trends 21* (1991) as 'living together as husband and wife without having legally married'. The following extract is from *Social Trends 32* (2002):

Partnerships
The pattern formation has changed since the mid-1970s, and although the majority of men and women still get married, the proportion of the population that are married is not as

large as it once was (Table 2.5). While the proportion of men and women who are married has been declining, the proportions who are cohabiting have been increasing, and the proportion living outside a partnership has also increased. In a combined estimation and projections exercise, undertaken by the Government Actuary's Department and the Office for National Statistics, it was estimated that there were just over one and a half million cohabiting couples in England and Wales in 1996 – representing about one in six of the adult non-married population. If current trends continue, the proportion of the population cohabiting would almost double from 12 per cent in 1996 to 22 per cent in 2021. The number of cohabiting men and women who are single is projected to increase by 130 per cent between 1996 and 2021.

Table 2.5 Proportion of the population by marital status[1] and gender[2]

Great Britain   Percentages

	1971	1981	1991	2000
Males				
Single	24	27	31	34
Married	71	66	60	53
Divorced	4	4	4	4
Widowed	1	3	6	8
All males[2]	100	100	100	100
Females				
Single	19	21	23	26
Married	65	61	56	52
Divorced	15	15	14	12
Widowed	1	4	7	9
All females[2]	100	100	100	100

1 Population estimates by marital status for 1971 are based on the 1971 Census and those for 1981 are based on the 1981 Census and have not been rebased using the 1991 Census.
2 Adults aged 16 and over.
Source: Office for National Statistics; General Register Office for Scotland

For non-married women aged under 60, the proportion cohabiting in Great Britain almost doubled from 13 per cent to 25 per cent between 1986 and 1998-99 and for men, more than doubled from 11 per cent to 26 per cent over the same time period. The longest time series on cohabitation exists for women aged 18 to 49. Between 1979 and 1998 the proportion of non-married women in this age group in Great Britain who were cohabiting almost tripled, from 11 per cent to 29 per cent. . . .

For some couples cohabitation may precede marriage, in the same way as a long engagement before marriage may have been customary in the past. Among couples about to marry, living together before marriage has become the norm rather than the exception and all but a few couples cohabit premaritally. Combined data from the 1996-97 and 1998-99 General Household Surveys show that for adults of all ages three in ten men and over a quarter of women in Great Britain who had ever been married had cohabited before their first marriage. The proportion who had cohabited with their future partner before their wedding increased with age at marriage. Around three-fifths of people who were aged 30 to 39 when they married for the first time had cohabited with their future partner (Chart 2.6).

An analysis undertaken using data from the British Household Panel Survey (BHPS) demonstrated that for women whose first partnership was a cohabitation which dissolved, almost all of those who repartnered cohabited in their second partnership. It was estimated that after a cohabiting first partnership had dissolved, the median duration to the next partnership was around five years.

Results from the 1998 BHPS indicate that nearly three-quarters of never married childless people aged under 35 who were cohabiting expected to marry each other (Table 2.7). Thus, for most people, cohabitation is part of the process of getting married and is not a substitute for marriage. About two-fifths of the cohabiting adults perceived advantages to just living together rather than marrying. Of the male cohabitants who did perceive there to be advantages, over half mentioned the idea of a trial marriage, compared with just over two-fifths of women. Around three in ten of both men and women mentioned the advantage of no legal ties. Only a small proportion (4 per cent of men and 8 per cent of women) reported the benefit of personal independence. Over half of the men and just over two-fifths of the women who perceived a disadvantage to cohabiting, cited financial insecurity as the reason. Almost a fifth of the women cited no legal ties as a perceived disadvantage of cohabiting, compared with less than a tenth of men. The social stigma of cohabiting was mentioned by less than 15 per cent of cohabiting men and women as a disadvantage.

Chart 2.6   Cohabitation prior to first marriage[1]: by age at first marriage and gender, 1996-1999[2]

Great Britain
Percentages

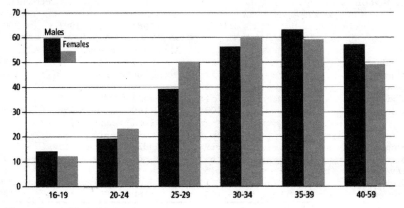

1   Those who cohabited with their future partner prior to their first marriage as a proportion of all ever married men and women.
2   Combined years: 1996-97 and 1998-99.
Source: General Household Survey, Office for National Statistics

Table 2.7   Marriage expectations of never married childless males and females aged under 35 in a cohabiting union, 1998

Great Britain   Percentages

	Males	Females
Planning to marry	30	25
Probably get married at some point	46	46
Probably just keep living together without marrying	14	18
Have not really thought about the future	8	8
Other[1]	3	4
All	100	100

1   Includes 'don't know' and refusals.
Source: British Household Panel Survey, Institute for Social and Economic Research

Cohabitation does not always result in marriage. In 1998-99 15 per cent of men and 13 per cent of women reported at least one cohabitation not leading to marriage. Cohabitation is not restricted not leading to marriage. Cohabitation is not restricted to periods before first marriage. Combined data from the 1996-97 and 1998-99 General Household Survey and Continuous Household Survey showed that 12 per cent of separated woman and 36 per cent of divorced women aged 25 to 34 were cohabiting.

Marriage in the European Union Today, a briefing of the National Family and Parenting Institute (March 2001), gives a European picture:

The European Picture
Who Marries When

United Nations research shows that in all parts of the world except the Caribbean, the percentage of adults under 50 who marry or cohabit as a partner in at least one relationship by the age of 49 is 85% or higher.

Interestingly, the United Nations figures for worldwide marriage include people who are in cohabiting partnerships. It seems that the vast majority of people in most of the world prefer to live as part of a couple for part of their lives. In Europe, though, there is a growing trend towards a longer lifespan with a larger proportion of years spent not living in a relationship – leaving individuals with more leisure time or the opportunity to pursue their own interests.

- In the European Union, the majority of couples with children are married while bringing up their children.
- In the UK, nine out of 10 couples living with their children are married, and just over half of the total adult population are married. Nearly a third of the adult population live alone or in a couple without children. As we move into the 21st century, most people will spend a much smaller part of their active life bringing up dependent children, more people will remain childless and the numbers of older people living alone will rise.
- In Scandinavia, 70% of families with children are married and 13% of families with children cohabit. In Finland, over half of all children are born into a family where the parents are married and over a third of children are born to cohabiting parents.

In the whole of the European Union, the numbers of people marrying each year has reduced by more than one-third since 1970 to five marriages per thousand of the population in 1998. The average age at which people first get married has increased over the same period – to almost 30 years of age for men and almost 27 years of age for women.

This recent trend represents a return to the picture in the pre-industrial Europe around 200 years ago, when the average age for a first marriage was about 27 years. In Britain, the generation of women born in the 1940s became brides at the earliest age ever recorded since registration began in 1837: 60% had married by the age of 23 years. In France, the average age for women to marry for the first time increased from 22 years in 1972 to 26 years in 1992. In Spain, there were 7.63 marriages per 1,000 people in 1972, but 5.55 marriages per 1,000 people in 1989.

The latest figures available for 1999 show that in England and Wales, the total number of marriages fell by 1.4% and the average age for marrying has increased to 28 years for women and 30 years for men.

However, marriage continues to be hugely popular.

Numbers of men and women marrying at least once in EU countries by the age of 49 as a percentage of the total population

Country	% men married at least once by age 49	% women married at least once by age 49
Austria	90.3	92.4
Belgium	91.3	94.7
Denmark	89.9	94.7
Finland	81.9	88.0
France	91.4	92.3
Germany	88.8	93.5
Greece	94.1	94.9
Ireland	83.8	89.9
Italy	90.2	92.5
Luxembourg	91.9	93.4
Netherlands	92.4	93.4
Portugal	95.4	93.1
Spain	89.9	91.9
Sweden	76.0	83.5
United Kingdom	91.2	95.1

Mary Ann Glendon, in 'Withering Away of Marriage' (1976), reflects on some of the reasons for the acceptance by society of informal arrangements:

Today, however, informal marriage is increasingly common among other social groups and, perhaps more significant, increasingly accepted. These two facts interact. The more persons in a particular group 'live together,' the more such behaviour becomes accepted. The more acceptance this alternative to formal marriage gains, the more people employ it. Thus, informal marriage has become a recurring subject in popular songs and cartoons and was discussed in the 1972 federal government report on population. Cohabitation is favored among young people, among pensioners and others receiving benefits terminable or reducible upon formal marriage, and increasingly among other diverse social groups. ...

Motivations to enter informal rather than legal marriage include economic advantages as in the case of many elderly people, inability to enter a legal marriage, unwillingness to be subject to the legal effects of marriage, desire for a 'trial marriage,' and lack of concern with the legal institution. This lack of concern is nothing new among groups accustomed to forming and dissolving informal unions without coming into contact with legal institutions. Among these groups legal marriage is but an aspect of the irrelevance of traditional American family law, law that is viewed as being property-oriented and organized around the ideals of a dominant social group. Lack of concern with marriage law has been growing, however, among many who definitely are not outside the mainstream of American life. Until recently these converts accepted unquestioningly the traditional structures of the enacted law, but they now find that on balance the enacted law offers no advantages over informal arrangements.

Helen Oppenheimer, in *Marriage* (1990), presents a thoughtful message from the liberal Christian viewpoint:

The harder moral argument is about relationships which are physical, emotional, social and even high-minded, but decline to be irrevocable. Once it is granted that sexuality is not as such unclean, why must it be confined so rigidly to matrimony? Why talk about 'fornication' at all, except perhaps for relationships which are irresponsibly ephemeral? Of course faithfulness is a good and life-enhancing thing, but must it be the only consideration? To answer these questions satisfactorily in a still traditional way one must keep one's head and consider the real good and the real harm in the partial commitments.

Sometimes what is missing is fairly clear: the relationship is simply one-sided and means more to one partner than to the other. Then we do well to wonder, though not triumphantly, whether somebody is being exploited or is presently going to be hurt. It is not moralistic to be convinced that such liberty to be unshackled does not constitute a moral breakthrough.

Nor is it moralistic still to look rather suspiciously for lopsidedness when the claim is made that options are being kept open: 'It would be nice if it lasted but if we get tired of one another it is nobody's else's business. So long as we are not irresponsible or inefficient enough to have a child, there is no question of blame or "immorality" if we live together for a while and then split up. Much better that than all the miserable struggle of divorce. We can try it out without getting too involved and see how we get on.' There is not much safeguard here for the emotionally weaker party against misery and bitterness not easily distinguishable from the misery and bitterness of divorce. To ask them how sure they really can be that they are totally at one in the degree of commitment is like asking a polygamist whether he can be quite sure of loving his wives equally. Practical experience is not altogether on their side.

Lovers sometimes part 'good friends'. They sometimes do after a broken marriage. But an advance promise of mature detachment is no more likely to be easy to keep in the end than an advance promise of faithfulness. How many people truly like it when their partners take care to keep their options open? This is the sort of freedom that is not so happy in the claiming as in the propounding. How many middle-aged women would want to allow the lovers of their youth to feel quite free to leave them, with no ill-feelings? Indeed how many fairly young women will go on being content with the condition they thought they could accept: no child?

Traditionalists who have taken the old morality for granted and lived contentedly by it all their lives torment themselves nowadays with the idea that this generation, maybe their own sons and daughters, are badly brought up and indeed immoral. They would be justified in forgetting the word 'fornication' but remembering these real questions about human happiness.

It is only fair to add, and even insist, that sometimes when people live together unmarried the commitment really is there, or is beginning to be there, and all that is lacking is the wedding ceremony. Instead of bandying about the idea of 'living in sin' a Christian would do well to consider honestly whether what we have here truly is a kind of marriage.

The standard way to make a marriage is a wedding. The couple take each other as husband and wife before witnesses. It is their consent that makes the marriage, not the ministrations of registrar or even priest. The wedding ceremony is a solemn way of making that consent public, and to ask for the blessing of family and friends and especially, for religious people, the blessing of God. But if what makes the marriage is consent, to dispense with the ceremony may not invalidate the consent.

There are a good many couples today who have seen the previous generation's notions about marriage and their ensuing ups and downs as hindrance rather than help. When people try to work out a different and more humanly satisfying way for themselves, it must be recognized that what they are engaged upon is a moral enterprise. At least in all seriousness let it not be nipped in the bud for the sake of respectability.

If we think, as well we may, that people who avoid formal commitment are living dangerously, we ought not to wash our hands of them but stand by to help pick up the pieces if necessary, which does not mean being ready to say 'I told you so'.

Question

Is this an argument in favour of providing cohabitation with the legal consequences of marriage?

Some cohabitants remain so simply because they do *not* want to become trapped with the legal implications of a marriage. But this is not the case for all.

Meade, in 'Consortium Rights of the Unmarried – Time for a Reappraisal' (1981), tends towards the view that there are a large number of interrelated reasons why couples opt out of traditional marriage. They include the following:

(1) a desire to avoid the sex-stereotyped allocation of roles associated with marriage;
(2) a belief that marriage is unnecessary or irrelevant if no children are involved;
(3) a reluctance to enter a supposedly permanent marriage;
(4) bohemian philosophy;
(5) a conscientious objection to state regulation of marriage;
(6) a desire to avoid the expense and trauma of a possible divorce;
(7) an insouciant outlook on legally sanctioned relationships;
(8) the desire for various forms of companionship;
(9) a trial period to test suitability for marriage;
(10) the need to share expenses in the face of long-lasting inflation.

One reason left out of Meade's list which will be relevant in some cases is simply that the parties are *unable* to marry because previous legal ties have not yet been broken.

Question

Do you think any of the reasons given by Meade to be more important than any other?

Susan McRae, in her book *Cohabiting Mothers* (1993), brings together the various factors influencing women's decisions *to* marry:

In contrast to the rising trend for cohabitation, the proportion of women aged under 50 who are married has slipped downwards at a steady pace – from 75 per cent in 1976, to just above one half – 53 per cent – in 1998, when the proportion cohabiting (amongst all women) appeared to increase at a faster rate.

To some extent this combination of rising and falling trends might be expected, since if the proportion of women who live in couples – whether married or cohabiting – remains roughly constant, an increase in the proportion cohabiting would be accompanied by a decline in the proportion married.

This feature, the proportion of all women who are either married or cohabiting, that is, the proportion of all women who are living in couples, is depicted in Figure 3. As may be seen, the trend is a moderately declining one, indicating that relatively fewer women have been living in a partnership in each successive year. Part of the explanation lies in the decline in the proportions of young men and women marrying – and amongst those who do marry, the postponement to older ages. Figure 3 indicates that the proportion of women aged under 50 who are single has grown from 17 per cent in 1976 to 30 per cent in 1998, a near doubling.

Percentage of women aged 18–49 who were: cohabiting; married; single, 1976–98, Great Britain

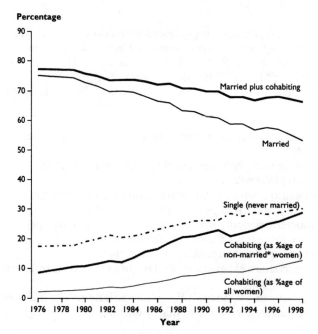

* Single + separated + divorced + widowed
Source: General Household Survey and 1976 Family Formation Survey

John Haskey's article, 'Co-habitation in Great Britain: past, present and future trends and attitudes' in *Population Trends 103* (Spring 2001), looks more closely at the married and cohabiting population by age:

Age

Cohabiting men and women are predominantly young – with the peak age-group for the number – and the *proportion* – cohabiting being the mid to late 20s. With cohabiting unions having grown at the expense of marriage, almost four in 10 non-married women aged between 25 and 29 were cohabiting in 1998, and over one third of those aged 30 to 34. The proportion was still over one quarter for women in their early 40s. The picture is broadly similar for men, although, age for age, the proportions are generally slightly higher ...

In order to consider long-term trends in cohabitation by age, it is easier to consider the numbers cohabiting out of the total number in the age group concerned – that is, including those who are currently married and living with their spouse. Proportions calculated on this alternative basis are inevitably lower, but with earlier estimates derived exclusively this way, comparisons are possible over a longer timespan.

Figures 5a and 5b depict the trends in these proportions (including estimates from the 1976 Family Formation Survey) – from which it may be seen that, in each age-group, for both men and women, there has been a consistent increase over the last quarter of a century. Furthermore, the *rate* of increase has in general been faster the younger the age-group, with the proportions cohabiting quintupling for women in their twenties. Just under one quarter – 23 per cent – of all women aged 20 to 24 were cohabiting in 1998, compared with 9 per cent in 1986. In addition, there is some evidence of a quickening of the rate of increase around 1993, although it is difficult to detect any changes at about that time in the proportions cohabiting by marital status.

One important factor which will have influenced these trends – particularly at the youngest ages – is the decline in the proportions of men and women who are married. Because, in the earlier years, relatively more in each age-group were married, the effect will be a greater 'dilution' of the numbers cohabiting in those years. This, in turn, will give the impression of a larger increase over the period in the proportion cohabiting than would be the case were the number cohabiting to be related to the number not currently married. Nevertheless, over the last 12 years, even on this latter basis, the proportion cohabiting has increased faster the younger the age-group – albeit not as fast as depicted in Figure 5.

Percentage of all women* who were cohabiting in each age-group, 1976–98, Great Britain

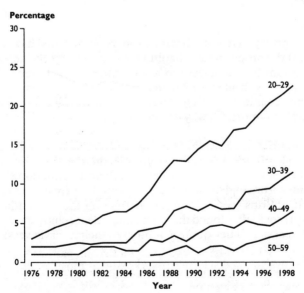

* all marital statuses, including married

Source: General Household Survey

Percentage of all men* who were cohabiting in each age-group, 1976–98, Great Britain

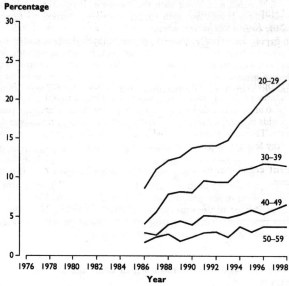

* all marital statuses, including married

Questions

(i)   Does it surprise you to note that the proportions married have consistently declined, whilst the proportions cohabiting have progressively increased?
(ii) Is it important for the lawyer to ask whether cohabitation is becoming: (a) institutionalised as an alternative to marriage; or (b) a new phase in a courtship process in which couples set up home before, rather than after, the 'paperwork'?
(iii) If you think it important, why do you think so?

   In *Family Affairs: Cohabitation, Marriage and the Law*, Anne Barlow, Simon Duncan, Grace Jones and Alison Park report on their research into attitudes to marriage and cohabitation, funded by the Nuffield Foundation (2002). They have found, not surprisingly, that there is increased acceptance of cohabitation across all strata of British society as both a partnering and a parenting structure. Equally unsurprisingly, they found that cohabiting relationships are most common among 25-34 year olds. They quote a number of their interviewees:

Melanie: '…Well, I don't know, after two marriages I feel that is what it's all about – it's you own me and I own you and what for? At least this way you know you're together because you love each other and you want to be together'.

Natasha: 'Living together you get on better. You really do – with marriage you own each other – with that bit of paper you are tied no matter what but living together it's easier…'

Pamela: 'It's like going to buy a car, you don't go and buy a car without test driving it, would you at the end of the day?'

Gail: '... the cost of everything stops us from getting married ... it's "what would you rather have, a new car or a wedding?" And now it's a conservatory'.

Some of their findings both confirm and challenge our assumptions; for example, in 'Just a piece of paper? Marriage and cohabitation', chapter 18 of *British Social Attitudes, the 18th Report: Public Policy, Social Ties* by A. Park, J. Curtice, K. Thomson, L. Jarvis and C. Bromley (eds.) (2001), Barlow and her colleagues report:

Earlier we saw that people's views about marriage and cohabitation vary according to social and demographic characteristics. So too does their behaviour. The next table shows the proportion of different groups who are either cohabiting or married. The most dramatic variation relates to age, with 25-34 year olds being the most likely to cohabit, over one in five doing so – more than twice the average rate. The very youngest are actually more likely to be cohabiting than to be married (although very few are either).

Table 2.10 Current cohabitation and marriage rates by age, religion and income source

	% cohabiting	% married	Base
All	9	56	3426
Age			
18-24	11	4	277
25-34	22	44	614
35-44	12	64	715
45-54	7	70	521
55-64	2	78	501
65+	1	55	791
Religion			
Church of England	7	63	1039
Catholic	8	55	331
Other Christian	5	59	560
Non-Christian	2	56	132
No religion	14	49	1344
Income source			
Earnings	13	61	1057
Pension	1	60	821
Benefits	7	30	213
Other	1	27	110

Not surprisingly, given its close association with attitudes to marriage, religion also makes a difference, with the non-religious being twice as likely as those belonging to religious groups to cohabit, and less likely to be married. The strength of this relationship is confirmed by multivariate analysis (shown in model C in the appendix to this chapter). This analysis also shows that the source of a household's income is associated with whether or not a person cohabits. In particular, those living in households whose main income source is earnings (as opposed to a pension or benefits) are more likely to cohabit than any other group.

Some commentators, especially those who argue that the family is 'breaking down', have claimed that cohabitation is concentrated among the less educated, less skilled and the unemployed (sometimes conceptualized as being part of a socially excluded 'underclass'). This in turn, it is argued, results in family breakdown and poor parenting. However, our results do not support this thesis. If anything, they contradict it, as we found that those whose income mainly comes from benefits are *less* likely than others to cohabit. Moreover, once we take account of age, religion and income source, there is no significant relationship between cohabitation and social class, education or whether a person is in work or not. Indeed, because of the relationship between age and qualifications, those who cohabit tend to be more highly qualified than those who do not.

Question

Why do you think people on benefit are *less* likely to be officially recorded as cohabiting?

Haskey goes on to look at future trends, and their implications:

Possible future growth in cohabitation

As has been noted earlier, there have been steady trends over the last quarter century, both in the increasing proportion cohabiting and the decline in the relative numbers married – and these trends seem set to continue ... A recent set of official projections of the population of England and Wales has been made by *de facto* marital status – that is, by both legal marital status and by whether or not cohabiting. The projections have a base year of 1996 and provide projected populations up to 2021...

The ... results can be brought together by considering the projected proportions of men and women in the different 'living arrangements': cohabiting; married, single and not cohabiting; and divorced or widowed and not cohabiting, for the adult population – those aged 16 and over... These show a projected increase in the proportions cohabiting and a continuing decline in the proportion married, accompanied by a slight increase in the proportion who are single and not cohabiting. In contrast, the proportion of those previously married who are not cohabiting is projected to remain virtually unchanged.

Another important implication of the projection results is the changing age profiles of those cohabiting, married, etc. Those who are cohabiting are projected to have an older profile – though the peak age group remains at 25 to 34 – as also are those who are married. ... In addition, the single who are not cohabiting are projected to become older, too. Of course, these results reflect the fact that the entire population is projected to age – what is of note is that the ageing applies to every group, no matter what their living arrangements.

Possible future numbers of cohabiting couples

The overall effect of the assumptions made is that the number of cohabiting couples, 1.56 million in 1996, is projected to rise to 2.93 million in 2021, an increase of almost 90 per cent. The best estimates of the numbers cohabiting in 1996 implied that 12 per cent, one in 8, of all couples were cohabiting, and the projection for 2021 implies that 22 per cent – more than one in 5 – of all couples will be cohabiting. ...

The implications of a growing number of cohabiting couples and their ageing

Until recently, we have become accustomed to thinking of cohabiting couples primarily as young couples without children, most of whom will either part company, or subsequently marry. Another group are those who have divorced and are living with a new partner, in an informal union. Many of these couples will not have any children at all, though some may have stepchildren either living with them or with a former spouse of one of the partners. Others will have children who are living with a former spouse or former partner.

The projections suggest that in the childbearing ages – those up to age 45 – the proportions of cohabiting men and women who are single will increase substantially, particularly amongst those in their thirties and early forties – and commensurately the proportion who are either separated or divorced will diminish. Such a trend may herald an increase in childbearing amongst cohabiting couples – resulting at least in a continuation of the trend towards relatively more families with dependent children being cohabiting couple families, and fewer being married couple families; possibly this trend could accelerate.

If this is so, issues such as the parental responsibility of unmarried fathers, contact by absent unmarried fathers with their children, and child support by unmarried fathers from cohabiting couples who have split up could become more important because of the increased numbers involved. In addition, there could be a trend towards relatively more stepfamilies being *cohabiting* couple stepfamilies, rather than married couple ones.

In addition, the projection results suggest that in the future, the proportion of all couples who are *cohabiting* couples will rise especially at the older ages – those over 50, and of pensionable age, for example. Issues such as pension entitlement, either on the death of one partner, or else at the time of the breakdown of the relationship could pose problems of equity, just as the corresponding issue of pension-splitting for divorced wives was one during the 1990s. Another current issue involving equity concerns the division of assets – and particularly property – in the event of relationship breakdown; the number of cohabiting couples with appreciable financial assets could increase as more reach the ages when mortgages have been paid off and capital accumulated.

Nevertheless, one factor that does not seem to weigh heavily – indeed, hardly to weigh at all – in the decision whether or not to marry is consideration of the legal consequences of marriage. In 'Why marry? perceptions of the affianced' (2001), Mary Hibbs, Chris Barton and Joanne Beswick record the following responses to their inquiries:

Table 7 – Influenced by legal consequences?

Influenced by legal consequences?	%
Influenced	3
Consideration	11
Not at all	86

Table 8 – Are cohabitants influenced by legal consequences of marriage?

Influenced by legal consequences?	Cohabitant %	Non-cohabitant %
Influenced	3	3
Consideration	11	11
Not at all	86	86

Table 9 – Are cohabitants influenced by legal consequences of marriage (gender)?

Influenced by legal consequences?	Male %	Female %
Influenced	2	4
Consideration	8	13
Not at all	90	83

The authors comment:

… we suspected that many respondents' indifference to the legal consequences of marriage arise from their view that by cohabiting they 'already have it all'. Another perception was that sharing household expenses resulted in property rights. One male respondent said that his cohabitant, who had moved into his property, had acquired an interest in the property because 'until we marry, she will be my common law wife. We have a daughter together. I intend to make a will before marriage, not after. A lawyer will not be necessary.'

Question

What advice would you give to that respondent? You might like to advise him generally, and specifically on s. 18 of the Wills Act 1837.

Cohabitants reveal equally disastrous ignorance of the law. Compare a respondent quoted by Ros Pickford, in *Fathers, marriage and the law* (1999):

Q: Do you have a pension?
A: Yes I do.
Q: And you get benefits on your death. Do you know who the benefits of that might go to when you die?
A: I think it would be my next of kin.
Q: Next of kin, and would you say that Kim [his partner] fell into that category under your pension scheme?
A: She probably would, I do have a will I must say at this point...
Q: And has that been made since you and Kim were living together?
A: No that was made before we were living together.
Q: So is she specifically provided for in your will?
A: No she's not actually.
Q: So, do you know what would happen to Kim financially if you did die?
A: Well actually, what actually happened was, everything is left, this was before I met Kim, to my parents...

2.2   The legal distinctions

Comprehensive advice to married and cohabiting couples about the legal consequences of their status would be quite lengthy. There are significant distinctions in the legal treatment of married and cohabiting partners, although we have of course come a long way from the position recorded by Blackstone in his *Commentaries on the Laws of England* (1765):

... By marriage, the husband and wife are one person in law: that is, the very being or legal existence of the woman is suspended during the marriage, or at least is incorporated and consolidated into that of the husband: under whose wing, protection, and *cover*, she performs every thing; and is therefore called in our law-french a *feme-covert, foemina viro co-operta*; is said to be *covert-baron*, or under the protection and influence of her husband, her *baron*, or lord; and her condition during her marriage is called her *coverture*. Upon this principle, of a union of person in husband and wife, depend almost all the legal rights, duties and disabilities, that either of them acquire by the marriage. ...

William Cobbett, in *Advice to Young Men and (incidentally) to Young Women* (1837) (quoted in A. MacFarlane, *Marriage and Love in England 1300-1840* (1986)) says:

[She] makes a surrender, an absolute surrender, of her liberty, for the joint lives of the parties: she gives the husband the absolute right of causing her to live in what place, and in what manner and what society, he pleases; she gives him the power to take from her, and to use, for his own purposes, all her goods, unless reserved by some legal instrument; and, above all, she surrenders to him her *person*.

As we can see from the quotations above, the common law 'incorporated and consolidated' the wife's legal existence into that of her husband. In *A Century of Family Law* (1957), Ronald Graveson sketched the legal position at common law in his introductory essay, 'The Background of the Century':

The English family in the years following Waterloo differed in many ways from the family of today. The husband was in a real sense the authoritarian head of the family, with very extensive powers over both person and property of his wife and children. But his right to inflict personal chastisement on his wife had greatly declined in importance since Blackstone had described it half a century before as one which the lower orders took seriously and cherished dearly. On marriage husband and wife became for many purposes one person in law, a doctrine of common law of great antiquity. In the words of a late nineteenth-century lawyer, 'The Creator took from Adam a rib and made it Eve; the common law of England endeavoured to reverse the process, to replace the rib and to remerge the personalities.' [de Montmorency (1897)]. On marriage all the wife's personal chattels became the absolute property of the husband, while the husband could dispose of the wife's leasehold property during his life and enjoyed for his own benefit her freehold estate during her life. Subject to the institution by the Court of Chancery of what was known as the wife's separate estate in equity, the married woman, both physically and economically, was very much in the position of a chattel of her husband. But her position was not completely black. The doctrine of the legal identity of husband and wife was never applied to its extreme limit. In the words of de Montmorency, 'The English judges were too reasonable to be logical, if they could possibly help it.'

In criminal law a presumption existed that a wife who committed a felony (other than the most serious ones) had been coerced by her husband. Civilly the husband was liable for torts, such as slander, committed by his wife, while rules of evidence prevented husband and wife bearing witness against one another in all but the most exceptional circumstances. Each of these aspects of the nineteenth-century relationship of husband and wife ... reflect the general position in the early nineteenth century when the relations of society were largely relations of status, that is, a legal position imposed by rules of general law by virtue of persons being in certain relationship with one another, such as husband and wife, parent and child, master and servant. The dominant character of these relationships was one of an often profitable guardianship to the person to whom the law gave control. But the idea of guardianship carried with it one of responsibility for the acts and defaults of what we may call the junior member of the relationship. Thus, while the husband obtained great economic advantages from marriage, he was liable to a great extent, both criminally and civilly, to suffer for the misdeeds of his wife, in a somewhat similar manner to that in which a master was and still is liable for the wrongful acts of his servant committed in the course of his employment.

It is clear that, so far as the law is concerned, one spouse no longer automatically predominates. However, the movement towards equality and joint responsibility has by no means been a simple process. It is worth reflecting upon the process by which the law eventually accepted that a man can be guilty of raping his wife:

R v Clarence
(1888) 22 QBD 23, 58 LJMC 10, 59 LT 780, 53 JP 149, 37 WR 166, 5 TLR 61, 16 Cox CC 511, High Court

Mr Clarence had been convicted of an assault upon his wife occasioning 'actual bodily harm' and of unlawfully and maliciously inflicting upon her 'grievous bodily harm'. It appears that Mr Clarence, to his knowledge, was suffering from a form of gonorrhea yet he nevertheless had marital intercourse with his wife without informing her of this fact. He infected her, and from this infection, it was claimed that his wife suffered grievous bodily harm. He was convicted, but he appealed successfully to the Queen's Bench Division against conviction. The case was considered by all of the thirteen judges: nine quashed the conviction and four dissented.

Hawkins J: ... The wife *submits* to her husband's embraces because at the time of marriage she gave him an irrevocable right to her person. The intercourse which takes place between husband and wife after marriage is not by virtue of any special consent on her part, but is mere submission to an obligation imposed upon her by law. Consent is immaterial.

A. L. Smith J: ... At marriage the wife consents to the husband exercising the marital right. The consent then given is not confined to a husband when sound in body, for I suppose no one would assert that a husband was guilty of an offence because he exercised such right when afflicted with some complaint of which he was then ignorant. Until the consent given at marriage be revoked, how can it be said that the husband in exercising his marital right has assaulted his wife? In the present case at the time the incriminated act was committed, the consent given at marriage stood unrevoked. Then how is it an assault?

The utmost the Crown can say is that the wife would have withdrawn her consent if she had known what her husband knew, or, in other words, that the husband is guilty of a crime, viz., an assault because he did not inform the wife of what he then knew. In my judgment in this case, the consent given at marriage still existing and unrevoked, the prisoner has not assaulted his wife.

Question

Would Mrs Clarence have been guilty of the offence charged against Mr Clarence if she had been suffering from venereal disease, or the AIDS virus, undisclosed to her husband?

The so-called 'marital immunity' to rape is allegedly based on the pronouncement of Sir Matthew Hale in *History of the Pleas of the Crown* (1976) vol. I, p. 629, where he said:

But the husband cannot be guilty of a rape committed by himself upon his lawful wife, for by their mutual matrimonial consent and contract the wife hath given up herself in this kind unto her husband, which she cannot retract.

In the Supreme Court of New Jersey in 1981, *State v Smith* 85NJ 193, 426A 2d 38 (1981), Pashman J commented on the issue of 'implied consent' in the following way:

... this implied consent rationale, besides being offensive to our valued ideals of personal liberty, is not sound where the marriage itself is not irrevocable. If a wife can exercise a legal right to separate from her husband and eventually terminate the marriage 'contract', may she not also revoke a 'term' of that contract, namely, consent to intercourse? Just as a husband has no right to imprison his wife because of her marriage vow to him, he has no right to force sexual relations upon her against her will. If her repeated refusals are a 'breach' of the marriage 'contract', his remedy is in a matrimonial court, not in violent or forceful self-help.

However, the Criminal Law Revision Committee, which produced its Report on *Sexual Offences* (15th Report) in 1984, recommended by a majority to retain the immunity in all cases except where the parties are living apart:

Arguments for retaining the present law in relation to married couples cohabiting at the time of the act of sexual intercourse

2.64 The majority of us, who would not extend the offence of rape to married couples cohabiting at the time of the act of sexual intercourse, believe that rape cannot be considered in the abstract as merely 'sexual intercourse without consent'. The circumstances of rape may be peculiarly grave. This feature is not present in the case of a husband and wife cohabiting with each other when an act of sexual intercourse occurs without the wife's consent...

2.66 There are also several grave practical consequences which would flow from an extension of the offence to all marriages and which might be detrimental to marriage as an institution. It is the common experience of practitioners in domestic violence cases that allegations of violence made by a wife against her husband are often withdrawn some days later or not pursued. Violence occurs in some marriages but the wives do not always wish the marital tie to be severed, whatever their initial reaction to the violence. Once, however, a wife placed the facts of an alleged rape by her husband before the police she might not be able to stop the investigation process if she wanted to. ... All of this, more likely than not, would be detrimental to the interests of any children of the family...

2.68 Nor would the actual investigation of the offence be easy. The fact of sexual intercourse having occurred would prove little unless it was allied to other evidence. ...

2.69 There are also other considerations ... Some of us consider that the criminal law should keep out of marital relationships between cohabiting partners – especially the marriage bed – except where injury arises, when there are other offences which can be charged.

The Law Commission, Working Paper 116, *Rape Within Marriage* (1990) find the view of the CLRC hard to accept:

4.20 First, and most fundamentally, if the rights of the married and the non-married woman are in this respect the same, those rights should be protected in the same way, unless there are cogent reasons of policy for taking a different course.

4.21 Second, it is by no means necessarily the case that non-consensual intercourse between spouses has less serious consequences for the woman, or is physically less damaging or disturbing for her, than in the case of non-consensual intercourse with a stranger. Depending on the circumstances the wife whose husband thrusts intercourse upon her may suffer pain from the act of intercourse itself; or the fear or the actuality of venereal or other disease; or the fear or the actuality of an unwanted pregnancy if because of the suddenness of the attack she has taken no contraceptive precautions or such precautions are unacceptable or impossible for medical reasons; and in the event of actual pregnancy a termination may be unavailable or morally offensive to her. All of these hazards may apply equally in the case of marital as of non-marital rape.

4.22 Third, we think that there is a danger that the CLRC underestimated the emotional and psychological harm that a wife may suffer by being subjected by her husband to intercourse against her will, even though on previous occasions she has willingly participated in the same act with the same partner...

4.23 Fourth, for a man to oblige his wife to have intercourse without her consent may be equally, or even more, 'grave' or serious as when that conduct takes place between non-spouses. In the case of the husband, he abuses not merely an act to which, as a matter of abstract principle, society attaches values, but the act that has been or should have been his means of expressing his love for his wife.

4.24 Fifth, in many cases where the husband forces intercourse on his wife they will be living in the same household, or at least she will be in some sort of dependent relationship with him. It is likely to be harder, rather than easier, for such a woman to avoid her husband's insistence on intercourse, since to do so she may for instance have to leave the matrimonial home. That is a further respect in which non-consensual intercourse by a husband may be a particular abuse.

The House of Lords eventually came to the rescue in *R v R* [1992] 1 AC 599. In this case, the appellant married his wife in 1984 and they had one son born in 1985. The wife left the matrimonial home in 1989 with their son as a result of matrimonial difficulties and went to her own parents' house. Three weeks later, the husband forced his way into his parents-in-law's house and attempted to have sexual intercourse with his wife against her will.

The husband pleaded guilty to attempted rape following the ruling by the trial judge that a man may rape his wife when the consent to intercourse has been revoked. His conviction was upheld by the Court of Appeal but he was granted leave to appeal to the House of Lords.

Lord Keith of Kinkel [After reviewing earlier case law, *R v Clarke* [1949] 2 All ER 448, *R v Miller* [1954] 2 QB 282, *R v O'Brien (Edward)* [1974] 3 All ER 663, *R v Steele* (1976) 65 Cr App R 22, *R v Roberts* [1986] Crim LR 188, and *R v Sharples* [1990] Crim LR 198, *R v C (Rape: Marital Exemption)* [1991] 1 All ER 755, *S v HM Advocate* 1989 SLT 469, *R v J (Rape: Marital Exemption)* [1991] 1 All ER 759, he concluded]: The position then is that that part of Hale's proposition which asserts that a wife cannot retract the consent to sexual intercourse which she gives on marriage has been departed from in a series of decided cases. On grounds of principle there is no good reason why the whole proposition should not be held inapplicable in modern times. The only question is whether section 1(1) of the Act of 1976 presents an insuperable obstacle to that sensible course. The argument is that 'unlawful' in the subsection means outside the bond of marriage. That is not the most natural meaning of the word, which normally describes something which is contrary to some law or enactment or is done without lawful justification or excuse. Certainly in modern times sexual intercourse outside marriage would not ordinarily be described as unlawful. If the subsection proceeds on the basis that a woman on marriage gives a general consent to sexual intercourse, there can never be any question of intercourse with her by her husband being without her consent. There would thus be no point in enacting that only intercourse without consent outside marriage is to constitute rape. ...

I am therefore of the opinion that section 1(1) of the Act of 1976 presents no obstacle to this House declaring that in modern times the supposed marital exception in rape forms no part of the law of England. The Court of Appeal (Criminal Division) took a similar view. Towards the end of the judgment of that court Lord Lane C.J. said, at p.1074:

> 'The remaining and no less difficult question is whether, despite that view, this is an area where the court should step aside to leave the matter to the Parliamentary process. This is not the creation of a new offence, it is the removal of a common law fiction which has become anachronistic and offensive and we consider that it is our duty having reached that conclusion to act upon it.'

I respectfully agree.

My Lords, for these reasons I would dismiss this appeal, and answer the certified question in the affirmative.

An attempt to take matters further to Europe spectacularly failed (*SW v UK; CR v UK* [1996] 1 FLR 434, [1996] Fam Law 275, ECtHR):

... the abandonment of the unacceptable idea of a husband being immune against prosecution for rape of his wife was in conformity not only with a civilised concept of marriage but also, and above all, with the fundamental objectives of the Convention, the very essence of which is respect for human dignity and human freedom.

Questions

(i)   What, if anything, do you think is meant by the phrase 'civilised concept of marriage'?

(ii)   Section 142 of the Criminal Justice and Public Order Act (1994) amends s. 1 of the Sexual Offences Act 1956 in the following way:

1. Rape of woman or man
(1)   It is an offence for a man to rape a woman or another man.
(2)   A man commits rape if —
(*a*)   he has sexual intercourse with a person (whether vaginal or anal) who at the time of the intercourse does not consent to it;
(*b*)   at the time he knows that the person does not consent to the intercourse or is reckless as to whether that person consents to it.
(3)   A man also commits rape if he induces a married woman to have sexual intercourse with him by impersonating her husband.
(4)   Subsection (2) applies for the purpose of any enactment.

Now that the House of Lords has spoken, why was there need for legislation?

The law of rape is just one area that has changed significantly in recent years. The issue today is three-fold: how much special status should be afforded to marriage? And how far should that status be extended to, or withheld from, co-habiting couples? And *which* co-habiting couples? Rebecca Bailey-Harris, in 'New families for a new society?' (in Stephen Cretney's *Essays for a New Millennium* (2000)) looks generally at the position of married couples and others:

The hierarchy of families in current family law
Not withstanding very considerable change in social patterns and an increasing recognition of moral pluralism, family law remains characterised by a hierarchy of family forms with differing levels of legal recognition. First position is retained by marriage, followed by heterosexual cohabitation, with the same-sex family a clear third. Unmarried cohabitation is usually confined by legislative definition to heterosexual cohabitation. Parliament has been coy and reluctant explicitly to recognise homosexual cohabitation per se, preferring to admit the partners' status (if at all) through some broader (and more neutral) categorisation of family relationship, or to leave the partners to their rights as single individuals. Conservative family values ideology did

not wholly disappear with the change of government which occurred in 1997. The present government finds itself on the horns of a perceived dilemma: how to promote equality and personal choice in family matters without appearing to undermine the sanctity of marriage? The dilemma manifests itself in a reluctance in government publications to be precise about policies towards different family forms as well as to introduce new primary legislation touching on 'family values' in the pre-election period. Considerable political difficulties (primarily in the House of Lords) have been encountered by the government in its attempts to modify the now notorious s 28 of the Local Government Act 1988 which prohibits the promotion of 'homosexuality as a pretended family relationship', although the problem may be short-lived if, as has been argued, the section breaches Art 10 of the ECHR (guaranteeing the right to freedom of expression).

Heterosexual cohabitation stands second in the legal hierarchy after marriage. However, heterosexual cohabitation outside marriage is not a *status* like marriage; rather, the approach of the legislature has been to confer certain consequences on the relationship. From a family law perspective, the recognition of unmarried heterosexual cohabitation is found in statutes governing inheritance, family provision, transfer of and succession to protected tenancies, and domestic violence. The statutory definition of the relevant relationship has to date drawn a strong analogy with the *consortium vitae* of marriage, making the de facto relationship the mirror equivalent of the de jure. Legislation uses the terminology of 'living together as husband and wife without being married to each other', a clear indication of intention to exclude same-sex cohabitation, although, as we shall see, same-sex partners may be recognised under an alternative (and broader) statutory definition within the same legislation.

Yet the policy of the current law is by no means coherent or consistent even in relation to heterosexual unmarried cohabitation; instead it displays confusion about the objectives of legal regulation and the State's attitude to this alternative to marriage. Where specific legislation exists, it sometimes confers rights virtually identical to those enjoyed by married couples; examples are found in fields of testator's family maintenance, protection from domestic violence by non-molestation orders and the transfer of certain protected tenancies. Moreover, under the child support legislation (strongly underpinned by the objective of protecting the public purse), the nature of the parents' relationship at the child's birth or conception is of little significance; the support obligation is founded simply on natural or adoptive parenthood, or on that arising from certain recognised procedures of assisted reproduction. In other instances, the statutory consequences conferred on unmarried heterosexual cohabitation differ (sometimes markedly, sometimes subtly) from those accorded to marriage. Thus, in relation to occupation orders under Part IV of the Family Law Act 1996 – in contrast to non-molestation orders within the same Part – there are statutory considerations which govern the exercise of the court's discretion to make orders in favour of non entitled cohabitants additional to those applying to spouses or former spouses, and there are further differences in the duration of the orders. For instance, in the absence of a marriage certificate or legal right to occupy, the nature and duration of a relationship is relevant, and no 'balance of harm test' applies. The general pattern of these seemingly complex provisions is to privilege at the same time both marriage and property or contractual rights. In relation both to occupation orders and to transfer of tenancies under the Family Law Act 1996, courts are required by s 41 to take into consideration the fact that cohabitants 'have not given each other the commitment involved in marriage' – a provision inserted at a late stage of the Act's troubled parliamentary history in order to secure its acceptance. The differences between marriage and heterosexual cohabitation are far less subtle when it comes to parental responsibility, one of the cornerstones of the Children Act 1989. Parental responsibility is not automatically conferred on the unmarried father, even one who has cohabited with the mother for many years before the child's birth; he must acquire it by registered agreement, or by court order. This apparent discrimination in the law (between married and unmarried fathers, and between unmarried fathers and mothers) has not escaped criticism; it is probable that a compromise reform will be introduced, giving automatic parental responsibility to those unmarried fathers who register at birth, but whether this happens before the coming election is open to doubt. It is unclear the extent to which reform will be compelled by the implementation of the Human Rights Act 1998; Strasbourg case-law has to date regarded some distinctions drawn in domestic law between married and unmarried fatherhood as justified.

There are significant aspects of the family rights of heterosexual cohabitants which the legislature has to date declined to address. In the areas of adoption and asset distribution on the breakdown of a relationship, heterosexual and homosexual cohabitants are in the same position of disadvantage. Only spouses are permitted to adopt jointly as a couple. An unmarried partner may adopt as a single person, and a residence order can confer parental responsibility on the other partner. The legislative restriction is founded on the assumption, simplistically stated in 1993 in the White Paper *Adoption: The Future*, that marriage is the preferred institution for the upbringing of children. Asset distribution between former cohabitants remains governed by the general law, with no equivalent of the adjustive ancillary relief jurisdiction exercisable on divorce under Part II of the Matrimonial Causes Act 1973. The situation is particularly unsatisfactory where property is not held in joint names (which gives rise to a presumption of equal beneficial ownership) and there is no written declaration of trust. The existence and quantum of the parties' beneficial interests are determined by equitable doctrines of trusts or proprietary estoppel. In the case of personal property, the trust may be express; for realty it must be resulting, implied or constructive. The fundamental problem in the context of family breakdown is that the equitable jurisdiction is by nature merely declaratory: its objective is the ascertainment of existing interests in property, not their fair distribution. Moreover the trust doctrines remain dominated by notions of agreement and common understanding, which can give rise to serious evidentiary problems. Both resulting and constructive trusts are restrictive in their recognition of the type of contribution which will bring an equitable interest into existence: there must be a financial contribution to the acquisition of property, and the wider range of contributions to family life is relevant only at the later stage of determining the quantum of the interest. The imperfections of these doctrines in reflecting the realities of a shared life are self evident. Furthermore, the general law, in contrast to Part II of the Matrimonial Causes Act 1973, does not take proper account of the future needs, nor of future resources such as pension entitlements. In sum, the general law governing property rights on the breakdown of unmarried cohabitation is inherently incapable of achieving the social objectives for which the statutory ancillary relief jurisdiction was designed more than three decades ago. The reluctance of successive governments to address the obvious need for reform is regrettable, and will be discussed further in the next section.

It is difficult to draw any conclusion other than that the current law lacks policy coherence or conviction...

When we turn to the homosexual family, the problem is not one of incoherence but of coyness and inaction by the legislature, which an orthodox conception of the judicial role is incapable of remedying. The homosexual family stands lowest in the hierarchy: its explicit recognition by legislation is very limited. Parliament has been reluctant to include the same-sex couple within the definition of cohabitation. In some limited contexts such as protection from violence and succession to tenancies, same-sex partnership (together with other relationships) has been included by statute within a category of association distinct from cohabitation. In other statutory contexts such as adoption, same-sex partners are treated as single persons. Asset distribution on the termination of same-sex partnership, along with heterosexual cohabitation, remains governed by the general law, the inadequacies of which have already been described. Occupation orders in favour of non-entitled applicants under Part IV of the Family Law Act 1996 are restricted to 'cohabitants' heterosexually defined, as is the transfer of tenancies. The judicial role in a field regulated by legislation is to interpret the law and not to make it. Nevertheless, within that constraint, judges in recent years have expressed recognition of the reality of personal commitment within the same-sex family, and have not been slow to draw the distinction between the interpretation of a statutory provision and the endorsement of its social policy.

Anne Barlow and her colleagues, in 'Just a piece of paper?' (see p. 45 above), report on the views of their respondents as to whether cohabitants (a) have and (b) should have the same rights in certain contexts as married partners. Their results are shown in the following table:

Table 2.11 Whether a cohabitant does and should have same rights as a married person in relation to financial support, property inheritance and parental consent

	Woman's right to Financial support after breakdown of relationship	Right to family home after death of partner	Father's right to consent to child's medical treatment
Current law	%	%	%
Does have	38	37	50
Does not have	54	53	38
Don't know	8	10	12

What should happen	%	%	%
Should have	61	93	97
Should not have	37	6	2
Don't know	2	1	1

Base: 3101

Note: England and Wales only

They comment:

One of the reasons given against reforming the law to give cohabitants the same rights as married couples is that it would be oppressive (Bailey-Harris, 1996; Freeman, 1984; Deech, 1980). Perhaps cohabitants are deliberately avoiding marriage-like regulation? If this is true, we would expect to find that cohabitants are *less* favourable than others of changes to the law. This is far from the case. In relation to financial support on marital breakdown and property inheritance, cohabitants were actually keener than others that cohabitants have the same rights as married people. For example, 70 per cent of current cohabitants thought that a cohabiting woman should have the same rights to financial support on relationship breakdown as a married woman, compared with 61 per cent of people overall. And a near unanimous 97 per cent of cohabitants thought that the woman living in the situation described in our second scenario should have the right to stay in the family home. There were no significant differences in the responses of men and women. Thus the wishes of cohabitants cannot be used as a particular obstacle to legal reform.

These findings show clearly that massive majorities believe the law should treat long-standing cohabitants in the same way as married couples and that this is particularly true among people who are themselves cohabiting. Disturbingly, substantial minorities believe the law already does so.

Questions

(i)   Do you think that cohabitants should be under a continuing duty to support each other?
(ii) If so, what form should that support take after the end of the relationship?

You should come back to this question when you have read Chapter 3 and considered the economic organisation of families.

2.3   The definition of marriage

Here we pause in our analysis of the different legal *consequences* of marriage and cohabitation, to ask 'what is a marriage, anyway?', and to remind ourselves that the answer to that question is not as straightforward as might appear in a jurisdiction with registry offices and marriage certificates.

C.C. Harris, in *The Family: an Introduction* (1979), expressed the problem in the following way: 'The inhabitants of Europe and America have an idea which they call marriage. People in other cultures have other ideas which are similar to, but not the same as, our ideas. Traditionally, the argument has been about how dissimilar the ideas have to get to force us to stop describing their ideas as "marriage".' E.R. Leach, in 'Polyandry, Inheritance, and the Definition of Marriage' (1955), argues that no definition can be found which applies to all institutions which ethnographers and anthropologists commonly refer to as marriage. Therefore he submits for consideration a definition based on a 'bundle of rights'. At least one part of the bundle must be present before the term 'marriage' can be used. The list, which according to Leach is not closed, is as follows:

A.   To establish the legal father of a woman's children.
B.   To establish a legal mother of a man's children.
C.   To give the husband a monopoly in the wife's sexuality.
D.   To give the wife a monopoly in the husband's sexuality.
E.   To give the husband partial or monopolistic rights to the wife's domestic and other labor services.
F.   To give the wife partial or monopolistic rights to the husband's labor services.
G.   To give the husband partial or total rights over property belonging or potentially accruing to the wife.
H.   To give the wife partial or total rights over property belonging or potentially accruing to the husband.
I.   To establish a joint fund of property – a partnership – for the benefit of the children of the marriage.
J.   To establish a socially significant 'relationship of affinity' between the husband and his wife's brothers.

In contrast with Leach, there are other scholars, of whom E. Kathleen Gough, in The 'Nayars and the Definition of Marriage' (1959), is representative, who argue that 'the status of children born to various types of union [is] critical for decisions as to which of these unions constitute marriage'. As a tentative definition that would have cross-cultural validity, and will fit the unusual cases such as that of the Nayar, Gough suggests: 'Marriage is a relationship established between a woman and one or more other persons which provides that a child born to the woman under circumstances not prohibited by the rules of the relationship, is accorded full birth-status rights common to normal members of his society or social stratum.' In a period before the British took control of India, Nayar women customarily had a small but not a fixed number of husbands. When a woman became pregnant, it was essential for one of those men to acknowledge probable paternity. The genitor, however, had no economic, social, legal or ritual rights, in nor obligations to, his children once he had paid the fees of their births. Their guardianship, care and discipline were entirely the concern of their matrilineal kinsfolk.

A slightly different way of looking at the problem is suggested by Harris (1979). He says that the major question is to consider *tasks*. The only significant question is the following: 'How do societies arrange for the orderly procreation and rearing of future generations and the transmission of material and cultural possessions?' Harris emphasises child rearing. We shall see later in Chapter 11 how judges in English courts have been preoccupied by similar considerations.

Question

How do you feel now about the different legal consequences of marriage and cohabitation in this jurisdiction?

Nevertheless, our legal system has been committed to a rigid distinction between partnerships that are and are not marriages. It is thus important to know what, in a formal sense, is and is not a marriage; the legal tool for that identification has been the law of nullity.

2.4 Void and voidable marriages; or, who can marry, and how not to marry

Sections 11 and 12 of the Matrimonial Causes Act 1973 (as amended) read as follows:

11. Grounds on which a marriage is void
A marriage celebrated after 31st July 1971 shall be void on the following grounds only, that is to say—
    (a) that it is not a valid marriage under the provisions of the Marriage Acts 1949 to 1986 (that is to say where—
        (i) the parties are within the prohibited degrees of relationship;
        (ii) either party is under the age of sixteen; or
        (iii) the parties have intermarried in disregard of certain requirements as to the formation of marriage);
    (b) that at the time of the marriage either party was already lawfully married;
    (c) that the parties are not respectively male and female;
    (d) in the case of a polygamous marriage entered into outside England and Wales, that either party was at the time of the marriage domiciled in England and Wales.
For the purposes of paragraph (d) of this subsection a marriage is not polygamous if at its inception neither party has any spouse additional to the other.

12. Grounds on which a marriage is voidable
A marriage celebrated after 31st July 1971 shall be voidable on the following grounds only, that is to say—
    (a) that the marriage has not been consummated owing to the incapacity of either party to consummate it;
    (b) that the marriage has not been consummated owing to the wilful refusal of the respondent to consummate it;
    (c) that either party to the marriage did not validly consent to it, whether in consequence of duress, mistake, unsoundness of mind or otherwise;
    (d) that at the time of the marriage either party, though capable of giving a valid consent, was suffering (whether continuously or intermittently) from mental disorder within the meaning of the Mental Health Act 1983 of such a kind or to such an extent as to be unfitted for marriage;
    (e) that at the time of the marriage the respondent was suffering from venereal disease in a communicable form;
    (f) that at the time of the marriage the respondent was pregnant by some person other than the petitioner.

We focus on three issues arising from this material, namely: who can marry? whom can I marry? and the questions surrounding voidable marriages under s. 12(b) and (c) of the Matrimonial Causes Act 1973.

2.4.1 Who can marry?

First, then, who can marry? Section 11(c), above, states that the parties must be respectively male and female. Same-sex marriage in this jurisdiction is not permitted. It was introduced in the Netherlands in 2001, along with legislation to enable a same-sex married couple to adopt a child (but not a child from outside the Netherlands). How did this come about? Kees Waaldijk, in 'How the road to same-sex marriage got paved in the Netherlands' (chapter 23 of R. Wintemute and Mads Andenas (eds.) *Legal Recognition of Same-Sex Partnership. A study of National European and International Law* (2001)) explains what he calls the 'law of small change':

Any legislative change advancing the recognition and acceptance of homosexuality will only be enacted,

- if that change is either perceived as small, or
- if that change is sufficiently reduced in impact by some accompanying legislative 'small change' that reinforces the condemnation of homosexuality.

Waaldijk goes on to explain the process in the Netherlands:

But even small changes take time. Originally the Government's aim was to let the marriage and adoption bills of 8 July 1999 become law by the end of 2000, so that they would enter into force in January 2001. The committee stages and plenary debates in both Houses of Parliament took a little more time than anticipated. The final vote in the Lower House was on 12 September 2000. The proposal to open up marriage was approved with a majority of 109 against 33 votes, and the adoption proposal with a similar but uncounted majority. On 19 December 2000, both bills gained an (uncounted) majority in the Upper House, and two days later the Queen and her State-Secretary for Justice, Mr M J Cohen, signed them into law.

In the meantime, a separate law was needed to adjust the language of other legislation to the opening up of marriage. This Adjustment Act introduces gender-neutral language into provisions that formerly used gender-specific words for parents and spouses (e.g. in the definitions of polygamy and half-orphans). The Act replaces the old rule, that the child benefit to which all parents are entitled is paid to the mother in the event of a disagreement between father and mother, by a gender-neutral rule; now the benefit office will decide to whom to pay the benefit in such circumstances. And the Act also specifies that an intercountry adoption will only be possible by different-sex married couples or by one individual (this is so because the authorities in the original country of the child would not allow it to be adopted by Dutch same-sex partners).

The Act on the Opening Up of Marriage, the Adoption Act and the Adjustment Act took effect on 1 April 2001. At the stroke of midnight the first four same-sex couples had their registered partnerships converted into full civil marriages. Later that month, 300 registered same-sex couples did likewise, and 82 unregistered same-sex couples married.

The passage of the marriage and adoption bills became possible because of the constant reduction in the Netherlands of the number of issues involved in the opening up of marriage, which made it into a topic that could be discussed in an orderly and reasonable fashion. In such an orderly discussion, it could more easily be established that there is hardly a reasonable argument against it. In fact, the debate could focus on whether there were any acceptable arguments against reducing the legal distinctions between same-sex and different-sex partners *a little further*.

The difference between the Netherlands and other jurisdictions in the world is that the debate in other jurisdictions remains burdened with all kinds of issues that really should be divorced from the notion of marriage: the position of churches, tax revenues, the burdens of social security, the influx of foreigners, the finances of pension funds, the upbringing of children, the plight of adoptive children, the integrity of family trees, etc. So what to mankind may seem a giant step—the opening up of the institution of marriage to same-sex couples—is, for the Dutch, only a small change.

Such a change seems still a long way off in this jurisdiction. Instead, debate has focused on the rights and needs of transsexuals.

In *Corbett v Corbett (otherwise Ashley)* [1971] P 83, [1970] 2 All ER 33, Ormrod J said: 'sex is clearly an essential determinant of the relationship called marriage, because it is and always has been recognised as the union of man and woman. It is the institution on which the family is built, and of which the capacity for natural heterosexual intercourse is an essential element.' Ormrod J defined a person's sex according to his birth, regardless of any sex change operation.

In *Rees v UK* (1986) 9 EHRR 56, [1993] 2 FCR 49, the applicant, who was born with all the physical and biological characteristics of the female sex, applied to the European Court of Human Rights contending that the UK Government was in breach of his right to respect for his private life under Art. 8 (see p. 27, above) and Art. 12 of the European Convention for the Protection of Human Rights and Fundamental Freedoms, in that the Registrar General refused to amend the birth certificate notwithstanding surgical sexual conversion under the National Health Service. Article 12 provides that: 'Men and women of marriageable age have the right to marry and to found a family, according to the national laws governing the exercise of this right.' The Court held that there was no violation of Art. 12 because that provision referred to the traditional marriage between persons of opposite biological sex.

Rees v UK was endorsed by the European Court of Human Rights in *Cossey v UK* (1990) 13 EHRR 622, [1991] 2 FLR 492, which was a male to female transsexual case. There were, however, strong dissenting opinions, in particular the joint dissent of Judges Palm, Foignel and Pekkanen:

5. When drafting Article 12 of the Convention the draftsmen probably had in mind the traditional marriage between persons of opposite biological sex as the Court stated in *Rees*. However, transsexualism was not at that time a legal problem, so that it cannot be assumed that the intention was to deny transsexuals the right to marry. Moreover, as we have tried to show above, there have been significant changes in public opinion as regards the full legal recognition of transsexualism. In view of the dynamic interpretation of the Convention followed by the Court, these social and moral developments should also be taken into account in the interpretation of Article 12.

Gender reassignment surgery does not change a person's biological sex. It is impossible for Miss Cossey to bear a child. Yet, in all other respects, both psychological and physical, she is a woman and has lived as such for years.

The fact that a transsexual is unable to procreate cannot, however, be decisive. There are many men and women who cannot have children but, in spite of this, they unquestionably have the right to marry. Ability to procreate is not and cannot be a prerequisite for marriage.

The only argument left against allowing Miss Cossey to marry a man is the fact that biologically she is considered not to be a woman. But neither is she a man, after the medical treatment and surgery. She falls somewhere between the sexes. In this situation a choice must be made and the only humane solution is to respect the objective fact that, after the surgical and medical treatment which Miss Cossey has undergone and which was based on her firm conviction that she is a woman, Miss Cossey is psychologically and physically a member of the female sex and socially accepted as such.

It should also be borne in mind that Miss Cossey has no possibility of marrying unless she is allowed to marry a man as she wishes. It would be impossible, both psychologically and physically, for her to marry a woman. There would certainly also be doubts as to the legality of a marriage of this kind.

6. For these reasons we are of the opinion that in the present case there is a violation of Articles 8 and 12 of the Convention.

Questions

(i) Is it only a matter of time before the European Court of Human Rights changes its mind about transsexuals? (Read *B v France* [1993] 2 FCR 145.)

(ii) And what do you think the Court would say about homosexuals having the right to marry?

(iii) Can transsexuals who are lesbian or gay after gender realignment marry? Should this be? (See C. Lind, 'Time for Lesbian and Gay Marriages' (1995) 145 New Law Journal 1553 and S. Whittle, 'An Association for as Noble a Purpose As Any' (1996) 146 New Law Journal 366.)

The latest UK case on transsexual marriage is *Bellinger v Bellinger* [2001] EWCA Civ 1140, [2002] 1 All ER 311, [2002] 2 WLR 411, [2001] 3 FCR 1, [2001] 2 FLR 1048, CA, where it was held that the law has not changed, and the criteria for the legal determination of gender remain those in *Corbett*. Note that such a marriage would be valid in some other jurisdictions, such as France, Germany and Italy. (Contrast the case of *W v W (Nullity: Gender)* [2001] 1 FLR 324, [2001] Fam Law 104; this was a case of physical inter-sex (ie where sex was indeterminate at birth), recognised in *Corbett v Corbett* as a situation that must be left until it came for decision. Charles J, in *W v W*, held that the respondent's marriage as a woman, following gender reassignment surgery, was not a nullity.) We give the last word on the issue of transsexual marriage to Thorpe LJ, in his dissenting judgment in *Bellinger*:

Conclusions
[144] The arguments for the Attorney General might be summarised into three principal propositions. (i) Expert medical evidence does not demonstrate that Mrs Bellinger is and always was female or that her medical treatment has changed her from male to female. (ii) The complexity of the issues surrounding transsexualism demand that the legislature bears the responsibility for introducing change rather than the judges. (iii) To accede to this petition would create enormous difficulties, even in the context of the transsexual's right to marry.[145] I will begin to express my conclusions on the present appeal by reviewing those three propositions.[146] The first may only be made good if regard is restricted to biological factors and physiological criteria. But in my view such a restricted approach is no longer permissible in the light of scientific, medical and social change. Leaving aside the possibility that one area of the appellant's brain may not be congruent with the other three biological factors that established her original sex, there can be no doubt that she suffered from gender identity disorder (within the DSM-IV and ICD-10 classifications) and has for many years been a psychological female. Her only remaining male feature is chromosomal. Post-operatively she has functioned sexually as a female having the capacity to consummate within the definition of sexual intercourse established by this court in *SY v SY (orse W)* [1963] P 37, [1962] 3 All ER 55. My approach reflects the views expressed in the sections above devoted to the expert evidence and the judgment of Ormrod LJ [in *Corbett*].[147] The second proposition demands a fuller response both because I have not touched on the point in earlier sections of this judgment and because it is in any event a point of real substance.[148] Of course judges must not usurp the function of Parliament ... But here we are asked to construe s 11(c), not previously construed (and so untrammelled by previous judicial effort) and to be construed in the light of moral, ethical and societal values as they are now rather than as they were at the date of first enactment or subsequent consolidation. Indeed the case rests on the construction of the single word 'female'. That Parliament intended some judicial licence seems clear to me from the absence of any definition within the statute and from the preceding debate ... (In my opinion nothing turns on the fact that Parliament adopted the words 'male' and ' female' instead of 'man' and 'woman' which the common law applied.)...
    ...My experience over the last ten years suggests how hard it is for any department to gain a slot for family law reform by primary legislation. These circumstances reinforce my view that it is not only open to the court but it is its duty to construe s 11(c), either strictly, alternatively liberally, as the evidence and submissions in this case justify.[152] I turn to Mr Moylan's third proposition, namely that any relaxation of the present clear-cut boundary would produce enormous practical and legal difficulties. I grant at once that to give full legal recognition to the transsexual's right to acquire (perhaps not irreversibly) his or her psychological gender gives rise to many wide-ranging problems, some profoundly difficult ... Indeed in reality such a development would almost certainly throw up additional problems as yet unforeseen. But we are not contemplating or empowered to contemplate such a fundamental development. That indeed can only be for Parliament. All we consider is whether the recognition of marriage should be denied to a post-operative male to female transsexual applying the decision in *Corbett v Corbett*. In that context difficulties are much reduced. We need concern ourselves only with those that arise from recognising marriages already celebrated and permitting the future celebration of marriages between parties one of whom is a transsexual seeking to satisfy the requirements of s 11(c) in his or her post-operative gender. The principal difficulty seems to me to stem from the emphasis that such a person will inevitably place on his or her psychological gender. If that, the fourth factor in the *Corbett* classification, is admitted to the decision making process, does it immediately become the trump factor? If so, why does it not operate immediately and without the reinforcement of medical treatment? Whilst conceding that any line can be said to be arbitrarily drawn and to lack logic, I would contend that spectral difficulties are manageable and acceptable if the right is confined by a construction of s 11(c) to cases of fully achieved post-operative transsexuals such as the present appellant. In assessing how formidable are the difficulties ..., we can surely take some comfort from the knowledge that within wider Europe many states have recognised the transsexual's right to marry in the acquired gender. Although different jurisdictions have adopted a widely differing range of responses... there seems to be no evidence that they have encountered undue difficulty in applying liberalised provisions. Furthermore we have the example of a common law jurisdiction, New Zealand, which has often legislated innovatively in the family law field ...

[155] Ormrod J's monumental judgment in *Corbett v Corbett* was undoubtedly right when given on 2 February 1970. It is only subsequent developments, both medical and social, that render it wrong in 2001. The major relevant medical developments are as follows. (i) In 1980 DSM-III introduced the diagnosis of transsexualism for gender dysphoric individuals who demonstrated at least two years of continuous interest in removing their sexual anatomy and transforming their bodies and social roles. In 1994 the DSM-IV committee replaced the diagnosis of transsexualism with gender identity disorder, denoting those with a strong and persistent cross-gender identification and a persistent discomfort with his or her sex or a sense of inappropriateness in the gender role of that sex. A similar classification is to be found in ICD-10. Gender identity disorder is a mental disorder, that is to say a behavioural pattern resulting in a significant adaptive disadvantage to the person causing personal mental suffering. The use of the formal diagnosis is an important step in offering relief, providing health insurance coverage, and generating research to provide more effective future treatments. All the above is derived from, and in the main directly quotes, the Harry Benjamin International Gender Dysphoria Association's Standards of Care for Gender Identity Disorders (Fifth Version, 1998) and provided for us in the Attorney General's bundle. (ii) The research of Professor Louis Gooren published in 1995 and 2000 suggests that gender dysphoria is not a purely psychological condition. His research suggests, but does not prove, that gender dysphoria has a physiological basis in the structure of the brain. The expert evidence in the present case suggests that support for the premise is growing in specialist medical circles... To make the chromosomal factor conclusive, or even dominant, seems to me particularly questionable in the context of marriage. For it is an invisible feature of an individual, incapable of perception or registration other than by scientific test. It makes no contribution to the physiological or psychological self. Indeed in the context of the institution of marriage as it is today it seems to me right as a matter of principle and logic to give predominance to psychological factors just as it seems right to carry out the essential assessment of gender at or shortly before the time of marriage rather than at the time of birth.

... Furthermore in 1989 the Parliamentary Assembly of the Council of Europe and the European Parliament adopted resolutions recommending that reclassification of the sex of a post-operative transsexual be made legally possible. In 1998 we introduced the European Human Rights Convention into our law. The Convention is founded upon the concepts of human dignity and human freedom. Human dignity and human freedom are not properly recognised unless the individual is free to shape himself and his life in accordance with his personality, providing that his choice does not interfere with the public interest...

[157] Of course social developments are scarcely capable of proof but judges must be sensitive to these developments and must reflect them in their opinions, particularly in family proceedings, if the law is to meet the needs of society. It is also, in my opinion, important that in this field law and medicine should move together in recognising and responding to disorder.

[158] Is there not inconsistency in the state which through its health services provides full treatment for gender identity disorder but by its legal system denies the desired recognition? As Judge Van Diijk pointed out in his dissenting judgment in *Sheffield and Horsham v UK* [1998] 3 FCR 141 at 168:

> 'Among the member states of the Council of Europe which allow the surgical re-assignment of sex to be performed on their territories, the United Kingdom appears to be the only state that does not recognise the legal implications of the result to which the treatment leads.'...

[160] The range of rights claimed by transsexuals falls across the divisions of our justice systems. The present claim lies most evidently in the territory of the family justice system. That system must always be sufficiently flexible to accommodate social change. It must also be humane and swift to recognise the right to human dignity and to freedom of choice in the individual's private life. One of the objectives of statute law reform in this field must be to ensure that the law reacts to and reflects social change. That must also be an objective of the judges in this field in the construction of existing statutory provisions. I am strongly of the opinion that there are not sufficiently compelling reasons, having regard to the interests of others affected or, more relevantly, the interests of society as a whole, to deny this appellant legal recognition of her marriage. I would have allowed this appeal.

2.4.2 Whom can I marry?

So much for 'Who can marry?' Now, whom can I marry? We turn our attention to prohibitions based on affinity and consanguinity. The Marriage Acts 1949 state that marriages between certain relatives are void. Rather than set out the wording of the schedule, we represent the prohibited degrees in diagram form. Note that the single lines refer to blood relationships only, while the double lines refer to relationships by blood *or adoption*:

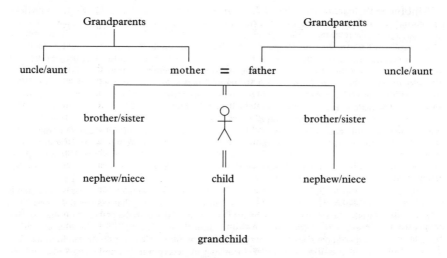

The surviving prohibitions based on affinity are laid down in the Marriage (Prohibited Degrees of Relationship) Act 1986, s. 1 and Sch. 1 as follows:

1.–(1) A marriage solemnized after the commencement of this Act between a man and a woman who is the daughter or granddaughter of a former spouse of his (whether the former spouse is living or not) or who is the former spouse of his father or grandfather (whether his father or grandfather is living or not) shall not be void by reason only of that relationship if both the parties have attained the age of twenty-one at the time of the marriage and the younger party has not at any time before attaining the age of eighteen been a child of the family in relation to the other party.

(2) A marriage solemnized after the commencement of this Act between a man and a woman who is the grandmother of a former spouse of his (whether the former spouse is living or not) or is a former spouse of his grandson (whether his grandson is living or not) shall not be void by reason only of that relationship.

(3) A marriage solemnized after the commencement of this Act between a man and a woman who is the mother of a former spouse of his shall not be void by reason only of that relationship if the marriage is solemnized after the death of both that spouse and the father of that spouse and after both the parties to the marriage have attained the age of twenty-one.

(4) A marriage solemnized after the commencement of this Act between a man and a woman who is a former spouse of his son shall not be void by reason only of that relationship if the marriage is solemnized after the death of both his son and the mother of his son and after both the parties to the marriage have attained the age of twenty-one.

(5) In this section 'child of the family' in relation to any person, means a child who has lived in the same household as that person and been treated by that person as a child of his family.

Part II
Degrees of affinity referred to in section 1(2) *and* (3) *of this Act*

Daughter of former wife	Son of former husband
Former wife of father	Former husband of mother
Former wife of father's father	Former husband of father's mother
Former wife of mother's father	Former husband of mother's mother
Daughter of son of former wife	Son of son of former husband
Daughter of daughter of former wife	Son of daughter of former husband

Part III
Degrees of affinity referred to in section 1(4) *and* (5) *of this Act*

Mother of former wife	Father of former husband
Former wife of son	Former husband of daughter

But most people do not marry their kin.

MacFarlane, in *Marriage and Love in England 1300-1840* (1986), provides historical background to the move from kinship marriages to what he refers to as 'free-floating' marriages:

... We may wonder when and how it originated. Is there any evidence in the period from the fifteenth to the nineteenth century of a transformation from the marriage system based on kinship rules, to the free-floating marriages based on psychology and economics which exist today? In answering the questions concerning the curious link between economics and demography raised by Malthus and Wrigley, we need to pursue this further. A marriage system embedded in kinship is close to biological restraints: marriage for women will very often be at or near puberty. Marriages will not adjust sensitively to economic changes, since they are mainly determined by kinship. Nor will there be space for personal psychological pressures. Likes and dislikes, love and passion, have no formal place where the decision about whom to marry is encoded in the kinship structure. ...

... Essentially one may marry all except members of the nuclear family and all those, including uncles and aunts, nephews and nieces, in the ascending and descending generations. First cousin marriage is now, as it was from 1540, legal, if often disapproved of. At marriage the couple became 'one blood'. Thus a man was forbidden from marrying the same range of wife's kin as of his own blood relatives. For instance, he could not marry his wife's aunt even though she was not a blood relative. The prohibitions continued after the spouse's death. Hence marriage with a deceased wife's sister was forbidden.

In the three centuries before 1540 the prohibitions were wider. By the decision of the Fourth Lateran Council of 1215, impediments of consanguinity and affinity were set at the fourth degree, according to the canonical computation. Thus a person could not marry his own or his wife's third cousin, or any nearer relative. Furthermore, wide rules of spiritual affinity prevented those related by godparenthood from marrying. On the other hand, dispensations were easily available, for a price, from the Church. There was a very limited prohibition in early Anglo-Saxon England, then a widening of the ring of prohibited persons, and then a narrowing again, so that England in 1540 returned to the situation that had prevailed in the seventh century. The change at the Reformation was important, but it was neither unprecedented nor indicative of a shift from 'elementary' to 'complex' structures. Indeed, by allowing all to marry first and second cousins without dispensation, the Reformers, if anything, encouraged a move towards the possibility of an elementary system. It is difficult to see how preferential kin marriages can have been enormously attractive and common when the whole weight of the Church forbade them.

More important in assessing the presence of kinship pressures are the positive rules. To prevent estates going out of the family, or to consolidate social, political and other ties, most societies are organized so that strong pressures are put on the individual stating which kin he should marry. To find a person standing in the right kinship relationship is one of the central tasks of an elaborate kinship vocabulary, as well as of the 'marriage brokers' who exist in many societies.

Questions

(i)   What do you see as the advantages of a preferential kin system?

(ii)   The criminal law prohibits only sexual intercourse between direct ascendants and descendants and brothers and sisters (Sexual Offences Act 1956, ss. 10 and 11): how would you account for the difference?

(iii)   Why should both parties to a marriage involving a step relationship have to be over 21 at the time of the marriage?

(iii)   'Child of the family' is defined as a child who has lived in the same household as that person and been treated by that person as a child of his family. Do you think that this restriction serves any useful purpose, and, if so, what purpose?

(v)   Do you agree that a marriage should only be possible between a man and his mother-in-law after the death of both the former wife and the father of the former wife? The father of the former wife may not necessarily have been married to the mother. Should this make a difference?

(vi) Do you believe that the changes which have been made to the bars based on affinity undermine the integrity of family life?

(vii) What justification is there for retaining any bars based on consanguinity or affinity?

The Law Commission, in their Report on *Nullity of Marriage* (1970), saw no need to change the law relating to consanguinity:

> 52(*a*) In so far as the question is biological, the answer depends on an evaluation of scientific evidence. The marriage of uncle and niece, or nephew and aunt is permitted in some countries and by some religions and it may well be that there is no such biological objection to these marriages as to justify legal prohibition. They may well be no more objectionable biologically than the marriage of a man with his grandparent's sister or of a woman with her grandparent's brother, which is not within the prohibited degrees.
>
> (*b*) Nevertheless, the question raises social and moral problems, the answer to which must depend on public opinion. Would public opinion tolerate or object to marriages between uncle and niece or nephew and aunt and, if it objects to such unions, does it wish to extend the prohibition to great-uncle and great-niece and great-nephew and great-aunt? Many people would no doubt instinctively hold the view that such marriages are unnatural and wrong, just as they would view with revulsion a marriage between brother and sister, even if there were no biological reasons against such a union. There are some matters of conviction on which men hold strong feelings of right and wrong though they cannot place their fingers on any particular reason for this conviction. It may be that such unions would be generally regarded as just as wrong as a marriage between adopter and adopted child – a union which is clearly considered objectionable although there cannot be any biological ground for this.

Question

Are there any objections to amending the law still further so as to permit marriages between uncle and niece or aunt and nephew?

2.4.3 Voidable marriages: s. 12(b) and (c)[1]

Singh v Singh
[1971] P 226, [1971] 2 All ER 828, [1971] 2 WLR 963, 115 Sol Jo 205, CA.

The wife was a 17-year-old girl from an orthodox Sikh family. She went through a ceremony of marriage in a Register Office with a 21-year-old Sikh boy. The marriage was arranged by her parents, and the bride had never seen the bridegroom before the actual ceremony of marriage. The plan was that there would be a religious ceremony of marriage and then the parties would commence living together. When the wife saw the husband at the Register Office, she did not like what she saw, and although she participated in the civil ceremony, she refused to go through with the religious ceremony or to live with the husband. She petitioned for a decree of nullity on two grounds, namely, duress and incapacity to consummate due to her invincible repugnance. Her petition was dismissed. Karminski LJ dealt with the issue of duress and continued:

> There is the alternative matter of repugnance. It is true that the wife never submitted herself to the physical embraces of the husband, because after the ceremony of marriage before the registrar it does not appear that she saw him again or went near him. Having taken the view which she did, that she did not want to be married to him, it is understandable that she did not want to have sexual intercourse with him; but that again seems to be a very long way from an

1. See p. 57 above.

invincible repugnance. True, as counsel for the wife argued, invincible repugnance can have a number of forms; and he reminded us of a decided case where the wife refused to undress when she went to bed so that the husband could not have intercourse with her. But here the wife abandoned the idea of her marriage altogether, and there is nothing of a psychiatric or sexual aversion on her part which is in any way established. In my view that ground of nullity fails completely.

Appeal dismissed.

In *Kaur v Singh* [1972] 1 All ER 292, the parties – both Sikhs – solemnised a civil ceremony of marriage which, in accordance with the custom of their community, was an arranged marriage. It was clearly understood by all that the civil ceremony would be followed by a religious ceremony, and that the parties would not cohabit prior to the religious ceremony. The husband failed to make arrangements for the religious ceremony, and the wife succeeded in obtaining a decree of nullity based on s. 12(b) of the Matrimonial Causes Act 1973, in that the husband's action (or inaction) amounted to wilful refusal to consummate the marriage.

Questions

(i) In *Kaur v Singh*, if the husband had attempted to consummate the marriage, would the wife have had a valid excuse?

(ii) Is there a difference between saying 'I can't' and 'I won't'?

(iii) What is the point of keeping alive, even for a short time longer, a marriage such as the one contracted in the *Singh v Singh* litigation?

(iv) It is clear that inability to consummate does not render the marriage void. Should it?

(v) Why should 'mistake' render a marriage merely voidable rather than void?

(vi) Should English law retain the concept of a voidable marriage in relation to s. 12(a) and (b) of the Matrimonial Causes Act 1973?

The Law Commission Report on *Nullity of Marriage* (1970) provides the following four reasons for retaining nullity of a voidable marriage:

24(*a*) It is not true to say that the difference between a nullity decree of a voidable marriage and a decree of divorce is a mere matter of form. It may be that the consequences of the two decrees are substantially similar, but the concepts giving rise to the two decrees are quite different: the decree of nullity recognises the existence of an impediment which prevents the marriage from initially becoming effective, while the decree of divorce records that some cause for terminating the marriage has arisen since the marriage. This distinction may be of little weight to the lawyer, but is a matter of essence in the jurisprudence of the Christian Church.

(*b*) The Church attaches considerable importance to consent as a pre-requisite to marriage. Consent to marriage includes consent to sexual relations and, hence, impotence can be regarded as having the effect of vitiating consent. Likewise, the grounds under section 9(1)(*b*), (*c*) and (*d*) of the Act of 1965 (mental disorder, epilepsy, pregnancy by another or venereal disease) can be considered to fall under the head of conditional consent [see now s. 12(*d*)(*e*)(*f*) Matrimonial Causes Act 1973] and are acceptable to the Church. Except with regard to wilful refusal to consummate, which the Church of England considers should cease to be a ground for nullity and be a ground for divorce, the Church is satisfied with the existing law of nullity. Therefore, so radical a change as is involved in the substitution of a decree of divorce for a decree of nullity in respect of matters which the Church regards as relevant to the formation of marriage and irrelevant to divorce, is likely to be unwelcome to the Church. It is also likely to be resented by people not necessarily belonging to the Church who associate a stigma with divorce and who would therefore prefer to see such matters as impotence and mental disorder, which are illnesses, remain grounds for annulling the marriage rather than causes for dissolving it.

(*c*) It may be that many people do not appreciate the distinction between divorce and nullity. They, presumably, would not oppose turning a nullity of a voidable marriage into a divorce. If, however, such a change is likely to cause offence to a substantial minority, then the proposal cannot be recommended unless some worthwhile advantage is to be gained from the change. The only advantage to be gained would be that one of the present voidable marriages (*i.e.*, one voidable for wilful refusal to consummate), might be thought by some to fit in more 'neatly' among divorces than among nullities.

(*d*)The assimilation of voidable marriages and dissolvable marriages could not be complete so long as we retained the bar on divorce within three years of the marriage. [This has now been changed: see p. 222 below.] Such a bar would be wholly inappropriate to nullity cases.

25.   We are therefore, opposed to the abolition of the class of voidable marriages and think that it should be retained. But the effect of the decrees of nullity of a voidable marriage should be modified so as to make it clear that the marriage is to be treated in every respect as a valid marriage until it is annulled and as a nullity only from the date when it is annulled.

On wilful refusal, in particular, they said:

(*a*)Wilful refusal to consummate is in most cases the alternative allegation to impotence as it is often uncertain whether the respondent's failure to consummate is due to one cause or the other; the petitioner may not know whether the respondent refuses to consummate the marriage because he is unable to have sexual intercourse or because, though able to have sexual intercourse, he does not want to have it; in such cases the court must draw an inference from the evidence before it and it seems unreal that the relief granted to the petitioner – nullity or divorce – should depend in any given case on the court's view as to which of the two reasons prevented the consummation of the marriage.

(*b*) Failure to consummate, whether it be because the respondent is unable or because he is unwilling to have sexual intercourse, deprives the marriage of what is normally regarded as one of its essential purposes. Parties would think it strange that the nature of the relief should depend on the court's decision whether non-consummation was due to the respondent's inability or whether it was due to his unwillingness. From the parties' point of view the relevant fact would be that the marriage had never become a complete one. To tell them that, in the eyes of the law, failure to complete it due to one cause results in their marriage being annulled, whereas such failure due to another cause results in their marriage being dissolved, would seem to them to be a strange result.

Questions

(i)   What advantages, other than those mentioned by the Law Commission, can you see for retaining the concept of nullity in this context?

(ii)   Do you agree with the four arguments referred to in the Law Commission Report generally?

(iii) Are the two arguments in relation to wilful refusal sufficient reasons by themselves to justify the retention of the present state of the law?

Hirani v Hirani
(1982) 4 FLR 232, CA

The wife was 19 and she was living with her parents. The family is Hindu. The girl became friendly with a young Indian Muslim, a Mr Husain. When the parents discovered this relationship, they immediately made arrangements for her to marry a Mr Hirani, who like them was a Hindu of the same caste and linguistic background. She had never seen this man nor had her parents. The judge recalled the pressure which was put on her by her parents to marry in this way: 'You want to marry somebody who is strictly against our religion; he is a Muslim, you are a Hindu. You had better marry somebody we want you to – otherwise pick up your belongings and go.' She married him, lived with him for six weeks and then left her husband and went to Mr Husain's house. Her petition for a decree of nullity on the ground of duress was dismissed. On appeal:

Ormrod LJ: The crucial question in these cases ... is whether the threats, pressure or whatever it is is such as to destroy the reality of consent and overbears the will of the individual. It seems to me that this case ... is a classic case of a young girl, wholly dependent on her parents being forced into a marriage with a man she has never seen in order to prevent her (reasonably from her parents' point of view) continuing in an association with a Muslim which they would regard with abhorrence. But it is as clear a case as one could want of the overbearing of the will of the petitioner and thus invalidating or vitiating her consent.
Appeal allowed.

Questions

(i)   Is it necessary to have genuine feelings of attraction or affection for a marriage to be valid in English law? What about arranged marriages?
(ii) The decision in *Hirani v Hirani* has not opened the floodgates to large numbers of nullity petitions on this ground; why not?

In August 1999 the Home Office Minister for Community Relations, Mike O'Brien MP, established a Working Group, chaired by Baroness Uddin of Bethnal Green and Lord Ahmed of Rotherham, to investigate the problem of forced marriage in England and Wales and to make proposals for tackling it effectively. The following short extracts from their report, *A choice by right*, give an indication of its scope and its message:

The difference between forced and arranged marriages
A clear distinction must be made between forced and arranged marriages. Many people expressed concern to the Working Group that this distinction was not being made, giving a false impression of arranged marriages.
The Working Group is clear that the distinction lies in the right to choose. In the tradition of arranged marriages, the families of both spouses take a leading role in arranging the marriage, but the choice whether to solemnize the arrangement remains with the spouses and can be exercised at any time. The spouses have the right to choose – to say no – at any time. In forced marriage, there is no choice.
The tradition of arranged marriage has operated successfully within many communities and many countries for a very long time and remains the preferred choice of many young people who spoke to the Working Group. This report is not about arranged marriage.

Cultural difference and forced marriage
In a multi-cultural, multi-faith society like the UK we must value and celebrate our diversity. Equally, we must not excuse practices that compromise or undermine the basic rights accorded to all people.
   'Multi-cultural sensitivity is not an excuse for moral blindness.'
   (Mike O'Brien, House of Commons Adjournment on Human Rights (Women) 10 February 1999)

Forced marriage in England and Wales
. . . The Working Group believes that forced marriage must be seen primarily as an issue of violence against women. It was clear from the consultations that it is women who most often live in fear and suffer violence as a result of forced marriage. The Working Group recognises that forced marriage affects men as well as women and that the experience of men who are forced

into a marriage should not be ignored. The Working Group also recognizes that both women and men perpetrate forced marriages.

Further work will be needed to address in more detail the needs of men who are forced into a marriage.

Most of the cases of forced marriage that the Working Group encountered involved young women, from teenagers to people in their early twenties. The Working Group heard of cases where girls under 16 years old were married abroad, despite not being legally capable of contracting a marriage in England and Wales. Many women forced into a marriage only sought help much later, when they had endured the relationship for several years. Family, social and economic pressures have all been cited as factors in a woman enduring an abusive relationship.

There is a spectrum of behaviours behind the term forced marriage, ranging from emotional pressure, exerted by close family members and the extended family, to the more extreme cases, which can involve threatening behaviour, abduction, imprisonment, physical violence, rape and in some cases murder. People spoke to the Working Group about 'loving manipulation' in the majority of cases, where parents genuinely felt that they were acting in their children and family's best interests.

> *'My parents said that I could go to University, but only if I agreed to marry a cousin from back home once I'd graduated.'*
> (*Young woman, Leeds*)

...

International dimensions

Forced marriages do not only happen in England and Wales. Several other countries are now looking at this issue. In April this year the Working Group met with representatives of the Norwegian Government who are currently implementing an action plan to tackle forced marriage. It is important that different countries are able to learn from each other as responses to forced marriage develop internationally.

Many of the cases brought to the Working Group's attention involved a spouse from overseas. A British national is either taken to live in their spouse's country (where they often have antecedents) or they are to act as a sponsor for their spouse's immigration to the UK.

Women described the fear that compelled them to support their spouse's immigration to the UK. Often family members had directly threatened them before their interview with an immigration officer. This fear prevented most women from putting on record that their marriage was forced.

Some women who had been brought to the UK for a forced marriage told the Working Group of the hardship they had suffered because of their unsound immigration status. Not being able to speak English and not having any family or friends to support them in the UK often added to these women's problems.

Some anecdotal evidence has been presented to the Working Group of cases where forced marriage has been deliberately used as part of a wider scheme to circumvent the immigration rules. These cases are not the norm.

The Working Group has heard of cases where a young woman has been taken (sometimes forcibly, sometimes through deception) overseas for the purposes of a forced marriage. Often these women reported having their documents, including passports, taken away from them on their arrival. In some cases, parents had taken the extreme action of drugging their daughter to ensure that she travelled overseas without complaint.

Cause and effect

While it is important to have an understanding of the motivations that drive parents to force their children to marry, this does not mean we should accept justifications for denying the right to choose a marriage partner. Motivations are complex and highly personal. It is important not to oversimplify when thinking about motivations – there will often be deeper reasons, which are not understood. These are some of the key motivations that the Working Group has heard about:
- peer group or family pressure
- attempting to strengthen family links
- protecting perceived cultural and religious ideals (which can often be misguided or out of date)
- preventing 'unsuitable' relationships (e.g. outside ethnic, cultural, religious or caste group)
- family honour
- long-standing family commitments
- controlling female behaviour and sexuality.

The Working Group has found that perspectives on motivations vary significantly between the parents themselves, their children and others outside of the immediate relationship.

Parents who forced their children to marry often justified their behaviour as building stronger families and protecting cultural or religious traditions – they did not see anything wrong with their actions. Many people felt that parents believed they were upholding the cultural traditions of their home country, when in fact practices and values there had moved on. They described a fossilization of cultural values within some families who had migrated to the UK. ...

Whatever the motivations, the consequences of a forced marriage can be devastating to the whole family. The victims of forced marriage suffer terribly, but parents, siblings, and the wider family members suffer too. Young women forced into a marriage often become estranged from their families. The impact on the children of a forced marriage is often that they themselves become trapped in the cycle of abuse with serious long-term consequences.

Preventing forced marriage
The Working Group has found that challenging and changing people's attitudes is the key to preventing forced marriage.

There is a general lack of awareness and understanding of individual's rights – both legal and religious – relating to marriage. Young people, their parents and families need to be educated about these rights and a dialogue needs to be facilitated between young people and their elders about their different expectations. For such a dialogue to be meaningful it would need to ensure that both young people and their parents are empowered to talk openly and safely about their expectations.

The Working Group acknowledges the importance of the role of opinion formers in developing an understanding of the right to choose. This includes anyone who is able to influence values, attitudes and behaviours. Religious and community leaders are key opinion formers, but the definition also takes account of local and national politicians, leaders of community and women's groups and many others who can make a difference.

The Working Group has heard people talk of their disappointment with many of these opinion formers who have failed to speak out against forced marriage because it was seen as a 'taboo' subject. People who have spoken to the Working Group have an expectation that opinion formers will send a clear and consistent message about the unacceptability of forced marriage. It is hoped that following this report, opinion formers will be in a more robust position to lead and send a clear message about the unacceptability of forced marriage.

A crucial area of misunderstanding that needs to be addressed is the effect on a family of a forced marriage. The Working Group has found that one of the main motivations for parents forcing their children into marriages is the desire to strengthen families and protect their cultures. In fact, the opposite is often the outcome, with families breaking apart and children turning against their cultural background because of their experiences. People who spoke to the Working Group felt that an understanding of the consequences of forced marriage would help prevent it happening.

Guiding principles for effective action to tackle forced marriage
The Working Group recommends these guiding principles that should be adopted in developing a response to forced marriage within any organization or area of service delivery.
- Commitment
- Safety and protection
- Sensitivity
- Involving communities
- Multi-agency working
- Monitoring
- Training
- Promoting awareness of rights and services.

Questions

(i) *A choice by right* notes that there are occasions ('not the norm') where forced marriages are used to circumvent immigration rules. Why do you suppose the Immigration and Asylum Act 1999 repealed s. 32 of the Marriage Act 1949, thus abolishing the concept of marriage by certificate after one day's notice, and substituting a requirement that all parties wanting to be married must give at least 15 days' notice to the registrar?

(ii) Section 24 of the Immigration and Asylum Act 1999 requires a marriage registrar to report to the Secretary of State if he has reasonable grounds for believing that a marriage will be, or is, a sham marriage; and a sham marriage is defined as one where at least one of the parties is not a British citizen nor a European national entitled to enter the UK, and entered into for the purpose of avoiding the effect of immigration law. How would the registrar spot such a marriage?

(iii) If a 'sham marriage' is solemnised, is it (a) valid, (b) voidable or (c) void?

2.5   Cohabitation: the options for the law

It should be obvious from what has been said already that neither marriage nor cohabitation is a monochrome institution; there are many different forms of partnership going under these two labels, and, across Europe, a number of different legal responses. The legal position is not static and there is constant pressure, from numerous lobbies, for change. In 'Displacing marriage – diversification and harmonisation within Europe' (2000), Rebecca Probert and Anne Barlow look at the options:

THE RANGE OF OPTIONS

At one end of the spectrum the law may insist that marriage alone should trigger legal rights. While this is no longer the predominant legal response, it does still find an echo in many legal systems. Even within those jurisdictions that have extended rights to cohabitants there remain certain rights that are reserved for married couples alone. At the opposite end of the range the law may take the approach that marriage by itself does not have any legal consequences and that it must be combined with other factors in order to have any effect on the legal rights of the parties. Within these two extremes, rights may be conferred on couples whose relationships display certain characteristics that are perceived as justifying the law's intervention, or upon those who have signified their commitment to one another by opting into a particular legal regime.

Marriage as the sole trigger for legal rights

The view that marriage should be the sole trigger for legal rights is encapsulated in the Napoleonic adage that 'cohabitants ignore the law, so the law ignores them'. Although the idea that cohabitation is 'immoral' has a dwindling number of adherents, there are many who believe that marriage forms the best basis for family life. It is possible to hold this view while tolerating the extension of rights to cohabitants, but it is often accompanied by a fear that this would undermine the status of marriage by encouraging more couples to cohabit. The extent of the influence of the Church is a major, although not always decisive, factor in the state's approach to this issue: religious opposition to the *pacte civil de solidarite* did not prevent the passage of legislation in France. However, such views are not confined to those with religious convictions... Such views continue to exert a strong hold. Certainly a single institution has the advantage of simplicity. However, the increase in couples choosing not to marry raises the question of how long this approach will remain feasible ... The argument that conferring rights on cohabiting couples causes the numbers of cohabitants to rise still further overlooks the fact that the legal change has generally followed demographic change. It also overstates the popular awareness of legal rights.

It should perhaps be noted that the idea that this is the 'traditional' approach of the law is rather misleading. Before the rise of the modern bureaucratic state made compliance with formal requirements an essential component of marriage, the laws of most countries elided marriage and cohabitation, in that cohabitation for a certain period was deemed to constitute a marriage. Thus, marriage only retained its claim to be the exclusive trigger for rights by converting certain relationships into marriages. It is also an argument that is sometimes selectively deployed, being used to justify the denial of rights in certain contexts, even though rights may have been granted to cohabitants in other areas of the law. Thus, in England and Wales the reliance that is placed on such arguments in justifying the lack of any adjustive regime to deal with property rights on the breakdown of the relationship overlooks the fact that rights are accorded where the relationship is terminated by death.

It is possible to reconcile the idea that marriage is the sole trigger for legal rights with some degree of protection of cohabitants, by employing status-neutral remedies under the general law. Thus the constitutional protection offered to marriage in Germany and Ireland does not preclude cohabitants acquiring property rights by means of an implied partnership or resulting trust. Cohabitants in England and Wales may also use trust law to claim rights over property. However, it would be an exaggeration to claim that such devices lead to the same results as if the parties had been married. Most demand either express agreement between the parties or financial contributions, which many cohabitants will be unable to establish.

Rights extended to those in relationships that resemble marriage

There is a long-standing debate concerning the weight to be given to the competing values of protection and respect for individual choice. Should rights and, more significantly, responsibilities be imposed on the basis that the relationship of a particular couple resembles the very relationship that they have chosen to avoid? ... While this argument has some validity, it assumes that an informed choice has been made. Given the widespread misunderstandings among cohabiting couples demonstrated in England and Wales – in particular a strong belief in mythical 'common law marriage' rights – this assumption perhaps needs to be reconsidered. ...

The requirement that couples should be living together 'as husband and wife' is often used to limit eligibility for certain rights. It offers both a justification for the extension of rights and a definition by which eligibility may be determined, namely the functional similarity between marriage and the cohabiting relationship under consideration. Even so, the extension of rights on this basis has tended to proceed in a piecemeal fashion. In particular, legislatures have tended to be less wary of extending rights to those whose relationships have been terminated by death, than those who have split up from their partner. In England and Wales a surviving cohabitant may apply for financial provision from the estate of a deceased partner or claim damages from the person who was responsible for the partner's death. The Portuguese Parliament has recently approved a proposal that deals with the ownership of the family home upon the death of the owner or tenant, and grants a survival pension to a person whose cohabitant is killed in a work accident. A bill dealing with inheritance rights was also debated in Italy recently.

Formulating eligibility in terms of the marriage model also means that same-sex couples have been excluded in the past ... The recent decision of the House of Lords in *Fitzpatrick v Sterling Housing Association Ltd* similarly indicates a willingness to recognise a same-sex couple as constituting a family, but not as a couple 'living together as husband and wife'.

Three reforms have taken a different approach on both of these points. Sweden and, more recently, the Spanish provinces of Aragon and Catalonia, have enacted wide-ranging reforms that deal with the issue of cohabitation in a holistic fashion and apply to both heterosexual and same-sex couples. All three pieces of legislation apply the terminology of marriage to both heterosexual and same-sex couples. In Sweden reform to this effect was achieved indirectly. The Homosexual Cohabitees Act 1987 simply provided that the provisions of the Cohabitees (Joint Homes) Act 1987 apply to homosexual couples without any further qualification. This presumably incorporates the requirement in the latter Act that the relationship of any couple claiming rights must be 'reminiscent of marriage'. The factors that the court will take into account in determining whether a relationship satisfies this definition include whether the parties have had children together, the length of time that they have been living together and whether they have shared daily housekeeping expenses. This imposes a higher threshold to be satisfied than a provision that merely conferred rights on cohabitants.

The approach taken by Aragon and Catalonia is rather more direct. The legislation confers rights on those in stable unmarried unions who live together as if they were married. It goes on to set out certain objective criteria by which this may be satisfied. In Aragon it is necessary to show either that the couple have made a notarised declaration in order to qualify for rights under the law, while rights will be accorded to a heterosexual cohabiting couple who have either lived together for two years, or have had a child together, or have made a declaration. In both cases the fact that the requirement of cohabitation for two years has been satisfied 'can be done through any means of proof admitted in law'. Thus these regimes combine elements of many of the reforms considered in this article, with it being possible to opt in to rights that may ultimately be conferred on account of the duration of the relationship.

These differences show that even where the same basic idea – the marriage model – underlies the way in which cohabitation is defined, there may still be substantial differences of approach. This impression is reinforced when one considers the substantive rights that are conferred upon cohabitants in each case. The idea of equality plays a far greater role in the Swedish legislation. Under the Cohabitees (Joint Homes) Act 1987, the value of property that was acquired for joint use will be divided equally between the parties at the end of the relationship. This principle of equal division is based on the idea that both parties are equally capable of earning their own living. It may be displaced by a written agreement between the parties, and a cohabitant may be entitled to retain more of his or her property if equal division would not be fair in the light of the duration of the relationship or other relevant circumstances. The needs of the parties play a relatively small role. The home or household goods will be allocated to the cohabitant who needs such property most, but there will be a corresponding deduction from his or her share if it is of any value. Moreover, where the property originally belonged to the other cohabitant it must also be considered whether it is reasonable for the property to be allocated in this way.

By contrast, while the legislation enacted in Aragon and Catalonia sets out certain minimum rights and responsibilities that the parties are to undertake and allows them to enter into agreements to regulate their financial and proprietary rights, there is no default provision of equal sharing. Instead, the emphasis is very much on protection of the weaker party at the end of the relationship. Compensation may be ordered upon the termination of the relationship during the lifetime of the parties if one party has been unjustly enriched. Economic and domestic contributions are accorded equal weight in determining whether one party has been enriched. Financial provision is also payable, for a limited period, to a partner who is unable to work while looking after children of the relationship, or whose earning power has been reduced as a result of the relationship. To a certain extent this reflects the weaker position of women in the employment market as compared to Sweden, as well as different opinions regarding the role of the state. Nor is there exact parity between the rights accorded to heterosexual and same-sex couples. Only heterosexual couples are entitled to adopt children jointly. On the other hand, in Catalonia the succession rights of same-sex couples are more generous. Heterosexual couples are dependent upon the will of the deceased for a share in the estate: the only automatic right is to reside in the home for at least one year and the right to retain the furniture and household goods. Same-sex couples are entitled to a proportion of the estate of the deceased, which may vary from one-quarter to the entire estate. The former is to be expected in view of the approach taken in virtually all other European countries. The latter is more interesting as it demonstrates awareness that homosexual couples do not have the option of marrying and that more extensive rights may thus be appropriate in certain circumstances.

Rights extended to cohabiting relationships without reference to the marriage model
A somewhat different approach is to extend rights to cohabitants without reference to the marriage model. This does not mean legislation that is premised upon a status-neutral concept such as 'dependency'. But legislation that actually acknowledges that the relationship of applying to a wide range of relationships, the law has to identify precisely which aspects of a relationship trigger the intervention of the law. One example is the definition of *concubinage* that has recently been inserted into the French Civil Code. It is described as '*une union de fait, caractérisée par une vie commune présentant un caractére de stabilité et de continuité, entre deux personnes, de sexe différent ou de même sexe, qui vivent en couple*'. [The authors' footnote translates this as 'a de facto union, characterised by a communal life which demonstrates stability and continuity, between two persons of the same or different sex, who live as a couple'.] While there may be some elements of tautology in such a definition – it may be doubted whether it is possible to have a de facto union without having some element of common life or living as a couple – it does at least illustrate that alternatives to the marriage model exist. Although the legislation does not confer new rights on cohabitants who meet this definition, its inclusion within the Civil Code means that all legislative references to *concubinage* will now be interpreted in this way.

Rights conferred on cohabitants who opt into a legal regime
So far the discussion has focused on the way in which cohabitation has been defined as a trigger for legal rights. A different approach is to allow cohabitants to decide for themselves whether they wish to assume certain rights and responsibilities and require them to opt in. Traditionally, this approach required couples to opt into marriage. In recent years, however, new institutions have been created. This marks a further retreat from the legal institution of marriage, all the more so if the new institution is open to those who are eligible to marry, rather than those who have no alternative. Thus, in the jurisdictions considered below, marriage is only one of a number of formal legal institutions that trigger legal rights. These new institutions fall into two categories. Those in the first category mirror marriage and are largely confined to same-sex couples. By contrast, those in the second category offer a substantive alternative to marriage for heterosexual couples, as well as a means by which same-sex couples may formalise their relationships.

The key example of the first approach is the registered partnership. Denmark was the first state to pass legislation allowing homosexual couples to enter into a registered partnership, in 1989, with Sweden following suit in 1994. Similar reforms have also been proposed in Finland and Germany but neither has passed legislation in this area so far. The legislation in those states that have enacted reform tends to follow the same pattern. Upon registration, partners are entitled to virtually the same rights as married couples, with the exception of the rules relating to adoption, custody and artificial insemination, and any provisions that involve special treatment on the basis of a spouse's sex. They are also subject to the same constraints as married couples, as it is necessary to obtain a divorce to terminate the relationship. Thus same-sex couples are entitled to opt into a marriage-like institution.

The legislation that has been passed in the Netherlands is also more concerned with conferring a status on same-sex couples than with dealing with cohabitation generally. Apart from the fact that partners may be of the same or the opposite sex, the approach of the Netherlands is very close to that taken in northern Europe, both in the terminology that has been adopted and in the rights that are conferred upon registered partners. Substantially the same rights are awarded to registered partners as to married couples, although there has been caution in extending rights relating to children to registered partners. Moreover, even though registered partners are not required to go through the same divorce procedure as their married counterparts, the requirement of either a court order or mutual consent means that there will be little difference in practice between the two procedures. In considering whether heterosexual cohabitants are likely to take advantage of the new legislation, the reasons why couples cohabit rather than marry should be considered. Those who are unwilling to assume the rights and responsibilities of marriage are unlikely to be any more willing to assume the same rights simply because they are offered by a different institution. It is perhaps only those couples who believe that the new institution will be free of the ideological baggage of marriage that will be willing to enter a partnership, rather than those who object to any form of state regulation of personal relationships. The fact that the registered partnership is open to same-sex and heterosexual couples means that it cannot by itself connote any particular gender-based division of labour. The fact that only a small number has chosen to register a partnership – 2822 in the first two years of the Act's operation – suggests that ideological objections of this kind are not a major motivating factor in the decision to cohabit.

By contrast, other institutions offer a real alternative to marriage. The concept of a civil union contract has been advanced in a number of European states and France, Belgium, Portugal and Spain have all debated Bills on this issue. It is intended that couples of the same or opposite sex should be entitled to enter into such an institution. The concept of a civil union contract goes beyond allowing couples to regulate their rights by means of a contract, although this is encouraged and in some cases required. It is similar to a registered partnership in that rights flow from registration of the relationship. However, these rights tend to be more limited than those attached to marriage. Concomitantly, less control is exercised over exit from the relationship. Thus the concept of a civil union contract offers an institutionally recognised form of relationship that does not require the parties to equate their relationship to that of marriage.

The concept has proved controversial. The attempts at reform in Spain and Portugal both failed and the legislation adopted in Belgium and France eschews the terminology of the civil union contract. However, both the Belgian *loi instaurant la cohabitation légale* (law establishing legal cohabitation) and the French *pacte civil de solidarité* (civil solidarity pact) follow the basic pattern outlined above. In each case the legislation details the formalities that have to be observed. In Belgium couples are required to make a declaration that they wish to cohabit legally, and mention must be made of any agreement that the parties have made. The French legislation has a slightly different emphasis. It is the contract governing the rights of the parties, rather than the relationship, that is registered. However, in both Belgium and France eligibility is limited to a certain extent in that only couples who do not have another formally recognised relationship and are capable of contracting will be able to make a declaration or register a *pacte*.

Little control is exerted over exit from the relationship, the main limitation being the requirement of compliance with certain administrative formalities. Similarly, the legislation essentially leaves the content of the obligations to be decided by the parties themselves. However, both *cohabitation légale and the pacte civil de solidarité* are more than institutionally recognised forms of cohabitation contracts. A minimum framework of rights is established. In Belgium cohabitants are given a degree of control over the family home and limited maintenance obligations apply on separation. Under a *pacte* the parties are exhorted to provide 'mutual and material' assistance for one another and there are certain provisions that property should be divided equally in default of agreement to the contrary. A *pacsé* couple will also be recognised as a unit for the purposes of tax and certain social security benefits. The fact that the institution offers an opportunity for couples to opt out of both the form of marriage and its substantive obligations within an institution that is recognised by the state, makes this a more radical option than those adopted in the Nordic countries and the Netherlands.

Marriage alone not sufficient to trigger legal rights

The logical end-point of an approach that emphasises such factors as the stability and duration of the relationship is to hold that marriage, by itself, is neither a necessary nor a sufficient trigger for the imposition of legal rights. This does not mean that marriage is thereby abolished, merely that it becomes a matter of personal or religious conviction without legal implications. Legal implications flow rather from incidents in life where rights or duties are judged to be appropriate, such as the birth of children, the breakdown of the relationship, or the death of one partner. Thus, if rules specify that certain rights should be conferred upon couples after a certain period of time, both married and unmarried couples should be required to satisfy that criterion. However, a rather different light is thrown on such arguments by the recent proliferation of alternative institutions. Opting in to such an institution is usually sufficient to confer certain rights upon the parties. Among the jurisdictions discussed above, France is the only one to introduce the idea of rights within an institution being 'graded': some being conferred automatically and others conferred after specific periods of time. Within this context, marriage as a sufficient – although not a necessary – trigger for the imposition of legal rights is perfectly justifiable.

The idea that marriage should not be an automatic passport to legal rights has found expression in a number of jurisdictions. In the case of Sweden, such ideas underpin the emphasis on individual responsibility and equality, and the rights attached to marriage have been reduced. The duration of the relationship is also taken into account in determining the distribution of property at the end of a marriage, a sliding scale of entitlement being used. The law in England and Wales also requires that the duration of the marriage is taken into account in assessing financial provision. Once the law begins to attach importance to the substance of the relationship, it becomes increasingly less tenable to continue to deny legal recognition to other relationships that are the same in substance if not in form.

Thus, although we are growing accustomed to the idea that there are registered partnerships for same-sex couples in the Scandinavian countries, and the PACS option for all couples in France, the full picture is immensely complex.

The PACS seems to stand alone in enabling the couple to construct their own contract and then register it, rather than constructing all the details of their legal status for them. In 'From lack of status to contract: assessing the French *Pacte Civil de Solidarité*' (2001), Rebecca Probert gives more detail:

The requirements of the *Pacte Civil de Solidarité*

A *Pacte Civil de Solidarité* is defined as a contract entered into by two persons, of the same or opposite sex, to organize their common life (CC art. 515-1). The institutional aspect of *PaCS* is illustrated by the restrictions on who can enter into a *Pacte* and the detailed instructions as to how registration should be effected. This is state-sanctioned private ordering for selected couples only. *Pactes* between those who are related or who are bound to third parties by marriage or an existing *pacte* are void (art. 515-2). Attempts to extend certain rights to siblings who shared a home were defeated in the National Assembly (Barlow and Probert, 1999). The legislation is thus concerned only with stable, adult, unrelated, monogamous dyads.

The circumstances in which it is possible to terminate a *pacte* are also set out. While they are less restrictive than the grounds on which a marriage may be ended, immediate unilateral termination is not permitted unless one of the partners marries a third party, which automatically brings the *pacte* to an end. Otherwise the *pacte* will officially subsist for three months after the desire to end the *pacte* has been notified to the relevant official. If both parties agree, the *pacte* can be terminated immediately (art. 515-7). Both the beginning and end of the relationship must be notified to and recorded by the appropriate official, as must any changes to the rights set out in the *pacte* itself (arts 515-3 and 515-7).

The second important institutional aspect of *PaCS* is the fact that it has consequences in public law, with fiscal and social security rights being conferred upon *pacsé* couples. Broadly, the longer the *pacte* subsists, the more advantages it will attract. Some rights are immediate: a partner may succeed to a tenancy in the name of the other (art. 14) and rely upon the other's health insurance and social security contributions (art. 7). Other rights are progressive: after the third anniversary of the *pacte* the couple will be taxed as if they are married, although this will only be a benefit where there is a significant disparity between the income of the partners (art. 4). There are no provisions for pensions, nor is a partner automatically entitled to any share of the estate of a deceased partner. The only advantage that a *PaCS* confers in the event of the death of one of the partners is tax relief on gifts: the first FF300,000 is not taxed; the next FF100,000 is taxed at 40 per cent and the rest at 50 per cent. Even this relief is only available where the couple have been *pacsé* for 2 years (art. 5).

The framework within which private ordering will take place is also set out. During the relationship, the parties will be jointly liable for debts that were contracted for the needs of their daily life and living expenses. They are exhorted to provide 'mutual and material assistance' for one another, but may stipulate what form this should take (art. 515-6). In default of agreement, property will be held jointly under the form of ownership termed *l'indivision*, although it is open to the parties to make alternative arrangements (art. 515-5). The division of property upon the breakdown of the relationship is also to be fixed by the parties. It is only if they cannot agree upon this, that the question may be referred to a judge (art. 515-7). A *pacte* thus offers a publicly recognized and delimited private space.

Question

Of the options available, which, if any, would you like to see introduced in this country for cohabitants?

Change is in the air here. The 2001-02 session of Parliament saw the introduction of two private members' Bills to introduce registered partnerships: the Civil Partnerships Bill in the House of Lords and the Relationships (Civil Registration) Bill in the Commons. In 'Registered Partnerships – coming soon?' (2002), Elizabeth Cooke described them as follows:

Particularly interesting is the form that each Bill takes. In each case, the status offered (a 'registered relationship' or 'partnership' in the Commons Bill, a 'civil partnership' in the Lords) is open to any couple, provided that they are not closely related. The status is available through registration; it may be ended by court order, made on joint or unilateral application. It is close to the Scandinavian registered partnership idea, in that the rights and responsibilities on offer are an off-the-peg, non-negotiable package (unlike the French Pacte Civil de Solidarité where it is the couple's own *pacte* that is registered), but differs from the Scandinavian model in being open to same-sex or heterosexual couples.

There the similarity ends; the two Bills exhibit sharply different drafting styles, and ideologies. The Commons Bill is short: five brisk sections, and a one-and-a-half page Schedule. Provision is made for a couple to register a relationship, provided they are not within the prohibited degrees of relationship set out in the Marriage Act 1949. Once registered, the parties have the same rights and responsibilities as spouses for the purposes of inheritance, housing succession, incapacity, pensions and social security, inheritance tax, compensation for fatal accidents, immigration and domestic violence. The provision on the latter point is typical: 'For the purposes of sections 30 to 37 and 45 to 47 of the Family Law Act 1996, a party to a registered relationship shall be treated as a spouse' (Schedule). On dissolution, the court is to give effect to any pre-registration agreement about their property rights on dissolution, provided that agreement has been lodged with the court, but otherwise is to decide an application for financial relief 'on the same terms as an application by a spouse in divorce proceedings'.

By contrast, the Lords Bill has 46 sections. It resolutely eschews every opportunity to define anything in terms of marriage. In each context – prohibited degrees of relationship, taxation, incapacity, social security, domestic violence etc – the couple's position is spelt out in detail. Domestic violence gets two long sections, replicating the relevant parts of the Family Law Act 1996 (including the 'balance of harm' test for occupation orders).

... The Lords Bill gives the registered partnership the dignity of its own, individually drafted, identity – although, once we get past the actual drafting, the effect is very similar. One startling difference of substance is that the Lords Bill provides for community of property in the dwelling-house that the parties occupy jointly, provided one or both of them is entitled to occupy it by virtue of a beneficial estate or interest, and any furniture or domestic items purchased for the purpose of living together. The communal property is to be treated as held 'jointly in equal shares' – this must mean a tenancy in common. The parties can opt out of this by registered agreement. There is a section-25-like power to make an 'intervention order' on cessation of the partnership, for financial provision (including periodical payments), in default of agreement at that stage on the question of the distribution of assets; there is even a general principle: 'that, so far as is reasonably practicable, the partners should not be reliant on each other financially after the cessation order is made'.

Neither Bill became law; the Lords Bill was withdrawn following the government's promise to institute a review of the issue of registered partnerships.

Questions

(i)   Given the choice between the two, why might cohabitants prefer one or other of the forms of partnership proposed by these Bills?
(ii) Would you have liked to see either Bill succeed? Why?
(iii) If the Civil Partnerships Bill had become law, how might a lawyer have advised an engaged couple on the question whether to proceed to marriage or to a civil partnership?

Meanwhile, perhaps despairing of legislation, the Greater London Authority has introduced the London Partnerships Register. Its legal purpose is evidential only, and it is not open to public inspection. *The Times* reported thus on 6 September 2001:

Gay couples make their love official
Two homosexual men yesterday became the first couple to have their relationship officially recognised under a scheme described as 'a step on the road to full equality' for same-sex couples.
    After 38 years together, Ian Burford, 68, a former member of the English Shakespeare Company, and Alex Cannell, 62, a retired nursing manager, formally declared their commitment to each other by signing the London Partnerships Register set up by Ken Livingstone, the Mayor of London.
    The couple, dressed in cream suits were joined at the Visitor's Centre of the Greater London Authority, by Linda Wilkinson, 49, and Carol Budd, 48, who also signed the register as a tribute to their 16-year relationship.
    Although the register will not confer any legal rights, Mr Livingstone hopes that it will be accepted as strong evidence in any dispute over tenancy, pension or immigration rights.
    In a ceremony lasting no more than 10 minutes, Mr Burford and Mr Cannell spoke of their delight at signing the register.
    'This is not a marriage but a recognition of the value of a partnership. For 38 years I have had the love, friendship and support of Alex and throughout whatever years are left to us he knows that he has my love, friendship and support,' said Mr Burford before receiving a bouquet of flowers from Mr Livingstone.
    Earlier he said: 'People in relationships which are not made legal through marriage face all sorts of problems. I hope this will be first step forward.'
    Miss Wilkinson and Miss Budd, of Bethnal Green, east London, then took the floor in the sparsely decorated room, with only a vase of flowers adding any romance to the occasion.
    'Love, trust and commitment, these are the reasons we have chosen to sign the partnership register,' said Miss Budd, an IT consultant.
    'We are not trying to ape a heterosexual marriage, we are doing this because we believe it's another nail in the coffin of prejudice that has denied our fundamental rights as human beings and makes us second-class citizens in our own country.'
    Under the scheme, heterosexual as well as homosexual and lesbian couples can have their relationships recognised. The ceremonies take place on Wednesdays and Saturdays with up to 25 guests allowed.
    For a fee of £85, couples will received a certificate marking the official declaration of their relationship. They can 'deregister' if they split up.
    The London Partnerships Register makes the GLA the first public organisation in Britain to offer recognition to same-sex couples, though the register will remain confidential.
    Peter Tatchell, the homosexual rights activist, welcomed the scheme but said it needed to be more than just symbolic.
    'The GLA should agree that registration will confer partnership rights on the lesbian and gay employees of GLA-controlled bodies including recognition as next of kin and pension inheritance,' he said.

2.6 Cohabitation contracts and 'pre-nups'

W. Weyrauch, in 'Metamorphoses of Marriage' (1980), writes:

The legal device of contract is particularly useful for women from the middle classes and of high educational attainment who are self-assertive and competitive in their relations with men. It is less adequate for parties of the lower classes and those who, because of continued differential treatment of the sexes, lack equal bargaining power. The courts may then fall back on traditional conceptions of marriage as status and emphasize the conjugal obligations of the husband. If there is no marriage, the courts may surreptitiously apply public policy by reading into a supposedly implied contract provisions that never occurred to the parties. A host of legal theories, equitable in nature, may also affect the obligations of parties to quasi-marital relationships. Thus, the courts may develop remedies akin to those in modern contract law when dealing with terms that are manifestly unfair and oppressive, and may borrow the reasoning from commercial litigation when deciding marital and quasi-marital disputes. They may refuse to enforce unconscionable terms that have been found to exist between the parties, married or not, and imply a duty of good faith and fair dealing.

The use of contract to regulate cohabitation has become a much more obvious planning vehicle in recent years, in spite of the continued absence of any decision by the courts as to their enforceability. Anne Barlow, in *Cohabitants and the law* (2001), explains:

1.35 Having examined some of the pitfalls of unmarried partnerships and families, what can be done to avoid the problems? Are cohabitation contracts detailing the agreed basis upon which the cohabitation is to operate the answer? It is popularly thought that such a contract would be binding upon the parties in the event of breakdown of the relationship, as is indeed the case in other jurisdictions. Unfortunately, in our jurisdiction, there is still no certainty that the courts would enforce such a contract. In fact, as will be illustrated, such precedents as there are point in the other direction. However, the issue has yet to be decided in a contemporary context, and it seems increasingly unlikely that a strict approach would now be adopted given the changed mores of our society. . . .

1.37 Whether or not a contract will be considered valid by the courts may depend on its contents as well as on a number of other factors. It is interesting to note that in 1988, the Council of Ministers of the European Community adopted the recommendation (No. R(88)3) that member states should not preclude cohabitation contracts dealing with property and money on the ground that the parties are not married to each other. Unlike the marriage contract, a cohabitation contract is a matter of a private rather than a public agreement, and thus the starting point is that the parties are free to agree the scope and nature of the terms themselves. Whether or not all or any of the terms of such a contract will be upheld by the courts may in any event not be the parties' only motive for having an agreement drawn up.

1.38 Couples are likely to want a cohabitation contract to cover their rights and obligations both during cohabitation and on breakdown of the relationship. Unlike their married counterparts who are thought to be prevented by public policy considerations from preparing for the contingency of breakdown, a cohabitation contract would not be void by reason of providing for such an eventuality. Interestingly, the Law Society's Family Law Committee has recommended that marriage contracts providing for the division of property on divorce should be enforceable where both parties have entered into them with the benefit of legal advice (see *Law Society's Gazette* 15 May 1991, page 2) and the government's 1998 consultation paper, *Supporting Families* similarly endorsed this idea. Both the 1997 Law Society and 2000 SFLA recommendations for reform of cohabitation law consider that cohabitation agreements should be enforceable. As noted above, there is a Council of Ministers' recommendation that cohabitation contracts dealing with property should be recognized. The Scottish Law Commission recommended that this type of approach should be adopted in reforming Scottish law and suggested that the following clause be enacted, a proposal endorsed by the recent Scottish Executive White Paper:

'A contract between cohabitants or prospective cohabitants relating to property or financial matters should not be void or unenforceable solely because it was concluded between parties in, or about to enter, this type of relationship.'

These developments bode well for the likely enforceability of a cohabitation contract made by heterosexual couples, where it is limited to issues of property, but before discussing enforceability in detail, the range of matters which cohabiting couples may wish to include in their contracts is considered.

(a) Contents

1.39 The exact content of each cohabitation contract is obviously a matter for the couple concerned. The advantage of drawing up a contract is that it requires the partners to consider, before there is any dispute, their respective expectations, both during the relationship and, in so far as can be foreseen, on breakdown.

1.40 It is also possible to have a contract that deals only with the eventuality of breakdown, without regulating the terms of the relationship itself. Some couples may wish to commit to writing every aspect of the agreements between them, down to the minutiae of the washing up rota, whilst others may find this unnecessary yet see the value of discussing, agreeing and recording in advance their respective rights in relation to property, maintenance and any children. The more romantic may wish instead to trust their partner sufficiently to feel sure that in the event of breakdown, a satisfactory agreement would be reached. However, sadly, the bitterness that breakdown usually engenders often means that such trust is misplaced. This is as true for cohabiting same-sex couples as it is for heterosexuals.

1.41 Some argue that to ask or advise couples to agree such matters in a formal legal document may raise problems within a relationship that were not previously present, and that accordingly matters are best left undocumented. However, it is submitted that if such an exercise reveals different understandings about the implications of a couple's arrangements, then surely this is a matter which merits discussion during the currency of the relationship where possible, rather than on breakdown when compromise or re-evaluation of the position may be much more difficult.

1.42 What should be the main tenets of a cohabitation contract? As previously indicated, it is perfectly possible to include the agreed rules upon which the cohabitation is founded; these include whether or not other relationships are permitted; how the household chores should be shared; and the amount of leisure time the parties will spend together. However, no court would ever compensate a breach of any such terms with an order for specific performance, as is the general rule with contracts for personal services. It is unlikely that a court would compensate a breach of the rules of the relationship (as opposed to the terms contained in the contract relating to property division), with damages, as it may be felt that the parties did not intend to be legally bound by such rules other than to provide evidence of breakdown of the relationship. Their inclusion can never be more than a record of the parties' intentions in those areas and should only be expressed as such in the contract.

1.43 Providing the contract meets the general criteria for an enforceable contract as set out below, contract terms which detail how property which is brought into the relationship or subsequently purchased individually or jointly by the parties, is to be treated on breakdown, may well be enforceable. At the very least it will be strong evidence of the parties' intentions at the time of the contract and will be valuable in case of dispute. Similarly, if a property is bought for occupation by the couple as a family home, a clause indicating that it is property which is to be beneficially jointly owned in stated shares may negative any contrary indication on the title documents, providing the cohabitation contract is executed as a deed. Provision can also be made for giving notice under the agreement to terminate the relationship and to provide for the agreed division of property at that juncture. A clause to pay maintenance on breakdown of the relationship to a partner who would otherwise have no right to maintenance will also prove enforceable if the contract is executed as a deed.

(b) Enforceability

1.44 The problems of enforcement have already been mentioned. The issues are raised by the law of contract, and are matters which courts must consider in relation to any contract the validity of which is challenged. There are as many as five hurdles at which a cohabitation contract may fall:

    (i)   it may be found illegal or void on grounds of public policy;
    (ii) an intention to create legal relations may be absent;
    (iii) it may be found void for uncertainty;
    (iv) consideration may be absent; or
    (v) it may be found voidable where there is undue influence.

(c) Illegality on grounds of public policy

1.45 Contracts for immoral purposes, which of course include sexual immorality, are illegal and consequently unenforceable. Contracts deemed to be prejudicial to the marital state are also contrary to public policy and void. Despite the changing tide towards recognition of cohabitation in some statutes, these common law principles of the law of contract remain unchanged. Thus, although current thinking is that no court today would strike down a cohabitation contract entered into by a cohabiting heterosexual couple on these grounds, this has not yet been tested in the courts. Accordingly the current legal position remains uncertain, although the recommendation by the Council of Ministers R(88)3 and its endorsement by the Scottish Law Commission discussed above, makes it highly unlikely a contract relating to property or financial matters between a cohabiting man and woman would be declared void on public policy grounds. The validity of a contract between a cohabiting gay couple may be significantly more vulnerable to an adverse finding that it promotes sexual immorality. . . .

(ii) Absence of intention to create legal relations

1.53 There is a rebuttable presumption that parties to an agreement regarding domestic arrangements do not intend to be legally bound. The principle was set out in the case of *Balfour v Balfour* [1919] 2 KB 571 where a promise by a husband who worked abroad, to his wife who had to stay behind on medical grounds, that he would pay her £30 per month was held to be unenforceable both because she had provided no consideration and also because the domestic nature of the agreement showed that there was no intention to create legal relations. Atkin LJ at page 578 said:

> 'Those agreements, or many of them, do not result in contracts at all . . . even though there may be what as between other parties would constitute considerations for the agreement . . . They are not contracts . . . because the parties did not intend that they should be attended by legal consequences.'

However, where there is a written agreement, especially if it has been drawn up by a legal advisor, this should be enough to rebut the presumption, as parties do not have agreements drawn up unless there is an intention that they should be legally binding (see *Merritt v Merritt* [1970] 1 WLR 1211, CA). . . .

1.55 The content of a contract may also influence the court's view. Thus the less domestic detail that is contained, and the more terms there are relating to more legalistic matters, such as a statement of respective interests in jointly owned property, the more likely a court would be to infer the requisite intention. In any event, this is a hurdle easily overcome by cohabitants who do wish to create a binding contract; an advisor drafting a contract can, to ensure the intention is unambiguous, specifically recite the intention to be bound.

(iii) Contract void for uncertainty

1.56 As with any contact, if the terms are so vague and uncertain that they are incapable of enforcement, then this will either be a term which the court ignores, or, if the uncertainty comprises terms which are fundamental to the operation of the contract, may vitiate the whole contract. Thus, a term agreeing to make financial provision without any indication of the nature or extent or the rules according to which such provision could be ascertained would be void for uncertainty. Thus, advisors drafting a cohabitation contract should have this potential problem in mind.

(iv) Absence of consideration

1.57 As with any contract, there must be consideration for a cohabitation agreement to be enforceable. In the case of cohabitation agreements, the consideration for one party's agreeing to make financial provision for the other may be the act of cohabiting with the other party; this risks being deemed immoral consideration, consequently rendering the contract illegal. There is a simple answer; if the agreement is in the form of a deed, no consideration for the bargain is necessary. Advisors should therefore recommend a deed be executed. With the introduction of the provisions of the Law of Property (Miscellananeous Provisions) Act 1989, even the mystery of the seal has been dispensed with, and, apart from the requirements that it be in writing and dated, a document merely needs to record that it is being signed as a deed in the presence of independent witnesses to the signatures.

(v) Contract voidable for undue influence?

1.58 A finding of undue influence exercised by one party over the other inducing that person to enter into the contract will vitiate the contract in its entirety. If the terms of a contract are heavily weighted in favour of one of the parties, it may be susceptible to such a finding. In contacts between spouses, there is no presumption of undue influence; to defeat a contract, it must be proved. In contrast, where a contract between an engaged couple substantially favours one party, there is a rebuttable presumption of undue influence and it must be proved that no such influence induced the less favoured party to enter into the bargain (see *Zamet v Hyman* [1961] 1 WLR 1442, CA). Whether or not there is a presumption of undue influence between cohabitants is unknown. As advisors may advise only one party to a contract (to avoid potential conflict of interest), it is obviously desirable, where there is any hint of inequality of bargaining power, to ensure that the less favoured party is urged to seek independent legal advice.

Barlow goes on to look at other jurisdictions – California, Minnesota, Canada – where cohabitation contracts are clearly enforceable. Here is a precedent from the leading practitioner text, *Cohabitation law and precedents* by Jane Craig and Philippa Pearson. Note that XX and YY are the partners and BB is their property; and that recital 6 is of course optional. Spot the provisions designed to ensure enforceability:

COHABITATION DEED

ON the   day of   2000, we YY ("YY"), and **XX** ("XX") ("BB") signed this agreement

BACKGROUND

1. We enter into this deed because we intend it to be legally binding upon us and for the Court only to be involved in making Orders supporting or endorsing the provisions we have laid out (though we accept that the court could be involved to make provision or arrangements for any children)
2. We have been advised to take legal advice on its terms and we have had the opportunity to do this before signing this deed and we sign the deed to express our intention to be legally bound by its terms
3. We have confirmed our financial circumstances and have attached copies of the disclosure that we have given each other summarizing our current circumstances
4. We have not been forced or put under pressure over the contents of this agreement or over signing it
5. The terms of this agreement
   i)   Operate from the date at the top of this page
   ii) are severable (so that even if any part of the agreement were declared void the remaining clauses would remain valid)
   iii) shall be interpreted by the courts of England and Wales, so that if there was an issue that had to be resolved by a court, we would intend a court in England and Wales to decide
6. We accept too that the court will have jurisdiction to consider our circumstances in the event of a separation following our anticipated marriage in [xxxxxxxxxxx]; however, we regard the arrangements that we have set out below as reasonable and would intend the provisions of this deed to be taken into account by any court and for it to provide the structure for any settlement at least pending a significant change in circumstances; specifically, we would expect the court to make a clean break settlement upon the arrangements in this deed being put into effect
7. **BB:**
   a)   We expect to purchase a property in the immediate future for the sum of £102,000, with the assistance of a mortgage ('the Mortgage') of £82,000;
   b)   The mortgage debt is underwritten by a policy which will pay on the first death, the amount of the Mortgage debt to the survivor (we make provisions about this in the deed, which we intend to operate as a declaration of trust of the policy fund)

   OR

   c)   The mortgage debt is underwritten by two policies, one in the name of each of us, which will pay to the survivor in the event of our death the amount of the Mortgage debt (we make provisions about this in the deed, which we intend to operate as a declaration of trust of the policy funds)
   d)   We intend to hold the property as joint tenants so that if either of us died that person's share would pass automatically to the survivor regardless of the terms of any Will or the rules of intestacy; however
   e)   We intend our shares in the property if we realise it during out life-times not to be equal but to be as set out below
   WE AGREE AS FOLLOWS:

Shares in BB

8. We will own BB *as joint tenants/tenants in common*;

Improvements and Contributions to BB

9. An "Improvement" is work (including repair) which increases the value of BB

10. We agree:
   a) to carry out improvements only by agreement between us or as is recommended by a chartered surveyor appointed (and paid for) by us together (and if we cannot agree then as appointed by the President for the time being of the Royal Institute of Chartered Surveyors)
   b) that we shall meet the cost of improvements with
      I) XX paying   %; and
      ii) YY paying   %

And see Appendix 2

Shares in the Policies

11. We agree that if one of us died then the proceeds of the Policy would be applied towards the mortgage debt and any surplus would form part of the estate of the deceased to be dealt with according to any Will that we had written;

OR

12. We agree that if we die within 28 days of each other, than:
   a) XX's policy will pay one half of the Mortgage debt; and
   b) YY's policy will pay one half of the Mortgage debt; and
   c) any surplus on either policy will be dealt with as part of our estate.

Meeting the outgoings

13. We will meet the outgoings as follows:

If	And if	Then	And
The other asks in writing	We are in the home together	We will pay equally the items at a) to f) below	
A sale request is given	"	"	
"	One of us moves out	The person who moves out pays • the items at a) for 3 months; and • continues to pay the items at b)-f) until a month after moving out	The Person remaining in the home will pay the remainder
"	We both move out, or the second of us also vacates after giving one month's written notice	We will share the items at a) to f) below relating to BB	We will share any income from the property equally, off-setting it against these outgoings

The outgoings are:
   a) on the property itself:
      · mortgage instalments
      · building insurance/service charge and ground rent
   b) the general bills
      · council tax, water rates,
      · gas, electricity, telephone,
      · the cost of agreed (or necessary) decoration and repairs,
      · any boiler servicing or alarm costs,
      · contents insurance, repair and replacement of white goods
      · tv licence/agreed satellite and cable charges

c) the following insurances:
- ·   premiums for the life cover on the mortgage
- ·   any unemployment insurance that we set up
- ·   the permanent health insurance (if any) that we set up

d) other home-related costs, eg
- ·   food
- ·   cleaner
- ·   pet
- ·   garden

e) transport costs, eg

f) the following financial costs
- ·   HP on xxxxxxxxxxx

g) (to the intent that we will keep separate and discharge from our separate resources for the time-being)
- ·   our respective work related costs
- ·   our savings and pension contributions; and
- ·   our other personal costs

And see appendix 2

Selling BB

14. We intend the following time-table to operate in disposing of BB

Date	For example	Event
At any time*	1 Jan	One of us asks in writing for the property to be sold
After 2 months	1 Mar	By this date we to have agreed, if possible, a figure for BB at which either of us would buy the interest of the other We would indicate our intention to proceed by paying a deposit
After three months	1 Apr	By this date, the completion by one of us of the share of the other should have taken place
At any time by agreement and otherwise after 2 months	1 Mar	We can market the property eg through estate agents
At any time	Say 15th Jan	One of us can vacate the property
1 month later	15th Feb	If the other remains in occupation then s/he becomes responsible for the general household expenditure (ie categories b) to f) above)
3 months later	15th Apr	If the other remains in occupation then s/he becomes responsible for the Outgoings
At any time	Say 15th Mar	The other can also vacate, but s/he must continue to pay the Outgoings and Household Expenditure, until: One month's notice has been given whereupon these costs are shared equally again until BB is disposed of

*   If either of us dies, then our joint holding of the property or our Wills may give rights to the other to remain in BB. Otherwise our personal representatives can give notice requiring a sale on the first anniversary of the death and will represent us in the detailed process of sale, set out in the appendix.

What to do with the proceeds of sale of BB

15. From the money received from the sale ("**the Sale Proceeds**") we will pay:
a) The Estate Agents fees or other marketing expenses; and

        b)   The legal cost of sale
16. We will then share what is left, with
        a)   XX receiving   %; and
        b)   YY receiving   %; and
17. From those shares,
        a)   XX will pay   % of the sum then outstanding on the Mortgage; and
        b)   YY will pay   % of the sum then outstanding on the Mortgage
18. If our combined shares of **the Sale Proceeds** are not enough to pay off the Mortgage entirely then
        a)   XX will borrow   % of the sum required to pay off the balance; and
        b)   YY will borrow   % of the sum required to pay off the balance; and
19. These sums will be paid to the Solicitor having conduct of the conveyancing not less than 7 days before the date on which the sale completes; and
20. See Appendix 2

Replacement Home
21. If we sell **BB** and move to another property we will enter into a declaration at the time of purchase setting out our interests in that property

Further promises about BB
22. Unless we agree in writing, we will not:
        a)   further mortgage **BB** nor our interest in it, nor increase the size of the **Mortgage**
        b)   lease it
        c)   grant any license in relation to it
        d)   allow any other person into occupation during such time as we shall share occupation of **BB**
        e)   assign or sublet **BB** or any part of it
        f)   do anything which makes the building or contents insurance cover lapse or terminate

Joint Accounts
23. We will make no unreasonable charge upon nor unusual withdrawal from any joint account that we operate (see Appendix 2)

The car
24. There is registered in XX's name a   car ("the Car"), purchased by her in February 2000 for the sum of £6,000 with the assistance of a hire purchase loan from Lloyds PLC
25. We agree that the Car is to be operated by us together for our joint benefit
26. The costs of running, repairing and maintaining the Car are to be met jointly
27. XX may purchase any interest YY has in the car by
        a)   paying to YY one half of the sum that the car would be reasonably likely to secure if sold by them privately after deducting firstly the sum of £300 to cover notional selling costs and inconvenience and secondly the amount of the Hire Purchase debt as at the Date of Separation; and
        b)   simultaneously securing the release of YY from any hire purchase liability in relation to the car; otherwise
28. The Car will be sold if we separate (XX to have conduct of the sale in default of other agreement) and the proceeds of sale after discharge of the hire purchase debt will be divided equally between XX and YY
(and see Appendix 2)

Other things
29. We will apply the following rules to things we will own or which are not mentioned specifically in this deed, if we need to decide who owns something or is responsible for discharging any claim:
        a)   If there is confirmation in writing by both of us, that will determine the point; otherwise:
        b)   We will each keep:
            i)   things we each owned prior to the commencement of our relationship
           ii)   things we use in connection with our respective work
          iii)   our respective clothing, jewellery and:
          iv)   anything else used by us personally;
        c)   The recipient of any gift will keep the item;

    d)   If one of us buys an item from her/his separate resources s/he will keep it (unless a gift—see item c) above). If both of us, we will share it in proportion to our contributions;

    e)   Loans from a family member will be discharged by the person whose family made the loan;

    f)   Gifts to both of us from a family member will be retained by the person whose family made the gift;

    g)   Items not falling into the above categories but acquired by us during our relationship shall be treated as owned by us equally.

30. During the time that we share the home, its contents shall be for the use of both of us.

31. If we separate then we will each be entitled to remove the things we own (as identified by the above principles).

32. If one of us vacates the home then the person remaining in occupation will be responsible for the safe keeping of the other's items and to ensure that those items are kept insured.

Other provisions concerning this agreement

33. We agree to review the provisions of this agreement:
    a)   If we sell BB and purchase an alternative home
    b)   If either or both of us had a dependent child living with us
    c)   After a period of [*five*] years
    d)   At the request of either of us
    e)   If either of us had been out of work for 3 months or were disabled

34. Even if those events happen, then we will continue with the arrangements as set out above, unless the Court makes an Order under the Children Act 1989 or the Child Support Agency becomes involved to raise a calculation

35. [This agreement will be brought to an end in any event by our marrying each other.] *or is to continue as a basis—ie as a pre-nuptial; ensure this corresponds with clause 6 in the recitals*

[Appendix 1 sets out arrangements for the eventual sale of the property; Appendix 2 deals with payment and interest where either party has not met the financial obligations in the deed.]

Consideration of cohabitation contracts leads us to think about the use of contract as a preliminary to marriage. Stuart Bridge, in 'Marriage and Divorce: the regulation of intimacy' (chapter 1 of Jonathan Herring (ed.) *Family Law: Issues, debates, policy* (2001)), has this to say:

Marital contacts and the contract of marriage: marriage private and public
The public/private divide
Few legal relationships present the public/private divide in as stark a contrast as marriage. It is on one level so public as to be an *institution*, a word which resonates with notions of church and state. On another, the individual marriage is the ultimate private arrangement the very intimacy of which is deserving of protection from the public eye. Marriage is more than a status: it is also a contract. We have already seen the terms and obligations which the state imposes, in the sense of legal consequences which flow from marriage. 'Traditional' marriage has changed. But it remains, for the most part, a contract of the standard form. The extent to which spouses can vary the marital obligations by negotiated agreement is doubtful, although it has become a central item on the current political agenda. Much recent consideration has been given to so-called 'pre-nuptial agreements' and the role they might play in the future regulation of marriage. The UK government has made statements supporting their utility as providing the spouses with a means of articulating their respective rights and obligations, and of enabling them to draw up their own marriage contract to deal with their own particular circumstances. Legislation has been contemplated to achieve this intended objective. The contractarians see the contractualisation of marriage as offering freedom of choice, enabling parties to exercise autonomy in negotiating and settling the terms of their own relationship, and perhaps persuading more to enter marriage by tailoring it to suit their individual needs and by allowing them to reject components which appear inappropriate or unduly onerous. It is not yet clear which way England and Wales will go. Here, we will briefly summarise the current legal position, and then consider the theoretical arguments for and against the advocacy of further contractualism. Should marriage be made-to-measure, or must it remain, as it has been to date, off-the-peg?

Types of marital contracts

Marriage contracts can take several forms. When a married couple purchase a house, they will agree between themselves that a certain regime will apply to that property. It is usual that it be held by the spouses as joint tenants at law, on trust for themselves as joint tenants in equity. An express declaration of trust to this effect will be binding on the parties. When one spouse dies, the property will pass by virtue of survivorship to the other. There is rarely any possibility of a successful challenge being made to the parties' agreement as contained in the documents of title. This kind of arrangement does not usually cause difficulties, as the operation of the principles of joint tenancy on death is accepted, and they have little impact as between the spouses on divorce.

More controversial is the agreement entered into before marriage (called the pre-nuptial or the pre-marital contract or agreement), which may purport to regulate a whole range of matters of mutual interest to the intending spouses. In the United States, such agreements may concern issues which will arise during the marriage itself, such as the place of residence, the effect of changes of employment, the requirement or waiver of marital fidelity, the frequency of sexual activity, as well as the more conventional issues such as the holding of property and the sharing of child-care. Pre-nuptial agreements are also likely to deal with the consequences of relationship breakdown, stipulating in advance who is to have primary care for the children, what contact would be available for the other spouse, and how the accumulated wealth or debt is to be distributed in the event of divorce. It is this final respect which has attracted the attention of our legislators. Should it be possible for spouses, before or during the marriage, to make a legally binding agreement dictating how the matrimonial property is to be divided up on divorce? The argument in favour of pre-nuptial contracts is that they can provide the parties with a freedom to dictate their own terms. On marital breakdown, the contract can be applied. The parties know where they stand. There is certainty, and less scope for dispute between the spouses, in particular about their respective rights to family property. With the destination of the family assets being otherwise determined by resort to a reallocative jurisdiction based on judicial discretion, any certainty is better than none.

The case for marital contracts

A leading proponent of contractarian marriage has been Professor Marjorie Shultz. In her major article ('Contractual Ordering of Marriage: A New Model for State Policy' (1982) 70 *California Law Review* 204) she argues the case for the promotion of marriage contracting. As 'traditional marriage' did not provide the diversity which was being sought by those in intimate relationships, and as the option of total deregulation of intimacy was unrealistic, contract offered an important contribution. While by no means a panacea, in that marital contracting could not be 'all things to all marriages', nevertheless its flexibility allows appropriate variation in accordance with the parties' personalities and predispositions. Moreover, changes in the laws relating to marriage have reduced the level of public control by treating spouses as private individuals capable of separate interests, injuries and remedies and recognising that legal dispute resolution in marriage may be desirable. The developments to which she refers include the articulation of the right to privacy (in the US Supreme Court), the tolerance of diverse sexual behaviour, the growth of no-fault divorce and the retreat from the doctrine of marital unity (the 'unit theory of marriage').

The model she ultimately advocates would involve the state leaving the most substantive marital rights and obligations to be defined privately by the parties, but making the legal system available to resolve disputes arising under the privately created 'legislation'. The diversity of marriage produces compelling pressures toward private rather than public ordering of marital obligations:

> Contract offers a rich and developed tradition whose principal strength is precisely the accommodation of diverse relationships. It is designed to regulate those arenas of human interaction in which the state recognises and defers to divergent values, needs, preferences, and resources. Indeed, the deference to individual choice is strengthened, the pluralistic choices themselves legitimized, by the state's readiness to enforce private expectations or resolve private disputes at the behest of one of the parties to the relationship.

There are limits to Shultz's enthusiasm. She accepts that terms in marital contracts which deal with 'non-economic' personal matters where the invocation of the court would be inappropriate should not necessarily be enforceable. Nevertheless, she does not believe that resort to the legal process should be proscribed merely because the parties are still cohabiting.

Objections to marriage contracts

A serious objection to marriage contracts is that they undermine the institution of marriage. Expressed colloquially, marriage contracts are 'not very romantic' in that they do not accord with a romantic notion of marriage. More fundamentally, by addressing the consequences of termination at the outset, the parties are implicitly accepting that marriage is finite and that their union may well not be life-long. This may give the spouses an unduly commercialist approach to their marital relationship and make them consider the severance of the matrimonial ties somewhat sooner than might otherwise be the case. It is easier to buy into divorce when the price is set in advance. As the English law considers the institution of marriage as in itself deserving of protection and support – the most recent divorce legislation laconically commences with a statement to this effect – it would be overtly hypocritical to enforce contracts entered into before or during the marriage which expressly contemplated its termination by divorce. The public interest in the sustenance of marriage as a worthwhile institution is thereby invoked as a reason for rejecting its private regulation. The counter-argument can be expressed succinctly. In so far as it cannot be denied that marriage is a legal relationship, with legal consequences, it is incongruent and unduly paternalistic for the law to disallow parties to a marriage who wish to do so from addressing those consequences and, possibly with the benefit of legal advice, extend, restrict or modify them.

Another public interest of importance is the ready enforceability of private support obligations – for spouses in particular, but also children of the marriage. To permit the mutual obligation of support, which is central to the concept of marriage, to be abrogated by an express contractual stipulation may result in the financial burden of marital breakdown falling on the public purse rather than the private pocket. A basic principle underlying support of families is that the primary responsibility should lie with the spouse, or parents as the case may be, and that the welfare system is a secondary resort where the private support scheme fails. While this is a powerful objection to allowing parties ultimate freedom of regulation, a state which wished to endorse and enforce parties' marital contracts in this respect could do so by denying recourse to public support systems for those who had agreed to the restriction or exclusion of their spouse's continuing financial liability. Whether it would be politically acceptable would be another matter, in particular where the welfare of children required the enforcement of personal liability as parent if not as spouse. The central tenet of the United Kingdom's legislation on child support is that the parent should not be able to assign their responsibility for their children onto the taxpayer.

The utility of contract as a fair method of regulating private obligations makes certain presuppositions. Contract may be an acceptable means, provided that the parties to the contract can bargain freely and with full recognition of the rights which they are conferring, restricting, moderating or giving up. The need for full disclosure of each party's income and assets will be essential if the bargain is to be fair. Where a pre-nuptial agreement is being negotiated, typically shortly before the wedding, there may be considerable pressure on one of the spouses to come to a final agreement, as the emotional and financial consequences of postponement of the ceremony and reception would be dire. . . .

The promulgation of effective marital contracts will place a considerable burden on the perspicacity and foresight of the parties' lawyers. Circumstances will change, and it will be very difficult for the parties to legislate for all eventualities. Children may be contemplated, but what about intervening incapacity, or redundancy, of one of the partners? How is the law to react to circumstances which the parties did not themselves envisage?

It could well be that widespread adoption of marital contracts could lead to more litigation rather than less. In the United States, where they are common-place, a litigation industry surrounds them, and the lawyers win both ways. They charge for advising upon and drafting the agreement at the inception of the relationship, or whenever the parties consider such an agreement useful. They then charge for unpicking it, for challenging it through the courts, following marital breakdown, either on points of construction or by invoking one of the vitiating factors listed above.

Question

Would you now contemplate the use of a contract before starting to live with a partner? Or before getting married?

The government explored the possibility of wider use of such agreements in its consultation paper *Supporting Families* (1998):

Agreements about property

4.20 Couples can already make agreements between themselves, under the ordinary laws of contract, which deal with the ownership and disposal of property during marriage. Some couples also seek to reduce the scope for conflict on divorce by making agreements which deal with the way their property would be divided if they did divorce. These are often called 'nuptial' or 'pre-nuptial' agreements. There is, however, no requirement for the courts to take any account of such an agreement in deciding how to award property on divorce. This lack of certainty may well discourage couples from making such agreements.

4.21 The Government is considering whether there would be advantage in allowing couples, either before or during their marriage, to make written agreements dealing with their financial affairs which would be legally binding on divorce. This could give people more choice and allow them to take more responsibility for ordering their own lives. It could help them to build a solid foundation for their marriage by encouraging them to look at the financial issues they may face as husband and wife and reach agreement before they get married.

4.22 Providing greater security on property matters in this way could make it more likely that some people would marry, rather than simply live together. It might also give couples in a shaky marriage a little greater assurance about their future than they might otherwise have had. Nuptial agreements could also have the effect of protecting the children of first marriages, who can often be overlooked at the time of a second marriage – or a second divorce.

4.23 There would be no question of written agreements being made mandatory for couples intending to marry. Also, we would protect the interests of a party to the agreement who is economically weaker and the interests of children through six safeguards. If one or more of the following circumstances was found to apply, the written agreement would not be legally binding:

- where there is a child of the family, whether or not that child was alive or a child of the family at the time the agreement was made
- where under the general law of contract the agreement is unenforceable, including if the contract attempted to lay an obligation on a third party who had not agreed in advance
- where one or both of the couple did not receive independent legal advice before entering into the agreement
- where the court considers that the enforcement of the agreement would cause significant injustice (to one or both of the couple or a child of the marriage)
- where one or both of the couple have failed to give full disclosure of assets and property before the agreement was made
- where the agreement is made fewer than 21 days prior to the marriage (this would prevent a nuptial agreement being forced on people shortly before their wedding day, when they may not feel able to resist).

Question

Given those qualifications to enforceability, how do you see the future of pre-nuptial contracts?

Bibliography

2.1   The factual background

We quoted from:

A. Barlow, S. Duncan, G. James and A. Park, *Family Affairs: Cohabitation, Marriage and the Law* (2002), Nuffield.

A. Barlow, S. Duncan, G. James and A. Park, 'Just a piece of paper? Marriage and cohabitation' in A. Park, J. Curtice, K. Thomson, L. Jarvis and C. Bromley (eds.) *British Social Attitudes, the 18th Report: Public Policy, Social Ties* (2001) London, Sage pp. 29, 15-16.

Central Statistical Office, *Social Trends 32* (2002) London, HMSO, pp. 42-43, and tables 2.5, 2.6 and 2.7.

M.A. Glendon, 'Withering Away of Marriage' (1976) 62 Virginia Law Review 663, 686.

J. Haskey, 'Co-habitation in Great Britain: past, present and future trends and attitudes', *Population Trends 103* (Spring 2001), pp. 8–10, 15–18.

M. Hibbs, C. and J. Beswick, 'Why marry? perceptions of the affianced' [2001] Family Law 197.

S. McRae, *Cohabiting Mothers* (1993) London, Policy Studies Institute, table 5.2.

D. Meade, 'Consortium Rights of the Unmarried – Time for a Reappraisal' (1981) 12 Family Law Quarterly 213.

National Family and Parenting Institute, *Marriage in the European Union Today* (2001), pp. 2–3.

H. Oppenheimer, *Marriage* (1990) London, Mowbray, pp. 32–34.

R. Pickford, in *Fathers, marriage and the law* (1999) Joseph Rowntree Foundation, p. 17.

Additional reading

E.M. Clive, 'Marriage: An Unnecessary Legal Concept' in J.M. Eekelaar and S.M. Katz (eds.), *Marriage and Cohabitation in Contemporary Societies: Areas of Legal, Social and Ethical Change* (1980) Toronto, Butterworths, p. 72.

2.2   The legal distinctions

We quoted from:

R. Bailey-Harris, 'New families for a new society?' in S. Cretney, *Essays for a New Millennium* (2000) Bristol, Family Law, pp. 67, 67–72.

A. Barlow, S. Duncan, G. James and A. Park, 'Just a piece of paper? Marriage and cohabitation' in A. Park, J. Curtice, K. Thomson, L. Jarvis and C. Bromley (eds.), *British Social Attitudes, the 18th Report: Public Policy, Social Ties* (2001), London, Sage, pp. 20-21.

W. Blackstone, *Commentaries on the Laws of England* (1765) 17th edn by E. Christian et al (1830) London, Tegg.

Criminal Law Revision Committee, *15th Report on Sexual Offences* (Cmnd. 9213) (1984) London, HMSO.

R. Graveson, 'The Background of the Century' in R.H. Graveson and F.R. Crane (eds.), *A Century of Family Law* (1957) London, Sweet & Maxwell, pp. 2–3.

Sir Matthew Hale, *History of the Pleas of the Crown* (1736) vol. I, p. 629 (ed. G. Wilson) (1778) London, Sollom Emlyn.

Law Commission, Working Paper 116, *Rape within Marriage* (1990) London, HMSO, paras. 4.20–4.24.

A. MacFarlane, *Marriage and Love in England 1300-1840* (1986) Oxford, Basil Blackwell, pp. 246–247.

2.3 A definition of marriage?

We quoted from:

E.K. Gough, 'The Nayars and the Definition of Marriage' (1959) 89 Journal of the Royal Anthropological Institute, pp. 23, 32.

C.C. Harris, *The Family: an Introduction* (1979) London, Allen and Unwin, p. 49.

E.R. Leach, *Polyandry, Inheritance, and the Definition of Marriage* (1955) Man, no. 199, p. 183.

2.4 Void and voidable marriages; or, who can marry, and how not to marry

We quoted from:
Law Commission, *Report on Nullity of Marriage,* Law Com. No. 33 (1970) London, HMSO, paras. 24, 25, 52.

A. MacFarlane, *Marriage and Love in England 1300-1840* (1986) Oxford, Basil Blackwell, pp. 246–247.

K. Waaldijk, How the Road to Same-Sex Marriage Got Paved in the Netherlands' in R. Wintemute and M. Andenas (eds.), *Legal Recognition of Same-Sex Partnership. A Study of National, European and International Law* (2001) Oxford, Hart Publishing, pp. 437–464, 440 and 452–453.

Working Group on Forced Marriage, *A choice by right* (2000) London, Home Office.

Additional reading
Cabinet Office, Women's Unit, *Living without fear: an integrated approach to tackling domestic violence* (1999).

S. N. Katz, 'State Regulation and Personal Autonomy in Marriage: How can I marry and whom can I marry?' in A. Bainham (ed.), *The International Survey of Family Law 1996*, p. 487.

C. Lind, 'Time for Lesbian and Gay Marriages' (1995) 145 New Law Journal 1553.

S. Whittle, 'An Association for as Noble a Purpose as Any' (1996) 146 New Law Journal 366.

Website of the Dutch Ministry of Justice on marriage and adoption: www.minjust.nl:8080/a BELEID/fact/fact.htm.

2.5 Cohabitation: the options for the law

We quoted from:
A. Barlow and R. Probert, 'Displacing marriage – diversification and harmonisation within Europe' (2000) 12 Child and Family Law Quarterly 153, 155–163.

E. Cooke, 'Registered Partnerships – coming soon?' [2002] Family Law 232.

R. Probert, 'From lack of status to contract: assessing the French *Pacte Civil de Solidarité*' (2001) 23(3) Journal of Social Welfare and Family Law 257, 258–259.

The Times 6 September 2001.

Additional reading
R. Bailey-Harris, 'Law and the unmarried couples – oppression or liberation?' (1996) 8 Child and Family Law Quarterly 137.

C. Bessant, 'Cohabitation, reform and the Human Rights Act 1998' [2001] Family Law 525.

A. Barlow and R. Probert, 'Addressing the Legal Status of Cohabitation in Britain and France: Plus ca change?' [1996] Web Journal of Current Legal Issues, issue 3.

M. Broberg, 'The registered partnership for same-sex couples in Denmark' [1996] 8 Child and Family Law Quarterly 149.

R. Deech, 'The Case Against Legal Recognition of Cohabitation' in J. M. Eekelaar and S. M. Katz (eds.), *Marriage and Cohabitation in Contemporary Societies: Areas of Legal, Social and Ethical Change* (1980) Toronto, Butterworths, pp. 309–310.

E. Steiner, 'The spirit of the new French registered partnership law – promoting autonomy and pluralism or weakening marriage?' (2000) 12 Child and Family Law Quarterly 1.

2.6   Cohabitation contracts and 'pre-nups'

We quoted from:

A. Barlow, *Cohabitants and the law* (2001), London, Butterworths, pp. 14–21.

S. Bridge, 'Marriage and divorce: the regulation of intimacy' in J. Herring (ed.), *Family Law: Issues, Debates, Policy* (2001) Devon, Willan Publishing, pp. 24–29.

J. Craig and P. Pearson, *Cohabitation law and precedents* (looseleaf) London, Sweet & Maxwell, 2–015.

Supporting Families (1998) London, Stationery Office, p. 33.

W. Weyrauch, 'Metamorphoses of Marriage' (1980) 13 Family Law Quarterly 436.

Additional reading

Barton, *Cohabitation Contracts, Extra Marital Partnerships and Law Reform* (1985) Aldershot, Gower, Coventry.

E. Hatley, 'Contractual Freedom within the Family' [1998] International Family Law 39.

D. Lush, *Cohabitation and Co-ownership Precedents* (1993) Bristol, Family Law.

Chapter 3

Family economics – income

3.1 **The economic evidence**

3.2 **Work and responsibility within the home**

3.3 **Women and employment**

3.4 **An ideological basis?**

The economic arrangements of a married or cohabiting couple do not exist in isolation. There is a need for a body of flexible rules within which the couple are free to regulate their affairs. These rules exist in all relationships; whether they be created by the parties themselves, by the society and the culture within which they live, or imposed upon them by judicial or other external intervention. The concern of the lawyer in this area tends to be expressed most often in terms of making a sensible allocation of the economic assets of the parties after the relationship has broken down. However, no legal solution to this particular problem can reflect a logical and realistic readjustment of the tangled affairs unless there is a clear understanding of the economic expectations of the parties during their relationship. Thus, the question 'what happens to property after divorce?' is closely interlinked with the question 'what were the economic arrangements of the husband and the wife when they were married?'; and a similar question must be asked in the context of a non-marital union. In addition, when considering what happens after divorce or separation, we must look ahead to what happens to those individuals in old age; how far have their financial arrangements, and the division of labour within the family, affected their ability to plan ahead and, in particular, to make adequate pension provision. Thus while this chapter examines how married and cohabiting couples organise their lives, there is an underlying theme as to how relevant these issues are to the resolution of financial affairs. There are also important ideological questions to be raised relating to support obligations of spouses or partners for one another and the state's involvement in the support of the family.

Professor Tony Honoré is fully aware of the link which we have just made between the dynamic and subsisting marriage and what has been described as the 'pathology of family law', when he categorises marriage ideologically into three distinct groups – as a partnership, as a contract, and thirdly as an arrangement by which a husband assumes the role of provider. The following extract is taken from *The Quest for Security: Employees, Tenants, Wives* (1982):

There are three main ways of viewing marriage. Some see it as a *partnership*. On a traditional view, it is a partnership, come what may, for life. In that case, after divorce the partnership notionally continues, and the wife is entitled to the support she would have received had the marriage not broken up, or at any rate to a standard of living which continues to be the equal of her husband's. ... More often, marriage is now seen as an equal partnership which lasts, like other partnerships, until it is dissolved. On that view there must on divorce be a fair division of the profits of the partnership, including property acquired during the marriage. ...

Another conception of marriage is that of an *arrangement* (a collateral contract?) *by which a husband induces his wife to change her career*. Had it not been for the marriage she might, for example, have had good earning prospects. She gives these up to marry. On divorce she must now retrain, sometimes late in life, with diminished prospects. If so, her husband must compensate her by keeping her, during a transitional period, while she brings up the children, if she wants to, and redeploys. If, after a long time together, she has become emotionally attached to her status as a wife, her husband may also be required to compensate her for the wrench.

Yet another conception views marriage not as a contract but *as an arrangement by which a husband assumes the role of providing for his wife's needs and those of their children*. This idea, more ancient and deeply rooted in genetics than the contractual ones, makes the husband to some extent the wife's insurer. If she is in need, it is to him, rather than the state, that she turns in the first instance. It is he who must see to her subsistence, and perhaps more, in ill-health, old age or disablement. It is only in this framework of anticipated security that childbearing and childrearing can flourish. But how far does the husband's responsibility extend? How far, in modern conditions does that of the state or community? [italics added]

These three categories must be borne in mind when we look, in this chapter, at the economic and sociological evidence for the ways in which families organise their work and the sources of their income.

We begin by looking at the economic evidence for the financial organisation of the family and, inevitably, at the roles men and women have assumed. Second, we look at the way household tasks are organised. This is an important aspect of the way in which families manage; and it has economic implications, both for the intact family and for the ways in which individuals cope when the family is disrupted or split. Next we focus on the employment of women and on the effect upon women of their modern, dual role as carers and workers. Finally, we look at the ideological evidence: how do people see themselves as individuals amidst all this?

3.1   The economic evidence

It is argued that the economic process of change in the family has proceeded through three stages, as explained by M. Young and P. Wilmot in *The Symmetrical Family* (1973):

Even though there is so much in common between family life at each stage, and even though the boundaries between one stage and another are somewhat arbitrary, the rough-and-ready division seems to us useful, as does the generalization, even though it cannot any more than most generalizations do justice to all the evidence. In the first stage, the pre-industrial, the family was usually the unit of production. For the most part, men, women and children worked together in home and field. This type of economic partnership was, for working-class people, supplanted after a bitter struggle by the Stage 2 family, whose members were caught up in the new economy as individual wage-earners. The collective was undermined. Stage 2 was the stage of disruption. One historian has pointed the contrast in this way (E.P. Thompson 1963).

'Women became more dependent upon the employer or the labour market, and they looked back to a "golden" period in which home earnings from spinning, poultry and the like, could be gained around their own door. In good times the domestic economy, like the peasant economy, supported a way of life centred upon the home, in which inner whims and compulsions were more obvious than external discipline. Each stage in industrial differentiation and specialisation struck also at the family economy, disturbing customary relations between man and wife, parents and children, and differentiating more sharply between "work" and "life". It was to be a full hundred years before this differentiation was to bring returns, in the form of labour-saving devices, back into the working woman's home. Meanwhile, the family was roughly torn apart each morning by the factory bell.'

The process affected most the families of manual workers (and not all of these by any means). The trends were different in the middle class family, where the contrasts for both husbands and wives were somewhat less sharp than they had been in the past. But as working-class people were preponderant most families were probably 'torn apart' by the new economic system. In the third stage the unity of the family has been restored around its functions as the unit not of production but of consumption.

It is clearly not possible, since social history is unlike political or military history, to do more by way of dating than to indicate in a rough manner when the successive waves of change started going through the social structure. The Stage 1 family lasted until the new industry overran it in a rolling advance which went on from the eighteenth well into the nineteenth century. The development of the new industry was uneven as between different parts of the country, coming much later to London than to the industrial north. It also outmoded the old techniques of production more slowly in some occupations than in others. But come it did, eventually, along with many other forms of employment which shared one vital feature, that the employees worked for wages. This led to the Stage 2 family. The third stage started early in the twentieth century and is still working its way downwards. At any one period there were, and still are, families representing all three stages. But as first one wave and then another has been set in motion, the proportions in Stage 2 increased in the nineteenth century and in Stage 3 in the twentieth.

The new kind of family has three main characteristics which differentiate it from the sort which prevailed in Stage 2. The first is that the couple, and their children, are very much centred on the home, especially when the children are young. They can be so much together, and share so much together, because they spend so much of their time together in the same space. Life has, to use another term, become more 'privatized'. ... This trend has been supported by the form taken by technological change.

The second characteristic is that the extended family (consisting of relatives of several different degrees to some extent sharing a common life) counts for less and the immediate, or nuclear, family for more. ...

The third and most vital characteristic is that inside the family of marriage the roles of the sexes have become less segregated.

Social historians, Louise Tilly and Joan Scott, describe each of these three stages in *Woman, Work and Family* (1978). They speak first of the family as the labour and consumption unit:

In both England and France, in city and country, people worked in small settings, which often overlapped with households. Productivity was low, the differentiation of tasks was limited. And many workers were needed. The demand for labor extended to women as well as men, to everyone but the youngest children and the infirm. Jobs were differentiated by age and by sex, as well as by training and skill. But, among the popular classes, some kind of work was expected of all able-bodied family members. ... But whether or not they actually worked together, family members worked in the economic interest of the family. In peasant and artisan households, and in proletarian families, the household allocated the labor of family members. In all cases, decisions were made in the interest of the group, not the individual. This is reflected in wills and marriage contracts which spelled out the obligation of siblings or elderly parents who were housed and fed on the family property, now owned by the oldest son. They must work 'to the best of their ability' for 'the prosperity of the family' and 'for the interest of the designated heir'. Among property-owning families the land or the shop defined the tasks of family members and whether or not their labor was needed. People who controlled their means of production adjusted household composition to production needs. For the propertyless, the need for wages – the subsistence of the family itself – sent men, women, and children out to work. These people adjusted household composition to consumption needs. The bonds holding the proletarian family together, bonds of expediency and necessity, were often less permanent than the property interest (or the inheritable skill) which united peasants and craftsmen. The composition of propertied and propertyless households also differed. Nevertheless, the line between the propertied and propertyless was blurred on the question of commitment to work in the family interest.

One of the goals of work was to provide for the needs of family members. Both property owning and proletarian households were consumption units, though all rural households were far more self-sufficient than urban households. Rural families usually produced their own food, clothing, and tools, while urban families bought them at the market. These differences affected the work roles of family members. Women in urban families, for example, spent more time marketing and less time in home manufacture. And there were fewer domestic chores for children to assist with in the city. In the urban family, work was oriented more to the production of specific goods for sale, or it involved the sale of one's labor. For the peasant family, there were a multiplicity of tasks involved in working the land and running the household. The manner of satisfying consumption needs thus varied and so affected the kinds of work family members did.

When the number of household members exceeded the resources available to feed them, and when those resources could not be obtained, the family often adjusted its size. Non-kin left to work elsewhere when children were old enough to work. Then children migrated. Inheritance systems led non-heirs to move away in search of jobs, limited positions as artisans forced children out of the family craftshop, while the need for wages led the children of the propertyless many miles from home. People migrated from farm to farm, farm to village, village to town, and country to city in this period. Although much migration was local and rural in this period, some migrants moved to cities, and most of these tended to be young and single when they migrated. Indeed, in this period cities grew primarily by migration; for urban death rates were high and deaths often outnumbered births, a result largely of the crowded and unsanitary conditions that prevailed.

In the second stage, the family wage economy, we enter a distributive period. As Kevin Gray says in *Reallocation of Property on Divorce* (1977): 'In the distributive stage, production occurs outside the family, and the family merely distributes among the family members the economic product of the labour performed by the provider husband, the house-maker wife of course playing a vital role in this secondary process of distribution.'

Tilly and Scott emphasise that this distributive period (the 'family wage economy', as they call it) developed gradually during the mid-nineteenth century:

Under the family wage economy married women performed several roles for their families. They often contributed wages to the family fund, they managed the household, and they bore and cared for children. With industrialization, however, the demands of wage labor increasingly conflicted with women's domestic activities. The terms of labor and the price paid for it were a function of employers' interest, which took little account of household needs under most circumstances. Industrial jobs required specialization and a full-time commitment to work, usually in a specific location away from home. While under the domestic mode of production women combined market-oriented activities and domestic work, the industrial mode of production precluded an easy reconciliation of married women's activities. The resolution of the conflict was for married women not to work unless family finances urgently required it, and then to try to find that work which conflicted least with their domestic responsibilities. ...

In general, married women tended to be found in largest numbers in the least industrialized sectors of the labor force, in those areas where the least separation existed between home and workplace and where women could control the rhythm of their work.

Question

The authors concentrate on working class families. Do you think that their comments might need modifying for the middle classes in the nineteenth century?

The authors then describe how the third stage, the consumer economy, developed:

By the early twentieth century the higher wages of men particularly and the availability of cheap consumer goods raised the target income of working-class families. Necessities now included not only food and clothing, but also other items that once had been considered luxuries. What we have termed the family consumer economy then was a wage earning unit which increasingly emphasized family consumption needs.

The organization of the family consumer economy was not dramatically different from that of the family wage economy. The management of money and of family affairs in an increasingly complex urban environment did, however, require additional time and a certain expertise. As a result, the household division of labor tended to distinguish even more sharply than in the past between the roles of husband and wife and of daughters and wives. Husbands and unmarried children were family wage earners, while wives devoted most of their time to child care and household management. Wives continued, however, to work sporadically in order to earn wages to help raise the family's level of consumption.

Tilly and Scott inform us that women who worked chose to do so not simply from individualistic motives and certainly hardly ever for financial independence. Rather the prime motive was to improve the financial position of the family and to raise its standard of living. The mother's work was a supplement to her domestic responsibilities.

The three models of family organisation described by Tilly and Scott and by Young and Wilmot have been criticised by Hudson and Lee in their introductory essay to *Women's Work and the Family Economy in Historical Retrospective* (1990):

The temporal sequence of organisational change from the traditional family economy to the family wage economy, and finally to the family consumer economy based on a 'symmetrical' marriage structure is of only limited usefulness. It is also problematic to view work at home for pay as constituting a 'transitional model', given both its traditional and contemporary prevalence. Even within the middle class, adherence to the Victorian cult of domesticity was not always translated into the reality of separate spheres of activity and maintaining the 'paraphernalia of gentility' was often financially impossible. With changing economic conditions participation by middle-class women in the public sphere became 'both respectable and necessary', and there is increasing evidence of their role in decision-making in relation to their husbands' careers and family businesses. ... Furthermore, despite the apparent pervasiveness of patriarchy in the later nineteenth century, there were certain industries, such as pottery, where the male breadwinner ethos failed to take root, and where women retained a strong presence, even in trade union organisations. A joint contribution to the family economy could also encourage mutuality in dealing with domestic responsibilities.

Diana Gittins in *The Family in Question* (1993) describes how the ideology of a single male breadwinner per family developed during the nineteenth century:

Although never an entirely secure institution, marriage in pre-industrial society had provided women with a reasonable means of economic survival involving both production and domestic work in and around the home, with a good chance of some minimal security in the event of widowhood. The growth of wage labour and the increasing separation of home from work put women more than ever before at the mercy of two increasingly unstable markets: the marriage market and the labour market. In both their position was weak, and economic survival was precarious whether a woman entered one or both.

In other areas the response to mechanisation, de-skilling and proletarianisation was different. Sometimes machine breaking was an immediate response, as in the Luddite and Captain Swing riots ... More often, men in skilled crafts or industries formed themselves into associations or unions. Their general purpose was to defend their members against further capitalist exploitation, mechanisation and wage cuts, and to protect themselves from cheap labour. Since most cheap labour was made up of women and children, the unions tended to contribute further to the already disadvantaged position of women. Until the second half of the nineteenth century, however, the majority of unions were made up of men from only the most skilled trades and crafts, and one of their main aims was to procure a 'family wage' – a single wage that was adequate to support a man and dependent wife and children on his work alone. This new emphasis on the father/husband as sole earner was a powerful factor in the development of modern notions of 'masculinity'. While the concept of a single male breadwinner had started with the rise of the middle classes in the late eighteenth century, this was the first time a sector of the working class – and a very small sector at that – did so.

... it is hard to know whether their argument for wanting to keep their wives and children out of the workforce was more a matter of conviction or a rationale for higher wages that they knew would appeal to middle-class ears. Whatever the rationale, the ideal of a family wage became increasingly important as an ideal of the organised trade union movement, and it was an ideal which coincided with the new middle-class ideology of women and children as dependants of the husband/father.

During the nineteenth century, however, the proportion of working-class families who could survive on the basis of the man's wage alone was very small. Nevertheless, the objective of a single male breadwinner per family was one of the most radical changes in family ideology of the modern era, and one that had dramatic effects on notions of fatherhood, masculinity, motherhood, femininity, family life and family policy, and still has. The ideal, then as now, was often very far removed from the reality, and the majority of working-class families in the nineteenth century still relied heavily on a household economy based on several wages. Working-class men and women, but women in particular, were therefore dependent on both wage labour in the labour market and a partner through the marriage market in order to survive economically. Both markets were insecure and in fact many individuals had to find extra economic support through children's or other kin's labour.

Questions

(i)   Do you feel that this campaign was one worth winning?

(ii) Think of your grandparents and great-grandparents. Do their household economies fit into the descriptions, so far as you know, provided by the previous extracts?

(iii) What about your parents and contemporaries – have we not moved on from the 'third stage' described above to an era where the economic demands upon the family, and in particular the cost of housing, mean that the 'family wage' is often an impossible ideal? (See the comments by Mary Ann Glendon, p. 111 – and note the date at which she was writing.)

(iv) You, our readers, are both men and women, and most of you expect to begin building a career in the near future. How do you feel about the 'family wage'?

3.2   Work and responsibility within the home

In 'Legal Regulation of Marriage: Tradition and Change' (1974), Lenore Weitzman writes:

The sociological data ... are closely related to the economic data ..., for in large part it is the changing position of women with respect to men in the larger society which has influenced and altered the position of the two sexes within the family. Thus the increased labor force participation of married women has probably been instrumental in causing a decline in the absolute authority of the husband, with a consequent growth in the wife's role in the family decision-making. With an expansion in women's roles, especially economic roles, outside the family, roles within the family have also become less strongly differentiated. Wives are assuming more responsibility for financial and domicile decisions, and husbands are assuming a greater share of the responsibility for housework and child care. In general, there is a strong trend toward egalitarian family patterns, those in which authority is shared and decisions are made jointly by the husband and the wife.

The spread in egalitarian family patterns may be briefly noted in several areas. First, there is an increase in the sharing of financial decisions within the family. As the wife's contribution to the total family budget assumes greater relative importance, financial responsibilities within the family are more equally shared. Decisions on family expenditures, savings, and the general 'struggle for financial security' are now made jointly or apportioned on a less sex-stereotyped basis. Second, the determination of the family domicile and the decision of when and where to move has become more of a family decision, with the needs and interests of the wife and children assuming a much greater importance than in the past. Although both of these trends represent a decline in the traditional authority of the husband, there is also a significant decline in the traditional authority of the wife as the husband assumes a more important role in household decisions and in household tasks. ...

A third area in which there is a significant trend toward more egalitarian patterns is that of sexuality. The current sexual revolution has focused increased attention and emphasis on the wife's participation and satisfaction in sexual relations, and consequently on more mutual and egalitarian sexual relationships. ...

A fourth and closely related trend is in the increased sharing of responsibility for birth control. Knowledge and use of some form of contraception has become nearly universal in the United States today. The most recently introduced and most highly effective methods of contraception, the pill and the I.U.D., are the first to give women independent control over their reproductive decisions, and the first to allow couples a real choice about the number and timing of children. With technological advances in effective methods of female contraception, the decision of when to have children, as well as the decision of when to have sexual relations, may be increasingly decided by the husband and wife together.

Fifth, and most important, is an extended range of family roles which are now being shared or alternated between husbands and wives.

Question

Is Weitzman saying that industrialisation and changes in women's labour force participation are responsible for changes in family patterns?

Although between the end of the Second World War and the beginning of the twenty-first century, the proportion of economically active women has risen dramatically (see p. 102, below), the evidence all points to the fact that women still bear the primary burden of domestic labour in the household. The following table is taken from *Social Trends 31* (2001):

13.1 Division of household tasks[1]: by gender, May 1999

Great Britain	Minutes per person per day		
	Males	Females	All
Cooking, baking, washing up	30	74	53
Cleaning house, tidying	13	58	36
Gardening, pet care	48	21	34
Care of own children and play	20	45	33
Maintenance, odd jobs, DIY	26	9	17
Clothes, washing, ironing, sewing	2	25	14
Care of adults in own home	4	3	4
All	143	235	191

[1] Main activities carried out by individuals who are married and living together or co-habiting couples.
Source: Omnibus Survey, Office for National Statistics

Question

Might some men cheat when answering the ONS's questions?

Susan McRae (1993) obtained the following information from her female sample:

Table 6.5 Household division of labour (I): Proportion who reported tasks shared equally

Column percentages

	Long-term cohabiting mothers	Cohabited pre-maritally Married after baby	Married before baby	Non-cohab. Married mothers
Cleaning	22	18	14	7
Washing up	34	33	35	29
Cooking	20	29	27	14
Washing clothes	12	6	4	1
Taking children to doctor	31	26	28	34
Painting/decorating	26	31	25	34
Car maintenance	8	14	10	5
Gardening	48	48	46	39
Helping children with homework	60	47	62	61
Base:	77	51	57	92

Table 6.6 Household division of labour (II): Proportion who reported tasks done entirely or mainly by women

Column percentages

	Long-term cohabiting mothers	Cohabited pre-maritally Married after baby	Married before baby	Non-Cohab. Married mothers
Cleaning	77	74	81	90
Washing up	57	50	51	60
Cooking	75	63	72	84
Washing clothes	87	94	96	97
Taking children to doctor	65	74	70	64
Painting/decorating	13	28	19	2
Car maintenance	5	11	4	4
Gardening	23	29	25	22
Helping children with homework	40	43	36	33
Base:	77	51	56	92

Question

If she had asked their male companions the same questions, how do you think they would have responded?

Consider the following table, also from *Social Trends 31* (2001):

13.4
Participation in home-based leisure activities: by gender and socio-economic group[1], 1996-97

United Kingdom

Percentages

	Professional	Employers and managers	Intermediate and junior non-manual	Skilled manual	Semi-skilled manual	Unskilled	All aged 16 and over[2]
Males							
Watching TV	99	99	99	99	98	99	99
Visiting/entertaining friends or relations	95	96	96	95	94	88	95
Listening to radio	93	92	93	87	85	83	89
Listening to records/tapes/CDs	83	80	85	74	73	67	78
Reading books	81	69	68	48	49	39	58
DIY	66	65	59	60	48	40	57
Gardening	62	63	50	52	46	42	52
Dressmaking/needlework/knitting	4	4	3	3	3	2	3
Females							
Watching TV	98	99	99	100	99	98	99
Visiting/entertaining friends or relations	100	98	97	95	97	96	97
Listening to radio	96	89	90	85	82	78	87
Listening to records/tapes/CDs	93	83	80	72	70	64	76
Reading books	91	80	77	63	61	54	71
DIY	41	36	32	30	27	22	29
Gardening	49	55	51	42	41	39	45
Dressmaking/needlework/knitting	30	36	39	40	36	36	36

1 Percentage of those aged 16 and over participating in each activity in the four weeks before interview. See also Appendix, Part 13 : Socio-economic group.
2 Includes full-time students, members of the armed forces, those who did not state their socio-economic group, and those whose previous occupation was more than eight years ago, or who have never had a job.

Source: General Household Survey, Office for National Statistics; Continuous Household Survey, Northern Ireland Statistics and Research Agency

The authors comment:

While watching television is the most common home-based activity for both men and women in the United Kingdom, participation in other activities varies by gender. For example, almost three-fifths of men had carried out some form of DIY in the four weeks prior to interview in 1996-97 compared with less than a third of women (Table 13.4). Women were more likely to read or do dressmaking, needlework or knitting than men. However, the overall popularity of dressmaking, needlework or knitting among women declined by 14 percentage points between 1977 and 1996-97.

Question

To what would you ascribe the decline of knitting?

Distribution of family income between its members is a difficult research field. Notwithstanding the difficulties, Jan Pahl in *Money and Marriage* (1984, 1990) attempts a structure for the research she and others have conducted in this field:

Patterns of allocation of money
There is an infinite variety of different allocative systems within the great variety of types of households. ... In reality, the proposed typology represents points on a continuum of allocative systems, but previous research suggests that the typology has considerable validity both within Britain and in other parts of the world. Two criteria are central in distinguishing one system from another: these are, first, each individual's responsibility for expenditure between and within expenditure categories, and second, each individual's access to household funds, other than those for which he or she is responsible.

The whole wage system
In this system one partner, usually the wife, is responsible for managing all the finances of the household and is also responsible for all expenditure, except for the personal spending money of the other partner. The personal spending money of the other partner is either taken out by him before the pay packet is handed over, or is returned to him from collective funds. If both partners earn, both pay packets are administered by the partner who manages the money. Where a whole wage system is managed by a husband, his wife may have no personal spending money of her own and no access to household funds.

The allowance system
In the most common form of this system the husband gives his wife a set amount, which she adds to her own earnings if she has any; she is responsible for paying for specific items of household expenditure. The rest of the money remains in the control of the husband and he pays for other specific items. Thus each partner has a sphere of responsibility in terms of household expenditure. If a wife does not earn she only has access to the 'housekeeping' allowance and, since this is allocated for household expenditure, she may feel that she has no personal spending money of her own: the same phenomenon can also be seen in the case of the whole wage system where the wife is responsible for all family expenditure but has no personal spending money. The allowance system has many variations, mainly because of the varying patterns of responsibility. At one extreme a wife may only be responsible for expenditure on food; at the other extreme she may be responsible for everything except the running of the car and the system may come close to resembling the whole wage system. The allowance system is also known as the 'wife's wage' and the 'spheres of responsibility' system, while the whole wage system is sometimes called the 'tipping up' system (Barrett and Mcintosh 1982).

The shared management or pooling system
The essential characteristic of this system is that both partners have access to all or almost all the household money and both have responsibility for management of the common pool and for expenditure out of that pool. The partners may take their personal spending money out of the pool. On the other hand one or both of them may retain a sum for personal spending; when

this sum becomes substantial the system begins to acquire some characteristics of the independent management system. ...

The independent management system
The essential characteristic of this system is that both partners have an income and that neither has access to all the household funds. Each partner is responsible for specific items of expenditure, and though these responsibilities may change over time, the principle of keeping flows of money separate within the household is retained.

The political economy of the household
Distinguishing different types of allocative system is, however, only a beginning. What are the variables which determine the allocative system adopted by any one couple at any one time? What are the implications for the couple as a whole, and for individuals, of adopting one system rather than another?

Pahl (1990) provides interesting information regarding the reasons given by her sample of wives and husbands for their system of money management.

Table 6.1 Reasons given by wives and husbands for their system of money management

		Number mentioning each reason	
		Wives	*Husbands*
	'Ideological' reasons		
1	System seemed natural/right/fair	41	53
	'Practical' reasons		
2	Seemed more efficient/'it works for us'	27	22
3	Response to way in which wages/salaries paid	22	19
4	More convenient/one partner able to get to bank	19	15
	'Psychological' reasons		
5	Wife 'better manager' so she manages money	23	15
6	Husband 'better manager' so he manages money	10	9
	'Generational' reasons		
7	Tried to avoid parents' mistakes	5	2
8	Money management similar to parents' system	4	1

Note: Numbers add up to more than sample because some individuals gave more than one reason.

Questions

(i) Are you impressed by the 'ideological' reasons given, or do you think that people simply drift into particular arrangements?

(ii) Is it more or less likely that parties to a marriage where one or both of them have been married before will opt for an independent management system?

(iii) Is it more or less likely that cohabitants will opt for an independent management system?

(iv) To what extent might age be a factor in this sort of decision? (Think again about your grandparents or great-grandparents – ask them if you can. Might they have operated a 'whole wage' or an 'allowance system'?)

3.3   Women and employment

Hudson and Lee, in *Women's Work and the Family Economy in Historical Perspective* (1990), describe the scale of married women's involvement in the formal labour market, which altered dramatically in the twentieth century:

...The post-1945 period in particular witnessed a rapid development in women's employment in advanced industrial economies despite the resurgence of a 'back to the kitchen ideology' in the 1970s fuelled by official concern about male unemployment. The abolition of the marriage bar in public-sector employment in Britain aided this trend. There were significant changes in a variety of areas, with women increasingly dominating such occupations as clerical work, retail sales, elementary teaching and nursing. The increasing importance of 'new industries' in the 1920s and 1930s, including rayon manufacture, light engineering, food processing, and white goods provided a boost for female employment in the formal sector, although on a regionally selective basis and with an emphasis on 'semi-skilled' and 'unskilled' work. Furthermore, the inter-war period generally was characterised by official restrictions on married women's employment as a reaction to male unemployment.

'New' female occupations in the service sector continued to expand after 1945, particularly in retailing, banking, public administration and other forms of clerical work. This trend was assisted by a variety of factors, including improved levels of female pay in certain sectors, shorter working hours, lower fertility, and the gradual provision of suitable, if still inadequate welfare support. ...Technological innovations in the production and conception of household consumer durables such as vacuum cleaners, cookers and electric irons were potentially a source of reduction of domestic burdens as they slowly percolated down the social scale, especially from the 1960s, but new higher standards of domestic cleanliness and decor put pressure on women to spend as much time as in the past on homemaking.

Despite growth in the employment of married women in the formal economy in the twentieth century, many of the factors which determined female labour force participation in the early stages of capitalist development continue to affect occupation choice, gender segregation and women's overall subordination in work. Married women frequently choose jobs which do not directly challenge the prevailing concept of a 'woman's proper place', and many people still 'view it unseemly and inappropriate for wives to work'. Women's occupational choices are clearly influenced by a variety of factors, both work and non-work related. The nature of the labour-market is important but persistently negative facets of women's employment, such as sex-typed jobs, low-ranking position and low comparative earnings, reflect the continued operation of more long-term and deep-seated factors. Married women are still not expected to express any dissatisfaction with their domestic status, so that a return to formal employment frequently has to be legitimised in a socially accepted fashion, with hours tailored to suit child care (for example, mothers' evening shifts in factories) and with earnings treated as 'pin money', or with work portrayed as an emergency measure. As important is the assertion that women have a different relationship to money and wages from men, a notion which has helped to cement the social construction of gender dependency.

Just as women's wage labour in the early phases of capitalist development was frequently an extension of home-based skills, so the general expansion of the service sector, particularly in the twentieth century, has tended to replicate a similar bond between the domestic and work environments. There has been an unprecedented expansion in nursing services since the nineteenth century, accompanied by the formation of professional nursing associations, but these have been based on women's 'traditional' role as carer. Moreover, gender segregation in the health sector as a whole has been associated with persistent low pay for nurses in comparison with other sections of the medical profession. Librarianship has also provided a fast-growing demand for low-paid, but educated, female recruits. Women librarians have frequently been employed because of their submissive attitudes or, as in Tsarist Russia, because of their function as 'guardians of traditional culture'. Even in the retail trades women have been employed not just because they were cheaper than men but because they had such positive virtues as 'politeness' and 'sobriety'. They could also function effectively in a 'world of women', linking women as workers with women as consumers.

In the long term, therefore, despite an unprecedented expansion in the employment of married women in the formal economy, many of the earlier facets of women's work have been retained, particularly in relation to economic marginalisation, pay discrimination, occupational segregation and trade union participation.

Hilaire Barnett, in *Introduction to Feminist Jurisprudence* (1998) has this to say about women's employment patterns:

In 1971, 44 per cent of women were 'economically active' (in either full time or part time employment); in 1994 53 per cent, and the figure projected for the year 2006 is 57 per cent. By contrast, between 1971 and 1994, the economic activity rate for men fell to 73 per cent, and is projected to fall to 70 per cent by the year 2006. Of mothers with children between the ages of five and 10, in 1994, 20 per cent were working full time, 44 per cent part time, six per cent were unemployed and 30 per cent were 'inactive'. The number of women working part time in the United Kingdom between 1984 and 1994 rose by 19 per cent, whereas the increase in women's full time employment was only 12 per cent. In 1994, 45 per cent of economically active women worked part time, nearly twice as many men as women worked full time, while five times as many women as men worked part time.

Childcare looms large in the explanations for economic activity, full or part time, or inactivity, and a woman's economic activity is also affected by the number of children she has. Of women with three or more children, over 50 per cent were economically inactive in 1994, compared with less than one-third of women with one child. Moreover, where there is more than one child the mother is most likely to be working part time, if at all. The number of places in registered day nurseries in the United Kingdom in 1993 was over 120,000, compared with 1981 when there were less than 20,000. The number of total day places available for children under five in 1993 was close to one million. Given the number of women who could potentially be in the workforce, and compared with the position in China, women's poverty and economic underactivity is most clearly explained by the failure of successive governments to invest in childcare facilities.

Women's earnings

Women remain lower paid than men in the United Kingdom according to the Government's statistics. In 1994, one-third of women earned £190 per week or less, compared with only 13 per cent of men. On the other hand, 75 per cent of men earned over £230 per week compared with only 50 per cent of women.

Occupational data

Clerical and secretarial remains the highest source of employment for women, with nearly 80 per cent of active women being in such employment. Personal and protective services is second, with just under 65 per cent, sales only slightly lower. Under 50 per cent of women are in associated professional and technical employment, and 40 per cent in professional employment. Just over 30 per cent of women are managers and administrators; 20 per cent plant and machine operatives, and approximately 10 per cent are in craft and related occupations. Women outnumber men by four to one in the health sector and by two to one in the education sector. However, when it comes to seniority of employment position, the statistics reveal another picture.

In primary schools in England, Wales and Northern Ireland in 1991-92, women represented 81 per cent of all teachers, but only 57 per cent of head and deputy head teachers. In secondary schools, women represent 49 per cent of all teachers, but only 30 per cent are head and deputy head teachers. In the police force, where women have traditionally been under-represented, 13 per cent (or nearly 20,000) of police officers in the United Kingdom in 1994 were female. In 1994, of Chief Constables, Deputy Constables and Assistant Chief Constables of approximately 42 police forces, only six were women. There were nine Chief Superintendents, 36 Superintendents, 70 Chief Inspectors, 285 Inspectors, 1,330 Sergeants and 18,245 Constables. Among the officers of the armed forces in the United Kingdom in 1995, seven per cent were women.

Question

Is there gender segregation in the legal profession? (Have a look at the statistics for women in the judiciary, at the Lord Chancellor's Department's website: www.lcd.gov.uk.)

Social Trends 32 (2002) provides a great deal of information about women's employment patterns. Chart 4.1 shows the movement of employment rates by gender over the past 60 years; compare table 4.6, showing economic activity rates, and the authors' comments:

Chart 4.1   Emploment rates¹: by gender

United Kingdom

Percentages

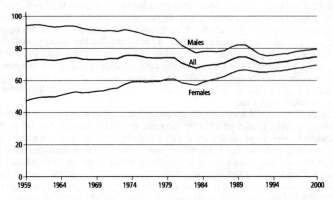

1   At Summer each year. In 1959 to 1971, males aged 15 to 64 and females aged 15 to 59; from 1972 onwards males aged 16 to 64 and females aged 16 to 59.

Source: Department for Work and Pensions

Chart 4.6   Economic activity rates¹: by gender

United Kingdom

Percentages

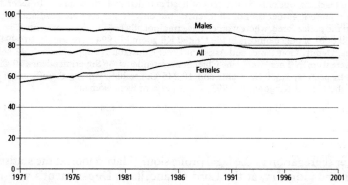

1   Males aged 16 to 64, females aged 16 to 59. The percentage of the population that is in the labour force. The definition of the labour force changed in 1984 when the former Great Britain civilian labour force definition was replaced by the ILO definition which includes members of the armed forces.

Source: Labour Force Survey, Office for National Statistics and Department of Enterprise, Trade and Investment for Northern Ireland

Economic activity rates for the population as a whole as well as for men and women separately, as shown in Chart 4.6, show broadly similar trends over the last 30 years as the employment rates illustrated in Chart 4.1. However, because the economically active population includes those who are unemployed as well as those who are employed, economic activity rates are less liable to be affected by economic cycle effects. Thus the trend in the male economic activity rate shows less marked peaks and troughs around a generally downward trend, falling from 91 per cent in 1971 to 84 per cent in 1997, the level at which it has remained over the succeeding four years. The female economic activity rate on the other hand has risen steadily, from 56 per cent in 1971 to 72 per cent from 1998 onwards. In 2001 therefore the gap between male and female economic activity rates was only 12 percentage points, compared with 35 percentage points 30 years earlier. Projections to 2011 indicate a further increase in female economic activity rates to reach 75 per cent and a fall in male rates to 82 per cent, narrowing the gap between the two even further, to only 7 percentage points.

Next, Table 4.10 sets this information in the context of the families, and particularly the children, of those women:

Table 4.10 Economic activity status of women[1]: by age of youngest dependent child, 1991 and 2001

United Kingdom   *Percentages*

	Age of youngest dependent child				No dependent children	All
	Under 5	5–10	11–15	16–18		
1991						
Working full time	14	21	31	38	50	38
Working part time	28	44	42	37	20	27
Unemployed[3]	6	6	4	3	5	5
Looking after family/home	47	22	15	13	6	17
Students[2]	1	1	..	..	6	4
Other inactive	4	5	7	8	11	9
All (=100%) (millions)	3.1	2.1	1.4	0.5	9.7	16.8
2001						
Working full time	18	26	37	44	49	39
Working part time	36	44	38	37	23	30
Unemployed[3]	3	3	4	2	3	3
Looking after family/home	38	18	12	7	4	13
Students[2]	1	2	1	..	8	5
Other inactive	3	6	8	10	13	10
All (=100%) (millions)	3.0	2.4	1.6	0.6	9.9	17.4

1 Aged 16–59. At spring each year.
2 Those in full-time education.
3 Based on the ILO definition. See Appendix, Part 4: ILO Unemployment.
Source: Labour Force Survey, Office for National Statistics

To this we must add the following table, which adds to our overall picture some information about working hours:

Chart 4.18   Distribution of usual weekly hours[1] of work: by gender, Spring 2001

United Kingdom

Thousands

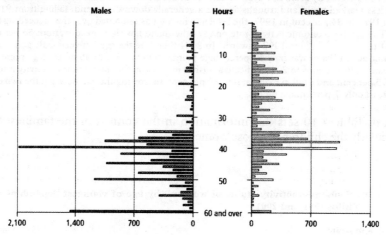

1   Figures based on valid hours.

Source: Labour Force Survey, Office for National Statistics

What about the rewards of this work? The following table, again from *Social Trends 32* (2002), gives a picture of men's and women's pay:

Chart 5.7   Gross earnings[1]: by gender and whether working full-time or part-time

Great Britian

£ per hour

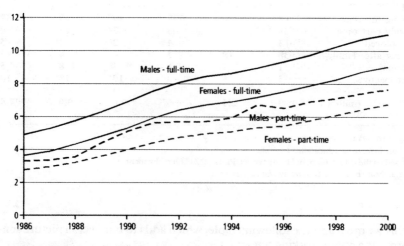

1   Average gross hourly earnings for employees on adult rates at April each year.
Source: New Earnings Survey, Office for National Statistics

Thus we can see that while women are participating more and more in the employment market, they are not reaping the same rewards as men are. The picture becomes more alarming when we look at women's working lifetimes. The Women's Unit of the Cabinet Office has carried out some research about this, and in particular about both the 'gender gap' and the 'mother gap'. Moreover, it emphasises the link between this and later chapters by considering the effect upon women of divorce and remarriage. The following is from the Cabinet Office's 'Briefing' (2000), summarising the research findings:

Women's incomes over the lifetime

In spring 1999 the Cabinet Office Women's Unit commissioned a research report into women's incomes over their lifetimes. The research set out to examine the key features of women's incomes over their lifetimes, and to identify, and quantify, the factors behind men's and women's lifetime incomes, drawing on existing research and undertaking new analysis, constructing illustrative biographies.

For the first time this research quantifies those parts of the lifetime earnings gap of equally–skilled men and women due to being female (the gender gap) and to motherhood (the mother gap). The overwhelming conclusion is that the level of a woman's educational achievement has the biggest single impact on her likely lifetime's earnings, but the hours she works, how many children she has and when she has them, and whether she divorces all have significant impacts on her lifetime income.

For example:

*   the mid-skilled childless woman is estimated to experience a lifetime gender earnings gap of £241,000. The mid-skilled mother of two experiences an additional earnings penalty (a mother gap) of £140,000;
*   the low-skilled mother of two is estimated to earn around half a million pounds less than her low-skilled husband;
*   women are likely to lose out financially as a result of divorce as they lose at least some access to the husband's income. For the mid-skilled mother of two the initial income loss of divorce is estimated to be £169,000 where the marriage is short (seven years) and £127,000 for a long marriage (17 years). Even with remarriage women can be net losers from divorce;
*   low-skilled mothers of two lose 42% of their earnings-related pension (84% if they have four children) as a result of having children, while the mid-skilled lose 21% if they have two children (69% with four children);
*   the low-skilled, never-married teenage mother of two children forgoes £300,000 in gross earnings, compared to what she is estimated to earn had she remained childless.

Background

It is nearly 30 years since the first anti-discrimination and equal pay legislation was introduced, and women's role in the economy has in many ways been transformed. But a number of key issues remain: women's and men's working lives continue to be very different as women are more likely to take time out of paid work to look after children; the pay gap is still an issue; and discrimination can still restrict women's opportunities. While we know quite a lot about income comparisons between individuals at particular moments in time, these do not tell us about the impact over women's lifetimes of the pattern and level of their earnings, the effect of the tax-benefit system and the importance to women's incomes of transfers within families.

Using a simulation model, the report estimates the lifetime incomes of women and men, examining closely the influence of differing educational attainment, the number and timing of children and other life events including early parenthood and divorce.

The findings relate to hypothetical individuals with given characteristics, not averages of all actual cases. A key characteristic is skill level, constructed at three levels:

*   'Mrs. Low-skill' who has no qualifications;
*   'Mrs. Mid-skill' who has qualifications at GCSE level; and
*   'Mrs. High-skill' who has a degree level qualification.

    ...

Summary of findings

1. THE EARNINGS GAP BETWEEN MEN AND WOMEN

The earnings gap measures the difference in total gross earnings and therefore is based on both hourly pay rates and the number of hours worked.

The lifetime gap has a number of components which this study quantifies for the first time.

The gender earnings gap

This represents the difference in lifetime earnings between equivalently-skilled childless women and men, at current rates of pay and patterns of work. Figure 1 shows estimates of this gap by education level. Mrs. Mid-skill is estimated to incur an earnings gap of £241,000 over her lifetime.

Around half of the gender earnings gap relates to the fact that married, childless women work fewer hours over their lifetimes than equivalent men; and around half is due to the hourly pay gap which exists between men and women.

The size of the gender earnings gap varies by educational level. For Mrs. Low-skill and Mrs. Mid-skill the gender gap represents over a third (37%) of their lifetime earnings, compared to Mrs. High-skill who experiences a shortfall of around an eighth (12%). In absolute terms, the gap is largest for Mrs. Mid-skill (241,000) with Mrs. Low-skill experiencing a gender earnings gap of £197,000 and Mrs. High-skill of £143,000.

The mother gap

In addition to the gender earnings gap, women who have children experience a 'mother gap' which represents the difference in lifetime earnings between equivalently-educated women with and without children. For two children these figures are: Mrs. Low-skill, £285,000; Mrs. Mid-skill, £140,000; and Mrs. High-skill, £19,000. Although there is some impact, high-skilled mothers forgo much less income than low- or mid-skilled mothers as they largely retain their place in the employment market.

However, they may incur very high childcare costs. (Childcare costs were left outside the scope of this study, along with all other expenditures on children.)

For Mrs. Mid-skill and Mrs. High-skill, motherhood has a smaller impact than that of being a woman. For Mrs. Low-skill, on the other hand, the effect of becoming a mother exceeds the already large impact of gender on her lifetime earnings.

Delaying childbirth has a significant, positive impact on lifetime earnings. For example, it is estimated that if Mrs. Mid-skill starts her family at 24 and has two children she forgoes more than twice the earnings than if she started her family at age 30. Figure 2 illustrates how Mrs. Mid-skill's mother gap is made up at different ages of first birth.

The parent gap

The combined effect of both the gender and the mother gap can be thought of as the difference in lifetime earnings between the mother and father in a family. The parent gap is substantial across the skills spectrum. Mrs. Low-skill with two children earns around half a million pounds less than her low-skilled husband. For Mrs. Mid-skill the equivalent figure is £380,000, and for Mrs. High-skill, £160,000.

However, the parent gap is much more significant for Mrs. Low-skill, whose husband has a lifetime earnings nearly double hers. Mrs. Mid-skill's husband has earnings 75% greater than her while Mrs. High-skill's husband has lifetime earnings just 14% higher.

Figure 1: Lifetime earnings of men, childless women and women with two children

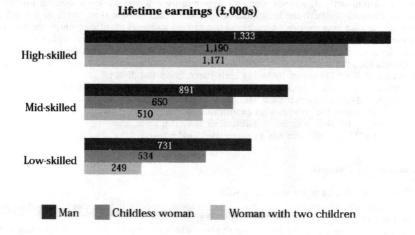

Lifetime earnings (£,000s)

High-skilled: 1,333 / 1,190 / 1,171

Mid-skilled: 891 / 650 / 510

Low-skilled: 731 / 534 / 249

■ Man   ■ Childless woman   ■ Woman with two children

2. Women's lifetime earnings and educational attainment

The most important source of variation on women's lifetime earnings is the level of educational attainment. The impact of educational level on lifetime earnings is illustrated in Figure 3. Looking from front to back, this shows the dramatic difference between women of different educational levels whatever the number of children they have. Looking from left to right, it also shows that having children has a very different impact on women of different educational levels.

These differences are a consequence of the levels of earnings commanded by women at different educational levels, and of the different labour supply behavior simulated for women at different educational levels. If Mrs. Low-skill has two children she takes nine years out of the labour market and works part-time for a further 28 years. Mrs. Mid-skill is out of the labour market for just two years and works part-time for a further 12. Mrs. High-skill works part-time for just one year, working full-time for the rest of her working life.

Figure 2: Breakdown of the mother gap for a mother of two children by age of mother at first birth: mid-skilled woman

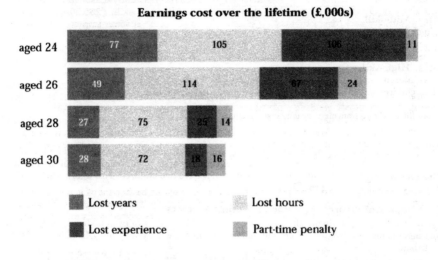

Earnings cost over the lifetime (£,000s)

Figure 3: Gross lifetime earnings

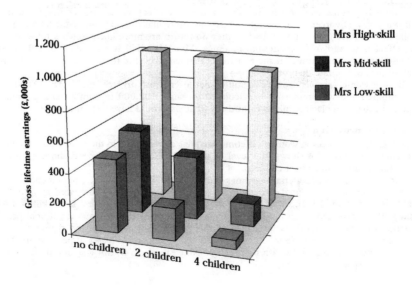

3. Partnership, divorce and income
Woman's contribution to family incomes

Table 1 shows the contribution women's earnings make to a couple's joint lifetime earnings. If Mrs. Mid-skill remains childless she contributes 42% of a couple's lifetime earnings; this figure is 41% and 49% for Mrs. Low-skill and Mrs. High-skill respectively. The percentage earned by the woman falls if she has children, most significantly for Mrs. Low-skill, again reflecting the large 'mother gap'.

Table 1: Average contribution of wife's earnings to couple's joint lifetime earnings

	Percentages
Mrs. Low-skill	
No children	41
Two children	24
Mrs. Mid-skill	
No children	42
Two children	35
Mrs. High-skill	
No children	49
Two children	47

Note: 'lifetime' runs from marriage until first retirement

Income sharing within families can be an important component of women's lifetime incomes. If couples share their incomes equally, then this family transfer can provide 30% of the lifetime incomes of Mrs. Low-skill and Mrs. Mid-skill if they have two children. This figure reaches 60% for Mrs. Low-skill during the childbearing years.

The impact of divorce on women's lifetime incomes

Many women lose out financially on divorce. If Mrs. Mid-skill with two children gets divorced, her income loss is £169,000 where the marriage is short (seven years) and £127,000 for a long marriage (17 years).

However, increased earnings and net transfers from the state and, if they are made, child support payments and a share in the ex-husband's pension, can make a big difference to the income loss due to divorce. In these examples, the income loss is reduced to £25,000 for the short marriage and £41,000 for the long marriage.

Compared to the women who remain married, the effect on earnings comes about in the following way. Divorcees who do not remarry are more likely to stay out of the labour market while their children are young but when they do return are more likely to work full-time. The net effect is to add to their lifetime incomes. Mrs. Mid-skill is estimated to end up with £28,000 more from earnings if she experiences an early divorce than either her non-divorced counterpart or the late divorcee.

Even if women remarry some can still be net losers from divorce. Mrs. Low-skill who has two children and who remarries is calculated to gain £102,000 in family transfer from her second husband, replacing only two-thirds of what she would have lost on divorce.

6. Pension provision

The notable differences in women's lifetime earnings are reflected in their individual income in retirement. As Figure 4 shows, the level of income in retirement depends both on level of education and the number of children.

Mrs. Low-skill's small lifetime earnings lead to a small individual retirement income – if she is childless she has an annual retirement income of around £4,900 compared to £9,600 for childless Mrs. Mid-skill and £20,700 for childless Mrs. High-skill. Mrs. Low-skill and Mrs. Mid-skill are assumed to be in SERPS, while Mrs. High-skill is in an occupational pension scheme. Low-skilled mothers lose 42% of their earnings-related pension if they have two children (84% if they have four). For Mrs. Mid-skill, comparable losses of pension are 21% if they have two children (69% with four). High-skilled mothers do not lose out at all.

The modelling of current trends build up a picture of growing polarisation among women – in retirement as in working life. Thus, as differences between men's and some women's lifetime incomes have narrowed, the differences appear to be growing among women.

Figure 4: Own net income in retirement

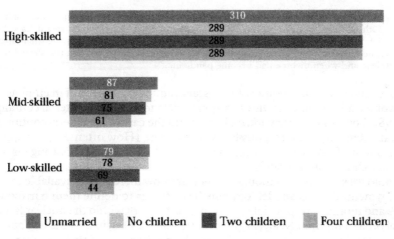

Total own net income in retirement (£,000s)

■ Unmarried ■ No children ■ Two children ■ Four children

Questions

(i)   Do you find these statistics alarming?

(ii) What should be the impact of this information upon the financial consequences of divorce?

(iii) But what about cohabitants?

3.4   An ideological basis?

Mary Ann Glendon, in *State, Law and Family: Family Law in Transition in the United States and Western Europe* (1977), emphasises the difficulties which appear when this question is explored.

The prevailing ideologies of marriage have never been alike for all groups of any large population. In Western society, however, one ideology has been dominant and until modern times has found universal expression in the law. The family law of Western legal systems has traditionally embodied ideas of separate spheres of activity appropriate for women and men. It has carried the image of the woman as principal caretaker of the home and children, the man as principal provider, and of a family authority structure dominated by the husband and father. This should not be understood as meaning that the woman's *exclusive* task has been to care for home and children. In pre-industrial society, the wife was often a co-worker with the husband on the farm, in the craft and in the shop. The exclusively housewife-marriage seems to be a phenomenon of the 20th century. Already this period is beginning to appear to have been a brief interlude in history. Today, as more and more women engage in economic activity outside the home, housewife-marriage is only one of many current marriage patterns. Where housewife-marriage exists, it is now more apt to be a phase of a marriage than a description of the marriage from beginning to end.

Organized around a hierarchical model, with a clear division of roles between the sexes, traditional family law placed primary responsibility for support of the family on the male partner and vested authority in him to determine the place and mode of family life and to deal with all the family property, including that of the wife. Among the wealthy, property matters could to some extent be arranged so that the interests of the wife (and her family of origin) could be protected. The law paid little attention to the needs of the poor, even when large numbers of women began to be employed outside the home in the early 19th century in England, and later in France and Germany. The set of legal rules organized along these traditional lines persisted in England, France, the United States and Germany well into the 20th century, long after behavior of many married people had ceased to correspond to the image enshrined in the laws.

This model was constantly adjusted, beginning in the late 19th century and in the first half of the 20th century, but at last the center could not hold. Laws which might have been appropriate for the family production community, or for the housewife-marriage when divorce was rare, no longer worked when many women's economic activity had been transferred to the marketplace and when divorce had become pandemic.

Although Glendon's point is a necessary reminder of the shift in emphasis of the women's economic activity, it is appropriate to recall the material contained at p. 98, above, that housework, child care and the care of the elderly continue to a great extent to be the responsibility of women. (How often do you suppose women move from years of caring for their children into years of caring for their parents? Or do both at once?)

Could we say that even though women are now increasingly available to seek employment, there is an ideology which continues to define them narrowly as wives and mothers, responsible for the domestic work within the nuclear family? Carol Smart and Bren Neale, in *Family Fragments* (1999), look at the way parents view themselves in relation to the home, their children, and their employment. Again, their findings provide a link between this and later chapters by looking at the impact of the couple's division of labour upon the divorced/separated family.

Identity

How many parents view themselves, and how much of their personal identity is bound up with their parenthood, has an important bearing on how parenthood operates in practice. People's biographies as parents assume importance because parental identities are not made instantly or ascribed but, much like other kin relationships, are negotiated and forged over considerable periods of time. From this perspective, parenthood can be seen as part of a nexus of life commitments. It is a matter of conscious choice, which must be weighed against competing life interests such as employment, leisure pursuits, geographical mobility and, following separation, the pursuit of new intimate partnerships. How this balancing is undertaken and to what extent parents make themselves available for their children in preference to other life chances will have a strong influence on how post-divorce parenthood is negotiated and established.

Where the activities of parental care are gendered then the parental identities which arise from them are also likely to be gendered. Motherhood and fatherhood are not perceived as identical subject positions. Many of the mothers in our sample had made their parenthood a central part of their lives:

> **Felicity Lessing:** I gave up my job in order to be their mother.... Basically my role is to be their mother.... I feel as if my role disappears if I've not got something to do with them... I am more available. I simply am.

> **Erica Dawson:** They are my life. My life revolves around what they do, what they need. They are my boys.... Where they go, I go. It was just never open to discussion.

> **Ann Black:** I've always looked after them.... I've always been there.... I don't work. I always took it for granted that she would stay with me, no matter what. Obviously he's working and he couldn't afford to give up work. But he weren't prepared to look after 'em anyway.... I think they automatically go to the mother, don't they, unless there are exceptional circumstances.

The strong identity as mothers which these parents express arises in part from dominant cultural constructions which idealize motherhood. It also arises, more concretely, from their experience as full-time parents who gave up their jobs when they had children. The employment patterns of mothers have undoubtedly shifted over the past decades with a small but growing percentage returning to work within a few weeks of their child's birth but even where the mothers in our sample were working full time in the early years of parenthood (nine out of thirty-one cases) they continued to take the main responsibility for the children's day-to-day care, for 'being there' when needed and for organizing substitute care. For these women, therefore, their maternal identity was (for a time at least) more significant than identities arising from their engagement in paid work.

The father's identity is less likely to be derived from such an intense focus on parenthood. As pointed out above, only one father in our sample gave up work to raise the children himself. But this does not mean that men do not have identities as fathers, but this is often linked to their work as financial providers. This work of financial provision is crucially important, yet it means deriving a sense of identity from outside the home and family. Although some fathers are now more actively involved in their children's lives, they are more likely to spend time sharing leisure pursuits with the children, rather than engaging in the basics of childcare. There is, therefore, a sense in which fathers have more freedom to opt in or out of such interactions and to choose how and when to balance fatherhood with their other commitments or interests. It is now quite acceptable for men to assume either the identity of the 'good provider' father or the 'new man' father. These fathers opted for the traditional identity.

Jim Walters: I'm a workaholic... [and] there's a lot of conflict in trying to follow a profession and being a parent.... It's a kind of balancing act, balancing my new relationship and my children... because they're not my partners' kids.... I think I probably put me first, my partner second and the children third.

Erica Dawson: He was a financial father. He wasn't one for picking them up or cuddling them .... On Sundays, he'd say, 'It's my day off'.

Gordon Fenton: You don't make parents, it's not something you study at or anything .... *you just are a parent.* How to behave is to be yourself ... I think we should stop analysing how to behave in front of children. (Our emphasis)

Colin Hanks: It wouldn't have been practical [for me to have the children], I had to work full time. She was looking after them full time because she's always been that sort of mum. I wouldn't have been able to look after them.

However, although only one father expressed his core identity as a caring parent during his marriage, we found that rather more shifted in this direction on divorce. Although we cannot generalize from our small, qualitative sample, we found that nine out of twenty-nine of our fathers were willing either to abandon their identities as earners and workers, or to reduce their commitment to their careers, in order to assume an identity as caring parent on divorce or separation. Most significantly, six of our fathers 'switched' identity at divorce either by giving up paid employment or, because they had been made redundant or taken early retirement (usually from military or police service), they decided not to seek new employment. These six fathers were all in manual or broadly working-class employment.

James Grant: I knew in my own mind that I could give the children the same or better care than Paula and I thought that we're in a modern world now and everyone's talking about 'new age men'. I'm a totally modern kind of parent.

Tim Muir: I think there's a big difference between a lot of fathers than there was twenty years ago. There's a lot more fathers now who are willing and able to look after their children and bring them up, whereas twenty years ago it was just assumed that men worked and women looked after children. Now I think it's changed.

None of these six fathers had been involved in childcare to any great extent before their divorce or separation. Their wives were housewives and had taken full responsibility for the children before the separation. But what is interesting in these cases is that these men were transformed into 'new' fathers almost overnight and they had a very strong commitment to their new identities, often seeing lone fathers as far superior to lone mothers because they were more organized and less likely to be over-emotional.

The other three fathers (out of a total of nine) who made this switch of identity were in positions which enabled them to have a good deal of control over the time they spent at work or outside the home. They were either self-employed or undergoing vocational training. In our sample of twenty-nine fathers, only two who had children living with them were in full-time, inflexible employment. These had support from their extended family.

Tentatively we would suggest that men's willingness to assume an identity as a caring parent is much more likely to be related to their position in the labour market than it is for women. Women may work full or part time, be students or be outside the paid labour market, but if they are mothers, then motherhood in the form of caring parenthood is a core identity. Fathers seem to assume this identity only if they leave the labour market (or are ejected from it) or if they have some degree of flexibility or control over their hours at work. Although the findings shown in table 3.1 are hardly surprising, they do reveal [the problem] in microcosm, ... which is particularly acute for fathers who are in full-time employment. The pressure to work long hours for a man whose identity is tied up with being a good employee or high achiever makes it virtually impossible to be involved to any great extent in his children's lives. Mothers have known this for a long time and as a consequence their life-chances in the employment market have diminished because they have typically opted to give priority to their identity as mothers. But now that the traditional gender contract is subject to change what once seemed like the 'natural' gender order becomes potentially problematic for both mothers and fathers. Fathers may be starting to make choices between the competing identities as 'new man' father and 'good provider' father. If they opt for the former then the time they are required to spend in the labour market becomes a problem which even having a new partner or help from an extended family cannot resolve.

Parenthood therefore still appears to have very different meanings for mothers and fathers, both before and after separation, although the meanings of both are currently subject to change.

Table 3.1 The relationship between gender, employment and children's residence

	Women		Men	
	Residential	*Non-residential*	*Residential*	*Non-residential*
Employed (full-time)	9	2	2	11
Unemployed	10	0	6	3
Flexible employment	9	1	3	4

Questions

(i)   Do you believe that society in the twenty-first century in the UK is ordered on a gender role basis, legitimising patriarchal power?
(ii) If you do believe this, should the law leave people free to arrange their lives thus, or should it encourage some different pattern?
(iii) If the latter, what and how?

Bibliography

Introduction

We quoted from:
   A. Honoré, *The Quest for Security: Employees, Tenants, Wives* (1982) London, Stevens, p. 62.

Additional reading
   J. Ginn and D. Price, 'Do divorced women catch up in pension building?', Bar Conference 2001.

3.1 The economic evidence

We quoted from:
D. Gittins, *The Family in Question* (1993) Basingstoke, Macmillan, pp. 27, 28.
K. Gray, *Reallocation of Property on Divorce* (1977) Abingdon, Professional Books, p. 176.
P. Hudson and W.R. Lee 'Women's Work and the Family Economy in Historical Perspective' in P. Hudson and W.R. Lee (eds), *Women's Work and the Family Economy in Historical Perspective* (1990) Manchester and New York, Manchester University Press, pp. 26, 27, 28, 31, 32.
L. Tilly and J. Scott, *Woman, Work and Family* (1987) New York and London, Methuen, pp. 21 et seq., 105, 123, 124, 176.
M. Young and P. Willmott *The Symmetrical Family* (1973) London, Routledge and Kegan Paul (1980) Harmondsworth, Penguin Books, pp. 28 et seq.

Additional reading
M. Anderson, 'Family, Household and the Industrial Revolution' in M. Anderson (ed.), *Sociology of the Family* (1980) Harmondsworth, Penguin Books.
N. Charles, *Gender in Modern Britain* (2002) Oxford, Oxford University Press, chapter 3.
O.R. McGregor, *Social History and Law Reform* (1981) London, Stevens.

3.2 Work and responsibility within the home

We quoted from:
Central Statistical Office, *Social Trends 31* (2001), London, HMSO, tables 13.1 and 13.4.
S. McRae, *Cohabiting Mothers* (1993) London, Policy Studies Institute, tables 6.5, 6.6.
J. Pahl, *Money and Marriage* (1989, 1990) Basingstoke and London, Macmillan, pp. 94, 108, 178.
J. Pahl, 'The Allocation of Money Within the Household' in M.D.A. Freeman (ed.), *State, Law and the Family* (1984) London and New York, Tavistock Publications, p. 36 at pp. 40–42, 44, 45.
L. Weitzman, 'Legal Regulation of Marriage: Tradition and Change' (1974) 62 California Law Review 1169.

Additional reading
M. Barrett and M. McIntosh, *The Anti-Social Family* (1982) London, Verso Editions.
J. Pahl, 'Patterns of Money Management Within Marriage' (1980) 9 Journal of Social Policy 313.
A. Oakley, *The Sociology of Housework* (1974) London, Martin Robertson & Co, pp. 122, 124.

3.3 Women and employment

We quoted from:
Cabinet Office, Women's Unit, *Briefing: Women's incomes over the lifetime.*
H. Barnet, *An Introduction to Feminist Jurisprudence* (1998) London, Cavendish, pp. 54–55.

Central Statistical Office, *Social Trends 31* (2001), London, HMSO, charts 4.1 and 4.6, 4.10, 4.18, 5.7, and p.72.

P. Hudson and W.R. Lee, 'Women's Work and the Family Economy in Historical Perspective' in P. Hudson and W.R. Lee (eds.), *Women's Work and the Family Economy in Historical Perspective* (1990) Manchester and New York, Manchester University Press.

Additional reading

J. Martin and C. Roberts, *Women and Employment: A Lifetime Perspective* (1984) London, HMSO.

H. Scott, *Working Your Way to the Bottom: the Feminisation of Poverty* (1984) London, Pandora Press.

3.4   An ideological basis?

We quoted from:

M.A. Glendon, *State, Law and Family: Family Law in Transition in the United States and Western Europe* (1977) Amsterdam, North Holland, p. 75.

C. Smart and B. Neale, *Family Fragments* (1999) Bristol, Polity Press, pp. 51–55.

Additional reading

C. Glendinning and J. Millar, *Women and Poverty in Britain* (1987) Brighton, Wheatsheaf Books.

C. Hakim, *Key Issues in Women's Work* (1996), London, Athlone.

H. Harman, *The Century Gap* (1993) London, Vermilion.

Chapter 4

State support and private support

4.1 State support for the family's income

4.2 Poverty and the lone-parent family

4.3 The private law obligation and the state – maintenance and income support

4.4 Support for families with elderly and/or disabled dependants

What does the family do – where does it turn for help – when the structures we looked at in Chapter 3 break down because its own income is inadequate or non-existent? This chapter considers the sources of financial support for the family, and addresses the complex questions which surround the question of state involvement in family income support. Of necessity, the chapter is concerned with priorities and with parity of treatment. It looks at lone-parent families, some of whom may well have forms of support other than the state; it looks at poor two-parent families, who may well have no other means of support; and it looks at those families where there is a dependent elderly adult living in the household.

We turn first to the basics of state support for the family, tracing its history from its post-war origins and looking at its nature today.

4.1 State support for the family's income

In her chapter on 'Income Maintenance for Families with Children', in *Families in Britain* (1982), Ruth Lister described the framework of the system of state support up until the reforms in the Social Security Act 1986:

The basic framework for today's income maintenance provisions was laid down in the Beveridge Report of 1942. The Beveridge Plan envisaged a comprehensive 'scheme of social insurance against interruption and destruction of earning power' combined with a 'general system of children's allowances, sufficient to meet the subsistence needs' of children. Family allowances (for all children but the first) and contributory national insurance benefits (such as unemployment and widows' benefits) were introduced after the war. The Beveridge Plan also included the safety-net of a means-tested national assistance scheme designed to protect the minority who fell through the meshes of the insurance scheme. It was intended that this safety-net would wither away until it was catering for only a tiny minority. Instead, because of the failure to pay adequate national insurance benefits, as recommended by Beveridge, the numbers claiming means-tested assistance (renamed supplementary benefit in 1966) trebled from one to three million between 1948 and 1978. Further, governments have attempted to bolster up inadequate income maintenance provisions for both those in and out of work through the introduction of a range of means-tested benefits, which have been much criticised. A classic example was the introduction, in 1971, of Family Income Supplement for poor working families, as an alternative to fulfilling an election pledge to increase family allowances. The failure to pay high enough national insurance benefits and family allowances was one reason for the growing dependence on means-tested benefits. The other was the exclusion from the Beveridge Plan of people such as the congenitally disabled who could not meet the contribution conditions attached to the insurance benefits. During the 1970s a number of non-contributory benefits were, therefore, introduced to help the disabled and those at home to care for disabled relatives.

The overall picture today is, thus, one of a confusing patchwork of contributory, non-contributory and means-tested benefits. Much of this patchwork has grown up in isolation from the other main element in our income maintenance provisions: the tax system. ... The system of personal tax allowances was supposed to ensure that 'there should be no income tax levied upon any income which is insufficient to provide the owner with what he requires for subsistence' (Royal Commission on the Taxation of Profits and Income, 1954). [However,] the personal tax allowances patently no longer perform this function. The value of the tax allowances has been so eroded since the war that people can now start to pay tax at incomes which are below the poverty line. ...

The most recent development in income maintenance provision for families has been the introduction of the child benefit scheme. This represented the fusion of two hitherto separate strands of financial support for children: family allowances and child tax allowances.

The Social Security Act 1986 replaced the supplementary benefit with a system known as income support, which remains the source of financial support for those, such as lone parents, who are not available for work (the Jobseekers Act 1995 introduced the jobseekers allowance, replacing unemployment benefit, for those available for work). A claimant is entitled to income support if he or she is aged 16 or over and not working, or working less than 16 hours a week and on a low income. No claim can be made if the claimant has capital of over £8,000, and his claim will be reduced on a sliding scale if he has £3,000 or more. The rates payable from April 2002 are shown in the following table published by the Department of Social Security:

Personal allowances for single people:

aged 16-17	£32.50
or depending on their circumstances	£42.70
aged 18-24	£42.70
aged 25 or over	£53.95

Personal allowances for couples:

both aged 18 or over	£84.65
where one or both partners are aged under 18, their personal allowance depends on their circumstances.	

Personal allowances for lone parents:

aged 16-17	£32.50
or depending on their circumstances	£42.70
aged 18 or over	£53.95

Personal allowances for dependent children:

from birth to September following 16th birthday	£33.50
from September following 16th birthday to the day before 19th birthday	£34.30

Premiums:

Family	£14.75
Family (one lone parent rate for people with preserved rights)	£15.90
Bereavement Premium	£21.55
Disabled child	£35.50
Carer	£24.40
Severe disability – paid for each	£41.55

Pensioner	£44.20 (single)
	£65.15 (couple)
Enhanced pensioner – aged 75-79	£44.20 (single)
	£65.15 (couple)
Higher pensioner	£44.20 (single)
	£65.15 (couple)
Disability	£23.00 (single)
	£32.80 (couple)
Enhanced disability premium	£11.25 (single)
	£16.25 (couple)
	£11.25 (child)

People who receive income support are also entitled to housing benefit, which will pay their rent, or, subject to significant limitations, mortgage interest.

Note that payment is made to one adult for the whole family; and that the income of cohabitants is amalgamated: thus, although they have no common law duty to support each other, social security legislation assumes they are doing so. When does living together mean cohabitation? In *Kimber v Kimber* [2000] 1 FLR 383, his Honour Judge Tyrer approved the following comment in *Rayden and Jackson on Divorce and Family Matters* (17th edn) on the definition of an unmarried couple for the purposes of income-related benefits to be found in s. 137(1) of the Social Security Contributions and Benefits Act 1992:

Three main factors have to considered in determining whether a man and a woman are living together as husband and wife: [1] their relationship in relation to sex; [2] their relationship in relation to money; [3] their general relationship.

No single factor is necessarily conclusive.

. . . six factors are still commonly cited by adjudication officers and social security appeal tribunals: [1] membership of the same household; [2] stability; [3] financial support; [4] sexual relationship; [5] children; and [6] public acknowledgement.

It is not necessary that all six aspects are found to point towards cohabitation for a couple to be found to be living together as man and wife, but they must in all cases be found to be members of the same household. It has been said that the concept (of the household) is a matter of common sense and common experience and that in practice if a person has exclusive occupation of separate accommodation from another person they do not live in the same household. However, in a case where there is not such a clear cut separation, the test will generally be whether there is a sufficiently shared domestic establishment for it to be said that there is one household.

Note that, for these purposes, an unmarried couple can only be a man and a woman; same-sex partners are not treated as a couple for social security purposes.

Question

Should same-sex couples be treated as a couple for this purpose?

There has been some attempt to allocate resources towards families with children. From 1945, there was in existence a system of family allowances. The philosophy behind this scheme was that the state should not meet the whole cost of the needs of children. The amount of the allowance, therefore, was based on the estimates of the cost of meeting physical needs only, for example, for food, clothing and housing. There was no notional account taken of items such as toys or books.

In particular, allowances were not payable for the first child of the family. Family allowances were subject to a tax 'claw-back'. But, under a child tax allowance scheme, tax payers could obtain exemption from a certain amount of their income from taxation for each dependent child. Tax allowances, of course, only benefited those subject to tax, and would hardly be of any value to those categories of persons who fall within or close to the poverty trap. Child benefit was phased in as from 1977, and provides a merger of child tax allowances and family allowances. Child benefit is a universal, non-means tested and tax-free cash benefit for all children. There is an additional payment, known as the one-parent benefit, for a lone parent. The benefit was seen by politicians from all parties as a way 'to put cash into the hands of mothers and to give a measure of independence to mothers' (Patrick Jenkin MP on 9 February 1977, in a debate on the Child Benefit Scheme in the House of Commons). In the same debate, the then Minister, Mr Stan Orme MP, said:

Child Benefit is non-means tested and non-taxable. The scheme has two big advantages over the present method of family support which relies on child tax allowances and family allowances. The child benefit will be paid to the mother, as it is typically the mother who is responsible for the housekeeping in raising the children. This contrasts with the child tax allowances, which typically go to the father. Thus, income is transferred within the family from father to mother. Wage earners who earn under the tax threshold do not get the benefit of the child tax allowances, but they will get the child benefit.

In addition to child benefit, there has been a series of different sources of support for families with children where one or both parents are in work but earnings are inadequate. Andrew Dilnot and Julian McCrae, in a paper produced for the Institute of Fiscal Studies in 1999, explain:

1   Introduction

There has been a system of support for working families with dependent children in the UK for almost 30 years. In 1971, as a supposedly temporary measure while policies to address the problem of family and especially single parent poverty were devised, Family Income Supplement (FIS) was introduced. FIS was a means-tested benefit for families with an adult working at least 24 hours a week, and with a dependent child. Initially numbers were quite low, but grew significantly through the 1970's and 1980's as shown in Table 1. There were three reasons for this growth – increased generosity of the benefit, higher take-up, and a growth in the eligible population, in particular that of single parents. In 1988, FIS was renamed Family Credit (FC), with some structural change, and an increase in generosity. Take-up continued to rise, as did the size of the eligible population and the generosity of the benefit, leading to further increases in numbers receiving. In the first half of the 1990's the hours requirement was cut to 16 per week, and a childcare disregard was introduced to encourage higher participation especially amongst mothers of young children. The take-up of the childcare disregard has been very small, but overall numbers have continued to rise, reaching more than three quarters of a million before the introduction of another reform, the replacement of FC by the Working Families Tax Credit, in October 1999. The government estimates that after the reform nearly twice as many families will be in receipt of WFTC as received FC.

Table 1: Number of individuals receiving FIS/FC/WFTC

	Number of recipients
1971	71,000
1985	199,000
1990	317,000
1995	600,000
1999	780,000
Post WFTC (gov est)	1,500,000

Figure 1: Increased generosity of in work support

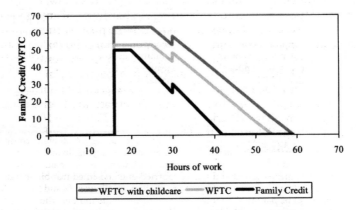

Starting in October 1999, Family Credit is to be replaced by the Working Families Tax Credit (WFTC). The WFTC will be substantially more generous than FC. By the end of the century, the government expects to be spending £5bn per year (1.5% of government budget, 0.6% of GDP) on the WFTC, almost £2bn more than was expected under FC. The WFTC will increase the generosity of in-work support relative to the FC system in four ways:

- a credit for children of between £19.85 and £25.95 per week
- an increase in the threshold from £80.65 to £90 per week
- a reduction in the taper from 70% to 55%
- a childcare credit of 70% of actual childcare costs up to £150 per week

The effects of these changes relative to FC are shown in Figure 1. Those currently receiving the maximum payment see a small increase in the level of their payment if they have children under 11. Those with net incomes between £80.65 and £90 move from being on the taper to receiving maximum support. The others on the taper see the taper rate fall from 70% to 55%. The largest cash gains go to those people who are currently just at the end of the taper. The increased generosity of in work support also creates new entitlement to in work support.

The National Family and Parenting Institute has produced a table comparing family support within Europe:

Benefits for married couples, families and children in European Union member states

EU Member Country	Benefits for Married Couples	Benefits for Families and Children
Austria	Optional joint taxation where advantageous eg in single earner households;	Family benefit paid for each child with the amount increasing with age; a direct payment is also given for each child, with the amount for each child increasing as the number of children in the household increases;
Belgium	Optional joint taxation and transfer of income from a higher or single income spouse to a non-earning or lower income spouse	Family allowance for each child, increasing in amount up to the third child. Age supplements paid at six, 12 and 16 years of age.

EU Member Country	Benefits for Married Couples	Benefits for Families and Children
France	Compulsory joint taxation for married couples and also for cohabiting couples registered under the new PACS law	Means-tested infant allowance paid up to three years of age; family allowance paid for second and subsequent children, with the amount increasing until the sixth child; means-tested schooling expenses allowance for age six to 18; Family allowance paid for each child up to 18 years and increases with each child born and with the age of each child.
Germany	Optional transferable tax allowances for married couples	Family allowances for all children up to age 16 are paid to anyone living in the country; family allowance is also paid for over 16s not married and still in education or training up to the age of 27.
Luxembourg	Compulsory joint taxation for married couples	Family allowances are paid for each child, with less for the first child than subsequent children; extra payments are made when a child reaches six and 12 years of age; a school expenses allowance is paid in August each year to children aged six and over.
Portugal	Compulsory joint taxation for married couples and a marriage grant payable to newly-married couples	Family allowance is paid for each child up to the age of 15; for over 15s, family allowance is only paid to children still in education; a nursing mother's allowance is paid for the first 10 months of a child's life.
Spain	Optional joint taxation linked to household income.	Family benefit paid for each child under 18,
United Kingdom	Each spouse taxed individually	Child benefit paid monthly with more paid for first child; family credit paid through tax system to parents on a low income; new Children's Tax Credit to be introduced in 2001; additional maternity benefits are paid to those on a low income through the Sure Start initiative.

Note: the Sure Start initiative provides services for families in areas where a high proportion of children are living in poverty, and aims to improve health, development and learning. See the website at www.surestart.gov.uk.

The Children's Tax Credit was introduced on 6 April 2001; it is non-means tested, and provides a tax credit of up to £520 per year for couples or single parents who have at least one child living with them for at least part of the tax year.

Question

Is there any merit in abolishing child benefit and using the money to target more help to more people through the tax credit mechanism or through means-tested benefits? Or would this mean that all the benefit went to the breadwinning head of the family rather than to the children's carer? Does that matter these days?

4.2 Poverty and the lone-parent family

The growth in the number of lone-parent families in Great Britain is apparent from the following table from *Social Trends 32* (2002).

Table 2.2 Households[1]: by type of household and family

Great Britain — *Percentages*

	1961	1971	1981	1991	2001[2]
One person					
Under state pension age	4	6	8	11	14
Over state pension age	7	12	14	16	15
Two or more unrelated adults	5	4	5	3	3
One family households					
Couple[3]					
No children	26	27	26	28	29
1-2 dependent children[4]	30	26	25	20	19
3 or more dependent children[4]	8	9	6	5	4
Non-dependent children only	10	8	8	8	6
Lone parent[3]					
Dependent children[4]	2	3	5	6	6
Non-dependent children only	4	4	4	4	3
Multi-family households[5]	3	1	1	1	1
All households[5]					
(=100%) (millions)	16.3	18.6	20.2	22.4	24.1

[1] See Appendix, Part 2: Households and Families.
[2] At Spring 2001.
[3] Other individuals who were not family members may also be included.
[4] May also include non-dependent children.
[5] Includes couples of the same gender in 2001, but percentages are based on totals excluding this group.
Source: Census, Labour Force Survey, Office for National Statistics

Households and families
The average household size in Great Britain was around 4.6 people for many years before falling to 3.1 in 1961. Since then it has reduced further to 2.4 people per household in 2000-01, as the number of households has grown at a faster rate than the population (Table 2.1). The population of Great Britain increased by a half over the 20th century, while the number of households tripled. Trends towards smaller families, and more people living alone, contribute to this increase in the number of households. The Continuous Household Survey estimated that at Spring 2001, the average household size in Northern Ireland was 2.7, slightly higher than in Great Britain.

Household composition has become more varied in recent decades, and increasing numbers of people are living alone. In Spring 2001 almost three in ten households in Great Britain comprised one person living alone, more than twice the proportion in 1961 (Table 2.2). The proportion of households consisting of a couple with dependent children fell from 38 per cent in 1961 to 23 per cent in Spring 2001, while the proportion of lone parent households with dependent children tripled, accounting for 6 per cent of all households in both 1991 and 2001. Multi-family households formed 3 per cent of all households in 1961, but have since declined to around 1 per cent. From the 1960s there was emphasis on the provision of first public, and then private, housing which encouraged the acquisition of separate accommodation. There is also evidence that lone parents, who historically were more likely than other families to live in multi-family households, increasingly became one-family households throughout the period.

Thus in 2001 lone parents comprised 29% of all households in Great Britain with dependent children; in 1961, the figure was about 14%. Who are lone parents? The following table comes from John Haskey's article, 'One-parent families and their dependant children in Great Britain', *Population Trends 91* (1998):

Fig. 1 Percentage of families with dependent children headed by lone mothers (by marital status) and lone fathers, 1971–1996

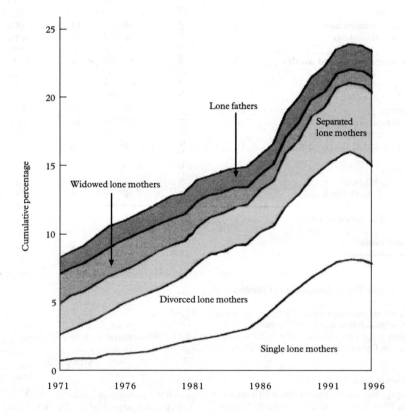

The National Council for One-Parent Families reports (on their website, www.ncopf.org.uk) in 2002:

Typically, lone parents' incomes are less than half those of two-parent families, with average net incomes a little over £100 a week.

   Fifty per cent of one-parent families live on gross weekly incomes of less than £150, compared to just 4% of married couples and 9% of cohabiting couples.

The following table from *Living in Britain: Results from the General Household Survey 1998* (Office of National Statistics) illustrates these figures:

Table 2 Usual gross weekly income by family type.[3]

**Families with dependent children Great Britain 1998 Usual gross
weekly household income**

Family type	£0.01-£150	£150.01-£250	£250.01-£350	£350.01-£450	£450.01 and over	Base = 100%
Married couple %	4	6	10	14	65	1,571
Cohabiting couple %	9	11	16	17	46	224
Lone mother %	51	21	13	6	9	542
Single %	64	17	6	6	6	205
Widowed %	18	18	23	5	37	22
Divorced %	45	24	15	8	9	195
Separated %	44	24	18	6	9	120
Lone father %	43	21	2	10	23	60
All lone parents %	5	21	11	6	11	602

Thus, a substantial proportion of lone parent families form a part of the lower income group of households on whom the bulk of state benefits are targeted. J. Bradshaw and J. Millar, in *Lone Parent Families in the UK* (1991), explain:

Lone parents are very different from other families with children in terms of both the sources and the level of their incomes. Unlike other (non-retired) households where earnings typically form the largest component of income, lone parents more often combine income from a variety of other sources, and benefits play a much larger role in the total. According to the 1989 Family Expenditure Survey the average gross weekly incomes of lone parent households were made up 49 per cent from earnings, 35 per cent from benefits and 29 per cent from other sources. By contrast the average gross weekly incomes of couples with two children were made up 81 per cent from earnings, five per cent from benefits and one per cent from other sources. Thus while benefits usually form a small addition to earnings for married couples, for lone parents they are often the major or sole source of income ...

The official statistics on 'low income' families and the new series on 'households below average income' also show lone parents significantly over-represented among the poorest families. In 1985 there were 540,000 lone parent families in receipt of supplementary benefit and a further 100,000 with incomes no higher than 40 per cent above supplementary benefit level – giving a total of 640,000 families (1.7 million adults and children) or 73 per cent of those in lone parent families at that time. This represents an increase of 40 per cent in the numbers of lone parents with incomes at that sort of level since 1979. The number of persons in lone-parent families with incomes below 110 per cent of supplementary benefit level increased by 67 per cent between 1979 and 1987. The 'households below average income' also show lone parents at the bottom end of the income distribution.

M. Maclean and J. Eekelaar in *Children and Divorce: Economic Factors* (1983), speaking of children of divorced parents, emphasise the importance of relating the problems of the poverty level for dependent children of lone-parent families to other children in comparable situations:

... but these children have potential sources of support not available to children of sick or unemployed fathers, or children in large families. On divorce there are essentially four sources from which support might be found to arrest the decline in the economic circumstances of the former family. The first comprises *the resources of the former family* as they stood at the moment of the dissolution. However, as most studies have shown, these are generally meagre ... But where an independent household existed, a dwelling, either owner-occupied or rented, is likely to be the most significant item. The second is *the earning capacity of the custodial parent* (which we assume for simplicity to be the mother). The third is *the earning capacity of the non-custodial parent* (the father). And the last resource is to be found in *State provisions*.

Questions

(i)   In spite of the overall growth in the number of lone-parent families, the number of widowed mothers has actually declined since the early 1970s. Why do you think this is? Could it be (a) remarriage rates? (b) divorce rates? (c) some other reason?
(ii)   Maclean and Eekelaar actually identify in their examination of potential sources of support for children of divorced parents a 'fifth and powerful economic resource'. What do you think they are referring to?

Two reports which are still of profound importance are Sir William Beveridge's report on *Social Insurance and Allied Services* (1942) and Sir Maurice Finer's *Report of the Committee on One-Parent Families* (1974).
Sir William Beveridge's report on *Social Insurance and Allied Services* (1942) had this to say of the divorced and separated:

347.   End of marriage otherwise than by widowhood
Divorce, legal separation, desertion and voluntary separation may cause needs similar to those caused by widowhood. They differ from widowhood in two respects: that they may occur through the fault or with the consent of the wife, and that except where they occur through the fault of the wife they leave the husband's liability for maintenance unchanged. If they are regarded from the point of view of the husband, they may not appear to be insurable risks; a man cannot insure against events which occur only through his fault or with his consent, and if they occur through the fault or with the consent of the wife she should not have a claim to benefit. But from the point of view of the woman, loss of her maintenance as housewife without her consent and not through her fault is one of the risks of marriage against which she should be insured; she should not depend on assistance. Recognition of housewives as a distinct insurance class, performing necessary service not for pay, implies that, if the marriage ends otherwise than by widowhood, she is entitled to the same provision as for widowhood, unless the marriage maintenance has ended through her fault or voluntary action without just cause. That is to say, subject to the practical considerations mentioned in the note below she should get temporary separation benefit (on the same lines as widow's benefit), and guardian or training benefit where appropriate.
   NOTE. – The principle that a married woman who without fault of her own loses the maintenance to which she is entitled from her husband should get benefit is clear. It is obvious, however, that except where the maintenance has ended through divorce or other form of legal separation establishing that the default is not that of the wife, considerable practical difficulties may arise in determining whether a claim to benefit, as distinct from assistance, has arisen. There will often be difficulty in determining responsibility for the break-up of the marriage. There will in cases of desertion be difficulty in establishing the fact or the permanence of desertion. There will in all cases be the problem of alternative remedies open to the wife. The point to which the principle of compensating a housewife for the loss of her maintenance otherwise than by widowhood can be carried in practice calls for further examination. It may for practical reasons be found necessary to limit the widow's insurance benefit to cases of formal separation, while making it clear that she can in all cases of need get assistance and that the Ministry of Social Security will then proceed against the husband for recoupment of its expenditure.

The proposal was not adopted. A major reason why the idea did not meet with approval, apart from the practical difficulties noted above, may lie in the need to reconcile the collective security involved in an insurance scheme with the concept of individual responsibility. In a welfare state, the moral virtue of contributing to a scheme which will provide relief against, for example, sickness and unemployment – both one's own and one's neighbour's – is, one hopes, self-evident. Contributing to a scheme which provides relief for the wives in other people's broken marriages, however, is not so easy to justify.

Question

Do you consider that the state has a responsibility to ensure that children do not spend most of their childhood living at the officially defined subsistence level? If you do think this way, should state resources be directed at (a) enforcing the 'liable relative' obligation (see p. 129, below), or (b) helping to alleviate the poverty of children and others in comparable situations?

The Finer Committee looked for an alternative state benefit to resolve the lone parent's problems, and opted for a 'guaranteed maintenance allowance' (GMA).

The ten main features of the proposed benefit are summarised in the Finer Report:

(1) The allowance would normally, in the hands of the lone parent, be a substitute for maintenance payments; maintenance payments would be assessed and collected by the authority administering the allowance; they would be offset against the allowance paid and any excess paid to the mother; the need for lone mothers to go to court to sue for maintenance awards would be largely eliminated;

(2) the level of the benefit would be fixed in relation to supplementary benefit payments, and, like them, would be reviewed regularly, so that, taken in conjunction with whatever family support was generally available (family allowances or tax credits) it would normally be sufficient to bring one-parent families off supplementary benefit even if they had no earnings;

(3) all one-parent families would be eligible for the benefit, including motherless families;

(4) the benefit would be non-contributory;

(5) the benefit would consist of a child-care allowance for the adult and a separate allowance for each child;

(6) the benefit would not be adjusted to the particular needs of individual families, except in so far as it would reflect the size of the family;

(7) for lone parents who are working or have other income the benefit would be tapered, after an initial disregard, so that it fell by considerably less than the amount by which income increased;

(8) the adult benefit would be extinguished by the time income reached about the level of average male earnings, but the child benefit would continue to be payable to all lone parents, whatever their income;

(9) once awarded, benefit would be fixed at that level for three months at a time, without in the normal way being affected by changes in circumstances. There would thus normally be no need for changes, including the beginning of a cohabitation, to be reported, until a fresh claim to benefit was made. Taken in conjunction with subparagraph (6) above this should much reduce the need for detailed enquiries;

(10) the benefit would be administered by post, on the lines of the family income supplements scheme.

Questions

(i) The Finer proposals have not been adopted: besides the obvious economic reasons, why do you think the Conservative and the Labour parties, for their differing reasons, have both been slow to support the scheme?

(ii) Do you think that public opinion nowadays would object to a *contributory* scheme for lone-parent families?

It is noteworthy that only a very small proportion of lone-parent families headed by widows are obliged to rely upon income support. This is because widowed mothers are entitled to a widowed mother's allowance if the deceased husband has paid the necessary contributions (and the contribution conditions are not very severe). The parent is entitled to a flat-rate benefit and an addition for each child. There is no reduction for earnings, or indeed for any other income, such as a pension from her deceased husband's occupational pension scheme, or from life insurance.

Question

Are there any arguments against extending this benefit to include unmarried, divorced and separated mothers? Or separated fathers?

From March 2001 the 'New Deal' scheme has provided help for lone parents to start work. The Department of Work and Pensions explains:
- From 9 April 2001, the first £20 of a lone parent's weekly earnings will not be counted when their Income Support is worked out.
- From 30 April 2001, lone parents on Income Support may receive an extra £15 a week while training for work through New Deal for Lone Parents. They can get this for a 12 month period.
- From 30 April 2001, anyone taking part in New Deal for Lone Parents can get help towards registered childcare costs if they start a job of less than 16 hours a week. They can get this for a 12 month period.

Question

What about the 'poverty trap'? Consider the single mother who is not working and who receives just enough from her children's father to take her off income support, but insufficient to compensate her for the loss of benefits that go with income support such as free school meals, free milk, etc?

That brings us to the issue of support for lone parents from their former partner.

4.3   The private law obligation and the state – maintenance and income support

Certain family members have a private law obligation to support each other. In particular, spouses must do so, during the marriage and, to some extent, after it has ended. Spousal support can be enforced both during and after the marriage; while the Matrimonial Causes Act 1973 is usually associated with divorce proceedings, a quick and relatively inexpensive procedure is available in the magistrates' court under the Domestic Proceedings and Magistrates' Courts Act 1978. Both statutes include provision for maintenance for children. Moreover, the Children Act 1989, in Sch. 1, expresses the duty of all parents, married or not, to provide for the maintenance and housing of their children.

Cohabitants have no private law obligation to make financial provision for each other.

However, the welfare state makes provision for all in times of financial hardship, whether or not that hardship is caused or accompanied by family breakdown. This section looks at the interplay between the private law obligation and the state's provision.

First, liable relatives. Section 78 of the Social Security Administration Act 1992 states:

> (*a*) a man shall be liable to maintain his wife and any children of whom he is the father, and
>
> (*b*) a woman shall be liable to maintain her husband and any children of whom she is the mother.

Section 107 of that Act extends this duty, so that unmarried or divorced parents of children under 16 are 'liable relatives', that is, they must reimburse the state if it has to pay means-tested benefits to support the other parent and their children.

Can a departing partner morally argue that his new responsibility is with a new liaison, leaving the state to provide support for his former partner and the children by that relationship? It is this question which lies at the heart of the *Report of the Committee on One-Parent Families*, the Finer Report (1974):

The dilemma of liable relatives

4.179   At this stage, it will be helpful to create the characters in an everyday drama. John, let it be supposed, contracted a marriage by which there are children of school age, or younger. He earns an average wage in a semi-skilled occupation. His marriage has broken down, and he has left home. He may or may not be divorced. Mary is John's former or deserted wife. Her lack of training, or the demands of the children, or both, prevent her from taking employment, or, at any rate, from earning more than a small amount in part-time work, insufficient for the needs of herself and the children. John is living with his second wife, or with his mistress. She and John have children of their own, or, it may be, she has children by a former marriage or association whom John looks after as his own. This woman also earns little or nothing. ...

4.181   ... Given John's earning capacity, however, it is clear that he cannot, when in work, earn enough money to maintain both the families. If he elects to do his duty by Mary's family, he will to that extent relieve the Supplementary Benefits Commission [now the DSS] from paying money to Mary, but the inevitable effect will be to deprive the family of which he is a current member of the means of subsistence in circumstances where, since he is in work, they will not themselves be eligible for benefit. If, on the other hand, he elects to maintain the latter family, then, with equal inevitability, he has to break his obligations towards Mary's family. But she, in that case, can claim supplementary benefit; in such circumstances neither family starves.

4.182   When a man is put in such a dilemma the solution he will lean towards is tolerably clear. He will feed, clothe and house those with whom he is living, knowing that the State will provide for the others.

This view of the dilemma and its solution is illustrated by the following cases.

Delaney v Delaney
[1991] FCR 161, [1990] 2 FLR 457, [1991] Fam Law 22, Court of Appeal

The parties married in January 1978. They separated in February 1987 and were divorced in March 1989. There were three children of the marriage – a boy aged eleven, a girl aged ten and another boy aged five. In February 1989 the wife applied for periodical payments for herself and the three children. On 8 September 1989 the deputy district judge ordered that the husband should pay £10 a week in respect of each child. He further made a nominal order for the wife of 5p a year. The husband appealed to the circuit judge. The husband and his girl friend had acquired a three bedroomed semi-detached house in conjunction with a housing association. They were paying a mixture of mortgage repayments and rent, amounting to £40.28 per week each. The judge found that this exceeded their needs and the husband had deliberately taken on unnecessary and excessive obligations after he had an obligation to the children. He dismissed the appeal.

The husband appealed. On appeal, Ward J noted that the wife's income, including the various state benefits to which she was entitled, amounted to £152 a week. He commented:

The Circuit Judge said this of her income and her need: 'After paying her rent and rates, she has left £50, with which to feed and clothe herself and her three children. This patently is not enough', and quite clearly it is not. ...

Ward J then considered the husband's outgoings, and reached this conclusion:

The real issue, therefore, is the extent to which the husband can meet that need for this wife and this family. ...

In my judgment the approach of this court in this case must be, firstly, to have regard to the need of the wife and the children for proper support. Having assessed that need, the court should then consider the ability of the husband to meet it. Whilst this court deprecates any notion that a former husband and extant father may slough off the tight skin of familial responsibility and may slither into and lose himself in the greener grass on the other side, nonetheless this court has proclaimed and will proclaim that it looks to the realities of the real world in which we live, and that among the realities of life is that there is a life after divorce. The respondent husband is entitled to order his life in such a way as will hold in reasonable balance the responsibilities to his existing family which he carries into his new life, as well as his proper aspirations for that new future. In all life, for those who are divorced as well as for those who are not divorced, indulging one's whims or even one's reasonable desires must be held in check by the constraints imposed by limited resources and compelling obligations. But this husband's resources, even when one adds to them the contribution made by his girl friend, are very limited indeed. He brings in £115 a week net and she brings in £97 a week net. Their joint income is £212 per week. Their expressed outgoings, as found by the Judge, ... were £179.39, and that took no account of food, clothing, entertainment, holidays, house repairs, car repairs, servicing, the television licence or the road fund tax. ... After meeting those expenses their joint income is then reduced to something in the region of £25 a week on which this man and his girl friend have to feed and clothe themselves and maintain the first family.

In my judgment this father was reasonably entitled to say that for the welfare of his children, ... he should have accommodation sufficient for proper access and so suitable to be able to offer them staying access. Two bedrooms may have been sufficient, but three bedrooms does not far exceed his need having regard to the fact that the wife herself lives in a three-bedroomed house. ... I find it difficult to say that this husband, in incurring these liabilities, was behaving in an extravagant fashion. That was the test applied in the case of *Furniss v Furniss* (1981) 3 FLR 46. The approach in *Barnes v Barnes* [1972] 1 WLR 1381 was to permit expenditure to a proper standard. The approach in *Preston v Preston* [1982] Fam 17 was to look at need within the context of s.25 of the Matrimonial Causes Act in terms of what was reasonably required. So whether one judges this man by a standard of extravagant expenditure or of living to an improper standard or of behaving unreasonably, I do not find it possible to judge him to have gone beyond the limit of what is permissible. His share of £40.28 per week is not out of proportion to the wife's rental of £33 per week. Consequently, I find that this expenditure as set out is reasonably incurred by him and I find, as a result, that the £25 a week or thereabouts left for himself and the girl friend to feed and clothe themselves is barely adequate to sustain any reasonable way of life.

In my judgment, therefore, this father would find it extremely difficult, if not impossible, to meet the obligation he has and which ordinarily he should honour to maintain his children. In paying him due credit, I observe that he has paid £10 a week to the children, being the most that he felt he could afford.

This court is entitled, as the authority of *Stockford v Stockford* (1981) 3 FLR 58 makes clear, to approach the case upon a basis that if, having regard to the reasonable financial commitments undertaken by the husband with due regard to the contribution properly made by the lady with whom he lives, there is insufficient left properly and fully to maintain the former wife and children, then the court may have regard to the fact that in proper cases social security benefits are available to the wife and children of the marriage; that having such regard, the court is enabled to avoid making orders which would be financially crippling to the husband. Benefits are available to this family of which the Judge was not made aware, and I have come to the conclusion that the husband cannot reasonably be expected to contribute at all to the maintenance of his previous family without financially crippling himself. In my judgment, it is far better that the spirit of effecting a clean break and starting with a fresh slate be implemented in this case, not by dismissing the claims of the wife and the children, but by acknowledging that now and, it is likely, in the foreseeable future he will not be able to honour the obligations he has recognised towards his children, and in my judgment the appeal should be allowed and I would substitute a nominal order to each of the children for the order of £10 which each of them is currently ordered to receive.

Appeal allowed; an order of £0.50 per annum per child substituted for the order made by the judge in the court below.

Questions

(i)   Do you agree with the proposition that a court should strive to avoid making orders that are financially crippling to the husband? Does not this approach encourage irresponsibility on the part of the husband? Or do you think that an order is justified so as to impress upon fathers that their primary obligation is to their own children and their first wives?

(ii)   Can you think of *any* advantages from the point of view of the wife in obtaining an order for nominal maintenance as in *Delaney* ?

(iii)   As a tax payer, can you see any justification for the use of public funding in such a case on behalf of the wife's applications?

(iv)   Do you see any value at all in sending a man to prison for non-payment of maintenance payments?

(v)   *Is* there a difference between failure to pay 'wife support' and failure to pay 'child support'?

Bradshaw and Millar (1991) (see p. 125 above) found that only 30% of lone mothers received regular payments of maintenance. They also found that maintenance formed less than 10% of lone parents' total net income compared with 45% for income support and 22% for net earnings. *Children Come First* (1990), 'The Government's Proposals on the Maintenance of Children' complains: 'The contribution made by maintenance to the income of lone-parent families therefore remains too low.'

Children Come First explains:

1.3.2   When a lone parent claims Income Support the DSS tries to ensure that the absent parent pays enough maintenance to remove his dependants' need for Income Support, or as much towards that amount as he can reasonably afford. A separated parent is asked to pay enough to support the claimant and the children fully so that payment of Income Support can stop. Divorced parents and parents who were never married who are not liable to maintain each other are currently asked to pay an amount equal to the personal benefit rates for the children they are liable to maintain plus the family and lone parent premiums payable under Income Support because there are children in the household. The Social Security Act 1990 has provided for courts to be able to include the amount to be recovered from the absent parent in recognition that it is responsibility for the care of the children which prevents the claimant working.

Children Come First proposed a major change in approach both by the courts and the DSS:

2.1   The Government proposes to establish a system of child maintenance which will be equally available to any person seeking maintenance for the benefit of a child and which will:

- ensure that parents honour their legal and moral responsibility to maintain their own children whenever they can afford to do so. It is right that other taxpayers should help to maintain children when the children's own parents, despite their own best efforts, do not have enough resources to do so themselves. That will continue to be the case. But it is not right that taxpayers, who include other families, should shoulder that responsibility instead of parents who are able to do it themselves;
- recognise that where a liable parent has formed a second family and has further natural children, he is liable to maintain all his own children. A fair and reasonable balance has to be struck between the interests of the children of a first family and the children of a second;
- produce consistent and predictable results so that people in similar financial circumstances will pay similar amounts of maintenance, and so that people will know in advance what their maintenance obligations are going to be;
- enable maintenance to be decided in a fair and reasonable way which reduces the scope for its becoming a contest between the parents to the detriment of the interests of the children;
- produce maintenance payments which are realistically related to the costs of caring for a child;
- allow for maintenance payments to be reviewed regularly so that changes in circumstances can be taken into account automatically;
- recognise that both parents have a legal responsibility to maintain their children;
- ensure that parents meet the cost of their children's maintenance whenever they can without removing the parents' own incentives to work, and to go on working;
- enable caring parents who wish to work to do so as soon as they feel ready and able;
- provide an efficient and effective service to the public which ensures that:
  - (*a*) maintenance is paid regularly and on time so that it provides a reliable income for the caring parent and the children and
  - (*b*) produces maintenance quickly so that the habit of payment is established early and is not compromised by early arrears;
- avoid the children and their caring parent becoming dependent on Income Support whenever this is possible and, where it is not possible, to minimise the period of dependence.

The proposal, put into effect in the Child Support Act 1991, was for an 'integrated package' involving a formula for the assessment of how much maintenance should be paid, a child support agency which has responsibility for tracing absent parents and for the assessment, collection and enforcement of maintenance payments, and changes in the rules of Social Security to encourage caring parents to go to work if they wish to do so. We might say that this was the only instance, during the Thatcher years, of nationalisation of what had previously been a private matter.

The Child Support Act 1991 in its original form was not a success. Perhaps its most notorious feature was the formula itself, requiring in some cases one hundred items of information for completion, and characterised by expressions such as:

$$MR = AG - CB$$

$$G = \frac{MR}{(A + C) \times P}$$

$$AE = (1 - G) \times A \times R$$

$$AE = Z \times Q \times \frac{A}{(A + C)}$$

Concerns, and protests, were generated by numerous aspects of the Act's operation, in particular the high levels of assessment generated by the formula, the complete lack of discretion in its operation, the Act's effect in families where a capital settlement had been made in partial satisfaction of child support obligations (see *Crozier v Crozier* [1994] 2 WLR 444, [1994] 2 All ER 362, [1994] 1 FLR 126) and the requirement that a person with care in receipt of income support co-operate with the agency in seeking maintenance from the absent parent.

The Secretary of State's *Guidelines on the Application of the Requirement to Co-operate* (1993) stated that: 'the PWC [parent with care] has a right to be believed unless what she says is inherently contradictory or implausible' and stresses the need for interviews to be 'handled with care and sensitivity' (para. 13). The Guidance lists as examples circumstances where it would be reasonable to conclude that a PWC had good cause not to co-operate in seeking maintenance:

- PWC fears violence;
- PWC a rape victim;
- the AP (absent parent) has sexually abused one of her children;
- child conceived as a result of sexual abuse (including incest).

It then lists, again as examples, 'circumstances in which the PWC will say that she or her children would suffer harm or undue distress, where there may be less of a *prima facie* case that this would be so', including:

- fears that the AP will want to see the child;
- PWC wishes to sever links with the AP;
- PWC wishes to protect the AP, 'usually because he is living in a stable relationship with someone else who is unaware of the child he shares with the AP';
- PWC wanted the child; AP did not.

Question

Would you mind being labelled an 'absent parent'?

Some minor changes were made in 1994, making the formula a little more generous to the paying parent. But the level of concern about the Act prompted the Select Committee to report on it, in its Fifth Report of the session in October 1994. Its report began by endorsing the principles and aims of the Act; but expressed grave concerns about the Act's operation. It went on to list a number of recommendations made in the light of detailed evidence given to the Committee.

As a result of the Committee's recommendations, a White Paper, *Improving Child Support*, was published in January 1995, announcing the following changes:

a. The introduction during 1996/7, following primary legislation, of some discretion to depart from the maintenance formula assessment in cases where the absent parent would otherwise face hardship or where certain property or capital transfers took place before April 1993. There will be closely specified grounds for the special circumstances that will be considered, and limits on the extent of the departure. Either parent will be able to apply for a departure, and both will be entitled to make representations.

b. Changes to the maintenance formula from April 1995:
   - no absent parent will be assessed to pay more than 30 per cent of his normal net income in current child maintenance, or more than 33 per cent in a combination of current maintenance and start-up arrears;
   - a broad-brush adjustment will be provided in the maintenance formula to take account of property and capital settlements;
   - an allowance will be made towards high travel-to-work costs;

- housing costs will be allowed for a new partner or step-children;
- the maximum level of maintenance payable under the formula will be reduced.

c. From April 1997, parents with care in receipt of Income Support or Jobseeker's Allowance will be able to build up a maintenance credit which will be paid as a lump sum when the recipient starts work of at least 16 hours a week.

d. Family Credit and Disability Working Allowance recipients will receive some compensation for loss of maintenance where the changes in b. above result in a reduction in their assessment during an award of benefit.

e. Fees will be suspended for a period of two years until April 1997; and interest payments will also be suspended, to be replaced after two years with a penalty for late payment.

f. Changes will also be made to improve the administration of the scheme.

These changes were put into effect, partly by Statutory Instruments and partly by the Child Support Act 1995, which substantially amends the Child Support Act 1991. Perhaps their most important feature is the reintroduction of discretion by making provision for 'departure directions'.

Nevertheless, satisfaction with the operation of the Child Support Act remained very low. Sweeping reform was effected by the Child Support, Pensions and Social Security Act 2001. A new formula has been introduced, which can make an assessment in many cases from only three items of information: the income of the non-resident parent (note the change in terminology); the number of his children; and the number of children he is living with. Nick Wikeley, in 'Child Support – the new formula' (2001), explains:

THE NEW RATES

CSPASSA 2000, s 1 and Sch 1 set out the basis for the new formula (replacing Child Support Act 1991, s 11 and Sch 1 respectively). The new scheme will have four rates: a basic rate, a reduced rate, a flat rate and a nil rate.

The normal or default rate will be the basic rate, under which the NRP will be liable to pay 15% of his net weekly income where he has one qualifying child. This will increase to 20% where he has two qualifying children and 25% where he has three or more such children. If the NRP has another child living with him, who is not a qualifying child (for example a stepchild or a child born in a relationship with a new partner), then his net weekly income is reduced by 15% before the basic rate is applied. This discount rises to 20% if he has two such children and 25% if he has three (or more) such children. As James Pirrie observes, 'step-children move centre stage for the first time' ('Changes to Child Support – The SFLA View' [1999] Fam Law 838, at p 839). This approach reflects that advocated in the White Paper over the alternative option canvassed in the green paper (simply calculating the child support for all the children and dividing by the number of children in each family) and reflects a 'slight preference' for first families.

A NRP is liable to pay a reduced rate of child support maintenance where his net weekly income is between £100 and £200 (these thresholds, as with all figures and percentages in the CSPASSA 2000, may be varied by regulations) and neither the flat rate nor the nil rate applies. The ... intention is that the child support liability will increase in proportion to the amount by which the net income exceeds £100. The reduced rate must not be less than the flat rate.

The flat rate (initially £5 per week, compared with the current minimum contribution of £5.30) will be payable in cases where the nil rate does not apply. In addition, the NRP must either have a net income of less than £100 per week or receive a prescribed benefit, pension or allowance or have a partner who receives a prescribed benefit...

The nil rate will apply where either the NRP has a net income of less than £5 per week or he falls into one of the prescribed categories of persons. These will include students in full-time education, children (ie using the social security definition of those under 16), people on income support who are aged 16 or 17 or who have been in hospital for more than one year, and prisoners. In appropriate but presumably rare cases (for example the full-time student NRP with extensive assets) it will be possible to seek a variation (see further below).

SHARED CARE AND APPORTIONMENT

As with the current scheme, the new child support system makes provision both for shared care (where the NRP shares care of the child(ren) with the parent with care (PWC)) and for apportionment of child support liabilities (for example where a NRP has qualifying children by two or more previous partners).

Under the current arrangements a reduction for shared care applies only if the child stays over with the NRP for at least 104 nights a year. In future, if the NRP has overnight care of one child for between 52 and 103 nights a year, his basic or reduced rate liability will be discounted by one-seventh. If the child stays over with the NRP for 104 to 155 nights a year, the fractional reduction will be two-sevenths, and for 156 to 174 nights a year it will be three-sevenths. If the shared care amounts to at least 175 nights, the reduction will be one-half (plus £7 for each such child). If more than one qualifying child of the same NRP live with the PWC, then for shared care purposes the relevant deduction will be the sum of the relevant fraction divided by the number of the children. Hence, if the NRP has overnight care of one child for one night a week on average, and that child's sibling for two nights a week on average, the child support liability will be reduced by three-fourteenths. The new rules provide plenty of scope for warring parents to continue their arguments over the extent of shared care.

The rules governing apportionment are best explained by an example. If Alan has two children from previous relationships, each of whom lives with their respective mother, Beth or Carol, then the aggregate child support liability (ie one of the four rates described above), is apportioned between the two PWC's. In this case Beth and Carol would each receive 50% of whatever rate applied. If, however, Alan had fathered three children, two with Beth and one with Carol, then Beth would receive two-thirds of the child support and Carol one-third.

INCOME

The fundamental point is that under the reformed scheme only the NRP's income is going to be relevant to the formula calculation. The PWC's income will have no effect on the assessment in future. According to Nicholas Mostyn QC (and others), this represents 'gross unfairness' ('The Green Paper on Child Support – Children First: a new approach to child support' [1999] Fam Law 95, at p 99). In practice, however, this makes eminently sound administrative sense: at present some 96% of NRPs with earnings have former partners who earn less than £100 per week. But there remains the very real risk that the general public's perception of the fairness of the new regime may be influenced by a minority of high profile cases in which the NRP's liability is unaffected by the fact that his former partner is earning £100,000 per year herself. At present there is no sign that such cases will be accommodated within the new variations scheme (see below)...

Contrary to the Government's original plans, there will be a cap on the NRP's net income that feeds into the formula calculation. Following intense pressure from peers and others, a Government amendment was introduced on third reading in the House of Lords, one week before Royal Assent. This provides that any net weekly income in excess of £2000 (an annual salary of just under £170,000 gross) is to be disregarded. The practical effect of this is that the liability of an NRP with a net weekly income in this range, who has one child to support and no children in his second family, will be capped at £300 per week. If he has two children, it will be capped at £400 per week (£200 per child) and if he has three or more children, £500 per week (£167 per child). The presence of any children in the second family will be taken into account against the capped income. Thus if there is one child in the second family, the £2000 capped net income will be reduced by 15% before the basic rate maintenance is calculated under para 2. This was hardly a major concession: according to Department of Social Security (DSS) estimates, it will affect about 50–100 parents in the CSA's caseload of 1.2 million. There is a consequential amendment to s 8(6) of the Child Support Act 1991 by CSPASSA 2000, Sch 3, para 11(5)(c), which enables courts to make top-up maintenance orders if the NRP's net weekly income exceeds £2000 per week...

VARIATIONS FROM THE FORMULA

Dissatisfaction with the rigidity of the formula under the Child Support Act 1991 led to the introduction of the complex departures scheme under the Child Support Act 1995... The new child support scheme is deliberately designed to be broad brush in nature, so avoiding the complexities inherent in the original legislation. This drive for (relative) simplicity is reflected in the provisions for 'variations', the new name for departures from the standard formula. The Government intends that variations from the new formula will very much remain the exception rather than the rule (in 1999 the CSA completed 270,000 maintenance assessments, of which just under 4000 came under the departures scheme)...

There are three general categories of case in which variations may be permitted. The first is where the NRP has 'special expenses', but these must be directly child-related. The legislation gives as one example contact costs. At present only direct travel-related costs (typically fares or petrol costs) are taken into account. However, the Government has announced a concession in that in future NRPs will be able to offset the cost of essential overnight stays if they have 'particularly difficult or arduous journeys' (Standing Committee F, 1 February 2000, col 281). The new legislation also makes express provision for boarding school fees and mortgage payments on the former matrimonial home where the NRP no longer retains an interest in it. The latter is an especially welcome innovation, as this has caused considerable frustration under the original scheme. It does not appear to deal with the situation where the NRP makes a payment of housing costs in relation to the home occupied by the PWC, but for which both remain liable. As with the current tolerance rules, the intention is that special expenses will be recognised only if they exceed £10 or £15 per week, depending on the NRP's net weekly income.

Secondly, the Government intends to carry forward unchanged into the new arrangements for variations the ground rules in the departures scheme for taking account of property or capital transfers. There will thus, at the margins, continue to be some recognition of pre-April 1993 'clean break' deals, although there will be no allowance in the formula itself.

Finally, variations may be applied for in so-called additional cases where the NRP's income, on which the maintenance calculation has been based, does not reflect his true ability to pay. Thus a variation may be allowed where the NRP has capital assets that exceed a prescribed level (the Government's intention is to prescribe the level of assets at £65,000, at least in the first instance). Similarly, a variation may be allowed where a person has income that is not taken into account in the standard maintenance calculation.

Questions

(i)   How would you order priorities between children and step-children?
(ii)   How do you feel about the fact that the income of the parent with care has no impact upon the formula?
(iii) Will non-resident parents now feel content with maintenance assessments?

The essence of the Child Support Act 1991 was to disable, while not repealing, the courts' powers to make periodical payment orders for children (s. 8(3)). One exception was when a 'top-up' order was made under s. 8(6). Another was where the adults had agreed a consent order; once the difficulties with the operation of the Child Support Act 1991 became apparent, s. 8(5) was activated by Statutory Instrument so as to make it possible for such orders to be both made and varied by the courts. There was thus a considerable incentive towards agreement (only, of course, in non-benefit cases). Under the new provision, from 2002, s. 8(6) will be irrelevant because of the much higher ceiling on the assessable income of the non-resident parent. Moreover, the amended s. 4(10) of the Child Support Act 1991 will provide that if a court order is made, an application can nevertheless be made to the Child Support Agency once the order has been in force for a year. This represents a dramatic reduction in the availability of court orders – unless some rather artificial tactics are used: see James Pirrie, 'Time for the courts to stand up to the Child Support Act?' [2002] Fam Law 115.

The courts' jurisdiction to order spousal maintenance is, of course, unaffected by all this. However, look back at Chapter 3, and at the evidence for the 'mother gap' (p. 107). Lone parents who are separated or divorced can obtain maintenance from their partners, in the magistrates' court under the Domestic Proceedings and Magistrates Courts Act 1978 and under the Matrimonial Causes Act 1973 (on which more in Chapter 8). Lone parents who have not been married to the other parent have no such recourse.

Question

How do you feel about the fact that the new Child Support Act formula includes no element of support for the parent with care?

4.4 Support for families with elderly and/or disabled dependants

We must now return to the question of priorities. The age structure of the population has changed in recent years. The proportion of children aged under 16 is falling, and the proportion of people over 60 is rising and projected to increase further as the tables from *Social Trends 32* (2002) illustrate:

Chart 1.2 Population: by gender and age, 1971 and 2000

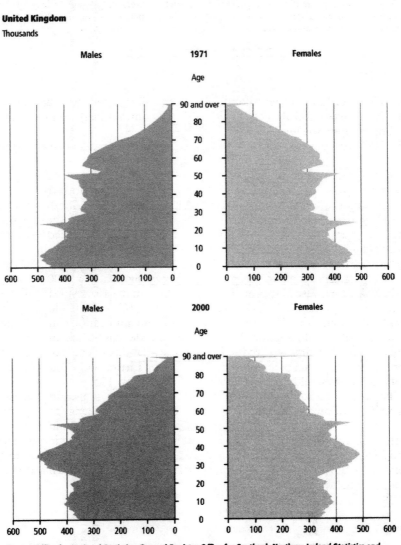

Source: Office for National Statistics; General Register Office for Scotland; Northern Ireland Statistics and Research Agency

Table 1.3 Population¹: by gender and age

United Kingdom

Percentages

	Under 16	16-24	25-34	35-44	45-54	55-64	65-74	75 and over	All ages (=100%) (millions)
Males									
1901²	34	20	16	12	9	6	3	1	18.5
1931²	26	18	16	13	12	9	5	2	22.1
1961²	25	14	13	14	14	11	6	3	25.5
1991	21	14	16	14	12	10	8	5	28.2
2000	21	11	16	16	13	10	8	5	29.5
2011	18	12	13	15	15	12	9	6	30.8
2025	18	10	13	13	13	14	10	9	32.3
Females									
1901²	31	20	16	12	9	6	4	2	19.7
1931²	23	17	16	14	12	9	6	2	24.0
1961²	22	13	12	13	14	12	9	5	27.3
1991	19	12	15	13	11	10	9	9	29.6
2000	19	10	14	15	13	10	9	9	30.3
2011	17	11	12	14	14	12	9	9	31.1
2025	17	10	13	13	12	14	11	11	32.5

1   Data for 1901 and 1931 are Census enumerated; data for 1961 to 2000 are mid-year estimates. Figures for Northern Ireland for 1931 relate to the 1937 Census. 2000-based projections.
2   Data for 1901, 1931 and 1961 for under 16 and 16 to 24 relate to age bands under 15 and 16 to 24 respectively.
Source: Office for National Statistics; General Register Office for Scotland; Governments Actuary's Department; Northern Ireland Statistics and Research Agency

The authors comment:

Historically, the ageing of the population structure was largely a result of the fall in fertility that began towards the end of the 19th century. Early in the 20th century lower mortality helped to increase the number of people surviving into old age, but the effects of improved survival were greater among younger people which operated as a counterbalance to the trend towards population ageing. More recently, there have been lower fertility rates and improvements in mortality rates for older people, both of which have contributed to the ageing of the population. The percentage of the population of both males and females for age groups over 55 are projected to continue to increase (Table 1.3). The assumptions underlying the projections for the United Kingdom mean that these trends will continue so that by 2014 it is expected the number of people aged 65 and over will exceed those aged under 16. The average age of the population is expected to rise from 38.8 years in 2000 to 42.6 years in 2025.

An ageing population is a characteristic the United Kingdom shares with the other countries in the European Union (EU). In the year 2000 the proportion of the total population that was aged 65 and over in the United Kingdom was 15.6 per cent, slightly lower than the EU average of 16.2 per cent. The percentage of the EU population aged 65 and over has increased by over half since 1960. The largest increases were in Finland and Spain, where the proportions doubled. Conversely, the proportion in the Irish Republic, the country with the lowest percentage of people aged 65 and over in the year 2000, has remained steady since 1960. Globally the number of people aged 60 years or over is expected to triple by 2050, increasing from 606 million currently to 2 billion.

These figures suggest that many more people than at present are likely to be involved in caring for dependent relatives. Indeed, *Social Trends 29* (1999) presents this fact in graphic form in its projection of the dependent population by age:

1.1 Dependent population: by age

United Kingdom

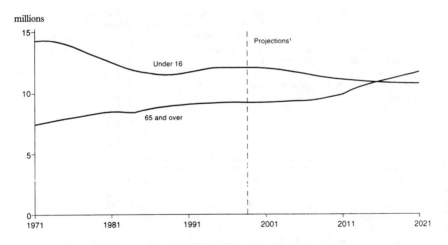

1   1996-based projections.
Source: Office for National Statistics; Government Actuary's Department; General Register Office for Scotland; Northern Ireland Statistics and Research Agency

Questions

(i)   Before 23 June 1986, the invalid care allowance (ICA), which is made available to the carers of the severely disabled, was not available to any married or cohabiting woman. In *Drake v Chief Adjudication Officer* 150/85 [1987] QB 166, [1986] 3 All ER 65, the European Court of Justice held that the original provision in s. 37(3)(*a*)(i) of the Social Security Act 1975 contravened the principle of equality of treatment set out in Council Directive 79/7 EEC. The Government changed the law (a day before the judgment!) so that the benefit is made available to such women. The rules for ICA state that a carer must provide care for at least 35 hours a week. The 'disregard' for part-time work is now £75 per week. These rules exclude many people, especially those who look after relatives who live in residential homes during the week and go to the carer's home at weekends. Why should these people be excluded from benefiting?

(ii) If you do not think that they should be excluded, would you welcome a universal non-means tested benefit such as child benefit, or would you prefer to see the introduction of a means-tested benefit? How about zero-rating VAT for the supply and delivery of goods and services for home carers?

(iii) What is the justification for the part-time earnings 'disregard' operated at present? Should it be abolished?

The issue of the value of caring is addressed by Jonathan Herring (2001):

Of particular interest is the state's support of those who care for elderly people and disabled adults. There is ample evidence that carers suffer great strain, both emotional and financial. The government has in recent years recognised the pressures that can be caused through caring for dependent relatives and has, following their report, *Caring About Carers*, set up a national strategy for carers. For example, the local authority has the power to make special grants to enable carers to have breaks. Further, there are special benefits available for those who spend significant time caring for dependent relatives, for example invalid care allowance. By offering these funds the state is recognising the benefits that carers provide not only to their dependants, but also to the state through saving the state the cost of providing the care. The details of these benefits are beyond the scope of this book, but three important points on a theoretical level can be made:

1. Parents who do not seek employment, and instead care for children, receive no special benefits in respect of their care. Further, the government has developed the New Deal, through which the benefits system and other forms of assistance are designed to encourage lone parents with children to find employment. So here the voluntary care by mothers (and especially lone mothers) of young children is not positively valued and encouraged by the state. By contrast, the care of older people is supported and encouraged through the benefits system, although many argue that the support given to such carers is inadequate. It may be that the government feels that carers of older people need financial incentives to provide care, which the parents of children do not need.

2. There are grave concerns that carers are inadequately valued within society. ... It is estimated that carers of dependent relatives save the state some £34 billion a year. However, there is a dark side to care of older people at home. The majority of carers described themselves as 'extremely tired' and some were depressed. Both the older people and carers were terrified about the possibility of having to move the older person into a nursing home. It should not be assumed that, once the older person is in residential care, their carers are then free from strain.

3. What is the state's obligation towards an older person who is wealthy enough to pay for support him- or herself? To what extent can the National Health Service and social services be expected to provide free care for an older person? There are large sums of money involved, with £10.5 billion being spent on long-term care in the year 2000. The government undertook a recent review of the funding of long-term care for the elderly following a Royal Commission report. The Royal Commission had argued that the state should be responsible for ensuring that older people receive the basic care necessary for their health, and therefore the state should provide the health and essential personal care without charge. They proposed distinguishing between care which involved touching the patient and care which does not: if it does, it should be provided free of charge. Other expenses, including housing and non-essential personal care, would not be provided without charge under the NHS. The government rejected this proposal, essentially on the ground that it would be too expensive. Instead, the government decided to distinguish between health care, which would be provided free of charge, and personal care (e.g. washing patients), which would only be provided free of charge if the patient had low income and

few assets. The distinction is problematic. As had been pointed out by the Royal Commission, a person would soon fall ill without washing. Further, if the inability to wash is caused by an illness, is it not a health issue? The government has supported its approach by arguing that there needs to be a 'fairer and lasting balance between taxpayers and individuals' over the financing of long-term care. It is clear that the approach proposed by the government will create artificial distinctions (between personal care and medical care), although this would happen wherever the line is drawn between what care is paid for and what is not. However, the idea that our society could accept that an older person who refuses to pay should be left unwashed seems unjustifiable in the light of the duty that society owes to all citizens to ensure that people do not suffer inhuman or degrading treatment under the Human Rights Act 1998.

Questions

(i) Does poverty in old age involve different issues from those raised by poverty among younger adults?

(ii) In particular, should we treat the old in the same way as the young, when many of them have a strong sense of independence and believe in self-sufficiency or social insurance rather than means-tested benefits, which in their minds replace the old poor law?

(iii) Would you agree with the view that we 'may make more fruitful efforts in tackling poverty [of various groups] if we look at the common factors which unite them rather than the more superficial aspects which distinguish their problems. In this way, we could perhaps develop strategies which encompass all who live in poverty, rather than seeking to exclude or differentiate by means of formal marital status or the accident of age'? (Douglas, 1988)

Bibliography

4.1 State support for the family's income

We quoted from:

A. Dilnot and J. McCrae 'Family Credit and the Working Families Tax Credit' (1999) Institute for Fiscal Studies, IFS Briefing Note Number 4. September 1999.

R. Lister, '*Income Maintenance for Families with Children*' in R. N. Rapoport, M. P. Fogarty and R. Rapoport (eds.), *Families in Britain* (1982) London, Routledge and Kegan Paul, p. 432.

A. Page, *Marriage in the European Union today* (2001) National Family and Parenting Institute briefing.

N. Wall et al, *Rayden and Jackson on Divorce and Family Matters* (17th edn), chapter 27, paras. 27.10, 27.11.

Website of the Department of Work and Pensions: www.dwp.gov.uk (in this section and in part 4.3 below).

4.2 Poverty and the lone-parent family

We quoted from:

Sir William Beveridge, *Social Insurance and Allied Services* (Cmd. 6404) (1942) London, HMSO, para. 347.

J. Bradshaw and J. Millar, *Lone Parent Families in the UK*, Social Security Research Report, no.6, (1991) London, HMSO, p. 18.

Central Statistical Office, *Social Trends 32* (2002) London, HMSO, table 1.2.
J. Haskey, 'One-parent families and their dependant children in Great Britain', *Population Trends 91* (1998) HMSO, London.
M. Maclean and J. Eekelaar, *Children and Divorce: Economic Factors* (1983) Oxford, SSRC, p.10.
Report of the Committee on One-Parent Families (Chairman: The Hon. Sir Morris Finer) (Cmnd. 5629) (1974) London, HMSO, paras. 4.179–4.183, 4.193, 4.207, 4.188–4.189, 5.104, 5.81–5.86 (in this section and in 4.3 below).
Office of National Statistics, Living in Britain: Results from the General Household Survey 1998, Website of the National Council for One-Parent Families: www.ncopf.org.uk.

Additional reading
J. Haskey, 'One-Parent Families and Their Children in Great Britain: Numbers and Characteristics' (1989) 55 Population Trends 27.
J. Lewis, 'The problem of lone-mother families in twentieth-century Britain' (1998) 20(3) Journal of Social Welfare and Family Law 251.

4.3   The private law obligation and the state

We quoted from:
Children Come First (Cm. 1264) (1990) London, HMSO: 'The Government's Proposals on the Maintenance of Children', vol. 1:1/16; Appendix C; vol. 2. 1.3.2.; 1.4.; 1.5.
Guidelines on the Application of the Requirement to Co-operation (1993) London, Department of Social Security, pp. 5, 9-10.
Improving Child Support (Cm 2745) (1995) London, HMSO, p. 8.
N. Wikeley, 'Child Support – the new formula' [2001] Family Law 820.

Additional reading
G. Davis, N. Wikeley and R. Young, *Child Support in Action* (1998) London, Hart.
N. Mostyn, 'The Green Paper on Child Support – Children First: a new approach to child support' [1999] Family Law 95.
S. Parker, 'Child Support in Australia: Children's Rights or Public Interest' (1991) 5 International Journal of Law and the Family, 24.
J. Pirrie , 'Changes to Child Support – The SFLA View' [1999] Family Law 838.
J. Pirrie, 'Time for the courts to stand up to the Child Support Act?' [2002] Family Law 115

4.4   Support for families with elderly and/or disabled dependants

We quoted from:
Central Statistical Office, *Social Trends 29* (1999), London, HMSO, table 1.1.
Central Statistical Office, *Social Trends 32* (2002), London, HMSO, tables 1.2, 1.3 (with text), 2.1
J. Herring, *Family Law* (2001), Harlow, Longman.

Additional reading
G. Ashton, *Elderly People and the Law* (1995) London, Butterworths.

G. Douglas, 'Individual Economic Security for the Elderly and the Divorced: A Consideration of the Position in England and Wales' in M. T. Meulders-Klein and J. Eekelaar (eds.) *Family, State and Individual Economic Security* (1988) Brussels, Story-Scientia, p. 491.

J. Eekelaar and D. Pearl (eds.) *An Aging World* (1989) Oxford, Oxford University Press.

Chapter 5

Family property

5.1 **Separate property for spouses**

5.2 **The field of choice**

5.3 **Property claims**

5.4 **Property claims for children**

5.5 **Legislative intervention**

In the last two chapters we have concentrated on income. In this chapter, we turn our attention to a discussion of family property. For many families, until comparatively recently, only the former question had much relevance. However, there has always been a substantial group who have enjoyed capital assets in the form of land, chattels and investments. Rules have developed to regulate and administer this property during the lives and after the deaths of its owners. In contrast to the modern concern for what was termed by the Finer Report 'the pathology of the family', traditional property law has been regarded as a law 'which fortifies and regulates an institution central to society'. Accordingly, the law's priorities in dealing with family property have shifted somewhat during recent years. Another change during the last quarter of the twentieth century and the beginning of the twenty-first has been the growth of the 'property owning democracy' and the spread of ownership of capital assets, so that the number of people owning their homes – not to mention other forms of wealth such as shares, pensions, annuities, life policies, etc – has expanded considerably.

The authors of *Social Trends 32* (2002) comment on that expansion:

From 1951 there were changes in the tenure of dwelling stock in Great Britain. Private renting decreased from 52 per cent in 1951 to 20 per cent in 1971. The period also saw an increase in the number of dwellings rented from local authorities as a result of the major housebuilding programme they had undertaken between the wars and after the Second World War. Renting from local authorities increased from 19 per cent in 1951 to 30 per cent in 1971. Owner-occupation increased from 29 per cent in 1951 to 50 per cent in 1971 and has continued to rise since. In 2000-01, 70 per cent of households owned their homes, either with a mortgage or outright; 21 per cent rented from the social sector, and 9 per cent rented privately.

In the two decades between 1981 and 2001 the number of owner-occupied dwellings in the United Kingdom increased by more than 40 per cent, while the number of rented dwellings fell by around 15 per cent (Chart 10.5). By 2001 the number of owner-occupied dwellings was over 17 million, which was more than double the number of rented dwellings.

Chart 10.5 – Stock of dwellings[1]: by tenure

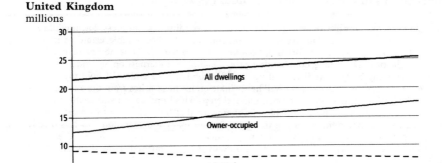

United Kingdom
millions

1 See Appendix, Part 10: Dwelling stock. Data are at 31 December from 1981–1990. Data for England and Wales are at 31 March from 1991–2001. Data for Scotland and Northern Ireland are at April based on Census outputs for 1991 and at 31 December of the previous year for 1992–2001.
Source: Department for Transport, Local Government and the Regions; National Assembly for Wales; Scottish Executive; Department for Social Development (Northern Ireland)

Thus although property law was developed in a different age by the land owners and the bourgeoisie, who in effect made their own laws by contracts, trusts and wills, there was a 'proletarianisation' during the last century. The only restraint on this expansion is the ever present shadow of state involvement (interference?) through taxation, social security law and death duties. Traditional property law was mainly concerned with devolution rules within the kinship group. Modern commercial activity now involves third parties: banks, building societies and other creditors. Courts are increasingly asked to adjudicate between competing claims. In examining these issues, this chapter straddles the boundary between property law and family law.

We begin our examination of family property by considering one of the earlier issues the law had to tackle, namely the ownership of property by married persons. The separate property regime is entrenched in our legal system, in contrast to the situation elsewhere, and we examine how that happened. In part 2 of the chapter we look at the available options for change. Then we move into the realms of strict property law, which determines the property rights of cohabitants, and of spouses in circumstances where the adjustive regime of the Matrimonial Causes Act 1973 is of no assistance – in particular, upon the bankruptcy or death of one of the partners. Next, we consider the one area where a discretionary, adjustive regime does apply to the property of cohabitants, namely property claims for children. Finally, we look at legislation for the property of cohabitants in other jurisdictions.

5.1   Separate property for spouses

5.1.1   Historical background

The law which at present governs the property of married persons is based on the principle of separate property: 'each spouse may acquire and deal with his or her property as if he or she were single' (Law Commission Working Paper on

Family Property Law 1971). But this was not always the case, as Sir Jocelyn Simon explains in *With all my Worldly Goods* (1964):

I invite you to accompany me to a village church where a wedding is in progress. The mellifluous cadences of the vicar's voice fall hypnotically on the ear – '... honourable estate ... mutual society, help and comfort ... comfort her, honour and keep her. ...' Now he has reached the ceremony of the ring. The bridegroom bends a gaze of ineffable tenderness on his bride – '... with this ring ... with my body ... and with all my worldly goods I thee endow.' I hold my breath, aghast. Will the vicar rend his cassock? Will he sprinkle on his head ashes from the ancient coke stove? Will he hurl the bridegroom from the chancel steps with imprecation and anathema? For the man has committed the most horrible blasphemy. In that holy place, at this most solemn moment, actually invoking the names of the Deity, he has made a declaration which is utterly false. He is not endowing the bride with a penny, a stick, a clod. Nor does he intend ever to do so. And yet the service proceeds as if nothing untoward has happened. How does this come about?

The phrase originates in the ancient Use of Sarum, where it is almost unique in liturgy. It reflects a mediaeval custom, the endowment of the bride at the church door, dower *ad ostium ecclesiae* itself a relic, I surmise, of a still more archaic usage, the payment of the brideprice negotiated between the families of bride and bridegroom.

Dower *ad ostium ecclesiae*, however, gave way to common law dower, where the law itself determined what interest the wife should have in her husband's property. That was a life estate after the death of her husband in one third of any land of which the husband had ever been solely seised at any time during the marriage for an estate of inheritance to which issue of the wife by the husband might possibly succeed.

But this was small compensation for the proprietary and personal rights that the wife lost at Common Law on her marriage.

In this country the feudal theory was, under the Norman kings, applied in all its rigour. The proper purpose of a tenement – and wealth at that time was largely to be measured in land – was the maintenance of a vassal in such a state that he could suitably perform his feudal services to his lord – not least military service. A married woman was considered to be generally incapable of performing the feudal services. Any freehold estate of which the wife was seised was therefore vested in the husband as well as the wife during coverture, and it was under his sole management and care. If there was any issue of the marriage born alive, the husband immediately gained an estate in the wife's freeholds corresponding to her dower in his lands, but extending to the whole estate, not merely to one third: this was significantly called the husband's estate by the courtesy of England. As soon as issue was born alive, he had therefore a life estate in his wife's land which he could charge to the full. Chattels being more evanescent than land, the Common Law took the simple course of letting the husband have them as his. Any goods, including money, in the wife's actual possession, came under his absolute ownership forthwith. Any property to which the wife might be entitled by bringing an action at law – her 'chose in action'; for example, any debt due to her – became the husband's if during coverture he recovered it or otherwise reduced it into possession. When leasehold interests began to be created, for the investment of money rather than for the enjoyment of land, the Common Law treated them largely as chattels: though they did not in theory become the husband's property, he might nevertheless sell them and take the proceeds as his own. During coverture the husband was entitled to the whole of the wife's income from any source, including her own earnings or the rent from her leasehold or freehold property. She could only bequeath her personal property with the consent of her husband; and such consent might be revoked by him at any time. On the wife dying intestate by virtue of this rule, all her personal property, including her leaseholds and her choses in action, passed to her husband. In such circumstances, it was a real triumph for 18th century self-satisfaction that Blackstone could write: 'Even the disabilities which the wife lies under are for the most part intended for her protection and benefit: so great a favourite is the female sex of the laws of England.' It could have been little less inconvenient to have been a favourite of Haroun-al-Raschid.

However, in mediaeval England, the wife did enjoy some limited rights. As Sir Jocelyn Simon says:

It is almost certain that in the 12th and 13th centuries our own law recognised, ... a reserved portion of a man's chattels of which he might not dispose by will if he left wife or child. After payment of debts the estate was divided into 'wife's part', 'bairns' part', and 'dead's part' (the two former were also called 'the reasonable parts'). Only over the 'dead's part' was there freedom of disposition.

Why did they not lead the lawyers to adopt a system of Community of Goods similar to that of our continental neighbours? Why, indeed, did it not survive in England, as it has in Scotland to this day? I think there were two reasons. First, with the invention of the English system of heirship in land, the heir took the whole of the freehold estate, the widow only a life interest and only in a third. Furthermore, she did not automatically enter the land as of right at the death of her husband: she had to wait to be assigned her portion by the heir. In the field of devolution which remained firmly within the view of the common lawyers, the widow, therefore, looked like a pensioner of the heir rather than a partner of the ancestor.

Secondly, in the eyes of the mediaeval Church intestacy was almost a sin: the 'dead's part' must be suitably devoted to such pious uses (especially ecclesiastic benefaction) as would mitigate the transcendental pains and penalties which would otherwise be the reward for the deceased's terrestrial shortcomings. In order to make sure that nothing went wrong about this, the Church – in this country alone – secured jurisdiction over probate of wills. The common lawyers became intensely jealous. Moreover, the interference of the Church courts with morals made them highly unpopular with laymen too. Thus neither common lawyers nor laymen were in the least disposed to follow the Church courts or their law. So it came about that in Edward III's reign the Lords in Parliament expressly disapproved the custom of the 'reasonable part' of the personal estate reserved from disposition by will – it was an intolerable interference with freedom. Under such disapprobation the custom had died out in the province of Canterbury by the end of the 15th century. In the northern province it lasted until 1692, but was then abolished by Act of Parliament. The excuse was that a system of jointuring widows had been invented, and if they enjoyed both jointure and 'wife's part' there would be too little left for the younger children; so it was helpfully arranged that a testator could thenceforward leave his children with nothing at all.

It is well known that equity intervened. Simon puts it in the following way:

During the Middle Ages the influence of the Church and the cults of chivalry and courtly love had brought about a steady rise in the status of women. ... But others besides the wife were interested in what happened to her property, not least her kinsfolk. They will wish to make suitable provision for her on her marriage, to ensure in particular that the children of the marriage, who will be their own blood relations, are properly advanced. But if there is no issue of the marriage the primary interest of the wife's kinsfolk is that the property which they have put into the marriage should return to them, rather than pass to the husband's family. This consideration was until quite modern times particularly potent among the ruling classes, where marriages were to be considered, at least partly, as political and economic alliances. But by the end of the Middle Ages ... the Common Law was too far committed to the interest of the husband to be able to recognise the claims of the wife and her kinship group. It had lost the flexibility to provide new remedies for new needs as they arose. ...

[But] a woman about to enter matrimony, or her kinsfolk, could transfer property to a trustee: at Common Law it was in his ownership; but in Chancery he was bound to deal with it according to the terms of the trust – which could, simply, be according to the married woman's wishes. Or the trust could provide that, in the absence of any issue of the marriage to take a vested interest in the property, it should after the wife's death or that of her husband revert to her kinsfolk. Moreover, if the husband had recourse to the Court of Chancery, with its superior remedies, for the purpose of asserting his common law rights over the wife's property, that Court would as a condition of its aid compel the husband to settle on his wife and children part of any such property; and ultimately the wife herself or the children could initiate the claim. Over the wife's interest acquired in these two ways Equity at last gave her nearly all the rights of a single woman: she could give it away or sell it, or leave it by will to whoever she wished, or charge it with her contracts. A married woman could thus possess separate property over which her husband had no control whatever, and against which neither he nor his creditors had any claim. But in safeguarding in this peculiar way the interests of the married woman and of her kinship group, Equity took a further and decisive step away from any system of Community of Goods between married people.

Equity created a regime of separate property for married women. This regime was limited, however, to the investment property of the wealthy. Simon explains how the doctrines of Equity were used in the late nineteenth century to deal with the needs of 'middle and lower middle classes':

First, the proponents of reform, led by John Stuart Mill, were principally interested in abrogating the subjection of women and in giving them equal political and civil rights with men. Men owned their own property, virtually untrammelled by any claims by their spouses. So women must be given similar rights. To entrench, say, the married woman's right to occupation of her husband's house would be to treat her as an unequal. ... Secondly, Mill was at this time in the full tide of his individualism. Indeed, there was as yet no significant movement of thought orientated towards the foundation of society on small voluntary groupings, such as the family, of which the law of property should take specific cognizance. Thirdly, together with Mill there was a vociferous group of emancipated women writers, who were acutely conscious that the Common Law delivered over to their husbands the fruits of their professional activities, but who were understandably less concerned with the claims of all the housewives and mothers whose real needs were security in the matrimonial home and the right to participate in the proprietary benefits which their husbands enjoyed through their own economic self-abnegation. Fourthly, comparative jurisprudence was virtually unstudied at this time; and there was in any event a tendency to regard French political and social institutions with a well-bred distaste. Lastly, and most important, legal reform proceeds largely on the principle of inertia, not least in countries where the rule of precedent colours legal thinking. A movement once started continues of its own momentum. We have already seen the Common Law operate in that way in this very field. And now Parliament. Equity had permitted married women of the wealthier classes to own their separate property: how could it be denied to the generality of married women? So the Married Women's Property Acts did not attempt to remove married women's incapacities in any general way; still less in their interests to put restriction on the freedom of disposition of married men. Statute merely followed Equity in permitting married women to hold and handle and bind themselves with regard to any property which might come to them.

Questions

(i)   Do you see similarities between the individualism of the nineteenth century and trends in the present generation which have led to the introduction of a system of independent taxation?

(ii) Modern feminists would regard chivalry and courtly love as the reverse of equalising the status of women. Why?

(iii) Do you think that a major reason why the Married Women's Property Acts were enacted could have been the tradesmen's difficulties in enforcing their debts?

5.1.2 Criticisms and survival of separation of property

Sir Jocelyn Simon made the following observation in his 1964 lecture:

But men can only earn their incomes and accumulate capital by virtue of the division of labour between themselves and their wives. The wife spends her youth and early middle age in bearing and rearing children and in tending the home; the husband is thus freed for his economic activities. Unless the wife plays her part the husband cannot play his. The cock bird can feather his nest precisely because he is not required to spend most of his time sitting on it.

In such a state of affairs a system of Separation of Goods between married people is singularly ill adapted to do justice. Community of Goods, or at the least community in acquisitions and accumulations, is far more appropriate. And as one leaves the sphere of those who enjoy investment property for that of those whose property largely consists of the home and its contents a regime of Separation is utterly remote from social needs.

The difficulties are taken up by the English Law Commission in 1971 in a Working Paper on *Family Property Law*:

0.12 It is said that equality of power, which separation of property achieves, does not of itself lead to equal opportunity to exercise that power; it ignores the fact that a married woman, especially if she has young children, does not in practice have the same opportunity as her husband or as an unmarried woman to acquire property; it takes no account of the fact that marriage is a form of partnership to which both spouses contribute, each in a different way, and that the contribution of each is equally important to the family welfare and to society.

The Law Commission give an example of how the principle works unfairly. This is what strict separation of property used to mean:

0.13 Mr Brown earns the family income. The home is in his name and he is responsible for the mortgage repayments and outgoings. Mrs Brown has given up her employment and earnings to attend to domestic affairs and to look after the family. She has no savings or private income, and cannot contribute in cash to the acquisition of property. If the marriage breaks down, the law regards the home, its contents, and any other property or savings acquired by Mr Brown in his name, as his sole property. Mrs Brown has a right to occupy the home and to be maintained, but she does not own the home or any other property acquired out of Mr Brown's earnings. On a decree of divorce, nullity or judicial separation she may apply to the court for property to be transferred to or settled on her [see Chapter 8, below]. If Mr Brown dies leaving a will which disinherits her (though this is relatively uncommon) she has a limited right of support, available only on application to a court and at its discretion: she has no right other than to ask for what is normally needed for her support. In short, she has no right of property in her dead husband's estate if he has made a will which disinherits her.

There are three reasons given for dissatisfaction with the principle of separation: (i) unfairness, (ii) uncertainty, particularly in relation to the matrimonial home, and (iii) that even when adjustments can be made, these adjustments depend on the discretion of the court after the termination of the marriage. As Sir Otto Kahn-Freund explains in *Matrimonial Property: Where do we go from here?* (1971):

0.15 Mr and Mrs Jones have been married for ten years and have three children. When they married they bought a house on mortgage. The deposit was paid partly from Mrs Jones' savings and partly from a loan from Mr Jones' employer. The mortgage instalments have usually been paid by Mr Jones. At the beginning Mrs Jones had a job; she went back to part-time work when the children were older. From her wages she paid a large part of the household expenses and bought some of the furniture. Occasionally she paid the mortgage instalments. A car and a washing machine were bought on hire-purchase in Mr Jones' name, but the instalments were sometimes paid by him and sometimes by her. Mr Jones has now left his wife and children and is living with another woman.
0.16 If, in the above situation, Mrs Jones asks what her property rights are so that she can make arrangements, she will receive no clear answer. In effect, the law will ask her what intentions she and her husband had about the allocation of their property, and to this she would only be able to reply that they had no clear intention.

Question

Which of the three reasons for dissatisfaction do you consider the most powerful reason for reform?

The reason why the ownership of the matrimonial home may be uncertain, and why the couple's intentions have to be discovered, is that in the absence of a system of community of property, a spouse whose name is not on the legal title must resort to the law of constructive trusts, or perhaps proprietary estoppel, in order to claim an interest in the property. Lord Denning had attempted to introduce an element of discretion, both through his interpretation of the courts' powers under s. 17 of the Married Women's Property Act 1882 (see below) and through his approach to the ownership of 'family assets'. This may have made the law even more uncertain, but in his view it certainly made it more fair. In the event, the House of Lords, in *Pettitt v Pettitt* [1970] AC 777, [1969] 2 All ER 385 and *Gissing v Gissing* [1971] AC 886, [1970] 2 All ER 780 (see pp. 150 and 165 below) overruled his interpretation of s. 17 and emphasised that the interests of husband

and wife in property must be determined in accordance with the ordinary rules of property law (as to which, see part 3 of this chapter, p. 164 below).

Pettitt v Pettitt
[1970] AC 777, [1969] 2 All ER 385, [1969] 2 WLR 966, 113 Sol Jo 344, House of Lords

The case was concerned with work carried out by a husband upon a matrimonial home which was owned by his wife. The facts appear in the speech of Lord Reid.

Lord Reid: My Lords, the appellant was married in 1952. For about nine years she and her husband lived in a house which she had inherited. During that time her husband carried out a number of improvements, largely redecorating, on which he says he spent some £80. In 1961 this house was sold and she acquired another. After this had been paid for there was a surplus of a few hundred pounds and he used this money, apparently with the consent of the appellant, in paying for his car. The spouses lived for about four years in the new house. Then the appellant left her husband, alleging cruelty, and she obtained a divorce in 1967. The husband then left the house and raised the present proceedings. He said that during those four years he carried out a considerable number of improvements to the house and garden and estimated that in doing so he performed work and supplied material to a value of £723. He sought a declaration that he was beneficially interested in the proceeds of sale of the house in the sum of £1,000 and an order on the appellant to pay. Then an order was made that she should pay him £300. The Court of Appeal reluctantly dismissed her appeal, holding that they were bound by the decision in *Appleton v Appleton* [1965] 1 All ER 44, [1965] 1 WLR 25. They gave leave to appeal.

For the last twenty years the law regarding what are sometimes called family assets has been in an unsatisfactory state. There have been many cases showing acute differences of opinion in the Court of Appeal. Various questions have arisen, generally after the break-up of a marriage. Sometimes both spouses have contributed in money to the purchase of a house; sometimes the contribution of one spouse has been otherwise than money: sometimes one spouse owned the house and the other spent money or did work in improving it: and there have been a variety of other circumstances. ...

Many of the cases have been brought by virtue of the provisions of section 17 of the Married Women's Property Act 1882. That is a long and complicated section: the relevant part is as follows:

> 'In any question between husband and wife as to the title to or possession of property, either party ... may apply by summons or otherwise in a summary way to any judge of the High Court of Justice ... and the judge ... may make such order with respect to the property in dispute ... as he thinks fit.'

The main dispute has been as to the meaning of the latter words authorising the judge ... to make such order with respect to the property in dispute as he thinks fit. They are words normally used to confer a discretion on the court: where discretion is limited, the limitations are generally expressed: but here no limitation is expressed. So it has been said that here these words confer on the court an unfettered discretion to override existing rights in the property and to dispose of it in whatever manner the judge may think to be just and equitable in the whole circumstances of the case. On the other hand it has been said that these words do not entitle the court to disregard any existing property right, but merely confer a power to regulate possession or the exercise of property rights, or, more narrowly, merely confer a power to exercise in proceedings under section 17 any discretion with regard to the property in dispute which has already been conferred by some other enactment. And other intermediate views have also been expressed.

I would approach the question in this way. The meaning of the section cannot have altered since it was passed in 1882. At that time the certainty and security of rights of property were still generally regarded as of paramount importance and I find it incredible that any Parliament of that era could have intended to put a husband's property at the hazard of the unfettered discretion of a judge (including a county court judge) if the wife raised a dispute about it. Moreover, this discretion, if it exists, can only be exercised in proceedings under section 17: the same dispute could arise in other forms of action; and I find it even more incredible that it could have been intended that such a discretion should be given to a judge in summary proceedings but denied to the judge if the proceedings were of the ordinary character. So are the words so unequivocal that we are forced to give them a meaning which cannot have been intended? I do not think so. It is perfectly possible to construe the words as having a much more restricted meaning and in my judgment they should be so construed. I do not think that a judge has any more right to disregard property rights in section 17 proceedings than he has in any other form of proceedings. ...

I would therefore refuse to consider whether property belonging to either spouse ought to be regarded as family property for that would be introducing a new conception into English law and not merely developing existing principles. There are systems of law which recognise joint family property or communio bonorum. I am not sure that those principles are very highly regarded in countries where they are in force, but in any case it would be going far beyond the functions of the court to attempt to give effect to them here.

As a result of this case, Parliament enacted s. 37 of the Matrimonial Proceedings and Property Act 1970:

It is hereby declared that where a husband or wife contributes in money or money's worth to the improvement of real or personal property in which or in the proceeds of sale of which either or both of them has or have a beneficial interest, the husband or wife so contributing shall, if the contribution is of a substantial nature and subject to any agreement between them to the contrary express or implied, be treated as having then acquired by virtue of his or her contribution a share or an enlarged share, as the case may be, in that beneficial interest of such an extent as may have been then agreed or, in default of such agreement, as may seem in all the circumstances just to any court before which the question of the existence or extent of the beneficial interest of the husband or wife arises (whether in proceedings between them or in other proceedings).

Questions

(i)   Mr Pettitt lost his case: would s. 37 have made any difference?
(ii) What interest would Mr Pettitt have acquired if he had spent his money on a new roof or on rewiring?

Look back now to p. 149, and the stories of Mrs Brown and Mrs Jones. There is nowadays more to say about these two. Mrs Jones is not left to the tender mercies of the constructive trust; on divorce, she can use the discretionary regime of the Matrimonial Causes Act 1973. Mrs Brown is now treated relatively generously by the Inheritance (Provision for Family and Dependants) Act 1975 (see p. 191, below); but she may be able to use the general law of property in order to strengthen her position by establishing her own independent property rights.

In part 3 of this chapter we examine those aspects of the law of property that regulate the rights both of cohabitants and of spouses, bearing in mind that spouses do not normally need to use property law when the relationship breaks down except in cases of death or bankruptcy. Cohabitants, of course, can only use property law principles to establish an interest in each other's property (except where a claim is made for children; see p. 199, below).

First, though, we conclude this section by looking at a right specific to spouses, namely the right to occupy the matrimonial home; and in part 2 of this chapter we look at the options for reform concerning spousal property.

5.1.3 The spouse's right of occupation

At common law, each spouse had a personal right, as against the other spouse, to occupy a matrimonial home to which that other was entitled. But this gave no rights against third parties to whom the owning spouse might seek to dispose of his interest. By selling the property, or defaulting on mortgage payments, he was therefore free to leave the other spouse homeless. This caused concern, and there were judicial attempts to create a 'deserted wife's equity', a right which she could enforce against, say, a mortgagee who was entitled to take possession of and sell the property. Such attempts were finally frustrated by the House of Lords' decision in *National Provincial Bank Ltd v Ainsworth* [1965] AC 1175, which reiterated the principle that a wife had only a personal right against her husband. To remedy the hardship to non-owning spouses, the Matrimonial Homes Act 1967 (later 1983) was passed. The relevant provisions are now to be found in Part IV of the Family Law Act 1996.

Section 30 defines the rights of the parties between themselves:

30. – (1) This section applies if
    (*a*) one spouse is entitled to occupy a dwelling-house by virtue of
        (i) a beneficial estate or interest or contract; or
        (ii) any enactment giving that spouse the right to remain in occupation; and
    (*b*) the other spouse is not so entitled.
    (2) Subject to the provisions of this Part, the spouse not so entitled has the following rights ('matrimonial home rights')—
    (*a*) if in occupation, a right not to be evicted or excluded from the dwelling-house or any part of it by the other spouse except with the leave of the court given by an order under section 33;
    (*b*) if not in occupation, a right with the leave of the court so given to enter into and occupy the dwelling-house.

An important part of the Act's function is to make available orders regulating the occupation of the home as between the spouses themselves (whether their right to occupy the home arises from their legal or beneficial ownership of it, or from s. 30). We shall have to consider these rights further in connection with protection from domestic violence and harassment in Chapter 9. Insofar as that protection is extended to cohabitants, we can say that they too have occupation rights of a purely personal nature in the house where the couple have lived together – and that includes, albeit on a temporary basis, cohabitants who have no property rights in that home (that has been the case since the enactment of the Domestic Violence and Family Proceedings Act 1976; *Davis v Johnson* [1979] AC 264). However, for spouses only, the Family Law Act 1996 enables the rights in s. 30(2) to be enforced against third parties, by providing that it shall be a charge on the other's estate or interest. The charge is registrable as a class F land charge in unregistered land, or as a notice in registered land (Land Charges Act 1972, s. 2(7), Family Law Act 1996, s. 31(10)); it cannot be an overriding interest in registered land.

The potential practical effects of the registrable right can be seen in one of the earliest cases following the 1967 Act:

Wroth v Tyler
[1974] Ch 30, [1973] 1 All ER 897, [1973] 2 WLR 405, 117 Sol Jo 90, 25 P & CR 138, High Court, Chancery Division

The wife registered a charge under the Matrimonial Homes Act 1967 after her husband, who was the sole legal and beneficial owner of the house, had signed a contract for the sale of the house. The registration of the charge meant that the sale with vacant possession could not be completed, and the husband was thus held liable in damages. It is not immediately apparent from the facts of the case why the husband did not seek an order under s.1(3) of the Matrimonial Homes Act 1967, as it then was, for the wife's right of occupation to be terminated so as to allow the completion to go ahead. It certainly appears on the face of it that the wife had led both the husband and the prospective purchasers, a newly married couple, reasonably to believe that she was not actively dissenting from the wish of the husband to move from Kent, where they had previously lived, so as to set up home in a cottage in Norfolk. Megarry J commented on the facts in the following manner:

Let me add that I would certainly not regard proceedings under the Act by the defendant against his wife as being without prospect of success. As the evidence stands (and of course I have not heard the defendant's wife) there is at least a real prospect of success for the defendant. He does not in any way seek to deprive his wife of a home; the difference between them is a difference as to where the matrimonial home is to be. In that, the conduct of the wife towards the plaintiffs and the defendant must play a substantial part.

Megarry J was not prepared to order specific performance of the contract, for to do so would be indirectly to force the husband to take proceedings under the Matrimonial Homes Act against his wife. This was a decision which only he could take. Perhaps therefore, one should not feel too concerned about the fate of the husband – who had to pay damages amounting to £5,500 – for after all the remedy was in his own hands. Certainly, on the result of *Wroth v Tyler*, the wife had the 'casting vote'.

Megarry J in *Wroth v Tyler* called the statutory right of occupation 'a weapon of great power and flexibility':

I can now say something about the nature of the charge and the mode of operation of the Act. First, for a spouse in occupation, the right seems to be a mere statutory right for the spouse not to be evicted. There appears to be nothing to stay the eviction of others. For example, if a wife is living in her husband's house with their children and her parents, her charge, even if registered, appears to give no protection against eviction to the children or parents. ... Nor if the wife takes in lodgers does there seem to be anything to prevent the husband from evicting them. If, for example, the husband is himself living in the house, it would be remarkable if the Act gives the wife the right to insist upon having other occupants in the home against his will. The statutory right appears in essence to be a purely personal right for the wife not to be evicted; and it seems wholly inconsistent with the Act that this right should be assignable or otherwise disposable. I may add that there is nothing to require the wife to make any payment to the husband for her occupation, unless ordered by the court under section 1(3) ...

Second, although the right given to an occupying wife by section 1(1) is merely a right not to be evicted or excluded 'by the other spouse', and so at first sight does not appear to be effective against anyone except that other spouse, section 2(1) makes the right 'a charge' on the husband's estate or interest; and it is this, rather than the provisions for registration, which makes the right binding on successors in title. The operation of the provision for registration seems to be essentially negative; the right is a charge which, if not duly protected by registration, will become void against subsequent purchasers, or fail to bind them. In this, the right seems not to differ from other registrable charges, such as general equitable charges or puisne mortgages. Yet there is this difference. For other charges, the expectation of the statute is plainly that they will all be protected by registration, whereas under the Act of 1967 there does not seem to be the same expectation.

Questions

(i) If statutory co-ownership were to be introduced (see p. 158, below), would the protection afforded under s. 30 of the Family Law Act 1996 be of any value?

(ii) What are the practical effects of the requirement of registration?

Another important third party to be reckoned with when the occupation of the home is in issue is the landlord, in the case of rented property.

Section 30(3), (4) of the Family Law Act 1996 is an important provision regarding rented property. If the tenancy is a protected or a statutory tenancy under the Rent

Act 1977 or a periodic assured tenancy under the Housing Act 1988 (private tenancies) or a secure tenancy under the Housing Act 1985 (council tenancies), an occupying spouse may keep the tenancy of the other spouse 'alive', even though the latter spouse is not living in the accommodation. In addition, Sch. 7 to the Family Law Act 1996 gives a spouse a right to seek a transfer of a protected, statutory or secure tenancy or assured tenancy on the granting of a decree of divorce etc., or at any time thereafter. (Unlike its predecessors ,the Matrimonial Homes Acts, the 1996 Act gives similar rights to cohabitants; see p. 206, below.)

Moreover, the tenant spouse cannot defeat the occupation rights of the wife by purporting to surrender the tenancy to the landlord (see *Middleton v Baldock* [1950] 1 KB 657, [1950] 1 All ER 708, CA). However, in the case of a periodic joint tenancy, when one of the tenants gives notice to quit, it seems that the tenancy terminates (see *Greenwich London Borough Council v McGrady* (1982) 81 LGR 288, 6 HLR 36, CA; *Hammersmith and Fulham London Borough Council v Monk* [1992] 1 AC 478). This may operate as a protection for a wife who has the support of a housing authority (consider *Harrow London Borough Council v Johnstone* [1997] 1 All ER 929, [1997] 1 WLR 459, [1997] 1 FLR 887, [1997] Fam Law 478), but equally it may enable one spouse to inflict on the other not only the loss of the tenancy but also the loss of any accrued right to buy. Helen Conway, in 'Protecting Tenancies on Marriage Breakdown' (2001) explores some of the issues in this area.

Bear in mind that an important aspect of public sector tenancies, of assured tenancies under the Housing Act 1988, and of those tenancies still current that were granted under the Rent Act 1977, is that they give security of tenure; the tenancy cannot simply be brought to an end by the landlord by notice to quit. But note that a tenancy granted by a private landlord since February 1997 is not an assured tenancy unless the landlord expressly makes it so. Thus private residential tenancies granted now do not normally give security of tenure.

Questions

(i)   The Finer Report (1974) stated that 'the protection which the wife and children may require when the family live in rented accommodation is protection in occupancy, which may be achieved irrespective of rights of ownership'. In the context of social housing, (a) do you think that it is appropriate that this protection should be exercised by the courts rather than by social landlords, and if so, (b) why do you have this view?

(ii)   A number of social landlords have introduced clauses into their tenancy agreements which state that violence or threats of violence constitute a breach of the tenancy agreement and can thus be grounds for possession giving the local authority the power to determine the tenancy. Do you feel that such clauses are appropriate, or would you deal with the problem of domestic violence in some other way? (See further, pp. 420ff, below.)

5.2   The field of choice

5.2.1   The issues

There are three possibilities: a complete freedom of choice for the parties with little or no judicial discretion available to the judges; a system of fixed property rights; and a freedom of choice but with a power for the courts to readjust the parties' rights either during the marriage or at the end of the marriage.

The distinction between the fixed and discretionary system is highlighted in the First Report on *Family Property – A New Approach* (1973), where the Law Commission acknowledge that there is a body of opinion that would oppose the introduction of any form of fixed property rights between husband and wife on the ground that this is unnecessary and in itself objectionable:

10 ... They believed that in so far as the existing law led to any injustice, the proper remedy was to allow the court to exercise its discretionary powers in matrimonial or family provision proceedings. It was claimed that all necessary reforms could be achieved by developing the traditional discretionary systems, which ensured great flexibility. The principal reasons for considering any form of fixed property rights undesirable were as follows:

(*a*)   fixed property rights would cause more dissension and injustice than they would alleviate;

(*b*)   the state should not interfere in the relations between spouses by imposing automatic rules regulating their property rights;

(*c*)   fixed property rights would deter marriage and compel people to take advice before marrying.

Question

Is advice before marriage a good thing which should be encouraged?

By contrast, the Canadian Law Reform Commission (1975) put the alternative point of view:

Another drawback to a discretionary system lies in its lack of fixed legal rights. Even were equality to be stated as a general legislative policy, the essential nature of judicial discretion would leave the court free to make whatever sort of property disposition seemed to be appropriate in any given case. A married person would not have a *right* to equality, but only a *hope* to obtain it. If no concept of equality were contained in the law establishing a discretionary system, then it would be accurate to say that a married person would have no property rights at all at the time of divorce. Our concern here is not limited to the way things would work out in practice, since the courts would do their best to ensure that arbitrary dispossession did not occur. Rather, it includes the psychological advantage that accrues to a person who knows he or she has a positive right that is guaranteed and protected by law.

But if there were to be a fixed system, what would it mean?

The following extract is taken from the Canadian Law Reform Commission (1975):

The community property concept of marital property rights is based upon the assumption that marriage, among other things, is an economic partnership. As such, the partnership, or community, owns the respective talents and efforts of each of the spouses. Whatever is acquired as a result of their talents and efforts is shared by and belongs to both of them equally, as *community property*.

Community property regimes exist in Quebec, in many European countries and in eight of the United States. Quebec's community property regime, like the separate property regime in that province, is an option available to married persons who choose not to be governed by the basic regime providing for separate ownership of property during a marriage, with fixed sharing upon divorce.

The essential idea of community property is very simple: the earnings, and property purchased with the earnings, of either spouse become community property in which each spouse has a present equal legal interest. Where the community is terminated – for example by divorce – the community property, after payment of community debts, is divided equally between the spouses. The community is also terminated by the death of a spouse, and in some jurisdictions, including Quebec, by an agreement between the spouses to switch to some other regime or to regulate their property relations by a contract. This simple formula conceals some rather complex rules. We can do no more in this paper than touch upon the general principles and a few of the major problem areas involved in community property systems without dealing with finer points in any great detail.

Under community regimes, there are three kinds of property: the separate property of the husband, the separate property of the wife, and community property. Typically, the property owned by either spouse before marriage is the separate property of that spouse, along with property acquired after marriage by a spouse by way of gift or inheritance. Separate property is not shared at the time of divorce, but rather is retained by the owner-spouse. All other property, however acquired, becomes community property, in which each spouse has a present interest as soon as it is purchased or obtained, and an equal share in its division upon divorce. In some jurisdictions, someone giving property to a married person must specify that the property is to be the separate property of the recipient. Otherwise it will be treated as a gift to both spouses, even though it is only given to one, and will become community property. In the Province of Quebec, some types of property owned before marriage become community property, but it is possible for persons giving such types of property to a single person to make the gift on the condition that it remain the separate property of the recipient should he or she thereafter marry under the regime of community property.

Under a community property regime, all property owned by either spouse at the time of a divorce is generally presumed in law to be community property unless it can be proved to be separate. In many marriages the spouses will not have adequate records of ownership or the source of funds used to acquire property. This produces the legal phenomenon of 'commingling' – that is, the separate property of each spouse eventually becomes mixed with that of the other spouse and with the community property, resulting in all the property being treated as sharable community property at the time of divorce. Commingling makes it impossible for the spouses to establish that certain items of property were owned before marriage, or otherwise fall into the classification of separate property. ...

Even assuming that the separate property of a spouse can in fact be kept identifiable, it is necessary to have rules governing the situation where community funds are expended with respect to such property. If, for example, a husband owns a house as separate property and has it repaired, using community funds, the community property is entitled to reimbursement at the time of divorce to the extent of the value of the repairs. Or if he sells the house and buys another, using for the purchase some community funds plus proceeds of the sale, the rule might be that if more than fifty per cent of the price of the second house came from the first house, it remains separate property subject to an appropriate compensation to the community upon divorce. If more than fifty per cent of the price of the second house came from community funds, then it loses its character as separate property and becomes community property. In the latter case there would be a compensation paid from the community at the time of divorce to the husband's separate property equal to the amount realized on the sale of the first house. When it is recognized that most families only have available the earnings of one spouse, which belong to the community, and that many items of separate property over the course of a marriage would be maintained and repaired out of these earnings, or sold and 'traded up' for newer property using the proceeds of the sale of the separate property plus community funds, then some of the practical difficulties in accounting during the marriage and sorting out community and separate property at its termination become readily apparent.

Deferred Community is described in detail in the Canadian Law Reform Commission's Working Paper (1975).

Deferred sharing, or deferred community of property as it is sometimes called, is based on the idea that there should be separate ownership of property during marriage, and an equal distribution of property on divorce. Deferred sharing, therefore, lies somewhere between the extremes of separate property on the one hand and full community of property on the other. Deferred sharing regimes exist in Denmark, Sweden, Norway, Finland, West Germany and Holland. In Canada, Quebec adopted a deferred sharing regime in 1970 – the 'partnership of acquests' – as its basic family property law, applicable to all married persons who did not make a positive choice of community property or separate property. ...

The basic theory of the deferred sharing system is simple. In general terms, all property acquired by either spouse during marriage is to be shared equally when the marriage partnership is dissolved.

The possibility of a deferred community regime was raised in the English Law Commission Working Paper (1971), and the Law Commission commented on the results of the consultation in the First Report (1973):

47. The proposals relating to such a system of 'deferred community' attracted far more interest and comment than did those relating to legal rights of inheritance. No clear view, however, emerged from the consultation. ... On balance, the majority did not support deferred community. Some thought that community would give effect to the partnership element in marriage and create definite property rights without the need to depend upon the exercise of the court's discretion; it was seen as a natural extension of the principle of co-ownership of the home into a wider field. Others thought that community could be unfair if applied arbitrarily without regard to the circumstances and to conduct, that it would be a cause of dissension and that it would be inconsistent with the independence of the spouses. ...

49. Very few took the extreme view that fixed principles of deferred community should replace the present discretionary powers exercisable on divorce or in family provision proceedings. The vast majority thought that existing discretionary powers should be retained.

53. The principle of deferred community should be considered in the light of the conclusions we have already reached in this Report, namely that the principle of co-ownership of the home is a necessary measure which would be widely accepted as better achieving justice than the present law, and that a system of fixed legal rights of inheritance is neither necessary nor desirable. Assuming, for the moment, that the principle of co-ownership of the home will be implemented, is the further step of introducing a system of community needed in order to attain the proper balance of justice?

54. The Working Paper pointed out that anomalies could arise if a fixed principle of sharing were limited to just one asset. It would apply only where there was a matrimonial home. Further, the spouse who acquired an interest in the matrimonial home under the co-ownership principle might own other assets of similar or greater value which did not have to be shared. It was suggested that a wider principle of sharing might appear fairer. The results of the Social Survey throw some light on both these points. The Survey confirms that spouses who do not own their home seldom have assets of any substantial value. It also indicates that where a home is owned, it represents a substantial proportion of the total value of the spouses' assets. For the majority of home-owners, sharing the home would, in effect, be sharing the most substantial asset of the family. How far is deferred community necessary as a means of eliminating the anomalies in other cases? ...

59. *Our conclusion* is that if the principle of co-ownership of the matrimonial home were introduced into English law much of what is now regarded as unsatisfactory or unfair would be eliminated, and the marriage partnership would be recognised by family property law in this very important context. Having regard to our conclusions regarding co-ownership of the matrimonial home, to the broad interpretation by the court of its powers to order financial provision on divorce, and to our conclusion that the court should have similar powers in family provision proceedings, we do not consider that there is at present any need to introduce a system of deferred community.

A system similar to deferred community has been introduced in Scotland by s. 10 of the Family Law (Scotland) Act 1985 and, to be honest with ourselves, in England as a result of case law developments (see Chapter 8, below).

Question

Is the introduction of deferred community good enough: (a) for women in the higher paid sectors of the employment market; (b) for women who do not work, or who work only part time? (See Chapter 8, below.)

5.2.2 The matrimonial home

The two areas which feature predominantly in Law Commission reports in England are the matrimonial home and household goods. We discuss each in turn. It is natural that discussions should centre around the home.

As we have seen (p. 145, above), problems invariably involve third party creditors.

The English Law Commission Working Paper, *Family Property Law* (1971) discussed the topic in detail, and formed the conclusion that a system of co-ownership should be introduced to meet many of the objections to the present law:

0.25 The matrimonial home is often the principal, if not the only, family asset. Where this is the case, if satisfactory provision could be made for sharing the home, the problem of matrimonial property would be largely solved. Under present rules, apart from any question of gift or agreement, ownership is decided on the basis of: (1) the documents of title, and (2) the financial contribution of each spouse. Part 1 of the Paper considers whether there should be alternative ways or additional considerations for determining ownership.

0.26 One possibility would be to allow the court to decide ownership of the home on discretionary grounds whenever a dispute arose between the spouses, taking into account various factors, including the contribution of each spouse to the family. ...

0.27 Another possibility would be to introduce a presumption that the matrimonial home is owned by both spouses equally. ...

0.28 A third possibility would be to go further than a presumption, which could be rebutted, and to provide that, subject to any agreement to the contrary, the beneficial interest in the matrimonial home should be shared equally by the spouses. We refer to this as the principle of co-ownership. There are advantages in this solution: it would in the absence of agreement to the contrary apply universally; it would acknowledge the partnership element in marriage by providing that the ownership of the principal family asset should be shared by the spouses; it would provide a large measure of security and certainty for a spouse in case of breakdown of marriage or on the death of the other spouse; and it would help to avoid protracted disputes and litigation.

0.29 ... The Paper proposes that a new form of matrimonial home trust should apply whenever the beneficial interest in the home is shared between the spouses, in order that they should have a direct interest in the property.

In their First Report on *Family Property – A New Approach* (1973) the Law Commission stated that the principle of co-ownership was widely supported:

21.   It emerged clearly from the consultation that the principle of co-ownership of the matrimonial home is widely supported both as the best means of reforming the law relating to the home, and as the main principle of family property law. The great majority who supported co-ownership included legal practitioners, academic lawyers, women's organisations and members of the public. Those who opposed co-ownership were those who were opposed to any form of fixed property rights, and they were relatively few in number.

23.   The opinions expressed favouring the co-ownership principle are supported by a change in the pattern of ownership of the matrimonial home in recent years. The Social Survey [Todd and Jones, 1972] analysed the pattern and found that 52% of couples owned their home; among the home owners 52% had their home in joint names. However, when the figures were broken down by the year of purchase of the home it was clear that a marked increase in the rate of joint ownership began in the middle 1960s and is continuing. ... In cases where the wife had made some financial contribution to the home the proportion of homes put into joint names was higher than in cases where there had been no such contribution. The rate of joint ownership was also very high in cases where the couple had owned more than one home.

Having examined this evidence, the Law Commission arrived at the conclusion that, subject to the proviso that a husband and wife remain free to make any arrangements they choose, the principle of automatic co-ownership of the matrimonial home should be introduced.

The Scottish Law Commission in their Report on *Matrimonial Property* (1984) disagreed with the English proposals:

(i) Statutory co-ownership of the matrimonial home would not be a good way of giving expression to the idea of marriage as an equal partnership. In some cases it would go too far, particularly if it applied to a home owned before marriage, or acquired by gift or inheritance during the marriage. These are not the results of the spouses' joint efforts. In other cases it would not go far enough and could produce results which were unfair as between one spouse and another. If the wife, say, owned the home and the husband owned other property, he could acquire a half share in the home without having to share any of his property. A spouse with investments worth thousands of pounds could allow the other to buy a home and then claim half of it without contributing a penny. The scheme would also work very unevenly as between different couples. If Mr A had invested all his money in the matrimonial home while his next-door neighbour Mr B had mortgaged his home to its full value in order to finance his business, the law would operate very unevenly for the benefit of Mrs A and Mrs B. It would, in short, be a hit or miss way of giving effect to the partnership ideal.

(ii) Statutory co-ownership of the matrimonial home would not be a good way of recognising contributions in unpaid work by a non-earning spouse. It would benefit the undeserving as well as the deserving. Extreme cases can be imagined. A man might marry a wealthy widow, encourage her to buy an expensive house, claim half of her house and leave her. Even in less extreme cases statutory co-ownership would be a poor way of rewarding unpaid work. Most housewives would get nothing from the new law because its effects would be confined to owner-occupiers. Only about 37% of married couples in Scotland live in owner-occupied accommodation. Even where the new law did apply, its effects would be totally arbitrary. Not only would the net value of the home vary enormously from case to case, and from time to time, but so too would the respective values of the spouses' contributions.

(iii) Statutory co-ownership of the matrimonial home would not necessarily bring the law into line with the views of most married people. We know that most married owner-occupiers in Scotland favour voluntary co-ownership of the matrimonial home.[1] We do not know that most married people in Scotland would favour forcing co-ownership on an unwilling owner regardless of the circumstances of the particular case.

(iv) It is not self-evident that property which is used in common should be owned in common. Even if this proposition were accepted, it would lead further than co-ownership between spouses. It would lead to co-ownership between the members of a household, including for example, children and parents.

(v) A scheme for statutory co-ownership of the matrimonial home would be very complex. The scheme we outlined in our consultative memorandum was as simple as we could make it, but even so it raised many difficult questions. Should, for example, co-ownership come about automatically by operation of law (in which case how would third parties, such as people who have bought the house in good faith, be protected) or should it come about only, say, on registration of a notice by the non-owner spouse (in which case would non-owner spouses bother to register before it was too late)? Should co-ownership apply to a house owned by one spouse before the marriage? Should it apply to a home which is part of commercial or agricultural property? Should it apply to a home bought by one spouse after the couple have separated? If not, should it make any difference if the spouses resume cohabitation for a short period? Should the spouses become jointly liable for any debts secured on the home? When should it be possible for one spouse, or both, to opt out of co-ownership and how should this be done? Should a spouse be able to claim half of the sale proceeds of one home, refuse to contribute to the purchase price of a new home, and then claim half of that one too? If not, how can this be remedied without forcing one spouse to invest in a home he or she does not want to invest in? These are just some of the less technical questions which would have to be answered.

(vi) Statutory co-ownership of the matrimonial home would not benefit many people. ... The majority of ... owner-occupier couples already have their home in joint names. Of those owner-occupiers who have their home in the sole name of one spouse, a number will have a good reason for this and would presumably opt out of a statutory scheme. In many cases a co-ownership scheme would confer no long-term benefit on the non-owner spouse because he or she would succeed to the house on the death of the other in any event, or would receive as much by way of financial provision on divorce as he or she would have received if the scheme had applied.

(vii) A scheme for statutory co-ownership of the matrimonial home would have to co-exist with the law on financial provision on divorce. It would make little sense, it might be said, to introduce a complicated scheme for fixed co-ownership rights in the home during the marriage if the whole financial circumstances of the spouses were to be thrown into the melting-pot on divorce. The supposed benefit of fixed rights would be illusory. It would be most useless when most needed.

(viii) Finally, a scheme for forced co-ownership could exacerbate matrimonial disputes. If co-ownership came about only when the non-owner spouse registered a notice, the act of registration might well be seen as a deliberate raising of the level of a domestic dispute. An intimation by one spouse that he or she was opting out of co-ownership would also be unlikely to promote good domestic relations.

---

1. A.J. Manners and I. Rauta, *Family Property in Scotland* (1981).

Questions

(i)   Which if any of these criticisms do you agree with, and why?

(ii) You may wish to look again at point (vii) above in the light of the law in Scotland on financial provision on divorce (Chapter 8, p. 329, below). Would statutory co-ownership fit better with the Family Law (Scotland) Act 1985 or with the Matrimonial Causes Act 1973? Is there any difference after the decision in *White v White* [2000] 2 FLR 981 (p. 322, below)?

(iii) The Law Commission proposal was that the legal estate would remain in the sole name of the spouse whose name was on the title. The spouses would therefore become equitable joint tenants. Why did the Law Commission not recommend joint legal ownership?

(iv) Why do you think the Law Commission's proposal has not been enacted?

(v)   Look back again at Chapter 2 and the description of the Civil Partnerships Bill (p. 75, above); how likely do you think it is that future registered partnerships legislation will include a provision for statutory co-ownership of property?

Brenda Hale, in *Family Law Reform:Wither orWhither?* (1995) comments:

The Commission's 1973 proposals for automatic joint ownership of the matrimonial home might have caught the same tide of public opinion which led to the Sex Discrimination Act 1975 and the Domestic Violence and Matrimonial Proceedings Act 1976. But by the time that the Commission's conveyancers had worked out a solution which satisfied them that tide had been missed. The experience of our later proposals on savings and chattels indicates the depth of opposition at official and political level to any alteration of the current rules on the acquisition of property rights, no matter how limited or subject to the contrary intentions of the parties. This seems particularly to occur with proposals [that] are thought to reflect a slightly different balance between the various interests and will be applicable to all couples rather than to those who separate or divorce. ... Continued examination and reform of the discretionary remedies on marital or family breakdown is more likely to bear fruit than attempts to introduce new rules of substantive law which will affect [the] whole population – especially in the property law area where, however misguidedly, this may be seen as benefiting certain (usually less powerful) groups at the expense of others (usually more powerful).

So it comes as something of a surprise to find in the Civil Partnerships Bill 2002 (see p. 75, above) a provision for statutory co-ownership of the homes of registered partners, and of anything bought by them for the purpose of living together, subject to contrary (registered) agreement. Clearly, the idea of community of property is by no means dead and we may yet see it revived as a possibility for spouses or others.

A final point here is the effect upon third parties of statutory co-ownership. The Law Commission in their Third Report on *Family Property* (1978) recommended that it should only give protection against third parties if the interest is registered, and that it would not be an overriding interest. However, since the House of Lords' decision in *Williams and Glyn's Bank Ltd v Boland* [1981] AC 487, [1980] 2 All ER 408, [1980] 3 WLR 138, 124 Sol Jo 443, [1980] RVR 204, 40P & CR 451 it is clear that beneficial interests in registered land are overriding interests where the holder of the interest is in actual occupation of the land. Thus they do bind a third party even though they do not appear on the register; nevertheless, if the land is sold by two legal owners, even if the holder of the beneficial interest in question is not one of them, the beneficial interest is overridden. This is now so much part of the fabric of land law that we do not comment upon it in detail here; the moral, for conveyancers, is never to accept a transfer from a sole married vendor and, in all cases, to ensure that all the adult occupiers of the property consent to the sale. *Boland* has thus resulted in better protection for adult occupiers of the home even if their names are not on the title, and may also have contributed to the rise in joint legal ownership among married and unmarried partners.

5.2.3 Family assets other than the matrimonial home

Professor Sir Otto Kahn-Freund was a strong advocate of an introduction of 'community' in the family assets, and we quote the following extracts from his Unger Memorial Lecture (1971):

What I suggest is a general rule that such assets as form the matrimonial aggregate – 'family assets' – should, in the absence of special circumstances, be shared by the spouses half and half. The special circumstances would have to be found by the court in the light of the facts of the case. It is here that the court should have a wide discretion, especially in assessing the significance in each case of various conflicting considerations. Some of the considerations enumerated in section 5 of the Matrimonial Proceedings and Property Act 1970 [now s. 25(1) of the Matrimonial Causes Act 1973 as amended; see Chapter 8, below] would be relevant, including above all, the value of pensions expectations which either spouse – in most cases the wife – stands to lose as a result of the termination of a marriage. Occasionally the court may also have to assess the value of the contributions made by either spouse to the welfare of the family, 'including any contribution made by looking after the home and caring for the family'. But this should only be done in exceptional cases – and normally the value of the contributions should be deemed to be equal. ...

But, of course, this leaves us with two fundamental problems: how should the assets which make up the aggregate be identified? And, equally important, is all this to affect the spouses themselves only, or also third parties?

Kahn-Freund answers his first question in the following manner:

I should identify the assets which are to constitute the aggregate not by reason of how, when, by whom and with whose resources they were acquired. My criterion of selection would not be their origin, but their purpose.

... An asset is a family asset if, at any given time it is by consent of the spouses, dedicated to the common use of the household family, irrespective of whether it was acquired before or after the marriage, or through the spouses' work or thrift or through inheritance or gift. It comprises the family home and its contents (furniture and equipment), but also a family car and other implements intended to be enjoyed by the family. It also includes such funds, however invested, as are, by the spouses' consent, at any given moment dedicated to future family expenditure... In the absence of proof to the contrary any house or flat used as a matrimonial home is presumed to be a family asset, and so are all chattels in common use. No other asset belonging to either spouse is presumed to be a family asset.

The major problem relating to family assets is whether any principle of co-ownership should affect third parties. The Law Commission, possibly aware of this difficulty, stated in their *First Report on Family Property* (1973) that in their view the primary consideration should be to devise a scheme which protected the 'occupation rights' of the spouses (see p. 151, above). However, the Law Commission's Working Paper, *Transfer of Money Between Spouses* (1985), recommended more extensive reform, as did the Second Consultation Paper (1986). Finally, in the Law Commission Report on *Matrimonial Property* (1988) they reviewed their earlier work:

1.4 There were two consistent themes running through all the Commission's earlier work. The first was the persistent observation that the present rules for determining the ownership of property during marriage were arbitrary, uncertain and unfair. The second was that the ownership of property while a marriage continues is important and that it is not right to consider marital property only in relation to what happens when a marriage ends. There are those who have said, and no doubt will continue to say, that since English law now provides for the discretionary re-allocation of property between spouses on various events, for example death or divorce, the precise detail of the ownership of property during marriage does not matter. It has also been said that in their attitudes to, and arrangements for, ownership of their property, married couples vary so greatly that it is impossible to generalise about the way in which such property would or should be regarded. If the parties did give thought to the ownership of property which they acquired for their joint use and benefit, they would not do so on any consistent or common basis. We cannot, however, accept these arguments, for the following main reasons:

(i)   To a partner who is the sole or main wage earner in the family, the present rules for determining ownership may seem as unimportant during the marriage as they are important when the marriage has broken down; to the partner who has no separate income, on the other hand, they may appear as unfair during the marriage as they do when it ends. Respondents to our Working Paper who represented the latter were unanimously of this view. ...

(ii)   It is a false dichotomy to split marriages into the happy and the unhappy, and to say that while the couple are happy, property ownership does not matter and that, if they are not, they will get divorced and that the court will reallocate the property. Most marriages do not end in divorce. There may be occasions during a marriage when knowledge of who owns what property is important to either or both spouses. We believe that a law which aims to reduce uncertainty and to reflect the intentions of both parties is more likely to further stability in the relationship of marriage than one which does not.

(iii) Although it is undoubtedly true that the attitude of the spouses to family property will vary enormously and will depend upon individual expectations, nevertheless the law already provides an extensive body of rules affecting the property rights of the spouses. Changes in the principles upon which these rules are based will not alter the fact that the law finds it necessary to make provision for such rules, which are just as much an intrusion into the private lives of the parties whether they are made by Parliament or by judges.

(iv)   It is clear that in some cases property rights during marriage are important when either spouse becomes bankrupt or dies...

The proposal made was as follows:

3.9   ... where money is paid by either spouse to the other or to buy property and the payment or purchase is for common purposes, the money or property will be jointly owned, subject to a contrary intention on the part of the purchasing spouse known to the other spouse.

...To expand a little, the purchase of property for common purposes would give rise to joint ownership, even though there had been no transfer of money to the other spouse and no expenditure on common purposes by the other spouse. This avoids the likely difficulties of the 'notional pool'. It might be thought that it would go too far and produce more joint ownership than is warranted. However, it would give way to a contrary intention which need not be communicated to the other spouse, so a spouse who wishes to retain sole ownership can do so. The main effect would be to produce co-ownership in household assets even though there was no thought given to it at the time... It might be thought that this proposal alone is sufficient. However, it makes no provision for ownership of money that is not spent, ... Hence we would retain the idea of making money paid by one spouse to the other for common purposes into jointly owned money.

However, the Law Commission did not speak with one voice on the question:

B. Davenport QC: I do not share the view of my colleagues that to give effect to the policy expressed in this report by enactment of the draft Bill in Appendix A would bring about an improvement in English Law. Some of my principal reasons are, in summary, as follows:–

(a)   Apart from making technical changes to the Married Women's Property Act 1964, I am not persuaded that there is any real need for reform in that area of the law. The reform suggested is as likely to lead to matrimonial quarrelling as to matrimonial concord.

(b)   Having regard to the almost infinite variety in relations between husbands and wives, the law should be very cautious before imposing any statutory regime of property rights upon them. The policy recommended in this report ... is to provide a series of rules which are intended positively to lay down when property is to be jointly owned. These rules are, I consider, too inflexible to be applied satisfactorily to every marriage. Indeed, it is not difficult to think of situations where an application of the rules can lead to consequences which many might regard as unjust.

(c) Assumptions made about household goods, generally of limited value, cannot safely be extrapolated to motor vehicles or to securities (both of which are excluded from the Scottish Act [see below]). The title to both vehicles and securities is likely to pass from person to person and claims for damages for wrongful interference or conversion by a spouse who had not consented to the sale would seem an almost inevitable consequence of giving effect to the draft Bill. Indeed, the sale of 'family' motor vehicles might become significantly more difficult, as might the sale of securities, unless special protection is given to *bona fide* purchasers.

Questions

(i)   What situations can you think of which might lead to unjust consequences?
(ii) With whom do you agree – Mr Davenport or his colleagues?
(iii) The Law Commission decided to exclude life insurance policies and to include motor cars. Why?
(iv) Why do you think the Law Commission's proposals have not been enacted?
(v)   The Family Law (Scotland) Act 1985, s. 25 states:

Presumption of equal shares in household goods

25.—(1) If any question arises (whether during or after a marriage) as to the respective rights of ownership of the parties to a marriage in any household goods obtained in prospect of or during the marriage other than by gift or succession from a third party, it shall be presumed, unless the contrary is proved, that each has a right to an equal share in the goods in question.

(2) For the purposes of subsection (1) above, the contrary shall not be treated as proved by reason only that while the parties were married and living together the goods in question were purchased from a third party by either party alone or by both in unequal shares.

(3) In this section 'household goods' means any goods (including decorative or ornamental goods) kept or used at any time during the marriage in any matrimonial home for the joint domestic purposes of the parties to the marriage, other than—

(a)   money or securities;
(b)   any motor car, caravan or other road vehicle;
(c)   any domestic animal.

Why the exception for pets? The Scottish Law Commission suspect that animals would often be regarded by the spouses as belonging fairly definitely to one of them. Are they right?

Contrast the provision in the Civil Partnerships Bill of 2001 (see Chapter 2, p. 75):

(1) 'Communal property', in relation to the partners in a civil partnership, means any of the following property, regardless of whether it was acquired before or after the civil partnership was registered—

(a)   any dwelling-house which either or both of them are entitled to occupy by virtue of a beneficial estate or interest and which the partners occupy (or have at any time occupied) jointly as their principal or only home:
(b)   any furniture or other functional domestic item which belongs to the partners and which they acquired (otherwise than by way of a gift to, or inheritance by, one of them separately) for the purpose of living together in the same household.

Question

The Civil Partnerships Bill was withdrawn in February 2002. Nevertheless, do you think that the idea of communal property, for spouses or for cohabitants, may soon become a feature of English law?

5.3 Property claims

We have explored the options for property regimes for married couples; nevertheless, the system of separate property is, as we have said, entrenched in our legal system. On divorce, matrimonial property is subject to a discretionary, adjustive regime, which enables the court to re-distribute it according to the needs and resources of the parties. Of course, it is useful to know who owns what as a starting point; but strict property law is not determinative of the outcome. Where spouses do need to know their property rights is when one of them becomes bankrupt, or dies, or when property is the subject of a charging order because debts have not been paid. By contrast, on the breakdown of cohabitation, where there is a dispute as to who owns what, the cohabitant's only recourse is to the principles of property law.

What are the relevant principles? To start from the very basics: one of the most distinctive features of English property law is the concept of the trust. The legal, or 'paper', owner of property may actually hold it for someone else's benefit – or, as is most often the case in family situations, for himself jointly with another. Trusts may be express (that is, declared and recorded) or implied (and therefore unrecorded); therefore, even when it is clear who is the legal owner of property (the name(s) on the deeds or the land register), the beneficial ownership may be unclear, and open to dispute. Thus the spouse or cohabitant who is not a legal owner of the family home may nevertheless say to the legal owner 'yes, but you hold it on trust for me, I have a proprietary interest in it, and I am entitled to all or part of the proceeds of sale'. And there is scope for detailed argument, because that trust may arise in a number of different ways. Where it is not possible to establish the existence of a trust, the claimant may seek to establish that the legal owner is estopped from denying her claim – whether that claim is to an interest in the property, to a right to live there, or to inherit it.

Thus there is a great deal of law here! In order to make it navigable in what is not, after all, a textbook on land law or trusts, we set out and illustrate the principles in six points, as follows:

5.3.1   The express trust
5.3.2   The resulting trust
5.3.3   The constructive trust
5.3.4   Estoppel claims
5.3.5   Bankruptcy and debt
5.3.6   Inheritance

We begin, then, with the express trust.

5.3.1 The express trust

Where the parties have made an express declaration of the trust upon which the property is held – for example, by stating in the purchase deed that they hold the property as joint legal owners, and that they hold the property for each other in stated proportions (equally, 72/25, etc) – then there is no scope for further dispute about the beneficial ownership of the property. The express trust trumps all other possibilities (*Goodman v Gallant* [1986] Fam 106).

5.3.2 The resulting trust

The principle of the resulting trust is that where A buys property using B's money, he normally holds the property on trust for B – the beneficial interest is said to 'result' or jump back to B – unless the money was a gift. The principle extends, of course, to the case where A buys the property partly with his own money but with a substantial contribution from B; he will then hold the property on trust for himself and B in the same proportions as their respective contributions. This is essentially the principle affirmed in *Pettit* (see p. 150, above); Mr Pettit's claim failed because only direct contributions would do.

This very simple form of implied trust may be complicated by the ancient rule that there is a presumption of advancement where a wife uses her husband's money, though not vice versa; ie it is presumed that the husband intended his money as a gift. Nowadays, the presumption is considered by many to be outdated, and will be rebutted relatively easily.

Resulting trust cases are rare in this context. More often, the claimant needs to bring himself within the principles of the constructive trust.

5.3.3 The constructive trust: existence

In *Gissing v Gissing* the House of Lords considered the mechanisms available in the law of trusts to assist the spouse who has no legal estate in the property and no formally created equitable interest.

Gissing v Gissing

[1971] AC 886, [1970] 2 All ER 780, [1970] 3 WLR 255, 114 Sol Jo 550, House of Lords

The facts are set out in the speech of Lord Diplock:

In the instant appeal the matrimonial home was purchased in 1951 for £2,695 and conveyed into the sole name of the husband. The parties had by then been married for some 16 years and both were in employment with the same firm, the husband earning £1,000 and the wife £500, per annum. The purchase price was raised as to £2,150 on mortgage repayable by instalments, as to £500 by a loan to the husband from his employers, and as to the balance of £45 and the legal charges was paid by the husband out of his own moneys. The wife made no direct contribution to the initial deposit or legal charges, nor to the repayment of the loan of £500 nor to the mortgage instalments. She continued earning at the rate of £500 per annum until the marriage broke down in 1961. During this period the husband's salary increased to £3,000 per annum. The husband repaid the loan of £500 and paid the mortgage instalments. He also paid the outgoings on the house, gave to his wife a housekeeping allowance of £8 to £10 a week out of which she paid the running expenses of the household and he paid for holidays. The only contribution which the wife made out of her earnings to the household expenses was that she paid for her own clothes and those of the son of the marriage and for some extras. No change in this arrangement was made when the house was acquired. Each spouse had a separate banking account, the wife's in the Post Office Savings Bank, and each made savings out of their respective earnings. There was no joint bank account and there were no joint savings. There was no express agreement at the time of the purchase or thereafter as to how the beneficial interest in the house should be held. The learned judge was prepared to accept that after the marriage had broken down the husband said to the wife: 'Don't worry about the house – it's yours'; but this has not been relied upon, at any rate in your Lordships' House, as an acknowledgment of a pre-existing agreement on which the wife had acted to her detriment so as to give rise to a resulting, implied or constructive trust, nor can it be relied upon as an express declaration of trust as it was oral only.

On what then is the wife's claim based? In 1951 when the house was purchased she spent about £190 on buying furniture and a cooker and refrigerator for it. She also paid about £30 for improving the lawn. As furniture and household durables are depreciating assets whereas houses have turned out to be appreciating assets it may be that she would have been wise to have devoted her savings to acquiring an interest in the freehold; but this may not have been so apparent in 1951 as it has now become. The court is not entitled to infer a common intention to this effect from the mere fact that she provided chattels for joint use in the new matrimonial home; and there is nothing else in the conduct of the parties at the time of the purchase or thereafter which supports such an inference. There is no suggestion that the wife's efforts or her earnings made it possible for the husband to raise the initial loan or the mortgage or that her relieving her husband from the expense of buying clothing for herself and for their son was undertaken in order to enable him the better to meet the mortgage instalments or to repay the loan. The picture presented by the evidence is one of husband and wife retaining their separate proprietary interests in property whether real or personal purchased with their separate savings and is inconsistent with any common intention at the time of the purchase of the matrimonial home that the wife, who neither then nor thereafter contributed anything to its purchase price or assumed any liability for it, should nevertheless be entitled to a beneficial interest in it.

Earlier in his speech, Lord Diplock looked at the role of the agreement in the creation of an equitable interest in real property.

A resulting, implied or constructive trust – and it is unnecessary for present purposes to distinguish between these three classes of trust – is created by a transaction between the trustee and the cestui que trust in connection with the acquisition by the trustee of a legal estate in land, whenever the trustee has so conducted himself that it would be inequitable to allow him to deny to the cestui que trust a beneficial interest in the land acquired. And he will be held so to have conducted himself if by his words or conduct he has induced the cestui que trust to act to his own detriment in the reasonable belief that by so acting he was acquiring a beneficial interest in the land.

This is why it has been repeatedly said in the context of disputes between spouses as to their respective beneficial interests in the matrimonial home, that if at the time of its acquisition and transfer of the legal estate into the name of one or other of them an express agreement has been made between them as to the way in which the beneficial interest shall be held, the court will give effect to it – notwithstanding the absence of any written declaration of trust. Strictly speaking this states the principle too widely, for if the agreement did not provide for anything to be done by the spouse in whom the legal estate was not to be vested, it would be a merely voluntary declaration of trust and unenforceable for want of writing. But ... [w]hat the court gives effect to is the trust resulting or implied from the common intention expressed in the oral agreement between the spouses that if each acts in the manner provided for in the agreement the beneficial interests in the matrimonial home shall be held as they have agreed.

An express agreement between spouses as to their respective beneficial interests in land conveyed into the name of one of them obviates the need for showing that the conduct of the spouse into whose name the land was conveyed was intended to induce the other spouse to act to his or her detriment upon the faith of the promise of a specified beneficial interest in the land and that the other spouse so acted with the intention of acquiring that beneficial interest. The agreement itself discloses the common intention required to create a resulting, implied or constructive trust.

But parties to a transaction in connection with the acquisition of land may well have formed a common intention that the beneficial interest in the land shall be vested in them jointly without having used express words to communicate this intention to one another; or their recollections of the words used may be imperfect or conflicting by the time any dispute arises. In such a case – a common one where the parties are spouses whose marriage has broken down – it may be possible to infer their common intention from their conduct...

The conduct of the spouses in relation to the payment of the mortgage instalments may be no less relevant to their common intention as to the beneficial interests in a matrimonial home acquired in this way than their conduct in relation to the payment of the cash deposit.

It is this feature of the transaction by means of which most matrimonial homes have been acquired in recent years that makes difficult the task of the court ... Where a matrimonial home has been purchased outright without the aid of an advance on mortgage it is not difficult to ascertain what part, if any, of the purchase price has been provided by each spouse. If the land is conveyed into the name of a spouse who has not provided the whole of the purchase price, ... the prima facie inference is that their common intention was that the contributing spouse should acquire a share in the beneficial interest in the land in the same proportion as the sum contributed bore to the total purchase price. This prima facie inference is more easily rebutted in favour of a gift where the land is conveyed into the name of the wife: but as I understand the speeches in *Pettitt v Pettitt* [1970] AC 777, [1969] 2 All ER 385 four of the members of your Lordships' House who were parties to that decision took the view that even if the 'presumption of advancement' as between husband and wife still survived today, it could seldom have any decisive part to play in disputes between living spouses ...

Similarly when a matrimonial home is not purchased outright but partly out of moneys advanced on mortgage repayable by instalments, and the land is conveyed into the name of the husband alone, the fact that the wife made a cash contribution to the deposit and legal charges not borrowed on mortgage gives rise, in the absence of evidence which makes some other explanation more probable, to the inference that their common intention was that she should share in the beneficial interest in the land conveyed. ... Where there has been an initial contribution by the wife to the cash deposit and legal charges which points to a common intention at the time of the conveyance that she should have a beneficial interest in the land conveyed to her husband, it would be unrealistic to regard the wife's subsequent contributions to the mortgage instalments as without significance unless she pays them directly herself. It may be no more than a matter of convenience which spouse pays particular household accounts particularly when both are earning ...

Even where there has been no initial contribution by the wife to the cash deposit and legal charges but she makes a regular and substantial direct contribution to the mortgage instalments it may be reasonable to infer a common intention of the spouses from the outset that she should share in the beneficial interest or to infer a fresh agreement reached after the original conveyance that she should acquire a share. But it is unlikely that the mere fact that the wife made direct contributions to the mortgage instalments would be the only evidence available to assist the court in ascertaining the common intention of the spouses.

Where in any of the circumstances described the above contributions, direct or indirect, have been made to the mortgage instalments by the spouse into whose name the matrimonial home has not been conveyed, and the court can infer from their conduct a common intention that the contributing spouse should be entitled to *some* beneficial interest in the matrimonial home, what effect is to be given to that intention if there is no evidence that they in fact reached any express agreement as to what the respective share of each spouse should be? ...

In such a case the court must first do its best to discover from the conduct of the spouses whether any inference can reasonably be drawn as to the probable common understanding about the amount of the share of the contributing spouse upon which each must have acted in doing what each did, even though that understanding was never expressly stated by one spouse to the other or even consciously formulated in words by either of them independently. It is only if no such inference can be drawn that the court is driven to apply as a rule of law, and not as an inference of fact, the maxim 'equality is equity,' and to hold that the beneficial interest belongs to the spouses in equal shares...

Difficult as they are to solve, however, these problems as to the amount of the share of a spouse in the beneficial interest in a matrimonial home where the legal estate is vested solely in the other spouse, only arise in cases where the court is satisfied by the words or conduct of the parties that it was their common intention that the beneficial interest was not to belong solely to the spouse in whom the legal estate was vested but was to be shared between them in some proportion or other.

Where the wife has made no initial contribution to the cash deposit and legal charges and no direct contribution to the mortgage instalments nor any adjustment to her contribution to other expenses of the household which it can be inferred was referable to the acquisition of the house, there is in the absence of evidence of an express agreement between the parties no material to justify the court in inferring that it was the common intention of the parties that she should have any beneficial interest in a matrimonial home conveyed into the sole name of the husband, merely because she continued to contribute out of her own earnings or private income to other expenses of the household. For such conduct is no less consistent with a common intention to share the day-to-day expenses of the household, while each spouse retains a separate interest in capital assets acquired with their own moneys or obtained by inheritance or gift. There is nothing here to rebut the prima facie inference that a purchaser of land who pays the purchase price and takes a conveyance and grants a mortgage in his own name intends to acquire the sole beneficial interest as well as the legal estate: and the difficult question of the quantum of the wife's share does not arise.

Lord Diplock concluded that he was unable to draw an inference that there was any common intention that the wife should have any beneficial interest in the matrimonial home.

Lord Dilhorne and Lord Morris were against indirect contributions entitling a spouse to some beneficial interest in the matrimonial home. Lord Reid and Lord Pearson would appear to permit a beneficial interest to be acquired through indirect contributions but do not elaborate this concept. Nevertheless, the decision in *Gissing* is regarded as the foundation for the 'common intention constructive trust'. It was followed by a series of decisions, of which we present a small selection, in which the courts explored this important and exciting concept.

Eves v Eves
[1975] 3 All ER 768, [1975] 1 WLR 1338, 119 Sol Jo 394, Court of Appeal

The plaintiff (referred to in the judgment of Lord Denning MR as 'Janet' because 'she has had four surnames already') met the defendant in 1968. The relationship lasted four and a half years and during this time she took his surname and had two children by him. He was a married man and they lived together initially in his house. In 1969, they moved to another house which was conveyed into the defendant's name, paid for in part by the sale of the former house and in part by a mortgage raised by the defendant. As in *Cooke v Head* [1972] 2 All ER 38, the plaintiff put in a lot of initial work on the renovation of the house. The couple separated in 1972, and she applied to the county court for a declaration of an interest in the house. On appeal to the Court of Appeal:

Lord Denning MR: ... Although Janet did not make any financial contribution, it seems to me that this property was acquired and maintained both by their joint efforts with the intention that it should be used for their joint benefit until they were married and thereafter as long as the marriage continued. At any rate, Stuart Eves cannot be heard to say to the contrary. He told her that it was to be their home for them and their children. He gained her confidence by telling her that he intended to put it in their joint names (just as married couples often do) but that it was not possible until she was 21. The judge described this as a 'trick,' and said that it 'did not do him much credit as a man of honour.' The man never intended to put it in joint names but always determined to have it in his own name. It seems to me that he should be judged by what he told her – by what he led her to believe – and not by his own intent which he kept to himself. Lord Diplock made this clear in *Gissing v Gissing* [1971]AC 886 at 906. It seems to me that this conduct by Mr Eves amounted to a recognition by him that, in all fairness, she was entitled to a share in the house, equivalent in some way to a declaration of trust; not for a particular share, but for such share as was fair in view of all she had done and was doing for him and the children and would thereafter do. By so doing he gained her confidence. She trusted him. She did not make any financial contribution but she contributed in many other ways. She did much work in the house and garden. She looked after him and cared for the children. It is clear that her contribution was such that if she had been a wife she could have had a good claim to have a share in it on a divorce: see *Wachtel v Wachtel* [1973] Fam 72 at 92–94.

Brightman J: The defendant clearly led the plaintiff to believe that she was to have some undefined interest in the property, and that her name was only omitted from the conveyance because of her age. This, of course, is not enough by itself to create a beneficial interest in her favour; there would at best be a mere 'voluntary declaration of trust' which would be 'unenforceable for want of writing': *per* Lord Diplock in *Gissing v Gissing* [1971]AC 886 at 905. If, however, it was part of the bargain between the parties, expressed or to be implied, that the plaintiff should contribute her labour towards the reparation of a house in which she was to have some beneficial interest, then I think that the arrangement becomes one to which the law can give effect. This seems to be consistent with the reasoning of the speeches in *Gissing v Gissing*.

The Court of Appeal decided that the defendant held the legal estate on trust for sale in the proportion one-quarter to the plaintiff and three-quarters to the defendant.

Similar reasoning is seen in the following case.

Burns v Burns
[1984] Ch 317, [1984] 1 All ER 244, [1984] 2 WLR 582, [1984] FLR 216, [1984] Fam Law 244, Court of Appeal

The plaintiff and the defendant set up house together in 1961. In 1963, when the plaintiff was expecting their second child, the defendant decided to buy a house.

This was purchased, and conveyed in the sole name of the defendant. He financed the purchase price out of his own money and paid the mortgage. The plaintiff remained at home in order to look after the two children and maintain the home. She did not go out to work until 1975. Subsequent to that date, she used some of her earnings to pay for the rates and telephone bills and buy certain items for the house. She also redecorated the interior of the house. The relationship deteriorated, and the plaintiff left the home in 1980. She claimed that she was entitled to a beneficial interest in the house by reason of her contributions to the household over the 17 years she had lived in the house with him. The judge dismissed her claim and she appealed.

Fox LJ rejected the proposition that there was any evidence of a payment or payments by the plaintiff which it can be inferred was referable to the acquisition of the house. He also felt that the redecoration gave no indication of a common intention that she had a beneficial interest. (*Pettitt v Pettitt* [1970] AC 777, [1969] 2 All ER 385, HL; see p. 150, above.) He then turned to the question of housekeeping and domestic duties.

There remains the question of housekeeping and domestic duties. So far as housekeeping expenses are concerned, I do not doubt that (the house being in the man's name) if the woman goes out to work in order to provide money for the family expenses, as a result of which she spends her earnings on the housekeeping and the man is thus able to pay the mortgage instalments and other expenses out of his earnings, it can be inferred that there was a common intention that the woman should have an interest in the house – since she will have made an indirect financial contribution to the mortgage instalments. But that is not this case.

During the greater part of the period when the plaintiff and the defendant were living together she was not in employment or, if she was, she was not earning amounts of any consequence and provided no money towards the family expenses. Nor is it suggested that the defendant ever asked her to. He provided, and was always ready to provide, all the money that she wanted for housekeeping. The house was not bought in the contemplation that the plaintiff would, at some time, contribute to the cost of its acquisition. She worked to suit herself. And if towards the very end of the relationship she had money to spare she spent it entirely as she chose. It was in no sense 'joint' money. It was her own; she was not expected and was not asked to spend it on the household.

I think it would be quite unreal to say that, overall, she made a substantial financial contribution towards the family expenses. That is not in any way a criticism of her; it is simply the factual position.

But, one asks, can the fact that the plaintiff performed domestic duties in the house and looked after the children be taken into account? I think it is necessary to keep in mind the nature of the right which is being asserted. The court has no jurisdiction to make such order as it might think fair; the powers conferred by the Matrimonial Causes Act 1973 in relation to the property of married persons do not apply to unmarried couples. The house was bought by the defendant in his own name and, prima facie, he is the absolute beneficial owner. If the plaintiff, or anybody else, claims to take it from him, it must be proved the claimant has, by some process of law, acquired an interest in the house. What is asserted here is the creation of a trust arising by common intention of the parties. That common intention may be inferred where there has been a financial contribution, direct or indirect, to the acquisition of the house. But the mere fact that parties live together and do the ordinary domestic tasks is, in my view, no indication at all that they thereby intended to alter the existing property rights of either of them. As to that I refer to the passage from the speech of Lord Diplock in *Pettitt v Pettitt* [1970] AC 777, 826 which I have already mentioned; and also to the observations of Lord Hodson in *Pettitt v Pettitt* at p. 811 and of Lord Reid at p. 796. The undertaking of such work is, I think, what Lord Denning MR in *Button v Button* [1968] 1 WLR 457, 462 called the sort of things which are done for the benefit of the family without altering the title to property. The assertion that they do alter property rights seems to me to be, in substance, reverting to the idea of the 'family asset' which was rejected by the House of Lords in *Pettitt v Pettitt* [1970] AC 777. The decision in *Gissing v Gissing* [1971] AC 886 itself is really inconsistent with the contrary view since the parties lived together for ten years after the house was bought. ...

The result, in my opinion, is that the plaintiff fails to demonstrate the existence of any trust in her favour.

May LJ agreeing with Waller LJ and Fox LJ referred to the unfortunate position that the plaintiff found herself:

> When one compares this ultimate result with what it would have been had she been married to the defendant, and taken appropriate steps under the Matrimonial Causes Act 1973, I think that she can justifiably say that fate has not been kind to her. In my opinion, however, the remedy for any inequity she may have sustained is a matter for Parliament and not for this court. *Appeal dismissed.*

Mrs Burns has become the paradigm of the cohabitant for whom the law on constructive trusts has nothing to offer, and a touchstone for reform proposals; of any new system proposed, we have to ask: 'will it have anything to offer another Mrs Burns?'

Grant v Edwards
[1986] Ch 638, [1986] 2 All ER 426, [1986] 3 WLR 114, [1987] 1 FLR 87, [1986] Fam Law 300, Court of Appeal

The plaintiff, a married woman who was separated from her husband, set up a home with the defendant. In 1969, the defendant purchased a house and moved into it with the plaintiff, their child and the two children of the plaintiff's first marriage. The house was conveyed into joint names of the defendant and his brother. It was alleged that the defendant told the plaintiff that her name was not included in the title simply because of possible difficulties in relation to her divorce. He paid the deposit and the mortgage instalments, although the plaintiff made substantial contributions to general household expenses. The parties separated in 1980 and the plaintiff claimed a beneficial interest in the house. The judge dismissed the claim, and the plaintiff appealed:

Nourse LJ: In order to decide whether the plaintiff has a beneficial interest in 96, Hewitt Road we must climb again the familiar ground which slopes down from the twin peaks of *Pettitt v Pettitt* [1970]AC 777 and *Gissing v Gissing* [1971] AC 886. In a case such as the present, where there has been no written declaration or agreement, nor any direct provision by the plaintiff of part of the purchase price so as to give rise to a resulting trust in her favour, she must establish a common intention between her and the defendant, acted upon by her, that she should have a beneficial interest in the property. If she can do that, equity will not allow the defendant to deny that interest and will construct a trust to give effect to it.

In most of these cases the fundamental, and invariably the most difficult, question is to decide whether there was the necessary common intention, being something which can only be inferred from the conduct of the parties, almost always from the expenditure incurred by them respectively. In this regard the court has to look for expenditure which is referable to the acquisition of the house: see *per* Fox LJ in *Burns v Burns* [1984] Ch 317, 328H-329C. If it is found to have been incurred, such expenditure will perform the twofold function of establishing the common intention and showing that the claimant has acted upon it.

There is another and rarer class of case, of which the present may be one, where, although there has been no writing, the parties have orally declared themselves in such a way as to make their common intention plain. Here the court does not have to look for conduct from which the intention can be inferred, but only for conduct which amounts to an acting upon it by the claimant. And although that conduct can undoubtedly be the incurring of expenditure which is referable to the acquisition of the house, it need not necessarily be so.

The clearest example of this rarer class of case is *Eves v Eves* [1975] 1 WLR 1338. That was a case of an unmarried couple where the conveyance of the house was taken in the name of the man alone. At the time of the purchase he told the woman that if she had been 21 years of age, he would have put the house into their joint names, because it was to be their joint home. He admitted in evidence that that was an excuse for not putting the house into their joint names, and this court inferred that there was an understanding between them, or a common intention, that the woman was to have some sort of proprietary interest in it; otherwise no excuse would have been needed. After they had moved in, the woman did extensive decorative work to the downstairs rooms and generally cleaned the whole house. She painted the brickwork of the front of the house. She also broke up with a 14-lb. sledge hammer the concrete surface which covered the whole of the front garden and disposed of the rubble into a skip, worked in the back garden and, together with the man, demolished a shed there and put up a new shed. She also prepared the front garden for turfing. Pennycuick V-C at first instance, being unable to find any link between the common intention and the woman's activities after the purchase, held that she had not acquired a beneficial interest in the house. On an appeal to this court the decision was unanimously reversed, by Lord Denning MR on a ground which I respectfully think was at variance with the principles stated in *Gissing v Gissing* [1971] AC 886 and by Browne LJ and Brightman J [in a different way, see before, p. 168].

About that case the following observations may be made. First, as Brightman J himself observed, if the work had not been done the common intention would not have been enough. Secondly, if the common intention had not been orally made plain, the work would not have been conduct from which it could be inferred. That, I think, is the effect of the actual decision in *Pettitt v Pettitt* [1970] AC 777. Thirdly, and on the other hand, the work was conduct which amounted to an acting upon the common intention by the woman.

It seems therefore, on the authorities as they stand, that a distinction is to be made between conduct from which the common intention can be inferred on the one hand and conduct which amounts to an acting upon it on the other. There remains this difficult question: what is the quality of conduct required for the latter purpose? The difficulty is caused, I think because although the common intention has been made plain, everything else remains a matter of inference. Let me illustrate it in this way. It would be possible to take the view that the mere moving into the house by the woman amounted to an acting upon the common intention. But that was evidently not the view of the majority in *Eves v Eves* [1975] 1 WLR 1338. And the reason for that may be that, in the absence of evidence, the law is not so cynical as to infer that a woman will only go to live with a man to whom she is not married if she understands that she is to have an interest in their home. So what sort of conduct is required? In my judgment it must be conduct on which the woman could not reasonably have been expected to embark unless she was to have an interest in the house. If she was not to have such an interest, she could reasonably be expected to go and live with her lover, but not, for example, to wield a 14-lb. sledge hammer in the front garden. In adopting the latter kind of conduct she is seen to act to her detriment on the faith of the common intention.

. ...

Was the conduct of the plaintiff in making substantial indirect contributions to the instalments payable under both mortgages conduct upon which she could not reasonably have been expected to embark unless she was to have an interest in the house? I answer that question in the affirmative. I cannot see upon what other basis she could reasonably have been expected to give the defendant such substantial assistance in paying off mortgages on his house. I therefore conclude that the plaintiff did act to her detriment on the faith of the common intention between her and the defendant that she was to have some sort of proprietary interest in the house. ...

For these reasons, I would allow this appeal.

Questions

(i) What if in *Burns v Burns*, the man had left and he had then tried to evict the woman?

(ii) Is *Burns v Burns* a different case, or do you think the decision simply reflects the consensus amongst the judiciary that Lord Denning had gone too far?

Windeler v Whitehall

[1990] FCR 268, [1990] 2 FLR 505, High Court, Chancery Division

The plaintiff went to live with the defendant in 1974. The defendant was very much in love with her and wanted to marry her, but she consistently refused and occasionally had affairs with other men. The defendant was a successful theatrical agent, first as an employee of an agency and then on his own with a partner. The plaintiff looked after his house and entertained for him, but the work of the agency was essentially done by the defendant in his office. In 1979 the defendant sold his house and bought a larger one. The plaintiff made no contribution to the purchase. She had no money of her own, never worked or earned money and was supported by the defendant. She supervised some minor building works carried out on the new house. In June of that year the defendant made a will leaving the plaintiff his residuary estate. By 1980 the relationship was deteriorating and in 1984 it ended. The plaintiff accepted some money from the defendant and removed her belongings from the house, together with some items belonging to the defendant. In January 1987 the plaintiff brought a claim for a proprietary interest in the house and the business:

Millett J: If this were California, this would be a claim for palimony, but it is England and it is not. English law recognises neither the term nor the obligation to which it gives effect. In this country a husband has a legal obligation to support his wife even if they are living apart. A man has no legal obligation to support his mistress even if they are living together. Accordingly, the plaintiff does not claim to be supported by the defendant but brings a claim to a proprietary interest in his business and his home. ...

The plaintiff, Victoria Windeler, claims a share in the house in which she formerly lived with the defendant, Michael Whitehall, and a share in his business as a successful West End theatrical agent. They never married. To succeed, therefore, it is not enough for Miss Windeler to persuade me that she deserves to have such a share. She must satisfy me that she already owns it. In each case legal ownership is vested in Mr Whitehall. Miss Windeler, therefore, must satisfy me that in equity she is a part owner. This depends on the intention of the parties and such intention must be proved directly or inferred from their conduct. But it is important to bear in mind, that it is to that narrow issue alone that the parties' conduct is relevant.

... Miss Windeler ... was essentially immature. She never shook off an adolescent desire to be free and to avoid being tied down. Her counsel submitted to me that she saw her life and future with Mr Whitehall. I do not think she did. I do not think she ever saw the relationship as a permanent arrangement. She saw it only lasting as long as she chose to make it last.

She told me in the witness box that she gave Mr Whitehall the stability necessary to pursue his career. I think that is the last thing she gave him. She had no stability herself. I think she gave him love and beauty and excitement. But, apart from her love, the greatest gift that a woman can bring to a man is security, tranquillity and peace of mind; something I think Miss Windeler was never able to give to Mr Whitehall.

Not only is there no direct evidence of any common intention but there is evidence which I accept that it was not Mr Whitehall's intention that Miss Windeler should have an interest in the house or, for that matter, in the business. That really is the end of the case.

But as to the business, Millett J went further:

This is not a case where a woman has worked full-time or for substantial periods in the business without wages and in a way which would lead anyone to believe that she must have been encouraged in the expectation that she had or would have an interest in the business. What Miss Windeler did was not work for which Mr Whitehall would have paid anyone to do in any circumstance whatever. In the present case Miss Windeler would not have been entitled even to a quantum meruit claim, and the idea that her conduct entitled her to a proprietary interest in the business is, in my judgment, ridiculous. I dismiss the action.

If it *were* California:

Marvin v Marvin
134 Cal Reptr 815, 557 P 2d 106 (1976), Supreme Court, State of California

Michelle Marvin contended that in 1964, she and the defendant, the film actor Lee Marvin, entered into an oral agreement that: 'while the parties lived together they would combine their efforts and earnings and would share equally any and all property accumulated as a result of their efforts whether individual or combined.' Furthermore, she said that they had agreed to hold themselves out to the general public as husband and wife, and that she would 'further render her services as a companion, housekeeper and cook'. She gave up what she said was a lucrative career as an entertainer and a singer to devote herself full time to Lee Marvin. She alleged that she lived with the defendant for six years and fulfilled her obligations under the agreement. When the relationship broke up, the plaintiff sought a declaration of constructive trust upon one-half of the property acquired during the course of the relationship:

Tobriner J: We base our opinion on the principle that adults who voluntarily live together and engage in sexual relations are nonetheless as competent as any other persons to contract respecting their earnings and property rights. Of course, they cannot lawfully contract to pay for the performance of sexual services, for such a contract is, in essence, an agreement for prostitution and unlawful for that reason. But they may agree to pool their earnings and to hold all property acquired during the relationship in accord with the law governing community property; conversely they may agree that each partner's earnings and the property acquired from those earnings remains the separate property of the earning partner. So long as the agreement does not rest upon illicit meretricious consideration, the parties may order their economic affairs as they choose, and no policy precludes the courts from enforcing such agreements.

In the present instance, plaintiff alleges that the parties agreed to pool their earnings, that they contracted to share equally in all property acquired, and that defendant agreed to support plaintiff. The terms of the contract as alleged do not rest upon any unlawful consideration. We therefore conclude that the complaint furnishes a suitable basis upon which the trial court can render declaratory relief.

The court went on to add that, in the absence of an express agreement, the court may look to a variety of other remedies in order to protect the parties' legitimate expectations:

The courts may inquire into the conduct of the parties to determine whether that conduct demonstrates an implied contract or implied agreement of partnership or joint venture ..., or some other tacit understanding between the parties. The courts may, when appropriate, employ principles of constructive trust ... or resulting trust. ... Finally, a nonmarital partner may recover in quantum meruit for the reasonable value of household services rendered. ...

We conclude that the judicial barriers that may stand in the way of a policy based upon the fulfillment of the reasonable expectations of the parties to a nonmarital relationship should be removed.

The mores of the society have indeed changed so radically in regard to cohabitation that we cannot impose a standard based on alleged moral considerations that have apparently been so widely abandoned by so many. Lest we be misunderstood, however, we take this occasion to point out that the structure of society itself largely depends upon the institution of marriage, and nothing we have said in this opinion should be taken to derogate from that institution. The joining of the man and woman in marriage is at once the most socially productive and individually fulfilling relationship that one can enjoy in the course of a lifetime.

There was further litigation in this case culminating in the California Court of Appeal (1981) 122 Cal App 3d 871 deleting the trial judge's rehabilitative award of $104,000 to the plaintiff. The Appellate Court held that there was no basis for a finding of damage or unjust enrichment, and there was no evidence of a wrongful act on the part of the defendant with respect to either the relationship or its termination.

Question

Perhaps the situation between England and California is not all that different?

Back to England now; the beginning of the 1990s saw another landmark decision.

Lloyds Bank plc v Rossett
[1991] 1 AC 107, [1990] 1 All ER 1111, House of Lords

The husband and wife bought a semi-derelict property as a family home. The acquisition was in the husband's sole name, apparently because of the insistence by the Swiss trustees of the husband's family trust. However, the wife carried out a considerable amount of the decorating work and generally supervised the builders. A lot of this work was done prior to exchange of contracts. The cost of the renovation was met by an overdraft on the husband's account. The husband signed the bank's form of legal charge. The husband left the house in 1984, and the loan was not repaid. In a claim by the bank for possession and an order for sale, the wife resisted the claim on the basis that she had a beneficial interest in the property under a constructive trust that qualified as an overriding interest under s. 70(1)(g) of the Land Registration Act 1925 (see p. 160, above) because she had been in actual occupation at the relevant date. The House of Lords, in following *Abbey National Building Society v Cann* [1991] 1AC 56, [1990] 1 All ER 1085, held that the relevant date for ascertaining whether an interest in registered land was protected by actual occupation so as to prevail against the holder of a legal estate as a overriding interest under s. 70(1)(g) was that of the transfer or creation of the estate rather than its registration. However, it was not necessary to determine whether she was in actual occupation at the relevant date, because the House was of the unanimous view that she did not possess a beneficial interest.

Lord Bridge of Harwich: The first and fundamental question which must always be resolved is whether, independently of any inference to be drawn from the conduct of the parties in the course of sharing the house as their home and managing their joint affairs, there has at any time prior to acquisition, or exceptionally at some later date, been any agreement, arrangement or understanding reached between them that the property is to be shared beneficially. The finding of an agreement or arrangement to share in this sense can only, I think, be based on evidence of express discussions between the partners, however imperfectly remembered and however imprecise their terms may have been. Once a finding to this effect is made it will only be necessary for the partner asserting a claim to a beneficial interest against the partner entitled to the legal estate to show that he or she has acted to his or her detriment or significantly altered his or her position in reliance on the agreement in order to give rise to a constructive trust or a proprietary estoppel.

In sharp contrast with this situation is the very different one where there is no evidence to support a finding of an agreement or arrangement to share, however reasonable it might have been for the parties to reach such an arrangement if they had applied their minds to the question, and where the court must rely entirely on the conduct of the parties both as the basis from which to infer a common intention to share the property beneficially and as the conduct relied on to give rise to a constructive trust. In this situation direct contributions to the purchase price by the partner who is not the legal owner, whether initially or by payment of mortgage instalments, will readily justify the inference necessary to the creation of a constructive trust. But, as I read the authorities, it is at least extremely doubtful whether anything less will do.

The leading cases in your Lordships' House are *Pettitt v Pettitt* [1970] AC 777 and *Gissing v Gissing* [1971] AC 886 [see pp. 150, 165, above]. Both demonstrate situations in the second category to which I have referred and their Lordships discuss at great length the difficulties to which these situations give rise.

...

Outstanding examples on the other hand of cases giving rise to situations in the first category are *Eves v Eves* [1975] 1 WLR 1338 (see p. 168, above) and *Grant v Edwards* [1986] Ch 638. In both these cases, where the parties who had cohabited were unmarried, the female partner had been clearly led by the male partner to believe, when they set up home together, that the property would belong to them jointly. In *Eves v Eves* the male partner had told the female partner that the only reason why the property was to be acquired in his name alone was because she was under 21 and that, but for her age, he would have had the house put into their joint names. He admitted in evidence that this was simply an 'excuse'. Similarly in *Grant v Edwards* the female partner was told by the male partner that the only reason for not acquiring the property in joint names was because she was involved in divorce proceedings and that, if the property were acquired jointly, this might operate to her prejudice in those proceedings. As Nourse LJ put it, at p. 649:

> 'Just as in *Eves v Eves* [1975] 1 WLR 1338, these facts appear to me to raise a clear inference that there was an understanding between the plaintiff and the defendant, or a common intention, that the plaintiff was to have some sort of proprietary interest in the house; otherwise no excuse for not putting her name on to the title would have been needed.'

The subsequent conduct of the female partner in each of these cases, which the court rightly held sufficient to give rise to a constructive trust or proprietary estoppel supporting her claim to an interest in the property, fell far short of such conduct as would by itself have supported the claim in the absence of an express representation by the male partner that she was to have such an interest. It is significant to note that the share to which the female partners in *Eves v Eves* and *Grant v Edwards* were held entitled were one quarter and one half respectively. In no sense could these shares have been regarded as proportionate to what the judge in the instant case described as a 'qualifying contribution' in terms of the indirect contributions to the acquisition or enhancement of the value of the houses made by the female partners.

I cannot help thinking that the judge in the instant case would not have fallen into error if he had kept clearly in mind the distinction between the effect of evidence on the one hand which was capable of establishing an express agreement or an express representation that Mrs. Rosset was to have an interest in the property and evidence on the other hand of conduct alone as a basis for an inference of the necessary common intention.

Appeal allowed.

Questions

(i) Is Lord Bridge saying the same as Lord Diplock in *Gissing v Gissing*? (See p. 166, above.)

(ii) Do you feel you can now construct a 'recipe' for a constructive trust, ie a list of the elements that must be proved in order to establish such a trust?

Nearly twenty years separate *Gissing* and *Rossett*, and as a House of Lords decision *Rossett* must be regarded as definitive in the sense that it finally settles the criteria for the existence of a constructive trust: there must be an agreement or common intention to share the property beneficially, together with detrimental reliance upon that agreement on the part of the claimant. The agreement, if not express, must be inferred from conduct, and that conduct must, it seems, consist in some kind of financial contribution. There is nothing here for the partner who stands most in need of a property interest because she has, and has always had, nothing. Alastair Hudson, in *Equity and Trusts* (2001), sums up the difficulties as follows:

> What Lord Bridge appears to forget is that people fall in love. And that when they fall in love they sometimes move in together, or get married, or have children. Or sometimes they don't fall in love but they have children and so have to move in together. And so on and so on. Hundreds of years of novels, plays and (latterly) films have shown us the perfidies of the human heart. Similarly, they have shown us that (to quote Shakespeare's *King Lear*) fate deals with us cruelly 'as flies to wanton boys are we to the gods / they use us for their sport'. It is not possible to create a strict test like that in *Rosset* and expect either that people will always sit down calmly in those glorious early days of a relationship and decide who is to have what equitable interest in the home, or that people will be able to form a common intention at the start of their relationship which will work perfectly throughout it without anyone becoming ill, being made redundant, falling out of love or whatever else. Life is just not like that. It is suggested that it is contrary to the very core of equity's flexible ability to do right on a case-by-case basis to use concepts like that in *Rosset* to attempt to fetter and bind the ability of the courts to see the right result in any particular case and ... to act with integrity to isolate the best possible outcome.

Something of an answer to this is found in the judgment of Waite LJ in *Midland Bank plc v Cooke* [1995] 4 All ER 562, CA; he had this to say about the creative role of the court:

Equity has traditionally been a system which matches established principle to the demands of social change. The mass diffusion of home ownership has been one of the most striking social changes of our own time. The present case is typical of hundreds, perhaps even thousands, of others. When people, especially young people, agree to share their lives in joint homes they do so on a basis of mutual trust and in the expectation that their relationship will endure. Despite the efforts that have been made by many responsible bodies to counsel prospective cohabitants as to the risks of taking shared interests in property without legal advice, it is unrealistic to expect that advice to be followed on a universal scale. For a couple embarking on a serious relationship, discussion of the terms to apply at parting is almost a contradiction of the shared hopes that have brought them together. There will inevitably be numerous couples, married or unmarried, who have no discussion about ownership and who, perhaps advisedly, make no agreement about it. It would be anomalous, against that background, to create a range of home-buyers who were beyond the pale of equity's assistance in formulating a fair presumed basis for the sharing of beneficial title, simply because they had been honest enough to admit that they never gave ownership a thought or reached any agreement about it.

Until recently, the focus of thinking on constructive trusts was on the ways to establish their existence. *Midland Bank plc v Cooke* offers valuable guidance on the issue of quantum: if there is a trust, how much does the applicant get? The facts of the case were complicated by a succession of mortgages. Suffice it to say that the matrimonial home was purchased in 1971, in the husband's sole name. It cost £8,500, of which £6,540 was provided by a mortgage loan, £1,100 by Mr Cooke's parents as a wedding gift, and the balance by Mr Cooke from his own savings. Mrs Cooke's claim to a beneficial interest in the property arose in the course of possession proceedings brought by a mortgagee in 1987. Looking at the contributions to the purchase price, the judge at first instance said: 'In the normal course of events, of course, if parents make gifts by way of wedding presents to their offspring, those gifts are considered to be gifts jointly to the husband and wife.' Accordingly, he held that Mrs Cooke was entitled to a beneficial interest of 6.47% of the property, since her half of the wedding gift (£550) represented that proportion of the total cost (£8,500). Mrs Cooke appealed, and Waite LJ rejected the argument that the interest in a property of a party who has proved a direct contribution to the purchase price is fixed at the proportion that contribution bears to the overall price of the property. He looked at the decisions in *McHardy Sons (a firm) v Warren* [1994] 2 FLR 338 and in *Grant v Edwards* (see p. 170, above) at Lord Diplock's reasoning in *Gissing* (see p. 165, above), and rejected the strictly mathematical approach seen in *Springette v Defoe* [1992] 2 FLR 288. He explained:

The general principle to be derived from *Gissing v Gissing* and *Grant v Edwards* can in my judgment be summarised in this way. When the court is proceeding, in cases like the present where the partner without legal title has successfully asserted an equitable interest through direct contribution, to determine (in the absence of express evidence of intention) what proportions the parties must be assumed to have intended for their beneficial ownership, the duty of the judge is to undertake a survey of the whole course of dealing between the parties relevant to their ownership and occupation of the property and their sharing of its burdens and advantages. That scrutiny will not confine itself to the limited range of acts of direct contribution of the sort that are needed to found a beneficial interest in the first place. It will take into consideration all conduct which throws light on the question what shares were intended. Only if that search proves inconclusive does the court fall back on the maxim that 'equality is equity'.

... No court is bound to deal with the matter on the strict basis of the trust resulting from the cash contribution to the purchase price, and is free to attribute to the parties an intention to share the beneficial interest in some different proportions.

It follows from the answers I have given to the last two questions that the judge was in my view in error when he proceeded to treat the cash contribution to the purchase price as wholly determinative of the issue of the current proportions of beneficial entitlement, without regard to the other factors emerging from the whole course of dealing between the husband and wife. That was an error of principle which entitles this court to intervene and reach our own conclusions as to how the proportions of beneficial interest should be assessed.

When the proper approach (that is to say the approach I have summarised in dealing with question B) is applied to the present case, I have little doubt as to what the answer should be. Mrs Cooke is a wife who in addition to bringing up three children (one of whom is still only 11) was working full or part-time as a teacher and paying out her earnings in relief on household bills. When a second charge was taken out on the property within a few months after the marriage, she undertook joint and several liability to repay it. When her husband wanted her to sign the consent form in respect of the mortgage to the bank for the benefit of his business, she did so, despite the anxiety and distress which provided part of the grounds for the judge's ruling that it had been obtained by undue influence. Thereafter she again undertook liability under a second charge on the property for the benefit of his business. One could hardly have a clearer example of a couple who had agreed to share everything equally: the profits of his business while it prospered, and the risks of indebtedness suffered through its failure; the upbringing of their children; the rewards of her own career as a teacher; and, most relevantly, a home into which he had put his savings and to which she was to give over the years the benefit of the maintenance and improvement contribution. When to all that there is added the fact (still an important one) that this was a couple who had chosen to introduce into their relationship the additional commitment which marriage involves, the conclusion becomes inescapable that their presumed intention was to share the beneficial interests in the property in equal shares. I reach this result without the need to rely on any equitable maxim as to equality. It is reinforced by the subsequent terms of their compromise of the Married Women's Property Act proceedings.

For all these reasons I would allow the appeal, dismiss the cross-appeal, and substitute for the declaration granted by the judge a declaration that Mrs Cooke has a beneficial one-half interest in the property.

Dianne Wragg, in 'Constructive trusts and the unmarried couple' (1996), represents the decision in diagrammatic form; she then explores its implications:

Figure 1
Stage 1 – Establishing a beneficial interest

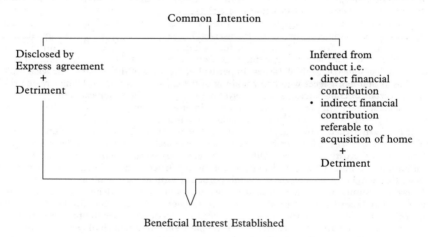

Stage 2 – Quantifying that interest

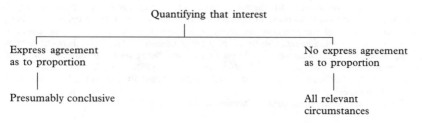

This would appear to allow wider contributions in terms of home-making and child-rearing to be taken into account in stage 2. What will be the effect of retaining a strict approach to stage 1, which specifically excludes such considerations? As suggested in figure 1, establishing a beneficial interest remains a narrow and difficult gateway through which a cohabitee must pass. Having done so, however, she now enters a liberal green pasture in which she may de facto enjoy rights in relation to the family home akin to those given to married couples by s 24 of the Matrimonial Causes Act 1973. The stakes having thus been raised, an increase in litigation must surely follow, coupled with a temptation on the part of the courts to find justification for assisting 'deserving' cases through the gateway.

... On this basis it would seem that a cohabitee who can show, perhaps, with the benefit of creative hindsight, that she made some very modest direct contribution, will get through the gateway to stage 2. *Halifax Building Society v Brown* [1996] 1 FLR 103 may provide an illustration. In that case a loan (as opposed to a gift) of the deposit by a parent was held to be capable of giving rise to the same inference of common intention, sufficient to satisfy stage 1 ... It would appear therefore that if, when an unmarried man and woman set up home, the man's father lends them the deposit, the woman will subsequently be able to meet the stage 1 criteria and the court will be able to take into account her wider, non-financial contributions in quantifying her interest. The possibly more 'deserving' cohabitee such as Mrs Burns (*Burns v Burns* [1984] FLR 216, CA), who had lived with a man for 19 years and brought up two children but had made no direct financial contribution, still remains on the wrong side of the gateway. It is suggested that this introduces an even greater element of 'lottery' into this area of law than already exists. If the law were to be that a 5% financial contribution results in a 5% beneficial interest this would be harsh, but would at least be clear and consistent. Arguably, it is counter-productive to liberalise stage 2 and introduce new criteria without a corresponding change to stage 1.

COHABITEES AND PROPERTY RIGHTS

What, then, are the objections to taking into account wider, non-financial contributions at stage 1? Is this, as some writers have argued, an unnecessarily reactionary and anti-feminist approach by male judges? It is suggested that the roots of the problem go far deeper and relate to inherent conceptual difficulties in using the model of the constructive trust to resolve property rights, particularly in relation to cohabitees.

In English law, a constructive trust is regarded as a substantive entity. It comes into existence as a result of the actions of the parties themselves. The courts' role is limited to stipulating the criteria which will 'trigger' its creation, for example, direct financial contribution. If the 'triggering' factors are very loosely defined, generalised criteria of wider contribution, there is a real danger of injustice to third parties. In particular, creditors of the owner of the legal estate, purchasers and mortgagees who know nothing of the existence of the informally created right may, in certain circumstances, find themselves bound by it. ... If a person can informally, and at an unspecified point in time, acquire an interest in property capable of ranking ahead of bona fide third parties, we are in the realms of palm tree justice.

It has been argued convincingly by Evans at [1989] Conv 418 that 'the evolutionary path taken by the *Gissing v Gissing* trust seems to have been dictated by the law's determination to avoid informal creation of rights'. Other writers have pointed out that this problem does not arise in other common law jurisdictions where the constructive trust is regarded as a remedy, rather than a right. In such jurisdictions this particular form of trust tends to be seen as part of the law of restitution, a remedy against various forms of 'unjust enrichment'. This issue was addressed by Dean J in the Australian case of *Muschinski v Dodds* (1985) 160 CLR 583 when he explained a constructive trust as 'an in personam remedy attaching to property which may be moulded and adjusted to give effect to the application and interplay of equitable principles in the circumstances of the particular case. In particular, where competing common law or equitable claims are or may be involved, a declaration of constructive trust by way of remedy can properly be so framed that the consequences of its imposition are operative only from the date of judgment or formal court order or from some other specified date'.

Injustice to third parties can, therefore, be avoided by ensuring that, where appropriate, their interests rank ahead of those of the constructive beneficiary. The same does not apply to the English model of the constructive trust. It is submitted that there are, therefore, valid reasons for not allowing wider, non-financial contributions to be taken into account in stage 1. In English law the constructive trust is the model currently being used to resolve two conceptually different issues:

    (1) disputes between spouses and third parties (typically the husband's creditors or mortgagees);

    (2) disputes between cohabitees themselves.

Having asserted in *Gissing v Gissing* and subsequent cases that the constructive trust in its 'substantive entity' English version is the appropriate model for both, the courts are faced with difficulty in any attempt to liberalise the position for cohabitees. Any principles devised to 'reward' deserving cohabitees for their non-financial contributions form a precedent equally applicable to claims between spouses and creditors. What is 'equitable' in the former situation may not necessarily be 'equitable' in the latter. Tinkering with the problem by introducing new criteria into stage 2 provides no real solution. Is there any alternative way forward?

The ideal solution would be statutory intervention. In theory, it would be possible to introduce legislation giving the courts power to make property adjustment orders between cohabitees comparable with those available for married couples. The courts have repeatedly made the point, from *Burns v Burns* onwards, that such change is a matter for Parliament. A possible model for such legislation is available in the New South Wales De Facto Relationships Act 1984. However, if the issue is to remain in the hands of the courts, it is suggested that it can be resolved only by a radical conceptual shift towards the constructive trust as a remedy, not a right. It could then become a flexible tool, providing a remedy against unjust enrichment, but still protecting the legitimate interests of third parties. Or is equity past the age of child-bearing after all?

5.3.4 Proprietary estoppel

Another fruitful device has been proprietary estoppel. This was described by Edward Nugee QC (sitting as a Deputy High Court Judge) in *Re Basham* [1987] 1 All ER 405 at 410 as follows:

Where one person, A, has acted to his detriment on the faith of a belief, which was known to and encouraged by another person, B, that he either has [been] or is going to be given a right in or over B's property, B cannot insist on his strict legal rights if to do so would be inconsistent with A's belief.

Thus we are looking at one person encouraging another, by words or actions, to act to his detriment, rather than at an agreement or common intention. Proprietary estoppel differs from the constructive trust, at least in theory, in that the interest awarded to the claimant is at the court's discretion. Patricia Ferguson, in 'Constructive Trusts – A Note of Caution' (1985), explains:

Conceptually the constructive trust is closer to the resulting trust than to proprietary estoppel. Both constructive and resulting trusts are mechanisms whereby the conduct of the parties leads by operation of law to the creation of a proprietary interest. ... Estoppel is conceptually different ..., the remedy for estoppel is discretionary and may be merely personal.

Pascoe v Turner
[1979] 2 All ER 945, [1979] 1 WLR 431, 123 Sol Jo 164, 9 Fam Law 82, Court of Appeal

In 1961, the plaintiff met the defendant, a widow. In 1963, the defendant moved into the plaintiff's home, at first as his housekeeper. In 1964, the plaintiff and defendant began to 'live in every sense as man and wife'. In 1965, they moved to another house. The plaintiff paid the purchase price and he also paid for the contents. In 1973, the plaintiff moved out. The defendant stayed on in the house and, in reliance upon the plaintiff's declarations that he had given her the house and the contents, she spent money and herself did work on redecorations, improvements and repairs. In 1976, the plaintiff tried to evict the defendant from the house. It was the man's determination to get her out of the house which persuaded the Court of Appeal to conclude that a fee simple rather than a life licence was the right answer.

Cumming Bruce LJ: ... The principle to be applied is that the court should consider all the circumstances and, the (defendant) having no perfected gift or licence other than a licence revocable at will, the court must decide what is the minimum equity to do justice to her having regard to the way in which she changed her position for the worse by reason of the acquiescence and encouragement of the legal owner. The defendant submits that the only appropriate way in which equity can here be satisfied is by perfecting the imperfect gift as was done in *Dillwyn v Llewelyn* (1862) 4 De GF & J 517.

This court appreciates that the moneys laid out by the defendant were much less than in some of the cases in the books. But the court has to look at all the circumstances. When the plaintiff left her she was, we were told, a widow in her middle fifties. During the period that she lived with the plaintiff her capital was reduced from £4,500 to £1,000. Save for her invalidity pension that was all that she had in the world. In reliance upon the plaintiff's declaration of gift, encouragement and acquiescence she arranged her affairs on the basis that the house and contents belonged to her. So relying, she devoted a quarter of her remaining capital and her personal effort upon the house and its fixtures. In addition she bought carpets, curtains and furniture for it, with the result that by the date of the trial she had only £300 left. Compared to her, on the evidence the plaintiff is a rich man. He might not regard an expenditure of a few hundred pounds as a very grave loss. But the court has to regard her change of position over the years 1973 to 1976.

We take the view that the equity cannot here be satisfied without granting a remedy which assures to the defendant security of tenure, quiet enjoyment, and freedom of action in respect of repairs and improvements without interference from the plaintiff. The history of the conduct of the plaintiff since 9 April 1976, in relation to these proceedings leads to an irresistible inference that he is determined to pursue his purpose of evicting her from the house by any legal means at his disposal with a ruthless disregard of the obligations binding upon conscience. The court must grant a remedy effective to protect her against the future manifestations of his ruthlessness. It was conceded that if she is granted a licence, such a licence cannot be registered as a land charge, so that she may find herself ousted by a purchaser for value without notice.

If she has in the future to do further and more expensive repairs she may only be able to finance them by a loan, but as a licensee she cannot charge the house. The plaintiff as legal owner may well find excuses for entry in order to do what he may plausibly represent as necessary works and so contrive to derogate from her enjoyment of the licence in ways that make it difficult or impossible for the court to give her effective protection.

Weighing such considerations this court concludes that the equity to which the facts in this case give rise can only be satisfied by compelling the plaintiff to give effect to his promise and her expectations. He has so acted that he must now perfect the gift.

Pascoe v Turner stands at the head of a long line of cases in which the courts have grappled with the meaning of the elements required to give rise to estoppel: the promise or assurance, the claimant's detrimental reliance, and the requirement that it be unconscionable to allow the defendant to go back on his promise. A number of these cases have concerned the 'abandoned mistress', similar to Mrs Burns or Mrs Grant; but they have also encompassed a wide range of family situations. Of course, neither estoppel nor trust claims are restricted to the enforcement of claims by women against men:

Walton v Walton
14 April 1994, CA (Lexis transcript)

This was a claim by Alfred Walton, who had worked on the farm that had belonged to his father and grandfather since he was 15 in 1960. His father died in 1962, and thereafter he worked for his mother; at some times of the year he worked a 70 hour week. When compared with the minimum agricultural wage for that period, his pay was very poor; he received considerably less than a farm worker who did no overtime. Hoffmann LJ explained:

From time to time he complained. His mother would tell him that he could not expect more because he was working for his future. 'You can't have more money and a farm one day,' was her stock phrase.

During that period he married and had two children. From 1977 his circumstances improved as his mother rearranged her business affairs so as to enable him to draw on the profits of the farm. In the years that followed

... he incurred expenditure ... by making improvements with his own labour and money which would otherwise have been profits which he could draw from the business. All these acts were to his detriment.

In 1988 Mrs Walton senior contracted to sell the farm to a neighbouring landowner; Alfred issued proceedings, and shortly afterwards his mother died. In her will she disposed of her property in such a way that the farm would have had to be sold to meet pecuniary legacies, leaving a small residue for the plaintiff's children and nothing for the plaintiff. He therefore pursued his claim on the basis of estoppel. Hoffmann LJ explained:

Mrs Walton's promise was not, of course, made under seal and ... I do not think that it was part of a contract. So if there was nothing more than the promise, she would have been free to change her mind. ... But the position is different if the person who has been promised some interest in the property has, in reliance upon it, incurred expense or made sacrifices which he would not otherwise have made. In such a case the law will provide a remedy. It can take various forms. It may order the maker of the promise to provide compensation for the expense which has been incurred. It may make payment of compensation a charge on the property. Or it may require the promise to be kept.

In this case, he concluded, there were various options:

The plaintiff says [the court should order] a transfer to him of the farm, subject to the existing mortgage. ... [Counsel for the defendant] puts forward various alternative proposals. One is that the transfer should be subject to a payment of £50,000, representing what Mrs Walton might have required to buy herself a house if she had moved off the farm during her lifetime. But Mrs Walton did not move off the farm and now has no need of a house. The only effect of the payment would be to provide money for the payment of the legacy to her niece. She seems to me to have no equitable claim superior to that of the plaintiff's right to take the farm in whatever state it was at the date of Mrs Walton's death. An alternative proposal is that the plaintiff should take a life interest (or, to avoid making him tenant for life under the Settled Land Act 1925, an agricultural tenancy for life) with remainder to his son Simon. ... There is no evidence that Mrs Walton ever told the plaintiff that he could expect only a life interest with remainder to Simon. ... In my judgment, therefore, the only way to satisfy the equity on the plaintiff's favour is to order a transfer to him of the farm subject to the mortgage.

In *Wayling v Jones* (1993) 69 P & CR 170, CA, the plaintiff, Paul Wayling, had lived with Daniel Jones as his homosexual partner from 1971 until Mr Jones' death in 1987. Throughout that time Mr Wayling worked for Mr Jones, helping him to run various hotel businesses; in return he received little more than pocket money. On more than one occasion Mr Jones promised Mr Wayling that he would leave him, in his will, the hotel they were running at the time. He did not do so. Mr Wayling's claim, based upon proprietary estoppel, foundered in the County Court on the issue of reliance. Balcombe LJ in the Court of Appeal set out the parts of Mr Wayling's evidence that were fatal to his claim at first instance:

In his affidavit evidence the plaintiff stated that he relied on the deceased's promises. In his oral evidence in chief he said:

Q: One question, Mr Wayling. Assuming you were in the Hotel Royal bar, before Dan's death and Dan was there, if Dan had told you that he was not going to give the Royal Hotel to you but to somebody else after his death, what would you have done?
A: I would have left.

... Later in cross-examination came the following questions and answers:

Q: If he had not made that promise to you, would you still have stayed with him?
A: Yes ... .
Q: Just to continue on from that. So far as you are concerned, from that reply you gave, you would have remained with the deceased whether or not he made the promises?
A: Whatever business venture he would have had, yes.
Q: The promises were not the reason why you remained with the deceased?
A: No, we got on very well together.

The Court of Appeal held that, nevertheless, Mr Wayling had relied upon the promises made to him. Balcombe LJ said that 'the only question that mattered' was the one asked in examination-in-chief, namely, 'What would you have done if the deceased had told you that he was no longer prepared to implement his promises?' The court was not concerned with the hypothetical question, 'What would you have done if the promises had not been made?' Accordingly, the plaintiff's claim succeeded. As the hotel had by the date of the hearing been sold, he was awarded the net proceeds of sale.

Question

What is meant by 'reliance upon a promise'? For some doubts on the views expressed by the Court of Appeal here, see Cooke (1995).

Compare with *Wayling* the following case:

Gillett v Holt
[2001] Ch 210, [2000] 2 All ER 289, [2000] 3 WLR 815, [2000] 2 FLR 266, Court of Appeal

This concerned a claim by Mr Gillett for satisfaction of his expectations based on assurances made to him over many years by Mr Holt in connection with the latter's farming business. The substance of Mr Holt's promises was that Mr Gillett and his wife would inherit the farm on Mr Holt's death, and Mr Gillett relied upon this, devoting himself to the farm business at less than a full wage and at the expense of other career prospects. What is the force of such a promise? We have seen a similar assurance in the case of *Wayling v Jones* (p. 181, above), where it seems the promise may have failed through the testator's inadvertence. In *Gillett v Holt* there was a deliberate change of mind.

At first instance, the judge held that a simple promise of an inheritance is by its nature revocable and cannot found an estoppel claim. He relied on the decision in *Taylor v Dickens* [1998] 3 FCR 455, where Judge Weeks QC said:

... it is not sufficient for A to believe that he is going to be given a right over B's property if he knows that B has reserved the right to change his mind. In that case, A must show that B has created or encouraged a belief on A's part that B would not exercise that right.

That decision attracted criticism. In the Court of Appeal, Robert Walker LJ quoted William Swadling, in (1998) Restitution Law Review 220:

The decision is clearly wrong, for the judge seems to have forgotten that the whole point of estoppel claims is that they concern promises which, since they are unsupported by consideration, are initially revocable. What later makes them binding, and therefore irrevocable, is the promisee's detrimental reliance on them. Once that occurs, there is simply no question of the promisor changing his or her mind.

In *Gillett v Holt*, Robert Walker LJ said:

In my judgment these criticisms of Taylor v Dickens are well-founded. The actual result in the case may be justified on the other ground on which it was put (no unconscionability on the facts); or (as Mr Swadling suggests later in his note) the gardener's unremunerated services might have merited some modest restitutionary relief. But the inherent revocability of testamentary dispositions (even if well understood by the parties, as Mr Gillett candidly accepted that it was by him) is irrelevant to a promise or assurance that 'all this will be yours'... Even when the promise or assurance is in terms linked to the making of a will ... the circumstances may make clear that the assurance is more than a mere statement of present (revocable) intention, and is tantamount to a promise.

... [I]t is notorious that some elderly persons of means derive enjoyment from the possession of testamentary power, and from dropping hints as to their intentions, without any question of an estoppel arising. But in this case Mr Holt's assurances were repeated over a long period, usually before the assembled company on special family occasions, and some of them (such as 'it was all going to be ours anyway' ...) were completely unambiguous ...I find it wholly understandable that Mr and Mrs Gillett, then ten years married and with two young sons, may have been worried about their home and their future depending on no more than oral assurances, however emphatic, from Mr Holt. The bitterly fought and ruinously expensive litigation which has ensued shows how right they would have been to be worried. But Mr Gillett, after discussing the matter with his wife and his parents, decided to rely on Mr Holt's assurances because 'Ken was a man of his word'. Plainly the assurances given on this occasion were intended to be relied on, and were in fact relied on. In any event reliance would be presumed (see *Greasley v Cooke* [1980] 3 All ER 710, [1980] 1 WLR 1306...).

How was the 'equity' raised by the estoppel to be satisfied in this case? The quantum of relief was somewhat difficult, because Mr Holt had other property and it was clear that the estoppel extended only to the farm. Moreover, it was not practicable to let him take the whole of the farming business, as tax and company law considerations imposed some constraints. Mr Gillett was therefore awarded the farmhouse, a large tract of farmland, and the sum of £100,000 to compensate him for exclusion for the rest of the farming business.

Question

In 'satisfying the equity', what special matters should the court take into account when the defendant is the promisor himself, rather than (as in *Wayling*) his successor in title?

Finally, we revert to the more typical case of a promise or arrangement made between lovers. Look back again at *Eves v Eves* and at *Grant v Edwards* (pp. 168, 170, above). These cases were decided on the principles of the constructive trust and therefore on the basis of an agreement between the parties. Gardiner (1993) has this to say about that finding:

In *Eves v Eves* and *Grant v Edwards*, the court found an *express* agreement that a woman should have a share in a house owned by her partner. In both, the woman's only hope of success lay with the finding of an express agreement, because she had not made the direct financial contribution needed to allow discovery of an implied agreement. But in both, the partner had explicitly told the woman that she was not to have a share. So on the face of it, there was most decidedly no agreement that she should. The courts based their contrary finding on the fact that in each case the man had added a reason for this refusal to let the woman share the house, which was in truth a bad reason. In one case, it was that at 20 years of age the woman was legally too young to have an interest in land; in the other, it was that any share she had would cause some prejudice in the matrimonial proceedings she was currently undergoing with her estranged husband. In each case the court characterised this as an *excuse*, and went on to say that the man's giving an excuse showed that he actually acknowledged the existence of an agreement that the woman should have a share.

But the fact that the men's statements were excuses (i.e. neither objectively valid nor even sincerely uttered) does not mean that the men were thereby acknowledging an agreement whereby the woman should have a share. If I give an excuse for rejecting an invitation to what I expect to be a dull party, it does not mean that I thereby agree to come: on the contrary, it means that I do not agree to come, but for one reason or another find it hard to say so outright. The fallacious quality of the reasoning in *Eves v Eves* and *Grant v Edwards* is thus clear. It is hard to think that the judges concerned really believed in it. One can only conclude that they too were engaged in the business of inventing agreements on women's behalf, but this time widening the catchment beyond merely those women who work outside the home.

The facts of *Hammond v Mitchell* [1991] 1 WLR 1127, [1992] 1 FLR 233, were that Mr H and Miss M began living together in 1977, and in 1979 Mr H bought a bungalow as a home for them both and their child. He explained to Miss M that the bungalow must be put in his name because of tax problems connected with his divorce, but assured her: 'Don't worry about the future because when we are married it will be half yours anyway and I'll always look after you and the boy.' Subsequently, Miss M participated in Mr H's business activities, including two speculative ventures which involved considerable financial risk. In proceedings between them when the relationship broke down after 11 years, Mr H's statements were taken as evidence of an understanding between the parties that Miss M was to have a beneficial interest in the property, as a result of which she acted to her detriment (by supporting the high risk business ventures). Linda Clarke and Rod Edmunds, in '*H v M*: Equity and the Essex Cohabitant' (1992), comment:

With respect, this could be seen as an ex post facto rationalisation, necessary in order to give the worthy claimant an interest in the property. Strictly speaking, the conduct in the present case (especially the words spoken after the bungalow had been acquired) looks less like a bilateral understanding or agreement and more in the nature of a unilateral assurance by Mr H that once married (an event which never took place) Miss M would have an interest in the bungalow. Such an assurance, like that made to the mistress in *Pascoe v Turner*, might then be relied upon to assert a successful proprietary estoppel claim.

5.3.5 Bankruptcy and debt

Bankruptcy is another example where there can be conflict between the rights of the spouse to occupy the matrimonial home and the rights of third parties to realise their interest. This is now regulated by ss. 336 and 337 of the Insolvency Act 1986.

336.(2)— Where a spouse's matrimonial home rights under Part IV of the Family Law Act 1996 are a charge on the estate or interest of the other spouse, or of trustees for the other spouse, and the other spouse is adjudged bankrupt—
  (a) the charge continues to subsist notwithstanding the bankruptcy and ... binds the trustee of the bankrupt's estate and persons deriving title under that trustee; and
  (b) any application for an order under section 1 of that Act shall be made to the court having jurisdiction in relation to the bankruptcy.
  (3) Where a person and his spouse or former spouse are trustees for sale of a dwelling house and that person is adjudged bankrupt, any application by the trustee of the bankrupt's estate for an order under section 30 of the Law of Property Act ... shall be made to the court having jurisdiction in relation to the bankruptcy.
  (4) On such an application as is mentioned under subsection (2) or (3) the court shall make such order under section 33 of the Act of 1996 or section 30 of the Act of 1925 as it thinks just and reasonable having regard to—
  (a) the interests of the bankrupt's creditors,
  (b) the conduct of the spouse or former spouse, so far as contributing to the bankruptcy,
  (c) the needs and financial resources of the spouse or former spouse,
  (d) the needs of any children, and
  (e) all the circumstances of the case other than the needs of the bankrupt.

(5) Where such an application is made after the end of the period of one year beginning with the first vesting ... of the bankrupt's estate in a trustee, the court shall assume, unless the circumstances of the case are exceptional, that the interests of the bankrupt's creditors outweigh all other considerations.

(Section 337 applies the principles of s. 336 to the situation where there are children under 18 who 'had their home' with the bankrupt. The needs of the children are to be taken into account but not the needs of the bankrupt himself. Section 337(6) is to the same effect as s. 336(5). Section 335A applies the same principles in cases where the application for sale is made by the trustee in bankruptcy under s. 14 of the Trusts of Land and Appointment of Trustees Act 1996.)

These provisions have their origin in *Insolvency Law and Practice* (The Cork Committee) (1982), which states:

1118: It would be consistent with present social attitudes to alleviate the personal hardships of those who are dependent on the debtor but not responsible for his insolvency, if this can be achieved by delaying for an acceptable time the sale of the family home.

Question

Would Mrs Rossett have fared better if her husband had been declared bankrupt?

In *Re Holliday (a bankrupt), ex p Trustee of the Bankrupt v Bankrupt* [1981] Ch 405, [1980] 3 All ER 385, the Court of Appeal decided that the interests of the wife and her children should prevail over the interests of the creditors to the extent that the sale of the house should be deferred for a substantial period.

Sir David Cairns: I reach that view because I am satisfied that it would at present be very difficult, if not impossible, for the wife to secure another suitable home for the family in or near Thorpe Bay; because it would be upsetting for the children's education if they had to move far away from their present schools, even if it were practicable, having regard to the wife's means, to find an alternative home at some more distant place; because it is highly unlikely that postponement of the payment of the debts would cause any great hardship to any of the creditors ...

However, in *Re Citro (a bankrupt)* [1991] Ch 142, [1990] 3 All ER 952, involving two bankrupts and their wives, the majority of the Court of Appeal distinguished the earlier case. At first instance, Hoffmann J imposed a provision for postponement of sale on the application of the trustee in bankruptcy until the youngest child in each case reached 16 years of age. He was of the opinion that if immediate orders for sale were made, the half shares to which each of the wives were entitled would be insufficient for them to acquire other accommodation in the area which would inevitably disturb the education of the children. In reversing the decision of Hoffmann J at first instance, Nourse LJ said:

Did Hoffmann J correctly apply [the law] to the facts which were before him? I respectfully think that he did not. First, for the reasons already stated, the personal circumstances of the two wives and their children, although distressing, are not by themselves exceptional. Secondly, I think that the judge erred in fashioning his orders by reference to those which might have been made in the Family Division in a case where bankruptcy had not supervened. ... Thirdly, and perhaps most significantly, he did not ask himself the critical question whether a further postponement of payment of their debts would cause hardship to the creditors. ...

Finally, I refer to section 336 of the Insolvency Act 1986 which, although it does not apply to either of these cases, will apply to such cases in the future. In subsection (5) of that section the court is required, in the circumstances there mentioned, to 'assume, unless the circumstances of the case are exceptional, that the interests of the bankrupt's creditors outweigh all other considerations'. I have no doubt that that section was intended to apply the same test as that which has been evolved in the previous bankruptcy decisions, and it is satisfactory to find that it has. I say that not least because section 336 only applies to the rights of occupation of those who are or have been married. The case law will continue to apply to unmarried couples, who nowadays set up house together in steadily increasing numbers. A difference in the basic tests applicable to the two classes of case would have been most undesirable.

Mark Pawlowski and Sarah Greer, in 'Undue influence – back door tactics' (2001), look at more recent developments:

...The case of *Re Holliday* [1981] Ch 405 appears to be the only reported bankruptcy decision prior to the 1986 Act in which a sale was not ordered. In that case, however, the bankruptcy petition had been presented by the husband himself as a tactical move to avoid a transfer of property order in favour of his wife at a time when no creditors were pressing for payment and he was in a position (in the next year or so) to discharge his debts. Not surprisingly, the circumstances were viewed as being exceptional, not least because no real hardship would be caused to creditors by postponing sale for a period of 5 years. Interestingly, Nourse LJ in *Re Citro* considered this to be the one 'special feature' of the case which distinguished it from the other bankruptcy cases. In his view, without that feature, the circumstances in *Re Holliday* would not have been treated as exceptional.

It is apparent also from the more recent authority that the wife's illness may qualify as an exceptional circumstance. In *Judd v Brown* [1998] 2 FLR 360 the wife was undergoing a course of chemotherapy which was likely to continue for 5 to 6 months, and she claimed that her chances of recovery would be damaged by stress if the matrimonial home was sold. Harman J, refusing an order for sale, held that the wife's sudden and serious attack of ovarian cancer was an exceptional event and clearly distinguishable from problems such as organising substitute housing and rearranging children's schooling, which were foreseeable and long-term conditions. Similarly, in *Re Raval* [1998] 2 FLR 718 the wife had suffered for many years from paranoid schizophrenia, and, although she was stable and living at home, her doctor advised her that 'adverse life events' (for example a move to a smaller property away from supportive friends and family) could cause a relapse in her condition. These circumstances were held to justify a postponement of the order for sale for one year to enable suitable alternative accommodation to be found for her by the local authority. The case is authority for the proposition that the wife's illness need not be sudden and short term to merit the exercise of the court's discretion in her favour. Indeed, Blackburn J opined that circumstances where a person who suffers from terminal cancer but whose life expectancy cannot be judged, and whose illness, therefore, could properly be described as long term and of indeterminate duration, could still be characterised as exceptional, justifying no order or, alternatively, a postponement of sale indefinitely. Reference may also be made to *Re Mott* [1987] CLY 212, where Hoffmann J postponed sale until after the death of the bankrupt's mother, who was 70 years old, in poor health and who had lived in the house for over 40 years. The evidence of her doctor was that she would deteriorate if she was forced to move from her home. His Lordship characterised the case as one of extreme hardship, especially as the son's creditors were largely the state in the form of the Inland Revenue and the Department of Health and Social Security.

CONCLUSION

It remains to be seen to what extent lending institutions adopt the practice of suing the husband debtor upon his personal covenant with a view to forcing a sale of the matrimonial home, notwithstanding the wife's equity arising from a successful *O'Brien* defence. What is evident is that the court's discretion to refuse (or postpone) sale is very limited in such cases and the lender will normally be able to achieve by the back door what it would not have been able to do by the front door; namely, force the wife to leave her home so as to realise its security. Only in extreme cases will the wife's voice prevail over that of the bank.

Question

Suppose that Harry is declared bankrupt, and he lives with his wife, Wendy, and their three children in a house which they jointly own. The eldest child is physically handicapped and the house has been adapted for her purposes. The other two children are gifted twins and attend a local school for gifted children. Harry is a self-employed builder and many of his creditors are local traders with families.

(a) Do you think that the court would make an immediate order for sale?
(b) If the application for sale is made after the end of one year beginning with the first vesting of the estate in Harry's trustee, would the court postpone the sale for a further period?
(c) In either (a) or (b) would it make any difference if Harry has the sole legal and beneficial interest?
(d) In either (a) or (b) would it make any difference if Harry and Wendy were not married?
(e) In either (a) or (b) would it make any difference if Harry and Wendy were not married and if Harry has the sole legal and beneficial interest?

Bankruptcy may arise when the family home has been used as security for a loan to the family business, or, indeed, to a business in which only one of the parties is involved. In this latter case, of course, it may be that only one party benefits from the loan, while the home of both is put at risk.

By contrast, where the owner or co-owner of the house is not bankrupt, but a sale is sought by a secured creditor, the full range of factors set out in s. 15 of the Trusts of Land and Appointment of Trustees Act 1996 is relevant and the interests of the creditor rank as just one among those factors.

15. Matters relevant in determining applications
(1) The matters to which the court is to have regard in determining an application for an order under section 14 include—
(a) the intentions of the person or persons (if any) who created the trust,
(b) the purposes for which the property subject to the trust is held,
(c) the welfare of any minor who occupies or might reasonably be expected to occupy any land subject to the trust as his home, and
(d) the interests of any secured creditor of any beneficiary.

Thus the principles applicable on bankruptcy do not apply, nor does the pre-1997 rule that the voice of the creditor will normally prevail, and the courts are far more willing to postpone sale in the interests of the debtor's family.

Another factor of growing importance in recent years has been the case where a spouse has been misled or pressurised into agreeing to the use of the family home as security for a loan to the other spouse. The law recognises that this is particularly likely to happen in the context of family relationships. At first sight, the wife in such a case is in difficulties because her husband's misrepresentation or undue influence would not normally affect her position vis-à-vis the creditor, where the latter was not involved in the husband's wrongdoing. The House of Lords' decision in *Barclays Bank plc v O'Brien* [1994] 1 AC 180, [1993] 4 All ER 417, [1993] 3 WLR 786, [1994] 1 FCR 357, HL establishes that the creditor may nevertheless be unable to enforce its security against the wife if it had constructive notice of the husband's wrong; however, the creditor can protect itself by ensuring that the wife receives legal advice on what she is doing.

The decision in *O'Brien* spawned a vast heap of case law; authoritative guidance has been given by the House of Lords in *Royal Bank of Scotland v Etridge (No 2)* [2001] UKHL 44, [2001] 4 All ER 449, [2001] 3 WLR 1021, [2001] 2 FLR 1364, HL, on the question as to when the bank is put on inquiry (quite simple: 'when a wife offers to stand surety for her husband's debts', Lord Nicholls of Birkenhead at [46]) and on the level of advice the bank must ensure the wife receives in order to protect herself.

In *O'Brien*, Lord Browne-Wilkinson stressed that although his judgment referred throughout to a wife being misled by her husband, the principle applied to 'all other cases where there is an emotional relationship between cohabitees', whether heterosexual or homosexual. In *Etridge*, at [47], Lord Nicholls of Birkenhead stated that the position is the same whether the parties are married or unmarried, heterosexual or homosexual, 'where the bank is aware of the relationship... Cohabitation is not essential'.

Questions

(i)   Should there be any restriction on the availability of the family home for use as security for a loan to one spouse (or cohabitant) alone?

(ii)   If cohabitation is not essential, would such a restriction help?

(iii)   You may like to have a look at the position of Mrs Coleman, one of the eight 'Etridge wives'; her case is discussed by Lord Scott of Foscote [2001] 3 WLR 1021 at 1099. Given Mrs Coleman's upbringing and cultural background, how could the legal system possibly have protected her?

5.3.6   Rights of inheritance

5.3.6.1   *A fixed share for the surviving spouse?*

In their Working Paper (1971) the Law Commission discussed a system of inheritance under which a surviving spouse would be entitled as of right to a fixed proportion of the estate of the deceased spouse whether he died intestate or testate and regardless of the terms of the will:

0.37   Such a system is to be distinguished from community of property and from the right to apply for family provision. Although theoretically it could co-exist with 'community', it would be a needless complication in a law which recognised and enforced a genuine community of property; accordingly we discuss it as an alternative or substitute for 'community'. It differs from the law of family provision in that an order for family provision is discretionary [see p. 190, below], and the amount of the order is assessed having regard to the means, needs and conduct of the applicant. A legal right of inheritance would be a property right in no way dependent upon the means, needs and conduct of the surviving spouse, all of which factors would be irrelevant. The system put forward for consideration is comparable with systems in certain other countries, including Scotland....

0.39. Questions which arise are: -

   (*a*)   what minimum amount or proportion of the estate should go, *as of right*, to the survivor,

   (*b*)   whether a spouse should be able to waive a right of inheritance,

   (*c*)   whether, and if so, how benefits received from the deceased during his life should be taken into account,

   (*d*)   how to deal with dispositions made by the deceased with the intention of defeating rights of inheritance,

   (*e*)   the relationship between rights of inheritance and the intestacy rules,

   (*f*)   whether children should enjoy rights of inheritance.

0.40   We make a number of tentative suggestions as to the way in which these questions might be answered. For instance, we reach the provisional view that children should not have a legal right of inheritance; we suggest £2,000 or one-third of the estate (whichever is the greater) for the surviving spouse; and we indicate that it may be better not to complicate the law by seeking a solution within a system of rights of inheritance of the problems of benefits received or dispositions made during the lifetime of the deceased. The appropriate context in which to consider these problems may well be that of family provision, where the courts will continue to have a discretion to set aside dispositions and to make such financial orders as are considered necessary for the support of the survivor.

Question

Would this raise problems similar to those of common law dower?

The Working Paper itself drew attention to a major disadvantage of fixed rights of inheritance:

4.71 A system of legal rights would be an imprecise way of protecting the survivor's interest in the family assets. It would take no account of the fact that the bulk of the family assets might already be vested in the survivor: the survivor's assets would be irrelevant unless derived from the deceased. It would not be limited to that part of the deceased's estate which could properly be regarded as family assets, and since it would operate only on death it would create a distinction between property rights on divorce and those on death.

The First Report (1973) noted the lack of support for the principle of legal rights of inheritance for a surviving spouse:

38. In the light of all the comments and views received we have considered again the principle of fixed legal rights of inheritance for a surviving spouse and its relation to family provision law. If one were starting from the position as it was in England before the introduction of family provision law [in 1939], it would be necessary to consider the best means of protecting the interests of the family of a deceased person and to weigh up the relative advantages and disadvantages of an automatic system of legal rights and a discretionary system of family provision operating through an application to the court. However, as the Working Paper suggested, and as the results of our consultation confirm, the issue now is whether it is necessary to supplement or reinforce family provision law by a system of legal rights.
39. Under family provision law the court can, in the exercise of its discretion, take into account the means and needs of all the parties concerned.

The Law Commission recommended substantial improvements to the family provision legislation, but rejected the introduction of a principle under which the surviving spouse would have a *legal* right to inherit part of the estate of the deceased spouse.

5.3.6.2 *Intestacy*

Legal rights of inheritance are seldom of significance when a spouse dies intestate. Under the present law, the surviving spouse inherits personal chattels, a statutory legacy of £125,000 of the estate and a life interest in half of any residue where there are children; or the personal chattels, a statutory legacy of £200,000 plus half the balance where there are no children but other close relatives. In other cases, the surviving spouse inherits the whole estate.

In 1989 the Law Commission, in their report *Distribution on Intestacy* (1989), considered the position of the surviving spouse on intestacy.

17. There was virtually unanimous agreement among respondents to our working paper that the present law is in need of reform. Consultees also agreed that its principal defect is the failure to ensure adequate provision for a surviving spouse. There are several reasons for this.
18. First, the statutory legacy is often insufficient to ensure that the surviving spouse is able to remain in the matrimonial home, even though the estate is otherwise large enough to enable him or her to do so. House values vary considerably in different parts of the country and also rise (or fall) at different rates. A figure which is large enough to cover the price of an average home in central London would give a substantial surplus to widows living elsewhere. Secondly, even if the legacy is sufficient to retain the home, it will often leave the survivor with very little on which to live or maintain the home.
19. This basic defect is compounded by two other, more technical problems. First, even supposing that the purpose of the statutory legacy is to enable the survivor to keep the home, the present rules make no distinction according to how the home is owned or tenanted. If the home was beneficially jointly owned by the couple, the survivor acquires the deceased's interest automatically and therefore receives the whole home and a full statutory legacy. If the couple were tenants in common, perhaps because they owned unequal shares or one had contributed to the purchase of the home in the other's name, the deceased's interest forms part of his or her

estate and thus counts towards the statutory legacy. If the home was wholly owned by the deceased, of course, it will count. ... Such disparities in what survivors receive will often seem arbitrary and unfair.

20. Secondly, the statutory legacies must from time to time be uprated by statutory instrument. The legacy applicable is that in force at the date of death. This can lead to gross disparity in the treatment of deaths taking place on either side of the date on which the legacy changed. Further, if the survivor has the house appropriated, in or towards satisfaction of the legacy, the legacy is that at the date of death, whereas the house is valued at the date of appropriation which could be years later.

21. If these rules can produce results which seem arbitrary or unfair in relation to the surviving spouse, the same can be said in relation to issue or other relatives. The children's expectations will depend, not upon how well their surviving parent is provided for, but upon the nature and tenure of their deceased parent's assets.

22. A further defect of the present rules is that, in places, they are complex and expensive to administer. ...

They therefore recommended that on intestacy the surviving spouse should receive the whole estate.

When the Law Reform (Succession) Bill was introduced in the House of Lords in February 1995, Lord Mishcon pointed out that the Bill as drafted did not implement this recommendation, and it was agreed that the question be discussed further at the Committee stage. However, the Bill was not amended.

Question

Why do you suppose the recommendation has not been enacted?

5.3.6.3 *Family provision*

Family provision legislation is a means of providing for family members for whom *either* the provisions of the deceased's will *or* the intestacy rules were not adequate.

Writing in 1974, Miller said that 'the aim of the present law of family provision is to ensure that reasonable provision is made for the *maintenance* of certain dependants of the deceased. It is not designed to enable members of the deceased's family to acquire a share in his estate without reference to their need for support, or in other words, dependency'.

The Law Commission at first advanced the belief that maintenance should remain as the governing factor. However, they subsequently had second thoughts and, so far as the wife is concerned, in their First Report (1973) recommended a change in objective:

41. At present, the aim, as expressed in the legislation, is to secure reasonable provision for the *maintenance* of the deceased's dependants, and this is clearly narrower in concept than the provision of a fair share (although in any particular case it may amount to much the same thing). 'Maintenance' is no longer the principal consideration in fixing the amount of financial provision for a spouse on divorce, and we have come to the conclusion that it would be anomalous to retain it as the main objective in determining family provision for a surviving spouse.

The recommendations of the Law Commission were enacted in the Inheritance (Provision for Family and Dependants) Act 1975 (as now slightly amended by the Family Law Act 1996):

1. Application for financial provision from deceased's estate

(1) Where after the commencement of this Act a person dies domiciled in England and Wales and is survived by any of the following persons—

(a) the wife or husband of the deceased;

(b) a former wife or former husband of the deceased who has not remarried;

(ba) any person (not being a person included in paragraph (a) or (b) above) to whom subsection (1A) below applies;

(c) a child of the deceased;

(d) any person (not being a child of the deceased) who, in the case of any marriage to which the deceased was at any time a party, was treated by the deceased as a child of the family in relation to that marriage;

(e) any person (not being a person included in the foregoing paragraphs of this subsection) who immediately before the death of the deceased was being maintained, either wholly or partly, by the deceased;

that person may apply to the court for an order under section 2 of this Act on the ground that the disposition of the deceased's estate effected by his will or the law relating to intestacy, or the combination of his will and that law, is not such as to make reasonable financial provision for the applicant.

(1A) This subsection applies to a person if the deceased died on or after 1st January 1996 and, during the whole of the period of two years ending immediately before the date when the deceased died, the person was living—

(a) in the same household as the deceased, and

(b) as the husband or wife of the deceased.

(2) In this Act 'reasonable financial provision'—

(a) in the case of an application made by virtue of subsection (1)(a) above by the husband or wife of the deceased (except where *the marriage with the deceased was the subject of a decree of judicial separation and at the date of death the decree was in force* [, at the date of death, a separation order under the Family Law Act 1996 was in force in relation to the marriage] and the separation was continuing), means such financial provision as it would be reasonable in all the circumstances of the case for a husband or wife to receive, whether or not that provision is required for his or her maintenance;

(b) in the case of any other application made by virtue of subsection (1) above, means such financial provision as it would be reasonable in all the circumstances of the case for the applicant to receive for his maintenance.

(3) For the purposes of subsection (1)(e) above, a person shall be treated as being maintained by the deceased, either wholly or partly, as the case may be, if the deceased, otherwise than for full valuable consideration, was making a substantial contribution in money or money's worth towards the reasonable needs of that person.

2. Powers of court to make orders

(1) Subject to the provisions of this Act, where an application is made for an order under this section, the court may, if it is satisfied that the disposition of the deceased's estate effected by his will or the law relating to intestacy, or the combination of his will and that law, is not such as to make reasonable financial provision for the applicant, make any one or more of the following orders—

(a) an order for the making to the applicant out of the net estate of the deceased of such periodical payments and for such term as may be specified in the order;

(b) an order for the payment to the applicant out of that estate of a lump sum of such amount as may be so specified;

(c) an order for the transfer to the applicant of any such property comprised in that estate as may be so specified;

(d) an order for the settlement for the benefit of the applicant of such property comprised in that estate as may be so specified;

(e) an order for the acquisition out of property comprised in that estate of such property as may be so specified and for the transfer of the property so acquired to the applicant or for the settlement thereof for his benefit;

(f) an order varying any ante-nuptial or post-nuptial settlement (including such a settlement made by will) made on the parties to a marriage to which the deceased was one of the parties, the variation being for the benefit of the surviving party to that marriage, or any child of that marriage, or any person who was treated by the deceased as a child of the family in relation to that marriage.

(2) An order under subsection (1)(a) above providing for the making out of the net estate of the deceased of periodical payments may provide for—

(a)   payments of such amount as may be specified in the order,
(b)   payments equal to the whole of the income of the net estate or of such portion thereof as may be so specified,
(c)   payments equal to the whole of the income of such part of the net estate as the court may direct to be set aside or appropriated for the making out of the income thereof payments under this section,

or may provide for the amount of the payments or any of them to be determined in any other way the court thinks fit.

(3) Where an order under subsection (1)(a) above provides for the making of payments of an amount specified in the order, the order may direct that such part of the net estate as may be so specified shall be set aside or appropriated for the making out of the income thereof of those payments; but no larger part of the net estate shall be so set aside or appropriated than is sufficient, at the date of the order, to produce by the income thereof the amount required for the making of those payments.

(4) An order under this section may contain such consequential and supplemental provisions as the court thinks necessary or expedient for the purpose of giving effect to the order or for the purpose of securing that the order operates fairly as between one beneficiary of the estate of the deceased and another and may, in particular, but without prejudice to the generality of this subsection—
(a)   order any person who holds any property which forms part of the net estate of the deceased to make such payment or transfer such property as may be specified in the order;
(b)   varying the disposition of the deceased's estate effected by the will or the law relating to intestacy, in such manner as the court thinks fair and reasonable having regard to the provisions of the order and all the circumstances of the case;
(c)   confer on the trustees of any property which is the subject of an order under this section such powers as appear to the court to be necessary or expedient.

3. Matters to which court is to have regard in exercising powers under s 2

(1) Where an application is made for an order under section 2 of this Act, the court shall, in determining whether the disposition of the deceased's estate effected by his will or the law relating to intestacy, or the combination of his will and that law, is such as to make reasonable financial provision for the applicant and, if the court considers that reasonable financial provision has not been made, in determining whether and in what manner it shall exercise its powers under that section, have regard to the following matters, that is to say—
(a)   the financial resources and financial needs which the applicant has or is likely to have in the foreseeable future;
(b)   the financial resources and financial needs which any other applicant for an order under section 2 of this Act has or is likely to have in the foreseeable future;
(c)   the financial resources and financial needs which any beneficiary of the estate of the deceased has or is likely to have in the foreseeable future;
(d)   any obligations and responsibilities which the deceased had towards any applicant for an order under the said section 2 or towards any beneficiary of the estate of the deceased;
(e)   the size and nature of the net estate of the deceased;
(f)   any physical or mental disability of any applicant for an order under the said section 2 or any beneficiary of the estate of the deceased;
(g)   any other matter, including the conduct of the applicant or any other person, which in the circumstances of the case the court may consider relevant.

(2) Without prejudice to the generality of paragraph (g) of subsection (1) above, where an application for an order under section 2 of this Act is made by virtue of section 1(1)(a) or 1(1)(b) of this Act, the court shall, in addition to the matters specifically mentioned in paragraphs (a) to (f) of that subsection, have regard to—
(a)   the age of the applicant and the duration of the marriage;
(b)   the contribution made by the applicant to the welfare of the family of the deceased, including any contribution made by looking after the home or caring for the family;
    and, in the case of an application by the wife or husband of the deceased, the court shall also, unless at the date of death a separation order under the Family Law Act 1996 was in force and the separation was continuing, have regard to the provision which the applicant might reasonably have expected to receive if on the day on which the deceased died the marriage, instead of being terminated by death, had been terminated by a divorce order.

(2A) Without prejudice to the generality of paragraph (g) of subsection (1) above, where an application for an order under section 2 of this Act is made by virtue of section 1(1)(ba) of this

Act, the court shall, in addition to the matters specifically mentioned in paragraphs (a) to (f) of that subsection, have regard to—

(a) the age of the applicant and the length of the period during which the applicant lived as the husband or wife of the deceased and in the same household as the deceased;

(b) the contribution made by the applicant to the welfare of the family of the deceased, including any contribution made by looking after the home or caring for the family.

(3) Without prejudice to the generality of paragraph (g) of subsection (1) above, where an application for an order under section 2 of this Act is made by virtue of section 1(1)(c) or 1(1)(d) of this Act, the court shall, in addition to the matters specifically mentioned in paragraphs (a) to (f) of that subsection, have regard to the manner in which the applicant was being or in which he might expect to be educated or trained, and where the application is made by virtue of section 1(1)(d) the court shall also have regard—

(a) to whether the deceased had assumed any responsibility for the applicant's maintenance and, if so, to the extent to which the basis upon which the deceased assumed that responsibility and to the length of time for which the deceased discharged that responsibility;

(b) to whether in assuming and discharging that responsibility the deceased did so knowing that the applicant was not his own child;

(c) to the liability of any other person to maintain the applicant.

(4) Without prejudice to the generality of paragraph (g) of subsection (1) above, where an application for an order under section 2 of this Act is made by virtue of section 1(1)(e) of this Act, the court shall, in addition to the matters specifically mentioned in paragraphs (a) to (f) of that subsection, have regard to the extent to which and the basis upon which the deceased assumed responsibility for the maintenance of the applicant, and to the length of time for which the deceased discharged that responsibility.

(5) In considering the matters to which the court is required to have regard under this section, the court shall take into account the facts as known to the court at the date of the hearing.

(6) In considering the financial resources of any person for the purposes of this section the court shall take into account his earning capacity and in considering the financial needs of any person for the purposes of this section the court shall take into account his financial obligations and responsibilities.

4. Time-limit for application

An application for an order under section 2 of this Act shall not, except with the permission of the court, be made after the end of the period of six months from the date on which representation with respect to the estate of the deceased is first taken out.

Questions

(i) Do you think that orders for periodical payments should cease on the remarriage of a *surviving* spouse?

(ii) Do you think that such orders should cease on the remarriage of a *former* spouse?

An examination of the special criteria applicable to claims by the surviving spouse is found in the following case:

Moody v Stevenson
[1992] Ch 486, [1992] 2 All ER 524, Court of Appeal

The applicant had married his wife in 1971 when he was 61 and she 66. In 1984 the wife went to live in a nursing home; she died in 1985, leaving all her property to her stepdaughter. More of the facts appear in the course of Waite J's judgment, when he considered the requirements of s. 3(2):

... the Act of 1975, when stripped down to its barest terms, amounts to a direction to the judge to ask himself in surviving spouse cases: 'What would a family judge have ordered for this couple if divorce instead of death had divided them; what is the effect of any other section 3 factors ...; and what, in the light of those two inquiries, am I to make of the reasonableness, when viewed objectively, of the dispositions made by the will and/or intestacy of the deceased?' If the judge finds those dispositions unreasonable, he will go on to ask himself: 'What, in the light of those same inquiries, would be a reasonable provision for me to order for the applicant under section 2?'

The result of applying that approach to the present case would be likely, in our judgment, to produce the following result at stage one. Looking first at the notional entitlement of the applicant on a presumed divorce at the date of death, it is necessary to visualise the probable reaction of a family judge when faced with a husband of 81 claiming from a wife of 86 financial relief in a case when he was still living in the former matrimonial home and she was permanently housed in a nursing home; where the only assets they had between them were £6,000 (his) and the former matrimonial home and £1,000 (hers); where the marriage had endured for 17 years, although for the last four years the parties had been separated through the wife's illness without contact with each other; where there were no children of the marriage as such, although the wife had an adult stepdaughter now living on her own; and where, this being a late marriage, the husband's contribution to the material welfare of the family unit had been limited to his earnings during the four years between the wedding and his retirement.

Applying his mind to those circumstances under section 25(1), and having regard to the various specific factors to which the court is required to have regard under section 25(2) of the Matrimonial Causes Act 1973, which of course closely resemble those set out in section 3 of the Act of 1975, a family judge would in our view be most unlikely to regard the case as one for refusing financial relief to the husband altogether. Periodic maintenance would clearly be inappropriate to a case where both sides were dependent on state benefit or state pension, or both. A lump sum order would be equally inappropriate because there would be no free capital to fund it. The most probable outcome, in our expectation, is that the court would make cross-orders under section 24 of the Act of 1973 directing on the one hand a settlement of the property on terms which, without going to the lengths of constituting him a life tenant, would give the husband a right of occupation so long as he was able and willing to exercise it; and on the other hand a transfer of part of the husband's £6,000 to, or for the benefit of, the wife, so that she might enjoy some small additional comforts in the nursing home in her last years.

Regard must next be had to those section 3 factors not already subsumed in that inquiry. It would, in particular, be necessary to consider the position of the respondent under section 3(1)(c) and (d), taking note of the fact that she lives in council accommodation with very limited financial resources, but at the same time could not be described as a person towards whom the deceased could be said to have had any obligations or responsibilities.

When the matter is approached in that way, and the stage one question is then asked, namely, whether the disposition of the deceased's estate was such, when viewed objectively, as to make reasonable provision for the applicant, who was of course wholly excluded from it, the answer must in our judgment be 'No'.

A settlement of the house for the husband's benefit was accordingly directed; in the end no order was made about any corresponding payment to the respondent, since it became apparent legal fees had left the husband without cash resources.

The fact that the surviving spouse's claim is not restricted to what is required for maintenance does not necessarily mean that he is entitled to capital provision.

Davis v Davis

[1993] 1 FLR 54, [1993] Fam Law 59, Court of Appeal

The widow, who was the second wife of the deceased and had been married to him for seven years, was left a life interest in his estate, which amounted at the time of his death to £177,000 and would later be increased to some £267,000 when the capital of the deceased's father (at present subject to a life interest in favour of his mother) became available. The estate included a house which the widow would be able to live in, although of course she did not own it absolutely. The judge at first instance said:

The Act of Parliament makes it plain that the court's powers only arise if the court is satisfied that the disposition of the deceased's estate by his will fails to make reasonable financial provision for the plaintiff. It seems to me that the plaintiff has manifestly failed to cross the threshold. It is not for this court to rewrite the testamentary provisions of deceased persons lightly.

The Court of Appeal saw no reason to interfere with that finding, and no further provision was made.

Apart from the surviving spouse, relatives and others may claim: s. 1(1)(*b*)–(*e*). The matter of maintenance is crucial here for two reasons. First, all claimants other than the surviving spouse may recover 'such financial provision as it would be reasonable ... for the applicant to receive for his maintenance'. Moreover, those who do not fall within s. 1(1)(*b*)–(*d*) may make a claim by virtue of the fact that they were already being maintained by the deceased. Thus, the question of maintenance governs eligibility in some cases, and quantum in all cases, except for the surviving spouse.

The effect of this on a child of the deceased is seen in the following case:

Re Jennings, deceased
[1994] Ch 286, [1994] 3 All ER 27, Court of Appeal

The plaintiff sought an order for family provision from the estate of his father. He was now 50 years old, and had been brought up by his mother and step-father since he was four. His father left his estate, worth about £300,000, mostly to charities. The plaintiff was married with two adult children; he and his wife owned a four-bedroomed house, subject to a mortgage, and ran two successful companies. The Court of Appeal held that he therefore had no need for maintenance, and his claim failed. The members of the court looked at the matters to be taken into consideration under s. 3(1)(*a*)-(*g*) and concluded that there was no reason why any provision should now be required, since the plaintiff appeared to have no financial needs beyond, perhaps, an unspecified need for better retirement provision. Under s. 3(1)(*d*) the question was whether or not the deceased's failure to provide for the plaintiff as a child gave rise to an obligation to make provision now. Nourse LJ said:

While it is true that [the subsection] requires regard to be had to obligations and responsibilities which the deceased 'had', that cannot mean 'had at any time in the past'. At all events as a general rule that provision can only refer to obligations and responsibilities which the deceased had immediately before his death. An Act intended to facilitate the making of reasonable financial provision cannot have been intended to revive defunct obligations and responsibilities as a basis for making it. Nor, if they do not fall within a specific provision such as section 3(1)(*d*), can they be prayed in aid under a general provision such as section 3(1)(*g*).

Question

As a matter of statutory interpretation, do you agree with Nourse LJ? Do you think that the plaintiff should have succeeded?

Cohabitants, of course, claim, not under s. 1(1)(*e*), as they did before 1995, but under s. 1(1)(*ba*), 1A and 2A, inserted by the Law Reform (Succession) Act 1995 following the Law Commission's recommendation in its report on *Intestacy* in 1989:

Cohabitants should be provided for, not under the intestacy rules, but where appropriate under the Inheritance (Provision for Family and Dependants) Act 1975:

(a) Cohabitants should be able to apply for reasonable financial provision ... without having to show dependence.
(b) The definition of a cohabitant should be the same as that used in s. 1(3)(b) of the Fatal Accidents Act 1976 ... .
(c) The definition of 'reasonable financial provision' should be what is reasonable for the applicant's maintenance but the relevant factors for the court to consider should be the same as those for spouses.

Questions

(i)   The plaintiff in *Wayling v Jones* (see p. 181, above) also made an application under the 1975 Act; this failed at first instance, and the Court of Appeal did not have to consider it in view of the conclusion on estoppel. If Mr Wayling had not had the estoppel claim, would the newly inserted subsections have been of any assistance to him?
(ii) Would you extend the provisions of the new subsections to include: (a) those who can benefit under the Ontario Family Law Reform Act (see p. 204, below); (b) those who would benefit under the reforms of the Alberta Law Reform Institute (1989) (see p. 204, below); (c) some other definition; or (d) leave well alone?
(iii) Why should not cohabitants be provided for under the intestacy rules?

Finally, what of those who fall within s. 1(1)(e): what does 'being maintained' mean? The following two cases show that the phrase may extend to quite unusual facts.

Rees v Newbery and the Institute of Cancer Research
[1998] 1 FLR 1041, Chancery Division

The deceased seems to have made most of his money from property investment, in partnership with the first defendant, but also worked as an actor at Covent Garden, where he met and became friends with the claimant, another actor. The headnote explains the facts:

In 1984 the plaintiff moved into a flat in the premises occupied and owned by the deceased at a rent of £200 per month. There was no written tenancy agreement. By 1993 the deceased had decided that the premises should be left to the Royal Opera House Covent Garden Benevolent Fund and used as lodgings for students and others working at Covent Garden who needed accommodation at modest rents ... In October 1993 the deceased gave instructions to his solicitors for a new will to be drawn up, whereby the premises were to be devised to the Fund, subject to the plaintiffs right to remain in the flat for his lifetime at the same rent adjusted to take account of inflation, the residue to go to four named charities. However, he died before the draft had been finalised and by the existing will, of which the first defendant was executor, the deceased's estate, consisting of some £250,000 in cash and the premises valued at £485,000, was left to the second defendant and other charities. The plaintiff applied under s 1(1)(e) of the Inheritance (Provision for Family and Dependants) Act 1975 for provision out of the estate, on the basis (1) that the rent he was paying was substantially below the market rent and that in all the circumstances he was a person 'who immediately before the death of the deceased was being maintained either wholly or in part by the deceased' within s 1(1)(e) and (2) of the Act; and (2) that the will had failed to make reasonable provision for his maintenance under s 3. He sought to be allowed to stay in the flat as had been the deceased's intention. The first defendant applied for a possession order on the counter-claim.

The claim succeeded. His Honour Judge Gilliland QC explained:

The first question which arises is whether the provision of accommodation under a tenancy at below the market rent is capable of constituting maintenance within the meaning of the Act. Mr Moor, counsel for the second defendant, has submitted that the existence of a formal legal relationship such as a tenancy under which a substantial rent is being paid shows that the relationship between the parties was a commercial one, which precludes Mr Evans-Rees from making any application under the Act.

In considering this submission it is necessary in my judgment to distinguish between the requirements of s 1(3) and those of s 3(4) of the Act. Under s 1(3), it is clear that the mere fact that consideration has been provided for a contribution towards the applicant's reasonable needs will not disqualify an applicant. The fact that a benefit may have been provided in the lifetime of a deceased person under a legally binding contract cannot in my judgment either, of itself, disqualify the recipient of the benefit from making a claim under the Act following the death of the provider of the benefit. If that were so, a mistress who had been in receipt of maintenance under a formal maintenance agreement would be unable to claim, and it could not in my judgment be suggested that such a person was not within the plain meaning of s 1(3) of the Act. The first question under s 1(3) of the Act is whether the applicant has given 'full valuable consideration' for the benefit received. In the present case, it is clear that Mr Evans-Rees, although he has given some consideration, has not given 'full' valuable consideration for his accommodation. The second question is whether accommodation is part of the reasonable needs of the applicant. Mr Moor has not suggested that accommodation was not part of Mr Evans-Rees's reasonable needs. I am satisfied that Mr Evans-Rees did need accommodation and that the deceased was in fact making a 'substantial' contribution in money's worth towards his reasonable needs by providing accommodation for him at a rate of £270 a month below the market rent. £270 a month is in my view a substantial amount. It is a substantial amount in itself and it represented a discount of 57.4% on the market rent and 38.5% of Mr Evans-Rees's total average net income. The provision of rent-free accommodation can clearly constitute maintenance for the purposes of the Act and there is nothing in s 1(3) in my judgment which would justify the inference that Parliament intended to exclude from the Act persons who were in occupation under a tenancy as such or who were paying more than merely a nominal rent.

As to s. 3(4):

In practice the evidence of the applicant will reveal the relationship with the deceased and if it shows an arrangement subsisting at the time of his death under which the deceased was making a substantial contribution in money or money's worth to the reasonable needs of the applicant, it will, as a general rule, be proper to draw the inference that the deceased has undertaken to maintain the applicant and thus 'assumed responsibility for the maintenance' within the meaning of section 3(4). It should not be necessary to search for any other overt act to demonstrate the 'assumption of responsibility'. If such an overt act were necessary, I suspect that most claims intended to be covered by the Act would fail.

That determined Mr Evans-Rees' eligibility to apply. The judge continued:

The next question is whether the will failed to make reasonable financial provision for Mr Evans-Rees's maintenance. In my judgment the answer to this question is 'yes'...

In the present case, the estate is a substantial one and the competition, if I may put it that way, is between a person who is a true dependant within the meaning of the Act and was a person whom the deceased wished to benefit and other persons or bodies to whom the deceased must also be taken to have wanted to benefit on his death. Each has claims upon his bounty, but in addition Mr Evans-Rees was actually dependent upon the deceased as the deceased was making a substantial contribution to the reasonable needs of Mr Evans-Rees by providing accommodation at substantially below the market rent. The deceased had also assumed responsibility for the maintenance of Mr Evans-Rees to the extent of providing what was in effect subsidized accommodation on a settled basis at the time of his death and clearly intended that it should continue after his death with any increases in rent being limited to the impact of inflation as indicated by the Retail Prices Index. These factors together with the difficulty which Mr Evans-Rees will have in obtaining suitable accommodation and his financial position provide an important distinction from the situation in *Re Coventry* and justify the conclusion that it is unreasonable that the will did not make any provision for Mr Evans-Rees, especially when it is remembered that the deceased was himself an actor and was aware of the precarious nature of Mr Evans-Rees's work and that he could not afford to pay a market rent for the flat. The present is a case where in my judgment it can properly be said, to use the words of Stephenson LJ in

Jelley v Iliffe [1981] Fam 128, 137, 138, that Mr Evans-Rees 'has been put by the deceased in a position of dependency upon him' and the object of the Act is to remedy the injustice of a dependant being deprived of that financial support 'by accident or design'. In the present case it cannot be said that he has been deprived of that support by design.

In *Re Coventry* [1980] Ch 461, 488, (1979) FLR Rep 142, 150 Goff LJ said:

> 'Indeed, I think any view expressed by a deceased person that he wishes a particular person to benefit will generally be of little significance, because the question is not subjective but objective.'

However where the competition is between on the one hand an applicant who has not been provided for under the will but who was intended by the deceased to benefit on his death and on the other hand those who have actually benefited under the will, it seems to me that the wishes of the deceased are of greater significance and can properly be given weight in considering what, objectively regarded, is in all the circumstances unreasonable. It is to be noted that in the passage referred to, Goff LJ used the word 'generally' and in my judgment the present is one of those exceptional cases in which the deceased's wishes should carry greater weight than would generally be the position. In all the circumstances, I am satisfied that the will did not make reasonable financial provision for the maintenance of Mr Evans-Rees.

Questions

(i)   How important do you think the wishes of the deceased should be in these 'family provision' cases?
(ii)   Is it unfair that the harder you work for your support the less likely you are to be held to be a dependant?

Sadly, the deceased could not have formed any wishes in *Bouette v Rose* [2000] 1 FLR 363, [2000] Fam Law 316. Louise Bouette had died at the age of 14 after suffering severe physical and mental disabilities due to negligence at her birth. She had received £250,000 damages from the relevant health authority, and the award was managed by her mother as receiver in the Court of Protection. Part of the award, with the court's approval, was used to provide three-quarters of the purchase price of a house for Louise and her mother, who provided the other quarter; the house was held upon trust for the two, in those relevant proportions. Moreover, of by a direction of the Court of Protection, regular payments were made from Louise's funds to Mrs Bouette for living expenses and for equipment for Louise.

On Louise's death her estate would pass by the rules of intestacy to her parents: Mrs Bouette, and her father Mr Rose, who left her mother shortly after her birth. Mrs Bouette's claim for family provision needed leave to proceed, as she made it after the time-limit of six months from the grant of letters of administration. At first instance her claim was struck out. She needed to prove that she had been maintained by Louise, that she had not given full valuable consideration for that maintenance, and the Louise had 'assumed responsibility' for her mother's maintenance within the meaning of s. 3(4) of the 1975 Act.

The Court of Appeal reinstated Mrs Bouette's application, and expressed the wish that a settlement might prevent further costs being incurred.

Robert Walker LJ explained:

[I]n my judgment the right general approach is that ... [w]hether one person makes a substantial gratuitous contribution to another person's needs is essentially a question of fact, and the benefactor's motives or intentions are irrelevant except insofar as s 3(4) makes them relevant to the court's task in deciding whether to make provision for the claimant, and if so in what form and on what scale. Even when s 3(4) is taken into account this court has taken the view that actions speak louder than words.

Question

Do you suppose that this was a situation that Parliament envisaged when the statute was enacted? If not, would they have minded this decision?

5.4 Property claims for children

When married parents divorce, the court can adjust the parents' property rights under the Matrimonial Causes Act 1973 (see Chapter 8, below), and will have as its 'first consideration ... the welfare while a minor of any child of the family who has not attained the age of eighteen' (s. 25(1)). The order made will provide a home for the children if possible. Unmarried couples cannot resort to this jurisdiction, and we have seen enough of the principles involved in property law to know that the party who is to look after the children may well be left homeless.

The Family Law Reform Act 1987 introduced a power for the court to make property adjustment orders in favour of children, following the recommendations made by the Law Commission in their report on *Illegitimacy* (1982). Paragraph 1(2)(*d*) and (*e*) of Sch 1 to the Children Act 1989 enables the court to make:

> (*d*) an order requiring a settlement to be made for the benefit of the child, and to the satisfaction of the court, of property—
>   (i) to which either parent is entitled (either in possession or in reversion); and
>   (ii) which is specified in the order;
> (*e*) an order requiring either or both parents of a child—
>   (i) to transfer to the applicant, for the benefit of the child; or
>   (ii) to transfer to the child himself,
> such property to which the parent is, or the parents are, entitled (either in possession or in reversion) as may be specified in the order.

This may enable the court to order the transfer of a council tenancy from one parent to the other, as in *K v K* [1992] 2 FLR 220, or to require one parent to settle a capital sum on a child, as in *H v P (Illegitimate Child: Capital Provision)* [1993] Fam Law 515. Such a settlement will be made so as to last for the child's minority or while he is in full-time education, rather than to make an outright transfer of a capital asset. In *A v A* [1994] 1 FLR 657, an application had been made for an order for the benefit of a child whose father was immensely wealthy; the settlement made for the child in *A v A* was described by Ward J as follows:

> The terms of the trust, the detail of which can be settled on further argument and if necessary with liberty to apply, should be that the property be conveyed to trustees, preferably ... the nominees of the mother and father to hold the same for A for a term which shall terminate 6 months after A has attained the age of 18, or 6 months after she has completed her full-time education, which will include her tertiary education, whichever is latest. I give her that period of 6 months to find her feet and arrange her affairs. The trustees shall permit her to enjoy a reasonable gap between completing her school education and embarking upon her further education. I have regard to para 4(1)(*b*) which requires me to consider the financial needs, obligations and responsibilities of each parent and also subpara (*c*) which requires me to have regard to the financial needs of the child. The mother's obligation is to look after A, and A's financial need is to provide a roof over the head of her caretaker. It is, indeed, the father's obligation to provide the accommodation for the live-in help which A needs. Consequently, it must be a term of the settlement that while A is under the control of her mother and thereafter for so long as A does not object, the mother shall have the right to occupy the property to the exclusion of the father without paying rent therefor for the purpose of providing a home and care and support for A.

Question

What would happen if the young lady decided, later in her teenage years, that she did object to her mother living in the house?

The facts of *A v A* are unrepresentative because of the father's great wealth. Nevertheless, similar provision could well be ordered in a family of more moderate means: see *T v S* [1994] 1 FCR 743, [1994] 2 FLR 883.

Obviously, the availability of these orders for children has an effect upon the housing position, and in some cases the property rights, of unmarried partners. Thus, while the mothers of the children concerned in *A v A* and *T v S* obtained, as a side-effect of the order, the right to live in the child's home until it was eventually disposed of, the mother in *K v K* (above) had the council tenancy transferred to her on a permanent basis.

Questions

(i)   How does a consideration of the orders available under Sch. 1 to the Children Act 1989 affect your view of the complex rules of property law to which cohabitants must resort when left without property on their separation?

(ii)   Where an order is made as in *A v A* or *T v T*, what will the mother do when the house is eventually sold?

Again, as we saw in our discussion of inheritance and, in particular, of family provision, the issue of disability may raise special considerations. In *C v F (Disabled Child: Maintenance Orders)* [1999] 1 FCR 39, [1998] 2 FLR 1, CA, a claim was made on behalf of a young man, T, for maintenance from his father extending beyond his nineteenth birthday. T was born severely disabled. He suffered from autism and hyperactivity, visual impairment, double incontinence and brain damage, so as to be dependent on others for the rest of his life. The Court of Appeal had no difficulty in holding that there was jurisdiction under the Children Act 1989 to make such an order, and that that jurisdiction was not impeded by the provisions of the Child Support Act 1991 (under which no maintenance assessment could be made beyond the child's nineteenth birthday). Thus, moving to different and more usual circumstances, it is practicable to use the Children Act 1989 to provide young people with support from one or both of their parents while they are at university.

Question

Can you think of another important difference between the Child Support Act 1991 and Sch 1 to the Children Act 1989? Look at para 16(2):

In this Schedule, except paragraphs 2 and 15, 'parent' includes any party to a marriage (whether or not subsisting) in relation to whom the child concerned is a child of the family...

Of course, part of the reason why Sch 1 to the Children Act 1989 is needed at all is the lack of any obligation upon cohabitants to support each other (let alone upon parents who have never cohabited) and the lack of any regime to adjust the property entitlements of cohabitants. We turn now to legislative interventions in other jurisdictions, where that situation has been changed:

5.5 Legislative intervention

Charles Harpum, in 'Adjusting Property Rights between Unmarried Cohabitees' (1982), states:

What is required is a broad statutory discretion (broader than that conferred by the Matrimonial Causes Act 1973 because the situations that exist are far more varied) to adjust the rights of cohabitees when they cease to live together. Already by statute, on the death of one cohabitee the other may have a claim against the estate of the deceased for reasonable financial provision, if the survivor was in some way economically dependent on the deceased: s.1(1)(e) of the Inheritance (Provision for Family and Dependants) Act 1975. If on death, why not in life? The example of the 1975 Act could be followed and the trigger for the discretion could be a situation of total or partial economic dependence by one cohabitee on the other. The sooner such legislation is enacted the better.

5.5.1 Australia

One of the most significant legislative interventions comes from New South Wales, where the De Facto Relationships Act 1984 was passed to put into effect the recommendations of the New South Wales Law Reform Commission (1983) relating both to property rights and to contractual claims. In 1999 the Act was re-named the Property (Relationships) Act, and now provides for rights of maintenance and property adjustment in a much wider range of relationships than it did originally, including same-sex couples. The sections reproduced below show both the obligation to pay maintenance and the jurisdiction to make a property adjustment order:

4. De facto relationships
(1) For the purposes of this Act, a de facto relationship is a relationship between two adult persons:
  (a) who live together as a couple, and
  (b) who are not married to one another or related by family.
(2) In determining whether two persons are in a de facto relationship, all the circumstances of the relationship are to be taken into account, including such of the following matters as may be relevant in a particular case:
  (a) the duration of the relationship,
  (b) the nature and extent of common residence,
  (c) whether or not a sexual relationship exists,
  (d) the degree of financial dependence or interdependence, and any arrangements for financial support, between the parties,
  (e) the ownership, use and acquisition of property,
  (f) the degree of mutual commitment to a shared life,
  (g) the care and support of children,
  (h) the performance of household duties,
  (i) the reputation and public aspects of the relationship.
(3) No finding in respect of any of the matters mentioned in subsection (2) (a) (i), or in respect of any combination of them, is to be regarded as necessary for the existence of a de facto relationship, and a court determining whether such a relationship exists is entitled to have regard to such matters, and to attach such weight to any matter, as may seem appropriate to the court in the circumstances of the case.
(4) Except as provided by section 6, a reference in this Act to a party to a de facto relationship includes a reference to a person who, whether before or after the commencement of this subsection, was a party to such a relationship.

5. Domestic relationships
(1) For the purposes of this Act, a domestic relationship is:
  (a) a de facto relationship, or
  (b) a close personal relationship (other than a marriage or a de facto relationship) between two adult persons, whether or not related by family, who are living together, one or each of whom provides the other with domestic support and personal care.

(2)   For the purposes of subsection (1) (b), a close personal relationship is taken not to exist between two persons where one of them provides the other with domestic support and personal care:
   (a)   for fee or reward, or
   (b)   on behalf of another person or an organisation (including a government or government agency, a body corporate or a charitable or benevolent organisation).

(3)   A reference in this Act to a child of the parties to a domestic relationship is a reference to any of the following:
   (a)   a child born as a result of sexual relations between the parties,
   (b)   a child adopted by both parties,
   (c)   where the domestic relationship is a de facto relationship between a man and a woman, a child of the woman:
      (i)   of whom the man is the father, or
      (ii)   of whom the man is presumed, by virtue of the Status of Children Act 1996, to be the father, except where such a presumption is rebutted,
      (iii)   a child for whose long-term welfare both parties have parental responsibility...

(4)   Except as provided by section 6, a reference in this Act to a party to a domestic relationship includes a reference to a person who, whether before or after the commencement of this subsection, was a party to such a relationship.

...

14. Applications for orders under this Part

(1)   Subject to this Part, a party to a domestic relationship may apply to a court for an order under this Part for the adjustment of interests with respect to the property of the parties to the relationship or either of them or for the granting of maintenance, or both.

(2)   An application referred to in subsection (1) may be made whether or not any other application for any remedy or relief is or may be made under this Act or any other Act or any other law.

...

17. Prerequisites for making of order length of relationship etc

(1)   Except as provided by subsection (2), a court shall not make an order under this Part unless it is satisfied that the parties to the application have lived together in a domestic relationship for a period of not less than 2 years.

(2)   A court may make an order under this Part where it is satisfied:
   (a)   that there is a child of the parties to the application, or
   (b)   that the applicant:
      (i)   has made substantial contributions of the kind referred to in section 20 (1) (a) or (b) for which the applicant would otherwise not be adequately compensated if the order were not made, or
      (ii)   has the care and control of a child of the respondent, and that the failure to make the order would result in serious injustice to the applicant.

18. Time limit for making applications

(1)   If a domestic relationship has ceased, an application to a court for an order under this Part can only be made within the period of 2 years after the date on which the relationship ceased, except as otherwise provided by this section.

(2)   A court may, at any time after the expiration of the period referred to in subsection (1), grant leave to a party to a domestic relationship to apply to the court for an order under this Part (other than an order under section 27 (1) made where the court is satisfied as to the matters specified in section 27 (1) (b)) where the court is satisfied, having regard to such matters as it considers relevant, that greater hardship would be caused to the applicant if that leave were not granted than would be caused to the respondent if that leave were granted.

(3)   Where, under subsection (2), a court grants a party to a domestic relationship leave to apply to the court for an order under this Part, the party may apply accordingly.

19. Duty of court to end financial relationships

In proceedings for an order under this Part, a court shall, so far as is practicable, make such orders as will finally determine the financial relationships between the parties to a domestic relationship and avoid further proceedings between them. Division 2 Adjustment of interests with respect to property

20. Application for adjustment

(1)   On an application by a party to a domestic relationship for an order under this Part to adjust interests with respect to the property of the parties to the relationship or either of them, a court may make such order adjusting the interests of the parties in the property as to it seems just and equitable having regard to:

(a) the financial and non-financial contributions made directly or indirectly by or on behalf of the parties to the relationship to the acquisition, conservation or improvement of any of the property of the parties or either of them or to the financial resources of the parties or either of them, and

(b) the contributions, including any contributions made in the capacity of homemaker or parent, made by either of the parties to the relationship to the welfare of the other party to the relationship or to the welfare of the family constituted by the parties and one or more of the following, namely:
(i) a child of the parties,
(ii) a child accepted by the parties or either of them into the household of the parties, whether or not the child is a child of either of the parties.

(2) A court may make an order under subsection (1) in respect of property whether or not it has declared the title or rights of a party to a domestic relationship in respect of the property.
...

26. No general right to maintenance between parties to relationship

A party to a domestic relationship is not liable to maintain the other party to the relationship, and neither party is entitled to claim maintenance from the other, except as provided in this Division.

27. Orders for maintenance

(1) On an application by a party to a domestic relationship for an order under this Part for maintenance, a court may make an order for maintenance (whether for periodic maintenance or otherwise) where the court is satisfied as to either or both of the following:

(a) that the applicant is unable to support himself or herself adequately by reason of having the care and control of a child of the parties to the relationship or a child of the respondent, being, in either case, a child who is, on the day on which the application is made:
(i) except in the case of a child referred to in subparagraph (ii) under the age of 12 years, or
(ii) in the case of a physically handicapped child or mentally handicapped child under the age of 16 years,

(b) that the applicant is unable to support himself or herself adequately because the applicant's earning capacity has been adversely affected by the circumstances of the relationship and, in the opinion of the court:
(i) an order for maintenance would increase the applicant's earning capacity by enabling the applicant to undertake a course or programme of training or education, and
(ii) it is, having regard to all the circumstances of the case, reasonable to make the order.

(2) In determining whether to make an order under this Part for maintenance and in fixing any amount to be paid pursuant to such an order, a court shall have regard to:

(a) the income, property and financial resources of each party to the relationship (including the rate of any pension, allowance or benefit paid to either party to the relationship or the eligibility of either party to the relationship for a pension, allowance or benefit) and the physical and mental capacity of each party to the relationship for appropriate gainful employment,

(b) the financial needs and obligations of each party to the relationship,

(c) the responsibilities of either party to the relationship to support any other person,

(d) the terms of any order made or proposed to be made under section 20 with respect to the property of the parties to the relationship, and

(e) any payments made, pursuant to an order of a court or otherwise, in respect of the maintenance of a child or children in the care and control of the applicant.

(3) In making an order for maintenance, a court shall ensure that the terms of the order will, so far as is practicable, preserve any entitlement of the applicant to a pension, allowance or benefit.

Sections 45–52 provide, moreover, for the ability of any two persons to make a domestic relationship agreement (what we would call a cohabitation contract; see pp. 77ff, above), which will be enforced by the court save where circumstances have changed so that enforcement would lead to serious injustice, and, of course, without prejudice to the courts' powers to make orders in respect of children.

Question

Is this what Harpum (see p. 201, above) was suggesting, in 1982, for England? Is it what the Law Commission is suggesting now? (See the discussion paper, *Sharing Homes* (2002).)

Note that a similar process has been seen in New Zealand, where the De Facto Relationships Act 1976 has been renamed the Property (Relationships) Act 1976, from February 2002, and definitions have been amended to cover a range of relationships including same-sex couples.

5.5.2 Scotland

The Scottish Law Commission's Discussion Paper on the *Effects of Cohabitation on Private Law* (1990) describes the New South Wales Act as well as other legislation from Australia and Canada.

5.2 Several Canadian provinces have enacted legislation which enables a cohabitant to apply to a court, during the cohabitation or within a specified period after its end, for an order for support against the other cohabitant. [Institute of Law Research and Reform, Alberta, *Towards Reform of the Law Relating to Cohabitation Outside Marriage* (Issues Paper No 2, 1987).] The details vary. In Ontario, for example, an application may be made by

'either a man or a woman who are not married to each other and have cohabited

(a) continuously for a period of not less than 3 years, or

(b) in a relationship of some permanence if they are the natural or adoptive parents of a child.'

[Family Law Act 1986, s.29. The New Brunswick Family Services Act 1980 s. 112(3) is broadly similar.]

In Manitoba the required period of cohabitation is 1 year if there is a child of the union and 5 years if there is not. [Family Maintenance Act 1978 (as amended) s. 2(3).] In British Columbia the required period of cohabitation is not less than 2 years, whether or not there is a child of the union. [Family Relations Act 1979, s. 1(c).] In Nova Scotia one year's cohabitation as husband and wife suffices [Family Maintenance Act 1980 (as amended) s. 2(m)], while in the Yukon Territory all that is required is cohabitation in a relationship of some permanence. [Matrimonial Property and Family Support Ordinance 1979 (as amended) s. 30.6.] In a recent report the Alberta Law Reform Institute has, by a majority, recommended that an order for the maintenance of one cohabitant by the other should be possible where

'(i) the applicant for maintenance has the care and control of a child of the cohabitational relationship and is unable to support himself or herself adequately by reason of the child care responsibilities; or

(ii) the earning capacity of the applicant has been adversely affected by the cohabitational relationship and some transitional maintenance is required to help the applicant to re-adjust his or her life.'

[*Towards Reform of the Law Relating to Cohabitation Outside Marriage* (Report No 53, 1989).]

5.3 There have also been interesting developments in Australia. One of them took place more than a hundred and fifty years ago. Tasmania has had since 1837 a provision [now in s. 16 of the Maintenance Act 1967] enabling a woman who has cohabited with a man for at least a year to obtain a maintenance order if the man, without just cause or excuse, leaves her without adequate means of support, or deserts her, or is guilty of such misconduct as to make it unreasonable to expect her to continue to live with him. More recently, New South Wales, following on a report by the New South Wales Law Reform Commission [1983] passed the De Facto Relationships Act of 1984. This allows a cohabitant, who must normally have cohabited with his or her partner for at least two years, to claim maintenance if he or she is unable to support himself or herself adequately and if the inability is due either to having the care of a child of the union or to having suffered a reduction in earning capacity as a result of the cohabitation. An order based on the applicant's reduced earning capacity resulting from the cohabitation ceases 3 years from the date of the order or 4 years from the end of the cohabitation, whichever

is earlier. The Act also gives the court power to make such order adjusting the interests of the cohabitants in their property as seems just and equitable, having regard to their contributions (financial or otherwise) to the property and to their financial resources. In Victoria, the Property Law (Amendment) Act 1988 enables a court in settling property disputes between cohabitants to take into account contributions of various kinds to the property of the cohabitants and the welfare of the family. The Northern Territory Law Reform Committee in its Report on *De Facto Relationships* [1988] recommended rules on maintenance and property adjustment similar, in their essential features, to those enacted in New South Wales.

The Scottish Discussion Paper (1990) identified a number of options for reform; the Scottish Law Commission's subsequent *Report on Family Law* (1992) reviewed these options and reported on the responses to consultation. The approach taken was to consider whether or not various aspects of the law on financial provision on divorce in Scotland should be made applicable to cohabitants (see p. 329, below):

16.15 We do not favour a comprehensive system of financial provision on termination of cohabitation comparable to the system of financial provision on divorce in the Family Law (Scotland) Act 1985. That would be to impose a regime of property sharing, and in some cases continuing financial support, on couples who may well have opted for cohabitation in order to avoid such consequences. Almost all consultees agreed with our provisional view that there was no adequate justification for applying to cohabitants the principle of equal sharing of property in section 9(1)(a) of the Family Law (Scotland) Act 1985. There was also general support for our provisional view that one cohabitant should not be ordered, on termination of the cohabitation, to make financial provision for the other on principles analogous to those in section 9(1)(d) or 9(1)(e) of the Family Law (Scotland) Act 1985. Section 9(1)(d) relates to an award of short-term financial support to enable one party to adjust, over a period of not more than three years from the date of the divorce, to the loss of financial support from the other. Almost all consultees considered that this would be inappropriate on the termination of a cohabitation, given that there would be no obligation of support during the cohabitation and that cases involving child care or compensation for contributions or sacrifices in the interests of the family could be otherwise covered. Section 9(1)(e) is concerned with the relief of long-term financial hardship which is likely *as a result of the divorce*. Again, this is linked to the loss of the obligation of support which exists during marriage and almost all consultees agreed with our provisional view that it would be inappropriate to apply it on the termination of a cohabitation. In the public opinion survey, respondents were shown a card saying

'Suppose that a couple cohabited for 5 years and then separated. They have no child. Should the one who is better off financially be bound to pay aliment (or maintenance) to the other?'

Over three-quarters (76%) of all respondents thought that the one who was better off should not be bound to pay aliment to the other. ... This ... was the only question which resulted in a negative response in relation to improved rights for cohabitants. We therefore do not recommend the introduction of principles for property-sharing or financial provision, on or after the end of a cohabitation, corresponding to the principles on section 9(1)(a), (d) or (e) of the Family Law (Scotland) Act 1985.

16.16 In the discussion paper we favoured the introduction of a principle designed to share the economic burden of child-care after the end of a cohabitation. ... In the event, this ... has been overtaken by the provisions in the Child Support Act 1991. ...

16.17 We asked in the discussion paper whether, on the termination of a cohabitation, a cohabitant should be able to apply to a court for an order for financial provision based on the principle in section 9(1)(b) of the Family Law (Scotland) Act 1985. This provides that

'fair account should be taken of any economic advantage derived by either party from the contributions of the other, and of any economic disadvantage suffered by either party in the interests of the other party or of the family'.

If this principle were applied to cohabitants it would enable some provision to be made for cases where, for example, one party has worked unpaid for years helping to build up the other's business or one party has given up a good pensionable career in order to look after the children of the relationship. ...

16.18 The principle on section 9(1)(b) could be applied, quite readily and appropriately, to cohabitants. The argument for applying it is that it would be unfair to let economic gains and losses arising out of contributions or sacrifices made in the course of a relationship of cohabitation simply lie where they fall. To allow a remedy for the type of situation covered by section 9(1)(b)

would not be to impose on cohabitants a solution based on a particular view of marriage. It would merely be to give them the benefit of a principle designed to correct imbalances arising out of the circumstances of a non-commercial relationship where the parties are quite likely to make contributions and sacrifices without counting the cost or bargaining for a return. ...

16.19 ... respondents to the public opinion survey ... were asked the following question.

'Suppose that a couple cohabited for some years. They do not have a child. They have now split up. During the cohabitation one of them worked unpaid to help build up the other's business. Should that person have any financial claim against the other because of this contribution to the other's wealth?'

Over four-fifths (85%) of respondents believed that a person should have such a financial claim.

...

16.23 We recommend that ...

(a) Where a cohabitation has terminated otherwise than by death, a former cohabitant should be able to apply to a court, within one year after the end of the cohabitation, for a financial provision on the basis of the principle in section 9(1)(b) of the Family Law (Scotland) Act 1985 – namely that fair account should be taken of any economic advantage derived by either party from contributions by the other, and of any economic disadvantage suffered by either party in the interests of the other party or of any child of the family.

...

(d) The court hearing an application should have power to award a capital sum (including a deferred capital sum and a capital sum payable by instalments) and to make an interim award.

Questions

(i)   How would you have responded to the questions quoted here from the public opinion survey?

(ii)   Do you agree with the Scottish Law Commission's recommendation and, if so, why?

(iii)   In England, different considerations apply because of the different basis of financial provision on divorce. Will it be necessary to introduce a law similar to the Family Law (Scotland) Act 1985 for divorcing couples prior to providing relief for former cohabitants, or would the extension of the principles in the Matrimonial Causes Act 1973 to former cohabitants suffice?

(iv)   The Law Commission has been investigating the property rights of unmarried cohabitants. Are there any suggestions that you would make on this topic?

(v)   Charles Harpum, in 'Cohabitation Consultation' (1995), wrote: 'Homesharers are not denizens of some black hole of outlawry. Is it better for the law that regulates their affairs to be developed by legislation after an exhaustive consideration of the issues or should it continue to be left to the chances of litigation?' What is your view?

Although this recommendation from the Scottish Law Commission's Report on Family Law has not been enacted, Scots law has taken one inconspicuous step that has been under discussion recently in this jurisdiction. It will be recalled (see p. 154, above) that the Family Law Act 1996 enables a spouse to seek a transfer of certain types of tenancy on the granting of a decree of divorce, etc, or at any time thereafter. The Matrimonial Homes (Family Protection) (Scotland) Act 1981, ss. 18 and 13 gives this right to cohabitants.

The Family Law Act 1996 makes similar provisions for cohabitants (again, only in respect of tenancies with statutory security of tenure), so that, say, a girlfriend living in her boyfriend's council house could apply for an order that the tenancy be transferred to her. The court is required to bear a number of

considerations in mind, including the housing needs and resources of each party, the health, safety and well-being of the parties and any child living with them, and the nature and length of the parties' relationship. The provisions are to be found in Part III of the Act, which is concerned both with occupation rights and with mechanisms for protection from domestic violence; but there is no requirement that there need have been any violence or misconduct before such an order can be made.

Question

This provision for cohabitants has given rise to considerable controversy. It was originally contained in the Family Homes and Domestic Violence Bill 1995, and it was partly because of objections to this provision that the bill was withdrawn. Why do you think it was so controversial? Why do you suppose it was nevertheless retained when the provisions of the Family Homes and Domestic Violence Bill 1995 were reproduced, with modifications, in Part III of the Family Law Act 1996?

We have seen (p. 75, above) that the Civil Partnerships Bill 2001 attempted to introduce a community property regime, linked with an opt-in status, for cohabitants.

Question

If legislation is introduced to regulate the property rights of cohabitants, which do you think more likely to happen: a community of property regime, or an adjustive regime on separation? Or both?

Bibliography

We quoted from:
Central Statistical Office, *Social Trends 32* (2002), HMSO, London, Table 10.5 and text.

5.1   Separate property for spouses

We quoted from:
O. Kahn-Freund, *Matrimonial Property: where do we go from here?* Joseph Unger Memorial Lecture, University of Birmingham (1974) pp. 11, 20–21, 22, 23, 25, 46–47.

Law Commission, Working Paper No. 42, *Family Property Law* (1971) London, HMSO, paras. 0.12, 0.13.

Report of the Committee on One-Parent Families (Chairman: The Hon Sir Morris Finer) (Cmnd. 5629) (1974) London, HMSO.

Sir J. Simon, *With All My Worldly Goods* (1964) Holdsworth Club, Presidential Address, University of Birmingham, pp. 1–4, 8–9, 10–13, 14–17, 100, 101, 102, 103.

Additional reading
H. Conway, 'Protecting Tenancies on Marriage Breakdown' [2001] Family Law 208.

5.2   The field of choice

We quoted from:

B. Hale 'Family Law Reform: Wither or Whither' (1995) Current Legal Problems 217, pp. 228–229.

O. Kahn-Freund, *Matrimonial Property: where do we go from here?* Joseph Unger Memorial Lecture, University of Birmingham (1974), pp. 11, 20–21, 22, 23, 25, 46–47.

Law Commission, Working Paper No. 42, *Family Property Law* (1971) London, HMSO, paras. 0.25–0.29

Law Commission, *First Report on Family Property: A New Approach*, Law Com. No. 52 (1973) London, HMSO, paras. 21–24, 38, 39, 41, 44, 47–59.

Law Commission, *Family Law, Matrimonial Property*, Law Com. No. 175 (1988) London, HMSO, para 1.4, etc, and footnote 21.

Law Reform Commission of Canada, *Family Property,* Working Paper No. 8 (1975) Ottawa, Information Canada, pp. 9–10, 18, 19–22, 27.

Scottish Law Commission, *Family Law: Report on Matrimonial Property* (Scot. Law Com. No. 86HC 467) (1984) Edinburgh, HMSO, para. 3.

Additional reading
Law Commission, *Third Report on Family Property: The Matrimonial Home (Co-ownership and Occupation Rights) and Household Goods*, Law Com. No. 86 (1978) London, HMSO, paras. 1.113–1.119.

A.J. Manners and I. Rauta, *Family Property in Scotland* (1981) Edinburgh, HMSO.

5.3   Property claims

We quoted from:

L. Clarke and R. Edmunds, '*H v M*: Equity and the Essex Cohabitant' (1992) 22 Family Law 523.

Review Committee, *Insolvency Law and Practice* (Report of the Review Committee, chaired by Sir Kenneth Cork) (Cmnd. 8558) (1982) London, HMSO, para. 1118.

P. Ferguson, 'Constructive Trusts – A Note of Caution' (1993) 109 Law Quarterly Review 114, pp. 124–125.

S. Gardiner, 'Rethinking Family Property' (1993) 109 Law Quarterly Review 263, pp. 264–265.

A. Hudson, *Equity and Trusts* (2nd edn, 2001) London, Cavendish.

Law Commission, Working Paper No. 42, *Family Property Law* (1971) London, HMSO, paras. 0.37–0.40 and 4.71

Law Commission, *First Report on Family Property: A New Approach* Law Com. No. 52 (1973) London, HMSO, paras. 38, 39, 41

Law Commission, *Distribution on Intestacy,* Law Com. No. 187 (1989) London, HMSO, paras 17–22.

M. Pawlowski and S. Greer, 'Undue influence – back door tactics?' [2001] Family Law 275.

D. Wragg, 'Constructive trusts and the unmarried couple' [1996] Family Law 298.

Additional reading
P. Clarke, 'The Family Home, Intention and Agreement' (1992) 22 Family Law 72.
E.J. Cooke, 'Reliance and Estoppel' (1995) 111 Law Quarterly Review 389.
Law Commission, *Second Report on Family Property: Family Provision on Death*
Law Com. No. 61 (1974) London, HMSO.
J.G. Miller, *Family Property and Financial Provision* (1974) (3rd edn, 1983)
London, Sweet and Maxwell.
W. Swadling, [1998] Restitution Law Review 220.
M.P. Thompson, 'Wives, Sureties and Banks' [2002] Conv. 174.

5.4   Property claims for children

Additional reading
E.J. Cooke, 'Property Adjustment Orders for Children' (1994) 6 Journal of
Child Law 156.
Law Commission, *Report on Illegitimacy*, Law Com. No. 118 (1982) London,
HMSO.

5.5   Legislative intervention

We quoted from
C. Harpum, 'Adjusting Property Rights Between Unmarried Cohabitees'
(1982) 2 Oxford Journal of Legal Studies 287.
Scottish Law Commission, *The Effects of Cohabitation in Private Law* (1990)
Scot. Law Com. Discussion Paper No. 86, Edinburgh, HMSO,
paras. 5.2, 5.3.
Scottish Law Commission, *Report on Family Law*, Scot. Law. Com. No. 135
Edinburgh (1992) HMSO, paras. 16.15–16.23.

Additional reading
C. Harpum, 'Cohabitation Consultation' (1995) 25 Family Law 657.
Parkinson, 'The Property Rights of Cohabitees – Is Statutory Reform the
Answer?' in A. Bainham, D. Pearl and R. Pickford (eds.), *Frontiers of Family
Law* (1995) Chichester, Wiley.
Law Commission, Discussion Paper, *Sharing Homes* (2002).

Chapter 6

Divorce

6.1 The history of English divorce law

6.2 The present law: the Matrimonial Causes Act 1973

6.3 The factual context

6.4 The Family Law Act 1996: a brighter future?

6.5 The Family Law Act 1996: stuck on the shelf

'Divorce is an institution only a few weeks later in origin than marriage.' [Voltaire, quoted in A. Alvarez, (1981).]

An American psychologist, Gerald Alpern, in *Rights of Passage* (1982), has tried to provide a guide to the emotional realities of divorce:

Some divorces are simple happenings, a graceful parting in which two people go off in different directions to new lives. Other divorces occur so gradually, over so many years, that the divorce process is not a deeply felt experience. For others, the marriage involved a connection so casual that a legal divorce is but a formality.

However, the majority of divorces are very powerful experiences which, for many, are devastating. For most people, divorce necessitates major revisions in life goals, expectations and personal identities. People involved in divorce find themselves acting in unfamiliar ways. They may behave irrationally, become vicious or promiscuous, or suddenly plan to desert loved children. These unfamiliar actions and feelings are very frightening and cause grave self-doubts which exacerbate the depression so common to divorcing men and women. The most disorienting experience is the wide mood swings which accompany the vacillating positive and negative feelings about the divorce. At one moment the person is high on thoughts of being independent, of being free of a spouse no longer loved. The next moment or day the same person may be crying, longing for the missing spouse and planning an attempt at reconciliation.

John Cleese and Robin Skynner, in *Families and How to Survive Them* (1993), remind us that we are perhaps asking for trouble by entering into the types of marriage expected of us in this period of our history:

John Let's start with an easy one ... Why do people decide to marry each other?
Robin Because they're in love.
John Oh, come on.
Robin No, I'm being serious.
John Well, perhaps, but this falling in love routine is very bizarre. You find perfectly ordinary, rational people like computer programmers and chartered accountants, and there they are, happily computing and chartering away, and suddenly they see someone across a crowded room and think, 'Ah, that person is made for me, so I suppose I'd better spend the rest of my life with them.' It borders on the occult.

210

Robin Perhaps you'd have preferred it three hundred years ago when parents arranged all the marriages for sensible reasons like land and money and social climbing. They all regarded 'falling in love' as the worst possible basis for marriage – a recipe for disaster.

John Yes, Samuel Johnson said that all marriages should be arranged by the Lord Chancellor without reference to the wishes of the parties involved.

Robin So the point I'm making is that nowadays we are free to marry the person we love, the one who can really make us happy.

John And of course we have the highest divorce rate in history.

Robin Since you and I have both made a contribution to those statistics, we'd better not sound too critical.

John I'm sorry if I did. Actually, I think divorce is underrated. It gives you insights into some of the trickier aspects of marriage, the more delicate nuances as it were, that couples who've been happy together for thirty years wouldn't begin to grasp. But nevertheless, divorced or not, here we are, millions upon millions of us, all blithely pairing off, thinking, 'This is the one for me.' So what's going on, Doctor?

Robin What do you think falling in love is about?

With that conundrum in mind we move into our discussion of the law of divorce.

We turn our attention first of all to the history of our divorce law up until the major changes of the Divorce Reform Act 1969; then we look at the current law, seen in the Matrimonial Causes Act 1973. Then we look at some of the empirical evidence about the use of that law. Next, we examine the reforms enacted in the Family Law Act 1996; finally, we ask why they are not to be implemented.

6.1 The history of English divorce law

We should first ponder on the important words of Lawrence Stone in *Road to Divorce* (1990). It is his view that there does not exist any single model of change which can explain the history of marital breakdown and divorce in a single country for all periods of time and for all classes of society. He writes:

Any historian who claims that either the law has always shaped marital practices or that marital practices have always shaped the law, or that the causes of change were at bottom either legal, or economic and social, or cultural and moral, or intellectual, is offering a simplistic solution which is unsupported by the evidence. History is messier than that.

The Gospel according to St Mark, in Chapter 10, lays the foundation for the Christian view of marriage and divorce which has influenced our law for so long:

2. And the Pharisees came to him, and asked him, Is it lawful for a man to put away his wife? tempting him.

3. And he answered and said unto them, What did Moses command you?

4. And they said, Moses suffered to write a bill of divorcement, and to put her away.

5. And Jesus answered and said unto them, For the hardness of your heart he wrote you this precept.

6. But from the beginning of the creation God made them male and female.

7. For this cause shall a man leave his father and mother, and cleave to his wife.

8. And they twain shall be one flesh: so then they are no more twain, but one flesh.

9. What therefore God hath joined together, let not man put asunder.

10. And in the house his disciples asked him again of the same matter.

11. And he saith unto them, Whosoever shall put away his wife, and marry another, committeth adultery against her.

12. And if a woman shall put away her husband, and be married to another, she committeth adultery.

An almost identical account appears in St Matthew's Gospel (Chapter 19, verses 3–9), but with the significant addition of the words 'except it be for fornication' in his version of Mark's verse 11.

A helpful summary of developments up until the second Royal Commission on Divorce (1912) appears in *The History of the Obligation to Maintain*, by Sir Morris Finer and Professor O.R. McGregor, which is Appendix 5 to the *Report of the (Finer) Committee on One-Parent Families* (1974):

The canon law of marriage

1. In medieval times most men, whether of high or low degree, married with the primary object of advancing their interests. For women, marriage was a protective institution. Monogamy did not require, or imply, that people should contract only one marriage in a lifetime, and remarriage was a frequent occurrence in all social groups thereby helping to fill the gaps among the married population which resulted from early deaths. Remarriage protected widows from the dangers of living alone in a violent society as well as feudal superiors from the risk that unmarried dependants would fail in the full performance of services due from them. Moreover, the medieval laity were motivated by a desire 'to place the satisfaction of the flesh under the shelter of the sacrament'.

2. From the middle of the twelfth century until the Reformation, the law regulating marriage in England was the canon law of the church of Rome administered in courts christian. The canon law was framed in the belief that marriage is a permanent union of the natural order established by God in the creation, and consequently it affirmed that marriage made man and woman one flesh and partook of the nature of a sacrament signifying the unity betwixt Christ and his Church. Medieval christendom regarded marriage as an eternal triangle within which spouses established unbreakable bonds not only with each other but also with God. For this reason, the church maintained that marriage was indissoluble and that no earthly power, not even the Pope himself, could break the bond of a christian marriage. ...

The canon law of nullity

4. In early English law, church and state recognised divorce *a vinculo matrimonii*. This was a divorce in the full sense. It dissolved the bond of marriage and left the parties free to marry again. The church of Rome, treating marriage as indissoluble, abolished divorce in this sense. Thereafter, the ecclesiastical courts granted in the case of a validly contracted marriage only a more limited form of relief. As against a spouse guilty of adultery, cruelty, heresy or apostasy, they might pass sentence of divorce *a mensa et thoro*. This had the effect of a modern judicial separation. It relieved the spouses of the obligation to live together – to share board and bed – but preserved intact the marriage tie.

5. Yet the practical realities of life in the middle ages demanded a method of legitimate avoidance of the rigours of the doctrine of indissolubility. The church provided such a method by developing an elaborate theory of nullity. It was argued that only a valid, consummated, christian marriage was indissoluble. If an impediment to the validity of a marriage had existed when it was contracted, then that marriage would be held by the ecclesiastical courts never to have taken place at all. Many impediments were soon established; the most important were the degrees of consanguinity and affinity within which marriage was prohibited. Before the Lateran Council of 1215, marriage was forbidden between persons to the seventh degree of blood relationship; afterwards, the prohibition was narrowed to the fourth degree, that is, to third cousins. To the impediments of blood were added those of affinity. Since sexual union made man and woman one flesh, it followed that all the blood kinswomen of a man's wife or even of his mistress, were themselves connected to him by affinity. To the impediments of sexual affinity the church then added yet another series created by the spiritual relationships of godchildren. ... [See further in Chapter 1, above.]

The effect of the Reformation

6. By the time of the Reformation, many reformers were rejecting the canon law of marriage developed by the medieval church. They no longer regarded virginity as superior to marriage; they abandoned sacerdotal celibacy; they urged that marriage should be treated as a civil contract regulated by the state; and they favoured the dissolubility of marriage, although differing as to the grounds on which a divorce *a vinculo* ought to be granted. Nevertheless, the protestant doctrines of divorce, though much discussed in the second half of the sixteenth century, did not become part of the law of the land. On the contrary, by the beginning of the seventeenth century, the new church of England had affirmed its belief in the indissolubility of

marriage mitigated only by divorce *a mensa et thoro*. ... At the same time, it rejected the extravagances of the canon law of nullity. Thus, ironically enough, the principal effect of the Reformation on marriage in England was the sealing up of the loopholes and the rejection of the evasions and absurdities by which the medieval system had been made tolerable in practice. Yet whatever formal respect the rich and powerful accorded to christian theology, they were no more prepared than were their ancestors to tolerate the inconveniences inseparable from a system of rigidly indissoluble marriage. In seventeenth and eighteenth century England, these classes both sustained monogamous marriage and encouraged the accumulation of private property. It was natural, therefore, for them to be more sensitive to the immediate damage which hasty and easily contracted marriages could inflict upon the orderly disposition of family property than to the remoter danger that sexual immorality might imperil their immortal souls. For these reasons, the state broke the exclusive familial jurisdiction of the ecclesiastical courts in two ways. First, it stepped in to regulate and formalise the procedure by which a valid marriage could be contracted. Secondly, it provided a machinery for the dissolution of valid marriages by Act of Parliament. ...

Parliamentary divorce[1]

13. As the ecclesiastical courts had no power to dissolve a valid marriage *a vinculo* and as the secular courts refused to invade the spiritual jurisdiction, only Parliament could break the indissoluble bond of marriage by intervening in particular cases through the procedure of sovereign legislation. The following Table shows the extent of its interference for this purpose by the passing of private Acts of divorce:

Period							Number	Percentage
Before 1714	...	...	...	...	...	...	10[2]	3
1715-1759	...	...	...	...	...	...	24	8
1760-1779	...	...	...	...	...	...	46	14
1780-1799	...	...	...	...	...	...	53	17
1800-1819	...	...	...	...	...	...	49	15
1820-1839	...	...	...	...	...	...	59	19
1840-1856	...	...	...	...	...	...	76	24
Total	...	...	...	...	...	...	317	100

Source: Adapted from PP 1857, Session 2 (106-I), Volume XLII, page 117.

[The table] shows how rare parliamentary divorces were before the accession of George I and how their use increased steadily thereafter, so that one quarter of all the private Acts were passed in the twenty years before the system was abolished in 1857. Before the eighteenth century the main reason for Parliament's willingness to grant the privilege of marrying again was to continue the succession to peerages in the male line. When the Duke of Norfolk successfully petitioned the House of Lords for his divorce bill of 1700, he stated that his wife had 'made full proof of her adultery' and that he 'hath no issue, nor can have any probable expectation of posterity to succeed him in his honours, dignities, and estate, unless the said marriage be declared void by authority of Parliament. ...'[3] This soon ceased to be the only circumstance in which Parliament would intervene. Later Acts were passed in favour of professional men (including seventeen clergymen) and people engaged in business; indeed, such folk accounted for half the Acts passed between the middle of the eighteenth century and 1857. Nevertheless all the promoters had one

---

1. See also Sybil Wolfram, 'Divorce in England 1700–1857', Oxford Journal of Legal Studies vol. 5 (1984) pp. 155–156, and S. Anderson, 'Legislative Divorce – Law for the Aristocracy' in G. Rubin and D. Sugarman (eds.) *Law, Society and Economy. Essays in Legal History* (1984).
2. The case of Lord Roos in 1670 is discussed in detail by Stone (1990). The case, described by Charles II as 'better than a play', apparently gave birth to the famous nursery rhyme 'Mary Mary quite contrary, how does your garden grow . . . pretty maids all in a row' after the alleged succession of extramarital liaisons of his wife Anne. Unlike 'Mary', 'Anne' does not rhyme with 'contrary'!
3. Stone (1990) informs us that Norfolk died in 1701 before he had had time to remarry so that the whole purpose of the Act was frustrated.

characteristic in common: they were very wealthy. They had to be, for the cost of a private Act and the related proceedings was formidable.

14.   After the adoption of a series of Resolutions framed by Lord Chancellor Loughborough in 1798, the House of Lords imposed a standard procedure upon all applications. Before coming to Parliament a petitioner had first to obtain both a decree of divorce *a menso et thoro* from the spiritual court, and an award of damages for criminal conversation against the wife's seducer in the secular court. The Resolutions further required that the petitioner should attend the House so that he might if necessary be examined as a witness, with reference both to collusion or connivance and also to another point which was always deemed of primary importance in judging divorce bills: whether at the time of the adultery he was living apart from his wife and had thereby contributed to her offence. ...

17.   This procedure, cumbersome, expensive and intricate as it was, could in practice be utilised only by aggrieved husbands. Only four wives were ever granted Acts and these were all passed in the nineteenth century. The first occurred in 1801. We quote Frederick Clifford's account of Mrs Addison's Act in full, both for its intrinsic interest and to show how, even at the close of the Age of Reason, the House of Lords could still be moved and bemused by arguments based upon the canonists' doctrine of the carnal affinities.

> 'Mr Addison had maintained a criminal intercourse with his wife's sister, a married woman. Her husband, Dr Campbell, obtained a verdict against him with £5,000 damages. Mrs Addison, after obtaining in the Ecclesiastical Court a divorce *a mensa et thoro*, applied to Parliament for a divorce *a vinculo*. Her husband did not appear. Lord Thurlow ... made a powerful speech for the Bill. Every principle of justice, he said, would be violated by its rejection. But Lord Thurlow did not assert a woman's general right to the same legislative relief as was given to an injured husband. He found his chief defence of the Bill upon the old doctrine of the canonists, that commerce between the sexes creates affinity. In this case, he argued, if Mr Addison had previously had illicit intercourse with her sister, he could not have married his present wife, because such marriage would have been tainted by incest, and might have been pronounced void by an Ecclesiastical Court. A like result occurred by reason of this incestuous adultery. It made reconciliation legally impossible, for, by the affinity it had created, renewed cohabitation between Mr and Mrs Addison would become incestuous.'

Lord Thurlow's subtleties prevailed upon the Lord Chancellor, Lord Eldon, to withdraw his intended opposition to the establishment of this precedent. There is no record of any opposition in the House of Commons, and Mrs Addison obtained her Act. But Parliament held thereafter to the principle that adultery without more by the husband was not a sufficient ground for a wife to obtain an Act. Of the three other instances, in Mrs Turton's case in 1830 the adultery was incestuous; in Mrs Battersby's case in 1840 there was adultery aggravated by cruelty and followed by bigamy for which her husband was transported; and in Mrs Hall's case in 1850 there was also bigamy.

18.   Two of the characteristics of the procedure of divorce by private Act of Parliament are now plain. It was so expensive that only the wealthy could avail themselves of it, and within the exclusive social sphere for which the procedure catered, it made a further discrimination between men and women. The discrimination which Parliament maintained between husbands and wives, in respect of the grounds on which it was prepared to dissolve a marriage, was justified in terms of the different effect of their adultery. As Lord Chancellor Cranworth explained to the House of Lords:

> 'A wife might, without any loss of caste, and possibly with reference to the interests of her children, or even of her husband, condone an act of adultery on the part of the husband but a husband could not condone a similar act on the part of a wife. No one would venture to suggest that a husband could possibly do so, and for this, among other reasons ... that the adultery of the wife might be the means of palming spurious offspring upon the husband, while the adultery of the husband could have no such effect with regard to the wife.'

R v Hall

(1845) 1 Cox CC 231

(cited by Stone (1990))

Maule J: Prisoner at the bar, you have been convicted before me of what the law regards as a very grave and serious offence: that of going through the marriage ceremony a second time while your wife was still alive. You plead in mitigation of your conduct that she was given to dissipation and drunkenness, that she proved herself a curse to your household while she remained mistress of it, and that she had latterly deserted you; but I am not permitted to recognise any such plea ... Another of your irrational excuses is that your wife had committed adultery, and so you thought you were relieved from treating her with any further consideration – but you were mistaken. The law in its wisdom points out a means by which you might rid yourself from further association with a woman who had dishonoured you, but you did not think proper to adopt it. I will tell you what that process is. You ought first to have brought an action against your wife's seducer, if you could have discovered him; that might have cost you money, and you say you are a poor working man, but that is not the fault of the law. You would then be obliged to prove by evidence your wife's criminality in a Court of Justice, and thus obtain a verdict with damages against the defendant, who was not unlikely to turn out pauper. But so jealous is the law (which you ought to be aware is the perfection of reason) of the sanctity of the marriage tie, that in accomplishing all this you would only have fulfilled the lighter portion of your duty. You must then have gone, with your verdict in your hand, and petitioned the House of Lords for a divorce. It would cost you perhaps five or six hundred pounds, and you do not seem to be worth as many pence. But it is the boast of the law that it is impartial, and makes no difference between the rich and the poor. The wealthiest man in the kingdom would have had to pay no less than that sum for the same luxury; so that you would have no reason to complain. You would, of course, have to prove your case over again, and at the end of a year, or possibly two, you might obtain a divorce which would enable you legally to do what you have thought proper to do without it. You have thus wilfully rejected the boon the legislature offered you, and it is my duty to pass upon you such a sentence as I think your offence deserves, and that sentence is, that you be imprisoned for one day; and in as much as the present assizes are three days old, the result is that you will be immediately discharged.

Question

As we can see from this sentence on the unfortunate Mr Hall, there was one law for the rich and another law for the poor. Could it be that only the rich needed to divorce? What social changes in the years leading up to 1857 might have made it necessary for others to seek this remedy?

The story is taken up by Sir Morris Finer and Professor O.R. McGregor:

The first Royal (Campbell) Commission on divorce
30.   In 1850 a Royal Commission, under the chairmanship of Lord Campbell, was appointed 'to enquire into the present state of the law of divorce'. The commission was an explicit response to the dissatisfaction with the existing law we have been describing: 'the grave objection,' as Lord Chancellor Cranworth explained, 'that such complicated proceedings were too expensive for the pockets of any but the richest sufferers, and that relief was put beyond the reach of all but the wealthiest classes.' It followed, as Lord Campbell himself said, that the object of the commission was not in any way to alter the law, but only the procedure by which the law was carried into effect. The same points were made repeatedly in the debates on the Matrimonial Causes Act 1857, whereby the recommendations of the Campbell Report were given effect. Thus, the Act of 1857 did not, as is sometimes mistakenly thought, introduce divorce into England or discard a hitherto sacred principle of indissolubility of marriage. The Act (apart from some minor innovations) did no more than consolidate and transfer to a civil

and more accessible court of law the jurisdictions that were already being respectively exercised by Parliament and the ecclesiastical courts. The only substantial change which it effected was to make more widely available matrimonial remedies which only the very few had until then enjoyed.

The Matrimonial Causes Act 1857

31.   The principal provisions of the Act of 1857 were, accordingly, as follows. The matrimonial jurisdiction of the ecclesiastical courts was abolished, but re-created in a new court called 'the Court for Divorce and Matrimonial Causes'. In exercising the transferred jurisdiction, the divorce court was to proceed on the same principles as had guided the ecclesiastical courts. The remedy which those courts had formerly granted under the name of a decree of divorce *a mensa et thoro* was henceforth to be called a decree of judicial separation. The divorce court would also deal with petitions for the dissolution of marriage. A husband could present a petition for divorce on the ground of his wife's adultery; a wife, on the ground of adultery aggravated by some other conduct (such as incestuous adultery, adultery coupled with cruelty or with desertion for two years or upwards) or on the ground of sodomy or bestiality. It is notable that Gladstone, while vigorously opposing the passage of the Act, was equally strong in contending that if it were passed at all it should not discriminate between the sexes:

> 'It is impossible to do a greater mischief than to begin now, in the middle of the nineteenth century, to undo with regard to womankind that which has already been done on their behalf, by slow degrees, in the preceding eighteen centuries, and to say that the husband shall be authorised to dismiss his wife on grounds for which the wife shall not be authorised to dismiss her husband. If there is one broad and palpable result of Christianity which we ought to regard as precious, it is that it has placed the seal of God Almighty upon the equality of man and woman with respect to everything that relates to these rights.' [See the extract from St Mark's Gospel at the beginning of this chapter.]. ...

The number of divorces

34.   The Act of 1857 opened the door to matrimonial relief for many whom the expense of the earlier procedures had excluded. In the four years following the passing of the Act 781 petitions for divorce and 248 petitions for judicial separation were filed in the new court. On the other hand, the Act, as these figures demonstrate, opened no floodgate. The highest number of decrees granted in any one year up to 1900 was 583 divorces (in the year 1897) and 57 decrees for judicial separation (in the year 1880). The new jurisdiction was wholly centralised in London, which acted as a deterrent to its employment by those who resided at a distance. Further, although the costs were not so wildly exorbitant as previously, they were still very considerable, and beyond the reach of people of ordinary means. It was not long before the criticisms which had preceded the Act regained currency. ...

The Second Royal (Gorell) Commission on Divorce

42.   In 1909, a Royal Commission was appointed, under the chairmanship of Lord Gorell 'to enquire into the present state of the law of England and the administration thereof in divorce and matrimonial causes and applications for separation orders, especially with regard to the position of the poorer classes in relation thereto.' By this time, while the High Court was dealing every year with some 800 petitions for divorce and judicial separation, the magistrates were dealing with some 15,000 applications for matrimonial orders. In the ten years 1897–1906 the magistrates made more than 87,000 separation orders. Almost all of the magistrates' clientele were the poor, whose problems the terms of reference expressly recognised. Indeed, the themes and anxieties which had dominated the discussion in the preceding century, and which the intervening reforms had not laid to rest, continued to be strongly reflected in the evidence given to the commission: discrimination between the sexes; discrimination against the poor. ... It continues ... to impress by a quality of vision and humanity which may be illustrated by a passage which refers to the obligation:

> 'to recognise human needs, that divorce is not a disease but a remedy for a disease, that homes are not broken up by a court but by causes to which we have already sufficiently referred, and that the law should be such as would give relief where serious causes intervene, which are generally and properly recognised as leading to the break-up of married life. If a reasonable law, based upon human needs, be adopted, we think that the standard of morality will be raised and regard for the sanctity of marriage increased.'

43.   As regards the law of divorce and its administration, the Gorell Report proposed, first, 'that the law should be amended so as to place the two sexes on an equal footing as regards the

grounds on which divorce may be obtained'. ... This recommendation was not followed until 1923. Next, the report proposed the broadening of the grounds on which either spouse might petition for divorce, by adding to adultery the offences of desertion for three years and upwards, cruelty, incurable insanity, habitual drunkenness and imprisonment under commuted death sentence. Extensions on these lines had to wait upon the Matrimonial Causes Act 1937. Thirdly, the Gorell Report recommended a decentralisation of procedure so that the High Court could sit and exercise divorce jurisdiction locally, for the benefit, in particular, of people of small means. It took another committee, in 1946, to produce any effective change in this respect.

The story since then is taken up in the main body of the Finer Report:

Lord Buckmaster's Act in 1923 had put husbands and wives on a footing of formal equality in respect of the grounds of divorce, by making it possible for each to petition against the other on the grounds of simple adultery. But it was not until the legal aid scheme of 1949 compensated wives for their lack of income or low earnings that they won practical equality of access to the court .[4]

The Third Royal (Morton) Commission on Marriage and Divorce
4.30 In 1951, Mrs Eirene White proposed, in a private member's bill, to permit divorce to spouses who had lived apart for seven years: that is to say, divorce which depended on the fact of separation over this period, and did not involve the proof, by one spouse against the other, of the commission of a matrimonial offence. Coming as it did, at the time when legal aid regarded as a social service was replacing help for the poor as a form of professional charity dispensed by lawyers, and the financial bar to the divorce courts was being lifted, Mrs White's bill was seen by its opponents as a measure to open the floodgates. Nevertheless, to the alarm of its opponents, and to the surprise of many of the supporters of the bill, it appeared as though the House might respond favourably. At this juncture, the government offered Mrs White a Greek gift in the shape of a Royal Commission. Mrs White accepted.
4.31 The Report of the Morton Commission in 1956, though divided, was decidedly against change. Reformers had urged that the doctrine of the matrimonial offence was out of step with people's actual behaviour and expectations in marriage, that the law was brought into contempt by the perjury thereby encouraged, and that the result was illicit unions and the birth of illegitimate children. The Church of England was the most influential opponent of change in the matrimonial law. It explained to the Royal Commission that the doctrine of the matrimonial offence was 'entirely in accord with the New Testament', asserted that divorce was 'a very dangerous threat to the family and to the conception of marriage as a lifelong obligation', and upheld its traditional view that, although much individual suffering and hardship might be relieved by making divorce easier to obtain, the damage to the social order must outweigh such benefits. ...

The pressure for reform
4.32 In 1956, it must have seemed that the Morton Commission and the Church of England had between them put the quietus on divorce law reform for many years to come. But the appearances were deceptive. The report proved to be little more than a ripple on the surface of a tide that was moving strongly in the other direction.

Nevertheless, it was a group set up in the 1960s by the Archbishop of Canterbury (under the chairmanship of the Rt. Rev. R.C. Mortimer, Lord Bishop of Exeter) that cleared the way for major reform. Its report was published in 1966, under the title *Putting Asunder – A Divorce Law for Contemporary Society*. It drew three main conclusions.

First, as Jesus himself had accepted the Mosaic law for those whose 'hardness of heart' made them unable to understand the truth of Jesus' own teaching about life-long fidelity, and today's secular society was full of such people:

---

4. This observation is based upon the respective proportions of husbands and wives who were subsequently legally aided (Gibson and Beer, 1971), but it should be recalled that part of the husband's common law duty to maintain his wife was to give security for her costs in litigation.

17.   There is therefore nothing to forbid the Church's recognizing fully the validity of a secular divorce law within the secular sphere. It follows that it is right and proper for the Church to co-operate with the State, and for Christians to co-operate with secular humanists and others who are not Christians, in trying to make the divorce law as equitable and as little harmful to society as it can be made. Since ex hypothesi the State's matrimonial law is not meant to be a translation of the teaching of Jesus into legal terms, but [to] allow properly for that 'hardness of heart' of which Jesus himself took account, the standard by which it is to be judged is certainly not the Church's own canon law and pastoral discipline. ...

18.   The only Christian interests that need to be declared are the protection of the weak and the preservation and strengthening of those elements in the law which favour lasting marriage and stable family life; and these are ends which Christians are by no means alone in thinking socially important. ...

Secondly, having considered the interpretation of the fault-based grounds; the stratagems to which these put couples who were determined on divorce; and the inconsistency of having some fault and some (like incurable insanity and cases of cruelty for which the respondent could not morally be blamed) no-fault grounds:

45(*f*)... We are far from being convinced that the present provisions of the law witness to the sanctity of marriage, or uphold its public repute, in any observable way, or that they are irreplaceable as buttresses of morality, either in the narrower field of matrimonial and sexual relationships, or in the wider field which includes considerations of truth, the sacredness of oaths, and the integrity of professional practice. As a piece of social mechanism the present system has not only cut loose from its moral and juridical foundations: it is, quite simply, inept.

Thirdly, the courts should be empowered, after an enquiry into every case, to recognise in law the fact that a marriage had irretrievably broken down:

55.   ... As we see it, the primary and fundamental question would be: Does the evidence before the court reveal such failure in the matrimonial relationship, or such circumstances adverse to that relationship, that no reasonable probability remains of the spouses again living together as husband and wife for mutual comfort and support? That is in line with Lord Walker's definition of a broken marriage as 'one where the facts and circumstances affecting the lives of the parties adversely to one another are such as to make it improbable that an ordinary husband and wife would ever resume cohabitation' (Morton Report, 1956). The evidence falling to be considered by the court would be all the relevant facts in the history of the marriage, including those acts and circumstances which the existing law treats as grounds for divorce in themselves. The court would then dissolve the marriage if, and only if, having regard to the interests of society as well as of those immediately affected by its decision, it judged it wrong to maintain the legal existence of a relationship that was beyond all probability of existing again in fact.

Immediately following the publication of *Putting Asunder*, the Lord Chancellor referred the matter to the Law Commission. Their report, entitled *Reform of the Grounds of Divorce – The Field of Choice*, was published only five months later. Their conclusions were summarised thus:

120.(1) The objectives of a good divorce law should include (*a*) the support of marriages which have a chance of survival, and (*b*) the decent burial with the minimum of embarrassment, humiliation and bitterness of those that are indubitably dead. ...

(2)   The provision of the present law whereby a divorce cannot normally be obtained within three years of the celebration of the marriage may help to achieve the first objective. ... But the principle of matrimonial offence on which the present law is based does not wholly achieve either objective. ...

(3)   Four of the major problems requiring solution are:
(*a*)   The need to encourage reconciliation. Something more might be achieved here; though little is to be expected from conciliation procedures after divorce proceedings have been instituted. ...
(*b*)   The prevalence of stable illicit unions. As the law stands, many of these cannot be regularised nor the children legitimated. ...

(c) Injustice to the economically weaker partner – normally the wife. ...

(d) The need adequately to protect the children of failed marriages. ...

(4) The field of choice for reform is circumscribed by a number of practical considerations and public attitudes, which cannot be ignored if acceptable and practicable reforms are to be undertaken. ...

(5) The proposals of the Archbishop's Group on Divorce made in *Putting Asunder*, though they are to be welcomed for their rejection of exclusive reliance on matrimonial offence, are procedurally impracticable. They propose that there should be but one comprehensive ground for divorce – breakdown of the marriage – the court being required to satisfy itself by means of a thorough inquest into the marriage that it has failed irretrievably. It would not be feasible, even if it were desirable, to undertake such an inquest in every divorce case because of the time this would take and the costs involved. ...

(6) However, the following alternative proposals, if any of them were thought desirable, would be practicable in the sense that they could be implemented without insuperable legal difficulty and without necessarily conflicting with the critical factors referred to in (4):

(a) *Breakdown without Inquest* – a modification of the breakdown principal [sic] advocated in *Putting Asunder*, but dispensing in most cases with the elaborate inquest there suggested. The court would, on proof of a period of separation and in the absence of evidence to the contrary, assume that the marriage had broken down. If however this were to be the sole comprehensive ground of divorce, it would not be feasible to make the period of separation much more than six months. If, as seems likely, so short a period is not acceptable, breakdown cannot become the sole ground, but might still be introduced as an additional ground on the lines of proposal (c) below.
...

(b) *Divorce by Consent* – This would be practicable only as an additional, and not a sole comprehensive, ground. It would not be more than a palliative and would probably be unacceptable except in the case of marriages in which there are no dependent children. Even in the case of childless marriages, if consent were the sole criterion, it might lead to the dissolution of marriages that had not broken down irretrievably.
...

(c) *The Separation Ground* – This would involve introducing as a ground for divorce a period of separation irrespective of which party was at fault, thereby affording a place in the law for the application of the breakdown principle. But since the period would be substantially longer than six months, it would be practicable only as an addition to the existing grounds based on matrimonial offence. The most comprehensive form of this proposal would provide for two different periods of separation. After the expiration of the shorter period (two years is suggested) either party, subject to safeguards, could obtain a divorce if the other consented, or, perhaps, did not object. After the expiration of the longer period (five or seven years) either party, subject to further safeguards, could obtain a divorce even if the other party objected. ...

(7) If any of these proposals were adopted, the following safeguards would appear to be necessary: –

(a) The three year waiting period should be retained. ...

(b) The court should have power to adjourn for a limited period to enable the possibilities of reconciliation to be explored. ...

(c) The court should have a discretion to refuse a decree if attempts had been made by the petitioner wilfully to deceive it; but the present absolute and discretionary bars would be inapplicable to petitions on these new grounds. ...

(d) Additional safeguards would be needed to protect the respondent spouse and the children. These should include: –

(i) A procedure to ensure that the respondent's decision to consent to or not oppose a divorce, had been taken freely and with a full appreciation of the consequences. ...

(ii) Retention, and possible improvement, of the provisions of the present law designed to ensure that satisfactory arrangements are made for the future of the children. ...

(iii) Provisions protecting an innocent party from being divorced against his or her will unless equitable financial arrangements are made for him or her. ...

(e) It is for consideration whether there should be a further discretionary bar based on protection of interests wider than those of the parties alone. If such a bar were introduced, it should be defined as precisely as possible so as to promote consistency in its exercise and to enable legal advisers to give firm advice to their clients. ...

Question

In the light of this summary, do you think that to title the Report *The Field of Choice* was 'inaccurate'?

The 'practical considerations and public attitudes' referred to in para. 120(4) above are of particular interest:

52. ...

(a) Public opinion would not accept any substantial increase in the difficulty of obtaining a divorce or of the time it takes, unless it could be shown that an appreciable number of marriages would be mended as a result.

(b) Experience shows that the chances of reconciliation between the parties have become almost negligible by the time that a petition for a divorce is filed.

(c) Whether a divorce is obtainable or not, husbands and wives in modern conditions will part if life becomes intolerable. The ease with which names can be changed under English law simplifies the establishment of a new and apparently regular 'marriage'; where the deception is not complete, the resulting children are the main sufferers because of the stigma that still attaches to the status of illegitimacy.

(d) Children are at least as vitally affected by their parents' divorce as are the parents themselves.

(e) Breakdown of a marriage usually precedes the matrimonial offence on which the divorce petition is based. Thus, an isolated act of adultery or isolated acts with different partners may be the grounds for divorce, but are likely to be the result of the breakdown of the marriage rather than its cause.

(f) Public opinion would be unlikely to support a proposal which had the effect of, say, doubling the amount spent on divorce proceedings; in so far as more Judges, more courts and more Legal Aid would impose a burden on public funds, it would be felt that the money could be better spent on other subjects, including, for example, marriage guidance and conciliation.

(g) Public opinion would be equally unlikely to support a great expansion of the Queen's Proctor's Office or the employment of additional public servants with the function of investigating the truth of the evidence given by parties to divorce proceedings. At the present time there is a shortage of trained welfare officers attached to the courts and no sudden addition to their numbers can be hoped for in the near future.

(h) Even where a marriage is childless, divorce granted automatically if the parties consent ('Post Office divorces') would not be acceptable; there must be an independent check if only to ensure that the economically weaker party really and freely consents to the divorce and to approve the financial arrangements worked out by the parties and their solicitors. The need for outside intervention is, of course, far greater where there are children.

Question

The Law Commission did not base these statements on any scientific opinion poll (although they were described as 'hard facts' in the Report) – how many of them would hold good today?

6.2 The present law: the Matrimonial Causes Act 1973

In this section we examine the current law under a number of headings:

The Divorce Reform Act 1969, by and large, translated the Law Commission's clear preferences into law. It came into force on 1 January 1971 and has since been consolidated with other relevant legislation in the Matrimonial Causes Act 1973, which remains the present law on divorce.

1. Divorce on breakdown of marriage

(1) Subject to section 3 below, a petition for divorce may be presented to the court by either party to a marriage on the ground that the marriage has broken down irretrievably.

(2) The court hearing a petition for divorce shall not hold the marriage to have broken down irretrievably unless the petitioner satisfies the court of one or more of the following facts, that is to say—

(a) that the respondent has committed adultery and the petitioner finds it intolerable to live with the respondent;

(b) that the respondent has behaved in such a way that the petitioner cannot reasonably be expected to live with the respondent;

(c) that the respondent has deserted the petitioner for a continuous period of at least two years immediately preceding the presentation of the petition;

(d) that the parties to the marriage have lived apart for a continuous period of at least two years immediately preceding the presentation of the petition (hereafter in this Act referred to as 'two years' separation') and the respondent consents to a decree being granted;

(e) that the parties to the marriage have lived apart for a continuous period of at least five years immediately preceding the presentation of the petition (hereafter in this Act referred to as 'five years' separation').

(3) On a petition for divorce it shall be the duty of the court to inquire, so far as it reasonably can, into the facts alleged by the petitioner and into any facts alleged by the respondent.

(4) If the court is satisfied on the evidence of any such fact as is mentioned in subsection (2) above, then, unless it is satisfied on all the evidence that the marriage has not broken down irretrievably, it shall, subject to sections 3(3) and 5 below, grant a decree of divorce.

(5) Every decree of divorce shall in the first instance be a decree nisi and shall not be made absolute before the expiration of six months from its grant unless the High Court by general order from time to time fixes a shorter period,[5] or unless in any particular case the court in which the proceedings are for the time being pending from time to time by special order fixes a shorter period than the period otherwise applicable for the time being by virtue of this subsection.

2. Supplemental provision as to facts raising presumption of breakdown

(1) One party to a marriage shall not be entitled to rely for the purposes of section 1(2)(a) above on adultery committed by the other if, after it became known to him that the other had committed that adultery, the parties have lived with each other for a period exceeding, or periods together exceeding, six months.

(2) Where the parties to a marriage have lived with each other after it became known to one party that the other had committed adultery, but subsection (1) above does not apply, in any proceedings for divorce in which the petitioner relies on that adultery the fact that the parties have lived with each other after that time shall be disregarded in determining for the purposes of section 1(2)(a) above whether the petitioner finds it intolerable to live with the respondent.

(3) Where in any proceedings for divorce the petitioner alleges that the respondent has behaved in such a way that the petitioner cannot reasonably be expected to live with him, but the parties to the marriage have lived with each other for a period or periods after the date of the occurrence of the final incident relied on by the petitioner and held by the court to support his allegation, that fact shall be disregarded in determining for the purposes of section 1(2)(b) above whether the petitioner cannot reasonably be expected to live with the respondent if the length of that period or of those periods together was six months or less.

(4) For the purposes of section 1(2)(c) above the court may treat a period of desertion as having continued at a time when the deserting party was incapable of continuing the necessary intention if the evidence before the court is such that, had that party not been so incapable, the court would have inferred that his desertion continued at that time.

(5) In considering for the purposes of section 1(2) above whether the period for which the respondent has deserted the petitioner or the period for which the parties to a marriage have lived apart has been continuous, no account shall be taken of any one period (not exceeding six months) or of any two or more periods (not exceeding six months in all) during which the parties resumed living with each other, but no period during which the parties lived with each other shall count as part of the period of desertion or of the period for which the parties to the marriage lived apart, as the case may be.

(6) For the purposes of section 1(2)(d) and (e) above and this section a husband and wife shall be treated as living apart unless they are living with each other in the same household, and references in this section to the parties to a marriage living with each other shall be construed as references to their living with each other in the same household.

---

5. The period is now fixed at six weeks.

(7)   Provision shall be made by rules of court for the purpose of ensuring that where in pursuance of section 1(2)(*d*) above the petitioner alleges that the respondent consents to a decree being granted the respondent has been given such information as will enable him to understand the consequences to him of his consenting to a decree being granted and the steps which he must take to indicate that he consents to the grant of a decree.

3.   Bar on petitions for divorce within one year of marriage

(1)   No petition for divorce shall be presented to the court before the expiration of the period of one year from the date of marriage.

(2)   Nothing in this section shall prohibit the presentation of a petition based on matters which occurred before the expiration of that period.

...

5.   Refusal of decree in five year separation cases on ground of grave hardship to respondent

(1)   The respondent to a petition for divorce in which the petitioner alleges five years' separation may oppose the grant of a decree on the ground that the dissolution of the marriage will result in grave financial or other hardship to him and that it would in all the circumstances be wrong to dissolve the marriage.

(2)   Where the grant of a decree is opposed by virtue of this section, then –

(*a*)   if the court finds that the petitioner is entitled to rely in support of his petition on the fact of five years' separation and makes no such finding as to any other fact mentioned in section 1(2) above, and

(*b*)   if apart from this section the court would grant a decree on the petition,

the court shall consider all the circumstances, including the conduct of the parties to the marriage and the interests of those parties and of any children or other persons concerned, and if of opinion that the dissolution of the marriage will result in grave financial or other hardship to the respondent and that it would in all the circumstances be wrong to dissolve the marriage it shall dismiss the petition.

So that we can see the English law in context, we reproduce Table 2 from Mary Anne Glendon in *Abortion and Divorce in Western Law* (1987). As Mary Ann Glendon explains, England was not alone:

Between 1969 and 1985 divorce law in nearly every Western country was profoundly altered. Among the most dramatic changes was the introduction of civil divorce in the predominantly Catholic countries of Italy and Spain, and its extension to Catholic marriages in Portugal. Other countries replaced or amended old, strict divorce laws. Most of these laws had been virtually unchanged since the grounds for ecclesiastical separation from bed and board became the basis for the secular institution of divorce. The chief common characteristics of all these changes were the recognition or expansion of nonfault grounds for divorce, and the acceptance or simplification of divorce by mutual consent. When California in 1969 became the first Western jurisdiction completely to eliminate fault grounds for divorce, the move was thought by some to prefigure the direction of reforms in other places. But it soon became clear that the purist approach was not to find wide acceptance. That same year England, too, passed a new divorce law which purported to make divorce available only when a marriage had irretrievably broken down. But since the English statute permitted marriage breakdown to be proved by evidence of traditional marital offences as well as by mutual consent or long separation, it did not really repudiate the old fault system. As it turned out, compromise statutes of the English type (resembling those already in place in Australia, Canada, and New Zealand) became the prevailing new approach to the grounds of divorce.

Glendon writes:

The changes in divorce law were themselves part of a more general process in which the legal posture of the state with respect to the family was undergoing its most fundamental shift since family law had begun to be secularized at the time of the Protestant Reformation. Beginning in the 1960s, movement in Western family law had been characterized, broadly speaking, and in varying degrees, by a withdrawal of much official regulation of marriage: its formation, its legal effects, and its termination. The removal of many legal obstacles to marriage; the effect of new attitudes of tolerance for diversity combined with older policies of nonintervention in the ongoing marriage; and the transformation of marriage itself from a legal relationship terminable

Table 2: Grounds for divorce in nineteen countries[a]

Mixed Fault and Non-fault Grounds			Non-fault Grounds Only	
Required waiting period of more than 1 year for contested unilateral non-fault divorce	Required waiting period of 1 year or less for contested unilateral non-fault divorce	Mutual consent required for non-fault divorce	Judicial discretion to deny contested unilateral divorce	No judicial discretion to deny divorce
Austria (1978)	Canada (1968–86)	U.S. (2 states)	Netherlands (1971)	Sweden (1973)
Belgium[b] (1974–82)	Switzerland[b] (1907)		West Germany (1976)	U.S. (18 states and D.C.)
Denmark (1969)	U.S. (22 states)			
England[b] (1969)				
Finland[c] (1929–48)				
France[b] (1975)				
Greece (1983)				
Iceland[b] (1921)				
Italy (1970–75)				
Luxembourg[b] (1975–78)				
Norway (1918)				
Portugal (1975–77)				
Spain (1981)				
U.S. (8 states)				

[a] This table classifies countries according to two criteria: the extent to which their divorce statutes have (1) abandoned the fault principle and (2) accepted the possibility of divorce by one spouse of a partner who opposes the divorce and has committed no marital 'fault.' The dates of the most recent major changes relating to the grounds of divorce are in parentheses. Countries vary, of course, in the extent to which these ideas are put into practice by the courts, the cost of implementing statutory rights, the opportunities offered for tactical delay, and so on. Ireland, which allows no divorce, is not included in table.

[b] In these systems of mixed grounds, the court has discretion to deny a divorce sought by one spouse against a non-consenting partner who has committed no 'fault' in the technical sense of the divorce laws.

[c] In 1986, the Finnish government introduced a bill to make marriage dissolution available on non-fault grounds only, with no discretion to deny divorce.

only for serious cause to one increasingly terminable at will, amounted to a dejuridification of marriage. This process of deregulation of the formation and dissolution of marriage, and of the relations of the spouses during marriage, was typically accompanied, however – again in varying degrees – by a continued, and sometimes intensified, state interest in the economic and child-related consequences of marriage dissolution.

Questions

(i)   Do you agree with Glendon's analysis of the fundamental shift, and if you do, do you welcome this process of 'deregulation' and 'dejuridification'?

(ii)   Does it surprise you to learn that the Divorce Act 1985 in Canada (still in force) provides for divorce after one year's separation, or for physical or mental cruelty, or for adultery?

(iii)   Does it surprise you to learn that the Scottish Law Commission concluded that adultery and behaviour should be retained as alternatives to the two separation 'facts'; these should be reduced to one year in the case of consent and two years where there is no consent (Report on *Reform of the Ground for Divorce* (1989))? (Divorce in Scotland is governed by the Divorce (Scotland) Act 1976, and the grounds for divorce are almost identical to those in the Matrimonial Causes Act 1973; the Scottish Law Commission's recommendations have not been implemented.)

To the international picture can now be added Ireland, where divorce became possible following an amendment to the Irish Constitution and the subsequent enactment of the Family Law (Divorce) Act 1996. The Act provides for divorce where the parties have 'lived apart' for a period amounting to four years of the preceding five and there is no 'reasonable prospect' of reconciliation. For a detailed account, see *The Law of Divorce in Ireland*, by Muriel Walls and David Bergin (1997).

6.2.1 The fault-based facts

At first sight, these provisions combine fault and no-fault 'grounds' for divorce in just the way so deplored by the Archbishop's group in *Putting Asunder*. In fact, as the following cases illustrate, the apparently fault-based 'grounds' are not always what they seem.

Cleary v Cleary
[1974] 1 All ER 498, [1974] 1 WLR 73, 117 Sol Jo 834, Court of Appeal

The wife left her husband and committed adultery. She then returned to her husband and they lived together for five or six weeks. She left again but did not repeat the adultery. She took proceedings unsuccessfully, in a magistrates' court, complaining of her husband's persistent cruelty and wilful neglect to maintain her. A few months later she petitioned for divorce on the basis of her husband's behaviour. The husband denied this and cross-prayed for divorce on the basis of her adultery. She withdrew her petition and the case proceeded undefended upon the husband's cross-prayer. The county court judge dismissed the suit and the husband appealed.

Lord Denning MR: ... [On the words of section 1(2)(*a*)] a point of law arises on which there is a difference of opinion between the judges. The question is whether the two facts required by section [1(2)(*a*)] are severable and independent, or whether they are interconnected. In other words, is it sufficient for the husband to prove (*a*) that the wife has committed adultery and (*b*) that he finds it intolerable to live with her? Or has he to prove that (*a*) the wife has committed adultery and (*b*) that *in consequence thereof* he finds it intolerable to live with her? Are the words 'in consequence thereof' to be read into section [1(2)(*a*)]?

On the one hand, in *Goodrich v Goodrich* [1971] 2 All ER 1340, [1971] 1 WLR 1142, Lloyd-Jones J quoted from *Rayden on Divorce*, 11th ed. (1971), p.175, where it was submitted that the two phrases are in the context independent of one another. The judge said: 'In my judgment that view is acceptable.' On the other hand, more recently in *Roper v Roper and Porter* [1972] 3 All ER 668, [1972] 1 WLR 1314, Faulks J took a different view. He said:

'I think that common sense tells you that where the finding that has got to be made is that the respondent has committed adultery, and the petitioner finds it intolerable to live with the respondent, it means, "*and in consequence* of the adultery the petitioner finds it intolerable to live with the respondent".'

So Faulks J would introduce the words 'in consequence thereof,' whereas Lloyd-Jones J would not. Which is the right view?

As a matter of interpretation, I think the two facts in section [1(2)(*a*)] are independent and should be so treated. Take this very case. The husband proves that the wife committed adultery and that he forgave her and took her back. That is one fact. He then proves that, after she comes back, she behaves in a way that makes it quite intolerable to live with her. She corresponds with the other man and goes out at night and finally leaves her husband, taking the children with her. That is another fact. It is in consequence of that second fact that he finds it intolerable – not in consequence of the previous adultery. On that evidence, it is quite plain that the marriage has broken down irretrievably. He complies with section [1(2)(*a*)] by proving (*a*) her adultery which was forgiven; and (*b*) her subsequent conduct (not adultery), which makes it intolerable to live with her.

I would say one word more. In *Rayden on Divorce*, 11th ed., p.175, it is suggested (referring to an extra-judicial lecture by Sir Jocelyn Simon [Riddell Lecture 1970, see *Rayden*, pp. 3227, 3234]): 'It may even be his own adultery which leads him to find it intolerable to live with the respondent.' I cannot accept that suggestion. Suppose a wife committed adultery five years ago. The husband forgives her and takes her back. He then falls in love with another woman and commits adultery with her. He may say that he finds it intolerable to live with his wife, but that is palpably untrue. It was quite tolerable for five years: and it is not rendered intolerable by his love for another woman. That illustration shows that a judge in such cases as these should not accept the man's bare assertion that he finds it intolerable. He should inquire what conduct on the part of the wife has made it intolerable. It may be her previous adultery. It may be something else. But whatever it is, the judge must be satisfied that the husband finds it intolerable to live with her.

On the facts of this case I think the judge could and should have found on the evidence the two elements required, (1) the adultery of the wife and (2) the husband found it intolerable to live with her. *Appeal allowed.*

Questions

(i) Husband and wife agree that they will live on the wife's earnings from prostitution; after some months of this the husband falls in love with a young virgin; he finds it intolerable to live with his wife; is he entitled to an immediate divorce?

(ii) The same husband leaves his wife to wait until he is free to marry his young virgin; is his wife entitled to an immediate divorce?

(iii) Do you find your answers to questions (i) and (ii) either (a) just, or (b) sensible?

(iv) If you are not happy with the answers to questions (i) and (ii), ought the result to be (a) that neither is entitled to an immediate divorce, or (b) that both are entitled to an immediate divorce?

(v) What difference, if any, would it have made to any of your answers if the husband's distaste for his wife had developed because she contracted the AIDS virus in the course of her prostitution?

(vi) But if 'adultery' and 'intolerability' need have nothing to do with one another, why is s. 2(2) expressed as it is?[6]

Livingstone-Stallard v Livingstone-Stallard
[1974] Fam 47, [1974] 2 All ER 766, [1974] 3 WLR 302, 118 Sol Jo 462, 4 Fam Law 150, High Court, Family Division

The husband and wife married in December 1969; they were then aged 56 and 24 respectively. Two months later, 'as the result of one of the few scenes of violence which took place during the marriage', the wife left. But in September 1970 they were reunited. The marriage ended for practical purposes in September 1972, when the wife left after the husband became enraged in the course of an argument. The wife petitioned on the basis of her husband's behaviour. Most of the incidents were 'trivial in themselves', and we quote only one of those described because of the significance attached to it by the judge. It took place shortly after the wedding and before the first parting.

Dunn J: ... The wife also complained about another incident which was, perhaps, the most illuminating incident so far as the husband's character was concerned. They had, naturally, had some photographs taken at their wedding, and not very long afterwards the photographer came round with the wedding album. The husband was out and the wife, exercising what one would imagine was normal courtesy and hospitality, offered the photographer a glass of sherry which he accepted and she had a glass of sherry too to keep him company. When the husband came home he went to his cocktail cabinet, took out the sherry bottle and said, 'You have drunk half a bottle of sherry. Don't you ever go to my cocktail cabinet again.' He asked her who she had been drinking with and she told him what had happened. He forbade her to 'give refreshment to trades people again.' He was naturally cross-examined about his attitude and it appeared to be that if his wife took a glass of sherry with a tradesman – and he apparently classed the photographer as a tradesman – then the glass of sherry might, as he put it, impair her faculties, so that the tradesman might make some kind of indecent approach to her; and that was the justification of his conduct on that occasion. To my mind, it is typical of the man. ...

I am quite satisfied that this marriage has broken down. The wife told me that in no circumstances would she continue to live with her husband, partly because he is so irresponsible with Jason [their son] and takes so little interest in him. I cannot, of course, dissolve this marriage unless I am satisfied that the husband has behaved in such a way that the wife cannot reasonably be expected to live with him. That question is, to my mind, a question of fact, and one approach to it is to suppose that the case is being tried by a judge and jury and to consider what the proper direction to the jury would be, and then to put oneself in the position of a properly directed jury in deciding the question of fact.

... I ask myself the question: Would any right-thinking person come to the conclusion that this husband has behaved in such a way that this wife cannot reasonably be expected to live with him, taking into account the whole of the circumstances and the characters and personalities of the parties? It is on that basis that I approach the evidence in this case.

The wife was young enough to be the husband's daughter and plainly considerable adjustment was required on both sides. Mr Reece submitted that she had known him a long time and that she knew exactly the kind of man that she was marrying; that the complaints which she made are trivial; and that she cannot bring herself within section 1(2)(*b*) simply because the character of her husband does not suit her. He further submitted that the reality of this case was that this young woman had simply got fed up and walked out, and walked out pretty soon too. I accept that the wife was a strong-minded young woman, but I am satisfied that she was anxious for the marriage to last and wished it to continue, that she wished to have children and bring them up and to have her own home, and that she did her best so far as she was able to adjust to her husband's character.

The husband was said, by Mr Reece, to be meticulous. I agree with Mr Beckman [for the wife] that more suitable adjectives would be self-opinionated, didactic and critical and I accept

---

6. A differently constituted Court of Appeal was troubled by this point in *Carr v Carr* [1974] 1 All ER 1193, [1974] 1 WLR 1534, but reluctantly accepted the *Cleary* interpretation of s. 1(2)(*a*).

that the husband's approach was to educate the wife to conform entirely to his standards. He, in my judgment, patronised her continually and submitted her, as I have found, to continual petty criticisms and his general attitude is well exemplified by the incident of the sherry and the photographer whom he called 'the tradesman.' I accept that many of the incidents were, or might appear to be, trivial in themselves and that there is a paucity of specific incidents between September 1970 and November 1972. But taking the facts as I have found them in the round in relation to the husband's character, in my judgment, they amount to a situation in which this young wife was subjected to a constant atmosphere of criticism, disapproval and boorish behaviour on the part of her husband. Applying the test which I have formulated, I think that any right-thinking person would come to the conclusion that this husband had behaved in such a way that this wife could not reasonably be expected to live with him. There will accordingly be a decree nisi under section 1(2)(b) of the Matrimonial Causes Act 1973.

Buffery v Buffery
[1988] FCR 465, [1988] 2 FLR 365, Court of Appeal

The parties were married in 1964. In December 1985 the wife petitioned for divorce under s. 1(2)(b) of the Matrimonial Causes Act 1973. The recorder considered that the conduct alleged against the husband had to be 'grave and weighty' and such that the wife could not reasonably be expected to continue to live with him. He concluded from the evidence that the cause of the breakdown of the marriage could not be blamed on the husband in the sense that he had been guilty of misbehaviour of a grave and weighty nature and that the breakdown could not be directed at either party since they had merely drifted apart. Accordingly, he held that the wife had failed to prove her case under s. 1(2)(b) and dismissed the petition. The wife appealed.

May LJ considered the meaning of s. 1(2)(b) and concluded that:

... on a proper reading of the statute and an assessment of the facts of a given case, the gravity or otherwise of the conduct complained of is of itself immaterial. What has to be asked ... is whether the behaviour is such that the petitioner cannot reasonably be expected to live with the respondent.

One considers a right-thinking person looking at the particular husband and wife and asks whether the one could reasonably be expected to live with the other taking into account all the circumstances of the case and the respective characters and personalities of the two parties concerned. ...

Looking at the facts in this case, May LJ went on:

The matters of which complaint is made in the original and supplemental particulars went, first, to the questions of finances between husband and wife and the way in which the husband had dealt with them and, secondly, to whether the husband ever took his wife out on social occasions, she contending that he did not. That failure on his part was at least part of the behaviour of which she complained, which led to the reasonable conclusion that she could not be expected to live with him.

In so far as going out together socially was concerned, the recorder made a more precise finding:

'I think the situation was this – the wife was not keen to go out when the children were growing up and they simply got to a stage when they did not go out socially except on rare occasions. By the time the children had grown up and they could have gone out socially, they were quite unable to communicate. In that respect, I do not think the blame is attached to one more than the other. As the wife put it on more than one occasion – we just do not communicate. We have nothing in common.'

Then, towards the end of his judgment, the recorder said:

'Although the [wife] has established that the marriage has irretrievably broken down, the cause of the breakdown cannot really be levelled at the [husband] in the sense that he has been guilty of misbehaviour of a grave and weighty nature. The [wife] has been quite candid about this; when asked she said the marriage has broken down; we cannot communicate;

we have nothing in common – and there lies, in my view, the crux of the matter. The situation is that neither is really at fault.'

Reading the judgment of the recorder in full, I conclude that in so far as any dissension over money matters was concerned, although the husband had been somewhat insensitive, nevertheless this did not constitute sufficient behaviour within the relevant statutory provision. In truth, what has happened in this marriage is the fault of neither party; they have just grown apart. They cannot communicate. They have nothing in common and there lies, as the recorder said, the crux of the matter.

It was submitted that if the matter went back to the recorder he could make various findings on the evidence about the sensitivity, for instance, of the wife in relation to these matters and various further findings of fact about the nature and extent of the husband's behaviour complained of. I, for my part, do not think he could. He heard all the relevant statutory and the conclusion to which he came was that nobody was really at fault here, except they both had grown apart. In those circumstances, in my judgment, clearly the wife failed to make out her case under s. 1(2)(b), although she satisfied the recorder that the marriage had broken down irretrievably. I do not think any advantage would be gained by sending this matter back for a retrial. The matter was fully investigated and the recorder made the findings to which I have referred. In those circumstances, I would reach the same conclusion as did the recorder, namely that the petition should be dismissed.

Appeal dismissed.

Questions

(i)   If Mr Livingstone-Stallard and Mr Buffery had petitioned for divorce based on s. 1(2)(b), what would have been the result?

(ii) The facts in *Pheasant v Pheasant* [1972] Fam 202, [1972] 1 All ER 587, to which Dunn J refers, were that a husband complained that the wife was unable to provide him with the 'spontaneous, demonstrative affection' which his character and personality demanded. This lack of affection made it impossible for him to live with his wife. The husband's petition was rejected by Ormrod J. If Mrs Pheasant had petitioned for divorce based on s. 1(2)(b) would she have obtained the same result as Mrs Livingstone-Stallard?

(iii) Desertion is leaving without consent or a good reason; the deserted party cannot petition for two years. Would a jury think it reasonable to expect her to live with a person who was no longer there to be lived with?

(iv) Should the test for 'unreasonable behaviour' be the same as the test for a good reason to leave?

Thurlow v Thurlow
[1976] Fam 32, [1975] 2 All ER 979, [1975] 3 WLR 161, 119 Sol Jo 406, 5 Fam Law 188, High Court, Family Division

The wife suffered from epilepsy and a severe physical neurological disorder. From June 1969, her mental and physical condition gradually deteriorated. Her husband made a 'genuine, sustained and considerable effort' to cope with her at home, but was forced to give up, and since July 1972 she had required full-time institutional care and would continue to do so for the rest of her life. In 1974, the husband petitioned on the basis of her behaviour.

Rees J: ... The husband's case therefore consists of allegations of both negative and of positive behaviour on the part of the wife. The negative behaviour alleged and proved is that between the middle of 1969 and 1 July 1972, she gradually became a bedridden invalid unable to perform the role of a wife in any respect whatsoever until she reached a state in which she became unfitted even to reside in an ordinary household at all and required to be removed to a hospital and there reside for the rest of her life. The positive behaviour alleged and proved is that during the same period she displayed bad temper and threw objects at her mother-in-law and caused damage by burning various household items such as towels, cushions and blankets. From time to time she escaped from the home and wandered about the streets causing alarm and stress to those trying to care for her.

I am satisfied that by July 1972 the marriage had irretrievably broken down and since the wife, tragically, is to spend the rest of her life as a patient in a hospital the husband cannot be expected to live with her. But the question remains as to whether the wife's behaviour has been such as to justify a finding by the court that it is unreasonable to expect him to do so. ...

Questions of interpretation of the words in section 1(2)(b) of the Act of 1973 which arise from the facts in the instant case include the following: Does behaviour which is wholly or mainly negative in character fall within the ambit of the statute? Is behaviour which stems from mental illness and which may be involuntary, capable of constituting relevant behaviour?

I consider these questions separately. As to the distinction which has been made between 'positive' and 'negative' behaviour I can find nothing in the statute to suggest that either form is excluded. The sole test prescribed as to the nature of the behaviour is that it must be such as to justify a finding that the petitioner cannot reasonably be expected to live with the respondent. It may well be that in practice such a finding will more readily be made in cases where the behaviour relied upon is positive than those wherein it is negative. Spouses may often, but not always, be expected to tolerate more in the way of prolonged silences and total inactivity than of violent language or violent activity. I find myself in respectful agreement with the views expressed by Davies LJ in the Court of Appeal in *Gollins v Gollins* [1964] P 32 at 58:

> '... I do not find the contrast between "positive" conduct and "negative" conduct either readily comprehensible or helpful, although these expressions are undoubtedly to be found in the decided cases. Almost any sort of conduct can at one and the same time be described both as positive and as negative. An omission in most cases is at the same time a commission.'...

I now turn to the question as to whether behaviour which stems from mental illness and which may be involuntary is capable of falling within the statute. ...

... I propose to follow the principle stated by Lord Reid in *Williams v Williams* [1964] AC 698 at 723 and cited by Sir George Baker P in *Katz v Katz* [1972] 3 All ER 219 at 224:

> 'In my judgment, decree should be pronounced against such an abnormal person ... simply because the facts are such that, after making all allowances for his disabilities and for the temperaments of both parties, it must be held that the character and gravity of his acts were such as to amount to cruelty.'

Sir George Baker P usefully suggested that this statement of principle may be adapted to meet the present law by substituting for the final words: '... the character and gravity of his behaviour was such that the petitioner cannot reasonably be expected to live with him.'

Accordingly the facts of each case must be considered and a decision made, having regard to all the circumstances, as to whether the particular petitioner can or cannot reasonably be expected to live with the particular respondent. If the behaviour stems from misfortune such as the onset of mental illness or from disease of the body, or from accidental physical injury, the court will take full account of all the obligations of the married state. These will include the normal duty to accept and to share the burdens imposed upon the family as a result of the mental or physical ill-health of one member. It will also consider the capacity of the petitioner to withstand the stresses imposed by the behaviour, the steps taken to cope with it, the length of time during which the petitioner has been called upon to bear it and the actual or potential effect upon his or her health. The court will then be required to make a judgment as to whether the petitioner can fairly be required to live with the respondent. The granting of the decree to the petitioner does not necessarily involve any blameworthiness on the part of the respondent, and, no doubt, in cases of misfortune the judge will make this clear in his judgment.

In the course of his most helpful submissions on behalf of the wife Mr Holroyd Pearce drew attention to some difficulties which he urged would arise if the law were such as to enable a decree to be granted in the instant case. It would mean, he said, that any spouse who was afflicted by a mental or physical illness or an accident so as to become a 'human vegetable' could be divorced under section 1(2)(b) of the Matrimonial Causes Act 1973. This was repugnant to the sense of justice of most people because it involved an implication of blameworthiness where none in truth existed and it was not what Parliament intended. The remedy was open to the petitioner in such cases to seek a decree of divorce on the ground of five years' separation under section 1(2)(e) of the Act of 1973 and if this were done no blame would be imputed to the respondent and also the special protection for the interests of the respondents provided by sections 5 and 10 of the Act of 1973 would be available whereas it would not if a decree were granted under section 1(2)(b). He cited two extreme examples to illustrate the point. One was the case of a spouse who was suddenly reduced to the state of a human vegetable as a result of a road traffic accident and was immediately removed to a hospital and there remained for life. The other was one in which supervening permanent impotency brought marital relations to an end.

There is no completely satisfactory answer to these submissions but what may properly be said is that the law as laid down in *Williams v Williams* [1964] AC 698, [1963] 2 All ER 994 does provide a remedy by divorce for a spouse who is the victim of the violence of an insane respondent spouse not responsible in law or fact for his or her actions and in no respect blameworthy. The basis for that decision is the need to afford protection to the petitioner against injury. So also in the insanity cases where the behaviour alleged is wholly negative and no violence in deed or word is involved but where continuing cohabitation has caused, or is likely to cause injury to health, it should be open to the court to provide a remedy by divorce. Before deciding to grant a divorce in such cases the court would require to be satisfied that the petitioner could not reasonably be expected to live with the respondent and would not be likely to do so in the case referred to by Mr Holroyd Pearce unless driven to it by grave considerations which would include actual or apprehended injury to the health of the petitioner or of the family as a whole. It is now common knowledge that health may be gravely affected by certain kinds of negative behaviour whether voluntary or not and if the granting of a decree under section 1(2)(*b*) is justified in order to protect the health of petitioners injured by violence so it should be in cases where the petitioner's health is adversely affected by negative behaviour. The safeguard provided for the interests of respondents is that it is the judge and not the petitioner who must decide whether the petitioner can reasonably be expected to live with the respondent; and that decision is subject to review upon appeal.

I do not propose to state any concluded view upon the case postulated in which a spouse is reduced to a human vegetable as the result of a road traffic accident and is removed at once to hospital to remain there for life ...

In reaching the decision the judge will have regard to all the circumstances including the disabilities and temperaments of both parties, the causes of the behaviour and whether the causes were or were not known to the petitioner, the presence or absence of intention, the impact of it upon the petitioner and the family unit, its duration, and the prospects of cure or improvement in the future. If the judge decided that it would be unreasonable to expect the petitioner to live with the respondent then he must grant a decree of divorce unless he is satisfied that the marriage has not irretrievably broken down.

Approaching the facts in the instant case upon the basis of these conclusions I feel bound to decide that a decree nisi of divorce should be granted. This husband has conscientiously and courageously suffered the behaviour of the wife for substantial periods of time between 1969 and July 1972 until his powers of endurance were exhausted and his health was endangered. This behaviour stemmed from mental illness and disease and no blame of any kind can be nor is attributed to the wife.

Questions

(i)   Is it possible for anyone nowadays to define the 'obligations of the married state'? How can a judge guess what a jury of 'right-thinking' people would think they were?

(ii)   The Family Law Sub-Committee of the Law Society, in *A Better Way Out* (1979), stated that, in undefended cases, 'the evidence presents little difficulty – after several years of marriage, virtually any spouse can assemble a list of events which, taken out of context, can be presented as unreasonable behaviour [sic] sufficient on which to found a divorce petition'. Does this surprise you?

(iii) If you were drafting a petition based upon the other's behaviour, would you be inclined to make it look as bad as possible (lest the court be tempted to probe more deeply) or as little as you think you can get away with (lest the respondent be goaded into defending either the petition itself or ancillary issues)?

(iv) How little do you think you can get away with?

A selection of newspaper cuttings on defended divorce petitions during the period 1984-1991 reveals successful petitions brought against the following:

(i)   a handyman husband who started many jobs in the house and garden, but seldom finished them. He was moody, aggressive and difficult (2 November 1984);

(ii)   a husband who deliberately annoyed his wife by hiding her underwear; if she did or said something he did not like he would become moody and not speak to her for days (17 April 1986);

(iii)   a husband who sat in the matrimonial home all day in his pyjamas shouting his opinions at anyone prepared to listen and even those not prepared to (1 March 1985);

(iv)   a wife who often forced her husband to sleep in the car and did not allow him to use the downstairs bathroom (14 February 1986);

(v)   a husband who was something of 'a martinet' and put his children on parade before him from time to time (17 June 1985);

(vi)   a wife who went to Athens where her husband was a diplomat, and attacked his mistress in a public cinema. Earlier, when they were stationed in Istanbul, where she was unhappy with the sewerage system, she had threatened to pour a pail of sewage over the Consul General's dining-room table if something was not done (25 March 1987);

And unsuccessful petitions against the following:

(vii)   an undemonstrative husband (16 April 1986);

(viii) a man of 'outstanding forbearance' who had shown 'patience and sympathy' for a wife who was 'cold, utterly self-centred and somewhat neurotic' (24 January 1985);

(ix)   a man who was alleged to be 'of dominant mind and character', especially in financial matters (18 January 1990).

The following feature in *The Times*, 19 February 1996, gives some more recent examples of particulars of 'unreasonable behaviour':

So what's unreasonable behaviour?

1. Allegation made by the petitioner – the husband – that his full-time working wife would only ever cook him 'microwave suppers' and not the 'real meals' his mother used to cook.

2. The allegation made by the petitioner – the wife – that her husband was an incompetent do-it-yourself fanatic who spent all his spare time constructing things around the house that would later fall down or – on one occasion – had caused actual structural damage to their home.

3. The wife who petitioned the husband on the ground that he would not speak to her for a year because he had been advised by a medium that he should not do so.

4. The wife who petitioned that her husband would count all the plants in the garden in an obsessive manner each night, making notes about how many blooms there were on each rose bush.

5. The wife who petitioned that her husband was obese and physically repugnant to her. On receiving the petition he was so upset that he lost four stone and they eventually became reconciled.

6. The husband who petitioned that his partner, a housewife, would spend all her evenings talking on the telephone to her friends, recalling every dull detail of her day.

7. The husband who alleged that his wife had claimed that she could not make love to him because she believed he was a reincarnated god and she should remain chaste.

8. The woman who petitioned that her husband would not give up control of the television zapper and would compulsively switch channels when she wanted to watch something. She could cope with this until he installed cable TV. With 24 channels to zap through, she finally left him.

9. The woman who claimed that her husband's problem with flatulence made it necessary for her to move into the spare room and eventually out of the marriage.

10.   The man who alleged that his wife was so concerned about being seen without makeup that she never took it off, even at night, and the sight of her clogged face was repugnant to him.

Questions

(i)   Was there really any point defending the petitions in the first six cases on p. 231, above?

(ii) Would you have advised the respondents in cases (vii) to (ix) to defend? What would have happened if they had been undefended?

(iii) Look back now to *Buffery* (p. 227, above). Do you think that, if the facts of that case were to recur today, the petition would be defended? In any event, do you think the petitioner would obtain a divorce?

(iv) Is 'adultery' or 'unreasonable behaviour' the more acceptable basis for a marriage to be terminated against (a) a male respondent, and (b) a female respondent?

6.2.2   The 'no-fault' facts

Santos v Santos

[1972] Fam 247, [1972] 2 All ER 246, [1972] 2 WLR 889, 116 Sol Jo 196, Court of Appeal

This was a wife's undefended petition on the basis of two years' separation and her husband's consent. The judge dismissed the petition because on three occasions since the separation the wife had stayed with her husband for a short while. These did not amount to more than six months and they had been apart for the requisite total of two years in all, but the judge's attention was not drawn to what is now s. 2(5) of the Matrimonial Causes Act 1973. The wife appealed and the Court of Appeal took the opportunity to consider a totally new point as to the meaning of 'living apart'. The judgment was that of the whole court.

Sachs LJ: ... The appeal first came before the court, differently constituted, on November 11, 1971. Then, after having heard the submissions of Mr Picard for the wife, it became apparent that it raised a very important issue as to the meaning of the words 'living apart' in section [1(2)(*d*)]. Does this relate simply and solely to physically not living under the same roof, or does it import an additional element which has been referred to in various terms – 'absence of consortium,' 'termination of consortium', or an 'attitude of mind' – phrases intended to convey either the fact or realisation of the fact that there is absent something which is fundamental to the state of marriage.

In the course of the argument before us reference was frequently made to the position of diplomats en poste in insalubrious foreign capitals, to those serving sentences in prison, to those in mental and other hospitals, and to prisoners of war – in the main, involuntary separations. None the less there are larger and no less important categories of separations which start voluntarily, such as business postings, voyages of exploration or recuperation trips when one party has been ill – all of which must also be looked at when endeavouring to determine what the legislature intended by the words 'living apart'.

Their Lordships then reviewed the Commonwealth authorities on comparable divorce legislation and the English authorities on similar expressions in English tax and criminal legislation:

The cogent volume of authority, to which we have been referred, makes it abundantly clear that the phrase 'living apart' when used in a statute concerned with matrimonial affairs normally imports something more than mere physical separation. This is something which obviously must be assumed to have been known to the legislature in 1969. It follows that its normal meaning must be attributed to it in the Act of 1969, unless one is led to a different conclusion either by the general scheme of the statute coupled with difficulties which would result from such an interpretation, or alternatively by some specific provision in that statute. ...

Obviously this element is not one which necessarily involves mutual consent, for otherwise the new Act would not afford relief under head (*e*) in that area where it was most plainly intended to be available – where the 'innocent' party adheres to the marriage, refusing to recognise that in truth it has ended, often despite the fact that the 'guilty' one has been living with someone else for very many years. So it must be an element capable of being unilateral: and it must, in our judgment, involve at least a recognition that the marriage is in truth at an end – and has become a shell, to adopt a much-used metaphor.

If the element can be unilateral in the sense of depending on the attitude of mind of one spouse, must it be communicated to the other spouse before it becomes in law operative? That is a question that gave particular concern in the course of the argument. There is something unattractive in the idea that in effect time under head (*e*) can begin to run against a spouse without his or her knowledge. Examples discussed included men in prison, in hospital, or away on service whose wives, so far as they knew, were standing by them: they might, perhaps, thus be led to fail to take some step which they would later feel could just have saved the marriage. On the other hand, communication might well be impossible in cases where the physical separation was due to a breakdown in mental health on the part of the other spouse, or a prolonged coma such as can occasionally occur. Moreover, need for communication would tend to equate heads (*d*) and (*e*) with desertion – which comes under head (*c*) – something unlikely to be intended by the legislature. Moreover, bowing to the inevitable is not the same thing as intending it to happen.

In the end we have firmly concluded that communication by word or conduct is not a necessary ingredient of the additional element.

On the basis that an uncommunicated unilateral ending of recognition that a marriage is subsisting can mark the moment when 'living apart' commences, 'the principal problem becomes one of proof of the time when the breakdown occurred'. ... Sometimes there will be evidence such as a letter, reduction or cessation of visits, or starting to live with another man. But cases may well arise where there is only the oral evidence of the wife on this point. One can only say that cases under heads (*d*) and (*e*) may often need careful examination by the first instance judge and that special caution may need to be taken. ...

... Therefore 'living apart' referred to in grounds (*d*) and (*e*) is a state of affairs to establish which it is in the vast generality of cases arising under those heads necessary to prove something more than that the husband and wife are physically separated. For the purposes of that vast generality, it is sufficient to say that the relevant state of affairs does not exist whilst both parties recognise the marriage as subsisting. ...

The case was therefore sent back for trial before a High Court judge.

Questions

(i) From the point of view of the innocent and loyal wife of the long-sentence prisoner, why is it 'absurd and unjust' if he makes up his mind to divorce her just before he is released, but apparently not if he makes up his mind five years earlier and tells her nothing about it?

(ii) Is the real reason not that this is absurd and unjust to her, but that such a recent decision is not conclusive evidence that the breakdown is irretrievable?

(iii) Suppose a couple whose marriage is going through a bad patch have a trial separation but keep returning to one another for brief periods until they finally decide that it is all over: is that decision any less likely to be 'irretrievable' than that of a couple whose initial separation was 'for good' but who kept changing their minds? (The logic of *Santos* coupled with s. 2(5) would appear to be that the second couple get their divorce whereas the first couple do not.)

However, the notion that 'living with each other in the same household' is as much an abstraction as a physical reality can be very helpful to those couples who are still under the same roof:

Fuller (otherwise Penfold) v Fuller

[1973] 2 All ER 650, [1973] 1 WLR 730, 117 Sol Jo 224, Court of Appeal

Husband and wife separated in 1964, when the wife left the matrimonial home, taking their two daughters, and went to live with a Mr Penfold in the latter's home. She took the name of Mrs Penfold and they lived together as husband and wife. Four years later, Mr Fuller had a coronary thrombosis and was no longer able to live alone. He therefore 'went and became a lodger in the house' where his wife lived with Mr Penfold. The wife gave him food and he ate with others in the house. The wife also did the washing. He paid a weekly sum for board and lodging. After four years of this, the wife petitioned for divorce on the basis of five years' separation and the husband did not defend. The judge refused the decree and the wife appealed.

Lord Denning MR: ... At the hearing the judge held that he had no jurisdiction to grant a divorce because he thought that when the husband came back to the house, he and his wife were not living apart. The judge referred to the cases under the old law, such as *Hopes v Hopes* [1949] P 227, [1948] 2 All ER 920; and also the cases under the new Act: *Mouncer v Mouncer* [1972] 1 All ER 289, [1972] 1 WLR 321 and *Santos v Santos* [1972] 2 All ER 246.

In *Santos v Santos* this court stressed the need, under the new Act, to consider the state of mind of the parties and, in particular, whether they treated the marriage as subsisting or not. Clearly they treated it in this case as at an end.

... In this case the wife was living with Mr Penfold as his wife. The husband was living in the house as a lodger. It is impossible to say that husband and wife were or are living with each other in the same household. It is very different from *Mouncer v Mouncer* where the husband and wife were living with the children in the same household – as husband and wife normally do – but were not having sexual intercourse together. That is not sufficient to constitute 'living apart'. I do not doubt the correctness of that decision. But the present case is very different. I think the judge put too narrow and limited a construction on the Act. I would allow the appeal and pronounce the decree nisi of divorce.

Stamp LJ: I agree. I can only say that to my mind the words 'living with each other in the same household' in the context of the Act relating to matrimonial proceedings are not apt to describe the situation where the wife is indisputably living with another man in the same household and her husband is there as a paying guest in the circumstances Lord Denning MR has described. 'Living with each other' connotes to my mind something more than living in the same household: indeed the words 'with each other' would otherwise be redundant.
Appeal allowed.

Questions

(i)   Until this case, we had all thought that the operative concept was that of a common 'household' – were they sharing such things as meals and television, and was the wife still doing some things for her husband, even if they were not sharing a bed? – but does it now seem that the operative words are 'with each other'? Does that make the words 'in the same household' redundant?

(ii) If that be so, why should not withdrawal to a separate bedroom, together with the state of mind envisaged in *Santos v Santos* [1972] Fam 247, [1972] 2 All ER 246, be sufficient?

(iii) Why do the judges apparently think that it is more important when a wife stops cooking and washing for her husband than when she refuses to share a bed with him?

(iv) Suppose a woman comes to you and explains that she and her husband have had little to do with one another for some time and would now like a divorce, although for convenience they are still living under the same roof: will you explain the law carefully to her before you seek further and better particulars of their circumstances?

(v) What questions would you then ask?

(vi) How do you think all this accords with the concern felt by the Archbishop of Canterbury's group for 'considerations of truth, the sacredness of oaths and the integrity of professional practice'?

We turn now to the s. 5 defence:

Le Marchant v Le Marchant
[1977] 3 All ER 610, [1977] 1 WLR 559, 121 Sol Jo 334, Court of Appeal

The husband was a post office employee and about to retire. He petitioned for divorce on the basis of five years' separation. The wife alleged that the possible loss of an index-linked widow's pension would cause her grave financial hardship. The judge granted a decree and the wife appealed.

Ormrod LJ: ... It would be quite wrong to approach this kind of case on the footing that the wife is entitled to be compensated pound for pound for what she will lose in consequence of the divorce. She has to show, not that she will lose something by being divorced, but that she will suffer grave financial hardship, which is quite another matter altogether. It is quite plain that, prima facie, the loss of the pension, which is an index-linked pension, in the order of £1,300 a year at the moment, is quite obviously grave financial hardship in the circumstances of a case like this unless it can be in some way mitigated. The learned judge, however, did not approach the case in this way. He said that s. 5 had to be read with s. 10 of the 1973 Act. Section 10 is the section which provides, in sub-s (3), that before a decree nisi is made absolute in cases such as the present, the court is required at the request of the wife to investigate the financial position and not to make the decree absolute until it is satisfied either that the petitioning husband should not be required to make any financial provision for the wife or that the financial provision made by him is reasonable and fair or (and these are the words which cause the trouble) is 'the best that can be made in the circumstances'. So, as counsel for the wife says, s. 10 offers an elusive or, perhaps better, an unreliable protection to a wife placed in the position in which this wife is placed. The marriage would have been dissolved by the decree nisi, there would have been therefore a finding of fact that she has not suffered grave financial hardship in consequence of the decree and she would then have to do the best she could under s. 10.

It is also right to point out that there are many cases, and this is one, in which the powers of the court, extensive as they are under ss. 23 and 24 as well as s. 10, are not wide enough to enable the court to carry out by order various things which a petitioner husband can do voluntarily, even if compelled to do it voluntarily, so s. 10 is not an adequate substitute. The learned judge, in a sentence, took the view that if he could see from the husband's financial position that he would be able one way or the other to alleviate sufficiently the financial hardship falling on the wife as a result of the loss of her pension, that was good enough. In the view of this court, that is not right. The right way to approach this problem is Cumming-Bruce J's approach in *Parker v Parker* [1972] Fam 116, [1972] 1 All ER 410, that is that the answer should set up a prima facie case of financial hardship, that the petition should be dismissed unless the petitioner can meet that answer in his reply by putting forward a proposal which is acceptable to the court as reasonable in all the circumstances and which is sufficient to remove the element of grave financial hardship which otherwise would lead to the dismissal of the petition. ...

Now, at the last minute, and this is really one minute to midnight, counsel for the husband has at least made an offer. The offer is this. His client offers to transfer the matrimonial home or his interest in the matrimonial home to the wife forthwith. Secondly, he offers to pay her £5,000 when he receives the capital sum under his pension scheme (his position has clearly improved since the figures in the document P1 were worked out) and in addition to that he proposes to take out a life insurance policy on his own life to provide on his death the sum of £5,000 which will be payable to the wife if she survives him and which she can then use as she thinks fit. That offer is without prejudice to any order for periodical payment which may be made hereafter by a registrar when the respective income positions have been investigated. ...

The view which I have formed is that the present offer is a reasonable one in the sense that it will, if implemented, remove the element of grave financial hardship so far as the wife is concerned, and remove therefore the defence which she has to the present petition. ...

I need only say that the decree absolute will not be made in this case until the matrimonial home has been transferred and the insurance policy has been taken out, and the lump sum paid over, to the satisfaction of the wife's advisers. In those circumstances, and in those circumstances only, would I be in favour of allowing a decree nisi to stand.

In *Reiterbund v Reiterbund* [1974] 2 All ER 455, [1974] 1 WLR 788, Finer J held that the possible loss of a state widow's pension to a woman of 52 who would have to rely, as she was then relying, on supplementary benefit was *not* a grave financial hardship.

The grave hardship does not, of course, have to be financial.

Rukat v Rukat
[1975] Fam 63, [1975] 1 All ER 343, [1975] 2 WLR 201, 119 Sol Jo 30, 4 Fam Law 81, Court of Appeal

The husband, a Pole, and the wife, a Sicilian, married in 1946. Both were Roman Catholics. They had not lived together since 1947, when the wife had visited Sicily with their daughter and the husband had written telling her not to return as he had fallen in love with another woman. Since then the wife had kept up the pretence that the marriage was still subsisting. In 1972, the husband petitioned for divorce on the basis of five years' separation. The wife alleged that this would cause her hardship on the grounds that: (i) the prospect of divorce was an anathema to her on religious and moral grounds because she was a Roman Catholic; (ii) because of the social structure of the area where she lived, divorce would cause serious repercussions for her and her child; and (iii) if a decree were pronounced she would not be accepted in her community in Sicily and would not be able to return to her home. The judge granted a decree and the wife appealed.

Lawton LJ: ... One has to start, I think, by looking at the context in which the phrase 'grave financial or other hardship' occurs. The word 'hardship' is not a word of art. It follows that it must be construed by the courts in a common sense way, and the meaning which is put on the word 'hardship' should be such as would meet with the approval of ordinary sensible people. In my judgment, the ordinary sensible man would take the view that there are two aspects of 'hardship' – that which the sufferer from the hardship thinks he is suffering and that which a reasonable bystander with knowledge of all the facts would think he was suffering. That can be illustrated by a homely example. The rich gourmet who because of financial stringency has to drink vin ordinaire with his grouse may well think that he is suffering a hardship; but sensible people would say he was not.

If that approach is applied to this case, one gets this situation. The wife undoubtedly feels that she has suffered a hardship; and the learned judge, in the passages to which Megaw LJ has referred, found that she was feeling at the time of the judgment that she could not go back to Sicily. That, if it was genuine and deeply felt, would undoubtedly be a 'hardship' in one sense of that word. But one has to ask oneself the question whether sensible people, knowing all the facts, would think it was a hardship. On the evidence, I have come to the conclusion that they would not, and for this reason. The wife has been separated from her husband now since 1947. She returned in that year to Sicily. She has been living in Palermo with her mother and father. Her relatives have been around her; they must have appreciated that something had gone wrong with the marriage. I make all allowances for the undoubted fact that many male Sicilians leave their country to work elsewhere, and wives may be left alone for months and years on end. Nevertheless, 26 years is a very long time; and such evidence as there was before the learned judge was to the effect that it was almost inevitable that her family and those who knew her would have appreciated that there was something wrong. There would be some social stigma attached to that; she might be thought to have failed as a wife. But she has lived that down; and the fact that there had been a divorce in some foreign country would add very little to the stigma. ...

Ormrod LJ: ... The court has first to decide whether there was evidence on which it could properly come to the conclusion that the wife was suffering from grave financial or other

hardship; and 'other hardship' in this context, in my judgment, agreeing with Megaw and Lawton LJ, must mean other *grave* hardship. If hardship is found, the court then has to look at the second limb and decide whether, in all the circumstances, looking at everybody's interests, balancing the respondent's hardship against the petitioner's interests in getting his or her freedom, it would be wrong to dissolve the marriage. ...
Appeal dismissed.

In *Balraj v Balraj* (1980) 11 Fam Law 110, Court of Appeal, another case where the wife's defence was based upon hardship arising from cultural and religious factors, the judge dismissed the defence. The wife appealed, and counsel for the wife submitted that the judge should have applied a subjective rather than an objective test. The Court of Appeal rejected this submission:

Cumming-Bruce LJ: ... in my view the President was right in taking the view that, having made that appraisal of the respondent's own expectation about her suffering, he must stand back and then look at all the circumstances and form an objective view as to whether the prospective situation for the lady would constitute grave hardship or not.
Appeal dismissed.

Questions

(i)   Can you describe a case, other than one such as *Le Marchant v Le Marchant* [1977] 3 All ER 610, [1977] 1 WLR 559 (see p. 235), in which a divorce would cause grave hardship to the respondent *and* it would be wrong to dissolve the marriage? (See *Johnson v Johnson* (1981) 12 Fam Law 116.)
(ii) Is it necessary for the 'grave hardship' to be caused by the divorce rather than by the breakdown of the marital relationship?
(iii) If it is necessary, why should this be?
(iv) What advice would you give to Mrs Balraj and Mrs Rukat? (Read MCA 1973, s.10(2)(3).)

6.2.3 The procedure under the 1973 Act

One feature which has militated against attempts to restrict divorce is the impossibility of forcing respondents to defend. By 1966, 93% of divorces were undefended, and the position now is that less than 1,000 cases a year are likely to result in a defended divorce hearing. (In 1989, only 285 defended divorces proceeded to a hearing.) A so-called 'special procedure' was invented for the very simplest of cases and extended to all undefended divorces in 1977. The 'special procedure' is described in Appendix C to the Law Commission's Report, *The Ground for Divorce* (1990):

26.   ... This requires the [district judge] to scrutinise the petition, supporting affidavit and any other evidence, in order to satisfy himself that the contents of the petition have been proved and that the petitioner is entitled to a decree. Thus the documents are checked both for their procedural regularity and for their sufficiency in substance to prove the petitioner's case. If they are found to be lacking in some way, the [district judge] may request further information or evidence. If the [district judge] is satisfied, he will issue a certificate that the petitioner is entitled to a decree and the judge will pronounce it formally in open court. If the [district judge] is not satisfied, he will remove the case from the special procedure list and require that it be heard before the judge.

Appendix C to the Report is a summary of a *Court Record Study* carried out by the Law Commission. One of the major aims of the study was to discover more about the circumstances in which district judges refused their certificates. This is what they reported:

31.   Procedural or administrative problems fell into the following broad categories: inaccuracies on the face of the documents, ... documents, for example the marriage certificate, not filed or the wrong document, for example an acknowledgement of service relating to the wrong fact, filed; disagreement or problems over costs; problems with service; and respondents under a disability for whom a guardian ad litem might have to be appointed ...

32.   Substantive problems arose where the [district judge] had questioned the method or sufficiency of proof of the fact asserted in the petition and whether the petitioner was entitled to a decree. These fell into the following broad categories: insufficient evidence of adultery ...; failure to name the person with whom the adultery was alleged to have been committed[7] ... and parties still living at the same address. ...

And in behaviour cases:

44.   It might have been thought that assessing behaviour cases would also cause some problems. [district judges] might have been unpersuaded, either that the behaviour complained of had in fact taken place or had the effect alleged, or that however accurately described it was such that it was unreasonable to expect the petitioner to live with the respondent. The files examined did not reveal evidence of this, apart from the problems arising where the couple were still living at the same address. The behaviour itself was generally proved by the assertions made in the petition and subsequently confirmed in the petitioner's affidavit.

The study concludes:

51.   It is certainly difficult to conclude from the files which we studied that the intervention of the courts, considerable though this may be, has a noticeable impact upon the outcome of cases. Of the cases which failed to proceed, far more did so because of the decisions of the parties themselves than because of the problems of proving the ground. Of the cases where there had been such problems, the great majority eventually reached a decree.

John Haskey in 'Divorce Statistics' (1996) presents the statistics for the duration of divorce proceedings in 1994, in the following table:

Table 2: Median interval of time, in months, between petition and decree absolute, 1994, England and Wales

						Months
Type of divorcing couple	Fact proven					
	Adultery	Unreasonable behaviour	Desertion	2 years' separation (with consent)	5 years' separation	Total
Decrees granted to wives with children aged						
under 16	7.1	7.6	9.3	6.4	7.7	7.3
all couples	6.8	7.3	8.3	5.9	6.6	6.8
Decrees granted to husbands with children aged						
under 16	6.8	7.7	7.3	6.2	7.5	6.9
all couples	6.3	7.0	6.8	5.7	6.7	6.3

Note: Calculated for single fact divorces granted to a single party. Intervals calculated using full dates of petition and decree absolute.

7. It is no longer necessary to do this: Family Proceedings Rules 1991, r. 2.7(1).

Questions

(i) Do you think the introduction and the extension of the 'special procedure' is a more radical departure than the introduction of irretrievable breakdown as the sole ground of divorce?

(ii) Is it necessary or desirable that the termination of the marriage be obtained in a formal or judicial manner?

(iii) In some circumstances, we recognise divorces obtained abroad by judicial or other proceedings and even, on occasions, in cases where the divorce is not accompanied by 'other proceedings' (Family Law Act 1986, s. 46(2)(*b*)). If we recognise such divorces obtained abroad, why not allow administrative divorces here?

(iv) Or do we already have that, given that almost all divorces are granted each year under the 'special procedure'?

Section 10A of the 1973 Act, added by the Divorce (Religious Marriages) Act 2002, addresses a problem discussed by Helen Conway in 'Divorce and Religion' (1995):

The failure of the legal system to allow a religious law influence in the dissolution of marriages has the potential to cause injustice to members of religious minorities.

A prime example of this is where a civil divorce is obtained but the Jewish Get is not forthcoming. In Jewish law a divorce can be obtained by consent without the commission of a matrimonial offence. A wife is divorced when a husband executes and delivers a Get to her, Get being the Aramaic word for a formal deed of severance. It is only the husband who may formally initiate the divorce. There are set grounds on which parties may compel the other to either execute or accept a Get. ...

... Problems occur when a civil divorce exists but one party refuses a Get. If the wife refuses to accept a Get, the husband has certain religious solutions. ... However, a wife is left in a position where she would be forbidden by religious law to contract a second Jewish marriage. Such women are known within their community as the *agunot* or 'the chained'.

... there is an argument to say that the English civil law ought to address this issue and offer some assistance to potential *agunot*.

Section 10A makes provision for this by enabling the court, on the application of either party where the marriage was of a Jewish nature, to require the parties to certify that they have fulfilled all the requirements for a religious divorce before the decree absolute is granted.

Question

(i) Can you foresee problems with this provision where either party has changed their religious views since the marriage?

(ii) Why make special provision for religions who *do* allow divorce on a discriminatory basis, and *not* for religions which do not allow it at all or only on limited grounds?

6.3 The factual context

We now turn to the facts behind the law, in order to look briefly at a number of different areas of research. We consider the use of the five facts; we ask why people divorce; and we look at the relationship between law reform and the divorce rate.

6.3.1 The use of the five facts

First, given the availability of divorce on proof of a single ground, which can only be proved by the use of one of the five facts set out in s. 1(2) of the Matrimonial Causes Act 1973, it is interesting to consider the use made of these facts by different people. The following table, from *Social Trends 30* (2000), shows the distribution of divorces by fact proven, granted to husbands and wives in 1997:

2.9 Decrees awarded: by fact proven, 1997

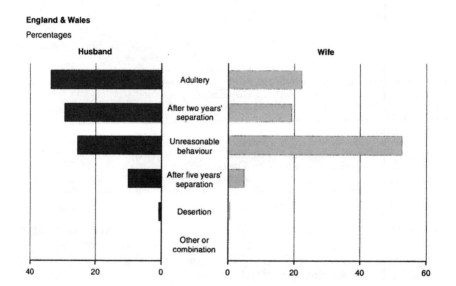

Source: *Office for National Statistics*

The proportion of petitions brought by husbands and wives has changed over the years, as the graph from John Haskey's 'Trends in Marriage and Divorce 1837–1987' (1987) makes clear (see facing page).

Question

In 1994, 71% of all divorce petitions were brought by wives. Do you think that (a) there is a greater desire among women for divorce or (b) there is a greater desire among women to be the petitioner? In either case, why might that be?

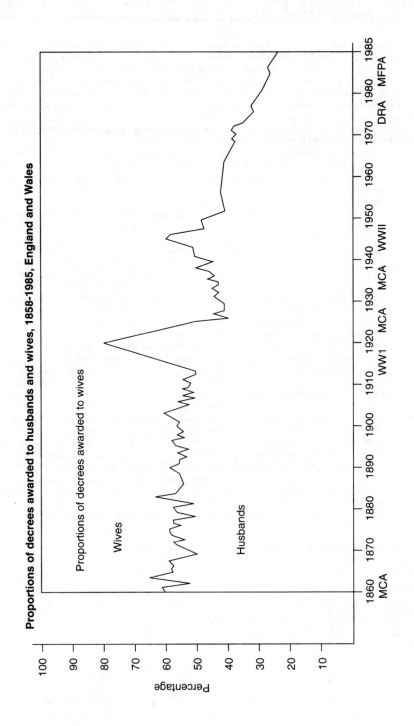

Proportions of decrees awarded to husbands and wives, 1858-1985, England and Wales

Some observations from these and other statistics, as well as more general arguments relating to questions of 'fault', are provided for us by the work of Gwynn Davis and Mervyn Murch in *Grounds for Divorce* (1988):

It is clear that choice of 'fact' is class-based. Social Classes I and II opt for 'adultery' in about 45 per cent of cases and have as many petitions based on two years separation as they have on 'behaviour'. The lower the social class, the more popular 'behaviour' petitions become until, in Social Class V, they comprise 57 per cent. Correspondingly, the proportion of 'adultery' petitions declines to the point where in Social Class V it is less than half that in Social Class I.

These patterns are confirmed by the larger (and more assuredly representative) study conducted by Haskey (1986). He also points out the parallels with the social class distribution under the old law, particularly in relation to the ground of 'cruelty' as analysed by Chester and Streather (1972). Those researchers found that amongst petitions based on the ground of cruelty, there was an over-representation of couples where the husband worked in a partly skilled or unskilled occupation, and a corresponding under-representation of Social Classes I and II.

Whilst it is possible to derive a degree of harmless amusement from speculating as to why adultery should be so popular amongst the upper classes, it is certain that we need to look for more broadly social (or extra-marital) explanations for these patterns, rather than regard them as reflecting (albeit with many distortions) the actual marital circumstances of couples within these social groups. They may reflect, for example, different social groups' tolerance of the stigma of fault, or commitment to an interactionist view of marital breakdown.

The class breakdown may also reflect legal practitioners' views as to what is an appropriate (or acceptable) basis for divorce for couples from a given social background. These days, 'adultery' provides an almost totally non-stigmatic route to divorce. This is especially true of those cases in which the third party is not even cited, it being alleged simply that the respondent has committed adultery with a person unknown to the petitioner. 'Behaviour' ... has not been sanitized in this way. Middle class people, perhaps more aware of the various options, or more anxious to preserve their dignity, tend to avoid it; or else their solicitors, alive to the social cost which a 'behaviour' petition entails, avoid it on their behalf.

As with the evidence relating to the parties' age or to the sex of the petitioner, one possible conclusion to be drawn from this breakdown of 'fact' by social class is that it undermines any case for the continued existence of the present legal categories. This is on the assumption, difficult to establish empirically, that social class variation in the choice of 'fact' does not reflect an objective reality in terms of marital circumstances.

The variation in use of the five 'facts' across the social classes probably accounts for the different patterns which we observed *within each court*. In Table 13 we give this breakdown for each of the courts in which we conducted the Special Procedure survey, focusing on the three most commonly used 'facts' of adultery, behaviour, and two years separation. It can be seen that choice of 'fact' does vary quite significantly by court. ... The underlying influence of social class is suggested by the fact that Newport and Cardiff, which had the highest incidence of 'behaviour' petitions, also had considerably more men who were unemployed or working in unskilled occupations. It is doubtful, therefore, whether Yeovil is the hotbed of adultery that the figures might suggest, or whether one should regard intolerable behaviour within marriage as another manifestation of Welsh culture, along with fine singing voices and a genius for rugby football.

Table 13: 'Fact' cited by court (Special Procedure survey)

Court	No.	Adultery %	Behaviour %	2 year sep. %
Bristol	615	32	42	20
Cardiff	255	24	55	15
Gloucester	447	34	45	14
Newport	273	30	51	13
Swindon	268	37	37	20
Taunton	222	37	32	23
Yeovil	163	44	34	19

...

Despite the elements of collusion and contrivance which are readily apparent in present-day decree proceedings, we would not wish to suggest that the parties' marital history plays *no* part in the choice of 'fact', even if the relationship between the two is not clear-cut. For example, when in the course of the Special Procedure project we asked petitioners what had led them to start divorce proceedings, 31 per cent of those petitioning on adultery cited their former spouse's relationship with someone else; only 4 per cent of 'behaviour' petitioners give this as the main reason. We also asked petitioners whether there had been any incidents of physical violence in their marriage. Of those petitioning on 'behaviour', 55 per cent said that there had been violence, as compared with 35 per cent of those petitioning on 'adultery' and 32 per cent of those petitioning on two years separation. It is also possible that the more severe or repeated violence may have been experienced by 'behaviour' petitioners, although this cannot be determined on the basis of our quantifiable information.

But rather than trying to ascertain whether there is any objective relationship between behaviour in marriage and 'fact' cited in the divorce petition, it might be more fruitful to ask whether the parties regard it as appropriate that the law should allow scope for public recrimination in divorce: if the answer to that question is 'yes', it might be argued that the 'fault' element should be retained. In the Special Procedure survey we asked everyone whether the idea of 'the guilty party' had any relevance as far as they were concerned. Thirty-one per cent said that it did, with a further 16 per cent giving equivocal responses. Since the Special Procedure research focused on uncontested cases, amongst which questions of 'fault' might be thought to have less relevance, it is evident that questions of guilt or innocence are still important for many people. But it was also apparent that the listing of one spouse's marital failings, whilst giving expression to the resentment felt by the petitioner, often provoked a sense of profound injustice on the part of the respondent. This, indeed, was the reason given by some men for wanting divorce to remain a public matter: they wished to see these false allegations openly challenged.

Not surprisingly, petitioners and respondents who had experienced the fault-based 'facts' were more likely to regard the question of which party was responsible for the marriage breakdown as being an appropriate element in divorce law, although the variation across the five 'facts' was not very dramatic. In general, respondents were more likely than petitioners to say that the issue of guilt or blame mattered to them. This was particularly true of those who had experienced the 'behaviour' fact, with 60 per cent of respondents saying that they were concerned about questions of 'fault', as against only 33 per cent of petitioners. This might suggest that the experience of being on the receiving end of a 'behaviour' petition actually promotes this way of thinking, so that the respondent is prompted to defend the allegations, or perhaps to recriminate in turn. The 'adultery' group was the only one in which petitioners were more likely than respondents to say that questions of guilt or innocence still mattered to them (52 per cent as against 37 per cent).

Our informants advanced a number of arguments in favour of retaining the 'fault' element. The first was that the drift away from fault has undermined the significance of marriage, making it more akin to other types of relationship. As one male respondent put it, 'It [the question of responsibility for the breakdown] matters a hell of a lot to me. By getting away from that, they've taken a lot of the importance out of marriage.'

Secondly, there was the argument that the 'innocent' spouse should be protected against divorce; in other words, if you lead a blameless marital life, you should be able to feel secure in your marital status. As it was put by another man whom we interviewed, 'To my mind, if you've done something wrong – OK, let someone divorce you. But if you've done nothing at all wrong, how can the other person divorce you?' Whilst some 'innocent' petitioners regarded it as appropriate that their spouse should be identified as the person whose conduct ended the marriage, they might nevertheless feel very aggrieved that all the trauma and responsibility of obtaining the divorce fell to them, so that in that sense the 'guilty' party escaped scot-free.

Maybe where you live has something to do with it. It is interesting to contrast the picture in Scotland, where both development and present practice are significantly different from that in England (Alastair Bissett-Johnson and Chris Barton in 'The similarities and differences in Scottish and English family law in dealing with changing family patterns' (1999)):

The deeply misaligned English and Scottish *social* and *cultural histories* of the family can be seen by the two countries' divorce laws. Apart from the rare Divorce by Private Act of Parliament, divorce as we now know it, as opposed to divorce *a mensa et thoro,* came late to England in 1857 (see McGregor, 1957). In Scotland, divorce *a vinculo* on the ground of adultery was known from a 1563 Act of Queen Mary, which begins in a masterpiece of invective and concision:

Farsameikle as the abhomiabill and filthie vice and cryme of adulterie, has bene perniciously and wickedly used within this Realm ... hauand no regaird to the commandmentes of God. [It then continues with the superadded right of 'the innocent to be free to remarry and for their partner to suffer the death that God hath required'!]

.... In 1573, desertion as an additional ground for divorce was added by c. 55 of the Act of 1573.

Thereafter, these existing divorce laws, which in substance grew remarkably similar, operated differently, possibly because Scottish society has been different from that in England. Scottish society, at least until recently, and perhaps because of its smaller size, has been more uniform, more egalitarian and less stratified than in England. A side-effect of this has been a higher degree of shared values in which the effect of the Church in, and perhaps of, Scotland has been an important factor. Not only was the incidence of divorce higher in England than Scotland, but the proofs of irretrievable breakdown in marriage resorted to in England and Scotland are remarkably different. Thus, while behaviour was the most popular proof of breakdown in England (46 per cent), it was relied on in Scotland in only 30 per cent of cases. In Scotland, 2 years separation was the most popular breakdown proof (48 per cent), while this proof was relied on in only 19 per cent of cases in England *(see Looking to the Future,* Lord Chancellor's Department, 1993). Within these national figures there are local variations which are often difficult to explain. Thus it is not readily apparent why people in Hamilton, Ayr and Greenock were nearly twice as likely to invoke 'fault-based' proofs in divorce as people in Campbelltown, Domoch and Lerwick (General Register Office for Scotland Supplement to the Registrar for Scotland's Annual Reports).

Even more interesting is the picture in Northern Ireland, where divorce on the basis of the five facts was introduced in 1978. In 'Divorce law and divorce culture – the case of Northern Ireland' (1998), Claire Archbold, Pat McKee and Ciaran White examine the practice of divorce in Northern Ireland and show a system which, though formally very similar to that in England, has diverged markedly in practice. Among other things, they show that the relative popularity of the five facts is quite different from that in England:

Fact on which decree is based by court and gender of petitioner in Northern Ireland

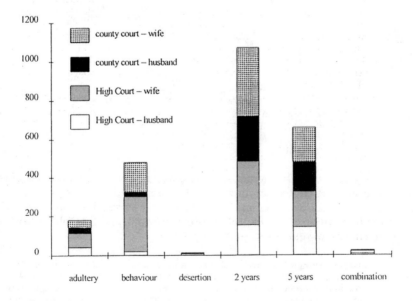

Source: Northern Ireland Judicial Statistics 1996, Table C3, County Court Table 11

Question

How would you account for the different patterns in England, Scotland and Northern Ireland?

6.3.2 Why divorce?

The more fundamental question why people divorce is a remarkably difficult one. Martin Richards, in 'Divorce Research Today' (1991), makes some suggestions:

The incidence of divorce

After a lull in the 1950s, divorce rates in Britain and, indeed, through most of the industrialised world, began to rise steeply in the early 1960s. This increase persisted until the late 1970s when the curve flattened out and it has remained more or less stable ever since. The fact that this pattern of change is so widespread, geographically, means that we should not look for its causes in local factors. Clearly, attitudes to marriage have undergone a very widespread change in the post-war years.

While it is widely believed that increasing rates of divorce are the consequence of reducing the legal hurdles involved in ending a marriage, the evidence suggests the opposite process is the more important: that as divorce has become more common, jurisdictions have found it necessary to reform their divorce law and to simplify the process in order to accommodate the growing numbers.

There have been many suggestions about how we might account for the rising rates. Rising expectations for marriage and a growing feeling that, if you do not succeed at first, you should try again, seem part of the pattern. Rising divorce rates, at least until very recently, have been associated with parallel increases in rates of remarriage, so the increasing divorce rates seem more to reflect a disenchantment with a particular partner, rather than any more general flight from marriage. But in recent years there may have been a change in this pattern and in many countries there has been an increase in cohabitation, especially for those who have been previously married. As the great majority of divorces are initiated by women, it is reasonable to assume that they most often make the decision to leave the marriage, so it is not surprising to find evidence that divorce rates are associated with the ease, or difficulty, with which women with children can support themselves financially on their own. Housing is probably of great importance and it has been suggested that the housing shortage and, especially the lack of council housing, may currently be acting to depress divorce rates especially in South-East England.

Regional differences in rates remain significant, so that, within the UK, we have very low rates in Northern Ireland, among the lowest in Europe, while those in England are towards the upper end of the European distribution.

It is often suggested that divorce is contagious. There may well have been an effect of this kind while rates were rising rapidly. As people saw those around them divorce and were increasingly likely to have friends or relatives who had been through the process, they may have been encouraged to use this means of trying to alleviate their own domestic problems. In the 1960s the literature on divorce tended to emphasise its potential positive results for adults and had little to say about the difficulties. But in recent years there have been indications of an opposite kind of influence. As the negative effects of divorce, in both personal and economic terms, become much more widely appreciated, people may be much more reluctant to leave a marriage and instead may try to make greater efforts to keep it going.

In 'Private Worlds and Public Intentions – the Role of the State at Divorce' (1995), Richards makes some further points:

There is a belief, especially among some of those associated with the law, that if divorce was made harder to obtain, the numbers would be reduced and some of the attendant consequences for children would therefore be avoided. ...

All these kinds of arguments seem to miss two basic points. The first is that marriage rates are now dropping and cohabitation is increasing. It is probable that cohabitation is being transformed from a prelude to marriage to its alternative. Perhaps we are moving towards the

Scandinavian model which is approaching a situation where only a minority of the population marries. In Britain approaching a third of all children are born outside marriage and in two thirds of these cases the birth registration is made jointly. It seems reasonable to assume that many of these are cohabiting couples. As yet we lack any information about the consequences of the ending of a cohabitation for children but there seem to be few reasons to believe that they will be any more benign than the ending of a marriage. Given the relative lack of institutionalised processes for dispute resolution at the ending of cohabitation, outcomes could be worse. Attempts to regulate marriage – either at entry or exit – seem likely to increase cohabitation. If we provide legal processes for regulating the exit from marriage partly on the grounds that they may serve to protect the welfare of children, should we not do the same for the ending of cohabitation?

The second point concerns the reason for the increased rates of divorce. The rise in divorce is associated with the development of companionate marriage. ... Expectations for marriage have risen as have the range of functions it is expected to fulfil. Spouses are now seen as friends, lovers, helpmates and companions for leisure time as well as lifelong marital partners. These extended functions, the high ideals of what marriage should provide, have made marriage relationships both more exclusive and more vulnerable. This vulnerability is further increased by the growing extent to which close relationships among the unmarried are now sexual and most spouses enter marriage with the experience of several earlier sexual relationships. This changing nature of marriage has meant that increasing numbers of spouses, especially women, find that their satisfaction with their marriages may fall quite steeply after the early years. This is particularly true after the arrival of children. I suggest that reasons for divorce in many cases are different for men and women. I believe that if men initiate a divorce it is more often because they have another partner to go to, while women are more likely to be motivated by a desire to leave an unsatisfactory marriage. The great majority of divorces are now initiated by women, a point to which I will return. ...

The influences that have led to the present day style of marriage have a long history and may be traced back to developing ideals of domestic life early in the nineteenth century ... They have been shaped by complex social and economic forces and seem most unlikely to be directly controllable by the action of any government. Leaving aside the effects of world wars which produced marked peaks in the marriage and divorce rates, there are a number of other factors which in the short-term do seem to influence divorce rates and probably lie behind some of the fluctuations in recent years. The following all seem likely to depress divorce rates: high house prices and a shortage of state housing, low rates of welfare support for poor single parent households, lack of child care facilities and high cost of child care in relation to the earning abilities of women. It seems undesirable to try and manipulate any of these factors in order to try to influence the divorce rate, not least because all of them are damaging to the welfare of children.

Another aspect of the relationship between cohabitation and the divorce rate is reflected in the table produced by John Haskey in 'Pre-marital Cohabitation and the Probability of Subsequent Divorce' (1992) (see facing page).
Haskey comments:

Of course, these results do not establish a *causal* link between pre-marital cohabitation and divorce; there may be other factors common to both. For example, couples who marry with a civil ceremony are more likely than those who marry with a religious ceremony to have cohabited pre-maritally; and marital breakdown rates are higher amongst the former group of couples than the latter. The type of marriage ceremony probably reflects not so much the presence or absence of religious belief or church affiliation, but more the commitment to – and the likely extent of external support for – the union; it is generally easier and quicker and involves far fewer family members and friends to marry with a civil, rather than a religious, ceremony.

Possibly couples who cohabit pre-maritally view marriage in a different light to those who do not; certainly the evidence we do possess – from the British Social Attitudes Survey, albeit based on a small sample size – suggests that, compared with those who are married, cohabitees have the most liberal views towards marriage and divorce and 'are emphatically against making divorce more difficult to obtain and markedly less sympathetic to the notion that society ought to do more to protect marriage'. In view of these differences, it would be understandable if those who pre-maritally cohabit were less likely – compared with those who do not pre-maritally cohabit – to think of marriage as a life-long commitment.

A number of other considerations could have a bearing on the observed results. For the most part, the pre-marital cohabitation of the couples included in the 1989 GHS sample took place in earlier decades when pre-marital cohabitation carried much greater social stigma than today.

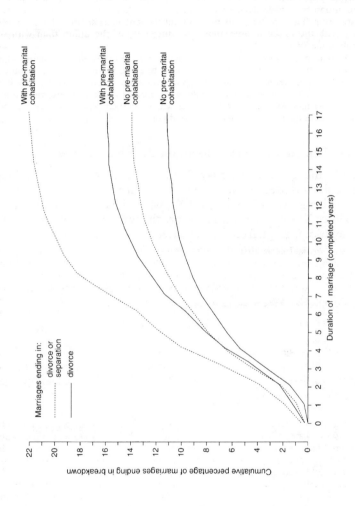

Fig. 3: Cumulative percentages of first marriages, from a hypothetical standard population, ending in (*a*) divorce, (*b*) divorce or separation, by duration of marriage, and by whether or not there was pre-marital cohabitation, based on data for 1970–89, Great Britain

As a result, these marriages may have been under greater strain, and the couple not so completely accepted in their local community, compared with the 'traditional' married couple. In addition, given that, historically, pre-marital cohabitation was a socially unconventional pattern of behaviour, partners who so cohabited before marriage may have been unconventional in their expectations of – and behaviour within – marriage. Possibly individuals who were divorce-prone might be 'selected into' marriages which were preceded by pre-marital cohabitation.

It should also be borne in mind that results from the GHS depend upon the respondents' statements about pre-marital cohabitation; there could be an association between the willingness to mention pre-marital cohabitation and of having subsequently divorced or separated. Another possible mechanism could operate as follows. Couples who were unsure about the stability of their union may have decided to cohabit for a short period before marriage to test their relationship. The greater probability of subsequent marital breakdown could be associated more with the initial doubts about the durability of the union than with the pre-marital cohabitation itself.

Overall, most authors tend to think that there are two main explanations for the observed phenomenon. One is that pre-marital cohabitation reflects a weaker commitment to the institution of marriage and that the higher rates of marital breakdown result from that weaker commitment. The other is that cohabitation attracts those who are more unconventional in their beliefs and lifestyles – characteristics which, by their very nature, tend to be held by those who are more likely to consider and seek divorce.

6.3.3   The effect of law reform on the divorce rate

Finally, then, what can we say about the numbers and rate of divorces, and in particular the effect upon the divorce rate, if any, of changes in the law? The last major change was, of course, in 1971 when the Divorce Reform Act 1969 came into force. The possible impact of that change upon numbers is demonstrated by the following graph from Richard Leete's study of *Changing Patterns of Family Formation and Dissolution 1964–76* (1979):

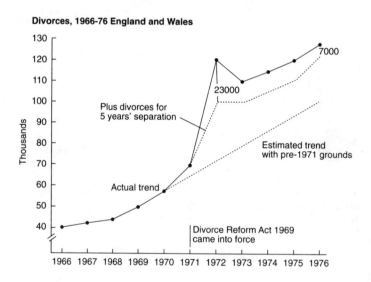

Questions

(i)   If in 1976 there were 7,000 more divorces than might have been expected from an extrapolation of the pre-1971 trend together with the five year cases,

how would you account for the increase? Is it (a) that the law was allowing more already broken marriages to be dissolved; or (b) that more marriages were breaking down than even the pre-1971 trend would have suggested; or (c) a bit of both?
(ii) If you are inclined to favour explanation (b), does the increase of 7,000 (in a total of 126,000 in 1976) strike you as being large or small?
(iii) If you think that the law contributes to an attitude of mind, do you think that this is most potent when the law is changed? Does the trend in the 1980s and 1990s support this?
(iv) How many *other* reasons can you think of for the rise in the divorce rate?

Ira Ellman, in 'Divorce in the United States' (2000), has this to say about the relationship between divorce reform and divorce rates:

Figure 15.1 shows, for the three states for which we have data, that the divorce rate began climbing long before no-fault divorce was adopted. An increase in the divorce rate followed Arizona's adoption of no-fault, but only for a few years, after which the rate declined. A short-term rate increase is precisely what one would expect from a legal reform that made divorce simpler and quicker to obtain, but which had no fundamental impact on the likelihood of divorce: such a reform would speed up divorces already in the pipeline, leading to a transitory one-time increase, followed by a resumption of the basic trends. This pattern is common, and also appears to be what happened after Utah's more recent adoption of no-fault, not even for the short term. The general pattern shown by these three states is typical – nationally, divorce rates have been stable or declining since 1981 – and is very difficult to reconcile with any claim that no-fault caused any important increase in divorce rates.

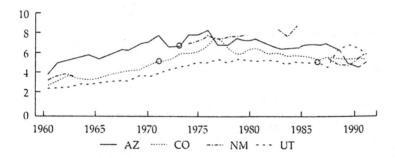

FIGURE 15.1. Divorce rates, in divorces per 1,000 population, for three states, 1960 to 1992 (plus partial data from New Mexico, for which other data is missing). For the three states with complete data, the circle marks the date of enactment of a law which added irremediable breakdown as grounds for divorce and adopted property and alimony rules that excluded consideration of fault.

Ellman goes on to suggest that more potent factors in the rising rates may be mobility (she finds a high correlation between the divorce and moving from one state to another) and the employment of wives. On the latter, she comments:

A second cultural force which most observers believe played an important role in increasing divorce rates is the enormous increase in the participation of married women in the paid labor force. Reviewing the literature, Cherlin concludes that while the evidence that the increase in women's participation in the labor force contributed to the 1960-80 rise in divorce rates is necessarily 'circumstantial, ... it is stronger and more suggestive than that linking any other concurrent trend with the rise in divorce' [Andrew Cherlin, *Marriage, Divorce, Remarriage* 53 (rev. edn 1992)]. Not mentioned by Cherlin, but supporting his conclusion, is the fact that most divorces today are sought by women. Indeed, the increase in divorce rates between 1950 and 1980 occurred over a period of time during which the proportion of divorces instigated by wives appears to have increased from a minority of the cases to two-thirds of the cases. It thus seems logical to suggest that anyone seeking to explain the increase in divorce rates during this period should look for changes in factors likely to affect the motivation of wives. Their increasing rates of employment is such a factor. Economists suggest simply that such employment, being associated with a decline in marriage role specialization, leads to a decline in the benefits derived by the spouses from their marriage. A more feminist-friendly take on the same phenomenon argues that rising female employment commands a wide consensus in the social science literature, although methodological difficulties have presented some challenge to those seeking empirical support for it. One can perhaps argue that rising divorce rates encouraged women to seek market labor, or that other phenomena caused changes in both women's economic behaviour and their choice to divorce.

In 'Formation and Dissolution of Unions in the Different Countries of Europe' (1993), John Haskey produces tables showing the divorce rate in various countries (see pp. 251–252, below). In 'Patterns of Marriage, Divorce and Cohabitation in the Different Countries of Europe' (1992) he comments:

The trend in divorce in many countries in the early 1950s still showed some evidence of the aftermath of the War. Immediately after the War there had been a large surge in divorce, followed by a decline to a level which nevertheless still exceeded that which had existed before the War. Levels were fairly steady during the 1950s, although somewhat erratic for some of the Eastern European countries. There was a large variation in the level of divorce between different countries – even between countries in the same part of Europe. Thus, throughout the 1950s, Denmark's TDR was more than double that of England and Wales, Austria's was twice Belgium's, and Poland's was more than double Hungary's.

Between the mid-1950s and the mid-1960s, the level of divorce was remarkably level in most Northern and Western European countries, but was already increasing slowly in many of the Eastern European countries. In general, divorce was very low or virtually non-existent in the countries of Southern Europe; indeed, there were no provisions for divorce in Italy, Spain, or Portugal. In the mid-1960s, the pace of increase in divorce rates quickened in the Northern and Western European countries, and also in some of the countries of Eastern Europe.

In the period 1965 to 1975, the increase in divorce in all the Northern European countries was substantial; the TDR doubled in Norway and Denmark and trebled both in Sweden and in England and Wales. The increase was generally smaller in the Western European countries; although the TDR doubled in Luxembourg and West Germany, it increased by only about 50 per cent in France, Austria, and Switzerland. Divorce tended to be resorted to at younger ages in countries where divorce rates were high, and at older ages in countries where divorce rates were comparatively low.

The decade 1965-75 was an extremely busy one as far as new divorce legislation was concerned – very few countries in Europe did not amend their law on divorce, and Italy, Spain, and Portugal introduced divorce legislation for the first time. Festy has examined the timing of the revision in divorce law and pointed out that countries which introduced legislation early in the 1970s – Denmark, England and Wales, and Sweden – saw a much greater increase in divorce than in those countries which introduced it later, such as France and West Germany. In addition, divorce had started to increase *before* the enactment of the new legislation, in those countries which had changed the law in the early 1970s.

After 1975, the rate of growth in divorce slowed down considerably in the Northern European countries. The level of divorce actually fell in Sweden after 1974, but this decline followed a massive rise of 70 per cent between 1973 and 1974 after the implementation of a radical reform of the law on divorce. In contrast, the rate of growth in the TDR for the countries of Western Europe continued at much the same pace as had occurred in the previous decade, 1965-75. The large fall in the rate for West Germany resulted from a complete overhaul of the law in 1976, which gave rise to uncertainty regarding the validity of a large number of cases which were temporarily suspended. Between 1975 and 1988, the level of divorce rose by about 50 per cent in Austria, Switzerland, and West Germany, and by about 90 per cent in France and The

Figure 2a: Total period divorce rate for selected countries of Eastern Europe, 1950–1988

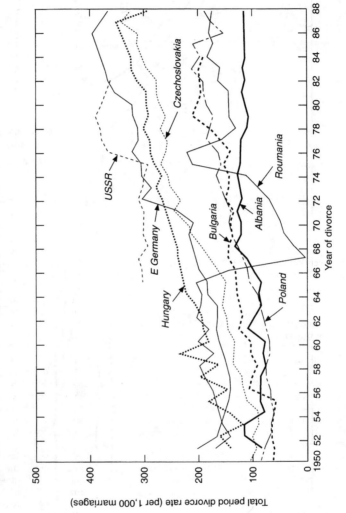

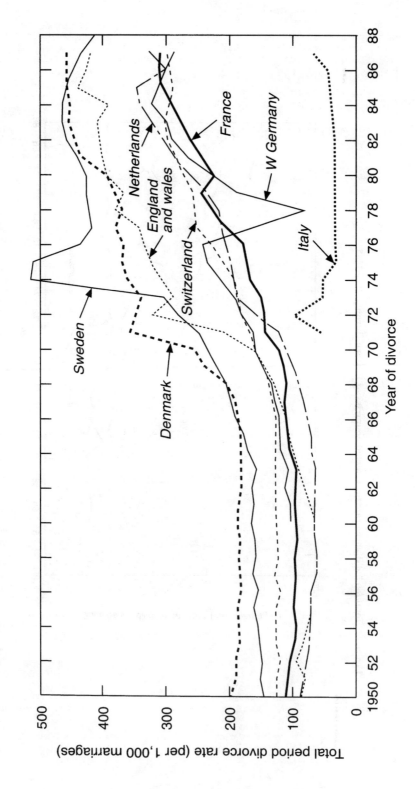

Figure 2b: Total period divorce rate for selected countries of Northern and Western Europe, 1950–1988

Netherlands. The picture for the Eastern European countries was somewhat mixed: for one group of countries, including Albania and Poland, the TDR scarcely changed, or else increased only slightly; whereas for another group of countries, such as East Germany and Czechoslovakia, it increased by a larger amount.

The most recent trends in divorce numbers in this country are seen in the following table from the *Judicial Statistics 2000*:

Dissolution of Marriage: Petitions Filed and Decrees Granted, 1991–2000

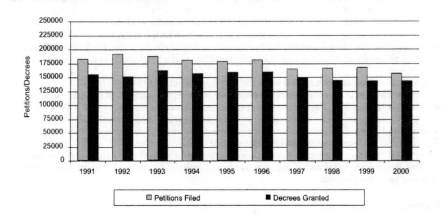

Question

Why do you suppose the numbers have gone down?

6.4   The Family Law Act 1996: a brighter future?

In 1996 a new divorce law was passed by Parliament, in Part II of the Family Law Act 1996. It was always clear that it would take some time for the Act to be brought into force; but we know now that it never will be. In this part of the chapter we look at the Law Commission's proposals, at the law as it was enacted, and at some of the aspirations revealed by the debate surrounding the enactment of the new law. In part 5 of this chapter we ask why the new law will not be brought into force, and what should be done next.

6.4.1 The Law Commission's proposal

In 1988, the Law Commission published *Facing the Future: A Discussion Paper on the Ground for Divorce*. In *Family Law: A Ground for Divorce* (1990) the Law Commission report on their inquiries and the responses to the discussion paper:

1.5 Our inquiries have made three things absolutely plain. First, of the existence of the problem there can be no doubt. The response to Facing the Future [1988] overwhelmingly endorsed the criticisms of the current law and practice which it contained. The present law is confusing and unjust. It now fulfils neither of its original objectives. These were, first, the support of marriages which have a chance of survival, and secondly, the decent burial with the minimum of embarrassment, humiliation and bitterness of those that are indubitably dead.

1.6   Secondly, it is clear that those basic objectives of a 'good' divorce law, as set out by our predecessors in 1966, still command widespread support, difficult though it may be to achieve them in practice. In 1990, however, any summary would include two further objectives: to encourage so far as possible the amicable resolution of practical issues relating to the couple's home, finances and children and the proper discharge of their responsibilities to one another and their children; and, for many people the paramount objective, to minimise the harm that the children may suffer, both at the time and in the future, and to promote so far as possible the continued sharing of parental responsibility for them.

1.7   Thirdly, there was overwhelming support for the view expressed in Facing the Future that irretrievable breakdown of the marriage should remain the fundamental basis of the ground for divorce. This means, first, that divorce should continue to be restricted to those marriages which have clearly broken down and should not be available for those which are capable of being saved; and secondly, that any marriage which has broken down irretrievably should be capable of being dissolved. The criticism is not of the principle itself, but of the legal rules and processes by which the irretrievable breakdown of a marriage is at present established in the courts.

1.8   Our consultations have led us to the firm conclusion that there is one particular model for reform which is to be preferred. It has not only received the support of the great majority of those who responded to Facing the Future, but has also been shown by our public opinion survey to be acceptable to a considerable majority of the general population. This was the model described in Facing the Future as divorce as a 'process over time' but here described as divorce after a period of consideration and reflection, colloquially a 'cooling-off' period or breathing space. [Our recommendations] constitute in many ways a radical departure from the present law: one designed to retain what are seen as the strengths of the present system while meeting the most serious criticisms.

They identify six criticisms of the present law and practice:

(i)   *It is confusing and misleading*

2.8   There is a considerable gap between theory and practice, which can only lead to confusion and lack of respect for the law. Indeed, some would call it *downright dishonest*. There are several aspects to this. First, the law tells couples that the only ground for divorce is irretrievable breakdown, which apparently does not involve fault. But next it provides that this can only be shown by one of five 'facts', three of which apparently do involve fault. There are several recent examples of divorces being refused despite the fact that it was clear to all concerned that the marriage had indeed irretrievably broken down.[8] The hardship and pain involved for both parties can be very great.

2.9   Secondly, the fact which is alleged in order to prove the breakdown need not have any connection with the *real reason* why the marriage broke down.[9] The parties may, for example, have separated because they have both formed different associations, but agree to present a petition based on the behaviour of one of them, because neither wishes their new partner to be publicly named. The sex, class and other differences in the use of the facts make it quite clear that these are chosen for a variety of reasons which need have nothing to do with the reality of the case. This is a major source of confusion, especially for respondents who do not agree with the fact alleged. As has long been said, 'whatever the client's reason for wanting divorce, the lawyer's function is to discover grounds'.

2.10   The behaviour fact is particularly confusing. It is often referred to as 'unreasonable behaviour', which suggests blameworthiness or outright cruelty on the part of the respondent; but this has been called a 'linguistic trap',[10] because the behaviour itself need be neither unreasonable nor blameworthy: rather, its *effect* on the petitioner must be such that it is unreasonable to expect him or her to go on living with the respondent, a significantly different and more flexible concept which is obviously capable of varying from case to case and court to court. Although the test is to be applied by an objective reasonable outsider, the character and personality of the petitioner are particularly relevant in deciding what conduct he or she should be expected to bear.[11]

---

8. *Buffery v Buffery* [1988] FCR 465, [1988] 2 FLR 365 (see p. 227, above).
9. *Stevens v Stevens* [1979] 1 WLR 885.
10. *Bannister v Bannister* (1980) 10 Fam Law 240 per Ormrod LJ.
11. *Astwood v Astwood* (1981) 131 NLJ 990.

2.11 Finally, and above all, the present law pretends that the court is conducting an inquiry into the facts of the matter, when in the vast majority of cases it can do no such thing. This is not the fault of the court, nor is it probably any more of a problem under the present law and procedure than it was under the old. It may be more difficult to evaluate the effect of the respondent's behaviour from the papers than from the petitioner's account in the witness box, but it has always been difficult to get at the truth in an undefended case. Moreover the system still allows, even encourages, the parties to lie, or at least to exaggerate, in order to get what they want. The bogus adultery cases of the past may have all but disappeared, but their modern equivalents are the 'flimsy' behaviour petition or the pretence that the parties have been living apart for a full two years. In that 'wider field which includes considerations of truth, the sacredness of oaths, and the integrity of professional practice',[12] the present law is just as objectionable as the old.

(ii) *It is discriminatory and unjust*

2.12 83% of respondents to our public opinion survey thought it a good feature of the present law that couples who do not want to put the blame on either of them do not have to do so, but these couples have to have lived apart for at least two years. This can be extremely difficult to achieve without either substantial resources of one's own, or the co-operation of the other spouse at the outset, or an ouster order from the court. A secure council house tenancy, for example, cannot be re-allocated between them without a court order which is only obtainable on divorce or judicial separation.[13] The law does recognise that it is possible to live apart by conducting two separate households under the same roof. In practice, this is impossible in most ordinary houses or flats, especially where there are children: it inevitably requires the couple to co-operate in a most unnatural and artificial lifestyle. It is unjust and discriminatory of the law to provide for a civilised 'no-fault' ground for divorce which, in practice, is denied to a large section of the population. A young mother with children living in a council house is obliged to rely upon fault whether or not she wants to do so and irrespective of the damage it may do.

2.13 The fault-based facts can also be intrinsically unjust. 'Justice' in this context has traditionally been taken to mean the accurate allocation of blameworthiness for the breakdown of the marriage. Desertion is the only fact which still attempts to do this: it requires that one party has brought about their separation without just cause or consent. Desertion, however, is hardly ever used, because its place has been taken by the two year separation fact. A finding of adultery or behaviour certainly need not mean that the respondent is any more to blame than the petitioner for the breakdown of the marriage. If one has committed adultery or behaved intolerably there is usually nothing to stop the other obtaining a divorce based upon it, even though that other may have committed far more adulteries or behaved much more intolerably himself or herself. Nor does the behaviour fact always involve blame: it may well be unreasonable to expect a petitioner to live with a spouse who is mentally ill or disabled[14] or has totally incompatible values or lifestyle.[15] Even when the catalogue of complaints contained in the petition includes violence or other obviously blameworthy behaviour, this might look different if weighed against the behaviour of the other. In a defended case, the petitioner's own character and conduct may be relevant in determining the effect of the respondent's conduct upon her, but if his conduct is sufficient, it is irrelevant that she may have behaved equally badly in some other way. In an undefended case, of course, the matter will appear even more one-sided.

2.14 This inherent potential for injustice is compounded by the practical problems of defending or bringing a cross-petition of one's own. It is extremely difficult to resist or counter allegations of behaviour. Defending them requires time, money and emotional energy far beyond the resources of most respondents. Even if the parties are prepared to go through this, what would be the point? If the marriage is capable of being saved, a long-fought defended divorce, in which every incident or characteristic that might amount to behaviour is dragged up and examined in detail, is not going to do this. It can only serve to make matters worse and to consume resources which are often desperately needed elsewhere, particularly if there are children. Legal aid will only be granted if the case cannot be disposed of as an undefended suit without detriment to the interests of either party. As the basis on which the divorce is granted is usually irrelevant to ancillary issues, the parties' *legal* positions are unlikely to be affected whatever their personal views. Small wonder, then, that lawyers advise their client not to defend and that their clients feel unjustly treated.[16]

---

12. *Putting Asunder* (1966) (see p. 218, above).
13. Unless it is a joint tenancy and one of them voluntarily surrenders it, but this brings the whole tenancy to an end. See *Greenwich London Borough Council v McGrady* (1982) 81 LGR 288 (see p. 154, above).
14. *Thurlow v Thurlow* [1976] Fam 32 (see p. 228, above).
15. *Livingstone-Stallard v Livingstone Stallard* [1974] Fam 47 (see p. 226, above).
16. See particularly the work of Davis and Murch (see p. 242, above).

(iii) *It distorts the parties' bargaining positions*

2.15 Not only can the law be unjust in itself, it can also lead to unfair distortions in the relative bargaining positions of the parties. When a marriage breaks down there are a great many practical questions to be decided: with whom are the children to live, how much are they going to see of the other parent, who is to have the house, and what are they all going to live on? Respondents to Facing the Future told us that the battles which used to be fought through the ground for divorce are now more likely to be fought through the so-called ancillary issues which in practice matter so much more to many people. The policy of the law is to encourage the parties to try and resolve these by agreement if they can, whether through negotiation between solicitors or with the help of a mediation or conciliation service. Questions of the future care of children, distribution of family assets, and financial provision are all governed by their own legal criteria. It is not unjust for negotiations to be affected by the relative merits of the parties' cases on these matters. Yet negotiations may also be distorted by whichever of the parties is in a stronger position in relation to the divorce itself. The strength of that position will depend upon a combination of how anxious or reluctant that party is to be divorced and how easy or difficult he or she will find it to prove or disprove one of the five facts. That might not matter if these represented a coherent set of principles, reflecting the real reasons why the marriage broke down; but as we have already seen, they do not. The potentially arbitrary results can put one party at an unfair disadvantage.

(iv) *It provokes unnecessary hostility and bitterness*

2.16 A law which is arbitrary or unjust can exacerbate the feelings of bitterness, distress and humiliation so often experienced at the time of separation and divorce. Even if the couple have agreed that their marriage cannot be saved, it must make matters between them worse if the system encourages one to make allegations against the other. The incidents relied on have to be set out in the petition. Sometimes they are exaggerated, one-sided or even untrue. Allegations of behaviour or adultery can provoke resentment and hostility in a respondent who is unable to put his own side of the story on the record. We are not so naive as to believe that bitterness and hostility could ever be banished from the divorce process. It is not concerned with cold commercial bargains but with the most intimate of human relations. The more we expect of marriage the greater the anger and grief when marriage ends. But there is every reason to believe that the present law adds needlessly to the human misery involved. Our respondents confirmed this.

(v) *It does nothing to save the marriage*

2.17 None of this is any help with the law's other objective, of supporting those marriages which have a chance of survival. The law cannot prevent people from separating or forming new relationships, although it may make it difficult for people to get a divorce. The law can also make it difficult for estranged couples to become reconciled. The present law does make it difficult for some couples – in practice a very small proportion – to be divorced, but does so in an arbitrary way depending upon which facts may be proved. It also makes it extremely difficult for couples to become reconciled. A spouse who wishes to be divorced is obliged either to make allegations against the other or to live apart for a lengthy period. If the petitioner brings proceedings based on behaviour, possibly without prior warning, and sometimes while they are still living together, the antagonism caused may destroy any lingering chance of saving the marriage. The alternative of two or five years' separation may encourage them to part in order to be able to obtain a divorce, when their difficulties might have been resolved if they had stayed together. From the very beginning, attention has to be focused on how to prove the ground for divorce. The reality of what it will be like to live apart, to break up the common home, to finance two households where before there was only one, and to have or to lose that day-to-day responsibility for the children which was previously shared, at least to some extent: none of this has to be contemplated in any detail until the decree nisi is obtained. If it had, there might be some petitioners who would think again.

2.18 It is a mistake to think that, because so few divorces are defended, the rest are largely consensual. There are many, especially behaviour cases, in which the respondent indicates an intention to defend, but does not file a formal answer, or files an answer which is later withdrawn. Some of these are a reaction to the unfairness of the allegations made against them, but some reveal a genuine desire to preserve the marriage. A defended suit is not going to do this, and if a case is, or becomes, undefended, there is little opportunity to explore the possibility of saving the marriage. An undefended decree can be obtained in a matter of weeks. If both parties are contemplating divorce, the system gives them every incentive to obtain a 'quickie' decree based on behaviour or separation, and to think out the practical consequences later.

(vi) *It can make things worse for the children*

2.19 The present system can also make things worse for the children. The children themselves would usually prefer their parents to stay together. But the law cannot force parents to live amicably or prevent them from separating. It is not known whether children suffer more from their parents' separation or from living in a household in conflict where they may be blamed for the couple's inability to part.[17] It is probably impossible to generalise, as there are so many variables which may affect the outcome, including the age and personality of the particular child. But it is known that the children who suffer least from their parents' break-up are usually those who are able to retain a good relationship with them both. Children who suffer most are those whose parents remain in conflict.[18]

2.20 These issues have to be faced by the parents themselves, as they agonise over what to do for the best. However regrettably, there is nothing the law can do to ensure that they stay together, even supposing that this would indeed be better for their children. On the other hand, the present law can, for all the reasons given earlier, make the conflict worse. It encourages couples to find fault with one another and disputes about children seem to be more common in divorces based on intolerable behaviour than in others. The alternative is a long period of separation during which children can suffer from the uncertainty before things can be finally sorted out or from the artificiality of their parents living in separate households under the same roof. This is scarcely an effective way of encouraging the parents to work out different ways of continuing to discharge their shared parental responsibilities. It is often said that couples undergoing marital breakdown are too wrapped up in their own problems to understand their children's needs. There are also couples who, while recognising that their own relationship is at an end, are anxious to do their best for their children. The present system does little to help them to do so.

Conclusion

2.21 These defects alone would amount to a formidable case for reform. The response to Facing the Future very largely endorsed its conclusion that 'Above all, the present law fails to recognise that divorce is not a final product but part of a massive transition for the parties and their children'. It is all too easy to think of divorcing couples in simple stereotypes. In fact they come in many different shapes and sizes. But for most, if not all, the breakdown of their relationship is a painful process, and for some it can be devastating. It affects each party in different ways: one may be far ahead of the other in withdrawing from the relationship before the other even realises that there is a problem. The anger, guilt, bitterness and regret so often felt have little to do with the law, which can seem an irrelevant game to be played by the lawyers. But the law does nothing to give the parties an opportunity to come to terms with what is happening in their lives, to reflect in as calm and sensible a way as possible upon the future, and to re-negotiate their relationship. Both emotionally and financially it is better for them and their children if they can do this by agreement rather than by fighting in the courts. There are always going to be some fights and the courts are there to resolve them. But the courts should be kept to their proper sphere of adjudicating upon practical disputes, ensuring that appropriate steps are properly taken, and enforcing the orders made. They should not be pretending to adjudicate upon matters they cannot decide or in disputes which need never arise.

Questions

(i)   Do you accept these criticisms?

(ii)   Can you think of other criticisms which can be levelled at the present law and practice of divorce?

(iii) Those are the criticisms. What are the strengths of the present law?

---

17. That there are adverse effects upon some children from some divorces cannot be doubted: see, eg J.S. Wallerstein and J.B. Kelly, *Surviving the Breakup* (1980); however the claims of J.S. Wallerstein and S. Blakeslee in *Second Chances* (1989) as to the high risks of such effects, have to be treated with some caution. One difficulty is distinguishing the effects of divorce itself from the poverty and consequent disadvantages which so often result; see M. Maclean and R.E.J. Wadsworth 'The Interests of Children after Parental Divorce: A Long-Term Perspective' (1988) 2 Int J of Law and the Family 155.

18. M.P.M. Richards and M. Dyson, *Separation, Divorce and the Development of Children: a Review* (1982).

The Law Commission rejected the retention of 'fault'; the introduction of a full judicial inquest into the marriage and the possibility of saving it; immediate divorce either unilaterally or by mutual consent; and a divorce after a fixed minimum period of separation. They recommended a divorce after a fixed minimum period for reflection and consideration of the arrangements: the process over time.

3.29 Several features particularly commended themselves to respondents. One was the recognition that divorce is not a single event but a social, psychological and only incidentally a legal process, which takes place over a period of time. Relate Marriage Guidance considered that acknowledging the time people need to adapt emotionally, socially and psychologically to their new circumstances could have far reaching – and beneficial – effects, not only for the parties and their children, but also for any new families formed through re-marriage. It is thought that one reason why so many re-marriages fail is the unresolved legal and emotional legacy of the first.

3.30 Another advantage emphasised was the encouragement given to focus upon the practical consequences of separation and divorce and to work these out *before* rather than after the divorce itself. Several respondents, including Relate, the Law Society, and the Association of Chief Officers of Probation, believed that the encouragement to look to the future instead of attacking the past would foster constructive rather than destructive attitudes towards the practical issues. The removal of the need to allege fault should reduce the temptation to adopt hostile and adversarial positions in the parties' discussions. This was seen as an incentive for the parties to recognise and meet their responsibilities towards the family, and therefore as a protection for the children and the financially weaker party. The financial position of the weaker spouse would also be improved by the power to make orders during this period. The period itself would assist in negotiations by providing a clear beginning and end to the process.

3.31 The potential for the increased use of conciliation and mediation, in order to resolve practical issues in a more constructive atmosphere, was also favoured, not only by professionals who are currently engaged in conciliation or mediation, including the Association of Chief Officers of Probation, the National Family Conciliation Council, and the Family Mediators' Association, but also by the legal profession and many others. One advantage seen was that the parties could set their own pace for the proceedings, giving time for a person who was less ready to cope emotionally, rather than progress at a pace dictated by one of them. The more constructive environment which this proposal would bring to the provision of counselling services was also welcomed by many respondents, including Relate Marriage Guidance.

3.32 Several features were thought likely to increase rather than decrease the chances of reconciliation. First was the removal of the need to separate or allege fault, with all the accompanying stigma and bitterness. Second was the encouragement to work out the practical consequences of a divorce before committing themselves to it. Third was the period of time itself, which would prevent hasty divorces and discourage people from rushing into remarriage. One respondent thought that it might even be sufficiently onerous to act as a deterrent to divorce itself.

3.33 Finally, it was thought that all these features would foster more constructive and co-operative attitudes towards the children's future and reduce the damage which they can suffer from prolonged uncertainty and hostility.

3.34 This model therefore received very substantial support from a wide variety of quarters. There is also good reason to believe from our public opinion survey that it would be acceptable to the general public. 87% of respondents to our public opinion survey thought a model along these lines might be 'acceptable', but that was alongside other models. More importantly, it was approved as the sole ground for divorce by 67% and disapproved by 15%, an 'acceptability' rate well above that for separation as the sole ground for divorce. If the law is to be reformed, as respondents to Facing the Future clearly thought that it should, then this is evidently the model to be preferred.

3.35 However, there was understandable concern among some of our respondents about the details of how it would work in practice. We ... should point out here the central features which were implicit, or in some cases explicit, in the support which it received. First, a substantial period of time should be required to elapse, in order to demonstrate quite clearly that the marriage has irretrievably broken down. There can be no better proof of this than that one or both parties to the marriage have stated their belief that their marital relationship has broken down and that either or both of them persist in that belief after the lapse of a considerable period. This must be longer than the present interval between petition and decree, which is six months or less in a substantial proportion of cases. It must also give the parties a realistic timescale within which, in the great majority of cases, the practical questions about the children, the home and the finances can be properly resolved. It must avoid rushing them towards a resolution of those issues, so that they can go at their own pace and draw back if they wish. It must discourage hasty and ill-thought-out applications. In our views, an overall period of one year would be required to achieve all these objectives. ...

3.36 Secondly, there should be an orderly but unhurried procedural timetable during the period, for the exchange of information and proposals, the negotiation of those matters which can be resolved by agreement, and the adjudication of those which cannot, together with the possibility of making orders to have effect during the period, and of extending it where matters have not been properly resolved.

3.37 Many respondents also attached particular importance to the provision of adequate counselling and conciliation services during this time. The National Campaign for the Family, for example, argued that there should be professionally monitored counselling and conciliation services available in all localities, with trained staff and a firm funding base. ... counselling and conciliation are two very different things: counselling may either help a couple who wish to try to save their marriage or give support to one or both of them, or to a child, who is suffering particular trauma or distress from the breakdown of a marriage which cannot be saved. Conciliation or mediation provide a neutral figure who helps both parties to negotiate an agreed solution to the issues concerning their children, and sometimes their property and finances, which will have to be resolved if the divorce proceeds. It was considered important that both such services should be available for all couples (and their children) who want them and that opportunities to make use of them should be built into the procedure itself.

3.38 We share our respondents' views of the importance of both counselling and conciliation services. Indeed, we think this just as great whether or not the law of divorce is to be changed. Similarly, we would consider our proposals a great improvement upon the present law, whether or not more resources were to be made available for these services; but there is no doubt that, just as our proposals would provide a much more constructive and less damaging context for both counselling and conciliation to be successful, so would our proposals greatly benefit from increased provision for them. We say this because we believe that it is by the provision of these services, to the people who want and need them, that the most harmful emotional, social and psychological effects of marital breakdown and divorce can best be avoided or mitigated. The law and legal processes cannot do this, although they can, and at present do, make matters worse. The law's processes are principally designed to adjudicate disputes and to oblige people to meet their financial and legal liabilities. This is an important element in the model which we propose.

3.39 There were of course some respondents who specifically rejected this model. It is necessary, therefore, both to explain their objections and if possible to attempt to meet them.

3.40 Some objections centred round the removal of fault from the ground for divorce. Two different types of advantage are claimed for retaining fault. The first is that it provides a moral base for conduct within marriage. The main difficulty with this is that, logically, it can only be done by returning to a system based wholly on fault. The present mixed system of fault and no-fault 'grounds' is, as the authors of *Putting Asunder* recognised in 1966, incapable of supplying a coherent and consistent moral base. ... Furthermore, granting or withholding the divorce itself is an inappropriate and ineffective sanction against marital misbehaviour; the real and effective sanction is the unwanted breakdown of the marriage. Conduct still has a part to play in determining the practical consequences of that breakdown.

3.41 Secondly, it is argued that the retention of fault provides a public affirmation of 'guilt' and 'innocence' within the marriage which enables the innocent party to feel vindicated in his or her decision to end it. This is an important psychological point. However, one of the difficulties with the whole concept of divorce for fault is that it assumes that fault is the only possible justification for divorce. People who hold this belief, whether for religious or other reasons, may well need to feel that they are morally justified in what they have done. Unfortunately for them, experience has shown the law cannot accurately allocate moral blameworthiness, for there are always two sides to every marital history and different people assess these in different ways; nor do the great majority of divorcing couples want it to do so. They may wish that something could have been done to stop the other spouse behaving as he or she did, or even for the other to be publicly branded in some way, but they shrink from the detailed examination of their marital lives which would necessarily be involved in making a proper assessment in every case. The human as well as the financial costs in making the attempt would be enormous. If that is so, then the sometimes (although obviously not invariably) inaccurate allocation which takes place at present is itself morally wrong, quite apart from the other problems it can cause.

3.42 Another objection was that this model amounts to divorce by unilateral demand, albeit not immediately. This is the inevitable consequence of any system based on irretrievable breakdown of the marriage, including the present one. The present law expressly provides for unilateral divorce after five years' separation, and 71% of respondents to our public opinion survey thought this period too long. In practice, it also provides for divorce by unilateral demand a great deal more quickly, because of the practical and legal problems of defending a petition based on behaviour or, sometimes, adultery.

3.43 It is also the case that this model does not supply an opportunity for one spouse to contest the other's allegation that the marriage has broken down. There are many divorces where one party believes that the marriage can be saved. Sometimes both may do so. Contests in court, however, cannot be the way to do this. As the Booth Committee observed, 'The court itself discourages defended divorce not only because of the futility of trying a contention by one party that the marriage has not broken down despite the other party's conviction that it has, but also because of the emotional and financial demands that it makes upon the parties themselves and the possible harmful consequences for the children of the family'. A reasonably long period of delay, where each party has every opportunity to reflect upon the position and explore the alternatives, coupled with the availability of counselling services if need be, and the removal of the necessity to make damaging allegations against one another, stand a better chance of helping those marriages which can and should be preserved.

3.44 However, it is one thing to accept that the marriage has irretrievably broken down once one party has become convinced, after a considerable period of delay, that it has done so. It is another thing to conclude that that person should 'be able to switch resources to a new family' irrespective of the hardship caused to the first. Under the present law, it is possible to resist a divorce, although only if based on five years' separation, on the ground that the divorce will cause the respondent grave financial or other hardship. In the vast majority of marriages, of course, it is the break-up and separation which cause the hardship, rather than the divorce as such. However, it would be both possible and logical to combine this model with such a hardship bar, if this were considered appropriate. [See p. 266, below.] ...

3.45 On the other hand, there were some respondents who objected that this model would in fact make divorce more difficult, particularly for couples who are agreed upon divorce and for petitioners who need a speedy decree for other reasons. Both groups would, however, be catered for by the availability of ancillary remedies at the outset, so that all they have to wait for is the decree itself, with its consequent permission to remarry. While we appreciate that there are young and childless couples who realise early in their marriage that they have made a mistake, it does not seem unduly intrusive to require a period of delay before granting what is, in effect, a licence to remarry.

Easier or harder?

3.46 This debate indicates quite clearly how impossible it is to characterise any particular divorce system as 'too easy' or 'too difficult'. 'Easy' may mean short or painless, whereas 'hard' may mean long or painful. For some, the model we are recommending might provide 'easier' divorce, in that they would not have to separate for years before proceeding; for others, for example most of those who now rely on adultery or behaviour, it would be 'harder' because they would have to wait for longer than they do at present. For some, it might be 'easier', because they would no longer, justly or unjustly, be branded the wrongdoer; for others, it might be 'harder', because they would have to disclose their financial circumstances and confront their responsibilities towards their families before they could obtain a decree.

3.47 The emotional pain which many people feel at the breakdown of their marriages is not necessarily linked in any way to the ease or difficulty of the legal process. Divorce is almost always painful for their children, but if there is to be a divorce at all, the system should certainly try to make it as easy for them as it can. This was the unanimous view of all those organisations whose principal concern is the welfare of children.

Conclusion

3.48 For all these reasons, we therefore *recommend*:
  (i)   that irretrievable breakdown of the marriage should remain the sole ground for divorce; and
  (ii) that such breakdown should be established by the expiry of a minimum period of one year for consideration of the practical consequences which would result from a divorce and reflection upon whether the breakdown in the marital relationship is irreparable.

Ruth Deech is no supporter of the Law Commission's work in this area. She puts her point in the following article in *The Independent* (1990):

Marriage as a short-term option

The last time divorce law was reformed, we all still believed that human behaviour was rational and could be shaped by legal rules.

The Law Commission said its 1969 Act, which introduced simpler divorce by separation, would promote marriage stability and reconciliation. It would encourage spouses to omit recriminations from their petitions.

Twenty-one years later, the inaccuracy of the reformers' predictions about the new law's effect on people's lives is striking.

Cohabiting couples would regularise their unions, they said, the illegitimacy rate would drop as a result of the freedom to remarry, and the divorce rate would not rise. Instead, we find a marked increase in cohabitation and a divorce rate that has trebled to some 190,000 petitions each year.

So why are we about to embark on another reform, and why is the Law Commission ... implicitly repeating naive claims that a new law will improve the lot of children?

Liberalised divorce law has not, so far, resulted in a greater sum of human happiness. It has given us over one million unremarried divorcees, many of whom are largely dependent on social security.

Feminists have remained largely silent on the question of easier divorce, presumably because women have diametrically opposed personal interests: one woman's bitter divorce and abandonment is another woman's freedom to claim the man or liberty she wants. Yet it could be argued that, if women as a sex ought to be protesting about anything, it is about this issue.

The public at large does not seem to want any change in the law, including the latest proposal to rid it of fault-based grounds and allow a couple to divorce after working out arrangements over children and finances. Neither is there any pressing need to liberalise the law, because all those whose marriages have broken down can readily obtain their divorces under the existing arrangements.

The reason for reform is one given several times before: that the law should reflect social reality and the fact that many divorces are undefended and uninvestigated.

On each occasion the law has been brought into line with practice, however, it has simply made divorce easier. Once the rate rises it never drops back to its previous level. The resulting increased faith in divorce as a solution to marital problems leads to increased willingness to use it, which in turn leads to a relaxation of divorce procedure and then a fresh call for further changes to bring the law into line with reality.

That happened in 1937, 1949 and 1969 and is about to happen again. It is a spiralling process that Parliament should not encourage, for the sake of children, if no one else.

Common sense, as well as academic research, has shown us that the children of divorce (unlike widows' children) suffer from the divorce itself. It results in lower educational achievement and worse employment and emotional prospects for the children.

From the research, it seems that the most hurtful episode for children in the divorce process is the time of separation. The proposals for a more effective maintenance system and for civilised agreements between parents about access can have no remedial effect: most children want their parents to stay together. Any change in divorce law is irrelevant to children's post-divorce suffering and we should not delude ourselves otherwise.

Rational lawyers, such as the Lord Chancellor, are reported to believe that something can be built into a new divorce process to encourage parents to concentrate on their children's welfare, and maybe to change their minds for the sake of their offspring.

That is much wishful thinking because, by the time a couple has initiated the divorce process, it is too late. In the great majority of cases, the children will remain with their mother and there are no real alternatives on offer. Many fathers soon stop visiting, and recent research by Newcastle University shows that conciliation services have little lasting impact.

The law reformers' argument is that divorce law should bury a dead relationship; it is never conceded that the law itself might have played a part in infecting the couple with a fatal virus.

Everything except the law, has been blamed for the breakdown of marriage – housing shortages, shotgun marriages, youthful marriages, unions, unemployment, living longer and legal aid.

My own hypothesis is that the most important element in divorce law is the *message* it conveys to the public. We all absorb the prevailing divorce ethos long before we ourselves ever seriously consider ending a marriage, and it is that earlier influence which counts in determining our response. ...

Everything points to the desirability of leaving the law of divorce unchanged. It would be better for the reformers to focus their efforts on informing teenagers and married couples of the harm done by divorce. It is far too late in a relationship to rely on the divorce law to do so.

Deech makes a further point, about the economic aspects of divorce, in *Divorce Dissent: Dangers in Divorce Reform* (1994):

We cannot afford serial marriage in our society: poverty is as inevitable as the damage to children from the emotional state of their parents. Yet it seems to be an unspoken political decision that attempts to make divorce more difficult are totally unacceptable. Even while public debate focuses on the plight of single parents and their children, the fact that over half of them are created by divorce and separation is overlooked. It is astonishing that any government should seriously contemplate easing divorce law while simultaneously expressing anxiety about single parents, their children and society's health.

She concludes:

1. The Government should abandon plans to reform the ground of divorce.
2. No decree absolute should be granted until at least twelve months have elapsed from service of the petition.
3. An education for marriage programme should be drawn up for school use.
4. The statutory provisions giving legal status to cohabitation and unmarried fathers should be reviewed.

The final recommendation refers to provisions such as the opportunities under the Children Act 1989 for unmarried fathers to obtain parental responsibility for their children (see p. 557), inheritance rights for unmarried partners (p. 196) and the protection of unmarried non-owning partners under Part IV of the Family Law Act 1996 (p. 412).

In *Divorce and the Lord Chancellor* (1994) Andrew Bainham comments:

I must take issue with Ruth Deech who suggests that there is a correlation between divorce reform and the rate of marriage breakdown. Deech confuses the rate of marriage breakdown with the rate of *divorce*. For while it is indisputable that the rate of dissolution is connected to the ease with which the law allows that dissolution to be obtained, it is quite another matter to suggest that divorce law has any significant influence on the *quality* of relationships within marriage – surely the factor most likely to determine whether those relationships end or survive.

Questions

(i)   Ruth Deech is concerned about the message the new law conveys to the public. Can you write a short paragraph describing that message? Now write another short paragraph describing the message the Matrimonial Causes Act 1973 conveys to the public.

(ii)   Do you think it is possible to establish any connection between the divorce rate, the provisions of divorce law, and the rate of relationship breakdown within the community?

(iii) Do you agree with Ruth Deech that to take away those elements of legal recognition given to unmarried fathers would support the institution of marriage? Would that have any effect upon the rate of relationship breakdown?

6.4.2 Divorce under the Family Law Act 1996

In 1993 the Green Paper, *Looking to the Future: Mediation and the Ground for Divorce* sought views and reactions to proposals for the reform of divorce law, including the Law Commission's recommendations but also a number of other possibilities ranging from a return to a system based on matrimonial offences to divorce by consent or immediate divorce on unilateral demand. The White Paper of the same title in 1995 set out the Government's proposals for reform, largely following the Law Commission's proposals, and these have been enacted in the Family Law Act 1996.

The conditions for the making of a divorce order are set out s. 3 of the Act:

3.—(1) If an application for a divorce order or for a separation order is made to the court under this section by one or both of the parties to a marriage, the court shall make the order applied for if (but only if)—

(*a*) the marriage has broken down irretrievably;

(*b*) the requirements of section 8 about information meetings are satisfied;

(*c*) the requirements of section 9 about the parties' arrangements for the future are satisfied; and

(*d*) the application has not been withdrawn.

(2) A divorce order may not be made if an order preventing divorce is in force under section 10.

These conditions are further defined as follows:

5.—(1) A marriage is to be taken to have broken down irretrievably if (but only if)—

(*a*) a statement has been made by one (or both) of the parties that the maker of the statement (or each of them) believes that the marriage has broken down;

(*b*) the statement complies with the requirements of section 6;

(*c*) the period for reflection and consideration fixed by section 7 has ended; and

(*d*) the application under section 3 is accompanied by a declaration by the party making the application that—

(i) having reflected on the breakdown, and

(ii) having considered the requirements of this Part as to the parties' arrangements for the future,

the applicant believes that the marriage cannot be saved.

(2) The statement and the application under section 3 do not have to be made by the same party.

...

6.—(1) A statement under section 5(1)(*a*) is to be known as a statement of marital breakdown; but in this Part it is generally referred to as 'a statement'.

(2) If a statement is made by one party it must also state that that party—

(*a*) is aware of the purpose of the period for reflection and consideration as described in section 7; and

(*b*) wishes to make arrangements for the future.

(3) If a statement is made by both parties it must also state that each of them—

(*a*) is aware of the purpose of the period for reflection and consideration as described in section 7; and

(*b*) wishes to make arrangements for the future.

...

7.—(1) Where a statement has been made, a period for the parties—

(*a*) to reflect on whether the marriage can be saved and to have an opportunity to effect a reconciliation, and

(*b*) to consider what arrangements should be made for the future,

must pass before an application for a divorce order or for a separation order may be made by reference to that statement.

(2) That period is to be known as the period for reflection and consideration.

(3) The period for reflection and consideration is nine months beginning with the fourteenth day after the day on which the statement is received by the court.

...

(6) A statement which is made before the first anniversary of any marriage to which it relates is ineffective for the purposes of any application for a divorce order.

(10) Where an application for a divorce order is made by one party, subsection (13) applies if—

(*a*) the other party applies to the court, within the prescribed period, for time for further reflection; and

(*b*) the requirements of section 9 (except any imposed under section 9(3)), are satisfied.

(11) Where any application for a divorce order is made, subsection (13) also applies if there is a child of the family who is under the age of sixteen when the statement is received by the court.

(12) Subsection (13) does not apply if—

(*a*) at the time when the application for a divorce order is made, there is an occupation order or a non-molestation order in force in favour of the applicant, or of a child of the family, made against the other party; or (*b*) the court is satisfied that delaying the making of a divorce order would be significantly detrimental to the welfare of any child of the family.

(13) If this subsection applies, the period for reflection and consideration is extended by a period of six months, but without invalidating the application for a divorce order.

8.—(1) The requirements about information meetings are as follows.

(2) A party making a statement must (except in prescribed circumstances) have attended an information meeting not less than three months before making the statement.

...

(5) Where one party has made a statement, the other party must (except in prescribed circumstances) attend an information meeting before—

(*a*) making any application to the court—
  (i)   with respect to a child of the family; or
  (ii) of a prescribed description relating to property or financial matters; or
(*b*) contesting any such application.

(6) In this section 'information meeting' means a meeting organised, in accordance with prescribed provisions for the purpose—

(*a*) of providing, in accordance with prescribed provisions, relevant information to the party or parties attending about matters which may arise in connection with the provisions of, or made under, this Part of Part III; and
(*b*) of giving the party or parties attending the information meeting the opportunity of having a meeting with a marriage counsellor and of encouraging that party or those parties to attend that meting.

...

9.—(1) The requirements as to the parties' arrangements for the future are as follows.

(2) One of the following must be produced to the court—

(*a*) a court order (made by consent or otherwise) dealing with their financial arrangements;
(*b*) a negotiated agreement as to their financial arrangements;
(*c*) a declaration by both parties that they have made their financial arrangements;
(*d*) a declaration by one of the parties (to which no objection has been notified to the court by the other party) that—
  (i)   he has no significant assets and does not intend to make an application for financial provision;
  (ii) he believes that the other party has no significant assets and does not intend to make an application for financial provision; and
  (iii) there are therefore no financial arrangements to be made.

...

(5) The requirements of section 11 must have been satisfied.

(6) Schedule I supplements the provisions of this section.

(7) If the court is satisfied, on an application made by one of the parties after the end of the period for reflection and consideration, that the circumstances of the case are—

(*a*) those set out in paragraph 1 of Schedule 1,
(*b*) those set out in paragraph 2 of that Schedule, or
(*c*) those set out in paragraph 3 of that Schedule, or
(*d*) those set out in paragraph 4 of that Schedule,

it may make a divorce order or a separation order even though the requirements of subsection (2) have not been satisfied.

10.—(1) If an application for a divorce order has been made by one of the parties to a marriage, the court may, on the application of the other party, order that the marriage is not to be dissolved.

(2) Such an order (an 'order preventing divorce') may be made only if the court is satisfied —

(*a*) that dissolution of the marriage would result in substantial financial or other hardship to the other party or to a child of the family; and
(*b*) that it would be wrong, in all the circumstances (including the conduct of the parties and the interests of any child of the family), for the marriage to be dissolved.

[Section 11 sets out the duty of the court to consider whether or not its powers under the Children Act 1989 should be exercised with respect to any child of the family.]

Schedule 1, paragraphs 1–4, read as follows:

The first exemption

1. The circumstances referred to in section 9(7)(*a*) are that—
  (*a*) the requirements of section 11 have been satisfied;

(b) the applicant has, during the period for reflection and consideration, taken such steps as are reasonably practicable to try to reach agreement about the parties' financial arrangements; and

(c) the applicant has made an application to the court for financial relief and has complied with all requirements of the court in relation to proceedings for financial relief but—

    (i) the other party has delayed in complying with requirements of the court or has otherwise been obstructive; or

    (ii) for reasons which are beyond the control of the applicant, or of the other party, the court has been prevented from obtaining the information which it requires to determine the financial position of the parties.

The second exemption

2. The circumstances referred to in section 9(7)(b) are that—

(a) the requirements of section 11 have been satisfied;

(b) the applicant has, during the period for reflection and consideration, taken such steps as are reasonably practicable to try to reach agreement about the parties' financial arrangements;

(c) because of—

    (i) the ill health or disability of the applicant, the other party or a child of the family or (whether physical or mental), or

    (ii) an injury suffered by the applicant, the other party or a child of the family,

      the applicant has not been able to reach agreement with the other party about those arrangements and is unlikely to be able to do so in the foreseeable future; and

(d) a delay in making the order applied for under section 3—

    (i) would be significantly detrimental to the welfare of any child of the family; or

    (ii) would be seriously prejudicial to the applicant.

The third exemption

3. The circumstances referred to in section 9(7)(c) are that—

(a) the requirements of section 11 have been satisfied;

(b) the applicant has found it impossible to contact the other party; and

(c) as a result, it has been impossible for the applicant to reach agreement with the other party about their financial arrangements.

The fourth exemption

4. The circumstances referred to in section 9(7)(d) are that—

(a) the requirements of section 11 have been satisfied;

(b) an occupation order or a non-molestation order is in force in favour of the applicant or a child of the family, made against the other party;

(c) the applicant has, during the period for reflection and consideration, taken such steps as are reasonably practicable to try to reach agreement about the parties' financial arrangements;

(d) the applicant has not been able to reach agreement with the other party about those arrangements and is unlikely to be able to do so in the foreseeable future; and

(e) a delay in making the order applied for under section 3—

    (i) would be significantly detrimental to the welfare of any child of the family; or

    (ii) would be seriously prejudicial to the applicant.

In spite of the simplicity of the Law Commission's conception of the basis for divorce, there is a great deal of complexity here. The bare bones of the process, greatly over-simplified, are:

1. Attend an information meeting. Wait three months and then:

2. Make a statement under s. 5. Wait a fortnight (s. 7(3)) and then wait for a period of nine months (in some circumstances fifteen months, s. 7(10)–(13)).

3. Apply for a divorce order.

Among the issues that may arise within that process are the retention of the hardship bar, s. 10; the purpose of s. 9; the use of the period for reflection and consideration; and the resolution of the parties' financial arrangements. Taking these in order:

Questions

(i)   Given that the Law Commission has rejected the philosophy of the fault-based divorce, why retain the hardship bar in s. 10?
(ii) Do you think the retention of the bar will be (a) the last recourse of the bloody-minded or (b) provide much needed protection for dependants and spouses who would otherwise be discarded at will?
(iii) Is pension splitting an answer? (See pp. 363ff, below.)

Section 7(3) states that the period for consideration and reflection which must elapse between the making of a statement of marital breakdown and the making of the divorce order is nine months. However, the effect of sub-ss. (10)–(13) is that the period is extended by a further six months if either party so requests or if there are children of the marriage under 16. In these circumstances, it may nevertheless be reduced to one year if there is in force a domestic violence injunction (see Chapter 9, below), or if the court considers that the longer period would be significantly detrimental to the children. (It remains the law that divorce proceedings cannot be initiated during the first year of marriage.)

In *Family Law:A Ground for Divorce* (1990) the Law Commission explained that the period:

> 5.25 ... is primarily designed to provide convincing proof that the breakdown in the marital relationship is indeed irreparable. It should also give the parties a realistic time within which to resolve the practical questions and to decide whether or not they wish to be reconciled.

They then considered the length of the period:

Length

> 5.27 There was overwhelming agreement amongst respondents to Facing the Future that these objectives could not be achieved in less than nine months. The great majority favoured a period of nine or twelve months, with only a few suggesting longer. It was pointed out that a twelve month period would make divorce a significantly more lengthy process for a substantial number of people. Respondents to our public opinion survey chose periods ranging from six months to over two years, with the highest number (35%) choosing one year. We *recommend* an overall period of twelve months. This should give sufficient time to enable all but the most difficult and complex matters to be decided and to establish that the breakdown is indeed irreparable. It should also allow sufficient time for the benefits of conciliation or mediation to be explored. We also *recommend* that the actual application for a separation or divorce order should not be made until at least eleven months of the period have elapsed. However, there would be no compulsion to apply for an order upon expiration of this time. Parties could take longer if they wished, as an order should not be made unless it is actually applied for. Once applied for, it would not be granted for a further month, making a minimum total of one year overall.
>
> 5.28 A few respondents to Facing the Future suggested that the period should be longer if there were children. Most, however, did not support this. A child's sense of time is quite different from an adult's and considerable harm can be done by prolonged uncertainty. Harm may also be done by the additional bitterness which can be caused by having to wait longer on their account. The general view, both on this and on previous occasions, has been that to make divorce inevitably more difficult for those who have children will not benefit the children themselves and could make matters worse. Thus, 'it would amount to a denial that childless marriage is real marriage. ... Unhappy motives would be introduced for having, or not having, children; and a child once there could become a focus of bitterness for the parent who wanted to be free.' We *recommend*, therefore, that the period should not automatically be longer where there are children. The parties and the court will, however, have to consider what arrangements should be made for them and, if it is desirable to prolong the period in their interests, this should be done.

Although the Family Law Bill, as originally drafted, imposed a one-year period in all circumstances, it was amended in the House of Commons and s. 7(10)–(13)

added. The aim of the amendment was, in the words of Edward Leigh, MP in the House of Commons Debate, to:

... send the important message that, if there are children in a marriage, that should also make a difference to the divorce process. In such circumstances, the parties should think not just of themselves but of the interests of the children.

He also expressed concern that:

... if the period is as short as 12 months, it is simply impossible to have a meaningful period of reconciliation – there is not enough time because there is so much to sort out. If children are involved and if there is not consent to the divorce, reconciliation will not be effective.

Questions

(i) Do you agree that there should be a longer period for reflection and consideration where there are children of the marriage?
(ii) Do you think that the extension of the period to 15 months increases the chance of reconciliation?
(iii) Bearing in mind the provisions of s. 7(10)(*a*), how could a couple with children ensure that they only had to wait nine rather than 15 months?

Another departure from the Law Commission's recommendations is contained in s. 3(1)(*c*): the requirement that financial arrangements be settled before a divorce order can be made. Brenda Hale, in 'The Family Law Act 1996 – Dead Duck or Golden Goose' (2000), explains:

The waiting period is intended to enable the parties 'to consider what arrangements would be made for the future'. The Law Society had tried to persuade the Law Commission that the couple should actually have made those arrangements before they could be divorced. The obligations of a first marriage should be identified before moving on to another. An economically weaker spouse and the children should be provided for before the stronger one is free.

The Law Commission argued that to insist on this in every case would play into the hands of an unreasonable, spiteful or malicious spouse who could delay the resolution of disputes for a long time knowing that this would prevent the divorce. Sometimes this would be in the hope of obtaining a larger financial settlement, but sometimes in the hope of avoiding making any settlement at all. It would hand a formidable bargaining chip to the more powerful or determined party. Under the Law Commission's scheme, a divorce application would automatically be granted after the minimum period had gone by, but on application the court would have power to postpone the divorce in the interests of the children or to allow time for the financial arrangements to be made.

The Lord Chancellor, however, was convinced that the couple should have sorted out the responsibilities from the first marriage before being free to embark upon another. ...

This greatly complicated the original timetable. No one embarking upon the divorce process can know how long it will take (even if the other party does not try to invoke the expanded hardship defence). Enthusiastic implementation of the new procedures for ancillary relief, with effective court management to outlaw the scandalous delays of the past, would be a much better solution.

Question

What effect do you think this requirement would have upon (a) the use made of the period for reflection and consideration, or (b) the chances of the parties' concluding, upon reflection, that the marriage has not irretrievably broken down?

Stephen Cretney, in 'The Divorce White Paper – Some Reflections' (1995), comments:

The Government commissioned a MORI poll which, apparently, showed that divorce on demand by one partner without having to give a reason was widely thought to be unacceptable. The requirement to deal with financial and child upbringing issues before the divorce order is made may be thought significantly to reduce the force of the criticism ... that divorce by repudiation was, in substance, on offer. But the White Paper seems curiously naive about what is likely to happen during the 'period of reflection'. Far from spending the evenings, as the White Paper, para 4.16 suggests, 'reflecting on whether their marriage can be saved and, if not to face up to the consequences of their actions and make arrangements to meet their responsibilities' some, at least, of those concerned seem likely to spend the time in the far more pleasurable activity of conceiving – necessarily illegitimate – babies. Some will spend the time exploiting their emotional or financial advantage; others will brood on their grievances.

Finally, the title to the Green and the White Papers, *Looking to the Future: Mediation and the Ground for Divorce*, draws one's attention to the fact that the ground for divorce is not the only concern of the reforms. We have seen that the Law Commission recommended that the use of mediation be encouraged (see p. 258, above). One of the questions raised in the Green Paper was whether or not mediation should be compulsory; responses to the consultation process indicated that it should not, and this was accepted in the White Paper. At the same time, the Government was encouraged by the positive conclusions of the *Rowntree Report* (discussed further in Chapter 7). Accordingly, the Act contained provision for the court to adjourn proceedings in order for the parties to resolve matters, and to direct that they attend a meeting to have the available mediation facilities explained to them (ss. 13 and 14); Part III of the Act amended the Legal Aid Act 1988 so as to make legal aid available for mediation in family matters.

6.4.3 Aspirations for a brighter future

We began this chapter with a comment on the emotional realities of divorce. During the debate about the new law, before it was enacted, there were frequent expressions of concern about the emotional and practical effects of divorce on the parties and their children, and about the stability of marriage.

Cardinal Basil Hume in *The Times*, 20 January 1996, suggested that:

... any necessary reform of the divorce law can only be part of a larger project of strengthening the institution of marriage and family life.

One urgent need is for better marriage preparation to be available to all. I am often struck by the thought that a monk has to wait five years before being allowed to take solemn vows. Monastic vows are no more solemn than the vows of marriage. And monks do not have the grave responsibility of bringing new life into the world and nurturing young children. We are spending too much money and energy focusing on the ending of marriages, when what is needed is more investment on preparing for marriage and sustaining couples, especially in the early years. Maybe we should make entry into marriage more difficult. ...

Questions

(i)   Is it (a) practicable or (b) desirable for the law to make entry into marriage more difficult?

(ii)   If more people cohabit instead of marrying, who loses – the man, the woman, their children, or all of us?

(iii) In a secular context, what form might 'better marriage preparation' take?

What about the effect of divorce upon children? In spite of widespread views that it is damaging, Maire Ni Brolchain, in '"Divorce Effects" and Causality in the Social Sciences' (2001), sounds a note of caution. She argues that the fact that divorce may be shown to be followed by adverse outcomes for children (poor performance at school, for example) does not mean that such outcomes have been shown to be *caused* by divorce. She comments:

That parental divorce is more often associated with adverse outcomes than parental death is widely cited as confirmation of the adverse impact of 'divorce itself' whereas it may of course signify that, for example, the discordant relationships preceding divorce, and that are unlikely to precede parental death, may be the true differentiating factor. The essence of good science is the capacity to identify competing hypotheses and to devise ways of putting them to the test. This in turn requires ... a dispassionate approach, and investigative imagination. There is much to be learned from existing clinical research on the subject, particularly in designing studies to test competing hypotheses and to disentangle supposed mechanisms.

We might study what happens when a supposed risk factor is removed. An example of such a reversal effect in the divorce context is to examine outcomes among children whose custodial parent remarries. A move into a stepfamily and the resulting family reconstitution appears not to be associated with improved outcomes, a finding that has, however, several interpretations. One might investigate outcomes among children whose parents go through a separation and later return to live together, if such a sample could be found. On the other hand, a causal process may be asymmetric so that changes in one or other direction are irreversible.

Corresponding to the dose-response idea, one might examine whether adverse outcomes were, for example, proportional to the level of father-absence that a child has experienced or, perhaps, proportional to the level of contact after divorce (in the latter case, the answer appears to be 'no'). In the case of parental conflict hypothesis, the relationship between the frequency of adverse outcomes and the degree of marital conflict could be examined.

Thelma Fisher, in 'Impressions of the Family Law Bill in the House of Lords' (1996), commented that the debate in the House of Lords gave the impression—

... of a grandparent generation's deep anxiety about marriage breakdown. There have been speeches about the effects of divorce at a personal level (several peers have given accounts of their own and others' experiences), about the effects of divorce upon children ... and about a 'throwaway' culture of relationships. The elders of the tribe have been grieving and casting about for explanations. However, the retention of the fault clauses has seemed a misguided way of tackling these issues. ... Lord Habgood made one of the most telling speeches, positively arguing the principle of the period of a year:

'Surely this Bill strikes at the right point by giving legal significance to the passage of time. It says "Slow down. What is wrong is precisely that you do want everything immediately". Time is itself important. Time is important not just for what can be done in it – reflection, negotiation, mediation, although they are important. *Time is important as a public assertion that marriages are not easily undone.*'

These concerns and aspirations are reflected in s. 1 of the Family Law Act 1996, added to the Family Law Bill as a House of Lords amendment:

1. The court and any person, in exercising functions under or in consequence of Parts II and III, shall have regard to the following general principles—
   (a) that the institution of marriage is to be supported;
   (b) that the parties to a marriage which may have broken down are to be encouraged to take all practicable steps to save it;
   (c) that a marriage which has irretrievably broken down and is being brought to an end should be brought to an end—
      (i)   with minimum distress to the parties and to the children affected;
      (ii) with questions dealt with in a manner designed to promote as good a continuing relationship between the parties and any children affected as is possible in the circumstances; and
      (iii) without costs being unreasonably incurred in connection with the procedures to be followed in bringing the marriage to an end; and

(*d*) that any risk to one of the parties to a marriage and to any children, of violence from the
other party should, so far as reasonably practicable, be removed or diminished.

(Part II of the Act is concerned with divorce and separation orders, Part III with
Legal Aid for mediation in family matters.)

Questions

(i) Can the reform of the law of divorce contribute to the support of the
institution of marriage?
(ii) Do you think that the provisions of the Family Law Act 1996 have
contributed to the achievement of the ideals set out in s. 1(*c*)?

6.5   The Family Law Act 1996: stuck on the shelf

The provisions of Part II of the Family Law Act were clearly going to take a
great deal of work to implement. Pilot schemes for the information meetings
were set up, and research was commissioned to assess their effectiveness. In
June 1999 the Lord Chancellor announced that the preliminary research results
were 'disappointing' and that implementation of Part II of the 1996 Act would
be delayed. The particular cause for disappointment was said to be the fact that
only 7% of those attending pilot information meetings had been diverted into
mediation and 39% of those attending had reported that they were more likely
than before to go to a solicitor. Stephen Cretney, at the UK Family Law
Conference (reported at [1999] Fam Law 517), expressed the reactions of
many:

...I am one of those who, until last Thursday, believed that the Family Law Act was to be
implemented in the year 2000; and I was indeed surprised – astonished might be the better
word – not only at the fact that this was not to happen but at the way in which the announcement
was made. In common with many other people, I had a strong – indeed legitimate – expectation
of implementation in 2000 for the very simple reason that, over and over again, with repeated
emphasis, the Lord Chancellor and his Department have told us so. ...

We are now told that the Government's decision has been taken because of research findings.
I have read all that has been published. There is *nothing* in them which would come as any
surprise to those who have taken even the most superficial interest in this subject over the years:
in particular, I know of no one who believed that as many as four out of ten of those attending
information meetings would be diverted into mediation.

The thousands of people who have invested huge amounts of capital – human in all cases,
financial in some – in preparing the mediation and other structures needed for implementation
will certainly be delighted to have heard from the Lord Chancellor that the Government only
acts on the basis of hard factual evidence and not on 'well meaning hypothesis or assumptions'
much less on 'wishful thinking'...

Let there be no mistake about it. There are many, many questions to be asked; and many,
many answers to be given. ... No democratic government – and certainly no government which
constantly reminds us of its commitment to consultation, openness, transparency – should
believe that it can get away with what the Lord Chancellor has said so far.

Nevertheless, in December 2000, the Lord Chancellor announced that the new
divorce provisions would not be implemented at all. *The Times* on 18 December
2000 reported as follows:

The Lord Chancellor is expected to announce this week that he is scrapping reforms that would
have enabled married couples to obtain a 'no fault' divorce.

Lord Irvine of Lairg has decided not to proceed with the main plank of the ill-fated Family Law Act 1996 after research has shown it to be unworkable and likely, if implemented, to cost up to £50 million a year.

Now ministers are expected to announce plans to strengthen support for families and marriage, including an enhanced role for marriage registrars in counselling couples. Couples would have more time to reflect before they marry, with both parties attending the register office to make the first arrangement. Marriage counselling and support services would also be boosted.

At the same time, a current review of the Children Act 1989 is likely to lead to stronger powers for courts to refuse divorces where arrangements for children are not in place.

The 1996 Family Law Act liberalised divorce by allowing couples to obtain a termination of their marriage without the need to cite adultery or some other fault-based ground. Divorce would be granted after one year or 18 months in the case of children, provided the couple had first sorted out arrangements over both children and money.

The reforms were one of the last acts of John Major's Government. But the original plans for 'no fault' divorce were criticised by traditionalists who said that they weakened marriage.

The result was a series of concessions which, according to lawyers, have made the package unworkable. The key concession, which has now forced the Lord Chancellor to rethink the whole idea, was a new compulsory information meeting for all people wanting to start a divorce.

The idea was that a meeting would identify 'saveable marriages' and steer couples who were uncertain to counselling. Those who did want to take part would be encouraged to use mediation services, rather than lawyers. But research has found that the meetings served only to reinforce in people's minds the need for legal advice and the need to consult a lawyer.

It has been estimated that it could cost between £40 million and £50 million to arrange information meetings for everyone who gets divorced, money which could be better spent on support and counselling.

Last year Lord Irvine announced that he was shelving the reforms for one year, pending the final outcome of research findings. The Family Law Act, which amounted to the biggest reform of divorce for decades, has been the butt of widespread criticism despite wide support for its aim of removing some of the bitterness from divorce. The Labour minister Paul Boateng, when he was opposition legal affairs spokesman, condemned it as a 'dog's dinner'.

Ministers have been nervous about proceeding with implementation of its main provisions, but equally there is concern that to leave a key reform passed by Parliament unimplemented may lay them open to legal challenge.

Mark Harper, a member of the Law Society family law committee, said that the law as passed was clearly unworkable but that scrapping the 'No-fault divorce would reduce unnecessary bitterness and antagonism which exists under the current law by having to make up allegations of unreasonable behaviour'.

The full report of the research into the family mediation pilot can be found at the Legal Services Commission website, www.legalservices.gov.uk, by clicking on the 'News' button. More of mediation in the next chapter.

Meanwhile, what of divorce? In September 1999 the Third Inter-disciplinary Conference on Family Law was held at Dartington Hall. The proceedings of that conference are published under the title *No fault or flaw: the future of the Family Law Act 1996* (2000), edited by Lord Justice Thorpe and Elizabeth Clarke. In his introduction, Lord Justice Thorpe summarised the message of the conference to the government as this: 'the introduction of no-fault divorce is the highest legislative priority for the family justice system.' Contributions to the conference discussed the Family Law Act, Part II; mediation; marriage support; the participation of children; mental health services; legal services; the judiciary; and national support structures. In the final chapter of *No fault or flaw*, Brenda Hale summarised the resolutions of the conference and added her own concluding comments:

The 1996 Act was emphatically not concerned with making divorce either easier or harder for the families involved. One wise observer of the Parliamentary debates commented how cleverly the opponents of no fault divorce had combined to produce a scheme which might be seen as well nigh unworkable. They cannot all have been unaware that the present law permits one party to obtain a very speedy divorce whether or not the other party wants it and then to delay the working out of the practical and financial consequences almost indefinitely. Participants in this conference were only too well aware that in doing so it is letting down everyone involved, not only the parties, but also their children and the wider community.

Even within the present law, there is much we could do to offer them a better service. The idea of offering the public a service is commonplace in many other areas of activity but something of a novelty in this context. It is nevertheless the clearest message to come out of this conference.

The conference was full of thoughts about information and mediation services, all of which could be improved within the present legislative framework. The main messages here are that we need to help rather than preach at the adults and that we need to consider the children as real people and active participants rather than passive recipients of the adults' decisions.

The conference was less full of thoughts about how we could better adapt the present court processes to the needs of the people rather than the professionals involved.... The present system allows and even encourages the parties to spend a quite disproportionate amount of their resources (or the resources of the legal aid fund which will usually be recouped from them) upon legal proceedings. Small wonder that many of those who have been through it once are reluctant to risk it again by remarrying. More and more young people are choosing to postpone or even reject marriage altogether. It may already be too late to halt that trend, but they are deluding themselves if they think that living together without marriage carries any less risk of legal proceedings. If anything, their problems are even more complex. The price of keeping the individualised discretionary approach to resolving family problems is that we must make the process as genuinely user friendly and as cost effective as we possibly can.

Questions

(i)   Having read this far, how do you feel about marriage?
(ii) What should the government do next?

Bibliography

Introduction

We quoted from:

G. Alpern, *Rights of Passage* (1982) Aspen, Colorado, Psychological Development Publications, p. 19.

A. Alvarez, *Life after Marriage: Love in an Age of Divorce* (1981) New York, Simon and Schuster.

J. Cleese and R. Skynner, *Families and How to Survive Them* (1993) London, Cedar, pp. 15, 16.

6.1   The history of English divorce law

We quoted from:

Sir Morris Finer and O.R. McGregor, 'The History of the Obligation to Maintain' Appendix 5, *Report of the Committee on One-Parent Families* (Cmnd. 5629-1) (1974), London, HMSO, paras. 1, 2, 4, 5, 6, 13, 14, 17, 18, 30, 31, 34, 42, 43.

Report of the Committee on One-Parent Families (Chairman: The Hon. Sir Morris Finer) (Cmnd. 5629) (1974), London, HMSO, paras. 4.29–4.32.

Law Commission, *Reform of the Grounds of Divorce – The Field of Choice* (Cmnd. 3123) (1966), London, HMSO, paras. 11, 15, 19, 52, 120.

Report of a Group appointed by the Archbishop of Canterbury (Chairman: The Rt Rev. R.C. Mortimer, Lord Bishop of Exeter), *Putting Asunder – A Divorce Law for Contemporary Society* (1966) London, Society for Promoting Christian Knowledge, paras. 17, 18, 45(f), 55, 69.

L. Stone, *Road to Divorce: England 1530-1987* (1990) Oxford, Oxford University Press, pp. 27, 310.

St. Mark, 'Gospel according to St. Mark' *Holy Bible* Authorised King James version, ch. 10.

Additional reading

Report of the Royal Commission on Marriage and Divorce (Chairman: Lord Morton of Henryton) (Cmd. 9678) (1956), London, HMSO.

6.2   The present law: the Matrimonial Causes Act 1973

We quoted from

H. Conway, 'Divorce and Religion' (1995) New Law Journal, p. 1618.

M.A. Glendon, *Abortion and Divorce in Western Law* (1987) Cambridge (Mass) and London, Harvard University Press, pp. 63–64, 66–68.

J. Haskey, 'Divorce Statistics' (1996) 26 Family Law 301, table 2.

Law Commission, *Court Record Study* Appendix C to *The Ground for Divorce*, Law Com. No. 192 (1990) London, HMSO, paras. 26, 31, 32, 44, 51.

'So What's Unreasonable Behaviour?', *The Times*, 15 February 1996, p. 15.

Additional reading

Law Society, Family Law Sub-Committee, *A Better Way Out: Suggestions for the Reform of the Law of Divorce and Other Forms of Matrimonial Relief; for the Setting Up of a Family Court; and for its Procedure* (1979) London, The Law Society, paras. 33, 35–38, 40, 42, 44, 46–52, 58, 69, 70.

The Scottish Law Commission, *Report on Reform of the Ground for Divorce*, Scot. Law Com. No. 116 (1989) Edinburgh, HMSO.

Sir Jocelyn Simon, 'Recent Developments in the Matrimonial Law' Riddell lecture, 1970. Reproduced in *Rayden on Divorce* (11th edn, 1971) London, Butterworths.

M. Walls and D. Bergin, *The Law of Divorce in Ireland* (1997) Family Law.

6.3   The factual context

We quoted from

C. Archbold, P. McKee and C. White, 'Divorce law and divorce culture – the case of Northern Ireland' (1998) 4 Child and Family Law Quarterly 377.

A. Bissett-Johnson and C. Barton, 'The similarities and differences in Scottish and English family law in dealing with changing family patterns' (1999) 21(1) Journal of Social Welfare Law 1.

Central Statistical Office, *Social Trends 30* (2000) London, HMSO, table 2.9.

G. Davis and M. Murch, *Grounds for Divorce* (1988) Oxford, Clarendon Press, pp. 78–85.

I. Ellman, 'Divorce in the United States' in S. Katz, J. Eekelaar and M. Maclean, *Cross Currents* (2000) Oxford, Oxford University Press.

J. Haskey, 'Trends in Marriage and Divorce 1837-1987' (1987) 48 Population Trends, pp. 11, 17, fig. 6.

J. Haskey, 'Pre-marital Cohabitation and the Probability of Subsequent Divorce' (1992) 68 Population Trends 10, pp. 17–18 and fig. 3.

J. Haskey, 'Formation and dissolution of unions in the different countries of Europe' in A. Blum and J.-L. Rallu (eds.) *European Population, vol. II: Demographic Dynamics* (1993) Paris, John Libbey Eurotext, figs. 2a and 2b.

R. Leete, *Changing Patterns of Family Formation and Dissolution in England and Wales 1964–1976,* OPCS Studies on Medical and Population Subjects No. 39 (1979) London, HMSO, tables 36, 38, figs. 19, 20.

Lord Chancellor's Department, *Judicial Statistics – Annual Reports* (2000), p. 49.

M.P.M. Richards, 'Divorce Research Today' (1991) 21 Family Law 70–72.

M.P.M. Richards, 'Private Worlds and Public Intentions – The Role of the State in Divorce' in A. Bainham, D. Pearl and R. Pickford (eds.), *Frontiers of Family Law* (1995) Chichester, John Wiley and Sons.

Additional reading

A.J. Cherlin, *Marriage, Divorce and Remarriage* (1981, revised 1992) Cambridge, Massachusetts, Harvard University Press.

R. Chester and J. Streather, 'Cruelty in English Divorce: Some Empirical Findings' (1972) 34 Journal of Marriage and the Family 706.

J. Haskey, 'Social Class and Socio-economic Differentials in Divorce in England and Wales' (1984) Population Studies 38.

J. Haskey, 'Recent Trends in Divorce in England and Wales: the Effects of Legislative Changes' (1986) 44 Population Trends 9.

J. Haskey, 'Regional Patterns of Divorce in England and Wales' (1988) 52 Population Trends 5, p. 13, table 6.

J. Haskey, 'Patterns of Marriage, Divorce, and Cohabitation in the Different Countries of Europe' (1992) 69 Population Trends 26, pp. 29–31, figs. 2(a) and 2(b).

L. Weitzman and R.B. Dixon, 'The Transformation of Marriage through No Fault Divorce – The Case of the United States' in J.M. Eekelaar and S.N. Katz (eds.), *Marriage and Cohabitation in Contemporary Societies: Areas of Legal, Social and Ethical Change* (1980) Toronto, Butterworths.

6.4   The Family Law Act 1996: a brighter future?

We quoted from:

A. Bainham, 'Divorce and the Lord Chancellor: Looking to the Future or Getting Back to Basics?' (1994) 53 Cambridge Law Journal 253, p. 256.

M. N. Brolchain, '"Divorce Effects" and Causality in the Social Sciences' (2001) 17(1) European Sociology Review 33, p. 49.

S. Cretney, 'The Divorce White Paper – Some Reflections' (1995) Family Law 302, p. 304.

R. Deech, 'Marriage as a Short-term Option' (1990) *The Independent,* 2 November 1990.

R. Deech, *Divorce Dissent: Dangers in Divorce Reform* (1994) London, Centre for Policy Studies, pp. 14, 20–21.

T. Fisher, 'Impressions of the Family Law Bill in the House of Lords' (1996) 6(1) Family Mediation 3.

B. Hale, 'The Family Law Act 1996 – Dead Duck or Golden Goose' in S. Cretney (ed.), *Family Law: Essays for the New Millenium* (2000) Family Law.

Hansard, House of Commons, vol. 276 (24 April 1996) cols. 502, 505.

Cardinal B. Hume, 'Why We Need a Change of Heart on Divorce Law' *The Times,* 20 January 1996, p. 20.

Law Commission, *The Ground for Divorce,* Law Com. No. 192 (1990) London, HMSO, paras. 1.5–1.8; 2.8–2.21; 3.29–3.48; 5.25; 5.27; 5.28; 5.75–5.77.

Additional reading

J. Eekelaar, *Regulating Divorce* (1991) Oxford, Clarendon Press.

J. Eekelaar, 'The Family Law Bill: The Politics of Family Law' (1996) 26 Family Law 46.

J. Haskey, 'Children in Families Broken by Divorce' (1990) 61 Population Trends 34, p. 35, fig. I, table I.

Looking to the Future: Mediation and the Ground for Divorce. A consultation paper (Cm. 2424) (1993) London, HMSO, paras. 9.28–9.30.

Looking to the Future: Mediation and the Ground for Divorce. The Government's proposals (Cm. 2799) (1995) London, HMSO.

M. Maclean and R.E.J. Wadsworth, 'The Interests of Children after Parental Divorce: A Long-term Perspective' (1988) 2 International Journal of Law and the Family 155.

M.P.M. Richards and M. Dyson, *Separation, Divorce and the Development of Children: a Review* (1982) London, DHSS.

S.D. Sugarman and H.H. Kay, *Divorce Reform at the Crossroads* (1990) New Haven and London, Yale University Press.

6.5 The Family Law Act 1996: stuck on the shelf

We quoted from:

S. Cretney, extract from a speech at the UK Family Law Conference 1999 [1999] Fam Law 517.

F. Gibb, 'Irvine will scrap "no fault" divorce', *The Times,* 18 December 2000.

B. Hale, conclusion, in M. Thorpe and E. Clarke (eds.), *No fault or flaw: the future of the Family Law Act 1996* (2000) Family Law.

Additional reading

L. Tottie, 'The Elimination of Fault in Swedish Divorce Law' in J.M. Eekelaar and S.N. Katz (eds.), *Marriage and Cohabitation in Contemporary Societies: Areas of Legal, Social and Ethical Change* (1980) Toronto, Butterworths.

Chapter 7

Adjudication and mediation

7.1 The family courts debate

7.2 Public regulation or private ordering?

7.3 Marriage mending or marriage ending?

7.4 Mediation: development and the way ahead

This chapter looks at the role of the courts and other agencies in the resolution of family disputes. It is now widely acknowledged that family disputes are different from others and may demand a different approach from all who are concerned with them. But quite how different that approach should be is controversial. We have placed this discussion immediately after our examination of divorce. This is partly because, for many people, divorce marks their first encounter with the legal system, and may prompt them to question its operation; and partly because it is in that context that legislative attempts have been made to introduce a new approach.

7.1 The family courts debate

The first comprehensive official discussion of family courts came in the *Report of the Committee on One-Parent Families* (the 'Finer Report') in 1974. The dilemma is highlighted in its discussion of the fundamental principle:

THE FAMILY COURT AS A JUDICIAL INSTITUTION

4.285 The fundamental principle which must govern the family court is that it shall be a judicial institution which, in dealing with family matters, does justice according to law. This may seem to be so obvious a point as hardly to be worth mentioning; but the need to emphasise it arises from the nature of a jurisdiction which aims to do good as well as to do right. To promote welfare is an unusual function for a court of law. To some extent, the courts which deal with matrimonial disputes and with children are already familiar with that function through references in the statutes to reconciliation in husband and wife disputes, and through the statutory obligation in many forms of proceedings which involve children to have first and paramount regard, in any decision the court may reach, to their welfare. But the deliberate attempt to expand and systematise the welfare function, which is an essential part of the family court concept, carries risks, as well as potential advantages, which can be eliminated only by clear thinking and firm practice regarding boundaries and priorities. The court must remain, and must be seen to remain, impartial. This is of particular importance now that local authorities and governmental agencies of various kinds have powers and duties imposed on them which bring them into the proceedings, either as interested parties or as advisers to the court. The object of achieving welfare must not be permitted to weaken or short cut the normal safeguards of the judicial process – the dispassionate examination of evidence properly adduced to the court, regular procedures which promote an orderly and fair hearing, and the allowance of legal representation. The court must not see the men, women and children with whom it is concerned as 'clients', and still less as 'patients' for whom the court process is one form of, or a preliminary to, 'treatment'. Professional staff serving the court, including any who are responsible for assisting the court to reach sound conclusions on welfare issues, must be answerable to the court for what they do and how they do it. The aim must be to make adjudication and welfare march hand in hand, but there should be no blurring of the edges, either in principle or in administration. Through the family court it should be possible to make a new and highly beneficial synthesis between law and social welfare, and the respective skills, experience and efforts of lawyers and social workers; but the individual in the family court must in the last resort remain the subject of rights, not the object of assistance.

Family disputes are still (mainly) dealt with in the ordinary courts. But in more than a quarter of a century since the Finer Report, we have learned a great deal more about the differences between them and other cases heard by the civil courts and about the 'synthesis' between law and social work. Gillian Douglas explains in *Resolving Family Disputes* (2002), a discussion paper for the Nuffield Foundation's Seminars in Civil Justice (following up Hazel Genn's survey of 'what people do and think about going to law', *Paths to Justice* (1999)):

It may be helpful to begin by setting out certain distinctive features that family disputes have, and which should be considered in determining how research and policy should be developed. The paper focuses on five such features here. In identifying these, it is not suggested that they are unique to family disputes; it is clear that they may be found in other contexts. But the particular constellation of these features does render family disputes different from other matters that may be dealt with by the civil courts and therefore shapes what we need to know.

1. Family disputes usually concern future arrangements rather than past events
There is probably no other type of civil proceeding so heavily concentrated upon making an assessment about future circumstances as that relating to family disputes. Although, as Mr Justice Wall is reported as saying, it will always 'be necessary to have the court for fact finding and for imposing sanctions where they are necessary', the focus of the proceedings is primarily on what is to happen next – who is to care for the child, should the house be sold, how long should maintenance for the spouse continue? These questions are not amenable to being resolved through traditional forensic legal expertise. They involve guesses as to the future, based on common sense, past experience or an appeal to experts for guidance. They may mean that, when circumstances develop differently to what had been expected, the case may return to court for re-assessment. The potentially open-ended nature of family litigation is a source of frustration for all concerned. Where the dispute concerns the children, judges may increasingly resent the seeming inability of some parents to 'come to terms' with the reality of the situation as their children grow up. Parents may be criticised for failing to recognise the need to compromise, and revise the terms of any previous arrangement they have agreed or which has been imposed by the court. . . .
    At least, in litigation concerning children, the court's continuing jurisdiction to hear the parties' dispute is clear (even though the courts do all they can to discourage them from making use of that jurisdiction). In the sphere of finance and property, this is not always the case. Except in the case of an order to pay continuing periodical payments to a former spouse, there is no continuing jurisdiction to revise settlements reached on the divorce. 'Property adjustment orders' (such as for the transfer of one spouse's interest in the home to the other) are one-off orders which cannot be subsequently varied. This may be unfortunate given the impossibility of predicting the future, such as the likely variation in house prices (both up and down), the performance of the stock markets, the vagaries of employment trends and the uncertainties of health and wellbeing. The case-law offers numerous examples of how such factors have falsified the assumptions upon which orders have been made. Yet that same case-law also confirms the courts' general reluctance to re-open settlements in such situations. Instead, the 'clean break' financial settlement, whereby there is no continuing financial obligation to support the dependent spouse, and the parties' claims on each other are satisfied from the available capital assets, is strongly favoured. The preference for the clean break (which, it must be acknowledged, is apparently shared by the majority of divorcing spouses as well) may reflect a recognition of this

lack of clairvoyant power possessed by the legal system, and a wish nonetheless to bring the marriage – and the litigation – to a final conclusion.

The problem is that when things *do* subsequently turn out differently from what was expected, the sense of grievance may be very strong. It is not surprising that Paths to Justice found that those with divorce or separation problems who had settled by agreement were significantly more likely than others to think this agreement was unfair. The 'divorce' respondents were also the most likely to regret how they had handled their problem and less likely to feel they had achieved their objectives.

The emphasis on how matters should be resolved for the future is linked to the well-known fact that divorce, or any relationship breakdown or re-alignment (such as in adoption), is a 'process' and not an event. Coming to terms with change and adjusting to new circumstances over time inevitably means that the nature and perception of problems relating to the family situation will also change. This may explain Professor Genn's finding that family disputes frequently involved clusters of problems, either simultaneously or spread out over time. The study found that respondents involved in divorce proceedings during the previous five years were very likely also to report family problems (59%), children problems (19%) and money problems (19%). These 'clusters' of problems appear to indicate respondents having to confront these different problems, as and when they arise and have to be faced. This represents a major challenge for the legal system, which suffers from what might be described as 'happy ever after' syndrome – the assumption that once the legal case has been dealt with, the 'problem' has been solved. On the contrary, Paths to Justice suggests that service providers must be alive to the need to respond over what may be a very long period of time to the range of problems which family breakdown and consequential readjustment may produce.

2. Family disputes frequently involve the interests of a third party

Around half of divorces each year involve couples who have one or more children under the age of 16. In 1999, of the 148,000 children under 16 whose parents divorced, around one in four children was aged under 5 years old, and seven out of ten were aged 10 or under. On the assumption that the breakdown of the marriage may place such children in a vulnerable position, the legal system has for the past fifty years attempted to take account of the interests of these children even though they may not be the subjects of legal proceedings themselves. For example, before a divorce can be granted, s 41 of the Matrimonial Causes Act 1973 requires the court to scrutinise the arrangements proposed by the petitioner for the children's care and upbringing. The court may make orders under the Children Act 1989 if required, or in exceptional cases delay grant of the decree absolute if dissatisfied with what is proposed. Not all divorces in fact result in a court order concerning the children's upbringing. However, a court dealing with the *financial* consequences of the divorce must give 'first consideration' to the welfare of the children in determining what orders it should make. Recent guidance issued to practitioners also emphasises the need to consider the interests of the children when handling matrimonial litigation. . . .

In proceedings relating to children, there are special mechanisms intended to provide the court with information as to their welfare, wishes and feelings. In contested private law proceedings, they may be the subjects of a welfare investigation and report compiled by a children and family reporter, in public law proceedings for care or adoption, a children's guardian is appointed to represent their interests. These mechanisms have been brought into effect over the past thirty years because of a growing recognition that parents may not always be able to represent their children's best interest themselves and that a conflict of interests may result. This recognition has accompanied the more general 'discovery' of children as social actors with their own interests and concerns epitomised by adoption of the United Nations Convention on the Rights of the Child. But it is the incorporation of the European Convention on Human Rights into English law that has perhaps brought the issue of how the legal system can best take account of the position of children most sharply to the forefront of legal, if not policy makers', attention. Children have the same human rights as adults, including the right under Art 6 of access to an independent court or tribunal for the determination of their civil rights and obligations, and the right under Art 8 to respect for their private and family life. The question for the courts and lawyers is how such rights are to be adequately protected when, in the usual case, the child is not a party to the legal proceedings between the adults. Whether a bare appeal to 'take account of the child's interests' adequately meets the obligation on the state is an important question. It is currently being slowly worked out through case-law and developments at the European level through, for example, the European Convention on the Exercise of Children's Rights – a convention which, as yet, the UK has not signed. . . .

When a family relationship breaks down, others may also be affected. At present, no special notice is taken of grandparents or other family members in this situation, although there are means whereby they can, for example, challenge parental decisions to curtail contact with their children. But as the population ages, and the middle generation find themselves taken up as much with the support needs of their parents as of their children, the impact of a divorce or relationship breakdown on the financial situation of an elderly relative may come to assume increasing significance.

3. Family disputes are associated with a relatively high level of involvement with courts and lawyers
Of particular importance to our understanding of how family problems are handled in the legal process is the finding in the Paths to Justice study that people with such problems were the most likely to resort to legal advice and legal action, as compared with other types of justiciable problems. 92% of those in the survey with divorce/separation problems took legal advice, and 82% saw a solicitor. 61% used a solicitor as their first point of contact for advice about their divorce or separation. Not only did people with family problems resort to legal advice, but they also, according to the study, used the courts to a significant extent. Professor Genn showed that divorce and separation problems had the highest percentage resolved by court decision or order, at 56% (and note, again, the findings relating to the apparently increasing number of disputes over children, considered above).

There would appear to be two reasons for this relatively high level of resort to the courts in family disputes. First, and most obviously, where the issue entails a change of legal status (such as on divorce), the parties *have to* take legal proceedings as only the court can make the change and terminate the marriage. But the second reason may be cultural expectation – coupled with good sense. Marriage breakdown has become associated with the courts in the general public's consciousness, largely because of the need for court sanction of change of status. It follows that most litigants are likely to feel that they will be better off having an expert who knows the courts and the law to advise or act for them in such disputes, if they can afford to do so. While they may later feel that they could have handled matters just as well without the lawyer, research does suggest that lawyers continue to fulfil an important role in offering reassurance and acting as 'passage agents' for those who are unfamiliar and uncomfortable with the legal process. . . .

Moreover, it is important to recognise and find out more about the 'dark figure' outside the statistics of use of legal proceedings, as the Paths to Justice study itself did. Indeed, there are two types of 'dark figure' to be considered here. First, there are those who, although they must engage with the legal system at some point (eg to obtain a divorce decree), do not use a lawyer to assist them to do so, or who only use a lawyer for certain stages in the process and who do not obtain a court order alongside the decree. For example, only a minority of those divorcing appear to obtain any kind of financial order, and, of course as is well known, a very small minority of these obtains such an order as a result of full adjudication of their dispute. Further, while publicly-funded legal assistance remains a possibility for a large number of litigants caught up in family disputes, there seems to be an increasing number of unrepresented litigants, often involved in the most intractable of family cases, to the despair of the judiciary and opposing counsel. . . .

Secondly, there is an unknown number of people who, because they are not married, do not have to go to the courts to terminate their relationship, and appear to be less likely to use the courts – or lawyers – to resolve problems arising when their relationship breaks down. We still know very little about the circumstances in such cases, and about how people manage without the use of the legal process. . . .

4. The courts are seen as an undesirable forum for the resolution of family disputes
Ironically, given the high level of resort to the courts as compared with other types of dispute, the legal process is regarded as an undesirable forum for the resolution of family disputes, and there is strong pressure throughout the system to avoid resort to adjudication. This is a complex matter. First, the legal system is seen as inappropriate for handling family matters because these often – perhaps even usually – concern 'non-legal' issues related to adjusting to life after separation. The law, lawyers and the courts, may be regarded as ill-equipped to deal with these matters. For example, there appears to be a strongly-held view among family solicitors that they have no particular expertise to offer to parents on, for example, how to help children come to terms with the divorce. Judges' reliance upon the views of experts may reflect a similar lack of confidence in their ability to make better decisions than parents on what is in a child's best interests. Secondly, the legal system may be seen as actually making family relationships *worse* because of its traditional adversarial character and procedures. As is well-known, such a view permeated the former government's thinking when it was proposing the divorce reforms which emerged in the Family Law Act 1996. Notwithstanding research (Eekelaar, Maclean and Beinart, 2000) suggesting that many family lawyers are, to the contrary, non-adversarial almost to a fault, there is also a view among a number of respondents in studies of divorce that lawyers either do, or may, antagonise the other party and make matters worse during negotiations.

These attitudes have resulted in the development of 'family courts' in some jurisdictions, of specialist family judges, and of alternative methods of dispute resolution, most importantly through family mediation.

It is worth noting here too, the valuable insights offered by the psychoanalytic perspective of divorce offered by Brown and Day Sclater (1999). They argue that the undermining of the adversarial approach and the idealisation of mediation as an alternative

'can thus be seen as an attempt to deny the uncomfortable fact of family breakdown . . . denying the psychological realities of loss and neglecting the psychological significance of the need to rebuild the self. . . . The focus of dispute resolution and mediation should, therefore, be on containing conflict, which means creating structures which can metabolise and transform it, rather than thinking quantitatively in terms of a reduction or denial of it.'

It may tentatively be suggested that the attraction of the 'clean break' settlement to lawyers and parties is another example of this denial of the messiness of divorce and of the need to 'work through it' rather than draw a neat line underneath the marriage as soon as possible. . . .

5. 'Justice' and 'rights' have little place in the legal resolution of family disputes
This leads to a final feature of family dispute resolution. This is the extent, perhaps not matched in any other area of the law, to which ideas of justice and rights have been driven from the lexicon when it comes to resolving disputes through the legal process. The process began with the diminution of emphasis upon matrimonial fault in the Divorce Reform Act 1969. The judiciary, most famously through the judgments of Lord Denning in the Court of Appeal in the 1970s, carried the new ethos, which had been created for the grant of the divorce itself, over into their handling of the consequences of the divorce. Both as regards finance and property disputes and custody and access decisions, it was soon laid down as a matter of law that matrimonial misconduct would usually be regarded as irrelevant to the court's determination of the dispute. . . .

One should not make the mistake of confusing the allocation of blame with the accomplishment of 'justice' between litigants. However, it is clear that ideas about 'fairness', entitlement and obligation do still underpin family members' own notions of how family disputes should be resolved (or at least, how their *own* dispute should). And indeed, in the context of financial settlements on divorce, the House of Lords has recognised that, in the words of Lord Nicholls, 'Everyone would accept that the outcome on these matters, whether by agreement or court order, should be fair'. This appeal to fairness seems to be an aspect of the psychological dimension discussed by Day Sclater (above). In attempting to understand the reasons for the failure of the relationship, a person must make sense of the past in order to move on to the future. This may entail having one's own account of the 'rights and wrongs' vindicated and 'heard' by the legal system, or at least by one's lawyer. Perhaps this is why clients appreciate the 'partisanship' of their lawyers and may distrust mediators. If one regards 'justice' as importing an idea of restoring a *balance* between the parties, one might certainly argue that family members' sense or grievance, either before, or at the end of, legal proceedings is stoked by an apparent asymmetry in their legal positions. Perhaps if there were more of an apparent willingness to grant the parties space to represent 'either side' of the story first, it would be easier for them to move on and to leave their sense of grievance behind them.

As with the position regarding children's participation in legal proceedings, how the Human Rights Act will affect this situation must remain to be seen. Appeals to rights have become more common as part of the legal arguments in family disputes, and are inevitably being confronted and addressed more directly by the judiciary. The courts' initial approach, as revealed through reported case-law, has been one of caution and a desire to find compatibility rather than conflict between domestic and Convention law. But one might expect, in future discussions on family policy matters, that Articles 6 and 8 of the Convention will colour the terms of the debate and the acceptability of the solutions proposed.

Questions

(i) Is it the function of the courts to channel and contain feelings such as anger, bitterness and aggression or allow them to be expressed?

(ii) Is it a good thing or a bad thing that many family lawyers are 'non-adversarial almost to a fault'? What sort of lawyers would you most want if your relationship broke up?

(iii) Do you think that family judges should have different skills from other judges? Should they be stricter and sterner or kinder and gentler? Should they have training in other disciplines and if so which (eg adult or child psychology, the sociology of the family, gender equality, ethnic issues)?

Even in the ordinary courts, most family cases are treated rather differently from others. In particular, all disputes about children, occupation of the family home and protection from violence or other forms of molestation, and about property and financial provision between spouses, or under the Inheritance (Provision for Family and Dependants) Act 1975 are heard in private. Article 6(1) of the European Convention on Human Rights, however, provides that:

Right to a fair trial
1. In the determination of his civil rights and obligations or of any criminal charge against him, everyone is entitled to a fair and public hearing within a reasonable time by an independent and impartial tribunal established by law. Judgment shall be pronounced publicly but the press and public may be excluded from all or part of the trial in the interest of morals, public order or national security in a democratic society, where the interests of juveniles or the protection of the private life of the parties so require, or to the extent strictly necessary in the opinion of the court in special circumstances where publicity would prejudice the interests of justice.

The English practice was challenged in Strasbourg by two fathers who had wanted their applications for residence orders in respect of their children heard in public:

B v United Kingdom; P v United Kingdom
[2001] 2 FLR 261, European Court of Human Rights

[36] The Court recalls that Art 6(1) of the Convention provides that, in the determination of civil rights and obligations, 'everyone is entitled to a fair and public hearing'. The public character of proceedings protects litigants against the administration of justice in secret with no public scrutiny; it is also one of the means whereby confidence in the courts can be maintained. By rendering the administration of justice visible, publicity contributes to the achievement of the aim of Art 6(1), a fair hearing, the guarantee of which is one of the foundations of a democratic society (see *Sutter v Switzerland* (1984) 6 EHRR 272, para 26).
[37] However, the requirement to hold a public hearing is subject to exceptions. This is apparent from the text of Art 6(1) itself, which contains the proviso that 'the press and public may be excluded from all or part of the trial . . . where the interests of juveniles or the private life of the parties so require, or to the extent strictly necessary in the opinion of the court in special circumstances where publicity would prejudice the interests of justice'. Moreover, it is established in the Court's case-law that, even in a criminal law context where there is a high expectation of publicity, it may on occasion be necessary under Art 6 to limit the open and public nature of proceedings in order, for example, to protect the safety or privacy of witnesses or to promote the free exchange of information and opinion in the pursuit of justice (see, for example, *Doorson v The Netherlands* (1996) 22 EHRR 330; *Jasper v United Kingdom* (2000) 30 EHRR 441; *Z v Finland* (1998) 25 EHRR 371; and *T v United Kingdom* (2000) 30 EHRR 121).
[38] The proceedings which the present applicants wished to take place in public concerned the residence of each man's son following the parents' divorce or separation. The Court considers that such proceedings are prime examples of cases where the exclusion of the press and public may be justified in order to protect the privacy of the child and parties and to avoid prejudicing the interests of justice. To enable the deciding judge to gain as full and accurate a picture as possible of the advantages and disadvantages of the various residence and contact options open to the child, it is essential that the parents and other witnesses feel able to express themselves candidly on highly personal issues without fear of public curiosity or comment.
[39] The applicants submit that the presumption in favour of a private hearing in cases under the Children Act 1989 should be reversed. However, while the Court agrees that Art 6(1) states a general rule that civil proceedings, inter alia, should take place in public, it does not find it inconsistent with this provision for a State to designate an entire class of case as an exception

to the general rule where considered necessary in the interest of morals, public order or national security or where required by the interests of juveniles or the protection of the private life of the parties (see *Campbell and Fell v United Kingdom* (1984) 7 EHRR 165, paras 86-87), although the need for such a measure must always be subject to the Court's control (see, for example, *Riepan v Austria* (Case 35115/97) (unreported) 14 November 2000). The English procedural law can therefore be seen as a specific reflection of the general exceptions provided for by Art 6(1).

[40] Furthermore, the English tribunals have a discretion to hold Children Act 1989 proceedings in public if merited by the special features of the case, and the judge must consider whether or not to exercise his or her discretion in this respect if requested by one of the parties. . . .

[41] In conclusion, therefore, the Court does not consider that the decision in each applicant's case to hold the hearing of his application for the residence of his son in chambers gave rise to a violation of Art 6(1) of the Convention.

[42] In addition, the applicants complained that the county courts' residence judgments were not pronounced publicly.

[43] The Government submitted that to pronounce the judgment in public would invalidate the purposes for holding the hearing in private.

[45] The Court recalls its long-standing case-law that the form of publicity given under the domestic law to a judgment must be assessed in the light of the special features of the proceedings in question and by reference to the object and purpose of Art 6(1) (see the above-mentioned *Sutter* judgment, para 33). Thus in the *Sutter* case, for example, it found that the publicity requirement under Art 6(1) was satisfied by the fact that anyone who could establish an interest could consult or obtain a copy of the full text of judgments of the Military Court of Cassation, together with the fact that Court's most important judgments were published in an official collection (ibid, para 34).

[46] The Court further recalls its above finding that, in view of the type of issues requiring to be examined in cases concerning the residence of children, the domestic authorities were justified in conducting these proceedings in chambers in order to protect the privacy of the children and the parties and to avoid prejudicing the interests of justice. It agrees with the Government that to pronounce the judgment in public would, to a large extent, frustrate these aims.

[47] The Court notes that anyone who can establish an interest may consult or obtain a copy of the full text of the orders and/or judgment of first instance courts in child residence cases, and that the judgments of the Court of Appeal and of first instance courts in cases of special interest are routinely published, thereby enabling the public to study the manner in which the courts generally approach such cases and the principles applied in deciding them. It is noteworthy in this respect that the first applicant, despite his desire to share information about his son with the child's grandparents, never made any application either for the grandparents to be present in the County Court or for leave to disclose the residence judgment to them.

[48] Having regard to the nature of the proceedings and the form of publicity applied by the national law, the Court considers that a literal interpretation of the terms of Art 6(1) concerning the pronouncement of judgments would not only be unnecessary for the purposes of public scrutiny but might even frustrate the primary aim of Art 6(1), which is to secure a fair hearing (see, mutates mutandis, the above-mentioned *Sutter* judgment, para 34).

[49] The Court thus concludes that the Convention did not require making available to the general public the residence judgments in the present cases, and that there has been no violation of Art 6(1) in this respect.

There was, however, a dissenting opinion from Judges Loucaides and Tulkens:

In our view, it is evident from the working of Art 6 . . . that private hearings can take place only in respect of specific proceedings pending before a court if, in the opinion of that court, the conditions set out in Art 6 for a private hearing are actually met, with reference to the nature and circumstances of the specific case.

Private hearings, then, apart from being an exception to the general requirement for public hearings, can be justified only if the needs of a particular case so demand; and this has to be decided by the court in any specific case where such an issue arises. It follows that the exceptional decision to hold a private hearing cannot be decided in abstracto or by reference to a category of cases; it must be determined in concreto by reference to the particular facts of a case. This, we believe, is the only interpretation which is compatible with the terms of Art 6. For how can the possibility of excluding the press and public from part of the trial, for example, be implemented in abstracto or by reference to a category of cases without regard to the facts and circumstances of any concrete case before the court? This is also true for the other conditions for a private hearing under Art 6. . . .

We believe that the general legal rule against public hearings applied in [children's] cases is incompatible not only with the wording but also with the basic objective and philosophy of the requirement for public hearings under Art 6, namely the protection of litigants against the administration of justice in secret with no public scrutiny and the maintenance of confidence in the courts. As pointed out in the *Sutter v Switzerland* judgment of 22 February 1984 ((1984) 6 EHRR 272, para 26):

> 'By rendering the administration of justice visible, publicity contributes to the achievement of the aim of Article 6(1), namely a fair trial, the guarantee of which is one of the fundamental principles of any democratic society, within the meaning of the Convention.'

Questions

(i) What are the advantages and disadvantages of private hearings for (a) adult parties, (b) children, or (c) courts?

(ii) If the advantages outweigh the disadvantages, should the same protection be extended to property disputes between unmarried couples?

(iii) Cases about children or financial provision between spouses which are heard in private cannot be reported in the media unless the court allows this; other cases, for example for occupation orders under the Family Law Act 1996, can be reported even if heard in private: see *Clibbery v Allen* [2002] EWCA Civ 45, [2002] 1 All ER 865, CA. What, if any, restrictions should there be on the reporting of family cases?

(iv) Are there reasons for protecting the privacy of adults and children involved in family proceedings over and above the protection (such as it is) of their private lives under Article 8 of the European Convention? (Consider the case of Flitcroft, the philandering footballer: *A v B (a company)* [2002] EWCA Civ 337, [2002] 2 All ER 545.)

A recurring theme of discussions about family courts has been the need for greater informality and for inquisitorial rather than adversarial procedures. The Finer Report (1974) had this to say:

4.404 We are impressed by the unanimity of the commentators in favour of greater informality in family matters. But we are impressed, too, by the lack of studies of the effect of legal ritual upon citizens who use the courts. We do not know how representative a figure is the trade union leader who observed of the Industrial Relations Court that, if his members are to be sent to prison for contempt of court, he desires it to be done by a judge properly robed in scarlet and ermine. On these aspects of court procedure, we think that decisions should be delayed until they can be based on knowledge of what will best satisfy the citizen user's desire for fairness and dignity in the determination of matrimonial cases.

Question

Should a judge dress up in purple dressing gown and curly wig (a) to grant an adoption order to which the birth parents have agreed, or (b) to try a hotly contested parental dispute about where the children are to live, or (c) to decide whether or not a ten-year-old girl has been sexually abused, or (d) to grant or enforce an ouster injunction against a violent man, or (e) to decide whether a child should be called by a new surname, or (f) in any family law case?

Finer continued:

4.405 Another much canvassed procedural question is how far the hearings in the family court should be inquisitorial rather than adversary in nature. In the accusatorial or adversary form of procedure, as it characterises our civil litigation, the parties not only choose the issues which form the subject matter of the dispute, but also determine what evidence shall be brought before the court. The court has no right and no means to act as its own fact-gatherer. In the inquisitorial form of procedure, the court is not confined to acting as a referee, but may, so far as it has the means, take steps of its own to inform itself of the facts and circumstances it considers it ought to know in order to make a just determination. But the two forms of procedure are not, in truth, mutually exclusive. In the divorce jurisdiction, the court has always been charged with the duty of being 'satisfied' that it can grant relief, which must involve, in appropriate cases, a duty to enquire into matters as to which the parties themselves may not be in dispute. So again, in matters affecting custody of and access to children the court has to have regard to the child's paramount interests, which is a matter which the views of the parties, even to the extent that they coincide, do not determine. The proper balance of the two forms of procedure in the family court should, in our view, be determined by the following considerations. It is desirable that the court itself should not come into the arena. To the extent that the court requires assistance by way of investigation or expert assessment of circumstances which it considers material, this function should be discharged by ancillary services which are attached to or can be called upon by the court, but whose personnel are not themselves members of the court. The bench of the family court is to consist only of judges, professional or lay, and experts or assessors should not be constituents. On the other hand, the bench as so constituted should, in every aspect of its jurisdiction, be able to call upon the aid of a competent person to make social and welfare enquiries and reports.

As we shall see further in Chapters 12 and 13, the Child and Family Courts Advisory and Support Service (CAFCASS) was set up in April 2001 to combine three separate services: the Family Court Welfare arm of the probation service, which provided reports and other services to courts hearing disputes between private individuals about the future of their children; the guardian ad litem and reporting officer service provided by local social services authorities to represent children involved in care proceedings brought by local authorities and make reports in adoption cases; and the service provided by the Official Solicitor in representing children in wardship and other particularly sensitive or difficult cases. Despite the existence of these specialist services designed to help the courts obtain the information which the parties would be unable or unwilling to put before them, the use of expert witnesses has escalated since the Children Act 1989, as Pat Munro explains in 'Expert Witnesses', in *Delight and Dole, The Children Act 10 years on* (2002) (the 2001 proceedings of the biennial Interdisciplinary Conference held by the President of the Family Division):

There was no widespread use of expert witnesses in public law proceedings before the Children Act. The majority of care cases were conducted in the juvenile court. Until May 1984, when the panels of guardians ad litem and reporting officers were established, the 'expert' evidence in the majority of cases was given by social workers employed by the local authority bringing the proceedings. . . .

Complex cases, particularly those that involved an assessment of future risk to a child, were heard in the High Court, where the Official Solicitor would be appointed to represent the child. Since his staff were civil servants, with no training or expertise which enabled them to make social work assessments or to assess the plans for the child concerned, he would tend to instruct an expert witness to provide a report. This would inevitably be a child psychiatrist. It has never been entirely clear why experienced social workers were not instructed in appropriate cases, unless it was because of the attitude of the judiciary, who were generally not persuaded that social workers were 'experts'. . . .

Significant changes to this system were brought about with the implementation of the Children Act. A guardian ad litem was appointed to safeguard the interest of the child who was the subject of proceedings, unless it was not necessarily in her interest. Although the pattern of appointment varied enormously over England and Wales, guardians were to be found in the majority of proceedings. The regulations did not specify the qualifications expected of a panel member, but the DHSS Circular LAC 83(83)21 stated that they should be 'persons with qualifications in social work plus sufficient relevant experience'. . . .

The child now had a welfare representative who would be regarded as an expert in relation to matters of general child care and development, and who had a right of access to local authority records (Children Act 1989, s 42). Where cases required specialist knowledge which might be beyond the competence of the guardian, it was hoped that a parent wishing to challenge the local authority case would accept an expert appointed by the guardian, instead of seeking to instruct his or her own expert.

However, the use of expert witnesses increased. In 1999 BAAF published research into the use of experts in care proceedings. It found that all parties had increased their use of experts. The reasons for guardians doing so were identified as follows:

- some of the concerns about the undervaluing of social work expertise by the courts had contributed to guardians' increased use of experts;
- the policies and practices adopted by some local authorities had contributed to the increased use of experts by guardians;
- complexity of cases;
- the case demanded the diagnosis of a mental health state.

Contrary to popular debate, guardians in the survey did not identify the 'spiral' or 'domino' effect as a major reason for the increase in use of experts.

The BAAF research was by Julia Brophy, Christopher Wale and Phil Bates. In *Myths and Practices* (1999), they discuss whether there should be multiple or single experts (either jointly instructed by all parties or appointed by the court):

i) The "hired gun" syndrome and experts appointed by parents

A common theme in discussions about the use of experts in care proceedings has been that many experts appointed by parents are already known to be biased in their favour. In effect, they continue to represent the "hired gun" syndrome associated with practices prior to the Children Act. However, not all experts instructed by parents necessarily support the cause of parents. . . .

When we compared [parents' experts' views] with the levels of agreement or disagreement between experts in cases where guardians commissioned a second report . . . the survey also showed that there was also a level of disagreement between the experts in these cases. This applied with regard to both the assessment and the appropriate recommendations. Just under a third of experts instructed by guardians disagreed with both the assessment and recommendations of a previous expert. Moreover, if cases where there was partial disagreement are included, this figure rises to over half of those cases.

In summary, it is not simply experts appointed by parents who disagree about issues, there is evidence of a divergence of views between experts appointed by guardians and those appointed by local authorities. That experts disagree over the most appropriate recommendations to make in a case and the fact that disagreement is not *necessarily* dependent on which party instructs them is an important finding.

ii) Competing paradigms make complex cases

Since the introduction of the Children Act, the debate on instructing experts in care proceedings has focused increasingly on the advantages of joint instructions. Perceptions of the proliferation of expert evidence have given rise to criticisms based on the high costs of experts, delay, duplication of evidence and overloading of some experts. Some guardians have also expressed difficulties in assessing competing reports. For example, should equal weight be given to a report based on an observation of a child compared with a report based on an "interactive" interview with a child? Joint instructions to a single expert has been seen as the solution to a considerable range of financial and practical problems.

However, little discussion has focused on the benefits of more information, or on problems of ensuring that the full range of available child welfare knowledge is made available to courts. We lack data on the full range of differences between experts addressing the same issues. The survey identified that a considerable degree of difference existed between experts addressing the same issues and concerns, resulting in different recommendations being made. What we do not know is the magnitude of differences and how these are underscored by both clinical judgment and experience and the best available research evidence.

iii) Competing expert evidence and future policy

One question which these data raise is that if the preferred trend in this field is towards joint instructions of a single expert, how will that change ensure that the best available child welfare knowledge remains available to the court? Will the reports of appointed experts reflect both their own clinical views and judgments *and* those of different schools of thought? Limited data to date suggest that experts do not routinely use research findings or other perspectives in their reports for courts. Some experts have questioned whether it is appropriate for them to undertake that exercise; they do not see it as part of their responsibility to assess the available research evidence or to present the views or perspectives of other clinicians.

We do not know how widespread this view is amongst experts currently providing reports for courts. Some practitioners increasingly argue that evidence-based medicine is about integrating individual clinical expertise with the best external evidence from systematic research. At the level of individual decision making in legal proceedings, the role of research is viewed as, at least, problematic. General principles derived from research may not be seen as especially helpful although views are divided on this.

The use of research also raises questions about how to assess its comprehensiveness, validity and relevance, and indeed about whose responsibility it is to undertake that exercise. Nevertheless, if decisions are to be informed by the best available child welfare knowledge, it is important to keep two factors to the forefront. First, child welfare knowledge is not a uniform category. Second, that lack of uniformity may be a positive characteristic. Human behaviour is immensely complex and subject to individual and environmental influences. The dialectic process of scientific research and writing allows for continual assessment and re-assessment in understanding, explaining and, if necessary, "treating" certain behaviours. The existing body of child welfare knowledge is thus neither static nor uniform. If decisions concerning the future care and welfare of children are going to benefit from this developing body of knowledge, mechanisms should be retained which allow for the full breadth of available knowledge, alternative perspectives and systematic research to be available to the court. Solutions which, in effect, limit this information may serve the needs and concerns of professionals for speed and simplicity. However, such an approach will not necessarily ensure that a more informed exploration of the issues and available options is undertaken. Limiting the range of child welfare knowledge which reaches the legal arena may have an effect on the quality of final decision making and may limit the options available to courts when considering the future care of some children. This caution applies to a range of solutions currently posed in this field, for example, the possibility of restricting the use of experts through the development of a system of court appointed experts. The same is true of joint instructions if involvement in such instructions would remove or reduce a party's right to question the subsequent report and, if necessary, seek a second opinion.

Questions

(i) In 1993/4 an ExpertWitness Group, chaired by Dr EileenVizard, Consultant Child Psychiatrist, recommended to the Children Act Advisory Committee:

That one expert should, wherever possible, be appointed with the agreement of all parties. The Group was divided on the issue of court appointed experts with all the experts favouring a move in this direction and most lawyers opposing this or expressing reservations.

Would you side with the lawyers or the experts?
(ii) The Committee, in its 1993/94 report, recommended that in giving leave for papers to be shown to an expert (who should always be named, never merely 'an expert') the court should:

–   Provide for the disclosure of any written expert report both to all parties and to the other experts in the case. When a report is disclosed it should include a copy of the letter of instruction.
–   Provide for discussions between experts following mutual disclosure of reports and for the filing of further evidence by the experts stating the areas of agreement and disagreement between the experts. Parties should only instruct experts who are willing to meet in advance of the hearing. When granting leave, the court must make this a condition of the appointment.

Why is it desirable for the letter of instruction to an expert to be disclosed?

(iii) In *Re L (minors) (police investigation: privilege)* [1997] AC 16, [1996] 2 All ER 78, the House of Lords, by a majority, held that in care proceedings (unlike other litigation) experts' reports are not privileged; the court may therefore order that they be disclosed to the other parties (and even to a non-party such as the police). Is this (a) desirable in the interests of the children? or (b) a fundamental inroad into the right to seek legal advice? (NB Complaints under Arts. 6(1) and 8 were held manifestly unfounded by the European Court of Human Rights: *L v United Kingdom*, Application 34222/96, [2000] 2 FLR 322.)

(iv) In *M v London Borough of Islington and L* [2002] 1 FLR 95 at 102, Dame Elizabeth Butler-Sloss P said this:

> . . . family judges should continue to play as full a part as possible in the evolution of child and family matters in as wide a spectrum of situations as possible. Judges are and should be part of advisory committees. There is, however, a difference between general interdisciplinary contacts, on conferences and committees, including family court business committees where local protocols may be developed, and participation in a child-care agency's novel scheme for handling individual cases which are bound to come before one's own court.

Are you pleased or shocked that the President of the Family Division holds a biennial Interdisciplinary Conference for 'judges, directors of social services, mental health professionals, academics, guardians . . . and other professionals'? Should the consumers of the family court service also be involved? And who are they?

Behind all these questions lies the essential role of the court in family cases: is it there to regulate and supervise family life, to help solve family problems, to resolve disputes by adjudication or by other means, or all of these things? We shall look at each of them in turn.

7.2 Public regulation or private ordering?

Robert Mnookin's celebrated article 'Bargaining in the Shadow of the Law – The Case of Divorce' (1979) begins:

> I wish to suggest a new way of thinking about the role of law at the time of divorce. It is concerned primarily with the impact of the legal system on negotiations and bargaining that occurs *outside* of court. Rather than regard order as imposed from above, I see the primary function of contemporary divorce law as providing a framework for divorcing couples themselves to determine their respective rights and responsibilities after dissolution. This process, by which parties to a marriage are empowered to create their own legally enforceable commitments, I shall call *'private ordering'*.

In 'Divorce Bargaining: The Limits on Private Ordering' (1984), he explains both the advantages and the disadvantages which have to be countered:

The advantages of private ordering
Let me begin with the arguments supporting the presumption in favour of private ordering. The core reason is rooted in notions of human liberty. Private ordering is supported by the liberal ideal that individuals have rights, and should largely be left free to make of their lives what they wish. In Charles Fried's words, a regime of law that 'respects the dispositions individuals make of their rights, carries to its logical conclusion the liberal premise that individuals have rights'.

Private ordering can also be justified on grounds of *efficiency*. Ordinarily, the parties themselves are in the best position to evaluate the comparative advantages of alternative arrangements.

Each spouse, in the words of John Stuart Mill, 'is the person most interested in his own well-being: ... with respect to his own feelings and circumstances, the most ordinary man or woman has means of knowledge immeasurably surpassing those that can be possessed by anyone else.' Through negotiations, there are opportunities for making *both* parents better off than either would be if a court or some third party simply imposed a result. A consensual solution is, by definition, more likely to be consistent with the preferences of each spouse than would a result imposed by a court. Parental preferences often vary with regard to money and child-rearing responsibilities. Through negotiations, it is possible that the divorcing spouses can divide money and child-rearing responsibilities to reflect their own individual preferences.

Finally, there are obvious and substantial *savings* when a couple can resolve the distributional consequences of divorce without resort to formal adjudication. The financial cost of litigation, both private and public, is minimised. The pain of the formal adversarial proceedings is avoided. A negotiated settlement allows the parties to avoid the risks and uncertainties of litigation, which may involve all-or-nothing consequences. Given the substantial delays that often characterize contested judicial proceedings, agreement can often save time and allow each spouse to proceed with his or her life. In short, against a backdrop of fair standards in the shadow of which a couple bargains, divorcing couples should have very broad powers to make their own arrangements. Significant limitations are inconsistent with the premises of no-fault divorce. Parties should be encouraged to settle the distributional consequences of divorce for themselves, and the state should provide an efficient and fair mechanism for enforcing such agreements and for settling disputes when the parties are unable to agree.

Capacity

On an abstract level, I find the general defence of private ordering both appealing and persuasive. But it is premised on the notion that divorce bargaining involves rational, self-interested individuals – that the average adult has the intelligence and experience to make a well-informed judgment concerning the desirability of entering into a particular divorce settlement. Given the tasks facing an individual at the time of divorce, and the characteristics of the relationship between divorcing spouses, there are reasons to fear that this may not always be the case.

...

Some might think that the stresses and emotional turmoil of separation and divorce undermine the essential premise of private ordering – the idea that individuals are capable of deliberate judgments. I disagree. After all, for most persons the emotional upheaval is transitory, and the stresses are an inevitable consequence of having to make a new life. Temporary incapacity does not justify state paternalism for an extended period of time. Nonetheless, safeguards are necessary, and the wooden application of the traditional contract defence of 'incompetence' may not provide sufficient protection. ...

Professor Eisenberg recently suggested a concept of 'transactional incapacity' to capture the notion that 'an individual may be of average intelligence and yet may lack the aptitude, experience, or judgmental ability to make a deliberative and well-informed judgment concerning the desirability of entering into a given complex transaction.'. . .

An analogous concept could be applied to divorce bargaining within a system that encourages private ordering at the time of divorce. When one spouse knows or has reason to know of the diminished capacity, and exploits this incapacity, a court should reopen the agreement. Proof of exploitation is essential, however. For this I would require a showing that the terms of the agreement considered as a whole fall outside the range of what would have been acceptable to a competent person at the time of the settlement. By providing a remedy only if a party exploited the other side's incapacity by securing an unusually one sided bargain, this test will not create uncertainty in most cases.

A second prophylactic to guard against transitory diminished capacity would involve a 'cooling-off' period, during which either party would be free to rescind a settlement agreement. In a commercial context, this period is often very short – typically three days. In the divorce context, I would make it considerably longer – perhaps sixty or ninety days. Like any safeguard, this one has costs. Some agreements may come apart even though they involve no exploitation whatsoever, simply because of ambivalence or a change of heart. Moreover, this cooling-off period might be used strategically by a party – a tentative agreement may be reached, only to be later rescinded, in order to wear an opponent down.

...

Unequal bargaining power

Let me now turn to a second possible justification for imposing limits on private ordering – the basic idea is simple; in negotiations between two competent adults, if there are great disparities in bargaining power, some bargains may be reached that are unconscionably one-sided.

The notion of bargaining power has intuitive appeal, but turns out to be very difficult to define. Without a complete theory of negotiations, it is hard to give precise substantive content to the notion of bargaining power, much less define precisely the idea of 'relative bargaining power'. Nonetheless, by briefly analyzing the five elements of the bargaining model I described in an earlier article, it is possible to suggest why some divorcing spouses may be seen as having unequal bargaining power.

First, there are *the legal endowments*. The legal rules governing marital property, alimony, child support, and custody give each spouse certain claims based on what each would get if the case goes to trial. In other words, the outcome the law will impose if no agreement is reached gives each parent certain bargaining chips – an endowment of sorts.

...

Second, a party's bargaining power is very much influenced by his or her *preferences* – i.e., how that party subjectively evaluates alternative outcomes. These preferences are not simply matters of taste – they can depend upon a party's economic resources and life circumstances.

...

A third element that effects bargaining power has to do with uncertainty, and the parties' attitudes towards risk. Often the outcome in court is far from certain, and the parties are negotiating against a back-drop clouded by substantial uncertainty. Because the parties may have different risk preferences, this uncertainty can differentially affect the bargaining power of the two spouses. ...

A fourth element that can create differences in bargaining power relates to the differential ability to withstand the transaction costs – both emotional and economic – involved in negotiations. ...

A fifth element concerns the bargaining process itself, and strategic behaviour. In divorce bargaining, the spouses may not know each other's true preferences. Negotiations often involve the attempts by each side to discern the other side's true preferences, while making credible claims about their own, and what they intend to do if a particular proposal is not accepted. Some people are more skilled negotiators than others. They are better at manipulating information and managing impressions. They have a more refined sense of tactical action. These differences can create inequalities in negotiations.

Externalities – third party effects

Third party effects provide the last set of reasons that justify limiting private ordering. ...

A divorce settlement may affect any number of interests not taken into account in the spouses' negotiations. The state's fiscal interests can be affected, for example. The economic terms of the bargain between the two spouses may substantially affect the odds that a custodial parent will later require public transfer payments. The most important third party effects concern the children, although there can be externalities with respect to other family members as well. At a conceptual level, it is easy to see how a negotiated settlement may reflect parental preferences but not the child's desires or needs. ...

Concerns about the effects of the divorce on the children underlie many of the formal limitations on private ordering – e.g., the requirement of court review of private agreements relating to custody and child support; the legal rules prohibiting parents from making nonmodifiable and binding agreements concerning these elements. ...

I believe divorcing parents should be given considerable freedom to decide custody matters – subject only to the same minimum standards for protecting the child from neglect and abuse that the state imposes on *all* families. The actual determination of what is in fact in a child's best interests is ordinarily quite indeterminate. It requires predictions beyond the capacity of the behavioural sciences and involves imposition of values about which there is little consensus in our society. It is for this reason that I conclude that the basic question is who gets to decide on behalf of the child.

Because primary responsibility for child-rearing after divorce does and *should* remain with parents there should be a strong presumption in favor of the parental agreement and limits on the use of coercive state power by judges or other professionals to force parents to do what the professional thinks is best. On the other hand, I think the state has an important interest in encouraging parents to understand that the responsibility for their children extends beyond the divorce, that children are in many ways at risk during the divorcing process, and that in deciding about the child-rearing arrangements, the parents have an important obligation to meet their children's needs. Moreover, there is reason to think that by facilitating parental agreement, and helping the parents transform their old relationship into one in which they can now do business together with respect to the children's future needs, the interests of the children are being served.

Questions

(i) Why are significant limitations on private ordering 'inconsistent with the premises of no-fault divorce'?

(ii) Would the Family Law Act 1996 have taken us further towards or further away from Mnookin's model?

(iii) Do the arguments in favour of allowing people to make their own arrangements when they separate or divorce apply equally to allowing them to make pre-marital or pre-cohabitation contracts? (See p. 77, above.)

(iv) What if the parties find it difficult to make their own arrangements? What help should they be given? (See p. 302 below.)

(v) Does the concept of private ordering help us to decide what sort of court would be best suited to adjudicating upon those issues which the parties cannot decide for themselves?

(vi) Consider the following comment by a young person consulted by Christina Lyon, Edward Surrey and Judith Timms, reported in *Effective Support Services for Children and Young People when Parental Relationships Break Down* (1998):

I tried to tell both my mum and dad who I wanted to see and when. I tried to work everything out so it would be fair to everyone including my nanna's and grandad's from both sides of the family and my aunties and uncles, but no one listened by me and everything afterwards was just such a mess.

Should his parents have been allowed to 'order' things for themselves?

This brings us to the question whether the court's role is to help solve family problems or simply to resolve disputes.

7.3 Marriage mending or marriage ending?

The Finer Report (1974) recounted the English experience of court-based attempts at 'marriage mending':

4.298 It may, indeed, be said to be the virtually unanimous opinion of those who have the relevant experience that there is little room for optimism when the court to which the parties have presented themselves to formalise or regulate the breakdown of the marriage seeks to use that occasion for mending it. The Denning Report [1947] concluded on the evidence it received:

'The prospects of reconciliation are much more favourable in the early stages of marital disharmony than in the later stages. At that stage both parties are likely to be willing to co-operate in an effort to save the marriage; but if the conflict has become so chronic that one or both of the parties has lost the power or desire to co-operate further, the prospects sharply diminish. By the time the conflict reaches a hearing in the divorce court, the prospects are as a rule very small. It is important therefore that the general public should be brought to realise the importance of seeking competent advice, without delay, when tensions occur in marriage.'

4.299 The Morton Royal Commission on Marriage and Divorce [1956] which took a good deal of evidence on this subject, recorded:

'If matters are allowed to develop into a condition of chronic disharmony one or perhaps both of the spouses will probably have lost the ability or desire to make any attempt to restore the marriage, and by the time steps have been taken to institute divorce proceedings the prospects of bringing husband and wife together again are greatly reduced. This view won a wide measure of support from our witnesses.'

4.300 The Law Commission [1966] considered that reconciliation procedures started after the filing of the petition achieve little success and 'have tended to become pointless and troublesome formalities'.

The Law Society took a similar view in *A Better Way Out* (1979):

178. ... It is generally accepted that, by the time either spouse reaches the stage of consulting a solicitor about divorce proceedings, the breakdown of the marriage has reached the point of no return and it is too late for there to be any real prospect of reconciliation. If the spouses wanted help in saving the marriage, they will have sought it before then from family, friends or marriage guidance counsellors.

Gwynn Davis and Mervyn Murch, however, in *Grounds for Divorce* (1988), reported that:

The results of our 'consumer' interviews indicate beyond doubt that this assessment is seriously wide of the mark. In particular, it fails to take account of the fact that the whole divorce process has speeded up, with many petitions being filed whilst the parties are still living together.

Earlier, they point to the evidence suggesting that, nowadays, the possibility of reconciliation may exist in a great many cases:

Our own research also suggests that there is a potential for reconciliation in a significant number of divorce cases. Even in the course of the Special Procedure survey (from which initially defended cases were excluded) 39 per cent of respondents and 23 per cent of petitioners claimed that they would have preferred to remain married to their former partner. In at least 50 per cent of these cases it appeared that the marriage breakdown reflected the will of only one party. Given that our interviews usually took place some months after the award of the decree nisi – and in some cases, several years after the initial separation – it is likely that the number wishing to continue with their marriage had, at the outset of proceedings, been even greater.

... we also asked respondents whether they believed that their own marriage had 'irretrievably broken down'. Fifteen per cent denied that it had done so, with a further 10 per cent saying that they were 'uncertain'. Few, if any, of those interviewed in the course of this research had attempted to defend the divorce petition.

This evidence of *doubt* or *regret* should not be taken as an indication that a great many of these marriages could have been 'saved'. ...

The findings of the Law Commission's *Court Record Study* (1990) also lent support to the view that there is more scope for reconciliation during divorce proceedings than had previously been acknowledged:

13. The original 477 files resulted in one nullity decree, five judicial separation decrees, 433 decrees nisi of divorce and 418 decrees absolute. One decree nisi was later rescinded. Thus 53 cases (11.1% of the total) fell by the wayside at some stage, 28 without any decrees at all, and 15 between decree nisi and decree absolute. These included one case (mentioned earlier) where the fact was not recorded. Otherwise, Table 6 shows the facts relied on in the unsuccessful petitions:

Table 6   Facts relied on in unsuccessful petitions

	No.	(%)	% of petitions on that fact
Adultery	13	(24.5%)	9.3%
Behaviour	30	(56.6%)	16.2%
Desertion	0	(0%)	0%
Two years	6	(11.3%)	5.4%
Five years	4	(7.5%)	11.1%
Total:	53	(99.9%)	

14. The behaviour cases did tend to run into more difficulty than the others, but it is significant that more than a quarter of these couples were still living at the same address at the date of the petition. This in itself was associated with a higher rate of failure to proceed.

15. It was not always possible to deduce the reason why a case had failed to reach decree or decree absolute. It was rarely associated with, let alone attributable to, the intervention of the court. The most common reason appeared to be reconciliation; there were also some who had obtained non-molestation or ouster injunctions but apparently gone no further, some where the proceedings on the file had been superseded by a new petition in that or another court, and some which proceeded no further than notification of an intention to defend.

Questions

(i) Do you find it worrying that a higher proportion of behaviour cases fell by the wayside?

(ii) Davis and Murch nonetheless concluded:

It would be absurdly facile to assume, just because some couples decide, in the end, to remain together, that *courts* have much (if any) role in the marriage mending business. Perhaps the most we can ask of courts and legal procedure is that they do not make life *even more difficult* for couples facing these decisions.

(a) Do you agree? (b) In what respects might (i) the present divorce law or (ii) the divorce law enacted in the Family Law Act 1996 (with its 'period for reflection and consideration' for the parties '(a) to reflect on whether the marriage can be saved and to have an opportunity to effect a reconciliation, and (b) to consider what arrangements should be made for the future') make life 'even more difficult'?

Mervyn Murch and his colleagues nevertheless have a vision of a different kind of role for the courts in divorce proceedings, as G. Douglas, M. Murch, L. Scanlan and A. Perry explain in 'Safeguarding Children's Welfare in Non-Contentious Divorce – Towards a New Conception of the Legal Process' (2000):

At present, there seem to be two basic models of using the courts as a forum for handling divorces. On the one hand, one can postulate a strongly 'inquisitorial' system, with the role of the court being to investigate the circumstances in issue and forming a judgment on them – often a moral judgment. . . . As we have shown, however, this has never been how the system has worked, and in an era of mass divorce, it is probably practically unattainable even if it were regarded as appropriate.

An alternative model, which appears closer to the reality of the current system, is a 'managerial' one. Here, the court's function is to process the parties' change in legal status, tidy up the implications and consequences of the change and 'bang the parties' heads together', where necessary, to induce them to accept what is happening and prepare them to move on in their lives. It recognises that the legal aspects of divorce are but a small part of the overall experience of marriage breakdown and family change. The divorce process is made as administrative as possible – the divorce itself is a bureaucratic and documentary process obviating the need for the parties to come near the court. The hard work is done by the parties, mostly through negotiation, with or without the assistance of lawyers, though, if the Government had its way, mediation would become the preferred medium for settlement. . . . But [this model] remains adult-centered and still basically adversarial, and fits awkwardly with a concern for children, who are not parties in the proceedings and thus have no obvious means of contributing to or participating in the negotiations leading to the agreement endorsed by the court.

It is doubtful, therefore, that either the inquisitorial or the managerial model provides a process which meets the needs and wishes of either parents or children. . . . This study, together with companion work and findings from other researchers shows that many children are kept in the dark about what is happening between the parents and how their lives may change. This can lead to dangerous misunderstandings and needless anxieties putting stress on children's emotional wellbeing. The need to obtain the legal licence to remarry, which is embodied by the divorce, and the resulting necessary engagement by the parties with the legal system, can be used as an opportunity to make available to them the range of supports which they, and their children, might wish to use throughout the breakdown process, in an attempt to reduce these harmful consequences.

To achieve this objective, a third model of the legal process needs to be developed, which one might describe as 'supportive'. This sees the legal system as a point of contact between the family and the state, . . . However, the purpose of making contact is not to 'scrutinise' and judge the parties' proposals, but to make available to families – and individual family members including children – on a *voluntary* basis, the opportunity to receive advice, support and assistance in coping with the consequences of relationship breakdown. The court would serve to channel those seeking help toward the appropriate agencies. To this extent, the supportive model fits the managerial ethos of the legal system by accepting that the 'real' focus of attention is not the legal consequences of the divorce, but the personal ones, which the law may be ill-fitted to tackle. However, instead of seeking to ignore or side-step these dimensions, as the current process does, it could provide a means, early in the legal process, and with the co-operation of the parents, of identifying and offering support to parents, and to children who are experiencing difficulties in adjusting to their parents' marriage breakdown. The court could act as an initial information resource and referral point in order to utilise a range or related community services such as family court welfare officers (and possibly guardians ad litem), mediators, school counsellors, health visitors, GPs and where necessary more specialist mental health practitioners.

There has long been a tendency to confuse the different kinds of non-legal professional help which may be available to people in relationship difficulties. In their Report on *The Ground for Divorce* (1990), the Law Commission tried to summarise the different kinds of processes and their objectives:

Counselling, conciliation and mediation

5.29 ... The umbrella term 'counselling' is used in Australia and New Zealand to encompass a variety of different types of help. All share the characteristic of keeping an open mind about the eventual outcome, while helping the couple or individuals involved to gain a greater understanding of their situation and to reach their own decisions about the future. The focus and method, however, can differ sharply, as can the organisational context in which the service is offered.

5.30 Broadly speaking, there are three different types of activity which may be involved:

(i) Marital counselling is offered, either to a couple or to an individual spouse, with a view to helping the couple to strengthen or maintain their marital relationship. If they are estranged or separated, the aim is to reconcile or reunite them. Historically, attempts at reconciliation were part of the role of 'police court missionaries' who became the probation and divorce court welfare service of today. Generally speaking, however, such services are offered by voluntary organisations, principally Relate Marriage Guidance. Relate counsellors are carefully selected and trained, but do not hold any particular professional qualification and offer their services voluntarily;

(ii) Divorce counselling and other forms of therapy aim to assist individuals, couples, and their children, to come to terms with the fact that their relationship is breaking down, to reduce the sense of personal failure, anger and grief, to disengage from and negotiate a new relationship with the former spouse and with the children, and eventually to move on to new relationships with confidence, avoiding the mistakes of the past. In other words, it seeks to minimise the harm done to either partner and to their children by the breakdown of their marriage. Once again, this is generally offered by voluntary organisations such as Relate, although some probation services offer divorce experience courses, and specialist therapy may be available privately or in some parts of the health service;

(iii) Conciliation or mediation is a way of resolving disputes without resort to traditional adjudication. The aim is to help the couple to reach their own agreements about the future, to improve communication between them, and to help them to co-operate in bringing up their children. Conciliation in this country developed first in the context of resolving disputes about children, often through the efforts of registrars and divorce court welfare officers at the court where a custody or access dispute was to be tried, but also through independent conciliation services, most of which are now affiliated to the National Family Conciliation Council. Conciliators generally hold professional qualifications in social work, undergo specialist training in family conciliation, and are paid for their services. The costs and benefits of various conciliation services have recently been the subject of a major research study conducted by the University of Newcastle. This has revealed that conciliation is indeed effective, both in reducing the areas of conflict and in increasing the parents' well-being and satisfaction with the arrangements made. In general, these benefits are greater when the service is provided away from the courts. The problems with conciliation conducted by or at the court, valuable and effective though it can often be, include the inevitable pressure to reach a settlement quickly, the inevitable authority of the registrar or court welfare officer conducting it, which may unconsciously or consciously dictate the outcome, and the risks of confusing the welfare officer's different roles of reporting to the court and assisting the couple to reach agreement. However, this is a fast-moving field in which developments are taking place all the time. For example, the independent sector is beginning to develop methods of comprehensive mediation, covering property and finance as well as child-related issues.

The Commission concluded that reconciliation attempts should *not* be a mandatory part of the divorce process:

5.33 . . . There are several reasons for this. First, there are the views of the organisations at present involved in providing these services. They would of course like there to be a properly funded network of services readily available to all who wish to use them. But such counselling is a two-way process which can only be offered to volunteers, not conscripts. The hostility and bitterness induced by conscription is unlikely to lead to a real and lasting resolution. Secondly, and perhaps more importantly, there are some marriages which it would be wrong in principle to attempt to save. A wife who is regularly subjected to violence or abuse from her husband needs rescuing from her marriage, not pressure to return to it. A system of mandatory reconciliation could not be justified without some attempt to distinguish between marriages, which would only reintroduce the very inquiry into past misbehaviour which it is the object of these proposals to avoid. Thirdly, it would be impossible to justify the enormous public expenditure which would be involved in requiring such attempts in every case, without a better prospect of success than can be demonstrated at present. Finally, it was felt by some respondents that *conciliation* might, paradoxically, be more likely to result in reconciling some couples, by encouraging them to find a way through their difficulties relating to future arrangements while they were still amenable to discussion.

Nevertheless, The Law Society's new *Family Law Protocol* (2002) requires:

Reconciliation

  1.2 When instructed by clients facing family breakdown the first step (unless it is clearly inappropriate to do so), is to discuss with clients whether the relationship is over or whether there is a possibility of saving the relationship.
  1.3 Solicitors must keep an up-to-date list or referral agencies including local marriage guidance agencies, counsellors, Relate, etc. and refer clients to them where appropriate. Solicitors need to bear in mind their clients' ethnic, cultural and/or religious background when considering referral agencies and should be aware of the benefits of referring clients to agencies with knowledge of their particular background.
  1.4 The prospect of saving the relationship and/or the benefits of family or personal counselling or marriage guidance should be kept under review throughout the case.

Questions

(i) When would it be 'clearly inappropriate to do so'? Should (a) a husband be invited to consider going back to an unfaithful wife, or (b) a wife be invited to consider going back to a violent husband, or (c) an unmarried parent be invited to consider going back to the other parent whom s/he no longer found sexually or socially congenial?
(ii) Do you think that it is the role of the state to provide any of the services identified by the Law Commission? If so, which?

(iii) If you do, should it be done by the Lord Chancellor's Department (responsible for the courts and legal services), the Department of Health (responsible for health and social services) or the Home Office (responsible for the police, prisons, immigration and asylum and 'everything else')?

(iv) And how might it be funded? Would a levy on marriage banns, licences, and certificates to marry be appropriate? If not, why not?

7.4 Mediation: development and the way ahead

The term 'mediation' is now generally used instead of 'conciliation'. In 1993 the National Council for Family Conciliation was renamed National Family Mediation (NFM); NFM and the Family Mediators Association (FMA) are the two specialist organisations offering family mediation in the voluntary and private sectors respectively. In *Mediation: the Making and Remaking of Co-operative Relationships* (1994) by Janet Walker, Peter McCarthy and Noel Timms (the 'Rowntree Report') mediation is defined as follows:

Family mediation is a process in which an impartial third person, the mediator, assists couples considering separation or divorce to make arrangements, to communicate better, to reduce conflict between them, and to reach their own agreed joint decisions. The issues to be decided may concern separation, the divorce, the children, finance and property.

The mediator has no stake in any disputes, is not identified with any of the competing interests, and has no power to impose a settlement on the participants, who retain authority to make their own decisions.

Couples enter mediation voluntarily, to work together on the practical consequences of family breakdown, and to reach proposals for settlements which may then be endorsed by their legal representatives and the court, wherever appropriate. Mediation offers an alternative to negotiation by solicitors and to adjudication through the court, but is not a substitute for legal advice and representation.

An outline of its history in this country is given in the University of Newcastle's Conciliation Project Unit's Report to the Lord Chancellor on the *Costs and Effectiveness of Conciliation in England and Wales* (1989) (the 'Newcastle Report'):

Early Forms of Family Conciliation

2.21 Conciliation in the area of family disputes has been a relatively recent development in England and Wales. It is difficult to trace its precise source simply because the further one delves into the past the greater the confusion between 'conciliation' and 'reconciliation' (Eekelaar and Dingwall (1988)). 'Conciliation' is reported to have been widely practised in the magistrates' courts before the Second World War – and not only by the probation service – but the context makes it clear that the primary aim was to preserve the marriage relationship and, in particular, to persuade wives not to pursue legal claims against their husbands. ...

2.23 The notion that divorce procedures should enable parties to resolve their differences with the minimum of bitterness and conflict, once the breakdown of the marriage was irretrievable, can be discerned in the change of attitude to collusion which, in 1969, became a discretionary, rather than an absolute bar to divorce (see the remarks of Lord Scarman in *Minton v Minton* [1979] AC 593, 608). The first official, explicit recognition of the distinction between 'conciliation' and 'reconciliation' would appear to be the Practice Direction of the President of the Family Division, issued on 27 January 1971 (*Practice Note (Divorce: Conciliation)* [1971] 1 WLR 223), and which coincided with the coming into force of the Divorce Reform Act 1969:

'Where the Court considers that there is a reasonable possibility of reconciliation *or that there are ancillary proceedings in which conciliation might serve a useful purpose*, the Court may refer the case, or any particular matter or matters in dispute therein, to the Court Welfare Officer.'

The Court Welfare Officer would then, if he decided that conciliation 'might assist the parties to resolve their dispute', refer the case on to a probation officer, a marriage guidance counsellor or 'some other appropriate person or body indicated by the special circumstances ... of the case'.

The Finer Report and its Aftermath

2.24 The impact of the 1971 Practice Direction on the divorce courts is unclear, but when the Finer Committee investigated the question it found that the court welfare services had concentrated almost exclusively on reconciliation rather than conciliation ...

2.25 Having reviewed conciliation and reconciliation practices both in Britain and in some foreign jurisdictions, the committee concluded that, whereas reconciliation procedures undertaken at the time when parties seek to formalise their marriage breakdown have small success, 'conciliation procedures conducted through the court at this same stage have substantial success in civilising the consequences of the breakdown'. In its view, the policy of the law should be that:

> 'dead marriages should be decently buried. Decency in this connection involves diagnosing the practical needs of the family at the time when the court assumes control over the relationship between its members and their affairs, invoking the help of other appropriate agencies to minister to those needs, and encouraging the victims of the family breakdown to wind up their failure with the least possible recrimination, and to make the most rational and efficient arrangements possible for their own and their children's future'.

The Committee envisaged that the 'agencies' referred to would comprise not only the court welfare service but also other bodies, including the social services and specialised organisations offering marriage guidance.

2.26 These suggestions for conciliation were made in the context of the Finer proposals for a family court and this may help to explain why they elicited no centralised response. Instead, initiatives were taken at a local level by different groups with different aims. Indeed, the very breadth of the Finer definition of conciliation encouraged a multitude of approaches. ... Parkinson [1986] lists six concerns which, in her view, fuelled the rapid growth of conciliation in Britain from 1975:

   (i)   to provide an alternative to the adversarial system in the divorce courts;
   (ii) to protect children involved in their parents' divorce;
   (iii) to give people more control over their own affairs and reduce their reliance on formal institutions;
   (iv) to achieve greater administrative efficiency by processing contested cases more quickly;
   (v)   to reduce public expenditure, particularly on legal aid;
   (vi) to stem the rising tide of divorce.

The Development of In-Court Conciliation

2.27 The first attempt to institute a formal conciliation service within the court process took place at the Bristol County Court. The Avon Probation Service, as a response to the Finer proposals, had organised a specialist civil work team and, following discussions with the judiciary, a system of preliminary appointments in defended divorced cases was set up in 1976. In 1978, the service was extended to cases of disputes over custody or access, the term 'mediation' being used to describe appointments in cases of this kind.

... [It] is clear ... that growth has been very rapid, particularly in areas where the enthusiasm of the probation service was matched by that of local judges or registrars. ...

2.29 Legally, it is clear that parties cannot be compelled to attend conciliation appointments (*Clarkson v Winkley* [1987] FCR 33) but there is evidence that they perceive the process to be compulsory (Davis and Bader (1985)). As will be revealed elsewhere in this Report, both the style of the conciliation appointment and the procedure of referral vary considerably. In some courts, once the existence of a dispute has been located, the parties are invited to an appointment with a court welfare officer. In others, the process is initiated by a registrar who seeks to identify the area of disagreement and then encourages the parties to meet with the conciliator in a separate room, with the possibility of a further appointment should this be necessary.

2.30 It was this approach to conciliation which the Booth Committee, reporting in July 1985, found to be so appealing, for it squared with its own view that much of the difficulty and cost associated with matrimonial litigation could be reduced by earlier institutional interventions, primarily through an 'initial hearing' which would take place as soon as practicable after the filing of the petition ...

The Development of Independent Conciliation Services

2.34 It has been argued by some that conciliation is most effective when undertaken independently of the judicial process (Davis and Bader (1985)). As recognised by the Booth Committee (para 3.12), this is, in part, based on a belief that the earlier the intervention the better, and court services can, of course, only be used when proceedings have begun. But other advantages are also regarded as important (Parkinson (1986): p76), such as quick accessibility in crisis situations and availability to unmarried as well as married couples and to those who wish to avoid court proceedings. It has also been argued (Roberts (1983)) that the essence of conciliation being to enable the parties themselves to make joint decisions on disputed matters, the process may be seriously inhibited by its location within the institutional framework of the courthouse or any connection with it.

2.35 Arguments such as these were deployed by those, including lawyers, who helped to launch the independent conciliation services. As with court schemes, Bristol took the lead with the establishment of the Bristol Courts Family Conciliation Service in 1979 (the word 'Courts' was abandoned in 1987 to avoid confusion with the court-based service). Perhaps the other most important pioneering service was the South-East London Family Conciliation Bureau, established also in 1979 at Bromley. ...

The debate about whether mediation should be provided as part of the court's own processes, or by an independent agency, has swung in favour of the latter. The Newcastle Report drew the following broad policy conclusions:

20.19 Our identification of the factors which, as regards existing services, seem to hinder the effectiveness of conciliation leads us to the view that conciliation:
  (a) should not be mandatory for all couples;
  (b) should not focus exclusively on child issues;
  (c) should not be surrounded by ambiguous terminology; and
  (d) should not overlap with other legal and welfare processes.
More positively, for effectiveness to be maximised, we believe that:
  (e) conciliation should be recognised as an alternative mechanism to legal, adjudicatory procedures for the resolution of disputes and be identifiable as a discrete, unambiguous process;
  (f) its distinguishing feature should be to enable couples to retain control of the decision-making process consequent on separation and divorce, encouraging them to reach their own agreements; and
  (g) the arena in which it takes place should be conducive to civilised discussion with an appropriate degree of informality.

These findings led the Law Commission to make the following recommendations in their Report on *The Ground for Divorce* (1990):

5.34 A more difficult question . . . is whether conciliation or mediation should be mandatory, if not in all cases at least in those which the court identifies as suitable for it. Once again, however, the majority of our respondents thought it should not. The professionals practising in the field said that mandatory conciliation or mediation was unlikely to be successful and indeed might be counter-productive. The Newcastle research indicated that the greatest benefits came from independent conciliation which was clearly distinguished from the coercive setting of the court. It is also clear that, whatever its benefits in some cases, there are many issues or relationships in which it is quite unsuitable. If so, the aim must be to ensure that adequate services are available to those who wish to use them, and to secure efficient information and referral machinery, rather than coercive sanctions to achieve this. There are also dangers in relying too heavily upon conciliation or mediation instead of more traditional methods of negotiation and adjudication. These include exploitation of the weaker partner by the stronger, which requires considerable skill and professionalism for the conciliator to counteract while remaining true to the neutral role required; considerable potential for delay, which is damaging both to the children and often to the interests of one of the adults involved; and the temptation for the court to postpone deciding some very difficult and painful cases which ought to be decided quickly. It is important that, whatever encouragement is given by the system to alternative methods of dispute resolution, the courts are not deterred from performing their function of determining issues which require to be determined. Where time permits, alternative methods can be explored so as to enable the parties to try and reach their own agreements away from the pressures of the court door. Where, however, an immediate decision is needed in the interests of either party or of their children, the courts should be prepared to give it.

5.35 We therefore *recommend* that undertaking . . . mediation should be purely voluntary.

5.36 We further *recommend* that opportunities and encouragement to resolve matters amicably should be built into the system where appropriate. . . .

5.37 Furthermore, although participation in conciliation or mediation should be voluntary, we *recommend* that the court should have two additional powers to encourage it. Neither of these powers should be seen as placing any pressure on the parties to participate. They are designed to ensure that the parties are better-informed and to facilitate participation if they wish. They are also designed to some extent to regulate what happens informally at present. ...

Referral for an explanation of conciliation or mediation

5.38 It is likely that in a number of cases one spouse, or perhaps both spouses, will not appreciate the nature and effectiveness of conciliation or mediation, or even if aware have a totally closed mind on the subject. Many people are confused about the distinctions between counselling, reconciliation and conciliation and are instinctively resistant to reconciliation. We therefore *recommend* that the court should have power, whether on application or of its own motion, to give a direction that the spouses meet a specified conciliator or mediator, in order to discuss the nature and potential benefits of conciliation or mediation in their case. ...

Adjournment for participation

5.39 We further *recommend* that, where the parties are in dispute about any issue arising in the context of divorce or separation, the court should have power, whether on application or of its own motion, to adjourn the hearing of that issue, for the purpose of enabling them to participate in conciliation or mediation, or generally with a view to the amicable resolution of the dispute. In deciding to do this, the court should take the interests of any children into account (whether, for example, they will be more helped by the amicable resolution or harmed by the delay). It should, of course, be open to the parties not to participate and if either of them feels unable to do so this should not affect the handling of the case thereafter.

The Newcastle Report had proposed the development of 'comprehensive' or 'all issues' mediation, dealing with money and property as well as child-related questions, while recognising that this would have far-reaching implications for charitable mediation services set up principally to produce better outcomes for children, in particular by requiring some legal input. NFM responded to the challenge with five pilot schemes, which were compared and evaluated by the Rowntree Report. No simple conclusions are drawn, but the following extract gives something of the flavour of clients' reactions to the process:

'I think it has moved us into this frame of mind to try to be co-operative which might not have happened if we had gone through this hostility that people often get going through solicitors. ... The children have been put first an awful lot of the time and conciliation has helped with that.' (F)

The benefits would seem to relate to mediation as preventing tension –

'I feel it has helped to keep me from getting tense and wound up and I have been able to keep things happier for the children.' (M)

– or managing it more effectively and over a shorter time period:

'Because of the way we have done it we are still quite friendly.' (F)

'At the worst time of the post-separation period my wife and I were able to meet and not scream at one another and I thought that was quite impressive and it didn't come from us I am sure.' (M)

'I think it has reduced the amount of bitterness over a shorter period than perhaps would have been the case. ... A plus, but not one that I had considered beforehand.' (M)

Even when feelings were largely negative between partners, the majority did not see themselves in a state of high conflict with each other. Several questioned whether they would have been suitable candidates for mediation if this had been the case:

'Overall I felt it was a very valuable exercise. It did help to reduce the tension because of having to talk about something in not a formal atmosphere, but with third parties present. It does tend to concentrate the mind far better than two of you sitting over a table. Although there were a few areas of disagreement it was more of establishing what had to be done and how we could best do it, both in a practical manner and also in an emotional manner. Providing a couple are not coming to blows at the service I would thoroughly recommend it to anyone else. ... I find it very difficult to envisage that situation being handled by the mediators.' (M)

'Had we been spitting blood I don't know how they would have coped. Certainly the one who was not quite so confident – I think she would have run out of the room screaming.' (M)

'I can see that the downfalls in that [mediation] would be that if you got two people sitting there and they really are at loggerheads then that must be one of the biggest problems because it then starts to get personal.' (M)

'Everything was amicable anyway and whether or not it would be different if you had a couple who were at loggerheads and trying to sort things out I can't say. In many ways we were giving the mediators a fairly easy ride.' (M)

Indeed, one client commented:

'Had there been a dispute no doubt we would have had to go elsewhere.' (M)

This view does seem rather odd to a process of which the main objective is dispute resolution, but it introduces what might become a major debate in divorce reform, namely the extent to which mediation can helpfully be considered as 'assisted decision-making' in which couples manage their own divorce with a mediator rather than through advising solicitors. Or does the concept of *dispute* resolution dominate, thus restricting the service to couples with identifiable disputes about which they need to reach agreement before the divorce can be finalised? The broader objectives associated with mediation could be viewed as equally important as resolving actual disputes, but this would raise a theoretical conceptual argument about the nature and meaning of mediation.

'It's a very good way of sorting out troubles in a friendly way without involving judges and courts and it didn't cost as much. It seemed more friendly and logical.' (F)

'Sorting out troubles' is somewhat removed from dispute resolution, yet would be said to be very valuable, particularly in relation to wider concerns to protect children from the experience and consequences of parental conflict:

'It gave me peace of mind where I'd been afraid and it freed me to concentrate on the children and on looking after myself. I don't think I'd have been able to deal with it as well as I did if I hadn't gone there. ... It's left me free to focus on the children, learn to do finances, look after the house, adjust my identity to being a single person and things like that.' (F)

The theme of 'assisted decision-making' is one to which we return since it seems to fit well with the ideal of encouraging a 'civilised' approach to marriage breakdown.

The most common response from mediation clients to the question of what they did not like about the outcome related quite clearly to the failure to meet *any* of the expected objectives. The majority of clients were satisfied with the service provided, and this was not dependent on either the reaching of agreements or the time spent in mediation.

'I haven't got a bad word to say about them. I thought it was brilliant.' (F)

'I think there would have been a big void if there hadn't been comprehensive mediation.' (F)

'The conciliation process was excellent. I cannot praise it highly enough. I know that if it hadn't been for the service, I would be still now feeling and manifesting considerable anger all the time over the separation. The availability of this service providing a non-confrontational, non-adversarial mechanism for dealing with issues at a time when both parties are suffering extreme emotional anguish was opportune, soothing, comforting and helpful. I am not certain whether, without it, my wife and I would have been able to come to any agreement at all.' (M)

One user was especially keen to ensure we had recorded his satisfaction:

'Just to make sure, in case you haven't got it down, that if the funding for this place doesn't carry on it would be a big mistake because I can't see how we would have got by without it. It made it very clean. I cannot think of any criticism of the way it was run.' (M).

Lord Habgood (former Archbishop of York and patron of NFM) sums it up neatly in a letter to *The Times* (6 April 1996):

It is a basic principle of mediation that couples must reach their own decisions, which are then given legal force by being referred to a lawyer. The task of the mediator is to provide a controlled, supportive and yet searching context in which a couple can face the practical implications of divorce together.

Not all couples are suitable for this, especially when there has been violence, and mediators are alert to the dangers of coercion. When the conditions for mediation are inappropriate they advise couples to seek independent legal advice. Alternatively if the couple show signs of changing their minds about divorce they are advised to use the reconciliation services.

Question

Go back to the child quoted on p. 290. What should a mediator do if the couple appear to be ignoring their children's wishes and feelings? How is he to know?

Anne Bottomley, in 'Resolving Family Disputes: a Critical View', her contribution to Michael Freeman's collection on *The State, the Law and the Family: Critical Perspectives* (1984), is more sceptical about who is in charge:

Other forms of dispute resolution share the objective of agreement rather than judgment; however in conciliation it is the parties who are deemed to be in control. The presence of a third party is simply to further face-to-face negotiations by 'assisting in' helping communication (the language here slips often into a quasi-therapeutic discourse) and, when necessary, to give technical assistance with the symbols of social recognition of an agreement having been reached, whether by eating and drinking or by the drafting of a document. The anthropological literature has long alerted us to the need to look behind the presentation of such a form of dispute resolution and ask two questions. First, is there equality of power in the relationship between the parties, and between the parties and the mediator? Such an 'open' process is open to manipulation. To be persuaded may be an invidious form of judgment and control. Second, despite the presentation of the mediator in terms of neutrality and objectivity the mediator may be the purveyor of a particular pattern of beliefs that would tend to favour a particular 'resolution' to which the parties give their formal agreement.

[T]he conciliator is clearly not neutral but the purveyor of certain ideologies and practices. Psychology, therapy, or social policy are not neutral bodies of knowledge. ... Social workers and probation officers tend to share a common belief in the functionalism of the family, and a particular familial ideology in which roles are cast and those who do not fit are deemed not to be fit. They also share a concern with the increase in divorce and the need somehow to 'normalize' divorce so that it becomes less challenging to the images of stability and continuity that remain at the core of the family image. Much emphasis is placed on the fact that parents never divorce, only spouses: 'The court is asked in a divorce petition to dissolve the legal bonds of marriage, not the bonds of parenthood'.

What we are experiencing at the moment is a pincer movement. On the one hand family law is being squeezed out of the formal legal system on arguments of cost and on the other hand it is being enticed out with promises of more fruitful pastures elsewhere. This shift towards de-legalization must not be simply accepted but must be more closely examined. We need to recognize that the process of de-legalization is not one of de-regularization but is a shift from one form of social discipline to another. While the articulate middle classes will continue to buy the services of professional groups, others will become more and more the subjects of control by 'welfarism'. Those who are most vulnerable will be caught between the unequal power relations of private ordering and a familial ideology rendered benign by welfarism in informal dispute resolution

In 'Involvement of Lawyers in the Mediation Process' (1996), Peter McCarthy and Janet Walker report on a survey of mediators and their views on the involvement of lawyers in mediation. They conclude:

The practice of all-issues mediation in England and Wales has involved considerable participation from lawyers, either as mediators or as legal advisers to couples who use mediation. In some services operating under the auspices of National Family Mediation, lawyers also act as consultants to mediators. Although mediation which is attended by the parties' legal advisers is practised in other jurisdictions, it is not an approach which would be welcomed by most FMA mediators. On the other hand, there is considerable support for suggestions that parties using mediation should have access to independent legal advice at all stages of the process and especially at the conclusion of mediation. ... Most respondents accept that the lawyer's legal knowledge and experience regarding financial issues make an important contribution to the mediation process, although lawyer mediators also seem to appreciate the contributions of family mediators. It is the balance that the sharing of skills brings to mediation which is valued, allowing mediation to deal with all issues and help mediators to cope with stress. Most survey respondents ... regard legal expertise as an essential component to the mediation process. Indeed, 83% of lawyer mediators, and 61% of family mediators, suggest that lawyers ought to be able to offer mediation as part of their legal practice. Moreover, 40% of ... mediators ... suggest that mediation training should be compulsory for all lawyers practising family law.

Questions

(i) Is mediation simply a form of alternative dispute resolution in family cases or is it yet another cloak for yet another type of professional to take over?
(ii) How far might Bottomley's concerns be dismissed as lawyers' special pleading?
(iii) Do you now have a clear perception of what mediation is and what it can achieve? How would you describe it to a client?

The Government increasingly saw mediation as an alternative, not only to conventional litigation, but also to lawyer-led negotiation and settlement. Part III of the Family Law Act 1996 provided for public funding of mediation in 'family matters', not just divorce, and was brought into force independently of the divorce reforms in Part II. More controversially, by s. 29 a new s. 15(3F), (3G) and (3H) was inserted into the Legal Aid Act 1988:

(3F) A person shall not be granted representation for the purposes of proceedings relating to family matters, unless he has attended a meeting with a mediator—
  (a) to determine—
    (i) whether mediation appears suitable to the dispute and the parties and all the circumstances, and
    (ii) in particular, whether mediation could take place without either party being influenced by fear of violence or other harm; and
  (b) if mediation does appear suitable, to help the person applying for representation to decide whether instead to apply for mediation.
(3G) Subsection (3F) does not apply—
  (a) in relation to proceedings under—
    (i) Part IV of the Family Law Act 1996;
    (ii) section 37 of the Matrimonial Causes Act 1973;
    (iii) Part IV or V of the Children Act 1989;
  (b) in relation to proceedings of any other description that may be prescribed; or
  (c) in such circumstances as may be prescribed.
(3H) So far as proceedings relate to family matters, the Board, in determining under subsection (3)(a) whether, in relation to the proceedings, it is reasonable that a person should be granted representation under this Part—
  (a) must have regard to whether and to what extent recourse to mediation would be a suitable alternative to taking the proceedings; and
  (b) must for that purpose have regard to the outcome of the meeting held under subsection (3F) and to any assessment made for the purposes of section 13B(3).

Question

Do you agree with the exclusions in s. 15(3G)?

Any publicly funded mediator is required to comply with a code of practice with the minimum requirements set out in s. 13A of the 1988 Act:

(7) The code must require the mediator to have arrangements designed to ensure—
(a) that parties participate in mediation only if willing and not influenced by fear of violence or other harm;
(b) that cases where either party may be influenced by fear of violence or other harm are identified as soon as possible;
(c) that the possibility of reconciliation is kept under review throughout mediation; and
(d) that each party is informed about the availability of independent legal advice.
(8) Where there are one or more children of the family, the code must also require the mediator to have arrangements designed to ensure that the parties are encouraged to consider—
(a) the welfare, wishes and feelings of each child; and
(b) whether and to what extent each child should be given the opportunity to express his or her wishes and feelings in the mediation.

Question

Is this enough to answer the critics?

In his Joseph Jackson Memorial Lecture in January 1996, Stephen Cretney commented caustically upon what was *not* to be in the Act, comparing the requirements in statutes such as the Chiropractors Act 1994 and the Osteopaths Act 1993 for accreditation, indemnity insurance and so on:

So you have expectations of the kind of provision you would expect to find in a statute concerned with the provision of mediation and other related services. I am afraid the Family Law Bill is unlikely to meet these expectations. You look for the duty to provide mediation services or at least a duty to ensure that mediation services are provided. There is none. You look for the duty – or even the power – to ensure that proper professional standards are maintained amongst all mediators; so that – for example – a mediator who abuses his or her position of trust can be prevented from offering such services in the future. There is no such provision.

In January 1996 the UK College of Family Mediators was founded by NFM, FMA and Family Mediation Scotland to become the single regulatory body for mediators, but without any statutory basis for its operations. The Legal Services Commission (LSC), however, is in a position to decide what it will and will not fund. It has piloted various ways of delivering publicly funded family mediation which were evaluated by a research team led by Gwynn Davis (see *Monitoring Publicly Funded Family Mediation, Final Report to the Legal Services Commission* (2000)). He has since offered the following 'Reflections in the aftermath of the family mediation pilot' (2001):

In very brief summary, some of the 'headline' conclusions were:
• the overall volume of mediation activity remained quite low, with a few suppliers continuing to do the bulk of the work;
• solicitor providers of mediation contracted to the LSC grew to outnumber the 'not for profit' providers, although the latter continued to undertake most of the business;
• the pilot (and particularly section 29 of the Family Law Act 1996) led to considerably increased activity around 'intake', but the number of actual mediations rose only very gradually;
• many of our informants who lacked experience of mediation considered it to be a good idea in theory, but doubted whether it would work in their case;
• those prospective legal aid applicants who were referred for mediation intake under section 29 appeared compliant, but not obviously enthusiastic; many displayed high levels of mistrust of their former partner;

- those couples who embarked upon mediation found it, for the most part, a positive experience which contributed significantly to the resolution of their disputes;
- the response to the help provided by solicitors was, on the whole, even more enthusiastic;
- solicitors modify their partisanship very considerably; most display strongly 'pro-family' values;
- mediation does not appear to reduce the number of applications for legal aid to support lawyer negotiation and representation (although the number of these applications is falling quite significantly as a result of declining eligibility and, secondly, a fall in the number of 'outlets' – solicitor firms contracted to the LSC to undertake legal aid work);
- nor does mediation reduce expenditure on lawyers (in other words, it seems to operate for the most part as an additional service, rather than as an alternative). . . .

THE NATURE OF MEDIATION

. . . Mediation is often described in terms that highlight the presumed contrast with late-stage litigation. For example, it is associated with reasonableness, with a commitment to negotiation rather than adjudication, with an explicit focus upon the interests of children, and with outcomes that are not only agreed, but enduring. Sometimes, in the transformations that are envisaged, it seems reasonable to characterise mediation as having 'therapeutic' effects. . . .

Encouragement to be 'reasonable' is not itself the problem (although it is certainly no solution, either). It can readily be conceded that separated parents will continue to be connected to one another through their children, and that this, in turn, places a premium upon their reaching understandings that both can live with. But we need always to bear in mind that mediation is a form, not an outcome. This means that the association between mediation and co-operation is a recurring *non sequitur*. In many of the accounts offered by practitioners, emphasis is laid upon the outcomes – by and large, and highly desirable outcomes – which can flow from mediation. It does not follow from this that were mediation to be applied to a range of issues and a range of disputants who do not, at present, volunteer for this way of tackling their problems, the same happy outcomes would result. Good outcomes may be expected to follow where the form meets the need.

. . . I want to focus, for the moment, on the differences between out-of-court mediation and the other, still dominant model of dispute resolution within the family arena, which is lawyer negotiation.

KEY CHARACTERISTICS

There seem to me to be two fundamental differences between these forms of professional intervention. The first concerns the locus of authority. In mediation this rests with the parties. It is their values and understandings that count. In lawyer negotiation, on the other hand, the key reference points are external to the parties, supplied by the lawyers. They reflect whatever principles are contained within statute, plus the influence of judicial decisions arrived at in what are supposedly like cases.

The second difference is one of form. Mediation is generally understood (at least in the family arena) to involve direct engagement with the other party, with the mediator acting as a facilitator. Lawyers, on the other hand, engage in representative negotiation in the course of which, typically, the parties are not present.

AN UNFAMILIAR CONCEPT?

. . . I have some experience as a mediation 'client'. My brother and I are 14 months apart in age, and we quarrelled, and our parents helped us to resolve those quarrels. Thereafter, in the world of work, I can recall at least two instances when a colleague and I have sought, or been offered, mediation. In each case we benefited from it. . . .

Little attention has been paid to this experience of informal mediation. In the family arena commentators have tended to focus upon the difficulties that are presented by the relationship between the parties – the separating couple – and their perhaps limited capacity to negotiate together. But consideration of our wider experience invites us to view mediation from another angle, from the perspective of the relationship between the mediator and those whom he is trying to help. And what do we find? I believe we find, first of all, that the mediator generally has a *prior relationship* with the disputants, and that his capacity to engage with them reflects this previously established intimacy and trust. Secondly, it is a *private* relationship, not a professional one. And thirdly, the mediator will probably be someone whom the disputants regard as *authoritative* – he will be a person of some standing in their eyes.

Family mediation has, necessarily, sought to develop a very different model. First, the mediator, generally speaking, is not familiar to the parties. Indeed, he is likely to be completely unknown. Secondly, he is someone who is accorded professional status, his claim to professionalism residing in his skills in the practice of mediation and, these days, in his adherence to a Code of Practice developed by one of the professional associations. And thirdly, he will probably explicitly repudiate any suggestion that he exercises any authority over the parties (other than the 'authority' that resides in a presumed working knowledge of family law and procedure). So, unfamiliar, professional, and without authority. . . .

Does any of this matter? I think it does, because it suggests that the modest take-up of family mediation (over at least 20 years) reflects not the unfamiliarity of the concept, but a fairly widespread reluctance to embrace its professionalised form in the context of relationship breakdown. This in turn suggests that we ought to be cautious before introducing procedural arrangements that privilege this form of negotiation over others which, to date, have attracted a more immediate, intuitive response.

This is not to deny the value of mediation for some couples. The evidence on this is clear and consistent: most couples who are referred, or who refer themselves, to a family mediation service derive benefit from it. But we also have to respect people's choices. We accept the principle of freedom of choice in most areas of life where the choices that can be made do not obviously harm others. But debates concerning the ending of intimate relationships are given a moral overlay that seeks to close off some choices and promote alternatives. That would be understandable if the focus were upon the decision to end the relationship in the first place, but it is less easy to see why separating couples should not be allowed to trust their own instincts when it comes to coping with the aftermath. Simon Roberts' writings provide a useful reference point here because he has been such a determined champion of the 'transition', as he refers to it, from lawyer negotiation to mediation. He appears in no doubt that his 'transition' is taking us in the right direction. All he is prepared to concede is that 'too little thought was perhaps given to detailed planning of the transition; particularly to the provision of appropriate support for the large proportion of parties who might have wanted to continue relying on representative negotiations at first' [Roberts, 2000]. . . .

KEY DISTINCTIONS

. . . Roberts . . . refers to 'a huge philosophic divide between those who see mediation as fundamentally an intervention supportive of party negotiation, and those who see it as an additional component in the existing regime of professional management. While the first of these directions moves away from a culture of litigation, the latter sustains it. While the first appears to offer a means of escape from professional domination (although, *paradoxically*, it involves the formation of a new professional group), the latter contemplates just another intervention'. Paradoxically'? In that case it is a paradox that Roberts declines to elucidate . . . This is because the drive to professionalise family mediation is unremitting. There may be a few family mediators who have resisted the embrace of the professional organisations, but they are being hunted down.

Secondly, Roberts surely knows that the degree to which the parties determine the outcome of mediation is fiercely, even bitterly contested. As Dingwall and Greatbatch [2001] put it in a recent article:

> 'Family mediators are required to remain impartial between clients and neutral as to the outcome. They are also supposed to intervene in order to redress, as far as possible, imbalances of power between clients. The logical inconsistency between these objectives has been widely discussed.'

Dingwall and Greatbatch confirmed, through their most recent work, that mediators certainly had views about outcomes, and that those views were conveyed to the parties. Naturally enough, the separating couple retained considerable room for manoeuvre, but this was within bounds set by the mediator – referred to by Dingwall and Greatbatch as 'parameters of the permissible'. This probably surprises no one by now, and it still seems reasonable to conclude that the parties retain a greater measure of control than when 'instructing' solicitors to negotiate on their behalf. . . .

WHY DO PEOPLE CHOOSE LAWYERS?

Then we come to our other difficulty, which is the recalcitrant behaviour of the population in question. It is beyond argument that separating couples are drawn to seek lawyers' help. Is this because divorce is still a legal process, giving rise to a natural assumption that one needs specialist legal help in order to negotiate it? I guess this must be true, at least in part. It may also be the case, as both King [1999] and Roberts seem to suggest, that family lawyers are a brilliantly adaptive life form and that they have transformed themselves to meet changed conditions. But this is not sufficient in itself to explain lawyers' popularity. There are many other difficult life circumstances that have, potentially, a legal dimension, but none give rise to this same, apparently almost automatic assumption that legal help is required. So I would prefer to start from the proposition that people go to solicitors – which cannot be an easy thing to do – because they have a genuine need for the kind of help that, in their judgment, only a lawyer can provide. Now what is this 'need' and what is the proposed remedy? I do not believe that the need is represented simply by 'a dispute'. After all, lawyers are not very good at resolving disputes, and I think people know this. The lawyer negotiation model was analysed, for example, in *Simple Quarrels* [1994] and found to be protracted, sporadic, sometimes unprincipled, and reliant upon attrition. It is also, of course, expensive.

Legal argument seldom culminates in judicial determination, as must by now be well known (it cannot be, as Roberts suggests, 'clandestine'). Arguably, settlements negotiated by lawyers offer the worst of all worlds, in that they represent *neither* judicial determination *nor* consensual decision making. They are a kind of hybrid which, in many cases, appears to satisfy neither party. And yet demand is unceasing. We have to ask ourselves why this is, and whether mediation can be an effective alternative provider of whatever it is that separating couples seek from lawyers – and not only seek, but also receive, because if they did not receive it the news would surely get out. . . .

There is plentiful evidence that people do not behave 'reasonably' in the immediate aftermath of separation. In public policy debates mediation has been characterised as involving 'constructive negotiation' that has a 'rational' basis, but such language conveys little sense of why it is that people may choose to consult lawyers rather than mediators. Almost certainly it is not because the problems they face can only be resolved within a legal framework. It is more likely that they make this choice because their relationship with their former partner has deteriorated to a point where, for a time at least, they feel that negotiation is no longer feasible. Mediation may not be able to respond effectively to conflict on this level – or, at least, that may be the perception of the parties. It is not that they necessarily reject the option of a reasoned negotiation with a fair-minded person; it is, rather, that they do not believe that those conditions exist. In other words, lawyers may offer the only hope of tackling, not 'disputes', but behaviour that is wholly uncivilised and unreasonable.

There is also the troubling question of whether, in requiring the parties to be reasonable, we are giving the message that we somehow expect them to turn their backs on principles of fairness that guide all of us in our responses to perceived injustice. All relationships, including intimate relationships, rest on a bedrock of perceived fairness. When love recedes, fairness may be all that we have left. So negotiations have to reflect this value. This is, in essence, what lawyers represent. They offer a framework – a set of rules, of which they say, in effect, 'these are fair; you will have to abide by them'. Mediators do not offer this. For example, one aspect of the 'civilised' nature of mediation, certainly in the family arena, is a reluctance to spend time reviewing the past (with its scope for blaming and for differing interpretations) and a preferred concentration upon future arrangements. Lawyers, on the other hand, are interested in the past; that is where evidence comes from. . . .

Law cannot cope with complex human emotions – indeed, it appears wholly uninterested in them – but law connotes *authority* and it can provide *containment* for what may otherwise appear overwhelming feelings of anger and loss. That containment may need to be exercised over a considerable period. Arguably, it is at the heart of the service that is provided by family lawyers. Their role as negotiators and as framers of compromise solutions may be less important than the physiological function that they serve in containing ungovernable, destructive emotion at a time of crisis in people's lives.

CONCLUSION

The above analysis suggests that family lawyers and family mediators do not provide a parallel service. They are not alternatives. Mediators negotiate, and so do lawyers, but lawyers provide something that mediators cannot replicate, and that 'something' is authority – and through authority, containment. Insofar as mediators provide this at all (and they probably do to some extent), they do so by investing the performance of their role with features that are not intrinsic to it and that do not figure in any ideal type characterisation. The fact that mediation has inserted itself in the marketplace as an alternative to lawyer negotiation is a wholly welcome development. Some people will prefer direct engagement. And they will prefer a form of negotiation in which legal signposts are present as a background feature, rather than being assumed to be determinative. I would have thought that it is for the parties, and no one else, to judge whether the conditions for mediation apply in their case. Even where they are disposed to negotiate, mediation may not be the preferred route. But it will be a viable option for some, and it is important, therefore, to have procedures that contain the flexibility to allow mediation to be chosen if and when the time is right.

Questions

(i) How would you rank the following explanations for the continuing popularity of family lawyers: (a) they are a 'brilliantly adaptive life form'; (b) breakdown in the family usually coincides with breakdown in trust; (c) it is not reasonable to expect reasonable behaviour from separating couples; (d) they do a good job at a fair price?
(ii) Do you still want to be a family lawyer?

Bibliography

7.1   The family courts debate

We quoted from

J. Brophy, C. Wale and P. Bates, *Myths and Practices: A national survey of the use of experts in child care proceedings* (1999) London, British Agencies for Adoption and Fostering, pp. 54–56.

G. Douglas, *Resolving Family Disputes: a discussion paper* (2002) London, Nuffield Foundation, pp. 1–9.

P. Munro, 'Expert witnesses', in M. Thorpe and C. Cowton (eds.), *Delight and Dole: The Children Act 10 years on* (2002), Bristol, Jordan, pp. 100–101.

Report of the Children Act Advisory Committee 1993/94 (1994) London, HMSO, pp. 13–14.

Report of the Committee on One-Parent Families (Chairman: The Hon Sir Maurice Finer) (Cmnd. 5629) (1974) London, HMSO, paras 4.285, 4.404, 4.405.

Additional reading

J. Brown and S. Day Sclater, 'Divorce: A Psychodynamic Perspective', in S. Day Sclater and C. Piper (eds.), *Undercurrents of Divorce* (1999) Ashgate.

J. Eekelaar, M. Maclean and S. Beinart, *Family Lawyers: The Divorce Work of Solicitors* (2000), Oxford, Hart Publishing.

H. Genn, *Paths to Justice: what people do and think about going to law* (1999) Oxford, Hart Publishing.

7.2   Public regulation or private ordering?

We quoted from:

C. Lyon, E. Surrey and J. Timms, *Effective Support Services for Children and Young People when Parental Relationships Break Down* (1998) Liverpool, University of Liverpool, National Youth Advocacy Service, Calouste Gulbenkian Foundation, p. 43.

R. Mnookin, 'Bargaining in the Shadow of the Law: The Case of Divorce' [1979] Current Legal Problems 65, p. 65.

R. Mnookin, 'Divorce Bargaining: The Limits of Private Ordering', in J.M. Eekelaar and S.N. Katz (eds.), *The Resolution of Family Conflict: Comparative Legal Perspectives* (1984) Toronto, Butterworths, pp. 366–372, 376–379.

Additional reading

C. Lyon, 'Children's Participation in Private Law Proceedings', in M. Thorpe
and E. Clarke (eds.), *No Fault or Flaw: The Future of the Family Law Act
1996* (2000) Bristol, Jordan.

N. Lowe and M. Murch, 'Children's participation in the family justice system
– Translating principles into practice' (2001) 13 Child and Family Law
Quarterly 137.

7.3 Marriage mending or marriage ending?

We quoted from:

G. Davies and M. Murch, *Grounds for Divorce* (1988) Oxford, Clarendon
Press, pp. 53–56.

G. Douglas, M. Murch, L. Scanlan and A. Perry, 'Safeguarding Children's
Welfare in Non-Contentious Divorce – Towards a New Conception of the
Legal Process?' (2000) 63 Modern Law Review 177, pp. 192–194.

Law Commission, *Report on the Ground for Divorce* Law Com. No. 192 (1990)
London, HMSO, paras. 5.29, 5.30, 5.33 and App C, *Court Record Study*,
paras. 13–15.

The Law Society, *Family Law Protocol* (2000) London, The Law Society, paras.
1.2–1.4.

The Law Society Family Law Sub-Committee, *A Better Way Out* (1979)
London, The Law Society, para. 178.

Report of the Committee on One-Parent Families (Chairman: The Hon Sir Maurice
Finer) (Cmnd. 5629) (1974) London, HMSO, paras. 4.298–4.300.

Additional reading

Law Commission, *Reform of the Grounds of Divorce – The Field of Choice*,
Law Com. No. 6 (1966) London, HMSO.

Lord Chancellor's Advisory Group on Marriage and Relationship Support,
*Moving Forward Together: A Proposed Strategy for Marriage and Relationship
Support for 2002 and Beyond* (2002) London, Lord Chancellor's
Department.

Report of the Royal Commission on Marriage and Divorce (Chairman: Lord
Morton of Henryton) (Cmd. 9678) (1956) London, HMSO.

7.4 Mediation: development and the way ahead

We quoted from:

A. Bottomley, 'Resolving Family Disputes: A Critical View', in M.D.A.
Freeman (ed.), *The State, the Law and the Family: Critical Perspectives*
(1984) London, Stevens, pp. 294–298.

S. Cretney, 'Family Law – "A Bit of a Racket"?', Joseph Jackson Memorial
Lecture 1996 (1996) 146 New Law Journal 91, p. 94.

G. Davis, 'Reflections in the aftermath of the family mediation pilot' (2001)
13 Child and Family Law Quarterly 371, pp. 371–381.

Law Commission, *Report on the Ground for Divorce*, Law Com. No. 192 (1990)
London, HMSO, paras. 5.34–5.39.

P. McCarthy and J. Walker, 'Involvement of Lawyers in the Mediation Process' [1996] Family Law 154.

University of Newcastle Conciliation Project Unit, *Report to the Lord Chancellor on the Costs and Effectiveness of Conciliation in England and Wales* (1989) Newcastle upon Tyne, University of Newcastle, paras 2.21–2.35, 20.19.

J. Walker, P. McCarthy and N. Timms, *Mediation: The Making and Remaking of Co-operative Relationships* (1994) Newcastle upon Tyne, Relate Centre for Family Studies, pp. 8, 81–84.

Additional reading

Report of the Matrimonial Causes Procedure Committee (Chairman: The Hon Mrs Justice Booth DBE) (1985) London, HMSO.

G. Davis, *Monitoring Funded Family Mediation, Final Report to the Legal Service Commission* (2000) London, Legal Services Commission.

G. Davis, *Partisans and Mediators* (1988) Oxford, Clarendon Press.

G. Davis and K. Bader, 'In Court Mediation: The Consumer View' (1985) 15 Family Law 42.

G. Davis, S. Cretney and J. Collins, *Simple Quarrels* (1994) Oxford, Clarendon Press.

R. Dingwall and D. Greatbatch, 'Family Mediators – What are They Doing?' [2001] Family Law 378.

J. Eekelaar and R. Dingwall, 'The development of conciliation in England', in R. Dingwall and J. Eekelaar (eds.), *Divorce Mediation and the Legal Process* (1988) Oxford, Clarendon Press.

J. Eekelaar, M. Maclean and S. Beinart, *Family Lawyers: The Divorce Work of Solicitors* (2000) Oxford, Hart Publishing.

L. Parkinson, *Conciliation in Separation and Divorce: Finding common ground* (1986) London, Croom Helm.

S. Roberts, 'Mediation in Family Law Disputes' (1983) 46 Modern Law Review 537.

S. Roberts, 'Family Mediation after the Act' (2001) 13 Child and Family Law Quarterly 265.

L. Webley, *A Review of the Literature on Family Mediation For England and Wales, Scotland, the Republic of Ireland, France and the United States*, prepared for the Lord Chancellor's Advisory Committee on Legal Education and Conduct (1998) London, Institute of Advanced Legal Studies.

Chapter 8

Maintenance and capital provision on divorce

8.1 The historical background

8.2 The Matrimonial Causes Act 1973

8.3 A question of principle

8.4 A Scottish alternative

8.5 Section 25 in action

8.6 Empirical evidence

In this chapter we examine the process of re-distributing the family finances after divorce. After looking at the historical background to the process, and the way the Matrimonial Causes Act 1973 is drafted, we consider the principles upon which it is operated. This is particularly exciting following the decision of the House of Lords in *White v White* [2001] 1 AC 596, [2000] 3 WLR 1571, [2000] 3 FCR 555, [2001] Fam Law 12, which marks a fresh start. Does it go far enough, and in the right direction? We pause to look northwards at the Scottish system by way of comparison. Next we look at s. 25 of the Act in action, and consider cases involving families in a number of different types of situation. Finally, in 'Empirical evidence', we ask what it is like to go through the process, and how people manage both during and after the re-distribution of assets.

8.1 The historical background

At common law the wife acquired the right to be supported by her husband throughout the marriage, albeit how and when the husband chose (see Chapter 3, above). When divorce was introduced into English law in 1857, it was thought to be only correct that the wife would have the right to apply to a court to obtain an order for support to substitute the voluntary payments to which she would have been entitled had the marriage continued.

Until 1969, English law was dominated by a system of divorce based on the doctrine of the matrimonial offence (see Chapter 6, above). It necessarily followed that the court would attempt to make awards which kept an 'innocent' wife in the position in which she would have been had her husband properly discharged his marital obligations towards her. The Law Commission discussion paper entitled

The Financial Consequences of Divorce: the Basic Policy (1980) reminds us of the following never to be forgotten words of Sir James Wilde (later Lord Penzance) in the Victorian case *Sidney v Sidney* (1865) 4 Sw & Tr 178, 34 LJPM & A 122:

... If, it was said, a man can part with his wife at the door of the Divorce Court without any obligation to support her, and with full liberty to form a new connection, his triumph over the sacred permanence of marriage will have been complete. To him marriage will have been a mere temporary arrangement, conterminous with his inclinations, and void of all lasting tie or burden. To such a man the Court may truly say with propriety, 'According to your ability you must still support the woman you have first chosen and then discarded. If you are relieved from your matrimonial vows it is for the protection of the woman you have injured, and not for your own sake. And so much of the duty of a husband as consists in the maintenance of his wife may be justly kept alive and enforced upon you in favour of her whom you have driven to relinquish your name and home.'

Further,

It is the foremost duty of this Court in dispensing the remedy of divorce to uphold the institution of marriage. The possibility of freedom begets the desire to be set free, and the great evil of a marriage dissolved is, that it loosens the bonds of so many others. The powers of this Court will be turned to good account if, while meting out justice to the parties, such order should be taken in the matter as to stay and quench this desire and repress this evil. Those for whom shame has no dread, honourable vows no tie, and violence to the weak no sense of degradation, may still be held in check by an appeal to their love of money; and I wish it to be understood that, so far as the powers conferred by the section go, no man should, in my judgment, be permitted to rid himself of his wife by ill-treatment, and at the same time escape the obligation of supporting her.

Question

Do you think that the knowledge that there is no escape from the financial ties and obligations of a marriage would operate today as a deterrent against divorce and a buttress to the institution of marriage?

What of a 'guilty' wife? Historically, a wife who had deserted her husband or committed adultery lost her common law right of maintenance. Although the position was ameliorated to a certain extent, the function of divorce was seen to be that of giving relief where a wrong had been done. This inevitably deprived many women of support after a divorce.

Finer and McGregor describe the position in the following way in 'The History of the Obligation to Maintain' (Appendix 5 to the Finer Report (1974)):

Alimony in the ecclesiastical courts
26. A right to maintenance in the strict sense – meaning a claim for the payment of money directly enforceable against the husband – was available to the wife only in the ecclesiastical courts, and even there was only ancillary to the power of these courts to pronounce a decree of divorce *a mensa et thoro*. Such a decree, if granted on its own, might have left the wife without the means of survival. The court would therefore at the same time pronounce a decree of alimony, under which the husband would be required to pay his wife an annual sum, calculated as a proportion of his income, or, if the wife had separate estate, a proportion of their joint incomes. It was common to award one third, sometimes less, sometimes – especially where the husband's property had come substantially from the wife – more. A decree of alimony could not be made separately from a decree of divorce *a mensa et thoro*, from which it followed that a wife who could not establish one of the offences on which such a decree could be granted could not be granted alimony either. Moreover, the means of enforcing an award of alimony were of more theoretical than practical utility. Alimony could not be sued for as a debt in the civil courts. Just as the common law courts refused to award maintenance on the grounds that this would have

interfered with the ecclesiastical jurisdiction, so on the same grounds they refused to enforce the awards made in that jurisdiction. Before 1813, the only sanction for non-payment of alimony was excommunication or other ecclesiastical censure. Thereafter, a machinery for the imprisonment of the defaulting husband on a writ of *de contumace capiendo* became available, but there is little evidence to suggest that the threat of punishment here and now proved to be any more effective than the threat of punishment in the hereafter.

Maintenance after parliamentary divorce

27. A second species of maintenance attached to divorce by private Act of Parliament. The women who benefited from these awards of maintenance were very few in number. But the parliamentary practice is of cardinal historical importance because it established the principles that were adopted by the legislature as governing the right to maintenance when it established for the first time, in 1857, a system of divorce in the civil courts. The earliest Divorce Acts contained express provisions to ensure that the divorced wife should not be left in a state of destitution. Subsequently, a different practice prevailed:

'In the House of Commons there was a functionary called "The Ladies' Friend", an office generally filled by some member interested in the private business of Parliament, who undertook to see that any husband petitioning for divorce made a suitable provision for his wife. No clause to this effect was inserted in the Bill, lest it should be rejected in the other House, but, as a condition of obtaining relief, a husband was made to understand that, before the Bill passed through Committee, he must enter into a bond securing some moderate income to his wife.'

Two features of this practice call for special note. First, unlike the practice in the ecclesiastical court, which granted alimony only to an innocent wife, Parliament deliberately saw to it that a man could not use its process to rid himself of his wife, whatever her matrimonial misconduct might have been, without making some financial provision for her. Secondly, also in contrast with alimony, the provision which had to be made was not for the periodic payment of a sum of money. A husband seeking divorce by Act of Parliament had to make secured provision: that is to say, he had to make property available which, under the terms of an appropriate deed, was permanently set aside to secure whatever gross or annual amount he was to pay.

Finer and McGregor describe the beginning of the divorce court (as to which see Chapter 6, above) and then continue:

Maintenance for wives under the new procedure

32. ... The new divorce court could grant alimony ancillary to a decree of judicial separation on the same principles as alimony could previously attach to a decree of divorce *a mensa et thoro*. It could also in granting a decree of divorce dissolving the marriage, insist on the husband making financial provision for the wife of the kind which the Ladies' Friend, under the parliamentary divorce procedure, had previously secured for her benefit. In this connection, the Act provided that on any decree of dissolution of marriage the court might order the husband to secure to the wife such gross sum of money, or such annual sum of money for any term not exceeding her own life, as having regard to her fortune (if any), to the ability of the husband, and to the conduct of the parties, the court should deem reasonable.

33. The use which the divorce court made of its powers of securing maintenance to the wife when dissolving her marriage took rather a curious course. Despite the fact that the distinctive feature of the parliamentary procedure which the court was supposed to have inherited was precisely that it guaranteed provision for the guilty (respondent) wife, the divorce court at first ruled that it would do this only in the rarest of cases. More than that, by 1861 (*Fisher v Fisher* (1861) 2 Sw & Tr 410, 31 LJPM & A 1) Sir Cresswell Cresswell, the first Judge Ordinary of the court, was saying that a wife petitioner should be awarded less by way of maintenance on being granted a decree of divorce than she would have been granted by way of alimony had she sought a judicial separation, for this would tend towards the preservation of the sanctity of marriage. Four years later, this view of the law was rejected by the court (*Sidney v Sidney* (1865) 4 Sw & Tr 178, 34 LJPM & A 122), which indicated in the same case that it would welcome a power, in dissolving a marriage, to make financial provision for the wife by way of an order for periodical payments, as well as by way of a secured sum. This power was granted by the Matrimonial Causes Act 1866, which provided that if a decree for dissolution of marriage were obtained against a husband who had no property on which the payment of a gross or annual sum could be secured, he might be ordered to pay such monthly or weekly amounts to his former wife, during their joint lives, as the court should think reasonable. By about the 1880s, the maintenance jurisdiction in divorce had come to be exercised to the following broad effect: the

guilty wife, as under the old parliamentary practice, would have some modicum awarded to her; the innocent wife, as under the old ecclesiastical practice, would be granted a proportion, almost always one third, of the joint income, and, in addition, an amount in respect of any children committed to her custody.

37. In 1873, as part of the general re-organisation of the superior courts which then took place, the jurisdiction of the Court for Divorce and Matrimonial Causes, set up in 1857, was transferred to the High Court of Justice to be exercised in the Probate, Divorce and Admiralty Division of the High Court.

38. ... the court began to state that the rule, borrowed from the ecclesiastical jurisdiction, of awarding one third of the joint income to the innocent wife was not a rule of thumb, and that in awarding maintenance it had to take into account all the circumstances of the particular case. Secondly, signs emerged of a recognition that the moral blame, if there was any, for the breakdown of a marriage might not be coincident with the finding of guilt in the divorce suit. It followed that an adulterous wife might in justice be entitled to a larger award than the sustenance which, following the former Parliamentary practice, the divorce court had conceded to her. As ultimately established, the rule was stated to be:

> 'Nowhere ... is there to be found any warrant for the view that a wife who had committed adultery thereby automatically loses her right to maintenance regardless of the other circumstances of the case. ... In practice a wife's adultery may or may not disqualify her from succeeding in her application for maintenance and may or may not reduce the amount allotted. At one end of the scale her adultery may indeed disqualify her altogether. It may do so, for example, where it broke up the marriage, where it is continuing and where she is being supported by her paramour. At the other end of the scale, her adultery will not disqualify her and have little, if any, influence on the amount' (*Iverson v Iverson* [1967]P 134, [1966] 1 All ER 258).

Nevertheless, the discretionary nature of the jurisdiction gave ample opportunity to judges so inclined to take an idiosyncratic view on these matters.

The Divorce Reform Act 1969 altered completely the conceptual basis of divorce (see Chapter 6, above). Necessarily, the preconceptions inherent in the legal status of the husband and the wife, especially in relation to the doctrine of unity and the concept of lifelong support obligation unless the wife committed a matrimonial offence – all this could no longer form the underlying philosophy of a marriage. At the same time, there was awareness that in reality, certainly in conventional marriages and perhaps also in dual career marriages (see p. 102, above) a wife's performing the 'domestic chores' *was* a significant contribution in its own right towards the resultant value of the family assets. There was also a view, although perhaps it did not play a major role in the reform, that marriage itself was a substantial impediment to a woman's self-sufficiency in many cases. All this resulted in the enactment of the Matrimonial Proceedings and Property Act 1970. That Act permitted all financial orders to be made in favour of either husband and wife, enabling the court to rearrange all the couple's assets through periodical payments (secured and unsecured), lump sum payments and property adjustment orders.

The Act also set out detailed guidelines designed to assist the court in the exercise of its powers. These guidelines were simply that; for the basic philosophy inherent in the Act was to permit a broad discretion within the framework of the legislative target. It is to that target that we must turn.

8.2   The Matrimonial Causes Act 1973

The 1970 Act was consolidated in the Matrimonial Causes Act 1973. Section 25, relevant to both maintenance and capital provision, provided that it was the duty of the court to:

... exercise those powers as to place the parties, so far as it is practicable and, having regard to their conduct, just to do so, in the financial position in which they would have been if the marriage had not broken down and each had properly discharged his or her financial obligations and responsibilities towards the other.

The Law Commission, in their discussion paper *The Financial Consequences of Divorce: the Basic Policy* (1980), identified four specific complaints:

(a) Inconsistency with the modern law of divorce

24. A fundamental complaint is, we think, that the underlying principle of the law governing the financial consequences of divorce is inconsistent with the modern divorce law. The law (it is said) now permits either party to a marriage to insist on a divorce, possibly against the will of the other party, regardless of the fact that the other party may have honoured every conceivable marital commitment. Why (it is asked), if the status of marriage can be dissolved in this way, should the financial obligations of marriage nevertheless survive – particularly in cases where divorce has been forced on an unwilling partner, or where a wholly innocent partner is required to support one whose conduct has caused the breakdown? Instead (it is argued), divorce ought to provide a 'clean break' with the past in economic terms as well as in terms of status, and, so far as possible, encourage the parties to look to the future rather than to dwell in the past.

(b) Hardship for divorced husbands

25. We have been told that the continuing financial obligations imposed by divorce often cause severe economic hardship for those who are ordered to pay, normally of course the husband. It is not uncommon for a man to be ordered to pay as much as one-third of his gross income to his ex-wife until she either remarries or dies, and to be deprived of the matrimonial home (which may well represent his only capital asset) at least during the minority of the children. Unless she remarries this obligation to maintain an ex-wife can put divorced husbands under financial strain not only over a very long period of years but even into retirement. The obligation to maintain an ex-wife is particularly resented if the husband feels that it is his wife who is really responsible for the breakdown of the marriage; and such feelings are further exacerbated where he believes that his ex-wife has either chosen not to contribute toward her maintenance by working, or has elected to cohabit with another man, who might be in a position to support her but whom she has decided not to marry so as not to be deprived of her right to maintenance from her first husband.

(c) Hardship for second families

26. ... Particular resentment seems to be felt by men who have remarried after a divorce, and by their second wives. The burden of continuing to provide for a first wife can involve financial deprivation for a man who does not remarry, but the burden may well be acute if he remarries and has a second family. In such cases the impoverishment caused by the first wife's continuing claim upon her husband may well fall on all the members of his new family. ... In particular the effect on a man's second wife is a frequent source of comment. It is claimed that she is invariably forced to accept a reduced standard of living by reason of the fact that part of her husband's income is being diverted to support his first wife; it is also claimed that a second wife may be forced, notwithstanding family commitments, to work, even although her husband's first wife, who possibly has no family commitments, chooses not to do so. Indeed some second wives have told us that they feel that they are being required personally to support their husband's first wife because the courts take a second wife's resources into account when assessing a husband's financial circumstances and his capacity to make periodical payments to a former spouse.

(d) Hardship suffered by divorced wives

27. ... There is no doubt that many divorced wives feel that the law still fails to make adequate provision for them. Not only is the starting point for assessing the provision to be made for a divorced wife only one-third [see *Wachtel v Wachtel* [1973] Fam 72, [1973] 1 All ER 829, CA, p. 322, below] (as opposed to one-half) of the parties' joint resources, but in practice divorced wives often face great difficulty in enforcing any order which the court has made. The law, it is true, requires that so far as practicable, the wife should be kept in the position she would have been in had the marriage not broken down, but, as the Finer Committee remarked in 1974, private law is not capable of providing the 'method of extracting more than a pint from a pint pot'. We have seen that economic realities often make it difficult for a husband to provide for his second family. The same economic factors also make it difficult for him to provide for his former wife. ...

One particular aspect of the debate still relevant today is the question of whether married women are justified in looking primarily to their husbands for support if their marriages break down. After all, so the argument goes, emphasis is now placed on equality of opportunity for men and women, and it is indeed a fact that most women are employed outside the home for at least some period during their married lives. The argument has been forcefully presented by Ruth Deech. We quote here from 'The Principles of Maintenance' (1977):

For some time now there have been available to married women reliable contraception, education and full legal status. Legislation provides for equal opportunities and equal pay: 40% of the working force of employees are female, of whom two-thirds are married and 85% of married women have been in employment at some time during their marriage. But the concept of female dependency on the male continues to permeate the maintenance laws and in addition the comparatively recent state pensions and tax provisions are based on sexual stereotypes of the husband as provider and the wife as full-time housekeeper and child-rearer. This legal supposition of female dependency tends to deny freedom of choice to married and formerly married persons; it is widely considered degrading to women and it perpetuates the common law proprietary relationship of the husband and wife even after divorce. While they express the superiority of the male the maintenance laws are at the same time an irritant to the increasing number of divorced men who have always to be able to provide and who suffer the perpetual drain on their income represented by a former wife. Maintenance awards are emotionally charged with the desire on the part of the wife for retribution and by their nature are unlikely to be readily enforceable because of the hostility surrounding their creation and the fact that the ex-husband is paying money without getting anything in return.

Deech concludes by stating that maintenance should be rehabilitative and a temporary measure confined to spouses who are incapable of work because of infirmity or child care.

Question

Do you think that Deech has appreciated the lifelong effect of caring for children – the 'mother gap' identified by the Cabinet Office Women's Unit (see Chapter 3, p. 107)?

A different view, however, is presented by Katherine O'Donovan in 'The Principles of Maintenance: An Alternative View' (1978):

Whilst it cannot be denied that laws based on sexual stereotypes are undesirable and ought to be eliminated what both Deech and Gray (1977) fail to see is that the current organisation of family life is premissed on the assumption that one partner will sacrifice a cash income in order to rear children and manage the home. The dependence of the non-earning spouse on the wage-earner is inevitable under present family arrangements. This leads in turn to inequality of earning power of spouses. Without a major change in social and family structures the Deech or Gray proposals merely serve to perpetuate an already unfair situation and will not ensure equality.
...
...The idea of a family wage adequate to support a wife and children with the addition of child benefit has been built into wage structure since the nineteenth century. So the expectation of society is that a wife's work is covered by her husband's wages. On divorce, without maintenance, the housewife will have little or no income from wage-earning and no National Insurance benefits to fall back on. If she does get a job, as already pointed out, her earning ability will be low.

For the majority of couples there will be a period in their marriage when their major asset, other than possible ownership of the matrimonial home, is the earning ability of the husband. This is why the law gives dependants a right of support after [divorce], and not the fact that they are parasites – as suggested by Deech. ...

Ruth Deech's argument is ultimately against marriage itself. If the spouse who undertakes housekeeping and child care should not consider marriage as (in part) an alternative career to one which is economically productive, then the answer is either not to marry, or to engage in paid work during marriage. But society does not seem ready for marriages in which both spouses work full-time. The present provision for nursery and pre-school facilities is inadequate. Children are prone to illness and are naturally dependent. Schools are not open for a full working day. And at present there is high unemployment. Participation in the workforce is not necessarily the answer, where there are young children; at least not without major changes in society, with the provision of communal laundries, cheap family restaurants, full-time nurseries etc. And male work attitudes would have to change to enable fathers to share equally in child care functions. It seems unlikely that this will happen. Deech argues that mothers with children should receive maintenance on divorce, and that it is only those who could earn who should be deprived. But withdrawal from the labour market at any time, current or past, affects earning ability, and it is fair that this diminution in earning ability be shared by both spouses.

Carol Smart, in *The Ties That Bind* (1984), points to the difficulty of both positions in the context of a feminist viewpoint:

The question that proponents on either side of this debate have posed is, 'Should individual husbands support their ex-wives after divorce?' This question does not allow for a 'feminist answer' as such because whichever side of the debate a woman supports she does a disservice to feminist arguments. Basically feminists have argued for the financial independence of women, hence dependency on men either during or after marriage is recognised as a major problem. But equally feminists have argued for a recognition of the value of domestic labour which benefits not only the state but also individual men. Hence it can be argued that if domestic labour has a value to both the state and individual men, *both* should recompense the woman who has lost material benefits whilst individual men and the state have been reaping them. If we consider these conflicting principles within the existing framework of family law there is no satisfactory solution. Abolishing maintenance for ex-wives does not give women their financial independence, it just means that even more women have to rely on inadequate supplementary benefit (assuming they cannot work outside the home or cannot earn a living wage). On the other hand arguing that individual men should pay for their privileges ignores the fact that many simply cannot afford to pay. But in addition this argument has the deleterious effect of containing the 'problem' within the private sphere, with the consequence that women's dependency remains a private issue and a personal conflict, and does not become a matter of public policy. It is an untenable situation for feminists *precisely* because the original question was framed outside feminist priorities.

Questions

(i)   Notice that O'Donovan argues that Deech's argument is ultimately against marriage itself. We know Deech's views about the divorce law reforms (see p. 260, above). Can her argument on maintenance in her 1977 article be reconciled with her views on divorce law reform, and if so, how?

(ii)   Why is the idea that men should be able to avoid all financial responsibility for their own children through realistic child benefits attractive to an 'emergent feminist policy'?

(iii)   Should an able-bodied house-husband be expected to support himself after divorce?

(iv)   What do you suppose Carol Smart means by the phrase 'feminist priorities'?

(v)   Do you think that the main question is really about how women can advance in the labour market?

Deech thinks that matters will only improve when the ideological basis of a support-dominated maintenance law is abolished; O'Donovan believes that a support-dominated maintenance law can only be abolished after the infrastructure of employment laws, support services for child care, pension and social security laws, and taxation provisions have all been reorganised to permit a woman to survive without the need for support from her former provider.

Questions

(i)   Which of these two views do you believe to be *politically* realistic?
(ii) Are they asking the right questions?

And what does the divorce(e) in the street think about this? Davis, Cretney and Collins, in *Simple Quarrels* (1994) (see below, p. 371), record an interview with one couple which revealed the following disagreement:

For example, Mrs Merton did not consider that she should be expected to work to support the children post-divorce given that Mr Merton had not wanted her to work whilst they were married. ... Mr Merton on the other hand made a very clear distinction between his wife's working when they were married and her doing so once they had separated. According to Mr Merton: 'There's no reason, other than her own choice, why she cannot get work and help to support herself. The marriage is over. The children are looked after. I don't see why she should, for the rest of her days, sit down on her bum. I've provided and supported her all these years. She's going to have to support herself now – we're no longer married. And as far as I'm concerned I'm not, morally, legally, or in any other way, obliged to keep her at the level I did when I was responsible for her because I was married to her.'

The authors identify a number of 'folk myths' which make for a gulf between the parties' thinking and the lawyer's assumptions:
   –   The man's belief that it is his money because he has earned it.
   –   The presumption of a 50:50 split (the authors comment that this is hardly a myth in Scotland, where it is the principle upon which Scots law is based).
   –   The man's reluctance to pay maintenance on the basis that his former wife and children are provided for by the state.
   –   The belief that 'conduct', especially in opting to terminate the marriage, should have a bearing upon the financial resolution.

Questions

(i)   Why are these 'folk myths' so prevalent?
(ii) Do you think it desirable that people's perceptions and expectations be changed? If so, how can this be accomplished? Do you think it a likely outcome of the way the law is developing at present?

In Part IV of their discussion paper, *The Financial Consequences of Divorce: the Basic Policy* (1980), the Law Commission describe seven models which might form the basis of a law to govern the financial consequences of divorce. These are discussed as separate options, and more briefly in combination. It should be recalled that the Commission were dealing mainly with the parties' finances and only incidentally with reallocation of their property. We summarise below the major characteristics of each model:

Model 1: Retention of section 25 of the Matrimonial Causes Act 1973
59 ... Whilst it is true that the failure of the Act to give any indication of the weight to be attached to any particular circumstance, or indeed to 'the circumstances' as a whole, can make it difficult for practitioners to advise clients on how a case is likely to be decided, it is claimed that any such disadvantage is more than outweighed by the advantage to be gained from the court having a discretion which cannot only be adapted to the infinitely varied facts of each case (which can be foreseen neither by a judge nor by the legislature) but also to changing social circumstances. Moreover, in this view it is not only inevitable, but indeed desirable,

that it should be left to case law to provide the coherent but evolving guidance on how to deal with such specific problems ...

Model 2: Repeal of the direction to the court in section 25 to seek to put the parties in the financial position in which they would have been had the marriage not broken down

66 ...We consider the most fundamental issue raised by the present controversy over section 25 to be whether or not it is desirable to retain the principle of life-long support which that section seems to embody. It might therefore be argued that the simplest solution to the criticisms of the present law would be for Parliament to repeal the specific direction at the end of section 25(1), but otherwise to leave the section intact; the court would simply be directed to make whatever order it considered appropriate in the light of all the circumstances, including the circumstances listed in sub-sections (*a*) to (*g*) of section 25(1). This would enable the courts to adopt a flexible approach, taking into account not only all the relevant individual circumstances of the parties, but also changing economic factors such as the availability of housing and changing attitudes to the proper purpose of financial provision. ...

Model 3: The relief of need

70 Under this model, the economically weaker party would be eligible to receive financial assistance from the economically stronger party if, and so long as, he or she could show that, taking into account his or her particular social and economic conditions, there is actual need of such assistance. The principle adopted would thus be one of individual self-reliance: after a marriage had broken down neither of the parties would have any automatic right to support, but rather only a qualified right insofar as it could be justified by special circumstances. ...

Model 4: Rehabilitation

73 ...The concept of rehabilitative financial provision has been explained in a recent American case as:

> 'sums necessary to assist a divorced person in regaining a useful and constructive role in society through vocational or therapeutic training or retraining, and for the further purpose of preventing financial hardship on society or the individual during the rehabilitative process' *Mertz v Mertz* (1973, 287 So 2d 691 at 692).

The onus is therefore firmly placed on the spouse in receipt of a rehabilitative award to take steps to become self-sufficient, and in this respect we think that such an approach might often result in the wife having to accept a significantly lower standard of living after divorce than that which she enjoyed before. She would be given an opportunity to develop such skills as she possessed, but ultimately she would be expected to fend for herself. ...

75 ... The rehabilitative period might be limited by statute, to a maximum of two or three years or to the duration of some course of training, or it might lie in the discretion of the court. ...

Model 5: The division of property – the 'clean break'

77 The essence of this model is the analogy of partnership. Where a partnership is dissolved, the partnership property is divided amongst the partners and that is the end of the matter. This, it is said, should also be the case where a marriage is dissolved (Grey, 1977). The principle might be adopted in one of a number of forms. At the one extreme it would involve no continuing financial relationship between ex-spouses: their rights and duties inter se would be resolved at the time of the divorce by dividing the matrimonial property between them. Such division might involve using a fractional approach (e.g. both parties would be entitled to half of the property available for distribution) or it might reflect some other principle such as the 'rehabilitative' or 'needs' models suggested above. Alternatively, the division might be effected solely on the basis of the court's discretion in each individual case. However, other variations on the basic theme that the financial consequences of divorce ought to be resolved by means of a division of the matrimonial property might also be possible. Thus a law based on this model might provide, for instance, for a delay in the division where the matrimonial home is needed to accommodate a growing family, or for additional payments of maintenance on a rehabilitative or needs basis. ...

Model 6: A mathematical approach

80 ... On this approach the spouses' financial rights and duties inter se on divorce would be resolved by reference to fixed mathematical formulae which might then be adjusted to take into account particular factors such as the care of children or the length of the marriage. The result, it is said, would be two-fold. First, the parties and their legal advisers would in most cases be

able to save time and money by negotiating a settlement in the knowledge that it accurately reflected current practice. Secondly, adjudicators would be able to decide cases in an entirely consistent fashion. ...

Model 7: Restoration of the parties to the position in which they would have been had their marriage never taken place
84 On this view (e.g. Gray) the court should seek to achieve 'not the position which would have resulted if the marriage had continued, but the position which would have occurred if the marriage had never taken place at all'. The model is therefore a guiding principle, and might be carried into effect either by imposing an obligation to make periodical payments or by a once and for all division of the parties' capital (or a combination of both) which would be designed to compensate the financially weaker spouse for any loss incurred through marriage. ...

A combination of models
86 ... It might be argued however that many of the problems which could result if a particular model were to be adopted as the sole governing principle might be avoided if the law were to be based on a combination of these models. For instance, elements of the needs or rehabilitative approaches could be used to temper some of the difficulties that might arise if the division of property model were to be adopted by itself. Alternatively it would no doubt be possible, whilst maintaining the main structure of the existing law, to amend the guidelines at present contained in section 25, so as to direct the court's attention more specifically to certain matters, for example the possibility that a wife should be expected to rehabilitate herself after divorce.

In *The Financial Consequences of Divorce* (1980), the Law Commission make the following recommendation:

17. We have come to the conclusion that the duty now imposed by statute to seek to place the parties in the financial position in which they would have been if the marriage had not broken down is not a suitable criterion; and in our view it should be removed from the law.

The Report goes on to recommend that the guidelines in s. 25(1) should be revised to give greater emphasis: (a) to the provision of adequate financial support for children which should be an overriding priority, and (b) to the importance of each party doing everything possible to become self-sufficient. The latter should be formulated in terms of positive principle and weight should be given to the view that, in appropriate cases, periodical financial provision should be primarily concerned to secure a smooth transition from the status of marriage to the status of independence. Thus, of the models advanced in the discussion paper, the English report argues for the retention of a discretion-based framework.

The proposals were introduced into law by the Matrimonial and Family Proceedings Act 1984 replacing the old s. 25 and adding a new s. 25A of the Matrimonial Causes Act 1973:

25. Matters to which court is to have regard in deciding how to exercise its powers under ss 23, 24 and 24A
(1) It shall be the duty of the court in deciding whether to exercise its powers under section 23, 24, 24A or 24B above and, if so, in what manner, to have regard to all the circumstances of the case, first consideration being given to the welfare while a minor of any child of the family who has not attained the age of eighteen.
(2) As regards the exercise of the powers of the court under section 23(1)(a), (b) or (c), 24, 24A or 24B above in relation to a party to the marriage, the court shall in particular have regard to the following matters—
   (a) the income, earning capacity, property and other financial resources which each of the parties to the marriage has or is likely to have in the foreseeable future, including in the case of earning capacity any increase in that capacity in which it would in the opinion of the court be reasonable to expect a party to the marriage to take steps to acquire;
   (b) the financial needs, obligations and responsibilities which each of the parties to the marriage has or is likely to have in the foreseeable future;
   (c) the standard of living enjoyed by the family before the breakdown of the marriage;

(d) the age of each party to the marriage and the duration of the marriage;

(e) any psychical or mental disability of either of the parties to the marriage;

(f) the contributions which each of the parties has made or is likely in the foreseeable future to make to the welfare of the family, including any contributions by looking after the home or caring for the family;

(g) the conduct of each of the parties, if that conduct is such that it would in the opinion of the court be inequitable to disregard it;

(h) in the case of proceedings for divorce or nullity of marriage, the value to each of the parties to the marriage of any benefit (for example, a pension) which, by reason of the dissolution or annulment of the marriage, that party will lose the chance of acquiring.

(3) As regards the exercise of the powers of the court under section 23(1)(d), (e) or (f), (2) or (4), 24 or 24A above in relation to a child of the family, the court shall in particular have regard to the following matters—

(a) the financial needs of the child;

(b) the income, earning capacity (if any), property and other financial resources of the child;

(c) any physical or mental disability of the child;

(d) the manner in which he was being and in which the parties to the marriage expected him to be educated or trained;

(e) the considerations mentioned in relation to the parties to the marriage in paragraphs (a), (b), (c) and (e) of subsection (2) above.

(4) As regards the exercise of the powers of the court under section 23(1)(d), (e) or (f), (2) or (4), 24 or 24A above against a party to a marriage in favour of a child of the family who is not the child of that party, the court shall also have regard—

(a) to whether that party assumed any responsibility for the child's maintenance, and, if so, to the extent to which, and the basis upon which, that party assumed such responsibility and to the length of time for which that party discharged such responsibility;

(b) to whether in assuming and discharging such responsibility that party did so knowing that the child was not his or her own;

(c) to the liability of any other person to maintain the child.

25A. Exercise of court's powers in favour of party to marriage on decree of divorce or nullity of marriage

(1) Where on or after the grant of a decree of divorce or nullity of marriage the court decides to exercise its powers under section 23(1)(a), (b) or (c), 24, 24A or 24B above in favour of a party to the marriage, it shall be the duty of the court to consider whether it would be appropriate so to exercise those powers that the financial obligations of each party towards the other will be terminated as soon after the grant of the decree as the court considers just and reasonable.

(2) Where the court decides in such a case to make a periodical payments or secured periodical payments order in favour of a party to the marriage, the court shall in particular consider whether it would be appropriate to require those payments to be made or secured only for such term as would in the opinion of the court be sufficient to enable the party in whose favour the order is made to adjust without undue hardship to the termination of his or her financial dependence on the other party.

(3) Where on or after the grant of a decree of divorce or nullity of marriage an application is made by a party to the marriage for a periodical payments or secured periodical payments order in his or her favour, then, if the court considers that no continuing obligation should be imposed on either party to make or secure periodical payments in favour of the other, the court may dismiss the application with a direction that the applicant shall not be entitled to make any future application in relation to that marriage for an order under section 23(1)(a) or (b) above.

The court's powers to make financial provision and property adjustment orders are set out in ss. 23, 24 , 25B and 25C of the 1973 Act:

23. Financial provision orders in connection with divorce proceedings, etc

(1) On granting a decree of divorce, a decree of nullity of marriage or a decree of judicial separation or at any time thereafter (whether, in the case of a decree of divorce or of nullity of marriage, before or after the decree is made absolute), the court may make any one or more of the following orders, that is to say—

(a) an order that either party to the marriage shall make to the other such periodical payments, for such term, as may be specified in the order;

(b)   an order that either party to the marriage shall secure to the other to the satisfaction of the court such periodical payments, for such term, as may be so specified;

(c)   an order that either party to the marriage shall pay to the other such lump sum or sums as may be so specified;

(d)   an order that a party to the marriage shall make to such person as may be specified in the order for the benefit of a child of the family, or to such a child, such periodical payments, for such term, as may be so specified;

(e)   an order that a party to the marriage shall secure to such person as may be so specified for the benefit of such a child, or to such a child, to the satisfaction of the court, such periodical payments, for such term, as may be so specified;

(f)   an order that a party to the marriage shall pay to such person as may be so specified for the benefit of such a child, or to such a child, such lump sum as may be so specified;

subject, however, in the case of an order under paragraph (d), (e) or (f) above, to the restrictions imposed by section 29(1) and (3) below on the making of financial provision orders in favour of children who have attained the age of eighteen.

(2)   The court may also, subject to those restrictions, make any one or more of the orders mentioned in subsection (1)(d), (e) and (f) above—

(a)   in any proceedings for divorce, nullity of marriage or judicial separation, before granting a decree; and

(b)   where any such proceedings are dismissed after the beginning of the trial, either forthwith or within a reasonable period after the dismissal.

(3)   Without prejudice to the generality of subsection (1)(c) or (f) above—

(a)   an order under this section that a party to a marriage shall pay a lump sum to the other party may be made for the purpose of enabling that other party to meet any liabilities or expenses reasonably incurred by him or her in maintaining himself or herself or any child of the family before making an application for an order under this section in his or her favour.

(b)   an order under this section for the payment of a lump sum to or for the benefit of a child of the family may be made for the purpose of enabling any liabilities or expenses reasonably incurred by or for the benefit of that child before the making of an application for an order under this section in his favour to be met; and

(c)   an order under this section for the payment of a lump sum may provide for the payment of that sum by instalments of such amount as may be specified in the order and may require the payment of the instalments to be secured to the satisfaction of the court.

(4)   The power of the court under subsection (1) or (2)(a) above to make an order in favour of a child of the family shall be exercisable from time to time; and where the court makes an order in favour of a child under subsection (2)(b) above, it may from time to time, subject to the restrictions mentioned in subsection (1) above, make a further order in his favour of any of the kinds mentioned in subsection (1)(d), (e) or (f) above.

(5)   Without prejudice to the power to give a direction under section 30 below for the settlement of an instrument by conveyancing counsel, where an order is made under subsection (1)(a), (b) or (c) above on or after granting a decree of divorce or nullity of marriage, neither the order nor any settlement made in pursuance of the order shall take effect unless the decree has been made absolute.

(6)   Where the court—

(a)   makes an order under this section for the payment of a lump sum; and

(b)   directs—

(i)   that payments of that sum or any part of it shall be deferred; or

(ii)   that that sum or any part of it shall e paid by instalments,

the court may order that the amount deferred or the instalments shall carry interest at such rate as may be specified by the order from such date, not earlier than the date of the order, as may be so specified, until the date when payment of it is due.

24. Property adjustment orders in connection with divorce proceedings, etc

(1)   On granting a decree of divorce, a decree of nullity of marriage or a decree of judicial separation or at any time thereafter (whether, in the case of a decree of divorce or of nullity of marriage, before or after the decree is made absolute), the court may make any one or more of the following orders, that is to say—

(a)   an order that a party to the marriage shall transfer to the other party, to any child of the family or to such person as may be specified in the order for the benefit of such a child such property as may be so specified, being property to which the first-mentioned party is entitled, either in possession or reversion;

(b) an order that a settlement of such property as may be so specified, being property to which a party to the marriage is so entitled, be made to the satisfaction of the court for the benefit of the other party to the marriage and of the children of the family or either or any of them;

(c) an order varying for the benefit of the parties to the marriage and of the children of the family or either or any of them any ante-nuptial or post-nuptial settlement (including such a settlement made by will or codicil) made on the parties to the marriage, other than one in the form of a pension arrangement (within the meaning of section 25D below);

(d) an order extinguishing or reducing the interest of either of the parties to the marriage under any such settlement, other than one in the form of a pension arrangement (within the meaning of section 25D below);

subject, however, in the case of an order under paragraph (a) above, to the restrictions imposed by section 29(1) and (3) below on the making of orders for a transfer of property in favour of children who have attained the age of eighteen.

(2) The court may make an order under subsection (1)(c) above notwithstanding that there are no children of the family.

(3) Without prejudice to the power to give a direction under section 30 below for the settlement of an instrument by conveyancing counsel, where an order is made under this section on or after granting a decree of divorce or nullity of marriage, neither the order nor any settlement made in pursuance of the order shall take effect unless the decree has been made absolute.

(Sections 25B and 25C are reproduced at p 365, below, under 'Pensions'.)

8.3 A question of principle

So there we have it: guidelines in s. 25, the possibility of a clean break in s. 25A, and the details of what can actually be ordered in ss. 23, 24, 25B and 25C. Note that what can be *achieved* in the context of a court order is wider than this, because one or both parties may undertake to do something that the court cannot actually order; for example, to make mortgage re-payments or to purchase an annuity. An undertaking is enforceable in the same way as an order, ultimately by committal. As we shall see (in part 5 of this chapter, p. 334ff, below), a package of complex and flexible re-structuring of the family's finances can be put together. But to what end are the courts aiming?

To some extent, the question of principle was addressed in the debate recorded above, which resulted in the 1984 amendments to the 1973 Act and the removal of the requirement that the court endeavour to place parties in the financial position in which they would have been had the marriage not broken down. But when that requirement was removed, nothing was put in its place. What sort of outcome is the court to produce, or approve, having taken into consideration all the s. 25 factors and within the ambit of its powers under the surrounding sections?

Two factors have perhaps contributed to the masking of the existence of this issue. One is the fact that in so many cases there is no money to spare, and that the only thing the parties and the court can hope to achieve is a position where everyone has enough to manage. Another is the longevity of the 'one-third rule'. This was the notion – or principle, or starting point – that on divorce, the wife's entitlement to maintenance would be such as to give her one third of the joint gross incomes of the parties (or one third of the husband's gross income where she has no income of her own). The very statement of the 'rule' alerts us to the fact that it rests on outdated assumptions; Lord Denning's explanation of it in *Wachtel v Wachtel* [1973] Fam 72, [1973] 1 All ER 829, [1973] 2 WLR 366, 117 Sol Jo 124, CA nowadays raises a smile, though perhaps rather a sad one:

In awarding maintenance the divorce courts followed the practice of the ecclesiastical courts. They awarded an innocent wife a sum equal to one-third of their joint incomes. Out of it she had to provide for her own accommodation, her food and clothes, and other expenses. If she had any rights in the matrimonial home, or was allowed to be in occupation of it, that went in reduction of maintenance.

There was, we think, much good sense in taking one third as a starting point. When a marriage breaks up, there will thenceforward be two households instead of one. The husband will have to go out to work all day and must get some woman to look after the house – either a wife, if he remarries, or a housekeeper, if he does not. He will also have to provide maintenance for the children. The wife will not usually have so much expense. She may go out to work herself, but she will not usually employ a housekeeper. She will do most of the housework herself, perhaps with some help. Or she may remarry, in which case her new husband will provide for her. In any case, when there are two households, the greater expense will, in most cases, fall on the husband than the wife. As a start has to be made somewhere, it seems to us that in the past it was quite fair to start with one third.

We have come a long way since that judgment was given, and it is now well established that the one-third rule has no relevance. Again, then, a rule (or principle, or expectation) disappeared, with apparently nothing to take its place.

To some extent, where there is nothing to spare, that does not matter except to the lawyers (who are uncomfortable without principles). But what are the courts supposed to do where there is something, or perhaps lots, to spare? What should the wife of a millionaire be awarded on divorce, if she had not directly generated the millions? From this situation grew up the jurisprudence of 'reasonable requirements': the idea that the wife (as it usually was) in those circumstances should recover more than the bare minimum, more than her 'needs', but not more than her 'reasonable requirements'. She would have sufficient to keep her in something not too far from the style to which she was accustomed; she would not be given capital or income provision beyond what she required to do that. Nor would she take capital with a view to passing it on to her children. The discriminatory nature of the situation is obvious; where, for the benefit of all the family, the wife has stayed at home to look after the children rather than engaging in business, the operation of financial provision on divorce penalises her. A powerful criticism of the 'reasonable requirements' approach was delivered by Peter Singer QC, as he then was, in his address to the Family Law Bar Association in 1992 (reproduced in 'Sexual Discrimination in Ancillary Relief' (2001)).

Things changed dramatically in October 2000, when the House of Lords gave its judgment in *White v White* [2001] 1 AC 596, [2000] 3 WLR 1571, [2000] 3 FCR 555, [2001] Fam Law 12. Lizzie Cooke in '*White v White*: a new yardstick for the marriage partnership' (2001), summarised the facts, and the decisions at first instance and in the Court of Appeal:

THE FACTS OF *WHITE*

Briefly, *White* concerned the ancillary financial relief consequent upon the divorce of Mr and Mrs White after 34 years of marriage. Both husband and wife had a farming background, and had farmed together as business partners throughout the marriage. By the time of the divorce the children had grown up and left home and there was no dispute that a clean break was appropriate. The matrimonial home was Blagroves, a farm with some 160 acres of land in Somerset. It was purchased jointly a year after the marriage, with the aid of a mortgage; Mr White's father assisted them with the deposit and some working capital, making a gift of £14,000 altogether. In addition a neighbouring farm, Rexton, of over 300 acres, was held in Mr White's sole name but farmed by the partnership. The two partners held a single joint capital account.

At first instance the couple's assets were found to be:
- Mrs White's sole property: £193,300 (mostly pension provision)
- Mr White's sole property: £1,783,500 (including Rexton, worth £1.25million)
- Mrs White's share of jointly owned property: £1,334,000
- Mr White's share of jointly owned property: £1,334,000

The family assets were thus worth around £4.6 million. Neither the total, nor the above breakdown, were agreed; there was considerable dispute about the value of the partnership assets and in particular the milk quota.

THE DECISION OF HOLMAN J

The application for financial provision was made by Mrs White. Her sole assets amounted to just over four per cent of the family's wealth; she was therefore looking for a transfer to herself from the jointly held assets and/or from Mr White's assets. At first instance Holman J assessed her reasonable requirements at £980,000, and awarded her a payment of £800,000. Given the value of the jointly owned assets, Holman J's decision actually deprived her of property. His reasoning was that it would be wrong to break up the successful farming business in order to release capital to enable Mrs White to farm on her own account. What she actually needed was *Duxbury* provision for income, together with a farmhouse type property and 25 acres of land for her horses. Mr White was thus left with far more than he needed in terms of home and income; but Holman J felt that Mr White reasonably required to be able to continue the farming business, justifying this inequality by the initial contribution to the farming business made by Mr White's family.

It is hard to feel comfortable with this decision. Given the tiny scale of the White family contribution to the now huge farming enterprise, one has the impression that in reality Mrs White was being penalised for being the wife and not the husband.

THE DECISION IN THE COURT OF APPEAL

The Court of Appeal did considerably better for Mrs White, awarding her a lump sum of £1.5million. The leading judgment was given by Thorpe LJ.

His first point was that although there is no hierarchy among the section 25 factors, 'there is as it were a magnetism which draws the individual case to attach to one, two or several factors as having a decisive influence upon its determination.'[1] In this case, the dominant factor was the partnership. Therefore although it was well settled that in a 'big money' case 'where the husband's fortune is immense and wife's contribution unexceptional'[2], the wife's award should be limited to her reasonable requirements, in a case like this the wife's contribution to the fortune as a business partner put her in a very different position and the award at first instance was wrong.

The partnership, he pointed out, was a legal mechanism for determining the parties' shares. That legal mechanism fed into the section 25 exercise. He explained:[3]

'In my opinion the first fundamental issue was what is the financial worth of each of the parties on the immediate dissolution of the partnership? Secondly should the court exercise its powers under ss 23 or 24 to increase the wife's share? Thirdly, if no, should the court exercise its powers to reduce the wife's share?'

Thorpe LJ went on to conclude that it was wrong to reduce the wife's share, and indeed discriminatory. She was as entitled as was Mr White to require to continue farming; the extra contribution made by the White family could be reflected in the different amount given to each. However, he was not prepared to go beyond the figure of £1.5 million and award a half share of the family's wealth, because of the White family contribution.

Butler-Sloss LJ agreed that the 'reasonable requirements' approach was not appropriate in cases of working partners, or where both spouses are directors of a family business. The starting point in such cases must be the parties' financial positions in their business relationship, though without the necessity of taking a detailed partnership account. She stressed that reliance on the *Duxbury* approach was inappropriate in such a case and would result in far too limited an award; the correct approach was to determine the partnership shares and then make any adjustment necessary in individual circumstances, particularly where there are children. In this case, 'the wife is entitled to an additional sum to recognise the contribution she made to the family as wife and mother over and above her partnership role in the farming business'[4]; hence the award of £1.5 million rather than £1.34 million.

The Court of Appeal's decision rests on the fact of the business partnership between two partners. What of the spouse who is not legally a partner, as Mrs White was, but makes just as much practical contribution to the business? Will the courts be astute to spot that contribution? And what of the wife who has no opportunity to engage in the family business – she has not the skills, or she and

---

1. [1998] 2 FLR 310, CA, at 317.
2. *Ibid* at 317.
3. *Ibid* at 318.
4. *Ibid* at 325.

her husband have, in happier times, been well content for her to be the homemaker? There seems no room in the Court of Appeal's decision for any value to be given to that contribution so as to take her beyond her 'reasonable requirements'; in such a case the businessman is still left with the lion's share.

The *Duxbury* approach, incidentally, is the method of providing a capital sum in order to generate income. The principle is referred to by Ward J in *B v B (financial provision)* [1990] FCR 105, [1990] 1 FLR 20 in this way:

> ... accountant or investment consultants calculate from a computer program the lump sum, which, if invested on assumptions as to life expectancy, inflation, return on investments, growth of capital and incidence of income tax, would produce enough to meet the recipient's needs for life.

The crucial assumption is that both capital and income would be used so that, at the end of the recipient's life, the lump sum would be exhausted. Note that this produced the '*Duxbury* paradox', whereby a young wife, after a relatively short marriage, would receive a higher sum, on a *Duxbury* calculation, than an elderly wife after a long marriage.

The legal profession waited on tenterhooks for the House of Lords' decision in *White*. Negotiations, and lives, were put on hold. There was a feeling that this case was going to be different, partly because of the momentum of concern that had built up over the 'reasonable needs' approach, and partly because this case stood out as one where that approach was unfair. When the House of Lords gave its decision, lawyers hungry for new law were not disappointed, although Mrs White herself probably was. The following extract is from the judgment of Lord Nicholls of Birkenhead:

> My Lords, Divorce creates many problems. One question always arises. It concerns how the property of the husband and wife should be divided and whether one of them should continue to support the other. Stated in the most general terms, the answer is obvious. Everyone would accept that the outcome on these matters, whether by agreement or court order, should be fair. More realistically, the outcome ought to be as fair as is possible in all the circumstances. But everyone's life is different. Features which are important when assessing fairness differ in each case. And, sometimes, different minds can reach different conclusions on what fairness requires. Then fairness, like beauty, lies in the eye of the beholder.
>
> So what is the best method of seeking to achieve a generally accepted standard of fairness? Different countries have adopted different solutions. Each solution has its own advantages and disadvantages. One approach is for the legislature to prescribe in detail how property shall be divided, with scope for the exercise of judicial discretion added on. A system along these lines has been preferred by the New Zealand legislature, in the Matrimonial Property Act 1976. Another approach is for the legislature to leave it all to the judges. The courts are given a wide discretion, largely unrestricted by statutory provisions. That is the route followed in this country. The Matrimonial Causes Act 1973 confers wide discretionary powers on the courts over all the property of the husband and the wife. This appeal raises questions about how the courts should exercise these powers in so-called 'big money' cases, where the assets available exceed the parties' financial needs for housing and income. The powers conferred by the 1973 Act have been in operation now for 30 years. This is the first occasion when broad questions about the application of these powers have been considered by this House. The House considered the statutory provisions recently, in *Piglowska v Piglowski* [1999] 3 All ER 632. But there the main issue concerned how appellate courts should approach appeals from trial judges' decisions, rather than the principles trial judges should apply when hearing applications for financial relief in this type of case. It goes without saying that these principles should be identified and spelled out as clearly as possible. This is important, so as to promote consistency in court decisions and in order to assist parties and their advisers and mediators in resolving disputes by agreement as quickly and inexpensively as possible. The present case is an unhappy, if extreme, example of how the parties' resources can be eroded significantly by legal and other costs.

His Lordship summarised the facts, and the decisions below, and went on:

Equality

Self-evidently, fairness requires the court to take into account all the circumstances of the case. Indeed, the statute so provides. It is also self-evident that the circumstances in which the statutory powers have to be exercised vary widely. As Butler-Sloss LJ said in *Dart v Dart* [1997] 1 FCR 21, 38–39, the statutory jurisdiction provides for all applications for ancillary financial relief, from the poverty stricken to the multi-millionaire. But there is one principle of universal application which can be stated with confidence. In seeking to achieve a fair outcome, there is no place for discrimination between husband and wife and their respective roles. Typically, a husband and wife share the activities of earning money, running their home and caring for their children. Traditionally, the husband earned the money, and the wife looked after the home and the children. This traditional division of labour is no longer the order of the day. Frequently both parents work. Sometimes it is the wife who is the money-earner, and the husband runs the home and cares for the children during the day. But whatever the division of labour chosen by the husband and wife, or forced upon them by circumstances, fairness requires that this should not prejudice or advantage either party when considering para (f), relating to the parties' contributions. This is implicit in the very language of para (f):

'... the contribution which *each* has made or is likely to make to the *welfare of the family*, including any contribution by looking after the home or caring for the family.' (See s 25(2)(f). Emphasis added.)

If, in their different spheres, each contributed equally to the family, then in principle it matters not which of them earned the money and built up the assets. There should be no bias in favour of the money-earner and against the home-maker and the child-carer. There are cases, of which the Court of Appeal decision in *Page v Page* (1981) 2 FLR 198 is perhaps an instance, where the court may have lost sight of this principle. A practical consideration follows from this. Sometimes, having carried out the statutory exercise, the judge's conclusion involves a more or less equal division of the available assets. More often, this is not so. More often, having looked at all the circumstances, the judge's decision means that one party will receive a bigger share than the other. Before reaching a firm conclusion and making an order along these lines, a judge would always be well-advised to check his tentative views against the yardstick of equality of division. As a general guide, equality should be departed from only if, and to the extent that, there is good reason for doing so. The need to consider and articulate reasons for departing from equality would help the parties and the court to focus on the need to ensure the absence of discrimination. This is not to introduce a presumption of equal division under another guise. Generally accepted standards of fairness in a field such as this change and develop, sometimes quite radically, over comparatively short periods of time. The discretionary powers, conferred by Parliament 30 years ago, enable the courts to recognise and respond to developments of this sort. These wide powers enable the courts to make financial provision orders in tune with current perceptions of fairness. Today there is greater awareness of the value of non-financial contributions to the welfare of the family. There is greater awareness of the extent to which one spouse's business success, achieved by much sustained hard work over many years, may have been made possible or enhanced by the family contribution of the other spouse, a contribution which also required much sustained hard work over many years. There is increased recognition that, by being at home and having and looking after young children, a wife may lose for ever the opportunity to acquire and develop her own money-earning qualifications and skills. In *Porter v Porter* [1969] 3 All ER 640 at 643–644, [1969] 1 WLR 1155 at 1159–1160 Sachs LJ observed that discretionary powers enable the court to take into account 'the human outlook of the period in which they make their decisions'. In the exercise of these discretions 'the law is a living thing moving with the times and not a creature of dead or moribund ways of thought'. Despite these changes, a presumption of equal division would go beyond the permissible bounds of interpretation of s 25. In this regard s 25 differs from the applicable law in Scotland. Section 10 of the Family Law (Scotland) Act 1985 provides that the net value of matrimonial property shall be taken to be shared fairly between the parties to the marriage when it is shared equally or in such other proportions as are justified by special circumstances. Unlike s 10 of the Family Law (Scotland) Act 1985, s 25 of the 1973 Act makes no mention of an equal sharing of the parties' assets, even their marriage-related assets. A presumption of equal division would be an impermissible judicial gloss on the statutory provision. That would be so, even though the presumption would be rebuttable. Whether there should be such a presumption in England and Wales, and in respect of what assets, is a matter for Parliament. It is largely for this reason that I do not accept Mr Turner's invitation to enunciate a principle that in every case the 'starting point' in relation to a division of the assets of the husband and wife should be equality. He sought to draw a distinction between a presumption and a starting point. But a starting point principle of general application would carry a risk that in practice it would be treated as a legal presumption, with formal consequences regarding the burden of proof. In contrast, it should be possible to use equality as a form of check for the valuable purpose already described without this being treated as a legal presumption of equal division.

Question

What do you understand to be the difference between a principle, a presumption, a starting point and a yardstick? (We are *not* suggesting that there is no difference, but would like you to consider how these different terms maybe used.)

Lord Nichols went on to consider a number of cases in the 1970s and 1980s where the 'reasonable requirements' approach had been developed. He concluded that:

[A]s matters stand, there is a degree of confusion. I venture to think this has arisen because the courts have departed from the statutory provisions. The statutory provisions lend no support to the idea that a claimant's financial needs, even interpreted generously and called reasonable requirements, are to be regarded as determinative. Another factor to which the court is bidden to have particular regard is the available resources of each party. ... [S]ection 25(2) does not rank the matters listed in that subsection in any kind of hierarchy. The weight, or importance, to be attached to these matters depends upon the facts of the particular case. But I can see nothing, either in the statutory provisions or in the underlying objective of securing fair financial arrangements, to lead me to suppose that the available assets of the respondent become immaterial once the claimant wife's financial needs are satisfied. Why ever should they? If a husband and wife by their joint efforts over many years, his directly in his business and hers indirectly at home, have built up a valuable business from scratch, why should the claimant wife be confined to the court's assessment of her reasonable requirements, and the husband left with a much larger share? Or, to put the question differently, in such a case, where the assets exceed the financial needs of both parties, why should the surplus belong solely to the husband? On the facts of a particular case there may be a good reason why the wife should be confined to her needs and the husband left with the much larger balance. But the mere absence of financial need cannot, by itself, be a sufficient reason. If it were, discrimination would be creeping in by the back door. In these cases, it should be remembered, the claimant is usually the wife. Hence the importance of the check against the yardstick of equal division. There is much to be said for returning to the language of the statute. Confusion might be avoided if courts were to stop using the expression 'reasonable requirements' in these cases, burdened as it is now with the difficulties mentioned above. This would not deprive the court of the necessary degree of flexibility. Financial needs are relative. Standards of living vary. In assessing financial needs, a court will have regard to a person's age, health and accustomed standard of living. The court may also have regard to the available pool of resources. Clearly, and this is well-recognised, there is some overlap between the factors listed in s 25(2). In a particular case there may be other matters to be taken into account as well. But the end product of this assessment of financial needs should be seen, and treated by the court, for what it is: only one of the several factors to which the court is to have particular regard. This is so, whether the end product is labelled financial needs or reasonable requirements. In deciding what would be a fair outcome the court must also have regard to other factors such as the available resources and the parties' contributions. In following this approach the court will be doing no more than giving effect to the statutory scheme.
...

The next generation

I must mention a further matter on which, through her counsel, Mrs White advanced submissions. It arises out of observations made in *Page v Page* (1981) 2 FLR 198. Ormrod LJ (at 201), expressed the view that when assessing the amount of a lump sum provision under s 25 it is not legitimate to take into account the wife's wish to be in a position to make provision by will for her adult children. ... I agree with this proposition to a strictly limited extent. I agree that a parent's wish to be in a position to leave money to his or her children would not normally fall within para (b) as a financial need, either of the husband or of the wife. But this does not mean that this natural parental wish is wholly irrelevant to the s 25 exercise in a case where resources exceed the parties' financial needs. In principle, a wife's wish to have money so that she can pass some on to her children at her discretion is every bit as weighty as a similar wish by a husband. ... In my view, in a case where resources exceed needs, the correct approach is as follows. The judge has regard to all the facts of the case and to the overall requirements of fairness. When doing so, the judge is entitled to have in mind the wish of a claimant wife that her award should not be confined to living accommodation and a vanishing fund of capital earmarked for living expenses which would leave nothing for her to pass on. The judge will give to that factor whatever weight, be it much or little or none at all, he considers appropriate in the circumstances of the particular case.

Inherited money and property

I must also mention briefly another problem which has arisen in the present case. It concerns property acquired during the marriage by one spouse by gift or succession or as a beneficiary under a trust. For convenience I will refer to such property as inherited property. Typically, in countries where a detailed statutory code is in place, the legislation distinguishes between two classes of property: inherited property, and property owned before the marriage, on the one hand, and 'matrimonial property' on the other hand. A distinction along these lines exists, for example, in the Family Law (Scotland) Act and the (New Zealand) Matrimonial Property Act 1976. This distinction is a recognition of the view, widely but not universally held, that property owned by one spouse before the marriage, and inherited property whenever acquired, stand on a different footing from what may be loosely called matrimonial property. According to this view, on a breakdown of the marriage these two classes of property should not necessarily be treated in the same way. Property acquired before marriage and inherited property acquired during marriage come from a source wholly external to the marriage. In fairness, where this property still exists, the spouse to whom it was given should be allowed to keep it. Conversely, the other spouse has a weaker claim to such property than he or she may have regarding matrimonial property. Plainly, when present, this factor is one of the circumstances of the case. It represents a contribution made to the welfare of the family by one of the parties to the marriage. The judge should take it into account. He should decide how important it is in the particular case. The nature and value of the property, and the time when and circumstances in which the property was acquired, are among the relevant matters to be considered. However, in the ordinary course, this factor can be expected to carry little weight, if any, in a case where the claimant's financial needs cannot be met without recourse to this property.

The decision of Holman J

I turn now to the decision of Holman J. In a careful and lucid judgment, he faithfully followed the approach of Thorpe LJ in *Dart v Dart* [1997] 1 FCR 21. He assessed the parties' reasonable requirements and on that basis made his award. That was the determinative factor. For reasons already given, I consider that, through no fault on his part, he was mistaken in taking this course. Indeed, the present case is a good illustration of the unsatisfactory results which can flow from the reasonable requirements approach. Even if Rexton were excluded, Mr and Mrs White's financial resources exceeded their financial needs. But Mrs White's award was confined to her financial needs, while Mr White, whose financial needs were no greater, scooped the entirety of the rest of the pool of resources. Even if Rexton were wholly left out of account, Mr White still received roughly two-thirds of their assets. The initial cash contribution made by Mr White's father in the early days cannot carry much weight 33 years later.

The decision of the Court of Appeal

In my view, therefore, the judge misdirected himself. Accordingly, the Court of Appeal was entitled to exercise afresh the statutory discretionary powers. Both parties criticised the manner in which the Court of Appeal did so. Mr White's primary complaint was that the Court of Appeal wrongly departed from the reasonable requirements approach prescribed in *Dart v Dart*. For reasons already given, I do not accept this criticism. His next criticism was that the members of the Court of Appeal placed undue emphasis on the financial worth of each party on the dissolution of the partnership. This was a wrong approach, as was the view that the court should not exercise its statutory powers unless there was a 'manifest case for intervention'. I agree that both Thorpe and Butler-Sloss LJJ did attach considerable importance to the wife's entitlement under the partnership. There are observations, particularly in the judgment of Thorpe LJ, which, read by themselves, might suggest that in this regard the clock was being turned back to the pre-1970 position. Then courts often had to attempt to unravel years of matrimonial finances and reach firm conclusions on who owned precisely what and in what shares. The need for this type of investigation was swept away in 1970 when the new legislation gave the court its panoply of wide discretionary powers. ... The wisdom of this approach is confirmed by the substantial body of additional evidence produced for the first time in your Lordships' House. The new material included the Whites' partnership agreement. From this evidence it emerged that, if a strict valuation of the parties' shares on a dissolution of the partnership were needed, several disputes would have to be resolved: disputes about the assets and liabilities of the partnership, a dispute about the value of the milk quota, and a dispute over the proper interpretation of the somewhat obscure retirement provisions in the partnership agreement. I do not think any of these differences need be resolved. The House can, and should, proceed on the basis of the factual findings of Holman J. A further contention advanced for Mr White was that there was no basis on which the court could increase Mrs White's award to an amount substantially in excess of her share of their joint assets. Here again, I am unable to agree. As one would expect, both Thorpe and Butler-Sloss LJJ had in mind all the available assets. They had in mind that the contribution made by Mr White's father was significant. Both of them referred to Mrs White's dual role as business partner and as wife and mother. They also had in mind the overall goal of fairness, a consideration specifically mentioned by Thorpe LJ. The amount of their award was well within the ambit of the discretion which the Court of Appeal was exercising afresh. For the same reason, I cannot accept Mrs White's contrary contention that the assets should have been divided equally. Mrs White advanced the further argument that if proprietorial interests were to be looked at, the court should have conducted a full and detailed investigation. I have already stated that such an investigation was not called for. Her next submission was that the Court of Appeal should not have adopted a selective revaluation of only one of the assets, the milk quota, and then without proper evidence. This criticism lacks substance. The Court of Appeal was understandably anxious to make any necessary major adjustments in the figures but without putting the parties to further expense. As matters have since turned out, the judge's figures have to be adjusted downwards, by a substantial amount, in any event. The parties' untaxed costs of their appeals to this House are estimated at the appalling sum of £530,000. This exceeds Thorpe LJ's estimate of the reduction in value of milk quota since the decision of Holman J. Whatever may be the rights and wrongs of the amount of the milk quota revaluation, the course taken by Court of Appeal did not prejudice Mrs White. Finally, Mrs White criticised the use of net values, arrived at after deducting estimates of the costs and capital gains tax likely to be incurred if the farms were sold. Mr White still owns and uses the farms. The farms have not been sold. Counsel submitted that the use of net values in this situation should be discontinued. I do not agree. As with so much else in this field, there can be no hard and fast rule, either way. When making a comparison it is important to compare like with like, so far as this may be possible in the particular case. In the present case a comparison based on net values is fairer than would be a comparison of Mrs White' cash award and the gross value of the farms. Under her award Mrs White will have money. She can invest or use it as she pleases. Mr White's equivalent, as a cash sum, is the net value of the farms. The farms have to be sold before he can have money to invest or use in other ways. What will be his financial position if he is able to retain the farms or parts of them? Will he better off financially? Dairy farming is currently languishing in the doldrums. On the evidence there is no reason to suppose that the farms are likely to yield a better financial return at present than the investment return to be expected if Mr White sold up and invested the net proceeds.

My conclusion is that ... there is no ground entitling this House to interfere with the Court of Appeal's exercise of discretion. I would dismiss the appeals of both Mr and Mrs White.

Questions

(i)   Given Lord Nicholls' reasoning, were you surprised by the result?

(ii)   How would you expect the 'yardstick of equality' to function on a divorce following a very short marriage?

(iii)   How might it operate where the applicant spouse had contributed (see s. 25(2)(f)) neither business activity nor homemaking?

(iv)   What might be the effect, if any, of *White* in a family where resources are scarce?

White thus swept away a lot of the earlier case law, and marks something of a fresh start. How fresh has yet to be seen. Our discussion of the English case law must be read with *White* in mind, and decisions subsequent to *White* are beginning to give us a sense of how the law will develop. First, though, we digress for brief look at the Scottish system, which Lord Nicholls mentioned.

8.4   A Scottish alternative

Proposals from the Scottish Law Commission in *Aliment and Financial Provision* (1981) and the resultant legislation in Scotland provides an interesting contrast:

Need for balance between principle and discretion

3.62 One of the main criticisms made of the present law on financial provision is that it leaves too much to the unfettered discretion of the court. We think that this criticism is justified. On the other hand we have no doubt that the courts must be left with considerable discretion to take account of the great variety of circumstances in cases which come before them. One of our main concerns in this Report has been to try to strike the right balance between principle and discretion. We take as our starting point the proposition that an order for financial provision should be made if, and only if, it is justified by an applicable principle. ...

FAIR SHARING OF MATRIMONIAL PROPERTY

A principle of quantification

3.65 When we refer to the principle of fair sharing of matrimonial property we are not talking about the division of specific items of property. How the value of a spouse's share would be satisfied would depend on the resources available at the time of the divorce. The court's powers would not be limited to matrimonial property (as defined) but would extend to all of the spouses' resources at the time of the divorce. ... The basic idea is that it covers property acquired by the spouses, otherwise than by gift or inheritance, in the period between the marriage and their final separation.

The norm of equal sharing

3.66 It would be too vague to empower the courts to award simply a 'fair share' of matrimonial property. One of the major criticisms of the present law is that it provides no guidance on the amount of a capital sum which can be expected on divorce. It would, on the other hand, be too rigid to lay down a fixed rule of apportionment for all cases. We think that the best solution is to provide that matrimonial property should normally be divided equally between the parties but that the court should be able to depart from this norm of equal sharing in special circumstances. ... [We] can see no good reason for giving either spouse, whether legal owner or not, whether wife or husband, less than half of the matrimonial property. The underlying idea is that of partnership in marriage and the only fair solution seems to us to be an equal division of the 'partnership' assets as the norm. ...

3.68 Where there are special circumstances justifying a departure from equal sharing ... we think that the court should be directed to share the matrimonial property in such proportions as may be fair in those circumstances. It would be impossible to provide with precision for the infinite variety of special circumstances which may arise. We therefore recommend:

> 32.(*a*) The principle of fair sharing of matrimonial property is that the net value of the matrimonial property should be shared equally or, if there are special circumstances justifying a departure from equal sharing, in such other proportions as may be fair in those circumstances. ...

Having defined matrimonial property essentially in terms of property acquired during marriage and discussed the special circumstances justifying the departure from equal sharing, they turn to a discussion of the recognition of contributions:

3.92 The first is where the contributions of one spouse have contributed to an improvement in the other's economic position. A husband, for example, may have paid off a loan over a house owned by his wife before the marriage, or he may have worked for years extending and improving her house. Similarly a wife may have worked for years, unpaid, in a small business owned by her husband before the marriage and may have helped to build up its value. In all these cases one spouse has contributed to an increase in the capital of the other and we think it reasonable that the court should be able to award some financial provision on divorce in recognition of the contributions. The position is essentially the same where one of the spouses has contributed to an increase in the other's earning potential. ... A husband may have worked overtime to pay his wife's fees for some special course of further education or training. A wife may have helped her husband with his work on an unpaid basis ... but because of the nature of his work (e.g. author, doctor, advocate, professional sportsman, entertainer) the result of her contributions may be an increase in his earning potential rather than in the capital value of a business. Again, there may be cases where one spouse's unpaid services as a housekeeper, hostess, domestic manager and child-minder could be shown to have contributed directly or indirectly to an improvement in the other spouse's economic position. ... In all these cases, ... it seems to us that there is a strong case for enabling the contribution to be recognised where this is not already done by means of a share in matrimonial property.

3.93 The position becomes more difficult, however, if there is no link between the contributions and any improvement in the other spouse's economic position. Suppose, for example, that three men all started work in the same employment at the age of 20. The first married a wife who assumed the traditional housewife's role and did all the domestic work. The second married an idle woman and did most of the domestic work himself. The third remained unmarried and did all his own domestic work. All three lived in rented accommodation. None accumulated any savings. All advanced remorselessly up their salary scale. If the first man was divorced at the age of 40 it would certainly not be obvious that his wife's contributions over the years had contributed to any improvement in his economic position, although they may well have contributed to an increase in the time available to him for leisure activities. Should an industrious wife receive more than an idle wife in this case? Should the principle of fair recognition of contributions extend to contributions to the welfare of the family even if they have not improved the other spouse's economic position? One submission made to us was that such contributions were made voluntarily and should therefore be ignored. The same point could, however, be made about many contributions which have directly improved the other spouse's economic position. Another view put to us was that the law should take a hard line on the question of a housewife's contributions in order to encourage women to preserve their economic independence during marriage. In our view, however, it is not the function of financial provision on divorce to encourage people to adopt any particular life style during marriage. ... We therefore reject these two arguments. We think, however, that there are other grounds for not recognising a claim based on contributions which have not resulted in any improvement in the other spouse's economic position. First, such contributions will often be evenly balanced. If, in the traditional type of marriage, a housewife could make a claim on the basis of contributions in work towards the welfare of the family, her husband could often do the same. ... Moreover, if a wife could make a claim on the basis of her contributions in work, her husband could often make a claim on the basis of his contributions in money to the welfare of the family. In some cases (for example the lazy wife, the wife with domestic help) the husband would be able to make a claim on this basis for a payment out of the wife's separate property. We doubt whether this would be acceptable. Secondly, an attempt to work out which spouse had contributed more to the welfare of the family during the marriage would often involve an unproductive examination and investigation of conduct over many years. Thirdly, and more fundamentally, the purpose of financial provision on divorce is not, in our view, the punishment of bad conduct or the reward of good conduct. In our view its concern should be with the economic effects of marriage and divorce ...

3.94 There is a further problem. One spouse may have sustained an economic disadvantage in the interests of the other party or of the family. The standard illustration is the well-qualified woman who married, say, 20 or 30 years ago and who gave up her own career prospects, perhaps with the encouragement or passive approval of her husband, in order to look after and bring up the family. There are other illustrations. A husband may have given up career prospects (for example the chance of a lucrative post abroad) in his wife's interests. An older woman may have given up a good position on marriage in order to look after her husband and may be unable to obtain employment again after divorce. One of the parties may have given up a tenancy in order to live with the other party on marriage. In all such cases there should in our view be the possibility of financial provision on divorce in recognition of the economic disadvantages sustained. ...

FAIR PROVISION FOR ADJUSTMENT TO INDEPENDENCE
The principle

3.107 In many cases divorcing spouses will already be economically independent by the time of the divorce. In many cases an award of financial provision under one of the principles discussed above would be sufficient to provide for any necessary adjustment to post-divorce independence. In other cases, however, we think that a reasonable objective of an award of financial provision on divorce is to enable a spouse to adjust, over a relatively short period, to the cessation on divorce of any financial dependence on the other spouse. Depending on the circumstances, the purpose of the award might be to enable the payee to undertake a course of training or retraining, or to give the payee time to find suitable employment, or to enable the payee to adjust gradually to a lower standard of living. It would be essential to specify a maximum time over which the adjustment would have to be made because otherwise there would, in many cases, be no way of ensuring that a transitional provision did not become permanent life-long support. We think that a period of three years from the date of divorce would be an adequate maximum period, given that in most cases the final separation between the parties would be some considerable time before that. We considered whether an adjustment provision ought to be available for, say, three years after the termination of a period of childcare after divorce. We have concluded, however, that this would not be justified. The main purpose of a provision under this principle is to provide time to adjust. ...

Factors to be taken into account

3.108 In addition to the usual factors such as the needs and resources of the parties, we think that it would be desirable to refer specifically, in relation to this principle, to the earning capacity of the payee, to the duration and extent of the payee's past dependency on the payer and to any intentions of the payee to undertake a course of education or training. ...

3.109 We therefore recommend as follows:

35.(*a*) The principle of fair provision for adjustment to independence is that where one party to the marriage has been financially dependent on the other and the dependence has come to an end on divorce, the dependent party should receive such financial provision as is fair and reasonable to enable him to adjust, over a period of not more than three years from the date of divorce, to the cessation of that dependence.

(*b*) In deciding what financial provision is fair and reasonable under this recommendation the court should have regard to the age, health and earning capacity of the applicant, to the duration and extent of the applicant's past dependency on the payer, to any intention of the applicant to undertake a course of education or training, to the needs and resources, actual or foreseeable, of the parties, and to the other circumstances of the case. ...

RELIEF OF GRAVE FINANCIAL HARDSHIP

Purpose and scope

3.110 It could be argued that the ... principles which we have discussed so far are adequate to cover all cases where financial provision on divorce is justified. This would mean that if there was no matrimonial property, if there was no claim based on contributions or disadvantages, and if there were no dependent children, then a divorced spouse could be awarded at most a provision designed to ease his or her adjustment to independence over a period of not more than three years. Thereafter he or she would have no claim against the former spouse. While there is much to be said for this approach, we have rejected it. The ... principles discussed already would not always ensure that a spouse who suffered severe financial hardship as a result of the marriage and the divorce could recover some financial provision in appropriate cases. A wife might, for example, have gone with her husband to some tropical country and might have contracted a disabling disease. Or she might have been permanently disabled as a result of injury in childbirth. We think that in such cases financial provision on divorce would be justified if it were reasonable having regard to the parties' resources. We have more doubt about whether a former spouse should ever be expected to relieve the hardship of the other if the hardship does not arise in any way from the marriage. If we were approaching the matter as one of pure principle we would be inclined to reject such a proposition as contrary to the idea that divorce ends the marriage. Financial provision on divorce is not, however, simply a matter of abstract principle. It is essential that any system should be acceptable to public opinion and it is clear from the comments we have received that many people would find it hard to accept a system which cut off, say, an elderly or disabled spouse with no more than a three-year allowance after divorce, no matter how wealthy the other party might be. We have concluded therefore that the law ought to provide, as a 'long-stop', for the case where one spouse would suffer grave financial hardship as a result of the divorce. In such a case the court should be able to award such financial provision as is fair and reasonable in the circumstances to relieve the hardship over such period as the court may determine. We do not intend this principle to be a gateway to support after divorce in all cases just as if the marriage had not been dissolved. We do not think, for example, that a man who suffers hardship on being made redundant at the age of 52 should have a claim for financial provision against a former wife whom he divorced thirty years before. We think that the general principle should be that after the divorce each party bears the risk of *supervening* hardship without recourse against the other. It should therefore be made clear in the legislation that it is only where the likelihood of grave financial hardship is established at the time of the divorce that a claim will arise under this principle.

Questions

(i)   Does the approach of the Scottish Law Commission differ substantially from that of the English Law Commission?
(ii) If so, whose approach do you prefer?

The Family Law (Scotland) Act 1985 states:

Principles to be applied

9.—(1) The principles which the court shall apply in deciding what order for financial provision, if any, to make are that

   (*a*)   the net value of the matrimonial property should be shared fairly between the parties to the marriage;
   (*b*)   fair account should be taken of any economic advantage derived by either party from contributions by the other, and of any economic disadvantages suffered by either party in the interests of the other party or of the family;
   (*c*)   any economic burden of caring, after divorce, for a child of the marriage under the age of 16 years should be shared fairly between the parties;
   (*d*)   a party who has been dependent to a substantial degree on the financial support of the other party should be awarded such financial provision as is reasonable to enable him to adjust, over a period of not more than three years from the date of the decree of divorce, to the loss of that support on divorce;
   (*e*)   a party who at the time of the divorce seems likely to suffer serious financial hardship as a result of the divorce should be awarded such financial provision as is reasonable to relieve him of hardship over a reasonable period.

(2)   In subsection (1)(*b*) above and section 11(2) of this Act—
        'economic advantage' means advantage gained whether before or during the marriage and includes gains in capital, in income and in earning capacity, and 'economic disadvantage' shall be construed accordingly;
        'contributions' means contributions made whether before or during the marriage; and includes indirect and non-financial contributions and, in particular, any such contribution made by looking after the family home or caring for the family.

Sharing of value of matrimonial property

10.—(1) In applying the principle set out in section 9(1)(*a*) of this Act, the net value of the matrimonial property shall be taken to be shared fairly between the parties to the marriage when it is shared equally or in such other proportions as are justified by special circumstances.

(2)   The net value of the matrimonial property shall be the value of the property at the relevant date after deduction of any debts incurred by the parties or either of them—

   (*a*)   before the marriage so far as they relate to the matrimonial property, and
   (*b*)   during the marriage,

which are outstanding at that date.

(3)   In this section 'the relevant date' means whichever is the earlier of—

   (*a*)   subject to subsection (7) below, the date on which the parties ceased to cohabit;
   (*b*)   the date of service of the summons in the action for divorce.

Question

Note that 'grave' financial hardship recommended by the Scottish Law Commission has been replaced by 'serious' financial hardship. Is there a difference?

Criticisms of the Scottish legislation are summarised by the Family Law Committee of the Law Society in their memorandum on *Maintenance and Capital Provision on Divorce* (1991):

2.17 The principles in the Scottish legislation were subject to criticism at the time of the legislation's enactment and this criticism has been borne out in research into the effect the

Act has had on advice given by solicitors to their clients (see Wasoff, Dobash and Harcus 'The *Impact of the Family Law Scotland Act 1985 on Solicitors' Divorce Practice'* (1990)).

2.18 At the time the Act was passed [Stephen] Cretney argued in *'Money After Divorce – The Mistakes We Have Made'* (1986) that although the Scottish system does seem to reduce judicial discretion nevertheless three criticisms can be made of it. First, that although certainty has been achieved through the implementation of a framework of principles, scope for uncertainty still exists. If you take the judge's discretion under the existing English law as being as long as a piece of string, and replace it by five pieces of string each of indeterminate length, as under the Scottish legislation, it is far from clear that the position has been improved. Secondly, he argues that the Scottish legislation is unfavourable to women as the court cannot make an order for periodical payments unless it is satisfied that an order for the payment of a capital sum or transfer of property would not by itself be appropriate or sufficient to give effect to the five principles embodied in the legislation. Thirdly, if the court does order periodical payments they must not be for a longer period than three years from the date of divorce unless these payments are required in order to satisfy the two principles of fair sharing of the burden of child care or relief from serious financial hardship. In addition, another limitation on any settlement is the fact that spouses are entitled to receive 'fair recognition of contributions and disadvantages'. There is also a proviso that claims are only to be accepted under this heading if they have resulted in an improvement in the spouse's economic position.

2.19 Under the Scottish Code there is no reference to the welfare of the child(ren) because claims in respect of the child(ren) are dealt with independently of claims of parents in divorce proceedings. Thus, when considering the allocation of income and property, attention is not specifically directed to the interests of the children although the court must have regard to the economic burden of child care. It is the Family Law Committee's view that any set of principles dealing with maintenance and capital provision on divorce should include within it recognition that the interests of any children should be the first consideration.

2.20 The Committee believes that the principles in the Scottish legislation have the potential to produce arbitrary results. This concern is backed up ... by A R Dewar *'The Family Law (Scotland) Act 1985 in Practice'* (1989) in which he stated that the courts were relying on the fifth principle of relief from serious financial hardship to an unexpected degree in order to avoid this. The results of the research carried out by Wasoff, Dobash and Harcus [1990] also lend support to this argument as well as revealing a number of other problems experienced by solicitors in their interpretation of the legislation.

2.25 Difficulties encountered by English solicitors can be attributed to a lack of principles. However, it is clear from the analysis set out above that while a set of principles is a useful tool it does not represent the complete answer. Indeed, the use of principles seems to introduce a new problem of when and how to apply them. The Committee was particularly concerned about the problems experienced when a conflict between different principles arose and the possible adverse effect on the former wife's financial position. The Committee's view, therefore, is that their introduction would not greatly increase certainty – particularly if the effect is merely to shift an argument from the issue of which principles should be applied to when and how to apply them.

Emily Jackson, Fran Wasoff, Mavis Maclean and Rebecca Dobash, in their article 'Financial Support on Divorce: the Right Mixture of Rules and Discretion?' (1993), report on their research project, examining the practice of solicitors dealing with financial matters after divorce in England and Scotland. The aim was to study solicitors' views and behaviour in the context of the tension between rules and discretion, and not principally to compare the workings of the two systems; the researchers acknowledge that the two legal frameworks are different, but found, 'sufficiently similar themes to justify tying the two projects together'. This is their description of a legal practitioner's approach in Scotland:

Their collective approach can best be summarised as primarily needs-based within the wide constraints set by a framework of rules and rights codified in the main by the Family Law (Scotland) Act 1985. There was no evidence that they sought to use a formula or even a particularly systematic approach to quantifying awards. To a great extent, they sought to secure individualized justice, using discretion not simply for its own sake but in order to re-allocate (usually) scarce resources by giving first priority to meeting the needs of the custodial parent and dependent children, and, secondly, providing for the basic needs of the non-custodial parent/husband, only after that redistributing the remaining matrimonial resources.

Question

Do you see anything in such an approach that reflects the Scottish rather than the English legal principles?

This research was carried out before the implementation of the Child Support Act 1991 took the issue of maintenance for children out of the discretionary system; it is now, of course, a fixed amount, in the light of which all other issues, such as housing and spousal maintenance, have to be calculated. Jackson and her colleagues comment that its introduction is a sign of 'an international trend towards the use of rules within family law', and that 'although the divergence between English and Scottish legislation will remain when a nationwide Child Support Agency is in place, it will be of less significance'.

8.5   Section 25 in action

When considering the effect of the legislation upon real families in the throes of reorganising and rebuilding their lives after divorce, we have to bear in mind that in the majority of cases no order is made for financial provision, and that, of the orders made, the most are by consent. Nevertheless, where the parties make or agree their own arrangements, with or without the help of a mediator, they are influenced by what the courts *would* do if the issue were litigated.

This section has eight parts. First, we look at the court's starting point and basic methodology. Next, we consider the outcomes where there are substantial assets and therefore money to spare; and again, at cases where resources are limited and public funding is an issue. We look at the effect upon outcomes of the length of the marriage and of the parties' conduct; finally we examine the courts' approach to housing, the clean break, and pensions.

8.5.1   The starting point

Faced with a family, not specially wealthy, not specially poor, how is the court to approach the exercise of considering the s. 25 factors and arriving at a fair redistribution of assets? We now know that the court must test its findings against the 'yardstick of equality' of which Lord Nicholls spoke in *White*. But how to make a start towards those findings? The current approach to periodical payments is to ascertain the net incomes of both husband and wife and to look at the net effect of the order on both parties.

An example of the 'net-effect' approach is seen in *Allen v Allen* [1986] 2 FLR 265, CA. It is described by Jill Black, Jane Bridge and Tina Bond in *A Practical Approach to Family Law* (1994) in the following way:

It is very helpful to the court to work out how a proposed order (be it a one-third order or an order arrived at on a different basis) would work in practice.

To do this it is necessary to calculate each party's tax liability on the basis of the proposed order. From the payer's gross income is then deducted the tax he would have to pay, and his expenses of earning it. What is left is his spendable income – is it enough to enable him to meet his reasonable expenses? If not, the proposed order may well be too high. If he would have a significant sum over after meeting his expenses, the order may be too low. The position of the payee must also be considered. From her gross income, including the proposed maintenance, child benefit and one-parent benefit, must be deducted tax and her earning expenses. Is her spendable income sufficient for her reasonable expenses?

The net effect approach can be a very valuable way of showing up inequalities between the parties that might not otherwise be apparent; for instance, if the proposed order leaves the husband with £200 a month to spend and the wife with minus £10, the proposed order will obviously have to be adjusted so that the husband pays more. It may well be, however, that *both* parties are left with too little to cover their expenses – an all too common situation following the breakdown of a marriage. In such a case there is no possibility of carrying out a fine balancing exercise to distribute surplus income – the court must do the best it can and may have to work on the basis that one or the other party (or both) will require state benefits.

District Judge Roger Bird, in 'Ancillary relief outcomes' (2000), speaks of the 'hierarchy of needs' which the court will try to meet:

Housing is normally the most important issue; the housing of the parent with care of the children normally takes priority over that of the other parent, although his/her needs must be met wherever possible. Once housing has been disposed of the reasonable needs of the parties should be considered. The clean break should only be imposed where there is no doubt that the parties will be self-sufficient. Attention must be given to pensions. Where the reasonable needs of the parties have been met there is no justification for further adjustment by the court.

That last sentence, of course, no longer holds good following *White*, but of course in so many cases there is no surplus to play with. Sometimes there is some leeway; occasionally (in the 'big money cases' considered under our next heading) there is a lot. In the light of *White*, it is particularly interesting to look back at the unreported first instance decision in *B v B* (Fam Div, 17 March 1995) as an illustration of the modern approach to financial provision:

Hale J: These are cross applications for all forms of ancillary relief. I shall call the parties husband and wife although they are now divorced. The wife is 51, a doctor, a partner in an eleven partner general medical practice. The husband is 50, a solicitor, a senior partner of a three partner firm. They were married in May 1969. They have three children: Helen, aged 24, who is a final year medical student; Lynne, aged 22, who is a fifth and penultimate year medical student; and Michael, aged 18, who is in his first of four years as a student of law and criminology. All three were educated at top flight independent schools. Sadly, since the breakdown of the marriage, all three children have become estranged from their father and look to their mother for financial and moral support.

It has been a typical dual career family. The husband worked full-time throughout the marriage. The wife continued to work during the early years of the marriage but only part-time while the children were young. She joined her present practice in 1980, at first part-time and then full-time a year later. For three and a half or four years when she first became full-time the family had a housekeeper. They have had a series of matrimonial homes in their joint names; the most recent is an attractive four bedroom house with an extension forming a separate flatlet. It was bought in 1976 and extended when the wife returned to full-time work.

The marriage went seriously wrong in 1992. No issue is now raised as to matrimonial conduct by either party; nor am I asked to take the conduct of this litigation into account in the assessment of ancillary relief.

I now turn to the consideration of the factors in section 25(2) of the Matrimonial Causes Act 1973. Paragraph (*a*) requires me to consider the resources which each of the parties has or is likely to have in the foreseeable future.

Firstly, the husband: the husband's share of the profits of his firm has fluctuated quite dramatically from £47,000 in 1987, up to £53,000 and £54,000 in 1988 and 1989, down to £47,000 in 1990 and then down to an all time low of £22,000 in 1991; up to £35,000 in 1992, back down to £26,000 in 1993, and last year it was £36,000.

He has a profession which will give him a reasonable income, more than adequate for the needs of a single man, for the rest of his working life. He works hard and the firm's turnover is still considerable. His evidence was that he would not expect to retire until 65 and possibly not even then. He thought that solicitors never retired.

The problem with the husband's position is that he has built up a deficit on his capital account with the firm of £73,000 and he has promised the bank to pay £60,000 out of the proceeds of these proceedings into the firm in order to reduce the firm's borrowings and thus enable the firm to continue in business. The reason for the deficit is that since 1990 his drawings have exceeded his share of the profits. ...

His initial explanation for the difficulties was that the wife was spending too much. He initially also contended that as a result the overdraft on their joint account was increasing, but this was not so. He then contended that he was drawing more out of the firm in order to meet their expenditure. Again this is not obviously demonstrated because his drawings have been comparable over the whole of the period under discussion. Also the allegation of excessive expenditure by the wife, although it has featured extremely heavily in the evidence in the case, is not maintained before me and on the evidence before me it could not possibly be. ...

The truth of course is that the family's expenditure was inevitably heavy. They were maintaining three children at expensive schools and university; they were amassing, although most of it was before this period, a collection of paintings, porcelain and antiques, and of course the general expenditure of a household of this nature is in itself heavy. ...

The capital position of the firm, according to the most recent accounts before me, is that the liabilities exceed the assets by £106,000 and the husband values the firm at nil. He is very pessimistic about the future of high street solicitors' firms. However he is a hard worker and he has a marketable skill which has brought him a good living in the past. I cannot speculate one way or another how his business will go over the next ten to fifteen years or whether by the time the husband comes to retire there will be any goodwill for him to sell. He may, of course, as he has been thinking of doing, go into another business in any event.

The husband has other assets of more limited value: guns, shares, premium bonds and cash totalling approximately £12,000 in value. He has recently acquired, presumably through the firm, an L registration Volvo estate worth approximately £18,000, presumably thinking it appropriate to continue to run the same sort of family car that he ran while the family were united. The husband also has a personal pension which at the moment has a value, depending on the method chosen of £97,500 or £106,000. The husband's parents are very elderly; their estate is worth about £80,000. In due course it will be shared between the husband and his sister. It cannot at the moment be foreseen whether his parents will soon both die leaving the estate intact or whether one or both will require expensive residential care. Very properly, the husband says he has no hopes of an inheritance from them.

As to his liabilities, I have already mentioned the loan account with his firm, in effect of £73,000, and his promise to repay £60,000 of it. However, it is now agreed that there are many items belonging to his firm which are currently housed in the matrimonial home. ...They must have made a sizeable contribution to the firm's loan account. Their sale could obviously go some way towards reducing it. ...The husband has also incurred actual costs of £28,200 up to the date of the trial of which £21,100 has been paid, leaving him with a debt of £7,100. ...

Turning now to the wife, the wife's drawings from her practice range from £39,000 in 1991 to £71,000 last year. They have never exceeded her share of the profits. She also has a capital account, put at £101,000 in the recent partnership accounts, which she will be able to take out when she leaves. ...

The precise value of a partner's capital account is worked out by reference to the partnership's assets at the time of leaving. The practice owns a surgery, an annex, which is let to various other practitioners and a chemist's shop, and four semi-detached properties; they get rent for these from the health authority and from tenants. They are currently building an extension to the surgery to improve the facilities for patients and nurses. There is a dispute about the valuation of these properties. The valuer used by the partnership gave two different valuations last year: one for the bank and one for the purpose of buying out a doctor leaving the practice. There is some discrepancy between them, but it has been agreed to take the higher figure which is £1,250,000. Of course the rental for the doctor's premises is to some extent notional because they could not be let for any other purpose which would attract such a rent and in any event they are not going to be sold. This is the only GP practice in the town and these are purpose built premises. The valuer instructed by the husband on the basis of the same information about rentals assumes the rental to represent about 10 per cent of the capital value and so values the whole at £1,745,000. When additional borrowings for the extension are taken into account the discrepancy is only put at some £80,500, which is not a great deal when divided amongst ten and a half partners, but in any event the rental figures have not yet been agreed and it is not clear what the effect will be of the new extension on the one hand and the lettings to the other practitioners on the other. ...

She no longer hopes to retire before she is 60. However when she does retire, she can expect a capital sum which, at the moment, is in the region of £100,000. On retirement she will also have an NHS pension. The amount accrued in her 14 years' service to date would yield, when she is 60, a pension of approximately £8,500 and a lump sum of approximately £25,500 but this will increase with each year of service. The present transfer value is £109,000. ...

The wife does have a residuary interest in her father's estate which is a share in a house worth on recent values around £29,400 plus securities of £29,100. Unlike her husband's expectations, this is an absolute and indefeasible interest but it will only come to her on the death of her father's widow who is now a fit 66-year-old with a life expectancy, I am told, of some 18 years.

The wife has other current assets: jewellery, stocks and shares, which again came from her father's estate; a building society account; insurance policy and premium bonds totalling in all approximately £39,600. She also has debts amounting in all to around £26,500. These include a legal expenses loan of £20,000; a debt to a family friend for Michael's school fees of over £2,000, and a debt of a similar sum to repay grant paid in error to Lynne, as well as normal fluctuating credit card purchases. ...

Thirdly their joint assets: this is a family in which until the marriage broke down the assets were pooled. The matrimonial home is worth something between £275-300,000. It has been agreed to take its value at £285,000. There is a mortgage of some £63,000 which with the cost of sale will bring this down to around £215,000.

Its contents are more than usually valuable because the couple enjoyed collecting water colours, porcelain and antiques. ... Together these valuables total approximately £61,000. The antiques and silver have been valued by antique dealers at just over £14,000, making a total of just over £75,000 worth of chattels. Those then are the assets and the debts of the parties.

I turn to paragraph (*b*), their respective financial needs obligations and responsibilities. Both have the needs of a single middle aged professional person. They will each need a home. The only special factor here is that the children are estranged from their father and he is not providing for them at all. The wife pays Helen's rent of £235 per month to the hospital and other sums when they are needed which she puts in all at about £500 per month. The wife also pays Lynne's hall fees of £250 per month and more if she is finding things difficult. Of the four terms of Michael's school fees left after the proceedings began she paid two full terms and two half term fees. The husband paid one half term and a friend lent the other. That is the debt that I referred to earlier. On a strict reading of the school fees account, therefore, this leaves the husband one and a half terms in deficit which would be some £6,600. She now pays Michael's hall fees of between £500 and £700 at the beginning of each term and some extra when she can. Whereas the girls of course can expect to become self-supporting within the relatively near future, Michael will be dependent for some years yet. It is of course to be hoped that the children will in due course be reconciled with their father but they will undoubtedly look to her for a home base. She needs at least a three bedroomed house and she also needs it ... either within the practice boundaries or within a reasonable distance of the surgery. Even if this were not a legal requirement, it is obviously necessary for the reasonable operation of a general practitioner who has to spend periods of time on-call.

The husband's housing needs as a single man are not quite so great, nor is he so restricted as to area, although of course he has to balance proximity to his practice against the problems of living too close to his clients.

Paragraph (*c*) refers to the standard of living enjoyed by the family while it was together and that of course was a good standard of living of the sort to be expected in these circumstances. Paragraph (*d*) refers to their ages and the duration of the marriage. The parties are in their early fifties, they are now well established in life, and it was a long marriage.

Paragraph (*e*) refers to the contributions that each has made and is likely to make in the foreseeable future to the welfare of the family. This was, as I have said, a typical dual career family in which both worked hard and contributed financially what they could at the time. They regarded themselves as a partnership. The husband worked throughout and of course contributed more financially when he was working full-time and the wife was not. He also put in extras from time to time, cashing in insurance policies and extra drawings from his firm to finance the extension and he also put in a sum of money received from his parents which was a result of the profit that they made on moving house. The wife bore and cared for the children but she also worked and everything she acquired went into the joint account; not only her earnings, but also the cash which she received immediately from her father's estate, amounting to some £41,000. They both did their best for the welfare of the family. Their contributions in the past are obviously equal. The wife's contributions since the breakdown and into the foreseeable future are undoubtedly greater, both financially and as to the welfare of the family, and this will continue for some time.

I have already pointed out that paragraph (*g*), conduct, is not an issue in this case, nor has any issue been made of paragraph (*h*), the loss of potential benefits which in the case of parties who each have their own profession and provision for retirement is no doubt appropriate.

Having considered all those factors, what conclusion should be drawn? No-one suggests that there should be periodical payments for either party or the children. The wife argues that their current joint assets, the house and the valuables, should be shared equally between them. Assuming that all the valuables were sold this would give them each roughly £145,000. The wife can get a suitable house for £175,000 with the help of a manageable mortgage. She has a little in hand after the payment of her debts, including legal fees, but not a great deal and she will still have to furnish and equip the house.

The husband also has a little in hand, but he has to reduce the firm's borrowing from the bank and this may take up to £60,000 from the proceeds. Some, of course, could be taken by the firm's valuables which will no longer be in the matrimonial home. If they are not sold to reduce the firm's debts, presumably they will remain on loan to him and will be of help to him in decorating his new home. He does not need quite such a large house and so he could manage with a similar sized mortgage.

In the future they will have their own incomes and pensions. The husband is free of commitments to the children. Their pension schemes are roughly equivalent in value at the moment and each will no doubt go on contributing between now and then. The husband's retirement plans are very far in the distance. Neither party has any plan to remarry or cohabit, although the husband does have a relationship with one of the other witnesses.

The husband argues that the wife should only have £30,000 and he should have the balance, on my figures, of £260,000. The way that he justifies this, on the face of it, entirely inequitable result is: firstly, his debt to the firm, which would bring it down to £200,000; secondly, that the wife has current extra resources that he does not; thirdly, that they both need the same sort of house, and fourthly, above all, that the wife can afford a huge mortgage now because of her expectations from the firm which will pay it off when she retires.

It seems to me in a case like this where there has been a long partnership marriage, and both have careers of their own, the Court should in principle seek to divide their current assets equally and let each go their separate ways into the future. Of course where one spouse has an income and pension and the other does not, or only has a very limited one, one has to take into account pension entitlements falling due in the foreseeable future as a resource and a lump sum order or other adjustment, or even an adjournment for the application of a lump sum, may be appropriate to take account of it. (See cases such as *Milne v Milne* (1981) 2 FLR 286; *Priest v Priest* (1980) 1 FLR 189 and *Davies v Davies* [1986] 1 FLR 497.) However these cases do not come anywhere near saying that the Court should be seeking to achieve equality of results, not only now but also in the future. The statutory injunction to seek to put the parties in the position that they would have been had the marriage not broken down was repealed in 1984. ...

The strongest argument in favour of the husband is that the wife was enabled to build up her capital account because she did not increase her drawings at the time when the husband was beginning to become overdrawn. I accepted the wife's evidence that she would have done so if asked, but I do not accept that all the husband's deficit is due to his family responsibilities. ... The wife also contributed to the assets which are now to be shared a very substantial extra cash sum, which she might have kept separately, to be weighed in the balance now. In reality, the main reason for their different prospects, if that is how they turn out to be, is that the wife is a doctor and the husband is a solicitor.

I have been very properly urged by Miss Ball to consider what the position would be in reverse. This is indeed an important discipline, but in this case it merely serves to re-enforce my conclusions. I find it difficult to accept that on a clean break settlement, if the husband were in a profession where he earned more and had better pension prospects than his wife, he would be expected to take less than his half share of the accumulated joint assets just because the wife was also in good employment, but somewhat less well paid with less good prospects on retirement. This is all the more the case where the future in relation to the husband's practice is so difficult to predict. Above all, however, the wife has the extra burden of the children to support and this is more than enough to compensate for the eventual differences there may be in the parties' positions if life for solicitors continues to be as gloomy as the husband fears.

I therefore propose to order that the house be sold and the net proceeds be divided equally and that the valuables listed be divided by agreement in equal shares by value and in default of such agreement within a short period – as to which of course I will hear further argument but I will put it at one month – they should be sold and the proceeds of sale equally divided. ...

The husband appealed. In the Court of Appeal (*Burgess v Burgess* [1996] 2 FLR 34, [1997] 1 FCR 89, [1996] Fam Law 465) counsel for the husband argued that Hale J's approach had been incorrect because she appeared to have applied a rule of equal division of assets for dual career families, expressed in the sentence in her judgment beginning 'It seems to me that in a case like this ...'. Dismissing the appeal, Waite LJ (with whom Morritt LJ agreed) said:

... I would accept that, as a matter of grammatical interpretation, the judge's remarks – read in isolation – would be capable of being construed as applying a precept that the interests of working spouses in joint assets acquired through their combined efforts are to be treated equally. If that is the correct interpretation, then the judge would certainly be in error. ... But in my view, when her words are read in the context of a judgment which demonstrably seeks to apply s. 25 of the Act to the letter, and which produced nothing in its result which betrays the least sign of error or misplaced emphasis, it becomes clear that the judge was really intending to say no more than this. When the Court is dealing with the joint assets of working spouses, common sense and equity require that equality of interest should be adopted as a starting point. It is, however, only a starting point, and will yield to the requirements of all the circumstances of the case including the specific factors to which s. 25(2) requires regard. That is an unexceptionable approach.

Following the decision in *White*, would an appeal have even been contemplated? In this area, at least, law and common sense seem to be joining forces.

8.5.2 Substantial assets

Whatever the scale of the family's finances, in all cases the level of child support must, of course, be determined not by the court but by the Child Support Agency; s. 8(3) of the Child Support Act 1991 provides that in any case where the child support officer has jurisdiction under the Act, 'no court shall exercise any power which it would otherwise have to make, vary or revive any maintenance order in relation to the child and absent parent concerned'. However, in very wealthy cases s. 8(6) may come into effect, which provides that if the absent parent's income is above a certain level (determined by the formula), the court may nevertheless order the absent parent to make periodical payments for the child in addition to the maintenance assessment carried out by the Agency, if 'the court is satisfied that the circumstances of the case make it appropriate' for him to do so.

The so-called 'big money' cases are the ones where we feel most immediately the effects of the House of Lords' decision in *White v White* (see above, pp. 322–325). They include: *D v D (Lump Sum Order: Adjournment of Application)* [2001] 1 FLR 633; *N v N (Financial Provision: Sale of Company)* [2001] Fam Law 347; and *Dharamshi v Dharamshi* [2001] 1 FLR 736. We want to know, of course, to what extent the yardstick of equality may be stretchy; how special must be the circumstances for it to be departed from?

The Court of Appeal had the opportunity to tackle this in *Cowan v Cowan* [2001] EWCA Civ 679, [2002] Fam 97, [2001] 3 WLR 684, [2001] 2 FCR 331, [2001] 2 FLR 192. The headnote (at [2001] 2 FLR 192) sets out the facts, and the problem, as follows:

The husband and wife married in 1959 and had two sons, born in 1959 and 1963. During the marriage the husband worked hard and used his entrepreneurial flair and drive to build up an extremely successful business. The wife had initially contributed to the business though the degree of her contribution was disputed. Her involvement ceased in the mid or early 1970s. In 1992, the wife filed a divorce petition, although it was not served until six years later. The parties separated in 1994, and the wife remained in the matrimonial home. Following the separation the husband paid the wife a monthly allowance of £6,600, increased to £8,900 in September 1995 when the wife acquired a flat in Florida for her use as a winter home. Thereafter the husband experienced some difficulties, both with the Inland Revenue and with his business, and reduced the wife's monthly allowance to £5,000, which led to service of the divorce petition and an application for ancillary relief. At the hearing in July 2000 total net assets were greater than £11.5 million and it was submitted that the wife was entitled to an equal share of those assets, all of which had been acquired during the course of a 35 year marriage throughout which the wife had been an unstinting contributor. The judge gave significant weight to the length of the marriage and to the balance of the contributions made by each spouse during the marriage. He found that the wife's contribution was not insignificant but that it was not as significant as the husband's contribution, which consisted not only of hard work but of entrepreneurial skills, technical knowledge and inventiveness. He decided the matter on the basis of the wife's reasonable requirements and assessed the wife's income needs at £100,000 per annum net, which he capitalised by use of the Duxbury table at £1.58 million. To that he added £200,000 to enable the wife to discharge the mortgage on the Florida flat making a lump sum payment of £1.775 million. Together with her pension fund and other assets this elevated the wife's wealth to approximately £3.2 million. The wife applied for permission to appeal in August 2000. In November 2000 ... the wife applied to amend her notice of application to increase the lump sum sought from £2.7 million to £4.6 million. She submitted that the decision of the House of Lords [in *White*] fully vindicated the outcome of equality in division of assets for which she had unsuccessfully argued at the hearing.

This applicant, then, was unlike Mrs White because she had not (apart from the initial start-up) taken an active part in the business. That, according to Lord Nicholls' reasoning, should not disadvantage her. But Mr Cowan's argument was that his contribution was so outstanding – of 'stellar quality'! – as to justify departure from equality. The Court of Appeal was, at least in part, swayed by this. Mrs Cowan's lump sum was increased, to £3m, so that (taking the value of properties into account) she would have altogether about £4.4m, while Mr Cowan would have assets totalling over £7.1m. Thorpe LJ had this to say about the application of *White*:

[43] I accept [the] submission that the ratio of the judgments in White is that the judge's objective is not equality but fairness. ...

[52] ... But as Lord Nicholls emphasised fairness is a subjective standard. An appeal for fairness is an appeal to the heart as well as to the mind. Individual judges are likely to have widely differing responses to the appeal. In so far as there may be said to be 'a generally accepted standard of fairness' how is the individual judge to ascertain or perceive it? There can be no doubt that the specialist profession is looking to this court to suggest ways and means of applying the principles and guidance in Lord Nicholls' speech to present and future cases during their preparation or negotiation. What then can be said with confidence?

[53] The decision in White's case clearly does not introduce a rule of equality. The yardstick of equality is a cross check against discrimination. Fairness is the rule and in its pursuit the reasons for departure from equality will inevitably prove to be too legion and too varied to permit of listing or classification. They will range from the substantial to the faint but that range can be reflected in the percentage of departure. However it would seem to me undesirable for judges to be drawn into too much specificity, ascribing precise percentage points to the various and often counterbalancing reasons which the facts of individual cases render relevant.

[54] Furthermore the decision in White's case is directed to the abnormal case. In his introductory paragraph, Lord Nicholls said:

'This appeal raises questions about how the courts should exercise these powers in so-called "big money" cases, where the assets available exceed the parties' financial needs for housing and income.' (See [2000] 3 FCR 555 at 558, [2001] 1 All ER 1 at 4.)

[55] When recording the three features of the case he said:

'The available assets substantially exceeded the amounts required by Mr and Mrs White for their financial needs, in terms of a home and income for each of them. The general observations I make later should be read with this in mind.' (See [2000] 3 FCR 555 at 560, [2001] 1 All ER 1 at 6.)

[56] The present case is far more evidently a big money case. It is common ground that the assets in contention are almost three times the value of the assets of Mrs and Mrs White. Any consideration of the application of the principles in White to the sort of case that is decided daily by district judges up and down the country, and which may therefore be loosely described as average or normal, will no doubt arise and is better deferred to a case prepared and tried since October 2000.

[57] But even within the relatively narrow sphere of the big money case the infinite variety of facts and circumstances thrown up in individual cases makes it dangerous to generalise or to attempt to distil principles. It is clearly safer to apply the decision in White's case to the facts and circumstances of the present appeal. In so doing some guidance will emerge for the negotiation or decision of cases broadly similar on their facts or within which there is some clearly identifiable common ingredient.

[58] In summary therefore these seem to me to be the consequences of the House of Lords' recent review of the ancillary relief cases in this court. Approved is the frequent theme

of decisions in this court that the trial judge must apply such
Approved also is the almost inevitable judicial conclusion t
the exercise is to arrive at a fair solution. Disapproved is any
traditional role of the woman as home-maker and of the man i
the destination of family assets amongst the next generation. A
the result of equal division is a necessary cross-check against such
is any evaluation of outcome solely or even largely by reference to i
so far as the yardstick of reasonable requirements was a judicia
negotiators and judges respectively to predict and calculate cone
element of predictability and accordingly curtailed the width of the jud
by Parliament. Thus the prohibition on the future use of the tool exten
at the very moment when government policy has seemingly moved in
in harmony with international trends, academic and specialist commentaries and such research
as is available. Therein lies the heightened case for legislation. If that case was clear when
judges applied the yardstick of reasonable requirements measured in part by Duxbury tables,
it must be considerably clearer when the only yardstick is a subjective judicial perception of
fairness after a careful appraisal of the s 25 criteria.

Question

Did you read *White* as a widening of judicial discretion?

Thorpe LJ went on to describe the factors that weighed with him in assessing
Mrs Cowan's award. Among them was Mr Cowan's capacities:

[67] … in my opinion fairness certainly permits and in some cases requires recognition of
the product of the genius with which one only of the spouses may be endowed. Indeed Miss
Baron conceded the proposition, whilst contending that this husband was not in the category,
since she submitted that he was no more than a hard working businessman. That submission
does not seem to me to do justice to the husband's achievements, which clearly for their scale
depended upon his innovative visions as well as upon his ability to develop those visions. It is
a factor that in the present case deserves some recognition. I do not regard it as discrimination
by the back door. Whilst no doubt the husband's capacity to devote himself to the expansion
of the companies depended in part upon the stability and security of the home and family life
which the wife created and sustained, his creativity was not so dependent to the same or
perhaps to any degree.

Question

Does s. 25 need another re-write?

See also *S v S (Financial provision: Departing from equality)* [2001] 2 FLR 246,
a decision of Peter Collier QC, who pointed out that equality may be unfair
where the parties have different needs – in particular, where one and not the
other has a second family. Note that in both *White* and *Cowan* the courts were
looking at families without dependant children

Legislation may be a possibility. In 1998 the Green Paper, *Supporting families*,
suggested the amendment of the law on ancillary relief so as to provide for an
'overarching objective', namely that the court should 'Exercise its powers so as
to endeavour to do that which is fair and reasonable between the parties and
any child of the family' (para. 4.49). The suggestion in the paper was that after
meeting the needs of the family, any surplus would be divided 'so as to achieve
a fair result, recognising that fairness will generally require the value of the
assets to be divided equally between the parties'.

...at circumstances is equality not fair? You might like to return to this question when you have read the whole of section 5 of this chapter.

The UK has not yet ratified Protocol 7 of the European Convention on Human Rights, of which Art. 5 reads as follows:

Spouses shall enjoy equality of rights and responsibilities if a private law character between them, and in their relations with their children, as to marriage, during marriage, and in the event of its dissolution. This article shall not prevent states from taking such measures as are necessary in the interests of the children.

In *Cowan v Cowan*, it was argued on Mrs Cowan's behalf that this article pointed towards equality of division of property on divorce. Her argument was rejected (for a consideration of the possible impact of Art. 5 on ancillary relief, see Stewart Leech and Rachel Young, 'Marriage, Divorce and Ancillary Relief under the Human Rights Act 1998' (2001)). The Home Office's website tells us that the Protocol will be ratified 'when [the UK] has legislated to amend some provisions of family law that are incompatible with the rights in protocol 7' (see www.homeoffice.gov.uk.)

Question

Can you think which provisions might be incompatible?

8.5.3 Limited resources

Where the family as a whole has limited resources, it is unlikely that an application will come to trial; still less likely that the case will be reported. In many typical cases the family's only or main asset is the matrimonial home, and we consider later the way the courts deal with this.

In other cases, however, the applicant has limited resources but is seeking a share of his or (usually, still) her spouse's wealth. She may well need help with the cost of legal advice. Public funding is available, subject, as ever, to a means test. Where funding has been granted, we have to consider the application of the statutory charge. Here is an extract from the leaflet, *The Statutory Charge*, produced by the Legal Services Commission, explaining the operation of the charge:

In April 2000 the Legal Aid Board was replaced by the Legal Services Commission (LSC), which runs two schemes – the civil scheme for funding civil cases as part of the Community Legal Service, and a scheme for funding criminal cases, the Criminal Defence Service.

Where you gain or keep money or property with the help of public funding from the LSC in a civil case, you may have to repay all or some of your legal costs out of that property. In this way funding can act as a loan. The money you repay will be put towards what the LSC has spent on your case. This is known as the statutory charge.

It is important that you understand the statutory charge before your case begins. This leaflet should answer most of your questions, but if in doubt ask your lawyer or adviser.

How does the Statutory Charge work?
The money or property you get with the help of public funding will be used first to repay your legal costs to the Legal Services Commission and you will receive anything left over. For example, if you recovered £10,000 and the cost of your case was £2,000 you would have to

repay £2,000 to the Legal Services Commission and you would be left with £8,000. Your solicitor cannot pay money out to you until the statutory charge has been dealt with.

Does the Statutory Charge apply in every case?
No. The statutory charge does not apply in the following cases:
- If you do not gain or keep money or property that was in dispute.
- If you recover all your costs from the other side (if you recover some costs the statutory charge applies only to the difference).
- Maintenance payments.
- To the first £2,500 of any money/property you gain or keep in divorce cases and most other family proceedings.

...

When does the Statutory Charge have to be paid?
Normally the statutory charge must be paid as soon as the money or property comes through from the other side. Most payments must be made through your solicitor and cannot be made to you directly.

If you recover a home, or money to buy a home, it may be possible to delay payment of the charge. If so, the charge will be registered on the house (like a mortgage) in the full amount of the outstanding costs. Interest will be added. The rate of interest is set by Parliament and is currently 8% simple.

Can the Statutory Charge be reduced?
No. The Legal Services Commission cannot reduce the statutory charge.

Questions

(i) Do you think the matrimonial home should be freed from the statutory charge?
(ii) Do you think that the present system of the statutory charge places a fetter on the discretion of the judges in publicly funded cases? (Consider the effect of awarding a publicly funded applicant a lump sum of, say, £4,000.)

8.5.4 The length of the marriage

The duration of the marriage is one of the factors listed under s. 25(2) of the Matrimonial Causes Act 1973, and before *White*, at least, it was clear that the claimant following a short marriage would suffer something of a 'discount'. Examples include *Foley v Foley* [1981] Fam 160, [1981] 2 All ER 857, [1981] 3 WLR 284, 125 Sol Jo 442, CA; *H v H (Financial Provision; Short Marriage)* (1981) 2 FLR 392; *Attar v Attar (No 2)* [1985] FLR 653; and *Robertson v Robertson* (1982) 4 FLR 387. John Eekelaar's note on *Cowan*, 'Asset Distribution on Divorce – the Durational Element' (2001), questions the operation of *White* and takes a close look at how we value the short and the long marriage.

The problem [with *White* and *Cowan*] that, even though Lord Nicholls' principle requires the evaluation of each parties' contributions to start at the same baseline (homemaking is to rank equally with earning in the marketplace), it is still necessary to evaluate against each other the degree of effort or skill each spouse has put into those activities. It seems implausible that such an evaluation can be made, except in very extreme circumstances, and in any event the extent and type of evidence necessary make such a quest impracticable. The American Law Institute expressed the problem in the following way: 'the difficulty of measurement may make it sensible for the law to presume irrebuttably that the spouses contributed equally to their entire relationship, even though the presumption will sometimes be incorrect. To determine whether the presumption is correct in any particular case would require a retrospective examination of the parties' marital life that would be impractical if not impossible' (see *Principles of the Law of Family Dissolution: Analysis and Recommendations, Proposal Final Draft*, Part I, February 14, 1997, p. 198). ...

But once you allow such evaluations in, parties will try to make them. Even if you successfully keep them out, you need an alternative basis of making the allocation. What is it to be? It is suggested that a solution is possible within the ambit of the present statutory framework. For the reason why evaluation of contributions has loomed so large has been that there appears to be little alternative basis for allocation, other than an apparently mechanical presumption in favour of equality. But there is an alternative, and that lies in a careful analysis of the significance of the duration of the marriage. This is one of the considerations, alongside contributions, to which the Matrimonial Causes Act 1973 requires the court to have 'particular regard' (s. 25(2)(d)). Courts have generally referred to this factor when deciding that long-term maintenance would not be suitable for a young wife after a short marriage (*Frisby v. Frisby* (1983) 14 Fam Law 19). But its relevance to asset distribution has been obscured by the practice of looking first and foremost to assessing, and then providing for, the parties, 'reasonable requirements'. So in *Attar v Attar (No. 2)* [1985] FLR 653, a case concerning a six-month childless marriage (with seven weeks' cohabitation) between a woman (aged 27) of moderate means and a very wealthy husband worth at least £2 million, Booth J. was unconcerned to establish the husband's exact wealth, because she thought that the wife's reasonable requirements would be met by a sum (£20,000) sufficient to provide her with two years' maintenance. *Leadbeater v Leadbeater* [1985] FLR 789 concerned a second marriage for both parties lasting four years, at the end of which the husband had assets of £250,000, and the wife had assets of £80,000. Balcombe J. set about deciding the wife's reasonable requirements, which took into account her standard of living both before and after her marriage. Having considered, among other things, the size of house she should have, the cost of furnishing it and her income requirements, he decided she needed an extra £50,000. But at this point the shortness of the marriage kicked in. The judge discounted that £50,000 by 25 per cent, saying that 'like all these things, it is a somewhat arbitrary test'. This left the wife with (£80,000 + (0.75 x £50,000) = £117,500). While the judge no doubt did his best to weigh all the factors, this methodology is rather hard to defend. It is quite possible that a person's needs may be affected by the length of the marriage. But that is because factors such as time spent out of the labour market will reduce an individual's earning capacity. Those matters will be germane to calculating what a person's needs actually are. But, having made that calculation, it seems very odd to say that, because the marriage was a short one, they should only partially be met. That would be to make the shortness of the marriage count twice. The judge's approach could be defended, however, by saying that he sought to meet the parties' *reasonable requirements*, and matters such as contributions, conduct and length of marriage were subsumed into that concept. But this approach has now been disowned in *White*. 'Needs' are to replace 'reasonable requirements', and each factor considered separately. Now, in a case such as *Leadbeater*, the question will be whether an assessment of *needs* can be discounted on the ground of the shortness of the marriage. For reasons that will be explained below, it is submitted that this would be wrong in principle.

We need to consider one further case before addressing that principle. In *Page v Page* (1981) 2 FLR 198 at the end of a 41-year marriage the husband was left with £359,000 capital and the wife with capital of £29,000. Ormrod LJ rejected this 'arithmetical' approach and proceeded to the usual exercise of deciding, in the manner of someone dispensing charity, what were the needs of this 78 year-old woman, deliberately excluding her wish to provide for her children in her will. He settled on a lump sum of £90,000, giving her a total of £120,000, enough to meet her needs. It is true that this case has been disapproved of in *White* and in *Cowan* in so far as Ormrod LJ expressly ruled out treating the wife as having made any contribution towards the husband's business because she had not been 'actively engaged' in it. Nevertheless, the general strategy of seeking only to meet the wife's needs is exactly the same as that used in *Attar* and in *Leadbeater*. But while in the latter case a discount was made for the shortness of the marriage, there was no discount in *Page*. Nor, however, was there any premium to recognise the length of the marriage. The length of the marriage played no independent role. That explains the *Duxbury* paradox, well observed in *White*, whereby a wife of a long marriage can be awarded a smaller capital sum than the wife of a shorter one because her needs, which have to be met from the income, are less.

White, of course, indicated that the approach leading to the *Duxbury* paradox may be wrong. But how can you avoid it? The answer lies in a proper appreciation of the part played by marriage duration: the 'durational element'. The reason why it is wrong in principle to discount from the amount required to meet needs on the ground of shortness of the marriage is that such a discount is levied against the wrong thing. The length of marriage is relevant, *in and of itself* (as distinct from being an element of some other feature, such as extent of contributions) to the amount allocated because it is defensible to hold that parties who share their lives together *earn a share in one another's assets relative to the length of time they have shared their lives*. So the discount in *Leadbeater* should have been against the share which would have been built up had the marriage lasted longer, not against the significance that this was a 4-year marriage: after such a period, parties will surely have built up the maximum share possible against one another's assets. That is why the *Duxbury* rule is not so much a paradox but wrong. It confines the basis of the award to needs, ignoring the entitlement built up through the durational element. ...

But how should we deal with marriages of different lengths? ... The initial question will be: at what stage, and on what principle, should each party be held to have earned an equal share in the other's assets? What will be this 'target' period? The average, or the median, lengths of marriages of people who married at the same age as the couple in question might provide a guide. We could separate those marriages which end in divorce from those which end in death. Such information would be difficult to extract, but not impossible. But why should it be relevant? Is one to assume that parties should be held to have earned an equal share only at the point when most marriages in their age cohort are likely to end? If one looks only at marriages ending by death, a young couple would take many years to reach the target period, and an elderly couple would reach it much quicker. There seems no reason which could justify that. If one looks only at those marriages which end in divorce, the matter is not improved. People marrying young tend to divorce quicker than those who marry when older. But it is unlikely that we would think that, for that reason, they should reach equality quicker.

In considering the durational element we should remember here the linkage between marriage and family. We should not forget that most disputes here are between *parents*. About 85 per cent of children are born to parents who are either married to one another or are living at the same address. ... So parental partnerships are still the major contexts into which children are born and, to a large extent, raised. While this is not the only social purples why adults cohabit, it is clearly a very significant one. One might therefore take the time necessary for raising a child as a yardstick by which to measure the minimal period of parental collaboration necessary to achieve the core aim of (most) adult partnerships. By the time that period is over, one might say that the adults have achieved, through their joint efforts, the primary social task of the partnership. They should therefore by that time have earned an equal share in each other's assets. Of course some will raise more children, but that just extends the task they set themselves, and which was first achieved (thought not, for them, completed) when the first child became independent. The period suggested by this analysis would be about 20 or 25 years of actual cohabitation. For couples who do not have children the rationale does not of course apply. Nevertheless, it can be used as a proxy for deciding the appropriate durational element in their case. Notice that this does not apply a general presumption of equality from the mere fact of marriage. It provides a principled reason why, in some cases, equal sharing should apply. But, equally, it is not the *only* element in the award. For example, as a matter of principle, one or the other party's needs, or the needs of the children, would provide grounds for one to receive an enhanced share or to make a reduced transfer. Length of marriage (or actual cohabitation) should be seen as establishing a baseline, which can be departed from if some other factor becomes sufficiently compelling.

If the target period is 20 years, the 'durational factor' (the rate by which the spouses earn a share in each other's property) would be 2.5 per cent per year. Claims before, say, two or three years of cohabitation had passed might be excluded so as to avoid having to make small adjustments in very short relationships. Following this method, no claim would have been allowed for the durational element in *Attar*. The durational element would have yielded Mrs Leadbeater only (0.1 x £170,000 = £17,000), giving her a total of £97,000, £20,500 less than she actually received. It would not, in the light of *White*, be open for the wife to argue that her 'reasonable requirements' entitled her to an enhanced share. She would need to put her claim on a 'needs' basis. But since her needs would be likely to be met out of the award to which she was entitled through the durational element, she should get no more. People might judge for themselves whether they think the outcome indicated here is more defensible that the one attained in the case itself. ...

And it also should be emphasised that the durational element remains, under section 25, only one of the factors to be taken into account. It would be quite proper for courts to give guidance as to how it should be weighed against other factors. It has already been stated that 'needs' would normally override it. There would still be a role for contributions, as required by the statutory framework, but it is suggested that these would have a much reduced role since the durational element largely replaces them. The courts could bring this reduction about in much the same way as they have diminished (but not removed) the relevance of 'matrimonial' misconduct. How, then, would *White* and *Cowan* be decided under the suggested approach? Both marriages lasted over 20 years, so the assumption would be that the spouses had earned an equal share in each other's property. Mrs White's assets were £1.57 million, and Mr White's were £3.12 million (these assets including their half shares in jointly owned property). She would have received half of the difference: *i.e.* £775,000, leaving each with £2.34 million. In fact she was left with no change in her capital position, the Court of Appeal increasing the trial judge's award of £800,000 to £1.5 million, and the House of Lords retaining it. In *Cowan* the wife was awarded £3 million from total available assets of £11.5 million, although the couple had lived together for 37 years. A substantial reason for giving the husband more than the wife was the recognition it was thought necessary to give to his 'innovative visions [and] his ability to develop those visions'. Although the length of the marriage was referred to, especially by Mance LJ, this factor was given little independent attention. Had this been done, it would have provided a substantial reason for equal division. It would then have been necessary to consider whether this reason for equal division was stronger than the reason given (the husband's business talents) for justifying departure from it. This will inevitably be a somewhat subjective matter, but, given that the marriage lasted well beyond a possible 'target' period of 20 years, it is suggested that it fell well short of doing so. One could imagine rare cases where the nature of the spouses' respective contributions were so out of balance that they should affect the outcome: perhaps the effect of exceptional artistic creativity. But innovation goes with successful business practice. It is one among many talents. But whatever one's views on this issue, it is submitted that it lies within the powers of the courts to restructure the manner in which the discretion is exercised in a principled way. Should they choose to do so, the approach outlined above is one option before them.

Questions

(i) If Eekelaar's suggestion is right in principle, do you agree with him as to the length of time it takes to achieve equality?

(ii) As things stand, the court's response to a short marriage may be to order periodical payments for a limited period to enable the financially weaker party to adjust and to get back on her feet. What should happen if she fails to get back on her feet during that period? (See *Richardson v Richardson* [1994] 1 FLR 286.)

8.5.5 Conduct

You will recall that s. 25(2)(*g*) of the Matrimonial Causes Act 1973 states that the court shall have regard to the conduct of each of the parties if that conduct is such that it would in the opinion of the court be inequitable to disregard it. Lord Denning MR, in *Wachtel v Wachtel* [1973] Fam 72, [1973] 1 All ER 829 (p. 322, above), used the phrase 'obvious and gross' when describing that conduct which would justify the court in departing from the then statutory objective. Sir George Baker P, in *W v W* [1976] Fam 107, [1975] 3 All ER 970, said that he would be entitled to take account of conduct in a case which would cause an ordinary mortal to throw up his hands and say 'surely that woman is not going to be given any money!' The problem with a definition such as that is that 'ordinary mortals' *are* ordinary mortals, and might be tempted to throw up their hands in cases where the judges would consider that some financial provision was appropriate. Consider some of the 'folk myths' identified by the authors of *Simple Quarrels* (p. 316, above).

Examples of cases where the ordinary mortal would throw up his hands include *Kyte v Kyte* [1988] Fam 145, [1987] 3 All ER 1041, [1987] 3 WLR 1114, [1988] FCR 325, [1988] 1 FLR 469, CA, where the wife helped her husband commit suicide so that she could inherit his estate and go to live with her lover; her lump sum award was reduced on appeal from £14,000 to £5,000. Perhaps the most conspicuous of recent cases is *Clark v Clark*.

Clark v Clark
[1999] 3 FCR 49, [1999] 2 FLR 498, [1999] Fam Law 533, Court of Appeal

Mr Clark was born in 1913, whilst Mrs Clark was born in 1949. Mr Clark had had a successful career as an insurance broker and, although retired, continued to work actively as a consultant.

Mrs Clark had not worked for some years, having developed phobias which had led her to live off capital since about 1984. Mr Clark was a rich man. Amongst other things he had about £2m on the stock exchange, about £1m on deposit and a home that was worth about £0.5m. By contrast, Mrs Clark's financial circumstances were desperate. Her home, which was worth about £170,000, was heavily mortgaged and overall her liabilities exceeded her assets.

...

On 17 February 1992 he purchased Thatch Cottage in Romsey for £195,000 and rapidly spent a further £85,000 on its embellishment. He agreed to a transfer into joint names. He discharged Mrs Clark's debts. Two letters that he wrote on 17 February 1992 referred to 'my thrill and privilege to have helped you see your enemies off.' One of those letters expressed his gratitude at her agreement to marry on 16 April 1992. In fact the ceremony took place on 7 April 1992.

...

The wedding day was not auspicious. The wife left at the start of the small reception. When she returned later she did not permit the consummation of the marriage. The next day she left and did not thereafter permit cohabitation. On 19 June 1992 the husband presented a nullity petition, which was subsequently dismissed by consent on 5 October 1992. Although that reconciliation did not herald cohabitation, it did signal a good deal of expenditure. The husband spent £146,000 redeeming the mortgage on the wife's own home. At his wife's prompting he purchased three London flats. It was his understanding that one of them would be for their use. At about the same time the wife's home was sold. Although the husband received almost all the proceeds of sale, they fell short of what the husband had paid to settle the wife's debts to the extent of approximately £30,000. For the following 18 months the wife lived at Thatch Cottage refusing to join the husband in Highgate, even when he was unwell. She barely tolerated his weekend visits to Thatch Cottage. Only once did she admit him to her bedroom. The marriage was in fact never consummated. Before long she relegated him to a caravan in the garden.

...

In July 1994 the wife induced the husband to purchase another property in Romsey, named Wellow Park.

On the day following completion the wife induced the husband to spend £28,500 on the purchase of a shop at Winchester Street in Romsey which she said would be business premises for her son, then a 19-year-old student. To partly finance these acquisitions, the husband sold his Highgate home and the wife arranged for him to stay at a geriatric nursing home. Meanwhile, she embarked on substantial expenditure on Wellow Park despite her assurances prior to purchase that it did not need money spending on it. The extent of that expenditure was assessed by the judge at £100,000. The wife's immediate object was to divide the property into two unequal parts. She intended the husband to live in the smaller part which was separated from her part of the house by connecting doors on the ground floor and first floor, with locks only on her side.

There followed further expensive property acquisitions for the wife, while the husband was virtually imprisoned in his part of the property. In 1997 he attempted suicide, and spent a short time in a psychiatric hospital. Not long after his return home, as Thorpe LJ put it:

the husband's niece and nephew removed him from Wellow Park with the assistance of the police. A petition for divorce was filed almost immediately and ancillary relief proceedings got under way. Thus ended one of the most extraordinary marital histories that I have ever encountered.

The judge at first instance awarded Mrs Clark £552,500. This was reduced on appeal to £175,000, to include the value of properties she retained.

Question

Why should Mrs Clark have received anything at all?

A different approach was taken in the next case:

A v A (Financial Provision: Conduct)
[1995] 2 FCR 137, [1995] 1 FLR 345

The parties in this case were married in 1968 and divorced in 1992; they had three children, daughters aged over 21 and 18, and a son of 14. At the time of the financial provision application the matrimonial home was worth about £52,000, and was not subject to a mortgage, so that it would be worth about £50,000 after deducting the cost of sale. At the time of the marriage the husband was a carpenter and the wife a civil servant, but when their son was about 10 she decided to retrain as a teacher. Thorpe J described the husband's reaction:

Prior to that development the husband had no relevant medical history and his reaction to the wife's ambition was therefore peculiarly extreme. He became depressed and suicidal, a state which continues unalleviated by continuing medical supervision. During the course of the last 3 years he has made approximately 12 suicide attempts. More seriously on 4 September 1991, after an absence from the home of some months, he appeared at the door of a neighbour's house which the wife and the son were visiting. Although offered no provocation, he advanced on the wife and struck her a forceful blow on the chest with a kitchen knife. Fortunately he was overpowered by the neighbour, who disarmed him. He ran off and attempted suicide on a nearby railway line. The physical damage sustained to both the husband and the wife on that day proved to be relatively trivial. The knife inflicted a surface wound at the top of the wife's left breast which was only a quarter of an inch deep and which required no treatment other than cleansing. She was left with a minimal scar. The husband suffered severe bruising after being struck by a train. Criminal proceedings followed. The husband was charged with unlawful wounding and, after conviction at the Crown Court, received a sentence of 18 months' imprisonment suspended for 2 years and subject to probation. It seems that for a time he moved to the Midlands and then returned to the West Country. He now lives in the West Country and receives supplementary benefit. ... Since this extremely frightening episode on 4 September 1991 neither the wife nor the son has received any further molestation, although there was an incident in the district judge's chambers when the husband exploded and left the room leaving a piece of paper on which he had written, 'I will fight on. I will kill'.

At first instance, the district judge made an order settling the husband's half share in the property upon the children; the wife now appealed. Thorpe J explained why this order was incorrect, and substituted a different arrangement:

I reject his discretionary conclusion for three reasons:
(1) There is no doubt that he over-estimated the significance and effect of the disgraceful episode of 4 September 1991. I agree that it constitutes conduct which it would be inequitable to disregard not only as an incident of aggravated violence but also in its long-standing effects on both the wife and the children, particularly the son. But it is only one of the factors to be reflected in the s. 25 exercise and it is not one which in my judgment should drive the court to conclude that the husband must be deprived of his entire capital. ...
(2) He seems not to have considered the wife's claim or potential claim to the Criminal Injuries Compensation Board. ...
(3) The application of capital from a spouse to children is not a permissible objective of the statutory powers. It may have been intended as a sop to the husband but as a matter of principle, it cannot be supported.
What discretion should I then exercise? For my part the starting-point is the joint entitlement to the property at the net value of £50,000. But that starting-point needs to be adjusted to reflect the combination of conduct, responsibility, needs and contribution. The wife has the overall responsibility for the care and upbringing of the children until they reach independence. ... The extent of that responsibility and contribution is exacerbated by the husband's conduct. However, his responsibility for that conduct may be attributed in part to his uncontrollable psychological state. Applying all these considerations, I would reduce his proprietary entitlement from a half to a third and would unhesitatingly say that its realisation must be deferred until the wife has completed the responsibility for the children, particularly the responsibility to provide them with a secure home. ... But ... it would be unwise to perpetuate a financial relationship between the husband and the wife over the course of years to come. If ever there was a case in which it was desirable for both the husband and the wife that the order be clear and final, it is

this. ... I come to the conclusion that, in substitution for the district judge's provision that the wife enter into a settlement of one-third of the property on the children, the order to transfer by the husband to the wife of all his share in the former matrimonial home be balanced by a lump sum payment of £15,000. A date for the payment of that lump sum need not be specified. There will be liberty to both parties to apply as to the date of payment. There are a number of possible sources from which the lump sum might be discharged, namely proceeds of sale, the wife's borrowing capacity and the wife's prospective award from the Criminal Injuries Compensation Board. ... It is in the interests of both that it should be paid sooner rather than later. But in view of the wife's responsibilities and the uncertainty of her resources, it would be wrong to impose any time for payment today.

Questions

(i)   Do you suppose that a different order would have been made if the husband's psychiatric disorder had been more serious and consequently his conduct more violent?

(ii)   Why is it regarded as incorrect to settle property on children in these circumstances? (Compare the approach to property adjustment orders under the Children Act 1989, p. 199, above.)

The term 'financial misconduct' may relate to the dissipation or mismanagement of assets during or after the marriage, or to failure to disclose assets or other improper behaviour during the ancillary relief proceedings. The following cases show two contrasting approaches:

Beach v Beach
[1995] 2 FCR 526, [1995] 2 FLR 160

The background is given by Thorpe J:

This ... is an unusual and a sad case, and its conclusion depends very much on findings of fact and upon the assessment of the evidence of the parties.

The husband is 53 and the wife is 51. Throughout, the husband was a dairy farmer, his principal unit being the farm at Selborne in Hampshire. He acquired the farm in 1969 and at that date his first wife acquired a proprietary interest in some proportion. When that marriage was dissolved in 1979, it was agreed that she should receive the sum of £100,000 in settlement of that share. There were two children of that marriage. The wife also had a previous marriage by which she had one son.

The marriage between these parties was celebrated on 21 October 1980 and an arrangement was worked out whereby the wife should step into the proprietary shoes of the former wife, providing the consideration of £100,000 from the proceeds of sale of her home.

The entitlement of the former wife was not the only burden on the farm and the business. It had been incurring losses and there were secured creditors for liabilities in the region of £300,000. The arrangement between the parties at marriage was that if the wife were to invest her capital in the venture she should be entitled to repayment by sale if the trade had not been turned into profit within a period of 3 years.

Unfortunately, the farm business went from bad to worse. This was largely due to the husband's irrational optimism and tendency to spending sprees. In addition, in 1983 the dairy herd was struck by a plague of leptospirosis. Mr Beach blamed this on the veterinary profession, and embarked upon a course of disastrous litigation, from which he emerged in 1989 without recovering damages, and liable for his own and his opponent's costs of £180,000. In February 1990 the husband and wife entered into an agreement, after legal advice on both sides, that the farm would be sold and that she would receive, on sale on or before 29 September 1990, £450,000 in respect of her interest in it. But the farm was not sold within that period, due to the husband's continued refusal to co-operate in a sale and his insistence that he would be able to continue running the farm. He was declared bankrupt in December 1990. The farm was sold by the trustee in bankruptcy. The wife, as a secured creditor, received about £412,000 on account of her interest and was still owed about £44,000 at the time of the husband's application for a lump sum. Thorpe J summarised the arguments on both sides:

The present position of the parties is that the husband resides with his parents. He is on income support. ... The wife's position contrasts strongly. With the money received from the sale of the commercial property, together with the money received from the trustee, she has assets of about £820,000. ...

The case for the husband is opened by Mr. Moor, who says that all the history is irrelevant to the decision that I have to take. The agreement of 20 February 1990 is an agreement that I am not bound to uphold. The principles contained in the judgment of Ormrod LJ in the root case of *Edgar v Edgar* (1980) 2 FLR 19 allow me to make proper provision for the husband. In particular, he says that the February 1990 agreement should be disregarded because of:

   (1) pressure on the husband;

   (2) change of circumstances; and

   (3) gross disparity.

He says that I should simply do the s. 25 exercise upon the parties' positions as they now are, and that a fair, discretionary decision would give his client a lump sum of £270,000, being a third of the wife's capital.

Inevitably Miss Ralphs for the wife places the greatest stress on the history. She emphasises the agreement of 20 February 1990, freely entered into on independent advice. It is not asserted that that advice was bad or unsatisfactory, and the agreement protects the wife from any claim since she has not yet received her entitlement under its terms.

Alternatively, if this is a case to be assessed on the s. 25 criteria, it is a case of manifest financial misconduct and in the exercise of discretion the application for lump sum should be dismissed: the husband has nobody but himself to blame for his present circumstances.

Thorpe J had this to say about the 1990 agreement:

Against those findings, what is the fair conclusion? I do not regard this as being an *Edgar* case in simple classification. The classic *Edgar* case contains a litigant who seeks to depart unreasonably or capriciously from a fairly negotiated formal settlement. Here, in February 1990 both the husband and the wife concede that the net proceeds of sale left to the husband after paying the wife £450,000 would be some greater sum. Here I am not concerned with a contracting party who wilfully or capriciously seeks to depart from a formal agreement, freely negotiated. Here I contemplate circumstances which are totally different from the circumstances contemplated by the contracting parties. ... My conclusion, therefore, is that although the agreement of 20 February 1990 is of importance, it is only of importance as part of the developing history. My essential duty is to determine this application upon the criteria contained in s. 25, as amended.

After considering the s. 25 factors, Thorpe J concluded:

... the crux of the case is really the responsibility for the present near-destitution of the husband. How has this come about? Who is responsible for this state of affairs? Is it the product of the husband's misconduct?

I have already recorded the developments and find the history as the wife presents it. I utterly reject Mr. Moor's submission that this history is irrelevant to the outcome of this case. I think Miss Ralphs is fully entitled to suggest that the husband's conduct amounted to conduct which it would be inequitable to disregard.

He obstinately, unrealistically and selfishly trailed on to eventual disaster, dissipating in the process not only his money but his family's money, his friends' money, the money of commercial creditors unsecured and eventually his wife's money, insofar as the disaster that eventually developed did not even pay for her specified agreed sum. It would have been in her interest, it would have been in his interest, had she forced him into accepting a properly marketed sale in the 1980s. She cannot be blamed for having failed to achieve that result. She secured formal agreement, she obtained orders in Chancery. But I can understand how difficult it must have been for her, living under the same roof with somebody so deluded. The responsibility is, in my judgment, not shared, not hers, but his.

So, on one view, why should he have anything when she has not even had what should have been her due under the freely negotiated contract? My first impression was to dismiss this claim as Miss Ralphs invited me to do. However, on further reflection I have concluded that the disparity between the present position of the husband and the wife is so great that that would not be a fair application of the s. 25 criteria. ...

I have reached the conclusion that the sum that would enable him to obtain some basic accommodation without at the same time removing from the wife the return of her basic financial contribution is £60,000, and I order the wife to pay the husband a lump sum in that amount within 28 days.

T v T (Interception of Documents)
[1995] 2 FCR 745, [1994] 2 FLR 1083, [1995] Fam Law 15

In this case the wife anticipated – correctly, as it turned out – that the husband would not give full disclosure of his assets during the financial provision proceedings. She therefore engaged in some detective work of her own, and the husband retaliated in kind, intercepting her mail and at one point breaking into her premises and removing a large number of documents. He now claimed that her conduct was such that it would be inequitable to disregard it. Wilson J's decision was as follows:

[Counsel for the wife] implied that, since each party had behaved similarly in relation to the other's documents, the issue was of little moment. I cannot accept his submission: although I cannot condone the husband's actions ... they were the result of acute provocation and I do not propose further to consider them.

The first question, which is not straightforward, is to what extent the wife's activities in relation to documents were reprehensible. The fact is that the husband had not made a full and frank presentation to the court of his financial resources and that a few of the documents taken by the wife (or, like the diaries, scrutinised by her and then called for) have enabled this to be made clear. The wife anticipated – and I find that she reasonably anticipated – at the outset of the litigation that the husband would seek to reduce the level of her award by understating his resources in breach of his duty to the court. On balance, I consider that in those circumstances it was reasonable for the wife to take photocopies of such of the husband's documents as she could locate without the use of force and, for that matter, to scour the dustbin. But the wife went far beyond that. She:

(a) used force to obtain documents;
(b) intercepted the husband's mail; and
(c) kept original documents.

The timing of the wife's production of some of the documents through the solicitors is also unacceptable. The original and copy documents which she had taken were discoverable documents and all those that she had in her possession at the discovery stage of the litigation should have been disclosed at that time, i.e. at the time of the delivery of her questionnaire, or earlier upon request. Those coming into her possession at a later stage should have been disclosed forthwith. Instead the wife suppressed her possession of some of the documents for many months, producing one or two of them piecemeal and then a substantial number, like a rabbit from a hat, just prior to the hearing.

The next question is whether the reprehensible activities of the wife in relation to documents amount to relevant 'conduct' or to a relevant 'circumstance' within the subsections. I appreciate that it has been held that a spouse's behaviour in the ancillary litigation, specifically a dishonest failure to make full disclosure, amounts to such conduct: *Desai v Desai* (1982) 13 Fam Law 46 and *B v B (Real Property: Assessment of Interests)* [1988] 2 FLR 490. But I agree with Thorpe J in *P v P (Financial Relief: Non-Disclosure)* [1994] 2 FLR 381 at p.392F-H that a dishonest disclosure will more appropriately be reflected in the inference that the resources are larger than have been disclosed (in which case it will fall within s. 25(2)(a)) and/or in the order for costs; indeed that is how I intend to approach the husband's disclosure in this case. I am also firmly of the view that the wife's activities in relation to documents should not be brought into my reckoning of the substantive award, whether as conduct or as a circumstance, but should prima facie have some relevance in respect of costs. The extent of their relevance will depend on the potency of other factors. Although the wife's activities may not have caused significant increase in the costs, the court's discretion is wide enough to permit their inclusion in its survey of the litigation.

Question

Do you now have a clear idea of what constitutes conduct which it would be 'inequitable to disregard', and of the effects of not disregarding it?

8.5.6 Housing

Jackson and her colleagues, in 'Financial Support on Divorce: the Right Mixture of Rules and Discretion?' (1993), describe the reasoning process of English solicitors when dealing with financial provision on divorce as follows:

The solicitors' first question was always directed at the needs of the two households. And since the interviewer was explicitly asking about the advice that would be given to a divorcing mother who would be seeking to retain custody, the highest priority was the needs of the first family. Indeed, it was their access to housing which was the primary concern; as one solicitor said 'I want to know how much the custodial parent needs to keep a home going'. Here, questions relating to the home will be separated from those concerning division of income. The home will be dealt with first, since it became clear, as in Scotland, that this is the order in which solicitors approach financial issues on divorce. Once a decision has been taken on the home, other resources and needs are assessed, but this secondary decision-making process is necessarily shaped by the prior resolution of the housing issue.

It will have been apparent from the cases already discussed that one of the most significant problems concerns what is to be done with the matrimonial home. In this section we consider the different legal forms that the solution to that problem may take. There are a number of options available to the court. First, the court may decide to allow the husband to retain an interest in the matrimonial home even though the former wife remains in the home with the children. It may be considered appropriate for the sale of the home to be postponed until the youngest child has completed his or her education

Mesher v Mesher and Hall
(1973) [1980] 1 All ER 126n, Court of Appeal

The marriage took place in 1956 and the one child of the marriage (aged 9) lived with the mother. The house was in joint names. The judge ordered that the house be transferred to the wife, and the husband appealed.

Davies LJ: ... Counsel for the husband submits that it would be quite wrong to deprive the husband of the substantial asset which his half-interest in the house represents ..., one has to take a broad approach to the whole case. What is wanted here is to see that the wife and daughter, together no doubt in the near future with Mr Jones [whom the wife intended to marry], should have a home in which to live rather than that she should have a large sum of available capital. With that end in view, I have come to the conclusion that counsel's submission for the husband is right. It would, in my judgment, be wrong to strip the husband entirely of any interest in the house. I would set aside the judge's order so far as concerns the house and substitute instead an order that the house is held by the parties in equal shares on trust for sale but that it is not to be sold until the child of the marriage reaches a specified age or with the leave of the court.

Harvey v Harvey
[1982] Fam 83, [1982] 1 All ER 693, [1982] 2 WLR 283, 126 Sol Jo 15, Court of Appeal

The parties were married in 1960. They had six children. The marriage broke down in 1979 and it was dissolved in May 1981. The judge made an order in the form used in *Mesher v Mesher,* namely that the home should be held in joint names of husband and wife on trust for sale in equal shares and that the sale of the property should be postponed until the youngest child attained 16 or completed her full-time education, whichever was later, when the wife should be at liberty to purchase the husband's share in the property at a valuation then made. The wife appealed.

Purchas J: ... I am of the opinion that the wife is entitled to live in this house as long as she chooses so to do, ... I do that on the basis that was adopted in *Martin v Martin* [1978] Fam 12, [1977] 3 All ER 762, that, had the marriage not broken down, that is precisely what she would have been entitled to do.

I would vary the judge's order, first of all to say that the asset (the matrimonial home) be transferred into the joint names of the wife and the husband on trust for sale in the shares two-thirds to the wife and one-third to the husband; and further that such sale shall be postponed during the lifetime of the wife, or her remarriage, or voluntary removal from the premises, or her becoming dependent on another man. I have in mind that if she begins to cohabit with another man in the premises, then obviously that man ought to take over the responsibility of providing accommodation for her. Until one or other of those events occur, she should be entitled to continue to reside at these premises, but after the mortgage has been paid off, or the youngest child has reached the aged of 18, whichever is the later, she should pay an occupation rent to be assessed by the [district judge].

Ormrod LJ: I agree. This is another case which illustrates very aptly the proposition which has been stated many times in this court, that the effect of making a *Mesher v Mesher* order is simply to postpone the evil day to avoid facing the facts now.

Questions

(i) Are you attracted by this solution? In *Carson v Carson* [1983] 1 All ER 478, [1983] 1 WLR 285, Ormrod LJ said that the facts of that case, where the judge had made the type of order in *Mesher v Mesher,* were 'a very good example of the chickens coming home to roost'. What exactly does he mean?

(ii) Why should a new man take over responsibility of providing accommodation for an ex-wife remaining in the former matrimonial home?

(iii) Assume the ex-wife is disabled and unable to contemplate moving out of a purpose built bungalow which is the former matrimonial home There are no children. Is her disability a sufficient reason by itself to transfer the matrimonial home into her name alone? (Read *Chadwick v Chadwick* [1985] FLR 606, [1985] Fam Law 96, CA.) What if the former spouse is terminally ill? (Consider *M v M (Property Adjustment: Impaired Life Expectancy)* [1993] Fam Law 521.)

In contrast, the court may decide not to postpone sale but rather to transfer title to the wife absolutely (*Hanlon v Law Society* [1981] AC 124). The husband may be ordered to continue to pay the mortgage. Or the wife may be ordered to pay a lump sum to the husband; in effect to buy him out. The deciding factor in determining whether to postpone sale or to transfer ownership is often whether the court considers that the husband cannot or will not pay periodical payments. However, the court is bound to think hard before it deprives the husband of the only real capital asset he has; and it will think even harder now that the Child Support Act 1991 may in the future deprive him of more of his income than can be envisaged at present (see Chapter 4, above).

Comparative merits of *Mesher* orders, *Harvey* orders (or *Martin* orders as they are generally known) and orders transferring the home absolutely are discussed in the following case:

Clutton v Clutton

[1991] 1 All ER 340, [1991] 1 WLR 359, Court of Appeal

The parties, who were married in 1964, had two children, now aged 23 and 16. In 1970 the husband bought the matrimonial home in his sole name for about £4,500, subject to a small mortgage. The parties separated in 1984 and a decree absolute dissolving the marriage was granted in 1985. The husband remarried in that year. In 1984 the wife had applied for ancillary relief, seeking transfer of the matrimonial home into her sole name or at least an order that she be allowed to remain there with the children and be not required to sell the house until death or remarriage 'or such order as the court shall think fit.' The district judge made an order transferring the house to the wife, subject to a charge in the husband's favour for £7,000, not to be enforced until 1 January 1991. In addition he awarded the wife maintenance of £10 per week, arrears of maintenance and maintenance of £25 per week for the younger child. On appeal by the husband the judge was told that the matrimonial home was the sole capital asset of the parties, the equity being worth £50,000; that the husband, whose debts amounted to £17,000, had a net disposable income, taking account of debt repayments, of £127 per week, while his second wife ran a small business which brought in £2,000 per annum; and that the wife, who had a stable sexual relationship with another man but had declared her intention of not remarrying or cohabiting, earned £66 per week from part-time work. The judge held that it was a clear case for a 'clean break' and ordered that the charge over the matrimonial home in the husband's favour should be set aside and that the husband should pay maintenance of £25 per week for the younger child until the end of the July following her sixteenth birthday so long as she remained in full-time education. He made no order for payments of maintenance to the wife. The judge refused the husband's application for leave to appeal against the order transferring the matrimonial home to the wife absolutely.

Lloyd LJ: An order whereby the sale of the matrimonial home is postponed until the youngest child of the family is 18, or some other age, is usually known as a *Mesher* order: see *Mesher v Mesher and Hall* [1980] 1 All ER 126n. An order whereby the sale is postponed until the wife dies, remarries or cohabits with another man, is usually known as a *Martin* order: see *Martin (BH) v Martin (D)* [1978] Fam 12. It will be seen that while, in 1984, the wife was asking for an out-and-out transfer of the matrimonial home, she would have been content, in the alternative, with a *Martin* order.

The principle of the clean break was, of course, well established long before the Matrimonial and Family Proceedings Act 1984: see for example *Minton v Minton* [1979] AC 593, *per* Viscount Dilhorne, at p.601, and *per* Lord Scarman, at p.608. It is now enshrined in section 25A(1) of the Matrimonial Causes Act 1973 by virtue of section 3 of the Act of 1984. But there is perhaps a danger in referring to it as a 'principle', since it might lead courts to strive for a clean break, regardless of all other considerations. This is not what section 25A requires. It requires the court to consider the appropriateness of a clean break, neither more nor less. It is salutary to remind oneself from time to time of the language of section 25A(1):

> 'it shall be the duty of the court to consider whether it would be appropriate so to exercise those powers that the financial obligations of each party towards the other will be terminated as soon after the grant of the decree as the court considers just and reasonable.'

Another danger is that 'clean break' may mean different things to different people. In origin it referred to an agreement whereby the wife abandoned her right to claim maintenance in return for a transfer by the husband of a capital asset, usually, though not always, the matrimonial home, thus encouraging the parties to put the past behind them, and, in the words of Lord Scarman in *Minton v Minton,* at p.608, 'to begin a new life which is not overshadowed by the relationship which was broken down.'

...

Where the judge went wrong, and plainly wrong in my opinion, was in refusing to make a *Martin* order. As I have pointed out, this is what the wife was originally content to accept.

It is also what the husband was asking for. Why then did the judge not make a *Martin* order? We cannot tell, because we do not know his reasons. It cannot surely have been because a *Martin* order would offend against the principle of the clean break. A charge which does not take effect until death or remarriage could only be said to offend against the principle of the clean break in the most extended sense of that term. The only clue we have is the argument on behalf of the wife that she did not want to be spied on.

I see some force in that argument, although it was scarcely pressed before us. Indeed it was not mentioned at all until it was raised by the court. Whatever the force of the argument, it is far outweighed by the resentment which the husband will naturally feel if the wife remarries within a year or two and continues thereafter to occupy the matrimonial home. She says she has no intention of marrying Mr. Davidson. But it remains a distinct possibility. In *Leate v Leate* (1982) 12 Fam Law 121 Ormrod LJ recognised that it is 'very galling' for a husband if the family assets are handed over to the wife, who then remarries. He said:

'Some provision as to the wife's remarriage was reasonable and there ought to be a charge enforceable by the husband in the event of her death or remarriage.'

In *Simpson v Simpson* (16 March 1984, unreported), Court of Appeal (Civil Division) Transcript No. 119 of 1984, Lincoln J, giving the first judgment of the Court of Appeal, said:

'Such then was her intention. On that evidence the judge was entitled to conclude that on the balance of probability she did not then intend to and might never marry Mr. Cook, and that he was no more than a man friend employing her at £25 a week as his secretary and helping with petrol for the car and its insurance. But the matter does not stop there. Such a finding, if it had been expressly made, would not be inconsistent with a further finding that there was still a real possibility that she might marry him. She accepts that her feelings for him have deepened recently, she had been considering marriage with him and his relationship with her was clearly a close one. In the circumstances her intention, though truly and genuinely described today as negative, could change with the passage of time. If it did and if the present order for an out-and-out transfer remained, then the wife would be joined in her occupation at the matrimonial home by her second husband or cohabitee, the latter having contributed nothing to its original acquisition, and meanwhile the husband would have lost his half interest. I agree with the husband's contention that this would scarcely appear to be a just and fair solution. A trust for sale in which the power of sale becomes exerciseable on remarriage or permanent cohabitation would remedy that unfairness. An out-and-out order by definition cannot do so.'

In *Hendrix v Hendrix* (27 January 1981, unreported), Court of Appeal (Civil Division) Transcript No. 57 of 1981, where the facts were very similar to the present, a court consisting of Ormrod LJ and Purchas J ordered that the matrimonial home be transferred into the name of the wife, on her paying the husband a capital sum of £3,000, and further ordered that the house stand charged in favour of the husband as to 25 per cent of the proceeds of sale, payable on the wife's death or remarriage, or on her cohabiting. In other words, the court made a *Martin* order.

It is true that, in the present case, the husband's earning capacity is very much greater than that of the wife. In due course, when he has paid off his debts, he will be able to get back on to the property ladder without insuperable difficulty. But the same was also true in *Hendrix v Hendrix*. The question is whether the difference in earning capacity, and the severance of the maintenance tie, justified an out-and-out transfer of the sole capital asset to the wife. In my judgment it did not. The very least which the judge should have done was to order a charge in favour of the husband in the event of the wife's death or remarriage.

Cohabitation raises a separate problem. But if, as Lord Scarman said in *Minton v Minton* [1979] AC 593, the reason underlying the principle of the clean break is the avoidance of bitterness, then the bitterness felt by the husband when he sees the former matrimonial home occupied by the wife's cohabitee must surely be greater than the bitterness felt by the wife being subject, as she fears, to perpetual supervision.

Not to have made a *Martin* order in this case was therefore in my opinion manifestly unfair to the husband. It deprived him forever of any share in the sole capital asset of the marriage, without any sufficient corresponding benefit to the wife.

...

I would be happy to leave the matter there. But Mr. Mostyn is not now content with a *Martin* order, as was his instructing solicitor, who appeared in this case in the court below. He asks us to consider making a *Mesher* order so that the charge would become effective on Amanda attaining the age of 18 or some other age.

The rise and fall of the *Mesher* order has been charted in many previous decisions of this court. Though decided in 1973, the case was not reported until 1980: *Mesher v Mesher and Hall*

[1980] 1 All ER 126n. It caught on very quickly, so much so that by the time of *Martin (BH) v Martin (D)* [1978] Fam 12 Ormrod LJ felt it necessary to say that the *Mesher* order was never intended to be a general practice.

> 'There is no magic in the fact that there are children to be considered. All it means is that the interests of the children take priority in these cases, so that often there can be no question of sale while the children are young. But the situation that will arise when the children reach the age of 18 requires to be carefully considered. Otherwise a great deal of hardship may be stored up in these cases by treating it as a rule of thumb that the matrimonial home should then be sold. It is not a rule of thumb.'

Ormrod LJ went on to say, however, that in some cases a *Mesher* order might be the only way of dealing with the situation.

The dangers of the *Mesher* order were emphasised in a number of cases in the early 1980s. In *Mortimer v Mortimer-Griffin* [1986] 2 FLR 315 Sir John Donaldson MR said, at pp.318–319:

> 'It does seem to me that both orders suffer from the defects to which Ormrod LJ drew attention, that "chickens come home to roost" at an unpredictable time and in unpredictable circumstances; and that while an adjustment based on percentages seems attractive at the time, experience shows that it is subject to all kinds of difficulties and objections when it is worked out in the event.'

Parker LJ said at p.319:

> 'I would also add that I wholly endorse what my Lord, the Master of the Rolls, has said with regard to what is known as a *Mesher* order. It has been criticised since its birth; it is an order which is likely to produce harsh and unsatisfactory results. For my part, I hope that that criticism, if it has not got rid of it, will at least ensure that it is no longer regarded as the "bible"'

It seems to me, with respect to Parker LJ, that there are still cases where, if only by way of exception, the *Mesher* order provides the best solution. Such a case might be where the family assets are amply sufficient to provide both parties with a roof over their heads if the matrimonial home were sold, but nevertheless the interests of the children require that they remain in the matrimonial home. In such a case it may be just and sensible to postpone the sale until the children have left home, since, ex hypothesi, the proceeds of sale will then be sufficient to enable the wife to rehouse herself. In such a case the wife is 'relatively secure': see the judgment of Ormrod LJ in *McDonnell v McDonnell* (1976) 6 Fam Law 220, CA.

But where there is doubt as to the wife's ability to rehouse herself on the charge taking effect, then a *Mesher* order should not be made. That is, as I see it, the position here. The split suggested by the husband would give the wife two thirds of £50,000. It must be very uncertain whether this would be sufficient to enable the wife to rehouse herself in a few years' time when Amanda leaves home. That is no doubt the reason why the [district judge] declined to make a *Mesher* order. I would agree with him. But the *Martin* order does not suffer from the same disadvantages.

In conclusion I would reject Mr. Mostyn's submission that we should make a *Mesher* order, but accept his submission that we should make a *Martin* order. The split which he suggests seems about right. Accordingly, I would grant leave and allow the appeal to that extent.

Ewbank J: I agree. It is of course important to retain flexibility to meet the circumstances of individual cases and changes in social conditions. On the other hand, justice and the provisions of the statute usually indicate that an asset which has been acquired by the joint efforts of the spouses should eventually be shared. Where the only asset is a jointly acquired home of modest value it is often necessary to give its occupation to the parent with custody of children or to the spouse with the greater need. The clean break principle does not, however, mean that the other spouse is to be deprived for all time of any share. Experience has shown that postponing such an interest until the children are grown up often merely postpones and exacerbates the problems in re-housing that the occupying spouse will have. This is why the *Mesher* type of order is regarded as unsuitable unless there is going to be sufficient capital available to provide a suitable alternative home. But postponement until death, remarriage or cohabitation does not produce the same problem and is not generally disadvantageous to the occupying spouse. It does ensure that the other spouse receives eventually an appropriate share in the jointly acquired asset.

This is such a case. The judge was wrong, in my view, in depriving the husband of all interest in the house. The proper order would be for proceeds of sale of the house to be divided in the proportions of one third [to the husband] to two thirds [to the wife] on the death, remarriage or cohabitation of the wife.

Questions

(i)   As a woman living in the former matrimonial home with your children, which would you prefer: (a) the knowledge that the house has to be sold when the youngest of your children goes to university and you receive one half of the equity; (b) the knowledge that the house has to be sold when you commence a 'permanent cohabitation' with your boyfriend so as to provide your husband with one third of the equity. Would your answer differ in either case according to whether you were in receipt of maintenance payments?

(ii)   What would amount to evidence of 'permanent cohabitation' if that fact were in dispute?

(iii)   Should property adjustment orders be capable of variation? (Read s. 31 of the Matrimonial Causes Act 1973 and *Thompson v Thompson* [1986] Fam 38, [1985] 2 All ER 243.)

(iv)   What happens when a property adjustment order is made, and circumstances subsequently change so as to make that order inappropriate (for example, the matrimonial home is transferred to the wife, to be a home for her and the children, and she dies soon after the order is made)? (See *Barder v Caluori* [1988] AC 20, [1987] 2 FLR 480; and consider 'Is *White v White* a *Barder* event', by Eleanor Hamilton QC (2001).)

We now consider the question of tenancies. Whereas orders of the court regulating the occupation of the home can be made under the Family Law Act only during the marriage, there is jurisdiction to order the transfer of a private or council tenancy if there is security of tenure from one spouse to the other in a case where the marriage is terminated by divorce or a decree of nullity (Family Law Act 1996, Sch. 7). The court has the power to order the transfer, on granting a decree of divorce, nullity or judicial separation, or, with leave of the court, at any time thereafter. The landlord's consent is not required, but he does have a right to be heard before an order is made.

Questions

(i)   Do you think (a) that this provision is an unnecessary interference in the powers and responsibilities of local authorities to determine housing priorities in their area; or (b) that to allow a housing authority to reallocate the home before the judicial decision was made would prejudge the matter and hamper the ousted party's chances of having the children?

(ii)   But what is a local authority to do if (as is now usual) there is a joint tenancy and neither party will risk surrendering it (see *Hammersmith London Borough Council v Monk*, p. 154, above)?

(iii)   There has been evidence that women are sometimes unable to obtain the children without housing and unable to obtain housing without the children. If this is correct, who should break this vicious circle, the court or the housing authority?

What of women who leave home because they find the relationship intolerable although there is no question of violence? Indeed, one reason why courts are asked to make orders may be because housing authorities often treat childless women or women who have left their children behind as intentionally homeless under the Housing Act 1996 and therefore not under a duty to rehouse. Rosy Thornton (1987) discovered that 54% of housing authorities in her survey (more than 100) would find such women intentionally homeless.

8.5.7 The clean break

The doctrine of the clean break has emerged from the haze of the judicial involvement as a major target.

Minton v Minton
[1979] AC 593, [1979] 1 All ER 79, [1979] 2 WLR 31, 122 Sol Jo 843, House of Lords

In this case, the House of Lords collectively, and Lord Scarman in particular, stressed the requirement that the parties put the past behind them and begin a new life which is in no way overshadowed by a former relationship:

... There are two principles which inform the modern legislation. One is the public interest that spouses, to the extent that their means permit, should provide for themselves and their children. But the other – of equal importance – is the principle of 'the clean break.' The law now encourages spouses to avoid bitterness after family break-down and to settle their money and property problems. An object of the modern law is to encourage each to put the past behind them and to begin a new life which is not overshadowed by the relationship which has broken down. It would be inconsistent with this principle if the court could not make, as between the spouses, a genuinely final order unless it was prepared to dismiss the application. The present case is a good illustration. The court having made an order giving effect to a comprehensive settlement of all financial and property issues as between spouses, it would be a strange application of the principle of the clean break if, notwithstanding the order, the court could make a future order on a subsequent application made by the wife after the husband had complied with all his obligations.

Questions

(i)   Is Lord Scarman being cruel to be kind?
(ii) Is the clean break approach consistent with the interests of the children?

Suter v Suter and Jones
[1987] Fam 111, [1987] 2 All ER 336, [1987] 3 WLR 9, 131 Sol Jo 471, Court of Appeal

The husband and wife, who had married in 1971, were divorced in 1985, on the husband's petition, on the ground of the wife's adultery with the co-respondent. Care and control of the two children of the marriage, born in 1972 and 1978, was awarded to the wife who continued to live with them in the former matrimonial home. The co-respondent, who earned £7,000 per annum, paid rent to his mother for a room in her house and had his meals there, but spent most nights with the wife, who neither sought nor received any contribution from him towards the expenses of running the home. The husband remarried. On the wife's application for financial provision, the district judge in the county court ordered, inter alia, the husband to transfer to the wife all his interest in the former matrimonial home, subject to the mortgage, together with the surrender value of two insurance policies, and to make periodical payments of £100 per month to her until she remarry or both children attain the age of 18 and periodical payments of £110 and £90 per month respectively to the children during their respective minorities. Without the periodical payments to her, the wife's outgoings would have exceeded her income by £570 per annum. The circuit judge dismissed the husband's appeal against the periodical payments order in favour of the wife, on the basis that a 'clean break' could not be ordered, under s. 25A(2), where there were children under 18, that s. 25(1) of the 1973 Act made the welfare of the children the paramount consideration in deciding whether to make a periodical payments order and its amount, and that the children's welfare required the order to be made so as to ensure that they continued to have a roof over their heads.

On the husband's appeal:

Sir Roualeyn Cumming-Bruce: This appeal raises questions about the meaning and application of section 25(1) of the Matrimonial Causes Act 1973, as amended by section 3 of the Matrimonial and Family Proceedings Act 1984, and the correct exercise of the powers and duties conferred on the court by section 25A of the Act of 1973.

...

Counsel for the appellant husband's first submission was that the judge misdirected himself in that he never carried out the exercise prescribed as a mandatory duty upon the court by section 25A. By section 25A(1) it is the duty of the court to consider whether it would be appropriate to exercise the powers so that financial obligations of each party towards the other will be terminated as soon after the grant of the decree as the court thinks just and reasonable. By subsection (2), where the court decides to make a periodical payments order in favour of a party to a marriage, the court shall in particular consider whether it would be appropriate to require those payments to be made for such term as would in the opinion of the court be sufficient to enable the party in whose favour the order is made to adjust without undue hardship to the termination of his or her financial dependence on the other party.

Those provisions, introduced by the Act of 1984, enshrine in statute law the principle that after dissolution of marriage a time may have come, or can be foreseen in the future, when the party in whose favour financial provision has been made can so adjust his or her life as to attain sufficient financial independence to enable that party to live without undue hardship without any further dependence on the other party. This has been described as the principle of a 'clean break,' the phrase used by Lord Scarman in his speech in *Minton v Minton* [1979]AC 593, 608. In a number of cases which were decided before the new legislation came into force the court observed that where there were children for whom the parties shared a continuing obligation there is likely to be little or no room for the father and mother to have a clean break from each other: see, for example, *Pearce v Pearce* (1979) 1 FLR 261 and *Moore v Moore* (1980) 11 Fam Law 109, in which Ormrod LJ observed at p.109:

'It is one thing to talk about a 'clean break' when there are sufficient financial resources to make a comprehensive settlement. Where there are no capital resources, as here, it is unrealistic to talk about a 'clean break' if there are children. It is not possible for the father and mother of dependent children to have a clean break from one another. ... So, in my judgment, the so-called principle of the 'clean break' has no application where there are young children.'

I agree with the submission of counsel that the new section 25A imposes a mandatory duty in every case to apply itself to questions set out in section 25A(2) whenever a court decides to make a periodical payments order in favour of a party to the marriage. The judgments in the cases before 1984 have to be read with that in mind. Though the parties may have to co-operate with each other over children still dependent upon them, it may be possible on the facts to recognise a date when the party in whose favour the order is made will have been able to adjust without undue hardship to the termination of financial dependence on the other party. I also agree that the judge appears to have been influenced by the earlier cases to approach the question of termination of financial dependence without specifically addressing himself to the question whether this wife could and should find a way of adjusting her way of life so as to attain financial independence of her husband. So this court is entitled to consider the facts for itself and to carry out the statutory duty prescribed by section 25A. Having said that, I am clear that on the facts it is not possible at this date to predict with any more confidence than the [district judge] when the wife will have been able to make the adjustment which leads to the inference that it will then be just and reasonable to terminate her right to claim periodical payments from her husband. The children are growing up. It is likely that it will become progressively easier for the wife to organise and increase her earning capacity. But there are too many uncertainties to predict the development of events over the next 10 years. Likewise in connection with the financial advantages which on the judge's finding she can expect to derive, if she wishes, from her association with the co-respondent. It is their declared intention at present not to marry. There has already been one interruption in the continuity of their cohabitation, if that is the right description of their present arrangements, as I think it is. She may become increasingly and permanently financially dependent on the co-respondent. She may not. Consideration of the facts in evidence before the [district judge] does not at this date enable the court to predict with any confidence whether she will in the next 10 years have had the opportunity so to adjust herself that her claim for periodical payments can be terminated without undue hardship. The [district judge] warned her that such would be the position once the younger child reached the age of 18. It may be that that situation will be attained earlier. It is not impossible that even after the younger child is 18, consideration of the wife's needs and earning capacity will still make it just and reasonable for her to claim some support from her husband, though I would expect it to be unlikely. For those reasons I reject the submission that the judge was wrong in refusing to make an order terminating the husband's financial obligations towards his wife.

I do not however found that conclusion upon the judge's reasoning and approach. I am satisfied for the reasons that I have stated, that he misdirected himself by failing to apply the test prescribed in section 25A(2). This court is therefore entitled to consider the facts in the way that section 25A(2) has enjoined, and then to exercise the discretionary power itself. So directing myself I come to the conclusion that it would be premature to make an order terminating the wife's claim for periodical payments for her support from her husband.

The second submission made on behalf of the husband is that the judge, following the approach of the [district judge], misdirected himself upon the proper construction and effect of section 25 of the Act of 1973, as amended by section 3 of the Act of 1984.

By section 25(1):

'It shall be the duty of the court in deciding whether to exercise its powers under section 23, 24 or 24A above and, if so, in what manner, to have regard to all the circumstances of the case, first consideration being given to the welfare while a minor of any child of the family who has not attained the age of 18.'

This subsection is new, and in effect replaces the words formerly enacted in section 25 at the end of the list of matters in paragraphs (*a*) to (*g*) of section 25(1) and paragraphs (*a*) to (*e*) of section 25(2) to which the court had to have regard amongst all the circumstances of the case.

The husband submits that both the judge and the [district judge] treated the welfare of the children as first and paramount, in the sense in which that phrase was interpreted by Lord MacDermott in the context of section 1 of the Guardianship of Infants Act 1925: see *J v C* [1970]AC 668, 711. There Lord MacDermott considered the two adjectives in the phrase, and said:

'That is the first consideration because it is of first importance and the paramount consideration because it rules upon or determines the course to be followed.'

I agree with the submission that counsel culled from a commentary by a distinguished commentator [F.A.R. Bennion (1976)] that the phrase 'first and paramount' means simply 'overriding,' and that if the draftsman had omitted the adjective 'first' the meaning and effect of the single adjective 'paramount' would have been the same. We are faced with the problem of discovering the intention of Parliament when it used the phrase 'the first consideration' without the conjunction of the adjective 'and paramount' which gave the phrase in section 1 of the Guardianship of Infants Act 1925 its dominant force and effect.

The duty of the court under section 25(1), as amended, is to have regard to all the circumstances, first consideration being given to the welfare while a minor of any child of the family under the age of 18. As regards the exercise of the powers in relation to a party to the marriage, the court shall in particular have regard to the matters set out in section 25(2) in the subparagraphs lettered (*a*) to (*h*). Sub-paragraph (*g*) introduces a matter not previously included: 'the conduct of each of the parties, if that conduct is such that it would in the opinion of the court be inequitable to disregard it; ...'

Having regard to the prominence which the consideration of the welfare of children is given in section 25(1), being selected as the first consideration among all the circumstances of the case, I collect an intention that this consideration is to be regarded as of first importance, to be borne in mind throughout consideration of all the circumstances including the particular circumstances specified in section 25(2). But if it had been intended to be paramount, overriding all other considerations pointing to a just result, Parliament would have said so. It has not. So I construe the section as requiring the court to consider all the circumstances, including those set out in subsection (2), always bearing in mind the important consideration of the welfare of the children, and then try to attain a financial result which is just as between husband and wife.

Consideration of the judge's judgment, taken in conjunction with paragraphs 15 and 16 of the judgment of the [district judge] which he clearly approved, shows that the judge treated the consideration of the children's welfare as paramount; and controlling the effect of the interplay of all other matters. Though the [district judge] and the judge gave some effect by way of reduction of the periodical payments to the financial contribution of the co-respondent to the wife's finances, which the judge held would be substantial, the order was calculated in such a way as to provide the wife with a periodical payments order which would enable her to make all the mortgage payments. And the reasoning thus proceeded because it was considered that the children's welfare required that solution, although the [district judge] for the reasons that he gave thought that ordinary people would regard the result as unjust. In my view the judge fell into error in treating section 25(1) as requiring him to give effect to a consideration of the children's welfare as the overriding or paramount consideration. This was a misdirection, and this court is entitled to review the facts, apply the statute on its proper construction, and decide how to determine the wife's financial claim for periodical payments.

The judge then considered the position of the co-respondent.

... the wife has invited her lover to live for the foreseeable future in the former matrimonial home with herself and the children, without seeking or receiving any contribution to the expenses of maintaining that house. He is a bachelor aged 21 with a gross income of not less than £7,000, subject to tax. The figures demonstrate that the payment of the mortgage amounts to £2,148 per annum, and that after payment thereof she has a deficit of £570 per annum. It is reasonable to infer that the co-respondent is in a position to contribute at least £12 per week for the privileges which he enjoys in the furnished residence which, as a consequence of the husband's transfer of property, now belongs wholly to the wife, subject to the mortgage. It is material to bear in mind that since he moved to reside in the wife's house the co-respondent has continued to pay £6 per week to his mother for the room in which he no longer sleeps. As the wife is now for practical purposes living with the co-respondent in the former matrimonial home, it is just and reasonable to make an order on the basis that she require him to contribute not less than £600 per annum for the expenses of the house which she has invited him to enjoy. On that basis I would not think it just that the husband should do more than he has done by making the capital transfers already completed and by continuing to make payments to the children amounting to £200 per month. In that situation the wife's and children's needs are met, she can afford to run the home and pay the mortgage, and the husband and wife can expect to enjoy a comparable standard of living in the accommodation in which they respectively live.

I would move that the appeal be allowed and that the husband's obligation to contribute to her support be reduced to a nominal order of £1 per year.
Appeal allowed.

Questions

(i)   Purchas LJ described a 'clean break' in *Scallon v Scallon* [1990] FCR 911, [1990] 1 FLR 194, CA, as follows:

Finally, I wish to say a word about 'clean break' which is a phrase which arises since the amendments to the 1973 Act were introduced to ensure that, where there were short-term marriages, one party should not get what is described as 'a meal ticket for life' upon the dissolution of such a marriage. Furthermore, it was to encourage spouses who hitherto had not earned their living to face up to the fact that after the dissolution they should earn their living.

But if the husband insisted that the wife remained at home during the marriage, is it really fair on her that she should now be encouraged to 'face up to the fact ... that she should earn her living?' Perhaps it is too late?
(ii)   When making a 'clean break' should the emphasis be on 'need' or 'earned share'? (See *B v B (financial provision)* [1990] FCR 105, [1990] 1 FLR 20.)

The ideology of the clean break is discussed in 'Indissolubility and the Clean Break' (1985) by Pamela Symes:

The Logic of the Clean Break Principle
The limitations of the old section 25 directive were soon apparent and therefore a realistic and workable alternative needed to be found. The clean break principle is arguably a logical step forward in the long march towards liberal divorce and sexual equality but it is possible that in principle, it carries almost as much potential conflict and inconsistency as the old directive – equally capable of producing unjust and inequitable results, but for different reasons. The former section 25 directive embodied an *inherent* contradiction ('to place the parties ... in the financial position in which they would have been if the marriage had not broken down'). By contrast, the clean break principle has an inherent logic about it based, as it is, on the assumption that the marital relationship is ending rather than being continued. The potential contradictions are not inherent – rather they are *internal* to the legislation (for example, trying to reconcile the clean break with the other policy objective of giving priority to children's needs) and *external*, such as when the clean break is not recognised by the D.H.S.S., for instance, who may still require contributions from an ex-husband after a clean break settlement. (*Hulley v Thompson* [1981] 1 All ER 1128.) [See now the Child Support Act (Chapter 4, above).]

After looking at the English and the Scottish proposals, Symes raises the basic issue of 'who pays'?

One very fundamental question was never satisfactorily answered before the Divorce Reform Act 1969 was enacted – namely, how is it going to be paid for? Divorce and remarriage it was realised would involve the creation of many new households; where were the extra resources to come from to finance this exercise? The wider fiscal implications of such a change in the divorce law seem to have been largely ignored ...
The husband's obligation to maintain his wife, is the very nub of the problem. It is debatable whether such an obligation should arise during marriage, but if it does not end on divorce then what does divorce mean? This leads to the second basic question which has still not been satisfactorily answered: does divorce constitute the termination of the marital relationship, or merely a readjustment of it? These two questions have chased one another in a kind of conundrum for the last 15 years. Unable to accept the full logic of the position that divorce should constitute a complete and final termination of the parties' legal and financial relationship with the parties reverting to being 'legal strangers,' we have been forced to accept that it must therefore be a readjustment of their former marital relationship. Our present law is still ambiguous; while apparently signalling the end of the marital relationship, the financial provisions point to its readjustive function. But in one respect the law is quite clear and unambiguous: it incorporates a licence to remarry.

She argues that marriage 'as it has been traditionally practised, is not intended to be ended by divorce':

Indeed, traditional housewife marriage has a most potent feature of indissolubility built right into it – dependency. When that dependency is reinforced in the social infrastructure (both explicitly through social security and taxation laws and implicitly in the underlying assumptions about marriage) then the marriage bond becomes practically indissoluble. The accumulation of responsibilities and obligations, the consequences of an unequal partnership based on dependency – all mean that an absolute severance of the bond without massive adjustment would be manifestly unjust, more likely impossible.

She ends her article in this way:

Conclusion
Present divorce is so often merely a readjustment of the former marital relationship. It results in the parties being released from the obligation to share bed and board but they are still saddled with the ongoing financial obligations of the marriage, not unlike judicial separation. Thus the licence to remarry is something of an illusion. In so many ways the parties are *not* free to remarry, as the evidence from numerous pressure groups will testify. Thus divorce, as granted in

most cases, is only *a mensa et thoro* simply because most marriages are still indissoluble. True divorce *a vinculo matrimonii* can only be granted when, because the marriage is short, childless or the parties are sufficiently rich, the bond can be truly severed and a clean break imposed – the marriage is, by practical definition, dissoluble. This is because, at the time the reformed divorce law came into operation, we failed to introduce simultaneously the effective means whereby the *vinculum*, the marriage bond could be broken (*i.e.* the necessary changes in the infrastructure). The ongoing marriage tie is reflected in the continuing support obligation which is imposed – admittedly imposed but often not met ... If the support obligation is met, there is financial strain where remarriage follows as limited resources are spread between two families; if it is ignored or only partly met, then usually the resort is to subsistence on state benefit for the first family.

This was the inevitable result of attempting the impossible, of trying to introduce divorce for indissoluble marriage. With the passing of the Matrimonial and Family Proceedings Act 1984 the clean break principle now has embryonic statutory form. While it remains unsupported by a reformed social policy it will at best be a non-event, at worst, it will simply open the way to more injustice and suffering. For only when a radical change in the marital relationship takes place, when it becomes a partnership of two economically independent individuals through the abolition of marital dependency and when the corresponding changes in the social infrastructure are brought about, will there be any chance of formulating a coherent, clean break divorce law.

Questions

(i) After reading this, are you inclined to give up searching for a coherent policy?
(ii) Do you think that the policy of the 'clean break' is consistent with the principles behind the Child Support Act 1991? (See Chapter 4, above.)
(iii) Will a 'clean break' be harder to achieve following implementation of the Child Support Act 1991?

8.5.8 Pensions

Section 25(2)(*h*) requires the court to have regard to 'the value to each of the parties to the marriage of any benefit (for example, a pension) which, by reason of the dissolution or annulment of the marriage, that party will lose the chance of acquiring'. Maggie Rae, in her article 'Pensions and Divorce: Time for Change' (1995), explains why pensions have posed such a problem on divorce:

Almost a third of all marriages in the United Kingdom end in divorce. About half of all those in work are members of occupational pension schemes and many others now invest in personal pensions. It follows that many of those who divorce are members of pension schemes or married to those who are. They constitute a major family asset but commonly, one spouse will have a much larger pension than the other one. The link between pension provision and divorce ought to be obvious. Equally obvious to divorce lawyers is the need to reform the law so that pensions can be dealt with on divorce in the same way as other family assets.

The core of the problem is that the courts usually have no power to divide pensions on divorce. This is because the Inland Revenue will not approve pension schemes which permit the assignment, charging or allocation of acquired pension rights to third parties including spouses. In addition, almost all occupational schemes and an increasing number of personal pensions contain 'Protective' or 'Spendthrift' trusts which mean that were a court to make an order against a member in relation to his/her pension rights, those pension rights would be forfeited.

This produces unfair results in a significant number of cases. Take for instance the couple who divorce in their early fifties when the children have grown up. The wife may not have worked for a decade or more while the children were young and after that only worked part-time. If she has a pension at all it will only be a small one, and much smaller than her husband's. In happier times both of them looked forward to a secure old age. Divorce changes all of that. Suddenly the wife finds herself unsure of what the future will bring. In the ensuing division of the assets, the family's largest potential asset cannot be the subject of division by the court. Widows' pensions and entitlements to death in service benefits are also affected and also outside the court's jurisdiction.

In this family, as in many others the decision that the wife should stay at home and then only work part-time, was one taken jointly – a family decision. The only fair way to look at this couple's pension provision is as a joint family asset. In some marriages that treatment would not necessarily be right. Nonetheless it ought to be available.

The Law Society Memorandum, *Maintenance and Capital Provision on Divorce* (1991), identifies six benefits which require consideration:

3.3(*a*) the payment of a lump sum on retirement;
  (*b*) the pension the husband will become entitled to on retirement;
  (*c*) a widow's pension which may be payable following the husband's death after retirement;
  (*d*) a lump sum which could be payable to the husband's estate should he die in service;
  (*e*) a widow's pension payable should the husband die in service; and
  (*f*) the possibility of substantial life cover which would be payable to the husband's estate in the event of his death.

In 1992 the Pensions Management Institute (PMI) set up a working group, in conjunction with the Law Society; its report, *Pensions and Divorce*, was published in May 1993. The report summarised the possible ways of dealing with pensions on divorce as follows:

We have looked at four ways of reallocating the value of pension rights when divorce takes place before the pension comes into payment:
  (*a*) pension rights continue undisturbed but their value is taken into account – any reallocation of resources between the couple is made by adjustment of non-pension assets;
  (*b*) earmarking – pension rights continue undisturbed, but a specified amount of whatever benefit eventually becomes payable to or in respect of the scheme member is earmarked for payment direct to the former spouse when the time comes;
  (*c*) pension splitting within a scheme – a scheme member's pension rights are reduced by the specified amount mentioned in (*b*), and the resources so released are used to provide, within the scheme, a package of benefit rights for the former spouse as an entirely separate member of the scheme;
  (*d*) transfer – a scheme member's pension rights are reduced as in (*c*), and the resources so released are made available to the former spouse in the form of a transfer payment to another pension arrangement.
Method (*a*) is in use at present, particularly in Scotland, but it is effective only if there are adequate non-pension assets, and there are difficulties in comparing the value of pension assets, which enjoy favourable tax treatment, with the value of other assets. Methods (*b*), (*c*) and (*d*) would need changes in the law. We favour method (*d*). ...

In addition, the working group favoured the earmarking approach (*b*), coupled with life assurance, in cases where the marriage broke down after retirement.

Question

Can you see why these two different methods are appropriate in the two different situations?

In September 1993 the Pension Law Review Committee, chaired by Professor Roy Goode QC, reported its findings on occupational pension schemes in *Pensions and Law Reform* (Cm. 2342) and endorsed the recommendations of the PMI group. Nevertheless, in its White Paper *Security, Equality, Choice: The Future for Pensions* (June 1994) the Government's response to the question of pension rights on divorce was (para. 1.45):

As the PLRC recognised, the issue of pension rights on divorce is extremely complex. Any change to the current position could have significant implications for pension schemes. ... In any event, there is at present no clear evidence of the extent of the problem. A detailed research programme will be undertaken to ascertain the extent of the problem before the issue is considered further.

The Pensions Bill contained nothing about the problem when it was introduced in the House of Lords in January 1995. As a result of pressure in the House of Lords, debate amendments were made to the Pensions Bill, making additions and amendments to the Matrimonial Causes Act 1973 so as to allow the earmarking of pensions. Richard Malone, president of the Pensions Management Institute, commented in *The Times*, 26 August 1995, that the effect of earmarking a pension is:

The husband has all the usual rights of moving the pension around. The divorced partner has no say in that. She may not ever know. She also has to wait until her ex-husband retires to receive an income. He may retire early and get a reduced level of pension. Worse still, he might die, in which case the ex-wife's pension is cut off altogether.

Question

How can concern about pension rights on divorce be consistent with the wish to achieve a clean break wherever possible? Which is more consistent with the clean break, earmarking or splitting?

Finally, as a result of an amendment made to the Family Law Bill during its passage through the House of Lords, the Family Law Act 1996 has made a further amendment to the Matrimonial Causes Act 1973 so as to allow pension splitting, now called pension sharing. Sections 25B and 25C of that Act now provide as follows:

25B. Pensions
 (1) The matters to which the court is to have regard under section 25(2) above include—
 (a) in the case of paragraph (a), any benefits under a pension arrangement which a party to the marriage has or is likely to have, and
 (b) in the case of paragraph (h), any benefits under a pension arrangement which, by reason of the dissolution or annulment of the marriage, a party to the marriage will lose the chance of acquiring,
and, accordingly, in relation to benefits under a pension arrangement, section 25(2)(a) above shall have effect as if 'in the foreseeable future' were omitted.
 (3) The following provisions apply where, having regard to any benefit under a pension arrangement, the court determines to make an order under section 23 above.
 (4) To the extent to which the order is made having regard to any benefits under a pension arrangement, the order may require the person responsible for the pension arrangement in question, if at any time any payment in respect of any benefits under the arrangement becomes due to the party with pension rights, to make a payment for the benefit of the other party.
 (5) The order must express the amount of any payment required to be made by virtue of subsection (4) above as a percentage of the payment which becomes due to the party with pension rights.
 (6) Any such payment by the person responsible for the arrangement—
 (a) shall discharge so much of his liability to the party with pension rights as corresponds to the amount of the payment, and
 (b) shall be treated for all purposes as a payment made by the party with pension rights in or towards the discharge of his liability under the order.
 (7) Where the party with pension rights has a right of commutation under the arrangement, the order may require him to exercise it to any extent; and this section applies to any payment due in consequence of commutation in pursuance of the order as it applies to other payments in respect of benefits under the arrangement.

(7A) The power conferred by subsection (7) above may not be exercised for the purpose of commuting a benefit payable to the party with pension rights to a benefit payable to the other party.

(7B) The power conferred by subsection (4) or (7) above may not be exercised in relation to a pension arrangement which—

(a) is the subject of a pension sharing order in relation to the marriage, or

(b) has been the subject of pension sharing between the parties to the marriage.

(7C) In subsection (1) above, references to benefits under a pension arrangement include any benefits by way of pension, whether under a pension arrangement or not.

25C. Pensions: lump sums

(1) The power of the court under section 23 above to order a party to a marriage to pay a lump sum to the other party includes, where the benefits which the party with pension rights has or is likely to have under a pension arrangement include any lump sum payable in respect of his death, power to make any of the following provision by the order.

(2) The court may—

(a) if the person responsible for the pension arrangement in question has power to determine the person to whom the sum, or any part of it, is to be paid, require him to pay the whole or part of that sum, when it becomes due, to the other party,

(b) if the party with pension rights has power to nominate the person to whom the sum, or any part of it, is to be paid, require the party with pension rights to nominate the other party in respect of the whole or part of that sum,

(c) in any other case, require the person responsible for the pension arrangement in question to pay the whole or part of that sum, when it becomes due, for the benefit of the other party instead of to the person to whom, apart from the order, it would be paid.

(3) Any payment by the person responsible for the arrangement under an order made under section 23 above by virtue of this section shall discharge so much of his liability in respect of the party with pension rights as corresponds to the amount of the payment.

(4) The powers conferred by this section may not be exercised in relation to a pension arrangement which—

(a) is the subject of a pension sharing order in relation to the marriage, or

(b) has been the subject of pension sharing between the parties to the marriage.

We are now seeing some case law on pensions earmarking. The first is *T v T* [1998] 1 FLR 1072. We quote from Eleanor Ingham's analysis in '*T v T*: Pensions Earmarking' (1998):

The parties had been married for 15 years. There were no children of the family. The parties separated in late 1995. The husband had a substantial income. The wife had not worked since 1988, being entirely supported by the husband. She had deferred pension rights accrued during her employment. The joint assets were the house, the net equity of which was approximately £150,000, and a joint bank account (balance £36,000). In addition the husband had in his sole name capital of £90–100,000.

It was agreed that this was not an appropriate case for a clean break. The wife's application was for periodical payments, a capital lump sum and specific provision for her in relation to the husband's pension rights...

Singer J [made] orders for capital provision and periodical payments for the wife, having done the usual s 25 'balancing' exercise, taking into account the parties income, assets, needs and other factors. He then turned to the issues arising from the wife's application for earmarking orders. First he dealt with two preliminary points of principle which were submitted by counsel for the wife.

The first and most significant was the argument that the provisions of the 1973 Act showed an intention on the part of the legislature to 'require, and not just to enable, a spouse in the position of this wife to be compensated for her actual or potential loss of pension benefits'. The wife further argued that this 'compensatory principle' entitled her to be compensated not only for loss of a widow's pension were she to survive him on his death, but also her 'share' of the pension income she would have derived as his wife on retirement.

Singer J specifically rejected the suggestion that the provisions imposed any duty on the court to provide for the wife from the pension fund. He concluded that if this were the case 'it would have the effect of turning on its head the court's established approach under s 25', as pension provision would have to be considered 'uniquely as a matter of right and entitlement'... Singer J concluded that the language of the statutory provisions was 'clearly permissive rather than mandatory as to the exercise of the powers provided.'

It was argued on the wife's behalf that the orders which could be made against pension providers were 'distinct' from any other orders which could be made under s 23, and therefore an earmarking maintenance order would not end on the wife's remarriage. Singer J rejected this argument, stating that s 25B clearly referred to the usual type of financial order under s 23 of the 1973 Act, rather than any new or distinct species. An earmarking order would therefore continue like any other periodical payments order (subject to variation) during the payer's lifetime, until the recipient's death or remarriage.

Having established these principles, Singer J turned to the three forms of earmarking order which it was suggested that the court could make in favour of the wife:- ...

Counsel for the wife maintained that the court should make a deferred earmarking maintenance order in relation to the husband's pension once he commenced drawing it. Singer J declined to make such an order, citing several disadvantages and complications. For example, it was impossible at this stage to predict what the quantum of the wife's potential maintenance dependence would be, if any, when the husband reached 60. It was also impossible to know when the payments would become due, given the husband's discretion to defer drawing his pension until age 75. Singer J took into account the scope for both parties to apply for a variation of the order before it came into effect. The court would also be far better informed if consideration of the quantum and form of periodical payments was left until much nearer the time when the husband took his pension. Lastly, bearing in mind the periodical payments order already made in favour of the wife, Singer J concluded that there were no grounds for supposing that the husband would not be able to meet an appropriate periodical payments order, if applicable, from his pension after retirement.

The wife contended that she should have an earmarked lump sum of £60,000 to compensate for the potential loss of widow's pension, to be deferred until the date at which the husband started to draw his pension... Singer J declined to make such an order in the context of this case, taking into account the parties' life expectancy and having regard to the provision already awarded to the wife. He indicated that, although there may be cases in which such an order would be appropriate, this was not one of them. The wife would be able to raise a claim against her husband's estate under the Inheritance (Provision for Family and Dependants) Act 1975 were he to die post-retirement and if she was still dependent on him at that time.

Finally, death in service benefits were considered. It was open to the court under s 25(c)(i) to make an order requiring the trustees to pay an amount to the wife, to take effect in the event of the husband's death during employment. Singer J was clear that s 25(D) enabled an earmarking order for death in service benefits to be made in the form of a lump sum only, and not periodical payments. He ordered that the pension scheme trustees should be required to pay the wife a lump sum from any death benefits which arose prior to the husband's retirement. This was to be an amount equal to a multiple of 10 times the maintenance payable annually pursuant to any periodical payments order in force at the date of the husband's death.

Singer J therefore formulated an overall order under which the wife was protected as to maintenance and provided for in terms of capital, with only extremely limited use of the court's earmarking powers. He highlighted the weaknesses of earmarking orders in cases where retirement is not imminent and the value of pension benefits and the parties' entitlement to them is uncertain. A similar approach is seen in *Burrow v Burrow* [1999] 1 FLR 549, [1999] Fam Law 83; see comments by Rebecca Bailey-Harris (1999). Valuation is a besetting difficulty with pensions. Antony Dnes, in 'Pension splitting in England and Wales' (1999), explains:

Valuation of pensions in divorces
There are broadly two methods used to value pensions at divorce: current equivalent transfer value (CETV) and past service reserve (PSR). Where valuation enters a divorce settlement, CETV is the most commonly used method (Prior and Field, 1996) and it is the method specified by the 1995 Act for earmarking pensions. Neither method of valuation raises any particularly difficult economic issues if the question is simply one of valuing a pension at a particular point in time.

Valuation methods
It is worth emphasizing that pensions cannot usually be cashed in to obtain funds in the present. This is because Inland Revenue rules give tax exemption for income spent as pension contributions up to defined limits. Therefore, pension schemes generally do not allow cashing in, as the

money must be kept for retirement; only transfers between schemes are possible. It is wrong to think of the pension as a current source of transferable liquid wealth. Attention should properly be focused on the value in the present of the expected receipt of pension benefits in the future.

What is the value in the present of a future pension benefit? Money placed in investment schemes, including pensions, normally grows at a compound rate of interest as fund managers or trustees invest the payments. Thus, benefits anticipated at some future date, the heart of the pension valuation question, must be discounted at a compound rate of interest to arrive at a present value. As an example, if the prevailing interest rate is 6 per cent, £100 expected in 10 years time is only worth £56 now. This is because we could invest £56 and it would grow at 6 per cent compound interest to equal £100 in 10 years time. Therefore, care must be taken to avoid overvaluing pension benefits by regarding future payments as money 'up for grabs' in the present. Rather, it is the lower present value that measures the benefit to be divided in the present, although distribution would be from other non-pension assets (because the pension may be valued in the present but cannot itself be cashed in). However, it would be in order to earmark *future* payments at their terminal value.

How about the effects of anticipated inflation? The discounting of future pension figures should strictly be based on a real compound interest rate, which has lenders' assessments of expected inflation rates removed. One way to achieve this is to increase future expected payments for anticipated inflation and then to discount using a nominal interest rate (which should incorporate the same inflation rate). Fortunately, it is easier and equally correct to remove current inflation forecasts from nominal rates and then not to adjust payments for inflation. The interest rates we see in banks, pension funds and other financial institutions are nominal ones. A good candidate for an interest rate to be used in calculating discounted present values would be the Clearing Banks' Base Rate, which has averaging properties and the benefit of being widely understood, but the inflation component must either be removed from the interest rate or added to the payments. When adjusting for expected inflation, calculations should do better than use a rule of thumb (e.g. the courts' practice of adding 5 per cent) and should, rather, seek published estimates from economic forecasting groups.

A third fundamental point in examining pension values is that the pension will be paid for the lifetime of the scheme member, usually followed by a survivor benefit for the spouse, and possibly for children, that is also governed by their life or dependency expectation. A proper calculation should use standard estimates of life expectancy to allow for uncertainty. Thus, if we know that a scheme member is expected to draw a pension for 9 years (e.g. male life expectancy is 74 years and he retires at 65) and that his widow is expected to draw a widow's pension for a further 2 years, we could calculate the present value of the pension for each of the 11 years and sum the discounted values to give the expected present value of the pension. Estimating life expectancy and discounting to present values are crucial elements of valuing pensions.

The life expectancy issue is important because courts have struggled with the problem that the pension is uncertain. Traditionally, prior to the impact of the 1995 Act, courts took the view that distant pensions (certainly those due over 10 years hence) were too remote to be taken into account as assets in a divorce settlement. What they could have done was simply to use standard life-expectancy tables to determine the number of pension benefit receipts and discounted those amounts to a present value. The courts were probably too shy of this approach. Technically, using life expectancy gives a present value assuming risk neutrality (i.e. one values a risky prospect by weighting the nominal value by the probability of occurrence, but with no further adjustment for the fact that it is risky). People may often be willing to accept lesser amounts to know they have the money for certain (the 'certainty equivalent'), in which case they are risk-averse.

Under a CETV approach, the pension company provides an estimate of the amount it would pay for the scheme member to transfer into a different scheme based on the retirement lump sum and expected annual pension. The calculation is inherently in present-value terms, although it is likely to be based on the market value of underlying investment of the scheme member's payments to date minus the pension company's costs in making the transfer. Current equivalent transfer value unambiguously answers the question: 'What is the *transfer* value of this pension asset to this individual now?' The CETV would therefore be the correct method to value a pension to be split at the point of divorce, where (part of) the transfer is still made but it goes to the former spouse, either within the member's pension scheme or to a different scheme. The rule focuses on the pension asset as a source of transferable 'wealth', where the transfer could be for any purpose (e.g. in lieu of lost housing, savings or pensions)...

The Past Service Reserve (PSR) approach examines the amassed entitlement of a member of a defined benefit scheme and allows for anticipated salary growth in estimating the value of the pension that is likely to be paid. It is important to realize that this approach does not really extend the pension value beyond the current entitlement. The approach asks what has been paid into the scheme and how anticipated salary increases will affect that entitlement in determining the final pension benefits. One should then discount back to a present value over the expected period of the pension. The PSR approach is likely to be a more generous measure than CETV, as some short-term administrative cost factors are ignored and allowance is made for the impact of salary growth. Strictly, PSR overestimates the present value of the member's pension entitlements to date.

Awarding a share of the pension impact of salary growth, following the PSR method, might be viewed as a rough effort at measuring the value of a former spouse's support in early stages of the member's career, or possibly as reflecting promised retirement support from the member. It would indeed be a rough measure, and clearly the government has not chosen this path. In general, awarding a proportion of a pension, including the impact of anticipated salary increases, could underestimate or overestimate the value of, for example, the support from the ex-spouse. Anyway, one could always award an increased proportion of the CETV to allow approximately for these additional factors.

CETV vs PSR

The CETV and PSR approaches will continue to be the principal valuation methods available to the courts. In a general sense, neither method raises controversies from an economic perspective, but also neither is an ideal measure. An ex-spouse's share of a pension should ideally be based on the present value of the benefits paid over the life expectancies of the member and the ex-spouse, allowing either for support given (taking a restitutionary or reliance view) or allowing for promises made (an expectation approach). So, whether using PSR or CETV, a proportion would be awarded from these imperfect measures to reflect the true estimate based on a present value calculation adjusted for risk. However, if forced to choose between simplifications, a case can be made that pension division at the point of divorce, (i.e. 'splitting') should use CETV, whereas division at retirement (i.e. 'earmarking') should adopt a PSR method (which it implicitly does). In general, we should expect the award of a split or of earmarking to define the property rights in the pension and to act as a basis for subsequent bargaining. It is also worth remembering that division will usually transfer *shares* in a pension; therefore, it is always possible for a court to hold that a share of CETV is equivalent to a different share of a PSR-based valuation. Similarly, negotiating ex-spouses could bargain across the two measures in that way.

It is clear that pension splitting and pension earmarking involve very difficult financial considerations and are not for the arithmetically challenged. David Salter's 'A Practitioner's Guide to Pension Sharing' (2000) gives some detailed guidance. Equally difficult are the moral/practical problems. At what point is one trying to achieve fairness? At the point of separation? At the time of the hearing? For the foreseeable future? Until death? Until those questions are answered, we suggest, it is not possible to develop a coherent approach to pension earmarking or sharing.

Equally, it may be impossible to get this right until we have taken more seriously the consequences, for women, of child-bearing and divorce. In 'Do divorced women catch up in pension building?' (2002), Jay Ginn and Debbie Pearce argue that even the present legislation does not do enough to compensate women for what they have lost as a result of the termination of the marriage, because divorced and separated women are not able to catch up:

Despite the general rise in women's employment, mothers' employment rates remain substantially less than for childless women. Over 85% of British women who have ever married have had children, generally restricting their employment while children are young. Despite the Government's national childcare strategy, the constraint on mothers' hours of paid employment remains far more severe in Britain than in those European countries where affordable quality child care services are widely available. In Britain, the net cost of child care for an average income family with two children under the age of three was 28% of their income, compared with 9% in France, 11% in Denmark and 16% in Sweden. The UK system of subsidising child care through tax credits to low income families has fuelled demand for limited services, so that the cost of a nursery place for a child aged under two has rocketed, typically to £120 per week nationally and nearly £150 per week in inner London. For a lone parent, the cost of paying for child care while employed and travelling is generally prohibitive. Many partnered mothers find it impossible to manage full-time employment, but for divorced/separated mothers living alone, the lack of a partner to share the care of the children or to help pay for market child care makes full-time employment even more difficult.

Part-time employment, a common strategy used by partnered mothers, may bring no financial gain to lone mothers, compared with claiming means-tested income support. Moreover, part-time employment is of limited value in pension building. Part-timers are less likely than full-timers to have access to an occupational pension; most part-timers, therefore, lack the advantage of an employer's contribution to their pension. Many part-timers earn below the lower earnings limit for national insurance, so will not be required to contribute to SERPS or a contracted out private pension. Even part-timers who earn above this threshold are unlikely to be able to contribute more than the minimum required. Where part-timers do contribute to an occupational or personal pension, their typically low earnings generate only small pension entitlements. As a result, their eventual retirement income may be insufficient to exceed the means-tested minimum income guarantee. In this case, their efforts will have been wasted, as they will fall foul of the pensions poverty trap and gain no financial benefit from their investment. Whether this perverse outcome occurs depends, of course, on the duration of part-time employment, the level of earnings and the quality of the pension scheme.

SUMMARY AND CONCLUSIONS

Women's ability to earn and build private or SERPS pensions is substantially less than men's and leads to the well-known concentration of poverty among older women. However, divorced/separated women fare worse than other women in later life, with only a low proportion receiving any income from a private pension and a high likelihood of dependence on means-tested benefits.

Among working age divorced/separated individuals, women are half as likely to work full time as men, have only half of men's median earnings and have substantially lower private pension coverage, with no compensating advantage in their range of home ownership. Divorcees of working age are, of course, a diverse group, differentiated by educational qualifications and occupational experience at the time of divorce and, as our analysis highlights, by whether they have had children. While childless divorced/separated women are able to build their own pensions just as well as childless single women, divorced/separated mothers of dependent children have even lower private pension coverage than married mothers. Although divorced/separated women's rates of full-time employment and pension coverage rise to exceed those of married women once their children are aged over 16, many years of earnings and pension contributions are lost during the years of lone childbearing. As a result, most divorced/separated women cannot make adequate pension provision for themselves and face a high risk of dependence on means-tested benefits in later life, unless policies are implemented to improve their situation.

This research indicates both the need and the scope for pension transfers from ex-husbands to ex-wives through the Pensions and Welfare Act of 1999. However, despite misleading media reports, the Act does not give divorcing women the right to a share of their husband's pension, only the right to argue they should have such a share as part of an overall financial settlement. For owner-occupier couples, past practice has been to allow divorcing mothers to keep the family home while husbands keep their pensions, which are often crudely seen as of comparable value. Since the housing needs of children in the ten years following divorce will remain a priority, the practice of offsetting home against pension may continue, limiting the effectiveness of the legislation in protecting divorced women from poverty-level incomes in retirement.

Even if divorced women with children were routinely awarded half of their husband's pension entitlement at the date of divorce, which would certainly help, substantial disparities in retirement income would remain between ex-spouses. While men are able to earn and accumulate a good pension after the divorce, the constraints on the divorced mother's employment and pension building continue. If the debate about fairness in ancillary relief cases is really about achieving equity between divorcing spouses, then it should encompass the longer-term effects of motherhood in reducing lone mothers' earning capacity, and the fact that a money purchase pension started only in mid-life has insufficient time to mature into a reasonable pension.

8.6   Empirical evidence

Our survey of the empirical evidence is divided into three parts. First, we consider how people arrive at the financial settlement following divorce; next, we ask how people manage pending that settlement. Finally, we look at the empirical evidence for the financial outcomes of divorce; how are divorced people getting on, one year, five years, or more, after divorce.

8.6.1 Working things out

Research in recent years has examined not only what actually happens to individuals after divorce, but also how that outcome is arrived at. There are three principal ways of reaching a financial settlement following divorce: using lawyers, using a mediator, and do-it-yourself.

The behaviour of divorce lawyers has been a particular focus of interest. The conclusion of Jackson and her colleagues in their study of English and Scottish solicitors, 'Financial Support on Divorce: the Right Mixture of Rules and Discretion?' (1993), was:

> It is clear that the role of solicitors in post-divorce financial arrangements is characterized by a high level of negotiation and compromise. ... [W]e found universal concern for the position of the other side and a strong desire for compromise. Whether this amounts to legal practitioners assuming the role of mediators is a question too broad for the ambit of this paper. Nonetheless, it would seem that family law represents a highly distinctive branch of legal practice, and the significance of the practitioners' role should not be underestimated.

In *Simple Quarrels* (1994), Gwynn Davis, Stephen Cretney and Jean Collins undertook an extensive study of the conduct of litigation on financial questions in divorce, and of the expectations and attitudes of solicitors and of their clients. The picture that emerges reinforces the impression that here is a 'distinctive branch' of the legal profession; it also reveals the diversity within it, and perhaps some unexpected features.

Compare these two views of the relevance of the law in this area (the authors have changed the names of clients studied in the book):

> This was how Mr Daniels's solicitor assessed the situation when we first spoke to him:
>> 'Let's just say the equity is £42,000 – it's probably a bit more – as a starting point, two thirds/one-third – automatic starting point. So if we divide that, that comes to about £14,000 for him, taking one third. We know that she can raise £16,000, so I will immediately go to the chap on the other side, and perhaps ask for ... I'll ask for £16,000, hoping I'll end up with £14,000, and then I can sell it to Mr Daniels and say : "Look, that's what the court will give you." I may be wrong here, because I think if I were him [the other solicitor] I'd come back and say: "Look, in normal circumstances I can see the approach you're adopting, but here we have [handicapped son] who is different, and this is a complication. We can't say, but [son] could put off somebody wanting to marry my client, [son] could really stop her getting full-time work, [son] may be a liability until he's 25-30, he may need a home for the rest of his life." I've said to Mr Daniels already: "Don't be too sure that you're going to get something."'
>
> Whilst this solicitor could not predict the final outcome (Mr Daniels's barrister agreed a lump sum of £7,500, in fact) and whilst he recognized and to some extent relished the bargaining element in the negotiation, he none the less regarded it as bargaining within narrow limits. The fact that there was an element of uncertainty did not dissuade him from making proposals. ...
>
> Many solicitors with whom we discussed this point likewise implied, or revealed in their case management, that as far as they were concerned the outcome of ancillary relief proceedings was wholly unpredictable. It was almost as if legal doctrine had no impact upon the actual administration of family law. This was the view of one solicitor, based in Newport:
>> 'I suppose it's a terrible reflection of how many things are done on the basis of nothing more than rough horse-trading, with only a very passing shadow of reference to case law. When one reads the models, the ways in which you should really deal with financial relief, they are so technical and so precise. In 999 cases out of a thousand it's all down to a wing and a prayer and what you can deal with off the back of a truck.'

Question

From what you have read so far, which of these two was right? Can we say that either was right or wrong?

Turning to the mediator's role in this context, John Haynes in *The Fundamentals of Family Mediation* (1993) describes this as 'being a mediator and not a judge', and as 'helping clients define a solvable problem':

When people have an intractable dispute that appears unresolvable, the mediator enters to assist them to settle the dispute by negotiating a mutually acceptable agreement. However, a significant part of the problem is the inability of parties to agree on the content of the dispute. Indeed, they often have quite different versions of its nature and history.

When the mediator first meets with the disputants each person has a story to tell. These stories consist of three parts – a version of the events, a complaint about the other, and a problem definition.

In specific versions of the events and of the past, the basic data may be similar, or even the same, but the interpretation each places on the facts colours their view of the situation. Each version is designed to show the mediator how good he or she is; how each is the innocent victim of the situation.

The second part, the complaint, is designed to show the mediator how bad the other is.

The hallmark of the definition of the problem is that each person defines it in such a way that it can be solved only by a change in the behaviour or position of the other. A's problem can only be solved by a change in B, and B's problem can only be solved by a change in A.

These three elements represent each party's definition of the problem. Their inability to agree on the content of the dispute means that the mediator's role in the early stages is to obtain agreement on the problem to be resolved. She helps the clients to arrive at a mutual and neutral definition of a problem which, when solved, benefits all participants.

Neither A nor B will change unilaterally, nor will either change to conform with the other's definition of the problem. The mediator's task is to help them discard their individual problem definitions and adopt a mutual and common definition. Only then can problem solving begin. ...

While mediators cannot avoid all legal questions or emotive behaviour, they can limit the non-useful dialogue. Their primary method is to focus on what they believe is relevant to the clients. Mediators test and clarify the difference between relevant and non-useful information. They clarify for the clients what is important, directing them away from emotive behaviour towards self-interests contained in the information about the problem and solutions to it. ...

Figure 1.2: Sorting information in mediation

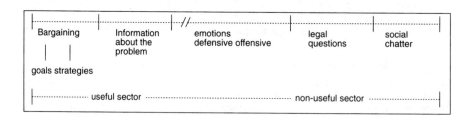

The client behaviour is divided into sectors. The right-hand sector is non-useful client information and the left-hand sector is useful client information. The mediator looks for useful data – information about the problem, the clients' bargaining goals and strategies. These data are collected and noted and form the basis of the next line of questioning. Client information that falls into the right-hand sector is ignored unless the client is persistent. Faced with client persistence, the mediator attempts to deal with the behaviour by acknowledging it and using other strategies to limit it.

Questions

(i) Why is legal material regarded as irrelevant in this process? Should it be?
(ii) Imagine yourself involved in a dispute about maintenance and capital provision on divorce. By what procedures would you like it to be resolved?

In 'The declining number of ancillary financial relief orders' (2000), Chris Barton and Alastair Bissett-Johnson demonstrate how prevalent the do-it-yourself option has become:

The purpose of this article is to analyse the net decline in ancillary financial relief (AFR) orders made for spouses since 1985 (following the Matrimonial and Family Proceedings Act 1984 (MFPA 1984)) and for children since 1993 (when the Child Support Act 1991 came into force). Amongst other revelations, the figures give the lie to the popular assumption that spousal periodical payments orders (PPOs) – now commonly called maintenance, and once called alimony – are still a key factor in divorce, but that court-ordered child maintenance is not. In 1998, for example, there were only 3920 county court spousal PPOs made until further order, in contrast to the 8136 PPOs made for children. ...

Chart 1 – Main decrees 1985–98 (county courts)

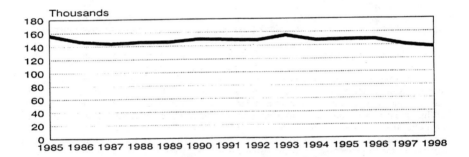

Chart 1 sets the scene by showing the numbers of main decrees (divorce, judicial separation and nullity) granted in the county courts. This information confirms what *Family Law* readers already know but *Any Questions?* panelists do not, namely that this number has remained comparatively stable, with some gentle downwards undulation, for the last 14 years: 156,000–137,000. A more important reason for mentioning these main relief figures is that their very stability has not been reflected in AFR usage over the same period, during which time there has been a modest rise in lump sum and property orders (see Chart 2) and a severe drop in PPOs both for spouses ... and for children ... These AFR trends are, of course, all explicable on the basis of parliamentary intentions in 1984 and 1991 respectively.

Chart 2 – AFR lump sum and property orders 1985–98 (county courts)

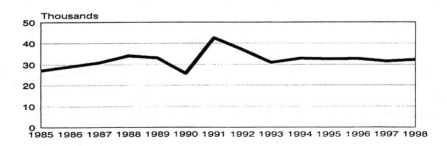

Another reason for including Chart 1 is that it evinces something markedly less explicable, namely the large, growing, gap between the number of divorces etc, and the number of – necessarily concomitant – AFR orders. We will discuss the significance and desirability of these trends later.

As mentioned, Chart 2 traces the usage of capital AFR, ie lump sum and property adjustment orders (irritatingly, *Judicial Statistics* lumps them both together) made under ss 23 and 24 respectively of the Matrimonial Causes Act 1973 (MCA 1973). Together, these orders have 'enjoyed' a modest 19%, 27,216–32,257, increase over the last 15 years. This upturn in their fortunes, or rather in the applicants' fortunes, is in line with the policy inherent in s 25A(1) of the 1973 Act, as inserted by the MFPA 1984:

> 'If the court decides to exercise any of its [AFR] powers ... it shall be the duty of the court to consider whether it would be appropriate so to exercise those powers that the financial obligations of each party towards the other will be terminated as soon after the grant of the decree as the court considers just and reasonable.'

The assiduous reader of *Family Law* will not have failed to notice the dramatic, one-off, 65% increase which came and (almost) went between 1990 and 1993. Below, we proffer the Child Support Act 1991 (the 1991 Act) as the reason why the same thing happened to AFR PPOs for both spouses and children ... But this 65% increase in capital orders is harder to understand: perhaps lawyers at that time were – understandably – unclear about the 1991 Act. ...

Maintenance for Spouses

... Charts 4.3 and 4.4 show the uses of spousal PPOs 'until further order' and for a 'fixed term' respectively. These charts thereby demonstrate the county courts' responses to what is now s 25A(2) of the MCA 1973:

Charts 4.3 and 4.4 – AFT periodical payments orders 1985–98 (county courts)

Spousal orders made for fixed term

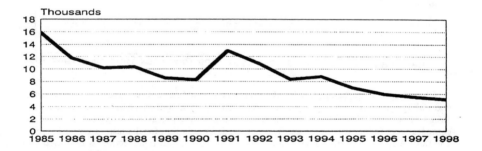

Spousal orders made pending further order

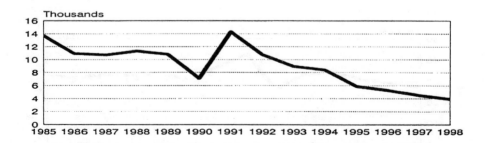

'the court shall in particular consider whether it would be appropriate to require those payments to be made ... for such term as would ... be sufficient to enable the [payee] to adjust without undue hardship to the termination of ... her financial dependence on the other party.'

Charts 4.3 and 4.4 show that there has been a consistently even recourse to these two possibilities. We will firmly bypass the issue of what might constitute due hardship, and why it should be disregarded, by concentrating instead on something once thought synonymous with divorce: permanent maintenance for former wives. Whether or not there have ever been many 'alimony drones', there certainly aren't too many people today who are obtaining AFR PPOs 'until further notice'. Quite apart from such orders dropping by 250% (from 13,724 to 3920) since the MFPA 1984, the number made in the county courts in 1998 was less than 3% of the number of main decrees granted in the same year. The presumably higher percentage of such orders made in the few High Court cases cannot justify – although it may, together with media and fictional accounts, help to explain – the continuing association in the public mind of divorce and spousal maintenance. Student tests and exam questions, based on untypical 'scenarios', are probably nearly as misleading.

In the light of these figures, we wonder how the 50-year-old former wife is expected to maintain herself, at a time when firms are reluctant to employ older people. It should be remembered that when firms do employ such people, they often prefer to lay them off with an early retirement package which may discriminate against those with interrupted work service and lower salaries – ie 50-year-old former wives! ...

Conclusion – Why are there so many more divorces than there are ancillary financial relief orders?

Chart 6 looks like the final part of a fairground ride, culminating in the pull-in to the station. Between 1991 and 1992 it looks like all the other charts above, perhaps because the 1991 legislation triggered a Corporal Jones-like burst of running round and 'not' panicking. But why, today, are AFR orders restricted to fewer than half the number of main decrees? The rate is even less than it appears from a causal glance at the chart, because a significant number of divorces, etc must each elicit multiple AFR orders (for example, capital orders and child maintenance). Furthermore, Chart 6 includes those spousal PPO applications which were dismissed. ...

Chart 6 – Percentage of all AFR orders per number of main decrees 1985–98 (county courts)

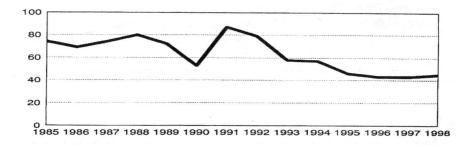

But why is it that only a minority of divorces now leads to money and property orders? One suspects many petitions, at least, have ticks in the AFR application boxes. Yet there a number of factors which may go some way to explaining the shortfall. They include remarriage, no assets other than local authority housing, and a literal recourse to private ordering. (No doubt the last must present a dilemma to any lawyers involved, whose dutiful admiration of the parties' conciliatory approach must have been at odds with their own wish to avoid action for professional negligence should one party subsequently win the lottery and/or the other become disabled: perhaps some of the main decree/AFR carefully filed gaps have been closed by disclaimers.) But perhaps there are two major factors. The first is the number of short-marriage, child-free divorces involving parties who had not built up much equity in their – anyway equally owned – family home: a young couple with similar salaries where no claim is likely to succeed. Finally, the drop since 1993 may mean that in those cases which previously attracted token spousal PPOs tacked on to child maintenance orders, the financially badly off parent is simply not issuing proceedings (perhaps as an adjunct to DIY divorce).

Is this declining usage a welcome trend? On the face of it, some spouses are acting like cohabitants in giving up their divorce rights. Some sort of a gap, at least, was within the contemplation of the Family Law Act 1996. Section 9, in normally requiring financial arrangements to be made pre-divorce, would have accepted:

(c) a declaration by both parties that they have made their own financial arrangements;

(d) a declaration by one of the parties (to which no objection has been notified to the court by the other party) that—

    (i) he has no significant assets and does not intend to make an application for financial provision;

    (ii) he believes that the other party has no significant assets and does not intend to make an application for financial provision; and

    (iii) there are therefore no financial arrangements to be made.

What would happen (today) if one of them, not to mention the taxpayer, later regrets her inaction? The Children Act 1989 plus the Child Support Acts 1991–95 would take care of her children and, under s 26 of the Matrimonial Causes Act 1973 she could seek leave to apply for herself. Whilst there are no statistics on the use of s 26, anecdotal evidence suggests that recourse is rare: how many would-be – unremarried – applicants know about it? Whatever the explanation for the falling numbers of ancillary financial relief orders, the decline does not seem to be worrying the parties. Perhaps the essential point of all these figures is the drive towards settlement; positive because of non-adversarial lawyers and mediators and negative because of the prohibitive costs for some people.

Question

Would the process of resolving the financial outcome of divorce, and/or the outcomes of the process, be improved at all by giving greater emphasis to pre-nuptial agreements made by the couple?

In the Green Paper, *Supporting Families* (para 4.20 ff), the Government advocates that 'pre-nups' should be legally binding except in six circumstances: where a child has been born; where the agreement is unenforceable under the general law of contract; where one or both parties did not receive prior independent legal advice; 'where the court considers that the enforcement of the agreement would cause significant injustice'; incomplete disclosure; agreement made less than 21 days before marriage. Do you see some potential for litigation here? See the comments by Chris Barton, in 'Spending more time with their families – the Government's consultation document' (1999) and Jane Lewis, in 'Relationship Breakdown, Obligations and Contracts' (1999).

8.6.2 Coping

However the financial settlement is reached, it takes time to get there. How do people cope in that interim period, between separation (or even desertion), before a financial agreement or order takes effect? This question was addressed in a study conducted by Cardiff Law School and sponsored by the Joseph Rowntree Foundation, carried out by a team led by Gillian Douglas and Mervyn Murch. A summary of their findings, published by the JRF in April 2000, sets out the objectives and findings of the project:

Background

The impact of separation and divorce upon family finances and living standards has been the subject of attention from both academic researchers and policy-makers over the years. There is considerable evidence demonstrating the often substantial drop in the standard of living likely to be experienced by carers (usually mothers) and children when the family is broken up and the extent to which such families depend on social security benefits. The working of the legal process has also been studied, and data collected on how financial settlements are handled by lawyers and the courts.

However, less is known about the shorter-term effects of marriage breakdown, and how families adjust to separation. When a marriage breaks down, there will be many immediate financial matters to deal with, which cannot wait for the divorce process to reach a conclusion. This study investigated the range of issues which parents have to deal with during this interim period and how they responded to them. It also collected information on the divorce settlements which parents finally reached, exploring their motivations and objectives in reaching them and their attitudes to the law and legal process.

Changes in income and expenditure

The mothers in the study were much more likely to experience a drop in the level of income available to them after separation than the fathers, reflecting their previous dependence upon their husbands for the bulk of the family's support. The income of the majority of men was unchanged or only temporarily affected by their separation, but nearly half the women had not recovered to their pre-separation level by the time of the interview.

In the short term, even where the father had left, he continued to provide the main source of the mother's income in nearly a third of the cases, yet this was rarely categorised by either party as 'maintenance'. Parents who left the home, especially men, had extra expenses to meet because they remained liable (practically as well as legally) to continue to pay for at least some of the costs of the family they left behind. Mothers were much more likely than fathers to make up their income from a variety of sources.

Effects on housing

Over half of the parents in the sample had left the matrimonial home since the marriage broke down. Women, and those with care of the children, were more likely to stay in the home. Only a quarter of homes were put up for sale, perhaps reflecting the state of the housing market at the time of their separation. Men – who were less likely to have children living with them – were much more likely to move several times in search of a secure home. Just under half the women who had moved had done so only once, while this was true of only 9 per cent of the men who had moved. Nearly half of parents, and over half of *mothers* reported difficulties in meeting housing costs.

Difficulties in coping with expenses

Three-quarters of the parents reported experiencing difficulty in making ends meet after separation. One-off expenses, such as holidays, birthdays and special occasions, were particularly problematic. Mothers were much more likely to face difficulties than fathers, due to their generally lower levels of income and their childcare responsibilities. One mother, reflecting on Christmas, said:

> 'I just try to put something away every month throughout the year to pay for it. But this year I only just managed ... I said to some people this year "Do you mind if we just give cards?" and they were very understanding, but it wasn't very nice to have to say it.'

Ways of coping

Parents used a wide range of measures to cope with their financial difficulties. Fathers, already usually in full-time work, might take advantage of overtime. Mothers, less likely to be working full-time before the separation, either took up such work or increased their part-time hours. The other side of the coin was to cut back on expenditure. Paring back spending could have a considerable impact upon the children's standard of living, especially affecting their ability to take part in school trips and leisure activities outside school. Parents learned to budget carefully, but many had to run down their savings, and resorted to borrowing, sometimes with detrimental results.

Support from the other spouse

The study confirmed that 'spousal maintenance' is now rare. Child maintenance, in the form of a court order or child support assessment, was also relatively infrequent. Much more commonly, a parent seemed to support the child through a voluntary arrangement, even where the carer was receiving social security benefits.

Forms of support other than regular maintenance were common, both for mothers and children. These ranged from continuing to pay the mortgage, to meeting school fees or the costs of holidays, clothes and leisure activities. No association was found in this study between paying child maintenance and exercising contact with the child.

Support from others

For one-off cash, and other forms of essential financial assistance, parents were likely to turn to their family. Friends provided an important source of emotional and practical support, although were less likely to be used for direct financial aid.

'My parents kept me going basically, with 'Red Cross' parcels. And now and again they used to send me a cheque to top up the freezer, pay the gas bills and things like that.'

Advice and assistance

Whether parents obtained what they regarded as adequate professional advice and assistance in charting a course through the murky waters of separation and divorce appeared a matter of good luck and individual circumstances.

'There's nobody to advise you, and that's where I think the whole thing goes 'phtt' because if it weren't for my brother, I think I'd have had a bum deal all the way down the line.'

Parents' experiences of dealing with banks and lenders varied widely. They appeared to need appropriate advice early on, but found that Citizens' Advice Bureaux, though useful in offering general advice, were unable to provide specific and sufficiently detailed help.

The legal process

Solicitors were usually not approached until the time came for what the parents saw as the 'legal side' of the separation to be dealt with. Parents seemed to use solicitors to handle the formal aspects of this, and to spell out the range of options open to them, but often negotiated the terms of the settlement between themselves. Only a minority of parents obtained legally binding orders settling their finances.

'Apart from making if official, it was all between ourselves. The solicitor complained he had nothing to do.'

The final settlement

Although the courts have wide powers to allocate property between the spouses, regardless of which spouse is the legal owner, the couples themselves tended to think that, apart from the house, entitlement to assets on divorce followed ownership. This was particularly so in relation to the pension. Mothers were much more concerned to secure their immediate housing needs (and those of their children) than to worry about their old age, and they traded off any claim to a share of the pension return for staying in the home or a larger share of the equity. Meeting the needs of the children, and the wish to avoid arguments, were the primary factors influencing the details of the settlement.

'That's why I gave him the car, I gave him the house. It wasn't worth the emotional trauma. I just wanted it to stop.'

Nearly a quarter of parents felt that the settlement had been unfair to them or to their children. They were fairly evenly divided as to whether a pre-nuptial agreement would be a good idea. Some felt that this could protect their existing children in any future divorce, but others were worried that it would be impossible to foresee how circumstances might change. Fathers were more likely to favour such agreements than mothers.

Implications for policy and practice

The researchers conclude that the deep financial difficulty into which families may be plunged when parents separate needs to be directly addressed through a review by both the private sector and the social security system of the ways in which they respond to parents' needs. There is also a need for reliable, accessible and appropriate advice and support to families facing marital breakdown, which provides detailed and individual assistance as and when they need it, and across the whole range of issues arising on marriage breakdown. The legal system, and the services provided by lawyers, cannot and should not be expected to meet this need entirely. However, the law can set out more clearly the objectives and the approach which should be taken when settling family finances which would aid couples in negotiating a settlement.

Question

Do you think that the case for reform of the law is made stronger by the project's findings?

8.6.3 Settling up, settling down

We now consider the outcomes of these procedures. We mentioned earlier in this chapter some of the 'folk myths' that persist about the financial outcomes of divorce. In a seminar paper, 'Settling Up: the views and values underpinning financial separation' (2000) Jane Lewis and Sue Arthur make the following points:

There were a number of important factors that shaped people's approach to reaching agreement about financial arrangements. One of the dominant factors was a pragmatic consideration of the financial needs of the two parties and the relative resources available to meet them. Children's needs were generally emphasised over and above the need of either parent. There was a greater emphasis on i) current rather than future need and resources, and ii) capital rather than income provision, for example a greater focus on the provision of a home than on the means to support the home.

There was a reluctance to see income as in any way joint following separation, except in relation to financial support for children, which was generally seen as a moral obligation. Items which had been funded out of the income of one partner also tended to be seen as no longer joint on separation, in the same way as items which had been inherited or acquired prior to the marriage. The clear exception here was the family home, where non-financial contributions (the running of the home, and caring for children) appeared to play a key role in a sense of entitlement. There were mixed views about the role that the assets or needs of new partners should play in a couple's financial division, and again differences in views about income and capital.

Underpinning these views were strong and widely held feelings about equality and a 'clean break'. An equal division was seen as an underlying principle, but one which did not apply in a range of circumstances. Interestingly, the idea of equality of *impact* did not appear to be important in influencing people's approach. The attribution of fault for instigating the break up of the relationship was another key factor underlying people's approaches to financial arrangements.

While some of these factors reflect the legal situation and others do not, it was notable that people's views did not appear to be based strongly on any knowledge or understanding of legal entitlement. Rather they were underpinned by pragmatism, emotional preferences, financial constraints, and moral principles or understandings (such as equal partnerships, or moral obligations to support children). Also interesting was the apparent lack of a systematic approach in applying these factors, for example in assessing needs, or in valuing all assets. ...

Pensions appeared not to have been taken into account in most of the cases involved in this study. They remained with the person in whose name they were held, but this was not seen as part of the arrangements or settlement and there was no compensation, offsetting or other provision for the future for the other party. People were sometimes not aware they had an entitlement to pension rights, or believed the values to be too low to consider, or were resistant to making a claim. The fact that the pension was derived from the husband's earnings appeared to remove any sense of entitlement, even though couples generally had shared access to the husband's earning during the marriage, and to the house which may have largely derived from them. ...

Ultimately, women – and to a lesser extent men with substantial caring responsibilities – traded off housing against income, capital and future provision.

(See the full research report, *Settling Up: making financial arrangements after divorce or separation* (2002).)

Question

Look back at the observations on pensions made by Jay Ginn and Debbie Price (p. 369, above); can you see any way to prevent women making this trade-off?

Hard evidence of what actually happens began to emerge in the 1980s. Eekelaar and Maclean in *Maintenance after Divorce* (1986), undertook to describe the present financial circumstances of a nationally representative sample of those who have divorced in England and Wales since the introduction of no-fault divorce in 1971. They chose an 'omnibus survey' which approached a quota sample of 8,000 individuals in England and Wales in May 1981; from this they were given permission to approach 92 of the men and 184 of the women. As the researchers admit:

our final sample of 276 individuals is, of course, relatively small. It was, however, central to our strategy that it should be as closely representative of the divorcing population at large as we could make it. We therefore chose not to distort our original sample by interviewing additional cases with particular characteristics.

They comment in detail on the housing position:

A distinction needs to be drawn between occupants of local authority housing at the time of separation and those enjoying other types of housing provision. In the former case, the childless invariably left the accommodation. But where there were children, 79 per cent of the women interview respondents (n = 52) and 30 per cent of the men (n = 21) stayed; all but one of the men having custody of the children. ... Of the few women who left, three returned (with their children) to their own families, four moved into a house with their new partners; and in one case both parents left and were re-housed by the local authority. For these people, then, housing circumstances in themselves played no significant role in altering their living standards on divorce. The effects of divorce would primarily be felt in respect to income. A similar pattern was found among the long-term mothers interviewed in 1984. Eight out of the ten in local authority housing at separation stayed there, the other two moving into owner-occupation (one with married children and one buying her council house).

But when we look at the housing outcome with respect to the owner-occupiers, a more complex picture emerges. ... childless and children divorces share one feature regarding the home. In almost half of each category, the owner-occupied home was sold on divorce. In the case of the childless, the reason for the sale seems to have been to allow the wife to realize her half-share in the house, for half the homes of such couples which were in their joint names were sold. If the house was not sold, it was much more likely that the husband would stay on in the home than the wife, but in the event the wife would invariably leave with a lump sum payment; the husband had bought her out. In the three cases (13 per cent) where the wife left without a share, she went straight into a home provided by another man. If the house was in the husband's name alone, he was overwhelmingly likely to remain in it and the wife to leave without any lump sum payment. It is possible that in some of those cases the wife went uncompensated for any beneficial interest she may have acquired in the home by reason of direct or indirect monetary contributions to its acquisition. The advantage, from a wife's point of view, of joint legal ownership is clear, and the message of these findings seems to be that for childless marriages, a lump sum payment made to the wife is likely to be in the form of strict compensation for the transfer to the husband of a property interest.

It is striking that owner-occupied homes are just as likely to be sold in the case of divorces involving dependent children as where the marriage was childless, despite the well-established policy of the courts that one of the primary goals of divorce settlement is to secure accommodation for the children, usually by keeping them in the matrimonial home. [See *H v H (family provision remarriage)* [1975] Fam 9, [1975] 1 All ER 367.] Are the children of divorcees who live in the owner-occupier sector subject to greater disruption than those of divorcees who live in public-sector housing?

In a number of cases it might be unnecessary to keep the home for the children because they and the wife will be moving into accommodation provided by another man. In four (28 per cent) of the cases where the house was sold the woman moved in with a new partner. So in over a quarter of the cases where the home was sold, no accommodation problem for the children arose. What of the other cases? It seems that the sales in these cases might either have been desired by the caregiving parent wanting to move from the area, or forced on her by the financial situation. This can be deduced from the fact that the wife stayed on in the house only once (3 per cent) in the childless cases, but did so in *one-quarter* of the children cases, irrespective of whether the house was in joint names or in the husband's name alone. Put another way, the wife stayed in half of the cases where the home was not sold. The reason for this is undoubtedly to provide accommodation for the children, and there is no reason to believe that this would not have happened in those cases where the house was sold were it not for the fact that the wife desired the sale or had it forced on her. Indeed, a small number of the sales (10 per cent) were in fact the result of foreclosure by the mortgagee. Others may well have taken place to prevent this eventuality.

It is at this point, of course, that the difficulties which the families with children experience over income have direct impact on their housing conditions. Yet, about three-quarters of the divorced mothers, still single and with dependent children, who had been in owner-occupation at the time of their separation were still living in *the private sector* at the time of interview. The lump sum acquired by the sale, or support from the former husband, or payments of mortgage interest by the supplementary benefit authorities, cushioned the *extent* of the deterioration in their housing circumstances; or, at least, the degree to which they needed to go to the public housing authorities for assistance. It is plausible to suppose that a move from the private sector will frequently cause greater social disruption, especially as regards the children's school environment, than moves within a sector. Our data showed that, of the women who moved, half (seven) were able to buy in the private sector (three of them later remarried). Only three (21 per cent) moved into public housing.

Our findings regarding the housing circumstances of divorcing men fail to show any disturbing degrees of hardship. In the childless cases, the man either kept the house or sold it, taking his share. Even where there were children, he stayed on in the house in one-quarter of the cases. Where the wife stayed, we found no evidence that she was joined by a cohabitee or new husband. The pattern seems clearly to be that, where a new partner enters the scene, he will provide a home for the wife and children. Where, in the divorces involving dependent children, the home was sold, the husband invariably took his share. There were, however, a few cases (thirteen (22 per cent) of those where either the house was sold or the wife remained in it) where the husband left without any apparent immediate compensation for his capital loss. However, four involved a 'Mesher' arrangement whereby the house is settled on trust for sale for both parents but sale is postponed until the youngest child reaches a certain age (usually eighteen or on completion of full-time education), or until a court order is made. Thus the husband is not deprived of his capital; his enjoyment of it is simply postponed. Of the seven cases where the husband left without taking any share of the asset, three forewent their share in discharge of their support obligation, one went to a new partner with a house and we had no information on the others. It should be remembered, of course, that when it is the man who leaves, it will usually be very difficult for the wife to raise sufficient capital to pay him a lump sum. Her inferior earning power and commitments to the children effectively preclude such a course.

The long-term mothers in owner-occupation at the time of separation were perhaps more firmly established in this sector. Even so, in half of the cases the home was sold and the proceeds shared enabled the women to buy a smaller property. Of the cases where the house was not sold, in half the house was occupied in lieu of maintenance (in one case with a 'Mesher' agreement), and in the two remaining cases the wife purchased her husband's interest, one with her own resources and the other with parental help.

We should conclude this review of the economic conditions of families after divorce by remarking on the significance of housing provision. Were it not for the relative security provided by public-sector housing, the position of many divorced single mothers would be far worse than it is. As we have seen, there is no potential in income transfers to substitute for its absence. We might make the same observation with respect to health care. It is fortunately not essential for these mothers to rely on income provision, from the state or from the absent parent, to meet the medical expenses of their children. These fall on the community through the national health service. But even outside the ambit of community-financed services, we note that, as far as accommodation is concerned, the position of mothers living in the private sector is not totally bleak. Most managed to stay in that sector, even if precariously. The attention given to the accommodation of children by judicial policy seems, according to our data, to have borne some fruit and, in so far as it has done so, has reduced the extent to which the receipt of income maintenance is critical to the most fundamental needs of these families [see Chapter 4, above]. The Social Security Review of 1985 revealed that the government was concerned about the burden which housing-related benefit (whether by way of rate rebates, payment of rent and mortgage interest, and of water and heating charges) was placing on the social security budget *(Reform of Social Security* (1985)). The implications of any erosion of these benefits for families broken by divorce do not seem to have been considered. The result might be to throw them into greater dependence on maintenance from the absent parent to undermine the already precarious degree to which stability in housing those in owner-occupation has been achieved and to put new pressure on the public sector.

Questions

(i)   What conclusions do you draw from Eekelaar and Maclean's work?
(ii) Is dependence on maintenance from the absent parent a good thing or a bad thing? (See Chapter 4, above.)

The *General Household Survey 1993* (published 1995) considers first the general pattern of housing tenure over the previous two decades (fig. 3A, below), and then the relationship between divorce, re-marriage and housing tenure. It is claimed that:

Almost two-thirds of divorced people who were owner-occupiers prior to separation were also owner-occupiers one year after divorce and almost three-quarters of those whose matrimonial home was rented were still living in rented accommodation one year after divorce. ... Twenty per cent of former owner-occupiers and 22% of former tenants had ceased to be householders in their own right one year after divorce. ... Men were more likely than women to have changed their tenure. ... Those whose tenure was unchanged a year after divorce, were unlikely to have changed their tenure later.

Figure 3A Tenure: Great Britain, 1971–93

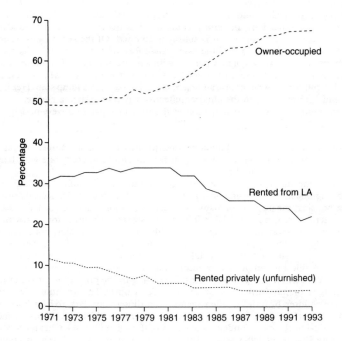

Question

Do these data shed any more light upon the questions considered by Eekelaar and Maclean?

Finally, we consider the major recent research undertaken by a team led by Gwynn Davis at the University of Bristol. He and his colleagues (Julia Pearce, Roger Bird, Hilary Woodward and Chris Wallace) presented their findings in 'Ancillary relief outcomes' (2000); the picture is, to say the least, complex:

QUESTIONS FOR THIS STUDY

We undertook this research because we felt we lacked detailed evidence of family financial circumstances matched to outcome in specific cases. We attempted, therefore, to analyse outcomes of ancillary relief applications by reference to specific case characteristics as reflected in the various documents on the court file. We wanted to describe the range of outcomes arrived at in respect of like cases, and to explore the reasons for such differences as emerged. Overall we were seeking to establish whether there was, broadly speaking, congruity of outcome in like circumstances; if not, why not; and whether decisions in leading cases determine settlements and lower court adjudications in the way everyone imagines...

ANALYSING FAMILY FINANCES

In was necessary for us, in recording information from the court files, to develop systems of classification in order to try to make sense of what otherwise would have appeared a mass of detail. We divided the family financial information into five categories:

- family type;
- family home;
- other assets;
- husband's income;
- wife's income.

By family type we meant whether the couple had dependent children, and – if there were no dependent children – whether the marriage had been long or short. The breakdown amongst the 285 cases analysed is presented in Table 2 below. We would be the first to admit that this is a very crude (and limited) categorisation. In particular, to group together all those cases which involved dependent children is about as 'broad brush' as one could get – and only justifiable on the basis that the way that courts and lawyers approach these cases is similar to the extent that the children's interests, and in particular their need for a 'roof', will be the first consideration. But of course there is a vast difference between, say, having three children under five and having one teenager on the verge of financial independence (as the parents may fondly hope). Such differences will, of course, be reflected in the ancillary relief orders which are negotiated by lawyers or determined by the court. To that extent it is important to recognise in all that follows that our various categorisations greatly under-represent the complexities which are involved in arriving at a fair – or 'appropriate' – financial outcome in these cases.

Table 2 – Family type

Marriage up to seven years, no children	63	22%
Marriage over seven years, no children	27	9.5%
Marriage with dependent children	157	55%
Marriage with adult children (only)	38	13%
Total	285	

As can be seen, 55% of the cases analysed involved dependent children; 22% involved short marriages (less than seven years), not producing children; and the other 23% either involved longer marriages without children, or, if children had resulted, they were no longer dependent.

Our second category of information concerned the family home. Here we distinguished cases in which (as far as we could discern) there was no home to assign, council tenancies; and three categories of private ownership, with the divisions being based on the amount of equity in the property. The breakdown amongst our 285 cases is contained in Table 3 below.

Table 3 – Family home

Council tenancy	15	5%
Private (equity up to £5000)	64	22.5%
Private (equity £5000 – £20,000)	77	27%
Private (equity over £20,000)	111	39%
No home to assign	18	6%
Total	285	

As can be seen, of the 285 cases, 252 (88.5%) included amongst the assets a privately owned family home. In many of these cases, as previously explained, the home would have been assigned *prior* to a consent application being filed. The three categories of equity were chosen simply on the basis that they generated three roughly equal divisions within the private ownership category. It is perhaps worthy of note that an equity of more than £20,000 was a feature of only 111 cases – which is just 39% of the total sample, or 44% of cases in which there was a privately owned home to assign. It has been observed that following the last Conservative administration's encouragement to local authority tenants to purchase their properties, and especially following house price inflation in the 1980s, many separating couples found themselves 'property rich but income poor'. Most of these divorcing couples were 'income poor', but the majority do not appear 'property rich'.

Our third category was that of 'other assets' – savings in any form, including insurance policies and pension entitlement. As can be seen from Table 4 (below), in over 50% of cases these 'other assets' totalled, as far as we could judge from the file, less than £5000. Just over one-quarter of our sample had assets (other than the family home) in excess of £20,000. Given the inevitable tendency for academic commentators to focus their attention upon cases which reach the higher courts, some of which involve assets running into millions of pounds, it is salutary to note the scale of the assets in the common run of divorce cases.

Table 4 – Other assets (including pensions)

Up to £5000	147	51.5%
£5000 – £20,000	60	21%
Over £20,000	78	27%
Total	285	

Our final two categories of financial information concerned the incomes of husband and wife respectively. Here again we determined income bands simply on the basis that they created roughly equal divisions within our case sample. Thus we find that the main income band for men was between £9000 and £15,000 (42%), which is significantly below average earnings. Only 8% of these divorced men had an income in excess of £25,000.

One-quarter of the women in the sample had no income other than state benefits. Only 6% had an income in excess of £15,000 and so might be considered, on that simple yardstick, financially independent. It has been pointed out to us that the time at which the parties' incomes were recorded may be critical. A Cardiff University study of parents' financial arrangements in the immediate aftermath of separation found that women's incomes often 'recovered' to some extent in the period following separation. This might explain some aberrant or apparently unfair outcomes.

Table 5 – Husband's income

Benefits only	37	13%
Income up to £8000	39	14%
Income £9000-£15,000	119	42%
Income £16,000-£25,000	66	23%
Income over £25,000	24	8%
Total	285	

Table 6 – Wife's income

Benefits only	73	25.5%
Income up to £5000	41	14.5%
Income £6000-£10,000	105	37%
Income £11,000-£15,000	49	17%
Income over £15,000	17	6%
Total	285	

Having presented these basic components of family financial information in five categories, we can now move to examine the relationship *between* the various elements. Our first step towards this is contained in Table 7 (below), which gives a breakdown of financial information relating to the home matched against family type.

Table 7 – Tabulation of family type by family home

Marriage up to seven years, no children
Council tenancy	1	0%
Owned – equity to £5000	24	8%
Owned – equity £5000-£20,000	19	6.6%
Owned – equity over £20,000	13	4.5%
No home to assign	6	2%

Marriage over seven years, no children
Owned – equity to £5000	4	1.4%
Owned – equity £5000-£20,000	11	4%
Owned – equity over £20,000	8	3%
No home to assign	4	1.4%

Marriage with dependent children
Council tenancy	13	4.5%
Owned – equity to £5000	33	11.5%
Owned – equity £5000-£20,000	43	15%
Owned – equity over £20,000	63	22%
No home to assign	5	1.7%

Adult children
Council tenancy	1	0%
Owned – equity to £5000	3	1%
Owned – equity £5000-£20,000	4	1.4%
Owned – equity over £20,000	27	9.5%
No home to assign	3	1%
Total	285	

There are marked differences between the various 'family types' in terms of home ownership – and in terms of the equity in the property. For example, if we take an equity in excess of £20,000 as our yardstick, the position is as given in Table 8 (below).

Table 8 – Percentage of cases in which the equity in the home exceeded £20,000

Marriage up to seven years, no children	20%
Marriage over seven years, no children	30%
Marriage with dependent children	40%
Adult children only	71%

It is striking, we think, how few divorcing couples with children, in the mid-1990s, had significant equity in the family home. The majority had the bricks and mortar, but for the most part these properties were heavily mortgaged. As we have already said, few of these couples were 'property rich', and this is important in that it allows little room for manoeuvre in assigning the property. On this evidence there can seldom be much scope for selling the home and re-housing the children and their mother in a cheaper property in order to free up capital for the husband...

Our final computing exercise involved bringing together the five components of our analysis, incorporating the breakdowns within each category as previously determined. In the resulting table our 285 cases generated 192 separate case categories – mostly, of course, with a single case in each...

ANALYSING OUTCOME

It seemed to us that there were three possible approaches to the task of analysing ancillary relief orders by reference to family financial circumstances as revealed on the court file:

(1) we could start with our case data and try to examine the relationship between case characteristics and outcome, employing whatever categorisations emerge from the data;

(2) we could identify, on the basis of our own experience of these matters, what we believe to be key factors in terms of family relationship, assets/income etc, and then construct a series of categories, each of which should lead to an outcome within a fairly narrow range (in other words, whilst approach (1) would be purely empirical, (2) would involve an element of prior conceptualisation); or

(3) we could forget case classification and focus instead on apparently aberrant outcomes. This would require us to judge cases intuitively, consigning most to a 'non-aberrant' category and then scrutinising the remainder in some depth in order to try to understand the factors which had led to a departure from the norm.

We thought that any of the above was defensible, and would probably lead to similar findings at the end of the day. However, a breakdown of our cases by the five very basic features previously outlined hardly encouraged us to extend this approach to incorporate court orders. Even this very limited set of variables generated 192 distinct categories, rendering comparisons within each case type somewhat impractical. It would obviously have been futile to add more variables, and nor did it seem feasible to superimpose the terms of the court order upon the analysis.

The other difficulty which we faced – and this would have applied whatever approach we took in analysing our data – was that the information available on the file was often insufficient for us to feel confident in judging the appropriateness of the order. The greatest variation in outcome (or the greatest unpredictability of outcome) was in consent applications, with the parties quite often appearing to settle on terms which we doubted a court would have ordered following a trial.

Although we found some variation of order in apparently similar circumstances, commonly, where *additional* information was provided, the order would seem perfectly sensible. What we are saying therefore is that the number of *potentially* relevant factors is enormous, and it would have been impossible for us to incorporate all these factors into our analysis, even if the information had been available…

Our final attempt to solve the conundrum of how to devise a system for matching orders to family finances involved homing in on what appeared – judging these matters intuitively – to be aberrant outcomes. There were in fact quite a few cases which appeared on the face of it to diverge from the norm – either because the children's housing needs were not obviously met, or because there appeared to be inequity between the parties. These comprised perhaps 5% of the case sample – although in each instance the order may not have seemed at all odd had we known the full facts. In what follows we focus on three categories of apparently aberrant outcomes:

(1) apparent inequity between the parties;
(2) possibly inappropriate clean breaks; and
(3) oddities associated with cohabitation.

APPARENT INEQUALITY

- Three-year marriage; no children; equity in the home of £2000. Both the home and a life policy to go to the husband; nothing to the wife.
- Short marriage; no children; £7000 equity in the home; husband and wife earning similar amounts. Home to the wife; nothing to the husband.
- Thirty-year marriage; adult children; both cohabiting; £35,000 equity in the home; wife earns £14,000 per annum; husband earns £9000 per annum. Home to the husband; wife to receive £10,000.
- Twenty-eight-year marriage; adult children; £45,000 equity in the home; husband has a pension valued at £225,000; he currently earns over £3000 per month; wife earns £850 per month. Husband to pay £50,000 to the wife; all insurance policies to the husband; home to the husband (in this case the Bill of Costs revealed that the wife went against her solicitor's advice).
- Fourteen-year marriage; three children aged 12, 10 and six – all to live with the wife; £23,000 equity in the home; husband earning £19,000 per annum; wife earning £1200 per annum. Wife to have the home; husband to pay £100 per month per child; wife to have the life policy and a £2000 lump sum.
- Five-year marriage; one child; husband and wife both earning £16,000–17,000; £73,000 equity in the home; neither party cohabiting. Wife to transfer her interest in the home to the husband in return for £20,000; he also to have the life policies, valued at £1400; no reference to where the child is to be housed.
- Husband and wife both earning approximately £16,000 per annum; three teenage children – to live with the wife; equity of £60,000 in the family home. Home to the wife, plus substantial child maintenance; husband to receive £6500.
- Two children aged 16 and 18 to live with the wife; she is disabled and earning £500 per month; husband earns £16,000 per annum (or more – this is disputed) and has other assets valued at £8000, including a life policy; equity of £24,000 in the home. Home to be sold and wife to receive 60% of its value, plus the life policy (valued at £6000); clean break order.

QUESTIONABLE CLEAN BREAKS

- Twenty-seven-year marriage with adult children; equity of £4000 in the home; husband earns £10,500 per annum, wife on benefits. Wife to have the home; clean break order.
- Sixteen-year marriage; two teenage children; husband earns £400 per month; wife also earns, and receives family credit. Council tenancy transferred to wife; clean break order.

- Six-year marriage; two children aged four and two; husband earns £1400 per month; wife on income support; negative equity in the property. Wife to get the home; not stated whether Child Support Agency involved; clean break order.
- Husband earns £1350 per month; wife on benefits; four-year-old disabled child with mother; husband has 12-year contribution to pension scheme. Home (with £2000 equity) to the wife; clean break order.
- Husband earns £1000 per month; eight-year-old child to live with wife; £26,000 assets in total, including equity in the home. Assets to be split 50/50; husband to pay £30 per week for child; clean break order.

IMPACT OF COHABITATION

- Five-year marriage; four-year-old child to live with wife; equity of £6000 in the home; husband earns £10,000 per annum; wife on incapacity benefit; both parties cohabiting. Wife agrees that she has no interest in the home; life policy divided equally.
- Wife has purchased new property with equity of £11,000; £20,000 equity in former matrimonial home; nine-year-old child living with wife; both parties cohabiting. Former matrimonial home to go to husband; life policy (value not specified) also to go to husband; apparently nothing for the wife, other than new home already purchased.
- Three children aged three, seven and eight all living with the wife; equity in family home £25,000; husband earns £230 per week and has pension valued at £25,000; wife earns £120 per week; wife cohabiting. Husband to have home and life policy (value not stated on file); wife to have £10,000.
- Six-year marriage; no children; husband cohabiting; equity of £9000 in the home; also an insurance policy valued at £1500. Home and insurance policy to the wife; nothing to the husband.
- Eleven-year marriage; no children; both cohabiting; £20,000 equity in the home; wife earns £8500 per annum; husband on Income Support. Husband to have the home; £2000 to the wife.

There were a few other cases which might have been included in these lists, but these were the most obvious ones. As we say, some of them might not appear at all 'odd' were we in possession of the full facts. That aside, it is a difficult policy issue to determine how much leeway the court *ought* to allow in giving its imprimatur to consent applications freely negotiated. Of course one or other party (but usually the wife) may have been subject to a variety of pressures which the court would wish to protect her against. But the possibility of coercion aside, and assuming that the children's interests are safeguarded, it is a moot point how far the court should seek to intervene.

Discussion...

The former Parliamentary Secretary in the Lord Chancellor's Office announced in 1998 that the Government intended to 'deliver a greater sense of certainty for the parties, without preventing the courts from ensuring that the outcome of cases is, as far as possible, fair and just to all concerned'. In keeping with that objective, the Government consultation paper, *Supporting Families*, suggested that – once the children's needs had been met – 'fairness will generally require the value of the assets to be divided equally between the parties'.

This proposal was presumably intended to achieve greater predictability in the determination of these cases. Whether it would promote fairness, or generate a greater sense of satisfaction with the resulting outcomes, is another question. ... In England and Wales we do not at present have an explicitly identified hierarchy of objectives, but it presumably would not hurt were this to be provided, if only as an aid to public understanding. It is not sufficient for experienced practitioners to understand these things: the parties directly concerned need help in penetrating the mysteries. Why should they not be told the basis upon which the finances are meant to be decided? If we really are concerned to provide the separating population with 'information' – and if we mean information, not indoctrination – we might start with a plain man's account of the basis upon which the court expects the financial cake to be apportioned. It is about the most important piece of information people could have – the rest is mainly preaching.

The evidence of the court files, limited as it is, does not encourage us to go further than this. Proposals to achieve greater predictability through, for example, a presumption of equal sharing – perhaps as a kind of 'third tier' principle, following upon those earlier alluded to – would almost certainly be unfair in their effects unless vitiated by yet further 'principles', even the most subtle proposals, such as those contained in Eekelaar's recent article, seem likely to run into definitional problems. If the objective is fairness it is difficult to know precisely when to stop along the road to rendering the whole thing formulaic. It is a paradox of formulae that they generate complexity. It would be our contention, on the evidence of the files, that most of these cases are fairly straightforward – they are simple, but they are idiosyncratic. That calls for individually tailored solutions – but these individual solutions should not require the expenditure of vast amounts of professional time.

What tends to take time is, first, achieving full disclosure, and secondly, an approach to negotiation which rests mostly upon bargaining and attrition. Any steps which limit the scope for bargaining and which place less reliance on attrition are, in principle, to be welcomed, although there are clearly limits to what can be achieved in this regard through the provision of a hierarchy of objectives. When we began this study one of the questions at the forefront of our minds was whether ancillary relief might be rendered more predictable than at present, thereby limiting the scope for unfair pressure of various kinds. As has been seen, our five-way breakdown of family financial information produced nearly 200 separate categories amongst 285 cases. That in itself was not a surprise – any breakdown which employs five variables, each of which has five possible 'values', will generate roughly this number of case categories – it is a statistical inevitability. The problem lies not with the differences which are revealed in our tables, but with all that has been excluded. Our various categories omitted a huge amount that was relevant, for example, cohabitees, debts, mortgage arrears, negative equity, marriage duration, parental support, compensation sums awarded, children from a previous relationship, and so on. The eventual orders – most of which were 'by consent' – could never have been predicted, in all their detail, from the financial pictures in the files. The specific case circumstances were such that whilst the main outlines of the eventual 'solution' were indeed predictable, the precise details were infinitely variable. Most of the bargaining, we presume, is about this detail, rather than about the main themes.

There is also the difficulty that the more we attempt to make ancillary relief formulaic, the more we lock the parties into patterns of division which may not make sense to them and which they would not choose as a reflection of their particular relationship history – or of their residual obligations and financial needs.

Questions

Where should ancillary relief go from here?

Bibliography

8.1   The historical background

We quoted from:

Sir Morris Finer and O.R. McGregor, 'The History of the Obligation to Maintain', App. 5, *Report of the Committee on One-Parent Families* (Cmnd. 5629-1) (1974) London, HMSO, paras. 26–27, 32–33, 35–38.

Additional reading

M.A. Glendon, *The New Family and the New Property* (1981) Toronto, Butterworths.

8.2   The Matrimonial Causes Act 1973

We quoted from:

R. Deech, 'The Principles of Maintenance' (1977) 7 Family Law 229, pp. 230–232.

Law Commission, *The Financial Consequences of Divorce: the Basic Policy: a Discussion Paper* (Cmnd. 8041) (1980) London, HMSO, paras. 24–27, 59, 66, 70, 73, 75, 77, 80, 84, 86.

Law Commission, *The Financial Consequences of Divorce,* Law Com. No. 112 (1980) London, HMSO, para. 17.

K. O'Donovan, 'The Principle of Maintenance: an Alternative View' (1978) 8 Family Law 180–184.

C. Smart, *The Ties that Bind* (1984) London, Routledge and Kegan Paul, pp. 223, 224, 227, 228.

G. Davis, S. Cretney and J. Collins, *Simple Quarrels* (1994), Oxford, Clarendon Press.

8.3   A question of principle

We quoted from:

E. Cooke, '*White v White*: a new yardstick for the marriage partnership' (2001) Child and Family Law Quarterly 81.

Additional reading:

G. Brasse, DJ, '*White v White* – A Return to Orthodoxy? [2001] Family Law 191.

S. Cretney, 'Black and White?' [2001] Family Law 3.

P. Duckworth and D. Hodson, '*White v White* – bringing section 25 back to the people?' [2001] Family Law 24.

J. Eekelaar, 'Should section 25 be reformed?' [1998] Family Law 469.

S. Ross, 'The Implications of *White v White* for Inheritance Act Claims' [2001] Family Law 547.

Singer, Mr Justice, 'Sexual Discrimination in Ancillary Relief' [2001] Family Law 115.

8.4   A Scottish alternative

We quoted from:

E. Jackson, F. Wasoff, M. Maclean and R.E. Dobash, 'Financial Support on Divorce: the Right Mixture of Rules and Discretion?' (1993) 7 International Journal of Law and the Family 230, p. 245.

The Scottish Law Commission, *Report on Aliment and Financial Provision,* Scot. Law Com. No. 67 (1981) Edinburgh, HMSO, paras. 3.18–3.22, 3.62, 3.65–3.68, 3.92–3.94, 3.107–3.110.

Additional reading

S. Cretney, 'Money After Divorce – The Mistakes We Have Made?' in M.D.A. Freeman (ed.), *Essays in Family Law 1985* (1986) London, Stevens.

E. Clive, 'The Financial Consequences of Divorce: Reform from the Scottish Perspective' in M.D.A. Freeman (ed.), *State, Law, and the Family* (1984) London, Tavistock.

A.R. Dewar, 'The Family Law (Scotland) Act 1985 in Practice' (1989) 42 Journal of the Law Society of Scotland.

E. Wasoff, R.E. Dobash and J. Harcus, *The Impact of the Family Law Scotland Act 1985 on Solicitors' Divorce Practice* (1990) Scottish Office, Central Research Unit Papers.

8.5   Section 25 in action

We quoted from:

R. Bird, District Judge, 'Ancillary relief outcomes' [2000] Family Law 831.

J. Black, J. Bridge and T. Bond, *A Practical Approach to Family Law* (3rd edn, 1994) London, Blackstone.

A. Dnes, 'Pension splitting in England and Wales' [1999] 21(1) Journal of Social Welfare and Family Law 41.

J. Eekelaar, 'Asset Distribution on Divorce – the Durational Element' [2001] 117 Law Quarterly Review 552.

J. Ginn and D. Price, 'Do divorced women catch up in pension building?' (2002) 14(2) Child and Family Law Quarterly 1, pp. 8 and 13–14.

E. Ingham, '*T v T*: Pension Earmarking' (1998) 148 New Law Journal 1484.

E. Jackson, F. Wasoff, M. Maclean and R.E. Dobash, 'Financial Support on Divorce: the Right Mixture of Rules and Discretion?' (1993) 7 International Journal of Law and the Family 230, p. 245.

Law Society, *Maintenance and Capital Provision on Divorce* (1991) London, The Law Society, 3.3.

S. Leech and R. Young, 'Marriage, Divorce and Ancillary Relief under the Human Rights Act 1998' [2001] European Human Rights Law Review 300.

Legal Services Commission's leaflet: *The Statutory Charge.*

R. Malone, letter to *The Times*, 26 August 1995.

M. Rae, 'Pensions and Divorce – Time for Change' (1995) New Law Journal 310.

Security, Equality, Choice: The Future for Pensions (Cm. 2594–I & II) (1994) London, HMSO, para. 1.45.

Supporting Families (1998) London, HMSO.

P. Symes, 'Indissolubility and the Clean Break' (1985) 48 Modern Law Review 44, pp. 46, 47, 51, 52, 53, 57, 59, 60.

Additional reading

R. Bailey-Harris, note on *Burrow v Burrow* [1999] 1 FLR 508, [1999] Family Law 83.

A. Dnes, *The Division of Marital Assets following Divorce with Particular Reference to Pensions* (Lord Chancellor's Department, Research Series no. 7/1997).

S.J. Glover, 'Pension sharing procedure' [2001] Family Law 691.

E. Hamilton QC, 'Is *White v White* a *Barder* event?' [2001] Family Law 135.

J. Harcus, 'Periodical Payments – End of Term' [1997] Family Law 340.

Home Office website: www.homeoffice.gov.uk.

D. Salter, 'A Practitioner's Guide to Pension Sharing' [2000] Family Law 489 and 543.

Singer, Mr Justice, 'Sexual Discrimination in Ancillary Relief' [2001] Family Law 115.

R. Thornton, 'Homelessness Through Relationship Breakdown: The Local Authorities' Response' [1987] Journal of Social Welfare Law 67.

Thorpe LJ 'The English System of Ancillary Relief' in R. Bailey-Harris (ed.), *Dividing the Assets on Family Breakdown* (1998) Family Law.

8.6   Empirical evidence

We quoted from:

Ch. Barton and A. Bissett-Johnson, 'The declining number of ancillary financial relief orders' [2000] Family Law 94.

J. Bradshaw and J. Millar, *Lone Parent Families in the UK,* Social Security Research Report, no. 6 (1991) London, HMSO, p. 98.

G. Davis, S. Cretney and J. Collins, *Simple Quarrels* (1994), Oxford, Clarendon Press, pp. 105–106.

G. Davis, J. Pearce, R. Bird, H. Woodward and C. Wallace, 'Ancillary relief outcomes' [2001] Child and Family Law Quarterly 43.

G. Douglas and M. Murch, *Findings*, a summary of research findings (April 2000) Joseph Rowntree Foundation.

J. Haynes, *The Fundamentals of Family Mediation* (1993) Tonbridge, Old Bailey Press, pp. 6–7, 11.

E. Jackson, F. Wasoff, M. Maclean and R.E. Dobash, 'Financial Support on Divorce: the Right Mixture of Rules and Discretion?' (1993) 7 International Journal of Law and the Family 230, p. 245.

J. Lewis and S. Arthur, 'Settling Up: the views and values underpinning financial separation', seminar paper (September 2000) (unpublished).

J.M. Eekelaar and M. Maclean, *Maintenance After Divorce* (1986) Oxford, Clarendon Press, p. 62.

Office of Population Censuses and Surveys, *General Household Survey 1993* (1995) London, HMSO, fig. 3A and text.

Additional reading

S. Arthur, J. Lewis, M. Maclean, S. Finch, R. Fitzgerald, *Settling Up: making financial arrangements after divorce or separation* (2002) National Centre for Social Research.

Australian Law Reform Commission, *'Matrimonial Property'*, Report no. 39 (1987) Sydney, Australian Law Reform Commission, pp. 41, 65, 68, 73–75, 80, 85, 86, 106.

C. Barton, 'Spending more time with their families – the Government's consultation document' [1999] Family Law 136.

S. Bridge, 'Marriage and divorce: the regulation of intimacy' in J. Herring (ed.), *Family Law: Issues, Debates, Policy* (2001) Devon, Willan Publishing.

J. Eekelaar and M. Maclean, 'Property and Financial Adjustment after Divorce in the 1990s – Unfinished Business' in K. Hawkins (ed.), *The Human Face of Law: essays in honour of Donald Harris* (1997) Oxford, Clarendon Press.

Home Office, *Supporting Families*, London, The Stationery Office.

J. Lewis, 'Relationship Breakdown, Obligations and Contracts' [1999] Family Law 149.

P. McDonald (ed.), *Settling Up; Property and Income Distribution on Divorce in Australia* (1986) Institute of Family Studies' Family Reformation Project, Sydney, Prentice-Hall of Australia.

A. Perry, G. Douglas, M. Murch, K. Bader and M. Borokowski, *How parents cope financially on marriage breakdown* (2000) Family Policy Studies Centre.

L. Weitzman, *The Divorce Revolution* (1985) New York, The Free Press.

Chapter 9

Dangerous families

9.1 What are the dangers?

9.2 The search for explanations

9.3 But is it not a crime?

9.4 Developing civil law remedies

9.5 Non-molestation orders

9.6 Occupation orders

9.7 What about the children?

Home is generally regarded as a place of safety, but in this chapter we examine some of the dangers which can face family members. We shall look first at the different kinds of abuse and ill-treatment which can be suffered, and then at some of the research into explanations, before turning to the remedies in criminal and civil law. We shall deal here only with the 'private law' remedies available to victims (usually women). Although these remedies are available to protect children (see p. 412, below), the abuse of children will usually require the involvement of local authority social services departments, or the NSPCC, exercising 'public law' powers under the Children Act 1989. These will be considered in Chapter 13, after we have looked generally at the legal relationship between parents, children and the state.

9.1 What are the dangers?

I have had ten stitches, three stitches, five stitches, seven stitches, where he has cut me. ... I have had a knife stuck through my stomach; I have had a poker put through my face; I have no teeth where he knocked them all out; I have been burnt with red hot pokers; I have had red hot coals slung all over me; I have been sprayed with petrol and stood there while he has flicked lighted matches at me. ...

When I was carrying he used to start hitting me a bit more, you know. He wanted me to have an abortion, but I would not – I kept on refusing. He kept punching me in the stomach.

So said two of the women who gave evidence to the House of Commons Select Committee on Violence in Marriage (1975). Susan Edwards (1996) describes some of the brutality which has reached the criminal courts:

In *R v Davies* (1986) 8 Cr App Rep (S) 97, a husband struck a wife on the back of the head with a hammer and rendered two further blows to the face fracturing the bridge of her nose and the upper part of the bony cavity of the eye. He also fractured the jaw bone and the eyeball had to be removed. The court conceded, 'Indeed she was lucky to have survived', sentencing him to seven years' imprisonment. ... In *R v Bedford* (1992) 14 Cr App Rep (S) 336-337, the wife was doused with petrol and ignited when she refused to sleep with the appellant. She said she would sleep on the settee. The appellant left the room and returned with a container of petrol he kept in the car. He set her alight and when she tried to leave the burning room he held the door shut against her. She sustained 40 per cent burns. When arrested he said to police, 'You know what it's like, you know what women are like. I just snapped.' . ... In *R v Dearn* (1990) 12 Cr App Rep (S) 527, the husband admitted tying a piece of electric flex around his wife's neck. Medical evidence estimated that the flex must have been held for at least five minutes causing irreparable brain damage. The husband explained that she had been, ' ... nagging him all that day' and he had tried to shut her up by using the flexible cord of the vacuum cleaner cable. A sentence of fifteen years was reduced to twelve years.

Civil courts also encounter many cases of domestic violence. In the year 2000, there were 15,734 applications to civil courts for non-molestation orders, and 10,295 applications for occupation orders (Judicial Statistics, 2000). However, many cases of domestic violence may never reach the courts, either civil or criminal. The House of Commons Home Affairs Committee recognised the difficulties in its report on *Domestic Violence* (1993):

9. Domestic violence is common, and its direct and indirect costs are high. There is clearly need for proper statistical information on which policy priorities can be set. Neither the Criminal nor the Judicial Statistics will ever provide a full picture of the incidence of domestic violence since many victims will neither report the violence to the police nor take action in the civil courts. Nor will the British Crime Survey (which involves asking a sample of the population about their experience of crime, whether they reported it or not) necessarily be entirely accurate, because of the shame which some victims may feel and which may discourage them from being frank. This may be particularly true of men – and one reason why statistics of male abuse by females appear insignificant.

Question

Can you think of any reasons, besides male shame, why the overwhelming majority of applications for injunctions in domestic violence cases are made by women? Is it because men are more violent?

There might be other explanations. In *Domestic Violence: Findings from a new British Crime Survey self-completion questionnaire* (1999) it was found:

Current levels of domestic violence
- 4.2% of women and 4.2% of men said they had been physically assaulted by a current or former partner in the last year. 4.9% of men and 5.9% of women had experienced physical assault and/or frightening threats. ...
- Women were twice as likely as men to have been injured by a partner in the last year, and three times as likely to have suffered frightening threats. They were also more likely to have been assaulted three or more times.
- In total it is estimated that there were about 6.6 million incidents of domestic physical assault in 1995. 2.9 million of these involved injury. In addition, there were about 7 million frightening threats.

Life-time experience
- Women were far more likely to say they had experienced domestic assault at some time in their lives: 23% of women and 15% of men aged 16 to 59 said they had been physically assaulted by a current or former partner at some time. The inclusion of frightening threats increases these figures to 26% and 17% respectively.
- At least 12% of women and 5% of men had been assaulted on three or more occasions. They were termed chronic victims.

- Young women aged 20 to 24 reported the highest levels of domestic violence to the survey: 28% said that they had been assaulted by a partner at some time, and 34% had been threatened or assaulted. Although the higher risk for young people tends to suggest domestic violence is increasing, it may also reflect a greater reluctance on the part of older victims to mention domestic assaults to the survey, or that incidents longer ago are less likely to be recalled in the survey context.

...

The assaults
- Pushing, shoving and grabbing are the most common type of assault. But kicking, slapping and hitting with fists took place in nearly half of incidents.
- The victim was injured in 41% of incidents. Women were more likely to be injured (47%) than men (31%). Although injury was usually restricted to bruising, 9% of incidents resulted in cuts and 2% in broken bones.
- Nearly all victims admitted they were upset by the experience, with women more likely to say so than men. The majority of female victims said they had been very frightened, compared to a minority of men.
- Of victims who had children in the household, about a third said the children had been aware of the last assault they had experienced.
- Chronic victims experienced more serious types of attack: they were more likely to be physically injured and were more emotionally affected by their experience. Three-quarters of the chronic victims were women.

The assailants
- Virtually all incidents against women reported to the survey were committed by men (99%). 95% of those against men were committed by women.
- The assailant was said to be under the influence of alcohol in 32% of incidents, and of drugs in 5%.
- Half of life-time incidents were committed by a current or former spouse compared to 43% of last-year incidents, probably reflecting lower rates of marriage amongst the younger age groups.
- The majority of life-time victims were living with their assailant at the time of the most recent assault: older victims more often so than younger ones.
- A half of those who were living with their assailant were still doing so at the time of the [research]. Women were less likely to still be living with their assailant than men, and chronic victims less likely than intermittent.

Victims' perceptions of their experiences
- Although the questions asked about incidents that would meet the legal definition of an assault, only 17% of incidents counted by the survey were considered to be crimes by their victims. Virtually no male victims defined their experience as a crime, while only four in ten chronic female victims did so.
- Victims were more likely to agree their experience made them 'a victim of domestic violence' than a victim of a crime – overall, one-third did so. Women, and in particular chronic female victims, were much more likely to say so than men.
...
- Victims' perceptions of their experiences influence willingness to take up available services. Respondents who believed they had experienced a crime or were victims of domestic violence were far more likely to have told others about it. For instance, incidents perceived as 'crimes' were more likely to be reported to the police: 34% were, compared to an overall reporting rate of 12%. Also, victims who felt to blame in some way were the less likely to report incidents to the police.

Question

Are you surprised that victims did not regard violence as criminal? What implications does this have for the law's response to domestic violence?

Before we consider the responses of the criminal justice system and the family justice system, we will briefly consider some of the possible explanations for domestic violence.

9.2 The search for explanations

In *Domestic Violence: Action for Change* (1993), Gill Hague and Ellen Malos review some of the different types of explanation which have been developed:

Individual pathological models of explanation

This kind of explanation is based on the idea that the individual using violence suffers from a pathological condition which leads to deviance from a non-violent norm. In practice it might only be quite extreme forms of violence or repeated violence that would be included in this kind of diagnosis. A certain kind of 'low-level' aggression might be seen as 'normal' at least in some families. Pathological deviance, however, might be thought to be based on either psychiatric illness or faults of temperament of one or both partners. Often it has been regarded as a sign of inadequacy, of an inarticulate person who had not learned to assert himself in non-violent ways.

When violence within families began to be perceived as a major problem in the early 1970s, it was in the context of medical evidence of the physical abuse of children in the United States. Initial explanations of violence within families at that time arose from concern about child abuse and focused on 'abusive families'. Women, as mothers, were viewed as colluding in the abuse of their children and also colluding in, or provoking, violence against themselves. The early research into 'family violence' in the United States in particular, where most of the large-scale studies have been carried out, was often based on this kind of assumption.

Such ideas are still current in psychiatry and psychology. They also persist in certain kinds of therapeutic social work, most notably in family therapy, where individualistic explanations shade over into theories of group pathology in which those who experience the violence are themselves often seen as helping to cause it. Certain kinds of psychotherapy too involve the idea that violence arises from 'issues' which the individuals concerned have not 'worked through' in their relationship. In recent years, some researchers with such views have been moving towards other types of explanation as they have asked more sophisticated questions.

Cycles of violence

The 'cycle of violence' theory suggests that there is a direct transmission of violence down the generations by learned behaviour, creating a cycle in which the violence continuously reproduces itself. This theory has a variant in which it is argued that the behaviour is learned by children who either witness or experience violence within an individual family. There is also a 'sub-cultural model' in which the use of violence is learned as part of a wider way of life, either in neighbourhoods in criminal sub-cultures or gangs, or in certain professions such as the police and the army.

There is certainly some evidence that violence can be learned, but these theories cannot explain why some individuals who observe such behaviour or live in such environments are not violent, or why some people are violent who do not live in this kind of family or social setting. Nor can they explain why, according to a rather indiscriminate lumping together of different kinds of learned behaviour, it ends up that boys both observing and experiencing violence should, according to the theory, become perpetrators of violence whereas girls apparently learn to choose violent partners and 'enjoy', or passively put up with, violent assault.

The theory rests ultimately on assumptions about the natural aggressiveness of boys and men, and the passivity of girls and women. This kind of explanation also loses force if violence, and violence against women in particular, is both very common and often accepted in the whole society, as suggested by Elisabeth Wilson in *What's to be Done about Violence Against Women?* (1983):

> 'If you are one of only 500 [abused] women in a population of 50 million then you have certainly been more than unlucky and there may perhaps be something very peculiar about your husband, or unusual about your circumstances, or about you; on the other hand, if you are one of 500,000 women then that suggests something very different – that there is something wrong not with a few individual men, or women, or marriages, but with the *situation* in which *many* women and children regularly get assaulted – that situation being home and the family.'

Yet, as we will see in later chapters, the cycle of violence is still a very popular kind of explanation. One possible reason for its popularity is that it seems to suggest that those men who attack their wives or partners, and those women who experience violence, are not 'people like us' – but rather belong to a special deviant group of 'violent families', who are completely different from the rest of us. Even if the violence happens more often than we would like to think and is much worse than we ever imagined, it has been explained. And, using the theory, it can be dealt with, perhaps by removing children from the violent family or violent sub-culture – and thus 'breaking the cycle'.

As to the adults, it might be too late to change the ingrained pattern. Perhaps all you can do is to recognize that, or perhaps you can help the women and children to get away. Perhaps you prosecute the man, or break the cycle by re-educating the parents or the perpetrator (in more optimistic variants of the theory which think it is actually possible to change what happens). Ultimately, though, if you believe that this is why domestic violence takes place, all you can probably hope to do is to minimize the transmission of violence, because it is all a result of some unexplainable situation in the violent past. It is not about the present situation of many families, as Elisabeth Wilson suggests. Some people are 'just like that', even if there are a large number of them.

...

Social-structural explanations

This is another kind of explanation of 'family violence'. It bases itself on the stress caused by lack of access to money, housing and education common to both men and women in the family. This view was expressed very succinctly in a discussion document drawn up by the British Association of Social Workers in 1975:

> 'Economic conditions, low wages, bad housing, and isolation; unfavourable and frustrating work conditions for the man; lack of job opportunities for adolescent school leavers, and lack of facilities such as day care (e.g. nurseries), adequate transport, pleasant environment and play space and recreational facilities, for mother and children were considered to cause personal desperation that might cause violence in the home.'

This kind of explanation usually assumes that violence occurs mainly in working-class and poor families. There is a 'middle-class' version in terms of financial pressures and stressful careers, but more commonly in this view the greater resources of middle-class families or, in some cases, the ability of middle-class men to maintain dominance without resorting to violence are thought to explain what is believed to be the relative lack of violence in these families.

However, as Michael Freeman (1987) and others point out, it is likely that violence in middle-class families can more easily remain hidden from neighbours and public agencies like the police and social services. Borkowski, Murch and Walker found in their study *Marital Violence* (1983) that the more significant class differential was not in whether violence occurred but in the kind of agencies consulted, the middle class being more likely to use lawyers and the divorce courts than the police, social services or women's refuges. Although it seems very likely that the pressures of poverty might increase the occurrence of violence or make it worse, this type of analysis fails adequately to account for the predominant direction of serious violence from men towards women or the fact that it occurs in all social classes.

...

Feminist explanations

... In the feminist view, domestic violence arises out of men's power over women in the family. This male power has been built into family life historically, through laws which assume that men have the right to authority over both women and children within families, where this does not conflict with public policy and the interests of the state. Rebecca and Russell Dobash in *Violence Against Wives* (1980), for example, describe the inferior historical position of women in British and North American society and in marriage, which arose from laws and customs which excluded women from public life and placed them under the authority of their husband or their father within the private sphere of the family.

As Susan Schechter has pointed out in *Women and Male Violence* (1982), this does not necessarily mean that feminists are 'dismissing psychology or ignoring violent individuals'. Rather:

> 'They are stressing the need for a psychology that analyses wife beating in its proper contexts, accounts for power differentials, and asks why women have been brutalized. Rather than label battering as pathology or a family systems failure, it is more conceptually accurate to assume that violence against women, like that directed towards children, is behaviour approved of and sanctioned in many parts of the culture. Extreme cases in which women are mutilated by psychotic men are only one end of a continuum of violent behaviour the more moderate forms of which are viewed as normal. Many in this culture approve of hitting women.'

Many feminists would use the kind of explanation which stresses the need to examine the historical position of women in particular societies and the way in which it was, and still is, embodied in law and custom. However, some forms of feminist explanation, basing themselves on the male-dominated nature of most known forms of society, come close to arguing that inherent biological differences between men and women are at the core of male violence and female non-violence. Others argue that there can be no such definite, undifferentiated categories as 'men' and 'women', but that we live among conflicting or intersecting sets of inequalities and differences in power.

Most feminist accounts draw attention to the economic position of women. They point to the way in which the responsibility that society assigns to women for looking after children often places them in a position of enforced financial dependency on their partners or ex-partners, a situation which will be reinforced in Britain by the new Child Support Act. It is also used as an excuse for paying women low wages or minimal state income support. Some feminists would also want to argue that class and racial oppression, and social stresses such as unemployment, bad housing and poverty, are likely to increase violence and make it harder to escape. Yet they would point out that this does not explain why it is that it is predominantly men who become violent in these circumstances, or why so much of the violence is directed towards women whom the men would profess to love.

Lorna Smith expands upon the nature of feminist explanations in *Domestic Violence: an overview of the literature* (1989):

Feminist explanations

At the core of feminist explanations is the view that all violence is a reflection of unequal power relationships: domestic violence reflects the unequal power of men and women in society and also, therefore, within their personal relationships. It is a view propounded by sociologists (for example, Dobash and Dobash, 1980; Edwards, 1985), psychologists (for example, Walker, 1984), lawyers (for example, Freeman, 1979; 1984) and practitioners in the criminal justice system (for example, Pence, 1985) alike.

Dobash and Dobash (1980, 1984) employ the notion of patriarchy to explain women's subordinate status. Patriarchy comprises two elements: the structural – that is those societal institutions which define and maintain women's subordinate position and thus prevent them from influencing or changing the social order – and the ideological – that is the socialisation process which ensures acceptance of that order. Both the Dobashes' (1981) historical analysis of legal sources and their empirical 'context specific' study (1980, 1984) demonstrate how husbands have sought and still seek to control their wives by violence.

Pahl (1985) has explicitly pointed out that the 'taken-for-granted assumptions' about marriage and the role of the family shape the ways in which the roles of women are defined, the ways in which domestic violence is perceived and thus also agencies' response to domestic violence. The ideology of the family and the privacy accorded the family in our society mean that women are, and are seen to be, subordinate to the men they live with. Men are expected to assume their 'natural' role as the dominant adult within the family. Indeed, Wilson (1983) has argued that domestic violence can be better understood if it is seen as an extreme form of normality – an exaggeration of how society expects men to behave as the authority figure in the family – and both Freeman (1980) and Edwards (1985) argue that the legal system both reflects and sustains this male supremacy. The pathology is, therefore, moved from that of the individual or even of the individual family to the family structure itself and its unequal power structure. Moreover, the family is seen as a microcosm of an unequal society. Domestic violence thus becomes a symptom of the more general demonstration of male violence, a demonstration of the male ethos and the male domination of women.

A number of writers have drawn attention to the economic dependency of women... Pahl's empirical study (1985) attests to the importance of the allocation of the control of money within the household. Although Pahl, herself, did not see this as important when she began her study, the women in her sample drew such consistent attention to it that she systematically investigated it: more than three quarters of the women named money a problem area. Husbands seemed to use the control of money as part of a more general attempt to control and subordinate wives. It appeared to be the key element in a marital relationship in which the husband assumed he would be the dominant partner. This finding is consistent with other studies. The Dobashes (1980) found that the majority of arguments preceding violence focused on husband's jealousy, differing expectations regarding the wife's domestic duties and the allocation of money. Roy (1977), in her American study, found that the four factors most often leading to violence were, in order of importance, arguments over money, jealousy, sexual problems and alcohol. Evason (1982), too, paid particular attention to financial arrangements within marriage. Her sample compared groups of women who had been victims of domestic violence with those who had not: those who had experienced violence were more likely to have had husbands who kept control over finances and who gave their wives money as and when they thought fit. Non-violent husbands were more likely to have opted for joint management of money. Assumptions and expectations about wives' appropriate behaviour were also identified as important by

Evason (1982) and Klein (1982). Evason, for example, found that although there were no differences between her violent and non-violent groups in terms of education, social class, age at marriage or length of courtship prior to marriage, wives who had been abused were particularly likely to have had husbands who favoured a traditional model of marriage in which the husband was 'master in his own home'. Any attempt by wives to assert themselves or question that authority was interpreted as wives 'getting above themselves' and, therefore, they had to be 'put back in their place'.

Morash (1986) has pointed out that socio-structural cultural explanations and feminist explanations are not necessarily antithetical despite their use of different paradigms for theory building. ... Moreover, some feminists (for example, Dobash and Dobash, 1980) would not reject the relevance of family history, social stresses, use of alcohol, sexual problems and so on, but argue rather that their explanatory power is not sufficient. Emphasising such factors leaves the question unanswered: why are women most frequently the victim?

Questions

(i) In the last section, we looked at the Home Office Research Study (1999), which found that men and women were equally likely to have suffered domestic violence in the previous year, but that women were twice as likely to have been injured, three times more likely to have faced serious threats and were more likely to have been assaulted at least three times. Does this evidence make the feminist explanations more or less convincing?

(ii) If the legal system fails to respond effectively to domestic violence, is it helpful to explain these failures in terms of discrimination against women?

In *Islam v Secretary of State for the Home Department, R v Immigration Appeal Tribunal, ex p Shah* [1999] 2 AC 629, [1999] 2 All ER 545, [1999] 2 WLR 1015, HL, the House of Lords considered whether women who were victims of domestic violence in Pakistan could claim refugee status in the UK:

Lord Hoffmann: In Pakistan there is widespread discrimination against women. Despite the fact that the constitution prohibits discrimination on grounds of sex, an investigation by Amnesty International at the end of 1995 reported that government attempts to improve the position of women had made little headway against strongly entrenched cultural and religious attitudes. Women who were victims of rape or domestic violence often found it difficult to obtain protection from the police or a fair hearing in the courts. ...

These appeals concern two women who became victims of domestic violence in Pakistan, came to the United Kingdom and claimed asylum as refugees. ...Both women were given limited leave to enter the United Kingdom as visitors. Afterwards they claimed the right to remain as refugees under the 1951 Geneva Convention relating to the Status of Refugees as amended by the 1967 Protocol. ... The Convention defines a refugee in article 1A(2) as a person who:

> 'owing to well founded fear of being persecuted for reasons of race, religion, nationality, membership of a particular social group or political opinion, is outside the country of his nationality and is unable, or owing to such fear is unwilling, to avail himself of the protection of that country . . .'

The question for the special adjudicators was whether Mrs Islam and Mrs Shah came within this definition.

Domestic violence such as was suffered by Mrs Islam and Mrs Shah in Pakistan is regrettably by no means unknown in the United Kingdom. It would not however be regarded as persecution within the meaning of the Convention. This is because the victims of violence would be entitled to the protection of the state. The perpetrators could be prosecuted in the criminal courts and the women could obtain orders restraining further molestation or excluding their husbands from the home. ... What makes it persecution in Pakistan is the fact that according to evidence which was accepted by the special adjudicator in Mrs Islam's case and formed the basis of findings which have not been challenged, the State was unwilling or unable to offer her any protection.

Question

Mrs Shah and Mrs Islam were able to claim refugee status in the UK because their own Government had failed to protect them from domestic violence. If a victim of domestic violence in the UK is unable to obtain effective protection, would this be a breach of her human rights? What remedy could she seek?

9.3 But is it not a crime?

According to Erin Pizzey, in the book which first alerted the public to the modern realities of wife-beating, *Scream Quietly or the Neighbours will Hear* (1974):

> The police attitude to wife-battering reveals an understandable but unacceptable schizophrenia in their approach to violence. Imagine that Constable Upright is on his beat one night and finds Mr Batter mugging a woman in the street. Mr Batter has already inflicted heavy bruises to the woman's face and is just putting the boot in when Constable Upright comes on the scene. The constable knows his duty and does it. He arrests Mr Batter, who is charged with causing grievous bodily harm and goes to prison for ten years.
>
> Ten years later Constable Upright is on his beat when he is sent to investigate screaming which neighbours have reported coming from the home of the newly released Mr Batter. Mr Batter is mugging his wife. He's thrown boiling water at her, broken her nose, and now he's trying for her toes with a claw hammer. When Constable Upright arrives what does he do? Does he make an arrest? Of course not.
>
> He knocks on the door and Mr Batter tells him to 'sod off'. He tells Mr Batter that the neighbours are complaining and he wishes to see his wife. Mr Batter says they have been having a minor row and he gets his wife who is looking bruised round the face and crying. The policeman will not arrest. In one case the husband even assaulted his wife in front of a policeman but still there was no arrest. All that he did was to advise her to go to the local magistrates' court the next morning and take out a summons against her husband, but he knew that she was unlikely to do this because she would have to live in the same house as her husband while she was taking him to court.

Confirmation for what she said came from the evidence of various police bodies to the House of Commons Select Committee on Violence in Marriage (1975). The Association of Chief Police Officers (ACPO) said this:

> ... Whilst such problems take up considerable Police time ... in the majority of cases the role of the Police is a negative one. We are, after all dealing with persons 'bound in marriage', and it is important, for a host of reasons, to maintain the unity of the spouses. Precipitate action by the Police could aggravate the position to such an extent as to create a worse situation than the one they were summoned to deal with. ...

Questions

(i) This was borne out by Jan Pahl's research (1982), which indicated that the police were far more likely to take action themselves if (a) the woman had already left for a refuge, or (b) although still under the same roof, the woman was not married to the man: can you list the 'host of reasons' why this might be?
(ii) How many of the reasons which might disincline a policeman to intervene appear to you to be valid?
(iii) What powers does Constable Upright have, if told to 'sod off' by a man who is apparently beating his wife inside the matrimonial home? (Consult *R v Thornley*

(1980) 72 CrApp Rep 302, and also the Police and Criminal Evidence Act 1984, s. 17(1)(*e*) and (6).)

In the past, police intervention was sometimes based upon powers to prevent a 'breach of the peace' (eg, *McLeod v Metropolitan Police Comr* [1994] 4 All ER 553). However, this approach was criticised by the European Court of Human Rights in *McLeod v United Kingdom* [1998] 2 FLR 1048. See also *Foulkes v Chief Constable of Merseyside* [1998] 3 All ER 705, in which the police responded to a call from a husband who had been locked out of the house by his wife and adult children. The officers established that the wife did not want to allow the husband into the house, and suggested that the husband should go for a cup of tea until tempers had cooled. When the husband continued his attempts to re-enter the house, he was arrested. He was released the next morning when his wife decided that she did not want him to be taken before a magistrate to be bound over to keep the peace. The Court of Appeal found that the husband's arrest had been unlawful. Thorpe LJ said that the wife's exclusion of the husband was wrongful in the light of his statutory rights of occupation (see p. 152), and that the police should have pointed out to the wife that she was not entitled to resolve the dispute by a lock out. He said ([1998] 3 All ER 705 at 712):

It is only in the most extreme cases that conflict between spouses results in imprisonment, absent some criminal act. The imprisonment of a spouse has a profound effect on the future family dynamics. In my experience the invariable response of the police if called to a domestic dispute in a family uncontrolled by orders made in the family justice system is to decline involvement in the absence of a criminal act or the apprehension of a criminal act. I find it hard to envisage a situation in which the power of arrest for an apprehended breach of the peace would be an appropriate management of a dispute between husband and wife within the matrimonial home.

Questions

(i) If a husband and wife are engaged in a heated argument but there has not yet been any violence, is it sensible to attempt to resolve the situation by explaining the husband's statutory rights of occupation to the wife? Should the police response differ where the parties are not married, and therefore have no statutory rights of occupation?

(ii) How should the police decide which situations are likely to escalate into violence? What should they do if they believe that violence is likely to occur?

The police may be the only agency which is available to provide an immediate response to incidents of violence or threatened violence. However, Mildred Dow put her finger on one difficulty in 'Police Involvement', her contribution to *Violence in the Family* (edited by Marie Borland in 1976):

... it has become obvious to the writer, through years of police experience as a practical officer, that however often one says to a wife, 'Your rights are ...' she will invariably be re-influenced by her husband and refuse to give the necessary evidence. Whether this is basically due to personal fear or to an essentially sexual attraction and influence or to fear for the children of the union, it is difficult to determine. I only know how frustrating it is for a police officer who has taken much care and trouble in the preparation of the presentation of the case at court to be let down because his principal witness has had 'second thoughts'... From a practical viewpoint it would appear better to charge the husband and keep him in custody, rather than to follow the practice in some few police areas where the husband is reported for summons, thus giving him time to influence his wife. If some aggressive husbands are, by these means, kept away from the matrimonial home, more wives may be prepared to give the relevant evidence.

Dobash and Dobash argue in *Women, Violence and Social Change* (1992) that it is the police themselves who are responsible for the problem:

Police officers continue to see victims as fundamentally 'unreliable and capricious', 'inadequate people', who are unworthy of police response. In light of such perceptions it is not surprising that arrest, even in areas of pro-arrest policies, is an unlikely outcome of police contact. ... Observations of police reactions and interviews with officers reveal that they discourage women from filing formal complaints, often give strong advice against arrest, present victims with all the potential 'negative effects of and barriers to pursuing a prosecution' and pressure women not to press charges [eg Sanders (1988)]. In this way the justice system helps create the reality of dropped charges and reluctant witnesses about which it complains.

In any event, both Dobash and Dobash (1980) and Wasoff (1982) in Scotland found that claims about wives dropping charges were 'greatly exaggerated', as did Tony Faragher, discussing 'The Police Response to Violence against Women in the Home' (1985):

The degree of police concern over possible withdrawal of the complaint is not matched, however, by the frequency with which this occurs in practice. Only one in ten women in a local study were found to have withdrawn their complaint (Dawson and Faragher, 1977, 142). The only way in which this low level of withdrawal can be accounted for is that the police are extremely selective about who they sponsor to take legal action. This is borne out by observation at the scene of 'domestics' – women are time and again asked whether they really want to take legal action. Alternatively women are given time to 'think it over' in the belief that an 'unemotional' decision made the next day will be more realistic. In this sense the police abrogate their protective role, for their judgment is heavily influenced by prognoses of the woman's reliability as a witness in court proceedings.

But things may have begun to change in the late 1980s (see Cretney and Davis (1996), p. 404, below). Morley and Mullender, in 'Hype or Hope?' (1992), argued that, after the 1975 Select Committee Report:

... the issue of domestic violence largely disappeared from the public agenda until the second half of the 1980s. When it re-emerged, it did so in the context of an increasing tendency to view the police, and criminal justice system generally, as being in the forefront of solutions to the problem. And within policing, the new emphasis was firmly on domestic violence as a *criminal* act, and on *arrest* as the primary response to assailants.

In contrast to its view in 1975, the Association of Chief Police Officers' evidence to the Home Affairs Committee (1993) said that, during the late 1980s, 'the Police Service changed its focus from one of conciliation to intervention'. This development is demonstrated by the Home Office Circular (60/1990) on *Domestic Violence*:

Nature and extent of problem
2. Chief officers will be aware of the wide range of abuse which is covered by the term 'domestic violence'. It encompasses all aspects of physical, sexual and emotional abuse, ranging from threatening behaviour and minor assaults which lead to cuts and bruises to serious injury, and sometimes even death. (In about 44% of homicide cases where the victim is a female the suspect is or was married to or lived with her.)...
4. Domestic violence is not simply a challenge for the criminal justice system. Victims will often need assistance which is beyond the capacity of the police to provide, requiring close co-operation with medical, social work and housing authorities and with victim support groups. Domestic violence is, however, a crime and it is important that the police should play an active and positive role in protecting the victim and that their response to calls for help is speedy and effective.
...

Force policy statements

11. The Home Secretary recommends that chief officers should consider issuing a force policy statement about their response to domestic violence. ... Central features of the force policy statement should be:
  – the overriding duty to protect victims, and children, from further attack;
  – the need to treat domestic violence as seriously as other forms of violence;
  – the use and value of powers of arrest;
  – the dangers of seeking conciliation between assailant and victim;
  – the importance of comprehensive record-keeping to allow the chief officer to monitor the effectiveness of the policy in practice.

Initial police response to incidents

(a) *Distinguish violent/non-violent incidents*

12. The first contact between a victim and the police is likely to be by telephone when a victim seeks police intervention or protection. The first priority for police officers answering such calls is to find out whether immediate police help is required, or whether there is no imminent danger of an assault. Even if immediate help is not sought, the call must be recorded and there should always be some sort of positive action to investigate the case – for instance, an interview with the victim to establish in more detail what prompted her call and whether it was part of a history of violence.

(b) *Check previous history of relationship*

13. All complaints of domestic violence by victims or witnesses should be properly recorded in the same way as similar incidents involving strangers. The seriousness of an incident should not be downgraded because it takes place in a domestic context and no incident should be 'no-crimed' unless the police conclude, after investigation, that the report was inaccurate or false.
...

(c) *Action at the scene of the incident: the victim*

14. In the past, police officers arriving at the scene of domestic violence have often tried to smooth over the dispute and reconcile the partners. Research suggests that this is not necessarily the best course of action and that what victims want is the enforcement of the law. Police officers should rarely attempt conciliation if the victim has been, or claims to have been, violently assaulted (bruises may not develop for some time after the incident so the absence of obvious injury may not be significant). Wherever possible, it is desirable for a woman police officer to be available to attend the incident so that the victim may be given a choice about the sex of the officer who assists her. If the victim is interviewed on the spot, the interview should not take place in the presence of her alleged assailant so that she does not feel pressurised into relating the incident in front of him. However, if she *chooses* to repeat the allegation in his presence and hearing, it may be given in evidence by the police at any subsequent court hearing. The victim should never be asked in the alleged assailant's presence whether she will be prepared to give evidence against him. In some cases, however, the immediate priority will simply be to remove her (and any children) to a place of safety.
...

(d) *Action at the scene of the incident: the assailant*

16. Police officers should be aware of their powers in respect to domestic violence. ... Experience in other countries suggests that the arrest of an alleged assailant may act as a powerful deterrent against his re-offending – at least for some time – and it is an important means of showing the victim that she is entitled to, and will receive, society's protection and support. The arrest and detention of an alleged assailant should therefore always be considered, even though the final judgement may be that this is inappropriate in the particular case.

(e) *Action at the scene: witnesses*

17. In view of the difficulties in bringing a prosecution in cases of domestic violence, there is a particular need to establish whether there are witnesses such as other members of the family or neighbours who can give evidence.

Action after the incident

(a) *Charging the suspect*

18. In considering whether or not to initiate criminal proceedings, police officers will wish to take into account the same factors as those which are relevant in the case of attacks by strangers. The fact that some women, having made a complaint, subsequently decide that they are not

prepared to give evidence at court should not affect a police officer's decision to charge in a case in which the evidence justifies that course of action. Many women will be in a state of shock when the police first arrive, and unable to contemplate the prospect of a court case. With proper support, however, they may gain in confidence and, following discussion of all the aspects of their case, they may well come to recognise that prosecution is in their own interest. When there is sufficient evidence to justify a prosecution the police should charge the suspect and refer the case to the Crown Prosecution Service.

...

(c) *Reports to the Crown Prosecution Service*

21. Just as police officers will find it essential to have background information about the nature and history of the relationship readily to hand in order to deal with an incident, so Crown Prosecutors need the same information in order to prosecute the case effectively and ensure the protection of the victim and any children by the imposition of bail conditions or a remand in custody. In particular, Crown Prosecutors need to be kept informed if circumstances change. ...

...

Withdrawal of victim's complaint

24. In the past, the likelihood of the victim's withdrawing her complaint has often been used to justify not taking criminal proceedings against the alleged assailant. Recent research has established, however, that withdrawal of complaint is less common than has been supposed. The victim's refusal to testify against her partner may considerably lessen the prospect of a conviction, however. The CPS has power, under section 97 of the Magistrates' Courts Act 1980 or section 80 of the Police and Criminal Evidence Act 1984 to seek to compel a spouse or partner to attend court for the purpose of giving evidence. The power is used infrequently and a decision to use it can only be taken in the light of the circumstances of the case, including the reasons why the complainant does not wish to give evidence and the views of the officer in the case. This underlines the need to give close support to the victim during the pre-trial period, so that she will feel sufficiently self-confident to give evidence.

Although the Circular is merely advisory, and its implementation may vary from area to area, it does indicate a change of attitude among senior police officers and Government officials. But are these new attitudes shared by the officers who actually respond to incidents of violence? A Home Office Research Study, *Policing Domestic Violence in the 1990s* (1995) by Sharon Grace, addressed this issue:

The general police response

Virtually all forces have developed policies on domestic violence which closely adhere to the recommendations in Home Office Circular 60/1990. However, the findings in this report suggest that the translation of this policy into practice has been limited. Just over half of the forces had a specialist unit with *some* responsibility for domestic violence but only five forces had domestic violence units dedicated solely to this offence. While there was a general awareness among officers about how domestic violence *should* be policed, this awareness was not always reflected in the way they dealt with such cases. It appeared that managers were overly optimistic about how effective they had been in getting the message across to their operational colleagues and were somewhat out of touch about what was happening at ground level.

Most officers felt that the policing of domestic violence had improved and that such incidents were now being taken more seriously with more positive intervention and more support and advice available for victims. There was evidence that officers had increased their awareness of domestic violence issues and showed a greater understanding and sympathy for victims. However, a third of operational officers had not heard of Circular 60/1990 at all and over half said that they had not received any new guidelines on domestic violence – despite their managers' confidence that the guidance had been successfully disseminated.

...

Although most officers were aware that arrest should be a priority in domestic violence cases, almost half of them put it below all other considerations (e.g. the safety of the victim and any children) when asked to prioritise their actions at a domestic violence scene. Their decision to arrest appeared to be heavily influenced by whether a complainant would support any police action. However, the use of informal responses to domestic violence incidents appeared from interviews to be unsatisfactory both for officers – who will usually have to return to that address at a later date – and for victims – who feel the police have not taken their plight seriously enough. If they are to follow the guidance in Circular 60/1990, officers need to consider arrest more often in domestic violence cases. In addition, it may be worth placing less emphasis on Breach of the Peace as a solution and making more use of assault charges. This will reassure the victim that her situation is being taken seriously, and may also have more of a long term impact on her assailant. CPS lawyers did say that, while Breach of the Peace was a speedy way of dealing with domestic violence cases, it probably did not help the victim in the long term nor was it likely to act as a deterrent.

Questions

(i)   Are you surprised that operational police officers are more concerned about the safety of women and children than about making arrests?

(ii)   Are these objectives incompatible?

Another Home Office study (Liz Kelly, *Domestic Violence Matters: An Evaluation of a Development Project*, Home Office Research Findings No. 91 (1999)) found that even in cases where there were visible injuries and the perpetrator was present, arrest occurred in only 45% of cases. The researchers suggested that 'a proportion of police officers were still making decisions on the basis of stereotypes (especially who was a 'deserving' victim) rather than the facts of the case'.

However, research by Antonia Cretney and Gwyn Davis (1996) suggests that domestic assaults are now much more likely to be prosecuted than in the past. A study of 448 assaults prosecuted in the Bristol courts between January 1993 and October 1993 found that 46% were 'domestics'. On this basis, the authors concluded that 'this is a hidden crime no longer'. However, they found that more than half of these prosecutions were discontinued (52%), whereas only 29% of the non-domestic cases were discontinued. They also found that the victim withdrew support for the prosecution in 30% of domestic cases, compared with 7% of non-domestic cases. A similar picture emerges from Home Office Research Study 185, *Entry into the criminal justice system: a survey of police arrests and their outcomes* (1998), which examined 4,250 people, arrested between September 1993 and March 1994 at ten police stations in seven forces. The study found that 6% of these suspects were arrested for offences arising from incidents of domestic violence, that there was a higher than average rate of charging domestic violence suspects, but that these cases were three times more likely to be terminated by the CPS because complainants frequently withdrew their allegations or were reluctant to give evidence in court, possibly through fear of intimidation.

In its evidence to the Home Affairs Committee (1993), the Association of Chief Police Officers highlighted some of the special problems attached to the investigation of domestic violence:

–   Witnesses are likely to be related to one or more of the parties and are, therefore, likely to take sides.

–   In many cases, there are no witnesses. Therefore abuse involving anything less than serious physical assault is unlikely to be referred to the court.

–   Close relationships inhibit reporting until repeated extreme behaviour has occurred, by which time positions have become firmly entrenched.

–   For a victim to report, takes courage. It may well result in the 'loss' of a partner, home and way of life, which could be replaced by near poverty line existence in hostel accommodation.

–   Assuming there is sufficient evidence to arrest a suspect at the time a complaint is made, in most cases the Bail Act will ensure freedom within a short space of time.

–   Conditions attached to bail/injunctions are regularly broken, resulting in considerable stress to the victim and increased work for the police. When the offender is returned to

court, it is common practice to admonish the offender, then release him on the same conditions. This practice does little for the confidence of the victim.
– Regardless of the outcome of criminal proceedings, a very high percentage of those involved in domestic violence continue their relationship.
– A longer term consideration is the accommodation and welfare of the victim and her children. This tends to inhibit the reporting of any incidents.

Questions

(i)   Why is it significant that a 'very high percentage' continue their relationship?
(ii) The Bristol study found that prosecutions were much more likely to be discontinued where the parties continued cohabiting (Cretney and Davis, 1996). How many reasons can you think of why a woman might withdraw support for prosecution in these circumstances?
(iii) Under what circumstances should prosecutions be continued against the wishes of the woman concerned?

The Police and Criminal Evidence Act 1984 made wives competent and compellable witnesses against their husbands in respect of certain offences including an assault or injury, or threat of injury, to the spouse or any person under 16 or a sexual offence against someone under 16. Before that, the House of Lords had held in *Hoskyn v Metropolitan Police Comr* [1979] AC 474, [1978] 2 All ER 136, HL, that a wife could not be compelled to give evidence against her husband in these cases. Lord Edmund Davies, who dissented, summed up the opposing viewpoints thus:

The noble and learned Lord, Viscount Dilhorne, has spoken of the repugnance created by a wife being compelled ' ... to testify against her husband on a charge involving violence, no matter how trivial and no matter the consequences to her and to her family'. For my part I regard as extremely unlikely any prosecution based on trivial violence being persisted in where the injured spouse was known to be a reluctant witness. Much more to the point, as I think, are cases such as the present ... , arising from serious physical maltreatment by one spouse of the other.

Such cases are too grave to depend simply on whether the injured spouse is, or is not, willing to testify against the attacker. Reluctance may spring from a variety of reasons and does not by any means necessarily denote that domestic harmony has been restored. A wife who has once been subjected to a 'carve up' may well have more reasons than one for being an unwilling witness against her husband. In such circumstances, it may well prove a positive boon for her to be directed by the court that she has no alternative but to testify. But, be that as it may, such incidents ought not to be regarded as having no importance extending beyond the domestic hearth. Their investigation and, where sufficiently weighty, their prosecution is a duty which the agencies of law enforcement cannot dutifully neglect.

The current policy of the Crown Prosecution Service is described in their *Policy On Prosecuting Cases Of Domestic Violence* (2001):

4. Is there enough evidence to prosecute?
4.1 Domestic violence nearly always happens in private. The victim is often the only witness. This means that unless the defendant pleads guilty, or there is strong supporting evidence, it will usually be necessary for the victim to give evidence in court. We know that some victims will find this very difficult and may need practical and emotional support which agencies such as Women's Aid, Refuge, Victim Support or the Witness Service can give. ...
4.2 We will not automatically assume that calling the victim is the only way to prove a case. We will actively consider what other evidence may be available, either to support the victim's evidence or as an alternative to the victim's evidence.
4.3 If it is necessary to call the victim, we will consider all options available to us to help victims give their best evidence in court.

What happens when the victim withdraws support for the prosecution or no longer wishes to give evidence?

4.4 Sometimes a victim will ask the police not to proceed any further with the case, or will ask to withdraw the complaint. This does not necessarily mean that the case will therefore be stopped – we will first consider what other evidence is available.

4.5 As a general rule we will prosecute all cases where there is sufficient evidence and there are no factors preventing us from doing so.

4.6 If the victim has decided to withdraw support, we have to find out why. ...

4.8 If the victim's statement after withdrawing the complaint is not the same as the earlier statement, the police will ask the victim to explain why it has changed.

4.9 If we suspect that the victim has been pressured or frightened into withdrawing the complaint, we will ask the police to investigate further. If necessary, we will ask the court to delay any hearing so that a thorough investigation can take place before we decide about the future of the case.

4.10 If the victim confirms that the complaint is true but still wants to withdraw that complaint, we will consider first whether it is *possible* to continue with the prosecution without it (the evidential test) and then, if it is possible, whether we should continue with the case against the victim's wishes (the public interest test).

4.11 We will explore all of these options fully, before we decide whether or not to proceed with a prosecution. The safety of the victim, children or any other potentially vulnerable person will be a prime consideration in reaching our decision.

Continuing with a prosecution against the victim's wishes or requiring a witness to go to court against the witness's wishes.

4.12 In some cases the violence is so serious, or the previous history shows such a real and continuing danger to the victim or the children or other person, that the public interest in going ahead with a prosecution has to outweigh the victim's wishes...

4.14 We can require a husband or wife to give evidence about an assault or threat of injury by their partner (section 80 of the Police and Criminal Evidence Act 1984). In the same way, unmarried partners or members of the family can be required to give evidence under section 97 of the Magistrates' Courts Act 1980.

4.15 If we decide that the victim must go to court to give evidence against their wishes, that decision will only be taken by an experienced prosecutor after consultation with the police.

Using the victim's statement as evidence under Section 23 of the Criminal Justice Act 1988 so that the victim does not have to give evidence in person at court.

4.16 Section 23 of the Criminal Justice Act 1988 allows us to use the victim's statement as evidence without calling the victim to court, *but only in very limited circumstances.*

4.17 We have to prove beyond reasonable doubt that the person who made the statement is afraid to give evidence or is being kept out of the way.

4.18 The victim does not have to give evidence to prove that he or she is afraid. This proof can come from someone else, for example a police officer or doctor or sometimes it can be seen from the victim's behaviour in court.

4.19 If the court decides that the statement *can* be used under section 23, it must then decide whether, in the interests of justice, the statement *should* be used in this way.

4.20 If the victim is the only witness to the offence, it is very difficult to satisfy the court that justice is being served when the defence cannot cross-examine the only witness against them.

5. Is it in the public interest to prosecute?

5.1 We always think very carefully about the interests of the victim when we decide where the public interest lies. But we prosecute cases on behalf of the public at large and not just in the interests of any particular individual.

5.2 There are often difficulties in striking this balance. ..

5.3 In cases of domestic violence, if the evidential test is passed and the victim is willing to give evidence, we will almost always prosecute.

5.4 If the victim withdraws support for the prosecution but we have enough evidence to proceed, we have to decide whether or not to prosecute.

5.5 Some examples of what helps us to decide this are:
- the seriousness of the offence;
- the victim's injuries – whether physical or psychological;
- if the defendant used a weapon;
- if the defendant has made any threats since the attack;
- if the defendant planned the attack;

- the effect (including psychological) on any children living in the household;
- the chances of the defendant offending again;
- the continuing threat to the health and safety of the victim or anyone else who is, or may become, involved;
- the current state of the victim's relationship with the defendant;
- the effect on that relationship of continuing with the prosecution against the victim's wishes;
- the history of the relationship, particularly if there has been any other violence in the past;
- the defendant's criminal history, particularly any previous violence.

...

5.7 Generally, provided we have sufficient evidence, the more serious the offence or the greater the risk of further offences, the more likely we are to prosecute in the public interest – even if victims say they do not wish us to do so.

On the basis of their research in Bristol, Cretney and Davis (1996) conclude:

It now appears that offenders are being arrested and charged where once they would only have been 'advised', and that in general women who seek police help are receiving a better service, both in terms of the immediate response and in the support which they receive during the prosecution process.

We would suggest that further thought now be given to the management of those cases in which the woman indicates that she no longer wishes to proceed. It does not seem to us that the issue of intimidation and pressure has been effectively addressed. Much that police, prosecutors and courts currently do to ensure that a retraction is properly made appears designed to protect the prosecuting authorities rather than to uncover coercion. The fact that coercion is seldom if ever revealed by these means forces this conclusion. We would suggest therefore that the courts and the CPS abandon the practice of requiring withdrawal from the witness-box. Instead, the emphasis should be on facilitating private consultation between victim and prosecutor, a policy which we recognise does present certain difficulties for the CPS although it is managed well enough by some prosecutors. A second issue which we would identify is the tendency to *blame* the woman. It has been part of police culture to regard victims of domestic violence as vacillating women who in the end deserve what they get because they are unable to make a break with their abuser. With an apparent increase in the number of domestic violence cases coming before the courts there is a tendency to regard the woman who withdraws at this stage as failing all those (police, CPS and court) who have put themselves out on her behalf. ... We consider there to be very good reasons why some women withdraw, whether this withdrawal be early or late. Furthermore, withdrawal does not necessarily denote failure on anyone's part.

Questions

(i)   Do you agree that the withdrawal of a prosecution should not necessarily be regarded as a failure?

(ii)   What are the 'very good reasons' why some women withdraw support for prosecutions?

The arguments for and against 'diverting' cases out of the criminal justice system are put by Susan Maidment in 'The Relevance of the Criminal Law to Domestic Violence' (1980):

Strong arguments can be put forward why the criminal law should be used in all cases of domestic violence. It would be a clear affirmation of social values, of condemnation by society, and a clear statement of the personal responsibility and accountability of the offender. We know that the criminal law can provide an effective and prompt protection for the victim. The criminal law can at least attempt to prevent an escalation of violence either through incarceration, or by making at the outset the strongest statement that society can make denouncing the act. The police are in any case often involved in emergency calls, and they may be the only agency with the authority and ability to cope with such volatile situations.

On the other side there are arguments against the use of the criminal law. It is a blunt tool. It misplaces emphasis on the offender, not the victim. There is no facility for treatment within the system, for example, for understanding and attempting to control aggression, except probation, but then the husband is still at large. No attempt is made to improve the marital relationship, to develop mutual respect between husband and wife. On a more technical level, there are problems of proof in criminal law, as compared with the easier standard of proof for an injunction. This may lead to some acquittals purely on technical grounds. For the wife however this means a lack of protection.

In more general terms a criminal conviction and sentence for the husband may be counterproductive for the wife in many ways. There may be financial disadvantage to the wife, emotional loss to the children. It may only escalate the problem because of the husband's anger and grudge against her; imprisonment is only a temporary respite (though this argument could equally apply to injunctions). It may not be what the wife really wants – she would like to have him treated. She may feel guilty and responsible for him being punished or locked away. Indeed her initial call to the police may not be a cry for criminal action at all; it is simply the only place she knows to turn to in an emergency.

Indeed the present operation of the criminal law, when it is invoked in these cases, makes a mockery of the criminal process, because of the derisory sentences that are passed, even for example where the charge is actual bodily harm (House of Commons, 1975; Pizzey, 1974). The basic problem to which the use of the criminal law gives rise has been well expressed in the following statement:

> 'Of all the areas in which an alternative to criminal treatment seems justified, the area of marital disputes is the most obvious. This is not to say that violence, theft or neglect between spouses should be ignored, but it does appear that these cases deserve different treatment than they are now given. Whether prosecution is decided upon or not, it would seem that beyond the point of immediate police response to danger, the criminal process is largely irrelevant in these cases. If anything, its very invocation may exacerbate poverty related and/or psychological problems. The summary, rather shallow treatment given these complainants does not answer the need that they have expressed for help.' (Subin, 1966)

Nevertheless there are some cases where the criminal law has to be used. These cases should be restricted to those occasions when there is a need present for coercive prevention of violence in view of serious physical or emotional danger to the wife. It is all the other cases, where there is a choice between the civil and criminal remedy, which give rise to problems of decision-making. At present the choice of remedy is, as already described, haphazard. It depends partly on the wife's choice as to whether she goes to a solicitor or to the police, and on the police as to whether they are willing to prosecute. In practice the choice will effectively be made by the police since they will usually be involved in the very initial stages. But the fact is that the choice of remedy can and ought to be a professional principled decision. There are some clear issues to be considered, and serious arguments for and against the use of the criminal law as already described. A professional decision needs to be arrived at after full consideration of the alternative remedies available.

Questions

(i)   Which professionals might those be? Why should they be better qualified to decide than the police or the woman herself?
(ii)   Do we need to distinguish between what Constable Upright does when called to the house in the middle of the night and what Inspector Morse or the Crown Prosecution Service do the next day?

Sharon Grace's study (1995) considered the views of victims of domestic violence:

What do victims want?

The clearest message to emerge from interviews with victims was that they wanted the police to treat their situations seriously and to take into account their needs and wishes when deciding what action to take. An understanding, sympathetic attitude from the police seems to help ensure that victims feel satisfied with the response they receive. The police should be able to offer long-term support to victims regardless of whether victims decide to pursue a criminal solution to their problems. To offer this support, officers need to know about the various non-criminal options available to victims and support them in whatever decision they decide to take.

Question

Are the police the most appropriate agency to give this type of long-term support?

9.4 Developing civil law remedies

In its evidence to the Home Affairs Committee (1993), the Women's Aid Federation England points out some of the reasons why victims of domestic violence might prefer to use civil remedies, rather than the criminal law:

From the point of view of the woman experiencing the abuse, it may seem preferable to apply for protection in the civil courts rather than to give evidence in a criminal prosecution of her partner. Firstly, the process seems to be more under her control: she instructs the solicitor, who will represent her in court, or will instruct a barrister on her behalf. Secondly, in most cases the hearing will be in a closed court or in the Judge's chambers, and there will be no publicity. Thirdly, her partner will not acquire a criminal record, which could hamper his employment prospects and hence indirectly affect the economic situation of the woman and her children. For all these reasons it is important that the process of obtaining injunctions or personal protection orders should be as straightforward as possible, and that the orders, once obtained should be effective and if breached, should be strictly enforced.

The victim's control over the process is a strength of the civil law, but it may also be a limitation. Jenny Clifton points to some of the difficulties which women face in taking action in her account of 'Factors Predisposing Family Members to Violence', in the Scottish Social Work Services Group's collection of papers on *Violence in the Family* (1982):

It is important to view the battered wife in the context of a family network which may tacitly or explicitly support the husband's position. The problems of the wife who does not think she will be believed if she tells how her apparently normal husband is a batterer ... represent a crucial component of the explanation for women remaining in a violent relationship. Women's own hopes and expectations of marriage and family life, added to the pressures from others to keep the family together, the very real hardships of life alone and the social disadvantages of divorced status offer plenty of scope for the explanation of women's apparent tolerance of a violent relationship without recourse to suppositions that women must need the violence in a pathological way (for example, Marsden 1978). This is not to say that conflict which may occasionally spill into violence does not sometimes become an integral part of a marital relationship (Cade 1978) but the consistent picture from research studies is that women who are beaten do not come to need or enjoy their victimisation (Dobash and Dobash 1980). Neither are conflict-ridden marriages and relationships which occasionally involve physical combat quite the same as marriages in which the wife is frequently and brutally subjected to physical force.

Dobash and Dobash (1992) also explain some of the reasons why women may return to violent men:

Women return for a myriad of reasons: because men promise to reform; they are concerned about the welfare of their husband and children; they accept the powerful ideals associated with an intact family; they do not wish to discard their emotional and material investment in the relationship; they have no accommodation and few prospects for meaningful employment; and they fear the violent reprisals of men who are often at their most dangerous when women leave.

As John Stuart Mill pointed out in 1869, 'it is contrary to reason and experience to suppose that there can be any real check to brutality, consistent with leaving the victim still in the power of the executioner'. The first step had therefore to be to improve and extend the procedures for releasing wives from their lifelong promise and legal duty to live with their husbands. But it is one thing to be told that you need no longer live with your husband, and another thing to pluck up the courage to live through the interim before the divorce and to find somewhere to live both then and thereafter.

The law in this area has been comprehensively reformed by the Family Law Act 1996, reflecting the recommendations of the Law Commission in their Report on *Domestic Violence and the Occupation of the Family Home* (1992). The Commission examined the various remedies which had been developed, and concluded (at para. 2.24) that '[t]he fact that different remedies are available to different applicants on different criteria in different courts with different enforcement procedures has resulted in a vastly complicated system, made even more confusing by the complex inter-relationship between the statutory remedies and the general principles of property and tort law'. Apart from this complexity, reform was also necessary to extend protection to certain family members (such as former spouses and former cohabitants), and to give greater weight to the needs of children. The Law Commission's recommendations were intended to address these problems, and led to the Family Law Act 1996, the effectiveness of which will be considered below. However, as the Law Commission's Report (1992) pointed out, it is not just the law's substantive defects which can reduce its effectiveness:

2.8 Domestic violence is not simply a legal problem which can be eradicated by the appropriate legal remedies. It is also a social and psychological problem which can be eliminated only by fundamental changes in society and in attitudes to women and children. While legal remedies are an attempt to alleviate the symptoms of domestic violence, they can do little to tackle the causes. Also, their effectiveness can be hampered by various factors [see Women's National Commission, *Violence Against Women: report of an ad hoc Working group*, 1985]. First, they have to operate in an area where there is a constant tension between the need for instant protection to be given to the victim and the need to observe due process in the conduct of proceedings against the alleged perpetrator. A balance has to be struck between the victim's need and the rights of other people, although there is, of course, room for argument about what the correct balance should be. Also, legal remedies can be undermined by the gap which exists between the letter and spirit of the law and the law in practice. It has been said that those who work in this area, including solicitors, barristers, police, court staff and judiciary, can, perhaps unconsciously, deter applicants from pursuing their proceedings or prevent the law operating as effectively as it might, if their reactions are affected by particular perceptions of male and female roles or an ambivalence about the propriety of legal or police intervention within the family [for example, Edwards and Halpern, 1991; Maidment, 1977]. As a recent study has concluded, 'whatever legal reforms may be made, and whatever changes may be made to court procedures, without effective enforcement by police officers and by courts, injunctions and protection orders will continue to be "not worth the paper they are written on"' [Barron, 1990].

Some of the reasons why women found that non-molestation orders were 'not worth the paper they were written on' are illustrated by Erin Pizzey (1974):

Joan took her husband before the High Court eleven times before she finally got him put in prison with a one-year sentence. The first time he broke in the police refused to come as they said there was nothing they could do on a High Court injunction. He beat her up and she came to Women's Aid. After that the poor woman yo-yoed back and forth with her three children using us as a refuge when her husband was around. Eventually she went back and tried to live in the home that the court said was hers when the divorce had been granted. He broke in, beat her up, punctured her ear-drum and raped her at the point of a knife. When she got him back into the High Court, the judge did not appear to have read the previous judges' notes and accepted the husband's story that he dropped in for some urgent papers at 3 a.m. and his wife had refused to let him have them. The judge gave him seven days and told him in effect that he was a naughty boy.

Part of Joan's problem was that whenever she took her husband to court they appeared in front of a different judge, and none of the judges bothered to read the file of her husband's atrocities, which was steadily getting thicker and thicker.

She gave up trying to live in 'her' home and moved in with us. Her husband broke our windows, screamed and raged outside the house, pestered the school and tried to snatch the children. We took him back to court and this time saw the same judge twice. He did read the case and was appalled enough to put him inside for a year. It was too late for Joan to claim her council house, though – the rent arrears had mounted up and the council had taken it back.

Other problems are demonstrated by a woman whose experience was described in the evidence of Welsh Womens' Aid to the Home Affairs Committee (1993):

In May 1989, I was hospitalised for eight weeks by my partner's violence. Whilst I was in hospital, my ex-partner was allowed out of prison on bail. The bail conditions were that he stayed away from the hospital and the village where the 'matrimonial home' was. However, no one bothered to tell me this and I only found out by 'pestering' the police.

About four to five weeks after I returned home from hospital, my ex-partner simply walked in on me – he literally didn't even bother to knock on the door. He said that he had been back to court and the bail conditions no longer applied. He had been given two years probation. Again, no one had bothered to let me know when the hearing was or what the decision was. I was very shocked and frightened and managed to escape with great difficulty, using a zimmer frame, to my neighbour's.

I phoned the Probation Officer and was told that I would have to take out an injunction myself despite the fact that my partner was supposedly under the direction and control of this Probation Officer.

I applied for an injunction and it took nearly three weeks to come to court. I asked for an injunction with a power of arrest attached. This I did not get, in fact I only got an undertaking which was negotiated in the corridor whilst I was sitting in the courtroom waiting for my application to be heard. After the hearing, I had to come into contact with my ex-partner because there was only one way out. He asked me if I wanted a lift 'home' from court – the 'home' that he had just undertaken to stay away from! The charge for this ended up on my Legal Aid bill.

When the undertaking ran out, I sought another injunction. I was told that as I had suffered no further assaults, it would be very unlikely that I would be granted one. During this time, he had called up to my house every weekend to see the children and to work on me. He wanted to move back into the house permanently. I felt harrassed and under threat.

By June 1990, I gave way and agreed for him to move into the house for one week because he had to leave his accommodation and his new accommodation was not ready. However, once he moved back in he would not leave. In order to get an 'ouster', I would have had to wait until I was assaulted again. With my last experience of hospitalisation in my mind and knowing that if I did get an 'ouster', it would only last three months anyway, I decided to leave. I felt that I had no real choice, I didn't want to leave my home.

At the end of September 1990, I moved to Aberystwyth. In November, my ex-partner found me and threatened me with a knife. I had to run to the Women's Aid office and from there, moved into a Refuge. I was granted an emergency *ex-parte* non-molestation order which lasted until 20 December. Again, this ended up on my Legal Aid bill.

On 20 December, I got another non-molestation order but I had to move from the Refuge into hiding because my ex-partner had found the Refuge and was calling there. He was also going to the children's school and into lecture theatres in the University looking for me. For three weeks, the non-molestation order was void as it had not been served. Therefore, I could not even use the limited power of the order to take my ex-partner back to court for contempt. I had extensions to the injunction and so on and similar things happened.

It seems to me that I was a victim of someone else's violent and irresponsible behaviour and yet it has always been me that has had to pay. Somewhere along the line, I had a property put into my joint name. My name should have been on the property in the first place if it were not for my ex-partner's irresponsible behaviour. I have had to respond to my ex-partner's actions in order to seek protection, but the costs go on to my Legal Aid bill as a charge on my house which I must pay when the house is sold.

I feel that I should have been told when the hearings would be and of the sentence. My feelings should have been considered when the bail conditions (my only protection) were lifted.

And I feel extremely let down by the Probation Service to whom I was an irrelevance. Every time I attended court no one met my eye. I was ignored. The judge would usually have a little joke with my ex-partner. I think I made them all feel uncomfortable. I am now a law student and, when they know this, they treat me very differently. I am no longer a victim but 'one of us'.

When I really needed protection I did not get it. If I knew then what I know now, I would not have bothered with all the distress of hours spent in solicitors' offices and court waiting rooms.

Although reform of the law cannot be a complete solution to the problem of domestic violence, it is important that the law should be as clear and comprehensible as possible. The Family Homes and Domestic Violence Bill 1995 was based upon the Law Commission's recommendations. However, these proved unexpectedly controversial, particularly in relation to the availability of orders to unmarried applicants. The Bill was withdrawn, but an amended version of its provisions eventually became Part IV of the Family Law Act 1996. The Act provides for 'non-molestation orders' and 'occupation orders' to be available at all levels of the court system, replacing the various orders and injunctions which were available under the previous law. We will consider the provisions relating to each of these orders, beginning with non-molestation orders.

9.5   Non-molestation orders

Section 42 of the Family Law Act 1996 deals with non-molestation orders:

42.—(1) In this Part a 'non-molestation order' means an order containing either or both of the following provisions—
>   (*a*)   provision prohibiting a person ('the respondent') from molesting another person who is associated with the respondent;
>   (*b*)   provision prohibiting the respondent from molesting a relevant child.
>   (2)   The court may make a non-molestation order—
>   (*a*)   if an application for the order has been made (whether in other family proceedings or without any other family proceedings being instituted) by a person who is associated with the respondent; or
>   (*b*)   if in any family proceedings to which the respondent is a party the court considers that the order should be made for the benefit of any other party to the proceedings or any relevant child even though no such application has been made.
>   ...
>   (5)   In deciding whether to exercise its powers under this section and, if so, in what manner, the court shall have regard to all the circumstances including the need to secure the health, safety and well-being—
>   (*a*)   of the applicant or, in a case falling within subsection (2)(*b*), the person for whose benefit the order would be made; and
>   (*b*)   of any relevant child.

'Relevant child' is defined by s. 62(2) as:

>   (*a*)   any child who is living with or might reasonably be expected to live with either party to the proceedings;
>   (*b*)   any child in relation to whom an order under the Adoption Act 1976 or the Children Act 1989 is in question in the proceedings; and
>   (*c*)   any other child whose interests the court considers relevant.

The category of 'associated persons' is defined in s. 62(3):

62.—... (3) For the purposes of this Part, a person is associated with another person if—
>   (*a*)   they are or have been married to each other;

(*b*) they are cohabitants or former cohabitants;
(*c*) they live or have lived in the same household, otherwise than merely by reason of one of them being the other's employee, tenant, lodger or boarder;
(*d*) they are relatives;
(*e*) they have agreed to marry one another (whether or not that agreement has been terminated);
(*f*) in relation to any child, they are both persons falling within subsection (4); or
(*g*) they are parties to the same family proceedings (other than proceedings under this Part).
(4) A person falls within this subsection in relation to a child if—
(*a*) he is a parent of the child; or
(*b*) he has or has had parental responsibility for the child.
(5) If a child has been adopted or has been freed for adoption by virtue of any of the enactments mentioned in section 16(1) of the Adoption Act 1976, two persons are also associated with each other for the purposes of this Part if—
(*a*) one is a natural parent of the child or a parent of such a natural parent; and
(*b*) the other is the child or any person—
(i) who has become a parent of the child by virtue of an adoption order or has applied for an adoption order, or
(ii) with whom the child has at any time been placed for adoption.
(6) A body corporate and another person are not, by virtue of subsection (3)(*f*) or (*g*), to be regarded for the purposes of this Part as associated with each other.

'Cohabitants' is defined by s. 62(1):

(*a*) 'cohabitants' are a man and a woman who, although not married to each other, are living together as husband and wife; and
(*b*) 'former cohabitants' is to be read accordingly, but does not include cohabitants who have subsequently married each other.

and 'relative' is defined by s. 63(1) as:

(*a*) the father, mother, stepfather, stepmother, son, daughter, stepson, stepdaughter, grandmother, grandfather, grandson or granddaughter of that person or of that person's spouse or former spouse, or
(*b*) the brother, sister, uncle, aunt, niece or nephew (whether of the full blood or of the half blood or by affinity) of that person or of that person's spouse or former spouse,
and includes in relation to a person who is living or has lived with another person as husband and wife, any person who would fall within paragraph (*a*) or (*b*) if the parties were married to each other.

Question

Do these provisions allow for non-molestation orders between: (a) a gay or lesbian couple living together; (b) a heterosexual couple who have separate homes, but frequently spend nights together; (c) a group of students sharing a house, which one of them sub-lets to the others; (d) an uncle and his niece's ex-cohabitant; (e) between two women, one of whom is now cohabiting with the ex-cohabitant of the other? Should they?

Even where it is clear that a particular type of relationship is within the scope of 'associated persons', there may be a dispute about whether the facts of the particular case are sufficient to establish the existence of the relationship. In relation to s. 62(3)(e) (people who have agreed to marry), s. 44 of the 1996 Act deals with 'evidence of agreement to marry' and provides as follows:

(1) Subject to subsection (2), the court shall not make an order under section . . . 42 by virtue of section 62(3)(e) unless there is produced to it evidence in writing of the existence of the agreement to marry.

(2) Subsection (1) does not apply if the court is satisfied that the agreement to marry was evidenced by—

(a) the gift of an engagement ring by one party to the agreement to the other in contemplation of their marriage, or

(b) a ceremony entered into by the parties in the presence of one or more other persons assembled for the purpose of witnessing the ceremony.

Those who have agreed to marry are likely to form a relatively small proportion of applicants for non-molestation orders. A larger number of those who are not married, are likely to apply as cohabitants or ex-cohabitants, or as homesharers (under s. 62(3)(b) or (c)). The proper approach to such cases is illustrated in the following case:

G v F (non-molestation order: jurisdiction)
[2000] 2 FCR 638, sub nom G v G [2000] 2 FLR 532

Wall J. ... This unusual appeal arises from the refusal of the justices sitting in the Wimbledon Family Proceedings Court on 2 February 2000 to entertain an application by a woman, 'LG', the applicant, for a non-molestation order against a man, 'DF', the respondent. The justices' refusal to hear the application was based on their finding that the applicant and the respondent were not 'associated' persons within s 42(1)(a) of the Family Law Act 1996. The applicant challenges that conclusion. She argues that the justices misdirected themselves in several material respects.
...

The facts

... The parties met in November 1996. The applicant has a daughter, J, born on 18 May 1993, of whom the respondent is not the father. The parties were never married and the respondent does not have parental responsibility for J ... The respondent had been previously married and his wife had died of cancer in August of 1996. The applicant says that very early in their relationship he said he wanted to marry her and adopt her daughter. According to the applicant they soon formed a 'strong attachment'. However, in February 1997 the applicant says that the respondent was violent to her for the first time. If she is right, it was a serious assault which required medical attention, but she did not inform the police. The applicant says, however, that three days later the respondent apologised and they were reconciled. The applicant alleges further incidents in 1998, which include both physical violence and threats to herself and the child. However, the events which led to the making of the application to the court on 21 December 1999 were, according to the applicant, a series of incidents over the preceding weekend, culminating on Monday, 20 December.

As to the status of the relationship between the parties, the applicant says:

'Strictly speaking, we did not live together, but the respondent would often stay over for two or three nights in the week, and then I would go to his flat at the weekends. During this time he was not only verbally abusive to me, but also threatening.'

...

Following the justices' reasons in the bundle is a document entitled 'Selected cases', which was before the justices and is clearly an in-house aide-memoire for justices dealing with cases under Pt IV of the 1996 Act. ... Under the heading 'Cohabitation', there is a reference to *Crake v Supplementary Benefits Commission, Butterworth v Supplementary Benefits Commission* [1982] 1 All ER 498, of which the summary is as follows:

'In order to establish that the man and woman were "living together as husband and wife" it was not sufficient merely to show that they were living together in the same household. Although in many circumstances that might be strong evidence to show that they were living together as husband and wife, it is necessary in each case to go on to ascertain the manner in which and why they were living in the same household. If the reason for someone living in the same household as another person is to look after that person because they are ill, or incapable for some other reason of managing their affairs, then that in ordinary parlance is not what one would describe as living together as husband and wife. Once one has established the relationship to exist, then it is much easier to show that it continues, even though many of the features of living together between husband and wife have ceased, perhaps because of advancing years or for other reason. This would be the position even though a court will have come to a different conclusion as to whether the paragraph applied, if at the outset all that existed was that state of affairs. As one of "signposts" which will assist in coming to a decision as to whether parties should be regarded as living together as man and wife are: (1) whether they are members of the same household; (2) whether the relationship is stable; (3) whether there is financial support; (4) whether there is a sexual relationship; (5) whether they have children; (6) whether there is public acknowledgment.'

The aide-memoire then goes on to consider *Re J (income support: cohabitation)* [1995] 1 FLR 660 and summarises that case as follows:

'The six "admirable signposts" placed a wholly inadequate emphasis on the parties "general relationship". The parties' sexual and financial relationship is relevant only for the light it throws on this general relationship between them. Where there has never been a sexual relationship between the parties, there must be strong alternative grounds for holding a relationship to be akin to that of husband and wife.'

...

It is plain that the justices were influenced by the applicant's statement that 'strictly speaking, we do not live together', that the respondent would often stay over for two or three nights in a week, 'and then I would go to his flat at weekends'. ...

In my judgment, the evidence is sufficient to support the proposition that the applicant and the respondent were cohabitants within the meaning of s 62(3)(b) of the 1996 Act. Of the 'admirable signposts' set out in *Crake v Supplementary Benefits Commission, Butterworth v Supplementary Benefits Commission,* three are present. There was plainly a sexual relationship; there is evidence that they lived in the same household, and there was substantial evidence from the respondent, not disputed on the papers before the justices by the applicant, that the applicant and the respondent operated a joint account into which the proceeds of sale of the respondent's previous property were paid. The respondent asserts also that money was spent on the applicant's property. In my judgment therefore the respondent's evidence taken as a whole is sufficient to demonstrate that he and the applicant were, indeed, cohabitants. It is true that the relationship was not stable, although in one way or another it appears to have lasted from November 1996 to December 1999.

In my judgment, therefore, viewed as a whole, there was evidence before the justices on which they could and should have found that the applicant and the respondent were former cohabitants within s 62(3)(b), and if they were advised by their clerk that as a matter of law such a finding was not open to them, that advice was, with all respect, wrong. Plainly, if that is what happened, the justices cannot be criticised for following the advice they were given, although they make no mention of the advice in their reasons. In any event, I am satisfied that on the material before them they should have found that the parties were associated and have assumed jurisdiction.

In my judgment, the message of this case to justices is that where domestic violence is concerned, they should give the statute a purposive construction and not decline jurisdiction, unless the facts of the case before them are plainly incapable of being brought within the statute. Part IV of the 1996 Act is designed to provide swift and accessible protective remedies to persons of both sexes who are the victims of domestic violence, provided they fall within the criteria laid down by s 62. It would, I think, be most unfortunate if s 62(3) was narrowly construed so as to exclude borderline cases where swift and effective protection for the victims of domestic violence is required. This case is, after all, about jurisdiction; it is not about the merits.

If on a full inquiry the applicant is not entitled on the merits to the relief she seeks, she will not get it. But it is at the lowest arguable that if the justices had accepted jurisdiction and made a further order on 2 February, the incident on 8 March, which appears to have been sufficiently serious to result in a conviction for criminal damage, would not have occurred.

In these circumstances, it does not seem to me to be necessary to consider the other limbs of s 62(3). I do, however, think there is some force in Miss Amaouche's point that it would have been preferable for the justices to have considered s 62(3)(b) first. By deciding the s 62(3)(c) point first and by rejecting it, they effectively precluded themselves from making a different finding under s 62(3)(b). Plainly, if the applicant and the respondent had never lived in the same household, they could not be former cohabitants. However, if the justices had taken the cohabitation point first, they would have been able, even if they had rejected it, to have considered whether or not the parties had lived together in the same household.

... In the light of my finding that these parties are former cohabitants, ... I do not think it necessary to consider s 62(3)(e), although it is at lowest arguable that the respondent's statements to the court provide sufficient 'evidence in writing' for the purposes of s 44(1).

Question

Why should a victim of violence, harassment or molestation have to demonstrate that he or she is 'associated' with the perpetrator of the molestation before he or she can seek a remedy?

In its Report (1992), the Law Commission considered the possibility of allowing anyone to seek a non-molestation order, but decided against:

3.19 ... We do not think it is appropriate that this jurisdiction should be available to resolve issues such as disputes between neighbours, harassment of tenants by landlords or cases of sexual harassment in the workplace. Here there is no domestic or family relationship to justify special remedies or procedures and resort should properly be had to the remedies provided under property or employment law. Family relationships can, however, be appropriately distinguished from other forms of association. In practice, many of the same considerations apply to them as to married or cohabiting couples. Thus the proximity of the parties often gives unique opportunities for molestation and abuse to continue; the heightened emotions of all concerned give rise to a particular need for sensitivity and flexibility in the law; there is frequently a possibility that their relationship will carry on for the foreseeable future; and there is in most cases the likelihood that they will share a common budget, making financial remedies inappropriate.

However, in addition to the categories eventually included in the Family Law Act 1996, the Law Commission (1992) had recommended that non-molestation orders should be available between people who 'have or have had a sexual relationship with each other (whether or not including sexual intercourse)'. The inclusion of this category was supported by the Home Affairs Committee (1993):

109 ... People must be protected against harassment, violence and abuse from those with whom they have or have had close emotional and sexual relationships. Not all intense relationships between partners result in marriage or cohabitation – there are, for example, 'visiting' or adulterous relationships where the parties still live with their spouses or simply lovers who choose not to live together. Nor do we believe that sexual intercourse should be a determining factor because not all cohabitees, let alone non-cohabitees, have sexual intercourse with each other. We therefore think it inappropriate to attach any special significance here to the sexual act.

On the other hand, His Honour Judge Fricker QC (1995) supported the exclusion of this group:

... when a 'family' breaks down, it is likely that further contact between the members will be needed in relation to practical and continuing arrangements for their children, or adjustments to their finances or housing needs. Therefore a right to be protected from molestation is related to a likely continuing practical nexus in many situations. The problems arising in disentangling previous shared commitments based on family membership involving a mixture of personal and legal relationships.

If the [Act] were extended to cover persons who have had an intimate sexual relationship without having created a child, ... would there be a continuing practical nexus? The continuing nexus in most cases would, I suggest, be substantially an inability to 'let go' the relationship. Usually there will not be a practical need to adjust to a change in existing financial or housing arrangements.

...

One form of harassment which has recently been publicised is 'stalking', e.g. an obsessional admirer harasses someone in the entertainment world. People who are unfairly harassed do need protection.

I suggest that extending the [Family Law Act] beyond a sensible family nexus would create an anomalous legal right not founded on legal principle other than convenience. It would create what would be in effect a right not to be harassed under a stretched umbrella of family law, with an arbitrary boundary. The nettle should be grasped and the right not to be harassed should be founded in the law of tort, where it belongs.

The eventual form of the legislation reflected the view of Judge Fricker that 'family law' remedies should not be available between people who are not relatives, and have never married, or agreed to marry, or lived together in the same household, or had children together. However, a wider remedy was provided by the Protection from Harassment Act 1997:

1 Prohibition of harassment

(1) A person must not pursue a course of conduct—
(a) which amounts to harassment of another, and
(b) which he knows or ought to know amounts to harassment of the other.

(2) For the purposes of this section, the person whose course of conduct is in question ought to know that it amounts to harassment of another if a reasonable person in possession of the same information would think the course of conduct amounted to harassment of the other.

(3) Subsection (1) does not apply to a course of conduct if the person who pursued it shows—
(a) that it was pursued for the purpose of preventing or detecting crime,
(b) that it was pursued under any enactment or rule of law or to comply with any condition or requirement imposed by any person under any enactment, or
(c) that in the particular circumstances the pursuit of the course of conduct was reasonable.

2 Offence of harassment

(1) A person who pursues a course of conduct in breach of section 1 is guilty of an offence.

(2) A person guilty of an offence under this section is liable on summary conviction to imprisonment for a term not exceeding six months, or a fine not exceeding level 5 on the standard scale, or both.

...

3 Civil remedy

(1) An actual or apprehended breach of section 1 may be the subject of a claim in civil proceedings by the person who is or may be the victim of the course of conduct in question.

(2) On such a claim, damages may be awarded for (among other things) any anxiety caused by the harassment and any financial loss resulting from the harassment.

(3) Where—
(a) in such proceedings the High Court or a county court grants an injunction for the purpose of restraining the defendant from pursuing any conduct which amounts to harassment, and
(b) the plaintiff considers that the defendant has done anything which he is prohibited from doing by the injunction,
the plaintiff may apply for the issue of a warrant for the arrest of the defendant.

...

(6) Where—
(a) the High Court or a county court grants an injunction for the purpose mentioned in subsection (3)(a), and
(b) without reasonable excuse the defendant does anything which he is prohibited from doing by the injunction,
he is guilty of an offence.

(7) Where a person is convicted of an offence under subsection (6) in respect of any conduct, that conduct is not punishable as a contempt of court.

(8) A person cannot be convicted of an offence under subsection (6) in respect of any conduct which has been punished as a contempt of court.

(9) A person guilty of an offence under subsection (6) is liable—
(a) on conviction on indictment, to imprisonment for a term not exceeding five years, or a fine, or both, or
(b) on summary conviction, to imprisonment for a term not exceeding six months, or a fine not exceeding the statutory maximum, or both.

This legislation uses both civil and criminal law to provide protection to victims of harassment. However, the Act requires a 'course of conduct'. The meaning of this phrase was considered in *R v Hills* [2001] 1 FCR 569, [2001] 1 FLR 580, CA:

26. The whole thrust of the prosecution case—and indeed the evidence from the complainant herself—centred on two separate and individual incidents, namely the assault in April and the

assault in October. They were a considerable distance apart. On their face and on the evidence there was a clear prima facie case which would have justified counts in the indictment alleging actual bodily harm on each occasion.

27. The Divisional Court in February 2000 considered the case of *Lau v DPP* [2000] 1 FLR 799, which concerned two incidents between a girlfriend and a boyfriend. It was held that although incidents to be proved in relation to harassment need not exceed two incidents, the fewer the occasions and the wider they were spread the less likely it would be that a finding of harassment could reasonably be made. It was possible to conceive of circumstances where incidents as far apart as a year could constitute a course of conduct and harassment, namely racial harassment taking place outside a synagogue on a religious holiday and repeated each year or a threat to do something once a year on a person's birthday. Nevertheless the broad position had to be that if one was left with only two incidents it was necessary to see whether what happened on those two occasions could be described as a course of conduct. It was not possible to answer that question, adopting an essentially mathematical approach by saying that there were two incidents and that showed that there was a course of conduct. The root question on which the magistrates ought to have concentrated was whether or not, bearing in mind that they had only found two of the incidents proved, separated as they were by some four months, and in the absence of any other relevant finding, that could reasonably be described as a course of conduct by the defendant. As the facts did not reveal sufficient material to have enabled the magistrates to convict the appellant of harassment the conviction would be quashed.

...

31. It is to be borne in mind that the state of affairs which was relied upon by the prosecution was miles away from the 'stalking' type of offence for which the Act was intended. That is not to say that it is never appropriate so to charge a person who is making a nuisance of himself to his partner or wife when they have become estranged. However, in a situation such as this, when they were frequently coming back together and intercourse was taking place (apparently a video was taken of them having intercourse) it is unrealistic to think that this fell within the stalking category which either postulates a stranger or an estranged spouse. That was not the situation when the course of conduct relied upon was committed.

32. In those circumstances, we have come to the conclusion that, when the evidence crossed over the threshold from a mere putting in fear to a substantive count of actual bodily harm, the prosecution might have been wiser to have abandoned the harassment count and to have concentrated on the two substantive counts of violence, and with more prospects of success. They insisted, for reasons which are not entirely clear, on proceeding with harassment counts, where, in the events leading up to the arraignment at least, they were put on notice that the chances of securing a conviction on the single count of harassment alone in the indictment were fast receding. We have come to the conclusion, therefore, that the conviction is not safe. We must allow the appeal and it must be quashed.

Questions

(i) Are injunctions under the Protection from Harassment Act available to people who are 'associated' under the Family Law Act 1996? Can you think of any reasons why an associated person might choose to use the 1997 Act instead of seeking a non-molestation order under the Family Law Act? Or vice versa?
(ii) Would it be possible to obtain a 'restraining order' under the Protection from Harassment Act after a single incident of domestic violence? Is there a 'course of conduct' or an 'anticipated' course of conduct in such circumstances?
(iii) Part IV of the Family Law Act 1996 was intended to reduce confusion by providing a single set of remedies for domestic violence under a single statute. Is there a danger that similar confusion could develop as a result of the use of the Protection of Harassment Act in domestic violence cases?

Under the Family Law Act 1996, a non-molestation order may be made for a specified period or until further order (s. 42(7)) and may be 'expressed so as to refer to molestation in general, to particular acts of molestation, or to both' (s. 42(6)). As the Law Commission point out in their Report (1992):

2.3 Domestic violence can take many forms. The term 'violence' itself is often used in two senses. In its narrower meaning it describes the use or threat of physical force against a victim in the form of an assault or battery. But in the context of the family, there is also a wider meaning which extends to abuse beyond the more typical instances of physical assaults to include any form of physical, sexual or psychological molestation or harassment which has a serious detrimental effect upon the health and well-being of the victim, albeit that there is no 'violence' involved in the sense of physical force. Examples of such 'non-violent' harassment or molestation cover a very wide range of behaviour [*Vaughan v Vaughan* [1973] 1 WLR 1159]. Common instances include persistent pestering and intimidation through shouting, denigration, threats or argument, nuisance telephone calls, damaging property, following the applicant about and repeatedly calling at her home or place of work. Installing a mistress into the matrimonial home with a wife and three children [*Adams v Adams* (1965) 109 Sol Jo 899], filling car locks with superglue, writing anonymous letters and pressing one's face against a window whilst brandishing papers [*Smith v Smith* [1988] 1 FLR 179] have all been held to amount to molestation. The degree of severity of such behaviour depends less upon its intrinsic nature than upon it being part of a pattern and upon its effect on the victim. Acts of molestation often follow upon previous behaviour which has been violent or otherwise offensive. Calling at the applicant's house on one occasion may not be objectionable. Calling frequently and unexpectedly at unsocial hours when the victim is known to be afraid certainly is. Such forms of abuse may in some circumstances be just as harmful, vicious and distressing as physical injuries.

The courts are usually able to recognise molestation when they see it, but the concept was examined by Sir Stephen Brown P in *C v C (Non-Molestation Order: Jurisdiction)* [1998] Fam 70, [1998] 1 FCR 11, [1998] 1 FLR 554:

Sir Stephen Brown P: Mr C has applied to the court for a non-molestation order under the provisions of s 42 of the Family Law Act 1996. ... The complaint which gives rise to this application is that on Sunday, 12 October 1997, the People newspaper published an article which related to the former marriage and the relationship between Mr C and his former wife. On 16 October a further article was publicised in the Daily Mail in a similar context, headed 'A Champion Cheat, by the women he deceived'. In it, the article purported to give details of complaints about Mr C's conduct made by two former wives. ...

The respondent submits that even though the articles are unflattering and, indeed, unpleasant so far as Mr C is concerned, none the less she has not 'molested' him and has done nothing which could bring her within the purview of s 42.

It is pointed out, on behalf of Mr C, that there is no legal definition of 'molestation'. Indeed, that is quite clear from the various cases which have been cited. It is a matter which has to be considered in relation to the particular facts of particular cases. It implies some quite deliberate conduct which is aimed at a high degree of harassment of the other party, so as to justify the intervention of the court. There is no direct communication, as I have said, between the former wife and the former husband in this case. ...

Endeavours have been made, in my view, to widen the concept of molestation. It does not include enforcing an invasion of privacy per se. There has to be some conduct which clearly harasses and affects the applicant to such a degree that the intervention of the court is called for.

It is further significant that in s 42(5), the 1996 Act provides as follows:

'In deciding whether to exercise its powers under this section, and if so, in what manner, the court shall have regard to all the circumstances including the need to secure the health, safety and well-being—(a) of the applicant ...'

It is significant, in my judgment, that s 42 is to be found in Part IV of the 1996 Act, which is concerned with the general topic of domestic violence. In this particular case the marriage between these parties has been finally ended; they are quite separate individuals, and the material complained of is some alleged revelations by the former wife of what she regarded as her former husband's misconduct.

In my judgment, it comes nowhere near molestation as envisaged by s 42 of the 1996 Act. ... It is not 'molestation' as such but damage to his reputation with which he is concerned. ...

Question

Perhaps the courts should not be expected to prevent one ex-spouse from maligning the other in the media, but might it be too restrictive to require 'some quite deliberate conduct which is aimed at a high degree of harassment of the other party'? (Compare the Protection from Harassment Act 1997, which applies where the person knows, or ought to know, that his conduct amounts to harassment.)

9.6   Occupation orders

In addition to non-molestation orders, the Family Law Act 1996 also provides for a variety of 'occupation orders'. The Law Commission (1992) recognised the importance of such orders in cases of domestic violence:

4.6 ... where the parties live together, an occupation order ousting the respondent from the home will often be the only way of supporting a non-molestation order and giving the applicant effective protection.

However, the Law Commission's Report (1992) also drew attention to the effect of such orders on the other party:

2.48 In principle, there must be a distinction between an order not to be violent towards or molest another family member, which can be obeyed without prejudice to the interests of the person concerned, and an order to leave or stay away from the home (or part of it), which obviously does prejudice those interests, however temporarily or justifiably.

The following story by Frances Gibb, Legal Correspondent, in *The Times* (1997), illustrates the impact of an occupation order:

Husband who snapped told to leave home
A Deputy headmaster who temporarily lost control and pushed his wife against a door after she confessed to an affair with one of his 'best friends' was ordered yesterday to give up his home to her. Despite expressing sympathy for the man's plight, two Court of Appeal judges yesterday refused to overturn an earlier ruling ordering the husband out of the family home, although they said that his estranged wife had 'created the situation'. The husband, from the Portsmouth area, had vowed not to harm his wife again and had offered to sleep in a separate room and stay out of the main part of the house.
    After dismissing his appeal Lady Justice Butler-Sloss and Lord Justice Phillips gave him until noon on September 6 to leave so that his wife and their three children, aged nine, seven and five, and who are currently living in a women's refuge, can move back in. In June this year the wife confessed that she had had a brief affair with a family friend. Her husband later admitted that he had reacted badly over the following three or four days, pushing her against the door once and gripping her wrists hard enough to leave a mark on two other occasions. But he was stunned when his wife took the children and fled, claiming she was too frightened to return while he was in their home. In July she won a ruling from Portsmouth County Court that her husband should leave the house by August 8 despite his promise not to harm her. But the order was stayed when the husband applied for leave to appeal against the decision.
    Lady Justice Butler-Sloss said: 'Members of the public might be forgiven for thinking that when a man finds his wife has committed adultery with one of his best friends and she tells it to him his reaction is likely to be uncontrolled.' But to have been violent on three occasions had been 'over the top' and although she had no doubt that the husband's promise not to harm his wife was genuine, to allow them to live under the same roof would create a situation 'fraught with emotional turmoil' leading to the risk of further violence.

Before the Family Law Act 1996, the criteria for 'ouster orders' were settled by the House of Lords:

Richards v Richards
[1984] AC 174, [1983] 2 All ER 807, [1983] 3 WLR 173, [1984] FLR 11,
13 Fam Law 256, House of Lords

The wife petitioned for divorce, relying upon allegations of behaviour, but remained in the matrimonial home for nearly three months performing 'wifely duties' but not sleeping with her husband. She then left taking the children, a girl of six and a boy of four, to a friend's cottage. She sought and obtained an order, inter alia, for the husband to leave the home. She then returned with the children; the parties had since arranged that she lived with them there during the week and the father lived with them there at weekends. The husband's appeal to the Court of Appeal was dismissed and he appealed to the House of Lords. The House of Lords decided that the judge had been wrong to give priority to the interests of the children. Instead, he should have applied the criteria in the Matrimonial Homes Act 1967 (later consolidated as the Matrimonial Homes Act 1983).

Lord Brandon of Oakbrook: ... That subsection requires the court to make such order as it thinks just and reasonable having regard to a number of specified matters. The matters so specified are these: (1) the conduct of the spouses to each other and otherwise; (2) the respective needs and financial resources of the spouses; (3) the needs of any children; and (4) all the circumstances of the case. With regard to these matters it is, in my opinion, of the utmost importance to appreciate that none of them is made, by the wording of s.1(3), necessarily of more weight than any of the others, let alone made paramount over them. All the four matters specified are to be regarded, and the weight to be given to any particular one of them must depend on the facts of each case.

My Lords, I do not go so far as to say that the conduct of an applicant wife in the particular respect under discussion is necessarily and in all cases decisive, in a manner adverse to her of the question whether the order for which she has applied should be made or not. It is however, an important factor to be weighed in the scales, along with the other matters specified in s.1(3) of the 1967 Act; and in a substantial number of cases at any rate it will be a factor of such weight as to lead a court to think that it would not be just or reasonable to allow her application. ...

When the Law Commission reviewed the law in 1992, they outlined the criticism of these criteria:

4.23 ... They do not give priority to the applicant's personal protection, but require this to be balanced against all other factors, including hardship to the respondent. Thus the level of protection provided for an applicant suffering from violence may not be adequate. Also a requirement to decide upon occupation of the family home on the basis (at least in part) of fault, thus encouraging parties to make allegations about behaviour, sits uneasily with the general trend in matrimonial law towards reducing the need for recrimination and fault-finding, and enabling the courts to deal with problems of family breakdown without allocating blame, with a view to enhancing the possibility of agreement or even reconciliation between the parties. The test is also thought to give insufficient weight to the interests of children as the balancing exercise throws the children into the scales along with all the other factors and gives no priority to their welfare.

However, the Law Commission stopped short of recommending that the welfare of children should be the paramount consideration. Instead, they recommended a 'balance of harm' test should apply, so that a court should have a duty to make an order if it appears likely that the applicant or any relevant child will suffer significant harm if an order is not made and that such harm will be greater than the harm which the respondent or any relevant child will suffer if the order is made. They said:

4.34 ... It is likely that a respondent threatened with ouster on account of his violence would be able to establish a degree of hardship (perhaps in terms of difficulty in finding or unsuitability of alternative accommodation or problems in getting to work). But he is unlikely to suffer significant harm, whereas his wife and children who are being subjected to his violence or abuse may very easily suffer harm if he remains in the house. In this way the court will be treating violence or other forms of abuse as deserving immediate relief, and will be directed to make an order where a risk of significant harm exists. However, by placing an emphasis on the need for a remedy rather than on the conduct which gave rise to that need, the criteria will not actually put a premium on allegations of violence and thus may avoid the problems which would be generated by a scheme which focuses on it.

Question

Why was the Law Commission concerned not to put a premium on allegations of violence?

An amended version of the 'balance of harm' test appears in s. 33 of the Family Law Act 1996:

33.—... (3)   An order under this section may—
  (*a*) enforce the applicant's entitlement to remain in occupation as against the other person ('the respondent');
  (*b*) require the respondent to permit the applicant to enter and remain in the dwelling-house or part of the dwelling-house;
  (*c*) regulate the occupation of the dwelling-house by either or both parties;
  (*d*) if the respondent is entitled [to occupy the dwelling-house by virtue of a beneficial estate or interest or contract or by virtue of any enactment giving him the right to remain in occupation], prohibit, suspend or restrict the exercise by him of his right to occupy the dwelling-house;
  (*e*) if the respondent has matrimonial home rights in relation to the dwelling-house and the applicant is the other spouse, restrict or terminate those rights;
  (*f*) require the respondent to leave the dwelling-house or part of the dwelling-house; or
  (*g*) exclude the respondent from a defined area in which the dwelling house is included.
  ...
  (6) In deciding whether to exercise its powers under subsection (3) and (if so) in what manner, the court shall have regard to all the circumstances including—
  (*a*) the housing needs and housing resources of each of the parties and of any relevant child;
  (*b*) the financial resources of each of the parties;
  (*c*) the likely effect of any order, or of any decision by the court not to exercise its powers under subsection (3), on the health, safety or well-being of the parties and of any relevant child; and
  (*d*) the conduct of the parties in relation to each other and otherwise.
  (7) If it appears to the court that the applicant or any relevant child is likely to suffer significant harm attributable to conduct of the respondent if an order under this section containing one or more of the provisions mentioned in subsection (3) is not made, the court shall make the order unless it appears to it that—
  (*a*) the respondent or any relevant child is likely to suffer significant harm if the order is made; and
  (*b*) the harm likely to be suffered by the respondent or child in that event is as great as, or greater than, the harm attributable to conduct of the respondent which is likely to be suffered by the applicant or child if the order is not made.
  ...

'Harm' is defined in s. 63 of the Act to mean ill-treatment or the impairment of physical or mental health, and (in the case of children) impairment of development.

Question

Why does sub-s. (7) require that the harm likely to be suffered is 'attributable to the conduct of the respondent'?

An application under s. 33 of the Family Law Act 1996 is only possible where the applicant is entitled to occupy the home by virtue of a legal or beneficial estate or interest or a contractual or statutory right. Section 33 will, therefore, always be available between spouses since, in the absence of any other right, they will have a statutory right of occupation under s. 30 of the Family Law Act 1996 (see p. 152, above). Occupation orders will be available between unmarried people, provided that they are 'associated' in the same way as for non-molestation orders, but only if the applicant can establish that he or she has some entitlement to occupy the property in question (s. 33(1)).

An application for an occupation order by an unmarried 'entitled' applicant was considered by the Court of Appeal in *Chalmers v Johns* [1999] 1 FLR 392; [1999] 2 FCR 110, [1999] Fam Law 16. Thorpe LJ had this to say about s. 33:

... [Section] 33 of the Family Law Act 1996 ... applies to those cases where the applicant has an estate or interest in the family home. It is common ground that these two are joint tenants. In those circumstances the court may, under sub-s (3) order the prohibition, suspension or restriction of the exercise by the respondent of his right to occupy the residence. Equally under that subsection the court may require the respondent to leave the dwelling house.

Now the exercise of that power is ordinarily governed by sub-s (6). Subsection (6) is in these terms:

'In deciding whether to exercise its powers under subsection (3) and (if so) in what manner, the court shall have regard to all the circumstances including—(a) the housing needs and housing resources of each of the parties and of any relevant child; (b) the financial resources of each of the parties; (c) the likely effect of any order, or of any decision by the court not to exercise its powers under subsection (3), on the health, safety or well-being of the parties and of any relevant child; and (d) the conduct of the parties in relation to each other and otherwise.'

However, the following subsection, sub-s (7), is designed to cater for an altogether more extreme situation, where it appears to the court that any applicant or any relevant child is likely to suffer significant harm attributable to conduct of the respondent if an order under this section containing one or more of the provisions mentioned in sub-s (3) is not made. In that more extreme circumstance, the court's discretion is much confined. The statute says that in such a situation—

'the court shall make the order unless it appears to the court that—(a) the respondent or any relevant child is likely to suffer significant harm if the order is made; and (b) the harm likely to be suffered by the respondent or the child in that event is as great as, or greater than, the harm attributable to conduct of the respondent which is likely to be suffered by the applicant or child if the order is not made.'

So it seems to me that in approaching its function under this section, the court has first to consider whether the evidence establishes that the applicant or any relevant child is likely to suffer significant harm attributable to the conduct of the respondent if an order is not made. If the court answers that question in the affirmative, then it knows that it must make the order unless balancing one harm against the other, the harm to the respondent or the child is likely to be as great. If, however, the court answers the question in the negative, then it enters the discretionary regime provided by sub-s (6) and must exercise a broad discretion having regard to all the circumstances of the case, particularly those factors set out in the statutory check list within paras (a)–(d) inclusive. ...

...The gravity of an order requiring a respondent to vacate a family home, an order overriding proprietary rights, was recognised in cases under the Domestic Violence and Matrimonial Proceedings Act 1976 and a string of authorities in this court emphasise the draconian nature of such an order, and that it should be restricted to exceptional cases. I do not myself think that the wider statutory provisions contained in the Family Law Act 1996 obliterate that authority. The order remains draconian, particularly in the perception of the respondent. It remains an order that overrides proprietary rights and it seems to me that it is an order that is only justified in exceptional circumstances. ...

Question

Can this approach be reconciled with the Law Commission's desire to give greater weight to the need to protect victims of violence and children, rather than to the 'Draconian' effect of the order? Why do you think that the courts persist in an approach which is narrower than the words of the statute? Whose approach do you prefer?

One case in which the interests of a child had a dramatic impact was *B v B (Occupation Order)*.

B v B (Occupation Order)
[1999] 2 FCR 251, [1999] 1 FLR 715, [1999] Fam Law 208, Court of Appeal, Civil Division

Butler-Sloss LJ: ...
The essential facts are not in dispute, and can be stated quite shortly. Mr and Mrs B were married on 30 May 1996. From a previous relationship, Mr B has a son, MB born on 21 December 1992 and so now six. When Mr and Mrs B began their relationship in 1996, and indeed up to the time of his marriage to Mrs B, Mr B was living with MB, and MB's mother, Ms M. However, it appears that immediately after the marriage, Mr and Mrs B set up home together with MB as part of their household.
On 17 June 1996 Mr and Mrs B were given the tenancy of two-bedroomed council accommodation (the property) which became the matrimonial home. On 4 October 1997 their daughter, YB, was born.
The parties separated when Mrs B left the property on 21 July 1998, taking YB (then aged nine months) with her, but leaving MB in the care Mr B. Mrs B's case, accepted by the judge, was that Mr B had treated her with violence.
On 22 or 23 July the local authority rehoused Mrs B and YB in temporary bed and breakfast accommodation. On 1 September Mrs B applied to the county court for an ex parte non-molestation order and for an occupation order against Mr B. On 9 September Mr B gave an undertaking not to molest Mrs B and the latter, who originates from Ghana, gave an undertaking not to remove YB from the jurisdiction. On 21 September the question of Mr B's contact to YB was resolved by agreement.

The hearing before the judge
The hearing of Mrs B's application for an occupation order under s 33 of the 1996 Act took two days, concluding late in the day on 10 November 1998. As already indicated, the judge made the order sought by Mrs B, and refused leave to appeal.
The judge first of all dealt with Mrs B's application for an injunction. This involved a resolution of the factual issues between the parties on the subject of domestic violence and Mrs B's reasons for leaving the matrimonial home. The judge made a number of adverse findings against Mr B, and concluded:

'It seems to me that this is a situation where there has been substantial violence, and it is clearly apprehended that in the absence of some form of injunction that is likely to happen again.'

...

As the judge recognised, the critical subsections of s 33 for the purposes of this case are sub-ss (6) and (7). Both MB and YB are relevant children within s 33(6)(a) and (c) – see s 62(2)(a) of the 1996 Act which defines 'relevant child' as 'any child who is living with or might reasonably be expected to live with either party to the proceedings'. The judge also found, correctly, that on the facts of the instant case the reference in s 33(7) to 'harm' did not mean ill-treatment, but did mean 'impairment of health or development' within s 63(1) of the Act.

...

In our judgment, ... the judge's analysis of the 'housing needs and housing resources of each of the parties and of any relevant child' under s 33(6) led him into error. The respective housing needs of the parties are, in one sense, equal. Each needs two bedroom accommodation provided by the local authority; but the 'housing resources', using that term to include the duty owed to each by the local authority, were quite different. Unsatisfactory as Mrs B's current temporary accommodation is, there is every prospect that in the reasonably foreseeable future she and YB will be rehoused by the local authority in suitable two-bedroomed accommodation. There is no such prospect for Mr B and MB if the occupation order stands.

In our judgment the judge's mistaken analysis of the housing position is sufficient to vitiate the exercise of his discretion in making an occupation order. There is, however, in our view, an additional point which flows from it, and which reaffirms our conclusion that the order made by the judge was plainly wrong.

... Applying the terms of s 33(7) to the facts of this case, the judge was plainly entitled to find that Mrs B and YB were likely to suffer significant harm attributable to Mr B's conduct if an occupation order was not made. The judge thus had to make an occupation order unless Mr B or MB were likely to suffer significant harm if the order was made, and that the harm likely to be suffered by Mr B or MB was as great or greater than the harm attributable to Mr B's conduct likely to be suffered by Mrs B or YB.

In this context it seems to us, with great respect to the judge, that he paid no attention to the fact that if an accommodation order [sic] was made, MB would not only have the disruption of leaving home, but would also have to leave his school, at which he was doing well. The judge's statement that MB would at least have 'the respite during term-time of being off at school with his friends' takes no account of this fact.

In our judgment, and whilst in no sense under-estimating the difficulties and frustrations of living with and caring for a toddler in bed and breakfast accommodation, the essential security for a child of YB's age is being where her mother is. Furthermore, of course, on the evidence, Mrs B's residence in bed and breakfast accommodation is likely to be temporary.

For MB the position is much more complex. His security depends not just on being in the care of his father, but on his other day-to-day support systems, of which his home and his school are plainly the most important.

... In our judgment, if, on the facts of this case, the respective likelihoods of harm are weighed so far as the two children are concerned, the balance comes down clearly in favour of MB suffering the greater harm if an occupation order is made.

... This case turns on its own very special facts. We have no sympathy for Mr B. He has behaved towards his wife in a manner which the judge found to be disgraceful. He treated her with serious domestic violence. Such conduct is unacceptable, and plainly falls to be considered within s 33(6)(d). Thus, were it not for the fact that he is caring for MB, and that MB has particular needs which at present outweigh those of YB, an accommodation order would undoubtedly have been made.

The message of this case is emphatically *not* that fathers who treat their partners with domestic violence and cause them to leave home can expect to remain in occupation of the previously shared accommodation. Equally, such fathers should not think that an application for a residence order in relation to a child or children of the relationship will prevent accommodation orders being made against them.

Part IV of the 1996 Act is designed to protect cohabitants from domestic violence and to secure their safe occupation of previously shared property. Nothing in this judgment should be read as weakening that objective.

Each case will, of course, turn on its facts. The critical, and highly unusual facts in this case are (1) that MB is not a child of the parties;(2) that there is no question of MB being cared for by Mrs B or anyone other than Mr B;(3) that Mr B is thus the full-time carer of a child who is likely to suffer greater harm than the harm which will be suffered by Mrs B and YB if an occupation order is made. It is the position of MB alone which, in our judgment, makes it inappropriate for an occupation order to be made on the facts of this case.

The injunction against Mr B will remain in force, and he should not think that, by setting aside the occupation order made by the judge, this court has vindicated him or in any way condoned his behaviour.

Question

Apart from the difference in age between the two children, the availability of local authority housing appears to have been a significant factor in this case. How significant do you think this factor should be when deciding whether to grant occupation orders?

The facts of *B v B* are unusual, but what about the more commonplace situation where a relationship breaks down, and the parties find it impossible to continue living together. Are occupation orders available to resolve the situation?

Re Y (children) (occupation order)
[2000] 2 FCR 470, Court of Appeal, Civil Division

The facts, briefly, were that the wife began divorce proceedings in 1998 and continued to live in the matrimonial home with the husband and the two youngest children, R, who was 16 years old and pregnant, and J, who was 13 years old. It was a dysfunctional family with R and the mother allied against J and the father, and living in separate quarters. R and the father had a very bad relationship and there were frequent rows and fights between them. On 29 October 1999 the husband applied, inter alia, for an order restraining the wife from molesting him and an occupation order. On 14 December cross-undertakings were given by each of the parents not to molest the other. On 9 February 2000 the recorder observed that the family 'was a family divided among itself and at war with itself, with people taking sides', and that there had been violence. He concluded that harm was likely to be caused if both parties continued to live in the house and he applied s. 33(7) of the Family Law Act 1996. He then referred to the matters to be taken into account in the exercise of his discretion under s. 33(6) of the 1996 Act, and he observed that, according to the father's solicitors, the local authority's view was that were they to become involved they might more easily accommodate the mother and R, rather than the father and J. He ordered the mother to vacate the matrimonial home on the ground that he was satisfied under s. 33 that on balance greater harm would be caused by not making the order, given the existing antagonism and the children taking sides. The mother appealed.

Ward LJ:

...

26. ... the question turns on s 33(6). The housing needs and housing resources of each of the parties is a relevant matter. Here the matrimonial home could reasonably be divided to meet the housing needs of each of them. They had established their separate camps and there was no real reason, apart from the atmosphere that prevailed, why they could not share the house until the court could resolve matters under the ancillary relief jurisdiction. The financial resources of each were relevant. The judge made no finding about this, but there is nothing to suggest that the wife's modest earnings put her in such a strong position that she was able to go into the private housing market and rent accommodation. There was certainly no finding to that effect. The likely effect of the order on the health, safety and well-being of the parties and of any relevant child may in the judge's view have tipped the balance in favour of the husband because of his health. But upon analysis it seems difficult to see what misconduct by the wife leads to the deterioration of his health. His unhappiness stems, if anything, from his inability to establish a good and proper working relationship with his daughter. On the conduct of the parties in relation to each other, they are perhaps one as bad as the other. The actual finding of violence, as I have said, is against the husband and not specifically against the wife.

27. But the problem about the exercise of discretion under s 33(6) is that the eviction of a co-owner of a matrimonial home is a Draconian remedy. It is a last resort and is not an order lightly to be made. That was the position before the 1996 Act and it remains the position now, as this court has confirmed in the matter of *Chalmers v Johns* [1999] 2 FCR 110. I give it emphasis again. Reading the judgment as a whole, one cannot but infer that the recorder was unduly swayed by the atmosphere in the house. He described it variously as 'hatred in the house', 'constant fighting', 'an armed ... truce', 'a family divided amongst itself and at war with itself'. Reading between the lines, it is plain the recorder took the view that, no progress having been made with the ancillary relief proceedings, the situation had to end sooner rather than later; and better sooner than later. But that too is an impermissible approach to an exercise of discretion under s 33(6).

28. In my judgment the most salient facts emerging from this unhappy dispute are (a) each of the parties and the children in their camp can be satisfactorily accommodated in the matrimonial home and (b) the undertakings given not to molest each other were effective, as the judge himself recognised. In my judgment he misdirected himself on the application of s 33(7). It falls to us, therefore, to exercise the discretion under s 33(6). I am quite satisfied that we have the evidence available to us to conclude, despite Miss Meachin's very attractive submissions, that the right

order here is to dismiss the application for the requested order on the basis that the neutral undertakings against molestation will continue. I would allow the appeal accordingly.

Sedley LJ: ...

30. The purpose of an occupation order, however large its grounds may potentially be, is not to break matrimonial deadlocks by evicting one of the parties, much less to do so at the expense of a dependent, and in this case a heavily pregnant, child. Nor is it to use publicly-funded emergency housing as a solution for domestic strife—see *Warwick v Warwick* (1982) 3 FLR 393.

31. There is no finding, and no evidential basis for any finding, that J was likely to suffer significant harm attributable to his mother's conduct. For this reason alone, s 33(7) of the Family Law Act 1996 could never come into play. If it were to do so, it is clear that the consequent harm to R, who is a relevant child just like J, would be at least as great as to J. There is now, of course, a yet further relevant child, R's new baby. As to the harm which will result if no order is made, I agree with all Ward LJ has said of the significance of the father's health and the absence of any evidence that the mother will be a source of harm if she stays.

32. The more general power under s 33(6) is not at large, especially where the court is asked to deploy it to the Draconian end sought here. It is there to afford necessary protection which can be afforded in no better way.

...

39. The nearest one can come to finding the recorder's reason for his decision is in this passage in the judgment:

'... it is clear that harm is likely to be caused if both parties continue to live in the house... Making any order requiring one parent to leave the home inevitably causes some harm and some distress, certainly in the short term; but, in the long term, hopefully peace will break out.'

40. There is no finding, and in my view none was possible, as to who it was caused the supposed harm and to whom. In my view no occupation order should even have been contemplated in this situation, much less made. Indeed, I take leave to doubt whether it was responsible (presumably on legal aid) to seek it in the circumstances disclosed by the judgment.

41. To use the occupation order as a weapon in domestic warfare is wholly inappropriate. Parliament has made provision for it as a last resort in an intolerable situation, not as a move in a game of matrimonial chess. ...

Question

Remember that occupation orders were meant to deal with the deadlock which can occur between spouses with equal rights of occupation in the matrimonial home irrespective of any violence or misconduct between them. What should happen in these cases?

So far we have been considering applications for occupation orders by 'entitled applicants'. Of course, a person with no right to occupy the home may be just as much in need of protection, but under the Family Law Act 1996 such a person may only apply for an occupation order against a former spouse, cohabitant or former cohabitant, and there are different criteria for such applications. Sections 37 and 38 of the 1996 Act provide for occupation orders where neither of the parties has a right of occupation. A more common situation will be where a non-entitled applicant is seeking an occupation order against a former spouse, cohabitant or former cohabitant who is entitled to occupy the property. These applications are governed by s. 35 (for former spouses) and s. 36 (for cohabitants and former cohabitants).

It was established under the previous legislation that ouster orders could be made in favour of a cohabitant who had no right to occupy the home (*Davis v Johnson* [1979] AC 264). The Law Commission (1992) explained why it was, nevertheless, thought necessary to distinguish between 'entitled' and 'non-entitled' applicants:

4.7 ... the grant of an occupation order can severely restrict the enjoyment of property rights, and its potential consequences to a respondent are therefore more serious than those of a non-molestation order which generally only prohibits conduct which is already illegal or at least, anti-social. Such consequences may be acceptable when both parties are entitled to occupy, but they are more difficult to justify when the applicant has no such right. ... In the case of non-entitled applicants, particularly when the respondent is also entitled, an occupation has a purpose beyond short term protection, namely to regulate the occupation of the home until its medium or short term destiny has been decided, or in some cases, indefinitely. ... In the case of non-entitled applicants, an occupation order is essentially a short term measure of protection intended to give them time to find alternative accommodation, or, at most, to await the outcome of an application for a property law remedy.

Under ss. 35 and 36, there is a two-stage approach to non-entitled applicants. Under both sections, an applicant must first obtain an order under sub-ss. (3) or (4) which gives the applicant the right to enter the home (if not already in occupation), and to remain there without being evicted or excluded by the respondent.

Before making such an order, the court is required to have regard to:

(6) ... all the circumstances including—
(a) the housing needs and housing resources of each of the parties and of any relevant child;
(b) the financial resources of each of the parties;
(c) the likely effect of any order, or of any decision by the court not to exercise its powers under subsection (3) or (4) on the health, safety or well-being of the parties and of any relevant child; and
(d) the conduct of the parties in relation to each other and otherwise.

This checklist occurs in identical form in ss. 35(6) and 36(6). However, the remainder of each subsection is different. In cases involving former spouses the court must also consider:

35.—... (6)   ...
(e) the length of time that has elapsed since the parties ceased to live together;
(f) the length of time that has elapsed since the marriage was dissolved or annulled; and
(g) the existence of any pending proceedings between the parties—
(i) for an order under section 23A or 24 of the Matrimonial Causes Act 1973 (property adjustment orders in connection with divorce proceedings etc.);
(ii) for an order under paragraph 1(2)(d) or (e) of Schedule 1 to the Children Act 1989 (orders for financial relief against parents); or
(iii) relating to the legal or beneficial ownership of the dwelling-house.

In cases involving cohabitants or former cohabitants the court must consider:

36.—... (6)   ...
(e) the nature of the parties' relationship;
(f) the length of time during which they have lived together as husband and wife;
(g) whether there are or have been any children who are children of both parties or for whom both parties have or have had parental responsibility;
(h) the length of time that has elapsed since the parties ceased to live together; and
(j) the existence of any pending proceedings between the parties—
(ii) for an order under paragraph 1(2)(d) or (e) of Schedule 1 to the Children Act 1989 (orders for financial relief against parents); or
(iii) relating to the legal or beneficial ownership of the dwelling-house.

Furthermore, where the court is considering the 'nature of the relationship' of cohabitants or former cohabitants, the court is required by s. 41 to 'have regard to the fact that the parties have not given each other the commitment involved in marriage'.

Question

How helpful are these provisions, given that the court is obliged to consider 'all the circumstances'?

If a non-entitled applicant obtains an order under sub-ss. (3) or (4), the court may then consider whether to include a provision under sub-s. (5) to:

(*a*) regulate the occupation of the dwelling-house by either or both of the parties;
(*b*) prohibit, suspend or restrict the exercise by the respondent of his right to occupy the dwelling-house;
(*c*) require the respondent to leave the dwelling-house or part of the dwelling-house; or
(*d*) exclude the respondent from a defined area in which the dwelling-house is included.

In deciding whether to include such a provision, the court is once more required to consider the basic criteria in sub-s. (6)(*a*)–(*d*) (see p. 428, above). However, there are further additional criteria at this stage, which differ according to whether the non-entitled applicant is a former spouse (applying under s. 35) or a cohabitant or former cohabitant (applying under s. 36).

In the case of former spouses, s. 35(7) requires the court to consider the length of time that has elapsed since the parties ceased to live together. In addition, the 'balance of harm' test (see p. 421, above) applies at this stage.

In the cases of a non-entitled cohabitant or former cohabitant, the court is required by s. 36(7) and (8) to consider:

(*a*) whether the applicant or any relevant child is likely to suffer significant harm attributable to conduct of the respondent if the subsection (5) provision is not included in the order; and
(*b*) whether the harm likely to be suffered by the respondent or child if the provision is included is as great or greater than the harm attributable to conduct of the respondent which is likely to be suffered by the applicant or child if the provision is not included.

Finally, s. 36(10) provides that an occupation order in favour of a non-entitled cohabitant or former cohabitant must be limited to a period not exceeding six months, and may be extended on only one occasion for a further period not exceeding six months. Under the previous legislation, ouster orders were rarely made for longer than three months (see *Practice Note* [1978] 2 All ER 1056, [1978] 1 WLR 1123). The Law Commission (1992) recommended that occupation orders in favour of entitled applicants could be made for any specified period or until further order, but that orders in favour of non-entitled applicants could only be made for up to six months, but renewable any number of times for up to six months at a time. They were persuaded that there was a widespread problem of applicants being unable to find alternative accommodation in less than six months. Where an order is made at a full hearing after an initial ex parte order, the maximum period of the two orders taken together is six months (s. 45(4)(*b*)). However, in determining the number of renewals, the two orders are treated as a single order (s. 45(4)(*a*)) which may, therefore, be renewed once more.

Questions

(i) Why, contrary to the recommendations of the Law Commission (1992), does the balance of harm test not apply to applications by non-entitled cohabitants or former cohabitants?

(ii)   Many of the complexities in the criteria for occupation orders for different types of non-entitled applicants were introduced after the failure of the Family Homes and Domestic Violence Bill in 1995. Is the complexity of the provisions necessary or justifiable?

As well as needing to satisfy the criteria in the legislation, a victim of domestic violence who is seeking a remedy will face many practical difficulties. One problem is graphically illustrated by Erin Pizzey (1974):

Going to court is quite an ordeal. The High Court in the Strand is as awe-inspiring as it sounds. It is a massive crenellated building with white towers and spires outside and a huge arched hall inside. The place is honeycombed with narrow corridors that run off the central hall to the small courtrooms. Everywhere ant-like uniformed figures bustle around. Barristers stride along in their black flapping gowns and wrinkled white wigs, best-suited solicitors scurry in their wake, blue-suited ushers look officious. The people waiting in little knots look shabby and out of place in this impersonal palace of justice.

If the case is to be heard in the morning we have to be there by 10. Waiting to meet the solicitor is always an anxious time because if the husband has been told to attend the court too, it will be the first time that his wife has had to face him since she ran away.

If you manage to avoid meeting him before, you usually find him crouched on the hard little benches that line the ill-lit, crowded corridor outside the courtroom. There, knee to knee and face to face, the couple must wait, sometimes for hours, before they are called into court.

My first time was with Lesley. Pat had come along to hold her other hand and together we had to hold Lesley upright because she was in such a state of fear at the prospect of seeing her husband. He had a terrible reputation, and on the night she had left him, he'd gone to see her friends with a gang and broken into the house. The gang beat up the old couple upstairs and their two sons. It took ten policemen to get them out, and though he was charged he was released on bail. Now we were in court to ask for an injunction to give her custody of the three children, maintenance while her divorce petition went through and a non-molestation order to keep him from carrying out his threat to kill her.

Waiting to go into the courtroom, we were all frightened. The solicitor and the barrister were quite unperturbed, and the barrister gave the impression that Lesley was making an unnecessary fuss. We were due in court mid-morning, so we settled down on the little benches to wait, morosely contemplating the other silent people waiting, and gazing at the stained walls.

The tedium and the peace were disturbed by the arrival of Lesley's husband and his henchmen. Then began a cat-and-mouse shuffle as we moved round the narrow corridors trying to prevent him upsetting Lesley even more. By the time it was our turn Lesley was speechless with fright and we half carried her between us into the court.

Fairness to the respondent requires that he be given a chance to hear the applicant's case, and respond to it. However, in some cases, the risk to the victim will be such that she should be able to seek an immediate remedy, either without informing the respondent at all, or without giving him as much notice of the application as would usually be required. A Practice Note issued in 1978 ([1978] 1 WLR 925) stated that 'an *ex parte* application should not be made, or granted, unless there is real immediate danger of serious injury or irreparable damage'. The Family Law Act 1996 provides new criteria for *ex parte* orders:

45.—(1)   The court may, in any case where it considers that it is just and convenient to do so, make an occupation order or a non-molestation order even though the respondent has not been given such notice of the proceedings as would otherwise be required by rules of court.

(2)   In determining whether to exercise its powers under subsection (1), the court shall have regard to all the circumstances including—

(a)   any risk of significant harm to the applicant or a relevant child, attributable to conduct of the respondent, if the order is not made immediately;

(b)   whether it is likely that the applicant will be deterred or prevented from pursuing the application if an order is not made immediately; and

(c)   whether there is reason to believe that the respondent is aware of the proceedings but is deliberately evading service and that the applicant or a relevant child will be seriously prejudiced by the delay involved -
  (i)   where the court is a magistrates' court, in effecting service of proceedings; or
  (ii)   in any other case, in effecting substituted service.
(3)   If the court makes an order by virtue of subsection (1) it must afford the respondent an opportunity to make representations relating to the order as soon as just and convenient at a full hearing.
...

Question

Which is the more unjust: making an alleged batterer leave the home for a short while before he has an opportunity of defending himself against the allegations, or making the alleged victim leave for a short while before she has an opportunity of putting her case before a court?

It is one thing to obtain an order, but it must also be enforced effectively if it is to ensure the applicant's safety. Because of difficulties with purely civil enforcement methods, s. 2 of the Domestic Violence and Matrimonial Proceedings Act 1976 contained a provision allowing a 'power of arrest' to be attached to an order in certain circumstances. This allowed a police officer to arrest someone whom he had reasonable cause to suspect was breaching the court's order. However, such orders were rarely granted for more than three months (see *Practice Note* [1981] 1 All ER 224, [1981] 1 WLR 27). In *Violence Against Women* (1985), a Working Group of the Women's National Commission commented:

108.   The Working Group received evidence that these apparently helpful legislative measures have, in practice, achieved much less than was anticipated. ... Many battered women are wholly ignorant of the law and are deterred from consulting solicitors because too afraid or believing it would be too costly. The Courts have proved suspicious of the wide powers which can be taken against the allegedly violent partner including removing him from his own property, and if they agree to grant injunctions they may limit the period these remain in force. Practical difficulties for complainants and their solicitors have proved to be great: the procedures are cumbersome and time consuming; it is virtually impossible for the police to assist in enforcing an injunction with no powers of arrest attached, and, probably through lack of specific training and lack of serious concern with domestic matters, police have often proved ill-informed about what to do, and sluggish to act, even where powers of arrest exist. ...
111.   Parker (1985) refers to the fact that in 1980, out of 6,400 injunctions granted under Section 1 of the DVA, only 24% had powers of arrest attached to them (in the North East only 10%). Other authorities discuss in greater detail the practical difficulties solicitors for battered women and the women themselves may encounter in obtaining injunctions. Violent husbands can be clever and elusive. They may return during the night to the home from which they are excluded by injunction to attack their wife. Wives may have difficulty in establishing that a breach of the injunction has occurred. Injuries may need to be grave and obvious to convince sceptical authorities. If a power of arrest is attached, police may nevertheless be very reluctant to act and have to be convinced that a breach has occurred. Where there is no power of arrest, the battered wife has to apply to the Court for her husband to *be charged with contempt of court*, first ensuring notice is served on him. ... The period of any legal delays can be most dangerous for wives as violent men are often inflamed by wives taking legal steps. ...
113.   The Working Group accepts that there are intrinsic difficulties for the Courts in establishing when violent partners should be subject to injunctions, especially when this makes a man homeless. If injunctions were granted to women without enquiry, judges would be criticised with some justification for failing to give a fair hearing to husbands to whom the asset of their home and the stability this represents for them will normally be very important. However, the Working Group urge judges to consider the frequently desperate situation of battered wives, who are obliged to seek safety and redress for acts of what may be extreme violence through an inadequate mechanism. They would like to see powers of arrest attached to all injunctions made

under the DVA, unless the judge is satisfied that there is no danger of physical attack. It would be desirable if legislation could be amended to incorporate this principle.

Responding to concerns of this kind, the Family Law Act 1996 creates a presumption in favour of powers of arrest in cases of actual or threatened violence:

47.—... (2) If—
(a)   the court makes [an occupation order or a non-molestation order], and
(b)   it appears to the court that the respondent has used or threatened violence against the applicant or a relevant child,
it shall attach a power of arrest to one or more provisions of the order unless satisfied that in all the circumstances of the case the applicant or child will be adequately protected without such a power of arrest.

This presumption does not apply to *ex parte* orders, but a court may attach a power of arrest to such an order if it appears:

47.—... (3) ...
(a)   that the respondent has used or threatened violence against the applicant or a relevant child; and
(b)   that there is a risk of significant harm to the applicant or child, attributable to conduct of the respondent, if the power of arrest is not attached to those provisions immediately.

The court may accept an undertaking from any of the parties to the proceedings instead of making an occupation order or a non-molestation order (s. 46(1)). An undertaking may be enforced in the same way as an order (s. 46(4)). However, a power of arrest cannot be attached (s. 46(2)). Therefore, the court cannot accept undertakings in cases where a power of arrest would have been added (s. 46(3)).

In cases where a power of arrest has not been granted, there is a new procedure under s. 47(8), allowing the court to grant a warrant of arrest if the court has reasonable grounds for believing that the respondent has failed to comply with the order.

The purpose of the power of arrest was considered in the following case.

Re H (a minor) (occupation order: power of arrest)
[2001] 1 FCR 370, [2001] 1 FLR 641, Court of Appeal, Civil Division

Hale LJ:...
    1. The issue in this appeal is a simple one. Can or should a court attach a power of arrest to an occupation order made under Pt IV of the Family Law Act 1996 (the 1996 Act) when the respondent is aged under 18? The same question would also arise in relation to a non-molestation order.
    2. This is the respondent's appeal against the order of Judge Sleeman made in the county court jurisdiction of the Principal Registry of the Family Division on 8 June 2000. He ordered the respondent to vacate the property named by 4 pm on Friday, 16 June 2000 and not to return to the property or to enter or attempt to enter the property. The property was the home of the respondent's parents and his three-year-old sister. The judge also ordered that there be a power of arrest attached to that order and that both stay in force until 8 December 2000.
    3. The applicant is the respondent's father. The respondent was at the time aged 17 years and three months. His behaviour towards his parents and in the home was totally unacceptable. The judge made a series of findings of fact upon allegations of violent and abusive behaviour towards both the applicant father and the mother. The judge described that behaviour as despicable. It was accepted by the Official Solicitor as the litigation friend of the respondent that if an adult had so behaved there would be ample justification for an occupation order.
    4. On 15 June 2000, the day before the respondent had to vacate the property, I refused permission to appeal against the occupation order itself. The Official Solicitor does not renew any application for permission to appeal against that order. I did, however, grant permission to appeal against the power of arrest although I refused a stay of execution.

5. It appears that the respondent son was arrested pursuant to the power of arrest ordered on 8 June and was brought before Judge Pearlman on 17 July 2000. She made a further occupation order, together with an order not to go within a distance variously described as one kilometre or one mile of the property, and attached a further power of arrest, again to last until 8 December this year.

6. The power of arrest was attached under s 47(2) of the 1996 Act. This reads as follows:

'If—(a) the court makes a relevant order; and (b) it appears to the court that the respondent has used or threatened violence against the applicant or a relevant child, it shall attach a power of arrest to one or more provisions of the order unless satisfied that in all the circumstances of the case the applicant or child will be adequately protected without such a power of arrest.'

7. The principal ground advanced in the grounds of appeal was that the court cannot attach a power of arrest where the respondent is a minor. The subsidiary ground of appeal was that in this case the judge should have been satisfied that the applicant and the young child would be adequately protected without it, because the police had previously shown themselves willing to attend the premises and arrest the son for breach of the peace.

8. The argument, in essence, is that the power of arrest is a prelude to the exercise of the court's power to punish for contempt of court. The difficulty that arises where contempt of court is committed by a minor is that there is little or no sanction available for the court to impose, once the matter is brought before it. Attention was drawn to that problem in the well known case of *Wookey v Wookey*, *Re S* (*a minor*) (*injunction*) [1991] FCR 811, [1991] Fam 121, in which it was held that a non-molestation injunction under the previous law was not appropriate because there was no realistic method of enforcing it in the circumstances.

...

13. It is ... clear that, although there are some powers to deal with persons under 18 for contempt of court, those powers are extremely limited. This is a serious gap in the law which, in my view, requires the urgent attention of those who are in charge of policy in this area.

14. However, that does not necessarily answer the question in this case. The wording of s 47(2) is quite clear. Once the two preconditions in (a) and (b) have been made out, which they clearly were in this case, the court must attach a power of arrest to one or more provisions of the order unless the court is satisfied that in all the circumstances of the case the applicant or relevant child will be adequately protected without it. The primary argument in this case would seek to introduce an exception to that mandatory duty which is not provided for in the subsection.

15. I should point out that the mandatory terms of the subsection were deliberately recommended by the Law Commission in its report on *Family Law: Domestic Violence and Occupation of the Family Home* (Law Com No 207) (1992) paras 5.11 to 5.14. This was not the Law Commission's original recommendation but it was supported by an impressive variety of respondents to the Law Commission's consultations. Those respondents included the Magistrates' Association, the Institute of Legal Executives, the Family Law Bar Association, the National Council for One Parent Families, the Association of Chief Police Officers and the Metropolitan Police. They also included Rights of Women, the Women's Aid Federation and the Association of Women Solicitors. I mention that list in order to indicate that this recommendation did enjoy a very large measure of support. It was also considered with care by a special public committee in the House of Lords under the chairmanship of Lord Brightman where evidence was received and amendments to the Law Commission Bill were made: see *Re B-J* (*a child*) (*non-molestation order: power of arrest*) [2000] 2 FCR 599 at 601, 602 and 603, [2001] 1 All ER 235 at 237 and 238 (paras 5, 6 and 10).

16. Mr O'Brien, who appears for the appellant son, is seeking to introduce into that section something which it does not contain. He argues that the protection to which it is directed is the protection provided by the power to commit for contempt of court, which does not exist in this case. For my part I am unable to accept that argument. In the first place, it is not the sole purpose of a power of arrest to provide a convenient short route to the court's power to commit for contempt of court. That is one of its purposes and a very helpful one, but it also has the purpose of taking the person concerned away from the scene. In a case such as this, the immediate object was to ensure that the young man did indeed leave the family home and that objective can readily be secured by a power of arrest.

17. Mr O'Brien's second submission was that 'all the circumstances of the case' in s 47(2) must include the relationship of father and son between the parties and the young age of the son compared with the mature years of the father; and that must be extremely relevant in considering the question of adequate protection. I agree with him. It will in many cases be very relevant; but that is an argument directed to whether or not the court can be satisfied as required by the subsection; it is not an argument directed to whether the court is able to impose a power of arrest at all in circumstances such as this.

18. On the facts of this particular case Mr O'Brien does not seek to argue with any great force that it was not open to the judge to reach the conclusion that father and child would not be adequately protected without such a power of arrest. He does refer to the police's previous willingness to attend at the premises and arrest the son for breach of the peace; but it would be difficult merely to rely on that as a guarantee of adequate protection in the future, particularly in the light of the father's natural reluctance to pursue criminal proceedings against his son.

19. For my part, therefore, I am unable to accept the primary case that s 47(2) should be read in such a way that it does not apply to a minor. I am also unable to accept the secondary case that this was a case where all the circumstances should lead the judge to be satisfied that father and child would be adequately protected without it. I would dismiss this appeal.

Laws LJ and **Dame Elizabeth Butler-Sloss P** agreed.

Question

We saw earlier in this chapter that it is a criminal offence to breach an injunction that has been granted under the Protection from Harassment Act 1997. Is this a more effective way to involve the police in the enforcement of civil orders?

The provisions relating to powers of arrest should help to provide additional security for victims of domestic violence, but civil remedies will rarely provide a complete or permanent solution. Gill Hague and Ellen Malos discuss the difficulties in 'Children, Domestic Violence and Housing', in the collection *Children Living with Domestic Violence*, edited by Morley and Mullender in 1994:

For very large numbers of women and children escaping domestic violence, the only way to achieve a safe and secure life is to leave the violent perpetrator completely and begin again somewhere else.

In our study [Malos and Hague (1993)], however, we collected evidence that women and children attempting to escape violence and seeking rehousing in various local authorities were refused any assistance from the council once they had obtained a legal order against the violent perpetrator. ... But, for women and children to be safe and secure in this situation, there will need to be an as yet unachieved level of effective legal protection and enforcement, accompanied by multi-layered support within the community and community intolerance of domestic violence. At the moment, this is not the situation in this country, and many women and children escaping violence in the home do not wish, under any circumstances, to return to their former home.

The availability of alternative housing will be crucial in these circumstances. The Working Group of the Women's National Commission (1985) discuss the possibilities:

115. ... An alternative to restraining the man is to remove the woman to a place of safety where she can begin a new separate existence if she wishes. ... Women's Aid refuges serve a number of purposes admirably, and are an exceedingly welcome development which needs supporting. But women often return to violent husbands because of concern about the quality of their own and their children's lives in refuges, which are often overcrowded. This underlines the importance of the Housing (Homeless Persons) Act 1977, which defines women victims of domestic violence as in 'priority need' and obliges a local authority to find permanent accommodation for them. Women's Aid groups normally find that the existence of the Act now enables them to negotiate some permanent local authority accommodation for women living in their refuges. But local authorities tend to strictly ration what is available. The assumption sometimes made that a very high proportion of women in refuges return permanently to their violent partners is not true. One research study undertaken by Jan Pahl (1985) found that:

'Out of the 42 women, 20 (48%) never lived with their husbands again after leaving the refuge, while only two lived with their husbands continuously from the time they left the refuge until the time of the second interview (about two years later). The remaining 20 of the women (48%) made between one and nine attempts at reconciliation. ... Of these only nine couples were still together at the second interview. ...'

Lack of a housing offer amongst other factors has forced large numbers of women to try again with their husbands and to suffer further violence. The Working Group therefore urge Housing Authorities to accept their responsibilities in relation to battered wives. It has been suggested that if Housing Authorities had a policy of seeking to find some accommodation (temporary or permanent) for violent husbands they would enable battered wives and children to remain in the family home in family sized accommodation which would be under-utilised by the man himself. To effect this kind of sensible solution probably requires multi-agency working groups to be set up on which police, personal social services, housing authority, and women's organisations representatives could serve.

Questions

(i) Section 177(1) of the Housing Act 1996 states: 'It is not reasonable for a person to continue to occupy accommodation if it is probable that this will lead to domestic violence against him'; coupled with the definition of homelessness in s. 191(1), this means that a victim who leaves in circumstances covered by s. 177(1) cannot be treated as intentionally homeless. Given that, would you be more or less inclined to grant an order ousting her husband from the matrimonial council house?
(ii) Will the court be able to transfer the tenancy into her name (see p. 357, above)? What if the couple are not married?
(iii) As the House of Commons Select Committee on Violence in Marriage (1975) asked during its proceedings, why do we not create hostels to receive the battering men?

9.7 What about the children?

Researchers have begun to explore the links between domestic violence and child abuse (see Hester and Pearson, *From Periphery to Centre: Domestic violence in work with abused children* (1998)), and there are indications that the abuse of mothers and children frequently occur in the same family. In addition, the impact of domestic violence on children has been recognised in the context of child contact (see pp. 602, 604, below). We have already seen that an adult may seek a non-molestation order or occupation order to protect a 'relevant child' (pp. 412, above). It is also possible for a child to make an application under the Family Law Act 1996 him or herself. Section 43 of the Family Law Act 1996 provides for this:

43.—(1) A child under the age of sixteen may not apply for an occupation order or a non-molestation order except with the leave of the court.

(2) The court may grant leave for the purposes of subsection (1) only if it is satisfied that the child has sufficient understanding to make the proposed application for the occupation order or non-molestation order.

This section is based upon similar provisions of the Children Act 1989, which we will consider in the next chapter, but what if no member of the family is able or willing to make an application? Even if the children are not directly attacked, there will often be a risk that they will be physically injured during an attack on their mother. Besides the physical dangers, the impact on a child's emotional and psychological development may amount to 'significant harm' under s. 31 of the Children Act 1989. This raises the possibility of an application by the local authority for a care order which would allow for the children to be removed from the home. We will consider care proceedings in Chapter 13.

Questions

(i)   If a woman is aware that her children might be removed from her care if she continues to live with their violent father, is she (a) more likely to leave him, or (b) less likely to seek any form of assistance? Is this another example of 'blaming the victim'?

(ii)   Would it not be better to allow someone to apply for orders to protect both adults and children from domestic violence?

Section 60 was added to the Family Law Act 1996 at a late stage:

60.—(1) Rules of court may provide for a prescribed person, or any person in a prescribed category ('a representative'), to act on behalf of another in relation to proceedings to which this Part applies.

(2)   Rules under this section may, in particular, authorise a representative to apply for an occupation order or for a non-molestation order for which the person on whose behalf the representative is acting could have applied.

(3)   Rules made under this section may prescribe—

(*a*)   conditions to be satisfied before a representative may make an application to the court on behalf of another; and

(*b*)   considerations to be taken into account by the court in determining whether, and if so how, to exercise any of its powers under this Part when a representative is acting on behalf of another.

The Government spokesman explained the background to this provision (HC Official Reports (5th Series),Vol. 279, cols. 598–599, 17 June 1996):

The proposal to grant police powers to seek civil remedies on behalf of those suffering domestic violence has its origin in the Law Commission report of 1992. However the Homes Affairs Select Committee's inquiry into domestic violence in 1993 rejected the proposal, as did the House of Lords Special Public Bill Committee on the Family Homes and Domestic Violence Bill.

There was, and remains, concern that the police have neither the resources nor the expertise to take on this role. Interest groups were also divided on this issue, some fearing the further disempowerment of women already trapped in situations over which they have little control. In light of these considerations, it was decided not to include such a provision in the Bill. Whatever the pros and cons of the third party approach to attacking domestic violence, it is clear we are not yet in a position where it is wise to embark immediately on this course. ...

The Government remain of the view that there may need to be a good deal more thought, discussion and research before any rules are made under the new clause. ...

The Government also accept that ... the amendment does not prescribe that the police shall act as the representatives, and that others may more appropriately be able to do it in consultation with the police.

In 2002, s. 60 has still not been implemented. On 18 March 2002, the Parliamentary Secretary to the Lord Chancellor's Department announced that a research project had been commissioned at the University of Leicester, which would consider the effectiveness of all civil remedies currently available to survivors of domestic violence (Commons Hansard,Written Answers, col. 74W). In the light of the findings of this research, consideration would be given as to whether or not the implementation of s. 60 would fill any gaps identified by the research.

Questions

(i)   Can you think of any circumstances in which third party 'representatives' should be allowed apply for non-molestation orders and occupation orders?

(ii) Should the representatives be police officers, or from some other agency?
(iii) How much weight should the representative and the court be required to give to the wishes of the person on whose behalf the representative is acting?

Bibliography

9.1   What are the dangers?

We quoted from:

S.M. Edwards, *Sex and Gender in the Legal Process* (1996) London, Blackstone, pp. 182–183.

Home Office Research Study 191, *Domestic Violence: Findings from a new British Crime Survey self-completion questionnaire* (1993), 7–10.

House of Commons Select Committee on Violence in Marriage, Report, *Minutes of Evidence and Appendices* HC 553-11 (1974–75) (1975) London, HMSO, paras. 73, 74, 634; p. 366.

House of Commons Home Affairs Committee, Third Report, *Domestic Violence*, HC 245-I (1992–93) (1993), para 9.

9.2   The search for explanations

We quoted from:

G. Hague and E. Malos, *Domestic Violence: Action for Change* (1993) Cheltenham, New Clarion Press, pp. 54–56, 58, 61–62.

L. Smith, *Domestic Violence: an overview of the literature*, Home Office Research Study 107 (1989) London, HMSO, pp. 27–29.

Additional reading

R. Dobash and R. Dobash, *Violence Against Wives: A Case Against the Patriarchy* (1980) London, Open Books.

S.M. Edwards, 'A sociolegal evaluation of gender ideologies in domestic violence, assault and spousal homicides' (1985) 10 Victimology 186.

E. Evason, *Hidden Violence* (1982) Belfast, Farset Press.

M.D.A. Freeman, *Violence in the Home* (1979) Farnborough, Saxon House (now Aldershot, Gower).

M.D.A. Freeman, 'Legal ideologies, patriarchal precedents and domestic violence' in M.D.A. Freeman (ed.), *The State, the Law and the Family: Critical Perspectives* (1984) London, Stevens.

M.D.A. Freeman, *Dealing with Domestic Violence* (1987) Oxford, CCH.

D. Klein, 'Battered wives and the domination of women' in N.H. Rafter and E. Stanko (eds.), *Judge, Lawyer, Victim, Thief: Women, Gender Roles and Criminal Justice* (1982) Boston, Mass., Northeastern University Press.

D. Martin, *Battered Wives* (1976) San Francisco, Glide Publications.

D. Martin, 'Battered women: society's problem' in J.R. Chapman and M. Gates, *The Victimisation of Women* (1978) Beverley Hills, California, Sage.

M. Morash, 'Wife Battering' [1986] Criminal Justice Abstracts 252.

J. Pahl (ed.) *Private Violence and Public Policy. The needs of battered women and the response of the public services* (1985) London, Routledge and Kegan Paul.

E. Pence, *Criminal Justice Response to Domestic Assault Cases* (1985) Duluth, Minnesota, Domestic Abuse Intervention Project, Minnesota Program Development Inc.

S. Schechter, *Women and Male Violence* (1982) Boston, South End Press.

M.A. Strauss, 'A sociological perspective on the prevention and treatment of wifebeating' in M. Roy (ed.), *Battered Women* (1977) New York, Van Nostrand Reinhold.

L.E. Walker, *The Battered Woman Syndrome* (1984) New York, Springer.

E. Wilson, *What is to be done about Violence against Women?* (1983) Harmondsworth, Penguin.

9.3   But is it not a crime?

We quoted from:

A. Cretney and G. Davis 'Prosecuting "Domestic" Assault' [1996] Criminal Law Review 162, pp. 173–174.

Crown Prosecution Service, *Policy On Prosecuting Cases Of Domestic Violence* (2001), paras. 4, 5.

R.E. Dobash and R.P. Dobash, *Women, Violence and Social Change* (1992) London, Routledge, pp. 208–209, 231.

M. Dow, 'Police Involvement' in M. Borland (ed.), *Violence in the Family* (1976) Manchester, Manchester University Press, pp. 132–133.

T. Faragher, 'The Police Response to Violence Against Women in the Home' in J. Pahl (ed.); *Private Violence and Public Policy. The needs of battered women and the response of the public services* (1985) London, Routledge and Kegan Paul, p. 117.

S. Grace, *Policing Domestic Violence in the 1990s*, Home Office Research Study 139 (1995) London, HMSO, pp. 53–54, 56.

Home Office Circular (60/90), *Domestic Violence* (1990) London, Home Office, paras. 2, 4, 11–18, 21, 24.

House of Commons Select Committee on Violence in Marriage, Report, Minutes of Evidence and Appendices, HC 553-11 (1974-75) (1975) London, HMSO, paras. 73, 74, 634; p. 366.

House of Commons Home Affairs Committee, *Domestic Violence, Evidence and Appendices* HC 245-11 (1992-93) (1993), pp. 26, 104.

S. Maidment, 'The Relevance of the Criminal Law to Domestic Violence' [1980] Journal of Social Welfare Law 26, pp. 30–31.

R. Morley and A. Mullender, 'Hype or hope? The importation of pro-arrest policies and batterers' programmes from North America to Britain as key measures for preventing violence against women in the home' (1992) 6 International Journal of Law and the Family 265, p. 268.

E. Pizzey, *Scream Quietly or the Neighbours Will Hear* (1974) Harmondsworth, Penguin Books, p. 98.

Additional reading

B. Dawson and T. Faragher, *Battered Women's Project: Interim Report* (1977) Keele, University of Keele, Department of Sociology.

E. Finch, *The Criminalisation of Stalking* (2001) London, Cavendish.

Home Office Research Study 185, *Entry into the criminal justice system: a survey of police arrests and their outcomes* (1998).

Liz Kelly, *Domestic Violence Matters: An Evaluation of a Development Project*, Home Office Research Findings No. 91 (1999).

J. Pahl, 'Police Response to Battered Women' [1982] Journal of Social Welfare Law 337.

A. Sanders, 'Personal Violence and Public Order: The prosecution of domestic violence in England and Wales' (1988) 16 International Journal of the Sociology of Law 359.

I. Subin, *Criminal Justice in a Metropolitan Court; the Processing of Serious Criminal Cases in the District of Columbia Court of General Sessions* (1966) Washington, Office of Criminal Justice, US Department of Justice.

F. Wasoff, 'Legal Protection from Wife Beating: The Processing of Domestic Assaults by Scottish Prosecutors and Criminal Courts' (1982) 10 International Journal of the Sociology of Law 187.

9.4   Developing civil law remedies

We quoted from:

J. Clifton, 'Factors Predisposing Family Members to Violence', in Social Work Services Group, Scottish Education Department, *Violence in the Family – Theory and Practice in Social Work* (1982) Edinburgh, HMSO, p. 31.

R.E. Dobash and R.P. Dobash, *Women, Violence and Social Change* (1992) London, Routledge, pp. 208-209, 231.

House of Commons Home Affairs Committee, *Domestic Violence, Evidence and Appendices*, HC 245-11 (1992–93) (1993), pp. 87–88.

Law Commission, *Domestic Violence and the Occupation of the Family Home* Law Com. No. 207 (1992) London, HMSO, paras. 2.3, 2.8

J.S. Mill, *The Subjection of Women* (1869); reprinted in Everyman's Library (1929) London, Dent.

E. Pizzey, *Scream Quietly or the Neighbours Will Hear* (1974) Harmondsworth, Penguin Books, p. 120.

Additional reading

J. Barron, *Not worth the paper? … the effectiveness of legal protection for women and children experiencing domestic violence* (1990) London, Women's Aid Federation, England.

A. Cade, 'Family Violence: An Interactional View' (1978) 9 Social Work Today 26.

S.M. Edwards and A. Halpern, 'Protection for the victim of domestic violence: time for radical revision?' [1991] Journal of Social Welfare and Family Law 94.

S. Maidment, 'The Law's Response to Marital Violence in England and the U.S.A.' (1977) 26 International and Comparative Law Quarterly 403.

D. Marsden, 'Sociological Perspectives on Family Violence' in J.P. Martin (ed.), *Violence and the Family* (1978) Chichester, Wiley.

9.5   Non-molestation orders

We quoted from:

Judge Fricker QC, *Evidence to the Special Public Bill Committee on the Family Homes and Domestic Violence Bill*, HL Paper 55 (1994–95), pp. 73–74.

House of Commons Home Affairs Committee, *Domestic Violence, Evidence and Appendices*, HC 245-11 (1992-93) (1993), para 109.

Law Commission Report on *Domestic Violence and Occupation of the Family Home* (1992), para 3.19.

Additional reading

G. Ashton, 'Injunctions and Mental Disorders' [2000] Fam Law 39.

S. Parker, 'The Legal Background' in J. Pahl, *Private Violence and Public Policy. The needs of battered women and the response of the public services* (1985) London, Routledge and Kegan Paul.

9.6   Occupation orders

We quoted from:

F. Gibb, 'Husband who snapped told to leave home' (1997) *The Times*, 28 August.

G. Hague and E. Malos, 'Children, Domestic Violence and Housing' in R. Morley and A. Mullender (eds.), *Children Living with Domestic Violence* (1994) London, Whiting and Birch, pp. 131–132.

Law Commission Report on *Domestic Violence and Occupation of the Family Home* (1992), paras. 4.6. 2.48, 4.23, 4.34, 4.7.

E. Pizzey, *Scream Quietly or the Neighbours Will Hear* (1974) Harmondsworth, Penguin Books, pp. 120–121.

Women's National Commission, *Violence Against Women, Report of an ad hoc Working Group* (1985) London, Cabinet Office, paras. 108, 111, 113, 115.

9.7   What about the children?

We quoted from:

HC Official Reports (5th Series), Vol. 279, cols. 598-599, 17 June 1996.

Additional reading

M. Hester and C. Pearson, *From Periphery to centre: Domestic violence in work with abused children* (1998) Bristol, Polity Press.

P. Parkinson and C. Humphries, 'Children who witness domestic violence' (1998) 10 Child and Family Law Quarterly 147.

Chapter 10

Parents, children and family life

Relying on parents to bring up their children is seen as an essential feature of Western democratic society. But is this for the parents', the children's, or society's sake? Parents and children alike are entitled to respect for their private and family life; the Children Act 1989 focuses on the responsibility of parents and the welfare of children. So we begin this chapter with an examination of the differing demands of parental rights and children's welfare; we then look at the arguments for and against parental autonomy. Next we move on to consider the children's rights, and the United Nations Convention on the Rights of the Child. Finally, we look at parental responsibility, in preparation for our consideration of parental status in Chapter 11.

10.1 Parental rights and children's welfare

The concept of parental 'rights' achieved its greatest legal prominence in the nineteenth century. An example of eighteenth-century thinking is provided by Sir William Blackstone in the first volume of his *Commentaries on the Laws of England* (1765):

1. And, first, the duties of parents to legitimate children: which principally consist in three particulars; their maintenance, their protection, and their education.

   The duty of parents to provide for the *maintenance* of their children is a principle of natural law; an obligation, says Puffendorf, laid on them not only by nature herself, but by their own proper act, in bringing them into the world: for they would be in the highest manner injurious to their issue, if they only gave the children life, that they might afterwards see them perish. By begetting them therefore they have entered into a voluntary obligation, to endeavour, as far as in them lies, that the life which they have bestowed shall be supported and preserved. And thus the children will have a perfect *right* of receiving maintenance from their parents. ...

After discussing the relevant provisions of English law, including its deficiencies in the matter of education, he continues:

2. The *power* of parents over their children is derived from the former consideration, their duty; this authority being given them, partly to enable the parent more effectually to perform his duty, and partly as a recompence for his care and trouble in the faithful discharge of it. And upon this score the municipal laws of some nations have given a much larger authority to the parents, than others. The ancient Roman laws gave the father a power of life and death over his children; upon this principle, that he who gave had also the power of taking away. ...

The power of a parent by our English laws is much more moderate; but still sufficient to keep the child in order and obedience. He may lawfully correct his child, being under age, in a reasonable manner; for this is for the benefit of his education. The consent or concurrence of the parent to the marriage of his child under age, was also *directed* by our ancient law to be obtained: but now it is absolutely *necessary;* for without it the contract is void. And this also is another means, which the law has put into the parent's hands, in order the better to discharge his duty; first, of protecting his children from the snares of artful and designing persons; and, next of settling them properly in life, by preventing the ill consequences of too early and precipitate marriages. A father has no other power over his son's *estate,* than as his trustee or guardian; for, though he may receive the profits during the child's minority, yet he must account for them when he comes of age. He may indeed have the benefit of his children's labour while they live with him, and are maintained by him: but this is no more than he is entitled to from his apprentices or servants. The legal power of a father (for a mother, as such, is entitled to no power, but only to reverence and respect) the power of a father, I say, over the persons of his children ceases at the age of twenty one: for they are then enfranchised by arriving at years of discretion, or that point which the law has established (as some must necessarily be established) when the empire of the father, or other guardian, gives place to the empire of reason. Yet, till that age arrives, this empire of the father continues even after his death; for he may by his will appoint a guardian to his children. ...
3. The *duties* of children to their parents arise from a principle of natural justice and retribution. For to those, who gave us existence, we naturally owe subjection and obedience during our minority, and honour and reverence ever after; they, who protected the weakness of our infancy, are entitled to our protection in the infirmity of their age; they who by sustenance and education have enabled their offspring to prosper, ought in return to be supported by that offspring, in case they stand in need of assistance. Upon this principle proceed all the duties of children to their parents, which are enjoined by positive laws.

Questions

(i)   How much of this represents the modern law?
(ii) Do you think that Blackstone's account of the rationale underlying parental power is equally applicable today?

If parents have rights, there might be two ways of enforcing them: either by an action in tort against anyone who interfered or by an action to recover the child and impose the parental will upon him. There was a common law action in tort, but only if the third party, either by enticement, seduction or harbouring, or by a wrongful act against the child, caused a loss of services actually being rendered by the child to the father. These actions were abolished in 1970 and 1982 respectively. Hence in *F v Wirral Metropolitan Borough Council* [1991] Fam 69, [1991] 2 All ER 648, Stuart-Smith LJ announced that 'In my judgment [counsel's] submission that this court could now declare that a parent had an action for damages for interference with his or her right as a parent was wholly misconceived'. However, various remedies were available to recover a child and enforce the father's wishes as to his upbringing (see Pettitt, 1957). These reached their peak in a case which Lord Upjohn in *J v C* [1970] AC 668, [1969] 1 All ER 788 (p. 444, below) could 'only describe as dreadful'.

Re Agar-Ellis, Agar-Ellis v Lascelles
(1883) 24 Ch D 317, 53LJ Ch 10, 50LT 161, 32WR 1, Court of Appeal

A Protestant father agreed at his marriage that any children would be brought up Roman Catholics, but at the birth of the first child he changed his mind. The mother, however, taught the children Roman Catholicism and eventually they refused to go to a Protestant church. The father made them wards of court and the court (see (1878) 10 Ch D 49, 48LJ Ch 1) restrained the mother from taking them to confession or to a Roman Catholic church and left the father to do what he thought fit for their spiritual welfare. He therefore took the children from their mother and placed them with other people, allowing her to visit only once a month and censoring her letters. In 1883, the second daughter, then aged 16, wrote to the judge begging to be allowed the free exercise of her religion and to live with her mother. The father agreed to the former but not the latter. Accordingly, she and her mother petitioned the court to allow them a two-month holiday together and freedom of correspondence and access. The father opposed this because he feared that the mother would alienate his child's affections. Pearson J dismissed the petition. The petitioners appealed.

Brett MR: ... The rights of a father are sacred rights because his duties are sacred duties. ...

Bowen LJ: ... This is a case in which, if we were not in a Court of Law, but in a court of critics capable of being moved by feelings of favour or disfavour, we might be tempted to comment, with more or less severity, upon the way in which, so far as we have heard the story, the father has exercised his parental right. But it seems to me the Court must not allow itself to drift out of the proper course; the Court must not be tempted to interfere with the natural order and course of family life, the very basis of which is the authority of the father, except it be in those special cases in which the state is called upon, for reasons of urgency, to set aside the parental authority and to intervene for itself. ...
... Judicial machinery is quite inadequate to the task of educating children in this country. It can correct abuses and it can interfere to redress the parental caprice, and it does interfere when the natural guardian of the child ceases to be the natural guardian, and shews by his conduct that he has become an unnatural guardian, but to interfere further would be to ignore the one principle which is the most fundamental of all in the history of mankind, and owing to the full play of which man has become what he is. ... If that were not so we might be interfering all day and with every family. I have no doubt that there are very few families in the country in which fathers do not, at some time or other, make mistakes, and there are very few families in which a wiser person than the father might not do something better for that child than is being done by the father, who however has an authority which never ought to be slighted.
Appeal dismissed.

Questions

(i)   Take out the sex discrimination and apply these arguments to a couple's decision: (a) that their child shall not go on the school trip to France; (b) that their child shall go to Sunday school every week; (c) that their child shall not have the MMR vaccine; or (d) that their child should not receive sex education or attend 'peace studies' in school. Should the law interfere?
(ii)   How relevant to your view of the *Agar-Ellis* decision was it (a) that mother and father disagreed with one another, and (b) that the child was, by the hearing, aged 17?

The position between mother and father was radically changed by or before the Guardianship of Infants Act 1925, later consolidated in the Guardianship of Minors Act 1971. Section 1 of each required any court considering a question of the custody or upbringing of a child, or the use of his income or property, to regard his welfare as the 'first and paramount consideration' and not to take into consideration whether 'from any other point of view the claim of the father, or any right at common law possessed by the father ... is superior to that of the mother' or vice versa. The same principle was later applied to disputes between parents and non-parents:

J v C
[1970] AC 668, [1969] 1 All ER 788, [1969] 2 WLR 540, 113 Sol Jo 164, House of Lords

It is almost impossible to summarise the facts dispassionately, but Lord Guest perhaps comes closest to doing so:

The story began in the autumn of 1957 when the infant's parents came to Britain from Madrid for the purpose of bettering their financial position by entering domestic service. The father was at that time a very lowly-paid worker living in poor housing conditions in Madrid. They are both of the Roman Catholic faith. They left behind a daughter then aged 4 who lived with the maternal grandmother. The mother became pregnant shortly after their arrival in Britain and the infant was born in hospital on 8 May 1958. As the mother was found to be suffering from tuberculosis and had to remain in hospital for some considerable time a home was found for the infant through the kind offices of a married couple who have been called the 'foster parents'. The infant was taken care of, from the age of four days, by them in their house in Northamptonshire while the mother remained in hospital. The foster parents had been both previously married and between them have four children by their previous marriages and now have two by their own marriage. The infant continued to remain with the foster parents until the mother was discharged from hospital in April 1959. The infant's father remained in employment near the foster parents' house and visited the infant from time to time. The infant thereafter rejoined his parents who had obtained employment in Surrey. The foster parents had also moved to Surrey. The infant remained with his parents at C for about ten months: the foster mother assisted the mother in looking after the infant and the parents kept in touch with the foster parents' family. In February 1960, the mother again became pregnant. As she was afraid of having another baby in this country she and her husband went back to Madrid taking the infant with them.

During the infant's stay in Madrid in the summer of 1960 his parents lived in what has been described as little better than a 'hovel'. The father was still a lowly-paid worker and the family lived in what were virtually slum conditions. In the summer heat of Madrid the infant's health rapidly deteriorated due to malnutrition and the local conditions which did not suit him. He only remained in Madrid with his parents for 17 months. In July 1961, he returned to Britain to stay with the foster parents. This move was made at the specific request of the parents who, through the intermediary of a Spanish maid of the foster parents, M, conveyed their request to the foster parents. This request was made on the ground of the infant's health. On his return to this country the infant's health rapidly improved and he has continued thereafter to enjoy good health. He has not lived with his parents since July 1961, and has continued to live with the foster parents ever since. ...

Up to [February 1963] the parents had evinced no wish to the foster parents to have the infant back with them in Madrid apart from a suggestion for a holiday. But in July 1963, the foster mother wrote to the mother what has been described as a tactless and most unfortunate letter. In this letter she described how the infant had become integrated with their family; he had gone to an English school and he had grown up an English boy with English habits, and that it would be most disturbing for him to have to return to live with his parents in Madrid. She also made critical remarks about the infant's father. This letter produced the not unexpected reaction from the mother who, after some previous correspondence, wrote on 25 September 1963, to the Surrey County Council, in whose official care the infant was, asking for the infant's return. The local authority did not act with conspicuous consistency or good sense. After appearing to agree to the mother's request they subsequently, after receipt of a letter from the foster parents expressing their point of view, resolved, on the advice of counsel, to apply to the Chancery Division to have the infant made a ward of court, which was done on 16 December 1963.

The proceedings took some considerable time to reach the judge and the parents were unfortunately led to believe by a letter from the Surrey County Council that they would be represented by counsel at the hearing who would state their case for them. For this reason the parents only lodged written representations which had been prepared for them by a Spanish lawyer. These, however, did express their wish for the infant's return. Affidavits were lodged by various other parties. After a hearing on 22 July 1965, Ungoed-Thomas J ordered that the infant remain a ward of court, that the care and control be committed to the foster parents, that the infant be brought up in the Roman Catholic faith and in the knowledge and recognition of his parents and in knowledge of the Spanish language.

Two years were to elapse before the final stage of the proceedings took place before the same judge. This stage had been initiated by the parents' summons – asking that they should have the care and control of the infant. This was made on 10 May 1967. An application was also made by the foster parents in January 1967, that the infant be brought up in the Protestant faith. This request for a change in the boy's religious upbringing was prompted by a desire on the foster parents' part that he should enter a choir school so as to avoid expense. The most convenient school was a Protestant school. The official solicitor also entered the proceedings, having been appointed next friend. On this occasion the judge heard evidence from all the parties and his judgment was given on 31 July 1967. No order was made on either application. ...

... It may be that if more expedition had been exercised by the parties in bringing the case to trial and the full facts had been known at the time, the judge's decision might well have been different in 1963. In 1963 when the parents first asked for the infant's return he was only 5 years old and he had only been parted from his parents for a matter of two years. Even in 1965 he was only 7 years old, but at the time of the second hearing he was 9 and he is now 10 years old. He has been at school in England since January 1963. He has not seen his parents since 1961 when he was 3, and apart from a matter of 27 months he has been living continually in the home of the foster parents with their family. There is no doubt, as the learned judge found, that the infant lives in happy surroundings in a united and well-integrated family. The mixed families have made it particularly easy for him to become integrated. He speaks English and only pidgin Spanish. He is especially friendly with P the child of the marriage of the foster parents who is only a little younger than him.

It is right at this stage to say that the house in which the parents now live in Madrid is entirely suitable for the reception of the infant. It contains three bedrooms and is in a modern block of flats in quite different surroundings from the previous home. The father is in good steady employment at a weekly wage of about £18 and the mother's health has been completely restored.

The reason which has impelled the judge to take the unusual step of taking the care and control from the parents and giving it to strangers is that, in his view, the risk of plunging this boy of 10 years into a Spanish family, where he has not seen his parents since he was aged 3 and into a foreign country, would be too great to take and that the adjustment necessary might well permanently injure the infant's health at the impressionable age at which he has arrived. The judge has regarded the infant's welfare as the paramount consideration and he has decided that this demands that he should remain with his foster parents.

The account of the law which has been most frequently quoted in subsequent decisions is that of Lord MacDermott:

All parties were agreed that the courts had jurisdiction and a duty to interfere with the natural right of parents to have the care, control and custody of their child if the welfare of the child required and the law permitted that course to be taken. But there agreement ended. For the parents it was submitted that the courts were in law bound to presume that the welfare of the child was best served by allowing him to live with his parents unless it was shown that it was not for his welfare to do so because of their conduct, character or station in life. Counsel for the infant and counsel for the foster parents submitted, on the other hand, that there was no such presumption of law, that the paramount and governing consideration was the welfare of the child and that the claim of natural parents, although often of great weight and cogency and often conclusive, had to be regarded in conjunction with all other relevant factors, and had to yield if, in the end, the welfare of the child so required.

... I have already mentioned counsel for the parents' concession as to the position if his argument does not prevail. I may add here that if it does prevail the appeal, in my opinion, is bound to succeed since: (*a*) the evidence shows no defects of character or conduct on the part of the parents sufficient to disentitle them to custody; and (*b*) their position in life has so improved as to be no longer capable in itself of constituting an answer to their claim.

His Lordship then reviews the developments in case law and statute before 1925 and continues:

I have referred to these Acts because, as in the case of the authorities, they record an increasing qualification of common law rights and the growing acceptance of the welfare of the infant as a criterion. In this way, and like the trend of the cases, they serve to introduce the enactment which has been so closely canvassed on the issue of law under discussion. It is s.1 of the Guardianship of Infants Act 1925 [see above, p. 443].

The part of this section referring to 'the first and paramount consideration' has been spoken of as declaratory of the existing law. See *Re Thain, Thain v Taylor* [1926] Ch 676, 95LJ Ch 292 per Lord Hanworth MR (p. 689) and Sargant LJ (p. 691); and *McKee v McKee* [1951] AC 352 at 366 per Lord Simonds. There have been different views about this, but whether the proposition is wholly accurate or not, the true construction of the section itself has to be considered as a matter of prime importance.

Two questions arise here. First, is the section to be read as referring only to disputes between the parents of the child? In *Re Carroll* [1931] 1 KB 317, 100 LJKB 113, Slesser LJ appears to have approved such an interpretation for he said (p. 355):

'This statute, however, in my view, has confined itself to questions between the rights of father and mother which I have already outlined – factors which cannot arise in the case of an illegitimate child ...'

Now, the latter part of the section is directed to equalising the legal rights or claims of the parents, and the preamble speaks only of achieving an equality between the sexes in relation to the guardianship of infants. But these considerations, do not, in my opinion, suffice to constrict the natural meaning of the first part of the section. The latter part beginning with the words 'shall not take into consideration ...' does not call for or imply any such constriction for it does not necessarily apply to all the possible disputes which the earlier part is capable of embracing; and as for the preamble, it could only be used to restrict the applicability of the earlier part of the section if that part were ambiguous. See *A-G v HRH Prince Ernest Augustus of Hanover* [1957] AC 436 at 463 per Viscount Simonds. Having read the whole Act, I cannot find this important earlier part to be other than clear and unambiguous. On the contrary, its wording seems to be deliberately wide and general. It relates to *any* proceedings before *any* court, and as Eve J said in *Clarke-Jervoise v Scutt* [1920] 1 Ch 382 at 388: '"Any" is a word with a very wide meaning, and prima facie the use of it excludes limitation.'...

The second question of construction is as to the scope and meaning of the words '... shall regard the welfare of the infant as the first and paramount consideration.' Reading these words in their ordinary significance, and relating them to the various classes of proceedings which the section has already mentioned, it seems to me that they must mean more than that the child's welfare is to be treated as the top item in a list of items relevant to the matter in question. I think they connote a process whereby, when all the relevant facts, relationships, claims and wishes of parents, risks, choices and other circumstances are taken into account and weighed, the course to be followed will be that which is most in the interests of the child's welfare as that term has now to be understood. That is the first consideration because it is of first importance and the paramount consideration because it rules on or determines the course to be followed. It remains to see how this 'first view', as I may call it, stands in the light of authority.

After a review of the authorities, he concludes:

... I conclude that my first view construction of s.1 should stand, and that the parents' proposition of law is ill-founded and must fail. The consequences of this present little difficulty, but before coming to them I would add in summary form certain views and comments on the ground surveyed in the hope that they may serve to restrict misunderstanding in this difficult field. These may be enumerated as follows:

1.   Section 1 of the Act of 1925 applies to disputes not only between parents, but between parents and strangers and strangers and strangers.

2.   In applying s.1, the rights and wishes of parents, whether unimpeachable or otherwise, must be assessed and weighed in their bearing on the welfare of the child in conjunction with all other factors relevant to that issue.

3.   While there is now no rule of law that the rights and wishes of unimpeachable parents must prevail over other considerations, such rights and wishes, recognised as they are by nature and society, can be capable of ministering to the total welfare of the child in a special way, and must therefore preponderate in many cases. The parental rights, however, remain qualified and not absolute for the purposes of the investigation, the broad nature of which is still as described in the fourth of the principles enunciated by FitzGibbon LJ in *Re O'Hara* [1900] 2 IR 232 at 240. [I.e. the court should act cautiously, and in opposition to the parent only when judicially satisfied that the welfare of the child requires it.]

4. Some of the authorities convey the impression that the upset caused to a child by a change of custody is transient and a matter of small importance. For all I know that may have been true in the cases containing dicta to that effect. But I think a growing experience has shown that it is not always so and that serious harm even to young children may, on occasion, be caused by such a change. I do not suggest that the difficulties of this subject can be resolved by purely theoretical considerations, or that they need to be left entirely to expert opinion. But a child's future happiness and sense of security are always important factors and the effects of a change of custody will often be worthy of the close and anxious attention which they undoubtedly received in this case.

... The learned judge applied the appropriate principles of law and I can find no ground for interfering with the manner in which he exercised his discretion. On these grounds I am of opinion that the appeal fails and should be dismissed.

Their Lordships all concurred in dismissing the appeal. Lord Upjohn, however, had this to say:

My Lords, Eve J [in *Re Thain* [1926] Ch 676] said that among other considerations the wishes of an unimpeachable parent undoubtedly stand first, and I believe, as I have said, that represents the law. ... The natural parents have a strong claim to have their wishes considered first and principally, no doubt, because normally it is part of the paramount consideration of the welfare of the infant that he should be with them but also because as the natural parents they have themselves a strong claim to have their wishes considered as normally the proper persons to have the upbringing of the child they have brought into the world. It is not, however, a question of the onus being on anyone to displace the wishes of the parents; it is a matter for the judge ...

Lord Donovan's short, sharp speech contains the following:

I think the section means just what it says – no more and no less; and although the claim of natural parents to the custody and upbringing of their own children is obviously a most weighty factor to be taken into consideration in deciding what is in the best interests of the infant, yet the legislature recognised that this might not always be the determining factor, whether the parents were unimpeachable or not.

The Law Commission discussed the point of principle in their Working Paper on *Custody* (1986):

6.20 There may still be doubts whether the child's 'best interests' should determine the issue between parents and non-parents. Respect for family life is guaranteed under the European Convention on Human Rights [see p. 466, below] and parents may require protection from unwarranted interference. Local authorities are not permitted compulsorily to intervene in the care of children simply because they could provide something better, but only where specific shortcomings in the home or the parents can be proved. In adoption, parental agreement is required, unless it can be dispensed with on defined grounds, and the child's welfare is only the 'first' rather than the 'paramount' consideration. In relation to custody and upbringing, however, the House of Lords decided in *J v C* that there is no presumption in favour of even the 'unimpeachable' natural parents of the child, although their relationship with the child will often carry great weight as they 'can be capable of ministering to the total welfare of the child in a special way'.

6.21 Although we recognise that this is a difficult question, several arguments persuade us that the present position in English law should be maintained. First, the child may have a much closer relationship with someone other than his 'natural' parent. The emotional and psychological bonds which develop between a child (especially a very young child) and those who are bringing him up are just as 'natural' as are his genetic ties. To give preference over such a 'psychological' parent to one whose interest may be based solely on a blood tie could on occasion be highly detrimental to the child. Secondly, the analogy with intervention by local authorities is not exact. By definition, the authority cannot be or become such a 'psychological' parent. Whereas a non-parent applicant will usually be seeking to secure the child's existing home and an established relationship, the local authority will usually be seeking to remove him from such a home in favour of an unspecified alternative. Unlike a case between private individuals, the court is not faced with a choice between two (or more) identifiable homes. There are also strong objections in principle to the authority of the state being used to impose standards upon families unless it can be shown that the children are suffering, or are likely to suffer, unacceptable harm.

6.22 We conclude, therefore, that the welfare of each child in the family should continue to be the paramount consideration whenever their custody or upbringing is in question between private individuals.

The Children Act 1989 replaced s. 1 of the Guardianship of Minors Act 1971 as follows:

1.—(1) When a court determines any question with respect to—
  (*a*) the upbringing of a child; or
  (*b*) the administration of a child's property or the application of any income arising from it,
the child's welfare shall be the court's paramount consideration.

Questions

(i) Do you agree with the principle?

(ii) Does this principle mean that, in a dispute between a parent and a non-parent, a court should compare their relative parenting abilities, and decide which of them is best able to meet the child's needs? Or is there a presumption that it is in the child's interests to be brought up by the natural parent? (Note the often-quoted statement of Lord Templeman in *Re KD (A Minor) (Ward: Termination of Access)* [1988] AC 806, [1988] 1 All ER 577, HL: 'The best person to bring up a child is the natural parent. It matters not whether the parent is wise or foolish, rich or poor, educated or illiterate, provided the child's moral and physical health are not endangered.' See also *Re D (Care: Natural Parent Presumption)* [1999] 1 FLR 583, but compare the view of Thorpe LJ in *Re L (A Child Contact: Domestic Violence)* [2000] 2 FCR 404, [2000] 2 FLR 334.)

(iii) The facts of *J v C* were very similar to those in *Re M (Child's Upbringing)* [1996] 2 FCR 473, [1996] 2 FLR 441. The child concerned, Sifiso Mahlangu, was a 10-year-old Zulu boy who was looked after by his mother's employer and brought to this country with her consent. He had been living in England for four years, when his mother decided that she wanted him returned to her in South Africa. In the Court of Appeal Neill LJ stated that there was a 'strong supposition' that it was in the child's interests to be brought up with his natural parent. Sifiso was sent back to South Africa even though he wanted to stay here. However, he was unable to settle in South Africa, and eventually returned to England. In a later case, Thorpe LJ stated that 'subsequent developments in the life of the Zulu boy demonstrate that the endeavour to override his deep-seated attachment to his psychological mother proved disastrous in outcome' (see *Re B* [1998] 1 FLR 520, at p. 521). With the benefit of hindsight, do you think that the decision to send Sifiso home was flawed: (a) because the court gave too much weight to the need for children to be brought up by their natural parents; or because it gave too little weight to Sifiso's own wishes and feelings; or (b) because it gave too much weight to the view that Sifiso's development 'must be, in the last resort and profoundly, Zulu development and not Afrikaans or English development'?

The significance of a child's cultural background was also an issue in the next case:

Re P (a child) (residence order: child's welfare)
[2000] Fam 15, [1999] 3 All ER 734, [1999] 2 FLR 573, Court of Appeal

The child, N, was born in 1990, and she was diagnosed with Down's syndrome and serious respiratory problems. Her parents were orthodox Jews, and her father was a rabbi. The parents asked the local authority to accommodate the child, because they could not meet all of her needs. The child was placed with foster parents who were non-practising Roman Catholics. The local authority were unable to find an orthodox Jewish family to provide short-term foster care, or as a long-term placement. Meanwhile, the child became increasingly attached to the foster parents. In 1994, the parents sought the child's return, but a residence order was made in favour of the foster parents, with reasonable contact to the parents. In 1998 the parents applied for the child to be returned to their care. They argued that the child had a presumptive right to be brought up by her own parents and in her own religion and that the judge had failed to give sufficient weight to the child's religious and cultural heritage.

Butler-Sloss LJ: ...
The first and crucial point is that the application which we are dealing with on appeal was a variation application and the primary issue of residence had already been decided in 1994. The next point is that this is a child with Down's syndrome who will never have sufficient capacity to live her own independent life. She will always be dependent upon carers. Then we know that from the age of 17 months to eight and a half years she has lived with a couple whom she sees as her 'real' or psychological parents. When she was four a court decided that she should spend her childhood with this couple. The evidence is that if she was now moved to a family, whom she knows from regular monthly contact but does not see as her 'real' parents, she will not have the ability to understand why. At eight there have to be strong reasons to move any child who has inevitably put down strong roots from a family where she has lived for seven years. The sometimes overemphasised status quo argument has real validity in this case. For this child, with limited capacity to understand, the reasons to move have, in my view, to be even more cogent. There is no presumption in the statutory code of the 1989 Act which can displace s 1(1) that the welfare of the child is the paramount consideration. There is, in particular, no presumptive right on a variation application at this stage of N's life that her natural parents should be preferred to the foster parents. On the contrary, the first question is: if it was right to place her with the foster parents in 1994, why should she be moved in 1998? ...

Religion
25. In considering the relevance and importance of the religious element in this appeal, I agree with Mr Ryder that s 1(3)(d) of the 1989 Act, which requires a court to have regard to the background of a child, includes a child's religious and cultural heritage. It is a relevant consideration, the weight of which will vary according to the facts of each case. In the present case, it is an important factor. No one would wish to deprive a Jewish child of her right to her Jewish heritage. If she had remained with a Jewish family it would be almost unthinkable, other than in an emergency, to remove her from it. I have no doubt, like the judge, that the orthodox Jewish religion provides a deeply satisfying way of life for its members and that this child, like other Down's syndrome children, would have flowered and prospered in her Jewish family and surroundings if she had continued to live with them. But in the unusual circumstances of this case her parents were not able to accommodate her within her community. The combination of the family illness and difficulties together with N's real medical problems as a young child made it impossible for her to be cared for within her family circle and it was *then, not now,* that she was deprived of her opportunity to grow up within the Jewish community. ...
26. ... The undoubted importance for an orthodox Jew of his religion which provides in itself a way of life which permeates all activities, is a factor to be put in the balancing exercise, particularly in considering the welfare of the daughter of a rabbi. But N's religious and cultural heritage cannot be the overwhelming factor in this case for the reasons set out by the judge nor can it displace other weighty welfare factors.

Attachment and risks of move

...

28. The evidence of the exceptional attachment of N to her foster parents and of them to her is overwhelming. The evidence of the harm to her, and not just short-term harm, of a move is also overwhelming. Her perception of the foster parents as her real parents, her inability to understand why she would lose them and the reasons for the move, the impossibility of a structured and gradual handover, the adjustment to the new home where she has not lived since a baby, the move from school as well as home (the two pillars of her security) are powerful reasons against a move. This court cannot intervene in a child case where the judge has exercised his discretion, unless the judge was plainly wrong or has erred in his approach to the case. But in this case, having read all the papers and heard all the arguments, in my judgment, he was plainly right. I suspect that if the religious dimension had not been so predominant and the question was asked: 'do we move this child?' the answer would have been given very quickly: 'of course not'. It is patently obvious that this child cannot move'and the balance falls firmly and clearly on the side of refusing the variation application.

...

Ward LJ: ...

(4) That children have rights is acknowledged in international conventions ratified by the United Kingdom. They may not have the force of law but, as international treaties, they command and receive our respect.

Article A14 of the United Nations Convention on the Rights of the Child (New York, 20 November 1989, TS 44 (1992); Cm 1976), adopted on 20 November 1989, provides:

'1. States Parties shall respect the right of the child to freedom of thought conscience and religion. 2. States Parties shall respect the rights and duties of the parents ... to provide direction to the child in the exercise of his or her right in a manner consistent with the evolving capacities of the child. 3. Freedom to manifest one's religion or beliefs may be subject only to such limitations as are prescribed by law and are necessary to protect public safety by law and are necessary to protect public safety, order, health or morals, or the fundamental human rights and freedoms of others.'

It also provides: 'Article 3.1: In all actions concerning children ... the best interests of the child should be of primary consideration.' The Convention for the Protection of Human Rights and Fundamental Freedoms (European Human Rights Convention) (Rome, 4 November 1950; TS 71(1953); Cmd 8969) is to similar effect. Article 9 provides:

'1. Everyone has the right to freedom of thought, conscience and religion ... 2. Freedom to manifest one's religion and beliefs shall be subject only to such limitations as are prescribed by law and are necessary in democratic society in the interests of public safety, for the protection of public order, health or morals, or for the protection of the rights and freedoms of others.'

Those articles were considered by the European Court of Human Rights in *Hoffmann v Austria* [1994] 1 FCR 193 at 205–206, [1994] 17 EHRR 293, a case concerning the Jehovah's Witnesses. The majority of the European Court held:

'In assessing the interests of the children, the Supreme Court (of Austria) considered the possible effects on their social life of being associated with a particular religious minority and the hazards attaching to applicant's total rejection of blood transfusions not only for herself but – in the absence of a court order – for her children as well; that is, possible negative effects of her membership of the religious community of Jehovah's Witnesses. It weighed them against the possibility that transferring the children to the care of their father might cause them physiological stress, which in its opinion had to be accepted in their own interests. This court does not deny that, depending on the circumstances of the case, the factors relied on by the Austrian Supreme Court in support of its decision may in themselves be capable of tipping the scales in favour of one parent rather than the other. However, the Supreme Court also introduced a new element, namely the Federal Act on the Religious Education of Children. This factor was clearly decisive of the Supreme Court. The European Court therefore accepts that there has been a difference in treatment and that the difference was on the ground of religion; this conclusion is supported by the tone and phrasing of the Supreme Court's consideration regarding the practical consequences of the applicant's religion. Such a difference in treatment is discriminatory in the absence of an "objective and reasonable justification" that is, if it is not justified by a "legitimate aim" and if there is no reasonable relationship of proportionality between the means employed and the aim sought to be realised. The aim pursued by the judgment of the Supreme Court was a legitimate one, namely the protection of the health and rights of the children . . .'

In other words, in the jurisprudence of human rights, the right to practice one's religion is subservient to the need in a democratic society to put welfare first.

(v) So it is here. That was confirmed by the House of Lords in *Re KD (a minor) (ward: termination of access)* [1988] FCR 657 at 672–673, [1988] 1 AC 806 at 825, where Lord Oliver of Aylmerton said:

> 'The word "right" is used in a variety of different senses, both popular and jurisprudential. It may be used as importing a positive duty in some other individual for the non-performance of which the law will provide an appropriate remedy, as in the case of a right to the performance of a contract. It may signify merely a privilege conferring no corresponding duty on anyone save that of non-interference, such as the right to walk on the public highway. It may signify no more than the hope of or aspirations to social order which will permit the exercise of that which is perceived as an essential liberty, such as, for example, the so called "right to work" or a "right of personal privacy." [I interpose and add "a right to practice one's parents' religion".] Parenthood, in most civilised societies, is generally conceived of as conferring upon parents the exclusive privilege of ordering, within the family, the upbringing of children of tender age, with all that entails. That is a privilege which, if interfered with without authority, would be protected by the courts, but it is a privilege circumscribed by many limitations imposed both by the general law and, where the circumstances demand, by the courts or by the authorities upon whom the legislature has imposed the duty of supervising the welfare of children and young persons. When the jurisdiction of the court is invoked for the protection of children the parental privileges do not terminate. They do, however, become immediately subservient to the paramount consideration which the court has always in mind, that is to say, the welfare of the child.'

Those are the basic principles which must inform the court's approach.

...

Conclusions

... In this case, in the events which have happened and with the passage of time, the need for an uninterrupted settled life outweighs the need for a religious life. Having been party to the decision to grant leave to appeal because of the importance of the religious issue raised, and having given N's claim to her Jewish birthright most anxious consideration, I have in the end not the slightest hesitation in coming to the conclusion that N's welfare dictated that she should not be moved from those whom she regarded as her devoted parents. The psychological tie outweighs the blood tie. The judge was right to refuse to alter N's residence.

Appeal dismissed. Leave to appeal to the House of Lords refused.

Questions

(i) In *Hoffmann v Austria* (1993) 17 EHRR 293 the European Court of Human Rights decided that the Austrian Supreme Court should not have denied the mother custody on the basis of her religion (although they could take account of the impact of her religious practices on the child). Is a prohibition on discrimination between parents on the basis of religion the same as saying that 'the right to practise one's religion is subservient to the need in a democratic society to put welfare first'?

(ii) Is it possible to consider a child's welfare without taking account of issues of culture or religion? Should we take account of these factors even if the child is unable to appreciate their significance? Are we doing this for the sake of the child, or the parents, or in the interests of social pluralism and non-discrimination?

It is one thing to decide between competing sets of parents, one 'natural' and the other 'social', but what about interfering in a particular upbringing decision made by otherwise 'unimpeachable' parents?

Of course, some decisions are more important than others:

Re D (a minor) (wardship: sterilisation)
[1976] Fam 185, [1976] 1 All ER 326, [1976] 2 WLR 279, 119 Sol Jo 696,
High Court, Family Division

D, now aged 11, was born with 'Sotos syndrome', the symptoms of which included epilepsy, clumsiness, an unusual facial appearance, behavioural problems, and some impairment of intelligence. Her mother was convinced that she was seriously mentally handicapped and would be unable to care either for herself or a child of her own. The paediatrician who had taken an interest in her case from an early stage took a similar view. When she reached puberty, therefore, mother and paediatrician arranged with a gynaecologist that she should be sterilised immediately, because they were afraid that she might be seduced and bear an abnormal child. The people responsible for her education, however, thought that it would be wrong to perform an irreversible and permanent operation upon her; her behaviour and social skills were improving steadily; she was of dull normal intelligence and it was common ground that she had sufficient intellectual capacity to marry in due course. The educational psychologist therefore made her a ward of court and applied for an order continuing the wardship in order to delay or prevent the proposed operation. It was not proposed that D should be removed from the care and control of her widowed mother, who had looked after her 'splendidly'.

Heilbron J: ...

Is wardship appropriate?
I have first of all to decide whether this is an appropriate case in which to exercise the court's wardship jurisdiction. Wardship is a very special and ancient jurisdiction. Its origin was the sovereign's feudal obligation as parens patriae to protect the person and property of his subjects, and particularly those unable to look after themselves, including infants. This obligation, delegated to the chancellor, passed to the Chancery Court, and in 1970 to this division of the High Court.

The jurisdiction in wardship is very wide, but there are limitations. It is not in every case that it is appropriate to make a child a ward, and counsel for Mrs B has argued with his usual skill and powers of persuasion that, as this case raises a matter of principle of wide public importance, and is a matter which affects many people, continuation of wardship would be inappropriate.

In his powerful argument, counsel for the Official Solicitor, on the other hand, submitted that the court in wardship had a wide jurisdiction which should be extended to encompass this novel situation, because it is just the type of problem which this court is best suited to determine when exercising its protective functions in regard to minors. As Lord Eldon LC said many years ago in *Wellesley v Duke of Beaufort* (1827) 2 Russ 1, 5 LJOS 85:

'This jurisdiction is founded on the obvious necessity that the law should place somewhere the care of individuals who cannot take care of themselves, particularly in cases where it is clear that some care should be thrown around them.'

It is apparent from the recent decision of the Court of Appeal in *Re X (A Minor)* [1975] Fam 47, [1975] 1 All ER 697 that the jurisdiction to do what is considered necessary for the protection of an infant is to be exercised carefully and within limits, but the court has, from time to time over the years, extended the sphere in the exercise of this jurisdiction.

The type of operation proposed is one which involves the deprivation of a basic human right, namely the right of a woman to reproduce, and therefore it would, if performed on a woman for non-therapeutic reasons and without her consent, be a violation of such right. ... As the evidence showed, and I accept it, D could not possibly have given an informed consent. What the evidence did, however, make clear was that she would almost certainly understand the implications of such an operation by the time she reached 18.

This operation could, if necessary, be delayed or prevented if the child were to remain a ward of court, and as Lord Eldon LC, so vividly expressed it in *Wellesley's* case: 'It has always been the principle of this Court, not to risk the incurring of damage to children which it cannot repair, but rather to prevent the damage being done.'

I think that is the very type of case where this court should 'throw some care around this child', and I propose to continue her wardship which, in my judgment, is appropriate in this case.

The operation – should it be performed?

In considering this vital matter, I want to make it quite clear that I have well in mind the natural feelings of a parent's heart, and though in wardship proceedings parents' rights can be superseded, the court will not do so lightly, and only in pursuance of well-known principles laid down over the years. The exercise of the court's jurisdiction is paternal, and it must be exercised judicially, and the judge must act, as far as humanly possible, on the evidence, as a wise parent would act. As Lord Upjohn pointed out in *J v C* [1970] AC 668, [1969] 1 All ER 788 the law and practice in relation to infants—

> 'have developed, are developing and must, and no doubt will, continue to develop by reflecting and adopting the changing views, as the years go by, of reasonable men and women, the parents of children, on the proper treatment and methods of bringing up children; for after all that is the model which the judge must emulate for ... he must act as the judicial reasonable parent.'

It is of course beyond dispute that the welfare of this child is the paramount consideration, and the court must act in her best interests.

The judge then reviews some of the evidence and arguments, including the facts that D had as yet shown no interest in the opposite sex, and had virtually no opportunities for promiscuity; that other methods of contraception or even abortion would be available should the need arise; and that there was no therapeutic reason for performing the operation now. She continues:

Dr Gordon, however, maintained that, provided the parent or parents consented, the decision was one made pursuant to the exercise of his clinical judgment, and that no interference could be tolerated in his clinical freedom.

The other consultants did not agree. Their opinion was that a decision to sterilise a child was not entirely within a doctor's clinical judgment, save only when sterilisation was the treatment of choice for some disease, as, for instance, when in order to treat a child and to ensure her direct physical well-being, it might be necessary to perform a hysterectomy to remove a malignant uterus. Whilst the side effect of such an operation would be to sterilise, the operation would be performed solely for therapeutic purposes. I entirely accept their opinions. I cannot believe, and the evidence does not warrant the view, that a decision to carry out an operation of this nature performed for non-therapeutic purposes on a minor, can be held to be within the doctor's sole clinical judgment.

It is quite clear that once a child is a ward of court, no important step in the life of that child can be taken without the consent of the court, and I cannot conceive of a more important step than that which was proposed in this case.

A review of the whole of the evidence leads me to the conclusion that in a case of a child of 11 years of age, where the evidence shows that her mental and physical condition and attainments have already improved, and where her future prospects are as yet unpredictable, where the evidence also shows that she is unable as yet to understand and appreciate the implications of this operation and could not give a valid or informed consent, but the likelihood is that in later years she will be able to make her own choice, where, I believe, the frustration and resentment of realising (as she would one day) what had happened could be devastating, an operation of this nature is, in my view, contra-indicated.

For these, and for the other reasons to which I have adverted, I have come to the conclusion that this operation is neither medically indicated nor necessary, and that it would not be in D's best interests for it to be performed.

Questions

(i)   In what circumstances do you think that the court should allow the sterilisation of (a) a female child, or (b) a male child?

(ii) In *Re B (a minor) (wardship: sterilisation)* [1988] AC 199 at 205–206, [1987] 2 All ER 206 at 214, Lord Templeman observed:

In my opinion sterilisation of a girl under 18 should only be carried out with the leave of a High Court judge. A doctor performing a sterilisation operation with the consent of the parents might still be liable in criminal, civil or professional proceedings. A court exercising the wardship jurisdiction emanating from the Crown is the only authority which is empowered to authorise such a drastic step as sterilisation after a full and informed investigation.

Why would it otherwise be a crime or a tort? Apart from sterilisation, are there any other decisions which should require court approval even where both parents agree on what is in the child's interests?
(iii) What difference would it have made if an operation had been necessary to save D's life?

In cases where parents refuse life-saving treatment for religious reasons, the courts have consistently acted to override the parental decision (for example, *Re R (a minor) (blood transfusion)* [1993] 2 FLR 757). However, some life-saving problems are easier than others:

Re A (children) (conjoined twins: surgical separation)
[2001] Fam 147, [2000] 4 All ER 961, [2001] 2 WLR 480, [2000] 3 FCR 577, (2000) 57 BMLR 1, Court of Appeal

Jodie and Mary were born 'conjoined', linked together and sharing vital organs. The medical evidence was that an operation to separate them would cause the death of Mary within a very short time, but that Jodie might live a relatively normal life after separation. Without the operation, both girls would die, since Jodie's organs were too weak to sustain them both. The parents were opposed to the operation, at least partly for religious reasons.

Ward LJ: ... There has been some public concern as to why the court is involved at all. We do not ask for work but we have a duty to decide what parties with a proper interest ask us to decide. Here sincere professionals could not allay a collective medical conscience and see children in their care die when they know one was capable of being saved. They could not proceed in the absence of parental consent. The only arbiter of that sincerely held difference of opinion is the court. Deciding disputed matters of life and death is surely and pre-eminently a matter for a court of law to judge. ...

5. The effect of the parents' refusal.
Since the parents are empowered at law, it seems to me that their decision must be respected and in my judgment the hospital would be no more entitled to disregard their refusal than they are to disregard an adult patient's refusal. To operate in the teeth of the parents' refusal would, therefore, be an unlawful assault upon the child. ... There is, however, this important safeguard to ensure that a child receives proper treatment. Because the parental rights and powers exist for the performance of their duties and responsibilities to the child and must be exercised in the best interests of the child, "... the common law has never treated such rights as sovereign or beyond review and control", per Lord Scarman in *Gillick* at p. 184 A.

Overriding control is vested in the court. This proposition is well established and has not been the subject of any challenge in this appeal. Because of the comment in the media questioning why the court should be involved, I add this short explanation. Long, long ago the sovereign's prerogative to protect infants passed to the Lord Chancellor and through him to the judges and it forms a part of the inherent jurisdiction of the High Court. The Children Act 1989 now contains a statutory scheme for the resolution of disputes affecting the upbringing of children. If a person having a recognisable interest brings such a dispute to the court, the court must decide it.

There are abundant examples of this happening. One such case is *In Re B (A Minor) (Wardship: Medical Treatment)* [1981] 1 W.L.R. 1424. There a child who was born suffering from Down's Syndrome and an intestinal blockage, required an operation to relieve the obstruction if she was to live more than a few days. If the operation were performed, the child might die within a few months but it was probable that her life expectancy would be 20-30 years. Her parents, having decided that it would be kinder to allow her to die rather than live as a physically and mentally disabled person, refused to consent to the operation. The local authority made the child a ward of court and, when a surgeon decided that the wishes of the parents should be respected, they sought an order authorising the operation to be performed by other named surgeons. Templeman L.J. said at p. 1423/4:-

'On behalf of the parents Mr Gray has submitted very movingly ... that this is a case where nature has made its own arrangements to terminate a life which would not be fruitful and nature should not be interfered with. He has also submitted that in this kind of decision the views of responsible and caring parents, as these are, should be respected, and that their decision that it is better for the child to be allowed to die should be respected. Fortunately or unfortunately, in this particular case the decision no longer lies with the parents or with the doctors, but lies with the court. It is a decision which of course must be taken in the light of the evidence and views expressed by the parents and the doctors, but at the end of the day it devolves on this court in this particular instance to decide ...'

Dunn L.J. said at p. 1424:-

'I have great sympathy for the parents in the agonising decision to which they came. As they put it themselves, "God or nature has given the child a way out". But the child now being a ward of court, although due weight must be given to the decision of the parents which everybody accepts was an entirely responsible one, doing what they considered was best, the fact of the matter is that this court now has to make the decision. It cannot hide behind the decision of the parents or the decision of the doctors; and in making the decision this court's first and paramount consideration is the welfare of this unhappy little baby.'

So it is that at this point we move into the realm of family law.

IV Family Law.

1. The test for overriding the parents' refusal.

This is trite law. In *In Re B. (A Minor) (Wardship: Sterilisation)* [1988] A.C. 199, 202 Lord Hailsham of St. Marylebone L.C. said:-

'There is no doubt that, in the exercise of its wardship jurisdiction the first and paramount consideration is the well being, welfare, or interest (each expression occasionally used, but each, for this purpose, synonymous) of the human being concerned ...'

Insofar as these proceedings are brought under the inherent jurisdiction of the court, that is the test that governs. In any event the position is regulated by Section 1(1) of the Children Act 1989 under which these proceedings are also brought. That provides:-

'When a court determines any question with respect to -

(a) The upbringing of a child; ...

the child's welfare shall be the court's paramount consideration.'

The peremptory terms of this section should be noted. It places the court under a duty to do what is dictated by the child's welfare.

2. The meaning of welfare.

In *J. v C.* [1970] A.C. 668, 710 Lord MacDermott addressed the question of construction as to the scope and meaning of the words in the Guardianship of Infants Act, 1925, '... shall regard the welfare of the infant as the first and paramount consideration', and he said:-

'I think they connote a process whereby, when all the relevant facts, relationships, claims and wishes of parents, risks, choices and other circumstances are taken into account and weighed, the course to be followed will be that which is most in the interests of the child's welfare as that term has now to be understood."

In *Re M.B. (Medical Treatment)* [1997] 2 F.L.R. 426, 439 Butler-Sloss L.J. said:-

'Best interests are not limited to best medical interests.'

In *Re A (Male Sterilisation)* [2000] 1 F.L.R. 549, 555 Dame Elizabeth Butler-Sloss, as President, said that:-

'In my judgment best interest encompasses medical, emotional and all other welfare issues.'

...

9. Giving due weight to the parents' wishes.

9.1 The parents and the courts.

Since the parents have the right in the exercise of their parental responsibility to make the decision, it should not be a surprise that their wishes should command very great respect.

Parental right is, however, subordinate to welfare. That was the view of the House of Lords in *In Re K.D. (A Minor) (Ward: Termination of Access)* [1988] 1 A.C. 806, 824-5 where Lord Oliver of Aylmerton said:-

'My Lords I do not, for my part, discern any conflict between the propositions laid down by your Lordships' House in *J. v C.* and the pronouncements of the European Court of Human Rights in relation to the natural parent's right of access to her child. Such conflict as exists, is, I think, semantic only and lies only in differing ways of giving expression to the single concept that the natural bond in the relationship between parent and child gives rise to universally recognised norms which ought not to be gratuitously interfered with and which, if interfered with at all, ought to be so only if the welfare of the child dictates it. The word "right" is used in a variety of different senses, both popular and jurisprudential ... Parenthood, in most civilised societies, is generally conceived of as conferring upon parents the exclusive privilege of ordering, within the family, the upbringing of children of tender age, with all that that entails. That is a privilege which, interfered with without authority, would be protected by the courts, but it is a privilege circumscribed by many limitations imposed both by the general law and, where circumstances demand, by the courts or by the authorities upon whom the legislature has imposed the duty of supervising the welfare of children and young persons. When the jurisdiction of the court is invoked for the protection of the child the parental privileges do not terminate. They do, however, become immediately subservient to the paramount consideration which the court has always in mind, that is to say, the welfare of the child. That is the basis of the decision of your Lordships' House in *J. v C.* [1970] A.C. 668 and I see nothing in *R. v United Kingdom* (Case 6/1986/104/152) which contradicts or casts any doubt upon that decision or which calls now for any re-appraisal of it by your Lordships. In particular the description of those familial rights and privileges enjoyed by parents in relation to their children as "fundamental" or "basic" does nothing, in my judgment, to clarify either the nature or the extent of the concept which it is sought to describe.'

In *J. v C.* at p. 175 Lord MacDermott set out the rule which has served the test of time:-

'While there is now no rule of law that the rights and wishes of unimpeachable parents must prevail over other considerations, such rights and wishes, recognised as they are by nature and society, can be capable of ministering to the total welfare of the child in a special way, and must therefore preponderate in many cases. The parental rights, however, remain qualified and not absolute for the purposes of the investigation the broad nature of which is still as described in the fourth of the principles enunciated by FitzGibbon L.J. in In *Re O'Hara* [1900] 2 I.R. 232, 240.'

That fourth principle which itself was derived from *Reg. v Gyngall* [1893] 2 Q.B. 232, is stated thus:-

'4. In exercising the jurisdiction to control or to ignore the parental right the court must act cautiously, not as if it were a private person acting with regard to his own child, and acting in opposition to the parent only when judicially satisfied that the welfare of the child requires that the parental right should be suspended or superseded.'

Finally, it is perhaps useful to repeat the passage in the judgment of Sir Thomas Bingham M.R. in *In Re Z (A Minor) (Identification: Restrictions on Publication)* [1997] Fam. 1, 32, in accordance with which Johnson J. approached this part of the case. The Master of the Rolls said:-

'I would for my part accept without reservation that the decision of a devoted and responsible parent should be treated with respect. It should certainly not be disregarded or lightly set aside. But the role of the court is to exercise an independent and objective judgment. If that judgment is in accord with that of the devoted and responsible parent, well and good. If it is not, then it is the duty of the court, after giving due weight to the view of the devoted and responsible parent, to give effect to its own judgment. That is what it is there for. Its judgment may of course be wrong. So may that of the parent. But once the jurisdiction of the court is invoked its clear duty is to reach and give the best judgment that it can.'

That is the law. That is what governs my decision. That is what I am desperately trying to do. I do not discern any very significant difference between the law, as set out above, and the Archbishop's fifth overarching moral consideration which he expresses in these terms:-

'Respect for the natural authority of parents requires that the courts override the rights of parents only when there is clear evidence that they are acting contrary to what is strictly owing to their children.'

9.2 The role of the court: reviewer or decision-maker?

Is the court reviewing the parental decision as it reviews an administrative decision or does the court look at the matter afresh, in the round, with due weight given to the parental wish? If there was doubt about that, it has been resolved in favour of the latter approach by the decision of this court in *In Re T. (Wardship: Medical Treatment)* [1997] 1 W.L.R. 242. That was an agonising decision for the court to take. The baby, a year old, had a life threatening liver defect. An operation when he was 3½ weeks old was unsuccessful. The unanimous medical opinion was that without a liver transplant he would not live beyond the age of 2½ years. His parents refused to consent to that operation. Their wish eventually prevailed. On this particular point Butler-Sloss L.J. said at p. 250 F:-

'... The first argument of Mr Francis that the court should not interfere with the reasonable decision of a parent is not one that we are able to entertain even if we wish to do so. His suggestion that the decision of this mother came within that band of reasonable decisions within which a court would not interfere would import into this jurisdiction the test applied in adoption to the refusal of a parent to consent to adoption. It is wholly inapposite to the welfare test and is incompatible with the decision in *In Re Z.*'

Waite L.J. said at 254 C:-

'An appraisal of parental reasonableness may be appropriate in other areas of family law (in adoption, for example where it is enjoined by statute) but when it comes to an assessment of the demands of the child patient's welfare, the starting point – and the finishing point too – must always be the judge's own independent assessment of the balance of advantage or disadvantage of the particular medical step under consideration. In striking that balance, the court will of course take into account as a relevant, often highly relevant, factor the attitude taken by the natural parent, and that may require examination of his or her motives. But the result of such an enquiry must never be allowed to prove determinative. It is a mistake to view the issue as one in which the clinical advice of doctors is placed in one scale and the reasonableness of the parent's view in the other.

...

It can only be said safely that there is a scale, at one end of which lies the clear case where parental opposition to medical intervention is prompted by scruple or dogma of a kind which is patently irreconcilable with principles of child health and welfare widely accepted by the generality of mankind; and that at the other end lie highly problematic cases where there is genuine scope for a difference of view between the parent and the judge. In both situations it is the duty of the judge to allow the court's own opinion to prevail in the perceived paramount interest of the child concerned, but in cases at the latter end of the scale, there must be a likelihood (though never of course a certainty) that the greater the scope for genuine debate between one view and another the stronger will be that inclination of the court to be influenced by a reflection that in the last analysis the best interests of every child include an expectation that difficult decisions affecting the length and quality of its life will be taken for it by the parent to whom its care has been entrusted by nature.'

...

11. Conclusion on the Family Law aspect of this case.
I would grant permission for the operation to take place provided, however, what is proposed to be done can be lawfully done. That requires a consideration of the criminal law to which I now turn.

...

After consideration of difficult issues of the criminal law, the Court of Appeal authorised the operation. Mary died shortly after the separation, but Jodie was reported to be doing well.

Questions

(i) If you were the judge, would you have authorised the operation? If so, is this because you think Jodie's interests should be given more weight than Mary's? Why?
(ii) Are disputes about a child's medical treatment best characterised as 'private' disputes about a child's upbringing, or as interference in parental decision-making by public agencies? Should it be necessary to show that a parent's decision will

cause harm to the child before the courts can impose their own view of the child's welfare? Would this have made any difference in *Re A*? Is there any decision which the parents could have made which could not have been challenged on the basis that it would inevitably cause harm to one or both children?

(iii) Should parental decisions about life or death medical treatment be respected if the decision falls within a band of 'reasonable' decisions, or should the courts always have the final say if parents and doctors are unable to agree?

(iv) Can you think of any other situations in family law where two children have competing interests? In such situations, do you think that the interests of both children should be given equal weight, or do you think that it should depend upon which child is the subject of the litigation? (See, for example, *Birmingham City Council v H (A Minor)* [1994] 2 AC 212; and *Re T and E (Children's Proceedings: Conflicting Interests)* [1995] 3 FCR 260.)

(v) How, if at all, would you have reconciled this decision with Art 2 of the European Convention on Human Rights:

1. Everyone's right to life shall be protected by law. No one shall be deprived of his life intentionally save in the execution of a sentence of a court following his conviction of a crime for which this penalty is provided by law.
2. Deprivation of life shall not be regarded as inflicted in contravention of this article when it results from the use of force which is no more than absolutely necessary:
   (a) in defence of any person from unlawful violence;
   (b) in order to effect a lawful arrest or to prevent escape of a person lawfully detained;
   (c) in action lawfully taken for the purpose of quelling a riot or insurrection.

In *Re A,* Johnson J at first instance, and Robert Walker LJ in the Court of Appeal, considered that the interests of the twins might not be in conflict, since the operation would bring Mary's pain and suffering to an end. However, the majority in the Court of Appeal (Ward and Brooke LJJ) concluded that the operation was *against* Mary's interests, but should be performed because of the potential benefit to Jodie. Nevertheless, there are cases in which the courts have decided that it is not in a child's interests to be kept alive:

Re J (a minor) (wardship: medical treatment)
[1991] Fam 33, [1990] 3 All ER 930, [1991] 2 WLR 140, Court of Appeal

J had been born very prematurely. He suffered very severe and permanent brain damage at the time of his birth. He was epileptic and the medical evidence was that he was likely to develop serious spastic quadriplegia, would be blind and deaf and was unlikely ever to be able to speak or to develop even limited intellectual abilities, but it was likely that he would feel pain to the same extent as a normal baby. His life expectancy was uncertain but he was expected to die before late adolescence, although he could survive for a few years. He had been ventilated twice for long periods when his breathing stopped, that treatment being both painful and hazardous. The medical prognosis was that any further collapse which required ventilation would be fatal. However he was neither on the point of death nor dying. The judge made an order that J should be treated with antibiotics if he developed a chest infection but should not be reventilated if his breathing stopped unless the doctors caring for him deemed it appropriate given the prevailing clinical situation. The Official Solicitor appealed:

Lord Donaldson MR: ... No one can *dictate* the treatment to be given to the child, neither court, parents nor doctors. There are checks and balances. The doctors can recommend treatment A in preference to treatment B. They can also refuse to adopt treatment C on the grounds that it is medically contra-indicated or for some other reason is a treatment which they could not conscientiously administer. The court or parents for their part can refuse to consent to treatment A or B or both, but cannot insist on treatment C. The inevitable and desirable result is that choice of treatment is in some measure a joint decision of the doctors and the court or parents. ...

Taylor LJ: The plight of baby J is appalling and the problem facing the court in the exercise of its wardship jurisdiction is of the greatest difficulty. When should the court rule against the giving of treatment aimed at prolonging life?

Three preliminary principles are not in dispute. First, it is settled law that the court's prime and paramount consideration must be the best interests of the child. That is easily said but not easily applied. What it does involve is that the views of the parents, although they should be heeded and weighed, cannot prevail over the court's view of the ward's best interests. In the present case the parents, finding themselves in a hideous dilemma, have not taken a strong view so that no conflict arises.

Second, the court's high respect for the sanctity of human life imposes a strong presumption in favour of taking all steps capable of preserving it, save in exceptional circumstances. The problem is to define those circumstances.

Third, and as a corollary to the second principle, it cannot be too strongly emphasised that the court never sanctions steps to terminate life. That would be unlawful. There is no question of approving, even in a case of the most horrendous disability, a course aimed at terminating life or accelerating death. The court is concerned only with the circumstances in which steps should not be taken to prolong life.

Two decisions of this court have dealt with cases at the extremes of the spectrum of affliction. *Re C (a minor) (wardship: medical treatment)* [1990] Fam 26, [1989] 2 All ER 782 was a case in which a child had severe irreversible brain damage such that she was hopelessly and terminally ill. This court held that the best interests of the child required approval of recommendations designed to ease her suffering and permit her life to come to an end peacefully with dignity rather than seek to prolong her life.

By contrast, in the earlier case of *Re B (a minor) (wardship: medical treatment)* (1981) [1990] 3 All ER 927, [1981] 1 WLR 1421, the court was concerned with a child suffering from Down's syndrome, who quite separately was born with an intestinal obstruction. Without an operation this intestinal condition would quickly have been fatal. On the other hand, the operation had a good chance of successfully removing the obstruction, once and for all, thereby affording the child a life expectation of some 20 to 30 years as a mongol. The parents genuinely believed it was in the child's interests to refrain from operating and allow her to die. The court took a different view. ...

Those two cases thus decide that where the child is terminally ill the court will not require treatment to prolong life; but where, at the other extreme, the child is severely handicapped although not intolerably so and treatment for a discrete condition can enable life to continue for an appreciable period, albeit subject to that severe handicap, the treatment should be given. ...

This leads to the arguments presented by counsel for the Official Solicitor. His first submission propounded an absolute test, that, except where the ward is terminally ill, the court's approach should always be to prolong life by treatment if this is possible, regardless of the quality of life being preserved and regardless of any added suffering caused by the treatment itself. I cannot accept this test which in my view is so hard as to be inconsistent at its extreme with the best interests of the child. Counsel for the Official Solicitor submits that the court cannot play God and decide whether the quality of life which the treatment would give the child is better or worse than death. He referred to dicta in *McKay v Essex Area Health Authority* [1982] QB 1166, [1982] 2 All ER 771. ...

Despite the court's inability to compare a life afflicted by the most severe disability with death, the unknown, I am of the view that there must be extreme cases in which the court is entitled to say: 'The life which this treatment would prolong would be so cruel as to be intolerable.' If, for example, a child was so damaged as to have negligible use of its faculties and the only way of preserving its life was by the continuous administration of extremely painful treatment such that the child either would be in continuous agony or would have to be so sedated continuously as to have no conscious life at all, I cannot think counsel's absolute test should apply to require the treatment to be given. In those circumstances, without there being any question of deliberately ending the life or shortening it, I consider the court is entitled in the best interests of the child to say that deliberate steps should not be taken artificially to prolong its miserable life span.

Once the absolute test is rejected, the proper criteria must be a matter of degree. At what point in the scale of disability and suffering ought the court to hold that the best interests of the child do not require further endurance to be imposed by positive treatment to prolong its life? Clearly, to justify withholding treatment, the circumstances would have to be extreme. Counsel for the Official Solicitor submitted that if the court rejected his absolute test, then at least it would have 'to be certain that the life of the child, were the treatment to be given, would be intolerably awful'.

I consider that the correct approach is for the court to judge the quality of life the child would have to endure if given the treatment and decide whether in all the circumstances such a life would be so afflicted as to be intolerable to that child. I say 'to that child' because the test should not be whether the life would be tolerable to the decider. The test must be whether the child in question, if capable of exercising sound judgment, would consider the life tolerable. This is the approach adopted by McKenzie J in *Re Superintendent of Family and Child Service and Dawson* (1983) 145 DLR (3d) 610 at 620-621. ... It takes account of the strong instinct to preserve one's life even in circumstances which an outsider, not himself at risk of death, might consider unacceptable. The circumstances to be considered would, in appropriate cases, include the degree of existing disability and any additional suffering or aggravation of the disability which the treatment itself would superimpose. In an accident case, as opposed to one involving disablement from birth, the child's pre-accident quality of life and its perception of what has been lost may also be factors relevant to whether the residual life would be intolerable to that child.

Counsel for the Official Solicitor argued that, before deciding against treatment, the court would have to be *certain* that the circumstances of the child's future would comply with the extreme requirements to justify that decision. Certainty as to the future is beyond human judgment. The courts have not, even in the trial of capital offences, required certainty of proof. But, clearly, the court must be satisfied to a high degree of probability.

In the present case, the doctors were unanimous that in his present condition, J should not be put back on to a mechanical ventilator. That condition is very grave indeed. ... In reaching his conclusion, the judge no doubt had three factors in mind. First, the severe lack of capacity of the child in all his faculties which even without any further complication would make his existence barely sentient. Second, that, if further mechanical ventilation were to be required, that very fact would involve the risk of a deterioration in B's condition, because of further brain damage flowing from the interruption of breathing. Third, all the doctors drew attention to the invasive nature of mechanical ventilation and the intensive care required to accompany it. They stressed the unpleasant and distressing nature of that treatment. To add such distress and the risk of further deterioration to an already appalling catalogue of disabilities was clearly capable in my judgment of producing a quality of life which justified the stance of the doctors and the judge's conclusion. I therefore agree that, subject to the minor variations to the judge's order proposed by Lord Donaldson MR, this appeal should be dismissed.

Appeal dismissed.

Questions

(i)   *Re J* concerned artificial breathing. In *Airedale National Health Service Trust v Bland* [1993] AC 789 at 884, [1993] 1 All ER 821 at 883, Lord Browne-Wilkinson said that:

... the critical decision to be made is whether it is in the best interests of Anthony Bland to continue the invasive medical care involved in artificial feeding. That question is not the same as, 'Is it in Anthony Bland's best interests that he should die?'

Do you find this distinction helpful?

(ii) Guidance on the withdrawal of life-sustaining medical treatment has been issued by the Royal College of Paediatrics and Child Health (*Withholding or Withdrawing Life Saving Treatment in Children: A Framework for Practice* (1997)). The guidance suggests that the decision to withdraw life-sustaining treatment should normally be made by the medical team and the parents, without the need for involvement by the courts. Can you think of any situations in which doctors should ask a court to allow them to withdraw life-saving treatment from a child against the parents' wishes (see *Re C (Medical Treatment)* [1998] 1 FLR 384)? Should the doctors be able to withhold life-saving treatment without parental agreement, or court approval (see *R v Portsmouth Hospital NHS Trust, ex p Glass* [1999] 2 FLR 905, [1999] 3 FCR 145)?

(iii) In a second *Re J (a minor) (child in care: medical treatment)* [1993] Fam 15, [1992] 4 All ER 614, Waite J had ordered the health authority to provide artificial ventilation if this became necessary to prolong the child's life; allowing the appeal, Lord Donaldson MR (with whom Balcombe and Leggatt LJJ expressly agreed) repeated his views:

> The fundamental issue in this appeal is whether the court in the exercise of its inherent power to protect the interests of minors should ever require a medical practitioner or health authority acting by a medical practitioner to adopt a course of treatment which in the bona fide clinical judgment of the practitioner concerned is contra-indicated as not being in the best interests of the patient. I have to say that I cannot at present conceive of any circumstances in which this would be other than an abuse of power as directly or indirectly requiring the practitioner to act contrary to the fundamental duty which he owes to his patient. This, subject to obtaining any necessary consent, is to treat the patient in accordance with his own best clinical judgment, notwithstanding that other practitioners who are not called upon to treat the patient may have formed quite a different judgment or that the court, acting on expert evidence, may disagree with him.

But if a court can take a child away from parents who are not acting in his best interests, should it not take a child away from a doctor who is not doing so and give him to one who will?

(iv) Money may be the reason. In *R v Cambridge Health Authority, ex p B* [1995] 2 All ER 129, Laws J in judicial review proceedings had quashed the authority's decision not to fund further chemotherapy and a second bone marrow transplant for a child with leukaemia. Allowing the appeal, Sir Thomas Bingham MR said:

> I have no doubt that in a perfect world any treatment which a patient, or a patient's family, sought would be provided if the doctors were willing to give it, no matter how much it cost, particularly when a life was potentially at stake. It would however, in my view, be shutting one's eyes to the real world if the court were to proceed on the basis that we do live in such a world. ... Difficult and agonising judgments have to be made as to how a limited budget is best allocated to the maximum advantage of the maximum number of patients. That is not a judgment that the court can make.

Now do you understand why Bowen LJ said (p. 443, above) that 'judicial machinery is quite inadequate to the task of educating children in this country'?

(v) Do you agree that the test of 'best interests' in matters of life and death should be what the child himself would have wanted? Or should the court adopt the 'same attitude as a responsible parent ... in the case of his or her own child' (per Balcombe LJ in the earlier *Re J*)? What difference would it make?

(vi) In *Re A (conjoined twins)*, Ward LJ considered the impact of the child's right to life, and concluded:

> What the sanctity of life doctrine compels me to accept is that each life has inherent value in itself and the right to life, being universal, is equal for all of us. The sanctity of life doctrine does, however, acknowledge that it may be proper to withhold or withdraw treatment. ... I cannot believe that the [European Court of Human Rights] would reach any other conclusion for solving that dilemma than we have done.

Do cases like *Re J*, and the outcome of *Re A* itself, suggest to you that disabled children have an equal right to life with other children?

The cases considered in this section concerned a single, albeit vital, question about the child's upbringing. There was no dispute about where the child should live or who should bring him up. But when the state wishes to challenge the parents' claim to bring the child up at all, should it be enough to prove that the state will probably be able to provide the child with a better life than they can? The *Review of Child Care Law* (1985) thought not:

2.12 ...We have had to consider whether a simple welfare or 'best interests' test should now be adopted where the state, in the shape of local authority, is in conflict with the parents.
2.13 We are firmly of the opinion that it should not and that in cases where compulsory committal to local authority care is in issue the present balance between the welfare of the child and the claims of his parents should be maintained. Taken to its logical conclusion, a simple 'best interests' test would permit the state to intervene whenever it could show that the alternative arrangements proposed would serve the children's welfare better than those proposed by their parents. But 'the child is not the child of the state' and it is important in a free society to maintain the rich diversity of lifestyles which is secured by permitting families a large measure of autonomy in the way in which they bring up their children. This is so even, or perhaps particularly, in those families who through force of circumstances are in need of help from social services or other agencies. Only where their children are put at unacceptable risk should it be possible compulsorily to intervene. Once such a risk of harm to the child has been shown, however, his interests must clearly predominate. [Later on:]
15.11   We have considered whether it would be sufficient to qualify a broad welfare test by a requirement that, as in family cases, the responsible body should first be satisfied that there are exceptional circumstances making it impracticable or undesirable that the child should be entrusted to his parents or to some other person. In our view that criterion would add very little to the broad welfare ground, given that only in exceptional circumstances would a court or local authority even consider compulsory intervention and given the readiness of the courts in applying section 1 of the 1971 Act to assume that generally a child's welfare is best served by his being brought up by his parents [see *J v C* [1970] AC 668]. The judges of the Family Division in proposing the criterion agreed that it might leave too much to subjective interpretation by the courts. We did consider whether adding guidelines to the criterion might overcome its apparent drawbacks, as has been suggested to us. However we doubt that these would be sufficient to direct the court's mind to the principles underlying restrictions on state intervention.

Questions

(i)   We shall come to the 'threshold conditions' for state intervention in Chapter 13, but how would you define the cases where a child is 'put at unacceptable risk'?
(ii)   The threshold conditions apply before a child can be placed in care or under supervision, but not where a social worker, educational psychologist, doctor or other representative of the caring agencies of the state seeks a 'specific issue order' dealing with a particular aspect of how the child should be brought up, as happened in *Re A (conjoined twins)*: can this distinction be justified?
(iii) Do you think that this will make much difference to what courts actually do?

10.2 Parental autonomy and respect for family life

In *Before the Best Interests of the Child* (1980), Goldstein, Freud and Solnit employ psychological concepts of a child's development to support their argument for severe limitations upon the state's power to intervene between parent and child:

... Constantly ongoing interactions between parents and children become for each child the starting point for an all-important line of development that leads toward adult functioning. What begins as the experience of physical contentment or pleasure that accompanies bodily care develops into a primary attachment to the person who provides it. This again changes into the wish for a parent's constant presence irrespective of physical wants. Helplessness requires total care and over time is transformed into the need or wish for approval and love. It fosters the desire to please by compliance with a parent's wishes. It provides a developmental base upon which the child's responsiveness to educational efforts rest. Love for the parents leads to identification with them, a fact without which impulse control and socialization would be deficient. Finally, after the years of childhood comes the prolonged and in many ways painful adolescent struggle to attain a separate identity with physical, emotional, and moral self-reliance.

These complex and vital developments require the privacy of family life under guardianship by parents who are autonomous. The younger the child, the greater is his need for them. When family integrity is broken or weakened by state intrusion, his needs are thwarted and his belief that his parents are omniscient and all-powerful is shaken prematurely. The effect on the child's developmental progress is invariably detrimental. The child's need for safety within the confines of the family must be met by law through its recognition of family privacy as the barrier to state intrusion upon parental autonomy in child rearing. These rights – parental autonomy, a child's entitlement to autonomous parents, and privacy – are essential ingredients of 'family integrity.' 'And the integrity of that life is something so fundamental that it has been found to draw to its protection the principles of more than one explicitly granted Constitutional right.'...

Beyond these biological and psychological justifications for protecting parent-child relationships and promoting each child's entitlement to a permanent place in a family of his own, there is a further justification for a policy of minimum state intervention. It is that the law does not have the capacity to supervise the fragile, complex interpersonal bonds between child and parent. As *parens patriae* the state is too crude an instrument to become an adequate substitute for flesh and blood parents. The legal system has neither the resources nor the sensitivity to respond to a growing child's ever-changing needs and demands. It does not have the capacity to deal on an individual basis with the consequences of its decisions, or to act with the deliberate speed that is required by a child's sense of time. Similarly, the child lacks the capacity to respond to the rulings of an impersonal court or social service agencies as he responds to the demands of personal parental figures. Parental expectations, implicit and explicit, become the child's own. However, the process by which a child converts external expectations, guidance, commands, and prohibitions into the capacity for self-regulation and self-direction does not function adequately in the absence of emotional ties to his caretakers.

A policy of minimum coercive intervention by the state thus accords not only with our firm belief as citizens in individual freedom and human dignity, but also with our professional understanding of the intricate developmental processes of childhood.

Question

Would it trouble you if a child's belief that his parents are omniscient and all powerful is broken prematurely?

There is also the question of the role of the state where parent and child are at odds with one another. This issue has arisen in the United States in connection with the right of parents to 'volunteer' their children for treatment in a psychiatric hospital. The following anonymous discussion of the 'Mental Hospitalisation of Children and the Limits of Parental Authority' (1978) provides a summary of the arguments:

Five justifications are most often advanced to support parental authority. They may for convenience be termed *social pluralism, social order, parental privilege, family autonomy* and *child's welfare*. Once each of these proffered justifications have been considered, the constitutional limits on a parent's power to admit his child to a mental hospital will emerge.

A. Social pluralism

It is a 'fixed star in our constitutional constellation,' especially with respect to the education of children, that the state shall not impose an orthodoxy 'in politics, nationalism, religion, or other matters of opinion.' And, especially in matters that relate to families and childrearing, the Constitution also disfavors state practices that threaten to impose on all a single conception of a worthwhile way of life. The institution of parental authority, by fragmenting decisions about the goals and methods of childrearing, serves to militate against such an orthodoxy. This, historically, has been part of its rationale and is today one reason for treating parental authority, when asserted against the state, as a constitutional right. It is therefore not surprising that the Supreme Court has acted more readily to protect parental authority against state intrusion when the threat to social pluralism has been acute. [1]

...Yet where, as here, the conflict under consideration is between parents and their children, the social pluralism rationale offers little direct guidance. Although a rule favoring parents over the state will always be a bulwark against a state-imposed orthodoxy of social values, a rule favoring parents over their children may or may not have that effect. The goal of social pluralism might just as well be advanced by allowing children to decide for themselves. ...

B. Social order

Historically, the law recognized society's interest in having children reared so that as adults they would be economically self-sufficient and would conform their conduct to society's norms. Parents, according to one court, were ordinarily entrusted with this task 'because it [could] seldom be put into better hands,' but they were subject to state supersession if they failed. Parents are still, to some extent, viewed as child-socialization agents of the state. ...

To the extent that parents actually do admit their children to mental hospitals as a method of social control, they are acting in their role of child-socialization agents of the state and are, therefore, subject to the same constitutional constraints as would apply if the state had acted directly. ...

C. Parental privilege

It is not uncommon for parents to seek to express their own personalities through their children. This interest of parents may serve as the basis for the claim they advance to have 'the power to dictate their [children's] training, prescribe their education and form their religious opinions.' To the extent that the law protects this claim of parents, it creates a *parental privilege* – that is, a prerogative of a parent to rear his child to be a person whose conduct, character, and belief conform to standards of the parent's choosing. There can be no doubt that this interest of parents, when asserted against the state, is within the scope of liberty protected by the Constitution. ...

It is regarded by many as unjust for one adult to impose his conception of the good life on another and as demeaning to another's dignity not to respect his choice of his own life plan. Psychological studies show that at adolescence, children of normal intellect are in this respect substantially like adults: they have the basic cognitive capacities to choose intelligently among competing values and to formulate their own life plans. So, as applied to adolescents, parental privilege – the prerogative of parents to impose on their children values and styles of life that best express the *parents'* personalities – is especially hard to justify on moral grounds. ...

D. Family autonomy

The state's interest in preserving the family unit is often cited to justify state sanction of parental authority. But protecting the family from outside interference is quite distinct from fortifying the family's power over one of its members. ...

When a parent, in his role of family governor, exercises authority over the child, his action has a moral basis that the exercise of bare parental privilege lacks. But there are other criteria for the moral assessment of social institutions – whether an institution that makes claims against some provides some reciprocal benefit for each of those whose liberty it restricts, or whether it makes an equal relative contribution to the good life of each of its participants. Although family life may often require that some good of one individual be foregone for the well-being of the family

---

1. The author's footnote reads: Compare *Wisconsin v Yoder* 406 US 205 (1972) (invalidating state compulsory education law as applied to Amish children) and *Pierce v Society of Sisters* 268 US 510 (1925) (invalidating state law requiring parents to send their children only to public schools) with *Prince v Massachusetts* 321 US 158 (1944) (upholding statute prohibiting street solicitation by children as applied to Jehovah's Witnesses distributing religious literature). The Court in *Yoder* noted especially that the statute as applied 'substantially interfer[ed] with the religious development of the Amish child and his integration into the way of life of the Amish faith community' and 'carrie[d] with it a very real threat of undermining the Amish community and religious practice.' 406 US at 218. Enforcement of the statute in *Prince*, however, posed no such threat to the Jehovah's Witnesses' way of life; the Court in *Prince* took pains to note that its holding left parents free to accomplish the religious training and indoctrination of their children by all means 'except the public proclaiming of religion [by their children] in the streets.' 321 US at 171. More importantly, in *Yoder* and *Pierce* the effect of a holding in favour of the state would have been to compel children to confront daily a set of religious and social values antagonistic to those that their parents sought to foster.

as a whole, a family that excessively derogates the interests of one for the sake of the others undermines its own moral basis.

These moral considerations suggest a legal norm. The state need not intervene in every family dispute, but if it does, it must treat each family member affected as having a distinguishable interest, which is equally entitled to the protection of the state. ...

E. Child's welfare

The last of the proffered justifications of parental authority is that it serves the child's welfare. It has been suggested that allowing parents to be the supreme arbiters of their child's fate is justified because it is conducive to the child's long term psychological health. More commonly, parental authority is defended on the ground that someone must choose for children since they lack the capacity to choose for themselves; parents are assigned this role because they are presumed to be better able to perform the task than anyone else.

The legitimacy of parental authority based on the child's welfare rationale depends primarily on the child's capacity to choose for himself. This capacity will vary with age. Parental authority over preadolescents is justified because the assumption that children are not competent to make their own choices is, as applied to them, generally correct. Since, however, parents under this rationale are presumed to act as guardians of the child's interests, parental authority would lose its underlying legitimacy if exercised for purposes unrelated to the child's welfare or in ways that create for the child a substantial risk of harm. ...

For the adolescent, the situation is more complex. Psychologists agree that about the time of adolescence a major transformation occurs in the quality of a child's thought. As a consequence of a shift to what is called formal operational thought, the youngster is capable of abstract, logical, and scientific thinking, which enables him to see the practical possibilities of real-life situations and to anticipate and evaluate the consequences of his own conduct. Simultaneously, or perhaps as a consequence of the same underlying process, the individual acquires an appreciation for the social ramifications of individual conduct, and a capacity to formulate his own personal and social ideals.

When a person makes choices after having identified the likely consequences for himself and others and having evaluated those alternatives in light of an overall life plan, he has chosen intelligently, even if unwisely from someone else's point of view. By this criterion, the psychological evidence shows that the typical adolescent will have acquired a basic capacity for intelligent choice by about fourteen years old.

Questions

(i) In *R v Kirklees Metropolitan District Council, ex p C (a minor)* [1993] 2 FLR 187, CA, it was held that a local authority having the responsibilities of a parent could arrange for the admission of a 12-year-old child to a psychiatric unit against her will without any of the safeguards in the Mental Health Act 1983. Do you consider this (a) a proper way to meet their parental responsibility, or (b) an unjustified invasion of the rights of the child? (See also *Nielsen v Denmark* (1988) 11 EHRR 175, in which the European Court of Human Rights concluded that placing a child in a psychiatric hospital was a proper exercise of parental authority, and not a deprivation of the child's liberty requiring justification under Art 5 of the European Convention. Compare *Re K (a child) (secure accommodation order: right to liberty)* (p. 474, below).

(ii) Would it make any difference to your answer if the child had been 15 years old and able to choose 'intelligently, even if unwisely from someone else's point of view'?

In Chapter 1 we introduced Art. 8 of the European Convention for the Protection of Human Rights and Fundamental Freedoms, now part of our domestic law following the Human Rights Act 1998. The article is worth repeating here:

Article 8

1. Everyone has the right to respect for his private and family life, his home and his correspondence.

2. There shall be no interference by a public authority with the exercise of this right except such as is in accordance with the law and is necessary in a democratic society in the interests of national security, public safety or the economic well-being of the country, for the prevention of disorder or crime, for the protection of health or morals, or for the protection of the rights and freedoms of others.

In Chapter 1 we quoted from *Keegan v Ireland* (1994) 18 EHRR 342; look again at para. 50 of the court's judgment (p. 27) for an explanation of what is entailed in Art. 8(1).

What, then, is the meaning of Art. 8(2), which permits interference with this right to a limited extent? The following discussion is taken from the judgment of Hale LJ in *Re W and B (children) (care plan); Re W (children) (care plan)* [2001] EWCA Civ 757, [2001] 2 FCR 450, [2001] 2 FLR 582; the context is the court's power to make a care order, which is, of course, an interference with the right to respect for family life:

[54] Such an interference can only be justified under art 8.2 if three conditions are fulfilled. (i) It must be 'in accordance with the law'. This means more than that it must have a basis in domestic law; the domestic law must also be adequately accessible and formulated so that it is reasonably foreseeable; and there must be adequate and effective safeguards in that law to protect against arbitrary interference: see *Sunday Times v UK* (1979) 2 EHRR 245; *Silver v UK* (1983) 5 EHRR 347; *Malone v UK* (1984) 7 EHRR 14; and *Halford v UK* (1997) 24 EHRR 523. Subject to that, however, the need for flexibility and discretion are also recognised, particularly in child care cases: see *Olsson v Sweden (No 1)* (1988) 11 EHRR 259 at 283 (para 61); *Eriksson v Sweden* (1989) 12 EHRR 183 at 200-201 (paras 59-60); *Andersson v Sweden* (1992) 14 EHRR 615.

(ii) It must be in pursuit of one of the legitimate aims provided for in the article: compulsory measures of care can be justified for the protection of health or morals or for the protection of the rights of the child. The rights of a child are not confined to his Convention rights and in this context include his interests: see *Hendriks v Netherlands* (1983) 5 EHRR 223; *Andersson v Sweden* (1992) 14 EHRR 615; *Johansen v Norway* (1996) 23 EHRR 33.

(iii) It must be 'necessary in a democratic society' . . . that is to say, the reasons given for the interference must be 'relevant and sufficient'. It must correspond to a 'pressing social need' and be 'proportionate' to the legitimate aim pursued: see *Olsson v Sweden (no 1)* (1988) 11 EHRR 259. Thus, at least where there is no question of adoption, the care decision should be 'regarded as a temporary measure, to be discontinued as soon as circumstances permitted, and any measures of implementation should have been consistent with the ultimate aim of reuniting the . . . family' (at 290 (para 81)). The more serious the intervention, the more compelling must be the justification: see *Johansen v Norway* (1996) 23 EHRR 33. The most important question in most care cases is therefore whether the proposed interference with the right to respect for family life is proportionate to the need which makes it legitimate.

In the early days of the interpretation of the convention in the European Court of Human Rights, it appeared that the arguments for parental authority weighed more heavily than the arguments for children's welfare or children's rights – which are not always the same thing. But the latter have gained greater prominence in recent years, as the next two sections show.

10.3 Children's rights

That last point makes it clear that we are here considering a tri-partite relationship: between parents and the state (or other third parties) and between parents and children, but also between children and parents and children and the state.

Gillick v West Norfolk and Wisbech Area Health Authority
[1986] AC 112, [1985] 3 All ER 402, [1985] 3 WLR 830, [1986] 1 FLR 224,
House of Lords

The plaintiff, mother of five daughters under the age of 16, sought a declaration that the guidance issued by the Department of Health and Social Security, to the effect that in exceptional circumstances a doctor might give contraceptive advice and treatment to a girl under 16 without her parents' consent, was unlawful. She failed at first instance, but succeeded in the Court of Appeal. On appeal to the House of Lords:

Lord Fraser of Tullybelton:... Three strands of argument are raised by the appeal. These are: (1) whether a girl under the age of 16 has the legal capacity to give valid consent to contraceptive advice and treatment including medical examination; (2) whether giving such advice and treatment to a girl under 16 without her parents' consent infringes the parents' rights; and (3) whether a doctor who gives such advice or treatment to a girl under 16 without her parents' consent incurs criminal liability. I shall consider these strands in order.

1. The legal capacity of a girl under 16 to consent to contraceptive advice, examination and treatment

There are some indications in statutory provisions to which we were referred that a girl under 16 years of age in England and Wales does not have the capacity to give valid consent to contraceptive advice and treatment. If she does not have the capacity, then any physical examination or touching of her body without her parents' consent would be an assault by the examiner. One of those provisions is s. 8 of the Family Law Reform Act 1969, which is in the following terms:

'(1) The consent of a minor who has attained the age of sixteen years to any surgical, medical or dental treatment which, in the absence of consent, would constitute a trespass to his person, shall be as effective as it would be if he were of full age; and where a minor has by virtue of this section given an effective consent to any treatment it shall not be necessary to obtain any consent for it from his parent or guardian. ...

(3) Nothing in this section shall be construed as making ineffective any consent which would have been effective if this section had not been enacted.'

The contention on behalf of Mrs Gillick was that sub-s (1) of s. 8 shows that, apart from the subsection, the consent of a minor to such treatment would not be effective. But I do not accept that contention because sub-s (3) leaves open the question whether consent by a minor under the age of 16 would have been effective if the section had not been enacted. That question is not answered by the section, and sub-s (1) is, in my opinion, merely for the avoidance of doubt. ...
... It seems to me verging on the absurd to suggest that a girl or a boy aged 15 could not effectively consent, for example, to have a medical examination of some trivial injury to his body or even to have a broken arm set. Of course the consent of the parents should normally be asked, but they may not be immediately available. Provided the patient, whether a boy or a girl, is capable of understanding what is proposed, and of expressing his or her own wishes, I see no good reason for holding that he or she lacks the capacity to express them validly and effectively and to authorise the medical man to make the examination or give the treatment which he advises. After all, a minor under the age of 16 can, within certain limits, enter into a contract. He or she can also sue and be sued, and can give evidence on oath. Moreover, a girl under 16 can give sufficiently effective consent to sexual intercourse to lead to the legal result that the man involved does not commit the crime of rape: see *R v Howard* [1965] 3 All ER 684 at 685, [1966] 1 WLR 13 at 15, ...
Accordingly, I am not disposed to hold now, for the first time, that a girl aged less than 16 lacks the power to give valid consent to contraceptive advice or treatment, merely on account of her age.

2. The parents' rights and duties in respect of medical treatment of their child
... It was, I think, accepted both by Mrs Gillick and by the DHSS, and in any event I hold, that parental rights to control a child do not exist for the benefit of the parent. They exist for the benefit of the child and they are justified only in so far as they enable the parent to perform his duties towards the child, and towards other children in the family. If necessary, this proposition can be supported by reference to *Blackstone's Commentaries* (1 Bl Com (17th edn, 1830) 452),
...

From the parents' right and duty of custody flows their right and duty of control of the child, but the fact that custody is its origin throws but little light on the question of the legal extent of control at any particular age. ...

It is my view, contrary to the ordinary experience of mankind, at least in Western Europe in the present century, to say that a child or a young person remains in fact under the complete control of his parents until he attains the definite age of majority, now 18 in the United Kingdom, and that on attaining that age he suddenly acquires independence. In practice most wise parents relax their control gradually as the child develops and encourage him or her to become increasingly independent. Moreover, the degree of parental control actually exercised over a particular child does in practice vary considerably according to his understanding and intelligence and it would, in my opinion, be unrealistic for the courts not to recognise these facts. Social customs change, and the law ought to, and does in fact, have regard to such changes when they are of major importance. ...

Once the rule of the parents' absolute authority over minor children is abandoned, the solution to the problem in this appeal can no longer be found by referring to rigid parental rights at any particular age. The solution depends on a judgment of what is best for the welfare of the particular child. Nobody doubts, certainly I do not doubt, that in the overwhelming majority of cases the best judges of a child's welfare are his or her parents. Nor do I doubt that any important medical treatment of a child under 16 would normally only be carried out with the parents' approval. That is why it would and should be 'most unusual' for a doctor to advise a child without the knowledge and consent of the parents on contraceptive matters. But, as I have already pointed out, Mrs Gillick has to go further if she is to obtain the first declaration that she seeks. She has to justify the absolute right of veto in a parent. But there may be circumstances in which a doctor is a better judge of the medical advice and treatment which will conduce to a girl's welfare than her parents. ...

The only practicable course is, in my opinion, to entrust the doctor with a discretion to act in accordance with his view of what is best in the interests of the girl who is his patient. He should, of course, always seek to persuade her to tell her parents that she is seeking contraceptive advice, and the nature of the advice that she receives. At least he should seek to persuade her to agree to the doctor's informing the parents. But there may well be cases, and I think there will be some cases, where the girl refuses either to tell the parents herself or to permit the doctor to do so and in such cases the doctor will, in my opinion, be justified in proceeding without the parents' consent or even knowledge provided he is satisfied on the following matters: (1) that the girl (although under 16 years of age) will understand his advice; (2) that he cannot persuade her to inform her parents or to allow him to inform the parents that she is seeking contraceptive advice; (3) that she is very likely to begin or to continue having sexual intercourse with or without contraceptive treatment; (4) that unless she receives contraceptive advice or treatment her physical or mental health or both are likely to suffer; (5) that her best interests require him to give her contraceptive advice, treatment or both without the parental consent. ...

Lord Scarman: ... Parental rights clearly do exist, and they do not wholly disappear until the age of majority. Parental rights relate to both the person and the property of the child: custody, care and control of the person and guardianship of the property of the child. But the common law has never treated such rights as sovereign or beyond review and control. Nor has our law ever treated the child as other than a person with capacities and rights recognised by law. The principle of the law, as I shall endeavour to show, is that parental rights are derived from parental duty and exist only so long as they are needed for the protection of the person and property of the child. The principle has been subjected to certain age limits set by statute for certain purposes; and in some cases the courts have declared an age of discretion at which a child acquires before the age of majority the right to make his (or her) own decision. But these limitations in no way undermine the principle of the law, and should not be allowed to obscure it. ...

... The underlying principle of the law was exposed by Blackstone and can be seen to have been acknowledged in the case law. It is that parental right yields to the child's right to make his own decisions when he reaches a sufficient understanding and intelligence to be capable of making up his own mind on the matter requiring decision. Lord Denning MR captured the spirit and principle of the law when he said in *Hewer v Bryant* [1970] 1 QB 357 at 369, [1969] 3 All ER 578 at 582:

'I would get rid of the rule in *Re Agar-Ellis* (1883) 24 Ch D 317 and of the suggested exceptions to it. That case was decided in the year 1883. It reflects the attitude of a Victorian parent towards his children. He expected unquestioning obedience to his commands. If a son disobeyed, his father would cut him off with 1s. If a daughter had an illegitimate child, he would turn her out of the house. His power only ceased when the child became 21. I decline to accept a view so much out of date. The common law can, and should, keep pace with the times. It should declare, in conformity with the recent report on the Age of Majority, that the legal right of a parent to the custody of a child ends at the eighteenth birthday; and even up till then, it is a dwindling right which the courts will hesitate to enforce against the wishes of the child, the older he is. It starts with a right of control and ends with little more than advice.'

But his is by no means a solitary voice. It is consistent with the opinion expressed by the House in *J v C* [1970] AC 668, [1969] 1 All ER 788, where their Lordships clearly recognised as out of place the assertion in the *Agar-Ellis* cases (1878) 10 Ch D 49; (1883) 24 Ch D 317 of a father's power bordering on 'patria potestas'. It is consistent with the view of Lord Parker CJ in *R v Howard* [1965] 3 All ER 684 at 685, [1966] 1 WLR 13 at 15, where he ruled that in the case of a prosecution charging rape of a girl under 16 the Crown must *prove* either lack of her consent or that she was not in a position to decide whether to consent or resist and added the comment that 'there are many girls who know full well what it is all about and can properly consent'. And it is consistent with the views of the House in the recent criminal case where a father was accused of kidnapping his own child, *R v D* [1984] AC 778, [1984] 2 All ER 449. ...

In the light of the foregoing I would hold that as a matter of law the parental right to determine whether or not their minor child below the age of 16 will have medical treatment terminates if and when the child achieves a sufficient understanding and intelligence to enable him or her to understand fully what is proposed. It will be a question of fact whether a child seeking advice has sufficient understanding of what is involved to give a consent valid in law. Until the child achieves the capacity to consent, the parental right to make the decision continues save only in exceptional circumstances. Emergency, parental neglect, abandonment of the child or inability to find the parent are examples of exceptional situations justifying the doctor proceeding to treat the child without parental knowledge and consent; but there will arise, no doubt, other exceptional situations in which it will be reasonable for the doctor to proceed without the parent's consent.

Lord Bridge agreed with them both. For him, however, the main ground for decision was that the DHSS guidance could only be challenged through judicial review, whereas Lord Scarman held that private rights were involved. Lord Brandon of Oakbridge did not discuss the rights of parents or children because he concluded from the provisions of the Sexual Offences Act 1956 relating to unlawful sexual intercourse that the provision of contraceptive facilities was unlawful in any event.

Lord Templeman: ... I accept also that a doctor may lawfully carry out some forms of treatment with the consent of an infant patient and against the opposition of a parent based on religious or any other grounds. The effect of the consent of the infant depends on the nature of the treatment and the age and understanding of the infant. For example, a doctor with the consent of an intelligent boy or girl of 15 could in my opinion safely remove tonsils or a troublesome appendix. But any decision on the part of a girl to practise sex and contraception requires not only knowledge of the facts of life and of the dangers of pregnancy and disease but also an understanding of the emotional and other consequences to her family, her male partner and to herself. I doubt whether a girl under the age of 16 is capable of a balanced judgment to embark on frequent, regular or casual sexual intercourse fortified by the illusion that medical science can protect her in mind and body and ignoring the danger of leaping from childhood to adulthood without the difficult formative transitional experiences of adolescence. There are many things which a girl under 16 needs to practise but sex is not one of them. ...

... In my opinion a doctor may not lawfully provide a girl under 16 with contraceptive facilities without the approval of the parent responsible for the girl save pursuant to a court order, or in the case of emergency or in exceptional cases where the parent has abandoned or forfeited by abuse the right to be consulted. Parental rights cannot be insisted on by a parent who is not responsible for the custody and upbringing of an infant or where the parent has abandoned or abused parental rights. And a doctor is not obliged to give effect to parental rights in an emergency.
Appeal allowed.

Question

Are all three of their Lordships saying the same thing? Does parental right yield to the child's autonomy? Or does the child's autonomy allow a third party to take over the decision of what will be best?

But what if a 'Gillick-competent' child does not want treatment? In *Re R (a minor) (wardship: medical treatment)* [1992] Fam 11, [1991] 4 All ER 177, it was held that the court could authorise the administration of anti-psychotic drugs to a 15-year-old girl despite her refusal; Lord Donaldson MR went further: adopting a keyholder analogy, he stated that the consent of either the parents or a competent child could unlock the door to treatment. He went further still in the next case.

Re W (a minor) (medical treatment: court's jurisdiction)
[1993] Fam 64, [1992] 4 All ER 627, Court of Appeal

W was a 16-year-old girl in local authority care who suffered from anorexia nervosa. She was admitted to an adolescent psychiatric unit but her physical condition had deteriorated so much that it was proposed to move her to a hospital specialising in eating disorders. She did not wish to go. The local authority asked the court, in the exercise of its inherent jurisdiction, to authorise this. Thorpe J held that she was competent to make the decision but that the court could make the order sought. She appealed, arguing that the Family Law Reform Act, s. 8 (see p. 467, above) gave her the exclusive right to consent and therefore an absolute right to refuse treatment.

Lord Donaldson of Lymington MR: ... *Gillick's case*
    In *Gillick v West Norfolk and Wisbech Area Health Authority* [1986] AC 112 the central issue was *not* whether a child patient under the age of 16 could refuse medical treatment if the parents or the court consented, but whether the parents could effectively impose a veto on treatment by failing or refusing to consent to treatment to which the child might consent. Mrs. Gillick accepted that the court had such a power of veto and contended that the parents had a similar power. ...
    The House of Lords decisively rejected Mrs. Gillick's contentions and held that at common law a child of sufficient intelligence and understanding (the '*Gillick* competent' child) could consent to treatment, notwithstanding the absence of the parents' consent and even an express prohibition by the parents. Only Lord Scarman's speech is couched in terms which might suggest that the refusal of a child below the age of 16 to accept medical treatment was determinative. ...
    In the light of the quite different issue which was before the House in *Gillick's* case I venture to doubt whether Lord Scarman meant more than that the *exclusive* right of the parents to consent to treatment terminated, but I may well be wrong. Thorpe J having held that 'there is no doubt at all that J. is a child of sufficient understanding to make an informed decision,' I shall assume that, so far as the common law is concerned, Lord Scarman would have decided that neither the local authority nor W.'s aunt, both of whom had parental responsibilities, could give consent to treatment which would be effective in the face of W.'s refusal of consent. This is of considerable persuasive authority, but even that is not the issue before this court. That is whether *the court* has such a power. That never arose in *Gillick's* case, the nearest approach to it being the proposition, accepted by all parties, that the court had power to override any minor's consent (*not* refusal) to accept treatment. ...

The Latey Committee Report
It is common ground that the Family Law Reform Act 1969 was Parliament's response to the Report of the Committee on the Age of Majority (1967) (Cmnd 3342). The relevant part is contained in paragraphs 474-484. These show that the mischief aimed at was twofold. First, cases were occurring in which young people between 16 and 21 (the then age of majority) were living away from home and wished and needed urgent medical treatment which had not yet reached the emergency stage. Doctors were unable to treat them unless and until their parents had been traced and this could cause unnecessary suffering. Second, difficulties were arising concerning

> 'operations whose implications bring up the question of a girl's right to privacy about her sexual life. A particularly difficult situation arises in the case of a girl who is sent to hospital in need of a therapeutic abortion and refuses point blank to enter the hospital unless a guarantee is given that her parents shall not be told about it.'

The committee had recommended that the age of majority be reduced to 18 generally. The report, in paragraph 480, records that all the professional bodies which gave evidence recommended that patients aged between 16 and 18 should be able to give an effective consent to treatment and all but the Medical Protection Society recommended that they should also be able to give an effective refusal. The point with which we are concerned was therefore well in the mind of the committee. It did not so recommend. It recommended that:

> '*without prejudice to any consent that may otherwise be lawful*, the consent of young persons aged 16 and over to medical or dental treatment shall be as valid as the consent of a person of full age.' (My emphasis.)

Conclusion on section 8

I am quite unable to accept that Parliament in adopting somewhat more prolix language was intending to achieve a result which differed from that recommended by the committee.

On reflection I regret my use in *In re R (A Minor) (Wardship: Consent to Treatment)* [1992] Fam 11, 22, of the keyholder analogy because keys can lock as well as unlock. I now prefer the analogy of the legal 'flak jacket' which protects the doctor from claims by the litigious whether he acquires it from his patient who may be a minor over the age of 16, or a '*Gillick* competent' child under that age or from another person having parental responsibilities which include a right to consent to treatment of the minor. Anyone who gives him a flak jacket (that is, consent) may take it back, but the doctor only needs one and so long as he continues to have one he has the legal right to proceed. ...

Hair-raising possibilities were canvassed of abortions being carried out by doctors in reliance upon the consent of parents and despite the refusal of consent by 16- and 17-year-olds. Whilst this may be possible as a matter of law, I do not see any likelihood taking account of medical ethics, unless the abortion was truly in the best interests of the child. This is not to say that it could not happen. This is clear from the facts of *In re D (A Minor) (Wardship: Sterilisation)* [1976] Fam 185. ...

Thus far I have, in the main, been looking at the problem in the context of a conflict between parents and the minor, either the minor consenting and the parents refusing consent or the minor refusing consent and the parents giving it. Although that is not this case, I have done so both because we were told that it would be helpful to all those concerned with the treatment of minors and also perhaps the minors themselves and because it seems to be a logical base from which to proceed to consider the powers of the court and how they should be exercised.

W.'s case

... I have no doubt that the wishes of a 16- or 17-year-old child or indeed of a younger child who is '*Gillick* competent' are of the greatest importance both legally and clinically, but I do doubt whether Thorpe J was right to conclude that W. was of sufficient understanding to make an informed decision. I do not say this on the basis that I consider her approach irrational. I personally consider that religious or other beliefs which bar any medical treatment or treatment of particular kinds are irrational, but that does not make minors who hold those beliefs any the less '*Gillick* competent'. They may well have sufficient intelligence and understanding fully to appreciate the treatment proposed and the consequences of their refusal to accept that treatment. What distinguishes W. from them, and what with all respect I do not think that Thorpe J took sufficiently into account (perhaps because the point did not emerge as clearly before him as it did before us), is that it is a feature of anorexia nervosa that it is capable of destroying the ability to make an informed choice. It creates a compulsion to refuse treatment or only to accept treatment which is likely to be ineffective. This attitude is part and parcel of the disease and the more advanced the illness, the more compelling it may become. ...

There is ample authority for the proposition that the inherent powers of the court under its parens patriae jurisdiction are theoretically limitless and that they certainly extend beyond the powers of a natural parent: see for example *In re R (A Minor) (Wardship: Consent to Treatment)* [1992] Fam 11, 25B, 28G. There can therefore be no doubt that it has power to override the refusal of a minor, whether over the age of 16 or under that age but '*Gillick* competent'. It does not do so by ordering the doctors to treat which, even if within the court's powers, would be an abuse of them or by ordering the minor to accept treatment, but by authorising the doctors to treat the minor in accordance with their clinical judgment, subject to any restrictions which the court may impose.

...This is not, however, to say that the wishes of 16- and 17-year-olds are to be treated as no different from those of 14- and 15-year-olds. Far from it. Adolescence is a period of progressive transition from childhood to adulthood and as experience of life is acquired and intelligence and understanding grow, so will the scope of the decision-making which should be left to the minor, for it is only by making decisions and experiencing the consequences that decision-making skills will be acquired. As I put it in the course of the argument, and as I sincerely believe, 'good parenting involves giving minors as much rope as they can handle without an unacceptable risk that they will hang themselves'. ...

Balcombe LJ delivered a judgment agreeing with Lord Donaldson. The third judge, however, was more cautious.

Nolan LJ: ... The general approach adopted by the House of Lords to the weight which should be attached to the views of a child who has sufficient understanding to make an informed decision is clearly of great importance, but it is essential to bear in mind that their Lordships were concerned with the extent of parental rights over the welfare of the child. They were not concerned with the jurisdiction of the court. It is of the essence of that jurisdiction that the court has the power and the responsibility in appropriate cases to override the views of both the child and the parent in determining what is in the child's best interests. Authoritative and instructive as they are, the speeches in *Gillick's* case do not deal with the principles which should govern the exercise of this court's jurisdiction in the present case. In my judgment, those principles are to be found in section 1 of the Children Act 1989. ...

In ... the circumstances of the present case the wishes and feelings of W., considered in the light of her age and understanding, are the first of the factors to which the court must have regard, but the court must have regard also to such of the other factors as may be relevant when discharging its overall responsibility for W.'s welfare.

... I am very far from asserting any general rule that the court should prefer its own view as to what is in the best interests of the child to those of the child itself. In considering the welfare of the child, the court must not only recognise but if necessary defend the right of the child, having sufficient understanding to take an informed decision, to make his or her own choice. In most areas of life it would be not only wrong in principle but also futile and counter-productive for the court to adopt any different approach. In the area of medical treatment, however, the court can and sometimes must intervene.

... One must, I think, start from the general premise that the protection of the child's welfare implies at least the protection of the child's life. I state this only as a general and not as an invariable premise because of the possibility of cases in which the court would not authorise treatment of a distressing nature which offered only a small hope of preserving life. In general terms, however, the present state of the law is that an individual who has reached the age of 18 is free to do with his life what he wishes, but it is the duty of the court to ensure so far as it can that children survive to attain that age.

To take it a stage further, if the child's welfare is threatened by a serious and imminent risk that the child will suffer grave and irreversible mental or physical harm, then once again the court when called upon has a duty to intervene. It makes no difference whether the risk arises from the action or inaction of others, or from the action or inaction of the child. Due weight must be given to the child's wishes, but the court is not bound by them. ...

We are not directly concerned with cases in which the jurisdiction of the court has not been invoked, and in which accordingly the decision on treatment may depend upon the consent of the child or of the parent. I for my part would think it axiomatic, however, in order to avoid the risk of grave breaches of the law that in any case where time permitted, where major surgical or other procedures (such as an abortion) were proposed, and where the parents or those in loco parentis were prepared to give consent but the child (having sufficient understanding to make an informed decision) was not, the jurisdiction of the court should always be invoked. ...

Appeal dismissed with costs against Legal Aid Board. Order below varied. Leave to appeal refused.

Questions

(i)   Given what Lord Donaldson says about the girl's competence, how much of the rest of what he says is *ratio decidendi*?
(ii) Lord Donaldson points out that consent provides the 'flak jacket' against liability for administering the treatment; does it also follow that the consent of a parent or local authority with parental responsibility would provide a 'flak

jacket' against liability for holding the patient down while treatment is forcibly administered? Do you consider such a possibility fanciful? Do you consider it hair-raising?

(iii) What would you advise a doctor to do if a mother insists that her pregnant daughter (a) of 17 or (b) of 13 should have an abortion which she does not want?

(iv) What would you advise a doctor to do if a mother wanted her pregnant daughter (a) of 17 or (b) of 13 to have a caesarian section without which there was a risk that (a) the daughter or (b) the baby would die?

(v) Competent adults have a right to refuse treatment for physical illness, even if they might die as a result (see *Re C* [1994] 1 FLR 31). Where children are concerned, are you surprised that the courts are reluctant to allow this outcome, even for a child who is '*Gillick* competent'? If a child is suffering from a long-term medical condition which will require blood transfusions to which the child has religious objections, should the court keep the child alive until his 18th birthday, and then allow him to die?

(vi) On the other hand, under the Mental Health Act 1983 patients may be detained and treated for their mental disorders without consent, whatever their age, or ability to understand. If children are treated for mental disorder, should they not have the same safeguards which apply to adult patients?

(vii) The Government has recently proposed that there should be new statutory safeguards to protect the interests of children receiving treatment for mental disorder (see the White Paper: *Reforming the Mental Health Act* (2000) Cm. 5016-I, paras. 2.35–2.41, 3.67–3.72). In particular, it was suggested that the ability of parents to authorise the compulsory psychiatric treatment of 16- and 17-year-olds would be removed. Does it make sense to remove the power of parents to authorise psychiatric treatment for mentally disordered 16-year-olds, but retain their ability to consent to treatment of competent 16- and 17-year-olds for physical disorders? Would it be better to restrict parental authority once the child achieves sufficient understanding, rather than when he or she reaches a particular age?

Besides using mental health legislation to detain children, s. 25 of the Children Act 1989, 'Use of accommodation for restricting liberty', provides an alternative mechanism:

(1) Subject to the following provisions of this section, a child who is being looked after by a local authority may not be placed, and, if placed, may not be kept, in accommodation provided for the purpose of restricting liberty ('secure accommodation') unless it appears—
(a) that—
(i) he has a history of absconding and is likely to abscond from any other description of accommodation; and
(ii) if he absconds, he is likely to suffer significant harm; or
(b) that if he is kept in any other description of accommodation he is likely to injure himself or other persons.
(2) ...
(3) It shall be the duty of a court hearing an application under this section to determine whether any relevant criteria for keeping a child in secure accommodation are satisfied in his case.
(4) If a court determines that any such criteria are satisfied, it shall make an order authorising the child to be kept in secure accommodation and specifying the maximum period for which he may be so kept.

The next case considers whether this provision is compatible with the child's rights, under the Human Rights Act 1998.

Re K (a child) (secure accommodation order: right to liberty)
[2001] Fam 377, [2001] 2 All ER 719, [2001] 1 FCR 249, Court of Appeal

The child concerned was a 15-year-old boy, who had been showing disturbed behaviour since the age of two. Assessments suggested that he had learning difficulties, but that he was not mentally ill. In view of his aggressive and sexualised behaviour, he was considered to be extremely dangerous to other children, and also to staff involved in his care. A series of secure accommodation orders had been granted allowing the local authority to place him in accommodation for the purpose of restricting his liberty. The child argued that the secure accommodation order was incompatible with his right to liberty under Art. 5(1) of the European Convention on Human Rights. He sought damages and a certificate of incompatibility under s. 4(2) of the Human Rights Act 1998.

Dame Elizabeth Butler-Sloss P: ...
14.   [Article 5 of the European Convention on Human Rights] 'Right to liberty and security' states:

'1. Everyone has the right to liberty and security of person. No one shall be deprived of his liberty save in the following cases and in accordance with a procedure prescribed by law: (a) ... (b) ...(c) the lawful arrest or detention of a person effected for the purpose of bringing him before the competent legal authority on reasonable suspicion of having committed an offence or when it is reasonably considered necessary to prevent his committing an offence or fleeing after having done so; (d) the detention of a minor by lawful order for the purpose of educational supervision or his lawful detention for the purpose of bringing him before the competent legal authority; (e) the lawful detention of persons for the prevention of the spreading of infectious diseases, of persons of unsound mind, alcoholics or drug addicts or vagrants; (f) ...

5. Everyone who has been the victim of arrest or detention in contravention of the provisions of this Article shall have an enforceable right to compensation.'

...

20.   In the Children (Secure Accommodation) Regulations 1991, SI 1991/1505, secure accommodation is defined in para 2(1) as 'accommodation which is provided for the purpose of restricting the liberty of children to whom s 25 of the Act (use of accommodation for restricting liberty) applies'.
21.   The length of court orders is regulated by paras 11 and 12 of the regulations. The power of the local authority to keep a child in a secure unit for a maximum of 72 hours in any period of 28 days, in the absence of a court order, is to be found in para 10.

Deprivation of liberty

...

27.   It is clear that not every deprivation of liberty comes within the ambit of art 5. Parents are given a wide measure of discretion in the upbringing of their children. This was recognised by the European Court in *Nielsen*'s case, the case of a child committed to a psychiatric ward at the request of his mother. It said (11 EHRR 175 at 191–192 (para 61)):

'It should be observed at the outset that family life in the Contracting States encompasses a broad range of parental rights and responsibilities in regard to care and custody of minor children. The care and upbringing of children normally and necessarily require that the parents or an only parent decide where the child must reside and also impose, or authorise others to impose, various restrictions on the child's liberty. Thus the children in a school or other educational or recreational institution must abide by certain rules which limit their freedom of movement and their liberty in other respects. Likewise a child may have to be hospitalised for medical treatment. Family life in this sense, and especially the rights of parents to exercise parental authority over their children, having due regard to their corresponding parental responsibilities, is recognised and protected by the Convention, in particular by Article 8. Indeed the exercise of parental rights constitutes a fundamental element of family life.' (See also *T v Austria* (1990) 64 DR 176 at 180 following *Nielsen*'s case.)

28.   I recognise the force of the principles set out in the decisions in *Nielsen*'s case and *T v Austria*. There is a point, however, at which one has to stand back and say—is this within ordinary

acceptable parental restrictions upon the movements of a child or does it require justification? In *Guzzardi v Italy* (1980) 3 EHRR 333 at 362–363 (paras 92–93) the Court said:

'The Court recalls that in proclaiming the "right to liberty", paragraph 1 of Article 5 is contemplating the physical liberty of the person; its aim is to ensure that no one should be dispossessed of this liberty in an arbitrary fashion ... In order to determine whether someone has been "deprived of his liberty" within the meaning of Article 5, the starting point must be his concrete situation and account must be taken of a whole range of criteria such as the type, duration, effects and manner of implementation of the measure in question. The difference between deprivation of and restriction upon liberty is nonetheless merely one of degree or intensity, and not one of nature or substance. Although the process of classification into one or other of these categories sometimes proves to be no easy task in that some borderline cases are a matter of pure opinion, the Court cannot avoid making the selection upon which the applicability or inapplicability of Article 5 depends.'

29. Applying those principles to the application of a secure accommodation order upon a young person, it is clear that the purpose of s 25, as set out in the interpretation in the regulations dependent upon it, is to restrict the liberty of the child. The application of s 25 is not dependent upon the making of a care or interim care order. A child can be the subject of a secure accommodation order in circumstances in which the local authority does not share parental responsibility with the parents. It is a benign jurisdiction to protect the child as well as others, (see *Re W (a minor) (secure accommodation)* [1994] 3 FCR 248 at 253 per Ewbank J), but it is none the less restrictive. If a parent exercised those powers by detaining a child in a similar restrictive fashion and was challenged to justify such detention, for my part, I doubt whether the general rights and responsibilities of a parent would cover such an exercise of parental authority. It might be permissible for a few days but not for nearly two years. A court, under our domestic law, would be likely to intervene. The limit of 72 hours detention imposed by statute on a local authority without court authorisation, even in the most extreme case, is in my view significant support for the argument that this is a deprivation of liberty. The requirement for a court order, and for the court to find proved the relevant criteria before the authorisation to restrict the child's liberty beyond 72 hours can be made, underlines, in my view, that this is an extreme measure.

...

32. ... I am satisfied that a secure accommodation order is a deprivation of liberty within the meaning of art 5 and requires, therefore, to come within one of the exceptions set out in art 5(1) so as not to be incompatible with K's right to liberty under the Convention.

The exceptions under art 5.

...

35. Detention under the relevant part of the exception in art 5(1)(d) must be by lawful order and for the purpose of educational supervision. On the facts of this appeal K is receiving education which is carefully supervised, from which he is clearly benefiting, even though there is criticism of the lack of sufficient therapy. The submission advanced by Miss de Haas was not that the regime was in fact unsuitable, but that educational supervision did not form part of the relevant criteria in s 25 which, she submitted, had nothing to do with education and but were designed to restrict liberty. Since the criteria did not refer to education, the section was not in keeping with art 5(1)(d).

36. It is not necessary, in my judgment, for s 25 to refer to education since, by the provisions of the Education Act 1996, education is compulsory for any child under 16, (see s 7) and optional thereafter. Consequently at the secure unit to which K was sent in December 1998, there was a statutory obligation to provide him with education.

37. The decision in *Koniarska*'s case is helpful [*Koniarska v United Kingdom* (App No 33670/96, Decision on Admissibility) (Unreported, European Court of Human Rights, 12 October 2000)]. The facts were that the applicant was 17 at the time of the secure accommodation order that was the subject of the application to the European Court. She had been diagnosed as suffering from a psychopathic disorder and there was a danger of her injuring herself or other persons. The Court found that: 'There could thus be said to be both medical and social reasons for her detention.'

38. The Court then considered the applicability of art 5(1)(d), and whether it covered her detention under a s 25 order. The Court said that the only question was whether the detention was 'for the purpose of' educational supervision. It considered the decision in *Bouamar*'s case and noted that the orders were not isolated orders for detention but were made in the context of a long history of efforts to ensure the best possible upbringing of the applicant, and that the local authority considered that the applicant needed to be placed in secure accommodation. The Court next noted that—

'... The Court considers that, in the context of the detention of minors, the words "educational supervision" must not be equated rigidly with notions of classroom teaching. In particular, in the present context of a young person in local authority care, educational supervision must embrace many aspects of the exercise, by the local authority, of parental rights for the benefit and protection of the person concerned. The Court has no doubt that the orders made by the Magistrates Courts on the 23 November 1995 and 23 February 1996, on the application of the local authority, were capable of constituting part of the "educational supervision" of the applicant. ...'

39. All the other grounds were rejected and the application was declared inadmissible. It is interesting to note that the Court did not express any criticism of the statutory framework of a secure accommodation order. It found that the circumstances in which the secure accommodation order was made were covered by art 5(1)(d). Those circumstances bear in many ways a close resemblance to the facts of this appeal. In my view, the decision in *Koniarska*'s case is determinative of this part of the appeal and it is clear that art 5(1)(d) covers the making of a secure accommodation order in respect of K.

...

43. In each case where a secure accommodation order is applied for, the English court, at any level, must have the requirements of art 5(1)(d) in mind when it is considering the relevant criteria, and thereby ensure the compatibility of the section with the Convention right.

...

I would dismiss this appeal. ...

Judge LJ agreed, stating that 'normal parental control' over the movements of a child may be exercised by the local authority over a child in its care, but that the implementation of a secure accommodation order went beyond normal parental control. However, while agreeing that the appeal should be dismissed, Thorpe LJ took a different approach:

Thorpe LJ:
50. The first issue is ... whether K has been deprived of his right to liberty guaranteed by art 5(1). As a matter of first impression the answer must be yes. Secure accommodation is defined in the section itself as 'accommodation provided for the purpose of restricting liberty'. However the order authorising the restriction of K's liberty was made on the ground that, if kept in any other accommodation, he was likely to injure himself or other persons.

51. Thus the primary purpose of the restriction was protective, both of K and of others. The secondary purpose was corrective, to enable trained and skilled professionals to teach K to modify his anti-social tendencies. There is no punitive purpose or element. ....

...

53. ... [P]lainly not all restrictions placed on the liberty of children constitute deprivation. Obviously parents have a right and a responsibility to restrict the liberty of their children, not only for protective and corrective purposes, but also sometimes for a punitive purpose. So acting they only risk breaching a child's art 5(1) rights if they exceed reasonable bounds. Equally parents may delegate that right and responsibility to others. Every parent who sends a child to a boarding school delegates to the head teacher and his staff. A local authority may even send a child to a school that provides 52 week boarding facilities. Then restrictions on liberty imposed by the school do not amount to a breach of the pupil's rights under art 5(1) unless the school betrays its responsibilities to the family.

54. This reality is, it seems, well recognised in European based law. As was said in *Nielsen v Denmark* (1988) 11 EHRR 175 at 191–192 (para 61):

'The care and upbringing of children normally and necessarily require that the parents or an only parent decide where the child must reside and also impose, or authorise others to impose, various restrictions on the child's liberty. Thus the children in a school or other educational or recreational institution must abide by certain rules which limit their freedom of movement and their liberty in other respects. Likewise a child may have to be hospitalised for medical treatment. Family life in this sense, and especially the rights of parents to exercise parental authority over their children, having due regard to their corresponding parental responsibilities, is recognised and protected by the Convention, in particular by Article 8. Indeed the exercise of parental rights constitutes a fundamental element of family life.'

...

60. ... the restriction on K's liberty is the consequence of a professional judgment as to what sort of accommodation best meets his needs, a judgment subsequently scrutinised and approved by a judge in accordance with the statutory requirement.

61. For these reasons I accept ... that the order of 30 June did not breach K's art 5 rights since the deprivation of liberty was a necessary consequence of an exercise of parental responsibility for the protection and promotion of his welfare.

Questions

(i) What restrictions on a child's liberty would you consider to be within 'normal parental authority'? Should a father be able to prevent his daughter leaving the house, in order to stop her from meeting her boyfriend, or if he is concerned that she is taking drugs, or if he wants her to finish her homework? Practically, how could he prevent her leaving? Would your answers differ if she was 11, 15 or 17 years old? Is it reasonable to expect a father to obtain a court order if he wants to restrict his child's liberty?

(ii) At the end of her judgment in *Re K*, Dame Elizabeth Butler-Sloss P commented on the way in which the child had been given an opportunity to take part in the proceedings:

Having been assessed as having a mental age of eight, one might raise an eyebrow at his ability to give instructions and his separate representation at various proceedings including before this court. But there is no doubt that it has been very beneficial for him to be allowed to play a part, and to have some understanding of the legal procedures which have the effect of depriving him of his liberty. I should like to commend the local authority for its careful, conscientious and sensitive approach to this very difficult case and to ensuring that K has been able to play such a full part in it.

Does this suggest that there are other rights at stake when courts make decisions about a child? For example, is it necessary to consider whether the child has a right to participate by virtue of Art. 6 of the European Convention (right to a fair trial) or Art. 12 of the United Nations Convention on the Rights of the Child (see p. 484, below)? Are there any risks involved in allowing children to participate in legal proceedings?

The Children Act 1989 allows the child to make applications about his own care and upbringing. Usually he must first have leave.

Re SC (a minor) (leave to seek residence order)
[1994] 1 FLR 96, [1993] Fam Law 618, High Court, Family Division

S was a 14-year-old girl who had been in the care of a local authority under a care order for eight years. She was living in a children's home and wanted to apply for an order that she should live with a friend's family who were willing to provide her with a home. The local authority did not know whether they would oppose the eventual application but did not oppose letting her apply; her mother opposed the application for leave.

Booth J: ... Mr Petrou, the solicitor instructed by S and who has presented the application on her behalf, submitted that the first test which must be satisfied is that contained in s. 10(8) of the Act. Section 10(8) provides:

'Where the person applying for leave to make an application for a section 8 order is the child concerned, the court may only grant leave if it is satisfied that he has sufficient understanding to make the proposed application for the section 8 order.'

S approached Mr Petrou of her own initiative in February 1993. She has given him clear instructions and he assesses her to have a good understanding of the situation. She does not suffer from any psychiatric or mental disability. The issues to which the substantive application would give rise are not complex, and the mother does not contend that S could not properly deal with them.

In the circumstances I am satisfied that the child does have sufficient understanding to enable the court to grant her leave to make the application. It does not, however, follow that the court is bound to grant leave once the test of s. 10(8) is satisfied. The court still has a discretion whether or not to do so. Where the application is made by a child, no guidance is to be found in the Act or in the rules as to the matters which should be taken into account in the exercise of this discretion. Where the person applying for leave is not the child, s. 10(9) lists the matters to which the court must have particular regard. No equivalent check-list exists in the case of an application by the child.

Mr Petrou makes two submissions. First, he submits that the court must be satisfied that the application for a s.8 order might reasonably succeed. Such a test is analogous to that applied by the court in deciding whether to grant leave for an adoption application to be made in respect of a ward of court: see *F v S (Adoption: Ward)* [1973] Fam 203, CA. ...

I accept that submission. In my judgment it is right for the court to have regard to the likelihood of success of the proposed application and to be satisfied that the child is not embarking upon proceedings which are doomed to failure.

Secondly, Mr Petrou submits that the application for leave made by a child gives rise to a question with respect to the upbringing of the child and accordingly s. 1 of the Act applies. It would then follow that not only must the court have regard to the child's welfare as its paramount consideration, but that it must also have regard to the matters set out in the check-list in s. 1(3).

That submission I am unable to accept. In *Re A (Minors) (Residence Order: Leave to Apply)* [1992] Fam 182, [1992] 2 FLR 154. ... Balcombe LJ said (at pp. 191G and 160D respectively):

'In granting or refusing an application for leave to apply for a s. 8 order, the court is not determining a question with respect to the upbringing of the child concerned. That question only arises when the court hears the substantive application. The reasoning of this court in *F v S (Adoption: Ward)* [above] supports this conclusion.'

... Mr Brasse, on behalf of the mother, opposes the application on a number of grounds. He submits, first, that a child should not be permitted to apply for a residence order but that, as a matter of principle, the person in whom parental responsibility would vest under the order should make the application. If that person was not entitled to apply, he would have to seek leave to do so. On that application the court would then be bound to apply what Mr Brasse submits is the more stringent test of s.10(9) of the Act and to have regard, among the other matters set out in that subsection, both to the local authority's plans for the child's future as well as to the wishes and feelings of the child's parents.

Mr Brasse submits that the court should not permit that more stringent test to be by-passed by allowing the child concerned, to whom it does not apply, to make the application instead.

... In my judgment the court should not fetter the statutory ability of the child to seek any s. 8 order, including a residence order, if it is appropriate for such an application to be made. Although the court will undoubtedly consider why it is that the person in whose favour a proposed residence order would be made is not applying, it would in my opinion be wrong to import into the Act any requirement that only he or she should make the application.

The second ground on which Mr Brasse relies is founded upon the fact that since Mrs B is a friend of S, the local authority is bound to consider her as a carer in accordance with the duty imposed upon them by s. 23(6)(*b*) of the Act. Despite the fact that she has already been considered and rejected as a carer the local authority are in the process of carrying out a further assessment and are thereby fulfilling their statutory duty. The local authority are under a duty to safeguard and promote S's welfare. In those circumstances, Mr Brasse submits, it is unnecessary and inappropriate for an application to be made for a residence order in favour of Mrs B. The decision whether or not it is in S's interests to live with Mrs B should be left to the local authority.

Although, again, those clearly are factors to be taken into account by the court on the issue of granting leave to S, I do not consider that they are determinative of it. They must be balanced against other circumstances which include the length of time S has been in care, the fact that in care she has not had settled accommodation and her wish now to live with and be cared for by Mrs B, a wish to which the court is statutorily bound to have regard whereas the local authority is not. I think that it may safely be assumed by the court that a child of S's age will, understandably, prefer to have parental responsibility for her vested in a trusted friend, if not a parent, rather than to be subject to a care order with parental responsibility vested in a local authority. It is also a matter for consideration that the local authority do not take the point themselves and remain neutral on the application. I do not, therefore, think that this argument should stand in the way of leave being granted to S.

These are not the only circumstances in which a child may become a party to proceedings; she may be allowed to make an application about another child, for example, for contact with a sibling who is living with another family; or she may be joined as a party in proceedings between her parents about her own future; or she may be a respondent to proceedings brought by others about her own child; mainly because of the last situation, the Family Proceedings Rules 1991, r. 9.2A make an exception to the usual rules about child parties to litigation.

Re T (a minor) (child: representation)
[1994] Fam 49, [1993] 4 All ER 518, sub nom Re CT (a minor) [1993] 2 FLR 278, Court of Appeal

T was a 13-year-old girl who had been adopted at the age of seven but now wanted to resume her links with her birth family and live with her birth mother's sister. She was given leave to apply for a residence order and a solicitor agreed to represent her without a 'next friend'. Her adoptive parents were strongly opposed to her application and instituted wardship proceedings. The judge made her a ward of court and appointed the Official Solicitor as her guardian ad litem in those proceedings. T appealed against the imposition of a guardian to conduct the case for her.

Waite LJ: ...

2. The child as a party generally
Family proceedings are in general subject to the ordinary rules of disability, applying to all civil proceedings, which prevent a minor from bringing or defending any proceedings except by a next friend or guardian ad litem (as the case may be): see RSC Ord 80, r 2 and the Family Proceedings Rules 1991, SI 1991/1247, r 9.2. A next friend or guardian does not in those circumstances act merely as the child's representative. He has an independent function to perform, and must act in what he believes to be the minor's best interests, even if that should involve acting in contravention of the wishes of a minor who is old enough to articulate views of his own: see the authorities cited in the notes to RSC Ord 80, r 2 in *The Supreme Court Practice 1993* vol 1, paras 80/2/1-80/2/16. Those functions can be performed by anyone who has no interest in the proceedings ...: there is no need for a next friend or guardian ad litem in private law proceedings to be professionally qualified, or even a member of the panel of guardians recruited to discharge the public law functions established by s. 41 of the Children Act 1989. In practice, however, problems of representation and legal aid make it difficult for a lay person to act, and in the majority of private law cases the child's next friend or guardian ad litem will be the Official Solicitor, whose department has unrivalled experience in dealing with the problems to which such proceedings are apt to give rise. In function, however, he does not differ at all from any other next friend or guardian ad litem. He owes a loyalty which has by its very nature to be divided: to the child whose views he must fully and fairly represent; and to the court, which it is his duty to assist in achieving the overriding or paramount objective of promoting the child's best interests.

An exception to that long-established principle has been introduced, uniquely, into family law by r 9.2A of the 1991 rules (as amended by SI 1992/456) in certain specified instances. Those are: (1) where the court has given leave at the outset for a minor to begin or defend proceedings without a next friend or guardian ad litem. Such leave is only to be granted if the court considers that 'the minor concerned has sufficient understanding to participate as a party in the proceedings ... without a next friend or guardian ad litem' (r 9.2A(1)(a) and (6)). (2) Where a minor has a next friend or guardian ad litem in proceedings that are already on foot and applies successfully for leave to prosecute or defend the remaining stages of the proceedings without a next friend or guardian ad litem. Leave for that purpose is only to be granted if the court reaches the same conclusion as in case (1) (r 9.2A(4) and (6)). (3) Where a solicitor has accepted instructions from the minor to act in the proceedings, and where that solicitor 'considers that the minor is able, having regard to his understanding, to give instructions in relation to the proceedings' (r 9.2A(1)(*b*)(i) and (ii)).

3. *The child's 'understanding'*
This is a factor expressly to be considered by the court when considering whether to grant leave to apply under s.10(8) of the 1989 Act, and also when considering whether to grant leave to initiate or continue proceedings without a next friend or guardian ad litem under cases (1) and (2) above. It is also a factor expressly to be considered by the solicitor in considering whether to accept instructions in case (3). No definition of 'understanding' is attempted by the 1989 Act or the 1991 rules, but guidance was offered by this court in *Re S (a minor) (independent representation)* [1993] Fam 263 at 276, [1993] 3 All ER 36 at 43-44, where Sir Thomas Bingham MR said:

> 'Different children have differing levels of understanding at the same age. And understanding is not absolute. It has to be assessed relatively to the issues in the proceedings. Where any sound judgment on these issues calls for insight and imagination which only maturity and experience can bring, both the court and the solicitor will be slow to conclude that the child's understanding is sufficient.'

...

(1) Was the judge justified in directing or authorising the use of wardship proceedings – whether as a means of introducing the Official Solicitor or for any other reason?
No one aware of the facts of this case could fail to sympathise with T., who must feel herself prey to torn loyalties and is clearly in need of all the help that can be given to her, or with the adoptive parents, who have shown her love and kindness and are still ready to offer her a permanent and loving home. It is thoroughly understandable, in such circumstances, that the judge should have wished to provide T. with the most objective representation and the most appropriate medical assessment that could be devised for her, and should have favoured the involvement of the Official Solicitor as her guardian ad litem as being an appropriate means to that end. It may even be fairly said that in placing this vulnerable child under the protection of a prerogative jurisdiction of great antiquity, which until the coming into force of the 1989 Act had become refined by the courts into an effective instrument for achieving continuity and flexibility in judicial supervision of child care procedures, the court was giving her, in juridical terms, the most favourable treatment possible.
    The arguments [of counsel] have persuaded me, however, that the judge was wrong to have invoked the wardship jurisdiction. Rule 9.2A(1) gives T. exactly the same rights in wardship as she enjoys in proceedings under Pt II of the 1989 Act. Provided the conditions of that paragraph are satisfied, she can bring or defend wardship proceedings without a next friend or guardian ad litem, and the court would have no power to impose one upon her against her will. If, therefore, the judge believed that wardship provided a means of requiring T. to accept a guardian ad litem, he was mistaken. If he thought that wardship would secure for her, or for the adoptive parents, any advantage not available in ordinary family proceedings under Pt II of the 1989 Act, he was mistaken in that respect also. ...
Appeal allowed. Leave to appeal to the House of Lords refused.

Questions

(i)   Is the understanding required to make an application about yourself the same as the understanding required to conduct the proceedings by yourself?
(ii) What would you do about (a) an 11-year-old boy who wanted to instruct his own lawyer in a bitterly contested dispute between his parents (as in *Re S (a minor) (independent representation)* [1993] Fam 263, [1993] 3 All ER 36, CA); (b) a 12-year-old girl who had run away from home after an argument with her mother and wanted to live with her boyfriend's parents?
(iii) If a brother and sister are living in separate households, and the sister is seeking contact with her brother, whose welfare would be paramount: the applicant, the child who is the subject of the application, or should the court be required to balance their interests? (See *Re S (Contact: Application by Sibling)* [1998] 2 FLR 897.)

(iv) If a child is conducting the proceedings himself, should he be in court like any other party?

(v) In public law proceedings (see Children Act 1989, s. 41) a child of sufficient understanding will have a professional social worker as a 'child's guardian' who must represent his best interests and a solicitor who must represent his views if these are different (see Family Proceedings Rules 1991, rr. 4.11, 4.12): why is this system not adopted in private law proceedings?

(vi) How would you go about deciding whether what a child wanted was in his best interests?

In 'The Emergence of Children's Rights' (1986), John Eekelaar discusses the concept of children's rights, and distinguishes three different kinds of interest they may have:

We may accept that the *social perception* that an individual or class of individuals has certain interests is a precondition to the conceptualization of rights. But these interests must be capable of isolation from the interests of others. I might believe that it is in my infant daughter's interests that I (and not she) take decisions concerning her medical welfare. This may even be supportable by objective evidence. But my interest, or right, to take such decisions is not identical with her interests. I might make stupid or even malicious decisions. Her interest is that I should make the best decisions for her. I am no more than the agent for fulfilling her interests. Hence we should be careful to understand that when we talk about rights as protecting interests, we conceive as interests only those benefits which the subject himself or herself might plausibly claim in themselves. This point is of great importance in the context of modern assertions of the right to parental autonomy. This has been advanced as a fuller enhancement of children's rights. Goldstein, Freud and Solnit [see p. 462, above] construct the concept of 'family integrity' which is a combination of 'the three liberty interests of direct concern to children, parental autonomy, the right to autonomous parents and privacy'. But can we say the children might plausibly claim any of these things in themselves? If they are claimed (which they may be) it will be because they are believed to advance other desirable ends (perhaps material and emotional stability) which are the true objects of the claims. Observe that the formulation refers to claims children might plausibly make. Not, be it noted, what they actually claim. We here meet the problem that children often lack the information or ability to appreciate what will serve them best. It is necessary therefore to make some kind of imaginative leap and guess what a child might retrospectively have wanted once it reaches a position of maturity. In doing this, values of the adult world and of individual adults will inevitably enter. This is not to be deplored, but openly accepted. It encourages debate about these values. There are, however, some broad propositions which might reasonably be advanced as forming the foundation of any child's (retrospective) claims. General physical, emotional and intellectual care within the social capabilities of his or her immediate caregivers would seem a minimal expectation. We may call this the 'basic' interest. What a child should expect from the wider community must be stated more tentatively. I have elsewhere [Eekelaar, 1984] suggested the formulation that, within certain overriding constraints, created by the economic and social structure of society (whose extent must be open to debate), all children should have an equal opportunity to maximize the resources available to them during their childhood (including their own inherent abilities) so as to minimize the degree to which they enter adult life affected by avoidable prejudices incurred during childhood. In short, their capacities are to be developed to their best advantage. We may call this the 'developmental' interest. The concept requires some elaboration.

It seems plausible that a child may expect society at large, no less than his parents, to ensure that he is no worse off than most other children in his opportunities to realize his life-chances. Could a child also plausibly claim that he should be given a *better* chance than other children, for example, by exploitation of his superior talents or a favoured social position? As an expectation addressed to the child's parents, such a claim might have some weight. A child of rich parents might retrospectively feel aggrieved if those resources were not used to provide him with a better chance in life than other children. On the other hand, such an expectation is less plausibly addressed to society at large, except perhaps with respect to the cultivation of singular talents. But from the point of view of a theory of rights, it does not much matter whether we decide that a privileged child has an interest in inequality favourable to himself. For, if the interest is to become a right, it must be acknowledged in the public domain as demanding protection for its own sake. As far as the 'developmental' interest is concerned, therefore, societies may choose to actualize it in harmony with their overall social goals, which may (but not necessarily) involve creating equality of opportunity and reducing socially determined inequalities, but encouraging diversity of achievement related to individual talent.

There is a third type of interest which children may, retrospectively, claim. A child may argue for the freedom to choose his own lifestyle and to enter social relations according to his own inclinations uncontrolled by the authority of the adult world, whether parents or institutions. Claims of this kind have been put forward on behalf of children by Holt (1975) and by Farson (1978). We may call them the 'autonomy' interest. Freeman (1983) has argued that such interests might be abridged insofar as children also have a right to be protected against their own inclinations if their satisfaction would rob them of the opportunity 'to mature to a rationally autonomous adulthood ... capable of deciding on [their] own system of ends as free and rational beings'. This may be no more than a version of the developmental interest defined earlier. The problem is that a child's autonomy interest may conflict with the developmental interest and even the basic interest. While it is possible that some adults retrospectively approve that they were, when children, allowed the exercise of their autonomy at the price of putting them at a disadvantage as against other children in realizing their life-chances in adulthood, it seems improbable that this would be a common view. We may therefore rank the autonomy interests subordinate to the basic and the developmental interests. However, where they may be exercised without threatening these two interests, the claim for their satisfaction must be high.

'Basic' interests are served by care proceedings, now under s. 31 of the Children Act 1989 (p. 719, below):

... the statute does not confer rights to be free of deprivations suffered by parents which are reflected on the children. But it does, as applied in practice, seem to give children rights to be removed from the adverse consequences of care by parents who suffer social or personal inadequacy. The imposition of these duties is primarily perceived by the enforcement agencies as directed at advancing the interests of the rightholders, and represents a total reversal of earlier characterizations of the child-parent relationship. This reflects not only the social recognition of the basic interests of the rightholders as ends in themselves, but also a societal decision of the priority to be applied where those interests conflict with the interests of others, in this case, the parents.

'Developmental' interests present more problems:

When we turn to the developmental interests, there is more difficulty. The requirement to allocate resources so that an individual child does not suffer such deprivations during childhood that he is disadvantaged disproportionately, when compared to children generally, in the outset of his or her adult life, can for a large part be met only by the community at large. The cost appears in such areas as children's medical services and education. The duties lie primarily in the political domain and therefore become enmeshed in still broader considerations of public policy. Their legal articulation is at a very broad level of generality. ...

While children are resident with their parents, the law imposes no duty on the parents to fulfil the developmental interests, apart from ensuring their education. However we may justify it, the developmental interest for the vast majority of children is not protected as a right, but owes its satisfaction to the natural workings of the economies of families which are themselves dependent on the wider social and economic mechanisms of the community. Where, however, the family is split apart, the regulation of the distribution of resources between the families is thrown into the public domain. Failure to ensure some such distribution carries the risk of visible impoverishment of the mother and child, with attendant threats to social stability and community welfare funds. The developmental interests of children are also threatened in these circumstances, so it is of interest to discover how far the legal regulation of income distribution after family separation can be characterized as the protection of that interest. ...

Finally, he discusses the autonomy interest in the light of *Gillick*:

... Of the nine judges who gave a decision in this litigation, five were in favour of the plaintiff. This perhaps illustrates the ambiguity in current perceptions of the proper scope of children's autonomy interests. But the majority decision of the House of Lords has implications which extend beyond the parent-child relationship and into the scope of state power over the lives of children themselves. ...

The significance of Lord Scarman's opinion with respect to children's autonomy interests cannot be over-rated. It follows from his reasoning that, where a child has reached capacity, there is no room for a parent to impose a contrary view, *even if this is more in accord with the child's best interests.* For its legal superiority to the child's decision can rest only on its status as a parental right. But this is extinguished when the child reaches full capacity. ...

This recognition of the autonomy interests of children can be reconciled with their basic and developmental interests only through the empirical application of the concept of the acquisition of full capacity. This, as Lord Scarman made clear, may be no simple matter. The child must not only understand the nature of the transaction, but be able to evaluate its implications. Intellectual understanding must be supplemented by emotional maturity. It is easy to see how adults can conclude that a child's decision which seems, to the adult, to be contrary to his interests, is lacking in sufficient maturity. In this respect, the provision of the simple test of age to provide an upper limit to the scope of a supervisory, paternalistic power has advantages. We cannot know for certain whether, retrospectively, a person may not regret that some control was not exercised over his immature judgment by persons with greater experience. But could we not say that it is on balance better to subject all persons to this potential inhibition up to a defined age, in case the failure to exercise the restraint unduly prejudices a person's basic or developmental interests? It avoids judgments in which questions of fact and value will be impenetrably mixed. But the decision, it seems, has been taken. Children will now have, in wider measure than ever before, that most dangerous but most precious of rights: the right to make their own mistakes.

Questions

(i)   Where does the child's 'autonomy interest' now stand in the light of *Re W (a minor) (medical treatment: court's jurisdiction)* [1993] Fam 64, [1992] 4 All ER 627, CA (p. 470, above)?

(ii)   Might not recognising the child's 'autonomy interest' itself be a means of recognising his 'basic' and 'developmental' interests? (See, for example, Adler and Dearling (1986).)

(iii) To what extent would you give priority to any of these interests if they conflicted with those of adults?

(iv) Eekelaar acknowledges the political implications of society recognising the developmental interests of children: how far is it possible to go in a democracy?

(v)   'Is it not almost a self-evident axiom that the state should require and compel the education, up to a certain standard, of every human being who is born its citizen?' (Mill, 1859.)

(vi) The European Convention on Human Rights, Protocol 1, Art. 2 (see further p. 593, below) requires:

No person shall be denied the right to education. In the exercise of any functions which it assumes in relation to education and to teaching, the state shall respect the right of parents to ensure such education and teaching in conformity with their own religious and philosophical convictions.

Would you consider it a breach of this article: (a) to impose a national curriculum including evolution within its compulsory science teaching upon children of a family who believed in the literal truth of the book of Genesis (probably not: *Kjeldsen, Busk Madsen and Pedersen v Denmark* Applications 5095/71, 5920/72 and 5926/72 (1976) 1 EHRR 711); (b) to use corporal punishment to enforce school rules, contrary to the philosophical convictions of the parents (definitely: see *Campbell and Cosans v United Kingdom* Series A, No. 48, (1982) 4 EHRR 293); (c) to enforce a compulsory school leaving age of 16 against children whose parents believed that education over 14 would prejudice their upbringing in the Amish way of life (probably not: but see *Wisconsin v Yoder* 406 US 205 (1972))?

(vii) Is this article protecting the rights of the child or the rights of the parents?

(viii)   What happens if a child with special educational needs wants to go to a special school but his parents want him to go to an ordinary school or vice versa?

So far, we have been concentrating on the development of children's rights from the perspective of domestic law, and under the European Convention on Human Rights. However, there is another important international document in relation to children's rights which we need to consider.

10.4 The UN Convention on the Rights of the Child

The Convention on the Rights of the Child was adopted by the United Nations General Assembly on 20 November 1989 and came into force on 2 September 1990. There are only two countries in the world which are not parties to the convention (the United States of America and Somalia), although in some instances there are significant reservations. It has three overriding themes: the child's best interests; respect for the child's evolving capacities; and protection against all forms of discrimination. The UK Government ratified the Convention in December 1991. It made reservations, as we shall see.

Philip Alston and Stephen Parker in their introductory essay to *Children, Rights and the Law* (1992) point to the extraordinary commitment to the convention:

No other treaty, particularly in the human rights field, has been ratified by so many states in such an extraordinarily short period of time. The Convention has thus generated an unprecedented degree of formal commitment on the part of Governments and the task confronting children's rights advocates will be to ensure that this commitment is matched by action.

There are 54 Articles in the Convention. The following Articles are four of the most important:

Article 3
1. In all actions concerning children, whether undertaken by public or private social welfare institutions, courts of law, administrative authorities or legislative bodies, the best interests of the child shall be a primary consideration.
2. States Parties undertake to ensure the child such protection and care as is necessary for his or her well-being, taking into account the rights and duties of his or her parents, legal guardians, or other individuals legally responsible for him or her, and, to this end, shall take all appropriate legislative and administrative measures.
...

Article 9
1. States Parties shall ensure that a child shall not be separated from his or her parents against their will, except when competent authorities subject to judicial review determine, in accordance with applicable law and procedures, that such separation is necessary for the best interests of the child. Such determination may be necessary in a particular case such as one involving abuse or neglect of the child by the parents, or one where the parents are living separately and a decision must be made as to the child's place of residence.
...
3. States Parties shall respect the right of the child who is separated from one or both parents to maintain personal relations and direct contact with both parents on a regular basis, except if it is contrary to the child's best interests.

Article 12
1. States Parties shall assure to the child who is capable of forming his or her own views the right to express those views freely in all matters affecting the child, the views of the child being given due weight in accordance with the age and maturity of the child.

Article 18

1. States Parties shall use their best efforts to ensure recognition of the principle that both parents have common responsibilities for the upbringing and development of the child. Parents or, as the case may be, legal guardians, have the primary responsibility for the upbringing and development of the child. The best interests of the child will be their basic concern.

Questions

(i)   Keep these articles in mind as we look at the provisions and implementation of the Children Act 1989, especially in Chapters 12 and 13. Do you think that English law falls short of or goes beyond the principles laid down in these articles?

(ii)   Are there any dangers in a project which attempts to set out universal norms, and if so, what do you suppose these dangers to be?

(iii) Bettina Cass (1992) states that the convention disaggregates the rights of children from the rights of 'families', to constitute children as independent actors with rights vis-à-vis their parents and vis-à-vis the state. She goes on to say that 'the very crux of the conservative ideology of family as unified, private and inviolate is exposed' by the convention. Is that your view of a conservative ideology of the family? Is the convention undermining any such ideology?

(iv) Why do you think the United States of America has not ratified the convention? (See Kilbourne, 'The wayward Americans – why the USA has not ratified the UN Convention on the Rights of the Child' (1998)). Might the material in section 2 of this chapter provide an answer?

There is a growing literature about the convention. Some of this has been labelled 'feminist' and Francis Olsen (1992) discusses four different approaches in this literature. The first view, labelled by her as 'Legal Reformist', focuses on a doctrinal examination of the convention to determine how it might be interpreted to benefit women. The second approach she calls 'Law as Patriarchy', which she sees as a document in a move toward a fuller, more feminist view of rights. The third approach is the 'Feminist Critical Legal Theory' and the fourth approach is 'Post-Modern Feminism'. These last two share much in common, but the emphasis is different:

REFORMIST APPROACHES

Legal reformist is a broad category in which I intend to include probably most feminist lawyers and liberal legal scholars. The important shared view is that the current inequality between men and women could be changed by allowing women to enjoy the privileges currently all too much reserved to men. Some legal reformists would also like to see other societal changes, but the identifying characteristic is that the primary goal is to include women in the existing structure, not wait until some more global change takes place, and not base hopes for improving the role and status of women on any other major changes in values, technology, social systems or economics. Law is valued for its ability to abstract from particularistic situations and provide a relatively neutral playing field on which reason and principle may prevail over the dead hand of tradition and over a wide variety of forms of illegitimate power.

   Most of the legal reforms that have improved the role and status of women have taken place within a broad liberal legal reformist perspective. While I believe it is important to be critical of this perspective, it would be foolish not to recognize both its practical value and the widespread perception that liberal reformism is the approach that works 'in the real world'. From such a perspective, rights for children, and specifically the United Nations Convention on the Rights of the Child, can be seen to have both positive and negative potentials.

Positive

Rights for women and children are usually seen as complementary, not as a zero sum game. The patriarchal family is generally understood to have denied rights to both women and children.

The problem with the ideology of liberal rights is often seen to be that it is too limited in that it too often provides only for the 'Rights of Man'. The legal and social treatment of women and of children during much of the past two or three centuries has been criticized as 'feudal'. Thus, the extension of rights to children is in one sense simply a more or less logical next step after the extension of rights to women.

Negative

Yet there are also less positive evaluations of the Convention on the Rights of the Child to be made from a feminist liberal reform perspective. One of the most significant of these concerns is whether the Convention may be used to control and confine women. Children, and the expressed interest in their welfare (expressed often by people who show no other interest in children) have often been used to control women.

...

Although the provisions making *both* parents responsible for children would seem to be generally beneficial to women, who otherwise too often wind up solely responsible for children, the provisions may also work against the interests of women as a group. It may well be that the obligations placed 'equally' upon fathers will turn out to be unenforceable as a practical matter, but that the provisions can be used by 'father's rights' groups, composed often of recently-divorced, angry and misogynistic men, to harass the women who are taking care of 'their' children. ...

LAW AS PATRIARCHY

The 'Law as Patriarchy' approach is less familiar to most people than the legal reformist approach and seems to some to make less positive contribution. Nevertheless, it is important to understand this approach and particularly to understand the critique it presents of liberal feminist legal reform. Moderate versions of the 'Law as Patriarchy' approach may play a particularly important role in dealing with children's rights issues. Just as a legal reformist approach is associated with and resonates with liberal feminism, the 'Law as Patriarchy' approach is associated with and resonates with the feminist movement referred to (especially by those who do not consider themselves part of the movement) as 'cultural feminism'.

Cultural feminists criticize legal reformist demands for women's equality with men as settling for too little. Men do not represent an adequate aspiration. The greatest problem with society is not just the suppression of women, but the suppression of the values associated with women. Indeed, the effort to achieve legal and social equality could even contribute to the devaluation and suppression of those values.

... The primary evil of 'paternalistic' behaviour toward adults is really not that it treats an adult with the kind of care and concern that would be proper toward a child. As Onora O'Neill (1992) recognizes, the claim of fatherly concern by those exercising illegitimate power over women, minorities, colonial peoples, or other oppressed groups is generally not made in good faith but is 'highly political rhetoric'. The same kind of negative, bad faith 'paternalism' that oppresses adults is just as oppressive to children.

FEMINIST CRITICAL LEGAL THEORY

A ... dimension of the public/private distinction is the dichotomy between the 'private' family or domestic world, and the 'public' commercial world. A critical examination of this distinction allows us to 'denaturalize' the family, and to recognize the contingent character of family life. The Convention on the Rights of the Child is striking in its ability to bridge over different family forms found throughout the world. Someone whose only knowledge of life on earth came from a careful reading of the Convention would be puzzled by the occasional references to 'traditional practices' and 'those responsible for children' other than parents. Throughout most of the document, one would assume that all children were born into two-parent families that look a lot like the family of my first grade reader – Dick, Jane and Baby Sally, Mom baking cookies at home, Daddy coming home from the office in a nice suit and playing with the children. Although cookie baking is clearly *productive* work, this family displays a sharp split between productive work in the market and affective life at home with the family. The family is the private haven to which Dick and Jane return from the public world of school and Daddy from the public world of work. Baby Sally and Mom stay at home, non-productive. If Sally helps bake the cookies, we all know that this is not child labour.

In the family worlds of many societies, life is not so easy and pleasant. It is not always clear when a child is being allowed to participate in the life of the community, and when the child is being exploited. The radical separation of home from work place is taken for granted, and the separation is assumed to be a good thing. The alternative possibility of making work places healthy and educational environments for children seems never to have been considered.

... The distinction between Critical Feminism and Post-Modern Feminism is not a sharp or clear division, but rather more a matter of emphasis. Each challenges both the gendering of life and law, and the claimed differences between men and women. ...

The concerns of post-modern feminism that bear most closely on the Convention on the Rights of the Child include the whole notion of a universal document to deal with all children, throughout the world; the concern that such an effort will almost inevitably result in a western-oriented document that merely purports to be universal; and, more positively, the question of the category 'child' and the status of that category.

Universal standards have serious problems, however. One such problem is that they seem to overlook particular social meanings. The social meaning of a law forbidding abortion for sex selection, for example, is very different in India than in the United States. In the United States where there is no history of gender-specific abortion nor a realistic danger of the practice, such a law serves the purpose of chipping away at the woman's right to abortion by entitling the State to harass a woman with questions regarding why she is choosing to have an abortion. At some point, it may serve to drive women to overseas or back-alley abortions. In India, the meaning is different. There amniocentesis has been used specifically to determine the sex of a foetus and if the sex is female, the pregnancy is in most instances terminated. Moreover, in India the abortion decision is all too often forced upon women by their families.

Question

Olsen ends her discussion of the literature by the remark that the convention is not a document she would have drafted and chosen to focus her energies upon. Would you have followed Olsen's advice?

In contrast to Olsen, Geraldine Van Bueren is supportive of the convention. In 'The Challenges for the International Protection of Family Members' Rights as the 21st Century approaches', in Lowe and Douglas (eds.) *Frontiers of Family Law* (1996), she develops her theme:

The Convention ... has been criticised because it appears to place duties directly on individuals, thereby confusing the nature of duties and international law. However, such criticism fails to understand that ... family responsibilities and rights are interconnected like a double helix.

She continues:

By incorporating a reference to 'all matters affecting the child' there is no longer a traditional area of exclusive parental or family decision-making. Similarly by referring to two criteria of equal value, the age and maturity of the child, States Parties do not have an unfettered discretion as to when to consider and when to ignore the views of children when children disagree with the traditional family decision-makers. Hence the participation rights of children, which are essential to child empowerment, are consistent with the ideological basis of the Convention on the Rights of the Child which is based upon the principle that children have rights which 'transcend those of the family of which they are part.'

Despite being in force less than five years articles 12 and 13 of the Convention on the Rights of the Child have already had a significant impact on domestic family legislative policies. In the United Kingdom, for example, the impact has been both in relation to the provision of information, most recently as recommended in the review of adoption provisions, and in the Children Act 1989 on the participation of children in decisions.

A third approach is taken by Michael King (1994). He suggests that both the detractors and the supporters concentrate their minds on policy and the philosophical aspects of rights for children. He offers a different analysis, known as 'autopoietical theory':

Among all the prevailing images of 'the child', it is the child-as-victim which dominates the Convention. As we move from the national to the international stage, however, it is not evil individuals who are seen as the instigators and perpetuators of crimes against children, but the generalised scourges of injustice, intolerance, inequality and failure to respect fundamental human rights and dignity. The preamble to the Convention asks us to 'bear in mind' that 'the child by reason of his physical and mental immaturity, needs special safeguards and care, including appropriate legal protection' and recognise that 'in all countries of the world there are children living in difficult conditions and such children need special consideration.' It recognises also 'the importance of international cooperation for improving the living conditions in every country, in particular in developing countries.'

What is interesting from a socio-legal perspective is that the Convention is presented to the world, not as a declaration of intent by the governments of the different countries or as a blueprint for action by United Nations agencies such as UNICEF, but as international law. ...

1.   The child shall have the right to freedom of expression; this right shall include freedom to seek, receive and impart information and ideas of all kinds. ...

... By what authority, one may well ask, have these laws or non-laws been created? Although formally legitimated by its adoption by the United Nations as an international Convention, this authority finds its origins in no court or legislature. Unlike international treaties or accords between states, its evolution owes little to the activities of state governments pursuing national or party interests. It is embedded neither within the legislation of any of the nation-states of the Convention's signatories nor in any international treaties governing political relations between these states. Rather, the Convention is the product of a Working Group of national representatives, set up by the UN Commission on Human Rights. This is not the end of the story, for it is clear that the major influence over its final form was exercised, not so much by the government delegations who were able to exercise an effective power of veto, but by the non-governmental organisations (NGOs) who attended the meetings of the *Ad Hoc* Group on the Drafting of the Convention. According to one writer, from the United Nations Centre for Human Rights in Geneva, 'The Working Group in its ten-year history ... never had a recourse to voting, since all the decisions are reached by consensus.' This meant that there was no practical distinction between those State delegations, who were accountable to their governments, and those NGOs, who were accountable for the most part to no one but themselves. According to another commentator, the *Ad Hoc* Group's influence on the Working Group increased considerably as the drafting process progressed and as its 'influence grew, its activities became more completely integrated into the Working Group process.' What did these NGOs consist of? They appear to have been a collection of 32 supranational organisations as diverse as Amnesty International and the International Association of Juvenile and Family Court Magistrates, the Bahai International Community and the International Federation of Women's Lawyers. While it is true that before it could be treated as law within individual states the Convention had to be ratified, in practice the national governments were presented with a ready-made package which they could either accept, reject or accept with reservations on the application in their territories of certain of the Articles. In the United Kingdom there was certainly no detailed debate on the contents of the Convention in Parliament and one suspects that the same was true of the vast majority of those 151 countries which have now ratified the Convention.

...The phenomenon of the campaign by adults for children's rights may seem, at first sight, a strange one. On a rather simplistic psychological level, it may be explainable by the fact that many adults who have suffered as children wish to prevent future generations from having similar experiences. More sophisticated sociological explanations have pointed to the relatively recent social construction of the parent-child relationship as a combination of strong emotional bonds with due recognition of the child's autonomy. This autonomy is sustained and given a public form through the notion of children's rights. As a philosophical and political phenomenon, the rights perspective owes much to Kantian rationality, social hygienics and liberal theories of justice. It proceeds as if children represent an oppressed group, who are likely to suffer hardship, exploitation and lack of respect for their dignity as human beings and of their capacity for self-determination. Children are, in other words, denied those rights which would, if granted, reduce their suffering and enhance their dignity and allow them to seize some control over their own lives. They have no way of achieving these objectives unless rights are granted to them. As Onora O'Neill (1992) points out, however, the logic that is relevant to the provision of rights for oppressed *adult* groups – that the notion of rights provides the necessary capacity and rhetoric for such groups to exert the necessary 'pressure from below' and so improve their situation – does not apply or applies only to a limited degree to children. 'Childhood,' she explains, 'is a stage of life from which children normally emerge and are helped and urged to emerge by those who have power over them. Those with power over children's lives usually have some interest in ending childish dependence. Oppressors usually have an interest in maintaining the oppression of social groups.

Therefore, she argues, 'The analogy between children's dependence and that of oppressed groups is suspect.' ... The introduction into international law of the 'manifesto rights' or 'dignified statements' about interests of and 'pious hopes' for children is clearly seen by the promoters of the Convention as the first stage in a process of taking children's rights seriously. It is certainly true that the Convention is likely to have the effect of drawing the attention of governments and the mass media of post-industrial Western societies to the needs of children as a weak, vulnerable and sensitive group and to the harms that they may suffer if those needs are not met.

It is no startling conclusion to suggest that at the level of international law the mechanisms do not exist to force governments to comply with the demands which may involve the massive redeployment of resources and major changes in policy. Nor is it particularly surprising if we find that, at the level of individual states, campaigns for substantive rights for children may become obstructed by government inertia, poverty or indifference. What autopoietic theory is able to add, however, is the image of demands for substantive rights for children being reconstructed as legal communications which governments are then able to respond to and operate upon within the closed system of law and so avoid the complexities and, at times, embarrassment that these demands generate.

Reconstructing children's rights as law has the additional advantage for governments and the United Nations of giving the impression that something is being done for the children of the world. In its communications, the legal system provides society with an image of law as capable of providing order and structure in an unruly and disordered world. The United Nations in its Convention on the Rights of the Child offers us a vision of a three-tiered hierarchy consisting of international law at the top, state law in the middle, and those national institutions, agencies and organisations concerned with child protection and welfare at the bottom. In the exhortations to national governments to 'assure,' 'promote,' 'encourage,' 'undertake,' 'provide,' 'respect,' 'use their best efforts' and 'take all appropriate legislative, social and educational measures,' and in the impressive tally of countries that have ratified the Convention, the impression is conveyed of a direct line of command (or at least strong influence), from the United Nations to nation-state to citizen. As we have seen, this impression bears little relation to any realities except those created by law.

Any false hopes generated by the Convention are nobody's fault. One cannot blame those advocates of children's rights, stirred into action by the spectacle of widespread child suffering and the powerlessness of children in the face of adult tyranny, insensitivity or indifference, for being carried away on the magic carpet of excessive optimism. It was not they who misled us into believing that the law was capable of improving children's lives by the imposition of legal order, but law itself. They were themselves misled. Their hopes arose from a genuine misreading of the nature of law and legal operations. To enter into and operate within the communicative world of law is to talk and think like a lawyer, that is to commit oneself increasingly to a belief in law's version of the social universe where political, economic and moral statements are all represented as amenable to direct legal transformation and to enforcement by law. At times when people are reeling from the uncertainties and insecurities created by global political and economic upheavals of enormous proportions law's vision of itself and of society may prove particularly attractive. To see children, the hope for the future, as protected and respected for their human attributes by an all-embracing legal order, which offers them rights, is to give the impression that the rational control of that future is within our grasp, if only we were to take seriously children's rights, now reconstructed by law, by believing in them and their magic.

Question

Which if any of these various approaches do you support? Are they inconsistent with each other?

There are important articles in the convention on immigration, refugee children, and juvenile justice.

Article 10

1. In accordance with the obligation of States Parties under article 9, paragraph 1, applications by a child or his or her parents to enter or leave a State Party for the purpose of family reunification shall be dealt with by States Parties in a positive, humane and expeditious manner.

States Parties shall further ensure that the submission of such a request shall entail no adverse consequences for the applicants and for the members of their family.

2. A child whose parents reside in different States shall have the right to maintain on a regular basis save in exceptional circumstances personal relations and direct contacts with both parents. Towards that end and in accordance with the obligation of States Parties under article 9, paragraph 1, States Parties shall respect the right of the child and his or her parents to leave any country, including their own, and to enter their own country. The right to leave any country shall be subject only to such restrictions as are prescribed by law and which are necessary to protect the national security, public order (*ordre public*), public health or morals or the rights and freedoms of others and are consistent with the other rights recognized in the present Convention.

Article 22

1. States Parties shall take appropriate measures to ensure that a child who is seeking refugee status or who is considered a refugee in accordance with applicable international or domestic law and procedures shall, whether unaccompanied or accompanied by his or her parents or by any other person, receive appropriate protection and humanitarian assistance in the enjoyment of applicable rights set forth in this Convention and in other international human rights or humanitarian instruments to which the said States are Parties.

2. For this purpose, States Parties shall provide, as they consider appropriate, cooperation in any efforts by the United Nations and other competent intergovernmental organizations or non-governmental organizations co-operating with the United Nations to protect and assist such a child and to trace the parents or other members of the family of any refugee child in order to obtain information necessary for reunification with his or her family. In cases where no parents or other members of the family can be found, the child shall be accorded the same protection as any other child permanently or temporarily deprived of his or her family environment for any reason, as set forth in the present Convention.

Article 40

1. States Parties recognize the right of every child alleged as, accused of, or recognized as having infringed the penal law to be treated in a manner consistent with the promotion of the child's sense of dignity and worth, which reinforces the child's respect for the human rights and fundamental freedoms of others and which takes into account the child's age and the desirability of promoting the child's re-integration and the child's assuming a constructive role in society.

2. To this end, and having regard to the relevant provisions of international instruments, States Parties shall, in particular, ensure that:

    (*a*) No child shall be alleged as, be accused of, or recognized as having infringed the penal law by reason of acts or omissions which were not prohibited by national or international law at the time they were committed;

    (*b*) Every child alleged as or accused of having infringed the penal law has at least the following guarantees:

        (i) to be presumed innocent until proven guilty according to law;

        (ii) to be informed promptly and directly of the charges against him or her, and if appropriate through his or her parents or legal guardian, and to have legal or other appropriate assistance in the preparation and presentation of his or her defence;

        (iii) to have the matter determined without delay by a competent, independent and impartial authority or judicial body in a fair hearing according to law, in the presence of legal or other appropriate assistance and, unless it is considered not to be in the best interest of the child, in particular, taking into account his or her age or situation, his or her parents or legal guardians;

        (iv) not to be compelled to give testimony or to confess guilt; to examine or have examined adverse witnesses and to obtain the participation and examination of witnesses on his or her behalf under conditions of equality;

        (v) if considered to have infringed the penal law, to have this decision and any measures imposed in consequence thereof reviewed by a higher competent, independent and impartial authority or judicial body according to law;

        (vi) to have the free assistance of an interpreter if the child cannot understand or speak the language used;

        (vii) to have his or her privacy fully respected at all stages of the proceedings.

3. States Parties shall seek to promote the establishment of laws, procedures, authorities and institutions specifically applicable to children alleged as, accused of, or recognized as having infringed the penal law, and in particular:

    (*a*) the establishment of a minimum age below which children shall be presumed not to have the capacity to infringe the penal law;

(*b*) whenever appropriate and desirable, measures for dealing with such children without resorting to judicial proceedings, providing that human rights and legal safeguards are fully respected.

4. A variety of dispositions, such as care, guidance and supervision orders; counselling; probation; foster care; education and vocational training programmes and other alternatives to institutional care shall be available to ensure that children are dealt with in a manner appropriate to their well-being and proportionate both to their circumstances and the offence.

Questions

(i)   Does it surprise you to be told that the UK Government has entered reservations to all three of the above articles? Why do you think it has done so?

(ii) What are the areas of family law, other than those where there are reservations, which in your opinion most fall short of the principles of the convention?

(iii) What happens if the UK Government fails to live up to its obligations under the convention?

The Children's Rights Alliance for England (CRAE) is a coalition of over 180 organisations, mainly from the voluntary sector. The following is from the 'Overview' section in its *Report to the Pre-Sessional Working Group of the Committee on the Rights of the Child* (2002):

The UK has the fourth richest economy in the world, yet 32% of our children live in relative poverty.

It is plain that government has so far failed to get to grips with its human rights obligations to children. This is not to ignore recent progress, in government policies or structures. A Children and Young People's Unit has been established, with huge potential; but in over a year the Government has said nothing about its role in ensuring the CRC is fully implemented. The Unit is championing children's participation in government and public services but still in key legislation – such as in education and family law – children have no legal right to have their views considered when decisions are made that affect them. Across the UK, we are seeing the emergence of independent watchdogs for children but the Government continues to resist the repeated calls for a children's rights commissioner for England's 11.3 million children.

The Government has committed itself to eradicating child poverty by 2019 – almost 30 years after ratifying the Convention on the Rights of the Child. Meanwhile, it refuses to reintroduce grants to enable poor families to buy essential living items such as cookers, beds and blankets. It will not bring back social security benefits for 16 and 17 year-olds; and homelessness is at an all time high, with 100,000 children living in temporary accommodation. Poor children continue to fare badly in education, they are more at risk of early death and childhood accidents, they are more susceptible to mental ill health and their neighbourhoods are hardest hit by crime.

Between one and two children die every week in England and Wales as a result of abuse and neglect (there were 77 child homicides in 1999-2000, 48% of which were babies under one).

Violence towards children is an everyday sight in English streets and supermarkets. In the mid-1990s researchers found that 52% of one year-olds were hit/smacked at least once a week by their parents. A quarter of children had been hit with an implement and over a third punished 'severely'.

A Public Inquiry into the torture and murder of eight-year-old Victoria Climbié by her aunt and aunt's partner in London in 2000 is under way. There has been widespread condemnation of the failure of our child protection system to save Victoria from such a brutal death. Yet within two months of the Inquiry opening the Government announced it would not reform the law on physical punishment. In November 2001 a Health Minister explained that the Government wanted to avoid 'heavy-handed intrusion into family life'. At the same time, it promotes zero tolerance of domestic violence between adults.

The UK has one of the worst records in Europe for locking up children – figures are 51.3% higher than a decade ago. Conditions in our young offender institutions have been described as "unacceptable in a civilised society" and 'institutionalised child abuse'. Eleven children in custody have killed themselves in the last five years. There are constant reports of children being denied access to fresh air and of going to sleep cold and hungry. Bullying is a huge concern, as is children's lack of educational provision. The Department for Education and Skills has shown that of the 5,963 boys admitted to young offender institutions during 2000/2001 37.6% had the numeracy ability of a seven year-old and 31.36% had the literacy ability of a seven year-old. Yet successive education acts have specifically excluded detained children.

The support given to asylum seeking families is discriminatory and wholly inadequate: these destitute and often desperate families are given 24% less financial assistance than other poor families and are excluded from a range of welfare services and housing support. Unaccompanied minors too often are left to fend for themselves in bed and breakfast accommodation, where they face the prospect of being 'dispersed' to a different part of the UK once they reach 18. Asylum-seeking mothers are denied milk and vitamin vouchers, even when they have HIV/AIDS and breastfeeding risks their babies' health.

Legislation permits the exclusion of disabled children from mainstream schools on the grounds of resources or the perceived needs of other children. The UK enlists the largest number of under 18s into the Armed Forces of any European state. One in ten of our children have mental health problems requiring professional help. At the end of March 2000, 70% of children in care left school with no GCSE qualifications. In 2000/01 30% of young people using a homelessness support centre in London had been in care: 47% had run away from home before their 16th birthday. Vulnerable children still have no entitlement to independent and confidential advocacy services, despite concerns about the high levels of children in need that fail to approach statutory services.

This report charts the continuing breaches in children's human rights since the Committee last examined the UK Government in 1995. We hope it will assist the Committee in its questioning of the Government, but most of all we hope it will generate outrage and then action with and for children in our country.

In 'Children's Rights and the Impact of Two International Conventions' in *Delight and Dole* (2002), Jane Fortin says this about the difficulties of enforcement of the UN Convention:

It was hoped that the obligation on ratifying countries to produce periodic reports to the UN Committee and the knowledge that they would be subjected to criticisms would encourage states to implement the UNCRC effectively. Countries are expected to be candid over any difficulties they have in reaching the standards required. Unfortunately, the overall impression created by the UK's first and second reports to the Committee on the Rights of the Child is that the Government is relatively untroubled by fear of criticism by the UN Committee. A cynic might argue that a casual approach to the UNCRC will continue until there are improved enforcement procedures. Its lack of teeth means that, in reality, it is legally unenforceable. Its impact would be strengthened significantly were enforcement procedures to be grafted on to it. This would bring the UNCRC in line with the African Charter on the Rights and Welfare of the Child, which incorporates the right of individual petition for all children. Many also consider that the Government should stop dragging its feet over establishing a post of Children's Commissioner for this country. One of his or her tasks would be to promote children's rights and ensure that Convention infringements were investigated and remedied.

Questions

(i) Do you think that the lack of effective enforcement might be one of the reasons why so many countries were prepared to sign up for the convention in the first place?

(ii) There is a Children's Commissioner for one part of the UK, as a result of s. 72 of the Care Standards Act 2000 (further provision is made by the Children's Commissioner for Wales Act 2001). The Act provides that the principal aim of the Commissioner in exercising his or her functions is to safeguard and promote the 'rights and welfare of children'. Would the rights and welfare of English children be improved by a similar appointment in England?

10.5 Parental responsibility

The Children Act 1989 uses the basic concept of 'parental responsibility', defined as follows:

3.—(1) In this Act 'parental responsibility' means all the rights, duties, powers, responsibilities and authority which by law a parent of a child has in relation to the child and his property.

(2) It also includes the rights, powers and duties which a guardian of the child's estate (appointed, before the commencement of section 5, to act generally) would have had in relation to the child and his property.

(3) The rights referred to in subsection (2) include, in particular, the right of the guardian to receive or recover in his own name, for the benefit of the child, property of whatever description and wherever situated which the child is entitled to receive or recover.

(4) The fact that a person has, or does not have, parental responsibility for a child shall not affect—

(*a*) any obligation which he may have in relation to the child (such as a statutory duty to maintain the child); or

(*b*) any rights which, in the event of the child's death, he (or any other person) may have in relation to the child's property.

...

The reasons for what might be thought a purely cosmetic change appear in the Law Commission's Report on *Guardianship and Custody* (1988):

Parental responsibility

2.4   Scattered through the statute book at present are such terms as 'parental rights and duties' or the 'powers and duties', or the 'rights and authority' of a parent. However, in our first Report on Illegitimacy we expressed the view that 'to talk of parental 'rights' is not only inaccurate as a matter of juristic analysis but also a misleading use of ordinary language.' The House of Lords, in *Gillick v West Norfolk and Wisbech Area Health Authority* [[1986] AC 112, [1985] 3 All ER 402, HL (p. 467, above)] has held that the powers which parents have to control or make decisions for their children are simply the necessary concomitant of their parental duties. To refer to the concept of 'right' in the relationship between parent and child is therefore likely to produce confusion, as that case itself demonstrated. As against third parties, parents clearly have a prior claim to look after or have contact with their child but, as the House of Lords has recently pointed out in *Re KD (A Minor) (Ward: Termination of Access)* [1988] AC 806, [1988] 1 All ER 577, HL, that claim will always be displaced if the interests of the child indicate to the contrary. The parental claim can be recognised in the rules governing the allocation of parental responsibilities, but the content of their status would be more accurately reflected if a new concept of 'parental responsibility' were to replace the ambiguous and confusing terms used at present. Such a change would make little difference in substance but it would reflect the everyday reality of being a parent and emphasise the responsibilities of all who are in that position. ...

2.5   One further advantage is that the same concept could then be employed to define the status of local authorities when children have been compulsorily committed to their care. The reports of the inquiries into the deaths of Jasmine Beckford and Tyra Henry indicate how helpful this would be in emphasising the continuing parental responsibility of the local authority even if the child has been allowed to live at home.

(a) The scope of parental responsibility

2.6   The concept of 'parental responsibility' can be defined by reference to all the incidents, whether rights, claims, duties, powers, responsibilities or authority, which statute and common law for the time being confer upon parents. It would be superficially attractive to provide a list of these but those who responded to our Working Paper on Guardianship recognised the practical impossibility of doing so. The list must change from time to time to meet differing needs and circumstances. As the *Gillick* case itself demonstrated, it must also vary with the age and maturity of the child and the circumstances of each individual case.

2.7   Three points should, however, be made clear. First, the incidents of parenthood with which we are concerned are those which relate to the care and upbringing of a child until he grows up. This does include some power to administer the child's property on his behalf but it does not include the right to succeed to the child's property on his death (which will almost always be without leaving a will because children under 18 can only make wills in very exceptional circumstances). The right to succeed is a feature of being related to the deceased in a particular way and operates irrespective of who has responsibility for bringing him up. ...

2.8   Secondly, it might also be helpful to clarify the nature and extent of a parent's powers to administer or deal with a child's property, for the law on this is most obscure ... a particular uncertainty is whether the parents have the same powers as do guardians, for example to receive a legacy on the child's behalf. Our provisional proposal that parents should be in no worse position than guardians in this respect was approved on consultation and we so recommend.

2.9   Thirdly, the fact that a person does, or does not, have parental responsibility for the care and upbringing of a child does not affect the rights of the child, in particular to be maintained or to succeed to a person's estate. The principle that children should have the same rights whatever the marital status of their parents was an essential feature of our recommendations on illegitimacy [see p. 556 et seq, below] which have recently been implemented by the Family Law Reform Act 1987. ...

Question

What do you think the Commission meant when they argued that the concept of parental 'responsibility' would 'reflect the everyday reality of being a parent'?

John Eekelaar, in 'Parental Responsibility: State of Nature or Nature of the State?' (1991), has pointed out that the concept of parental responsibility can be used in two rather different senses:

It was ... in the context of appreciation that parental 'rights' needed to be exercised for the benefit of the child that the Law Commission (1982) first suggested that it might be more appropriate to talk about parental responsibilities than parental rights. Similarly, the Commission's confirmation in paragraph 1.11 of its 1985 Working Paper on Guardianship of its preference for speaking of 'powers and responsibilities' rather than 'rights and duties' follows the observation that a parent 'will not ... be permitted to insist upon action which is contrary to (the welfare of the child) or to resist action which will promote it' (Law Commission, 1985). The shift in terminology reflects a similar change made in West Germany as long ago as 1970, when 'parental power' (*elterliche Gewalt*) was replaced by 'parental care' (*elterliche Sorge*) (Frank, 1990) and the conception of 'parental responsibilities' recommended by the Committee of Ministers of the Council of Europe in 1984 (Recommendation No. R(84)4, February 28,1984), which states that 'parental responsibilities are a collection of duties and powers which aim at ensuring the moral and material welfare of the child, in particular by taking care of the person of the child, by maintaining personal relationships with him and by providing for his education, maintenance, his legal representation and the administration of his property.' I shall refer to this sense of 'responsibility' as *responsibility (1)*.

However, also in paragraph 1.11 of its 1985 Working Paper, the Commission introduced a different concept of responsibility. 'Further,' they wrote, 'to the extent that the law enables parents to decide how to bring up their children without interference from others or from the state, it does so principally because this is a necessary part of the parents' responsibility for that upbringing and in order thus to promote the welfare of their children'. 'Responsibility' does not here refer to the way in which a parent behaves *towards* his child (as is reflected in the references to duties and supervision over parental conduct made earlier) but rather to a role which is to be exercised by the parent rather than some other entity. Of course, the assumption of responsibility for a child in this sense is not necessarily inconsistent with the presence of duties towards the child (as we shall see, it is sometimes thought that it encourages their performance). But the focus is not upon those duties but rather upon the distance between the parent and others in making provision for the child; indeed, on the degree of *freedom* given to parents in bringing up their children. And the more scope that is given to parental autonomy, the less room there is for external supervision over the way duties (under *responsibility (1)*) towards children are discharged. This will be referred to as *responsibility (2)*.

Question

As various provisions of the Children Act 1989 appear, try to identify whether they owe more to responsibility (1) or responsibility (2).

In Scotland, the Children (Scotland) Act 1995, s. 1(1) provides a fuller list of parental responsibilities:

(a) to safeguard and promote the child's health, development and welfare;
(b) to provide in a manner appropriate to the child's stage of development, direction and guidance to the child;
(c) if not living with the child, to maintain personal relations and direct contact with the child on a regular basis and
(d) to act as the child's legal representative.

Furthermore, s. 2(1) of the Act provides that, in order to meet their responsibilities, parents have the following *rights*:

(a) to have the child living with him or otherwise to regulate the child's residence;
(b) to control, direct or guide in a manner appropriate to the stage of development of the child, the child's upbringing;
(c) if the child is not living with him, to maintain personal relations and direct contact with the child on a regular basis;
(d) to act as the child's legal representative.

Questions

(i) If you were trying to explain parental responsibility to someone, do you think that these provisions would be more useful than the English definition of parental responsibilities in s. 3(1) of the Children Act 1989 (see above)?
(ii) Do you think it is a good idea to include parental rights as well as parental responsibilities?
(iii) Although the Scottish legislation makes it clear that the exercise of parental rights and responsibilities is subject to the welfare principle, do you think that there might be any dangers in stating that a parents has a *right* 'to maintain personal relations and direct contact with the child on a regular basis'? Do you think that the *responsibility* to maintain direct contact creates a legally enforceable duty upon parents to stay in contact with their children if they no longer live together? Do you think that there should be such a duty? Look at the extract from Anne Heath-Jones' *Divorce and the Reluctant Father* (Chapter 12, p. 614, below).

Returning to English law, the Children Act 1989 deals with some important features of parental responsibility:

2.—... (5) More than one person may have parental responsibility for the same child at the same time.

(6) A person who has parental responsibility for a child at any time shall not cease to have that responsibility solely because some other person subsequently acquires parental responsibility for the child.

(7) Where more than one person has parental responsibility for a child, each of them may act alone and without the other (or others) in meeting that responsibility; but nothing in this Part shall be taken to affect the operation of any enactment which requires the consent of more than one person in a matter affecting the child.

(8) The fact that a person has parental responsibility for a child shall not entitle him to act in any way which would be incompatible with any order made with respect to the child under this Act.

(9) A person who has parental responsibility for a child may not surrender or transfer any part of that responsibility to another but may arrange for some or all of it to be met by one or more persons acting on his behalf.

(10) The person with whom any such arrangement is made may himself be a person who already has parental responsibility for the child concerned.

(11) The making of any such arrangement shall not affect any liability of the person making it which may arise from any failure to meet any part of his parental responsibility for the child concerned.

3.—... (5) A person who -

(a) does not have parental responsibility for a particular child; but

(b) has care of the child,

may (subject to the provisions of this Act) do what is reasonable in all the circumstances of the case for the purpose of safeguarding or promoting the child's welfare.

Once again, these are explained in the Law Commission's Report (1988):

(b) *The power to act independently*

2.10 ... We believe it important to preserve the equal status of parents and their power to act independently of one another unless and until a court orders otherwise. This should be seen as part of the general aim of encouraging both parents to feel concerned and responsible for the welfare of their children. A few respondents suggested that they should have a legal duty to consult one another on major matters in their children's lives, arguing that this would increase parental co-operation and involvement after separation or divorce. This is an objective which we all share. However, whether or not the parents are living together, a legal duty of consultation seems both unworkable and undesirable. The person looking after the child has to be able to take decisions in the child's best interests as and when they arise. Some may have to be taken very quickly. In reality ... it is that person who will have to put those decisions into effect and that person who has the degree of practical control over the child to be able to do so. The child may well suffer if that parent is prevented by the other's disapproval and thus has to go to court to resolve the matter, still more if the parent is inhibited by the fear that the other may disapprove or by the difficulties of contacting him or of deciding whether what is proposed is or is not a major matter requiring consultation. In practice, where the parents disagree about a matter of upbringing the burden should be on the one seeking to prevent a step which the other is proposing, or to impose a course of action which only the other can put into effect, to take the matter to court. Otherwise the courts might be inundated with cases, disputes might escalate well beyond their true importance, and in the meantime the children would suffer. We recommend, therefore, that the equal and independent status of parents be preserved and, indeed, applied to others (principally guardians) who may share parental responsibility in future. This will not, of course, affect any statutory provision which requires the consent of each parent, for example to the adoption of the child.

(c) *The effect of court orders*

2.11 Allied to this is the principle that parents should not lose their parental responsibility even though its exercise may have to be modified or curtailed in certain respects, for example if it is necessary to determine where a child will live after his parents separate. Obviously, a court order to that effect will put many matters outside the control of the parent who does not have the child with him. However, parents should not be regarded as losing their position, and their ability to take decisions about their children, simply because they are separated or in dispute with one another about a particular matter. Hence they should only be prevented from acting in ways which would be incompatible with an order made about the child's upbringing. If, for example, the child has to live with one parent and go to a school near home, it would be incompatible with that order for the other parent to arrange for him to have his hair done in a way which will exclude him from the school. It would not, however, be incompatible for that parent to take him to a particular sporting occasion over the weekend, no matter how much the parent with whom the child lived might disapprove. These principles form part of our general aim of 'lowering the stakes' in cases of parental separation and divorce, and emphasising the continued responsibility of both parents, to which we shall return [see p. 586, below]. However, they are equally important where children are committed to local authority care. The crucial effect of a care order is to confer parental responsibilities upon the authority and there will be detailed regulations about how these are to be exercised. But the parents remain the parents and 'it will continue to be important in many cases to involve the parents in the child's care'. Clearly, the order will leave little scope for them to carry out their responsibilities, save to a limited extent while the child is with them, because the local authority will be in control of so much of the child's life [see p. 727, below]. But the parents should not be deprived of their very parenthood unless and until the child is adopted or freed for adoption.

(d) *Arrangements and agreements with parents and others*

2.12 ...

2.13 It is clearly important to maintain the principle that parental rights or responsibility cannot be legally surrendered or transferred without a court order and we so recommend. Equally, it is always possible, and a common practice, for parents to delegate the exercise of some or all of their parental responsibilities either between themselves or to other people or agencies, such as schools, holiday camps, foster parents or local authorities. It would be helpful for the law to recognise this expressly, for two reasons. First, parents are now encouraged to agree between themselves the arrangements which they believe best for their children, whether or not they are separated. It is important, therefore, that they should feel free to do so. Secondly ... it is helpful if, for example, a school can feel confident in accepting the decision of a person nominated by the parents as a temporary 'guardian' for the child while they are away. ...

2.14 We do not recommend, however, that such arrangements should be legally binding so that the parents cannot revoke or change them. ... It would scarcely be in the best interests of children for parents to be bound by such arrangements should they wish to change them. No court would uphold them if they were contrary to the child's interests but the burden of taking the case to court should not lie with the parents. This is particularly important in the context of arrangements made with or through local authorities. Both the Review of Child Care Law and the Government's response to it have emphasised that these should always be voluntary and that court proceedings should be required before any compulsory interference with the parents' responsibilities.

2.15 ... As between those who share parental responsibility, ... a provision for legally binding agreements might inhibit them from making whatever arrangements seem best at the time for fear that it might later be difficult to change them. Any disagreement will eventually have to be resolved by a court and in practice the burden will still lie on the one wishing to change the agreed arrangements. The court, in deciding what is best for the child, will no doubt take account of the arrangements agreed, the reasons for them, and the risks of changing them. But if they have already been changed in fact it would be wrong for there still to be a bias in favour of the previous agreement. ...

(e) *The position of those without parental responsibility*

2.16 However, it would be helpful to clarify the position of those who have actual care of a child without having parental responsibility for him in law. ... There is criminal liability for, *inter alia*, ill-treatment, neglect and failure to educate, whether or not a person has legal custody. ... But there may be confusion about the power of such people to take certain decisions about the child. We therefore recommend that it be made quite clear that anyone with actual care of a child may do what is reasonable in all the circumstances of the case for the purpose of safeguarding or promoting the child's welfare. The obvious example is medical treatment. If the child is left with friends while the parents go on holiday, it would obviously not be reasonable to arrange major elective surgery, but it would be reasonable to arrange whatever was advised in the event of an accident to the child. ...

Questions

(i) Section 2(7) of the Children Act 1989 provides that each person with parental responsibility may act alone. Does this mean that one parent can change the child's school without consulting the other parent? (See *Re G (A Minor) (Parental Responsibility: Education)* [1995] 2 FCR 53, [1994] 2 FLR 964.) What will happen if he or she does so? (See p. 637.) Might this be another example of the courts' ignoring the plain words of the statute?

(ii) In *Re J (child's religious upbringing and circumcision)* [2000] 1 FCR 307, Dame Elizabeth Butler-Sloss P said:

31. There is, in my view, a small group of important decisions made on behalf of a child which, in the absence of agreement of those with parental responsibility, ought not to be carried out or arranged by a one-parent carer although she has parental responsibility under s 2(7) of the Children Act 1989. Such a decision ought not to be made without the specific approval of

the court. Sterilisation is one example. The change of a child's surname is another. Some of the examples, including the change of a child's surname, are based upon statute (see s 13(1) of the 1989 Act).

32. The issue of circumcision has not, to my knowledge, previously been considered by this court, but in my view it comes within that group. The decision to circumcise a child on grounds other than medical necessity is a very important one; the operation is irreversible, and should only be carried out where the parents together approve of it or, in the absence of parental agreement, where a court decides that the operation is in the best interests of the child. This requirement for a determination by the court should also apply to a local authority with parental responsibility under a care order.

Does sterilisation require court approval only where there is no parental agreement, or is court approval required in all cases (see p. 454, above)? What do male circumcision and changing the child's surname have in common, apart from being in this special category? Would you include anything else in this category? (iii) If a mother and father disagree about whether their child should have the Measles Mumps and Rubella (MMR) inoculation, should one parent be able to authorise this without the other's knowledge or agreement? Should one parent be able to authorise cosmetic surgery for the child without the other parent's knowledge? Is it practical to produce a list of 'major' and 'minor' decisions, according to whether parental agreement is required?

The Department of Health's *Introduction to the Children Act 1989* (1989) sums up the concept of parental responsibility like this:

1.4 The Act uses the phrase *'parental responsibility'* to sum up the collection of duties, rights and authority which a parent has in respect of his child. That choice of words emphasises that the duty to care for the child and to raise him to moral, physical and emotional health is the fundamental task of parenthood and the only justification for the authority it confers.

1.5 The importance of parental responsibility is emphasised in the Act by the fact that not only is it unaffected by the separation of parents but even when courts make orders in private proceedings such as divorce, that responsibility continues and is limited only to the extent that any order settles certain concrete issues between the parties. That arrangement aims to emphasise that interventions by the courts where there is family breakdown should not be regarded as lessening the duty on both parents to continue to play a full part in the child's upbringing.

Questions

(i) Do you really believe that parents are for children rather than children for parents?

(ii) If you do, would you introduce any controls over who is allowed to have children (see Chapter 11, below)?

(iii) Does the development of the concept of parental responsibility mean that the language of parental rights is now irrelevant? What about the human rights of parents, particularly under Art. 8 of the European Convention of Human Rights, which is incorporated into English law by the Human Rights Act 1998?

In the next and subsequent chapters, we will be considering the significance of human rights development for the law relating to parents and children in a variety of contexts. In particular, in the next chapter we will see that not everyone who has parental responsibility is a parent and that not all parents have parental responsibility.

Bibliography

10.1 Parental rights and children's welfare

We quoted from:

DHSS, *Review of Child Care Law – Report to Ministers of an Interdepartmental Working Party* (1985) London, HMSO, paras. 2.12–2.13, 15.11.

Sir William Blackstone, *Commentaries on the Laws of England* (1st edn, 1765) Oxford, Clarendon Press, book 1, pp. 434–435, 440–441.

Law Commission, Working Paper No. 91, *Review of Child Law: Custody* (1986) London, HMSO, paras. 6.20–6.22.

Additional reading

C. Bridge, 'Religion, culture and conviction – the medical treatment of young children' (1999) 11 Child and Family Law Quarterly 1.

R. Huxtable, 'Logical separation? Conjoined twins, slippery slope and resource allocation' (2001) 23 Journal of Social Welfare Law 459.

Royal College of Paediatrics and Child Health, *Withholding or Withdrawing Life Saving Treatment in Children: A Framework for Practice* (1997).

10.2 Parental autonomy and respect for family life

We quoted from:

Anon., 'Mental Hospitalisation of Children and the Limits of Parental Authority' (1978) 88 Yale Law Journal 186, pp. 194–208.

J. Goldstein, A. Freud and A.J. Solnit, *Before the Best Interests of the Child* (1980) London, Burnett Books, pp. 8–10, 11–12, 16–17, 92, 93–94.

Additional reading

C. Barton and A. Bissett-Johnson, 'The European Convention and Parental Rights' (1995) 25 Family Law 507.

B.M. Dickens, 'The Modern Function and Limits of Parental Rights' (1981) 97 Law Quarterly Review 462.

J. Fortin, 'Children's rights and the use of physical force' (2001) 13 Child and Family Law Quarterly 243.

J. Masson, 'Securing human rights for children and young people in secure accommodation' (2002) 14 Child and Family Law Quarterly 77.

M. Parry, 'Secure accommodation – the Cinderella of family law' (2000) 12 Child and Family Law Quarterly 101.

10.3 Children's rights

We quoted from:

J. M. Eekelaar, 'The Emergence of Children's Rights' (1986) 6 Oxford Journal of Legal Studies 161, pp. 169–174, 176, 180–182.

Additional reading

R. Adler and A. Dearling, 'Children's Rights: A Scottish Perspective' in B. Franklin (ed.), *The Rights of Children* (1986) Oxford, Basil Blackwell.

R. Farson, *Birthrights* (1978) Harmondsworth, Penguin Books.

B. Franklin (ed.), *The Rights of Children* (1986) Oxford, Basil Blackwell.

M.D.A. Freeman, *The Rights and Wrongs of Children* (1983) London, Frances Pinter.

J. Herring, 'The Human Rights Act and the welfare principle in family law – conflicting or complementary?' (1999) 11 Child and Family Law Quarterly 223.

J. Holt, *Escape from Childhood* (1974) New York, Dutton.

Report of the Committee on the Age of Majority (Chairman: Mr. Justice Latey) (Cmnd. 3342) (1967) London, HMSO.

White Paper: *Reforming the Mental Health Act* (Cm. 5016-I) (2000) London, HMSO.

C.A. Wringe, *Children's rights – A philosophical study* (1981) London, Routledge and Kegan Paul.

10.4   The UN Convention on the Rights of the Child

We quoted from:

P. Alston and S. Parker, 'Introduction' in P. Alston, S. Parker and J. Seymour (eds.), *Children, Rights and the Law* (1992) Oxford, Clarendon Press, p. viii.

B. Cass, 'The Limits of the Public/Private Dichotomy: A Comment on Coady & Coady' in P. Alston, S. Parker and J. Seymour (eds.), *Children, Rights and the Law* (1992) Oxford, Clarendon Press, p. 140.

Children's Rights Alliance for England, *Report to the Pre-Sessional Working Group of the Committee on the Rights of the Child* (2002), p. 1.

J. Fortin, 'Children's Rights and the Impact of Two International Conventions' in Thorpe LJ and C. Cowton (eds.), *Delight and Dole* (2002) Family Law.

M. King, 'Children's Rights as Communication: Reflections on Autopoietic Theory and the United Nations Convention' (1994) 57 Modern Law Review 385, pp. 388–389, 392, 400–401.

G. Van Bueren, 'The Challenges for the International Protection of Family Members' Rights as the 21st Century Approaches' in N. Lowe and G. Douglas (eds.), *Frontiers of Family Law* (1996) The Hague, Martinus Nijhoff Publishers.

Additional reading

S. Kilbourne, 'The wayward Americans – why the USA has not ratified the UN Convention on the Rights of the Child' (1998) 10 Child and Family Law Quarterly 243.

F. Olsen, 'Children's Rights: Some Feminist Approaches to the United Nations Convention on the Rights of the Child' in P. Alston, S. Parker and J. Seymour (eds.), *Children, Rights and the Law* (1992) Oxford, Clarendon Press, pp. 195–216.

O. O'Neill, 'Children's Rights and Children's Lives' in P. Alston, S. Parker and J. Seymour (eds.), *Children, Rights and the Law* (1992) Oxford, Clarendon Press.

G. Van Bueren, 'The Struggle for Empowerment: the Emerging Civil and Political Rights of Children' in *Selected Essays on International Children's Rights* (1993) Geneva, Defence for Children International.

10.5   Parental responsibility

We quoted from:

Department of Health, *An Introduction to the Children Act 1989* (1989) London, HMSO, paras. 1.4–1.5.

J. Eekelaar, 'Parental Responsibility: State of Nature or Nature of the State?' [1991] Journal of Social Welfare and Family Law 37, pp. 38–39.

Law Commission, *Report on Guardianship and Custody*, Law Com. No. 172 (1988) London, HMSO, paras. 2.4–2.16.

Additional reading

Brent Council, *A Child in Trust – The Report of the Panel of Inquiry into the Circumstances Surrounding the Death of Jasmine Beckford* (Chairman: L. Blom-Cooper QC) (1985) London, London Borough of Brent.

Lambeth London Borough Council, *Whose Child? The Report of the Inquiry into the Death of Tyra Henry* (1987) London, London Borough of Lambeth.

Chapter 11

Becoming a parent

11.1 Births in and out of marriage

11.2 How to become a father

11.3 How to adopt a child

11.4 Assisted reproduction and the 'social parent'

11.5 Illegitimate children or illegitimate parents?

Once upon a time there was only one way to become a mother, and to become a father you had to be married to a mother. Nowadays you can become a father without being married to the mother. You can also become a parent of someone else's child by adoption, by assisted reproduction, and by surrogacy, which is a mixture of the two. We shall look briefly at each of these in turn, before examining what difference it makes whether or not the parents are married to one another.

11.1 Births in and out of marriage

Women are having fewer children these days. The first graph, from *Population Trends 107* (Spring 2002) shows that the total period fertility rate in the United Kingdom is now well below the rate of 2.1 which is associated with long-term population replacement. The second graph, from the same volume, shows how a rapidly increasing proportion of children are being born outside marriage:

Total period fertility rate

TFR (average number of children per woman)

Live births outside marriage

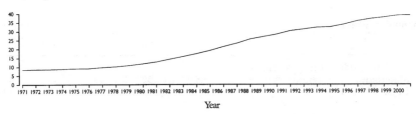

Percentage of all live births

The next table, from *Social Trends 32* (2002) gives information about the registration of births outside marriage:

Chart 2.14   Births outside marriage as a percentage of all live births

Great Britain

Percentages

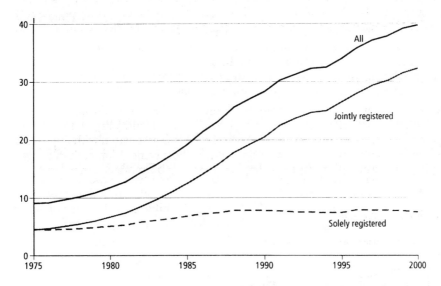

Source: Office for National Statistics; General Register Office for Scotland

The final table, again from *Social Trends 32*, looks at responses to pregnancy in recent years:

Table 2.10   Conceptions[1]: by marital status and outcome

England & Wales   Percentages

	1987	1991	1995	1998	1999
Conceptions inside marriage leading to					
Maternities	56	52	49	44	44
Legal abortions[2]	5	4	4	4	4
Conceptions outside marriage leading to					
Maternities inside marriage	5	4	3	3	3
Maternities outside marriage	20	25	28	30	31
Legal abortions[2]	14	15	16	18	18
All conceptions (=100%) (thousands)	850	854	790	797	774

1   See Appendix, Part 2: Conceptions.
2   Legal terminations under the 1967 Abortion Act.
Source: Office for National Statistics

Questions

(i) In 1971, the percentage of conceptions outside marriage leading to maternity inside marriage was 8.1%. Look at the latest rate in the table above. How would you account for the fall in 'shot-gun' marriages?
(ii) As these marriages have in the past been twice as likely to break down, does this strike you as a good thing or a bad thing?
(iii) But has it got anything to do with the rise in joint registrations?
(iv) Does this strike you as a good thing or a bad thing?

Of course, the children's situation may well change after their birth. If their natural parents later marry, for example, they are legitimated (Legitimacy Act 1976, s. 2) and can be re-registered as such. John Haskey's article 'Having a birth outside marriage: the proportion of lone mothers and cohabiting mothers who subsequently marry' (1999) looks at how lone mothers may cease to be lone mothers. Bear in mind that while the article speaks of the situation of mothers, their decisions have a very close effect upon their children, on the type of family those children grow up in, and upon the children's relationship with their parents and/or step-parents:

Introduction – Background and Purpose
... With the increase in the divorce rate since the 1960s and the accelerated rise during the last decade in the proportion of all births which have occurred outside marriage, it has been easy to assume that it was to be expected, indeed inevitable, that the numbers of divorced and single lone mothers would increase relentlessly. Whilst it was reasonable to expect the numbers to rise, it was far from inevitable, since another factor enters the equation, and one easily overlooked – the different ways existing lone mothers can cease to be lone mothers. Because of gaps or inadequacies in our regular data sources, or sample sizes which are too small, it has proved impossible to quantify these *outflows* from the stock of lone mothers. One important such

outflow is by marriage – since if a lone mother marries, the family ceases to be a one-parent family and instead becomes a married couple family, and possibly a stepfamily, too. (Another important outflow is by the lone mother starting to cohabit, a subject not studied in the present article.) Public attention has concentrated on the growth in the number (stock) of lone mothers, and lone parents generally, and also on the inflows, whilst at the same time ignoring, or at least overlooking, the outflows. One of the purposes of this study was to rectify the balance, and to indicate that, for many mothers, lone motherhood is not a long-term situation.

...

Selecting the sample

A systematic sample of just over 2½ thousand births outside marriage, from the total of 177 thousand such births, was selected from the 1988 births file for England and Wales, representing a 1.4 per cent sample.

...

   The mothers were traced in the marriage registers from the date of birth of the child up to the end of 1996. ... Also, Figure 1 gives a diagrammatic representation the different groups of mothers studied in this article. ...

Figure 1   Diagrammatic representation of the sample mothers in the study

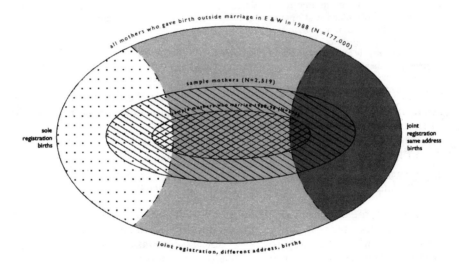

Note: diagrammatic only – not to scale

Representativeness of the sample

The sample of 2,519 births outside marriage closely resembles the entire set of births outside marriage during 1988, as measured by the profile of the mothers' age at birth and by the type of birth registration. Hence, 3 in every ten mothers had registered the birth by themselves without the father's details being recorded; 5 in every ten mothers had jointly registered the birth with the father, with both parents giving the same address, and the remaining two in every ten mothers had jointly registered the birth with the father, the parents living at different addresses. In addition, one in four sample mothers was a teenager, and two in five were in their early twenties, so that about two thirds of all the sample mothers were aged under 25. Given that the peak age group for women to marry in recent years has been the late twenties, it was expected, solely on the basis of age, that many of the lone and cohabiting mothers would marry in the subsequent 5 or so years. ...

Proportions of the mothers who married

Overall, one quarter of the sample mothers married between giving birth in 1988, and 1996; 633 of the sample of 2,519. This proportion varies considerably according to age of the mother at maternity and also by the type of birth registration. Perhaps not surprisingly, mothers who jointly registered the birth with the father, both living at the same address, married in proportionately largest numbers; 3 in every ten. The group of mothers to marry in the next largest numbers were those who jointly registered the birth with the father but lived at different addresses; about one in 4 such mothers subsequently married.

Mothers who registered the births by themselves – most often thought to be lone mothers – were least likely overall to marry subsequently; only one in 6 did so.

One in 4 teenage mothers subsequently married, and three in every ten mothers who were in their early twenties. The proportion of mothers who married declined with successively older ages at maternity, so that only about one in 8 mothers who gave birth at age 35 or over subsequently married. Mothers who had jointly registered their births with the fathers with whom they were residing were the most likely to marry, particularly those mothers who were in their early twenties; over one in 3 did so.

Table 4 considers the men whom the mothers married – and allows the proportions of mothers who subsequently married the fathers to be compared with the proportions marrying someone other than the father. Overall, one in 5 mothers married the father, with only 3 per cent definitely marrying someone other than the father. Mothers who jointly registered the births with the fathers, both living at the same address, were proportionately more likely to marry the fathers than the corresponding mothers whose residential addresses were different from those of the fathers; the ratio of marrying the father to marrying someone else was roughly 9 to 1 for the former group, but only 4 to 1 for the latter group. Overall, amongst the 25 per cent of mothers who married, 19 per cent married the fathers, that is, around three quarters of all mothers who did marry, married the fathers.

Inevitably, amongst mothers who had registered the birth of their child as a sole registration, there was a relatively high proportion of cases where it was uncertain whether or not the mother married the father of her child – 11 out of the total of 17 per cent. Interestingly, even amongst births which were solely registered by the mother, it was reasonably certain that at least one in 20 of the mothers married the child's father. Roughly half the number of such cases could be decided because the child's surname was different from the mother's, but the same as that of the man the mother married, and in the other half of cases the initial sole registration was replaced by a later joint registration, from which the father's name could be obtained. ...

Figure 2 shows the proportions of mothers who married the fathers, by both age of the mother at maternity, and also by type of birth registration ...

Figure 2   Percentage of mothers who married the fathers*, 1988–96, by age at maternity and type of birth registration, England and Wales

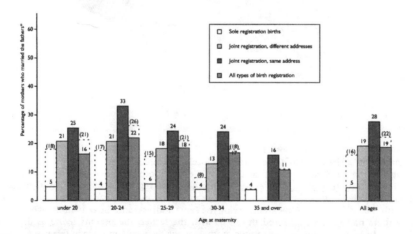

*   for sole registration births, the low solid histogram includes only those husbands where it is certain they were the fathers; the upper, dotted histogram represents the additional husbands where it is not sure whether they were the fathers or not.

†   no sample mothers married.

Time interval between maternity and marriage

During the first six months after having a birth outside marriage, relatively few mothers married (Figure 4), as has been confirmed elsewhere. Even amongst mothers who had jointly registered the birth with the fathers with the same address, only 5 per cent married, and the corresponding proportion was even smaller amongst mothers of jointly registered births with different addresses. Nevertheless, the same pace of marriage in the first half year was maintained throughout the two years following the birth for each of the three groups of mothers shown in Figure 4, so that about 19, 12, and 6 per cent of joint registration same address mothers, joint registration different address mothers, and sole registration mothers, respectively, had married within two years. After this period, the pace slackened somewhat, particularly for the first-mentioned group of mothers. However, it is notable that amongst each of the groups of mothers, the proportion marrying continued to rise, even after some 6 years or so. However, very few extra mothers with jointly registered births with different parental addresses married after about 7 years.

Figure 4 Cumulative percentage of mothers who married, 1988–96, by interval of time between maternity and marriage, by type of birth registration, England and Wales

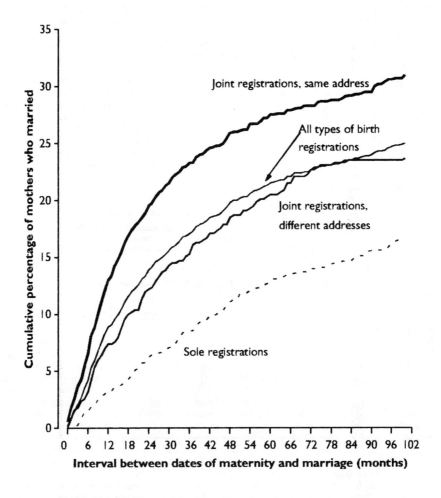

Of course, of equal interest are the corresponding patterns of marriage of the mothers to the fathers, and to others, by the length of time since the birth. Because for every sole registration birth where it was reasonably certain that the mother had married the father, there were two where it was impossible to tell, attention is best focused on the mothers of jointly registered births. Figure 5 shows the cumulative proportions of such mothers who married, by type of joint birth registration, that is, same or different parental addresses, and by whether or not the mother married the father.

Figure 5   For jointly registered births, cumulative percentage of mothers who married, 1988–96, by interval of time between maternity and marriage, by whether married the father and whether the parental addresses were the same, England and Wales

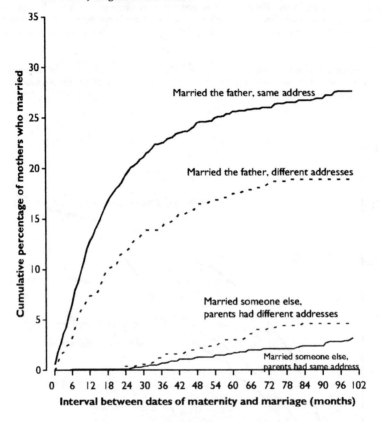

There is a fundamental difference in the timing of marriage between the mothers who married the father, and the mothers who married someone else. Mothers started marrying the fathers immediately after the birth of their child; indeed the cumulative proportion grew at its fastest rate during the first year. In contrast, virtually no mothers married men other than the fathers during the first two years – and the proportions were only 1 or 2 per cent by the end of the third year. Furthermore, this basic finding applies whether or not the father lived at the same address as the mother at the time of birth. Some fathers possibly wanted no further involvement after the birth of the child, and the mothers were too occupied looking after their babies during the first few years to have a full social life and meet potential husbands. Also, men other than the fathers are possibly less willing to marry women with young babies than those with older children. Alternatively the mothers may have been having an unsuccessful relationship with the father at the time of the birth, even though the father might be committed to her and their child. The very occurrence of the birth might have caused the relationship to founder, and so present the mother from marrying the father.

Some unmarried parents remain unmarried. Why might this be? Susan McRae, in *Cohabiting Mothers* (1993), addresses this question:

Why haven't they married and will they?

Our study identified three key reasons why long-term cohabiting mothers had not married: the high cost of weddings, a fear of divorce, and the wish to avoid the institution of marriage itself. In addition, a range of other reasons were identified which could be summarised as factors which were delaying marriage. Remaining unmarried was a complex process, and often seemed to stem as much from having decided not to marry, as from having not decided to marry. Cohabiting mothers sometimes reported more than one reason for remaining unmarried; and, of course, the impact of some reasons was likely to be greater than that of other reasons.

For example, about 1 in 5 long-term cohabiting mothers reported that they had not married *yet*; that is, something was delaying marriage, such as a not-yet-finalised divorce, the desire to finish a course of education, falling pregnant again, being too busy at work and so on. Among all the long-term cohabiting mothers we interviewed in 1992, these women had lived with their partners for the shortest period and seemed the most likely to join the flow from cohabiting-motherhood into married-motherhood. Indeed, they probably have done so already.

Similarly, just over 1 in 4 long-term cohabiting mothers cited the high cost of weddings as a reason for not marrying. Although we have no way of knowing for sure, it seems improbable that a lack of money would permanently deter long-term cohabiting parents from marriage: either the attraction of a big white wedding will fade as they get older (there are other ways of marrying) or the added years will bring enough money to foot the bill. Either way, it seems likely that these women also will join the flow from cohabiting-motherhood into married-motherhood.

Much less certain is the fate of almost 1 in 3 long-term cohabiting mothers who cited a fear or dislike of divorce as their reason for not marrying. Indeed, in speculating on the chances of these women marrying, we come up against a considerable irony: the trauma involved in the process of divorcing – the effects of which may last for many years afterwards – seemingly deter some cohabiting mothers from marrying. If the divorce process was less confrontational, or divorce perhaps easier to obtain, then it seems likely that more long-term cohabiting mothers would marry.

Finally, we come to long-term cohabiting mothers who reported that they were deterred from marrying by the idea of marriage itself. Just one half of the long-term cohabiting mothers we interviewed expressed a wish to avoid marriage. In the strong version (reported by 1 in 5), this appeared to be based upon an ideologically-informed aversion to marriage. In the weaker version (expressed by 30 per cent), women simply could see no advantages in marriage. Neither group, in other words, could find reasons to marry; it seems reasonable to assume that for the foreseeable future at least, they will remain *cohabiting* mothers.

Our speculations so far suggest that as many as one-half of long-term cohabiting mothers, perhaps more, will not marry their partners, at least in the foreseeable future. However, our conjectural analysis of their chance of marrying has left out the one aspect of their lives that is, arguably, the most likely to encourage them to marry: their children. The principal reason for marrying given by the large majority of women who became mothers while cohabiting – whether or not they had married – was to ensure the security of their children. A substantial minority (1 in 4) of cohabiting women who married *before* having children also cited their children's security as a reason for marrying. Again, while we have no way of knowing for sure, it is possible that even women who object to the institution of marriage might be tipped into it by the wishes of their children, or by their desire to protect their children's interests.

Question

Recall what you have read so far about the financial consequences of having children (Chapter 3, pp. 102–111) and the financial outcomes of divorce compared with those of cohabitation breakdown (Chapter 8). Would you advise cohabiting mothers to marry for their children's sakes, or for their own?

11.2 How to become a father

Until recently, proving paternity had always been thought to be a problem. Somehow it is easier to remember the first part of Lancelot's speech to Old Gobbo – 'It's a wise father, that knows his own child' – than the second – 'Truth will come to light; murder cannot be hid long, a man's son may; but in the end, truth will out'. Hence there is a presumption that any child born to a married woman is her husband's child. This used to be extremely difficult to rebut. There was also a procedure for conclusively determining a person's legitimacy. Both are illustrated by the following case:

Ampthill Peerage Case
[1977] AC 547, [1976] 2 All ER 411, [1976] 2 WLR 777, 120 Sol Jo 367, House of Lords' Committee of Privileges

In 1921, Christobel, wife of the man who was later to become third baron Ampthill, gave birth to Geoffrey, who had been conceived by external fertilisation while his mother was still a virgin. Her husband petitioned for divorce, alleging that this was the result of Christobel's adultery. At the trial, the husband gave evidence that he had had no sexual intimacy of any kind with his wife at the probable date of conception and was granted a decree. On appeal, the House of Lords decided that evidence of non-access by a husband or a wife was inadmissible both in legitimacy proceedings and in divorce proceedings (*Russell v Russell* [1924] AC 687, 93 LJP 97: the rule was subsequently reversed in the Law Reform (Miscellaneous Provisions) Act 1949, s. 7(1)). The divorce decree was rescinded. In 1925, the High Court made a declaration that Geoffrey was the legitimate child of Christobel and her husband. Under the Legitimacy Declaration Act 1858, such declarations were binding on all the world, but could not prejudice anyone who had not been given notice or made a party (or did not claim through such a person) or if obtained by fraud or collusion. The marriage was eventually dissolved in 1937. In 1950, a son John was born of the third baron's third marriage. The third baron died in 1973 and both Geoffrey and John claimed to succeed him. Geoffrey relied upon the declaration, but John alleged that this was not binding, inter alia, because it had been procured by fraud. Blood samples were available from Christobel and the third baron, but not from Geoffrey.

Lord Simon of Glaisdale: ... There is one status for which Parliament, in the wisdom of experience, has made special provision. This is the status of legitimacy. Status means the condition of belonging to a class in society to which the law ascribes peculiar rights and duties, capacities and incapacities. Such, for example, is the status of a married person or minor. Legitimacy is a status: it is the condition of belonging to a class in society the members of which are regarded as having been begotten in lawful matrimony by the men whom the law regards as their fathers. Motherhood, although also a legal relationship, is based on a fact, being proved demonstrably by parturition. Fatherhood, by contrast, is a presumption. A woman can have sexual intercourse with a number of men any of whom may be the father of her child; though it is true that modern serology can sometimes enable the presumption to be rebutted as regards some of these men. The status of legitimacy gives the child certain rights both against the man whom the law regards as his father and generally in society. Among the peculiar rights which a child is entitled to enjoy by virtue of the status of legitimacy is the right to succeed to a hereditary title of honour. If the hereditary title of honour is a peerage of the United Kingdom, the oldest legitimate son when of full age is entitled to be called to your Lordships' House on the death of the man whom the law regards as his father.

It was probably for two reasons that Parliament made special provision for judgment as to the status of legitimacy. First, no doubt, because, since fatherhood is not factually demonstrable by parturition, it is questionable; and it is generally in the interest of society that open questions should be finally closed. Second, no doubt, because since the legitimate child, by virtue of his legal relationship with the man whom the law regards as his father, is entitled to certain rights both as against the father and generally in society, it is desirable that the legal relationship between father and child should be decisively concluded.

His lordship then reviews the law and the evidence and concludes that the decree was not obtained by fraud or collusion, not least because, as the law stood in 1925, Geoffrey was entitled to the benefit of the presumption even if his mother had confessed to committing adultery at the relevant time.

Questions

(i) This case demonstrates the strength of the courts' traditional reluctance to bastardise a child, but now that most of the legal distinctions between birth in and outside marriage have been removed, is there any longer a need for this presumption? (ii) Is it so obvious these days who is a child's mother? (See p. 537, below.)

However, the position has since changed. The Family Law Reform Act 1969 now provides:

26. – Any presumption of law as to the legitimacy or illegitimacy of any person may in any civil proceedings be rebutted by evidence which shows that it is more probable than not that that person is illegitimate or legitimate, as the case may be, and it shall not be necessary to prove that fact beyond reasonable doubt in order to rebut the presumption.

The leading case on the meaning of this was decided shortly afterwards:

S v S; W v Official Solicitor
[1972] AC 24, [1970] 3 All ER 107, [1970] 3 WLR 366, 114 Sol Jo 635, House of Lords

Both were divorce cases in which the husband denied paternity of a child to whom the presumption of legitimacy applied. They are the leading authorities on whether or not the court should direct the use of blood tests to determine a child's paternity (as to which see the extracts quoted in *Re H (a minor) (blood tests: parental rights)*, p. 514, below). On the presumption of legitimacy:

Lord Reid: ... The law as to the onus of proof is now set out in s 26 of the Family Law Reform Act 1969 ...
    That means that the presumption of legitimacy now merely determines the onus of proof. Once evidence has been led it must be weighed without using the presumption as a make-weight in the scale for legitimacy. So even weak evidence against legitimacy must prevail if there is not other evidence to counterbalance it. The presumption will only come in at that stage in the very rare case of the evidence being so evenly balanced that the court is unable to reach a decision on it. I cannot recollect ever having seen or heard of a case of any kind where the court could not reach a decision on the evidence before it. ...

Compare Lord Reid's remarks with those of Lord Jauncey in *Re Moyniham* [2000] 1 FLR 113 at 119: 'I am content to accept [that the standard of proof] although not so high as proof beyond reasonable doubt is more stringent that the mere tipping of the scales in favour of probability.'

Questions

(i) Do you think that the approach of the House of Lords to the standard of proof in care proceedings (see *Re H (minors) (sexual abuse: standard of proof)* [1996] AC 563, [1996] 1 All ER 1, [1996] 2 WLR 8, HL, p. 722, below) has, or should have, any relevance here?

(ii) Do you think that the standard of proof of paternity should be the same (a) if the mother is applying for financial provision or a property settlement for her child, or (b) if the father is applying for a contact, residence or parental responsibility order, or (c) if the child is applying for a declaration of parentage?

The whole debate has now been overtaken by the scientific development known as 'DNA profiling' or 'genetic fingerprinting', explained by Alec Jeffreys in 'Genetic fingerprinting: applications and misapplications' (1993):

What is DNA fingerprinting?

While most of our DNA shows little variation, regions called 'minisatellites' scattered along our chromosomes can show extreme levels of variability. These minisatellites consist of 'stuttered' regions of DNA, in which a short chemical sequence of bases is repeated over and over again. If, for example, a normal DNA sequence is written … ABCDEFGH … then a minisatellite would appear as … ABCDEDEDEDEFGH … with multiple copies of the motif DE, variability arising from differences in the number of DE repeats. As a result, some minisatellites can show dozens or even hundreds of different length states and thus provide the most variable and informative genetic markers yet discovered.

In 1984, we showed that the repeat units (DE in the above example) of different minisatellites tend to share a similar sequence motif, which seems to predispose DNA towards this stuttering. Discovering of this shared motif allowed us to design a method for highlighting many of these minisatellite regions simultaneously in human DNA, thus producing the first DNA or genetic 'fingerprint'.

DNA fingerprinting is a complex process, taking perhaps a week to proceed from biological sample to final result. The first stage is to extract chemically the DNA from suitable sources such as blood (DNA is present in white blood cells), semen, hair roots or mouth swabs; other sources of DNA, such as saliva and urine, generally yield too little DNA for fingerprinting by this method. Next, the extracted DNA is checked to ensure that sufficient good-quality DNA has been recovered for subsequent typing. It is then cut with a restriction enzyme, a protein that cleaves the DNA strands at specific positions, to produce a complex set of millions of different DNA fragments, some of which contain the variable minisatellites. The length of these minisatellite fragments is determined by the number of repeats or stutters, and the next stage is, therefore, to separate the DNA fragments according to length by passage through a slab of gel in an electric field. The pattern of DNA fragments sorted by size is then transferred from the gel to a sheet of membrane, which is subsequently treated to separate the two strands of the double helix within each DNA fragments without disrupting the pattern on the membrane. Next, the membrane is reacted with a radioactive 'probe', a segment of stuttered DNA which seeks out and forms a double helix with any minisatellite fragments on the membrane. As a result, the variable minisatellites become radioactive and can be visualized on X-ray film.

The end result of this process is a pattern of 30 or so bands or stripes on X-ray film, resembling to some extent the bar code used on supermarket goods. These film patterns, examples of which are shown in Figure 1, have three critical properties:

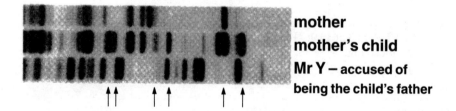

mother

mother's child

Mr Y – accused of

being the child's father

Figure 1 DNA fingerprint analysis of a paternity case. The child's pattern contains a number of bands not present in that of the mother, which must therefore have been inherited from the child's natural father. Most of these bands are not present in Mr Y (arrowed bands), proving that he could not be the child's father.

(1) The degree of pattern variation between individuals, even if they are closely related, is so extraordinary that we can legitimately refer to these patterns as DNA fingerprints, a unique biological identifier. Extensive comparisons of different people's patterns have shown that the odds against two people (other than identical twins) having the same patter is remote in the extreme, to the extent to that it would be very unlikely that *any* two people on earth would by chance share the same pattern.

(2) Despite this extraordinary variation, an individual's DNA fingerprint is essentially constant, irrespective of the source of DNA (blood, semen). Thus DNA fingerprinting can be applied to any appropriate source of DNA.

(3) DNA fingerprints show a simple pattern of inheritance, a child receiving approximately one-half of its bands from the mother and the remainder from the father. Occasionally, a new mutant band unattributable to either parent will appear in a child (these mutations are the ultimate source of this extraordinary variability), but extensive analysis of families has shown that the frequency of such mutant bands is low enough not to interfere significantly with the use of DNA fingerprinting in establishing family relationships.

There may be some concerns over quality control in the forensic context, but there is no doubt as to the reliability of the technique in the family law context, where good quality samples are readily available, either by court order under Part III of the Family Law Reform Act 1969, or more commonly by agreement. Thus it is now possible to ascertain for certain whether or not a given individual is a child's father, and ss. 20–23 of the Family Law Reform Act 1969 (as amended) set out the court's power to direct that tests be carried out:

20.—(1) In any civil proceedings in which the parentage of any person falls to be determined, the court may, either of its own motion or on an application by any party to the proceedings, give a direction—

(a) for the use of scientific tests to ascertain whether such tests show that a party to the proceedings is or is not the father or mother of that person; and

(b) for the taking, within a period specified in the direction, of bodily samples from all or any of the following, namely, that person, any party who is alleged to be the father or mother of that person and any other party to the proceedings;

and the court may at any time revoke or vary a direction previously given by it under this subsection.

...

21. Consents, etc, required for taking of [bodily samples]

(1) Subject to the provisions of subsections (3) and (4) of this section, a bodily sample which is required to be taken from any person for the purpose of giving effect to a direction under section 20 of this Act shall not be taken from that person except with his consent.

(2) The consent of a minor who has attained the age of sixteen years to the taking from himself of a bodily sample shall be as effective as it would be if he were of full age; and where a minor has by virtue of this subsection given an effective consent to the taking of a bodily sample it shall not be necessary to obtain any consent for it from any other person.

(3) A bodily sample may be taken from a person under the age of sixteen years, not being such a person as is referred to in subsection (4) of this section,

(a) if the person who has the care and control of him consents; or

(b) where that person does not consent, if the court considers that it would be in his best interests for the sample to be taken.

(4) A bodily sample may be taken from a person who is suffering from mental disorder within the meaning of the Mental Health Act 1983 and is incapable of understanding the nature and purpose of scientific tests if the person who has the care has certified that the taking of a bodily sample from him will not be prejudicial to his proper care and treatment.

(5) The foregoing provisions of this section are without prejudice to the provisions of section 23 of this Act.

...

23.—(1) Where a court gives a direction under section 20 of this Act and any person fails to take any step required of him for the purpose of giving effect to the direction, the court may draw such inferences, if any, from that fact as appear proper in the circumstances.

(2) Where in any proceedings in which the [parentage] of any person falls to be determined by the court hearing the proceedings there is a presumption of law that that person is legitimate, then if—

(a) a direction is given under section 20 of this Act in those proceedings, and

(b) any party who is claiming any relief in the proceedings and who for the purpose of obtaining that relief is entitled to rely on the presumption fails to take any step required of him for the purpose of giving effect to the direction,

the court may adjourn the hearing for such period as it thinks fit to enable that party to take that step, and if at the end of that period he has failed without reasonable cause to take it the court may, without prejudice to subsection (1) of this section, dismiss his claim for relief notwithstanding the absence of evidence to rebut the presumption.

(3) Where any person named in a direction under section 20 of this Act fails to consent to the taking of a bodily sample from himself or from any person named in the direction of whom he has the care and control, he shall be deemed for the purposes of this section to have failed to take a step required of him for the purpose of giving effect to the direction.

Note that the court directs, it does not order. But how does the court decide whether or not to make that direction? The typical scenario is where the child's mother has had an affair with a third party but is now reconciled to her husband; she may not know the truth, but she does not want the presumption of legitimacy, the status quo, and indeed the beliefs of her family members to be disturbed. The following is now the leading case on this issue:

Re H (a minor) (blood tests: parental rights)
[1996] 2 FLR 65, [1996] Fam Law 254, Court of Appeal

The mother's husband, Mr H, had a vasectomy in 1990. The mother became pregnant in March 1994. At the time she was having a sexual relationship with both her husband and the applicant, Mr B. The understanding then was that the husband would leave and the applicant move into the matrimonial home. The husband left in May 1994 but the mother changed her mind and ended the affair in July. A year later the mother and her husband were reconciled. The applicant applied for a blood test direction but the mother adamantly refused to agree that either herself or the child, Haydon, should be tested. The judge granted the application and the mother appealed.

Ward LJ: ... The mother is adamantly opposed to the use of blood testing to establish paternity. She is totally convinced that blood testing is likely to be detrimental to Haydon's welfare which she believes depends, for the foreseeable future, on his settled relationship in a happy family unit, the stability of which may be disturbed by a blood test and the pursuit of litigation by Mr B. which is doomed to fail. She saw no advantage in establishing the truth by science because, as she said:

'Haydon has a father, it is Mr H. ...'

'Even if a blood test or a DNA test were to show that B. is the father, I will never allow contact. ...'

'Even if H. died I would not let B. have any contact with Haydon. ...'

'Haydon will never know the truth. My husband's name is on the birth certificate as the father. He is Haydon's father. ...'

The following issues arise in this appeal:

1. Is refusal to undergo blood testing determinative of the application for a direction under section 20(1) of the Family Law Reform Act 1969?

2. Can an inference adverse to the refusing party be drawn only if the refusal is made after the court has directed the use of blood testing?

3. How does the child's welfare influence the decision?

4. How do the prospects of success in the proceedings influence the decision?

5. What are this child's best interests?

Issue 1 has now been resolved since this case was decided. Following the cases of *Re R (Blood test: constraint)* [1998] 1 FLR 745 and *Re O and J (Paternity: blood tests)* [2000] 1 FLR 418, s. 21(3) was amended, as shown above. Ward LJ continued:

2. Can an inference be drawn only if the refusal to give blood samples is made after the court's direction?

Mr Blair QC supports the judge's conclusion that, 'because of the existence of the statutory provision it must be only in the circumstances in which an adverse inference may be drawn as laid down in the Act that any such inference can be drawn and this cannot happen outside the Act'. ...

The question seems to me to be not so much whether the court is entitled to draw an adverse inference but what, if any, inference can be drawn from a refusal. That is the way the Law Commission approached the question. They said:

'43. So far as adultery is concerned the wife knows, as a fact, whether or not she has committed adultery. It is, therefore, proper that the court should be able to infer from her refusal to be tested that she is trying to prevent it from discovering a fact of which she herself has knowledge. On the question of the child's paternity however the position is different. Here she does not know which of the two men is the child's father; she is refusing to be tested, not in order to hide facts of which she has knowledge, but because she does not want to run the risk of her child being shown to be illegitimate. Her refusal has no bearing on whether or not the child is illegitimate and the court may well decide that it cannot draw any inference on the issue of paternity.

44. The problem is not confined to cases where the child's mother refuses to be tested. A husband can also take advantage of the presumption of legitimacy and refuse to be tested if he is anxious to have the child's legitimacy established. Let us take as an example the case where a husband is divorcing his wife on the ground of her adultery. The wife admits her adultery and it is clear that both the husband and the co-respondent had intercourse during the period of conception of the child concerned. The husband and wife are each applying for custody of the child. There is no way, apart from using blood test evidence, by which it can be established which of the men is the child's father. The wife, wanting custody and wanting to prove that the co-respondent, whom she is to marry, is the child's father, asks for blood tests. The husband also wanting custody, refuses to be blood tested because he wishes the child to be declared his. The court cannot properly draw from his refusal the inference that the child is illegitimate; neither the husband nor anyone else knows who is the child's father. The presumption of legitimacy is therefore applied and the husband is held to be the child's father.

45. How can parties be prevented from refusing to comply with a court order for blood tests, purely as a matter of tactics, so as to prevent the presumption of legitimacy being rebutted? We have already said that we do not think that it would be acceptable to force a person by physical compulsion to submit to an order for blood tests to be taken. We think it would be equally unacceptable to treat a refusal as contempt of court. ...

47. In our view the most effective way of dealing with this problem is to provide that where a direction for blood tests is made and a party to the proceedings is entitled to rely on the presumption of legitimacy in claiming relief, then if that party refuses to be tested the court may either draw inferences against him (if appropriate) or dismiss his application for relief.'

It should be remembered that at that time blood testing served only to exclude paternity: It did not establish it. It seems to me that a refusal to comply after the solemnity of the court's decision is more eloquent testimony of an attempt at hiding a truth than intransigent objection made as a forensic tactic. Science has now advanced. The whole truth can now be known... Common sense seems to me to dictate that if the truth can be established with certainty, a refusal to produce the certainty justifies some inference that the refusal is made to hide the truth, even if the inference is not as strong as when the Court's direction is flouted.

3. How do considerations of the child's welfare influence the decision?

The judge correctly directed himself that he should 'refuse the test if satisfied it would be against the child's interests to order it'. This is wholly in accordance with *S v McC*. There Lord Reid said at p.45D:

'I would, therefore, hold that the court ought to permit a blood test of a young child to be taken unless satisfied that would be against the child's interests.'

Lord Hodson said at p.58G:

'The court in ordering a blood test in the case of an infant has, of course, a discretion and may make or refuse an order for a test in the exercise of its discretion, but the interests of the other persons than the infant are involved in ordinary litigation. The infant needs protection but that is no justification for making his rights superior to those of others.'

It is clear, therefore, that whereas welfare is the paramount consideration in deciding the applications for parental responsibility and contact orders, welfare does not dominate this decision.

4. How do the prospects of success in the proceedings influence the decision?

In *Re F* it was held at p.32A that:

> 'If the probable outcome of those proceedings will be the same whoever may be the natural father of E., then there can be no point in exposing E. to the possible disadvantages of a blood test.'

The speeches in the House of Lords seem to take a somewhat different view. Lord MacDermott, at p.48E says:

> 'If the court had reason to believe that the application for a blood test was of a fishing nature, designed for some ulterior motive to call in question the legitimacy, otherwise unimpeached, of a child who had enjoyed a legitimate status, it may well be that the court, acting under its protective rather than its ancillary jurisdiction, would be justified in refusing the application. ...
>
> ... It would be a backward step to start to whittle down the effect of section 1, but it would be just as bad to have to apply its final criterion on a finding of fact which was not reached on the best available evidence, and even worse if that had to happen because the court, having spied a paternity issue, considered that it should not be fully explored.'

Reading those authorities together, it seems to me that the correct approach must be:

1. The paternity issue must be judged as a free standing application entitled to consideration on its own.

2. The outcome of the proceedings in which the paternity issue has been raised, insofar as it bears on the welfare of child, must be taken into account.

3. Any gain to the child from preventing any disturbance to his security must be balanced against the loss to him of the certainty of knowing who he is.

4. The terms of section 10(4) of the Children Act 1989 are explicit in giving parent a right to apply for contact because they provide:

> 'The following persons are entitled to apply to the court for any section 8 order with respect to a child—
>
> (a) any parent ... of the child; ... .'

There is no statutory justification for transforming the paternity issue into a disguised application for leave to apply and judging the paternity issue by the criteria set out in section 10(9).

5. Accordingly, whilst the outcome of the section 8 proceedings and the risk of disruption to the child's life both by the continuance of the paternity issue as well as the pursuit of the section 8 order are obviously factors which impinge on the child's welfare, they are not, in my judgment, determinative of the blood testing question.

In this case the judge's conclusion was that 'it would be rather unlikely that the court would make an order for contact'. That is a conclusion he was plainly entitled to reach, and one which I would support. He did not, however, expressly deal with the parental responsibility order. ...

5. What are the child's best interests?

The mother submits that 'pursuing contact would be to destabilise her own marriage which has only recently been put together again to the disadvantage of the child'. Miss Scotland QC submits accordingly that the case is indistinguishable from *Re F*.

I do not agree. ... The material facts of the case under appeal before us include these features which may or may not have applied in *Re F*:

1. As the judge found, Mr B. has a substantial case for his claim to be this child's father. That can be seen from:

    a.   The mother's clear belief, at least until she set eyes on her baby, that the child was born of her adulterous relationship. She now closes her mind even to the possibility that might be so.

    b.   The fact that Mr H. has had a vasectomy. He admitted thinking that it was 'unlikely that I would be the father'.

2. If Mr and Mrs H. were reconciled in that state of mind, having their worst fears realised is unlikely of itself to be the cause for the breakdown of a fragile reconciliation. ...

3. It may well be correct, as Miss Scotland submits, that denial of the truth is essential to this mother for the restoration of her self-esteem and for the expiation of her guilt. That creates a danger in putting her welfare to the forefront, not the child's. ...

4. This secret cannot be hidden forever. Mr H. knows the substantial difficulty of his position. Moreover, and most importantly, 14 year old Christopher knows, because his mother told him, that his father may not be Haydon's father. It is unrealistic to pretend that the time will not come when Haydon has to face these doubts about his paternity. If his peace of mind is likely to

be threatened, and if he has a right to know, the question then becomes one of when it is best he should learn the truth.

5. In my judgment every child has a right to know the truth unless his welfare clearly justifies the cover up. The right to know is acknowledged in the United Nations Convention on the Rights of the Child (Treaty Series No 44 of 1992) (Cm. 1976) which has been ratified by the United Kingdom and in particular Article 7 which provides 'that a child has, as far as possible, the right to know and be cared for by his or her parents'. In *Re F* the putative father submitted that the child's welfare included her right to know under this Article. Balcome LJ said at p.321A:

'Whether or not B is included in this definition of parent within the meaning of this Article, it is not in fact possible for E to be cared for by both her parents (if B is such). No family unit exists, nor has it ever existed, between B and Mrs F, and if B were able to assert his claims to have share in E's upbringing it would inevitable risk damaging her right to be cared for by her mother, Mrs F.'

That passage concentrates on the child's right to be cared for by his or her parents. I do not read it as refuting what to me seems the clear intent of the Article that there are two separate rights, the one to know, and the other to be cared for by, one's parents. ...

6. This is the whole tenor of the speeches in the House of Lords. Lord Reid (and Lord Guest) said at p.45D:

'The court must protect the child, but it is not really protecting the child to ban a blood test on some vague and shadowy conjecture that it may turn out to be to its disadvantage: it may equally turn out to be for its advantage or at least do it no harm.'

...

Lord Hodson at p.59B asked:

'Who is to say what is in the interest of the child and whether knowledge of true paternity would or would not favour his or her future prospects in life? How are these interests to be assessed? I find these questions especially difficult to answer in view of the fact that it must surely be in the best interests of the child in most cases that paternity doubts should be resolved on the best evidence, and, as in adoption, the child be told the truth as soon as possible.'

7. Lord Hodson's reference to adoption produces interesting parallels. The Houghton Committee reporting in 1972 called for greater openness in adoption. That call was heeded. Section 51 of the Adoption Act 1976 now enables adopted persons to obtain access to their birth records. The Inter-departmental Review of Adoption Law in 1992 expressed the opinion that 'it is fundamental to the welfare of the child that he or she is told (when of sufficient age and understanding) about his or her adoptive status'. It is a recognition that the child's shock at discovering the truth about his origins at a later stage in childhood will be increased by the realisation that his adopted parents have, to date, allowed him to believe in a falsehood that he was their child.

8. Section 56 of the Family Law Act 1986 gives Haydon the right to apply for a declaration—

'(a) that a person named in the application is or was his parent: or

(b) that he is the legitimate child of his parents.'

9. Given the real risk bordering on inevitability that Haydon will at some time question his paternity, then I do not see how this case is not concluded by the unassailable wisdom expressed Lord Hodson at p.57H:

'The interests of justice in the abstract are best served by the ascertainment of the truth and there must be few cases where the interests of children can be shown to be best served by the suppression of truth.'

If, as she should, this mother is to bring up her children to believe in and to act by the maxim, which is her duty to teach them at her knee, that honesty is the best policy, then she should not sabotage that lesson by living a lie.

10. If the child has the right to know, then the sooner it is told the better. The issue of biological parentage should be divorced from psychological parentage. Acknowledging Mr B.'s parental responsibility should not dent Mr H.'s social responsibility for a child whom he is so admirably prepared to care for and love irrespective of whether or not he is the father. If the cracks in the H. marriage are so wide that they will be rent asunder by the truth then the piece of paper which dismisses the application hardly seems adhesive enough to bind them together.

11. If Haydon grows up knowing the truth, that will not undermine his attachment to his father figure and he will cope with knowing he has two fathers. Better that than a time-bomb ticking away.

Conclusions

The judge concluded that it was not within his power to prevent this father pursuing his application. I agree. ...

Appeal dismissed. Order below varied to direct rather than to order taking of blood samples from applicant, mother and child.

Questions

(i) What would your answer have been if (a) it had been the applicant who had had the vasectomy, and/or (b) there was a strong physical resemblance between the child and the mother's husband?

(ii) If everyone has the right to know who their biological parents are, does this apply (a) to all adopted people, (b) to all people born of donated sperm, or (c) to all people born of donated eggs?

(iii) How easy is it to judge what will be in the child's best interests? Suppose, for example, that Miss B is brutally raped by Mr X, who is a very rich man, and a child Y results; 20 years later X is killed in a road accident having left no will. Should he have been registered as Y's father when his application for contact with the baby was refused?

(iv) Does the making of a direction under s. 20 of the Family Law Act 1969 amount to an interference with an individual's private and family life (European Convention on Human Rights, Art. 8), given the possibility that a test result may disturb or destroy a happy family?

Of course, there are a number of contexts in which a determination of paternity may be needed. As the Lord Chancellor's Department's Consultation Paper on *Procedures for the Determination of Paternity* (1998) puts it:

6. A determination of paternity may be needed for a variety of reasons, including those listed below.
   a.   A person may need to prove that he or she is a child of a specified person, for example in order to amend his birth certificate, to establish his or her right to inherit property, or to acquire nationality or citizenship (which may be relevant for immigration purposes).
   b.   A father may need to prove his relationship with his child, for example in order to seek a parental responsibility order, or an order for residence or contact, under the Children Act 1989.
   c.   The child's mother, or the Child Support Agency, may need to establish paternity so that the father can be required to contribute to the child's maintenance.
7. At present there is no single procedure, covering all these circumstances, for obtaining a determination of parentage from the court. Paternity may be established in one of three ways:
   a.   by a declaration of parentage under section 56 of the Family Law Act 1986, which is binding for all purposes but is available only on the application of the 'child' in question; or
   b.   by a declaration under section 27 of the Child Support Act 1991, which is effective only for child support purposes and is available on the application of the person with care of the child or the Secretary of State; or
   c.   by a direction from the court for blood tests under section 20 of the Family Law Reform Act 1969; this is only available when the court has to resolve a dispute about paternity in the course of existing civil proceedings, and no freestanding application can be made under section 20.

Section 56(1) of the Family Law Act 1986 allows a child to apply for a declaration: (a) that a person named in the application is or was his parent; or (b) that he is the legitimate child of his parents. Section 56(2) allows him to apply for a declaration that he has or has not become a legitimated person.

Questions

(i) Why should only the child himself be able to apply? Why not a grandchild? Why not a father? Why not a mother?

(ii) If you know who your parents are, in what circumstances might you also have to know whether you were legitimate or legitimated?

(iii) Do you think that a mother should be obliged to name a child's father (a) for the purpose of claiming benefits (so that steps can be taken to recover a contribution from him) or (b) in all cases?

(iv) Is your stereotype of the unmarried father a man who is anxious to avoid his responsibilities or a man who is anxious to assert his relationship in the face of the mother's determination to have nothing more to do with him? Should the law on establishing paternity be the same in each case?

11.3 How to adopt a child

Another way of becoming a parent is to adopt a child. Adoption means a great many different things. For a summary of the extraordinary diversity of the institution, we may turn to *Adoption: A Second Chance* (1977), Barbara Tizard's account of her study comparing the adoption or rehabilitation of children in care:

The essence of adoption is that a child not born to you is incorporated into your family as though he were your own. This practice can be found in some form in most cultures – one of the best-known early adoptions was that of Moses. But just as the family, although a constant feature of all societies, has assumed many different forms and functions, so the characteristics of adoption have varied enormously during history. Today most people think of adoption as a process in which a young child, usually an infant, is permanently incorporated into a family into which he was not born. Typically, the adoptive parents and the biological parents are strangers, and the adoption is arranged through an agency or other third party. Great stress is laid on keeping the two sets of parents from meeting or even knowing each others' identity. All links between the adopted child and his natural parents are severed, and the adopted child has all the rights, and is treated in the same way, as a natural child of his new family. The primary purpose of the adoption is seen to be the satisfaction of the desire of a married couple to rear a child; at the same time, a home is provided for a child whose natural parents are unable to rear it. ...

Perhaps the greatest contrast is with the custom of child exchange, or kinship fostering, formerly prevalent in Polynesia and parts of Africa. In these societies children were often not reared by their biological parents but sent to be raised by relatives, sometimes after weaning, sometimes from the age of 6 or 7. The exchange of children was arranged by the parents, who continued to maintain some contact with their biological child. It was believed that aunts, uncles and grandparents would bring children up and train them more effectively than their parents. This custom of child exchange seems to have been part of a system of mutual kinship obligations.

Adoption played a very different role in such ancient civilisations as the Babylonian, Chinese and Roman. There, its function was primarily to ensure the continuity of wealthy families by providing for the inheritance of property and the performance of ancestral worship. Roman law, for example, permitted adoption only in order to provide an heir to the childless, and laid down that the adopters must be past child-bearing age and the adoptee must be an adult. Until recently, the adoption laws of many European countries were influenced by Roman law; often adoptive parents had to be childless and over the age of 50.

Hindu law also recognised adoption as a method of securing an heir, both for religious purposes and for the inheritance of property. It specified, however, that the adopted child should be if possible a blood relative, and that the transaction must take place directly between the two sets of parents. For this reason, orphans could not be adopted. In most ancient civilisations adoption was only one among several possible ways of providing an heir, and often not the preferred one. In Islam, for example, divorce and remarriage, polygamy, and the legitimisation of children by maidservants were common practices, while adoption was not permitted.

In all these societies adoption was essentially concerned with preserving the property and the religious observances of the families of the ruling class. It was very much a service for the rich, and for men; it was men who wanted heirs, and for this purpose they wanted boys. The emotional needs of childless wives were not recognised; indeed if they did not produce an heir they were likely to be divorced or otherwise replaced. Nor was it a service for homeless children; the adoptees were often adult, or, if children, they were given to the adoptive parents by their biological parents in order to better their social status.

Question

It may be easy to see why the modern idea of providing a home for an illegitimate and often pauper child found little favour in medieval England, but how do you account for the fact that the great English families did not wish to do as the Romans had done – so that, even now, an adopted child cannot succeed to a peerage or other hereditary title?

Tizard adds that 'It is only relatively recently that adoption has become a recognised practice in Western society'. Certainly in England there was no legal form of adoption until the 1920s. In 1921, the Hopkinson Committee reported in favour of providing for legal adoption, but its recommendations proved so controversial that a second Committee was appointed, under the chairmanship of Mr Justice Tomlin. The Report of the Child Adoption Committee in 1925 is far from enthusiastic:

4. ... There have no doubt always been some people who desire to bring up as their own the children of others but we have been unable to satisfy ourselves as to the extent of the effective demand for a legal system of adoption by persons who themselves have adopted children or who desire to do so. It may be doubted whether any such persons have been or would be deterred from adopting children by the absence of any recognition by the law of the status of adoption. The war led to an increase in the number of de facto adoptions but that increase has not been wholly maintained. The people wishing to get rid of children are far more numerous than those wishing to receive them and partly on this account the activities in recent years of societies arranging systematically for the adoption of children would appear to have given to adoption a prominence which is somewhat artificial and may not be in all respects wholesome. The problem of the unwanted child is a serious one; it may well be a question whether a legal system of adoption will do much to assist the solution of it.
...
9. [Nevertheless] ... we think that there is a measure of genuine apprehension on the part of those who have in fact adopted other people's children, based on the possibility of interference at some future time by the natural parent. It may be that this apprehension has but a slight basis in fact notwithstanding the incapacity of the legal parent to divest himself of his parental rights and duties. The Courts have long recognised that any application by the natural parent to recover the custody of his child will be determined by reference to the child's welfare and by that consideration alone. The apprehension, therefore, in most cases has a theoretical rather than a practical basis. There is also a sentiment which deserves sympathy and respect, that the relation between adopter and adopted should be given some recognition by the community. We think, therefore, that a case is made out for an alteration in the law. ...

Having reluctantly reached that conclusion, the Committee went on to consider how adoption should take place, and to what effect. Some of their arguments cast an interesting light upon more recent debates:

11. ... some form of judicial sanction should be required. ...
15. ... Whichever be the tribunal selected it is important that the judicial sanction, which will necessarily carry great weight, should be a real adjudication and should not become a mere method of registering the will of the parties respectively seeking to part with and take over the child. To avoid this result we think that in every case there should be appointed ... some body or person to act as guardian ad litem of the child with the duty of protecting the interests of the child before the tribunal.
...

18. ... No system of adoption, seeking as it does to reproduce artificially a natural relation, can hope to produce precisely the same result or to be otherwise than in many respects illogical, and this is made apparent in the diversity of provisions in relation to succession and marriage which appear in the adoption laws of other countries.

19. We think that in introducing into English law a new system it would be well to proceed with a measure of caution and at any rate in the first instance not to interfere with the law of succession ... it does not require any profound knowledge of the law of succession to bring home to an enquirer (1) the impracticality of putting an adopted child in precisely the same position as a natural child in regard to succession, and (2) the grave difficulties which would arise if any alteration were to be made in the law of succession for the purpose of giving an adopted child more limited rights ... but ... the tribunal which sanctions the adoption should have power if it thinks fit, to require that some provision be made by the adopting parent for the child.

Question

What, if anything, was so different about the system of succession in classical Roman law that the complete absorption of the adopted child into his new family presented none of the difficulties apparently so obvious to English lawyers in 1925?

If these passages in the report betray (although they do not confess to) deep-seated attitudes about 'natural' and 'artificial' relationships, there is one point upon which the Committee's views have a decidedly modern ring:

28. ... Certain of the Adoption Societies make this feature an essential part of their policy. They deliberately seek to fix a gulf between the child's past and future. This notion of secrecy has its origin partly in a fear (which a legalised system of adoption should go far to dispel) that the natural parents will seek to interfere with the adopter and partly in the belief that if the eyes can be closed to facts the facts themselves will cease to exist so that it will be an advantage to an illegitimate child who has been adopted if in fact his origin cannot be traced. Apart from the question whether it is desirable or even admissible deliberately to eliminate or obscure the traces of a child's origin ... we think that this system of secrecy would be wholly unnecessary and objectionable in connection with a legalised system of adoption.

The first cautious steps were taken in the Adoption of Children Act 1926; the issue of succession was resolved following the Houghton Report (1972) so that, since 1975, there have been only three important exceptions to the principle that an adopted child is the same as a child born to married parents: he cannot succeed to peerages and similar dignities; the rules prohibiting marriages with certain relatives in his birth family remain and he is only debarred from marriage with his adoptive parent in the new family; and if he is adopted abroad he will not gain the same rights under nationality and immigration laws as would a child born abroad to United Kingdom parents or adopted here. That last point has disappeared for most overseas adoptions following s. 7 of the Adoption (Intercountry Aspects) Act 1999.

The principal Act is now the Adoption Act 1976, shortly to be replaced by what is now the Adoption and Children Bill, introduced in Parliament in 2001 and expected to become law late in 2002. Section 57 of the 1976 Act, and now clauses 93 and 94 of the Bill, preserve one principle which has been taken for granted from the start:

93. Prohibition of certain payments

(1) This section applies to any payment (other than an excepted payment) which is made for or in consideration of—

(a) the adoption of a child,

(b) giving any consent required in connection with the adoption of a child,

(c) removing from the United Kingdom a child who is a Commonwealth citizen, or is habitually resident in the United Kingdom, to a place outside the British Islands for the purpose of adoption,

(d) a person (who is neither an adoption agency nor acting in pursuance of an order of the High Court) taking any step mentioned in section 90(2),

(e) preparing, causing to be prepared or submitting a report the preparation of which contravenes section 92(1).

(2) In this section and section 94, removing a child from the United Kingdom has the same meaning as in section 84.

(3) Any person who—

(a) makes any payment to which this section applies,

(b) agrees or offers to make any such payment, or

(c) receives or agrees to receive or attempts to obtain any such payment,

is guilty of an offence.

(4) A person guilty of an offence under this section is liable on summary conviction to imprisonment for a term not exceeding six months, or a fine not exceeding £10,000, or both.

94. Excepted payments

(1) A payment is an excepted payment if it is made by virtue of, or in accordance with provision made by or under, this Act, the Adoption (Scotland) Act 1978 or the Adoption (Northern Ireland) Order 1987.

(2) A payment is an excepted payment if it is made to a registered adoption society by—

(a) a parent or guardian of a child, or

(b) a person who adopts or proposes to adopt a child,

in respect of expenses reasonably incurred by the society in connection with the adoption or proposed adoption of the child.

(3) A payment is an excepted payment if it is made in respect of any legal or medical expenses incurred or to be incurred by any person in connection with an application to a court which he has made or proposes to make for an adoption order, a placement order, or an order under section 25 or 83.

(4) A payment made as mentioned in section 93(1)(c) is an excepted payment if—

(a) the condition in section 84(2) is met, and

(b) the payment is made in respect of the travel and accommodation expenses reasonably incurred in removing the child from the United Kingdom for the purpose of adoption.

Questions

(i) What is so wrong about paying an unmarried mother to let you have her baby?

(ii) Can it be distinguished from paying a doctor to inseminate you with the semen of an unknown donor?

(iii) Or paying a woman to bear your child? (See p. 544, below.)

(iv) Wait a moment – is not that what husbands do?

At first, however, while payment was prohibited, adoptions could be arranged either by adoption societies, or by individual third parties (such as doctors or lawyers) or by the mother herself. Regulation of adoption societies was introduced in 1939 and improved in 1950. The increasing professionalism of adoption societies led to an increasing concern about the private placement of children for adoption, discussed in the *Report of the Departmental Committee on the Adoption of Children* (the Houghton Report) in 1972:

83. The Hurst Committee estimated that in 1954 more than one-third of non-relative adoptions resulted from placements by third parties or by the natural parents. The 1966 survey figures... show that the proportion was then very much less. Nevertheless there were some 1,500 children a year placed in this way. There are a number of reasons why people make independent arrangements without using agency services. One is the inaccessibility of agencies in some areas, which our recommendations are designed to remedy. Others are people's dislike of the idea of enquiries by an agency, a desire to keep control of the situation themselves, or their trust

in a person known to them, such as their family doctor. Some would-be adopters have been turned down by agencies, and others may seek independent placements because they realise that no adoption agency would consider them suitable.

84. Much concern has been expressed about these placements. The decision to place a child with a particular couple is the most important stage in the adoption process. Adoption law must give assurance of adequate safeguards for the welfare of the child at this stage, otherwise it is ineffective. This assurance rests mainly upon the skilled work of the adoption services, which includes preparation for adoptive parenthood. An independent adoption is one in which this assurance is lacking. We therefore suggested in our working paper that independent placements with non-relatives should no longer be allowed.

Clause 90 of the Adoption and Children Bill (the successor to s. 11 of the 1976 Act) provides:

90.   Restriction on arranging adoptions, etc.

(1)   A person who is neither an adoption agency nor acting in pursuance of an order of the High Court must not take any of the steps mentioned in subsection (2).

(2)   The steps are—

(a)   asking a person other than an adoption agency to provide a child for adoption,

(b)   asking a person other than an adoption agency to provide prospective adopters for a child,

(c)   offering to find a child for adoption,

(d)   offering a child for adoption to a person other than an adoption agency,

(e)   handing over a child to any person other than an adoption agency with a view to the child's adoption by that or another person,

(f)   receiving a child handed over to him in contravention of paragraph (e),

(g)   entering into an agreement with any person for the adoption of a child, or for the purpose of facilitating the adoption of a child, where no adoption agency is acting on behalf of the child in the adoption,

(h)   initiating or taking part in negotiations of which the purpose is the conclusion of an agreement within paragraph (g),

(i)   causing another person to take any of the steps mentioned in paragraphs (a) to (h).

(3)   Subsection (1) does not apply to a person taking any of the steps mentioned in paragraphs (d), (e), (g), (h) and (i) of subsection (2) if the following condition is met.

(4)   The condition is that—

(a)   the prospective adopters are parents, relatives or guardians of the child (or one of them is), or

(a)   the prospective adopter is a step-parent of the child.

...

By clause 91, contravening this, or receiving a child placed in contravention of this, or taking part in the management of a body which exists to arrange adoptions but is not an approved adoption agency, is an offence.

Questions

(i) Now that so few babies are offered for adoption here, many more couples are going abroad, often to South America or China, to adopt: what can we do to insist that restrictions on arrangements and payments are obeyed?

(ii) If they succeed in finding a child and bring him back here, should we allow them to adopt?

(iii) What can we do (a) to stop them or (b) to protect the children?

We look at inter-country adoptions later in this section. First, we look at the way in which the overall picture of adoption has changed over the years.

The fluctuating fortunes of adoption over the years are shown in the following graph taken from Nigel Lowe's 'English Adoption Law, Past, Present and Future' (2000):

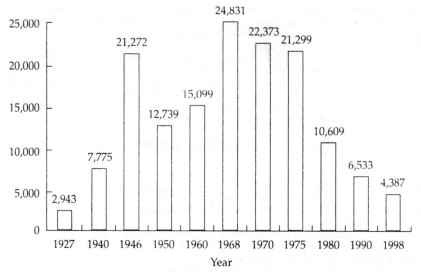

Figure 14.1.   The total number of adoptions in England and Wales.
Source: 1927–71: Houghton Committee Report – Appendix B. 1975–98: 1997 Marriage, Divorce and Adoption Statistics.

Question

Would you expect a continuing decline in the supply of babies and young children for adoption?

Nigel Lowe, in 'The changing face of adoption – the gift/donation model versus the contract/services model' (1997), comments:

... the 'mind set' which is, rightly or wrongly associated with the adoption of babies, still permeates thinking not only behind the law and, possibly to a lesser extent, practice, but also the attitudes of adopters themselves. Under this 'mind set'... adoption is seen very much as the last and irrevocable act in a process in which the birth parent – normally, of course, the mother – has 'given away' her baby via the adoption agency to the adopters, who are then left to their own devices and resources to bring up the child as their own. Associated with this model is the 'exclusive' view of adoption, ie that the child is both *de jure* and *de facto* transplanted *exclusively* to the adoptive family, with no further contact or relationship with the birth family. This model, however, sits uneasily with the adoption of older children, and it will be my contention that in these instances, at least, a different model is needed in which it is recognised that adoption is not the end of the process, but merely part of an ongoing and often complex process of family development.

Thus three quite different kinds of adoption have emerged: the voluntary, if deeply painful, surrender of a baby or young child to complete strangers; the adoption of a child by a step-parent or other member of his existing family network; and the compulsory removal from one family to another of a child who usually already has a family history of his own. We shall here concentrate on the first, dealing with the others in Chapters 12 and 14. Here we ask: in the once typical but now unusual 'baby adoption', who should be able to adopt? Is it right to continue the 'total transplant' model of adoption? What about open adoption?

Eligibility to adopt is discussed in the *Review of Adoption Law – Report to Ministers of an Interdepartmental Working Group* (1992):

26.4 We recommend that agencies should not be allowed to operate absolute rules governing people's eligibility for consideration as adopters. In other words, a person who meets the statutory criteria for an adoptive parent should not automatically be excluded from consideration on account, say, of his or her age. An agency may, however, decide that, having regard to the needs of the children for whom adoptive families are required and to agency guidelines on suitability, it would not be appropriate to accept that person for consideration.

...

Upper age limits

26.7 Agencies may not impose strict age limits on adopters, as there is no provision for this in legislation, but they do operate their own age guidelines in relation to people who want to adopt healthy infants. These vary from the early to late thirties, and few agencies will accept applicants over 40 for consideration as adopters for healthy infants. The guidelines reflect the view that it is better for very young children to be placed with adopters who are not older by too wide a margin than most couples starting a family.

26.8 We do not consider it appropriate to set down requirements or guidelines in relation to an upper age for adopters, or a maximum interval between the ages of adopter and child. Some children may benefit from having adoptive parents who do not differ greatly in terms of age from their birth parents or from the parents of their peers. But there may be circumstances where older applicants, by virtue of their maturity, experience, or other special qualities, are particularly well-qualified to provide a home for a child. Agencies should always be satisfied, however, that adopters have a reasonable expectation of retaining health and vigour to care for a child until he or she is grown up; age is one of a number of factors which should be taken into account in determining whether an applicant meets this criterion.

Marital status

26.9 At present, an adoption order may be made on the application of a married couple. A single person may also apply for an adoption order. However, a married person may only adopt alone if the court is satisfied that the spouse cannot be found or is incapable of applying by reason of physical or mental ill-health; or that the couple have separated and are living apart, and the separation is likely to be permanent.

26.10 In practice, some agencies assess and prepare unmarried couples together, although only one partner may apply for the order and become the child's legal parent. It has been asked whether an unmarried couple should be allowed to adopt jointly. Family structures are changing and more children are born to parents who are not married but are living in stable unions. Under section 4 of the Children Act 1989, an unmarried father may acquire the same parental status as one who is married. On the other hand, unmarried parents do not have the same legal obligations to one another as a married couple have. Should the relationship break down, the caring parent may therefore be less financially secure than if they were married. Furthermore, one of the special features of adoption is that it transfers a child from one family to another and gives the child a legal relationship with all members of the new family, including grandparents, aunts and uncles. However great the commitment of unmarried adoptive parents to a child might be, it is open to question how far their wider families would be willing to accept that child as part of their family.

26.11 It is also important to bear in mind Article 6(1) of the European Adoption Convention which prohibits adoption by unmarried couples. Although some unmarried couples might be suitable adoptive parents for a child, we feel that the security and stability which adopted children need are still more likely to be provided by parents who have made a publicly recognized commitment to their relationship and who have legal responsibilities towards each other. Taking into account also the United Kingdom's international obligations, we consider that it would not be appropriate to allow two unmarried people to adopt jointly.

26.12 The fact that two people are married to each other is not of course in itself a sufficient guide to the likely stability of their relationship. Agencies generally expect applicants to have been married for at least three years, although some are prepared to take into account periods of co-habitation preceding marriage, where there is evidence of it available. We consider that agencies should have flexibility to operate their own criteria in forming views on the likely stability of a marriage, and that this should be the subject of guidance.

26.13 We do not propose any changes to the law relating to single applicants, including lesbians and gay men. There are examples of extremely successful adoptions, particularly of older children and children with disabilities, by single adopters. Some children are only able to settle in single-parent households, as a result of experiences in their early lives.

26.14 Some agencies may place a child with a single applicant who is living with a partner. As a matter of practice, to safeguard the child, they also assess the suitability of the partner. We have suggested above that an unmarried couple should not be allowed to adopt jointly, ie that it should not be possible for them to have the same legal relationship towards a child which they would have if they were a married couple adopting together. We do not feel that this is necessarily incompatible with allowing a single person who has a partner to adopt. We recommend that, where assessing a single applicant, agencies should have a duty to assess any other person who is likely to act in a parental capacity towards the adopted child.

Health

26.15 There are no statutory requirements in respect of the health of adopters. Adoption agencies are required to obtain a report on the prospective adopters' health, covering matters such as personal and family health history and current state of health, and consumption of tobacco, alcohol and other habit-forming drugs.

26.16 Professionals, agencies and courts can face difficult decisions in relation to the extent to which health factors may influence a prospective adopter's suitability. Agencies appear to employ a variety of approaches, particularly in relation to smoking. Central guidelines on general principles might help to achieve a greater sense of fairness among prospective adopters and assist agencies in making difficult decisions.

In *Adoption – a new approach*, the White Paper published by the Department of Health in 2000, the issue of eligibility is addressed again. It is said that there is:

... little evidence of agencies using arbitrary criteria for assessment, [but] if these are used, children are the losers. There have been cases where potential adopters have been told they cannot adopt solely because they are too old or because they smoke. Blanket bans of this kind are unjust and unacceptable. Each case should be judged on its merits and the needs of children considered – the important thing is to ensure that adopters can offer children a safe, stable and loving home through childhood and beyond.

Questions

(i) Who do you think would be more suitable to bring up a little girl of two, recently released for adoption by her mother, who had found it impossible to cater for either her physical or her psychological needs: (a) a childless couple in their 30s, who have turned to adoption in desperation after unsuccessful attempts to cure the wife's infertility, or (b) a couple in their 40s whose own three children are now aged 18, 15 and 10 and who have been acting as short-term foster parents but would prefer a permanent placement?

(ii) Would you say the same if the child were of mixed race and couple (a) were white and couple (b) were black?

(iii) Parliament has agreed an amendment to the Adoption and Children Bill so as to allow unmarried couples to adopt. If a man and woman have chosen not to marry, why should they be able to enter a joint legal commitment to a child? Can you foresee problems for either the child or the full-time carer (usually the mother) in such circumstances?

(iv) What about same-sex couples, who of course cannot marry? Can you suggest any legal arrangements they might be required to make before being allowed to adopt?

Those last two questions reflect some of the controversy that has surrounded the Adoption and Children Bill 2001 which, as drafted, did not allow unmarried couples to adopt. At the point when this book goes to press, the final form of the Bill is uncertain; so, too, is the resolution of the current demand for the availability of registered partnerships for unmarried couples (see Chapter 2, p. 70).

But what should adoption mean? Is it simply a way of providing a home for a child who needs one, or is it a total transfer from one family to another? And can that transfer ever be quite complete? In fact this raises two issues. First, how far is adoption incompatible with a continuing relationship with the birth family, and the appropriateness of 'open adoption'; second, the question of access to birth records.

Open adoption is an issue because, despite the reservations expressed by the Tomlin committee (p. 521, above), secrecy has long been a feature of adoption. Nigel Lowe (1997) comments:

Today, the practice of so-called 'open adoption' is very much a fact of adoption life. Of the respondents to our family questionnaire we found that about half had met the birth mother, and 21 per cent the father. There were also a substantial number who had had some form of contact with other birth relatives, and nearly as many had ongoing contact after the adoption order. Indeed, considerable post-adoption work is involved with various forms of contact, whether it is direct or indirect – and, if the latter, through letter-box and telephone schemes. Reflecting this *de facto* growth in post-adoption contact and evident change of policy is the change of recruiting practice. As one social worker told to us:

'The whole issue of contact, letter-boxes, post-adoption work and that sort of thing has just come into our practice. It is also a standard feature of our assessment. There is a line in our agreement with prospective adopters which says Mr and Mrs Smith would be very happy for you to exchange information [ref to letter-box contact scheme]. That's just par for the course now. In fact if Mr and Mrs Smith weren't happy with that then we would wonder whether we should be approving them as adopters.'

This last point was echoed by another comment, 'Our agency has a policy of only recruiting prospective adopters who understand what openness means and are prepared to actively work with it'. This is not to say that we did not find consumer resistance to this; indeed, one adoptive couple questioned the whole rationale for contact and whether it is really helpful to a child's development, especially as the child has to hold in mind and understand so many relationships. When the couple sought to explain this to adoption agency staff they were told in no uncertain terms that their views were 'old fashioned' and unacceptable in the light of the agency's policy on open adoption and supporting contact. They had, therefore, in their own words 'to soft peddle' and keep their mouths shut. But, in fact, the couple accept letter-box contact with their adoptive daughter's half-brother and a great aunt in her eighties.

But in many cases, particularly baby adoption, there is no contact with the birth family. The effect of the transplant is an important issue, not only for many children today, but for many of today's adults who were adopted years ago. A total legal transplant does not mean a total physical or psychological transplant, as shown by these quotations from adopted adults who had sought their original birth certificates, as then permitted by Scottish but not English law, in John Triseliotis' study *In Search of Origins* (1973):

'You look at yourself in the mirror and you can't compare it with anybody. You're a stranger because you don't know what your real mother looks like or what your father looks like. ...'

'All through my life I had the feeling of unreality about myself; a feeling of not being real, something like an imitation antique ... I have been told that I was born in the Poor House and that my birth mother was a bad lot. This has been haunting me. I tried desperately to avoid being like her but then who am I like? I feel I have nothing to pass on to my children. ...'

'My parents were kind people but very isolated. We had few relatives calling and we had no habit of calling on others. My parents' relatives meant nothing to me and I must have meant nothing to them. ...When I was 15 or 16 I was very curious to know "who I was" and especially to know about my natural parents and their families. With your adoptive family you can only go as far back as they are and not beyond. But with your natural ones you feel you want to go further back. ...'

The adopted person's needs are discussed by Christine Walby and Barbara Symons in *Who am I?* (1990):

The need to know
A major task faced by adopted people is the development of a sense of separate identity out of what Sants in 1967 called 'genealogical bewilderment'. Triseliotis in 1974 posed the question of 'how far adopted people face similar or different developmental tasks from those who have not been adopted'. These 'growing-up' tasks may be seen as achieving a mature independence and a clear sense of identity, and being able to give and receive love. They are inextricably linked with knowledge and feelings about heritage and about how other people see us and behave towards us.

Thus while the growing-up tasks may be common to all, the adopted person's development may be hampered by lack of knowledge. Margaret Kornitzer described the situation graphically in 1971 when writing of the effect upon the adopted person's natural development of a sense of identity when there has been a failure to provide information about 'blood and bones':

'Background knowledge of one's family is like baby food – it is literally fed to a person as part of the normal nourishment that builds up his [or her] mental and emotional structure and helps the person to become acquainted with what he [or she] is so that he can seize his inheritance of himself.'

She goes on to discuss the importance of knowing what our (biological) parents were like in understanding much about ourselves, and of the reality being 'healthier' than the fantasy. The point is made that simply being honest with adopted children is not enough: 'Even those adopted children whose adopters have been quite honest with them do feel left out on a limb at a certain point in their development because they can have no visual or mental picture of the couple who gave them their physical continuity in the chain of life': a fact denied by many practitioners and adopters.

At a more mundane level, as McWhinnie [1970] reports, the simplest tasks of adult life, such as completing medical data on forms, can become an ordeal because of the adopted person's lack of very basic information about biological background which others possess as a matter of course.

An adopted person has, in Triseliotis' view, to base his or her identity on 'the concept of two sets of parents'. ...

The crucial issue, says Rowe, is that adopters should not pretend that being an adoptive parent is the same as being a biological parent, but should have a 'sturdy belief that their form of parenthood really is parenthood'. They also need to be able to feel 'some sense of kinship with the people who gave their child birth', and truly absorb the child's background into their family traditions.

Attitudes in the outside world

Unfortunately, as Triseliotis illustrated, the problems encountered by adopted persons in the maturation process are not limited to the resolution of attitudes, roles and relationships within the family. The community too has a subtle but profound effect: 'However successful adoptive parents are in their parental task, they cannot protect the child from the nuances of the outside world'. He also refers to 'covert negative messages', which are best illustrated by some of his examples from discussion with adopted people:

'When I told my fiance I was adopted his reply was "I do not know what my father and mother will feel ..."

When my boy was born and my mother-in-law visited me in hospital she exclaimed: "Thank God that he has taken from our side of the family." I know what she was getting at and it hurt.

Somehow I felt that my parents were ashamed to talk about it and they gave me the feeling that adoption was unnatural ...'

Thus the concept of access to birth records must be considered against a shifting foundation of confusion about the real nature of adoption. On the one hand we have absolute legal precision about the status of adoption and on the other, highly complex cultural and emotional uncertainty. It is in this context, and that of the complicated development of maturity and independence, that adopted people seek information on, and sometimes direct contact with, their origins.

Since 1975, adopted children have had the right to gain access to their birth certificates on reaching the age of 18. The Adoption Contact Register, set up under s. 51A of the Adoption Act 1976, enables adopted persons and their birth families to register a willingness to be contacted; and many adoption agencies are willing to assist adopted people in tracing their origins. The Children's Society, for example, has operated an Intermediary Service for this purpose. David Howe and Julia Feast's book, *Adoption, Search and Reunion* (2000) presents the results of a study carried out from 1997 by The Children's Society of adopted people's experience of search and reunion. The study was able to look both at adopted people who searched and at those who did not. Her analysis is as follows:

Why do adopted people search?

Explanations for the desire to search are broadly captured by two models – the normative and the pathological. The normative model sees searching as a natural outcome of adoption and not as a negative response to an adverse adoptive situation. This model stresses the fluidity of identity, and sees searching as an attempt to integrate one's roots and to develop a fuller understanding of who one is. The act of searching adds to, rather than replaces, one's existing identity. Adopted people's desire to know their roots is a universal phenomenon and is part of normal personality development. For adopted people, finding out who one is and where one comes from just happens to be a more complex process.

The pathological model suggests that the desire to search arises out of a dissatisfaction or difficulty with one's adoption. The adopted person is seeking a new, or reclaiming some lost, original identity. The model predicts that those with mental health or personality problems are more likely to search to fulfil a need. It is suggested that knowledge of one's origins is essential for mental health and identity formation. Triseliotis (1973) interviewed 70 people in Scotland who had sought further information about their parents. He found evidence of mental health problems and/or disturbed family relationship, concluding that the need to seek genealogical information and search for birth parents was activated by some deeply felt psychological need and rarely related to a matter-of-fact attitude (Triseliotis, 1973, p. 154).

The idea that adopted people have trouble with their identity is prevalent in the literature. Sorosky *et al.* (1974) believed that many adopted people cannot realise their full identity until they have information about their birth parents. 'For some, the existing block to the past may create the feeling that there is a block to the future as well' (Sorosky *et al.* 1974, p. 205). The authors describe feelings of 'genealogical bewilderment' caused by a lack of biological connection. The term genealogical bewilderment was first used by Sants (1964) to describe an adopted person not having access to information about their ancestry. Feeling a lack of connectedness is not necessarily caused by an unhappy adoption experience; it is simply a lack of knowledge about one's past that interferes with identity formation (see also Ryburn, 1995).

Supporters of the normative model argue that since adoption is essentially a social construct, and that adoption is constructed through interactions within a social environment, it is not useful to talk about adopted people being psychologically impaired. Being adopted marks people out *socially* as being either different and special; or different, disadvantaged, and in a sense not 'normal'. Searching, then, is seen as an attempt to account for this difference and establish a more complete social identity.

March (1995) formulated the idea that searching was associated with adopted people's feelings of stigma. In order to gain social acceptance, adopted people must neutralise their stigma. This they do by searching: normalising themselves by identifying a past that is theirs. In the study by March (1995, p. 658), adopted people's 'search and reunion activities were not symptomatic of adoption breakdown. They represented an attempt to neutralise the stigma trait by placing self within a biosocial context valued by their community.' In a similar vein, Haimes and Timms (1985) describe adopted people who search as trying to place themselves in a narrative framework. For adopted people, parts of their narrative are missing and by searching for birth relatives they seek to fill in the gaps.

Searching, therefore, can either be seen as a normal part of development or as an adverse response to adoption. Adopted people who search can be viewed as either psychologically impaired or mentally healthy, fully exploring their pasts in a positive manner. Searching for identity involves either trying to connect with one's biological past or seeking to place oneself in a social context. Adopted people also search to neutralise feelings of loss, cancel out the past, or connect the past to the future. Summing up her research of people who had sought access to their Barnardo's childcare record, Pugh (1999) identified three motivations to search: the wish to understand the meaning and significance of one's roots, the need to know about one's history, and the need to make sense of one's past.

Who is sought?

To some extent, who is sought appears to affect the outcome of the search and reunion process. The emotional agenda with birth parents, particularly birth mothers, is complex and often highly charged. In terms of issues of loss and rejection, meeting birth siblings is likely to be more neutral. In practice, most adopted people set out initially to search for their birth mother. However, Humphrey and Humphrey (1989) suggest that it is easier to build a more comfortable relationship with siblings than with birth parents. McMillan and Irving (1994, p. 24) echo this, saying 'starting from a position of loss without the responsibility for the loss, siblings are freer for their relationship to develop in a more normal way, on the basis of relatedness and compatibility' (see also Sachdev, 1992).

Sachdev (1992) reports that few of his respondents expressed a desire to meet their biological father. Only 10% said they ever thought about their biological father.

It is not always the adoptive person who searches for the birth relative. Sometimes the birth relative decides to search for the adopted person. The Children's Society has been providing an intermediary service for birth relatives since 1991. They found that search and reunion for this group was, in many ways, more complicated. Feast and Smith (1993, 1995) reported that contacts initiated by birth relatives had a number of positive effects for both adopted adults and birth parents in terms of identity fulfilment and reassurance about lost relatives.

Why do some adopted people not search?
Gaining research access to adopted people who do not search for their birth parents has proved difficult and many studies of the search and reunion process have omitted this group from their investigations. However, a small number of studies have looked at why some adopted people delay or forestall their search. The speculation is that the reasons for some adopted people stopping their search might be similar to the reasons that non-searches choose not to search at all.

Gonyo and Watson (1988) suggest that a decision to search is inhibited by three things: (i) a hesitancy to intrude on the life of the unknown party; (ii) fear of failure, discovering unforeseen problems, or upsetting the adoptive parents; and (iii) guilt or feeling disloyal to the adoptive family.

Feast records the accounts of Susie, who searched:

Searcher SUSIE
It was four or five years ago and I was discussing it with my partner, Les, and he said to me 'Have you ever thought of trying to find your blood mother?' And I think that everybody who is adopted, it always crosses their mind: 'I wonder if this bit's like her, or I wonder if that bit's like her?' I was about five or six months when I was adopted and I wanted to know what happened in that part of my life that nobody knew. Or just to ask the question, 'Why did you have me adopted? Why didn't she struggle?' Especially once I had my daughter, I thought, 'I couldn't give my daughter up. How could she give her child away?' And then my mum had a major clear out of her attic and she came across my adoption papers and she kept asking me if I wanted them and I said 'Yes' but then I conveniently kept forgetting to take them with me ... I kept leaving it because I think I didn't really want to know ... while I didn't have them I could accept my life the way it's been. Once I'd got them, you've got to read them ... It didn't really bother me until later on in life when I'd had my children and the oldest one had left home and so, as I say, she gave me the adoption papers and I came home and read them and that's when my partner said, 'Why don't we go and look – ask your mum to make sure she doesn't mind – and we'll see what we can find.'

and of Jessica, who did not:

Non-searcher JESSICA
When I was 18 I took that opportunity then to start trying to trace my natural mother. At the time you had to go through a social worker so that's what I did ... On the second meeting with him he actually had a piece of paper with the details surrounding the circumstances of my adoption. I always remember it was rather impersonal and upsetting at the time. It just basically said my mother was 5ft 5ins, brown hair, brown eyes, an art student – the purportive father was blonde, 6ft – and that they regretted having to give me up for adoption but they did. And there was also a note about my mother, at the time when she was carrying me, that she had actually attempted to commit suicide – and it all sounded really quite traumatic and sad ...

I decided then that it was just too big a thing for me to take on board and especially as the circumstances seemed quite traumatic for my natural mother. I started thinking, 'Maybe it's not right for me just to turn up in her life so many years later' – so I thought I'd just leave it.

Contact can be a wonderful experience; but it may be unwelcome. The way in which it is initiated may be crucial (consider the disastrous history related *Buchanan v Milton* [1999] 2 FLR 844).

Questions

(i) Is access to birth records a question of psychological welfare or of human rights (see p. 518, above)?
(ii) Recall Triseliotis' interviewee (p. 527, above) who looked in the mirror and had no one to compare. Now imagine looking, for the first time in your life, at the face of someone to whom you are physically related. How might you feel about this?

Finally, we have to look at inter-country adoption, mentioned briefly above. Some of the international complexities may be gleaned from David Rosettenstein's article on 'Trans-Racial Adoption in the United States and the Impact of Considerations relating to Minority Population Groups on International Adoptions in the United States' (1995):

The political considerations impinging on international adoptions are complex and multi-faceted. At the national level, they reflect the concerns of the foreign country, and of the United States. Not surprisingly, national interests are usually not couched in terms that necessarily reflect the interests of the child. Thus, traditional objections by source countries to these international adoptions are that they reveal or suggest an inability on the part of the foreign country to care for its children and thus undermine national pride, or constitute an insult or are symptomatic of an ailing society. They have also been seen as a vehicle for depriving the country of a future resource – citizens, even though the numbers are really not sufficiently large to constitute a meaningful threat. Foreign countries are also concerned that the financial rewards and incentives for facilitating an international adoption tend to corrupt the social service infrastructure of the source country as well as leading to kidnapping, coercion, baby-selling and fraud. The process is also seen as manifestly a form of neo-colonialist exploitation and inducing colonial values in the welfare delivery system. In some instances, because intercountry adoptions are seen as exploiting poor countries, indulging the wealthy, and reducing the guilt of rich countries, a refusal to allow such adoptions by potential source countries might be seen as aimed at heightening the discomfort of rich countries. In a similar vein, on occasion, the United States has manipulated its approach to intercountry adoptions with a view to discrediting the source country. Of interest to the policies of both the United States and the source country is the fact that the adoption of a child from a crisis area may only serve to disrupt the foreign country further. Sometimes the argument is made that the commercialism invites inattention to the question of whether the child is truly 'available' for adoption, although this concern has to be balanced against the knowledge that where a child is coming from a country where there is war, social disorder or even simply poverty, delays in evaluating the adoptability of the child may involve risks of harm to the child. A further concern of some countries is that intercountry adoptions distract attention away from the needs of domestic programmes in the source country. This may be a particularly difficult issue where the concept of adoption is culturally unknown in the source country. Thus, in a country such as India, where trans-ethnic adoption is an alien concept, such a consequence in the context of an intercountry adoption tends to produce suspicions about the adoptees' motives.

Earlier, he had described the objections to trans-racial placement within the United States:

In 1972 the National Association of Black Social Workers (NABSW) stated:

'Black children should be placed only with Black families whether in foster care or adoption. Black children belong physically, psychologically and culturally in Black families in order that they receive the total sense of themselves and develop a sound projection of their future. Human beings are products of their environment and develop their sense of values, attitudes and self concept within their family structures. Black children in white homes are cut [off] from the healthy development of themselves as Black people.

Our position is based on:

1. the necessity of self-determination from birth to death, of all black people.

2. the need of all young ones to begin at birth to identify with all Black people in a Black community.

3. the philosophy that we need our own to build a strong nation.

The socialization process for every child begins at birth. Included in the socialization process is the child's cultural heritage which is an important segment of the total process. This must begin at the earliest moment; otherwise our children will not have the background and knowledge which is necessary to survive in a racist society. This is impossible if the child is placed with white parents in a white environment.'

The impact of this statement on trans-racial adoptions in the United States was dramatic. The best information suggests that the numbers of trans-racial adoptions reached an all time high of 2,574 in 1971, the number of such placements then falling to 831 by 1975. Since that year, comprehensive national figures on adoption, whether same-race or trans-racial, have not been available. Two prominent authors [Simon and Altstein, 1987] in the field have stated that they and others believe that both public and private agencies are placing children trans-racially, but will not admit to doing so, because of political considerations.

He concluded that:

The overall irony of the role of race in adoption placements is that domestically minority children do not get placed because it is feared that trans-racial placement will harm them. As a consequence, adoptive parents are apparently driven to trans-racial adoptions from abroad. In this context, the children will be subjected to the same potential risks the domestic children were being shielded from, at the same time as being exposed to increased risks resulting from the international process.

Question

To what extent do you think that similar considerations would operate here? Is it right to call them political?

The other side of the coin is stated by William Duncan in 'Regulating Intercountry Adoption – An International Perspective' (1993):

By contrast, the figures for abandoned children in developing countries remain staggering. It is estimated by UNICEF [1991] that about 155 million children under five in the developing countries live in absolute poverty. There are about 100 million abandoned children who 'subsist only by back-breaking work, or turn to petty crime, prostitution or begging'. Every civil war or civil upheaval seems to add to this tragic picture. In Europe, much attention has been paid in the recent past to Romania where the official estimate of abandoned children is 67,339. But the scale of the problem is far greater in Latin America, Asia and Africa, where the fundamental causes remain poverty and, in some countries, continuing economic deterioration. The same economic conditions hinder the development of child care (including adoption) services in the developing countries, despite the widely accepted view that priority should always be given to placement of abandoned children in families in their own communities – a view eloquently expressed by the Indian Supreme Court in 1984 in *Laxshmi Kant Pandey v Union of India*. The development of adoption services in developing countries will no doubt continue to be a principal theme. It is obviously of great importance for those who come from the wealthier countries to appreciate the problems involved, and to avoid developments, especially in the context of intercountry adoption, which may frustrate efforts to build up local services and encourage domestic placements of children.

Kate Silverman, in 'The Hague Children's Conventions' (2000), explains the operation of the Hague Convention on Protection of Children and Co-operation in Respect of Intercountry Adoption, which the Adoption (Intercountry Aspects) Act 1999 enables the United Kingdom to ratify:

Background

The Hague Convention on Intercountry Adoption addresses another important aspect of the law relating to children. General concerns as well as a series of specific incidents about the trafficking of children and illegal buying of babies lie behind this Convention. Perhaps nothing crystallized the issue more than the Baby-Bazaar in Romania after the fall of the Ceausescu regime in 1989. Many individuals in the US and other countries were affected by the reports of children living in wretched conditions in Romanian orphanages and moved to adopt these children. Apparently, however, not all of the children adopted came from the orphanages, and, to some extent lack of controls led to a situation in which some prospective adoptive parents, or their representatives, walked the streets of Romanian offering cash and other inducements to parents in exchange for their babies. The Adoption Convention, by establishing certain minimum safeguards and promoting co-operation and communication between countries, is designed to expose and eliminate such abuses.

But regulation is only one aspect of the intercountry adoption picture. The other side of the adoption crisis is the tragic condition of unwanted children and the failure of any system to handle adoptions in a way that facilitates their placement. While critics of intercountry adoption view transnational and transracial placement of children as forms of imperialism and genocide, others argue that intercountry adoption offers the only viable opportunity for many of these children.

Without formal mechanisms of co-operation in place, intercountry adoption was plagued by an overly cumbersome process, in which prospective adoptive parents, as well as biological parents wishing to give up a child, were forced to undergo a series of duplicative, and sometimes conflicting determinations and processes. By allocating responsibilities between the 'sending' state and the 'receiving' states and instituting formal mechanisms for co-operation, the Adoption Convention seeks to avoid duplication and conflict.

The Structure of the Adoption Convention

Basic Premises

One important premiss of the Adoption Convention is its favorable view of intercountry adoption. Consistent with the UN Convention on the Rights of the Child's subsidiary principle of intercountry adoption, the Preamble to the Adoption Convention states that as a matter of first priority each state should take appropriate measures to ensure that a child remains in the care of his or her family of origin. However, the Convention deviates from the UN Convention's second priority of preferring that a child remain in the country of origin – even in institutionalized care – and provides that 'intercountry adoption may offer the advantage of a permanent family to a child for whom a suitable family cannot be found in the state of origin.'

The goals of the Adoption Convention are set forth in its first article: (1) providing a system of co-operation among contracting states, thereby deterring the abduction, sale of, and trafficking in children; (2) establishing minimum safeguards to ensure that an intercountry adoption is in the best interests of the child; and (3) securing the recognition of adoptions made in accordance with the Convention.

The Convention applies whenever a child habitually resident in one contracting state (the state of origin) has been, is being, or is to be moved to another contracting state (the 'receiving' state) either after adoption in the state of origin or for the purpose of such an adoption in the receiving state or in the state of origin. The Convention thus applies regardless of whether the adoption takes place in the state of origin or the receiving state, and, in fact, regardless of whether the adoption takes place at all; the Convention does not apply, however, unless the prospective adoptive parent(s) and the child are habitually resident in different contacting states.

The Adoption Convention applies not only to 'full adoptions' but also to 'simple adoptions', ie adoptions in which the pre-existing legal relationship between the child and family of origin is not completely severed. Given the widespread use of 'simple' adoptions in some countries, it was thought desirable to extend the Convention in this way.

Allocation of Functions

The Convention avoids many of the conflict of laws and jurisdiction problems that have plagued intercountry adoption by allocating responsibilities between 'sending' and 'receiving' states. But rather than adopting a formal conflict of laws approach to adoption as a whole, the Convention subdivides the adoption decision into discrete determinations and then allocates authority for certain issues between the two states. The Convention then gives each state a 'veto power' in Article 17(c), thus requiring both states to co-operate in and ultimately take joint responsibility for the adoption decision as a whole, regardless of where the final adoption takes place. Article 17(c) thus becomes the linchpin of the Convention.

Article 4 of the Convention is directed to the primary responsibilities undertaken by the state of origin. Before an adoption can be granted in any contacting state, the 'competent authorities' in the state of origin must determine that the child is adoptable; that an intercountry adoption is within the child's best interests, after possibilities for placement of the child within the state of origin have been given 'due consideration'; and that the relevant consents, including the child's if required, have been granted. The state of origin thus controls the issue of adoptability, although the receiving state will have a veto over that determination before any adoption may proceed.

Apart from allocating functions, the Convention also establishes minimum conditions that must be met in each state regardless of where the adoption takes place. One example of how the Convention imposes such standards is in the area of consents surrounding adoption. The applicable law in the state of origin will determine who must consent to an adoption, but the Convention provides that those persons are to be counseled and must be informed of the effects of their consents. The Convention also requires that the consent be given 'freely, in the required legal form, and expressed or evidenced in writing.'

Article 5 of the Convention addresses the responsibilities of the receiving state in regard to the adopting parents; once again, the Convention mandates certain minimum conditions that must be met, this time with respect to the qualifications of the adoptive parents. The receiving state determines, in accordance with its law, the eligibility and suitability of the adoptive parents; it also must ensure the adoptive parents have been counseled; and that the child is or will be authorized to enter and reside permanently in the state. While the receiving state will have primary responsibility for determining the eligibility of the adoptive parents, the sending state may withhold its agreement for the adoption under Article 17(c).

Proceeding with an Intercountry Adoption Under the Convention
It may be useful to consider how an intercountry adoption would proceed under the Convention. A person wishing to adopt goes to the appropriate authority in the state of habitual residence. That 'authority', which in the United States is likely to be an accredited adoption agency, will determine the eligibility and suitability of the applicant and provide information about the applicant for a report which will be issued and transmitted to the relevant authority in the state which has a child available for adoption. Authorities in the 'sending' state prepare a report on any child who may benefit from an intercountry adoption, even if there is no particular request for the child.

Once a 'sending' country receives the report on an applicant wishing to adopt, it makes a preliminary determination that a particular placement is in the best interests of the adoptable child, giving due consideration to the child's ethnic, religious, and cultural background. It then transmits to the receiving state the report on the child as well as proof that the necessary consents have been obtained, and the reasons for its determination that the envisaged placement is in the child's best interests. In some states of origin, the identity of the mother (and possibly the father) are not to be disclosed, and thus care must be taken not to reveal those identities.

The final steps in the adoption process involve the 'entrustment' of the child to the prospective adoptive parents and the transfer of the child to the receiving state. Article 17 of the Convention places primary responsibility on the state of origin for the entrustment decision; it is the state of origin that must ensure that the adopting parent agrees to the placement. No approval of the placement by the receiving state is necessary, unless either the receiving or sending state imposes such a requirement. However, authorities in both the sending and receiving states must agree that the adoption may proceed. Thus, any decision to go ahead with the adoption is made jointly, and either state is fully empowered – indeed obligated – to stop an adoption from going forward and withhold approval of the adoption if it appears that there is a legal bar to the adoption or its recognition in either state. Finally, the state of origin must verify that the prospective adoptive parents are eligible and suitable to adopt and that the child is or will be authorized to enter and reside permanently in the receiving state.

Both states involved in the intercountry adoption are required to 'take all necessary steps to obtain permission for the child to leave the state of origin and to enter and reside permanently in the receiving state'. Transfer of a child is authorized once all conditions have been satisfied; there is a preference to have the transfer take place in the company of the adoptive or prospective adoptive parents.

The issue of whether there should be a probationary period prior to adoption was again resolved by a Convention compromise. A receiving state may require that a child serve a post-placement probationary period with the prospective adoptive parents before a final adoption order is issued, but the state of origin can avoid such a probationary period by insisting that an adoption order be granted prior to the placement or transfer of a child habitually resident in that state.

The final order of adoption can be made in either the sending or the receiving state. An adoption certified as having been made in accordance with the Convention must be recognized not only by the sending and receiving states but also by all other contracting states. ...

Under the Convention, all adoptions result in the establishment of a permanent parent-child relationship between the child and the adoptive parents, with the adoptive parents assuming parental responsibility for the child. The status of the child with respect to pre-adoption parental relationships depends upon the effect of the adoption in the state where the adoption took place. For example, if the state of origin grants a full adoption – which terminates any pre-existing legal parent-child relationship – the receiving state must give the same effect to the adoption. However, in the situation where the state of origin grants only a simple adoption – an adoption which does not involve a complete severing of the legal ties between the adopted child and the birth family – the Convention permits the receiving state to convert the simple adoption into a full adoption if the law of the receiving state so permits and if the consents to the adoption were not limited. Thus, the receiving state does not have to obtain permission from the state of origin to convert the adoption; but the state of origin can withhold its agreement for the adoption to proceed under Article 17(c) if it wishes to prevent the conversion of a simple adoption into a full adoption.

The Convention leaves rules on confidentiality up to individual contracting states. It does require the preservation of information concerning the child's origin and in particular, the identity of the child's parents. However, access to that information is governed by the law of that state.

Question

Which do you prefer – the UN Convention's preference for a child to remain in its country of origin, even in institutional care, or the Hague Adoption Convention's willingness to acknowledge that intercountry adoption may be a good option where the first priority – care within the child's own family – cannot be fulfilled?

11.4 Assisted reproduction and the 'social parent'

Nowadays, one can become a parent, not by adopting the child, but by adopting the sperm or the egg which go to make up the child. The Law Commission considered the parentage of children born as a result of artificial insemination with sperm from a donor other than the mother's husband (now known as donor insemination or DI) in their Working Paper on *Illegitimacy* (1979):

10.9 The policy of the legislation, we are at present inclined to think, should therefore be that where a married woman has received A.I.D. treatment with her husband's consent, the husband rather than the donor should, for all legal purposes, be regarded as the father of a child conceived as the result. ...
10.11 The simplest way of implementing the policy which we have suggested would be a statutory provision deeming the husband to be the father of an A.I.D. child born to his wife; the only ground on which the husband could challenge the operation of this deeming provision would be that he had not consented to his wife receiving A.I.D. treatment. This approach seems to us to have the merit not only of simplicity, but also of giving effect to the likely feelings and wishes of the wife and husband. We note that statutory provision of the type we envisage has been made in several States of the USA. ...
10.17 Although there are many advantages to such a statutory deeming provision, there are two main objections to it. The first involves a major point of policy: it could be said that the proposal involves a deliberate falsification of the birth register. The second objection is more theoretical: that the proposal would involve a transfer of legal rights from the donor to the husband, and that the law should accurately mirror that transfer.

A comment upon the first objection may be taken from a Ciba Foundation Symposium on the *Law and Ethics of A.I.D. and Embryo Transfer* (1973):

McLaren [geneticist]: Even though the genetic register which Canon Dunstan proposed might not be very useful, through being erroneous (owing to the possibility that occasionally the supposedly infertile husband fertilizes the egg), our present registry system is itself erroneous in all those cases where the husband is not actually the father of the child. Are there any statistics on how common this is? This is probably more frequent than the cases where a supposedly infertile husband was really the father of an A.I.D. child.
Philipp [consultant obstetrician and gynaecologist]: We blood-tested some patients in a town in south-east England, and found that 30% of the husbands could not have been the fathers of their children ...

JH Edwards [geneticist]: ... Analysis of some blood group data, making allowance for the fact that one could not detect all the illegitimacies, showed that in the 1950s in the West Isleworth area about 50% of premarital conceptions were not fathered by the apparent father. As the apparent fathers were questioned while visiting their wives immediately after the birth, most of them obviously thought they were the father. I think the group Mr Philipp referred to is also highly biased. In spite of much talk about artificial insemination by donor and all the difficulties with genetics and so on, natural insemination by donor is practised on quite a substantial scale on an amateur basis.

Meanwhile, the Government had set up the Warnock Committee of Inquiry into Human Fertilisation and Embryology. This dealt with other techniques for counteracting infertility, which are usefully summarised in the DHSS Consultation Paper on *Legislation on Human Infertility Services and Embryo Research* (1986):

In vitro fertilisation
8. This technique is used mainly where a woman has no fallopian tubes or they are blocked. Currently about 1,000 births in the UK are thought to have involved IVF. It has also been used in dealing with some types of male infertility and where the cause of infertility is unknown. A ripe egg is taken from the woman's ovary shortly before it would have been released naturally. It is then mixed with sperm in a dish (in vitro) so that fertilisation can occur. Once the fertilised egg has started to develop it is transferred back to the woman's womb. If a pregnancy is to be established the embryo must then implant in the womb.
9. IVF although simple in concept is not an easy technique in practice. To increase the chances of success (currently the success rate is thought to be of the order of 15 per cent) it is usual to create and transfer to a woman more than one embryo. Several eggs are thus required. To obtain these eggs the woman is given superovulatory drugs which ensure that a number of eggs is produced in one menstrual cycle and these are available for fertilisation.
10. Fertilisation of these eggs may result in more embryos than it is appropriate to transfer to the woman's womb. These embryos can then be preserved by freezing for later transfer to the womb or scientific use or they may be left to perish. At present it is not possible for embryos to grow outside a woman's body for longer than 9-10 days.

Egg donation
11. The IVF technique allows a pregnancy to be achieved where the woman cannot produce an egg. An egg by another woman is fertilised with the husband's sperm in vitro and the resulting embryo is then transferred to the infertile woman. One case involving sisters was reported in this country in 1985.

Embryo donation
12. In this case donated eggs and sperm would be used to create an embryo for transfer to the infertile woman. The technique could apply where both partners are infertile. Embryo donation is thought not yet to have been used in the UK.

Surrogacy
13. This practice involves one woman carrying a child for another with the intention that the child be handed over after birth. Surrogacy can make it possible for a woman to obtain a child in cases where she cannot carry the pregnancy at all, or for long enough for the fetus to be capable of being born alive. Artificial insemination of the surrogate mother by sperm of the commissioning mother's husband makes it possible for that child to be conceived without the need for sexual intercourse. However, by means of IVF it may be possible in some instances for the commissioning mother's eggs to be used.

As the Warnock Committee pointed out in their *Report* (1984):

6.8. Egg donation produces for the first time circumstances in which the genetic mother (the woman who donates the egg), is a different person from the woman who gives birth to the child, the carrying mother. The law has never, till now, had to face this problem. There are inevitably going to be instances where the stark issue arises of who is the mother. In order to achieve some certainty in this situation it is our view that where a woman donates an egg for transfer to another the donation should be treated as absolute and that, like a male donor she should have no rights or duties with regard to any resulting child.

These proposals are all now implemented by the Human Fertilisation and Embryology Act 1990:

27.—(1) The woman who is carrying or has carried a child as a result of the placing in her of an embryo or of sperm and eggs, and no other woman, is to be treated as the mother of the child.

...

28.—(1) This section applies in the case of a child who is being or has been carried by a woman as a result of the placing in her of an embryo or of sperm and eggs or her artificial insemination.

(2) If—

(a) at the time of the placing in her of the embryo or the sperm and eggs or of her insemination, the woman was a party to a marriage, and

(b) the creation of the embryo carried by her was not brought about with the sperm of the other party to the marriage,

then, subject to subsection (5) below, the other party to the marriage shall be treated as the father of the child unless it is shown that he did not consent to the placing in her of the embryo or the sperm and eggs or to her insemination (as the case may be).

(3) If no man is treated, by virtue of subsection (2) above, as the father of the child but—

(a) the embryo or the sperm and eggs were placed in the woman, or she was artificially inseminated, in the course of treatment services provided for her and a man together by a person to whom a licence applies, and

(b) the creation of the embryo carried by her was not brought about with the sperm of that man,

then, subject to subsection (5) below, that man shall be treated as the father of the child.

(4) Where a person is treated as the father of the child by virtue of subsection (2) or (3) above, no other person is to be treated as the father of the child.

(5) Subsections (2) and (3) above do not apply—

(a) in relation to England and Wales and Northern Ireland, to any child who, by virtue of the rules of common law, is treated as the legitimate child of the parties to a marriage,

...

(6) Where—

(a) the sperm of a man who had given such consent as is required by paragraph 5 of Schedule 3 of this Act was used for a purpose for which such consent was required, or

(b) the sperm of a man, or any embryo the creation of which was brought about with his sperm, was used after his death,

he is not to be treated as the father of the child.

(7) The references in subsection (2) above to the parties to a marriage at the time there referred to—

(a) are to the parties to a marriage subsisting at that time, unless a judicial separation was then in force, but

(b) include the parties to a void marriage if either or both of them reasonably believed at that time that the marriage was valid; and for the purposes of this subsection it shall be presumed, unless the contrary is shown, that one of them reasonably believed at that time that the marriage was valid.

...

29.—(1) Where by virtue of section 27 or 28 of this Act a person is to be treated as the mother or father of a child, that person is to be treated in law as the mother or, as the case may be, father of the child for all purposes.

(2) Where by virtue of section 27 or 28 of this Act a person is not to be treated as the mother or father of the child, that person is to be treated in law as not being the mother or, as the case may be, father of the child for any purpose.

(3) Where subsection (1) or (2) above has effect, references to any relationship between two people in any enactment, deed or other instrument or document (whenever passed or made) are to be read accordingly.

(4) In relation to England and Wales and Northern Ireland, nothing in the provisions of section 27(1) or 28(2) to (4), read with this section, affects—

(a) the succession to any dignity or title of honour or renders any person capable of succeeding to or transmitting a right to succeed to any such dignity or title, or

(b) the devolution of any property limited (expressly or not) to devolve (as nearly as the law permits) along with any dignity or title of honour.

Questions

(i) How many arguments can you think of for making (a) the carrying mother, or (b) the genetic mother the mother in law?
(ii) Are the arguments for recognising 'social' rather than 'genetic' fatherhood stronger or weaker?
(iii) Does the widespread availability of donor insemination, whether by artificial or more conventional methods, on a 'do-it-yourself' basis, affect matters?
(iv) Why should not the same provisions apply when a husband accepts his wife's naturally born child by another man?
(v) What if the husband or partner consented to in vitro fertilisation of the woman's egg by a donor's sperm and the resulting embryo was frozen for some years before implantation? Should he be able to change his mind? But what if an unmarried couple split up after creation but before implantation of the embryos? Are they still being 'treated together'? Can or should the law make a 'father' of a man who is neither the genetic nor the social father of the child?
(vi) As donors can never be fathers, what do you think of the re-introduction of a class of children who are inevitably 'fatherless by law'?
(vii) Do you think that all this is, or is not, in the best interests of the children?

The Law Commission (1979) also considered a further problem raised by their basic approach:

10.25 A problem which would arise whichever method were used for dealing with A.I.D. is whether or not legal provision should be made so that the child would be entitled to ascertain the facts about his parentage. Under the present law and practice the truth about the child's genetic identity may well be concealed from him if he has been registered as the legitimate child of the mother and her husband; in any event it is up to his mother and her husband to decide whether or not to disclose the fact that he is an A.I.D. child. Even if they do decide to tell him what they know, they will not usually be able to tell him who the donor was.
10.26 The argument in favour of a procedure giving the child the right to know the facts about his conception is essentially that a person has the right to know the truth about his origins. This principle is now accepted in adoption law, and an adopted child is entitled to discover the recorded facts about his natural parentage on attaining his majority. It therefore seems logical that an A.I.D. child should have the same right. On the other hand, if the only fact which the child is able to discover is that he is not genetically the offspring of his mother's husband, but of a donor wholly unknown not only to him but to his mother and her husband, it is difficult to see that this would be of any real advantage to him. To go further, by giving the child the right to know the identity of the donor would involve a major, and probably unacceptable, change of policy and practice.

The Warnock Committee's Report (1984) took much the same view:

4.19 It is the practice of some clinics in the USA to provide detailed descriptions of donors, and to permit couples to exercise choice as to the donor they would prefer. In the evidence there was some support for the use of such descriptions. It is argued that they would provide information and reassurance for the parents and, at a later date, for the child. They might also be of benefit to the donor, as an indication that he is valued for his own sake. A detailed description also offers some choice to the woman who is to have the child, and lack of such choice can be said to diminish the importance of the woman's right to choose the father of her child.
4.20 The contrary view, also expressed in the evidence, is that detailed donor profiles would introduce the donor as a person in his own right. It is also argued that the use of profiles devalues the child who may seem to be wanted only if certain specifications are met, and this may become a source of disappointment to the parents if their expectations are unfulfilled.
4.21 As a matter of principle we do not wish to encourage the possibility of prospective parents seeking donors with specific characteristics by the use of whose semen they hope to give birth

to a particular type of child. We do not therefore want detailed descriptions of donors to be used as a basis for choice, but we believe that the couple should be given sufficient relevant information for their reassurance. This should include some basic facts about the donor, such as his ethnic group and his genetic birth. A small minority of the Inquiry, while supporting the principle set out above, and without compromising the principle of anonymity, consider that a gradual move towards making more detailed descriptions of the donor available to prospective parents, if requested, could be beneficial to the practice of AID, provided this was accompanied by appropriate counselling. **We recommend that on reaching the age of eighteen the child should have access to the basic information about the donor's ethnic origin and genetic health and that legislation be enacted to provide the right of access to this. This legislation should not be retrospective.**

4.22 We were agreed that there is a need to maintain the absolute anonymity of the donor, though we recognise that in privately arranged donation, for example between brothers, a different situation would of course apply; such domestic arrangements, however, fall outside any general regulation. Anonymity would give legal protection to the donor but it would also have the effect of minimising the invasion of the third party into the family. Without anonymity, men would, it is argued, be less likely to become donors ... We recognise that one consequence of this provision would be that AID children, even if informed about the circumstances of their conception would never be entitled to know the identity of their genetic fathers.

Questions

(i) What is the 'principle' which would prevent would-be parents from designing their own baby?

(ii) Should a white woman be able to ask for sperm from a black man?

(iii) Has this principle got anything to do with whether or not the child should later on know something about his genetic parents?

On the last point, the contrary view is succinctly put by Eric Blyth in his article, 'Assisted reproduction: what's in it for the children'? (1990):

However, available evidence serves to undermine justification of both donor anonymity and secrecy. Research conducted in Sweden, Australia and New Zealand indicates that sperm donors would be prepared to continue to donate in the absence of anonymity. A report prepared for the European Commission recommends the removal, for an evaluated trial period, of donor anonymity.

Empirical evidence concerning AR families is restricted to those brought about following DI, but this clearly reveals both the disadvantages of maintaining secrecy and the benefits of openness. Secrecy, it appears, can only be sustained at high psychological cost to the parent(s). It deprives them of social support, whilst inadvertent disclosure remains a potentially lifelong fear. Children who found out about their genetic origins by less than direct means often expressed bitterness about their experiences .

Conversely, children whose parents had been open with them valued their parents' honesty, experienced few emotional consequences of being told, and fears about the specific effect of openness on the father-child relationship were not substantiated. Parents who were open felt that they no longer had to carry the burden and guilt of secrecy and were able to obtain support from others. The task of telling children at an early age about the nature of their conception could be considerably lightened by the development of story books similar to those currently available for adopted children.

The positive experiences of 'open' AR families are supported by the experience of both traditional adoption and more recent practices of 'open adoption' where contact between the child and birth-parent(s) is maintained.

Nigel Bruce takes the argument a stage further in a later article, on 'The importance of genetic knowledge' (1990):

Adopted young people now have the legal right in Britain, on reaching maturity, to see their original birth certificates. Those conceived by means of DI do not as yet enjoy this legal right.

The main purpose of this article is to argue that, at least in the contemporary culture of Western Europe, such young people have strong moral claims to know their genetic identities; and that these moral claims should now be converted to legal rights.

In any civilised moral code, the truth is preferable to deception; without respect for truth, social institutions could not operate. Truth-telling is a basic legal, as well as moral, principle; the courts oblige us to swear or affirm to tell the truth, and they can punish us if we resort to deception.

In any civilised moral code, trustworthiness is more meritorious than unreliability. Sociologists say that society depends upon honesty and trustworthiness if it is to function properly. Psychologists say that trust is a basic component in the social development of the child.

In any civilised moral code, individual members of society have a prima facie right to personal autonomy. They must not be enslaved or imprisoned without trial; they must not be bought or sold; and they have legal rights not to be discriminated against or unjustly treated. In contemporary Western law, this personal autonomy also includes the right to personal information about themselves which may be held on official commercial or welfare files. ... Linked with this claim to autonomy is the need which we all have to possess and develop a personal identity. There are two aspects of the term 'identity': the objective identity perceived by authority, which we possess; and the subjective identity which we develop within our 'selves' and which is the way we perceive and come to terms with our 'selves'.

The United Nations Declaration of the Rights of the Child (1959) referred only to the objective aspect of identity when it declared in Principle 3: 'The child shall be entitled from his birth to a name and a nationality'. The new United Nations Convention on the Rights of the Child (1989) contains a broader concept of identity in Articles 7 and 8. Article 7 requires that:

> '... the child shall be registered immediately after birth and shall have the right to a name, the right to acquire a nationality, and as far as possible the right to know and be cared for by his or her parents.'

Article 8 requires the States Parties:

> '... to respect the right of the child to preserve his or her identity, including nationality, name and family relations as recognised by law, without unlawful interference.'

The Convention also contains an Article 13 on freedom of expression and of information, which must surely include the right to obtain medical information about one's conception and birth. Even if the release of such information may be seen as an infringement of the privacy of the adults involved, it is now well established in the law of most developed countries that when there is a conflict between the interests of children and adults, the interests of the children should be paramount. Principle 2 of the UN Declaration of the Rights of the Child states that 'in the enactment of laws for this purpose, the best interests of the child shall be the paramount consideration'. Article 3 of the UN Convention contains the less definitive statement that:

> '... in all actions concerning children, whether undertaken by public or private social welfare institutions, courts of law, administrative authorities or legislative bodies, the best interests of the child shall be the primary consideration.'

Thus the claim that children should be legally as well as morally entitled to know the facts of their conception and birth rests equally on the argument that it is in their best interests to be treated with honesty and respect and on the relevance of the legal provisions prohibiting traffic in children, protecting their mental health and guaranteeing free access to information.

Another article by Eric Blyth, 'Secrets and lies; barriers to the exchange of genetic origins information following donor assisted conception' (1999), reveals some of the practical problems facing clinics:

[Researchers have] examined the experiences of centres in obtaining information from donors. A number reported difficulties in obtaining further information. Among the reasons cited were: donors not being interested in, or not attaching any importance to, providing further information; donors being ambivalent about providing information about themselves; donors being unwilling to provide more than basic information about themselves; and donors fearing that ostensibly non-identifying information might, nevertheless, compromise their anonymity. Some respondents, however, indicated that it was possible to get further information from donors. Successful strategies that were identified included: explaining the rationale for requesting further information; providing encouragement; providing counselling, advice and guidance on what information could be supplied; and in one instance 'persuasion'.

Questions

(i) Should such persuasion be applied?

(ii) Section 31 of the Human Fertilisation and Embryology Act 1990 leaves it to regulations to specify what information about the donor should be given to people born as a result of licensed treatment services (ie egg or sperm donation or in vitro fertilisation) when they grow up, but insists that information identifying the donor cannot be released unless regulations provided for this at the time of the donation: should such regulations be made now or should they wait until public opinion has developed further?

(iii) If they should be made now, should they provide (a) for identifying information to be released if the donor consents, or (b) for such information to be released even if he or she does not consent, and (c) what other information about the donor should be provided to his or her offspring?

The concern here is with the long-term welfare and interests of a person who has been born as a result of licensed treatment. But what about the welfare of children who may be born if treatment is given? Section 13(1) of the 1990 Act provides that it shall be a condition of every licence to provide treatment service under the Act that:

13.—(5) A woman shall not be provided with treatment services unless account has been taken of the welfare of any child who may be born as a result of the treatment (including the need of that child for a father), and of any other child who may be affected by the birth.

The Lord Chancellor explained what this meant to the House of Lords (*Hansard* (HL), vol. 516, c.1097) thus:

I think everyone would agree that it is important that children are born into a stable and loving environment and that the family is a concept whose health is fundamental to the health of society in general. A fundamental principle to our law about children, including the legislation which this House considered in such detail last Session and which became the Children Act 1989, is that the welfare of children is of paramount consideration. I think that it is, for these general reasons, entirely right that the Bill should be amended to add that concept. It could be argued that the concept of the welfare of the child is very broad and indeed all-embracing. That I think is inevitable given the very wide range of factors which need to be taken into account when considering the future lives of children who may be born as a result of techniques to be licensed under the Bill. ...

...The amendment will place on clinicians in statutory form a responsibility which I believe most, if not all, of them already perform. I accept that that is an important responsibility and it may in particular cases be far from easy to discharge.

Among the factors which clinicians should take into account will be the material circumstances in which the child is likely to be brought up and also the stability and love which he or she is likely to enjoy. Such stability is clearly linked to the marital position of the woman and in particular whether a husband or long-term partner can play a full part in providing the child with a permanent family setting in the fullest sense of that term, including financial provision.

The House does not need to be reminded of the plight of childless people and the very strong and deeply felt emotions which those in that position experience. We may on the one hand pay the tribute which is due to the importance of ensuring that children are born into the family environment by specifically excluding from treatment women who are not married or have no stable partner to be involved in the decision about treatment and in counselling beforehand, but I wonder what will happen if we do that. Surely there is a risk that such women, driven by the very strong desire for a child, may turn elsewhere for treatment. I am advised that it is a relatively easy matter for AID to be carried out in clinically unsupervised conditions. It may be that the result of the amendment would be to encourage those few single woman who are infertile to seek unsuitable donors if we were to introduce such a restriction. Any children who may be born as a result of uncontrolled treatment are at risk of serious disease, including HIV infection.

On the other hand, if the law recognises that in a very small number of cases single women will come forward for treatment, it may be better to encourage them to seek clinical advice. With the child and welfare amendments we have just discussed there is a likelihood that through counselling and discussion with those responsible for licensed treatment they may be dissuaded from having children once they have fully considered the implications of the environment into which their child would be born for its future welfare.

Guidance on the welfare of the child is given by the Human Fertilisation and Embryology Authority in its *Code of Practice* (2001):

Welfare of the Child

3.8 One of the conditions of a treatment licence is that 'a woman shall not be provided with treatment services unless account has been taken of the welfare of any child who may be born as a result of the treatment (including the need of that child for a father), and of any other child who may be affected by the birth'. This applies to every woman whether or not she is resident in or a citizen of the United Kingdom. 'Any other child' includes children who already exist within the woman's household or family.

3.9 The condition applies only to centres with a treatment licence, but it covers any of the services they offer to assist conception or pregnancy, whether or not these require a licence. However, the degree of consideration necessary will be greater if the treatment is required to be licensed under the HFE Act and particularly if it involves the use of donated gametes.

3.10 Centres should have clear written procedures to follow for assessing the welfare of the potential child and of any other child who may be affected. The HFE Act does not exclude any category of woman from being considered for treatment. Centres should take note in their procedures of the importance of a stable and supportive environment for any child produced as a result of treatment.

Factors to be Considered

3.11 Centres should take all reasonable steps to ascertain who would be legally responsible for any child born as a result of the procedure and who it is intended will be bringing up the child. When people seeking treatment come from abroad, centres should not assume that the law of that country relating to the parentage of a child born as a result of donated gametes is the same as that of the United Kingdom.

3.12 People seeking treatment are entitled to a fair and unprejudiced assessment of their situation and needs, which should be conducted with the skill and sensitivity appropriate to the delicacy of the case and the wishes and feelings of those involved.

3.13 Where people seek licensed treatment, centres should bear in mind the following factors:
  a.   their commitment to having and bringing up a child or children;
  b.   their ability to provide a stable and supportive environment for any child produced as a result of treatment;
  c.   their medical histories and the medical histories of their families;
  d.   their health and consequent future ability to look after or provide for a child's needs;
  e.   their ages and likely future ability to look after or provide for a child's needs;
  f.   their ability to meet the needs of any child or children who may be born as a result of treatment, including the implications of any possible multiple births;
  g.   any risk of harm to the child or children who may be born, including the risk of inherited disorders or transmissible diseases, problems during pregnancy and of neglect or abuse; and
  h.   the effect of a new baby or babies upon any existing child of the family.

3.14 Where people seek treatment using donated gametes, centres should also take the following factors into account:
  a.   a child's potential need to know about their origins and whether or not the prospective parents are prepared for the questions which may arise while the child is growing up;
  b.   the possible attitude of other members of the family towards the child, and towards their status in the family;
  c.   the implications for the welfare of the child if the person providing the gametes for donation is personally known within the child's family and social circle; and
  d.   any possibility known to the centre of a dispute about the legal fatherhood of the child (see paragraphs 3.15, 3.17 and 7.27-7.29, below).

3.15 Further factors will require consideration in the following case:
  a.   where the child will have no legal father. Centres are required to have regard to the child's need for a father and should pay particular attention to the prospective mother's

ability to meet the child's needs throughout their childhood. Where appropriate, centres should consider particularly whether there is anyone else within the prospective mother's family and social circle willing and able to share the responsibility for meeting those needs, and for bringing up, maintaining and caring for the child.

b.   where it is the intention that the child will not be brought up by the carrying mother. In this case, centres should bear in mind that either the carrying mother and in certain circumstances her husband or partner, or the commissioning parents could become the child's legal parents. Centres should therefore consider the factors listed in paragraphs 3.13-3.14 as applicable in relation to all those involved, and any risk of disruption to the child's early care and upbringing should there be a dispute between them. Centres should also take into account the effect of the proposed arrangement on any child of the carrying mother's family as well as its effect on any child of the commissioning parent's family.

3.16 The application of assisted conception techniques to initiate a surrogate pregnancy should only be considered where it is physically impossible or highly undesirable for medical reasons for the commissioning mother to carry the child.

3.17 Centres should be aware of the Parental Orders (Human Fertilisation and Embryology) Regulations 1994 and the Parental Orders (Human Fertilisation and Embryology) (Scotland) Regulations 1994 that came into effect on 1 November 1994. Under these Regulations, parental rights and obligations relating to a child born from a surrogacy arrangement may be transferred from the birth parents to the commissioning parents. The conditions that *must* be fulfilled before an application can be made are set out in Annex D. Annex D also contains information about birth registration of children born through surrogacy arrangements.

3.18 When selecting donated gametes for treatment, centres should take into account each prospective parent's preferences in relation to the general physical characteristics of the person providing gametes for donation. This does not allow the prospective parents to choose, for social reasons alone, a donor of different ethnic origin(s) from themselves. People seeking treatment with donated gametes should be advised that the result of any attempt at matching physical characteristics cannot be guaranteed.

Enquiries to be Made

3.19 Centres should take a medical and social history from each prospective parent. They should be seen together and separately. This should include all the information relevant to paragraphs 3.8-3.15, above.

3.20 Centres should seek to satisfy themselves that the GP of each prospective parent knows of no reason why either of them might not be suitable for the treatment to be offered. This would include anything that might adversely affect the welfare of any resulting child.

3.21 Centres should obtain the client's consent before approaching the GP. However, failure to give consent should be taken into account in considering whether or not to offer treatment.

Questions

(i) Can you improve upon this? Would it also be useful in adoption placements?

(ii) What is the case for imposing these requirements upon couples who need IVF or other assistance but can use their own eggs and sperm?

(iii) Not all candidates for assisted reproduction are infertile: do you think that it should be available to a single, virgin or lesbian woman or to a woman who would like another child so that her first is not brought up alone?

(iv) Should it be available to a woman who is HIV positive?

(v) What difference, if any, does it make that treatment is more readily available for people who can pay for it? How rigorously do you think that the Code will be applied (a) in an NHS hospital and (b) in a private clinic?

(vi) Blyth (1990) points out that: 'the extent to which welfare principles might apply to children in the field of AR is questionable ... Firstly, it is hardly valid to claim that anyone would have been better off not having been born in the first place. Secondly, the implication that alternatives exist from which a choice may be made does not hold.' Do you agree?

Paragraph 3.15b of the HFEA *Code* refers to surrogacy, which may involve either sperm donation alone, or egg and sperm donation. The Warnock Committee's Report (1984) summarised the arguments like this:

Arguments against surrogacy

8.10 There are strongly held objections to the concept of surrogacy, and it seems from the evidence submitted to us that the weight of public opinion is against the practice. The objections turn essentially on the view that to introduce a third party into the process of procreation which should be confined to the loving partnership between two people, is an attack on the value of the marital relationship. Further, the intrusion is worse than in the case of AID, since the contribution of the carrying mother is greater, more intimate and personal, than the contribution of a semen donor. It is also argued that it is inconsistent with human dignity that a woman should use her uterus for financial profit and treat it as an incubator for someone else's child. The objection is not diminished, indeed it is strengthened, where the woman entered an agreement to conceive a child, with the sole purpose of handing the child over to the commissioning couple after birth.

8.11 Again, it is argued that the relationship between mother and child is itself distorted by surrogacy. For in such an arrangement a woman deliberately allows herself to become pregnant with the intention of giving up the child to which she will give birth, and this is the wrong way to approach pregnancy. It is also potentially damaging to the child, whose bonds with the carrying mother, regardless of genetic connections, are held to be strong, and whose welfare must be considered to be of paramount importance. Further it is felt that a surrogacy agreement is degrading to the child who is to be the outcome of it, since, for all practical purposes, the child will have been bought for money.

8.12 It is also argued that since there are some risks attached to pregnancy, no woman ought to be asked to undertake pregnancy for another, in order to earn money. Nor, it is argued should a woman be forced by legal sanctions to part with a child, to which she has recently given birth, against her will.

Arguments for surrogacy

8.13 If infertility is a condition which should, where possible, be remedied it is argued that surrogacy must not be ruled out, since it offers to some couples their only chance of having a child genetically related to one or both of them. In particular, it may well be the only way that the husband of an infertile woman can have a child. Moreover, the bearing of a child for another can be seen, not as an undertaking that trivialises or commercialises pregnancy, but, on the contrary, as a deliberate and thoughtful act of generosity on the part of one woman to another. If there are risks attached to pregnancy, then the generosity is all the greater.

8.14 There is no reason, it is argued, to suppose that carrying mothers will enter into agreements lightly, and they have a perfect right to enter into such agreements if they so wish, just as they have a right to use their own bodies in other ways, according to their own decision. Where agreements are genuinely voluntary, there can be no question of exploitation, nor does the fact that surrogates will be paid for their pregnancy of itself entail exploitation of either party to the agreement.

8.15 As for intrusion into the marriage relationship, it is argued that those who feel strongly about this need not seek such treatment, but they should not seek to prevent others from having access to it.

8.16 On the question of bonding, it is argued that as very little is actually known about the extent to which bonding occurs when the child is in utero, no great claims should be made in this respect. In any case the breaking of such bonds, even if less than ideal, is not held to be an overriding argument against placing a child for adoption, where the mother wants this.

The Committee were divided between those who wanted an almost complete ban on the practice and those who wanted only profit-making agencies banned. The Surrogacy Arrangements Act 1985 banned commercial agencies and advertising of and for surrogacy services. The Human Fertilisation and Embryology Act 1990 inserted a further provision making all surrogacy arrangements unenforceable (and see *A v C* (1978) [1985] FLR 445).

However, the 1990 Act provides a convenient method of avoiding its own rules about parentage and allowing the commissioning parents to take over:

30.—(1) The court may make an order providing for a child to be treated in law as the child of the parties to a marriage (referred to in this section as 'the husband' and 'the wife') if—

(a) the child has been carried by a woman other than the wife as the result of the placing in her of an embryo or sperm and eggs or her artificial insemination,

(b) the gametes of the husband or the wife, or both, were used to bring about the creation of the embryo, and

(c) the conditions in subsections (2) to (7) below are satisfied.

(2) The husband and the wife must apply for the order within six months of the birth of the child or, in the case of a child born before the coming into force of this Act, within six months of such coming into force.

(3) At the time of the application and of the making of the order—

(a) the child's home must be with the husband and wife, and

(b) the husband or the wife, of both of them, must be domiciled in a part of the United Kingdom or in the Channel Islands or the Isle of Man.

(4) At the time of the making of the order both the husband and the wife must have attained the age of eighteen.

(5) The court must be satisfied that both the father of the child (including a person who is the father by virtue of section 28 of this Act), where he is not the husband, and the woman who carried the child have freely, and with full understanding of what is involved, agreed unconditionally to the making of the order.

(6) Subsection (5) above does not require the agreement of a person who cannot be found or is incapable of giving agreement and the agreement of the woman who carried the child is ineffective for the purposes of that subsection if given by her less than six weeks after the child's birth.

(7) The court must be satisfied that no money or other benefit (other than for expenses reasonably incurred) has been given or received by the husband or the wife for or in consideration of—

(a) the making of the order,

(b) any agreement required by subsection (5) above,

(c) the handing over of the child to the husband or the wife, or

(d) the making of any arrangements with a view to the making of the order,

unless authorised by the court.

...

(9) Regulations may provide—

(a) for any provision of the enactments about adoption to have effect, with such modifications (if any) as may be specified in the regulations, in relation to orders under this section, and applications for such orders, as it has effect in relation to adoption, and applications for adoption orders, and

(b) for references in any enactment to adoption, an adopted child or an adoptive relationship to be read (respectively) as references to the effect of an order under this section, a child to whom such an order applies and a relationship arising by virtue of the enactments about adoption, as applied by the regulations, and for similar expressions in connection with adoption to be read accordingly.

and the regulations may include such incidental or supplemental provision as appears to the Secretary of State necessary or desirable in consequence of any provision made by virtue of paragraph (a) or (b) above.

Questions

(i) In *A v C* (1978) [1985] FLR 445, Ormrod LJ referred to a surrogacy arrangement (from which the mother had repented) as a 'quite bizarre and unnatural arrangement' and Cumming-Bruce J called it a 'kind of baby-farming operation of a wholly distasteful and lamentable kind': do you agree?

(ii) How much of the law relating to adoption would you apply to the procedure under s. 30?

(iii) (a) In 1987, Mrs Pat Anthony gave birth to triplets. Doctors in South Africa had implanted into her eggs from her daughter Karen which had been fertilised by Karen's husband's sperm. Mrs Anthony therefore became the world's first surrogate grandmother (see Reid, 1988). Should treatment be provided in such a case? (b) In 1989, an English husband, infertile as a result of mumps, was told that it was 'ethically impossible' for his wife to be artificially inseminated with his brother's sperm. Can you think what the ethical objection might be? (c) How relevant are the Houghton Committee's doubts (p. 633, below) about adoption by relatives?

(iv) Why do we not feel able to allow the carrying mother to decide what she finds 'inconsistent with [her] human dignity'?

The legal position today, and the Court of Appeal's views on whether or not surrogacy is contrary to public policy, is set out in the following case

Briody v St Helens and Knowsley Health Authority
[2001] EWCA Civ 1010, [2002] QB 856, [2001] 2 FLR 1094

Hale LJ:

[10] English law on surrogacy is quite clear: (a) Surrogacy arrangements are not unlawful, nor is the payment of money to a surrogate mother in return for her agreeing to carry and hand over the child. (b) The activities of commercial surrogacy agencies are unlawful. It is an offence for any person to take part in negotiating surrogacy arrangements on a commercial basis, ie for payment to himself or another (apart from the surrogate mother); for a body of persons negotiating surrogacy arrangements to receive payment from either the proposed surrogate mother or the commissioning parents; or for a person to take part in the management or control of a body of persons which negotiates or facilitates surrogacy arrangements: Surrogacy Arrangements Act 1985, s 2. (c) It is also a crime to advertise either for surrogate mothers or a willingness to enter into or make surrogacy arrangements: Surrogacy Arrangements Act 1985, s 3. (d) The surrogate mother is always the child's legal mother, irrespective of whose eggs were used: Human Fertilisation and Embryology Act 1990, s 27(1). (e) If the commissioning father supplied the sperm, he will be the child's legal father, unless s 28 of the Human Fertilisation and Embryology Act 1990 applies so as to make someone else the father. It should be possible, by treating him and the surrogate together, to avoid the exclusion from fatherhood of ordinary sperm donors: see 1990 Act, s 28(6)(a) and Sch 3, para 5. (f) If the child is born by IVF (in vitro fertilisation), GIFT (gamete intra-fallopian transfer) or artificial (but not natural) insemination to a married surrogate mother, her husband will be the legal father unless it is shown that he did not consent to the treatment: Human Fertilisation and Embryology Act 1990, s 28(2). If the treatment was given '. . . in the course of treatment services provided for her and a man together' by a licensed clinic, her partner will be the father: 1990 Act, s 28(3). But this can easily be avoided by her partner taking no part in the treatment. (g) No surrogacy arrangement is enforceable by or against any of the persons making it: Surrogacy Arrangements Act 1985, s 1A (see also Children Act 1989, s 2(9), reflecting the common law). (h) The future of any child born, if disputed, will always be governed by the paramount consideration of the welfare of the child: Children Act 1989, s 1(1). It is unlikely, although not impossible, that a court would decide that the child should go to the commissioning parents rather than stay with a mother who had changed her mind: see *A v C* [1985] FLR 445, [1984] Fam Law 241; *Re P (Minors) (Wardship: Surrogacy)* [1988] FCR 140, [1987] 2 FLR 421. If the mother does not want the child and the commissioning parents are able to offer a suitable home, the court is likely to allow them to do so: see *Re C (A Minor) (Wardship: Surrogacy)* [1985] FLR 846. (i) If the child is handed over in accordance with the arrangement, the court may be prepared retrospectively to authorise, under s 57(3) of the Adoption Act 1976, any payment made to the surrogate mother and grant an adoption order which would otherwise be prohibited by s 24(2) of the 1976 Act: see *Re Adoption Application AA212/86 (surrogacy)* [1987] FCR 161; *sub nom Re Adoption Application (Payment for Adoption)* [1987] Fam 81. (j) There is now a special procedure, similar to adoption, whereby the commissioning parents may become the child's legal parents: they must be married to one another, the child must be born as a result of IVF, GIFT or artificial (again not natural) insemination using the gametes of one or both of them, the child must be living with them, the surrogate mother (and any father of the child who is not the commissioning father) must agree, and no payment must have been made unless authorised by the court: Human Fertilisation and Embryology Act 1930, s 30; see *Re Q (a minor) (parental order)* [1996] 2 FCR 345, [1996] 1 FLR 369. (k) If a surrogacy arrangement involves treatment in a clinic licensed by the Human Fertilisation and Embryology Authority (which will be the case in this country unless natural or private artificial insemination is used), this must not be provided:

'. . . unless account has been taken of the welfare of any child who may be born as a result of the treatment (including the need of that child for a father), and of any other child who may be affected by the birth.' (Human Fertilisation and Embryology Act 1990, s 13(5).)

(l) Clinics must observe the Code of Practice promulgated by the Human Fertilisation and Embryology Authority (4th edn, 1998). This provides (para 3.20):

'The application of assisted conception techniques to initiate a surrogate pregnancy should only be considered where it is physically impossible or highly undesirable for medical reasons for the commissioning mother to carry the child.'

It also gives guidance on the factors to be considered when taking account of the child's welfare (para 3.17); and points out that in a surrogacy arrangement either the surrogate (and her husband or partner if any) or the commissioning parents may become the child's parents and so both should be assessed, along with any risk of disruption should there be a dispute, and the effect on any other children in either the surrogate's or the commissioning parents' family (para 3.19.b).

[11] These provisions do not indicate that surrogacy as such is contrary to public policy. They tend to indicate that the issue is a difficult one, upon which opinions are divided, so that it would be wise to tread with caution. This is borne out in the official publications which have considered the matter. If there is a trend, it is towards acceptance and regulation as a last resort rather than towards prohibition.

[12] The 'moral and social objections to surrogacy' weighed heavily with the majority of the Warnock Committee: see *Report of the Committee of Inquiry into Human Fertilisation and Embryology*, 1984 (Cmnd 9314), Ch 8; 'Expression of Dissent: Surrogacy'. They not only made the recommendations which resulted in the 1985 Act, but also recommended criminal liability '. . . for professionals and others who knowingly assist in the establishment of a surrogate pregnancy'. This would have resulted in the virtual abolition of safe surrogacy arrangements while leaving private do-it-yourself arrangements untouched. Two members dissented: they thought that public opinion was not yet fully formed on the question and that it would be a mistake to close the door on it completely. They wanted to ban profit-making agencies but regulate the practice of non-profitmaking agencies on the analogy of adoption. The 1985 Act took a minimalist course. Yet only six years later, Parliament made special provision for commissioning parents to become legal parents, in s 30 of the 1990 Act.

[13] There was renewed concern in 1997, when Professor Brazier and her colleagues were asked to review the current law and practice. They found 'that incomplete implementation of the recommendations of either the majority or the minority of the Warnock Committee created a policy vacuum within which surrogacy has developed in a haphazard fashion': see *Surrogacy, Review for Health Ministers of Current Arrangements for Payments and Regulations*, Report of the Review Team, 1998 (Cm 4068), 'Executive Summary', para 3. They recommended further regulation, through the registration of non-profit-making agencies, who would have to abide by a Code of Practice, the continued banning of commercial agencies, statutory limitations so that surrogate mothers could only be paid genuine expenses, and the tightening of the s 30 process, with no power retrospectively to authorise illegal payments. These recommendations have not, as yet, been implemented.

Question

Should the recommendations of the Brazier report be implemented? Why do you suppose they have not been?

11.5 Illegitimate children or illegitimate parents?

For centuries the law tried, with varying success, to deter parents from having children outside marriage. Deterrence began in the medieval ecclesiastical courts, but the secular authorities took a hand once it appeared that failures in spiritual control were likely to cost the community money. The following examples are offered by Peter Laslett in *The World We Have Lost* (1971):

Anyone who committed or tried to commit a sexual act with anyone not his spouse, whether or not conception took place, ran the risk of a summons to the archdeacon's court – the lowest in the hierarchy of spiritual courts – a fine, and then penance in church at service time, or in the market place. If a person about whom a fame of incontinency had got abroad (that is a suspicion of a sexual escapade) ignored the summons or refused the punishment, then excommunication followed. This meant exile from the most important of all social activities, isolation within the community.

The lay courts and lay authority could be invoked for the more serious offences, and this often happened for the begetting of bastards. ...

If the records of the church courts are filled with notices of sexual incontinence, those of the magistrates courts are studded with measures taken in punishment of unmarried mothers, and sometimes of unmarried fathers too, with provision for the upkeep of the child:

> 'Jane Sotworth of Wrightington, spinster, swears that Richard Garstange of Fazarkerley, husbandman, is the father of Alice, her bastard daughter. She is to have charge of the child for two years, provided she does not beg, and Richard is then to take charge until it is twelve years old. He shall give Jane a cow and 6s. in money. Both he and she shall this day be whipped in Ormeskirke.'

So ordered the Lancashire justices at the Ormskirk Sessions on Monday, 27 April 1601, though the language they used was Latin and lengthier. At Manchester, in 1604, they went so far as to require that Thomas Byrom, gentleman, should maintain a bastard he had begotten on a widow, and be whipped too. On 10 October 1604, he was whipped in Manchester market place. ...

The legal warrant for Thomas Byrom's punishment is explained by Elisofon in 'A Historical and Comparative Study of Bastardy' (1973):

The year 1576 was especially important in relation to rights of the bastard child; for this was the first time in English history that a duty of support was imposed upon the parents of an illegitimate child. The statute passed by Parliament read, in part:

> 'Concerning bastards begotten and born out of lawful matrimony (an offence against God's law and man's law), the said bastard being now left to be at the charge of the parish where they be born, to the great burden of the same parish, and in defrauding of the relief of the impotent and aged true poor of the same parish, and to the evil example and encouragement of lewd life; it is ordained and enacted that two justices of the peace, upon examination of the cause and circumstances, shall and may by their discretion take order as well for the punishment of the mother and reputed father of such bastard child, as also for the better relief of every such parish in part or in all, and shall make likewise by like discretion, take order for the keeping of every such bastard child, by charging such mother or reputed father with payment of money weekly or other substentation for the relief of such child and such ways as they think covenant. And if ... the reputed mother and father shall not observe and perform the order, then the party making the default in not performing the order, be committed to the common gayle.' (emphasis added) ...

Question

Which do you suppose was the more serious – the offence against God's law or burden of the parish?

If the penalties for such an offence were serious for the parents, they were worse for the child:

The bastard, like the prostitute, thief, and beggar, belongs to that motley crowd of disreputable social types which society has generally resented, always endured. He is a living symbol of social irregularity, and undeniable evidence of contramoral forces; in short, a problem – a problem as old and unsolved as human existence itself.

These are the opening words of Davis's seminal article, 'Illegitimacy and the Social Structure' (1939). But why should the child be the problem? Why not his parents? Why not marriage itself? Davis explains a sociological theory of illegitimacy thus:

... The gist of the theory is that the function of reproduction can be carried out in a socially useful manner only if it is performed in conformity with institutional patterns, because only by means of an institutional system can individuals be organized and taught to co-operate in the performance of this long-range function, and the function be integrated with other social functions. The reproductive or familial institutions constitute the social machinery in terms of which the creation of new members of society is supposed to take place. The birth of children in ways that do not fit into this machinery must necessarily receive the disapproval of society, else the institutional system itself, which depends upon favorable attitudes in individuals, would not be approved or sustained. ...

People are not supposed to have illegitimate children, but when they do an emergency machinery is set into operation to give the child a status (though an inferior one) and to define the positions of the parents. In this way society continues. No one ever completely transcends the institutional boundaries. If he did, he would not be human. On the other hand, no one ever remains completely within the narrowest institutional boundaries. If he did, he would not be human. The fundamental explanation of nonconformity to the marital institutions is the same as the explanation of institutional nonconformity in general. ...

The question as to why the child is punished for the sins of its parents is wrongly put. It assumes an explanation of what has yet to be explained. It should read: What is the status of the illegitimate child, and why is he given this status? Perhaps his status is partly explicable in terms of punishment, but not primarily. ... punishment for parental sin is not the sole motive for the treatment of illegitimate children and does not deserve the primacy generally given it. The inquiry must be pushed to a deeper level which will explain both the legal disabilities (concerning descent, inheritance, support, and domicile) and the social disabilities (concerning public opinion, folkways, and mores).

Turning back, then, to the parents: the deterrent approach was carried on through the poor law. Its more recent history is taken up by Sir Morris Finer and Professor O.R. McGregor, in *A History of the Obligation to Maintain*, printed as an appendix to the Report of the Committee on One-Parent Families (1974). They begin with the Report of the Royal Commissioners on the Poor Laws which led to the 'new' poor law of 1834:

56. In the case of such a mother, the report did not recommend any change in the methods of relief, but it urged the repeal of all legislation which punished or charged the putative father of a bastard who should become, the Commissioners said:

'what Providence appears to have ordained that it should be, a burden on its mother, and, where she cannot maintain it, on her parents. The shame of the offence will not be destroyed by its being the means of income and marriage, and we trust that as soon as it has become both burthensome and disgraceful, it will become as rare as it is among those classes in this country who are above parish relief. ... If we are right in believing the penalties inflicted by nature to be sufficient, it is needless to urge further objections to any legal punishment. ... In affirming the inefficiency of human legislation to enforce the restraints placed on licentiousness by Providence, we have implied our belief that all punishment of the supposed father is useless.'

Behind this extreme statement of the providential foundations of the double standard of sexual morality lay the experience of abuses under the old bastardy laws. Under these, if a single woman declared herself pregnant and charged a man with being responsible, the overseers of the poor or any substantial householder could apply to any justice of the peace for a committal warrant. This would issue unless the accused man could give security to indemnify the parish or to enter into a recognisance to appear at Quarter Sessions and to perform any order which might there be made. The Commissioners thought that poor men were at the mercy of blackmail and perjury by unscrupulous women, and that the bastardy laws promoted social demoralisation.

57. The bastardy clauses of the Act of 1834 were in line with the opinions of the Poor Law Commissioners. ...

However, not all sections of society took the same view of the problem:

59. With the dislike of Tories for the centralising tendency of Benthamite administrative reforms, went also a different view of sexual morality and obligation. The urban Victorians inherited a strict moral code. They got it from evangelical religious teachers who imposed it on

the new middle class, the executive agents of the expanding industrial economy; and they planted it, as far as they could, on their lower orders. Their bookshelves carried the weight of such typical products of the evangelical outlook as Thomas Bowdler's The Family Shakespeare, In which nothing is added to the Text; but those Words and Expressions are omitted which cannot with Propriety be read aloud in a Family. These ten volumes reached a sixth edition in 1831, six years before the adolescent Victoria came under the influence of her first prime minister, a cultivated Whig who had been heard to respond to an evangelical sermon with the observation that 'things are coming to a pretty pass when religion is allowed to interfere with private life'. 'That d – d morality' which disturbed Lord Melbourne did not result from religious enthusiasm only. Differing provisions for the inheritance of family property were an important factor, too. The sexual waywardness of the territorial aristocracy did not endanger the integrity or succession of estates which were regulated by primogeniture and entail. Countless children of the mist played happily in Whig and Tory nurseries where they presented no threat to the property or interest of heirs. But middle class families handled their accumulating industrial wealth within a system of partible inheritance which demanded a more severe morality imposing higher standards upon women than upon men. An adulterous wife might be the means of planting a fraudulent claimant upon its property in the heart of her family; to avoid this ultimate catastrophe, middle class women were required to observe an inviolable rule of chastity. Just as the new poor law of 1834 represented a political triumph for philosophic radicalism by establishing an effective means of policing poverty, so it imposed middle class morality upon pauper women by seeking to police their sexual virtue.

60. Despite protests, the Poor Law Commissioners remained stout, for a time, in their insistence that to afford the mother of an illegitimate child a direct claim against the putative father for its maintenance would, by extending the rewards of matrimony to the unqualified and undeserving, tend to the destruction of the institution. In their sixth annual report in 1840, they printed with approval a report on the law of bastardy submitted to them by Sir Edmund Head, an Assistant Commissioner. ...

'... We were told by many eminent members of the legislature that, to afford a woman who had once broken the marriage tie an opportunity of even seeing her children for a few minutes was an encroachment on the privileges of wives who had remained faithful, and in this way a direct encouragement to immorality. If this be so, what shall we say to the infringement of the exclusive privileges of the married state implied by conferring on the mother of a bastard that claim for its support from a definite father, which it is one great object of matrimony to secure? Does not the principle that anything short of marriage is sufficient to fix the paternity of the child involve in itself a direct attack on that institution?'

Against such arguments were set the findings of the Commissioners of Inquiry for South Wales who were appointed to investigate the Rebecca Riots. They reported in 1844 that the bastardy laws had:

'altogether failed of the effect which sanguine persons calculated they might produce on the caution or moral feelings of the weaker sex. (There was little prostitution in South Wales but) subsequent marriage – and that not a forced one – ... almost invariably wiped out the light reproach which public opinion attached to a previous breach of chastity. (Now subsequent marriage was becoming rarer and women were exposed to) all the temptations of a life of vice (while) the man evades or defies the law, with a confidence and effrontery which has outraged the moral feeling of the people to a degree that can hardly be described.'

61. In the end, the Poor Law Commissioners gave ground and recommended in their tenth annual report that a mother should be given a civil action for maintenance against the putative father of her child. The Poor Law Amendment Act 1844 made a complete change by taking bastardy proceedings out of the hands of the poor law authorities and turning them into a civil matter between the parents. ...

62. The Poor Law Amendment Act 1868 restored to the parish the power to recover from the putative father the cost of maintenance of a bastard child by providing that, where a woman who had obtained an order against the father of her child herself became a charge of the parish, the justices might order the payments to be made to the relieving officer. ...

64. If the history of the legal rules which determine responsibility for the maintenance of bastards and their mothers is complicated, their treatment under the poor law was entirely straightforward. The mother was regarded as an able-bodied woman of demonstrated immorality, and relief was accordingly provided on a strictly deterrent basis in the workhouse. Mothers and babies were separated after the confinement and initial period of nursing. Most unmarried mothers could only use the workhouse as an immediate refuge during childbirth, after which they abandoned their children within it. Such unfortunates shared the fate of orphans and other deserted children who suffered deprivation as pauper children. But girls suffered worse than

boys, because the workhouse served as a manufactory of prostitutes. Frances Power Cobbe's observation in 1865 remained true throughout the nineteenth century:

> 'The case of the girls is far worse than of the boys, as all the conditions of workhouse management fall with peculiar evil on their natures. ... Among all the endless paradoxes of female treatment, one of the worst and most absurd is that which, while eternally proclaiming "home" to be the only sphere of a woman, systematically educates all female children of the State, without attempting to give them even an idea of what a home might be. ...'

Workhouse children gained in the later decades of the nineteenth century from such advances in institutional care as cottage homes, sheltered homes and boarding out. But the need for change was only just beginning to be recognised in the early years of this century. ...

Question

Does the difference in patterns of inheritance between the landed aristocracy and the commercial bourgeoisie strike you as a plausible explanation for the difference in their attitudes to illegitimacy?

The primacy of succession is reflected in the view of Sir William Blackstone, in his *Commentaries on the Laws of England* (1765):

The incapacity of a bastard consists principally in this, that he cannot be heir to any one, neither can he have heirs, but of his own body; for, being nullius filius, he is therefore of kin to nobody, and has no ancestor from whom any inheritable blood can be derived. A bastard was also, in strictness, incapable of holy orders; and, though that were dispensed with, yet he was utterly disqualified from holding any dignity in the church: but this doctrine seems now obsolete; and in all other respects, there is no distinction between a bastard and another man. And really any other distinction, but that of not inheriting, which civil policy renders necessary, would, with regard to the innocent offspring of his parents' crimes, be odious, unjust, and cruel to the last degree.

In 1979, the differences at that time between children born in and out of wedlock were summarised thus in the Law Commission's Working Paper on Illegitimacy:

Discrimination directly affecting the illegitimate child

2.10 It may be that the biggest discrimination suffered by a person born out of wedlock is the legal characterisation of him as 'illegitimate': we deal with the perpetuation of this label in Part III of this paper. The main practical areas in which there is legal discrimination are:

    (i) the maintenance of an illegitimate child is subject to the restrictions affecting the jurisdiction of the magistrates' courts: no lump sum exceeding £500 can be awarded and financial provision cannot be secured;

    (ii) although an illegitimate child can now inherit on the intestacy of either of his parents, he cannot take on the death intestate of any remoter ascendant or any collateral relation. In effect, therefore, he is treated as having no grandparents, brothers or sisters;

    (iii) despite recent reforms, an illegitimate child cannot succeed as heir to an entailed interest or succeed to a title of honour; and

    (iv) an illegitimate child if born outside the United Kingdom is not entitled as of right to United Kingdom citizenship even if both his parents are United Kingdom citizens.

Discrimination affecting the father of an illegitimate child

2.11 From a strictly legal point of view, the father of an illegitimate child is today probably at a greater disadvantage than the child himself; and while many fathers may take little or no interest in their children born out of wedlock, other fathers who have lived with the mothers for perhaps many years are clearly affected by the discrimination. This discrimination takes a number of different forms:

    (i) the father has no automatic rights of guardianship, custody or access, even where an affiliation order has been made against him. Any such rights are obtainable by him only by court order or, if the mother has died, under the mother's will. The basic principle is set out in section 85(7) of the Children Act 1975: 'Except as otherwise provided by or under any enactment, while the mother of an illegitimate child is living she has the parental rights and duties exclusively'.

(ii) Even if the father is awarded custody, he (unlike the father of a legitimate child) cannot obtain maintenance for the child from the mother, whatever her means.

(iii) The father's agreement to the child's adoption is not required unless he has already been granted custody or has become the child's guardian by court order or by appointment under the mother's will. His position is therefore different from that of the mother, and of both parents of a legitimate child, whose agreement is required.

(iv) The father's consent to a change of the child's name is not required unless he has become the legal guardian of the child by court order or under the mother's will.

(v) the father's consent to the marriage of the child during the child's minority is not required unless he has been granted custody of the child or has become the child's guardian under the mother's will.

(vi) There is no legal procedure by which the father can establish his paternity without the consent of the child's mother.

Procedural discrimination

2.12 There are, in addition, a number of procedural matters which point to the illegitimate child as 'different':

(i) Maintenance for an illegitimate child involves the institution by the mother of a special form of proceedings (affiliation proceedings) which many people regard as involving a stigma.

(ii) The mother cannot obtain maintenance for the child unless she is a 'single woman' at the date of the application for maintenance, or was so at the date of the child's birth. The phrase 'single woman' includes not only an unmarried woman (spinster, widow or divorcee) but also a married woman who is living apart from her husband and who has lost the right at common law to be maintained by him.

(iii) Only the magistrates' court has jurisdiction in affiliation proceedings, whereas the High Court, the county court and the magistrates' court all have jurisdiction in cases where maintenance is sought for legitimate children.

(iv) Subject to certain exceptions, an application for maintenance by way of affiliation proceedings must be made within three years of the child's birth. There is no such time limit as respects legitimate children.

(v) There is a special rule of evidence applicable to affiliation proceedings: if the mother gives evidence, her evidence must be corroborated.

(vi) There is a special form of appeal from a magistrates' court in affiliation proceedings.

Questions

(i) Why, do you suppose, did the Law Commission choose the word 'discrimination' instead of, for example, 'distinction'?

(ii) Should the lack of an automatic relationship with the father be classified as 'discrimination affecting the father' or 'discrimination affecting the child' or both?

(iii) Why are the matters described in para. 2.12 not labelled discrimination against the mother?

The Law Commission went on to survey the basic question of discrimination in this way:

3.2 ... It is not now easy to put convincing arguments in favour of discrimination, because such arguments would logically justify a return to the strict common law position, and it is difficult to believe that there would be any substantial support for turning the clock back in this way. Nevertheless, arguments in favour of preserving the principle of discrimination may still be used by those who are prepared reluctantly to accept, as an accomplished fact, the changes which have already been made towards improving the legal status of the illegitimate child, but think that no further reform should be made. ...

3.3 First, it is said that the legal distinction between 'legitimacy' and 'illegitimacy' reflects social realities. This was certainly true at one time. The birth of an illegitimate child was regarded as bringing disgrace not only on the mother but also on her immediate family. The child could no more expect to be recognised as a member of the family and be received into the family home than he could expect to inherit family property. He was not a real member of the family group. However, although there may still be cases where the illegitimate child is in this position, the evidence suggests that a significant and increasing proportion of all illegitimate children born each year are recognised by both their parents, at least if the parents have a relationship of some stability. ...

3.4 Secondly, it is said that the distinction serves to uphold moral standards and also to support the institution of marriage. In relation to the preservation of moral standards, it is difficult to say how far the fear of producing illegitimate children influenced sexual behaviour in the past; since the risk of an unwanted pregnancy can now usually be avoided by contraceptive measures it seems improbable that such fears still influence sexual behaviour to any substantial extent. Support for the institution of marriage is of course of great importance, especially in the present context, because a married relationship between parents should in principle be more stable than an unmarried one, so creating a better environment for the child's upbringing. However, many marriages are not stable, and statistically it seems that marriages entered into primarily for the purpose of ensuring that an expected child is not born illegitimate are especially at risk. ...

3.5 The third argument in favour of preserving discriminatory treatment asserts that the legal relationship between the child's parents should be relevant in determining the child's legal status: that as the legal relationship of marriage results in legitimate status for the child, so a relationship which does not accord with the norm should not result in normal status for the child. On this view it is regarded as significant not only that a legitimate child is the issue of a legally recognised union, the incidents of which are fixed by law and which can only be dissolved by formal proceedings but also that marriage, at least in its inception, is intended to be permanent. The relationship of an illegitimate child's parents, on the other hand, is not in general legally recognised and may never have been intended to be more than transient. However this argument is based on the premise that a child's status ought to be affected by that of his parents. This is the proposition which we do not accept; it is, after all, the child's status, and the nature of the relationship between his parents need not and should not affect this.

Two further reasons for reform were put forward in the Scottish Law Commission's Consultative Memorandum on *Illegitimacy* (1982):

1.15 Reform would be in line with this country's treaty obligations. The United Kingdom has ratified the European Convention on the Legal Status of Children born out of Wedlock. The preamble to this Convention notes that in a great number of member States of the Council of Europe efforts have been, or are being, made to improve the legal status of children born out of wedlock by reducing the differences between their legal status and that of children born in wedlock which are to their legal or social disadvantage. It records that the signatory States believe that the situation of children born out of wedlock should be improved and that the formulation of certain common rules concerning their legal status would assist this objective. The Convention then binds each Contracting Party to ensure the conformity of its law with the provisions of the Convention. A State is, however, allowed to make not more than three reservations. The present law of Scotland [and England] does not conform to two provisions of the Convention and the United Kingdom accordingly reserved the right not to apply, or not to apply fully, those provisions in relation to Scotland.* The policy of the Convention is to allow 'progressive stages for those States which consider themselves unable to adopt immediately' all of its rules and reservations are valid for only five years at a time. It is clear that the general policy of the Convention is the reduction of legal discrimination against illegitimate children and that the United Kingdom's position would be more in accord with that policy if the reservations were unnecessary.

* The provisions in question are: – Art. 6(2) 'Where a legal obligation to maintain a child born in wedlock falls on certain members of the family of the father or mother, this obligation shall also apply for the benefit of a child born out of wedlock.'

  Art. 9 'A child born out of wedlock shall have the same right of succession in the estate of its father and its mother and of a member of its father's or mother's family, as if it had been born in wedlock.'

1.16 The United Kingdom is also a party to the European Convention on Human Rights. It has been held in the case of *Marckx v Kingdom of Belgium* that the provisions of Belgian law prohibiting an illegitimate child from inheriting from his close maternal relatives on their intestacy contravened Article 8 [see p. 27, above] and that these different inheritance rights of legitimate and illegitimate children lacked objective and reasonable justification. In Scots law, as in Belgian law, an illegitimate child has no such inheritance rights, so that changes are necessary to prevent the continuing breach of Article 8 by the United Kingdom.

Having concluded that there was no justification for retaining the status quo, the English Law Commission (1979) went on to discuss two possible models for reform:

(b) First model for reform: abolition of adverse legal consequences of illegitimacy
3.8 In this model the concepts of legitimacy and illegitimacy are preserved, but further steps are taken to remove by statute certain of the practical and procedural consequences of illegitimacy: in particular, all consequences which are adverse to the child. ...
3.9 The particular reforms for inclusion within such a scheme could be selective; and the model has what some may regard as the advantage of not necessarily involving the automatic removal of all discrimination against the father of an illegitimate child. ...

(c) Second model for reform: abolition of the status of illegitimacy
3.14 This model involves the total disappearance of the concept of 'legitimacy' as well as of 'illegitimacy', for the one cannot exist without the other. It goes beyond the mere assimilation of the legal positions of children born in and out of wedlock, since that solution, which has been considered above, would still preserve the caste labels which help artificially to preserve the social stigma now attached to illegitimacy.
3.15 The case for abolishing illegitimacy as a status is in our view supported by the fact that such a change in the law would help to improve the position of children born out of wedlock in a way in which the mere removal of the remaining legal disabilities attaching to illegitimacy would not. No change in the law relating to legitimacy would help to improve the economic position of a child born out of wedlock in so far as he suffers from being the child of a 'one-parent family'; but an illegitimate child suffers a special disadvantage which does not affect the child of a widow or divorcee. He has a different status, even if the incidents of that status do not differ greatly from those attached to the status of a legitimate child; attention is thus focused on the irrelevant fact of the parents' marital status. We believe that the law can help to lessen social prejudices by setting an example clearly based upon the principle that the parents' marital relationship is irrelevant to the child's legal position. Changes in the law cannot give the illegitimate child the benefits of a secure, caring, family background. They cannot even ensure the he does not suffer financially, since his father may not be in a position to support him. But they can at least remove the additional hardship of attaching an opprobrious description to him. ...
3.16 If the law were changed so that there was no longer a legal distinction between the illegitimate child, it would also follow that in principle there would be no distinction between parents: both parents would have equal rights and duties unless and until a court otherwise ordered. ... We have tentatively concluded that the advantages of removing the status of illegitimacy altogether from the law outweigh the disadvantages of giving all fathers parental rights.

The response of the National Council for One-Parent Families, *An Accident of Birth* (1980), supported the end but not the means:

In discussing the abolition of illegitimacy, we believe that it is necessary to draw a clear distinction between the rights of the child and the rights of the parents. We do not believe that the two models – that of abolishing the status of illegitimacy and that of preserving some distinction between the parental rights and duties of married and unmarried parents – are necessarily mutually exclusive. We believe that by giving all children equal rights, irrespective of the marital status of their parents, the status of illegitimacy is abolished. Any remaining difference in the custodial relationship of parents is a consequence of the status of marriage, of which we are not proposing the abolition. We recognise the need for reform in the area of parental rights, and would certainly support an increase in father's rights to encourage unmarried fathers to play a greater role in the upbringing of their children. However, we feel that there are strong arguments against giving all fathers automatic equal parental rights. ...
    (a) In our experience, the majority of illegitimate children during early childhood are living with and being cared for by their mothers alone, and either have no contact, or very erratic contact, with their natural fathers. We believe that giving fathers automatic rights will remove the existing protection and security an unmarried mother has in bringing up her child alone, and will lead to increased pressure and distress, caused not only in the event of intervention by an estranged father, but also by the uncertainty of never knowing whether or not the father will exercise his rights, unless the issue is decided by the court.

(b) If an unmarried father is to be given automatic parental rights, the question of establishing paternity takes on increased significance. We believe that many mothers will be deterred from entering the father's details on the birth certificate or will deny the identity of the father if automatic parental rights flow from paternity being established. This will act against the child's right to know the facts about his or her origins and will undermine the Law Commission's recommendation on this subject.

[However:] ... There is a need to provide a procedure available to all unmarried parents, whether cohabiting or not, to make a mutual declaration of parentage and joint custody, and to register it with the court. Simple forms could be available at the Municipal Offices where births are registered, where such a declaration could be formalised. This would give full custody rights to unmarried fathers where the mother consents. Although we believe that such a consensual arrangement is the only one having a reasonable chance of success, it could be viewed as giving an unjustifiable veto to the mother. We therefore recommend that a further amendment should be made to the Guardianship of Minors Act 1971, to allow unmarried fathers to apply to the court for joint custody if the mother should not agree to a mutual declaration. In reaching its decision, the court would have to apply the cardinal principle of family law in regarding the welfare of the child as paramount.

[Finally:] We deplore the Law Commission's statement that 'One-parent families remain a major social problem'. The one-parent family is not problematic per se and it is not a deviation from the two-parent family. Despite the fact that one-parent families suffer both economic and social discrimination we believe that a one-parent family is a normal and viable family form in its own right and is able to carry out required family functions such as parenting. Given such negative attitudes it is not surprising that laws developed to suit a two-parent family fit so awkwardly on a one-parent family.

Residual social stigma affects the confidence of single women in their undoubted ability to provide a satisfactory upbringing for their children. Attitudes towards illegitimacy are part of wider social and moral codes affecting sexual behaviour and particularly attitudes towards women. The sense of shame, of feeling different and inferior, which has been the experience of so many illegitimate children in the past, is the result of society's punishing attitude towards the mother for contravening the moral code. In our concern to give equality to all children, we should not overlook that in the early childhood years, the fate of many children will be in the hands of one custodian only, usually the mother. The law must strike a balance which protects and respects her as custodian whilst at the same time keeping open the channels of access to the father.

The Commission's Report on *Illegitimacy* (1982) therefore paid much greater heed to the arguments against according automatic rights to fathers:

4.26 ...

(a) It was said that automatically to confer 'parental rights' on fathers could well result in a significant growth in the number of mothers who would refuse to identify the father of their child. Mothers would be tempted to conceal the father's identity in order to ensure that in practice he could not exercise any parental rights. If this were to happen, it would detract from the desirable objective of establishing, recognising and fostering genuine familial links.

(b) It was said that to confer rights on the father might well be productive of particular distress and disturbance where the mother had subsequently married a third party, who had put himself in loco parentis to the child. The possibility – however unlikely in reality – of interference by the child's father could well engender a damaging sense of insecurity in the family; matters would be all the worse if the father did intervene. Some commentators argued that the result in such a case might be that the mother and her new partner would seek, for instance by an application for custody or adoption, to forestall any possible intervention by the natural father with the result that the child would be prematurely denied the possibility of establishing a genuine link with him.

(c) It was said that automatically to confer 'rights' on the father of a child born outside marriage could put him in a position where he might be tempted to harass or possibly even to blackmail the mother at a time when she might well be exceptionally vulnerable to pressure. In this context a number of commentators made what seems to us to be the valid point that what is in issue is not so much how the law is perceived by the professional lawyer or the experienced social worker, but how it might be perceived by a fearful and perhaps ill-informed mother. Sometimes what the law is thought to be may be almost as important as what it in fact is. Thus the parents of a child might well attach more significance to the fact that the law had given the father 'rights' than would a lawyer who is accustomed to the forensic process and able dispassionately to consider the likelihood of a court in fact permitting a father to exercise those rights, given its overriding concern to promote the child's welfare.

(d) It was also suggested that the experience of countries which have sought to abolish the discrimination affecting those born outside marriage is generally against automatically conferring 'parental rights' on the father of an illegitimate child. In most of those countries the father does not have the full range of parental rights unless he has obtained a court order or he falls within a delimited category of fathers in whom the law automatically recognises parental rights.

(e) Finally it was suggested that if all fathers automatically possessed parental authority over their illegitimate children, practical difficulties would be encountered where the child was in the care of a local authority. ... These would arise because a local authority is not entitled to keep a child in its care if a person having parental rights expresses a desire to take over the child's care. The result might therefore be either that the father would, contrary to its best interests, take the child out of care, or alternatively that long-term planning for the child's future would be delayed until the father's rights had been terminated. In such cases the child might well suffer.

Questions

(i) Which of the following do you think would be the best for most children: (a) abolishing the status and giving all fathers automatic parental responsibility; (b) abolishing the child's exclusion from his father's lineage, giving him the same claims to financial provision and property adjustment as any other child, but not giving the father automatic parental responsibility; or (c) abolishing the status and giving no fathers automatic parental responsibility?

In their First Report on *Illegitimacy* (1982), the Law Commission opted for a package of reforms corresponding to model (b):

4.44 ... Some commentators expressed the view ... that it would be perfectly possible to abolish the status of illegitimacy whilst preserving the existing rules whereby parental rights vest automatically only in married parents. We do not accept this view. The argument for 'abolishing illegitimacy' (rather than merely removing such legal consequences of that status as are adverse to the child) is essentially that the abolition of any legal distinction based on the parents' marital status would itself have an influence on opinion. The marital status of the child's parents would cease to be legally relevant, and thus the need to refer to the child's distinctive legal status would (in this view) disappear. This consequence could not follow if a distinction – albeit relating only to entitlement to parental rights – were to be preserved between children which would be based solely on their parent's status. There would remain two classes of children: first, those whose parents were married and thereby enjoyed parental rights; secondly, those whose parents were unmarried and whose fathers did not enjoy such rights. ...
4.49 In the result, we have come to the conclusion that the advantages of abolishing the status of illegitimacy are not sufficient to compensate for the possible dangers involved in an automatic extension of parental rights to fathers of non-marital children. ...
4.51 For almost all purposes the effect of the changes which we recommend will be that all children – irrespective of their parents' marital status – will be treated alike by the law. However, in a few areas (the most important of which is obviously the question of entitlement to parental rights) there will continue to be a difference between those children whose parents have married and those whose parents have not. To this extent it will be necessary to preserve the concepts of 'legitimacy', 'illegitimacy' and 'legitimation'. On the question of terminology, however, we would at this stage make one small, but we think important, recommendation: namely, that whenever possible the terms 'legitimate' and 'illegitimate' should cease to be used as legal terms of art. The expressions that we favour in their stead, and that we use generally in this Report and in the draft legislation attached hereto, are 'marital' and 'non-marital', which avoid the connotations of unlawfulness and illegality which are implicit in the term 'illegitimate'.

Question

Could they have gone further and purged the statute book of the concepts of legitimacy and legitimation altogether?

The Family Law Reform Act 1987 provides:

General Principle

1.—(1) In this Act and enactments passed and instruments made after the coming into force of this section, references (however expressed) to any relationship between two persons shall, unless the contrary intention appears, be construed without regard to whether or not the father and mother of either of them, or the father and mother of any person through whom the relationship is deduced, have or had been married to each other at any time.

(2) In this Act and enactments passed after the coming into force of this section, unless the contrary intention appears—

(a) references to a person whose father and mother were married to each other at the time of his birth include; and

(b) references to a person whose father and mother were not married to each other at the time of his birth do not include,

references to any person to whom subsection (3) below applies, and cognate references shall be construed accordingly.

(3) This subsection applies to any person who—

(a) is treated as legitimate by virtue of section 1 of the Legitimacy Act 1976;

(b) is a legitimated person within the meaning of section 10 of that Act;

(c) is an adopted child within the meaning of Part IV of the Adoption Act 1976; or

(d) is otherwise treated in law as legitimate.

(4) For the purpose of construing references falling within subsection (2) above, the time of a person's birth shall be taken to include any time during the period beginning with—

(a) the insemination resulting in his birth; or

(b) where there was no such insemination, his conception.

and (in either case) ending with his birth.

The Children Act 1989, however, provides:

2.—(1) Where a child's father and mother were married to each other at the time of his birth, they shall each have parental responsibility for the child.

(2) Where a child's father and mother were not married to each other at the time of his birth—

(a) the mother shall have parental responsibility for the child;

(b) the father shall not have parental responsibility for the child, unless he acquires it in accordance with the provisions of this Act.

(3) References in this Act to a child whose father and mother were, or (as the case may be) were not, married to each other at the time of his birth must be read with section 1 of the Family Law Reform Act 1987 (which extends their meaning).

(4) The rule of law that a father is the natural guardian of his legitimate child is abolished.

The 1989 Act also provides for several ways in which the father may come to share parental responsibility with the mother:

4.—(1) Where a child's father and mother were not married to each other at the time of his birth—

(a) the court may, on the application of the father, order that he shall have parental responsibility for the child; or

(b) the father and mother may by agreement ('a parental responsibility agreement') provide for the father to have parental responsibility for the child.

(2) No parental responsibility agreement shall have effect for the purposes of this Act unless—

(a) it is made in the form prescribed by regulations made by the Lord Chancellor; and

(b) where regulations are made by the Lord Chancellor prescribing the manner in which such agreements must be recorded, it is recorded in the prescribed manner.

(3) Subject to section 12(4), an order under subsection (1)(a), or a parental responsibility agreement, may only be brought to an end by an order of the court made on the application—

(a) of any person who has parental responsibility for the child; or

(b) with leave of the court, of the child himself.

(4) The court may only grant leave under subsection (3)(b) if it is satisfied that the child has sufficient understanding to make the proposed application.

...

12.—(1) Where the court makes a residence order in favour of the father of a child it shall, if the father would not otherwise have parental responsibility for the child, also make an order under section 4 giving him that responsibility.

...

(4) Where subsection (1) requires the court to make an order under section 4 in respect of the father of a child, the court shall not bring that order to an end at any time while the residence order concerned remains in force.

Note that the case law of the European Court of Human Rights is clear that the law as set out here does not offend against Art. 14 of the European Convention on Human Rights: see, for example, *Keegan v Ireland* (1994) 18 EHRR 342 (Chapter 1, p. 27).

Nevertheless, there has been a growing feeling that the law is not satisfactory. The Lord Chancellor's Department's Consultation Paper, *Procedures for the Determination of Paternity and on the Law of Parental Responsibility for Unmarried Fathers* (1998), includes the following comments:

56. One of the difficulties about legislating for the rights or responsibilities of unmarried parents is that they are not a homogeneous grouping. The very significant proportion of births outside marriage which are registered by both parents living at the same address seems to reflect the growing acceptance of long-term cohabitation as a preliminary or alternative to marriage. Many such relationships must be at least as stable as marriage. At the other end of the spectrum, however, there are still children who (despite the widespread availability of contraception and abortion) are born as a result of transient or coercive relationships. The underlying aim of the present law on parental responsibility is to protect women who are 'victims' of such circumstances by allowing the mother, in effect, to veto parental responsibility for an unmarried father unless he can persuade the court to override her objections.

57. The most radical option for the future would be to change the law to create an automatic link between biological parentage and parental responsibility, so that all fathers would have parental responsibility for their children, whatever their marital status at the time of the child's birth, without the need for any special registration procedures or for any court order. (There are, however, no plans to alter the Human Fertilisation and Embryology Act 1990 in relation to those who donate sperm or eggs.) The question of the father's 'merits' would not arise, but there would still need to be some provision for challenge by the mother, and perhaps by others, on the grounds that a man claiming parental responsibility was not in fact the father of the child concerned. It is possible that such a provision might lead to an increase in the number of cases of disputed paternity.

58. It would be open to consideration whether there should also be limited circumstances in which the mother's wishes should be allowed to override the father's automatic right to parental responsibility, even when his paternity was not in dispute. That might apply, for example, in cases where the child had been conceived as a result of rape, or where the father had a history of violence against the mother or other children. The need for exceptions to the normal rule would need to be carefully considered in the light of legal remedies already available, including those against domestic violence under Part IV of the Family Law Act 1996 as well as orders under section 8 of the Children Act 1989.

59. Another possible approach, falling short of automatic parental responsibility for all fathers, would be to limit the automatic conferment of parental responsibility to a defined category or categories of unmarried fathers, retaining the existing provisions for court orders and parental responsibility agreements for those who did not qualify automatically. The most obvious category would be those unmarried fathers who sign the birth register jointly with the mother. There would be the practical advantage that the birth certificate would provide proof of the father's status. In addition, joint registration could probably be assumed to imply the mother's agreement, and to demonstrate an appropriate degree of commitment to the child. It is open to question whether the same would apply in cases where the birth register is altered after the initial entry.

60. A further point for consideration is the scope for coercion by violent or abusive fathers, and whether vulnerable mothers would need the protection of a special provision for the revocation of parental responsibility acquired in this way.

61. Other categories of unmarried fathers who might be considered as candidates for automatic parental responsibility are those who are living with the mother at the time of the child's birth (whether or not they signed the register), and those in respect of whom the court has made a

declaration of parentage. A link between parental responsibility and a child maintenance order made by the Child Support Agency is also a possibility, but would be more controversial because it might deter mothers from applying to the CSA. The practical implications of any of these options which would probably require some form of registration process, would, in any event, need careful consideration.

Evidence of father's views comes from the report, *Fathers, marriage and the law*, by Ros Pickford (1999) (summarised by the Joseph Rowntree Foundation):

In 1996, while over 230,000 babies were born to unmarried parents, only about 3,000 couples made Agreements and around 5,500 more fathers got Court Orders for Parental Responsibility. There are, therefore, many thousands of families in this country where the father is not legally entitled to make important decisions about the everyday care and upbringing of his child.

The research set out to find out what today's fathers themselves think about the relationship between fatherhood and marriage, and whether there are any differences between those fathers who choose to marry and those who do not. It was also intended to discover what fathers know about the law on Parental Responsibility, why Agreements and Orders are being so little used, and what kind of problems fathers had encountered as a result of the current law. Fathers in the study were also asked for their views on a possible change in the law.

Fathers' knowledge of the law

Fathers were asked about a range of situations where the law on Parental Responsibility is relevant, such as fathers' liability for child support and whether a father is legally entitled to care for his child if the mother dies.

The research found that four out of five fathers, both married and unmarried, were aware that a father is liable for child support, irrespective of whether the father is married to the child's mother. However, on the question of what would happen if a child's mother died, three-quarters of fathers wrongly thought that an unmarried father would be legally entitled to look after his child.

There were two main reasons for these discrepancies in fathers' knowledge. First, there is a lack of accessible information about the law. There has been a great deal of publicity about the Child Support Agency; most fathers, even those who had never had any contact with the Agency, had heard about it and were aware of fathers' financial responsibilities. Very few, however, had heard anything about the law relating to Parental Responsibility, and most felt it was wrong that no information is offered to parents about it.

Secondly, the law is at odds with other areas of the law relating to the family with which people are familiar, such as child support and income support where it makes no difference whether parents are married. Most fathers, therefore, assumed that marriage would not be relevant to the role of a father. As one father put it:

'I mean I get the same, I get the tax relief on Lucy, get the same kind of benefits, that we would if we were married or not.'

Another father said:

'So much is now ... heard about the ... Child Support Agency, the, the fact that you are now so much more regarded as the father ... The father's role either inside or outside marriage is quite well defined, purely for the purposes of getting the child support money back so, there's a, you know, that the other side of the coin must be true.'

All this made the law difficult to understand, and fathers were often confused that the fact they had registered on the birth certificate as the father, or actually lived with the child, made no difference.

'I didn't think there was any difference. I thought like if the child's yours and you sign the birth certificate ... at the end of the day it's your child.'

Fathers' problems with the law

Fathers who had used the legal process to apply for Parental Responsibility reported a range of problems which had prompted their legal actions. The majority were involved in contact disputes with the mother, which had arisen after their relationship broke down. Other problems included hospitals refusing to allow fathers to give medical consent, schools refusing to provide information about the child's progress, and a battle with grandparents over who was to care for the child after the mother died.

This father had accompanied his child to a specialist hospital 50 miles away while the child's mother remained at home to look after their other baby.

'One of them's got heart problems. Last year I had to go to [hospital] with him. You know he's going to have his pacemaker changed, but when it come down to it, the first question they ask me is, was I married? And I said 'Well, no' – then they said to me I can't sign for it. Which is ridiculous, because I was there. The mother wasn't. They had to ring up, call up the mother to come down, right, you know, so that she can sign, right. Even though I'm the father like and you know I've been there all week.'

Fathers' views of the law

The majority of unmarried fathers in the study either found out about their lack of Parental Responsibility as a result of a problem arising or during the course of the research interview. Reactions ranged from disbelief and bewilderment through to anger and fear. Many thought that the current law undermines their role as fathers.

'Well I think, I think, it devalues fatherhood, you know, it, it's taking away some of my role of being her father. Just because the fact that I haven't, you know, I haven't signed a bit of paper.'

All those who were cohabiting or supporting their children said they could see no difference between their situation and that of a married father.

'I would base it on that except [for] a marriage certificate, I'm basically living a married kind of life. You know the full family life.'

There were many criticisms of Parental Responsibility Agreements not least where fathers thought that there should be equality between mothers and fathers. Others thought that having to raise the issue with the mother would be difficult because it might imply a lack of trust. This father, who had done so, said:

'It was difficult because I had to basically approach her from the point of view that it was something I was requesting, almost as a favour, and although she didn't have any theoretical objections to it, she was suspicious of the motives.'

...

Conclusion

The Lord Chancellor's Department has announced plans for the Government to bring forward legislation to give Parental Responsibility automatically to fathers who register on the birth certificate. This research indicates that because the law is at odds with many other aspects of family law and was seen by most respondents as illogical, unfair and out of date, there appear to be strong arguments in favour of such a change. However, the research also suggests the need to widen the scope of such legislation to include other groups of unmarried fathers. The researcher concludes that there is an urgent need for information to be provided about Parental Responsibility at appropriate places, such as antenatal clinics and birth register offices, not least because any change in the law will not affect the situation of existing unmarried fathers.

The Adoption and Children Bill provides, in clause 108, for an additional means for the unmarried father to acquire parental responsibility:

107   Parental responsibility of unmarried father

(1)   Section 4 of the 1989 Act (acquisition of responsibility by the father of a child who is not married to the child's mother) is amended as follows.

(2)   In subsection (1) (cases where parental responsibility is acquired), for the words after 'birth' there is substituted ', the father shall acquire parental responsibility for the child if—

(a)   he becomes registered as the child's father under any of the enactments specified in subsection (1A);

(b)   he and the child's mother make an agreement (a "parental responsibility agreement") providing for him to have parental responsibility for the child; or

(c)   the court, on his application, orders that he shall have parental responsibility for the child.'

(1)   After that subsection there is inserted—

'(1A) The enactments referred to in subsection (1)(a) are—

(a)   paragraphs (a), (b) and (c) of section 10(1) and of section 10A(1) of the Births and Deaths Registration Act 1953;

(b)   paragraphs (a), (b)(i) and (c) of section 18(1) of the Registration of Births, Deaths and Marriages (Scotland) Act 1965; and

(c)   sub-paragraphs (a), (b) and (c) of Article 14(3) of the Births and Deaths Registration (Northern Ireland) Order 1976 (S.I. 1976/1041 (N.I. 14)).

(1B) The Lord Chancellor may by order amend subsection (1A) so as to add further enactments to the list in that subsection.'

(4) For subsection (3) there is substituted—

'(2A) A person who has acquired parental responsibility under subsection (1) shall cease to have that responsibility only if the court so orders.

(3) The court may make an order under subsection (2A) on the application—

(a) of any person who has parental responsibility for the child; or

(b) with the leave of the court, of the child himself,

subject, in the case of parental responsibility acquired under subsection (1)(c), to section 12(4).'

Note that the following clause provides for step-parents to acquire parental responsibility by order or agreement.

The many reported cases on parental responsibility orders, including the often cited *Re H (minors) (local authority: parental rights) (No 3)* [1991] Fam 151, [1991] 2 All ER 185, CA, are conveniently summarised in the following case:

Re S (Parental Responsibility)
[1995] 3 FCR 225, [1995] 2 FLR 648, [1995] Fam Law 596, Court of Appeal

The parents lived together from 1985 and the child was born in January 1988. The parents separated when she was 18 months old. The father regularly paid the mother £500 per month. In 1990 he was convicted of possessing obscene literature. The mother stopped contact for a while but resumed it because of the child's distress. It developed into staying contact. The father applied for a parental responsibility order but was refused. He appealed. In the course of his judgment, Ward LJ pointed out the leading cases on this issue:

Ward LJ: The first important case on this subject... is *Re H (Minors) (Local Authority: Parental Rights) (No 3)* [1991] Fam 151, sub nom *Re H (Illegitimate Children: Father: Parental Rights) (No 2)* [1991] 1 FLR 214. Balcombe LJ ... suggested, and most helpfully, this test at pp. 158B and 218F respectively:

'In considering whether to make an order under s.4 of the 1987 Act, the court will have to take into account a number of factors of which the following will undoubtedly be material (although there may well be others, as the list is not intended to be exhaustive):

(1) the degree of commitment which the father has shown towards the child;

(2) the degree of attachment which exists between the father and the child; and

(3) the reasons of the father for applying for the order.'

...

In *Re G (A Minor) (Parental Responsibility Order)* [1994] 1 FLR 504, again a decision of the Court of Appeal, Balcombe LJ at p.508A said this ...:

'... I am quite prepared to accept that the making of a parental responsibility order requires the judge to adopt the welfare principle as the paramount consideration. But having said that, I should add that, of course, it is well established by authority that, other things being equal, it is always to a child's welfare to know and, wherever possible, to have contact with both its parents, including the parent with whom it is not normally resident, if the parents have separated.

Therefore, prima facie, it must necessarily also be for the child's benefit or welfare that it has an absent parent sufficiently concerned and interested to want to have a parental responsibility order. In other words, I approach this question on the basis that where you have a concerned although absent father, who fulfils the other test about which I spoke in *Re H*, namely having shown a degree of commitment towards the child, it being established that there is a degree of attachment between the father and the child, and that his reasons for applying for the order are not demonstrably improper or wrong, then prima facie it would be for the welfare of the child that such an order should be made.'

...

[I]t is my increasing concern, both from the very fact that there are so many reported cases on this topic and from my experience when dealing with the innumerable appeals from justices to the Family Division, that applications under s. 4 have become one of these little growth industries born of misunderstanding. Misunderstanding arises from a failure to appreciate that, in essence, the granting of a parental responsibility order is the granting of status. It is unfortunate that the notion of 'parental responsibility' has still to be defined by s. 3 of the Children Act to mean '... all the rights, duties, powers, responsibilities and authority which by law a parent ... has in relation to the child and his property', which gives outmoded pre-eminence to the 'rights' which are conferred. That it is unfortunate is demonstrated by the very fact that, when pressed in this case to define the nature and effect of the order which was so vigorously opposed, counsel for the mother was driven to say that her rooted objection was to the rights to which it would entitle the father and the power that it would give him. That is a most unfortunate failure to appreciate the significant change that the Act has brought about where the emphasis is to move away from rights and to concentrate on responsibilities. She did not doubt that if by unhappy chance this child fell ill whilst she was abroad, her father, if then enjoying contact, would not deal responsibly with her welfare. ...

Butler-Sloss LJ: I also agree. ...

It is important for parents and it is important, indeed, for these parents to remember the emphasis placed by Parliament on the order which is applied for. It is that of duties and responsibilities as well as rights and powers. Indeed, the order itself is entitled 'parental responsibility'. A father who has shown real commitment to the child concerned and to whom there is a positive attachment, as well as a genuine bona fide reason for the application, ought, in a case such as the present, to assume the weight of those duties and cement that commitment and attachment by sharing the responsibilities for the child with the mother. This father is asking to assume that burden as well as that pleasure of looking after his child, a burden not lightly to be undertaken.

Appeal allowed.

Questions

(i) If a father is granted a residence order, s. 12(1) insists that a parental responsibility order must also be made; there is no corresponding requirement whenever a contact order is made; did Parliament intend that all fathers who have contact should also have parental responsibility?

(ii) In *Re H (minors) (local authority: parental rights) (No 3)* [1991] Fam 151, the Court of Appeal held that a father should be granted parental responsibility, so that his agreement to the child's adoption was required, but then that this could be dispensed with on the ground that it was unreasonably withheld: what good did this do either the father or the child?

(iii) Do you think that the Law Commission had such cases in mind?

(iv) Ward LJ was mistaken about the position in Scotland. The Scottish Law Commission, in their *Report on Family Law* (1992), had concluded that:

2.48 The question is not whether there should be an unalterable recognition or denial of parental responsibility and rights. Whatever the initial position may be, a court order could alter it in the interests of the child. The question is whether the starting position should be that the father has, or has not, the normal parental responsibilities and rights. Given that about 25% of all children born in Scotland in recent years have been born out of wedlock, and that the number of couples cohabiting outside marriage is now substantial, it seems to us that the balance has now swung in favour of the view that parents are parents, whether married to each other or not. If in any particular case it is in the best interests of a child that a parent should be deprived of some or all of his parental responsibilities and rights, that can be achieved by means of a court order.

But the Children (Scotland) Act 1995, ss. 4 and 11, make provision equivalent to that in England and Wales. (a) Do you agree with the Scottish Law Commission? (b) Is opinion amongst you on this matter divided according to gender?

Section 4(1)(b) provides for parental responsibility agreements. We have already mentioned One-Parent Families' proposal for a voluntary sharing procedure (p. 554, above). The Law Commission's response in their first *Report on Illegitimacy* (1982) was this:

4.39 It may, however, be argued that the father should be entitled to parental rights in cases where both parents of the child agree that he should. After all (it might be argued) the law already accords parental rights to all married parents without any prior scrutiny of what is in the child's best interests. Why should it not equally accord such rights to unmarried parents who are in agreement? We see force in this argument, but have nevertheless rejected it. The most powerful factor influencing our decision was the strong body of evidence from those best acquainted with the problems of the single parent family about the vulnerable position of the unmarried mother in many cases. Such mothers may well be exposed to pressure, and even harassment, on the part of the natural father; and it would, in our view, give unscrupulous natural fathers undesirable bargaining power if they were to be placed in a position where they might more easily extort from the mother a joint 'voluntary' acknowledgement, having the effect of vesting parental rights in the father, perhaps as the price of an agreement to provide for the mother or her child, or even as the price of continuing a relationship with the mother. For this reason, we think it appropriate for the court to investigate and sanction even a joint request that parental rights vest in the father. In reaching this conclusion we have, as we have said, been particularly impressed by the need to protect single mothers from the risk of pressure. But we should make it plain that we do not, in any event, accept the argument that since a couple can acquire parental rights over their child by marriage they should be able to do so by some other formal act. Apart from the consideration (to which some will attach considerable importance) that to do so would debase the institution of marriage, it must be borne in mind that marriage is still, in principle, a permanent relationship. In contrast, there is no such unifying factor in the case of unmarried relationships, which are infinitely variable in their nature and in the intentions of the partners to them. This diversity suggests to us that scrutiny by a court is a not unreasonable protection for the interests of the child of unmarried parents.

Questions

(i) Is not the threat of legal proceedings just as much harassment for the mother, at least if her consent is not required for an order?

(ii) Does not a parental responsibility order debase the institution of marriage just as much as a voluntary agreement might do?

(iii) Why should a parent be able to appoint a guardian to share parental status with the other parent after her death, but not to share her own status while she is alive?

(iv) Will automatic parental responsibility for registered unmarried fathers (see p. 560, above) (a) encourage more joint registrations, or (b) deter more mothers from naming the father?

(v) Should fathers be able to acquire parental responsibility for their children without undertaking any responsibility towards mother(s)?

(vi) It will still be possible to remove parental responsibility from unmarried fathers, but not from married fathers nor from mothers, married or unmarried. (a) Can this discrimination be justified? (b) In what circumstances do you think this can or should be done?

The Commission were able to return to this question in the course of their review of the whole of the private law relating to the upbringing of children. In their *Report on Guardianship and Custody* (1988) they concluded:

2.18 ... In our Working Paper on Guardianship, we pointed out that such judicial proceedings may be unduly elaborate, expensive and unnecessary unless the child's mother objects to the order. We suggested, therefore, that the mother might be permitted to appoint the father guardian to share responsibility while she was alive. A large majority of those who responded, including the leading organisations representing single parents and children's interests, supported this suggestion. It was pointed out, however, that it would be more consistent with the primary concept of parenthood if the father were to acquire the same status by such an appointment as he would by a court order. We therefore recommend that mother and father should be able to make an agreement that the father shall share parental responsibility with the mother. This will have the same effect as a court order. Both, for example, will confer upon him the power to give or withhold agreement to the child's adoption or to appoint a guardian. More importantly perhaps, both an agreement and an order may only be brought to an end by a court order made on the application of either parent (or a guardian). The child should also be able to make such applications, but only if the court is satisfied that he has sufficient understanding to do so.

2.19 For this reason, we also recommend that the agreement be made in a prescribed form. ... The object is to ensure that, as far as possible, both parents understand the importance and effects of their agreement. Overall, this should provide a simple and straightforward means for unmarried parents to acknowledge their shared responsibility, not only for the support, but also for the upbringing of their child.

2.20 ... Given the serious concern about the pressures to which mothers may be subject, which was expressed at the time of our first Report on Illegitimacy, it is appropriate for the machinery for such sharing appointments to be different from, and more formal and deliberate than, the machinery for appointment of a guardian. However, although it is hoped that more and more unmarried parents will agree to share parental responsibility, there may still be cases in which they would prefer the mother to have sole responsibility during her life-time but for the father to assume it in the event of her death. It should therefore remain possible for the mother to appoint him guardian. ...

Questions

(i) Given the courts' attitude to making parental responsibility orders when the mother does not agree, how strict should the formalities be when she does agree?

(ii) What now are the advantages and disadvantages, from the father's point of view, of being married to the mother?

(iii) What now are the advantages and disadvantages, from the mother's point of view, of being married to the father?

(iv) What now are the advantages, from the child's point of view, of his mother being married to his father?

(v) Look at *Re B (a minor) (adoption: natural parent)* [2001] UKHL 70, [2002] 1 FCR 150, [2002] 1 FLR 196, HL. Would the result have been the same if the mother had applied to adopt?

(vi) The new s. 2A of the Children Act 1989 (p. 561, above) refers to the loss of parental responsibility. What do you think might be the criteria for its removal? Why should it be possible to remove parental responsibility from fathers and not from mothers?

Bibliography

11.1   Births in and out of marriage

We quoted from:

Central Statistical Office, *Population Trends 107* (2002), London, HMSO, p. 4.

Central Statistical Office, *Social Trends 32* (2002), tables 2.10, 2.14.

J. Haskey, 'Having a birth outside marriage: the proportion of lone mothers and cohabiting mothers who subsequently marry' (1997) *Population Trends 97*, pp. 6–17.

S. McRae, in *Cohabiting Mothers* (1993), London, Policy Studies Institute, pp. 101–102.

Additional reading

K. Kiernan, H. Land, J. Lewis, *Lone Motherhood in twentieth century Britain* (1998) Oxford, Clarendon Press.

11.2 How to become a father

We quoted from:

A. Jeffreys, 'Genetic fingerprinting: applications and misapplications' in B. Holland and C. Kyriakou (eds.) *Genetics and Society* (1993) London, Addison-Wesley, pp. 51–53.

Lord Chancellor's Department, *Procedures for the Determination of Paternity and on The Law on Parental Responsibility for Unmarried Fathers* (1998), p. 5.

11.3 How to adopt a child

We quoted from:

Department of Health, White Paper, *Adoption – a new approach* (2000) London, HMSO.

W. Duncan, 'Regulating Intercountry Adoption – An International Perspective' in A. Bainham and D. Pearl (eds.), *Frontiers of Family Law* (1993) London, Chancery Law Publishing, pp. 49-50, reprinted in A. Bainham, D. Pearl and R. Pickford (eds.), *Frontiers of Family Law* (2nd edn, 1995) Chichester, John Wiley and Co.

D. Howe and J. Feast, *Adoption, Search and Reunion* (2000) London, The Children's Society, pp. 16–18, 38, 58.

N. Lowe, 'The changing face of adoption – the gift/donation model versus the contract/services model' (1997) 9 Child and Family Law Quarterly 371.

N. Lowe, 'English Adoption Law, Past, Present and Future' in S. Katz, J. Eekelaar, and M. Maclean (eds.), *Cross Currents* (2000) Oxford, Oxford University Press, p. 314.

D. Rosettenstein, 'Transracial Adoption in the United States and the Impact of Considerations relating to Minority Population Groups on International Adoptions in the United States' (1995) 9 International Journal of Law and the Family 131, pp. 139–140, 142–143, 149.

K. Silverman, 'The Hague Children's Conventions' in S. N. Katz, J. Eekelaar and M. Maclean, (eds.), *Cross Currents* (2000) Oxford, Oxford University Press, pp. 606–614.

Report (first) of the Child Adoption Committee (Chairman: Mr Justice Tomlin) (Cmd. 2401) (1925) London, HMSO, paras. 4, 9, 11, 15, 18, 19, 28.

Report of the Departmental Committee on the Adoption of Children (Chairman: Sir William Houghton, later Judge F.A. Stickdale) (Cmnd. 5107) (1972) London, HMSO, paras. 83, 84.

Review of Adoption Law – Report to Ministers of an Interdepartmental Working Group (1992) London, Department of Health and Welsh Office, paras. 26.4, 26.7–26.16

B. Tizard, *Adoption: A Second Chance* (1977) London, Open Books, pp. 1, 3–8.

J. Triseliotis, *In Search of Origins: The Experiences of Adopted People* (1973) London, Routledge and Kegan Paul, pp. 84, 85, 101.

C. Walby and B. Symons, *Who am I? Identity, adoption and human fertilisation, Discussion Series No. 12* (1990) London, British Agencies for Adoption and Fostering, pp. 39–41, 68.

Additional reading

J. Feast and J. Smith, 'Working on behalf of birth families – The Children's Society experience' (1997) 21 Adoption and Fostering 8–15.

B. Gonyo and K.W. Watson, 'Searching in adoption' (1988) Public Welfare (Winter) 14–22.

E. Haimes and N. Timms, *Adoption, Identity and Social Policy: The Search for Distant Relatives* (1997) Aldershot, Gower.

M. Humphrey and H. Humphrey, 'Damaged identity and the search for kinship in adult adoptees' (1989) 62 British Journal of Medical Psychology 301–309.

K. March, 'Perception of adoption as a social stigma: Motivation for search and reunion' (1995) 57 Journal of Marriage and the Family 653–660.

R. McMillan and G. Irving, *Heart of Reunion: Some Experiences of Reunion in Scotland* (1994) Essex, Barnardo's.

G. Pugh, *Unlocking the Past: The Impact of Access to Barnardo's Childcare Records* (1999) Aldershot, Gower.

M. Ryburn, 'Adopted children's identity and information needs' (1995) 9 Children and Society 41–46.

P. Sachdev, 'Adoption reunion and after: a study of the search process and experience of adoptees' (1992) 71 Child Welfare 53–68.

H.J. Sants, 'Genealogical bewilderment in children with substitute parents' (1964) 37 British Journal of Medical Psychology 133–141.

A. Sorosky, A. Baran, R. Pannpr, 'The reunion of adoptees and birth relatives' (1974) 3 Journal of Youth and Adolescence 195–206.

J. Triseliotis, 'Identity and Adoption' (1974) 78 Child Adoption.

11.4   Assisted reproduction and the 'social parent'

We quoted from:

E. Blyth, 'Assisted reproduction: what's in it for the children?' (1990) 4 Children and Society 167, pp. 174–177.

E. Blyth, 'Secrets and lies; barriers to the exchange of genetic origins information following donor assisted conception' (1999) 23 Adoption and Fostering 49, p. 53.

N. Bruce, 'The importance of genetic knowledge' (1990) 4 Children and Society 183, pp. 191–192.

Ciba Foundation Symposium, No. 17 (new series), G.E.W. Wolstenholme and D.W. Fitzsimmons (eds.), *Law and Ethics of A.I.D. and Embryo Transfer* (1973) Amsterdam, Associated Scientific Publishers, pp. 63, 66.

DHSS, *Legislation on Human Infertility Services and Embryo Research, A Consultation Paper* (1986) (Cm. 46) London, HMSO, paras. 8–13.

Hansard (House of Lords), vol. 516, cols. 1097–1098.

Human Fertilisation and Embryology Authority, *Code of Practice* (2001), paras. 3.8–3.21.

Law Commission, Working Paper No. 74, *Illegitimacy* (1979) London, HMSO, paras. 10.9, 10.11, 10.17, 10.25, 10.26.

Report of the Committee of Inquiry into Human Fertilisation and Embryology (Chairman: Dame Mary Warnock) (Cmnd. 9314) (1984) London, HMSO, paras. 6.8, 4.19–4.22, 8.10–8.16.

Additional reading

D. Langridge and E. Blyth, 'Regulation of assisted conception services in Europe: Implications of the new reproductive technologies for "the family"' (2001) 23 Journal of Social Welfare and Family Law 45.

S. Millns, 'Reproducing inequalities: assisted conception and the challenge of legal pluralism' (2002) 24 Journal of Social Welfare and Family Law 19.

S. Reid, *Labour of Love: Story of the World's first Surrogate Grandmother* (1988) Oxford, Bodley Head.

11.5 Illegitimate children or illegitimate parents?

We quoted from:

Sir William Blackstone, *Commentaries on the Laws of England* (1st edn, 1765) Oxford, Clarendon Press, book 1, p. 447.

K. Davis, 'Illegitimacy and the Social Structure' (1939) 45 American Journal of Sociology 215, pp. 215, 216, 219, 221, 223.

H. Elisofon, 'A Historical and Comparative Study of Bastardy' (1973) 2 Anglo-American Law Review 306, p. 318.

Sir Morris Finer and O.R. McGregor, 'A History of the Obligation to Maintain' App. 5, Report of the Committee on One-Parent Families (Cmnd. 5629-1) (1974) London, HMSO, paras. 56, 57, 59–62, 64.

P. Laslett, *The World We Have Lost* (2nd edn, 1971) London, Methuen, pp. 137, 140–141.

Law Commission, Working Paper No. 74, *Illegitimacy* (1979) London, HMSO, paras. 2.10–2.12, 3.2–3.5, 3.8, 3.9, 3.14–3.16.

Law Commission, *Report on Illegitimacy*, Law Com. No. 118 (1982) London, HMSO, paras. 4.26, 4.39, 4.44, 4.49, 4.51.

Law Commission, *Report on Guardianship and Custody*, Law Com. No. 172 (1988) London, HMSO, paras. 2.18–2.20.

The Lord Chancellor's Department's Consultation Paper, *Procedures for the Determination of Paternity and on the Law of Parental Responsibility for Unmarried Fathers* (1998) London, HMSO.

National Council for One-Parent Families, *An Accident of Birth – A Response to the Law Commission's Working Paper on Illegitimacy* (1980) London, One-Parent Families, pp. 2–4, 9, 11–12.

R. Pickford, *Fathers, marriage and the law* (1999) Family Policy Studies Centre (summarised by the Joseph Rowntree Foundation at www.jrf.org.uk/knowledge/findings/socialpolicy/989.asp).

Scottish Law Commission, *Family Law – Illegitimacy*, Consultative Memorandum No. 53 (1982) Edinburgh, Scottish Law Commission, paras. 1.15, 1.16.

Scottish Law Commission, *Report on Family Law*, Scot. Law Com. No. 135 (1992) Edinburgh, HMSO, para. 2.48.

Social Trends 32 (2002), tables 2.20 and 2.21.

Chapter 12

When parents part

12.1 **Coping with change**

12.2 **The law**

12.3 **Who speaks up for the child?**

12.4 **Step-families**

12.5 **International child abduction**

Doreen: I feel very angry sometimes, that a man can literally decide that he wants to be free, free of responsibilities that somebody must take. Somebody needs to when children are involved. But men can just walk off. I think because they know that the woman is going to be the strong one, that she will not ... walk away.

Michael: The effects on my career have hurt. ... The company begins to assess you a bit lower perhaps because your mind has family welfare as a higher priority than it should be. ... I took Anne down to junior church as I always have done ... but I'd never brushed her hair before or tied ribbons, and this was actually impossible to me.

These two lone parents, and others, talked about their lives to Catherine Itzin for her book on *Splitting Up: Single Parent Liberation* (1980). The following extract is fictional, but it is interesting that it comes from a primary school reading book, *Ugly Mug* by Annie Dalton (1994):

Mum didn't want to stay married to Dad. She'd told them one terrible bedtime months ago. Dad didn't want to say married to her, either. She'd explained it very calmly. As if a family was some bit of old knitting people could unpick without hurting anyone.

Then, Ned and Rose had had to go and brush their teeth as usual. That didn't seem right to Ned. There should have been a smoking hole in the middle of Osborne Street. There should have been screams, ambulances, flashing lights. Not this careful niceness that left Ned feeling crazy inside.

The trouble was that Mum wanted Ned to treat Dad the same as before. Even though they lived in different streets and had to arrange to meet like strangers. Even though Ned woke every morning to a new scared feeling in his stomach.

But Ned would never be the same again. And it just wasn't fair of Mum to try to make him.

This chapter is concerned with how it is decided what should happen to the children when their parents part.

We shall look first at the circumstances in which these children find themselves and the effects of this upon them and their parents; then at the present law and the reasons for it, together with a few illustrative cases. We look at the role of CAFCASS in working with children; and then we consider what happens if the lone parent family is reconstituted into a step-family. Finally, we look at one of the most dramatic and disruptive features of the fractured family, international child abduction.

12.1 Coping with change

Everyone knows that the proportion of families with children where there is only one parent in the household has grown dramatically over the past 30 years (look again at the table in Chapter 4 (p. 123)). But there are many different kinds of lone-parent household, and the ways in which these have changed over the years are shown in the figure below, taken from David Utting, *Family and Parenthood – Supporting Families, Preventing Breakdown* (1995).

Number of one-parent families, Great Britain
Half all lone-parent families are headed by divorced or separated mothers, but in recent years the number of single mothers has grown more rapidly

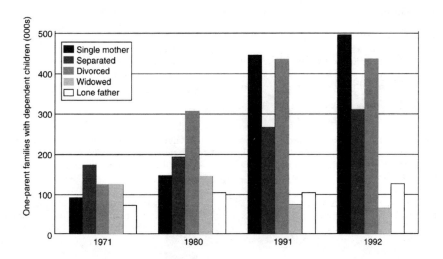

Source: Burghes, L (1994)/Haskey, J (1994b)
Note: 1992 figures are provisional estimates

The following table, from *Social Trends 32* (2002), brings up to date the proportions of one parent households headed by mothers and fathers, respectively:

Families with dependent children headed by lone parents[1]

Great Britain					Percentages
	1971	**1981**	**1991**	**1999**	**2001[2]**
Lone Mothers					
Single	1	2	6	8	9
Widowed	2	2	1	1	1
Divorced	2	4	6	6	6
Separated	2	2	4	4	4
All lone mothers	7	11	18	20	20
Lone fathers	1	2	1	2	2
All lone parents	8	13	19	22	22

1   Lone mothers (by their marital status) and lone fathers.
2   At Spring 2001.
Source: General Household Survey and Labour Force Survey, Office for National Statistics

But lone parents may re-partner. The following table from *Social Trends 31* (2001) illustrates this, with the following commentary:

Stepfamilies are one reflection of the diversity of family life that young people experience. Such family types may be formed when lone parents, whether single, separated or widowed, form new partnerships. According to the General Household Survey, in 1998-99, step-families (married and cohabiting) where the head of the family was aged under 60 accounted for about 6 per cent of all families with dependent children in Great Britain. There is a tendency for children to remain with their mother after a partnership breaks up. Almost nine in ten stepfamilies consisted of a couple with at least one child from a previous relationship of the female partner.

Stepfamilies[1] with dependent children[2]: by family type, 1998-99

Great Britain

Percentages

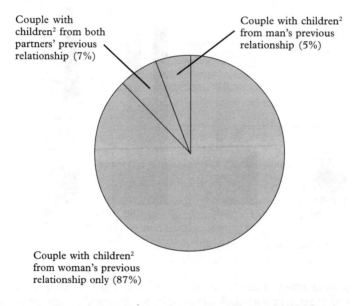

Couple with children[2] from both partners' previous relationship (7%)

Couple with children[2] from man's previous relationship (5%)

Couple with children[2] from woman's previous relationship only (87%)

1 Head of family aged 16 to 59.
2 One or more children.
Source: General Household Survey, Office for National Statistics

But, of course, because there are so many more lone mothers than lone fathers, children who are living with their fathers are more likely to have a step-mother than children who are living with their mothers are to have a step-father.

Questions

(i)   Why, do you think, has the proportion of lone-parent families headed by fathers gone up since 1971?

(ii) Why do you think the numbers now seem to have levelled off?

(iii) Why do we talk about 'lone-parent' rather than 'one-parent' families these days?

We still do not know quite how much impact the decisions of courts have on what happens to children whose parents part. In their research report, *Monitoring Private Law Applications under the Children Act*, for the Nuffield Foundation (1998), Rebecca Bailey-Harris and her colleagues found that in the majority of cases there is no court decision (compare the evidence in financial provision cases; Chapter 8, p. 373). Settlement, sooner or later or at the door of the court, seems to be the goal of many of the professionals involved, including the judges themselves. We shall look again at this report later in this chapter (p. 618, below). In this section we are concerned with the reactions of the parties themselves and their children, and one issue we can look at is the incidence of children staying with their fathers or mothers; we have seen that the majority of lone parents are mothers. Martin Richards, in his discussion of 'Post-Divorce Arrangements for Children: A Psychological Perspective' (1982), looks at some reasons why fathers might not seek to have their children living with them (remember that, before the Children Act 1989, writers would use the legal terminology of custody and access):

Mother or father?

Though the law itself does not favour mothers or fathers as potential custodial parents, if all else is equal and, especially if the children are young ('of tender years'), the mother is more likely to be granted custody in a dispute. Not all would concur with this point, but I think the weight of the evidence from reported cases and the surveys support a principle of a presumption that custody should be vested in the mother. Of course, I am not suggesting that the courts are entirely responsible for the fact that only in a small percentage of cases does a father have custody of his children after a divorce. In most cases the father has not sought custody and does not challenge his wife's claim. The main reason for this situation is that the general assumptions that are held about the sexual division of labour within marriage are extended to the post-divorce situation. Within most marriages, the prime responsibility for childcare falls on women and so it is after the marriage ends. A small and probably increasing proportion of men would like to have the custody and care and control of their children. In many of these cases it seems that they are so certain that this will not be granted to them that they do not bother to raise the issue with their solicitors. One man I interviewed recently thought that it was 'against the law' for men to have custody 'especially if they had daughters.' (He, incidentally, was looking after his children on his own and had consulted a solicitor. Later, after he received some counselling, he asked for and got the custody and care and control of his children.) In turn, solicitors are unlikely to suggest to their male clients that they might seek custody (or joint custody). If the client does bring it up the common advice seems to be that it is not worthwhile to proceed unless their partners will agree to the proposal. So [in] almost all cases where a man does get custody, it is because the spouses have agreed to this, or because the wife has left the matrimonial home and has not maintained contact with the children.

Question

But might there be another reason not to fight? As the *New English Bible* relates:

So they went on arguing in the king's presence. ... Then he said, 'Fetch me a sword.' They brought in a sword and the king gave the order: 'Cut the living child in two and give half to one and half to the other.' At this the woman who was the mother of the living child, moved with love for her child, said to the king, 'Oh! sir, let her have the baby; whatever you do, do not kill it.' The other said, 'Let neither of us have it; cut it in two.' Thereupon the king gave judgement: 'Give the living baby to the first woman; do not kill it. She is its mother.'

Can you think of less drastic ways in which a legal system might try to achieve the same?

For most children, therefore, the vital question is not where, or with whom, they will live but how their parents will resolve what Murch (1980) has called the 'fundamental dilemma facing divorcing parents. This is how to disengage from the broken marriage while preserving a sense of being a parent with a part to play in the children's future.' Many 'absent' parents lose touch with their children. Martin Richards, in 'Post Divorce Arrangements for Children' (1982), also addresses the question 'why do non-custodial parents disappear?'

Almost all the evidence we have is about absent fathers so I will discuss this. However, there is no reason to think that male non-custodial parents disappear any more or less often than female ones, although the reasons may differ somewhat in the two cases. I will list some of the reasons that have been uncovered in the research studies.

(a) Some men believe that it is in their children's interests for them to disappear. They may feel that their visits will upset the children or that their continued presence makes it less likely that their ex-spouses will settle down with a new partner. Often, and especially in the early days after separation, a child's upset at what has happened is most likely to be apparent before and after a visit from the father. This may lead either parent to try to reduce or stop the visiting. It is hardly surprising that the child's feelings are most likely to be expressed at these times as they will be the most vivid reminders of what has happened. Indeed, it would be odd if any child accepted such a radical change in their lives without upset and in the long term it is probably much better that these feelings are expressed at the time. The real issue here is the capacity of the parents to accept the expression of such feelings at a time when they are likely to be feeling very vulnerable and upset themselves.

(b) It is often said, not least by mothers with custody that some fathers are uninterested in their children. Doubtless this is sometimes true but I suspect that this reason is often used to cover others.

(c) Some men believe, incorrectly of course, that if they do not see their children they will not be required to pay maintenance. More realistically, others assume that if they have no contact with their old families it will be hard for them to be traced and forced to pay maintenance. Others connect maintenance and access in another way so that they see the money they pay as an entitlement to visit. If they can only afford a little, they see themselves as having little entitlement to visit.

(d) Some men are prevented from seeing their children by their ex-spouse. Preventing contact with children is the most obvious weapon available to a custodial parent and some use it. After a long journey the father arrives to find the house empty. Or perhaps a child may always turn out to be 'ill' on access days. More bluntly, a father may simply be told at the doorstep that he cannot see his children. As I have mentioned above, the sanctions are few in such cases and without persistence and the ability to find the right kind of help the situation may seem hopeless.

(e) Some men feel that after a separation they want to move away and start again. Particularly if their spouse has a new partner, they may not want to live nearby. Distance may then create too many problems for the visiting arrangements to survive.

(f) A new partner may be very resentful of the contact with the children of the first marriage and bring pressure to try to end it. Not infrequently the custodial parent will attempt to argue for access orders which try to prevent the children having contact with a new partner. Although it is not hard to understand the feelings that give rise to such attempts, these are unrealistic and unreasonable from the point of view of both the adults and children and, in general, courts have not sanctioned them. But pressures from both the new and old spouse may effectively reduce access.

(g) Access visits may be so painful and upsetting that a father cannot bear to continue with them. This may be because the visits involve meeting the ex-spouse or because the father finds it very difficult to readjust to a new kind of relationship with his children. The latter is particularly likely if access visits are brief. Sometimes the conditions in an access order are such that it seems impossible that any parent could conform, e.g. two hours a month in the old matrimonial home in the presence of the ex-spouse (and often her new partner). If access is brief and the father's home is far away there is the problem of where to take the children. There is also the 'father Christmas syndrome' – where the father seems only able to relate to his children by giving gifts and treats. Anything more realistic and normal may seem threatening to his relationship with the children. As one might expect the problems of access are most acute at the beginning and they usually resolve over time provided, of course, that access continues.

(h) Last among the reasons I shall mention, but certainly not least, is the point made to me by many men I have interviewed – that all too often continued contact is not supported or encouraged by anyone. Indeed, I have been told of men being advised by a whole variety of professional people that access was a kind of selfish private indulgence they should give up as soon as possible. Very few had received any sensible advice or help – if they had it was usually from a court welfare officer, one of the few solicitors who specialise in family law or from another parent who had experienced a divorce. ...

There is much debate about the effects of family disruption upon the children. There is also a large research literature. Something of the flavour of this may emerge from the summary in David Utting, *Family and Parenthood – Supporting Families, Preventing Breakdown* (1995):

Separation and divorce – the effects on children

'There is no indication that divorce is entered into lightly. Quite the reverse.'

If children were, miraculously, able to live through their parents' separation or divorce without experiencing any ill (or positive) effects, the personal and social consequences of relationship breakdown might be of limited interest. As it is, there is accumulated evidence that children whose birth parents separate run increased risks of adverse educational, health and behavioural outcomes when compared with those from similar social backgrounds whose parents stay together. Modest, but statistically significant, differences have been observed in terms of reading and arithmetic skills, general health, psychological adjustment, delinquency and personal relationships. Furthermore, where studies at one time suggested that ill-effects were mostly confined to the years immediately following relationship breakdown, it is now apparent that some consequences for some children continue into adult life. The chances have been shown to be greater, for example, of leaving school at the minimum age, failing to obtain educational qualifications, leaving home due to friction, cohabitation, marriage and childbearing at an early age, and of poor mental health.

Attempts to unravel the processes responsible for these effects are hampered by methodological difficulties, but few would nowadays deny their existence. There is, however, considerable disagreement over their scale and interpretation – a matter of no small importance if available research is to contribute to practical policy-making. ...[T]here is no single or straightforward relationship between family disruption and the consequences for children. Poorer outcomes can occur separately or in association with other factors such as low income, unemployment, reduced parental supervision, mental and physical illness and inadequate schooling. She has also emphasised the equally valid point that there is no inevitable path down which children who experience their parent's separation can be expected to travel.

Conflicting perspectives

'It makes good copy for the media to claim that divorce is either a disaster for children or that it does no harm at all. Neither case is true.'

Outcomes observed by comparison with children living in intact families may be less good on average, but that does not mean that every child whose parents divorce – or more than a small minority of children in many cases – is likely to experience a particular difficulty. If, for example, one-third of divorced parents report behaviour difficulties among their children compared with only a fifth of parents in intact families (as was the case in one American study), a seemingly impressive statistic emerges that problems were more than 50 per cent more prevalent among the children of divorce. Yet it is equally true that a large majority of children whose parents had divorced did not display behaviour problems. Is the policy-maker to conclude that the glass was, in this instance, an encouraging two-thirds empty or a worrying one-third full?

Louie Burghes has concluded that a wide range of psychological, economic and social factors are at work in families affected by parental separation whose subtle connections are only beginning to be understood. Others have warned their academic colleagues and the media against exaggeration and over-simplification when trying to unravel the processes involved. This has not deterred less prudent analysts from asserting the primacy of one set of influences over another. The rival theoretical perspectives can be considered under three broad headings:

- Father absence: these focus on the loss of one birth parent – in most cases the father – as the key to understanding the deficits associated with separation and divorce. In Britain, this approach has been given polemical force by Norman Dennis and George Erdos [1992] who argue its relevance to one-parent families whether they result from parental separation or births to single mothers. In their view: 'The longer the same father has been part of the child's life and the more effectively the father has taken part in the life of the family, the better the results for the child.'
- Child poverty: interpretations emphasising the economic disadvantage that commonly results from the breakdown of a parental relationship. Children growing up in families that are relatively poor are more likely to encounter health, educational and housing

problems. It is also self-evident that families which divide into two households are going to be poorer than they were before. Yet poverty is more obviously one of the consequences of breakdown – six out of ten separated or divorced lone mothers are, at any one time, receiving Income Support [Bradshaw and Millar, 1991] – than a cause.

- Parental conflict: a view that what children find most upsetting is high levels of conflict between their parents and that this can prove damaging regardless of whether it leads to separation. Hence the results obtained by the Cambridge Study in Delinquent Development which found similar rates of juvenile criminal involvement among children from 'broken homes' and from high conflict families that were intact; likewise, analyses of longitudinal studies in Britain and the United States showing that educational and behaviour deficits found among children aged 16 whose parents had divorced could also be observed before the divorce took place.

One attempt to measure the relative strengths of these perspectives, using the statistical technique of meta-analysis, has looked at results from 92 American and British studies concerned with the well-being of children affected by divorce. It concludes that there is evidence to support all three hypotheses, but that the strongest – or more accurately the 'least weak' – effects are associated with parental conflict.

New dimensions

'You cannot predict anything sensible about an adult's life from just knowing that his or her parents were divorced.'

Almost inevitably, further research will not only reinforce parts of the existing picture, but add new and sometimes unexpected dimensions. To take just one example, the researchers who traced behaviour problems among 16-year-old children whose parents had divorced back to a time before the break-up (see above) have since examined social handicaps and mental health problems among the same sample of children when they were interviewed at age 23. Their study shows that emotional disorders, leaving home due to friction and having a child outside marriage were found significantly more often among the children of divorce than those from intact families (although those affected were only a small minority in both cases). Intriguingly, however, these particular effects did not relate to what was observed about the children's emotional state and behaviour at age 7 before their parents' divorce. In other words, studying a different set of outcomes at a later age pinpointed a different group of children from divorce backgrounds whose particular problems had emerged during a different period of their lives. Those determined to characterise the available research in black and white, rather than multiple shades of grey should, once again, beware.

Re-ordered families

'It is critical that we address the way that an increasing number of children are moving through different family households.'

Understanding the events in children's lives before, during and after their parents' separation can be assisted by examining them as a sequence of events or 'process'. Research, as already seen, suggests that the behaviour and educational achievement of some children is affected by conflict between their parents long before it leads to divorce. Where children have been the unhappy witnesses of domestic violence between their parents, the consequences can be especially traumatic [see also p. 604, below]. It is also well-established that children whose parents divorce commonly go through a crisis period at the time of separation from which they recover with varying degrees of resilience and speed. For some (see above), there may be long-term consequences.

But that is only part of the story. While some children may remain living with one parent for many years, others will find themselves part of a step-family living with a new parent figure and, perhaps, his or her children from a previous relationship. Half-brothers and sisters may also be born. There is the possibility, too, that this second partnership will break down (if current trends are maintained, 50 per cent of re-marriages will end in divorce) to be followed by further transitions. The question which research has, in recent years, begun to consider is what influence this 're-ordering' of families exerts over children's lives, health and happiness.

According to one study, young people who have lived in a lone-parent family [headed by their mother] before the age of 16 as a result of divorce are more likely to leave school at the minimum age and to leave home by 18 compared with those in intact families. However, the chances of those events occurring among children who become part of a step-family following divorce are also significantly greater. In addition, there are increased risks (compared with intact families) of girls and boys in step-families leaving home due to friction, marrying before the age of 20 and becoming a parent by an equally young age.

Such findings could not be expected if children's outcomes after divorce were determined entirely by economic poverty, since a lone parent's re-partnering would normally increase rather than diminish family income. They would not, likewise, be expected if the outcomes depended on whether families were headed literally by one parent or two. The fact that children living in step-families following the death of one parent were generally not found to have been affected in the same way is further evidence that the particular reason for family disruption is relevant to the outcomes for children rather than disruption per se.

Bryan Rodgers and Jan Pryor, in *Divorce and Separation: The outcomes for children* (1998) comment:

Disadvantages among children of separated families
Typically, the areas of disadvantage identified by research only apply to a minority of those whose parents have separated during childhood. There is no simple or direct relationship between parental separation and children's adjustment, and poor outcomes are far from inevitable. As a rule of thumb many adverse outcomes are roughly twice as prevalent among children of divorced families compared with children from intact families. Outcomes which research suggests occur with a higher probability among children of separated families are listed in the box.

Children of separated families:
- tend to grow up in households with lower incomes, poorer housing and greater financial hardship than intact families (especially those headed by lone mothers);
- tend to achieve less in socio-economic terms when they become adult than children from intact families;
- are at increased risk of behavioural problems, including bedwetting, withdrawn behaviour, aggression, delinquency and other antisocial behaviour;
- tend to perform less well in school and to gain fewer educational qualifications;
- are more likely to be admitted to hospital following accidents, to have more reported health problems and to visit their family doctor;
- are more likely to leave school and home when young and more likely at an early age to: become sexually active; form a cohabiting partnership; become pregnant; become a parent; and give birth outside marriage;
- tend to report more depressive symptoms and higher levels of smoking, drinking and other drug use during adolescence and adulthood.

Although the differences in outcomes are clear, it cannot be assumed that parental separation is their underlying cause. The complexity of factors that impinge on families before, during and after separation indicates a process, rather than a single event, that merits careful examination. Much of the confusion seen in media coverage, and even academic debate, about 'the effects of divorce on children' reflects a failure to distinguish between separation as a process and separation as an event. An understanding of process and of the factors that influence this process is crucial if ways are to be found of optimising the chances that children experiencing the separation of their parents will emerge relatively unharmed.

Step-families and lone-parent families
There are many adjustments that children whose parents separate may have to make, most obviously that of no longer living with both parents. If their parents subsequently form new partnerships, they may experience a further transition into a household comprising one birth parent, another adult and, sometimes, step-siblings. Research findings for children from step-families suggest a number of ways in which they do not fare as well as those from intact families – and, in some instances, not as well as those from lone-parent families. The risk of adverse outcomes for young people in step-families compared with those in lone-parent families appears higher for older children, especially in areas of educational achievement, family relationships and sexual activity, partnership formation and parenthood at a relatively young age. Young children in step-families seem to fare better, possibly because it is easier to adapt to a new family structure at an age when they have had a relatively short period of living with either both or just one birth parent.

There is even more contention about what can be done to minimise any short- or long-term ill effects for children. In *Beyond the Best Interests of the Child* (1973), Joseph Goldstein, Anna Freud and Albert J. Solnit (respectively a lawyer, a psychoanalyst and a psychiatrist) collaborate in an attempt to use 'psychoanalytic theory to develop generally applicable guidelines to child placement'. That theory 'establishes, for example, as do developmental studies by students of other orientations, the need of every child for unbroken continuity of affectionate and stimulating experiences with an adult'. The authors develop three basic concepts. The first is that of the relationship between a 'psychological parent' and a 'wanted child', whom they later define as follows:

A wanted child is one who receives affection and nourishment on a continuing basis from at least one adult and who feels that he or she is and continues to be valued by those who take care of him or her.

A psychological parent is one who, on a continuing, day-to-day basis, through interaction, companionship, interplay, and mutuality, fulfills the child's psychological needs for a parent, as well as the child's physical needs. The psychological parent may be a biological ..., adoptive, foster, or common law ... parent, or any other person. There is no presumption in favor of any of these after the initial assignment at birth. ...

Secondly, they stress the need for continuity in this relationship:

Continuity of relationships, surroundings, and environmental influence are essential for a child's normal development. Since they do not play the same role in later life, their importance is often underrated by the adult world.

Physical, emotional, intellectual, social, and moral growth does not happen without causing the child inevitable internal difficulties. The instability of all mental processes during the period of development needs to be offset by stability and uninterrupted support from external sources. Smooth growth is arrested or disrupted when upheavals and changes in the external world are added to the internal ones.

Disruptions of continuity have different consequences for different ages:

In *infancy*, from birth to approximately 18 months, any change in routine leads to food refusals, digestive upsets, sleeping difficulties, and crying. Such reactions occur even if the infant's care is divided merely between mother and baby-sitter. They are all the more massive where the infant's day is divided between home and day care center; or where infants are displaced from the mother to an institution; from institutional to foster care; or from fostering to adoption. Every step of this kind inevitably brings with it changes in the ways the infant is handled, fed, put to bed, and comforted. Such moves from the familiar to the unfamiliar cause discomfort, distress, and delays in the infant's orientation and adaptation within his surroundings.

Change of the caretaking person for *infants and toddlers* further affects the course of their emotional development. Their attachments, at these ages, are as thoroughly upset by separations as they are effectively promoted by the constant, uninterrupted presence and attention of a familiar adult. When infants and young children find themselves abandoned by the parent, they not only suffer separation distress and anxiety but also setbacks in the quality of their next attachments, which will be less trustful. Where continuity of such relationships is interrupted more than once, as happens due to multiple placements in the early years, the children's emotional attachments become increasingly shallow and indiscriminate. They tend to grow up as persons who lack warmth in their contacts with fellow beings.

For *young children* under the age of 5 years, every disruption of continuity also affects those achievements which are rooted and develop in the intimate interchange with a stable parent figure, who is in the process of becoming the psychological parent. The more recently the achievement has been acquired, the easier it is for the child to lose it. Examples of this are cleanliness and speech. After separation from the familiar mother, young children are known to have breakdowns in toilet training and to lose or lessen their ability to communicate verbally.

For *school-age children*, the breaks in their relationships with their psychological parents affect above all those achievements which are based on identification with the parents' demands, prohibitions, and social ideals. Such identifications develop only where attachments are stable and tend to be abandoned by the child if he feels abandoned by the adults in question. Thus, where children are made to wander from one environment to another, they may cease to identify with any set of substitute parents. Resentment toward the adults who have disappointed them in the past makes them adopt the attitude of not caring for anybody; or of making the new parent the scapegoat for the shortcomings of the former one. In any case, multiple placement at these ages puts many children beyond the reach of educational influence, and becomes the direct cause of behavior which the schools experience as disrupting and the courts label as dissocial, delinquent, or even criminal.

With *adolescents*, the superficial observation of their behavior may convey the idea that what they desire is discontinuation of parental relationships rather than their preservation and stability. Nevertheless, this impression is misleading in this simple form. It is true that their revolt against any parental authority is normal developmentally since it is the adolescent's way toward establishing his own independent adult identity. But for a successful outcome it is important that the breaks and disruptions of attachment should come exclusively from his side and not be imposed on him by any form of abandonment or rejection on the psychological parents' part.

Adults who as children suffered from disruptions of continuity may themselves, in 'identifying' with their many 'parents,' treat their children as they themselves were treated – continuing a cycle costly for both a new generation of children as well as for society itself.

Thus, continuity is a guideline because emotional attachments are tenuous and vulnerable in early life and need stability of external arrangements for their development.

Thirdly, they discuss the child's sense of time:

A child's sense of time, as an integral part of the continuity concept, requires independent consideration. That interval of separation between parent and child which would constitute a break in continuity for an infant, for example, would be of no or little significance to a school-age youngster. The time it takes to break an old or to form a new attachment will depend upon the different meanings time has for children at each stage of their development.

Unlike adults, who have learned to anticipate the future and thus to manage delay, children have a built-in time sense based on the urgency of their instinctual and emotional needs. As an infant's memory begins to incorporate the way in which parents satisfy wishes and needs, as well as the experience of the reappearance of parents after their disappearance, a child gradually develops the capacity to delay gratification and to anticipate and plan for the future.

Emotionally and intellectually an infant and toddler cannot stretch his waiting more than a few days without feeling overwhelmed by the absence of parents. He cannot take care of himself physically, and his emotional and intellectual memory is not sufficiently matured to enable him to use thinking to hold on to the parent he has lost. During such an absence for the child under two years of age, the new adult who cares for the child's physical needs is latched onto 'quickly' as the potential psychological parent. The replacement, however ideal, may not be able to heal completely, without emotional scarring, the injury sustained by the loss.

For most children under the age of five years, an absence of parents for more than two months is equally beyond comprehension. For the younger school-age child, an absence of six months or more may be similarly experienced. More than one year of being without parents and without evidence that there are parental concerns and expectations is not likely to be understood by the older school-aged child and will carry with it the detrimental implications of the breaches in continuity we have already described. After adolescence is fully launched an individual's sense of time closely approaches that of most adults.

Finally, they point to the limits of the law's ability to supervise personal relationships and of knowledge to predict long-range outcomes:

While the law may claim to establish relationships, it can in fact do little more than give them recognition and provide an opportunity for them to develop. The law, so far as specific individual relationships are concerned, is a relatively crude instrument. It may be able to destroy human relationships; but it does not have the power to compel them to develop. It neither has the sensitivity nor the resources to maintain or supervise the ongoing day-to-day happenings between parent and child – and these are essential to meeting ever-changing demands and needs. Nor does it have the capacity to predict future events and needs, ... [However] placement decisions can be based on certain generally applicable and useful predictions. We can, for example, identify who, among *presently available adults*, is or has the capacity to become a psychological parent and thus will enable a child to feel wanted. We can predict that the adult most likely suited for this role is the one, if there be one, with whom the child has already had and continues to have an affectionate bond rather than one of otherwise equal potential who is not yet in a primary relationship with the child. Further, we can predict that the younger the child and the more extended the period of uncertainty or separation, the more detrimental it will be to the child's well-being and the more urgent it becomes even without perfect knowledge to place the child permanently.

Beyond these, our capacity to predict is limited.

These concepts lead the authors to propose the following guidelines for all child placement decisions:

As an overall guideline for child placement we propose, instead of the 'in-the-best-interests-of-the-child' standard, 'the least detrimental available alternative for safeguarding the child's growth and development.' The new standard has as its major components the three guidelines which we have already described. The least detrimental alternative, then, is that specific placement and procedure for placement which maximizes, in accord with the child's sense of time and on the basis of short-term predictions given the limitations of knowledge, his or her opportunity for being wanted and for maintaining on a continuous basis a relationship with at least one adult who is or will become his psychological parent.

However, the reasoning behind this proposal also reveals how unhelpful it is in the normal dispute between parents:

To use 'detrimental' rather than 'best interest' should enable legislatures, courts, and child care agencies to acknowledge and respond to the inherent detriments in any procedure for child placement as well as in each child placement decision itself. It should serve to remind decision-makers that their task is to salvage as much as possible out of an unsatisfactory situation. It should reduce the likelihood of their becoming enmeshed in the hope and magic associated with 'best,' which often mistakenly leads them into believing that they have greater power for doing 'good' than 'bad'.

The concept of 'available alternatives' should press into focus how limited is the capacity of decisionmakers to make valid predictions and how limited are the choices generally open to them for helping a child in trouble. If the choice, as it may often be in separation and divorce proceedings, is between two psychological parents and if each parent is equally suitable in terms of the child's most immediate predictable developmental needs, the least detrimental standard would dictate a quick, final, and unconditional disposition to either of the competing parents.

Questions

(i) Dingwall and Eekelaar (1986) state: 'Psychology is used selectively to legitimate an ideal of social organisation so that moral or political choices are made to appear matters of natural law.' How would you describe the moral and political choices of Goldstein, Freud and Solnit?

(ii) Goldstein, Freud and Solnit's footnote to the last passage quoted from their book suggests that 'a judicially supervised drawing of lots between two equally acceptable psychological parents might be the most rational and least offensive process for resolving the hard choice'. Do you agree?

Goldstein, Freud and Solnit's arguments, however, did lead to some firm and controversial conclusions on post-separation contact:

Children have difficulty in relating positively to, profiting from, and maintaining the contact with two psychological parents who are not in positive contact with each other. Loyalty conflicts are common and normal under such conditions and may have devastating consequences by destroying the child's positive relationships to both parents. A 'visiting' or 'visited' parent has little chance to serve as a true object for love, trust, and identification, since this role is based on his being available on an uninterrupted day-to-day basis.

Once it is determined who will be the custodial parent, it is that parent, not the court, who must decide under what conditions he or she wishes to raise the child. Thus, the noncustodial parent should have no legally enforceable right to visit the child, and the custodial parent should have the right to decide whether it is desirable for the child to have such visits. What we have said is designed to protect the security of an ongoing relationship – that between the child and the custodial parent. At the same time the state neither makes nor breaks the psychological relationship between the child and the noncustodial parent, which the adults involved may have jeopardized. It leaves to them what only they can ultimately resolve.

Martin Richards (1982), however, argues that continued contact is so much in the interests of the child that the system should try to encourage it. In discussing the needs of children, he first points to the lack of good direct evidence either way, and continues:

There are a couple of findings in the psychological studies which have turned up several times and are at least consistent with my hypothesis. The first is that some of the long-term disruptive effects on children whose parents divorce are most marked if the separation comes earlier (say before the age of five) rather than later. Several explanations are possible but one of these is that the likelihood of losing contact with the non-custodial parent will increase over time and so is most likely to be lost after an earlier separation. A similar explanation can be given of the evidence that divorce is more upsetting for children who remain with their mothers if those mothers remarry, as the presence of a step-father almost always reduces contact with the father.

The nearest we get to a direct study of the question of continuing contact is an American one where groups of children spending varying amounts of time with each of their divorced or separated parents were compared. Here the children (and parents) who spent at least 25% of their time with each of their parents seem to adjust best. However, in this study we cannot be certain that factors other than the post-separation arrangements determined the outcome. For instance, it could be that parents who decide to share their time with their children after separation are also parents who prepare their children for the separation and support them before it occurs. However, this evidence is in the same direction as the hints which can be found in all the recent studies of children of divorced parents that continuing relations with both parents are desirable from the point of view of the children's adjustment. ...

A continued relationship with the non-custodial parent would appear to offer many psychological advantages for children. One of the most obvious is that it offers a wider variety of experience; the experience of a relationship with a second parent. A child is not denied a close and continuing relationship with a parent of each gender. This may be of special value in the development of his or her own gender identity (which has been shown to be disturbed in some studies of children of divorce). With two parents a child is given the opportunity of learning how to move from one relationship to another. Often this is seen in a rather negative sense as something a child must learn to cope with. But I think we should see it much more positively as a very necessary skill for adult life that allows us to live within a whole network of relationships of differing kinds and qualities. It might be argued that these aspects of development should be satisfied equally by any two (or more) adults, not just a child's parents. To some extent this may be true, but there are many indications that parental relations are usually very special and cannot be replaced by other adults in any easy way. To say this is not to evoke any concept of a blood tie but one of a psychological parent. The potency of a psychological parent lies in the continuity of the relationship with their child and their symbolic position as a parent. A separation that does not involve the loss of one parent is likely to be much less disturbing of a child's social connections outside the immediate family. Friends and relatives of the non-custodial parent are not lost to the child. The child has a much better chance of maintaining links with both sets of grandparents.

At a separation, it is usual that among the many feelings a child is likely to experience is anger. This anger is associated with the wish or fantasy that the parents will come back together again and it is generally expressed towards the parent who spends most time looking after the child regardless of their role in the separation. If a child is able to maintain a relationship with both parents this anger gradually dissipates as the child begins to feel confident in the new kind of relationship that develops with both parents. The separation of the parents gradually ceases to be the total threat to the child's life it once had seemed. In a case where the child does not have contact with the non-custodial parent the resolution of the anger at the parents' separation may be much more complex and prolonged. The absent parent, just because he or she is absent, may be built up into a totally idealised figure while the custodial parent's role is seen as that of the person who has driven out the 'ideal' parent. Everything that goes wrong or frustrates the child may be laid at the door of the custodial parent. Under this emotional pressure even the strongest of parents begins to react so that the child may feel signs of rejection or anger in return. This in turn increases the child's anger and insecurity. Of course, not all children of divorce react in this way, but those who do are probably those who have lost contact with one parent.

It has been suggested that a continued relationship with both parents makes the acceptance of a step-parent much more difficult for a child. There is no evidence to support this idea, which is improbable in view of our understanding of a child's parental relations. The unlikely assumption here is that a child has the capacity for two parental relations and if both spaces are filled there will be no space for anybody else. In fact there is great variation in number and kind of relations that a child can maintain. It seems much more likely that if children feel confident that they are going to lose neither of their parents despite the marital separation, that they will accept a new adult more easily. Certainly, we need to move beyond the simplistic notion of very fixed parental roles which can be occupied by anybody that a parent or a court chooses to place in that position.

At the social level there are several very powerful arguments that can be given for the maintenance of ties with both parents.

For many, if not most children, a marital separation is followed by a permanent or temporary period in a single-parent family. We have abundant evidence that these families suffer from many disadvantages. Among these are the effects of a single person providing for all the children's needs day in and day out and the low incomes typical of such families. Both of these are likely to be reduced by continuing [contact] with the non-custodial parent. Such a parent not only provides the child with an alternative home but is also a relief for the custodial parent. These breaks allow the custodial parent to recharge emotional batteries and indulge in some adult life uninterrupted by the demands of childcare.

In principle, there is no connection between access and the payment of maintenance by non-custodial parents. However, this is not the way it is always seen by those involved. Parents who have regular contact with their children and maintain a close relationship are much more likely to want to pay maintenance and feel that it is fair and reasonable to do so. If the contact is maintained the needs of the children including financial ones will be more obvious and are likely to be more freely met.

One can also see the non-custodial parent as a kind of insurance policy for children. Lives of custodial parents cannot be predicted with certainty; changes may occur which make it very difficult or impossible for them to cope with children. If there is a disaster a second parent who is in close touch can often take the children and so avoid another major upheaval.

But what of the negative side – what arguments are there against the continuing involvement of both parents? There is a general belief, which is borne out by the research studies, that many difficulties are associated with access visits. However, the extent of these should not be exaggerated. Murch's study (1980), for instance, found a majority who are satisfied with their access arrangements and he also noted that initial difficulties often resolved in time. That difficulties occur around access visits is hardly surprising as this will often be the one point of contact between spouses (Eekelaar, 1982). The remedy of cutting off the contact may be superficially attractive, but in the long term is unlikely to help the adults to resolve their difficulties, apart from its likely effects on the children.

Part of our ambivalence about access is expressed in the common attitude that, though access is desirable, it can easily be overdone and so it is necessary to limit visits in terms of both their duration and frequency. Over-long or frequent visits are held to lead to confusions of loyalty for the children and to undermine their security in their main home. Clearly, if two parents are determined to continue their battles via their children, heavy pressures can be brought to bear which, if long-lasting, could make life a misery for children. However, such battles are usually relatively short-lived. As the separated parents begin to rebuild their lives and acquire new concerns and interests the old battles begin to lose their fire. Also children are surprisingly resourceful in avoiding situations which cause them pain.

One of the feelings that most concerns children at a parental separation is the fear of loss of both parents. If one parent has chosen to leave home and live elsewhere, why should not the other one make the same decision at a future date? The only way in which these fears can be countered is by a demonstration that there is continuity in the new arrangements. But it is not always understood that a child's fears are best countered if continuity is demonstrated in both parental relationships. Part of the mistaken fear that access visits are disturbing rests on the assumption that they may unsettle the relationship with the custodial parent. However, unless the child has a reasonable amount of time with the non-custodial parent there is no chance to regain confidence in that relationship.

Perhaps the most common cause of difficulties in access is that visits are too brief. We are well-used to descriptions of the Sunday afternoon access visit spent in the park and cafe. Only a moment's reflection is required to see how difficult or impossible it would be to recreate a normal parental relationship on that kind of basis. What children and adults need is the chance to share some of the very ordinary and routine aspects of life. Access visits must be long enough to remove the sense that they are a special occasion. Excessive gifts and the provision of 'treats' are sure signs that an ordinary relationship has not been recreated. The matter was summed up very clearly by a man I interviewed who told me that it was only after he had first got angry with his children during a visit that he began to feel that they were getting back to a reasonable relationship.

Given the many factors that will influence a particular situation and the practical constraints in making visiting arrangements I feel it would be unwise to try to lay down norms for the length of visits. However, I think it is fairly obvious that difficulties will be more common if overnight stays are not possible.

Sometimes it is felt important that things like rules about bedtimes should be as similar as possible in the two homes. Children often make comparisons and talk about any differences they have noted. In general, I would take the ability to talk openly about such differences as evidence that they were coming to terms with the separateness of their parents. Children will, of course, also try to exploit differences between the homes, supposed and real, to get what they want from a parent. But it is simple enough to make it clear to them that rules between the homes may differ and the fact that they are allowed to do X in the other house is no reason why they should do it here. Far from seeing differences in rules and routines in the two homes as confusing for children, I think there are good reasons for viewing them as advantages. They are ways of seeing something of variety in life and learning that there is not always a single answer to a problem. If different activities are possible in the two homes, just as the two relationships with the two parents will each have its own characteristics, so much the better for the children.

In 'Private Worlds and Public Intentions – The Role of the State in Divorce' (1993), Martin Richards suggests that the need for contact should dictate where the children are to live:

The principle of the primacy of the welfare of the children should still obtain in such situations but I suggest it should be given a single simple definition, that the children should reside with whichever parent is able to convince the court that they are the parent most likely to foster and maintain the children's links with the other parent. Such a criterion has a long history (Solomon, 1 Kings 3.16-28) and should ensure that attention is focused on the welfare of the children rather than the supposed moral worth of each parent. Here my argument directly contradicts that of those feminists who have argued for a system based exclusively on who was the primary caretaker within marriage (Smart and Sevenhuijsen, 1989). While such a system is attractive in its simplicity, it fails to take account of the changes in living arrangements and employment that divorce may bring and seems likely to reinforce further the expectation that child care should remain a mother's duty.

Question

Do you agree with this suggestion? You may like to bear this in mind when we look at some of the responses reported in *Making Contact Work* (p. 613, below), and also when you read the report by Sturge and Glasyer (p. 604, below).

This is how sociologist Carol Smart explains the argument about caring in *The Legal and Moral Ordering of Child Custody* (1990):

We are now in a position to recognise the complexity of the concept of 'care' and to appreciate that it is not simply a natural outpouring of instinctual love but a moral practice... [T]here is a distinction to be made between 'caring about' and 'caring for'. Typically we have taken 'caring about' to be a moral position. Hence caring about what happens to people is regarded as taking a moral stance. But 'caring for' has not been regarded as a moral stance, merely a maternal activity which arises from instinct which is, if anything, amoral.

Herein lies an important distinction between the moral claims that women and men make in relation to children. In relation to fathers it is common to hear the sort of statement that takes the form, 'He is their father after all'. What is meant by this and how does it compare with how both men and women typically talk about mothers' relationships to children?

'He is their father after all.'

This statement carries two quite contradictory meanings. The first is an assertion of a right arising from biological fatherhood. This is a statement which implies a legal or moral right arising out of a procreative act. But why isn't it sufficient to say 'He is their father' or 'I am their father'? Why is the 'after all' added? What does this add or take away? This 'after all', which men add as often as women, is a form of apology. It means 'I may not have done much but I am still their father'. It means 'I may not occupy the same moral terrain in terms of what I should claim, but I shall claim it anyway because of my biological status'.

Consider the following statement.

Maureen: He said he hadn't been a bad father and he didn't see why any judge would say to him that he couldn't have joint custody. I thought he had quite a good point really because he hadn't been a bad father. He had left them, but before that he wasn't cruel or vindictive and we didn't go short of anything so really I couldn't say that he had abused the children in any way.

In this construction it is enough for this mother that her husband has not done any harm for her to acknowledge his legal rights. But consider her reaction when asked how she might have felt if her husband had tried to gain care and control of their sons.

Maureen: I would have fought tooth and nail that he couldn't have them. There is no way he would have taken the children off me because I am a good mother and I love my children. ... Yes, I think mothers and fathers feel differently about their children and a mother's love is a strong deep love and even though they are boys, and boys are supposed to be closer to their father, I think in a stable background I would give them the best stability and love in their lives until they are old enough to go on their own.

Now, we can dismiss this as special pleading based on an outdated ideology of motherhood and mother love. It might even be that she is mistaken and that she can't give her sons what they most need and so on. But this is not the point. She was making a moral claim which had its foundations in the years of care she had given to her sons. If we say this is nothing, or that it counts for little, we are adopting a position which affirms that the act of 'caring for' has no (moral) value in our culture. We continue to place 'caring about' above 'caring for' and turn the moral content of acts of caring into self-interest.

In her statement Maureen is obviously associating the moral claim that arises out of caring with gender identity. That is to say she does use the language of the ideology of motherhood which is held as suspect in many quarters. Indeed one of the main claims of fathers' rights groups is that there is nothing intrinsic to being a woman/mother which means you can love deeply and care well. But this is not the end of the story as it is so often presumed. We can accept that there is nothing intrinsically caring about being a woman, but that does not mean we should reject the meanings that arise from providing care and nurture. Indeed, this research has indicated quite clearly that as soon as men begin to 'care for' children dramatic changes can occur. They become, metaphorically, 'born again'.

Smart also has something to say about the practical problems of sharing parenthood after separation:

... Maureen had been devastated when her husband left her and she remained extraordinarily sad at the turn of events she had endured. Notwithstanding her pain she was able to see how hard it was for her husband to (re)form and sustain his relationship to their sons and she was working hard to make this possible even though she was not prepared to include the 'other' woman in her efforts. Finally Tina was faced with a husband who was doubly dependent on drugs and alcohol. Her reaction was one of sympathy rather than mutual understanding, nonetheless she regarded her husband in a caring way and was prepared to work to sustain his role as father even though it had been entirely minimal until that time.

What comes as a shock to many parents who have had little involvement in 'caring for' children during a marriage is the emotional work that is required to sustain relationships after divorce. The parents who were successfully sharing parenting shared this work. That is to say they took on an extra dimension of planning and negotiating in order to make it work. This was arduous but regarded as essential. The parents who had 'cared about' but had done little 'caring for' often seemed angry at the emotional work that was required. One father remarked that he could not see why things could not be just like they were during their marriage. He did not want to do the emotional work that was necessary to keep things going. In other cases the mothers merely took on the work of keeping access going. They prepared the children emotionally for their fathers, they consoled the children when their fathers left, they kept up the flow of information and so on. The work of 'caring for' merely extended beyond the boundaries of divorce and dealing with access and sustaining their former husbands as adequate fathers became an additional task in the repertoire of care giving.

It is interesting that when mothers refuse to take on this extra work they become identified as bad or vindictive mothers. The work of sustaining access is like housework, it is only visible when it is not done. When it is done it is expected to be its own reward, but when it is not done the mother becomes blameworthy.

If we accept that sustaining parenting after divorce is hard work, that it adds a dimension to caring that is not an element of an ongoing marriage, we need to consider that there may be circumstances in which parents are reluctant to do the extra work without regarding this as a moral failure or as emotional immaturity.

Questions

(i) How would you define (a) a 'good father', and (b) a 'good mother'? And in each case (a) while they were living together, and (b) after they had separated? (ii) Smart (1990) also points out that:

there has grown up over time the argument that merely because a father does not pay child support a mother cannot deprive the child of the opportunity of seeing her father because the child's psychological needs are paramount – or at least can be separated from her substantive needs. Mothers who deny access because of maintenance arrears are therefore bad mothers.

Do you agree?
(iii) Do you believe that children mainly live with their mothers because it is better for them or because their mothers have earned the right to go on looking after them by doing so in the past?
(iv) Do you believe that children should go on seeing their fathers because it is better for them or because their fathers have a right to go on seeing them?

In 'Changing families and changing concepts – reforming the language of family law' (1998), Andrew Bainham comments on Smart's views:

Human experience and common sense do indeed dictate that contact be recognised as a *mutual* right or claim of parent and child, in each case subject always to the welfare principle...

This has not stopped some English courts from viewing the contact question exclusively from the child's perspective. Neither has it stopped commentators, most recently Smart and Neale, from challenging the proposition that contact is a fundamental right which the courts should attempt to enforce in the absence of a very good reason for not doing so. [They argue] form the perspective that contact has become accepted as a basic right of the *child*, and enforced as such, but the effect of failing to enforce it, as the authors must be aware, would be felt particularly by parents, usually the so-called 'absent fathers'. Indeed, it cannot be seriously doubted that the article is pushing a feminist agenda and that it is the interests of *mothers*, and not those of children, which preoccupy the authors. They are in reality crudely equating the interests of women and children and setting them up in opposition to those of men.

Question

Is this fair? Is it outrageous?

What about the children themselves? Carol Smart's article, 'Objects of concern? – children and divorce' (1999) found strong views among children about how contact might be organised and agreed. The conversations with children that she reports leave one in no doubt that, for these children at least, contact was immensely important (bear in mind that the children interviewed were living in shared care arrangements and so may be an unusual sample whose views may be untypical).

One of the ironies of [the] exclusion of children from open discussions about divorce and changes in family life is that they are a fount of knowledge and information themselves on what it is like, on how to cope, on how to intervene (even in limited ways) and what it all feels like. They may even have a very different perspective on the process when compared to parents, and they may even have solutions to some of the typical problems thrown up by parenting across households. We may have a lot to learn about divorce from children if we suspend the presumption that they are damaged goods in need of protection.

Here are some of the conversations Smart relates:

Q:	'Is there anything that you might like to change?'
Rosie (9):	'Yes. For there to be *eight* days in the week. That's the only thing.'
Q:	'What difference would that make?'
Rosie:	'Four days with both people.'

In the quotation above Rosie is performing a modern day version of the Judgement of Solomon. However, rather than envisaging an emotional and grim scenario of splitting a child into two, she seeks a more prosaic solution, namely to split the week equally into two halves to ensure fairness between parents. ...

Claudia, who was 12 years old, could sometimes feel like a referee in just the same way that many parents can:

Claudia:	'[T]hey always say I can say something but then, like, it's a bit hard you see because both of them want different things and if you agree with one, then the other one will feel a bit upset. I mean they won't say that to you, but you can sense it so it's a bit annoying. So even if you didn't want to do that, if you wanted to do something completely different, it's better to say [that] you want to do something completely different 'cos then neither of them wins, then they'll just find an argument about something else.'

...

Nick (14):	'It's almost made it easier though, our mum and dad not living together, because before there was arguments and things like that and it was really difficult really to live. But now that they've moved apart they're both much happier and much more relaxed. Like my mum, she comes in tense from work just 'cos her work's like that, but she comes home and she'll relax rather than before she would have come home and there would probably have been an argument about something.'
Emma (10):	'I think it works quite well for [my mother] because she likes to have a rest, so on a Friday night, well once every fortnight on a Friday night, she just has herself and she just sort of goes to sleep and enjoys having no children I think.' (co-parented, ESRC)

These children appreciate their parents as separate individuals with needs and interests – and even tastes:

Beth (14):	'it works for my mum 'cos she's got time with Ian, where they can have fish and stuff, 'cos I hate the smell of fish, and it gives her a break from like worrying about me all the time.'

Question

How might (a) the law and (b) parents tap into the resources of children's wisdom? We shall look, in the rest of the chapter, at some of the ways in which the law tries to do so.

12.2 The law

In this section we look at:
1. The orders available
2. The welfare principle
3. More about residence
4. More about contact
5. The non-intervention principle
6. The child's sense of time

12.2.1 The orders available

The Children Act 1989 replaced the old orders for custody, joint custody, care and control, access, and the resolution of disputes about the exercise of parental rights, as follows:

8.—(1) In this Act—

'a contact order' means an order requiring the person with whom a child lives, or is to live, to allow the child to visit or stay with the person named in the order, or for that person and the child otherwise to have contact with each other;

'a prohibited steps order' means an order that no step which could be taken by a parent in meeting his parental responsibility for a child, and which is of a kind specified in the order shall be taken by any person without the consent of the court;

'a residence order' means an order settling the arrangements to be made as to the person with whom a child is to live; and

'a specific issue order' means an order giving directions for the purpose of determining a specific question which has arisen, or which may arise, in connection with any aspect of parental responsibility for a child.

(2) In this Act 'a section 8 order' means any of the orders mentioned in subsection (1) and any order varying or discharging such an order.

As between parents (married or unmarried) these may be made in the following circumstances:

10.—(1) In any family proceedings in which a question arises with respect to the welfare of any child, the court may make a section 8 order with respect to the child if—

  (a) an application for the order has been made by a person who—

      (i)   is entitled to apply for a section 8 order with respect to the child; or

      (ii) has obtained the leave of the court to make the application; or

  (b) the court considers that the order should be made even though no such application has been made.

(2) The court may also make a section 8 order with respect to any child on the application of a person who—

  (a) is entitled to apply for a section 8 order with respect to the child; or

  (b) has obtained the leave of the court to make the application.

...

(4) The following persons are entitled to apply to the court for any section 8 order with respect to a child—

  (a) any parent or guardian of the child;

  (b) any person in whose favour a residence order is in force with respect to the child.

There are also various supplementary provisions:

11.—(3) Where a court has power to make a section 8 order, it may do so at any time during the course of the proceedings in question even though it is not in a position to dispose finally of those proceedings.

(4) Where a residence order is made in favour of two or more persons who do not themselves all live together, the order may specify the periods during which the child is to live in the different households concerned.

(5) Where—

  (a) a residence order has been made with respect to a child; and

  (b) as a result of the order the child lives, or is to live, with one of two parents who each have parental responsibility for him,

the residence order shall cease to have effect if the parents live together for a continuous period of more than six months.

(6) A contact order which requires the parent with whom a child lives to allow the child to visit, or otherwise have contact with, the other parent shall cease to have effect if the parents live together for a continuous period of more than six months.

(7) A section 8 order may—

(a) contain directions about how it is to be carried into effect:

(b) impose conditions which must be complied with by any person—

    (i) in whose favour the order is made;

    (ii) who is a parent of the child concerned;

    (iii) who is not a parent of his but who has parental responsibility for him; or

    (iv) with whom the child is living,

    and to whom the conditions are expressed to apply;

(c) be made to have effect for a specified period, or contain provisions which are to have effect for a specified period;

(d) make such incidental, supplemental or consequential provision as the court thinks fit.

...

13.—(1) Where a residence order is in force with respect to a child, no person may—

(a) cause the child to be known by a new surname; or

(b) remove him from the United Kingdom;

without either the written consent of every person who has parental responsibility for the child or the leave of the court.

(2) Subsection (1)(b) does not prevent the removal of a child, for a period of less than one month, by the person in whose favour the residence order is made.

(3) In making a residence order with respect to a child the court may grant the leave required by subsection (1)(b), either generally or for specified purposes.

These provisions are explained in the Law Commission's Report on *Guardianship and Custody* (1988):

Orders between parents

...

4.5 In framing a scheme of orders to replace the present law, we have had in mind throughout the clear evidence that the children who fare best after their parents separate or divorce are those who are able to maintain a good relationship with them both [eg Wallerstein and Kelly, 1980; Lund, 1987; Richards and Dyson, 1982; Maidment, 1984]. The law may not be able to achieve this – indeed we are only too well aware of the limits of the law in altering human relationships – but at least it should not stand in their way. Our respondents were generally agreed on three points. Where the parents are already able to co-operate in bringing up their children, the law should interfere as little as possible. Where they may be having difficulty, it should try to 'lower the stakes' so that the issue is not one in which 'winner takes all' or more importantly 'loser loses all'. In either case, the orders made should reduce rather than increase the opportunities for conflict and litigation in the future.

4.6 The scheme which we provisionally proposed in the Working Paper had three basic elements. The first, as we have already explained, [see p. 496, above] is that the parents should retain their equal parental responsibility and with it their power to act independently unless this is incompatible with the court's order. A parent who does not have the child with him would still be regarded in law as a parent. He should be treated as such by schools and others, so that he can be given information and an opportunity to take part in the child's education. He should not be able to exercise a power of veto over the other, but should be able to refer any dispute to the court if necessary. A parent who does have the child with him should be able to exercise his responsibilities to the full during that time.

...

4.8 The second element in our proposals was designed to reflect the practical reality that parental status is largely a matter of everyday responsibility rather than rights. It is 'a mistake to see custody, care and control and access as differently-sized bundles of powers and responsibilities in a descending hierarchy of importance'. Most parental responsibilities can only be exercised while the parent has the child, for only then can the parent put into effect the decisions taken. Equally, however, it is then that the parent must be in a position to meet his responsibilities as the circumstances and needs of the child dictate. Parental responsibilities, therefore, largely 'run with the child'. Clearly, in most cases, one parent carries a much heavier burden of that responsibility than does the other. The present system of orders, by concentrating on the allocation of 'rights', appears more concerned with whether one parent can control what the other parent does while the child is with the other, than with ensuring that each parent properly meets his responsibilities while the child is with him. The practical question in most cases is where the child is to live and how much he is to see of the other parent. Hence we provisionally proposed that custody and access orders should be replaced by a single order, possibly termed 'care and control', allocating the child's time between the parents.

...

4.10 However, several respondents who approved of the general thrust of our provisional proposals suggested different terminology from 'care and control' which still carries some of the proprietorial connotations of 'custody'. There is also a practical disadvantage in having only a single order which divides the child's time between his parents. Most children will live with one parent for most of the time and spend variable amounts of time with the other. The usual order at present is for 'reasonable' access. Our respondents did not think it desirable for orders to spell this out in any more detail unless and until disputes arose. Parents are usually able to agree upon their own arrangements, which have to be flexible enough to meet changing needs and circumstances. Rather than being required to specify the periods of time intended, therefore, the court should normally deal with where (or, more accurately, with whom) the child is to live, whom he should see, and any other specific matters which have to be resolved.

...

(a) Residence orders

4.12 Apart from the effect upon the other parent, ... the main difference between a residence order and a custody order is that the new order should be flexible enough to accommodate a much wider range of situations. In some cases, the child may live with both parents even though they do not share the same household. It was never our intention to suggest that children should share their time more or less equally between their parents. Such arrangements will rarely be practicable, let alone for the children's benefit. However, the evidence from the United States is that where they are practicable they can work well and we see no reason why they should be actively discouraged. None of our respondents shared the view expressed in a recent case [*Riley v Riley* [1986] 2 FLR 429] that such an arrangement, which had been working well for some years, should never have been made. More commonly, however, the child will live with both parents but spend more time with one than the other. Examples might be where he spends term time with one and holidays with the other, or two out of three holidays from boarding school with one and the third with the other. It is a far more realistic description of the responsibilities involved in that sort of arrangement to make a residence order covering both parents rather than a residence order for one and a contact order for the other. ...

4.14 The effect of a residence order is simply to settle where the child is to live. If any other conditions are needed they must usually be specified. However, the Matrimonial Causes Rules 1977 at present specify two conditions which must be included in divorce court custody orders unless the court otherwise directs. First, the parent with custody must not change the child's surname without the written consent of the other parent or the leave of a judge. The child's surname is an important symbol of his identity and his relationship with his parents. While it may well be in his interests for it to be changed, it is clearly not a matter on which the parent with whom he lives should be able to take unilateral action. ...

4.15 Secondly, a divorce court order for custody or care and control must provide for the child not to be removed from England and Wales without leave of the court except on such terms as the court may specify in the order. This means that, unless the court makes an exception at the outset, the child cannot be taken on holiday abroad (or even to Scotland), even if the other parent agrees, without the trouble and expense of an application for leave. This is clearly quite unrealistic these days and we suspect that the requirement is often ignored. Otherwise, an order for legal custody does not permit a person to arrange the child's emigration unless he is a parent or guardian but the order contains no more stringent requirement unless the court specifically prohibits removals and we understand that it rarely does so. The matter could be dealt with entirely by the criminal law [Child Abduction Act 1984, s. 1]. However, taking the child abroad indefinitely can obviously have a serious effect upon his relationship with the other parent and it may be important to remind the residential parent of this, and of the steps to be taken if she wishes to do so. A simple, clear general rule seems most likely to be remembered and observed.

...

(b) Contact orders

4.17 Where the child is to spend much more time with one parent than the other, the more realistic order will probably be for him to live with one parent and to visit the other. There are important differences between this and the present form of access order. It will not provide for the 'non-custodial' parent to have access to the child. It will provide for the child to visit and in many cases stay with the parent. While the child is with that parent, the parent may exercise all his parental responsibilities. He must not do something which is incompatible with the order about where the child is to live. The court may also attach other conditions if there are particular anxieties or bones of contention but these should rarely be required. If visiting is not practicable, the court may nevertheless order some other form of contact with the child, including letters or telephone calls or visits to the child. We would expect, however, that the normal order would be for reasonable contact, which would encompass all types. ...

(c) Specific issue orders

4.18 Specific issue orders may be made in conjunction with residence or contact orders or on their own. ... As with conditions attached to other orders, the object is not to give one parent or the other the 'right' to determine a particular point. Rather, it is to enable either parent to submit a particular dispute to the court for resolution in accordance with what is best for the child. A court can determine in the light of the evidence what decision will be best for the child at the time. It may equally be content for decisions to be taken by each parent as they arise in the course of everyday life in the future. It may even attach a condition to a residence or contact order that certain decisions may not be taken without informing the other or giving the other an opportunity to object. But to give one parent in advance the right to take a decision which the other parent will have to put into effect is contrary to the whole tenor of the modern law [eg the disapproval of the old form of 'split' orders, giving custody to one and care and control to the other, *Williamson v Williamson* [1986] 2 FLR 146]. A court can scarcely be expected to know in advance that the first parent's decision will be the best for the child.

4.19 However, a specific issue order is not intended as a substitute for a residence or contact order. There is obviously a slight risk that they might be used, particularly in uncontested cases, to achieve much the same practical results but without the same legal effects. We recommend, therefore, that it should be made clear that a specific issue order cannot be made with a view to achieving a result which could be achieved by a residence or contact order.

(d) Prohibited steps orders

4.20 Prohibited steps orders are also modelled on the wardship jurisdiction. The automatic effect of making a child a ward of court is that no important step may be taken without the court's leave. An important aim of our recommendations is to incorporate the most valuable features of wardship into the statutory jurisdictions. It is on occasions necessary for the court to play a continuing parental role in relation to the child, although we would not expect those occasions to be common. If this is in the best interests of the child, it should be made clear exactly what the limitations on the exercise of parental responsibility are. Hence, instead of the vague requirement in wardship, that no 'important step' may be taken, the court should spell out these matters which will have to be referred back to the court. We would expect such orders to be few and far between, as in practice the wardship jurisdiction is more often invoked to achieve a particular result at the time than to produce the continuing over-sight of the court. One example, however, might be to ensure that the child is not removed from the United Kingdom, especially in a case where there is no residence order and so the automatic prohibition cannot apply. As with specific issue orders, however, we recommend that these orders should not be capable of being made with a view to achieving a result which could be achieved by a residence or contact order.

(e) Supplemental provisions

4.21 The courts have interpreted their powers under section 42 of the Matrimonial Causes Act 1973 so flexibly as to enable them to make interim orders, delay implementation or attach other special conditions. The other legislation contains specific provisions for similar purposes. The object of our recommendation is to preserve the present flexibility of the divorce courts' powers within the new scheme of orders. We would not expect these supplemental powers to be used at all frequently, as most cases will not require them and all are subject to the general rule that orders should only be made where they are the most effective means of safeguarding or promoting the child's welfare.

Question

This scheme of orders has to be read in conjunction with the provisions on parental responsibility, and in particular the rule that each person with parental responsibility may act alone in meeting it, unless this is inconsistent with a court order (see pp. 497, above). Do you suppose that the scheme in the Children Act 1989 would appeal more to Martin Richards (see p. 579, above) or to Carol Smart (see p. 581, above) or would they both like or dislike it equally?

12.2.2 The welfare principle

The Children Act 1989 restates the welfare principle (first enacted in s. 1 of the Guardianship of Infants Act 1925, p. 443, above) with additions:

1.—(1) When a court determines any question with respect to—
  (a) the upbringing of a child; or
  (b) the administration of a child's property or the application of any income arising from it,
the child's welfare shall be the court's paramount consideration.
  ...
  (3) In the circumstances mentioned in subsection (4), a court shall have regard in particular to—
  (a) the ascertainable wishes and feelings of the child concerned (considered in the light of his age and understanding);
  (b) his physical, emotional and educational needs;
  (c) the likely effect on him of any change in his circumstances;
  (d) his age, sex, background and any characteristics of his which the court considers relevant;
  (e) any harm which he has suffered or is at risk of suffering;
  (f) how capable each of his parents, and any other person in relation to whom the court considers the question to be relevant, is of meeting his needs;
  (g) the range of powers available to the court under this Act in the proceedings in question.
  (4) The circumstances are that—
  (a) the court is considering whether to make, vary or discharge a section 8 order, and the making, variation or discharge of the order is opposed by any party to the proceedings; or
  (b) the court is considering whether to make, vary or discharge an order under Part IV [see Chapter 9, above].

Section 1(1), however, differs in two respects from the recommendations of the Law Commission:

3.13 We suggested, however, two modifications in the present formulation of the paramountcy rule. First, the interests of the child whose future happens to be in issue in the proceedings before the court should not in principle prevail over those of other children likely to be affected by the decision. Hence their welfare should also be taken into consideration. Secondly, the word 'first' had caused confusion in that it had in the past led some courts to balance other considerations against the child's welfare rather than to consider what light they shed upon it [eg *Re L (infants)* [1962] 3 All ER 1, [1962] 1 WLR 886]. Since *J v C* [1970] AC 668 [p. 444, above], that view has been decisively rejected in the courts [*Re K (a minor) (children: care and control)* [1977] Fam 179, [1977] 1 All ER 647, [p. 590, below] and a modern formulation should reflect this. These proposals were approved by all those who commented upon them.
3.14 It could be said that, given its recent interpretation in the courts, retaining the present formula does no harm. However, merely to drop 'first', as a piece of 'draftsman's duplicity (now obsolete)' [Bennion, 1976], does nothing to resolve the earlier confusion. Litigants might still be tempted to introduce evidence and arguments which had no relevance to the child's welfare, in the hope of persuading the court to balance one against the other. The whole aim of these proposals is to state the modern law simply and clearly. We recommend, therefore, that in reaching any decision about the child's care, upbringing or maintenance, the welfare of any child likely to be affected by the decision should be the court's only concern. ...

Questions

(i) Is there a difference between a 'paramount' and a 'sole' consideration?
(ii) If other considerations can be taken into account, should they include, for example, (a) the 'justice' of the matrimonial dispute, (b) the need to minimise public expenditure, or (c) the wishes and feelings of any of the adults involved?
(iii) What would an economist or utilitarian think of a law which, in theory, required that a small gain to the child's welfare, in living with the marginally more suitable parent, should outweigh a much greater detriment to the welfare of a parent who would be devastated by the loss of his or her child?

The position which the courts had already reached before the 1989 Act is well illustrated by the following case:

Re K (Minors) (Children: Care and Control)
[1977] Fam 179, [1979] 1 All ER 647, [1977] 2 WLR 33, 121 Sol Jo 84, Court of Appeal

The parents married in 1969. They had a son in 1971, who was now aged 5, and a daughter in 1974, who was now 2½. The father was a Church of England clergyman. Through church activities, the mother met a young man named Martin in 1973. By March 1975, their friendship had become adulterous. The father wished the mother to give up her relationship with Martin and be reconciled. The mother wished to leave the father and set up home in a house to be bought jointly with Martin, but she was unwilling to go without the children. Accordingly, in May 1976 she applied to the local magistrates' court for their custody. The father halted those proceedings by applying to make the children wards of court. Reeve J granted care and control to the mother and the father appealed.

Stamp LJ: Before turning to the facts of the case, I would make some introductory observations. In the first place the law which is to be applied is not in doubt. It is that the welfare of the children is, in the words of the statute, the first and paramount consideration. ... [T]his court in *S (BD) v S (DJ) (infants: care and consent)* [1977] Fam 109, [1977] 1 All ER 656 held that the earlier case of *Re L (infants)* [1962] 3 All ER 1, [1962] 1 WLR 886, where this court appears to have balanced the welfare of the child against the wishes of an unimpeachable parent or the justice of the case as between the parties, was no longer to be regarded as good law. ...

The second thing I would say at the outset is, ... that although one may of course be assisted by the wisdom of remarks made in earlier cases, the circumstances in infant cases and the personalities of the parties concerned being infinitely variable, the conclusions of the court as to the course which should be followed in one case are of little assistance in guiding one to the course which ought to be followed in another case.

Thirdly I would emphasise that where a judge has seen the parties concerned, has had the assistance of a good welfare officer's report and has correctly applied the law, an appellate court ought not to disturb his decision unless it appears that he has failed to take into account something which he ought to have taken into account or has taken into account something which he ought not to have taken into account, or the appellate court is satisfied that his decision was wrong; it is not enough that a judge of the appellate court should think, on reading the papers, that he himself would on the whole have come to a different conclusion. ...

The arrangements which the father would make if he were to have care and control and the mother in fact went to live with M were summarised by the judge thus:

> 'Moreover, I bear this matter in mind. That the arrangements which the father can make – I refer to the roster which is exhibited to one of his affidavits – is on the face of it satisfactory in that these children will be cared for by worthy persons at all hours of the day, nevertheless it is not a satisfactory way, through no fault of the father's, in having children cared for. As has been pointed out, during the course of one week there may be five different persons who may be responsible for looking after these children. There will be some continuity in the care that the father can lavish on them. Nevertheless there would be a succession of other persons who would be assisting in that regard. That, as I say, is not the fault of the father, he is making the best arrangements that he can.'

...

I agree with the learned judge that the arrangements are far from satisfactory and that if the matter rested there it could hardly be doubted that it would be for the benefit of these children that effect should be given to the dictates of nature which make the mother the natural guardian, protector and comforter of the very young. But, as the judge pointed out in a judgment which shows the greatest possible sympathy with the father – a sympathy which I would emphasise that I share – in considering the welfare of the children one has to look also to their moral and spiritual welfare.

The father, who naturally holds his beliefs very strongly, not only wants to live according to his faith, but wants his children to be brought up in that faith, to hold the same beliefs as he does and to live their lives as he intends to live his life.

...

But unfortunately, as the judge pointed out, if one yielded to that submission and committed the care of these children to the father, it would not in great measure protect them from the moral and spiritual harm which the father fears. The plain fact is that the children's mother intends to live with a young man who is not her husband. No one suggests that she should be denied access to the children and the judge thought, and I share that view, that it would have to be liberal access, including staying access. How could the children then fail to be aware, and constantly aware, that their mother was living with M in, to quote the judge's words 'blatant defiance of church doctrine and all that [the father] believes in'? And, if, as appears to be the case, the children are children who love their mother and are fond of M, to deprive them of her would, in my judgment, be as likely as not to cause a revolt against the very teaching that the father would have them imbibe and a revolt, so I would have thought, which in due course would be a revolt against the father himself. ...

...

The judge made it abundantly clear that if he were deciding the case by trying to do justice between the father and the mother, there could be only one way in which he could possibly decide it, and that was in favour of the father; but he correctly applied what was laid down in *J v C* and refused to set that consideration against the welfare of the children. ...

I can only say that I am quite unable to conclude that the judge came to a wrong conclusion; I agree with it and would dismiss this appeal.

Appeal dismissed.

Questions

(i) Do you consider that this decision was 'unfair' to the father?
(ii) If you do think it unfair, is that because: (a) the law requires the court to determine the case on the basis of the children's welfare and not upon the rights and wrongs of the marital dispute, or (b) the court gave effect to the 'dictates of nature which make the mother the natural guardian, protector and comforter of the very young'?
(iii) What do you think was best for these two children?

On the third point made by Lord Justice Stamp, the House of Lords affirmed a slightly wider view of the role of appellate courts in children cases:

G v G (Minors) (Custody:Appeal)
[1985] 2 All ER 225, [1985] 1 WLR 647, [1985] FLR 894, [1985] Fam Law 321, House of Lords

Lord Fraser of Tullybelton: ...We were told by counsel that practitioners are finding difficulty in ascertaining the correct principles to apply because of the various ways in which judges have expressed themselves in these cases. I do not think it would be useful for me to go through the cases and to analyse the various expressions used by different judges and attempt to reconcile them exactly. Certainly it would not be useful to inquire whether different shades of meaning are intended to be conveyed by words such as 'blatant error' used by the President in the present case, and words such as 'clearly wrong', 'plainly wrong', or simply 'wrong' used by other judges in other cases. All these various expressions were used in order to emphasize the point that the appellate court should only interfere when they consider that the judge of first instance has not merely preferred an imperfect solution which is different from an alternative imperfect solution which the Court of Appeal might or would have adopted, but has exceeded the generous ambit within which a reasonable disagreement is possible. The principle was stated in this House by my noble and learned friend Lord Scarman in *B v W (wardship: appeal)* [1979] 3 All ER 83, [1979] 1 WLR 1041: ...

> 'But at the end of the day the court may not intervene unless it is satisfied either that the judge exercised his discretion upon a wrong principle or that, the judge's decision being so plainly wrong, he must have exercised his discretion wrongly.'

The same principle was expressed in other words, and at slightly greater length, in the Court of Appeal (Stamp, Browne and Bridge LJJ) in *Re F (a minor) (wardship: appeal)* [1976] Fam 238, [1976] 1 All ER 417, CA ... Browne LJ said:

'Apart from the effect of seeing and hearing witnesses, I cannot see why the general principle applicable to the exercise of the discretion in respect of infants should be any different from the general principle applicable to any other form of discretion.'

... The decision in *Re F* is also important because the majority rejected, rightly in my view, the dissenting opinion of Stamp LJ, who would have limited the right of the Court of Appeal to interfere with the judge's decision in custody cases to cases 'where it concludes that the course followed by the judge is one that no reasonable judge having taken into account all the relevant circumstances could have adopted'. That is the test which the court applies in deciding whether it is entitled to exercise judicial control over the decision of an administrative body, see the well-known case of *Associated Provincial Picture Houses Ltd v Wednesbury Corpn* [1948] 1 KB 223. It is not the appropriate test for deciding whether the Court of Appeal is entitled to interfere with the decision made by a judge in the exercise of his discretion.

Questions

(i) 'But to say that the judge below is deemed to have "exceeded the generous ambit within which a reasonable disagreement is possible" is surely to say no more, nor less, than that his decision was one which no reasonable judge could make'? (Eekelaar, 1985)
(ii) How much importance should be attached to 'the effect of seeing and hearing witnesses' in children cases?
(iii) Do you think appeals should be encouraged or discouraged? Why?

The Law Commission went on to explain the 'checklist' in s. 1(3) like this:

3.18 The 'checklist' received a large majority of support from those who considered the matter. It was perceived as a means of providing a greater consistency and clarity in the law and was welcomed as a major step towards a more systematic approach to decisions concerning children. Respondents pointed out that it would help to ensure that the same basic factors were being used to implement the welfare criterion by the wide range of professionals involved, including judges, magistrates, registrars, welfare officers, and legal advisers. One respondent, for example, who is a magistrates' clerk, thought that the list would be particularly useful when advising magistrates in making decisions in contested custody cases and in formulating reasons in the event of an appeal. It would also provide a practical tool for those lacking experience and confidence in this area. Perhaps most important of all, we were told that such a list could assist both parents and children in endeavouring to understand how judicial decisions are made. At present, there is a tendency for advisers and their clients (and possibly even courts) to rely on 'rules of thumb' as to what the court is likely to think best in any given circumstances. A checklist would make it clear to all what, as a minimum, would be considered by the court. At the very least, it would enable the parties to prepare and give relevant evidence at the outset, thereby avoiding the delay and expense of prolonged hearings or adjournments for further information. Moreover, we were informed that solicitors find the checklist applicable to financial matters most useful in focusing their clients' minds on the real issues and therefore in promoting settlements. Anything which is likely to promote the settlement of disputes about children is even more to be welcomed. We recommend, therefore, that a statutory checklist similar to that provided for financial matters be provided for decisions relating to children.

Questions

(i) The list deliberately steers clear of statements like 'young children need their mothers', or 'boys need a masculine influence', or 'brothers and sisters need to stay together': is this a good thing?
(ii) Factor (g) was added later: why?

But how can the courts square the demands of s. 1(1) of the Children Act 1989 with those of the European Convention on Human Rights, which gives every member of the family a right to respect for his family life? Does the convention principle oblige the English courts to change their views? Aidan Vine (2000) asks 'Is the paramountcy principle compatible with Article 8?':

The argument for incompatibility

The argument for a fundamental difference of approach between the Convention and domestic law relies upon:

(1) the absence of an express guarantee in the Convention for the welfare of the child, unlike in domestic law;

(2) the existence of Convention case-law suggesting that the rights of both parents and children are in the balance under Art. 8; and

(3) dicta in a recent domestic decision of the Court of Appeal concerning the overlap of family and immigration law.

Point (1) is unarguable, but does not of itself establish that there is a fundamental difference between the Convention and the domestic law approach. In relation to point (2), it is also correct that Convention case-law, principally the case of *Johanssen v Norway* (Application 17383/90) (1996) 23 EHRR 33, at para 78, has concluded that 'a fair balance' has to be struck between the interests of the child and those of the parents. However, it is clear from the cases considered in more detail below, including the *Johanssen* case, that the interests of the child, including its welfare, are matters to which the Convention case-law attaches particular weight when assessing where the balance lies in decisions concerning children under Art. 8.

In relation to point (3), in *R v Secretary of State for the Home Department ex parte Gangadeen; R v Secretary of State for Home Department ex parte Khan* [1998] 1 FLR 762 the Court of Appeal considered two applications for leave to judicially review deportation decisions in circumstances where the interests of the applicants' children would be adversely affected by the resulting enforced separation from the non-custodial parent. Both applicants submitted unsuccessfully that the interest of the child should be the paramount consideration and relied upon Art. 8. In the lead judgment, Hirst LJ considered Convention case-law and particularly three cases concerning the interplay between the right to respect for family life and immigration decisions. He concluded, at pp. 773H-4A:

> 'In my judgment these three cases demonstrate quite clearly that, in their interpretation of Art. 8 *in the present context*, the Human Rights Court and the Commission approach the problem as a straightforward balancing exercise, in which the scales start even, and where the weight to be given to the considerations on each side of the balance is to be assessed according to the individual circumstances of the case; thus they do not support the notion that paramountcy is to be given to the interests of the child.' (Emphasis added.)

The significance of Hirst LJ's conclusion depends upon whether it is taken to be a statement of Convention case-law under Art. 8 in respect of the upbringing of children generally, or whether it is to be taken more narrowly as confined to the upbringing of children in the context of immigration decisions. The three cases considered by Hirst LJ in detail, together with the words italicised in the above extract from his judgment, suggest that he may have intended his conclusion to go no further than the latter, more narrow context of immigration. In any event, the Convention case-law shows that while the court may have adopted a discrete approach to Art. 8 in cases concerning immigration, reflecting the necessity for states to control immigration, in cases dealing squarely with the upbringing of children its approach is remarkably similar to that secured in domestic law by the paramountcy principle. ...

Article 8 and the upbringing of children

The significance of the interests of the child, including his welfare, in decisions concerning this upbringing has been considered in the Convention case-law a number of times, both in the private and public law contexts.

General principles

In a private dispute, in *Hokkanen v Finland* (Application 19823/92) (1994) 19 EHRR 139, at para 58, the court held that the interests, rights and freedoms of all concerned must be taken into account and more particularly the best interests of the child, but went on to observe that where contact with a parent might appear to threaten or interfere with the interests or rights of the child, it was for the national authorities to strike the right balance. In *Hendriks v The Netherlands* (Application 9427/81) (1982) 29 DR 5, at paras 95, 115 and 124, the Commission had earlier held that whilst contact with an absent parent should not be denied unless there were strong reasons, the interests of the child predominated and must prevail under Art. 8(2), it being a question of the overriding interest of the child.

The issue has arisen more often in the public law context of care measures, where the court has held, in the *Johansen* case, at para 78, that in carrying out the balancing exercise of the rights of all concerned, the court will attach 'particular importance' to 'the best interests of the child', which 'may override those of the parent'. On a number of occasions, in *Johansen*, at para 64, as well as in *Bronda v Italy* (Application 22430/93) [1998] EHRLR 756, at para 59, *Scott v UK* (Application 34745/97) [2000] 1 FLR 958, at p. 968G and *K and T v Finland* (Application 25702/94) [2000] 2 FLR 79, at p. 101E, the court has specifically described the interests of the child as of 'crucial importance' and held that it attached 'special weight' to 'the overriding interest of the child'. In the recent case of *L v UK* (Application 34222/96) [2000] 2 FLR 322, at p. 332H, concerning the admissibility of an expert report in care proceedings under s. 31 of the Children Act 1989, the court expressly concurred with the importance of the welfare of the child in cases concerning children.

Private disputes

In the *Hokkanen* case, where a 14-year-old child had lived with her grandparents for 7 years, despite the father's attempts to secure her return, and had strong attachments to them and felt that their home was her home, the court found, at paras 84-5, that the transfer of custody from the father to the grandparents was not a violation of Art. 8, even though there had been violations in respect of the domestic courts' failure to enforce the father's rights of access throughout the time the child had been with the grandparents.

In the *Hendriks* case, where on the facts contact would have led to tension in the family of the custodial parent and to a conflict of loyalties for the child, at paras 124-5 the Commission found that the refusal of contact to the father was not a violation of Art. 8, as contact would not have been in the interests of the child.

In *Söderbäck v Sweden* (Application 24484/94) [1999] 1 FLR 250, where the natural father had had infrequent and limited contact with the 7-year-old child and had never had custody or care, and where there had been de facto family ties between the child and her stepfather for 6½ years, the court found, at pp 257E–258D, that the making of an adoption order in favour of the stepfather was not a violation of the natural father's rights under Art. 8, given that its aim was to achieve the best interests of the child. By contrast, in *Keegan v Ireland* (Application 16969/90) (1994) 18 EHRR 342, at para 55, where the mother had been allowed to place the child for adoption without the knowledge or consent of the father, the court found that the absence of any reasons relevant to the welfare of the child to justify that step meant that there had been a violation of Art. 8.

In *Rogl v Germany* (Application 28319/95) (1996) 85-A DR 153, at para 2, where on the facts the 7-year-old child's interests lay in fully integrating her into her stepfamily and where the child had never lived with her father, had had a disturbed relationship with him and was attached to her stepfather, the Commission found that the making of an order permitting the child's surname to be changed to that of her stepfather was not a violation of the father's rights under Art. 8. ...

Conclusion

The right to respect for family life under Art. 8 of the Convention is not an absolute right and may be interfered with by national authorities if such an interference is justified under Art. 8(2). In assessing the need to interfere with that right, the national authorities enjoy a margin of appreciation. The weight to be attached to the interests of the child in justifying such an interference has been considered in Convention case-law on many occasions. While it seems clear that the Convention case-law concerning the right to respect for family life in the immigration context does not give paramountcy to the welfare of the child, the position in relation to cases concerning the upbringing of a child outside of the context is very different.

The Commission's concept of the 'prevailing' or 'overriding' interests of the child in the *Hendriks* case appears, if anything, to go further than the paramountcy principle applied in domestic law. The court's concepts of 'particular importance', 'crucial importance' and 'special weight' in relation to the interests of the child, which may 'override' the interests of the parent, in the *Johansen, Bronda, Scott* and *K and T* cases, are remarkably similar in effect to the principle in domestic law that the welfare of the child is the paramount consideration. The particular importance of the welfare of the child in Convention law is especially clear in the *Hokkanen* and *K and T* cases where, notwithstanding that violations of parental rights under Art. 8 had occurred in the past, for welfare reasons the court was not prepared to turn back the clock. It is particularly significant that in the *Scott* case there was no criticism from the court of a decision made in Children Act 1989 proceedings on welfare grounds in which the paramountcy principle had been applied. It is also significant that in *L v UK*, which also concerned Children Act 1989 proceedings, the court stated that it concurred with the importance of the welfare of the child in cases concerning children.

It would be tempting to conclude in absolute terms, particularly having regard to *Scott v UK* and *L v UK*, that there is no difference of approach between Art. 8 of the Convention and the domestic law's requirement that the welfare of the child is the paramount consideration. None the less, the Convention does establish rights, albeit rights subject to justifiable interference, which are not expressed in domestic law. As far as protection of the welfare of the child is concerned, however, to the extent that any distinction can be made out between Convention case-law and domestic law, it appears to be a distinction without a difference. It seems more than likely that, even if persuaded that there is a difference between Convention and domestic law, family courts in the future will hold that the requirement that the welfare of the child be the court's paramount consideration is consistent with Convention case-law, well within the margin of appreciation permitted to national authorities under Art. 8(2), and therefore compatible with the right to respect for family life.

Question

The prediction was accurate: see *Payne v Payne*, p. 639 below. Do you think the distinction between the terms of the convention and the requirements s. 1(1) of the Children Act 1989 is a distinction without a difference?

12.2.3 More about residence

We pause on the issue of residence in order to say a little about shared residence orders.

Re D (children) (shared residence orders)
[2001] 1 FCR 147, [2001] 1 FLR 495, [2001] Fam Law 183

The father and mother had married in 1986. There were three children of the marriage aged 13, 11 and 9 years. The marriage broke down in 1995. The pattern was quickly established of the children living with the mother, who obtained sole residence orders, but having very substantial contact with their father. There was an exceptionally high level of animosity between the parties, with frequent court appearances concerning child matters. The father complained that he had difficulty in gaining information about the children's education and medical treatment. The father brought an application to determine the contact schedule for 2000/01, for joint residence and for a prohibited steps order, to prevent the mother causing third parties to withhold information about the children from him. The judge found that the mother was using the sole residence order as a weapon in the war with the father. The judge considered the authorities and decided that the making of a shared residence order was a matter for his discretion. As a consequence, he ordered shared residence which he expected to reduce the conflict between the parties. The mother appealed on the ground that a shared residence order was not appropriate as there was no evidence of exceptional circumstances or that shared residence would be a positive benefit to the children.

Hale LJ [summarised the facts and then discussed the issue of shared residence]:
21. It may be helpful to go back to basics. Before the Children Act 1989 there was a Court of Appeal authority in *Riley v Riley* [1986] 2 FLR 429, to the effect that a shared residence order, which had been made and worked comparatively well in that case for five years, should never have been made at all. It is clear, as the court appreciated in the later cases, that the intent of the Act was to change that decision.
22. The background to the 1989 Act provision lies in the Law Commission's Working Paper No 96, Review of Child Law: Custody published in 1986, on custody and the Law Commission's Report, Review of Child Law: Guardianship and Custody (Law Com No 172),

published in 1988, on guardianship and custody. If I may summarise the basic principles proposed, the first was that each parent with parental responsibility should retain their equal and independent right, and their responsibility, to have information and make appropriate decisions about their children. If, of course, the parents were not living together it might be necessary for the court to make orders about their future, but those orders should deal with the practical arrangements for where and how the children should be living rather than assigning rights as between the parents.

23. A cardinal feature was that when children are being looked after by either parent that parent needs to be in a position to take the decisions that have to be taken while the parent is having their care; that is part of care and part of responsibility. Parents should not be seeking to interfere with one another in matters which are taking place while they do not have the care of the children. They cannot, of course, take decisions which are incompatible with a court order about the children. But the object of the exercise should be to maintain flexible and practical arrangements wherever possible.

24. Then dealing with residence orders the Commission said (Law Com No 172, para 4.12):

'Apart from the effect on the other parent, which has already been mentioned, the main difference between a residence order and a custody order is that the new order should be flexible enough to accommodate a much wider range of situations. In some cases, the child may live with both parents even though they do not share the same household. It was never our intention to suggest that children should share their time more or less equally between their parents. Such arrangements will rarely be practicable, let alone for the children's benefit. However, the evidence from the United States is that where they are practicable they can work well and we see no reason why they should be actively discouraged. None of our respondents shared the view expressed in a recent case [Riley's case] that such an arrangement, which had been working well for some years, should never have been made. More commonly, however, the child will live with both parents but spend more time with one than the other. Examples might be where he spends term time with one and holidays with the other, or two out of three holidays from boarding school with one and the third with the other. It is a far more realistic description of the responsibilities involved in that sort of arrangement to make a residence order covering both parents rather than a residence order for one and a contact order for the other. Hence we recommend that where the child is to live with two (or more) people who do not live together, the order may specify the periods during which the child is to live in each household. The specification may be general rather than detailed and in some cases may not be necessary at all.'

25. It is for those reasons that s 8(1) of the Act defines 'a residence order' as 'an order settling the arrangements to be made as to the person with whom a child is to live'.

26. 'Person' of course includes 'persons' on ordinary principles of statutory construction. It is, therefore, an order about where the children are to live. Section 11(4) of the 1989 Act specifically provides:

'Where a residence order is made in favour of two or more persons who do not themselves all live together, the order may specify the periods during which the child is to live in the different households concerned.'

27. Not long after the 1989 Act came into force in October 1991 the matter came before the Court of Appeal, on 1 December 1992, in *Re H*, Purchas LJ said:

'That such an order [which he referred to as a joint residence order] is open to the court, as has been said in the judgment of Cazalet, J., is clear from the provisions of s. 11(4) of the Children Act 1989, as was indicated during the debate on the Bill by the Lord Chancellor. But, at the same time, it must be an order which would rarely be made and would depend upon exceptional circumstances.' (See [1993] 1 FCR 671 at 682-683.)

28. He went on to refer to Riley's case.

29. The matter next came before the Court of Appeal on 3 February 1994, in *A v A (minors)*; Butler-Sloss LJ (as she then was) said:

'Miss Moulder, representing the father, accepts that the conventional order still is that there would be residence to one parent with contact to the other parent. It must be demonstrated that there is positive benefit to the child concerned for a s. 11(4) order to be made, and such positive benefit must be demonstrated in the light of the s.1 checklist : The usual order that would be made in any case where it is necessary to make an order is that there will be residence to one parent and a contact order to the other parent. Consequently, it will be unusual to make a shared residence order. But the decision whether to make such a shared residence order is always in the discretion of the Judge on the special facts of the individual case. [I suspect that when My Lady used the word "special" she meant "particular".] It is for him alone to make that decision. However, a shared residence order would, in my view, be unlikely to be made if there were concrete issues still arising between the parties which had not been resolved, such as the amount of contact, whether it should be staying or visiting contact or another issue such as education, which were muddying the waters and which were creating difficulties between the parties which reflected the way in which the children were moving from one parent to the other in the contact period.' (See [1995] 1 FCR 91 at 100.)

30. She went on to say:

'If a child, on the other hand, has a settled home with one parent and substantial staying contact with the other parent, which has been settled, long-standing and working well, or if there are future plans for sharing the time of the children between two parents where all the parties agree and where there is no possibility of confusion in the mind of the child as to where the child will be and the circumstances of the child at any time, this may be, bearing in mind all the other circumstances, a possible basis for a shared residence order, if it can be demonstrated that there is a positive benefit to the child.'

31. It is quite clear that in those words my Lady was moving matters on from any suggestion, which is not in the legislation, that these orders require exceptional circumstances. She was also recognising that it stands to reason that if it has not yet been determined where the children are to live, how much contact there is to be, or whether or not there is to be staying contact with the parent with whom they are not spending most of their time, then there could not be a shared residence order, because that would be an order that the children were to live with both parents.

32. If, on the other hand, it is either planned or has turned out that the children are spending substantial amounts of their time with each of their parents then, as both the Law Commission and my Lady indicated in the passages that I have quoted it may be an entirely appropriate order to make. For my part, I would not add any gloss on the legislative provisions, which are always subject to the paramount consideration of what is best for the children concerned.

33. This case is one in which, as the judge said, the arrangements have been settled for some considerable time. The children are, in effect, living with both of their parents. They have homes with each of them. They appear to be coping extremely well with that. I accept entirely what we have been told by the mother today, that she would never seek to turn the children against their father, because she herself so loves her own father that she could not possibly do that. It is greatly to her credit that her children have been able to maintain such a very strong and good relationship with both of their parents. Of course, it is to the father's credit as well that he has remained as dedicated to their interests as he has.

34. In those circumstances it seems to me that there is indeed a positive benefit to these children in those facts being recognised in the order that the court makes. There is no detriment or disrespect to either parent in that order. It simply reflects the reality of these children's lives. It was entirely appropriate for the judge to make it in this case and neither party should feel that they have won or lost as a result. I would, therefore, dismiss the appeal.

Questions

(i) Do you think there might be a connection between the use of shared residence orders and the so-called 'non-intervention' principle (see below)?

(ii) What do you think is the difference between (a) a shared residence order specifying that a child is to live with the mother during the week and with dad at the weekend and (b) a residence order in favour of the mother together with a contact order stating that the child is to have staying contact with the father at the weekend?

(iii) How would the practical arrangement reflected by either of those two orders interact with the Child Support Act 1991, as amended?

(iv) In the light of the recent research evidence (p. 579, above), do you think that there was 'wisdom' in the earlier decisions such as *Riley*?

(iii) What is the difference between a shared residence order and the pre-Children Act joint custody order? (Look at *Re A (children) (shared residence)* [2001] EWCA Civ 1795, [2002] 1 FCR 177.)

12.2.4 More about contact

Eekelaar (1973) was inclined to describe access as one of the few remaining 'rights' of parenthood, but now we would more readily describe it as the right of the child. We have seen in the first section of this chapter how divided are academic views about the benefits and importance of contact in different situations. The following case sets out the courts' approach:

Re H (minors) (access)
[1992] 1 FLR 148, [1992] Fam Law 152, Court of Appeal

The parents married in 1980 and had two daughters, born in 1984 and 1986. They separated in June 1987. The children had regular contact with their father until November 1987 when the mother stopped it because one of them had been upset by the father's remark that they might come to live with him. The father took no immediate action, but in March 1989 he applied for access and his parents joined in the application. It was refused in May 1990. The father applied again early in 1991. This was again refused and the father appealed.

Balcombe LJ: ... in most cases, by the time the matter comes to be decided by the court, it is more than likely that access has ceased because (as in this case) the custodial parent has taken the unilateral decision (whether rightly or wrongly matters not for this purpose) to terminate access to the non-custodial parent who then applies for access. ... Judge Heald said:

'... I am not asked to try that issue whether access should cease, access has ceased for a period now of over 3 years. What I am being asked to do is to reintroduce access.'

... He then continued:

'Now, quite clearly, the actual reintroduction on the first occasion may be somewhat upsetting for a child, but one has to consider it from the child's point of view. Is there anything positive to be gained by reintroducing access to the father at the present time?'

...

The judge says, in effect, that they can have contact with their father by writing and continues:

'... but the actual meeting of them is, of course, an upsetting experience. And I am by no means satisfied that contact access is of benefit in the circumstances in this case where there has been no access for such a long period. ...'

It seems to me that [counsel] is correct in her submission that Judge Heald applied the wrong test in this case and he should have asked himself the question: are there here any cogent reasons why this father should be denied access to his children?; or, putting it another way: are there any cogent reasons why these two children should be denied the opportunity of access to their natural father?

Accordingly, in my judgment, the decision to which Judge Heald came was wrong, and this court should set aside his order. The question then arises, what order should be made in its place? ... There must be an introductory period and, in the meantime, the court below should have the benefit of a welfare officer's report to indicate how access has gone – whether it has been successful or not.

I would propose three periods of visiting access between now and Christmas, in circumstances which will enable the welfare officer to observe the reaction of the children to access. A report should then be prepared, directed to the question of how access has taken place – whether it has been successful or not – and its future development. The matter should then be referred back to the Nottingham County Court as early in the new year as is possible.
Appeal allowed.

Sometimes face-to-face, or 'direct', contact is not possible:

Re O (contact: imposition of conditions)
[1995] 2 FLR 124, [1995] Fam Law 541, Court of Appeal

The parents did not marry but lived together for three and a half years, separating in July 1992. Their son was born in November 1992. The father undertook not to pester or molest the mother, and was punished for breaking that undertaking. Early on, the father made clear his wish to have contact with his son and the mother made clear her intention to resist this. There were orders for contact at a contact centre but the child became upset. The court welfare officer's view was that contact would only work if the mother was prepared to take part until the boy became acquainted with his father. An order was made for indirect contact with conditions that the mother send photographs every three months, inform the father if the child began at nursery or playgroup and send copies of all reports on his progress, inform the father of any significant illness and send copies of all medical reports, accept delivery of cards and presents from the father, read and show them to the child and give him any present. The mother objected to these conditions because she was not prepared to have any contact with the father.

Sir Thomas Bingham MR: ... It may perhaps be worth stating in a reasonably compendious way some very familiar but none the less fundamental principles. First of all, and overriding all else as provided in s. 1(1) of the 1989 Act, the welfare of the child is the paramount consideration of any court concerned to make an order relating to the upbringing of a child. It cannot be emphasised too strongly that the court is concerned with the interests of the mother and the father only insofar as they bear on the welfare of the child.

Secondly, where parents of a child are separated and the child is in the day-to-day care of one of them, it is almost always in the interests of the child that he or she should have contact with the other parent. The reason for this scarcely needs spelling out. It is, of course, that the separation of parents involves a loss to the child, and it is desirable that that loss should so far as possible be made good by contact with the non-custodial parent, that is the parent in whose day-to-day care the child is not. ...

Thirdly, the court has power to enforce orders for contact, which it should not hesitate to exercise where it judges that it will overall promote the welfare of the child to do so. I refer in this context to the judgment of the President of the Family Division in *Re W (A Minor) (Contact)* [1994] 2 FLR 441 at p. 447H, where the President said:

'However, I am quite clear that a court cannot allow a mother, in such circumstances, simply to defy the order of the court which was, and is, in force, that is to say that there should be reasonable contact with the father. That was indeed made by consent as I have already observed. Some constructive step must be taken to permit and encourage the boy to resume contact with his father.'

...

Fourthly, cases do, unhappily and infrequently but occasionally, arise in which a court is compelled to conclude that in existing circumstances an order for immediate direct contact should not be ordered, because so to order would injure the welfare of the child. In *Re D (A Minor) (Contact: Mother's Hostility)* [1993] 2 FLR 1 at p.7G, Waite LJ said:

'It is now well settled that the implacable hostility of a mother towards access or contact is a factor which is capable, according to the circumstances of each particular case, of supplying a cogent reason for departing from the general principle that a child should grow up in the knowledge of both his parents. I see no reason to think that the judge fell into any error of principle in deciding, as he clearly did on the plain interpretation of his judgment, that the mother's present attitude towards contact puts D at serious risk of major emotional harm if she were to be compelled to accept a degree of contact to the natural father against her will.'

I simply draw attention to the judge's reference to a serious risk of major emotional harm. The courts should not at all readily accept that the child's welfare will be injured by direct contact. Judging that question the court should take a medium-term and long-term view of the child's development and not accord excessive weight to what appear likely to be short-term or transient problems. Neither parent should be encouraged or permitted to think that the more intransigent, the more unreasonable, the more obdurate and the more unco-operative they are, the more likely they are to get their own way. Courts should remember that in these cases they are dealing with parents who are adults, who must be treated as rational adults, who must be assumed to have the welfare of the child at heart, and who have once been close enough to each other to have produced the child. It would be as well if parents also were to bear these points in mind.

Fifthly, in cases in which, for whatever reason, direct contact cannot for the time being be ordered, it is ordinarily highly desirable that there should be indirect contact so that the child grows up knowing of the love and interest of the absent parent with whom, in due course, direct contact should be established. This calls for a measure of restraint, common sense and unselfishness on the part of both parents. If the absent parent deluges the child with presents or writes long and obsessive screeds to the child, or if he or she uses his or her right to correspond to criticise or insult the other parent, then inevitably those rights will be curtailed. The object of indirect contact is to build up a relationship between the absent parent and the child, not to enable the absent parent to pursue a feud with the caring parent in a manner not conducive to the welfare of the child.

The caring parent also has reciprocal obligations. If the caring parent puts difficulties in the way of indirect contact by withholding presents or letters or failing to read letters to a child who cannot read, then such parent must understand that the court can compel compliance with its orders; it has sanctions available and no residence order is to be regarded as irrevocable. It is entirely reasonable that the parent with the care of the child should be obliged to report on the progress of the child to the absent parent, for the obvious reason that an absent parent cannot correspond in a meaningful way if unaware of the child's concerns, or of where the child goes to school, or what it does when it gets there, or what games it plays, and so on. Of course judges must not impose duties which parents cannot realistically be expected to perform, and it would accordingly be absurd to expect, in a case where this was the case, a semi-literate parent to write monthly reports. But some means of communication, directly or indirectly, is essential if indirect contact is to be meaningful, and if the welfare of the child is not to suffer.

...

The sixth submission in the skeleton reads:

'The court had no power to compel the mother to send photographs, medical reports and school reports to the father when she was unwilling to do so.'

Sections 8 and 11(7) of the Children Act 1989 are given as authority for that proposition. In my view they provide no such authority. The court has ample power to compel the mother to send photographs, medical reports and school reports in order to promote meaningful contact between the father and the child, which would almost certainly wither and die if the father received no information about the child's progress. It is in my view plain that the court does have power under these sections as a necessary means of facilitating contact. ...
Appeal dismissed.

Questions

(i) There is no hint in this, or any recent case, that it was relevant that the parents had not married one another: should there have been?

(ii) No mention is made of a parental responsibility order. Look back at pp. 562: should there have been?

(iii) In what circumstances would you consider that a parent's 'implacable hostility' to contact was justified?

Psychologist Kevin Hewitt makes a few suggestions in 'Divorce and Parental Disagreement' (1996):

In my own exposure (both as expert witness and as therapist) to the problems of children of divorced or separated parents, I have come across several cases where it seems that it is contact with the absent parent which appears to have become the paramount consideration, rather than what is in the best interests of the child. Although, generally speaking, contact with the absent parent is usually of value to the child, there are also cases which really do challenge and question whether or not any contact at all is in the child's best interests (for example non-resident parents who repeatedly break promises about when contact will occur; parents who use contact to expose the child to further hostility about the resident parent; parents who use contact as a means of winning a battle, rather than having the child's needs at heart once contact is finally obtained; parents who are frankly abusive to the child or expose the child to abuse of the mother as a result of contact). There are also situations where it seems that applications for contact are being used to perpetuate contact between the non-resident and the resident parent, perhaps, in the context of a perpetuation of some pre-existing power struggle in their relationship.

The courts have struggled with this dilemma: when the residential parent is opposed to contact, how can the court discern whether or not contact should nevertheless be ordered? The problem is particularly acute where there has been violence in the family, and by the late 1990s considerable concern had been voiced about cases where contact had been ordered in the face, not so much of hostility, as of well-founded fear. Felicity Kaganas and Shelley Day Sclater sum up the concern, and some of the developments, in 'Contact and Domestic Violence – the Winds of Change?' (2000):

In recent years there has been growing concern about the ways in which contact disputes are managed by *professionals* and decided by courts in cases involving domestic violence. This concern has developed as a result of an accumulating body of social scientific research about violence to mothers and children. In particular, researchers have suggested that separation and divorce may lead to an escalation of violence. Also, there is research drawing links between woman abuse and child abuse. Two major research studies by the research team led by Marianne Hester and Lorraine Radford highlighted the plight of those mothers and children who were expected to participate in contact arrangements despite the violence or abuse perpetrated by non-resident fathers (Hester and Radford *Domestic Violence and Child Contact Arrangements in England and Denmark* (Policy Press, 1996), and pointed to a number of deficiencies in professional practice in dealing with such cases (Hester, Pearson and Radford *Domestic Violence: A national survey of court welfare and voluntary sector mediation practice* (Policy Press, 1997). Both the legal process and mediation have been criticised as, at best, failing to meet the safety needs of women and children and, at worst, as perpetuating the abuse (see Piper and Kaganas 'Family Law Act 1996, Section 1(d) – how will 'they' know there is a risk of violence?' [1997] CFLQ 269; Kaganas and Piper 'Divorce and Domestic Violence' in Day Sclater and Piper (eds) *Undercurrents of Divorce* (Ashgate, 1999); Anderson *Contact Between Children and Violent Fathers: In Whose Best Interests?* (ROW, 1997); Smart and Neale 'Arguments Against Virtue – Must Contact be Enforced?' [1997] Fam Law 332; and Neale and Smart '"Good" and "Bad" Lawyers? Struggling in the Shadow of the New Law' [1997] 19 JSWFL 377). ...

... [M]others who oppose contact have been designated as 'implacably hostile'. During the 1990s, the courts took an increasingly dim view of such mothers. In *Re D (A Minor) (Contact: Mother's Hostility)* [1993] 2 FLR 1, at p. 7, while it was said to be 'well settled' that the implacable hostility of a mother towards contact was a factor that was capable of supplying a cogent reason for departing from the general principle that a child should grow up in the knowledge of both parents, the court made it clear where the mother's duty lay. It accepted that the mother's attitude to contact might, if contact were foisted on her, put the child at risk of emotional harm. However, the judge expressed the wish that she would come to realise the importance to the child of his father. Subsequent decisions have shown the courts willing to go beyond expressions of disapproval and attempts to persuade mothers; instead they have imposed coercive and punitive measures in the name of children's welfare. ...

The Winds of Change?
The first intimation of change came with the judgment of Hale J in *Re D (Contact: Reasons for Refusal)* [1997] 2 FLR 48. In that case the Court of Appeal dismissed an appeal by a father against a refusal of an order for direct contact, accepting that he posed a risk to the child, whether directly or indirectly through harm to the mother. Importantly, Hale J considered that the term 'implacable hostility' was sometimes misleadingly applied to cases where the mother's fears were 'genuine and rationally held'. Then, in *Re P (Contact: Discretion)* [1998] 2 FLR 696, Wilson J adopted a three-fold analysis of 'hostility' cases according to which 'rational' grounds for hostility might warrant a denial of contact. Even in the absence of 'rational' reasons, contact might be refused if, in the light of the mother's hostility, it could create a serious risk of emotional harm for the child. And, in cases where there are sound arguments both for and against contact the mother's hostility itself could, said Wilson J, prove decisive.

Subsequent reported decisions, particularly those of Wall J in the Family Division, also reveal an emerging tendency to treat the fears of abused mothers seriously.

The leading case is now the following, generally referred to as '*Re L*':

Re L (a child) (contact: domestic violence); Re V (a child) (contact: domestic violence); Re M (a child) (contact: domestic violence); Re H (children) (contact: domestic violence)

[2001] Fam 268, [2000] 4 All ER 609, [2001] 2 WLR 339, [2000] 2 FCR 404, [2000] 2 FLR 334, Court of Appeal (Civil Division)

Dame Elizabeth Butler-Sloss P: These four appeals on issues arising out of contact applications have certain features in common. In each case a father's application for direct contact has been refused by the circuit judge against a background of domestic violence between the spouses or partners. We are grateful to Wall J, the Chairman of the Children Act Sub-Committee of the Advisory Board on Family Law, for permission to look at their report on parental contact in domestic violence cases and their recommendations recently presented to the Lord Chancellor and now published (see The Advisory Board on Family Law Children Act Sub-Committee: A Report to the Lord Chancellor on the Question of Parental Contact in Cases where there is Domestic Violence (12 April 2000)). At our request, the Official Solicitor acted as amicus curiae in each case and we are most grateful to him for instructing Dr JC Sturge, consultant child psychiatrist in consultation with Dr Glaser, consultant child psychiatrist to provide a joint report and to advise on the four appeals and to Mr Posnansky QC, on behalf of the Official Solicitor, for the helpful arguments addressed to us. We heard the four cases together and reserved judgment in each case. I propose to comment on the report on domestic violence (the report), and the expert psychiatric evidence (the psychiatric report), presented to us before turning to the facts of each appeal.

THE REPORT

The report by the Children Act Sub-Committee underlined the importance of the question of domestic violence in the context of parental contact to children. Domestic violence takes many forms and should be broadly defined. The perpetrator may be female as well as male. Involvement may be indirect as well as direct. There needs to be greater awareness of the effect of domestic violence on children, both short-term and long-term, as witnesses as well as victims and also the impact on the residential parent. An outstanding concern of the court should be the nature and extent of the risk to the child and to the residential parent and that proper arrangements should be put in place to safeguard the child and the residential parent from risk of further physical or emotional harm. In cases where domestic violence is raised as a reason for refusing or limiting contact, the report makes it clear that the allegations ought to be addressed by the court at the earliest opportunity and findings of fact made so as to establish the truth or otherwise of those allegations and decide upon the likely effect, if any, those findings could have on the court's decision on contact...

THE PSYCHIATRIC REPORT

Drs Sturge and Glaser in their joint report to this court had the opportunity to see the responses to the Sub-Committee consultation paper and to read the report and recommendations. Their psychiatric report was read and approved by a number of other consultant child psychiatrists and incorporates the views of a distinguished group of consultants. We are extremely grateful to them for their wise advice. [For the substance of the report, see p. 604, below.]
...

GENERAL COMMENTS

There are however a number of general comments I wish to make on the advice given to us. The family judges and magistrates need to have a heightened awareness of the existence of and consequences (some long-term) on children of exposure to domestic violence between their parents or other partners. There has, perhaps, been a tendency in the past for courts not to tackle allegations of violence and to leave them in the background on the premise that they were matters affecting the adults and not relevant to issues regarding the children. The general principle that contact with the non-resident parent is in the interests of the child may sometimes have discouraged sufficient attention being paid to the adverse effects on children living in the household where violence has occurred. It may not necessarily be widely appreciated that violence to a partner involves a significant failure in parenting – failure to protect the child's carer and failure to protect the child emotionally.

In a contact or other section 8 application, where allegations of domestic violence are made which might have an effect on the outcome, those allegations must be adjudicated upon and found proved or not proved. It will be necessary to scrutinise such allegations which may not always be true or may be grossly exaggerated. If however there is a firm basis for finding that violence has occurred, the psychiatric advice becomes very important. There is not, however, nor should there be, any presumption that, on proof of domestic violence, the offending parent has to surmount a prima facie barrier of no contact. As a matter of principle, domestic violence of itself cannot constitute a bar to contact. It is one factor in the difficult and delicate balancing exercise of discretion. The court deals with the facts of a specific case in which the degree of violence and the seriousness of the impact on the child and on the resident parent have to be taken into account. In cases of proved domestic violence, as in cases of other proved harm or risk of harm to the child, the court has the task of weighing in the balance the seriousness of the domestic violence, the risks involved and the impact on the child against the positive factors, if any, of contact between the parent found to have been violent and the child. In this context, the ability of the offending parent to recognise his past conduct, be aware of the need to change and make genuine efforts to do so, will be likely to be an important consideration. Wall J in *Re M (minors) (contact: violent parent)* [1999] 2 FCR 56 at 68-69 suggested that often in cases where domestic violence had been found, too little weight had been given to the need for the father to change. He suggested that the father should demonstrate that he was a fit person to exercise contact and should show a track record of proper behaviour. Assertions, without evidence to back it up, may well not be sufficient.

In expressing these views I recognise the danger of the pendulum swinging too far against contact where domestic violence has been proved. It is trite but true to say that no two child cases are exactly the same. The court always has the duty to apply s 1 of the Children Act 1989 that the welfare of the child is paramount and, in considering that welfare, to take into account all the relevant circumstances, including the advice of the medical experts as far as it is relevant and proportionate to the decision in that case. It will also be relevant in due course to take into account the impact of art 8 of the Convention for the Protection of Human Rights and Fundamental Freedoms (the European Convention on Human Rights) (Rome, 4 November 1950; TS 71 (1953); Cmd 8969) on a decision to refuse direct contact....

The President went on to consider the first appeal:

Appeal in *Re L (a child) (contact: domestic violence)*

The child T is a little girl born on 29 June 1998 and is still under two years old. She lives with her mother. The parents did not marry or cohabit. The father was and remains married with a child by that marriage. T was registered in the father's name but is now known by her mother's name. There is no issue on the change of name. Contact ceased soon after the birth of the child. The father applied for a parental responsibility order and contact to the child. The applications came before Judge Allweis on 29 September 1999. He heard evidence of violence alleged by the mother both before and during the latter part of her pregnancy which included slapping, hitting her with an umbrella and trying to strangle her which caused bruising to her neck. An incident occurred when the baby was four weeks old. She was sitting naked on the bed feeding the child. The father pulled her hair and using foul language threatened to cut it off with scissors he was holding. He then cut off her pubic hair with the scissors. She was in tears and felt shaken, scared and degraded. She decided to leave him and did so three weeks later. On that occasion he collected her from her mother's home. He told him she wanted to stay with her mother because the child had colic. She locked herself into the bathroom and he kicked the door open and grabbed her and the baby in her baby seat so she felt she had to go with him. The next day she went to the police. She then received threatening telephone calls including threats to remove T. The police went to the mother's home on 19 August 1998 which they found had been vandalised and rendered uninhabitable. The father completely denied the violence and the vandalism of the mother's home. He continued to deny the violence at the contact hearing and on appeal. The judge gave judgment on 4 October 1999 and said that the allegations amounted to a catalogue of sadistic violence. He found the mother's account of violence to be true. He said:

'... this is a man who has mood swings and a temper ... I would add this: that a father who systematically went through and damaged partner's home, as he did, has a very real anger and control problem. It indicates a cruel streak, which suggests a significant psychological problem ...'

He then considered the mother's opposition to contact:

'I conclude that the mother's opposition to contact is implacable but reasonable. Her fear is genuine and based on rational grounds, namely actual violence and a genuine fear of him, and that [T] will in time witness violence. I believe that direct contact, if ordered, would trigger enormous anxiety which would affect the mother ... The mother's attitude towards contact would put [T] at serious risk of major emotional harm if she were to be compelled to accept a degree of contact to the father against her will, and indeed in time that heightened anxiety would be conveyed to the child . . .'

He made a residence order to the mother. He ordered indirect contact and made a family assistance order to help set up the indirect contact and dismissed the father's application for a parental responsibility order and granted permission to appeal. The father appeals to this court on both issues and raises arts 8 and 14 of the European Convention on Human Rights.

On the issue of contact, the judge found the mother's opposition to contact to be reasonable and that her fear of him was genuine and based on actual violence and that T would in time witness violence. ...

The risks to the child were obvious and the father, in refusing to face up to them, was clearly unable to reduce those risks. In her able submissions to the court, Miss de Haas QC, on behalf of the father, made the point that the mother was white and the father was black and, since the child was of mixed race, she needed to understand her roots and establish her identity, which would best be achieved by direct contact. In the circumstances of this case, in my view, it would certainly be possible to achieve that important objective by indirect contact. The judge applied the proper principles and the decision to which he came was not only well within his exercise of discretion, but on the facts of this case, clearly right.

Although a decision on the point is not yet strictly relevant, there was no failure, in my view, by the judge, under art 8(1), to have proper respect for family life. ... The observation by the Court in *Johanssen v Norway* (1996) 23 EHRR 33 is particularly apposite to this appeal. The Court said:

'In particular . . . the parent cannot be entitled under Article 8 of the Convention to have such measures taken as would harm the child's health and development.'

In the present appeal, there are very real risks of emotional harm that require the court to protect the child. I would dismiss the appeal on the issue of contact.

The report by Claire Sturge and Danya Glaser referred to by Dame Elizabeth Butler-Sloss, 'Contact and Domestic Violence – the Experts' Report' (2000), is worth quoting at some length:

For the cases *Re L (Contact: Domestic Violence); Re V (Contact: Domestic Violence); Re M (Contact: Domestic Violence); Re H (Contact: Domestic Violence)* [2000] 2 FLR 334 (and see p. 603 (above)) we were asked, by the Official Solicitor, to prepare a report giving a child and adolescent opinion on, amongst other matters, the implications of domestic violence for contact. We were asked to address a series of questions which we will take in order as headings. We approach this task with humility as much of what we say is self-evident, is clearly already part of the judiciary's thinking as is illustrated in so many judgments, and as we cite a literature that is well known to many in the legal profession involved with child care. ...

(1) What are the Psychiatric Principles of Contact Between the Child and the Non-Residential Parent?
The principles that guide the advice of child psychiatrists and psychologists are drawn from developmental and psychological knowledge, theory and research.

Knowledge base
These draw particularly on the following:

(i) Development: knowledge of children's cognitive, social and emotional development
The following needs of children have particular relevance to issues of contact.
- There are particular needs at particular times with critical times for forming basic relationships.
- There is the need for warmth and approval and the development of positive self-esteem.
- There is the need to increasingly explore and develop independence from a secure base.
- There is the need for a sense of security, stability, continuity and 'belongingness'.
- Cognitive development affects children's ability to remember and to hold people in their minds; it affects their ability to understand situations.

(ii) Interactional issues: knowledge, theory and research on such aspects are:
- attachment;
- relationships and interactions with carers, parents, siblings and the extended family;

- effects of loss when families are disrupted;
- effects of adverse care;
- the child's interaction with the environment; questions of resilience and vulnerability;
- significance of cultural factors.

All of the above hold different relevance for different children at different ages. A young child experiencing loss through separation or trauma through exposure to violence will express his or her feelings through behaviour such as agitation, sleep disturbance and 'naughtiness' rather than any coherent account of what he or she is feeling and why.

Older children and adolescents may also act out their distress and confusion through their behaviour rather than expressing this directly. The more emotionally mature and well adjusted the girl or boy is, the more able (but not necessarily willing) he or she will be to put their feelings and wishes into words.

(iii) Innate factors

These are the factors brought into the situation by virtue of the child's own unique make-up – genetic and temperamental factors including the sex of the child. ...

Principles drawn from this knowledge base relating to contact

These are seen as core principles that should guide decisions whatever the nature of the case.

(i) We see the centrality of the child as all important. There will be tensions around the child because, in disputed cases, the parents will hold differing positions. The needs of the adult positions obscure and overwhelm the needs of the child but promoting the child's mental health remains the central issue.

Decisions about contact must be child-centred and relate to the specific child in his or her specific situation, now. Every child has different needs and these also alter with the different needs at different stages of development. The eventual plan for the child must be the one that best approximates to these needs.

(ii) To consider contact questions the purpose of any proposed contact must be overt and abundantly clear.

Contact can only be an issue where it has the potential for benefiting the child in some way. Defining in what way this might be will help guide decisions about whether there should be contact and also its nature, duration and frequency.

The different purposes of contact include:

- the sharing of information and knowledge; curiosity is healthy; sense of origin and roots contribute to the sense of identity which is also important as part of self-esteem;
- maintaining meaningful and beneficial relationships (or forming and building up relationships which have the potential for benefiting the child; this may be particularly relevant to infants);
- experiences that can be the foundations for healthy emotional growth and development; children benefit from being the special focus of love, attention and concern and of loving and being concerned;
- reparation of broken or problematic relationships;
- opportunities for reality testing for the child; children need to balance reality versus fantasy and idealisation versus denigration;
- facilitating the assessment of the quality of the relationship or contact – most relevant where a return to a particular parent is being considered;
- severing relationships, for example, goodbye meetings.

(iii) Decisions must involve a process of balancing different factors and the advantages and disadvantages of each. This includes contact versus no contact and whether to accept or go against the wishes of a child.

Fathers

Contact with fathers, as opposed to other family members of people with whom the child has a significant relationship, brings the following, in particular, to bear, although the general principles remain the same:

- the father's unique role in the creation of the child;
- the sharing of 50% of his or her genetic material;
- the history of his or her conception and the parental relationships;
- the consequent importance of the father in the child's sense of identity and value;
- the role of modelling a father can provide of the father's and male contribution to parenting and the rearing of children which will have relevance to the child's concepts of parental role models and his or her own choices about choosing partners and the sort of family life he or she aims to create.

(2)(i) What are the benefits of (a) direct and (b) indirect contact with the non-residential parent?

Benefits of contact

Potentially, these are all the benefits referred to above and depend on the age and development of the child, the individual characteristics of the child and his or her situation, which is the present situation but includes the impact on that situation of past experiences and events. Central to potential benefits are also the capacity of the parent concerned to understand and respond appropriately to his or her child's needs.

In summary, the benefits include the meeting of his or her needs for:
- warmth, approval, feeling unique and special to a parent;
- extending experiences and developing (or maintaining) meaningful relationships;
- information and knowledge;
- reparation of distorted relationships or perceptions.

By way of summary a dimensional diagram is attached in Appendix 2. Direct contact can meet one or more or all of these needs. ...

Indirect contact can only meet a much more limited number of needs, amongst these in particular, are:

(i)   experience of the continued interest of the absent parent which, in a very partial way, will meet the need to feel valued and wanted, ie is not rejected, by that parent;

(ii) knowledge and information about the absent parent;

(iii) the keeping open of the possibility of the development of the relationship, for example, when the child is older or has some specific need of that parent;

(iv) there may be some opportunity, through letters or phone calls, for reparation.

Much depends, particularly with small children, on the manner in which the indirect contact is managed by the resident parent. ...

(2)(ii) What are the risks of (a) direct and (b) indirect contact with the non-residential parent?

Direct contact

The overall risk is that of failing to meet and actually undermining the child's developmental needs or even causing emotional abuse and damage – directly through the contact or as a consequence of the contact.

Specifically, this includes:

(i) Escalating the climate of conflict around the child which will:
  - (a) undermine her or his general stability and sense of emotional well-being;
  - (b) inevitably result in tugs of loyalty and a sense of responsibility for the conflict (except in the smallest of babies);
  - (c) affect relationships between the child and the resident and the non-resident parent. It may, for example, result in extreme polarisation with enmeshment with the resident parent and rejection of the non-resident parent as a result of the child's efforts to reduce the conflictual situation.

(ii) Direct experiences within the contact:
  - (a) Abuse: physical or sexual, or emotional, see below; neglect; dangerous situations include those in which the parent has delusional beliefs at the time of contact, ie is acutely mentally ill or is under the influence of alcohol or drugs.
  - (b) Emotional abuse through the denigration of the child directly or the child's resident carer, through using the contact as a means of continuing or escalating the 'war' with the resident parent, for example, seeking derogatory information, engendering secrets, making derogatory remarks in an attempt to undermine the resident parent. ...
  - (c) Continuation of unhealthy relationships, for example, inappropriately dominant or bullying relationships, controlling relationships through subtly or blatantly maintaining (or initiating) fear or through other means (for example bribes, emotional blackmail). ...
  - (d) Undermining the child's sense of stability and continuity by deliberately or inadvertently setting different moral standards or standards of behaviour. Rules for the child may be very different with the contact parent and the child may be allowed to do quite different things which are normally forbidden. This can affect his or her understanding of right and wrong and/or given him or her the means to then challenge or defy the resident parent. ...
  - (e) Experiences lacking in endorsement of the child as a valued and individual person, for example, where little or no interest is shown in the child himself or herself. Contact where the contact parent is unable to consistently sustain the prioritisation of the child's needs.

    (f)   Unstimulating experiences which are lacking in interest, fun or in extending the child and his or her experiences.

(iii) Other:
    (a)   Continuation of unresolved situations, for example, where the child has a memory or belief about a negative aspect of the contact parent, for example, abuse, and where this is just left as if unimportant. ...
    (b)   Unreliable contact in which the child is frequently let down or feels rejected, unwanted and of little importance to the failing parent. This also undermines a child's need for predictability and stability. ...
    (c)   The child is continuing to attend contact against his or her ongoing wishes such that the child feels undermined as someone in his or her own right whose feelings are considered and heeded.
    (d)   All significantly difficult contact situations for the child where there is little potential and prospect for change, for example, wholly implacable situations, contact which is failing to prioritise the child's needs.
    (e)   The stress on the child, on his or her resident carer and on the situation as a whole of ongoing proceedings or frequently re-initiated proceedings, of periods of contact and then no contact on and off also need taking into account. ...

Indirect contact

The above apply only inasmuch as the non-resident parent is able to convey undermining and distorting messages through whatever indirect contact medium is agreed. Obviously, there is greatest scope for harm in telephone contact and least in vetted contact such as letters.

    Other risks are that of the non-resident parent, in abduction risk situations, using the child's communications to establish details about the child that could lead to identifying the child's home address, school or routines, or as ammunition in legal proceedings or simply in undermining the resident parent.

    In summary: in contested contact cases it is unlikely that the best contact situation for the child can be established – one which both parents support and in which the child's needs are consistently met. Hence the balancing act between the potential benefit versus detriment of contact.

(3) What weight is to be placed upon the following factors in children contact cases?

(i) Where there is a history of significant intra-familial violence and the child has had a negative experience of the non-residential parent, for example, witnessing an incident of intra-familial violence or threats to the mother

We take the term intra-familial violence to refer to inter-partner violence and not to other forms of domestic violence such as direct child abuse per se. The child may, of course, be abused in inter-partner violence – directly and physically or emotionally. Research indicates that children are affected as much by exposure to violence as to being involved in it. The ongoing fear and dread of it recurring is also emotionally very damaging. ...

    Secondly, we take the position that all children are affected by significant and repeated inter-partner violence, even if this is only indirect, ie the child is not directly involved. Awareness is all but inevitable and even without this there will be the aftermath of the violence and the distorted inter-partner relationships, communication and behaviours. The research is entirely consistent in showing deleterious effects on children of exposure to domestic violence.

    It needs to be noted that research in this area is all in relation to the effects on children of domestic violence and not to either the changing circumstances of that violence, for example, if the violent partner leaves the relationship and other factors in such situations (contribution of mother's behaviour to the violence, the further relationships she makes and her overall competence as a parent), nor to the question of how previously exposed children fare according to whether or not contact continues.

    Thus views in this area are based on the generality of the research on the ill-effects of such exposure and experience and using this in a common sense way to inform opinion. However, findings in relation to children's fear and dread ... and the experience of those treating children psychotherapeutically after exposure to domestic violence that the persecutory fears are deep-seated and persistent, indicate that even when children do not continue in that violent situation, emotional trauma continues to be experienced; the memories of the violence continue as persecutory images.

    The context of the overall situation is highly relevant to decision making. The contribution of psychiatric disorders to situations of domestic violence and emotional abuse must be considered. Such disorders will have put enormous pressures not only on the child but on the other parent.

Depression and delusional disorders are obvious examples but personality disorders may be most relevant in this context. Where such a personality disorder, for example a borderline personality disorder, affects interpersonal relationships both the relationship with the partner and the child are likely to have been marked by unstable and intense relations on an inter-personal level with extremes of feelings, anger problems and other behavioural problems – for example, jealousy and irrational ideas, threats or acts of self-harm and marked impulsivity. This will have added to the emotional abuse of the child and is likely to continue. The reinforcing effects on some such people of continuing the inter-personal battles will complicate and prolong legal proceedings and may lead to frequent re-applications. The continuing complex and intense on/off relationships so often seen in domestic violence may further undermine arrangements. The child needs protecting from all this.

It needs to be remembered that the most extreme form of domestic violence is murder where one partner (usually the man) kills the other. The fear that one of their parents might be killed during the violence is often a significant part of the trauma to the child.

Domestic violence is relevant in the following ways with regard to contact (and all relate to the general principles already set out).

(a)   There may be a continuing sense of fear of the violent parent by the child.

(b)   The child may have post-traumatic anxieties or symptoms which the proximity of the non-resident violent parent may re-arouse or perpetuate.

(c)   There may be a continuing awareness of the fear the violent parent arouses in the child's main carer.

(d)   There are likely to be all or many of the issues referred to under 'risks of direct contact', some of which may not be directly the responsibility of the violent parent, for example, the mother's or resident parent's reaction and post-traumatic symptoms in relation to the past violence.

(e)   There is the important, but largely neglected area, of the effects of such situations on children's own attitudes to violence, to forming 'parenting' relationships and to the role of fathers in such relationships and in caring for and protecting their children …

Put in moral terms what is the view about encouraging children to have relationships with fathers who have behaved criminally and in a way that specifically denigrates the mother and specifically undermines and distorts the caring and protective roles of parents? …

(f)   Direct physical abuse: parents who are violent to each other are more likely to be violent to their children. The same review mentioned above, taking the research together, puts the risks as between three and nine times greater than in non-violent families.

We are not in these questions asked to address the issue of the mother's part in any domestic violence which complicates the picture but less so if the decision that she is to be the main carer is already taken and if she has successively extricated herself from that and other violent relationships.

(ii) Where the child is adamant that he/she does not wish to see the parent or contemplate contact

Eekelaar has produced a helpful approach to assessing how to weight children's wishes (see Appendix 1). The following need to be accepted:

(i)   the child must be listened to and taken seriously;

(ii)   the age and understanding of the child are highly relevant;

(iii)   the child, and the younger and the more dependent, either for developmental or emotional reasons, if in a positive relationship with the resident parent will inevitably be influenced by:
- that parent's views;
- their wish to maintain her or his sense of security and stability within that household.

(iv)   Going against the child's wishes must involve the following.
- Indications that there are prospects of the child changing his or her view as a result of preparation work or the contact itself; for example, there is a history of meaningful attachment and a good relationship; the none-resident parent has child-centred plans as to how to help the child overcome his or her resistance; there are some indications of ambivalence such as an adamant statement of not wanting to see that parent accompanied by lots of positive memories and affect when talking of that parent.
- Consideration of the effects on the child of making a decision that appears to disregard their feelings/wishes. It is damaging to a child to feel he or she is forced to do something against his or her will and against his or her judgment if the child cannot see the sense of it.

(v)   Unreliable contact: see (2)(iii)(b) above.

(iii) Where there is an absence of a bond between the child and the parent with whom he or she does not live

The following need to be taken into account.

(i) The age and developmental level of the child: infants invoke and promote parenting behaviour towards them by their own behaviour and interactions. The interactions and experience of the carer of the infant and the infant of the carer are necessary to the formation of attachment and bonds (positive and significant relationships in either direction) between them. The lack of attachment or bonds in a small baby should not therefore in itself be seen as a reason for not promoting contact.

Toddlers and older children remain capable of forming bonds and attachments although these will be of different quality and type according to the situation. A strong bond for years with a single carer is likely to result in a greater resource for forming future strong bonds and relationships. However, if they remain with the longstanding 'attachment' parent new bonds are unlikely to become as strong or meaningful as the basic one.

In adolescence, other significant developmental issues come into the situation. In relation to an absent bond with the non-residential parent, the seeking of a clear and separate identity may lead to greater interest in a little-known biological parent. The introduction of contact may, at the same time, because of the adolescent's seeking of independence, add complications which undermine the 'main' placement (for example expressing a wish or leaving to live with the non-resident parent as an act of defiance towards the resident parent and his or her controls).

(ii) The question, perhaps, needs to be looked at the other way around. If there is a strong relationship, bond or attachment that is a good reason to continue and promote contact as failure to do so will be an emotional loss for the child and much more likely to be experienced as an abandonment or rejection.

Lack of such a bond means there is not that argument for furthering contact but it is not, in itself, a reason not to try to build a new relationship.

In this last situation, other considerations may come into play, such as other emotional investments of the child, for example, in a step-parent and what specifically the new relationship might add to the child's life and well-being.

In the event that there is no meaningful relationship between the child and non-residential parent and an established history of domestic violence with or without opposition to contact by the resident parent, there would need to be very good reason to embark on a plan of introducing direct contact and building up a relationship when the main evidence is of that non-residential parent's capacity for violence within relationships.

(iv) Where there is a case of Parental Alienation Syndrome

Parental Alienation Syndrome does not exist in the sense that it is:

- not recognised in either the American classification of mental disorders (DSMIV) or the international classification of disorders (ICD10);
- not generally recognised in our or allied child mental health specialities.

We do not consider it to be a helpful concept and consider that the sort of problems that the title of this disorder is trying to address is better thought of as implacable hostility. The essential and important difference is that the Parental Alienation Syndrome assumes a cause (seen as misguided or malign on the part of the resident parent) which leads to a prescribed intervention whereas the concept (which no one claims to be a 'syndrome') is simply a statement aimed at the understanding of particular situations but for which there is no single and prescribed solution, this depending on the nature and individuality of each case.

The basic concept in the Parental Alienation Syndrome is a uni-directional one as if such situations are a linear process when they are, in fact, dynamic and interactional with aspects of each parent's relationship to the other interacting to produce the difficult and stuck situation.

There is an elegant rebuttal of such a syndrome by the highly reputable Kathleen Faller and we fully agree with the thrust of her arguments (see 'The Parental Alienation Syndrome: What Is It and What Data Support It?' (1998) 3(2) *Child Maltreatment* 100).

The possible reasons for a resident parent taking a position of implacable hostility (by implication to the ex-partner as much as to contact) are as follows:

(a) A fully justified fear of harm or abduction resulting from any direct contact with the non-resident parent.

(b) A fear of violence or other threat and menace to herself if the non-resident parent has indirect contact to her through the child, ie it could lead to direct contact.

(c) Post-traumatic symptoms in the custodial parent which are acutely exacerbated by the prospect or the fact of contact.

(d) The aftermath of a relationship in which there was a marked imbalance in the power exercised by the two parents and where the mother fears she will be wholly undermined and become helpless and totally inadequate again if there is any channel of contact between herself and the ex-partner, even when that only involves the child. The child can be used as a weapon in such a bid to continue to hold power over the mother. As in (a), (b), and (c) above this can be a sequelae of domestic violence.

(e) Wholly biased hostility which is not based on real events or experience. This may be conscious and malign or perceived to be true. The latter encompass the full continuum from misperceptions and misunderstandings through overvalued ideas to delusional states. The former may result from a simple wish to wipe the slate clean and start again and can be seen after relationships that were initially highly romantic or idealised and for the breakdown of which the woman can only account for by vilifying the partner in order to avoid facing the possibility that the breakdown in the relationship was her failure and amounts to rejection.

It is in this last situation (e), in which there are often sexual abuse allegations emanating mainly from the resident carer, which particularly exercise experts and the courts as the fathers may be well-functioning, well-meaning and represent a real potential for a good relationship with the child.

The term 'implacable' is used here to describe the intensity and unchanging nature of the hostility and the fact that any amount of mediation is unlikely to result in an alteration in the hostility felt by the parent. It is important to note it is often two-way, ie the non-resident parent as the other way around.

It is more often not directly expressed or camouflaged as the non-resident parent has 'more to lose' by its being obviously stated.

Implacability makes no difference to the general principles outlined in this document although it increases the complexity and difficulties and the prospects of solution finding.

(4) In what circumstances should the court give consideration to a child having no direct contact with the non-residential parent?

The core question

In our experience the judiciary takes careful account of all the relevant factors and comes to decisions based on the individual needs of the child in question.

From all that is written above, it will be clear that we consider that there should be no automatic assumption that contact to a previously or currently violent parent is in the child's interests; if anything the assumption should be in the opposite direction and the case of the non-residential parent one of proving why he can offer something of such benefit not only to the child but to the child's situation (ie act in a way that is supportive to the child's situation with his or her resident parent and able to be sensitive to and respond appropriately to the child's needs), that contact should be considered. We would go as far as to suggest, acknowledging our limited knowledge of the law, a position in which a father (or mother in certain circumstances) who has been found to have been domestically violent to the child's carer should need to show positive grounds as to why, despite this, contact in the child's interests in order for an application to be even considered. There could be a requirement that that parent sets out how he proposes to help the child heal and recover from the damage done.

In these situations, it is unlikely that the conditions outlined in (2)(i) above will be met and that contact will be in the child's interests. Domestic violence involves a very serious and significant failure in parenting – failure to protect the child's carer and failure to protect the child emotionally (and in some cases physically – which meets any definition of child abuse).

Without the following we would see the balance of advantage and disadvantage as tipping against contact:

(a) some (preferably full) acknowledgement of the violence;

(b) some acceptance (preferably full if appropriate, ie the sole instigator of violence) of responsibility for that violence;

(c) full acceptance of the inappropriateness of the violence particularly in respect of the domestic and parenting context and of the likely ill-effects on the child;

(d) a genuine interest in the child's welfare and full commitment to the child, ie a wish for contact in which he is not making the conditions;

(e) a wish to make reparation to the child and work towards the child recognising the inappropriateness of the violence and the attitude to and treatment of the mother and helping the child to develop appropriate values and attitudes;

(f) an expression of regret and the showing of some understanding of the impact of their behaviour on their ex-partner in the past and currently;

(g) indications that the parent seeking contact can reliably sustain contact in all senses.

...

Other general comments

We would like to see greater creativity in addressing ways of resolving contact difficulties. For example:

- Overcoming fear and resistance where this appears to be ill-founded: some children can overcome their fears of seeing a parent if able to see them in a safe situation in which they are in control – for example, a one-way screen with an interviewer programmed by them interviewing the parent on the other side. The child can control what is explored and whether or not he or she wishes to enter the room to face the parent.

- Proxy contact where a trained person acts as the 'go-between' who can read and discuss correspondence and even meet with the child and parent separately to discuss issues that come up and convey messages or raise issues that one or other wants raised with the other.

- Identified resources to be set up or new services prepared to continue work where there are, have been or are likely to be contact difficulties after the conclusion of a court case – possibly mediation services, the new amalgamated child advocacy service or social services family centres. In addition to the sorts of approaches mentioned just above, the resident parent may need support and advice in relation to any contact ordered and there may be work to be done with the child.

- **Contact and supervision**
  We recognise the considerable problems in deciding whether or not to order supervised contact where this appears to be a reasonably safe way of maintaining or foregoing some sort of relationship. The difficulties include:

  - The quality of such experiences for a child (or parent) if this is continued over a long time. It is an abnormal situation, it is often disliked by the child both because of its artificiality and because of the restricted opportunities for interest, fun and stimulation within it; such arrangements often make the child (and parent) feel tense and ill at ease and may result in the child simply holding that parent responsible for their having to put up with it. This may result in further alienation and no real benefit to the child.

  - There is a lack of resources: good contact centres with good facilities and good supervision are scarce and by and large not available for long-term arrangements; it is expensive.

  - It is unlikely to lead to improvements in a parent's sensitivity or parenting skills or to lead to a situation where it becomes safe for the child to be alone with that parent.

  - There are a few situations where it might be considered if a time-frame is set. These are situations where change in the short-term is seen as likely, for example, where a parent is recovering from a mental illness, where a parent with learning difficulties is thought to be capable of improved input with a programme of work. Or where there is a therapeutic purpose to the contact – see below.

- **Specified types of contact**
  We see the issue of supervision as needing specifying in any order or agreement. The supervision of contact can be looked on as having the following specific purposes.

  (i) Safety from physical harm and emotional abuse: this requires a very high level of constant supervision and the superviser needs to be experienced enough and confident enough to immediately and firmly intervene if anything of concern arises.

  (ii) Checks on the fitness of the parent at the start of contact and/or the availability of a supervisor to support the child if needed: this requires an intermediate level of supervision. The superviser might simply meet the parent and spend a little time with the parent at the beginning of contact to check the parent is, for example, sober or free from obvious mental disturbance and, thereafter, be at a distance or in and out.

  (iii) Therapeutic purposes in the widest sense: the contact might need to be managed so that the child is supported in resolving issues with the parent which he or she wishes or needs to understand; or to provide an opportunity for a parent to apologise or in other ways make amends; or to discuss an ending to contact. In managed contact the superviser can play a role in guiding the parent and improving the quality of the interactions and the parenting.

  (iv) Support for the child: supervision provided to make the child feel more at ease or safe, for example, the presence of the other parent, another familiar person or a superviser. This can be included in (ii).

...

Appendix 1 – Contact

TABLE – DIMENSIONS OF POTENTIAL BENEFIT AND DETRIMENT OF CONTACT

Likelihood of beneficial contact	Dimension	Likelihood of detrimental contact	Purpose of contact
if relationship has significant meaning for the child	meaning of relationship	if relationship is of no significance to the child	to maintain or further develop a relationship
if it is good	quality of attachment	if it is poor	to provide continuity of sense of emotional well-being
yes	absence of conflict in the relationship*	no	to support the child and promote his interests
if opportunities are good	opportunities for reality testing	if opportunities are poor	to reduce distortions/effect repair and to enhance self-knowledge and identity
strong likelihood	likelihood of a good experience	unlikely	to extend the child's experience and sense of worth

*   This includes the absence of conflict in relation to those around the child, ie the child's placement/situation is supported.

Relevance to frequency

The frequency of contact and its length and nature should be a direct reflection of its purpose. The age of the child is also relevant. For example, there is a need for high levels of contact if it is to build up a relationship, lower levels if it is to maintain a relationship and intermittent if it is simply for the sharing of information.

Appendix 2 – Considering children's wishes and feelings

Eekelaar draws attention to the many practical difficulties such an approach encounters. There are difficulties due to:

- distinguishing between wishes and
- deeper feelings;
- statements influenced by a specific context;
- separating out the incidental or transitory;
- pressure from disputing adults;
- risk of being burdened with guilt;
- risk of receiving hostility from others;
- decision affected by information quality and provider bias;
- articulation affected by age and how they might think it will be received;
- whether they have promised someone what or not to say;
- whether they have support;
- where and how they are asked;
- where it is difficult to explain the alternatives to children.

Clause 116 of the Adoption and Children Bill now reads as follows:

116. Meaning of harm

In section 31 of the 1989 Act (care and supervision orders), at the end of the definition of 'harm' in sub-section (9) there is inserted 'including, for example, impairment suffered from seeing or hearing the ill-treatment of another'.

But if an order for contact is made, how can it be enforced? Court orders are normally enforced by committal; but the damaging effect of that upon the child concerned is only too obvious. Equally obvious is the frustration of the non-residential parent who feels that the court will not enforce the order it has made. This was one of the problems discussed in *Making Contact Work*, a report to the Lord Chancellor by the Children Act Sub-Committee of the Advisory Board on Family Law. The Sub-Committee reported on the results of its survey of individuals and organisations, and, in the extract quoted below, considered some alternatives to committal (note that where earlier cases and writings have referred to court welfare officers, this report now refers to CAFCASS; see p. 621 ff, below):

What alternative to committal to prison do you think there should be in a case where the court finds that contact is in the best interests of the child but is being irrationally frustrated by the residential parent? Should the court be given broader powers to deal with recalcitrant residential parents – for example to require them to attend parenting classes?

14.21 This is, we think, the most important question in this part of the Consultation Paper, and it was the question which produced a substantial number of suggestions. There was widespread support for the proposition that the Court should be given the power to impose a range of alternative options.

14.22 In our view the most constructive suggestions were those which proposed either community penalties, or the attendance by the person in contempt at parenting classes or meetings designed to persuade that person that the order should be obeyed. Professor Walker summed up a number of responses here when she said:

> Parenting education would be an obvious option here. Yes – courts should be given broader powers to refer parents to such classes. The general rule ought to be to find 'therapeutic' approaches to the problem and to support parents to work through difficulties, hostilities, etc. The more rigid and punitive the responses/court orders, the more likely that contact will fail.

14.23 In this respect, many respondents were attracted, as were we by the thinking behind the Australian model, in which a three stage process is proposed as follows:-

> The first stage is preventative. It requires the court to include in its orders a clause which sets out the obligations the order creates and the consequences which follow should the order not be observed. The Court is also required to provide the parties with information about parenting programmes to assist the parties in meeting their new parenting responsibilities as well as information about the use of location and recovery orders. These measures are intended to improve the knowledge and understanding of parents leading to an increased rate of compliance.

> The second stage provides the court with a range of powers where a breach of the order first occurs. The court will have the power to order one or both parties to a programme termed a 'post separation parenting programme'. The aim of such referral is to enable the parties to explore the real or underlying reason for the breach so that as the parties come to terms with their new parenting responsibilities after separation, they are able to obtain professional assistance. Some of the parenting programmes are anger management programmes. In addition, the court will be able to order compensatory contact.

> The third stage arises where there has been a second or subsequent breach of the order. This stage provides the court with a range of sanctions extending from community service order, bond or fine, but in the most serious case, imprisonment. This third stage provides the court with discretion to return to stage 2 where further parenting program attendance may be warranted, such as where the first and second breaches were of a trivial nature and the more punitive sanctions are not warranted.

14.24 We were also very attracted by response on this point by *CAFCASS*, which summed up its approach by saying:-

What is proposed is an approach that gives practitioners more time to work with parents and children within a vision of a range of services such as supervised Contact Centres, child *counselling*, perpetrator programmes, information giving meetings, conciliation meetings prior to initial directions and psychological assessments. There will be cases where even this level of intervention will fail to bring about change in a situation. In such cases attempting to facilitate some form of indirect contact is more appropriate than resorting to fines or imprisonment.

14.25 For court in England and Wales to be given these powers would require legislation. Equally, there would be no point in giving the courts wider powers, if programmes of the type envisaged were not to be available. We are, however, convinced that this is the way forward.

Transfer of residence to the other parent

14.26 This was discussed in a number of responses. It was, however, clear that such a transfer would have to be in the interests of the children concerned, since such a course clearly fell within section 1 of the Children Act and when determining that question the welfare of the children concerned was paramount. In the large majority of cases, therefore, a transfer of residence is unlikely to be the appropriate response to a committal summons without a substantial degree of further investigation. Judge Richard Jenkins, we thought, described the dilemma well:-

> The dilemma is increased because a transfer of residence will very rarely be appropriate. On the advice of the Official Solicitor and a consultant psychiatrist I have had success in ordering a transfer of residence where contact was unreasonably being refused. An extensive investigation and lengthy evidence persuaded me that a change of residence would have been appropriate in any event. The mother of a seven-year-old boy had placed herself in a socially isolated position with the child and was thoroughly over-protective of him. He was sensible enough to realise as soon as transfer had taken place where his best interests lay. That was an isolated case and I disparage the use of a residence application as a tactical weapon.

14.27 We wholly endorse Judge Jenkins' disapproval of the use or threat of a residence application as a means of achieving contact. It is a legitimate complaint by Women's Groups that abused women are sometimes induced to agree to unsuitable and unsafe contact with violent fathers by their belief in unfounded threats that their children will either be transferred to the father or taken into care. At the same time there will be cases in which a refusal of contact will be sufficiently damaging to a child as to outweigh the trauma caused by removing the child from the care of the residential parent. Judge Jenkins gives one example. Others are where children are being brought up in the false belief that they have been sexually abused by the absent parent, or where children of mixed race are being brought up in the belief that the race to which the absent parent belongs consists of people who are dangerous and/or bad.

Question

The law reports are full of the problems of dealing with parents who are opposed to contact, but there is another side: if continued contact is the right of the child, how can the law enforce the corresponding duty of a parent to keep in touch?

In 'Divorce and the Reluctant Father' (1980), Anne Heath-Jones gives a vivid account of the problem and her solution to it:

When my husband and I separated 12 years ago, we had two children who were then one and three years of age with long years of childhood ahead of them. ...

James was never a doting father, which had been one of the problems of the marriage. In effect I had always been a single parent. The boys were very young and their awareness of, and attachment to, their remote father was slight. James was all set to vanish from our lives completely.

But somehow in all the mess, in all my own grief and loneliness, and in spite of all the bitterness I harboured against him, I knew that if I had strength to fight for anything it should be to maintain contact between the children and their father. ...

In those early years the fact that he saw them at all was due to every imaginable ploy. Persuasion, appeal, anger and tears. I met him more than half-way on any arrangement that he was prepared to concede. I would deliver them to his flat and collect them. If he refused to have them to stay overnight then I settled for one day – or half a day. I felt anything was better than that they should lose touch and become strangers.

Meanwhile, I kept James informed of progress at nursery and later primary school. I made sure the boys remembered his birthday; I showed him school reports. I begged him (swallowing large hunks of indigestible pride) to attend school open days, birthday parties and Guy Fawkes parties. Most important of all I kept his image intact for his children. They never heard from me any criticism of his character, or knew of my deep hurt and resentment that their father needed so much coercion to see them or be involved in their lives.

For many years all the initiative for contact came from us. He never 'phoned or wrote or asked to see them. Then slowly, very slowly, the years of effort began to pay off. The boys and I moved from London into the country. James came down occasionally for the weekend and I would clear off and leave the cottage to them. After he re-married a more or less regular arrangement was worked out for the school holidays.

We were lucky in his choice of a new wife. She was friendly and accepted her two step-sons, and in time they formed an easy relationship with her. Christmases were now peopled with a whole new branch of extended family. Instead of moping alone with me (and some Christmases were very mopey) they had a welcome at their father's and his relations and even at the big family gatherings of his new wife. ...

Now, 1967 seems a long time ago and their childhood is nearly over. The relationship with their father now is mutually warm, positive and spontaneous. At times the price to pay for nurturing that relationship has been high. If you idealise the absent parent you must be prepared for the consequences.

When life got tough for us, when the boys were unhappy with school or friends, or when they sobbed for the father whose contact I had so carefully preserved, the cry was 'I want to live with Dad.' It hurt of course because I had provided the years of love and security, it hurt because I knew their father wouldn't want them and it hurt because that was the last thing in the world that I could explain to the crying child.

In spite of the upheavals of those early years we have all survived. They now have a father they can respect and admire, a man they can talk to and learn from, and a model to emulate when they become husbands and fathers themselves.

But while it can be hard for the parent with whom the children are living, it can also be hard for the other one, as an anonymous mother explained in 'Saturday Parent' (1980):

One morning nine years ago, when she was seven years old, I watched my youngest daughter walk across the school yard, knowing that it would not be me who collected her at the end of school that day. I do not care to describe the pain of that moment, nor the many pains that followed in the years to come. The decision had been made in court the day before – henceforward she was to live with her father, my ex-husband, and his new wife and her two adopted children. From that day on I have been a 'Saturday Parent' – the one who has access – that part-time travesty of parenting that is shared by an increasing number of separated parents in our present society. For years I could not see the problems with any kind of objectivity – I merely experienced them. ...

It is this vexed question of management which I wish to highlight – by-passing all the aggravation of actually settling on mutually convenient times and places – a most flourishing battle ground for embittered ex-spouses. I would like to enumerate some of the areas of difficulty personally experienced.

Firstly, there is the passage of time. Access is usually fixed at one hearing at a given point in time when the child is of a certain age. Obviously times and frequency of contact negotiated then frequently become obsolete, a child passes rapidly from toddler, to schoolchild, to independent teenager, and unless there is good-will – a scarce commodity in the devastation of a broken marriage – the poor youngster is stuck with every second Saturday from 9 a.m. to 7 p.m. whether it will or no. Access is for the benefit of children. The law acknowledges this; many parents do not.

Then there is the vexed question of discipline and training – something which was an everyday part of living, suddenly becomes a major issue. There is no time to confront, disagree, sulk and make-up when all you have is a truncated week-end. One vacillates between turning a 'blind eye' to everything and jumping on the poor kid at every turn. Related to this is one's attitude to the 'other' set of parents – the real (?) parents – does one share their values, opinions, standards? It is all too easy to fall into the role of permissive Aunty who lets the kid go to parties and stay out late, only to find that a 10 p.m. ban is standard at home. (No one bothered to tell you, though – unless something goes wrong!)

Matters of loyalty to ex-spouses, towards whom one's feelings are, to say the least, ambivalent, arise continually. 'So-and-so (in my case, step-mother) would not let me do so-and-so, isn't she unfair?' 'Well no, actually. If you were with me all the time, I too would' ... etc.

One had to fight an overwhelming desire to put all one's frustrated love into the small parcel of time allowed – a present on the bed, a cake specially baked – one yearns to be perceived as loving and lavishing, for after all one has also to cope with one's own feeling of guilt about letting the child go. However it happened, and whatever your reasons, you did it. Recounting the story of Solomon's wise judgment to a colleague, he remarked sadly: 'Trouble is, there's no one around with Solomon's wisdom or his knowledge.' Too true. Judges have to make life decisions for people they hardly know and who are not likely to be presenting themselves in the best light anyway.

Question

Can you think why this chapter has contained so many references, from independent sources, to the judgment of Solomon?

12.2.5 The non-intervention principle

Section 1 of the Children Act 1989 contains another important, but novel, principle:

1.—(5) Where a court is considering whether or not to make one or more orders under this Act with respect to a child, it shall not make the order or any of the orders unless it considers that doing so would be better for the child than making no order at all.

The Law Commission's explanation, in its Report on *Guardianship and Custody* (1988), was this:

3.2 A tendency seems to have developed to assume that some order about the children should always be made whenever divorce or separation cases come to court. This may have been necessary in the days when mothers required a court order if they were to acquire any parental powers at all, but that is no longer the case. Studies of both divorce and magistrates' courts have shown that the proportion of contested cases is very small so that orders are not usually necessary in order to settle disputes. Rather, they may be seen by solicitors as 'part of the package' for their matrimonial clients and by courts as part of their task of approving the arrangements made in divorce cases [Priest and Whybrow, 1986, para. 8.2]. No doubt in many, possibly most, uncontested cases an order is needed in the children's own interest, so as to confirm and give stability to the existing arrangements, to clarify the respective roles of the parents, to reassure the parent with whom the children will be living, and even to reassure the public authorities responsible for housing and income support that such arrangements have in fact been made. However, it is always open to parents to separate without going to court at all, in which case there will be no order. If they go to court for some other remedy, they may not always want an order about the children. The proportion of relatively amicable divorces is likely to have increased in recent years and parents may well be able to make responsible arrangements for themselves without a court order. Where a child has a good relationship with both parents the law should seek to disturb this as little as possible. There is always a risk that orders allocating custody and access (or even deciding upon residence and contact) will have the effect of polarising the parents' roles and perhaps alienating the child from one or other of them.
3.3 For these reasons, the Working Paper proposed a more flexible approach, in which it was not always assumed that an order should be made, but the court would be prepared to make one even in uncontested cases if this would promote the children's interests. Most of those who responded agreed with this approach. Such a change would be consistent with the view that anything which can be done to help parents to keep separate the issues of being a spouse and being a parent will ultimately give the children the best chance of retaining them both. On the other hand, the impression should not be given that an application or an order is a hostile step between them. We therefore recommend that the court should only make an order where this is the most effective way of safeguarding or promoting the child's welfare.

Carol Smart, in *The Legal and Moral Ordering of Child Custody* (1990), exposes these arguments to a feminist critique:

The Law Commission report espoused a policy of non-intervention by the courts into matters of child care arrangements on the basis that parents are the best people to decide what is right for their children. This exalted principle was wisely underscored by the recognition that even if parents were not, there is not a great deal of evidence to suggest that judges or local authority social workers are much better equipped for the job (except in cases of actual harm or abuse). The legislation therefore seeks to allow parents to make their own decisions. In practice this is what happens in the vast majority of cases anyway and the courts merely legitimate arrangements which have occurred elsewhere (even though these agreements take place in the shadow of the law). On the face of it the Act simply acknowledges this, but at the same time it goes further and promotes a 'hands off' approach as the ideal. ...

The criticism which has been made of non-interventionist family law in general, and this provision in particular, is that non-intervention is really intervention by another name. In other words to stand outside the 'fray' and do nothing is to be just as influential as doing something. The classic examples are, of course, domestic violence and child abuse where critics of non-intervention have shown that 'inaction' is not a position which is somehow morally superior to intervention. Non-intervention is therefore not automatically good but, by the same token, research in both of these fields has also shown that some caution must be applied to rushing to embrace intervention as if it must be better. Olsen suggests that we really should abandon such terms as indications of political orientation rather than as objective statements of how the law operates in relation to the family and there is some merit in this.

There is, however, another side to this argument (and it is one which was reflected in the interviews for this research). Much, as long ago as 1980, pointed to the resentment caused to parents by the experience of state intervention into their lives at the point of marriage breakdown. It is also often remarked upon that if we allow parents to raise children according to their own values whilst a relationship is ongoing, there is no reason to assume that they become especially incapacitated in this respect just because the relationship ends. ... [We] do not require a judge to be satisfied with arrangements made for a child when a spouse dies or simply leaves. In other words there is no reason to draw the line between intervention and non-intervention at the point of divorce although we may still wish to draw it where violence occurs for example.

The non-intervention principle is closely linked to the role of the court in divorce cases where there are relevant children, even if the parties have agreed. As the Law Commission (1988) explain:

3.5 ... one possible reason why orders are almost always made at present is the divorce court's present duty under section 41 of the Matrimonial Causes Act 1973 to declare itself satisfied as to the arrangements made for the children of the family before making absolute a decree of nullity or divorce or making a decree of judicial separation. ...

3.6 The original main aims [Royal Commission on Marriage and Divorce 1951-1955, 1956, paras. 366 at seq.] of section 41 procedure were to ensure that divorcing parents made the best possible arrangements for their children and to identify cases of particular concern where protective measures might be needed. In our Working Paper on Custody we concluded that the procedure had not been successful in achieving either of these aims. The information currently available to the court is too limited, being based on a brief statement from the petitioner alone; the arrangements are usually discussed in a short interview with the judge, which cannot be other than perfunctory in many cases; and, most importantly, the practical power of the court to produce different outcomes is very limited, nor can it ensure that the approved arrangements are subsequently observed. Although there are undoubtedly exceptional cases in which protective measures of supervision or even care may be needed, the present process is not principally designed to discover these.

3.7 Hence the Working Paper provisionally proposed replacing the divorce court's present duty to declare that the arrangements are 'satisfactory' or 'the best that can be devised in the circumstances' with the domestic court's more modest duty to consider what order, if any, to make. ...

3.8 There was a large measure of support for these proposals ... But it was thought by some of our respondents that a duty invariably to have decided what order to make before granting the decree absolute went too far. We accept that this requirement would be too strong if it meant that no divorce could be granted while a custody dispute existed. This would create a serious risk of children becoming pawns in their parents' own battles. ...

3.9 We recommend, therefore, that once divorce, nullity or judicial separation proceedings have been initiated, the court should have a duty to consider the arrangements proposed for the children in order to decide whether to exercise any of its powers under this legislation. Where this is so, but only in exceptional circumstances, the court should also have power to direct that the decree absolute (or a decree of judicial separation) cannot be made until the court allows it.

The Children Act 1989 substituted a new s. 41 accordingly.

But how is s. 1(5) working in practice? Rebecca Bailey-Harris, Gwynn Davis, Jacqueline Barron and Julia Pearce, in 'Settlement culture and the use of the 'no order' principle under the Children Act 1989' (1999), report the following findings from their study (see p. 571, above):

Our study showed that section 1(5) receives a very mixed response in practice at county court level. These variations may simply reflect the width of discretion afforded to judges in children proceedings under the Act. Nevertheless, the evidence from our study could be interpreted as suggesting two themes. First, the 'no order principle' is invoked by judges to reinforce the concept of parental autonomy and the vigorous promotion of agreement, this results in the court declining or refusing to make an order even when parties have sought one. It is highly questionable whether this use of the principle accords with the original intention of the legislature, and we found that it could be productive of acute dissatisfaction on the part of parents who were expecting an adjudicated outcome. Secondly, and in complete contrast, the principle is very commonly breached or not observed by judges, particularly when legal practitioners press for resolution by consent order. There are various forms of outcome in which the principle can be reflected. The court can refuse or dismiss an application, or give leave for it to be withdrawn, or adjourn it not to be restored under certain conditions. Sometimes the court makes a formal 'order of no order'. Our file survey showed that, overall, a substantive order was made in 67 per cent of cases, no substantive order in 27 per cent, and an order of 'no order' in 5 per cent. The extent of non-observance of the principle by the courts we sampled is thus immediately apparent.

To pursue the first theme: it is possible to argue from the evidence of our study that in practice the courts are using the 'no order principle' in cases to which it was never intended to apply. In many cases where there is originally real conflict between parents who have invoked the court's jurisdiction specifically to resolve their dispute, the principle is invoked by judges to reinforce the promotion of parental autonomy and agreement as the preferred mode of resolution: the court asserts that no order is needed where parents can eventually agree, even though their preferred original intention was to obtain an order.

Our study reveals many examples of judges using the rhetoric of parental autonomy to justify the refusal to make an order, even in proceedings where there is real dispute and where proceedings are protracted. The judicial message delivered ranges through 'parents know better for their children than the court can' to 'your agreement is more likely to "stick" than a court order'. Examples abounded in each of the four courts we observed. In one, a particular district judge was notable for his strong messages regularly delivered to parties during the course of family days that the policy of the Children Act 1989 is that court is not there to tell parents how to bring up their children; parental co-operation is everything, parental agreement is the preferred option and that the court's role is to make a decision only when parents cannot agree. ... In another court ... a district judge frequently told parties on family days that anything he ordered would be strictly second best to anything the parties could decide themselves since they know their children far better than the court could. He commented to us in general discussion that 'The object of directions appointments is to get as much as possible solved without a contest – if parties get to a stage where they agree, it is more likely to stick'. ...

There is considerable evidence of the dissatisfaction of parents with the outcome of 'no order' when they consider that they have invoked the court's jurisdiction precisely for the exercise of its authority in a matter which they find difficult to resolve themselves. ...

[T]he case of the Daveys involves an application by grandparents for contact with their four-year-old grandson living with his mother. The grandmother told us: 'We wanted a court order. We were advised by the Grandparents' Support Organisation (sic); we wanted an order – it wasn't going to be just word of mouth any more ... we had got to the point when we wanted something legal'. The matter went through a number of directions hearings and was referred to mediation, which the mother did not attend. A year later no order had been made and the grandmother was a very dissatisfied 'customer' with the legal system. She wrote to us that she 'felt the court system abysmal' and now doubted whether she had been right to take the matter to court at all. Both these examples are cases of protracted disputes. In a different category of case, there may well be a widespread popular misconception of the nature of directions hearings in the early stages of proceedings, which are wrongly perceived by many parents as likely to finalise matters by adjudication.

Question

Why do you think some judges are so reluctant to decide these disputes?

12.2.6 The child's sense of time

There is one value judgment in the Children Act 1989 about what is good for children:

1.—(2) In any proceedings in which any question with respect to the upbringing of a child arises, the court shall have regard to the general principle that any delay in determining the question is likely to prejudice the welfare of the child.

The Law Commission (1988) are to blame:

4.55 ... Prolonged litigation about their future is deeply damaging to children, not only because of the uncertainty it brings for them, but also because of the harm it does to the relationship between the parents and their capacity to co-operate with one another in the future. Moreover, a frequent consequence is that the case of the parent who is not living with the child is severely prejudiced by the time of the hearing. Regrettably, it is almost always to the advantage of one of the parties to delay the proceedings as long as possible and, what may be worse, to make difficulties over contact in the meantime. At present, particularly in divorce courts, the responsibility for the progress of the proceedings lies principally with the adult parties, although a considerable source of delay is the time taken to prepare welfare officers' reports and sometimes to attempt conciliation between the parties.
4.56 ... there is serious concern, particularly among the judiciary, about the present delays and ... action is required to remedy the situation. There may be problems in preparing welfare reports, given the other constraints within which welfare officers have to work, and in some cases time may be beneficial in enabling an agreed solution to emerge, perhaps with the help of conciliation. Nevertheless, the 'child's sense of time' is quite different from the adults' and it is the child's interests which should prevail.
4.57 The most effective practical action which can be taken to remedy matters is to place a clear obligation upon the court to oversee the progress of the case and to ensure that the court regards all delay as prejudicial to the child's interests unless the contrary is shown. (An example might be where the benefit to the child from a thorough report outweighed the detriment of having to wait for it, but the Court of Appeal has said that if one has to wait as long as nine months it is better to do without one [*Re C (a minor) (custody of child)* (1980) 2 FLR 163].) This approach is something of a novelty within our legal system, which is generally content to leave such matters to the parties themselves.

Question

Look back at what Goldstein, Freud and Solnit said about the child's sense of time (alternatively, if you have the opportunity, try asking a two-year-old to wait for five minutes). Do you agree with the value judgment in s. 1(2)?

Again, Bailey-Harris and her colleagues (1999) report some significant findings:

Our study suggests that cases fall into two categories: those which achieve early settlement and those which fail to do so. The former are disposed of with considerable rapidity, the latter tend to be drawn out through a large number of directions hearings.

The court process undoubtedly starts with considerable momentum. Initial appointments generally take place within a short time of the filing of the application. Our file study showed that a quarter came to court on the day of the application, and three-quarters were in court within one month. A large number of cases are normally heard during the family day by the district judge in each of the county courts which we observed; 12 to 20 was the norm – a remarkable figure when one observes that most family day hearings are primarily concentrated in the morning. The momentum of the initial stages of the legal process results in rapid disposition of those cases which are capable of early agreement. Our file survey conducted across the four courts showed that 24 per cent of cases settled with only one appointment and a further 26 per cent with two; furthermore, 26 per cent of cases were resolved within one month and a further 20 per cent between one and three months. Our follow-up study revealed a similar pattern: of the 38 cases, five were resolved in a single appointment and a further eight in two. Eight of those 38 cases were concluded in less than three months, and 12 in between three and six months. However, we found that the initial momentum drops off rapidly if cases fail to settle at an early stage. The file study showed that 27 per cent of cases took between three and six months and 19 per cent from six months to one year. This pattern was reflected in the cases we observed and followed up, some of which involved very protracted disputes lasting many months or even years. Of the 38 cases in our follow-up study, 25 took three or more appointments, 14 of these over five. A total of 18 cases took in excess of six months to resolve.

In the more protracted cases the parties frequently expressed their frustration at the delays in the legal process. For example, to quote Mr Rose, a divorced father seeking contact: 'It's taken too long, basically. It's taken miles too long'. Similar were the sentiments of Mrs Miles involved in a prolonged dispute over the details of holiday contact: 'I thought (the legal process) would be a lot faster'. In the Twine's case we first interviewed the father, who was seeking contact with his daughter, in May 1996:

> 'I've tried to read up on the Children act ... I agree delay is bad. It's really bad in my case. The welfare bloke admitted on the phone that the quicker (my daughter) and I start seeing each other the better. I think it is being dragged out ... I think the law needs a real shake-up because I don't think I'm getting a very fair deal ... it's being dragged out. This has gone on now since last July. I made the application to court just after Christmas.'

Our final interview with him took place in June 1997 when he had recently received a letter from the court informing him that the case stood adjourned to be dismissed unless restored by September; in the meantime his daughter had gone to live with him. He told us that he had expected 'an answer' by now and that the case had dragged on and on. Parents are not the only ones who voice anxiety about delays. The occasional solicitor even expressed the view that the Children Act 1989 has actually been productive of delay. One welfare officer told us of the 'terrible delay' which often occurs in one of the courts within the main region we studied: 'You write the report and then wait months for a hearing. Usually whatever you have written in the report has been overcome by events'. One obvious cause of delay is the time required for the welfare report – 12 to 16 weeks was normal in the courts we observed – poses dilemmas for district judges. The file survey showed that in 26 per cent of cases the welfare report took up to three months to submit, and between three and six months in 13 per cent of cases. While the report obviously provides a unique opportunity for exploration of considerations in the 'welfare checklist' (section 1(3)), including the child's wishes, some district judges are understandably reluctant to order a welfare report because of the inevitable delays which will result, and try instead to manage the case judicially in an attempt to give maximum opportunity to parents to reach agreement, without the case being 'tracked' down the report route. The file survey showed that welfare reports were ordered in 49 per cent of cases. The problem of delay here is essentially one of under-resourcing of the service.

Question

Can you think of any other solutions, apart from money?

We have heard quite a lot about welfare reports in this section; in the next section we focus on the ways in which the court can ascertain the views of children.

12.3 Who speaks up for the child?

The Law Commission (1988) dealt with the 'wishes and feelings' of the child himself (item (a) in the Children Act checklist, p. 589, above) in this way:

3.23 The opinion of our respondents was almost unanimously in favour of the proposal to give statutory recognition to the child's views. Obviously there are dangers in giving them too much recognition. Children's views have to be discovered in such a way as to avoid embroiling them in their parents' disputes, forcing them to 'choose' between their parents, or making them feel responsible for the eventual decision. This is usually best done through the medium of a welfare officer's report, although most agreed that courts should retain their present powers to see children in private. Similarly, for a variety of reasons the child's views may not be reliable, so that the court should only have to take due account of them in the light of his age and understanding. Nevertheless, experience has shown that it is pointless to ignore the clearly expressed wishes of older children [*M v M (transfer of custody: appeal)* [1987] 1 WLR 404, [1987] 2 FLR 146]. Finally, however, if the parents have agreed on where the child will live and made their arrangements accordingly, it is no more practicable to try to alter these to accord with the child's views than it is to impose the views of the court. After all, united parents will no doubt take account of the views of their children in deciding upon moves of house or employment but the children cannot expect their wishes to prevail.
3.24 These considerations all point towards including the child's views as part of a statutory checklist, which in practice will be limited to contested cases, rather than as a separate consideration in their own right. This solution was generally favoured by our respondents and we so recommend....
3.25 ... The courts' present powers to make custody and access orders endure until the child reaches 18, although the court will rarely, if ever, make a custody order which is contrary to the wishes of a child who has reached 16 [*Hall v Hall* (1945) 175 LT 355]. Any other approach is scarcely practicable, given that this is the age at which children may leave school and seek full-time employment and become entitled to certain benefits or allowances in their own right. However, the matter goes beyond the question of what is practicable. There are powers of direct enforcement of custody orders which operate upon the child rather than the adults involved [eg s. 34 of the Family Law Act 1986]. The older the child becomes, the less just it is even to attempt to enforce against him an order to which he has never been party. As we explain below, it is usually thought unnecessary to accord party status to children in family disputes and in general we would not disagree. We recommend, therefore, that orders relating to the child's residence, contact or other specific matters of upbringing should not be made in respect of a child who has reached 16 unless there are exceptional circumstances and that orders made before that age should expire then unless in exceptional circumstances the court orders otherwise.

Question

(i) The Family Law Act 1996 provides for the Lord Chancellor to make regulations about the separate representation of children in divorce and other proceedings between the adults. Look back at pp. 584–620, above. When should children be separately represented in proceedings about their own futures? Should it depend upon whether or not there is a dispute between their parents? Should they be represented by a lawyer, a social worker, or both?

The usual way of ascertaining the child's views and protecting his interests in private law proceedings is to obtain a report from a professional formerly known as a court welfare officer. The family court welfare service formed part of the probation service. That service is now provided by the Children and Family Court Advisory and Support Service; as CAFCASS' own website explains:

CAFCASS was created by the Criminal Justice and Courts Services Act 2000... CAFCASS brought together all those groups of practitioners who provided advice to the courts about the wellbeing of children and their families. These services have previously been provided by three separate services: the Family Court Welfare Service, the Guardian ad Litem and Reporting Officer Service and the Children's Division of the Official Solicitor's Department. CAFCASS will be a non-departmental public body answering to the Lord Chancellor.

It is fair to say that the new arrangements have not yet settled down. Stephen Gerlis, in 'CAFCASS – Twisted Knickers' (2002), comments:

The Children and Family Court Advisory and Support Service (CAFCASS) has got off to a bad start. In fact, that is an understatement. It has had a diabolical start. Charles Prest, Director of Legal Services at CAFCASS, when addressing a recent meeting of family judges, described it as 'a child born prematurely'. Serious disputes over terms of employment, budget limitations (£4.8 million short in 2001 – rising in subsequent years) and divisions in philosophy contrive to give the impression of an organisation that has its knickers firmly in a twist.

A symptom of this is the changing of names of various personnel. It is frankly bewildering. The old court welfare officer is now a children and family reporter, but a report from the local authority under s 7(1)(b) of the Children Act 1989 is prepared by – a welfare officer. Even the title 'children and family reporter' is now seen to be problematical. Mr Prest reported that it has led some parents to believe either that the person has some connections with the press, or that it refers to the parent who has care and control of the children, who must then 'report' on their situation to the court. His advice was that a different title should be used in directions – but which?

There is a bewildering number of titles to choose from, some of which have replaced previous titles; some of which have not changed; and some of which have swapped with others. Take your pick: guardian ad litem, children's guardian, reporting officer, parental order reporter, litigation friend, Uncle Tom Cobley and all. Mr Prest has said that a generic name has been agreed – 'family court advisers' – but I have yet to see formal sanction or notice of such nomenclature.

The problems with titles pale into insignificance when set against an apparent change of policy by CAFCASS in certain areas of the UK, in relation to the impact of domestic violence. It has been common knowledge among judges that, recently, some CAFCASS officers have been refusing to prepare reports in children matters that have been ordered by the court where there is an allegation of domestic violence, unless and until the court has made a finding of fact on those allegations.

Now consider very carefully the effect of this policy. There is already a minimum period of 12 weeks in which a report is supposed to be prepared, and this varies widely across the UK. At a seminar for family judges in 2001, the President of the Family Division, Dame Elizabeth Butler-Sloss, announced that there were areas where it was taking much longer than that to get a report – in one particular instance the average was 40 weeks. On the basis that judgment delayed is judgment denied, any turn of events that contrives to further delay the resolution of children matters not only breaches the ethos of the Children Act 1989, it also runs the risk of running foul of Art 8 of the European Convention for the Protection of Human Rights and Fundamental Freedoms 1950.

Question

Is he being fair?

Be that as it may, the functions of the family reporters remain very much those of the court welfare officers. In addition to writing reports for the court, they may also help couples to reach agreement, or provide short-term family assistance (under s. 16 of the Children Act 1989) to help with difficulties, for example over contact arrangements. The mediation and reporting functions should be kept separate (*Re H (conciliation: welfare reports)* [1986] 1 FLR 476). Great weight is attached to a report and the court should not depart from a clear recommendation without explaining why (*Re T (A Minor) (welfare report recommendation)* (1977) 1 FLR 59). The courts' expectations of reports are spelled out by Johnson J in *Re P (a minor) (inadequate welfare report)* [1996] 2 FCR 285:

The whole point of the court welfare officer system is that, because in the nature of things the court cannot itself observe the relationships between the children and the parents, the welfare officer acts as the eyes and ears of the court and provides the court with an independent and objective assessment of the relationships involved. Here the report was inadequate. The welfare officer's inquiry was conducted in such a way as to make it impossible for her to form any view about the relationships involved.

Decisions such as this require a very delicate balance of a number of considerations, principal among which must surely be the relationships between the children and the parents. Such assessments cannot be made in an office, they have to be made in a natural environment. All that was done here was that the children went along to the welfare officer's office and were interviewed.

A better example is set by the following ideal specimen, formerly used by welfare officers for training purposes but rarely achieved in practice these days:

Specimen Welfare Report

BLANKSHIRE PROBATION & AFTER-CARE SERVICE

Wood & Wood

Applicant:	Mrs Jean Wood – 22 years
Respondent:	Mr John Wood – 35 years
Child concerned:	Richard Wood – 3 years
Child:	Amanda Forbes – 6 years
Respondent's cohabitant:	Janet Smith – 32 years
Children:	Mary Smith – 6 years
	Brian Smith – 5 years

1. Enquiries
I have read the Court file concerning this matter
I have had discussions with:
– the Applicant with Richard
– the Respondent and Cohabitant with Richard
– Richard by himself
I have had a telephone conversation with the Housing Department
I have had a telephone conversation with Dr Jones, the Respondent's Physician

2. Background relating to the child
I understand from both parties that initially their relationship was good though the Applicant claims the Respondent spent too much time with his mother. In March 1995 Mr Wood's father died and he invited his mother to live with him and his wife. The Applicant and her mother-in-law had never enjoyed a good relationship and there were immediate problems. Mrs Wood senior it is claimed assumed control of the family, gradually taking over responsibility for the housework and the care of both the Respondent and the child – Richard. There were constant quarrels and in November 1994 following a violent disagreement, the Applicant left the matrimonial home on an impulse and stayed for a short period with a relative. Being without accommodation she did not feel it fair to Richard to take him with her at that time. Within three weeks she had found accommodation in a very small bedsitting room sharing a kitchen and bathroom with a family of five people; again a situation she felt unsuitable for Richard.

3. Applicant mother
Mrs Jean Wood – Mrs Wood, a full time housewife, impressed as a bright, outgoing young woman who is obviously deeply attached to her son. She told me she had found the situation in the former matrimonial home quite intolerable from the time her mother-in-law moved in. She claimed Mrs Wood senior had undermined her discipline of Richard and had tried to cause difficulties between her and the Respondent. She said that her reason for staying had been the fear that she might lose Richard and that she left only when she felt she could no longer cope with the situation. I understand that Richard's behaviour was untypically bad from the time she left home causing the Respondent to contact the family doctor. I am told the child's behaviour returned to normal once contact with his mother was re-established in December 1994. Mrs Wood visits Richard twice weekly at the former matrimonial home. The Respondent has been quite adamant that he will not allow her to take the child away from the home. Until very

recently, there were no difficulties with contact. The Applicant feels, however, that the atmosphere has become tense since the Respondent's cohabitant moved into the home in January 1995 whereupon the grandmother left.

4. Of her own relationship with her cohabitant, Mr Forbes, the Applicant tells me she had known him some years ago and met him again soon after leaving her husband. She has lived with Mr Forbes since the beginning of January 1995 and has already formed an excellent relationship with his daughter, Amanda, who lives with them. The Applicant and Mr Forbes plan to marry as soon as both are free to do so.

5. The Applicant Mother feels very strongly that she is the appropriate person to have the day to day care of Richard. She feels he has already been subjected to too many changes and that she can now offer him the stability he needs. She has made tentative enquiries concerning a playschool for Richard, but if he comes to live with her would delay any decision until he was completely settled in his new home. Mrs Wood appears to fully appreciate the importance of the child having regular contact with the Father and would have no objection to reasonable contact which she suggests could be staying on alternate weekends.

6. Applicant's cohabitant

Mr Michael Forbes – Mr Forbes presented as a pleasant, mature personality. He told me he had married very young, that his wife had had difficulty in managing on a low income and the resulting debts had caused difficulties between them. He told me that his wife left him 2 years ago and he has not heard from her since. He has made enquiries concerning her whereabouts as he is anxious now to petition for divorce. Mr Forbes has had the care of his daughter since his wife left and has coped admirably with the help of a neighbour. He is employed as a clerk. He tells me that because of the demands made on him in caring for his daughter, he has not been able to take advantage of promotion. However, now that the Applicant is caring for his daughter Amanda, he feels his employment prospects are excellent. Because the Respondent has refused to allow Richard to leave the home with his mother, Mr Forbes has not met the child. He is realistic about the possible difficulties should Richard come to live with them but feels his experience with his own child will help.

7. Applicant's home

The home is a 2-bedroomed flat which is adequately furnished and well kept. Mr Forbes expects to move to a 3-bedroomed maisonette in the near future having negotiated an exchange with another family. I have contacted the Housing Department who confirm that there are no objections to this transfer.

8. Respondent

Mr John Wood – Mr Wood is a quiet, introspective man. He tells me he was the youngest son in a large family. He has always enjoyed a very close relationship with his mother who did not approve of his relationship with the Applicant. Mr Wood tells me that his wife coped well with the home and the child until his mother moved in with them. He claims that the Applicant then became lazy and lost interest in the home, leaving everything to the grandmother. The Respondent is employed as a Sales Manager. In the course of his work he travels extensively, often away overnight and sometimes travels abroad. His cohabitant – Mrs Smith – has lived with him since mid January 1995 and although he has not known her for very long, the relationship appears to be sound and based on mutual interests. The Respondent told me that Richard has caused him some anxiety since Mrs Smith arrived and the grandmother left the home. He has again consulted the family doctor but feels that if a firm line is taken with Richard, he will quickly adapt to the new situation. The Respondent tells me that he is asking Richard to stay with him as he does not wish to have another man involved in bringing up his son. He also feels he is in a better position to care for Richard's material needs than is the Applicant. He would have no objection to the present arrangement for contact being continued but would oppose staying visits.

9. Respondent's cohabitant

Mrs Janet Smith – Mrs Smith is a quiet, intelligent woman who is studying for a degree with the Open University and would like a teaching career. She talked frankly about her own children saying that she was not very maternal and although she very much enjoys her children's monthly visits, she does not wish to see them more often. She expressed some reservations about bringing up Richard, especially with the Respondent being often away from home. She told me however, that she is fond of Richard and is anxious to do whatever Mr Wood wishes.

10. Respondent's home

The home is a spacious, 4-bedroomed house where material standards are high. The property is owned by Mr Wood subject to a mortgage.

11. Child concerned

Richard Wood – Richard is a bright and lively child, obviously well cared for. I have seen him with the Applicant and also separately with the Respondent. When I saw Richard with the Respondent and Mrs Smith, he appeared to be anxious to do and say the right thing and was quieter and more subdued than when I interviewed him with the Applicant. With the Applicant, Richard was talkative and lively and very upset when the time came for her to leave. Although Richard is hardly 4, it appears that given the choice, he would wish to spend most of his time with his mother.

12. Conclusion

From my enquiries, it would appear that both parents care about Richard's welfare and either could offer him a good home. The Respondent is in a position to offer material advantages and wishes Richard to be privately educated. The Applicant Mother's means are more modest but the bond between mother and child is particularly close and the separation was of such short duration that it appears to have done no damage to the relationship. It has not been possible to see the Applicant's cohabitant with the child. On the other hand the child's relationship with the Respondent's cohabitant is not yet a close one. In fact, the child appears to be having some difficulty in relating to a third mother figure.

13. In view of the very close relationship between mother and child, it would appear to be in Richard's long-term best interests if he were to live with his Mother. The court will want, however, to ensure that he sees as much as possible of his father.

14. It is clear that whatever the decision Richard will experience problems in adjusting to the new step-parent. The Court may consider, therefore, that a short period of assistance would be of benefit to Richard in making this adjustment.

February 1996
Court Welfare Officer

Questions

(i) If you were counsel for the mother in this case, what features of the report would you emphasise to the court?

(ii) If you were counsel for the father, would you advise him to settle the dispute along the lines suggested by the welfare officer?

(iii) If the father wished to fight the case, which features would you as counsel emphasise to the court?

(iv) As counsel for the father, how would you go about challenging the suggestion in para. 11 of the report that 'although Richard is hardly four, it appears that given the choice, he would wish to spend most of his time with his mother'?

How do families, and particularly children, perceive the welfare inquiry process? Ann Buchanan, Joan Hunt, Harriet Bretherton and Victoria Bream have carried out research funded by the Nuffield Foundation; their findings are summarised in 'Families in Conflict – perspectives of children and parents on the family court welfare service' (2001):

Key Findings

- Parents were highly distressed (84% were above the threshold of the General Health Questionnaire (GHQ)). Distress was, in part, related to the court case and, to some extent, was alleviated once proceedings were over.
- Children were also highly distressed (46% had significant levels of emotional and behavioural difficulties). Levels for children who were interviewed were comparable with those reported for children subject to child protection proceedings and nearly twice the level expected in the general child population. Distress in children was linked to distress in the resident parent and to domestic violence. For boys, it did not alleviate once proceedings were over and it also remained high for girls.
- Most children believed that the family court welfare officer (FCWO) had listened to them and understood what they were saying. However, half did not feel that their voices had been heard, either by the court process or by their parents.

- Parents' perceptions of the preparation of the welfare report varied, but more than half were dissatisfied, voicing strong criticisms of the assessment process. The main criticism was that the investigation was not thorough enough. The best predictors of satisfaction were outcome and initial expectations.
- While satisfaction with welfare reporting was principally linked to outcome and initial expectations, some parents were particularly dissatisfied.
- Almost all parents, irrespective of outcome, were dissatisfied with the court process. Their reported experiences paralleled those of parents involved in care proceedings.
- Parents whose cases were settled before the court hearing were more likely to be satisfied with both the process and the outcome, and contact was more likely to progress over the next 12 months.
- Many parents were critical of a system that each gender saw as favouring the other, ignoring their own perspectives and needs.
- Comprehensive services are needed to prevent and alleviate the negative effects of conflict associated with parental separation. Some families where parents cannot agree on arrangements may have particularly complex social and emotional needs and require therapeutic, rather than primarily investigative services, to safeguard children's well-being.

...

The parents' experiences of welfare reporting

Many parents were highly anxious about the first meeting with the FCWO, which was often critical in that it altered their attitude to the process. The main criticism was that the investigation was not thorough enough, either in the amount of time spent, or the number of professionals and other family members who were contacted. Reading a 'negative' report was a very distressing experience.

Differing perspectives

A total of 56% of parents were dissatisfied or mainly dissatisfied with the process of welfare reporting. Gender, ethnicity and experience of domestic violence did not go far to explain different perceptions. The best predictors of satisfaction were negative expectations at the outset and positive reactions to the outcome. Both mothers and fathers (primarily those who were dissatisfied with the process) were critical of a system that each gender saw as favouring the parent of the opposite sex and ignoring their own perspectives and needs. Black parents' accounts of the FCWO's sensitivity to issues of ethnicity, culture and religion were mixed. Four out of the 20 interviewed believed that their race, culture or religion had counted against them.

Seven of the 11 mothers for whom domestic violence was an issue in the proceedings were dissatisfied with the process. However, in their view, violence was not the key factor in making a decision about the arrangements for their child. Many parents believed that their concerns about how the other parent looked after their child were discounted by the FCWO. ...

Children's' voices

Most of the children who were interviewed said that they knew why they were seeing the FCWO and what he did. They liked the FCWO and though they had been taken seriously by him, but this was not the same as feeling that their voices had been heard. Some children were worried that their parents would learn about what they had said to the FCWO.

Less than half the children thought they had been involved in the decision-making process. A total of 83% would have liked to have been involved, and half though children should be allowed to go to court. Up to half would have liked another family member or a friend involved.

Children described positive relationships with both parents. However, half were aware that their parents disagreed about contact arrangements and one-third had witnessed their parents pushing or shoving in an argument. Just under one-third of children said they would rather not see the parent they did not live with if this meant an end to the arguments.

Gillian Douglas, Mervyn Murch, Margaret Robinson, Lesley Scanlan and Ian Butler also write about children's views in their report of their research into 'Children's perspectives and experience of the divorce process' (2001). The following extract gives a sample of views about the legal process itself, and some conclusions about policy issues:

Abbie (11) said:

> 'I knew they were going to court and stuff like that 'cos I seen it in a film "Mrs Doubtfire". I asked my Dad about that, and he said, "No! We don't go to court at all". I said "I know you do 'cos I'd seen it on the telly".'

Interestingly, most of the children regarded the legal aspects of divorce as adult matters, which were private and confidential. In some cases they accepted that this spared them from learning details of marital misconduct. Even when children did want to know what was happening, they did not want to ask their parents for information because they often wanted to spare their parents' feelings. As Josie (13) explained:

> 'Well, my Mum told me that they were getting divorced and she explained that that's like through solicitors and all that ... I didn't really understand it. Like when Mum was upset, I didn't really want to worry her with it again.'

Some children would have welcomed an opportunity to speak up on behalf of a parent; others were fearful that greater involvement in the legal process might have led them to having to 'betray' one parent or another. Children did not see the relevance of legal proceedings to the more important practical and emotional tasks in hand. As Nicky (12) put it:

> 'I don't think I would have liked to know more ... I wouldn't have really minded if I didn't know anything about it ... It's more the emotional side – how other people feel about it.'

Children's feelings about involvement in the divorce process

Although the legal side aroused rather little interest, the question of involvement in critical decisions was of vital concern to the children. Like Libby (13), many of them reported feeling excluded from the changes that were occurring in their family:

> 'It was like, "Oh well, it's not really your problem, you're just not going to be affected by it. You don't have to go through all the divorce things." But, no one seemed to realise I was sort of THERE. They were all concerned with what they were doing.'

Fewer than half of the children (45%) had been asked whom they wanted to live with; more (55%) said they wished that they had been asked. The children were strong in their belief, expressed in terms of rights and fairness, that their opinion was important and should be considered when decisions were being made concerning their future. As Louise (12) explained:

> 'It would have been well ... not nice, but a GOOD thing to be ASKED. Because if they'd asked by parents I know my Dad would be saying "They've got to live with me" and my Mum would be saying "They've got to live with me". So I knew if I was ASKED I'd say my Mum. Still, I'd feel that I said it and they didn't MAKE me live with one of them.'

...

Policy Issues

This brief flavour of the findings in our study may help to highlight certain key policy issues. First, it is clear that many children and parents would have welcomed information and guidance on how to deal with each other during this stressful family situation. At present, there is a 'gap' in communication between them. Parents must be assisted to identify children's needs during the process of divorce. And, perhaps more importantly, parents and children need help to develop skills which will enable them to give, to receive and to request the information and support each require. It should not be seen as patronising or a sinister manifestation of the 'nanny state' for government or voluntary organisations to offer well-crafted information and guidance on how parents and children can communicate with each other during marital breakdown. The information meeting required under s. 8 of the Family Law Act 1996 has not translated into reality, but the immensely valuable work done in the pilot research should not be allowed to go to waste in helping to formulate future assistance for families in this situation. There is both a need and a desire for it.

Secondly, this assistance must be provided when families want and need it – not when the dictates of the legal system permit it. Parents and children need to have access to information and support at an early stage, and not simply when the legal process is invoked, which may be many months, even years, after the initial parental separation. This raises a much deeper policy question. In our view, the time has come to recognise that the legal system cannot carry the whole burden of dealing with family breakdown. This is a social phenomenon, and indeed a mental health question, which needs to be addressed on a broad front through a range of strategies and mechanisms. Lawyers, courts and even mediators can only be expected to handle a small part of the issues which parents and children have to face when a divorce occurs. The harmful impact of divorce could indeed be reduced if the facilities designed to address it could be accessed when families need them – which may be long before they finally resort to the legal system to tidy up the legal angles.

Finally, children often feel isolated, with limited avenues of social and emotional support beyond their parents. They may gain much from their friends, but friends may be ill-equipped to help them come to terms with what is happening in their lives. If parents are unable to provide the support they need, because of their own emotional difficulties and inability to communicate, it may be a matter of chance whether children find a suitable channel for their fears and feelings. Some are only left with 'talking to teddy' when things get too much for them. It might be thought that a society concerned for the well-being of children in this situation should be doing much more to provide a rather more reliable form of support than this.

Question

What sort of support is available to children when their parents, and the legal system, let them down?

12.4 Step-families

As every child knows, there have always been step-parents, but their stereotype is the wicked step-mother who invades the family after their real mother is dead. Nowadays, the more appropriate stereotype would be the divorced father who has gradually faded out of his own children's lives, and has now married a woman with children from a previous marriage or relationship. At the beginning of this chapter we presented some of the statistics (see p. 570. above). But what of the practical consequences for individuals?

The finances of a lone parent family may improve if the mother has a new partner, but the well-being of the children does not necessarily improve as well. The research is summarised by Louie Burghes in *Lone Parenthood and Family Disruption – The Outcomes for Children* (1994):

Repartnership
Step families may be formed after separation and divorce or following single motherhood. Some single mothers may form partnerships with their children's natural father. (Although strictly speaking this is a first partnership rather than a repartnership.)

Crellin et al [1971] showed that it is not always the case that children born 'illegitimately' who move from a single mother family to living with both natural parents fare better than those who remain with their lone mother (in some cases as part of a larger household).

Elliott and Richards [1991] found significantly more disruptive behaviour among children in step families than among those who remained with a lone mother (although all their caveats about the difficulties of these measures must be borne in mind). But there was no such difference on the 'unhappy and worried' score. Nor were there significant differences in achievement in maths and reading or in the chances of getting a university qualification by age 23 between those living with a lone mother or with their mother and a step father.

Maclean and Wadsworth [1988] and Kuh and Maclean [1990] found that repartnership following bereavement increased the chances of achieving educational qualifications. But this was not the case where it followed separation or divorce. Indeed, Maclean and Wadsworth found that likehood of higher educational qualifications increased where remarriage followed bereavement.

Kiernan [1992] found that just as there was little difference in the ages at which young people from intact and bereaved families made adult transitions, there was not a great deal of difference where the lone parent repartnered or remarried (following the bereavement).

By contrast, there were differences between transitions made by young people in intact families and for those whose lone parent had repartnered or remarried following separation or divorce.

The only exception was for young people in step families. They were more likely than those in intact families to leave home by 18 years whether the family disruption was due to separation, divorce or bereavement.

In her study of step children in the NCDS, Ferri [1984] found that overall:

'... the development of children with stepmothers did not differ very markedly from that of their peers in unbroken families or of those living with lone fathers.'

On the other hand,

'The results relating to children with stepfathers, however, were rather less reassuring. These children, and particularly the boys, frequently compared unfavourably with those in unbroken families, and differed little from children living with lone mothers.'

The outcomes from step-family life were generally less favourable when following the divorce of natural parents than the death of one of them.

But despite these observations, Ferri concludes that:

'For the majority of children we studied, there was no discernible adverse effect and little to distinguish them from their peers living with two natural parents.'

It was also true that

'... there was sufficient indication of unhappiness and development difficulties among a minority of stepchildren to suggest that remarriage should not be seen as an instant, all-purpose "cure" for the many problems faced by the one-parent family, especially if those problems are viewed from the child's perspective.'

Research in Australia of a cross-section of step-families looked at the relationships that 66 children had with their absent fathers and resident step-fathers. Children seemed to be happy at home where their step-father was involved with the family, but even more so where the step-father was well liked but slightly less involved. Moreover, good relations with their natural father seemed to be associated with better relations with their step-father. The researchers concluded that:

'Whatever the explanation, children tend to be involved with two fathers, or have little involvement with either.'

Some advice and help for step-parents on the complexities of the new relationship is given by Christine Webber and David Delvin on the 'NetDoctor' website:

Stepfamilies are very common nowadays. In fact it's been calculated that 18 million people in the UK are part of a stepfamily in some way or another. That's an awful lot of us.

And yet, most of us were not brought up in stepfamilies, so we don't know much about them. Furthermore, I doubt if many of us had any ambition to be a step-parent – and we've definitely had no training. Small wonder then that a lot of people today find the whole stepfamily set up very difficult.

The change from one relationship to another

Stepfamilies are created when one person who has children marries, or cohabits, again. Of course this can happen after a death, but nowadays it's much more common after divorce, or after the breakdown of a live-in relationship.

Splitting up

During this split between two co-habiting partners, there is usually a lot of trauma and bad feeling. And sometimes the adults concerned are so busy with all of their own upset and grief, that they don't have much time for their children – or for explaining things to them.

Unfortunately, the youngsters in such situations often feel completely bewildered. They have loyalties to both parents, but they are forcibly removed from one of them. They may also hear very strong criticism of each parent by the other, and yet they're expected to 'be a good boy' or to 'be a nice girl and don't make a fuss'. Meanwhile, they often feel they don't know exactly what's going on, but that they hate the changes. They also feel quite strongly that they have not asked for all this upset in their lives.

This is a very important point for adults to remember. No matter how difficult life is for the grown-ups in all of this, they should take on board that it can be absolutely terrifying for the children – and mostly that the kids would give anything for the split not to have happened.

Can you make the break any easier for the children?

You can certainly try.

First of all, try to fully comprehend just how important you and your partner are to your children. You are by far their biggest source of love. And they depend on it. In fact they frequently feel that Mum and Dad are their whole world. So a split between the two of you is just about the most frightening thing they can imagine. And it's important not to make light of it by saying something like: 'Mummy and Daddy are going to live in new houses. You'll stay with Mummy some of the time and go to Daddy's at weekends and in the holidays. It's all going to be great fun and you can have a bicycle and a computer in both houses.'

Of course, the new family set-up may be great fun – eventually. But putting this kind of gloss on a situation that is breaking a child's heart is irresponsible, and far too glib.

So both of you should talk to your children. And you should also reassure them that you both love them hugely – and that you will continue to love them even though you no longer want to live together.

Most important of all, do make sure they understand that the split is not their fault. Very often a break up in a relationship comes after months of quarrelling – and it's common for the children to become pawns in that situation with the parents disagreeing with each other on how the child should be brought up and disciplined. The memory of all these quarrels stays with such offspring – and they often grow up believing that they were somehow responsible for the break-up of their home.

Finally, during this traumatic time while parents are splitting up, it's a good idea to make sure that each child who is affected has an adult of his or her own with whom they can discuss what is going on and how they're feeling about it. Aunts, uncles or grandparents are possibilities. But relatives are only helpful if they don't take sides about the break-up. Other than a relative, a schoolteacher can be a good alternative, or a minister of religion, or a counsellor.

If the child is of school age, it is vital to tell the school that their parents are splitting up. Children frequently become quite badly behaved at such a time, or lose ground academically, and the teachers need to know what's going on so they can be sympathetic and helpful.

New partners

The next thing that happens for many families is that one parent finds a new love.

Of course in many situations, this new love has been around for a while, and may even have been a factor in the breakdown of the relationship.

But the realisation that one parent has a new boyfriend or girlfriend can be an enormous shock to a child.

Another scenario is when the children are living with a lone parent after a divorce or separation – and are just adjusting to that situation – when suddenly this live-in mum or dad meets someone new.

In this case the child has yet another adjustment to make after the initial upheaval. So it's hardly surprising that such a youngster might become clingy, or might resist going to school, or may well have curious tummy-upsets, or even insomnia.

A wise parent will understand that this kind of response from children is perfectly natural. After all:

- their home as they knew it has changed beyond recognition.
- one parent no longer lives in the home.
- there is now another grown-up to deal with.

So it's scarcely surprising that the child's behaviour alters.

But a parent who is newly in love – and who may be feeling very blessed and lucky to have found love again – very frequently gets cross and upset with a child who is 'acting up' and appearing to be doing everything possible to sabotage the new relationship. The parent feels vulnerable after the demise of the last relationship and anxious about sustaining a new one, but this should not blind them to the very real anxieties that the children are suffering.

If you are experiencing these feelings in this kind of situation, do try to remember that though you have fallen for this new and wonderful person, your child has not. In fact, the chances are that your child is feeling very strange about your new romance – and deeply worried about what it will mean about their own relationship with you, and with your ex.

Try to remember too that children often perceive the new person as a temporary measure. In fact, they often comfort themselves with this thought, so they certainly are not gong to make a tremendous effort to be likeable to your new lover, no matter how important this person is to you.

Once you have become a stepfamily by introducing a new live-in partner, do make sure that:

- you still have plenty of time with your child without your new partner being there all the time.
- your children are not forced into accepting the new person as a replacement parent.
- your children still get plenty of opportunities to see your ex.

Of course if your ex has disappeared into the blue yonder and is having nothing to do with the kids, that's a different matter. But even then, it is wise to try to speak well of your former spouse – even if you can't stand them. It is also sensible not to try to force the pace in encouraging your child to accept your new partner. Children very frequently form exceedingly good relationships with step-parents, but they do so in their own time – and not to order.

The family with two sets of children

Often nowadays a new family is formed between two adults who both have children living with them – so two lots of youngsters have to learn to share a home and to get on together.

Sometimes, of course, the two sets of kids only meet up at weekends or holidays because one lot lives with another parent much of the time.

Then there are situations where one set of children may be older and possibly living away from home, but return occasionally.

In all of these situations, it really helps if you don't expect too much too soon from anybody in the house!

I have heard new partners say that everything is going to be great because they both have kids under 10 years old and they're all bound to get along! Alas, such optimism is frequently misplaced.

In such a new family there is often trouble about territory. Sometimes the accommodation is crowded and there's not enough space for all the children to have their own room. But do try to make sure that they all at least have their own areas within a room, and that these areas are regarded as private to that individual.

Many kids may well have had their own rooms in a previous house, and it can take a while before they feel settled in the new place. So having somewhere where they can put their toys, books and clothes – and know that no one is going to interfere with these items – is vitally important.

Discipline is another big issue. It's essential that the two adults present a united front. Of course this isn't easy as kids will often try to play one grown-up off against the other.

Try not to rise to this. Just make sure that you and your new partner support each other wholeheartedly in front of the children, even if you need to settle some differences between you when the kids aren't around.

Then there's the question of love. Step-parents often worry that they don't feel they can love their partner's children as much as they love their own. Of course they can't! Not immediately anyway, so this is not something you should feel guilty about. In time you may very well come to love these new children very, very much indeed. But initially all you can do is strive to be fair in your dealings with two sets of children, and also to make a big effort to take a real interest in the children who are not yours by birth.

New baby

It's very natural for two people who love each other to want to produce their own child.

Frequently, a new baby is a very joyous event for the whole family. But it goes without saying that the happy, expectant parents should be acutely aware of the feelings and needs of their existing children at this time. Giving them extra hugs and attention is a very good idea. And involving them every step of the way with the new baby will help them to feel important and useful and excited: a family get-together to discuss names for the forthcoming arrival, for example, can help all the kids to feel part of this new family adventure.

With careful handling, the kids should come to feel very pleased and happy that there's to be a new baby. But if they're not helped though this, they can feel 'second best', or 'in the way'.

Step-parents who have no children of their own

Step-parents who have no children of their own have the advantage of not feeling torn between two sets of kids. But they have the disadvantage of never having brought up children – and frequently they're worried that they haven't a clue how to start!

Some people fall in love with someone who has children but spend their lives wishing that the youngsters would somehow disappear and leave them in peace. This kind of attitude is not just selfish; it's really stupid. And it commonly ruins the very relationship they want to keep so special and intimate.

Other new step-parents are so keen not to be seen as the 'wicked' stepmum or stepdad, that they go over the top in their bid to get the kids to love them – buying them expensive presents and giving them treats every time they meet, for example.

Laudable though it is to try to show kids that you want to love and care for them, most children are very suspicious of these tactics. They have no idea whether the new partner is going to be permanent. And they don't want to be forced to appreciate or love someone.

If you're a new step-parent, you should be aware that your stepchild may believe that loving and accepting you would be disloyal to your partner's ex. In fact, children often feel guilty if they have a good time with a step-parent – and just when you might think that progress has been made, they'll withdraw their smiles and their co-operation. This is awfully hard to put up with, but it doesn't feel quite so painful or personal if you remember the complexity of the child's feelings.

The best thing you can do as a new step-parent is to be genuinely interested in your stepchild and to learn the names of his or her friends and teachers – and to be aware of favourite books, pop groups, television programmes and so on. More than that you cannot do. So don't be pushy – just keep being kind and interested, and in time, the child will come to accept you.

Sometimes this process seems unending. In fact, it may be 10 years before some stepfamily arrangements really shake down and become comfortable and loving. But persistence pays off. And though many tears may be shed during this period, the rewards are usually great in the long run.

Part-time parents
Many stepfamily situations do not actually involve having children living with you all the time. You and your partner may have kids who just come at weekends, or in the holidays.

One of the common complaints of this kind of setup is that because the two partners work very hard all week, they would like to relax over the weekends – but they can't because that's when the children come.

If it's at all possible for some of the contact with these children to be made on weekdays so that weekends are not always taken up in this way, then do it.

Quite apart from your needs and feelings, as children get older they very frequently want to be at their main home at weekends, so that they can go out with their mates. Therefore, if the only contact is on Saturdays and Sundays you may well find that the children start refusing to come – and this can cause great problems.

But the other factor to remember is that if you are exhausted by the working-week and then have no time to relax because of visiting children at the weekends, you're likely to get very ratty and very fed up. This can damage your relationship with your partner as well as that with the visiting children.

All of us need some leisure time and some space of our own. So if you are a step-parent and the weekends are a nightmare of activity when all you really want to do is to have a lie-in, and some time to yourself, you should try to discuss this before it becomes a huge contentious issue.

If re-arranging things so that the children don't come every single weekend is impossible, do remember that kids want to have some time with their natural parent without the step-parent being present. This can give the step-parent time to visit friends or to catch up on sleep, but of course the natural parent is on the go the whole time!

If weekends are totally taken up with children, then the two adults should make sure they have some quality time for themselves and each other during the week to make up for it.

The other important issue here is that the children should have space in your home to call their own. If they don't, they will feel like unwelcome lodgers and their behaviour will probably reflect that. But if they have their own space, their own toys and books – maybe their own television – they will feel more at home and they will be happier. They will also amuse themselves some of the time – and then you and your spouse won't be at their beck and call 24 hours a day.

It's not all bad!
As I said earlier in this article, it can take anything up to 10 years for everyone to settle in a stepfamily situation. And the 'settling' process can seem fraught and difficult – and as if it's never, ever going to come right.

But it's not all bad. Gradually people accept individuals – and grow to love them. And wonderful new relationships can be developed.

A stepdaughter may find her stepmother easier to talk to than her own mum. A stepson might use a step-parent to get an important message through to his own dad.

There are plenty of bonuses in being in a stepfamily. It's just that you have to surmount a lot of obstacles before you notice them!

In *Making a Go of It* (1984), Burgoyne and Clark construct the following typology to reflect these variations:

Table 6.1: A typology of stepfamilies

1   *'Not really a stepfamily'*
The stepchildren of the family were young at the time of divorce and remarriage; within a short time they were able to think of themselves as an 'ordinary' family. Children of new marriage confirm this.

2   *'Looking forward to the departure of the children'*
Older couples with teenage children await departure of dependent children so that they can enjoy their new partnership more fully.
Too old for children in new marriage.

3   *The 'progressive' stepfamily*
Prototype 'new' stepfamily in which conflicts with ex-partners have been resolved. They stress the advantages of their circumstances.
Few barriers to additional children of new marriage.

4   *The successful conscious pursuit of an 'ordinary' family life together*
Stepparent becomes full 'social' parent transferring allegiance to stepchildren. Their initial problems are solved or successfully ignored.
Children of new marriage symbolise 'normality' of their family life.

5   *The conscious pursuit of 'ordinary' family life frustrated*
The legacy of their past marriage(s) frustrates their attempts to build an ordinary family life together.
Children of new marriage are unlikely because of continuing problems.

Step-families began increasingly to resort to adoption as a solution to these difficulties. In 1970, however, a Departmental Committee on the Adoption of Children published a Working Paper in which they voiced the doubts of many professionals about this practice and made a radical suggestion:

93. Just as openness about adoption and illegitimacy is desirable, so is it desirable to recognise openly the fact and the consequences of divorce and of death. One of the consequences of divorce is that many children are living with a parent and a step-parent and retain contact with, or even live for part of the time with, their other parent, who may also have remarried. Such a situation may well be disturbing to the child, but it is not appropriate to use adoption in an attempt to ease the pain or to cover up these consequences of divorce. The legal extinguishment of a legitimate child's links with one half of his own family, which adoption entails in such circumstances, is inappropriate and may well be damaging.

The Children Act 1975 accordingly introduced statutory discouragement of all types of step-parent adoption. The courts have always been reluctant to dispense with the agreement of an estranged father who does not want his children adopted, but they have had difficulty in working out when they ought to refuse an adoption which everyone wanted (see *Re D (minors) (adoption by step-parent)* (1980) 2 FLR 102, 10 Fam Law 246).

The numbers of step-parents have increased dramatically, but the numbers of step-parent adoptions have not. They remain, however, a sizeable proportion of the diminishing number of adoption orders, as the Judicial Statistics 2000 show:

During 2000, 4,438 orders for adoption were made (12% more than in 1999). Of these, 35% (1,551) were made to step-parents, 4% less than in 1999 (where 1,614 of the 3,962 orders were to step-parents).

Table 5.4 – Adoption of children: Summary of proceedings, 2000

Nature of proceedings	Family Proceedings courts[1]	County courts	High Court	Total
Applications:				
by step-parents	884	978	17	1,879
by others	953	2,052	112	3,117
Total	**1,837**	**3,030**	**129**	**4,996**
Orders made:				
to step-parents	691	852	8	1,551
to others	858	1,948	81	2,887
Total	**1,549**	**2,800**	**89**	**4,438**

1 Contains imputed data

Under the Children Act 1989, the court may make any s. 8 order instead of an adoption order whenever it wishes, although it has no duty to consider doing so. Step-parent adoptions are no longer expressly discouraged. If the child is treated as a 'child of the family' of the new marriage, the step-parent is always entitled to apply for a residence or contact order (s. 10(5)(a)). He may be ordered to make financial provision for the child, although he will not be automatically liable under the new child support scheme (see Chapter 4). The child may also apply for family provision from his estate (see p. 191, above).

Judith Masson, Daphne Norbury and Sandra Chatterton, in *Mine, Yours or Ours? A Study of Step-parent Adoption* (1983), found, as others have done, that step-parents are not very interested in an alternative to adoption. They discuss a new way of giving them some status:

Applicants we interviewed had little or no idea of the legal implications of adoption. They wanted to make the family like a 'proper family' but did not intend that the child be considered as 'adopted' rather than as 'their own'. Mothers did not want to become adoptive mothers and some were disturbed that the birth certificate had to be replaced with an adoption certificate. What they appeared to want was recognition for the step-parent, permission to change the child's name and something to reassure them that their family was secure. Adoption went far beyond this and legally made fundamental changes in the family structure. The belief that adoption is essential if members of the step-family are to be treated as belonging to a complete family unit or the step-parent is to enjoy legal rights arises largely from ignorance. ...

There is need for recognition of the step-parent during the life of his spouse: a need currently met, albeit inadequately for a minority, by adoption. The criticisms of the present and former laws suggest that whether or not there is a thorough investigation of the family, it has simply not been possible to assess families for a different status because there are no accepted criteria. If this is true, it follows that any new status should be available to all step-parents on demand. If there were no assessment and no selection then there would be no place for either a guardian ad litem or a judge. An administrative process could be used, just as adoption applicants themselves had expected in the past.

If a status is to be available without investigation to all who seek it, it should involve neither the exclusion of the other natural parent nor the creation of extra rights in the step-family. This could be achieved by a change in legislation enabling the step-parent to share those parental rights which his spouse has. There would be no need for the law to allocate these rights between the parent and the step-parent; this would be a matter for the parties, as it is in families of first marriage. Both parent and step-parent, and the other natural parent, would be able to challenge a decision or refer a dispute to the court, as can parents and guardians at present. Disputes would be settled applying the welfare principle. ... It would avoid the necessity of the natural parent naming the step-parent as guardian by will or deed if she wished him to act in the event of her death. The status which a step-parent can be given on the death of his spouse would exist during the marriage, thus problems would not arise as they do now merely because the natural parent dies intestate. ... This new status would not automatically provide for inheritance between the child and step-parent on intestacy; this would, perhaps, be too fundamental a change in English law. Nor would it permit the post-divorce parent and step-parent to change the child's name without the permission of either the other natural parent or the court. In fact, the status provided would be similar to the guardianship which the step-parent (or any other person) may obtain on the parent's death.

The *Review of Adoption Law – Report to Ministers of an Interdepartmental Working Group* (1992) took up the argument once more:

19.2 Adoption by a step-parent and parent severs the legal links between a child and the other side of his or her birth family. There may be circumstances in which this is appropriate, for instance where the other parent has never acted in a parental capacity and the child has never really known any member of that side of the birth family. But where the child has some relationship with the parent, or with his or her relatives, it is unlikely to be in the child's interests for their legal relationship to be extinguished. A parent may agree to adoption simply because he has no interest in the child, or even where he has such an interest and is keen to retain it but wishes to end the payment of maintenance. Where the other parent has died or is no longer in the picture, the possible benefits to the child of retaining a legal relationship with grandparents or other relatives may be overlooked. Of course, the adoption order need not mean severance of practical links. But where the prime motivation behind an adoption application is the wish to cement the family unit and put away the past, this may be confusing and lead to identity problems for the child, especially if (as is statistically not unlikely) the new marriage breaks down. It is also possible that the step-parent's family has little or no involvement or interest in the adopted child, so that the child loses one family without really gaining another. As divorce has become more common, it is less necessary for families to pursue step-parent adoption in order to avoid embarrassment and difficult explanations. We do not consider it appropriate to prevent step-parent adoptions; but there may be ways in which the law can help to discourage inappropriate applications.

Step-parent adoption orders
19.3 Where adoption by a step-parent is in a child's interests, we consider it anomalous that the parent who is caring for the child should also become an adoptive parent. It can be disturbing for a birth parent and child to have the birth certificate replaced by an adoption certificate on which the birth parent is shown as an adoptive parent. We therefore recommend that there should be a new type of adoption order, available only to step-parents, which does not make the birth parent (ie the step-parent's spouse) an adoptive parent but in almost all other respects resembles a normal adoption order. Application for the order would be by the step-parent with the agreement of his or her spouse. The order could not be made unless the child's other parent (if he or she had parental responsibility) – and the child (if 12 or over) – agreed to the adoption, or the court dispensed with agreement on one of the specified grounds [see p. 778, below]. The child's legal links with the other birth parent and family would be severed. Consideration would have to be given to an appropriate way of amending the adoption certificate and of recording the adoption on the Adopted Children Register. The order should only be open to a step-parent, not to an unmarried partner.
19.4 We are concerned by the relative incidence of breakdown of second and subsequent marriages. Where a step-parent who has adopted a child subsequently becomes divorced from the child's birth parent, it is possible that the parent and child may wish to have restored their legal relationship with the other side of the child's birth family. We therefore recommend that there should be provision for a step-parent adoption order to be undone where the marriage ends by divorce or death and the child is under the age of 18. Application would be by the birth parent whose parental responsibility had been extinguished by the adoption order. Agreement to the revocation of the order would be required from the step-parent, the parent who retained parental responsibility and the child if aged 12 or over. If any of these people did not agree to the revocation of the order, it would stand unless their agreement could be dispensed with. ... Consideration should also be given to whether, and if so in what circumstances, a child who has reached the age of 18 should be able to apply for the revocation of an order.

Alternative orders
19.5 We have already made clear our concern that some applications by step-parents appear to be made without full consideration of the needs of the child. It is likely that in many circumstances

a residence order would be a better way of confirming a step-parent's responsibility for a child, because it does not alter a child's legal relationship with his or her parents and family. ...
19.6 ... we do not feel it would be advisable to have a ... legislative presumption in favour of residence orders for step-parents. We have already recommended (see above, paragraph 6.3) that the court should have a duty to consider alternative orders, including residence orders. It is even more important that any step-parent who is considering applying for an adoption order should be encouraged to explore alternative orders before the application comes to court. ...

Acquisition of parental responsibility by step-parents
19.8 Inappropriate applications might also less frequently be made if step-parents were able to acquire parental responsibility without a court order by making an agreement with the birth parent, in the same way that unmarried fathers may now acquire parental responsibility under section 4 of the Children Act 1989. A person with parental responsibility has all the rights, duties, powers, responsibilities and authority which by law a parent of a child has in relation to the child and the child's property. A person with a residence order has parental responsibility but only while the residence order remains in force. ... It would therefore be a significant step to allow step-parents to acquire parental responsibility, but one which we feel is justified in view of the public relationship which the step-parent has with the child's parent and their entitlement to apply for an adoption order, which is likely to be far less appropriate. We therefore propose that a step-parent should acquire parental responsibility for a child if at any time he and both parents make an agreement to share parental responsibility (in a form prescribed under regulations made by the Lord Chancellor). We propose also that a court should have the power to make a parental responsibility order in favour of a step-parent. Where the other parent does not agree to the step-parent's acquisition of parental responsibility, the step-parent could apply for such an order. It would also be one of the alternatives available to a court (and which the court would have a duty to consider) when considering an application for a step-parent adoption order.
19.9 It should not be possible, under this system, for an unmarried co-habitant to acquire parental responsibility in respect of his or her partner's child, or for the court to grant it.

Two important changes are contained in the Adoption and Children Bill. First, adoption will be possible by one person who is the 'partner' of the child's natural parent, by virtue of clause 50(2), and the (mysterious) result is that the child is treated –

66 (1) ...
    (b) where the adoption is effected by an order made by virtue of section 50(2), as if the person had been born as a child of the marriage of the adopter and the person to whom the adopter is married (whether or not the person was in fact born after the marriage was solemnized)...

Clause 66 goes on to say:

    (2) An adopted person—
    (a) where the adoption is effected by an order made by virtue of section 50(2), is to be treated in law as not being the child of any person other than the adopter and the person to whom the adopter is married...
    but this subsection does not affect any reference in the Act to a person's natural parent

Moreover, clause 109 of the Bill would add a new section to the Children Act 1989:

4A Acquisition of parental responsibility by step-parent
    (1) Where a child's parent ('parent A') who has parental responsibility for the child is married to a person who is not the child's parent ('the stepparent')—
    (a) parent A or, if the other parent of the child also has parental responsibility for the child, both parents may by agreement with the step-parent provide for the step-parent to have parental responsibility for the child; or
    (b) the court may, on the application of the step-parent, order that the step-parent shall have parental responsibility for the child.
    (2) An agreement under subsection (1)(a) is also a 'parental responsibility agreement', and section 4(2) applies in relation to such agreements as it applies in relation to parental responsibility agreements under section 4.

(3) A parental responsibility agreement under subsection (1)(a), or an order under subsection (1)(b), may only be brought to an end by an order of the court made on the application—

    (a) of any person who has parental responsibility for the child; or

    (b) with the leave of the court, of the child himself.

(4) The court may only grant leave under subsection (3) (b) if it is satisfied that the child has sufficient understanding to make the proposed application.

Questions

(i) Suppose that your parents divorced, your mother remarried and your step-father adopted you; but some time after that your mother died and your step-father was no longer able to look after you; meanwhile your father had remarried and wanted you to live with him; and so did you: should it be possible for the adoption order to be revoked? (See *Re M (minors) (adoption)* [1990] FCR 993, [1991] 1 FLR 458, CA, and *Re B (adoption: jurisdiction to set aside)* [1995] Fam 239, [1995] 2 FLR 1, CA.)

(ii) The recommendations in para. 19.8 have been accepted: how do they differ from the proposals made by Judith Masson and her colleagues?

(iii) Would you have banned step-parent adoptions altogether?

So what does an adoption order do that a residence order in favour of parent and step-parent does not? Most of the cases concern emigration and change of surname, which are prohibited unless the other parent consents or the court gives leave (s. 13 of the Children Act 1989; see p. 586, above). These issues are not confined, of course, to step-families, but we deal with them here because, in practice, getting leave to change a name or to remove a child from the jurisdiction is easier when the primary carer has re-partnered than when she simply wants to go home to mum.

Question

Why do you suppose that is so?

The leading case on change of name is *Re W, Re A, Re B*:

Re W (A Child) (Illegitimate Child: Change of Surname); Re A (A Child); Re B (Children)
[2001] Fam 1, [1999] 2 FLR 930, Court of Appeal

In the first of these three cases the mother registered her illegitimate child, J, with her surname. She subsequently married the father and had another child who was registered with his surname. The parents applied to re-register J's name following their marriage but by the time the registrar contacted them the marriage had failed. The mother changed her own name by deed poll, reverting to her original surname. The father applied to change J's surname to his own. The judge refused the application and the father appealed.

Butler-Sloss LJ:

[1] These three appeals have one issue in common, the circumstances in which a child registered at birth in one surname may have that name changed by deed poll by one parent against the wishes of the other. Before turning to the individual facts and issues which arise on each appeal, following the decision of the House of Lords in *Dawson v Wearmouth*

[1999] 2 AC 308 it may be helpful to set out what appears to be the present position on change of name applications.

...

[5] In *Dawson v Wearmouth* the father was not married to the mother. After the birth of their child, without consulting the father, she registered him in the name of her former husband, by whom she had previously had two children. They had already separated. The father sought, various orders under the Children Act, including a parental responsibility order and a specific issue order to change the child's surname to his. The circuit judge made a contact and parental responsibility order and directed that the child be known by the father's surname. His decision was reversed by the Court of Appeal and their decision was upheld by the House of Lords [1999] 2 AC 308.

[6] In his speech Lord Mackay of Clashfern said, at p 321:

'The application of section 1 so long as they take account of the criteria there in question is a matter within the discretion of the Court of Appeal and I can see no ground for suggesting that they have erred in principle. The heavy emphasis on the registration is, I think, a reflection of the fact that they considered that the judge had wrongly left that out of account and that the application must be understood as for a change from a name already registered and therefore that in the light of section 1 of the 1989 Act some circumstances required to be pointed to which would justify making that change in the interests of the child's welfare. In fairness to the Court of Appeal it must be pointed out that, although they described the fact that the name sought to be changed was the duly registered name as 'all-important', they coupled that with the circumstances that the name Wearmouth was the mother's actual name at the time it was chosen by her, as well as being that of Alexander's half-brother and half-sister, in stating their view that their discretion should be exercised against the making of the order for change ... In my opinion on a fair reading of the decision of the Court of Appeal they were suggesting not that the registration was conclusive of the issue in the present case but that in order to justify changing the name from that which was registered circumstances justifying the change would be required and they concluded in the exercise of their discretion that there were no such circumstances of sufficient strength to do so in the present case.'

...

[9] The present position, in summary, would appear to be as follows. (a) If parents are married they both have the power and the duty to register their child's names. (b) If they are not married the mother has the sole duty and power to do so. (c) After registration of the child's names, the grant of a residence order obliges any person wishing to change the surname to obtain the leave of the court or the written consent of all those who have parental responsibility. (d) In the absence of a residence order, the person wishing to change the surname from the registered name ought to obtain the relevant written consent or the leave of the court by making an application for a specific issue order. (e) On any application the welfare of the child is paramount, and the judge must have regard to the section 1(3) criteria. (f) Among the factors to which the court should have regard is the registered surname of the child and the reasons for the registration, for instance recognition of the biological link with the child's father. Registration is always a relevant and an important consideration but it is not in itself decisive. The weight to be given to it by the court will depend upon the other relevant factors or valid countervailing reasons which may tip the balance the other way. (g) The relevant considerations should include factors which may arise in the future as well as the present situation. (h) Reasons given for changing or seeking to change a child's name based on the fact that the child's name is or is not the same as the parent making the application do not generally carry much weight. (i) The reasons for an earlier unilateral decision to change a child's name may be relevant (j) Any changes of circumstances of the child since the original registration may be relevant. (k) In the case of a child whose parents were married to each other, the fact of the marriage is important and I would suggest that there would have to be strong reasons to change the name from the father's surname if the child was so registered. (l) Where the child's parents were not married to each other, the mother has control over registration. Consequently on an application to change the surname of the child, the degree of commitment of the father to the child, the quality of contact, if it occurs, between father and child, the existence or absence of parental responsibility are all relevant factors to take into account.

[10] I cannot stress too strongly that these are only guidelines which do not purport to be exhaustive. Each case has to be decided on its own facts with the welfare of the child the paramount consideration and all the relevant factors weighed in the balance by the court at the time of the hearing. I turn now to the three appeals. The issue in the first appeal concerns the amendment of the register in relation to a child legitimated by the subsequent marriage of the parents. ...

Appeal in In re W

...

[14] In this case there has been no unilateral change of name so the child has always been called by her registered name of W. The judge directed himself that the approach was what is in the best interests of the child now. There had to be good and cogent reasons shown to allow a change. In applying the section 1(3) welfare checklist the likely effect of any change of circumstances (section 1(3)(c)), her present name should not be changed without good reason. He referred to the Court of Appeal judgments in *Dawson v Wearmouth* [1998] Fam 75 and the significance attached to registration. He did not, of course, have the speeches of the House of Lords cited to him. He concluded:

> 'When I come back to this case and consider the reasons advanced; first the maintenance of the link with the father and the question of the two girls attending the same school and having the same name. The maintenance of a link is not a matter of a name but a matter of contact how the father gets on [with it] and treats and cares for the girls. ... Change of name takes away from the family unit. In general those considerations balance out and favour no change. When I look to see good and cogent reasons I can find none. In this case I see no reason to disturb the little girl's name, state of mind or knowledge.'

...

[16]... But, for my part, in this case, which was not easy to decide, I cannot say that the judge fell into error by exercising his discretion in the manner in which he did. Appellate judges ought not to substitute their exercise of discretion for the judge's unless he erred in principle or was otherwise plainly wrong. I would dismiss the appeal in *In re W*.

Questions

(i) What weight should be given to the views of the children on this question?

(ii) There are many cases in which a child's surname might be changed without resort to litigation – for example, if any of these fathers had consented, or if they were dead, or if the children had used their names although the parents were unmarried – are the arguments against allowing this any less strong in such cases?

(iv) What do you think the answer would be if a divorced mother reverted to her maiden name and wanted her children to use it too? (See *Re F (child: surname)* [1993] 2 FLR 837n.)

What about the issue of emigration? The break-up of a family may prompt the desire to start afresh somewhere else; but there may be many different reasons and attitudes involved in such a decision.

Payne v Payne
[2001] EWCA Civ 166, [2001] Fam 473, [2001] 2 WLR 1826, [2001] 1 FCR 425, [2001] 1 FLR 1052, Court of Appeal

The mother of a four-year-old child applied to remove the child from the United Kingdom to New Zealand. The mother was originally from New Zealand but had met and married the father in England. The mother was not happy in England and the parties had discussed relocating to New Zealand. The father accepted a contract of employment in Kuala Lumpur and whilst he was there the mother and the child resided in New Zealand. The parties separated and the mother made an application for custody and an order that the father be prevented from removing the child from that jurisdiction, arguing that the move to New Zealand was intended as a permanent relocation of the family. The judge did not find the mother a convincing witness and ordered that the child be returned to the United

Kingdom, which was done. On arrival the mother disappeared with the child but was discovered within a few days by the father who had sought the assistance of the police. The mother applied for residence and to remove the child from the country permanently. In the county court the mother's application was successful. The father appealed on the basis that over the last 30 years the comparative importance of contact between the child and the absent parent had increased and that the body of case law was inconsistent with the Children Act 1989 as it created a presumption in favour of the applicant. Alternatively he argued that the court's approach was inconsistent with the Human Rights Act 1998 and that a new approach ought to be formulated which would properly recognise the father's human rights.

Thorpe LJ: ...
[16] The modern law regulating applications for the emigration of children begins with the decision of this court in *P (LM) (otherwise E) v P (GE)* [1970] 3 All ER 659; sub nom *Poel v Poel* [1970] 1 WLR 1469. I doubt that the judges deciding the case recognised how influential it would prove to be. Whilst emphasising that the court should have regard primarily to the welfare of the child, both Sachs LJ and Winn LJ emphasised the importance of recognising and supporting the function of the primary carer. That consideration was most clearly expressed by Sachs LJ when he said:

'When a marriage breaks up, then a situation normally arises when the child of that marriage, instead of being in the joint custody of both parents, must of necessity become one who is in the custody of a single parent. Once that position has arisen and the custody is working well, this court should not lightly interfere with such reasonable way of life as is selected by that parent to whom custody has been rightly given. Any such interference may, as Winn LJ has pointed out, produce considerable strains which would be unfair not only to the parent whose way of life is interfered with but also to any new marriage of that parent. In that way it might well in due course reflect on the welfare of the child. The way in which the parent who properly has custody of a child may choose in a reasonable manner to order his or her way of life is one of those things which the parent who has not been given custody may well have to bear, even though one has every sympathy with the latter on some of the results.'

[21] In the case of *Lonslow v Hennig* [1986] 2 FLR 378, Dillon LJ reviewed and applied the authorities in allowing a mother's appeal from the refusal of her application to emigrate with the children to New Zealand. Having reminded himself that so far as the law was concerned the first point was that the welfare of the children was the paramount consideration and secondly that previous cases decided on other facts could only provide guidelines, he noted that there was a consistent line of guidance throughout the decisions of this court since 1970.
[22] In *Belton v Belton* [1987] 2 FLR 343 at 349 Purchas LJ in allowing a mother's appeal against the refusal of her application to emigrate to New Zealand said:

'I sympathize and understand, where a lay person such as a father is concerned, the difficulty of reconciliation with the concept of such a separation being in the paramount interests of the child in the long term, but the long-term interests of the child revolve around establishing, as Griffiths LJ (as he then was) said in Chamberlain, a sound, secure family unit in which the child should go forward and develop. If that can be supported by contact with the father, that is an immense advantage, but, if it cannot, then that is no reason for diverting one's concentration from the central and paramount issue in the case.'

[23] He summarised the authorities by saying (at 349-350):

'. . . the authorities and the law which dictate the hard and difficult decision which must be made once it is established that the custodial parent genuinely desires to emigrate and, in circumstances in which there is nothing adverse to be found in the conditions to be expected, those authorities are quite clear in the course that the court must take, whatever the hardship and distress that may result.'

[24] In *Tyler v Tyler* [1990] 1 FCR 22 at 25 Kerr LJ, having been referred to virtually all the reported cases in which an issue of this kind had arisen, offered this summary:

'I also accept that this line of authority shows that where the custodial parent herself — it was the mother in all those cases — has a genuine and reasonable desire to emigrate then the court should hesitate long before refusing permission to take the children.'

...

[26] In summary a review of the decisions of this court over the course of the last 30 years demonstrates that relocation cases have been consistently decided upon the application of the following two propositions: (a) the welfare of the child is the paramount consideration; and (b) refusing the primary carer's reasonable proposals for the relocation of her family life is likely to impact detrimentally on the welfare of her dependent children. Therefore her application to relocate will be granted unless the court concludes that it is incompatible with the welfare of the children.

...

[31] Logically and as a matter of experience the child cannot draw emotional and psychological security and stability from the dependency unless the primary carer herself is emotionally and psychologically stable and secure. The parent cannot give what she herself lacks. Although fathers as well as mothers provide primary care I have never myself encountered a relocation application brought by a father and for the purposes of this judgment I assume that relocation applications are only brought by maternal primary carers. The disintegration of a family unit is invariably emotionally and psychologically turbulent. The mother who emerges with the responsibility of making the home for the children may recover her sense of well-being simply by coping over a passage of time. But often the mother may be in need of external support, whether financial, emotional or social. Such support may be provided by a new partner who becomes stepfather to the child. The creation of a new family obviously draws the child into its quest for material and other fulfilment. Such cases have given rise to the strongest statements of the guidelines. Alternatively the disintegration of the family unit may leave the mother in a society to which she was carried by the impetus of family life before its failure. Commonly in that event she may feel isolated and driven to seek the support she lacks by returning to her homeland, her family and her friends. In the remarriage cases the motivation for relocation may well be to meet the stepfather's career needs or opportunities. In those cases refusal is likely to destabilise the new family emotionally as well as to penalise it financially. In the case of the isolated mother, to deny her the support of her family and a return to her roots may have an even greater psychological detriment and she may have no one who might share her distress or alleviate her depression. ...

[32] Thus in most relocation cases the most crucial assessment and finding for the judge is likely to be the effect of the refusal of the application on the mother's future psychological and emotional stability. ...

[34] However with the commencement of the Human Rights Act 1998 on 2 October 2000 it was not hard to foresee that a father responding to a relocation application would submit that the emigration of his child to a distant land constituted a breach of his right to family life under art 8. This court indeed anticipated the development in its rejection of an application for permission to appeal reported as *Re G-A (a child) (removal from jurisdiction: human rights)* [2001] 1 FCR 43. Although the Convention for the Protection of Human Rights and Fundamental Freedoms (the European Convention on Human Rights) (Rome, 4 November 1950; TS 71 (1953); Cmd 8969) was not then of direct application and although the court was not determining an appeal, the opinions expressed are obviously persuasive. There has of course been some evolution in the application of the Convention over the course of the last nine months and the view expressed by Buxton LJ to the effect that the Convention has perhaps no place in this area of litigation seems no longer sustainable, in the light of the decision of the European Court in *Glaser v UK* [2000] 3 FCR 193 and the decision of this court on 21 December 2000 in the case of *Douglas v Hello Ltd* [2000] CA Transcript 2283.

[35] I am in broad agreement with the views expressed by Ward LJ to the effect that the advent of the Convention within our domestic law does not necessitate a revision of the fundamental approach to relocation applications formulated by this court and consistently applied over so many years ...

[39] As early as 1988, the House of Lords stated that the European Convention in no way conflicted with the requirements in English law that in all matters concerning the upbringing of a child, welfare was paramount (*Re KD (a minor) (ward: termination of access)* [1988] FCR 657, [1988] AC 806). This has been restated recently in *Dawson v Wearmouth* [1999] 1 FCR 625, [1999] 2 AC 308, *Re A (adoption: mother's objections)* [2000] 1 FLR 665 and *Re N (leave to withdraw care proceedings)* [2000] 1 FCR 258...

[40] However there is a danger that if the regard which the court pays to the reasonable proposals of the primary carer were elevated into a legal presumption then there would be an obvious risk of the breach of the respondent's rights not only under art 8 but also his rights under art 6 to a fair trial. To guard against the risk of too perfunctory an investigation resulting from too ready an assumption that the mother's proposals are necessarily compatible with the child's welfare I would suggest the following discipline as a prelude to conclusion. (a) Pose the question: is the mother's application genuine in the sense that it is not motivated by some selfish desire to exclude the father from the child's life? Then ask is the mother's application

realistic, by which I mean founded on practical proposals both well researched and investigated? If the application fails either of these tests refusal will inevitably follow. (b) If however the application passes these tests then there must be a careful appraisal of the father's opposition: is it motivated by genuine concern for the future of the child's welfare or is it driven by some ulterior motive? What would be the extent of the detriment to him and his future relationship with the child were the application granted? To what extent would that be offset by extension of the child's relationships with the maternal family and homeland? (c) What would be the impact on the mother, either as the single parent or as a new wife, of a refusal of her realistic proposal? (d) The outcome of the second and third appraisals must then be brought into an overriding review of the child's welfare as the paramount consideration, directed by the statutory checklist in so far as appropriate.

[41] In suggesting such a discipline I would not wish to be thought to have diminished the importance that this court has consistently attached to the emotional and psychological well-being of the primary carer. In any evaluation of the welfare of the child as the paramount consideration great weight must be given to this factor. ...

[56] The following conclusions result. (a) An analysis of the judgment reveals no misdirection or error of law. (b) The judge carried out an impeccable investigation of the relevant facts and circumstances as a prelude to clear findings on the mother's reliability, both as a parent and as a witness, as well as upon her proposals and the impact of their rejection both on her and on S. (c) The judge's discretionary choice of the option least damaging to S's welfare is not open to challenge in this court. ...

Appeal dismissed.

Questions

(i)   Why do you suppose that all the relocation cases Thorpe LJ has met (para. [31] above) have been brought by mothers?

(ii) Suppose the child's mother wishes to relocate from, say, Tyneside, where she has lived with his father, to Cornwall. What will be the effect of this upon the child's relationship with his father? What application could the father make to challenge that decision and what would be his prospects of success?

12.5 International child abduction

We do not know a great deal about parents who abduct their children, except that it appears to be on the increase. The law has struggled for a long time to reconcile the desire to deter abduction with the court's usual duty to do what is best for the particular child concerned. The 1983 Hague Convention on the Civil Aspects of International Child Abduction, implemented in English law by the Child Abduction and Custody Act 1985, imposes on contracting states reciprocal obligations to return abducted children to the country of their habitual residence almost irrespective of the welfare of the child. The most important articles are these:

Article 3
The removal or the retention of a child is to be considered wrongful where—
(a) it is in breach of rights of custody attributed to a person, an institution or any other body, either jointly or alone, under the law of the State in which the child was habitually resident immediately before the removal or retention; and
(b) at the time of removal or retention those rights were actually exercised, either jointly or alone, or would have been so exercised but for the removal or retention.
The rights of custody mentioned in sub-paragraph (a) above may arise in particular by operation of law or by reason of a judicial or administrative decision, or by reason of an agreement having legal effect under the law of that State.

Article 5

For the purposes of this Convention –

    (a) 'rights of custody' shall include rights relating to the care of the person of the child and, in particular, the right to determine the child's place of residence;

    (b) 'rights of access' shall include the right to take a child for a limited period of time to a place other than the child's habitual residence.

Article 12

Where a child has been wrongfully removed or retained in terms of Article 3 and, at the date of the commencement of the proceedings before the judicial or administrative authority of the Contracting State where the child is, a period of less than one year has elapsed from the date of the wrongful removal or retention, the authority concerned shall order the return of the child forthwith.

The judicial or administrative authority, even where the proceedings have been commenced after the expiration of the period of one year referred to in the preceding paragraph, shall also order the return of the child, unless it is demonstrated that the child is now settled in its new environment.

Where the judicial or administrative authority in the requested state has reason to believe that the child has been taken to another State, it may stay the proceedings or dismiss the application for the return of the child.

Article 13

Notwithstanding the provisions of the preceding Article, the judicial or administrative authority of the requested State is not bound to order the return of the child if the person, institution or other body which opposes its return establishes that –

    (a) the person, institution or other body having the care of the person of the child was not actually exercising the custody rights at the time of removal or retention, or had consented to or subsequently acquiesced in the removal or retention; or

    (b) there is a grave risk that his or her return would expose the child to physical or psychological harm or otherwise place the child in an intolerable situation.

The judicial or administrative authority may also refuse to order the return of the child if it finds that the child objects to being returned and has attained an age and degree of maturity at which it is appropriate to take account of its views.

In considering the circumstances referred to in this Article, the judicial and administrative authorities shall take into account the information relating to the social background of the child provided by the Central Authority or other competent authority of the child's habitual residence.

Article 19

A decision under this Convention concerning the return of the child shall not be taken to be a determination on the merits of any custody issue.

Article 21

An application to make arrangements for organising or securing the effective exercise of rights of access may be presented to the Central Authorities of the Contracting States in the same way as an application for the return of a child.

The Central Authorities are bound by the obligations of co-operation which are set forth in Article 7 to promote the peaceful enjoyment of access rights and the fulfilment of any conditions to which the exercise of those rights may be subject. The Central Authorities shall take steps to remove, as far as possible, all obstacles to the exercise of such rights. The Central Authorities, either directly or through intermediaries, may initiate or assist in the institution of proceedings with a view to organising or protecting these rights and securing respect for the conditions to which the exercise of these rights may be subject.

This may look simple but it has generated a great deal of law; and the law may only scratch the surface of the personal issues involved. In 'The view from Court 45' (1999), Brenda Hale wrote about her perceptions of the law:

Child Abduction

Child abduction cases are of two kinds: those which are brought under the Hague Convention on the Civil Aspects of International Child Abduction, implemented in the UK by the Child

Abduction and Custody Act 1985, and those which are not. It is generally agreed that the Hague Convention is a very good thing: more and more countries are joining the club. But we also know that a crucial change has taken place in the pattern of child abduction cases since the Hague Convention was implemented.

The original paradigm was of the parent who is not looking after the children taking or keeping them away from the parent who is doing so: sometimes kidnapping or spiriting them away (there was much talk of the school gates) and sometimes keeping them back after a visit. The public perception may well still be so.

The Hague Convention is capable of working very well in those cases. We can and do send the children back very quickly. Nigel Lowe and Alison Perry studied all incoming and outgoing cases handled by the Central Authority for England and Wales under both the Hague Convention and the European Convention on Recognition and Enforcement of Decisions concerning Custody of Children during 1996. They found that our average return time was six-and-a-half weeks with an amazing 34 per cent of incoming cases completed within four weeks. I have seen other countries act with even more speed but they found an average of 11½ weeks. This is still very quick by the standards of most cases concerning children.

The defence raised in snatching or keeping cases is usually the objections of the child. The advantage of having all proceedings issued and heard in the High Court in London is that we have specialist court welfare officers who are familiar with the Hague Convention issues and can operate very quickly.

But it was recognised at the Third Review of the Hague Convention in 1997 that the popular paradigm does not represent the majority of cases. David McClean reported to the 1997 All Souls seminar that 'something like two-thirds of abductions are now by the mother, the primary carer ... In a considerable number of such cases, the mother's decision is taken against a history of domestic violence during the marriage and sometimes after the separation of the parties'.

Lowe and Perry found that 70 per cent of abductors were mothers, 27 per cent fathers, with grandparents and others making up remaining three per cent. This compares with 45 per cent, 48 per cent and seven per cent respectively in 1987 (when the numbers were much smaller). If nationality is any guide to home country, more than half of abductors were taking the children 'home', although this tendency was stronger in incoming than outgoing cases and among fathers rather than mothers. Even so, 61 per cent of the mothers bringing children in were British nationals. They also found that 26 per cent of parents were still married, 24 per cent were divorced, eight per cent were currently divorcing, 17 per cent were separated and 22 per cent had never been marred to one another. It was not known how many of these were living together at the time but where it was known, they were evenly split. Hence the theory of mothers 'coming home to mum' in the context of an immediate family breakdown is not at all fanciful: there is good reason, apart from my own experience in Court 45, to think that it is quite common.

As Lowe and Perry say, we need more research into why parents abduct their children. An even more interesting question is why the other parent, particularly the father, pursues them. In my experience, I believe born out by that of Reunite, it is rarely because he wants to look after the children full time himself. More often he wants to establish his right to contact. The Hague Convention gives him little help with that and so he has to ask for the child's return. I am pleased that David McClean [(1997)] considered my decision in *S v H (Abduction: Access Rights)* to be correct: that is, the Hague Convention deliberately distinguished between custody and access rights and did not intend summary return to be the remedy to secure the latter. But that distinction is generally completely set at nought: first, by the completely understandable inclusion of 'travel restrictions' as 'rights of custody' within the meaning of the Hague Convention; and, secondly, by the equally understandable equality of parental status enjoyed by both married and unmarried parents in many Hague Convention countries, unless and until there is a court order modifying it. Often there has been a technical breach of 'rights of custody' but, in the view of Reunite, the remedy of peremptory return 'may be unnecessary, distressing and damaging'.

We need to know more about *why* some fathers pursue these mothers with such determination. Sometimes the pursuit is designed to put pressure on the mother, whether to make her return to him or to gain some other advantage in their matrimonial battles. In these cases automatic non-means-tested legal aid for the plaintiffs sits ill against non-automatic means-tested legal aid for the defendants. This is compounded by the Child Abduction Unit's use of a small number of expert solicitors for plaintiffs while defendants often go to inexpert high street solicitors who sell the pass in the first affidavit. It also sits ill against the frequent lack of legal aid for those same defendants in the countries to which we are obliged to return their children. It will be interesting to see whether any of these points are argued under Article 6 of the European

Convention for the Protection of Human Rights and Fundamental Freedoms when the Human Rights Act 1998 comes into force.

We could also do with knowing more about how the children feel and fare. Barristers and judges are prone to talk about the 'evil' of child abduction. There must be cases in which the sudden and secret uprooting from home, family, school and friends is indeed an evil for the children, as well as for the people they have left behind. There must be cases in which it will do them no harm at all to go back to the country where they have always lived, where they have a home to live in and an extended family to live with, whether or not their primary carer goes with them. The loss or destabilisation of their primary carer may be much less important than we think it is. The problem is that we cannot know, because no welfare inquiry takes place in the individual case and there is, as far as I know, no research which might give us the wider picture.

Over the years since the Child Abduction and Custody Act 1985 came into force we have undoubtedly learned to harden our hearts to such questions. Our dedication to the objects of the Hague Convention is strong and if anything getting stronger.

In the new paradigm 'home-coming' cases, the defence is sometimes objection but more often risk under the first paragraph of Article 13:

> 'the judicial or administrative authority of the requested State is not bound to order the return of the child if the person ... which opposes its return establishes that—
> (a) ...; or
> (b) there is a grave risk that his or her return would expose the child to physical or psychological harm or otherwise place the child in an intolerable situation.'

The test, recently re-emphasised by the Court of Appeal, requires clear and compelling evidence of grave risk of harm or other intolerability, substantial and not trivial, and much more severe than the inevitable disruption, uncertainty and anxiety following an unwelcome return. The most recent Court of Appeal case concerned a mother caught between two children, one subject to the Hague Convention, the other not. Once again the court regarded her as the author of her own misfortune. In *Re C (Abduction: Grave Risk of Physical or Psychological Harm)* [1999] 2 FLR 478 Thorpe LJ said this:

> 'In many cases a balanced analysis of the assertion that an order for return would expose the child to the risk of grave psychological harm leads to the conclusion that the respondent is in reality relying on her own wrongdoing in order to build up the statutory defence. In testing the validity of an Article 13(b) defence trial judges should usefully ask themselves what were the intolerable features of the child's family life immediately prior to the wrongful abduction? If the answer be scant to non-existent then the circumstances in which an Art 13(b) defence would be upheld are difficult to hypothesise. In my opinion Article 13(b) is given its proper construction if ordinarily confined to meet the case where the mother's motivation for flight is to remove the child from a family situation that is damaging to the child's development.'

Whatever the rights or wrongs of adding such a qualification to the words of the article, the outcome is very tough. We usually refuse to hear oral evidence for the very good reason that it puts the victim at a disadvantage: we cannot hear one without the other and the object is to return the child without the victim having to travel round the world. We therefore have to resolve conflicts on affidavit evidence alone. This is very difficult unless there is independent or documentary evidence to help. Nor is there much case-law on whether the situation fled from was indeed intolerable: abuse or neglect of the child is one thing, but what about abuse or neglect of the primary carer? I have expressed the view that violence to a necessary primary carer could fall within Article 13(b), but it remains to be seen whether others agree.

We are equally tough in outgoing cases, bending over backwards to find 'rights of custody' which have been interfered with so as to enable us to grant a declaration under Article 15 that the removal was 'wrongful within the meaning of Article 3 of the Convention', even in cases where the plaintiff father has no parental responsibility, no crime has been committed and no court order infringed.

We are even tough in non-Convention cases, where there is no comforting reciprocity in the countries to which we return the children. There has recently been some recognition that one reason why these countries are not party to the Hague Convention is that they apply a system of law very different from our own. But we remain better at sending children to such countries than regaining them.

Perhaps we are right to be so tough. We are certainly trying hard to give the Hague Convention the effect it was intended to have. Some reforms, such as improving the procedures for enforcing contact, or clarifying the effect of violence to the abducting carer, might mitigate our severity. But they would not help against vindictive or violent pursuers unless we were more adventurous in taking evidence across continents. The upshot is that it sometimes looks as though we are punishing the mother for her clandestine behaviour rather than saving her children from the evils of abduction. But perhaps these cases are troubling because we in the UK are generally more tender to primary carers, usually mothers, than other countries are. Or do they occur because we and others are still reluctant to look closely at the effect upon children of violence or other forms of abuse and oppression of their mothers?

We can cover only a few of the legal issues here, and only a little of the mass of case law. As Brenda Hale mentions, 'rights of custody' are protected under Art. 3, which are deliberately distinguishes them from the 'rights of access' protected only under Art. 21. This is not an easy issue. It arose in the following case, which also considered the extent to which Art. 13(b) can be used to protect the child's interests:

Re F (abduction: custody rights abroad)
[1995] Fam 224, [1995] 3 All ER 641, Court of Appeal

A US father and a British mother married in Colorado in 1987. Their son was born there in 1990. The whole family lived there until 1994. The mother alleged that the father had been violent towards her, her mother and the child. In June 1994, she obtained a temporary order ousting the father from the home and giving her care and control of the child. In July she brought the child to the United Kingdom. The expert evidence was that this was not in breach of the law of Colorado. The judge ordered the child's return and the mother appealed.

Butler-Sloss LJ: ... It is the duty of the court to construe the Convention in a purposive way and to make the Convention work. It is repugnant to the philosophy of the Convention for one parent unilaterally, secretly and with full knowledge that it is against the wishes of the other parent who possesses 'rights of custody', to remove the child from the jurisdiction of the child's habitual residence. 'Rights of custody' within the Convention are broader than an order of the court and parents have rights in respect of their children without the need to have them declared by the court or defined by court order. These rights under the Convention have been liberally interpreted in English law. Waite LJ said in *Re B (A Minor) (Abduction)* [1994] 2 FLR 249 at p. 260:

> 'The purposes of the Hague Convention were, in part at least, humanitarian. The objective is to spare children already suffering the effects of breakdown in their parents' relationship the further disruption which is suffered when they are taken arbitrarily by one parent from their settled environment and moved to another country for the sake of finding there a supposedly more sympathetic forum or a more congenial base. The expression "rights of custody" when used in the Convention therefore needs to be construed in the sense that will best accord with that objective. In most cases, that will involve giving the term the widest sense possible.'

Rights of custody

I am satisfied that the father and mother both enjoyed equal and separate rights of custody by Colorado law. Equally by Colorado law in the absence of a court order to the contrary either parent could remove the child from the State and from the USA without violating any principles of Colorado law. It cannot, however, be the case that the lawful removal of the child by one parent destroys the rights of the other parent nor did any of the Colorado lawyers suggest it. The removal of the child by the mother interfered with the rights of the father in that he was prevented from actually exercising them in the USA. Such interference with rights is recognised in the Convention and Art.3 includes in its definition rights which 'would have been exercised but for the removal'. In my judgment the father continued to enjoy 'rights of custody' subject to the effect of the orders of the Adams County Court.

... In my view the temporary order for care and control was of a limited nature and did not affect the father's 'rights of custody' nor was it suggested by the Colorado lawyers that it did. The answer to the first part of the question is therefore 'Yes'. ...

...

Having found that the father retains rights as a parent by Colorado law which fall within the Convention definition, as I have, equally it is a matter of English law whether the mother is in breach of those 'rights of custody' by her removal of the child. In applying the Convention we are not bound by the mother's right under Colorado law to remove the child from the USA and that information is in my judgment irrelevant to the decision the English court has to take whether the removal from the USA was wrongful. We are concerned with the mother's unilateral decision to remove the child without the consent of the father and with the knowledge that if he knew he would have opposed her removal of the child. By the removal she frustrated and rendered nugatory his equal and separate rights of custody, in particular that the child should reside in the USA. In so doing she was in my judgment in breach of the father's rights of custody under the Convention and the removal was wrongful.

...

Article 13(b)

When a court has found that the removal of the child is wrongful within the meaning of the Convention, Art.12 requires that the court 'shall order the return of the child forthwith' unless any of the provisions of Art.13 is established and the requested State exercises its discretion not to do so. It is asserted by the mother that Art.13(b) is established on the facts before us and that the judge was in error in finding that it was not proved. ...

[Counsel] recognised that a very high standard is required to demonstrate grave risk and an intolerable situation, but he has argued that the Convention envisaged that there would be cases in which the facts would meet that high standard. In the present case the mother and grandmother have made very serious allegations against the father, in particular of his violence towards the child and the extremely serious effect it has had upon him. ...

Admission of oral evidence in Convention cases should be allowed sparingly.

If the issues between the parties cannot be resolved on affidavit the Art. 13(b) criteria will not have been established. The child is returned pursuant to Art. 12 and it will be for the court of habitual residence to determine the disputes issues with the opportunity to hear oral evidence and the parties cross-examined. In many cases the absence of evidence from the other parent on the major issues would cause a court to hesitate to find the Art.13(b) threshold reached: see *Re E (A Minor) (Abduction)* [1989] 1 FLR 135. But I agree with the judge that the evidence adduced by the mother should be treated as true, particularly since the allegations affect this child, there was an opportunity to rebut them and the consequences for this child on the evidence before us are potentially very serious. ...

In looking at this evidence I have reminded myself of the difficulties inherent in proving grave risk of physical or psychological harm or of demonstrating that the child would be placed in an intolerable situation if returned to the country of habitual jurisdiction. ...

The child was, like so many other children, present at acts of violence and displays of uncontrollable temper directed at his mother or elsewhere, and at occasions of violence between the parents. These included assaults on his mother and one on his grandmother on 6 June 1994, and destruction of household items such as ripping the fridge door off its hinges. More important in my view was that the child was himself the recipient of the violence by the father. The judge was in error in finding only one occasion which directly affected the child when he suffered a nosebleed caused by the father in a temper throwing a cool box onto the back seat where the child was sitting which hit him in the face. There were other incidents. He destroyed the child's toys by stamping on them and smashing them when the child was present. This happened more than once. On several occasions he pinched the child on the legs causing bruising. One occasion of pinching was witnessed by the maternal grandmother. On 6 June 1994, C was thrown out of the house as well as his mother. On this occasion, which was immediately before the mother made her ex parte application to the county court, the police were called and took his father away. His father in his presence threatened to kill him and his mother. In these incidents the child was not a bystander to matrimonial discord but a victim of it. In addition other aspects of the behaviour of the father towards the child were unusual and inappropriate, such as waking up the child aged under 4 in the early hours of the morning, once to get him to help wash the jeep. In addition after the temporary restraining order was made and the father left the house, the father seems to have engaged in a campaign of intimidation and harassment directed at the mother, including following her about in his car and threatening her with a gun. He also camped in the jeep several doors away from the matrimonial home, which had a very adverse effect upon the child as well as upon the mother.

The child is asthmatic and the effect upon him of this behaviour was serious. He was present when his grandmother, who was recovering from surgery, was forcibly pushed out of the house and thrown against a wall. The child's reaction was to scream and to cry. He started to bedwet regularly and to have nightmares where he screamed out in his sleep. He became unusually aggressive at the child care centre as well as at home. The effect of the father camping nearby in the jeep made him scared and upset. He copied the tantrums, the yelling, the screaming and bad language of his father.

Since leaving the USA he has been living in Wales in his maternal grandfather's house. The misbehaviour, the bedwetting and the nightmares ceased after he settled down. But his mother told him after the start of the present proceedings that he might have to return to Colorado. He has had a disturbing resumption of the bedwetting and nightmares and has begun to wet himself during the day. He has become aggressive towards other children at the nursery school he is attending and towards grown-ups.

The extent to which the child has himself been drawn into the violence between his parents and the clear evidence of the adverse effect on him of his father's violent and intimidating behaviour would not in my view in themselves be sufficient to meet the high standard required in Art.13(b). The matters which I find most telling are:

(1) the actual effect upon the child of the knowledge that he may be returning to Colorado together with the unusual circumstances;

(2) that he would be returning to the very same surroundings and potentially the very same situation as that which has had such a serious effect upon him before he was removed.

There has to be concern as to whether the father would take any notice of future orders of the court or comply with the undertakings he has given to the judge. How is a child of 4 to have any security or stability or from his perception come to terms with a return to his former home? I have come to the conclusion on the unusual facts of this case that the extreme reaction of the child to the marital discord and the requirement by Art.12 to return him on the facts of this case to the same house with the same attendant risks would create a grave risk that his return would expose him both to psychological harm and would place him in an intolerable situation. ...

Appeal allowed.

Questions

(i) Should the question of whether the removal is in breach of custody rights be governed by English law or is it, as stated by Professor Carol Bruch (1993), 'the law of the child's habitual residence that controls this question under the Convention, not the law of the court hearing the return question'?

(ii) What if the abducting mother then claims that the father left behind is not in fact the father of the child?

(iii) By virtue of s. 1 of the Child Abduction Act 1984, and s. 13 of the Children Act 1989, it is contrary to English law for a mother to remove the child for more than one month without either the father's consent or the leave of the court, even if the court has ordered that the child is to live with the mother indefinitely and has made no order for contact with the father: is such a removal in breach of the father's 'rights of custody' for the purpose of the Convention?

(iv) The whole purpose of the Convention is to secure the return of the child without the wronged parent having to come to the country to which the child has been taken: how can the court decide about allegations of violence without hearing oral evidence?

(v) How can a removal be in breach of custody rights if proceedings about the future of a child are pending and the position as to residence is unresolved? (See *Re H (Abduction: Rights of Custody)* [2000] 1 FLR 374.)

(vi) Given that the court treated the mother's allegations as true, would you have had the slightest hesitation in finding Art. 13(b) applied in this case?

(vii) Would it place the child in an intolerable situation if his main carer either could not or would not return with him?

The English courts have responded to the last problem by extracting or accepting undertakings from the plaintiff. In *Re O (child abduction: undertakings)* [1994] 2 FLR 349, an English mother had removed two children aged six and five from Greece, where they had lived in comfortable circumstances all their lives. The following undertakings were given by their Greek father:

(1) Not to remove or seek to remove the children from the care and control of the mother.

(2) To provide a car for the mother and to pay all running costs, including petrol, maintenance and insurance.

(3) To provide as soon as possible for the mother a three bedroomed apartment ... for the sole occupation by her and the children and to pay all the running costs of such property and not to enter such property and until provision of such property to permit the mother to reside at [the matrimonial home] and not to enter [the matrimonial home].

(4) To pay all school fees including school books for the children and all medical expenses for the mother and children.

(5) To pay all travel costs for the return of the mother and the children ... together with the cost of the return of the mother's and children's personal belongings.

(6) Not to institute nor voluntarily support any proceedings for the punishment or committal of the mother in respect of any criminal or civil wrong which the mother may have committed by reason of the children's removal from Greece and to use his best endeavours to ensure that such proceedings do not happen.

(7) To pay maintenance to the mother at the rate of £1,000 per calendar month.

Questions

(i) Do you think that these two children would have been placed in an intolerable situation if ordered to return to their home, whether in the care of their mother or of their father and his relatives, without all or any of these undertakings?

(ii) The mother returned to Greece with the children, but left a few days later claiming that the father was in breach, in particular, of undertakings (3) and (7); the father denied this, but also claimed that the undertakings had been extracted under duress and went far beyond what the mother could reasonably expect in Greece; Hale J ordered her to return the children once more; what would you have done?

(iii) Do you get a sense that the English courts are bending over backwards to apply the convention?

(iv) At what age would you think it 'appropriate' to take account of the child's objection to being returned? What is an objection?

On that last question, consider the following story:

The mother had three children with her first husband. The oldest, a girl now nearly 15, had refused to see her father for some years. The youngest, a boy aged nearly 11, had never seen him. The middle one, a boy aged 13, had regular contact and a good relationship with him. The mother also had another child by her second marriage. This, she alleged, had been a violent and abusive relationship, as a result of which she was still very afraid of her second husband. She was also in considerable financial difficulties in her home country. She brought all the children secretly to this country. The Family Division judge refused the first husband's application for the return of his children on the ground that they would face an intolerable situation if their mother was ordered to return to a country in which she was in such dread of her second husband. All the children were opposed to returning, although the middle child was torn between his feelings for his father and his loyalty to the family group. The Court of Appeal, by a majority, reversed the judge's decision. The mother then decided that she would not return with the children, which intensified their opposition and distress, but the Court of Appeal declined to interfere with the earlier order. However, when the tipstaff arrived to take them to the airport, all the children adamantly refused to go, the two boys locking themselves in the bathroom making threats of self harm. The court had to admit defeat.

Question

Would you have ordered these children to be returned? What purpose(s) were being served in doing so?

The point of it all is, of course, that if we return children who are wrongly abducted to this country, other convention countries will return our children who have been wrongly abducted there. But what should we do if the other country is not a party to the convention? Non-convention countries are often those, such as Pakistan or Saudi Arabia, with a very different legal system from our own and where views about the welfare of the child may be different. And as Brenda Hale comments (p. 645, above) it is not so easy to retrieve our children from these countries; so why should we be ready to return children there?

Re JA (Child Abduction: Non-Convention Country) [1998] 1 FLR 231, [1998] 2 FCR 159 concerned a child whose father was a national of the United Arab Emirates, while the mother was English. J was born in 1995 in the Emirates and was of dual nationality. The family came to England in 1996 and later that year the mother indicated that she wished to remain in England. The mother issued divorce proceedings and the father issued an originating summons in wardship seeking the peremptory return of the child upon various undertakings. Hearing an appeal against an order that the child be returned, Ward LJ summarised the law concerning abduction from non-Convention countries as follows:

The decision to return the child must be justified by more than an adoption by analogy of the Hague Convention approach because in a Convention case welfare is not the paramount consideration or a consideration at all (save in the different guise of Art 13), nor can it be justified as an adoption of principles of forum conveniens which concept, 'as the phrase is used in other kinds of litigation, has no place in the wardship jurisdiction', per Ormrod LJ in *Re R (Minors) (Wardship: Jurisdiction)* (1981) 2 FLR 416, 426H. True it is that the interests of the child may ordinarily be thought to be better served if the court having direct knowledge of the conditions prevailing in the place where the child has his or her home is charged with the decision whether a change of that home should be ordered where the parents cannot agree about the matter between themselves. The only proper reason for returning the child without investigating the merits is that the child's welfare demands it...

[The] authorities seem to me clearly to establish that it is an abdication of the responsibility and an abrogation of the duty of this court to the ward under its protection to surrender the determination of its ward's future to a foreign court whose regime may be inimical to the child's welfare. If driven to it, I would reluctantly say that the decision of this court in *Re M (Abduction: Peremptory Return Order)* [1996] 1 FLR 478 was decided per incuriam. It is perhaps not necessary to suffer that embarrassment because in this case there is evidence of the law which will be applied in the Emirates. Here it is common ground that the child will reside ('Hadanah') with the mother but the guardianship ('Wilayah') remains with the father. After the age of 12 the Hadanah reverts automatically to the father. If the mother remarries the father has the right to request that the Hadanah return to him. The place of residence for the divorced mother is where the father of the child lives and the mother is restricted to living within 133 km of the father otherwise her right of residency is lost since the child needs the care and attention of the father as guardian. The court may give consent to the mother to accompany the child to spend her vacation in the mother's homeland on condition this is not permanent, otherwise the mother again loses Hadanah, the basis being that the child is always in need of the guardian, the father. ...

From that review of the law to be applied in the UAE, it seems clear the court's powers are limited and there is no indication that welfare is the test. If the mother returns to Sharjah with the child, there is no power in the court to permit her to return to this country with the child if the father objects to that move, whatever the best interests of the child dictate. Once the mother and child return to the Emirates, they are effectively locked in there. Those facts are not disputed.

This leads me to consider Mr Harrison's second objection. He submits that the judge failed to give proper weight to the disadvantage to the child if the mother came under such stress in the Emirates that her care of the child was imperilled. The scant evidence before the judge has been supplemented by a report of a consultant psychiatrist and once again we are better placed than he was ...

If the judge had had the benefit of this new material, I doubt whether he would have concluded that there was not a significant risk of harm to the child were she returned to the Emirates, even with the protection of the undertakings offered by the father. I doubt whether he would have held that the impetus for return outweighed this welfare consideration, a fortiori when the Emirates' court seems to have no discretion in the decisions that are to be taken and no power to permit the mother to leave the Emirates if that is necessary for the proper care of the child. When the judge observed that the 'personal disadvantages if an order for peremptory return is made are no greater than what was inherent in her situation, in any event, before she retained J in this country', he begged the question whether that entitled the court to ignore consequential harm to the child. In the light of the medical evidence, the risks to the mother's health and consequently the child's care by being locked into a life in the Emirates against her will, do take the case out of the ordinary: her health not merely her happiness is at risk. Furthermore, the lack of judicial remedy to alleviate that hardship does, in my judgment, make this case very different from those where this court knows that the foreign court will be guided by the best interests of the child.

Questions

(i)   If the children had been living here with their mother and their father had taken them to the Emirates without her knowledge or consent, do you think that the courts there would have ordered him to return them?

(ii)   What about a mother who abducts her child from a country where there is civil war because she is worried that the child will be caught up in the violence that exists on a day-to-day basis there. How can it be in the paramount interests of children to return them to a country where there is such a risk? Can the return of children in such circumstances be consistent with the United Nations Convention on the Rights of the Child? (see chapter 10, p. 484).

(iii)   Do you sympathise with this view expressed by David McClean and Kisch Beevers (1995): 'in a non-Convention case, let the welfare principle have full rein'?

Speaking of *Re JA* in *Re E (Abduction: Non-Convention Country)* [1999] 3 FCR 497, [1999] 2 FLR 642, [1999] Fam Law 610, Thorpe LJ said:

What weighed with Ward LJ in *Re JA* was not so much that child welfare would not be considered as that the mother would have no right to apply in Sharjah to relocate to this jurisdiction. The relationship between the wrongful international abduction of children and the rights of a parent to relocate on separation have always seemed to me to be intricately interconnected. In this jurisdiction we do not refuse the application of the parent with the residence order the right to exercise that responsibility in another jurisdiction, unless the decision is clearly shown to be incompatible with the paramount welfare consideration: see *Chamberlain v de la Mare* (1983) 4 FLR 434. ...

The Council of Europe has worked hard, and continues to work hard, for the harmonisation of family law amongst its membership. However, the number and diversity of the member States makes this a difficult if not impossible goal. Even the European Union has as yet made no endeavour to map out a common approach to family law, I have no doubt that the number and the diversity of the States that have joined the Hague club have made it impossible to formulate minimum standard requirements of other family justice systems before recognising accession. As a matter of logic, if we make no investigation and in litigation permit no criticism of the family justice systems operating in the member States, I am extremely doubtful of the wisdom of permitting the abducting parent to criticise the standards of the family justice system in the non-member State of habitual residence, save in exceptional circumstances, such as ... persecution, or ethnic, sex, or any other discrimination. I am equally doubtful of the principle enabling a judge in this jurisdiction to criticise the standards or paramount principles applied by the family justice systems of a non-member State save in such exceptional circumstances.

Question

Do you feel this affords sufficient protection for children abducted to this country from non-convention countries? Do you think that this approach in fact protects children from this country abducted to non-convention countries?

What about the practicalities? What should a parent do if there is a threat of abduction or if a child is actually taken away? The following is an extract from guidance published by the Official Solicitor; note the brevity of the passage on non-convention countries:

8. The Lord Chancellor is designated by the Child Abduction and Custody Act 1985 as the Central Authority for England & Wales and Northern Ireland; in Scotland the Secretary of State is the Central Authority. The duties of the Central Authority in England & Wales are carried out by the CAU, which has a full-time staff of two, and is under the administrative control of the Official Solicitor to the Supreme Court, an independent, quasi-judicial figure whose function is to give confidential advice to the judges, assist the court and represent the interests of those under legal disability. ...

Application to the Child Abduction Unit

9. Although there is no specified form for making an application to a Central Authority under the Hague or European Conventions, in outgoing cases applicants are provided with a *questionnaire* which enables the CAU to send an application which broadly follows the model suggested by the Hague Conference. An incoming application will be accepted in any form, provided that it contains sufficient information. Requests for advice and assistance are usually made by telephone or by letter, and sometimes come from or through a Member of Parliament.

Legal Representation

10. An applicant in a Convention case before an English court is represented by solicitors and counsel (a barrister) in private practice, not by the CAU or the Lord Chancellor's Department. Solicitors and counsel, unless instructed privately, are paid in European Convention cases and Hague Convention abduction cases by the Legal Aid Board. In access cases under Article 21 of the Hague Convention they may be paid either by the Legal Aid Board or the applicant (see below).

THE HAGUE CONVENTION – Operation

Incoming Abduction Cases (Articles 3 & 8)

11. All incoming cases are dealt with in London by a High Court judge of Family Division, and the High Court official responsible for listing cases, known as the Clerk of the Rules, ensures that they are listed for hearing very quickly – sometimes in two days. Adjournments are limited to a maximum of 21 days, so that the court exercises control over the progress of the case, and the litigants cannot allow it to 'drift'.

12. When the CAU receives an application for return, an experienced solicitor from a firm familiar with these cases is asked to take the case, and a letter sent certifying that the applicant is eligible for free legal aid (see below). The solicitor is then responsible for making the application for legal aid, for taking the applicant's (now his client's) instructions, assembling the evidence, if necessary with help from the CAU, and filing affidavits of fact and about foreign law. The solicitor will also instruct counsel and attend the hearing.

13. The solicitor will often obtain ex parte orders to protect the child immediately after the proceedings start, which could include orders requiring the surrender of passports, prohibiting the removal of the child from the jurisdiction or a specific address, or if the whereabouts of the child is not known, a seek and find or seek and locate order, or orders requiring the disclosure of information.

14. Applications are not normally required to attend the hearing.

Outgoing Abduction Cases

15. In outgoing abduction cases, the CAU discusses the case with the applicant or his solicitor, asks them to fill in the *questionnaire*, make a written statement if necessary, and provide copies of any court orders. An application is then sent off, with translations if necessary, to the Central Authority of the requested state or states. Thereafter, the CAU will monitor the progress of the case, liaise with the Central Authority of the requested state and the applicant, give advice about English law and do all that it can to help to bring the case to a successful conclusion. ...

Legal Aid

20. The United Kingdom has system of civil legal aid which is now set out in the Legal Aid Act 1988. Provided that they wish to institute or are involved in proceedings for which legal aid is available, any person, whether within the jurisdiction or not, can apply for legal aid. The applicant must, however, satisfy the Legal Aid Board, who administer the scheme, that they have reasonable grounds for taking or defending the proceedings (the 'merits' test) and that their means fall within the eligibility limits (the 'means' test). Depending on the extent of the applicant's means, he may be required to pay a contribution towards the costs of his solicitors and counsel. Although not applicable to Hague or European Convention cases, in other cases in which the legal aided litigant is successful in recovering or preserving property (for example, an award of damages), the Legal Aid Board has a first charge on the property recovered or preserved, so that the money paid out is 'clawed back', although the successful litigant may be awarded costs, which my offset the cost.

Hague Convention Cases

21. The United Kingdom has made a reservation under Article 42 of the Hague Convention in relation to Article 26, but free legal aid (that is, not subject to means and merits tests) is available to applicants seeking the return of a child under Articles 3 & 8. Legal aid is available for those seeking to organise or secure effective rights of access by way of an application for an order under section 8 of the Children Act 1989, but subject to tests of means and merits.

European Convention Cases

22. Applicants seeking the registration or enforcement of orders under the European Convention are entitled to free legal aid – that is, without means or merits tests.

Applications for Legal Aid by Non-UK Residents

23. Enquiries and applications about legal aid for those not resident in the United Kingdom should be made to the London office of the Legal Aid Board at 29/37 Red Lion Street, London WC1R 4PP.

Non-Convention Cases

24. The Child Abduction Unit may be able to give general advice, the Foreign and Commonwealth Office can provide lists lawyers in foreign countries, can try to obtain welfare reports and may offer informal assistance.

25. The Official Solicitor has considerable experience of acting for children who have been taken to non-convention countries; there is a charitable organisation, 'Reunite', which will offer help and advice.

26. The courts in England & Wales apply the principle of the Hague Convention to the cases of children who are brought into the jurisdiction from non-convention countries.

27. Abductions within the United Kingdom are dealt with by the Family Law Act 1986.

Enforcing English Court Orders

28. The orders made by the High Court are enforceable by the Tipstaff, a court official who can call on help from police. Failure to comply with an order for return is a civil contempt, which is punishable by imprisonment for a maximum of two years, sequestration or a fine.

PREVENTING CHILD ABDUCTION

Criminal Law

29. Apart from the common law offence of kidnapping (which can be committed by a parent), the Child Abduction Act 1984 makes it a criminal offence for a person connected with a child under the age of sixteen to take or send that child out of the United Kingdom without the appropriate consent. Persons connected with a child are parents (including a putative father), guardians and persons with a residence order or who have custody. The 'appropriate consent' is the consent of each of the mother, father (if he has parental responsibility), guardian and anyone with a residence order or custody, or the leave of the court. A person with a residence order may, however, take or send the child out of the United Kingdom without the appropriate consent for up to a month at a time.

Civil Law

30. If it is feared that a child might be abducted, then an application can be made for either a prohibited steps order and/or, a residence order under the Children Act 1989, or an injunction, or the child can be made a ward of the High Court, which imposes an automatic prohibition on taking the child out of the United Kingdom. Orders can, if necessary be made ex parte (without notice to the other side).

31. In addition, where there is a contact order (formerly known as 'access') in force, and it is feared that the child may be abducted by the person exercising contact, an application may be made for a variation of the order to provide for the contact to be supervised.

32. A wide range of orders may be made under the High Court's inherent jurisdiction with respect to children or within wardship proceedings, including 'Seek and Find' orders, orders restraining persons from leaving the jurisdiction and requiring the surrender of passports.

33. In the Family Law Act 1996 there are powers to order disclosure of a child's whereabouts, to order the recovery of a child, to restrict the removal of a child from the United Kingdom and to require the surrender of any passport containing details of a child.

34. The United Kingdom Passport Agency can be asked not to issue passports, and the police operate a 'Port Stop' system to prevent children being taken out of the country through the principal ports and airports.

35. If it is feared that a child might not be returned from a visit abroad, then it is possible to ask the court to allow the visit only on condition that the person taking the child abroad lodges a sum of money in court – a bond – or a charge on property, which will be forfeit if the child is not returned.

Bibliography

Introduction

We quoted from:

A. Dalton, *Ugly Mug,* (1994) Harmondsworth, Puffin.

C. Itzin, *Splitting Up: Single Parent Liberation* (1980) London, Virago, pp. 130, 138.

12.1   Coping with change

We quoted from:

A. Bainham, 'Changing families and changing concepts – reforming the language of family law' (1998) 10 Child and Family Law Quarterly 1.

Central Statistical Office, *Social Trends 31* (2001) London, HMSO, table 2.20.

Central Statistical Office, *Social Trends 32* (2002) London, HMSO, table 2.17.

New English Bible (1972) The Bible Societies, I Kings 3, vs. 22–27.

J. Goldstein, A. Freud and A.J. Solnit, *Beyond the Best Interests of the Child* (1973) London, Collier Macmillan, pp. 31–34, 37, 40–41, 49–50, 51, 53, 62–63.

M. Richards, 'Post Divorce Arrangements for Children: A Psychological Perspective' [1982] Journal of Social Welfare Law 133, pp. 135–136, 142–149.

M. Richards, 'Private Worlds and Public Intentions – The Role of the State at Divorce' in A. Bainham and D. Pearl (eds.), *Frontiers of Family Law* (1993) London, Chancery Law Publishing, pp. 26–27.

B. Rodgers and J. Pryor, *Divorce and Separation: The outcomes for children,* (1998) York, Joseph Rowntree Foundation.

C. Smart, *The Legal and Moral Ordering of Child Custody* (1990) University of Warwick, Department of Sociology, pp. 9–12, 82–85, 91–92.

C. Smart, 'Objects of concern? – children and divorce' (1999) 11 Child and Family Law Quarterly 365.

D. Utting, *Family and Parenthood – Supporting Families, Preventing Breakdown* (1995) York, Joseph Rowntree Foundation, pp. 22, 24, 45–47.

Additional reading

R. Bailey-Harris, G. Davis, J. Barron, J. Pearce, *Monitoring Private Law Applications under the Children Act* (1998) Nuffield.

J. Bradshaw and J. Millar, *Lone Parent Families in the UK,* Department of Social Security Research Report No. 6 (1991), London, HMSO.

R. Dingwall and J. Eekelaar, 'Judgements of Soloman: psychology and family law' in M. Richards and P. Light (eds.), *Children of Social Worlds* (1986) Cambridge, Polity Press.

J.M. Eekelaar, 'Children in Divorce: Some Further Data' (1982) 2 Oxford Journal of Legal Studies 62.

M. Murch, *Justice and Welfare in Divorce* (1980) London, Sweet & Maxwell.

C. Smart and S. Sevenhuijsen (eds.), *Child Custody and the Politics of Gender* (1989) London, Routledge.

12.2 The law

We quoted from:

Anon., 'Saturday Parent' (1980) 144 Justice of the Peace 353.

R. Bailey-Harris, G. Davis, J. Barron, J. Pearce, 'Settlement culture and the use of the 'no order' principle under the Children Act 1989', (1999) 11 Child and Family Law Quarterly 53, pp. 57–60.

Children Act Sub-Committee of the Advisory Board on Family Law, *Making Contact Work* (2002) Lord Chancellor's Department.

J.M. Eekelaar, 'Custody appeals' (1985) 48 Modern Law Review 704, p. 705.

A. Heath-Jones, 'Divorce and the Reluctant Father' (1980) 10 Family Law 75, p. 75.

K. Hewitt, 'Divorce and Parental Disagreement' (1996) 26 Family Law 368, p. 370.

F. Kaganas and S. Day Sclater, 'Contact and Domestic Violence – the Winds of Change? [2000] Family Law 630.

Law Commission, *Report on Guardianship and Custody,* Law Com. No. 172 (1988) London, HMSO, paras 3.2, 3.3, 3.5–3.13, 3.14, 3.18, 4.5–4.21, 4.55–4.57.

C. Smart, *The Legal and Moral Ordering of Child Custody* (1990) University of Warwick, Department of Sociology, pp. 82–85, 91–92.

C. Sturge and D. Glasyer, 'Contact and Domestic Violence – the Experts' Report' [2000] Family Law 615.

A. Vine, 'Is the paramountcy principle compatible with Article 8?' [2000] Fam Law 826.

Additional reading

F.R. Bennion, 'First consideration: a cautionary tale' (1976) 126 New Law Journal 1237.

E. Butler-Sloss, 'Contact and Domestic Violence' [2001] Family Law 355.

Children Act Sub-Committee of the Advisory Board on Family Law, *Contact Between Children and Violent Parents: the Question of Parental Contact in Cases where there is Domestic Violence* (1999) Lord Chancellor's Department.

J.M. Eekelaar, 'What Are Parental Rights?' (1973) 89 Law Quarterly Review 210.

J. Eekelaar and M. Maclean, *The Parental Obligation*, (1997) Oxford, Hart.

K. Faller, 'The Parental Alienation Syndrome: What is it and What Data Support It' (1998) 3(2) Child Maltreatment 100.

J. Herring, 'The Human Rights Act and the Welfare Principle in Family Law – Conflicting or Complementary?' (1999) 11 Child and Family Law Quarterly 223.

M. Hester, C. Pearson and L. Radford, *Domestic Violence: A national survey of court welfare and voluntary sector mediation practice* (1997) Bristol, Polity Press.

M. Hester and L. Radford, *Domestic Violence and Child Contact Arrangements in England and Denmark* (1996) Bristol, Polity Press.

Law Commission, Working Paper No. 96, *Review of Child Law: Custody* (1986) London, HMSO.

M. Lund, 'The non-custodial father', in C. Lewis and M. O'Brien (eds.), *Reassessing Fatherhood* (1987) London, Sage.

S. Maidment, *Child Custody and Divorce* (1984) London, Croom Helm.

S. Maidment, 'Parental Responsibility – Is There A Duty To Consult?' [2001] Family Law 518.

J. Masson, 'Thinking about contact – a social or a legal problem?' (2000) 12 Child and Family Law Quarterly 15.

B. Neale and C. Smart '"Good" and "Bad" Lawyers? Struggling in the Shadow of the New Law' (1997) 19 Journal of Social Welfare and Family Law 377.

C. Piper, 'Assumptions About Children's Best Interests' (2000) Journal of Social and Welfare Family Law 22(3).

C. Piper and F. Kaganas, 'Family Law Act 1996, Section 1(d) – how will "they" know there is a risk of violence?' (1997) 9 Child and Family Law Quarterly 269.

C. Piper and F. Kaganas, 'Divorce and Domestic Violence' in S. Day Sclater and C. Piper (eds.) *Undercurrents of Divorce* (1999) Aldershot, Ashgate.

J.A. Priest and J.C. Whybrow, *Custody Law in Practice in the Divorce and Domestic Courts*, Supplement to Law Commission W.P. No. 96, *Review of Child Law: Custody* (1986) London, HMSO.

M. Richards and M. Dyson, *Separation, Divorce and the Development of Children: A Review* (1982) Child Care and Development Group, University of Cambridge.

C. Smart and B. Neale, 'Arguments Against Virtue – Must Contact Be Enforced?' [1997] Family Law 332.

J.S. Wallerstein and J.B. Kelly, *Surviving the Breakup: How Children and Parents Cope with Divorce* (1980) London, Grant Mcintyre.

12.3   Who speaks up for the child?

We quoted from:

A. Buchanan, J. Hunt, H. Bretherton and V. Bream, 'Families in Conflict – perspectives of children and parents on the family court welfare service' [2001] Family Law 900, pp. 900–902.

CAFCASS, website: www.cafcass.gov.uk.

G. Douglas, M. Murch, M. Robinson, L. Scaulan and I. Butler, 'Children's perspectives and experience of the divorce process' [2001] Family Law 373, 375–377.

Law Commission, *Report on Guardianship and Custody,* Law Com. No. 172 (1988) London, HMSO, paras 3.23–3.25.

Probation and Aftercare Service, *SpecimenWelfare Officer's Report* (1981).

Additional reading

N. Fricker, 'The New Children and Family Courts Advisory Service' [2000] Family Law 102.

12.4 Step-families

We quoted from:

L. Burghes, *Lone Parenthood and Family Disruption:The Outcomes for Children* (1994) London, Family Policy Studies Centre, pp. 22–23.

J. Burgoyne and D. Clark, *Making a Go of It – A study of stepfamilies in Sheffield* (1984) London, Routledge and Kegan Paul, table 6.1.

Departmental Committee on the Adoption of Children (Chairman: SirWilliam Houghton), *Working Paper* (1970) London, HMSO, para. 93.

Lord Chancellor's Department, *Judicial Statistics 2000* (2000) London, HMSO.

J. Masson, D. Norbury and S. Chatterton, *Mine,Yours or Ours? A study of stepparent adoption* (1984) London, HMSO, pp. 84, 103–105.

Review of Adoption Law – Report to Ministers of an InterdepartmentalWorking Group (1992) London, Department of Health, paras. 19.2–19.9.

C. Webber and D. Delvin, at www.netdoctor.co.uk/sex_relationships/facts/stepfamilies.

Additional reading

E. Crellin et al., *Born Illegitimate, a Report by the National Children's Bureau* (1971) London, National Foundation for Educational Research.

B.J. Elliott and M. Richards, 'Children and Divorce. Educational Performance and behaviour before and after parental separation' (1991) 5 International Journal of Law and the Family 258.

K.E. Kiernan, 'The Impact of Family Disruption in Childhood onTransitions made inYoung Adult Life' (1992) 46 Population Studies 213.

D. Kuh and M. Maclean, 'Women's Childhood Experience of Parental Separation and their subsequent Health and Status in Adulthood' (1990) 22 Journal of Biosocial Science 121.

M. Maclean and M.Wadsworth, 'The Interests of Children after Parental Divorce: a long term Perspective' (1988) 2 International Journal of Law and the Family 155.

12.5 International child abduction

We quoted from:

B. Hale, 'The view from Court 45' (1999) 11 Child and Family Law Quarterly 377.

The Lord Chancellor's Child Abduction Unit, *International Child Abduction,* (1997, still current July 2002), at www.offsol.demon.co.uk/cauopefm.htm.

Additional reading

C. Bruch, 'Child Abduction and the English Courts' in A. Bainham and D. Pearl (eds.) *Frontiers of Family Law* (1993) London, Chancery Law Publishing, reprinted in A. Bainham, D. Pearl and R. Pickford (eds.) *Frontiers of Family Law* (2nd edn, 1995) Chichester, John Wiley and Co.

N. Lowe and A. Perry, *International Child Abduction – The English Experience* (1997) Nuffield.

D. Maclean, 'International Child Abduction – some recent trends' (1997) 9 Child and Family Law Quarterly 387.

D. McClean and K. Beevers, 'International Child Abduction – Back to Common Law Principles' (1995) 7 Child and Family Law Quarterly 128.

Chapter 13

Social services for children and families

13.1 Children in need

13.2 Out of the poor law

13.3 Services for children and families

13.4 Child protection inquiries

13.5 Assessment and protection orders

13.6 The threshold test

13.7 The choice of final order

In this chapter we shall consider the legal mechanisms that are available to local authority social services departments and to the National Care Standards Commission to meet the needs of children and their families. We shall consider the range of needs which must be met, and the influences which have shaped the law in this area, before considering the comprehensive code in the Children Act 1989 and the Care Standards Act 2000.

13.1 Children in need

In the Department of Health *Children in Need* Survey for 2000 (2002), the following findings emerged:

Executive summary: Key results
The following summarizes the main points:
Numbers of children involved
- There were nearly 400,000 Children in Need in England in February 2000;
- 64,000 of them were Children Looked After and the remaining 320,000 or so were other Children in Need;
- Social Services are providing services for nearly a quarter of a million Children in Need in a typical week;
- 92% of Children Looked After and 54% of other Children in Need receive a service or have money spent on their behalf in a typical week (either in terms of staff/centre time or in terms of cost of the Local Authority paying for provision needed – eg residential costs).

Characteristics of Children in Need
- The main need for social service intervention on children is cases of 'abuse and neglect' which account for just over half (56%) of all Children Looked After and 25% of other Children in Need;

659

- About 12% of the Children in Need population is disabled;
- At least 16% of Children in Need are from the ethnic minorities (which is about one and a half times the figure for the under 18 population as a whole from the census).

Costs and resources

- Services for Children in Need cost Social Services on average about £41m per week, £26m per week on Children Looked After, and £15m per week on other Children in Need;
- About half of these Childrens costs are accounted for by regular payments (on residential/fostering/adoption costs) for Children Looked After;
- The average Child Looked After costs Social services £435 per week; and other Children in Need costs £35 per week.

Activity

- The average Child Looked After receives 4.3 hours per week of service from Social Work staff either in teams or centres;
- Other Children in Need receive on average about 2.9 hours per week of staff or centre time.

In a sample week, it was estimated that some 229,300 children in need received services. This works out at 19 children out of 1,000 across the country. The regional variations are huge. For example, whereas 10 children out of 1,000 received services in North Tyneside, the figure was 28 out of 1,000 in South Tyneside.

Social workers are frequently confronted by some of the most horrifying aspects of family life:

I burned him later with the iron; I did it deliberately. I'd look at him, and think, oh you little bastard, you know? I just got hold of him and burned him on the back of the hand. I was so fed up! He'd been grizzling; he was tired out in the daytime because he didn't sleep at night. And of course I was tired too, and he wouldn't stop grizzling. I was ironing on the floor in the lounge because it was just something quick I wanted – I was kneeling down and he was sitting over by the window. I just got hold of his hand and I said, that'll make you sleep! It was all done in such a quick second, you know, that I didn't … it wasn't sort of premeditated; I just looked at him, had the iron in my hand, and did it.

Jasmine Beckford died at the age of 4 and a half, in Kensal Rise, North-West London, at the home of Mr Morris Beckford (her step-father) and Miss Beverley Lorrington (her mother) of cerebral contusions and subdural haemorrhage as a direct result of severe manual blows inflicted on the child's head shortly before death. At the time of her death, and for some months (if not years) before, Jasmine was a very thin little girl, emaciated as a result of chronic undernourishment. When she was discharged from hospital after being taken into care she weighed 18 lbs, 14 ozs. Seven months later, when she was reunited with her parents after being fostered, she weighed 25 lbs, 5 oz. She died, 27 months later, weighing 23 lbs. Apart from her stunted development, she had been subjected to parental battering over a protracted period, multiple old scars appearing both to the pathologist who conducted the post-mortem and to the consultant orthopaedic surgeon who gave evidence to us, as being consistent with repeated episodes of physical abuse, to say nothing of the psychological battering she must have undergone.

Samantha's mother died when she was very young and her father brought up her younger brother and herself singlehanded. He began to abuse her when she was 4. When she was little he covered her head and top half with a blanket and interfered with her vagina. By the age of 10 it was regular sexual intercourse and thereafter it included buggery and oral intercourse. 'He made me say that I enjoyed it, that I wanted it. He wouldn't like any disagreement.' As she got older she began to realise that this did not happen to other girls. She said that: 'it got to the stage that if I wanted a favour, to go out with a friend, or buy a new pair of shoes, I had to let him do it first.'

She had no-one to confide in, no-one to turn to: 'I thought any adult would not believe me – they would think I was making up a story. … I didn't know what might happen. For my brother's sake I didn't want my family split up. … I loved my father so much. I respected him as a father. But I was confused, didn't understand. I wanted it to stop. I hated that part of it so much.'

So said, respectively, the mother who told her story to Jean Renvoize for her investigation into *Children in Danger* (1974), the report of the panel of inquiry into the circumstances surrounding the death of Jasmine Beckford, *A Child in Trust* (1985), and 'Samantha', whose history is told in the Report of the *Inquiry into Child Abuse in Cleveland 1987* (1988). Understandably, tragic cases like these receive a great deal of professional and public attention. However, local authority social services departments are concerned with a much wider range of problems. Three broad types of children (the 'victims', the 'villains', and the 'volunteered') were identified by Jean Packman, John Randall and Nicola Jacques, in *Who Needs Care?* (1986):

... Admission to care is not a unitary concept: it clearly has several purposes, and is a response to a wide range of different problems and situations, as this study has underlined. At its simplest, there are at least three distinct sorts of public child care on offer. One is for families who are beset by difficulties or handicaps which interrupt or interfere with their capacity to look after their children. Their problems may be acute or chronic, one-dimensional or, more usually, multifaceted and interconnected, and they are likely to be short on supportive networks of relatives or friends to help out, and without the means to pay for child-care services outside these networks. For such families the local authority can provide – and, indeed, is legally obliged to provide (under the old 1948 Act and its [successors]) – a child-care service. Provided that it is judged to be in the interests of the child's welfare, no limits are set on the circumstances in which an admission can take place, nor (apart from an upper age limit) to the time the child may spend in care. Parents can and do request such admissions (more properly, 'receptions' into care), though they can also be effected in their absence. In the words of one commentator, it 'does not imply any criticism of parents who may seek care for their child as a solution to a crisis. It can be a very constructive move by the parents.' [Holden, 1980] It is therefore a type of admission that responds to parents as unfortunate rather than blameworthy, and casts the local authority in the role of the child's caretaker, acting on the parents' behalf. As such, it can be seen to be at one end of a continuum of services which includes domiciliary help and day care for children. It therefore forms, in our view, part of a range of child-care services for families and not, as the narrower interpretations of 'care' and 'prevention' would imply, a stark alternative to such services. Given the severity of poverty and disruption in most of the families with whom social services departments come into contact, and the undoubted increase in their number through rising rates of unemployment and divorce, it is disturbing that the provision of such a service seems to be shrinking, relative to other forms of public child care.

A second type of admission provides a protection and rescue service for children who are thought to be in danger, whether it be physical, sexual, moral, emotional or developmental. Here the emphasis is on parental faults and failings and on the child as a victim of inadequate or inappropriate parenting. The local authority intervenes on the child's behalf, and, more often than not, if an admission is arranged (and even if it is requested by the parents) the local authority itself takes over parental rights as well as duties. In essence, the child-care service offered is protection for very vulnerable children.

The third type of admission relates to the child whose own behaviour is causing problems. Children whose behaviour troubles no one but their own families, or who behave in ways which adults too easily overlook – depressed and withdrawn children, for example – are unlikely candidates for care. But children whose disruptive and antisocial behaviour spreads beyond the family, and is visible to schools, police, neighbours and strangers, may well be so. For them, admission to care has a more ambiguous meaning. The intentions of the 1969 Children and Young Persons Act were to cast admitted 'villains' in the role of 'victims' of another sort – vulnerable youngsters from difficult backgrounds who had succumbed to family, neighbourhood and societal pressures, and were in need of care or control not otherwise available to them. In practice, familiar elements of punishment, containment and deterrence are also in the minds of decision-makers and, it must be said, the parents themselves. In the event, the child-care service offered to this group is as much a retributive and protective service for the public as it is a 'care' service for the young people themselves.

Almost 59,000 children were looked after at 31 March 2001, and we reproduce below two of the alarming tables produced by the Department of Health in its *Bulletin 2001/26* (2001):

Table 4   Children looked after at 31 March 2001 by category of need

England   numbers and percentages

Category of need	Number	Percentage
Abuse or neglect	36,600	62
Disability	2,100	4
Parental illness or disability	3,800	6
Family in acute stress	4,100	7
Family dysfunction	5,900	10
Socially unacceptable behaviour	2,400	4
Low income	220	1
Absent parenting	3,700	6
Total all children[1]	58,900	100

1 Figures for children looked after in this table exclude agreed series of short term placements

Figure 4   Children looked after at 31 March 2001, by category of need

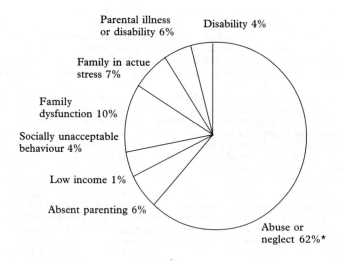

*   62% of looked after children were recorded with a need category of abuse or neglect' at 31 March 2001

The Department of Health's *Children Act Report for 2001* (2002) provides a further table with a breakdown of ethnicity against reasons for needing services.

Figure 3.3   Ethnicity of Children in Need by reason for needing services

numbers

Need code	White	Mixed	Asian	Black	Other	Not stated
Abuse or neglect	62,000	4,300	1,900	3,400	800	4,200
Child's disability	21,000	700	1,800	1,200	500	1,500
Parental illness or disability	8,700	700	400	1,000	200	700
Family in acute stress	16,500	1,100	800	1,200	400	1,900
Family dysfunction	20,700	1,100	600	1,100	300	2,000
Socially unacceptable behaviour	10,300	500	300	700	100	1,200
Low income	6,000	400	700	1,600	2,100	600
Absent parenting	4,200	300	500	1,600	800	300
Cases other than children in need	4,000	300	200	300	100	1,600
Not stated	8,000	400	600	800	1,000	9,900
Total	162,000	9,900	7,900	12,700	6,500	24,000

Percentages

Need code	White	Mixed	Asian	Black	Other	Not stated
Abuse or neglect	38	44	25	26	13	17
Child's disability	13	7	24	9	7	6
Parental illness or disability	5	7	6	8	4	3
Family in acute stress	10	11	10	9	7	8
Family dysfunction	13	11	8	8	5	9
Socially unacceptable behaviour	6	5	3	5	2	5
Low income	4	4	9	13	33	3
Absent parenting	3	3	6	12	13	1
Cases other than children in need	2	3	3	2	2	7
Not stated	5	4	7	6	15	41
Total	100	100	100	100	100	100

It is important to look at all these figures not only from the perspective of category of need, but also from that of placement and age. The next table provides the breakdown of the figures for 31 March 2001.

Table M   Children looked after at 31 March 2001 by placement and age

England   numbers

Placement	All Children	Age at 31 March 2001				
		Under 1	1-4	5-9	10-15	16 & over
All Children[1]	58,900	2,300	9,300	13,400	24,600	9,300
Foster placements	38,400	1,700	5,900	9,600	16,600	4,600
Foster placement inside Council boundary						
With relative or friend	5,100	120	930	1,500	2,000	560
With other foster carer						
provided by council	23,500	1,300	3,800	5,700	10,100	2,700
arranged through agency	670	20	60	140	360	90
Foster placements outside LA boundary						
With relative or friend	1,400	30	260	440	510	170
With foster carer						
provided by council	4,600	190	560	1,000	2,100	760
arranged through agency	3,000	70	330	780	1,500	350
Placed for adoption	3,400	210	1,800	1,200	210	–
Placement with parents	6,900	220	1,500	1,900	2,400	780
Other placements in the community	1,200	0	0	0	100	1,100
Living independently	1,200	0	0	0	100	1,100
Residential employment	10	0	0	0	0	10
Secure units, homes and hostels	6,800	20	80	430	4,300	1,900
Secure unit inside Council boundary	40	0	0	0	40	10
Secure unit outside Council boundary	140	0	0	0	110	30
Homes and hostels not subject to Children's Homes regulations						
inside Council boundary	3,700	10	30	230	2,500	930
outside Council boundary	2,300	10	40	200	1,500	560
Homes and hostels not subject to Children's Homes regulations	520	0	0	0	30	390
Other residential settings	680	90	40	40	240	270
Residential care homes	220	0	10	20	140	60
NHS Trust providing medical/ nursing care	100	10	10	–	20	50
Family centre or mother and baby unit	180	80	30	10	30	40
Youth Treatment Centres	20	0	0	–	10	10
Young offenders institution or prison	160	0	0	0	40	120
Residential Schools	1,100	0	0	70	750	280
Absent from agreed placement	190	0	10	20	70	90
Other accommodation	320	–	40	60	130	100

1 Figures for children looked after in this table exclude agreed series of short term placements

13.2 Out of the poor law

Jean Heywood explains the beginnings of the public service for the deprived child in her classic history of *Children in Care* (3rd edn, 1978):

In pre-Reformation England the orphaned or illegitimate child had a place in a feudal and employed community, though opportunities were open and found for human nature to exploit him. His safeguard, if it existed, lay in the communal nature of the society and its ethical canons, expressed – though not always observed – in the teaching against usury, on the duty of almsgiving, on the efficacy of the corporal works of mercy. In the fact that life was centred round the community rather than the family there lay the possibility of opportunity and protection for the unwanted child. In the community obligations of medieval society a way could be found to provide for him and the family setting was less vital to him than it is to us today. The medieval Church had exalted not the private family but rather the greater one, Christian society, endowing chastity, asceticism and celibacy with greater virtue than the sacrament of marriage. It was at the Reformation period when economic as well as religious changes were taking place, that men turned from the Church's teaching on celibacy, and as they found the social order crumbling away they discovered that in family life there could also be an opportunity to witness to the glory of God.

The ideal of the small home and personal family life could hardly be achieved until a middle class came into existence. The sixteenth century Tudor households of yeomen farmers, of small merchants and tradesmen provided the setting in which real family life became possible, and in a growing urban society, which was neither stable economically, nor ruled any longer by a philosophy of the good of a united community, the family became of major significance. Without it the individual was unsupported in society and became without identity.

The spread of destitution which followed the social and economic changes of the sixteenth century was the cause of the increasing legislation dealing with poor relief in the Tudor era. Vagrancy increased with unemployment, and everywhere the old order was breaking down and a new and as yet unstable society being formed.

The discharging of servants and apprentices increased the numbers of deprived children while the growth of poverty, vagrancy and unemployment made it more difficult for them to find a home or to be fitted in to the pattern of village life. Collections made for the poor in the parish churches were unable to meet the demand for alms. The dissolved houses of the monks and nuns were no longer able to provide out-relief, and the hospitals were falling into decay. In consequence laws were passed to make each parish responsible for providing a place where the sick, the old and the 'succourless poor child' could receive shelter and care. At this time, too, the right of destitute children to beg was recognised and they were given a licence.

... In 1530, authority was first given for the compulsory apprenticing of vagrant children between the ages of five and fourteen, though sixteen years afterwards further legislation had to reduce the severity of apprenticeship regulations and give justices power to liberate children badly treated by master and mistress.

The crowds of vagrants and unemployed at this time (which included the child 'unapt to learning') were seen not only as a chronic nuisance but a serious danger to society, as social failures for whom the community was now legally and financially responsible. ...

So many of the composite hospitals which were established at this time, at first by persuasive and finally by compulsory taxation, for the relief of the poor became also houses of correction and punishment for the idle, as well as technical schools for the young. The deprived child, in need of training, and old and sick people in need of care were accommodated together with vagrants sent for punishment. The degradation of the pauper had begun.

It was the Elizabethan statute, the Poor Relief Act of 1601, which set the pattern for our system of relief to the poor until 1948. Those responsible for the care of deprived children, the churchwardens and the parish overseers, were to take such measures as were necessary for setting them to work or binding them as apprentices. These bald embodiments of a constructive principle of care remained unaltered in our legislation for three hundred and forty-seven years, until the shadow of a grim farm-house fell across them, and darkened them for ever.

However, Heywood also notes that the *Report of the Committee on Parish Apprentices* (1815) stated that in London poor relief was 'seldom bestowed without the parish claiming the exclusive right of disposing, at their pleasure, of all the children of the person claiming relief'. The parental right of custody emerged as a powerful factor in upper class litigation during the nineteenth century (p. 442, above) and began to pose a challenge both for the poor law authorities and for the philanthropists seeking to rescue children from their supposedly corrupting environment:

In all the planning of the various systems of care for the deprived child, the natural family, where it existed, remained a problem which, if it was not being treated, was certainly to be reckoned with. Separating the child and the unfit parent or relative of bad influence was a definite attempt to prevent pauperism reproducing itself in the next generation, but the policy was often difficult to effect even if it was considered ethically sound. The constructive work which the poor law attempted by providing a better environment for the child was frequently brought to nothing by what was described as the 'pernicious influence of the child's relations' particularly when the children passed out of the guardians' care at 16. Two solutions were found for coping with this problem: ...

Boards of Guardians were empowered under the Poor Law Amendment Act of 1850 to emigrate orphan or deserted children under the age of 16 years, provided the child gave his consent. There were real opportunities, particularly in Canada where there was a shortage of labour and where food was cheap, and the guardians made use of these opportunities, though not to any great extent. In general voluntary organisations, such as Dr Barnardo's Homes or the Roman Catholic Emigration Agency, were used as agents, the fittest and most promising of the eligible pauper children being chosen for this new life.

The more difficult problem of the child and the unfit parent was grappled with by Acts of 1889 and 1899. These gave the boards of guardians in England and Wales authority to assume complete rights and responsibilities of a parent over a child in care until he reached the age of 18. Such rights could be assumed only in respect of deserted children at first, but in 1899 their application was widened to include orphans and children of parents who were disabled or in prison, or unfit to have the care of them. This power to assume parental rights by the state was an expression of the public interest in the welfare of children and was intended to lay down a definite standard of parental care. ...

However, the standard of care provided by the local authorities which became responsible for administering the poor law left a great deal to be desired. The 'grim farmhouse' to which Heywood refers was where Dennis O'Neill died in 1945, as recounted by Sir Walter Monckton in his Report (1945):

2. ... Dennis and Terence O'Neill were born respectively on the 2 March 1932, and the 13 December 1934, and were the children of Thomas John O'Neill, a labourer, of Newport, Monmouthshire, and Mabel Blonwyn O'Neill, his wife. On the 30 May 1940, Dennis and Terence were committed by the Newport Juvenile Court to the care or protection of the Newport County Borough Council, as a 'fit person' within the meaning of Sections 76 and 96 of the Children and Young Persons Act 1933, hereinafter referred to as the 1933 Act. Dennis was boarded out at Bank Farm, Minsterley, Shropshire, on the 28 June 1944. The foster-parents were Reginald Gough and Esther Gough, his wife, Terence joined Dennis at Bank Farm on the 5 July 1944. Dennis died there on the 9 January 1945. Terence was removed from Bank Farm to a place of safety on the 10 January 1945.

3. An inquest was held on the boy Dennis. The coroner's jury returned a verdict that his death was due to acute cardiac failure following violence applied to the front of the chest and back while in a state of under-nourishment due to neglect and added a rider that there had been a serious lack of supervision by the local authority. Reginald and Esther Gough were charged with manslaughter. At Stafford Assizes on the 19 March 1945, Reginald Gough was found guilty of manslaughter and was sentenced to six years' penal servitude. Esther Gough was found not guilty of manslaughter but guilty of neglect and was sentenced to six months' imprisonment.

The children had been boarded out with the Goughs in an emergency, but thereafter there had been no adequate inquiry into their suitability, no medical examination, and no proper supervision. Sir Walter concluded, however, that little change in the law was needed:

54. ... What is required is rather that the administrative machinery should be improved and informed by a more anxious and responsible spirit. ... The personal relation in which the local authority, which has undertaken care and protection stands to the child should be more clearly

recognized. ... It may well be that, in order to ensure that those who supervise are competent for the purpose, some training or instruction should be required; but this is a question which would need fuller consideration. The duty to be sure in the care of children must not be put aside, however great may be the pressure of other burdens.

By that time, however, plans were already afoot to abolish the poor law and a different approach was being urged to the care of children, as can be seen from this letter from Lady Allen of Hurtwood to *The Times* (1944):

Sir,
Thoughtful consideration is being given to many fundamental problems, but in reconstruction plans one section of the community has, so far, been entirely forgotten.

I write of those children who, because of their family misfortune, find themselves under the guardianship of a Government Department or one of the many charitable organisations. The public are, for the most part, unaware that many thousands of these children are being brought up under repressive conditions that are generations out of date and are unworthy of our traditional care for children. Many who are orphaned, destitute, or neglected, still live under the chilly stigma of 'charity'; too often they form groups isolated from the main stream of life and education, and few of them know the comfort and security of individual affection. A letter does not allow space for detailed evidence.

In many 'Homes', both charitable and public, the willing staff are, for the most part, overworked, underpaid, and untrained; indeed, there is no recognised system of training. Inspection, for which the Ministry of Health, the Home Office, or the Board of Education may be nominally responsible, is totally inadequate, and few standards are established or expected. Because no one Government Department is fully responsible, the problem is the more difficult to tackle.

A public inquiry, with full Government support, is urgently needed to explore this largely uncivilised territory. Its mandate should be to ascertain whether the public and charitable organisations are, in fact, enabling these children to lead full and happy lives, and to make recommendations how the community can compensate them for the family life they have lost. In particular, the inquiry should investigate what arrangements can be made (by regional reception centres or in other ways) for the careful consideration of the individual children before they are finally placed with foster-parents or otherwise provided for; how the use of large residential homes can be avoided; how staff can be appropriately trained and ensured adequate salaries and suitable conditions of work, and how central administrative responsibility can best be secured so that standards can be set and can be maintained by adequate inspection.

The social upheaval caused by the war has not only increased this army of unhappy children, but presents the opportunity for transforming their conditions. The Education Bill and the White paper on the Health Services have alike ignored the problem and the opportunity.
Yours sincerely,
Marjory Allen of Hurtwood.
15 July 1944. Hurtwood House, Albury, Guildford.

The public inquiry was conducted by the Care of Children Committee, chaired by Miss Myra Curtis, 'into the existing methods of providing for children who from loss of parents or from any cause whatever are deprived of a normal home life with their own parents or relatives'. This covered almost 125,000 children, some 57,000 of whom were cared for under the poor law. The Curtis Report (1946) paints a gloomy picture:

138. ... . It was clear that in some areas the workhouse served as a dumping ground for children who could not readily be disposed of elsewhere, and that in some districts where children's Homes provided insufficient accommodation, or boarding out had not been well developed, older children, for whom there had never been any properly planned accommodation, were looked after in the workhouse for a considerable length of time.
...
140. An example of this kind of motley collection was found in one century-old Poor Law institution providing accommodation for 170 adults, including ordinary workhouse accommodation, an infirmary for senile old people and a few men and women certified as either mentally defective or mentally disordered. In this institution there were twenty-seven children, aged 6 months to 15 years. Twelve infants up to the age of 18 months were the children of

women in the institution about half of them still being nursed by their mothers. In the same room in which these children were being cared for was a Mongol idiot, aged 4, of gross appearance, for whom there was apparently no accommodation elsewhere. A family of five normal children, aged about 6 to 15, who had been admitted on a relieving officer's order, had been in the institution for ten weeks. This family, including a boy of 10 and a girl of 15, were sleeping in the same room as a 3 year old hydrocephalic idiot, of very unsightly type, whose bed was screened off in the corner. The 15 year old girl had been employed in the day-time dusting the women's infirmary ward. These children had been admitted in the middle of the night when their mother had left them under a hedge after eviction from their house. No plan appeared to have been made for them.

...

144. One nursery which was structurally linked to the Public Assistance Institution had sunk to the lowest level of child care which has come under our notice. ... The healthy children were housed in the ground floor corrugated hutment which had been once the old union casual ward. The day room was large and bare and empty of all toys. The children fed, played and used their pots in this room. They ate from cracked enamel plates, using the same mug for milk and soup. They slept in another corrugated hutment in old broken black iron cots some of which had their sides tied up with cord. The mattresses were fouled and stained. On enquiry there did not appear to be any available stocks of clothes to draw on. ... The children wore ankle length calico or flanelette frocks and petticoats and had no knickers. Their clothes were not clean. Most of them had lost their shoes; ... Their faces were clean; their bodies in some cases were unwashed and stained.

This nursery was an exception, and some were very good, but even for the children who found their way into children's homes, conditions might not be much better:

171. ... In another Single Home with accommodation for 18 boys there were 24 present at the time of our visit. They had only one small sitting room for meals, reading and play. The dormitories were tightly packed and there was no room for any provision in the way of lockers or other receptacles for the boys' own possessions, though they were said to be on order. Outside was a small asphalt yard.

It was attitudes, as much as organisation and resources, which were to blame:

154. ... We do not mean to suggest that we found evidence of harshness for which the staff was responsible. Except in the one instance of the nursery unit described in paragraph 144 the ill-usage was of a negative rather than a positive kind and elsewhere sprang directly from unsuitability of buildings, lack of training and of appreciation of children's needs. Officials of local authorities suggested that the children suffered from the attitude of the public to children maintained under the poor law. This attitude had affected some members of the Public Assistance Committees, some of whom had survived as Committee members from the days of the old Boards of Guardians and still held old-fashioned views about what was suitable for a destitute child.

The Committee also visited some of the 27,800 children who were boarded out:

370. ... The contrast between the children in Homes and the boarded out children was most marked. The boarded out children suffered less from segregation, starvation for affection and lack of independence. They bore a different stamp of developing personality, and despite occasional misfits were manifestly more independent. For example, they were much more indifferent to visitors, were much better satisfied by their environment (by which we mean the special features of security and love). There was, we thought, much greater happiness for the child integrated by boarding out into a family of normal size in a normal home.

Question

Why was the fact that the children 'were much more indifferent to visitors' regarded as a good sign?

When it came to recommending solutions, the Committee assumed that most of the children would remain in public care for a long time. It was clear about what their substitute home should provide:

427. ... If the substitute home is to give the child what he gets from a good normal home it must supply –
  (i) Affection and personal interest; understanding of his defects; care for his future; respect for his personality and regard for his self esteem.
  (ii) Stability; the feeling that he can expect to remain with those who will continue to care for him till he goes out into the world on his own feet.
  (iii) Opportunity of making the best of his ability and aptitudes, whatever they may be, as such opportunity is made available to the child in the normal home.
  (iv) A share in the common life of a small group of people in a homely environment.
Some at least of these needs are supplied by the child's own home even if it is not in all respects a good one; it is a very serious responsibility to make provision for him to be brought up elsewhere without assurance that they can be supplied by the environment to which he is removed.

Hence:

447. ... Every effort should be made to keep the child in its home, or with its mother if it is illegitimate, provided that the home is or can be made reasonably satisfactory. The aim of the authority must be to find something better – indeed much better – if it takes the responsibility of providing a substitute home. The methods which should be available may be treated under three main heads of adoption, boarding out and residence in communities. We have placed these in the order in which, subject to the safeguards we propose and to consideration of the needs of the individual, they seem to us to secure the welfare and happiness of the child.

Question

Do you agree with this order to priorities?

The Committee's main solution was for new local authority Children's Departments to take responsibility for all kinds of children's homes, including approved (reform) schools, boarding out, and adoption, and for children found in need of care and protection by a court. At its head would be a universal mother:

441. ... We desire ... to see the responsibility for the welfare of the deprived children definitely laid on a Children's Officer. This may indeed be said to be our solution of the problem referred to us. Throughout our investigation we have been increasingly impressed by the need for the personal element in the care of children, which Sir Walter Monckton emphasised in his report on the O'Neill case. No office staff dealing with them as case papers can do the work we want done – work which is in part administrative, but also in large part field work, involving many personal contacts and the solution of problems by direct methods. ...
443. ... She (we use the feminine pronoun not with any aim of excluding men from these posts but because we think it may be found that the majority of persons suitable for the work are women) will of course work under the orders of her committee or board but she will be a specialist in child care as the Medical Officer of Health is a specialist in his own province and the Director of Education is in his; and she will have no other duties to distract her interests. She would represent the council in its parental functions. The committal of the child to the care of a council which takes over parental rights and duties is not without incongruity. To be properly exercised the responsibility must be delegated to an individual, and that individual one whose training has fitted her for child care and whose whole attention is given to it. ...

Hence the Children Act 1948 set up the new departments and gave them, among other things, the duty to care for orphaned, abandoned or deprived children, the power to assume parental rights over children in their care who had no parents or parents who were in some way incapable or unfit to look after them, and the duty to act as a fit parent for children compulsorily removed from home by a court. The compulsorily removed children fell into three different categories, which were eventually brought together in s. 1 of the Children and Young Persons Act 1969. John Eekelaar, Robert Dingwall and Topsy Murray in 'Victims or Threats? Children in Care Proceedings' (1982) explain how this came about:

... A significant report published in 1816 by an unofficial Committee of the Society for Investigating the Causes of the Alarming Increase of Juvenile Delinquency in the Metropolis, attempted a radical assessment of the problem. Although it is sometimes thought that the significance of the home and community environment among the causative factors of delinquency is a modern realisation, this is not so. The 1816 Report numbered 'the improper conduct of parents, the want of education and the want of suitable employment' as the first of the five most significant causes of delinquency. Here is a recognition of human nature as being a product of environment, of behaviour being socially caused. The work of the reformatory movement was inspired by the same idea and it received statutory recognition in the Youthful Offenders Act 1854. But the scope of reform schools in combating juvenile delinquency was restricted by the major limitation that children were committed there only after having been convicted of an offence. ...

[Nineteenth century reformers] maintained a distinction in classification between children who had committed offences and those who had not. They were to be kept in separate establishments. The industrial schools, which catered for the latter category, were a development of the 'ragged schools' of the eighteenth century which, as the Departmental Committee on Young Offenders of 1927 noted 'were an attempt to deal more radically with the problem of child welfare by providing education and industrial training for the class of children from whom delinquents were mainly drawn.' ...

Yet it is clear that the children in industrial schools were there at least as much because they were thought of as being a risk to society as being at risk themselves and already by 1870 the Inspector of Industrial Schools reported that those schools had been assimilated to reformatories 'in their necessary arrangements and regulations and the main features of their management.' The children were sent there by warrant of a magistrate. The schools had become 'houses of detention for the young vagabond and petty misdemeanant.' ...

The third source which makes up the composition of section 1(2) of the 1969 Act had its origin in the Prevention of Cruelty to, and Protection of, Children Act 1889. The most significant provision of this Act created an offence if anyone over 16 who had custody, control or charge of a boy under 14 or a girl under 16 wilfully ill-treated, neglected or abandoned the child in a manner likely to cause unnecessary suffering or injury to health. On conviction of a parent for this offence, the court could commit the child to the charge of a relative or anyone else willing to have the care of the child who would have 'like control over the child as if he were its parent and shall be responsible for its maintenance, and the child shall continue under the control of such person, notwithstanding that it is claimed by its parents'.

The necessity of conviction of the parent is significant, for it reflects the basis of the justification for state intervention on which this provision rests. This is that the parent's conduct offends against the moral conception of society held by the Act's proponents. The purpose for the intervention was, indeed, to protect children, but the method by which this was sought was morally to reform the parents. ...

But in 1933 this category of children was included in the category of children formerly covered by the industrial schools legislation as being 'in need of care and protection.' This was a highly significant move for, as we have seen, children found to be in need of care and protection could be committed to approved schools as young offenders could be. It seems odd to find children who, even more clearly than the 'neglected' category, were in need of protection from adults, being dealt with under the very same statutory provisions, and indeed, court procedure, as children from whom the community sought to protect itself. It is revealing therefore to discover how this happened. The 1927 Committee was required 'to inquire into the treatment of young offenders and young people who, owing to bad associations or surroundings require protection and training.' They considered that their inquiry was concerned not only with the 'young offender' but also with 'the neglected boy or girl who has not yet committed offences but who, owing to want of parental control, bad associations or other reasons needs protection and training.' ... However, the Committee went on to say: 'There are also young people who are the victims of cruelty or other offences committed by adults and whose natural guardianship having proved insufficient or unworthy of trust must be replaced.'

We may note here what has been characteristic of all these investigations into the condition of children, that the concern has primarily been with the problem of troublesome children, and the question of child protection has been tagged on very much as a subsidiary and secondary question. ...

There is no doubt that the result was to strengthen the provisions for protecting such children because local education authorities were now placed under a duty to inquire into such cases and bring them before a court and the courts were empowered to commit them into the care of local authorities. But these children had now become irredeemably intertwined with a group of children with entirely different problems and who were regarded by society as virtually inseparable from delinquent children.

In the meantime another significant development had been occurring in attitudes towards neglected and abused children. The evangelical movement had declined, but the growth of community health services provided an alternative model for intervention in family life. ... The immediate impetus arose from the prosecution by the NSPCC of a blind couple for neglecting their children, and in 1952 the Children and Young Persons (Amendment) Act removed the requirement of prosecution of parents as a condition precedent for finding a child to be in need of care and protection within the 1933 Act. Hence forward it would be enough if the child had no parent or guardian or if his parent or guardian was 'unfit to exercise care or guardianship or (was) not exercising proper care and guardianship' and 'he was being ill-treated or neglected in a manner likely to cause him unnecessary suffering or injury to health.' Failure (for whatever cause) in the parenting function leading to a specified condition in the child became a ground for intervention. Although the approach is now overtly welfarist, the requirement that the child's condition should arise from parental failure still serves to maintain a distinction between this class of children and those from whom society sought to protect itself. The distinction was not to last for long.

The Ingleby Committee (1960) and the 1969 Act

... In dealing with the general issue of the circumstances in which the state may properly intervene in proceedings against parents for child neglect, the Committee states that 'difficulty has not arisen for several years over the reasonable requirements for nutrition, housing, clothing and schooling' although there had been some cases where parents had refused to give their children proper medical attention. No mention is made at all by the Committee of child abuse cases and the Committee proceeds, throughout the rest of the chapter, to consider the issue solely in terms of delinquency cases. By 1960, then, our society had become blind to potential conflicts between family autonomy and child protection. Apart from a few troublesome cases involving unconventional religious sects, the resolution of welfarist child protection and family autonomy was considered simple and unproblematic. In fact, it had been obscured by the overwhelming preoccupation with delinquency. ...

The two Government White Papers, The Child, the Family and the Young Offender and Children in Trouble (Home Office, 1965 and 1968) were, as their titles indicate, wholly concerned with the problem of juvenile delinquents. They set the basis for the policy of the 1969 Act. One cornerstone of that policy was that children should progressively cease to be prosecuted for offences and should, instead, be made subject to care proceedings under the Act. Accordingly, the grounds for bringing care proceedings were to be extended to include a ground that the child had committed an offence (excluding homicide). Child offenders were now to be treated under (almost) exactly the same process as troublesome children who were not offenders. And, as we have seen, child victims had by now been assimilated into this category. The logic of this assimilation compelled the abandonment, for all categories of these children, of any reference to parental inadequacy among the conditions precedent to bringing care proceedings. For, as the Home Office observed in its official guide to the Act, such a provision 'meant that proceedings inevitably appeared to cast blame for the child's situation or behaviour directly into his parents or those looking after him' a fact which was quite irrelevant for the delinquent child (though, as will be argued below, crucially relevant in the case of the child victim). The Act, therefore, took the line originally proposed by the Ingleby Report and simply required that it be shown that the child was in need of 'care of control' which he would not receive if an order was not made.

Implementation of the 1969 Act, which tried to cater for the villains and the victims by the same process, coincided with the Local Authority Social Services Act 1970, which amalgamated the children's services with those provided for the old, the mentally disordered or handicapped, and the disabled, into new all-purpose social services departments. As Jean Packman explains in *The Child's Generation* (1981):

Developments in prevention and work with delinquency not only strained, modified and redefined the original aims and methods of the child care service; they also contributed to its eventual demise. The pursuit of both policies increased the children's departments' involvement with and dependence upon other agencies and threw into relief their relationship with one another and the illogical and wasteful effects of the fragmented pattern of personal social services. As the two policies drew closer together, with prevention of neglect being seen more and more as a key means of forestalling delinquency, the pressure to change that pattern and to provide an integrated 'family service' in its place mounted.

However, not everyone was delighted:

Oxfordshire's Children's Committee, in preparing its own evidence to Seebohm, said 'it would in our opinion, for instance, be damaging to the highly personal type of work done by the child care service to place it in such a large and general group of functions that the old pattern of the former Public Assistance Service might recur, with the disadvantages that would entail'. The spectre of the Poor Law still haunted the local councillors.

But there was another spectre, which soon came to haunt those responsible for local authority social services departments. There were some 18 reports of child abuse inquiries between 1973 and 1980 (see DHSS, 1982), beginning with Maria Colwell (1973) and including Susan Auckland (1975) and Wayne Brewer (1977). Between 1980 and 1989 there were at least 19 more (see DH, 1991), including Jasmine Beckford (1985), Heidi Koseda (1986), Tyra Henry (1987) and Kimberley Carlile (1987). The President of the Association of Directors of Social Services in 2001 reported that at that time there were nearly 100 large-scale ongoing police inquiries into allegations of sexual and physical abuse believed to involve about 2,500 children at more than 500 residential and care homes (*Guardian*, 8 January 2001).

The Cleveland Report (1988) dealt with the issue of child sexual abuse:

1. Child abuse, the non-accidental injury of a child, received increasing attention in this country in the 1960s, and followed upon its recognition in the United States. ... A parallel can be drawn between the reluctance to recognise physical abuse in the United Kingdom in the 1960s and the reluctance by many to accept the reality of certain aspects of child sexual abuse in the 1980s.
2. Child abuse has many forms; the concerns may centre upon physical abuse, sexual and emotional abuse, or upon neglect. Dr Cameron in discussing the 3 categories of active child abuse: physical, emotional, and sexual abuse, pointed out that, while it was helpful to the diagnostician to have distinct forms of child abuse in mind, not infrequently, in practice, a child is subject to more than one form of abuse. It is obviously important to recognise that the categories of the abuse are not closed. Experts gave us figures indicating that as much as 30% of children referred because of other forms of abuse may also show medical evidence of sexual abuse.

Definitions of child sexual abuse
4. The definition of child sexual abuse by Schechter and Roberge is widely quoted:

'Sexual abuse is defined as the involvement of dependent, developmentally immature children and adolescents in sexual activities that they do not fully comprehend and to which they are unable to give informed consent or that violate the social taboos of family roles.'

In other words it is the use of children by adults for sexual gratification. Dr Cameron described it as inappropriate behaviour which involved: 'the child being exploited by the adult either for direct physical gratification of sexual needs or for vicarious gratification'.
5. Child sexual abuse may take place within the family circle or outside, for example, by a neighbour or a complete stranger. According to Dr Paul (1986) abuse within the family is the most common form. The type of sexual abuse, its degree of seriousness, the age of the child and whether it is within the family all affect not only the presentation but also the response to it by the community and the action required of the professionals charged with the duty of protecting the abused child. It is essential in any consideration of child sexual abuse to be clear at all times as to the definition and description being used.

...

The children

12. The Inquiry was provided with evidence about Cleveland children primarily in respect of allegations of the most serious offences of incest, unlawful sexual intercourse and buggery of girls and buggery of boys and indecent assault almost all within the family, including digital penetration, fondling, mutual masturbation, anal and oral/genital contact. From the evidence presented to the Inquiry a majority of children sexually abused in the U.K. are girls but there are significant numbers of boys. ...

13. The abuse may be one incident, occasional, a gradual but escalating level of abuse; or it may be frequent and regular. For some children it may become a way of life and only in adolescence do they realise they have not enjoyed a 'normal' family life. At the time it may not necessarily be experienced as distasteful by the child and it is only later that the child realises it is what it is. On the other hand it may be coercive and frightening from the beginning.

14. Some children appear to be specially vulnerable, for example those with physical or mental handicaps, others treated as scapegoats, or those who are particularly immature. It may occur where the older child has a parenting role. Alcohol, drugs, absence of the other parent from home; a single parent with a succession of male partners, violence, marital or sexual difficulties may be factors. Other factors suggested include chaotic or inadequate families, or the sub-normality of a parent.

15. The children caught up in the crisis in Cleveland ranged in age from under a year to adolescence. It would be impossible to say how many sexually abused children in Cleveland were boys. But there were some boys sexually abused during the period and significant proportions in respect of whom allegations were made.

16. There were some unusual complaints, for example: one little girl of 7 complained that her father and girl friend squirted tea in a syringe up 'her front'; one little boy of 4 spoke of an iron bar being pushed up his bottom; one boy said he had a toilet roll pushed up as a punishment. In several instances children who were later found to have been abused at home engaged in sexualised behaviour towards each other or with other children at school.

Pressure to keep the secret

17. Many children who have been subject to sexual abuse are put under pressure from the perpetrator not to tell; there may be threats of violence to the child or that the perpetrator will commit suicide, of being taken away from home and put into care, threats that someone they love will be angry with them, or that no-one would believe them. Children may elect not to talk because of a genuine affection for the perpetrator and an awareness of the consequences to the perpetrator, to the partner, to the family unit, or for an older child an understanding of the economic considerations in the break-up of the family and the loss of the wage earner. The secretive element persists. Professor Sir Martin Roth in evidence said: 'There is a powerful disincentive to disclosing the fact that one has been subject to sexual abuse. The person who discloses this has fears that he may be regarded as having permitted himself, as having collaborated in it, as having been lastingly damaged in a sexual way. He is likely to fear ridicule, humiliation, obloquy and so on'.

18. This pressure upon the child not to tell and the desire of all to keep the secret is also apparent in the pressure brought upon children to retract once they have made a complaint. The pressure comes from the family, mother, siblings and the extended family as well as the abuser. The withdrawal of the complaint is a common situation with child complainants and presents particular difficulties for the police.

19. In Cleveland we heard of examples of pressure on children. A girl of 12 told the Official Solicitor that her step-father said no-one would believe her. A girl of 8 expressed relief at the death of her father who committed suicide after she revealed the abuse. One little girl of 5 told the police that her father had sexually abused her. According to a letter from her mother she explained why she had not told before: 'It was because my daddy told me I would lose my voice if I told anyone'. The mother wrote: 'These are the things she has told me: she was told, somebody will come and take her away, people would hit her for telling lies, Mammy will cry if you tell her'.

The children may become 'double victims'

20. Those who fear a child has been sexually abused naturally wish to protect the child from further assaults; to stop the abuser having the opportunity to abuse again. The ideal would be to protect the child within his or her home and neighbourhood, preferably after identifying and excluding the abuser. However, if, as is often the case, the perpetrator is unknown, or is suspected but denies the abuse, how can the child be protected? In practice, it is the child who

is taken away from home, friends and school and it is the child who is placed in hospital, in a childrens' home or in a foster home, in strange surroundings and among strangers.

21. The plight of the 'double victim' is well illustrated by what happened to one of the children in Cleveland. The girl told the police that she had been sexually abused by her father. She said that the threat from the perpetrator was that she would be taken away from home and placed in care if she told anyone what was going on. As it happened the effect of the complaint was a place of safety order and she was removed from home, and suffered twice over. That child retracted her story.

...

Relationships within the family

28. The mother, we are told, is by no means certain to be the protector of the child. Some may have themselves been abused as children. Some may be afraid of the man, inadequate personalities ill-equipped to give the child protection, or even prefer him to pay attention to the child rather than to themselves. Some mothers can not or will not believe it to be possible. There is a very acute dilemma for a mother in the conflict between her man and her child, in which the relationship with the man, the economic and other support which she received from him may disincline her to accept the truth of the allegation. Some mothers choose sexual offenders as partners more than once.

Again quoting Professor Sir Martin Roth: 'In many cases mothers play a role in the genesis of the sexual abuse of their daughters. They may be too physically ill or inadequate in personality to provide proper care and protection for their children. In other cases mothers elect the eldest or one of the oldest daughters to the role of 'child mother'. The girl in her early teens or even earlier is expected to take the responsibility for the caring of younger children whose mothering role is allowed to slide into a sexual relationship with the father. This is tolerated with little or no protest. I refer to lack of protest on the part of the mother for a variety of reasons and the mother may in such cases deny what is happening. She conceals the truth from herself as well as others; the relationship continues and when the situation is brought to light it may be insisted by the mother that it had been unknown to her'.

29. In the evidence presented to the Inquiry several children who described abuse indicated that their mothers either were present or knew what was going on.

The lasting effects of sexual abuse in childhood

30. We have been provided with a considerable amount of written material on various aspects of the long term effects on the abused child. ...

33. Professor Sir Martin Roth told us in evidence of the serious harm sexual abuse had done to some of his patients. He warned that 'Those who have been intimidated by threats into incestuous relationships in childhood proved to be at high risk of abusing their own children thus transmitting the effects of deprivation. The ill effects are not confined to feelings of guilt, self-reproach and humiliation aroused after incest has begun or when its character has come to be appreciated. Emotional development may be seriously deranged or arrested and ability to form normal personal and sexual relationships to be fulfilled and happy in marriage and to prove emotionally equal to the responsibility of rearing children suffer lasting impairment. Although it is the more intrusive and more aggressive forms of abuse that cause the most grave damage, forms of incestuous relationship that leave no sign may inflict a lasting wound.'

Question

Before Cleveland, all of the other public inquiries concerned the authorities' failure to protect children from physical abuse or neglect either at home or in care. In Cleveland the concern was that the authorities might have been too anxious to protect the children. Is it significant that Cleveland involved allegations of sexual abuse?

The Department of Health's summary of research, *Child Protection – Messages from Research* (1995), suggests the importance of seeing child protection issues within the wider context of social services functions:

Protection issues are best viewed in the context of children's wider needs. It is important to ensure that inappropriate cases do not get caught up in the child protection process, for this could have several undesirable consequences. Of particular concern is the unnecessary distress caused to family members who may then be unwilling to co-operate with subsequent plans. Professionals have to weigh up which stages in the protection process are relevant to each case. They may have to rebuild a sense of trust with family members to enable them to participate. Ultimately, it will be necessary to decide when and how to permit a case to leave the child protection arena. ... The Children Act 1989 requires local authorities to provide a range of services for children in need and intends that only extreme cases will require adjudication by courts. For all but the most serious cases there are many intermediate stages between a child first coming to the notice of welfare agencies, the removal of the child from home and/or a court hearing being necessary. The child protection process encompasses some of these stages. The idea of a 'threshold' which includes the criteria for moving a child from one stage in the process to another has been introduced. In the following pages several thresholds for action are described, as are the criteria on which they are based.

...

Psychological evidence suggests that while children suffer in an environment of low warmth and high criticism, the intervention of professionals in these situations is seldom necessary or helpful. If, however, family problems endure, some external support, perhaps using Section 17 services [see p.584, below], will be required to ensure that the health and development of the child is not significantly impaired. If the child's fraught situation endures, then he or she is likely to suffer significant harm and may need to be looked after away from home. There are, in addition, a small proportion of cases in which the abuse is extreme and will not be reduced by family support alone. For children who have been grossly injured or sexually abused, swift child rescue, sometimes using emergency powers, will be necessary. However, the research evidence suggests that, for the majority of cases, the need of the child and family is more important than the abuse or, put another way, the general family context is more important than any abusive event within it. This message applies when defining maltreatment, designing interventions or assessing outcomes.

Thus, in addition to the considerable burden of child protection work, professionals also offer family support and provide child welfare for the small proportion who live away from home. For a child-care system to be effective, some overlap between these services is inevitable. But the research studies have questioned whether the balance between child protection and the range of supports and interventions available to professionals is correct. This is an issue Area Child Protection Committees and professionals associated with this group must constantly raise about services in their region.

The research studies suggest that too much of the work undertaken comes under the banner of child protection. ...

A more balanced service for vulnerable children would encourage professionals to take a wider view. There would be efforts to work alongside families rather than disempower them, to raise their self-esteem rather than reproach families, to promote family relationships where children have their needs met, rather than leave untreated families with an unsatisfactory parenting style. The focus would be on the overall needs of children rather than a narrow concentration on the alleged incident.

One of most important recent reports is the *Report of the Tribunal of Inquiry into the abuse of children in care in the former county council areas of Gwynedd and Clwyd since 1974*, chaired by a former High Court judge, Sir Robert Waterhouse, '*Lost in Care*' (2000). The report runs to some 937 pages. The tribunal of inquiry found that there was widespread sexual abuse of boys in children's residential establishments in Clwyd between 1974 and 1990. It found also that physical abuse in the sense of unacceptable use of force in disciplining and excessive force in restraining residents occurred in most of the residential establishments that the inquiry examined. It concluded that the quality of care provided in all the local authority homes and private residential establishments examined was below an acceptable standard throughout the period under review, and in most cases far below the required standard. It made 72 recommendations, and we reproduce (1) to (38):

	Recommendation	Source[1]

The detection of, and response to, abuse

Children's Commissioner	(1) An independent Children's Commissioner for Wales should be appointed.	**1 to 21 45 to 58**
	(2) The duties of the Commissioner should include:	
	(a) ensuring that children's rights are respected through the monitoring and oversight of the operation of complaints and whistleblowing procedures and the arrangements for children's advocacy;	
	(b) examining the handling of individual cases brought to the Commissioner's attention (including making recommendations on the merits) when he considers it necessary and appropriate to do so;	
	(c) publishing reports, including an annual report to the National Assembly for Wales.	
Children's Complaints Officer	(3) Every social services authority should be required to appoint an appropriately qualified or experienced Children's Complaints Officer, who should not be the line manager of residential or other staff who may be the subject of children's complaints or complaints relating to children.	**18 to 21 58(i) to (iii)**
	(4) Amongst the duties of the Children's Complaints Officer should be:	
	(a) to act in the best interests of the child;	
	(b) on receiving a complaint, to see the affected child and the complainant, if it is not the affected child;	
	(c) thereafter to notify and consult with appropriate line managers about the further handling of the complaint, including:	
	(i) any necessary interim action in relation to the affected child, the complainant and the person who is the subject of complaint, including informal resolution of the complaint, if that is appropriate;	
	(ii) consideration of the established procedures to be implemented, such as child protection and disciplinary procedures and including any necessary involvement of the police and/or other agencies;	
	(d) to ensure that recourse to an independent advocacy service is available to any complainant or affected child who wishes to have it;	
	(e) to keep a complete record of all complaints received and how they are dealt with, including the ultimate outcome;	
	(f) to report periodically to the Director of Social Services on complaints received, how they have been dealt with and the results.	
Response to complaints	(5) Any decision about the future of a child who is alleged to have been abused should be made in that child's best interests. In particular, the child should not be transferred to another placement unless it is in the child's best interests to be transferred.	**19,58(ii)**

[1] Where the source is stated to be a plain number in the range of 1 to 95 it is a Conclusion set out in para 55.10 of the report. Other sources cited are paragraphs in the report.

	Recommendation	Source[1]
Complaints procedures	(6) Every local authority should promote vigorously awareness by children and staff of its complaints procedures for looked after children and the importance of applying them conscientiously without any threat or fear of reprisals in any form.	
	(7) Such complaints procedures should: (a) be neither too prescriptive nor too restrictive in categorising what constitutes a complaint; (b) encompass a wide variety of channels through which complaints by or relating to looked after children may be made or referred to the Children's Complaints Officer including teachers, doctors, nurses, police officers and elected members as well as residential care staff and social workers; (c) ensure that any person who is the subject of complaint will not be involved in the handling of the complaint.	
Whistleblowing procedures	(8) Every local authority should establish and implement conscientiously clear whistleblowing procedures enabling members of staff to make complaints and raise matters of concern affecting the treatment or welfare of looked after children without threats or fear of reprisals in any form. Such procedures should embody the principles indicated in recommendation (7) and the action to be taken should follow, as far as may be appropriate, that set out in recommendation (4).	**20,58(iii), 62(v)**
Duty to report abuse	(9) Consideration should be given to requiring failure by a member of staff to report actual or suspected physical or sexual abuse of a child by another member of staff or other person having contact with the child to be made an explicit disciplinary offence.	
Field social workers	(10) An appropriate[2] field social worker should be assigned to every looked after child throughout the period that the child remains in care and for an appropriate period following the child's discharge from care.	
	(11) Field social workers should be required by regulation to visit any looked after child for whom they are responsible not less than once every eight weeks[3]. In the case of older children, they should be required also to see the child alone and at intervals away from their residential or foster home.	**30,58(vi)**
	(12) Any arrangements made for the provision of residential care or fostering services should expressly safeguard the field social worker's continuing responsibilities for supervision of the placement and care planning.	**59**

---

[2] "Appropriate" in this recommendation and in succeeding recommendations means a social worker with specific training in working with looked after children.

[3] See Sir William Utting, People Like Us, 1997, The Stationery Office at para 3.46 in relation to visits to foster homes.

	Recommendation	Source[1]
Awareness of abuse	(13) Area Child Protection Committees should arrange training in sexual abuse awareness for social services staff and for those from other departments, agencies and organisations in their area.	
	(14) Steps should be taken through training and professional and other channels periodically to remind persons outside social services departments who are or may be in regular contact with looked after children, such as teachers, medical practitioners, nurses and police officers, of their potential role in identifying and reporting abuse, the importance of that role and the procedures available to them.	
Police log	(15) A log of all incidents, disturbances, reports, complaints and absconsions at a children's home should be kept at an appropriate nearby police station and made accessible, when required, to officers of the Social Services Department.	19, 29
Absconders	(16) Police officers should be reminded periodically that an absconder from a residential care or foster home may have been motivated to abscond by abuse in the home. They should be advised that, when apprehended, an absconder should be encouraged to explain his reasons for absconding and that the absconder should not automatically be returned to the home from which he absconded without consultation with his field social worker.	75
	(17) It should be a rule of practice that any absconsion should be reported as soon as possible to the absconder's field social worker and that the absconder should be seen on his return by that social worker or by another appropriate person who is independent of the home.	
Strategy on investigation of complaint	(18) When a complaint alleges serious misbehaviour by a member of staff, the Director of Social Services should appoint a senior officer to formulate an overall strategy for dealing with the complaint, including such matters as liaison with the police in relation to investigation and with other agencies as appropriate, the impact on the child and other residents, any links with other establishments, the handling of any disciplinary proceedings, treatment of any looked after children who are or may become abusers themselves, the management of information for children and parents, staff, elected members and the public.	**Paras 15.15 to 15.18, 16.06 to 16.19**
Liaison with police	(19) Whenever a police investigation follows upon a complaint of abuse of a looked after child, the senior officer referred to in recommendation (18) or another senior officer assigned for the specific purpose should establish and maintain close liaison with the senior investigating officer appointed by the police for that investigation and the local authority's officer should be kept informed of the progress of the investigation.	76, 77

	Recommendation	Source[1]
Disciplinary proceedings	(20) Any disciplinary proceedings that are necessary following a complaint of abuse to a child should be conducted with the greatest possible expedition and should not automatically await the outcome of parallel investigations by the police or the report on any other investigation. In this context it should be emphasised to personnel departments and other persons responsible for the conduct of disciplinary proceedings within local authorities that: (a) police or any other independent investigation does not determine disciplinary issues; (b) disciplinary proceedings may well involve wider issues than whether a crime has been committed; (c) the standard of proof in disciplinary proceedings is different from that in criminal proceedings; and (d) statements made to the police by potential witnesses in disciplinary proceedings, including statements by a complainant, can and should be made available to local authorities for use in such proceedings, if consent to this is given by the maker of the statement.	21, 39, 62(v)

(21) Personnel departments and other persons responsible for disciplinary proceedings within local authorities should be reminded that:
(a) in deciding whether or not a member of staff should be suspended following an allegation of abuse to a looked after child, first consideration should be given to the best interests of the child;
(b) suspension is a neutral act in relation to guilt or innocence;
(c) long periods of suspension are contrary to the public interest and should be avoided whenever practicable;
(d) depending upon the gravity of the allegation of abuse, the employment of a member of staff in another capacity not involving contact with children or other vulnerable persons may be an appropriate decision at the time of suspending or finally, having regard to the importance of protecting looked after children from abuse.

	Recommendation	Source
Review of procedures in major investigations and guidance	(22) In the light of the recent experience gained in both England and Wales in major investigations of alleged wide ranging abuse of children in care/looked after children, an inter-agency review of the procedures followed and personnel employed in those investigations should now be arranged with a view to issuing practical procedural guidance for the future. In any event guidance is required to social services departments and police forces now in relation to: (a) the safeguarding and preservation of social services files;	82

Recommendation	Source[1]

(b) the safeguarding and preservation of police records of major investigations, including statements and the policy file;

(c) access by the police to social services files;

(d) the supply of information about alleged and suspected abusers by the police following an investigation; and

(e) the sharing of information generally for criminal investigation and child protection purposes.

The prevention of abuse

Recruitment of staff

(23) Social Services Departments should be reminded periodically that they must exercise vigilance in the recruitment and management of their staff in strict accordance with the detailed recommendations of the Warner committee[4]; and compliance with them by individual local authorities should be audited from time to time.

25 to 27

Approval of foster parents

(24) Similar vigilance should be mandatory in relation to all applications for approval as foster parents. In particular, any application to foster by a member of a local authority's child care staff should be stringently vetted by a social worker who is not known to the applicant.

27
Paras 26.05
to 26.15

Introduction training

(25) Social Services Departments should ensure that appropriate and timely induction training is provided for all newly recruited residential child care staff.

28

Training generally

(26) The Tribunal endorses all five of the most recent recommendations of Sir William Utting in "People Like Us"[5] in relation to the content and provision of training for staff in children's homes and the care units of residential special schools and recommends that they should be implemented as expeditiously as possible.

(27) It should be a requirement that senior staff of children's homes (including private and voluntary homes) must be qualified social workers or, if that is not practicable before appointment, that it should be a condition of their appointment that they undertake qualifying training within a specified period.

26

(28) Central government should take the initiative to promote and validate training in safe methods of restraint with a view to making such training readily available for residential child care staff and foster parents.

12, 28, 49

(29) Suitable specialist training in child care at post-qualifying level should be made widely available and, in particular, to the senior residential care staff of children's homes and to field social workers.

Attracting suitable staff

(30) There should be a national review of the pay, status and career development of residential child care staff and field social workers to ensure as far as possible that there is a sufficient supply of candidates for such posts of appropriate calibre.

---

[4] Choosing with care, 1992, HMSO.

[5] Sir William Utting, op cit, at paras 12.22, 12,28, 12,31, 12.34 and 12.37.

	Recommendation	Source[1]

The quality of care

Assessment

(31) Whenever it is possible to do so, an appropriate social worker should carry out a comprehensive assessment of a child's needs and family situation before that child is admitted to care. — **31, 58(vii)**

(32) All emergency admissions should be provisional and should be followed, within a prescribed short period, by a comprehensive assessment of the child's needs and family situation. — **37, 62(iii)**

Care planning

(33) The comprehensive assessment referred to in recommendation (31) and (32) should form the basis for the preparation of a care plan in consultation with and for the child within a prescribed short period after the child's admission to care. — **31, 58(vii)**

(34) An appropriate social worker should be designated as the person responsible for the implementation of the care plan and supervision of the looked after child.

Foster carers

(35) Foster carers should receive continuing support and have access as necessary to specialist services. In this context we endorse the recommendations of Sir William Utting in relation to training in "People Like Us"[6].

Leaving care

(36) The daily regime in residential establishments and foster homes should encourage and provide facilities for the acquisition of skills necessary for independent living. — **32, 58(viii)**

(37) A leaving care plan should be prepared for each looked after child, in consultation with that child, a year in advance of the event and should be reviewed periodically thereafter until the child ceases to require or be eligible for further support. — **58(viii)**

(38) The duty upon local authorities under section 24(1) of the Children Act 1989 to advise, assist and befriend a child with a view to promoting his welfare when he ceases to be looked after by them should be extended so as to ensure that placing authorities provide the level of support to be expected of good parents, including (where appropriate) help to foster parents to provide continuing support[7].

[6] Sir William Utting, op cit, at paras 12,23 and 12,34.
[7] Sir William Utting, op cit, at para 8,64.

Questions

(i) Given what you have read, do you think that children should be kept out of care at all costs?

(ii) Is it possible to support families in a non-threatening way, and also protect children effectively?

(iii) We now have a Children's Commissioner for Wales as recommended in *Lost in Care* (Care Standards Act 2000, s. 72, see Chapter 10, above). We asked the question in Chapter 10, p. 492 whether you see arguments in favour of a Commissioner for England. Having read the sections of Chapter 13 so far, what is your view now?

13.3 Services for children and families

The Department of Health's guide, *Working Together* (1991), emphasises the importance of working in 'partnership' with parents:

1.4   Local authorities have, under the Children Act 1989, a general duty to safeguard and promote the welfare of children within their area who are in need and so far as is consistent with that duty to promote the upbringing of such children by their families. As parental responsibility for children is retained notwithstanding any court orders short of adoption, local authorities must work in partnership with parents, seeking court orders when compulsory action is indicated in the interests of the child but only when this is better for the child than working with the parents under voluntary arrangements.

The key provisions of the Children Act 1989 are these:

17.—(1) It shall be the general duty of every local authority (in addition to the other duties imposed on them by this Part)—
   (a)   to safeguard and promote the welfare of children within their area who are in need; and
   (b)   so far as is consistent with that duty, to promote the upbringing of such children by their families,
by providing a range and level of services appropriate to those children's needs.
   (2) For the purpose principally of facilitating the discharge of their general duty under this section, every local authority shall have the specific duties and powers set out in Part I of Schedule 2.
   (3) Any service provided by an authority in the exercise of functions conferred on them by this section may be provided for the family of a particular child in need or for any member of his family, if it is provided with a view to safeguarding or promoting the child's welfare
   ...
   (10) For the purposes of this Part a child shall be taken to be in need if —
   (a)   he is unlikely to achieve or maintain, or to have the opportunity of achieving or maintaining, a reasonable standard of health or development without the provision for him of services by a local authority under this Part;
   (b)   his health or development is likely to be significantly impaired, or further impaired, without the provision for him of such services; or
   (c)   he is disabled,
and 'family', in relation to such a child, includes any person who has parental responsibility for the child and any other person with whom he has been living.
   (11) For the purposes of this Part, a child is disabled if he is blind, deaf or dumb or suffers from mental disorder of any kind or is substantially and permanently handicapped by illness, injury or congenital deformity or such other disability as may be prescribed; and in this Part –
      'development' means physical, intellectual, emotional, social or behavioural development; and
      'health' means physical or mental health.
17A.—(1) The Secretary of State may by regulations make provision for and in connection with requiring or authorising the responsible authority in the case of a person of a prescribed description who falls within subsection (2) to make, with that person's consent, such payments to him as they may determine in accordance with the regulations in respect of his securing the provision of the service mentioned in that subsection.
   (2) A person falls within this subsection if he is—
   (a)   a person with parental responsibility for a disabled child,
   (b)   a disabled person with parental responsibility for a child, or
   (c)   a disabled child aged 16 or 17,
and a local authority ('the responsible authority') have decided for the purposes of section 17 that the child's needs (or, if he is such a disabled child, his needs) call for the provision by them of a service in exercise of functions conferred on them under that section.
   (3) Subsections (3) to (5) and (7) of section 57 of the 2001 Act shall apply, with any necessary modifications, in relation to regulations under this section as they apply in relation to regulations under that section.
   (4) Regulations under this section shall provide that, where payments are made under the regulations to a person falling within subsection (5)—
   (a)   the payments shall be made at the rate mentioned in subsection (4)(a) of section 57 of the 2001 Act (as applied by subsection (3)); and

    (b)   subsection (4)(b) of that section shall not apply.

(5) A person falls within this subsection if he is—

    (a)   a person falling within subsection (2)(a) or (b) and the child in question is aged 16 or 17, or

    (b)   a person who is in receipt of income support, working families' tax credit or disabled person's tax credit under Part 7 of the Social Security Contributions and Benefits Act 1992 (c 4) or of an income-based jobseeker's allowance.

(6) In this section—

    'the 2001 Act' means the Health and Social Care Act 2001;

    'disabled' in relation to an adult has the same meaning as that given by section 17(11) in relation to a child;

    'prescribed' means specified in or determined in accordance with regulations under this section (and has the same meaning in the provisions of the 2001 Act mentioned in subsection (3) as they apply by virtue of that subsection).

Part I of Sch. 2 lists many specific services for children living at home or elsewhere. Day care is dealt with in ss. 18 and 19. Section 20 deals with the provision of accommodation:

20.—(1) Every local authority shall provide accommodation for any child in need within their area who appears to them to require accommodation as a result of —

    (a)   there being no person who has parental responsibility for him;

    (b)   his being lost or having been abandoned; or

    (c)   the person who has been caring for him being prevented (whether or not permanently, and for whatever reason) from providing him with suitable accommodation or care.

(2) Where a local authority provide accommodation under subsection (1) for a child who is ordinarily resident in the area of another local authority, that other local authority may take over the provision of accommodation for the child within—

    (a)   three months of being notified in writing that the child is being provided with accommodation; or

    (b)   such other longer period as may be prescribed.

(3) Every local authority shall provide accommodation for any child in need within their area who has reached the age of sixteen and whose welfare the authority consider is likely to be seriously prejudiced if they do not provide him with accommodation.

(4) A local authority may provide accommodation for any child within their area (even though a person who has parental responsibility for him is able to provide him with accommodation) if they consider that to do so would safeguard or promote the child's welfare.

(5) A local authority may provide accommodation for any person who has reached the age of sixteen but is under twenty-one in any community home which takes children who have reached the age of sixteen if they consider that to do so would safeguard or promote his welfare.

(6) Before providing accommodation under this section, a local authority shall, so far as is reasonably practicable and consistent with the child's welfare—

    (a)   ascertain the child's wishes regarding the provision of accommodation; and

    (b)   give due consideration (having regard to his age and understanding) to such wishes of the child as they have been able to ascertain.

(7) A local authority may not provide accommodation under this section for any child if any person who—

    (a)   has parental responsibility for him; and

    (b)   is willing and able to—

        (i)   provide accommodation for him; or

        (ii)   arrange for accommodation to be provided for him,

objects.

(8) Any person who has parental responsibility for a child may at any time remove the child from accommodation provided by or on behalf of the local authority under this section.

(9) Subsections (7) and (8) do not apply while any person—

    (a)   in whose favour a residence order is in force with respect to the child; or

    (b)   who has care of the child by virtue of an order made in the exercise of the High Court's inherent jurisdiction with respect to children,

agrees to the child being looked after in accommodation provided by or on behalf of the local authority.

(10) Where there is more than one such person as is mentioned in subsection (9), all of them must agree.

(11) Subsections (7) and (8) do not apply where a child who has reached the age of sixteen agrees to being provided with accommodation under this section.

The 'continuum' of services provided under the Act can be traced back to the ideas in the Curtis Report (p. 667, above). Jean Packman, in *The Child's Generation* (1981), explains the development, after the 1948 Act, of the concept of 'prevention':

Research studies of the period [principally Bowlby (1953)] stressed the importance of the mother-child relationship and the damaging effects on a child's mental, emotional and even physical development, if the relationship were inadequate, disturbed or broken. Most studies examined the latter – deprivation by separation – the phenomenon in its most readily observable form. The emphasis therefore tended to rest on the temporary, or even irreversible damage caused to children by removing them from home. To these studies were added the observations of the child care workers themselves. Seeing, at first hand, the unhappiness and distress of many children in care, they were naturally spurred to seek ways of avoiding admissions. Depressingly, too, they saw that many deprived children themselves grew up to be inadequate parents whose children were, in turn, deprived. A 'cycle of deprivation' was acknowledged long before it became a political catchphrase.

To this central concern to avoid separating children from their parents, was added the complicating factor that some families were clearly incapable of providing even a minimum of physical or emotional care and stability for their children. Social workers were therefore faced with decisions about whether or not the deprivations suffered by a child within his family were worse and more hazardous than those he would suffer by removal from home. Such decisions were also affected by estimates of their own skills and the resources available to them, to intervene and improve the family situation, to the child's benefit; and by the standards of substitute care that might offset and compensate the child for the effects of separation.

Prevention thus came to be a two-pronged concept; prevention of admission to care; and prevention of neglect and cruelty in the family. A variety of methods of working towards each of these ends can be seen emerging, in response to the differing circumstances of the families concerned. With some families the work was clearly directed to their weaknesses, whether these were problems of poor home management and low standards of hygiene, or of disturbed and volatile relationships. ...

In other situations more stress was laid on family and community strengths. Child care workers were aware that many children came into care at a time of family crisis, for lack of any alternative. It was their task to explore and encourage links with kin or with neighbours who could offer care for the children in a familiar environment. ...

A third dimension to preventive work grew from the knowledge that some families collapsed through external pressures which were beyond their control, yet were within the power of children's departments to influence. A prime example lies in the field of housing. As early as 1951 concern was expressed at the effects on children, separated from their parents because of homelessness. ...

The *Review of Child Care Law* (1985) and the Government's White Paper on *The Law on Child Care and Family Services* (1987), which led to the 1989 Act, emphasised the importance of preventative services:

18. It is proposed to give local authorities a broad 'umbrella' power to provide services to promote the care and upbringing of children, and to help prevent the breakdown of family relationships which might eventually lead to a court order committing the child to the local authority's care. Within this power the local authority will be able to provide services to a child at home, for example a family aide to assist within the home; at a day centre, for example a day nursery for pre-school children, an after school scheme for school age children or placement with a childminder; or residential facilities allowing a child to stay for short or long periods away from home, say with a foster family or in a children's home. The local authority will also be able to offer financial assistance in exceptional circumstances. ...

20. Local authorities have a duty under current legislation to receive children into their care in special circumstances, generally where there is a need to care for the child away from home because of the absence or incapacity of parents. This duty will be maintained broadly as at present. So will the duty to return the child to his family where this is consistent with his welfare.

21. The Government wish to emphasise, however, that the provision of a service by the local authority to enable a child who is not under a care order to be cared for away from home should

be seen in a wider context and as part of the range of services a local authority can offer to parents and families in need of help with the care of their children. Such a service should, in appropriate circumstances, be seen as a positive response to the needs of families and not as a mark of failure either on the part of the family or those professionals and others working to support them. An essential characteristic of this service should be its voluntary character, that is it should be based clearly on continuing parental agreement and operate as far as possible on a basis of partnership and co-operation between the local authority and parents.

Hence the abolition of the power to assume parental rights by administrative resolution and the insistence (in s. 20(8), (9) and (10)) that any person who is entitled to have the child living with him may remove the child from local authority accommodation at any time. One reason for this emphasis on the voluntary provision of services was the recommendation of the *Review of Child Care Law* (1985) that child care legislation should be combined with the health and welfare legislation, under which services are provided for mentally handicapped and disabled children, to embody the best features of both. The White Paper agreed:

16. The health and welfare legislation generally makes no provision for the supervision of the welfare of individual children provided with services. Thus, for example, under this legislation a child may remain away from home for long periods without any legal requirement for the caring agency to review his case, or to give first consideration to his welfare or to consult him where practicable in taking any decisions about him all of which are requirements under child care law. Nor are there any provisions about local authority responsibilities to children when they leave facilities provided under this legislation. This again contrasts with child care law. There are also inconsistencies between health and welfare legislation and child care law over such matters as charging for services.

17. The Government therefore propose the unification of these two sets of legislation as recommended by the Review. In reaching this decision the Government considered carefully the reservations expressed by some that this would cause concern to those parents of handicapped and disabled children who provide expert and devoted care but from time to time need respite care provided by the local authority. This concern it was said flowed from the perception that reception into care by local authorities under the present legislation was frequently associated with parental shortcomings. ... The intention of the Government is to ensure that in all cases the children concerned receive the standard of care and protection and professional review appropriate to their needs and that those ends are achieved where possible in a partnership with parents.

A clear distinction should therefore be drawn between children 'in care', who are the subject of care orders (see p. 719, below), and other children who are simply provided with accommodation by the authority. A sharp eye, however, is needed to recognise the differences in the sections of the 1989 Act dealing with all children being 'looked after':

22.—(1) In this Act, any reference to a child who is looked after by a local authority is a reference to a child who is—
  (a) in their care, or
  (b) provided with accommodation by the authority in the exercise of any functions (in particular those under this Act) which stand referred to their social services committee under the Local Authority Social Services Act 1970.
  (2) In subsection (1) 'accommodation' means accommodation which is provided for a continuous period of more than 24 hours.
  (3) It shall be the duty of a local authority looking after any child—
  (a) to safeguard and promote his welfare; and
  (b) to make such use of services available for children cared for by their own parents as appears to the authority reasonable in his case.
  (4) Before making any decision with respect to a child whom they are looking after, or proposing to look after, a local authority shall, so far as is reasonably practicable, ascertain the wishes and feelings of—

(a) the child;
(b) his parents;
(c) any person who is not a parent of his but who has parental responsibility for him; and
(d) any other person whose wishes and feelings the authority consider to be relevant, regarding the matter to be decided.

(5) In making any such decisions a local authority shall give due consideration—
(a) having regarded to his age and understanding, to such wishes and feelings of the child as they have been able to ascertain;
(b) to such wishes and feelings of any person mentioned in subsection (4)(b) to (d) as they have been able to ascertain; and
(c) to the child's religious persuasion, racial origin and cultural and linguistic background.

(6) If it appears to a local authority that it is necessary, for the purpose of protecting members of the public from serious injury, to exercise their powers with respect to a child whom they are looking after in a manner which may not be consistent with their duties under this section, they may do so.

(7) If the Secretary of State considers it necessary, for the purpose of protecting members of the public from serious injury, to give directions to a local authority with respect to the exercise of their powers with respect to a child whom they are looking after, he may give such directions to the authority.

(8) Where any such directions are given to an authority they shall comply with them even though doing so is inconsistent with their duties under this section.

Questions

(i) Subsections (6) to (8) of s. 22 stem from the Children and Young Persons Act 1969, when local authorities were given responsibility for most juvenile offenders: now that committal to local authority accommodation is no longer available as a disposal in criminal cases (except on remand or as a six month maximum residential condition in a supervision order[1]), can they still be justified?
(ii) Why are they not limited to 'children in care'?

23.—(1) It shall be the duty of any local authority looking after a child—
(a) when he is in their care, to provide accommodation for him; and
(b) to maintain him in other respects apart from providing accommodation for him.

(2) A local authority shall provide accommodation and maintenance for any child whom they are looking after by—
(a) placing him (subject to subsection (5) and any regulations made by the Secretary of State) with—
  (i) a family;
  (ii) a relative of his; or
  (iii) any other suitable person,
on such terms as to payment by the authority and otherwise as the authority may determine;
(aa) maintaining him in an appropriate children's home; or
(f) making such other arrangements as—
  (i) seem appropriate to them; and
  (ii) comply with any regulations made by the Secretary of State.

(2A) Where under subsection (2)(aa) a local authority maintains a child in a home provided, equipped and maintained by the Secretary of State under section 82(5), it shall do so on such terms as the Secretary of State may from time to time determine.

(3) Any person with whom a child has been placed under subsection (2)(a) is referred to in this Act as a local authority foster parent unless he falls within subsection (4).

(4) A person falls within this subsection if he is—
(a) a parent of the child;
(b) a person who is not a parent of the child but who has parental responsibility for him; or
(c) where the child is in care and there was a residence order in force with respect to him immediately before the care order was made, a person in whose favour the residence order was made.

(5) Where a child is in the care of a local authority, the authority may only allow him to live with a person who falls within subsection (4) in accordance with regulations made by the Secretary of State.

---

1. Powers of Criminal Courts (Sentencing) Act 2000, Sch. 6, para. 5.

(5A) For the purposes of subsection (5) a child shall be regarded as living with a person if he stays with that person for a continuous period of more than 24 hours.

(6) Subject to any regulations made by the Secretary of State for the purposes of this subsection, any local authority looking after a child shall make arrangements to enable him to live with—

(a) a person falling within subsection (4); or
(b) a relative, friend or other person connected with him,

unless that would not be reasonably practicable or consistent with his welfare.

(7) Where a local authority provide accommodation for a child whom they are looking after, they shall, subject to the provisions of this Part and so far as is reasonably practicable and consistent with his welfare, secure that—

(a) the accommodation is near his home; and
(b) where the authority are also providing accommodation for a sibling of his, they are accommodated together.

(8) Where a local authority provide accommodation for a child whom they are looking after and who is disabled, they shall, so far as is reasonably practicable, secure that the accommodation is not unsuitable to his particular needs.

(9) Part II of Schedule 2 shall have effect for the purposes of making further provision as to children looked after by local authorities and in particular as to the regulations that may be made under subsections (2)(*a*) and (*f*) and (5).

(10) In this Act—

'appropriate children's home' means a children's home in respect of which a person is registered under Part II of the Care Standards Act 2000; and

'children's home' has the same meaning as in that Act.

The Children Act 1989 provides for three types of children's homes: community homes (Part VI), voluntary homes (Part VII), and registered homes (Part VIII). All these homes are now regulated by the National Care Standards Commission for England and the National Assembly for Wales, as a result of the Care Standards Act 2000. The new Act defines a children's home as an establishment which provides care and accommodation wholly or mainly for children. The definition covers private, voluntary and local council children's homes, and both mainstream and special boarding schools accommodating or arranging accommodation for any child for over 295 days a year. The new regulation authorities have taken on the regulation and inspection functions that hitherto were split between local authorities, health authorities, and the Department of Health. Registration will only be granted if the registration authority is satisfied that the applicant has complied with all the relevant requirements and the authority has power to cancel registration of a person where a condition of registration has been breached. There is a right of appeal under the Care Standards Act 2000 to the Care Standards Tribunal against a decision of the authority under Part II of the Care Standards Act 2000.

'National Minimum Standards' for children's homes have now been issued pursuant to the Care Standards Act 2000, s. 23 and the Children's Homes Regulations, SI 2001/3967. We reproduce below *Standards 7,8, and 22* relating to support for individual children, quality of care and behaviour management:

Support to Individual Children
Outcome
Children receive individual support when they need it.

Standard 7

7.1 All children are given individualised support in line with their needs and wishes, and children identified as having particular needs receive help, guidance and support when needed or requested.

7.2 The registered person ensures, so far as is feasible, the provision of individually appropriate personal, health, social and sex and relationship education for each resident child, including disabled children.

7.3 The registered person actively promotes the involvement of all children in the home's social group, counters isolation of individuals by others, nurtures friendships between children, and supports those children who for any reason do not really 'fit in' to the resident group.

7.4 Support is provided for any child for whom English is not their first language (or who use alternative methods of communication), enabling them to communicate their needs, wishes and concerns, and to communicate with staff and other children within the home.

7.5 Children are able to approach any member of the home's staff with personal concerns, not only their key worker.

7.6 The registered person ensures, as far as possible, that professional services are provided where necessary to help children develop individual identity in relation to their gender, disability, religious, racial, cultural or linguistic background or sexual orientation.

7.7 Support and advice is provided to any child in the home who is, or has been, involved in abuse or prostitution, whether as a victim of abuse or in abusing others, and the child is involved in the planning of any such programme of support.

7.8 Each child has at least one person, independent of the home and the child's placing authority, whom they may contact directly about personal problems or concerns at the home (such a person may for example be an advocate, children's rights officer, adult family member, personal adviser, befriender, visitor on behalf of an organisation carrying on the home, independent visitor, or mentor).

7.9 Children are supported to take controlled risks (appropriate to their age and understanding) that are relevant and necessary to negotiating their place in the community. Significant risks are defined in the placement plan and an appropriate risk assessment is made and recorded.

7.10 Children whose placement plan requires specialist external services for them (eg for recreation, health or education) receive those services in practice. Staff co-operate in implementing any programmes associated with specialist services such as speech and language therapy or physiotherapy programmes.

7.11 Subject to the agreement of the placing authority, relevant personal, educational and health information concerning each child is passed on to that child's subsequent placement.

7.12 Any specific therapeutic technique is only used with any child at the home if specified in the child's placement plan and specifically approved by the child's placing authority and, where the placing authority does not have parental responsibility, by the child's parent (or parent if the child is not placed by a local authority or voluntary organisation), and if the safe and effective use of the technique is known to be supported by evidence. It is carried out only by, on the directions of, or under the supervision of a member of staff or other practitioner holding a current recognised qualification in the therapy concerned, whose qualification the home has verified as valid and appropriate directly with the awarding body or relevant register. Any member of staff using such a technique is subject to supervision in using the technique by a person outside the home and not responsible for the home, who is qualified and experienced in the therapy concerned.

7.13 Appropriate support is provided for children who are refugees and for asylum seeking children, taking into account the particular circumstances of each child's flight from his or her country of origin and the advice of specialist agencies where necessary.

[Children's Homes Regulations 11, 20, Children Act 1989, Sections 22, 61, 64.]

2 Quality of Care
Consultation
Outcome

Children are encouraged and supported to make decisions about their lives and to influence the way the home is run. No child is assumed to be unable to communicate their views.

Standard 8

8.1 Children's opinions, and those of their families or others significant to the child, are sought over key decisions which are likely to affect their daily life and their future. There are systems in place for doing this, such as written agreements, private interviews, key worker sessions, children's or house meetings. The systems reflect children's differing communication needs.

8.2 Staff take into account the religious, racial, cultural and linguistic backgrounds of children and their families and any disabilities that they may have.

8.3 Significant views, discussions and expressed opinions are recorded promptly.

8.4 The opinions and views of children on all matters affecting them, including day to day matters, are ascertained on a regular and frequent basis and not taken for granted.

8.5 Children, their families and significant others receive feedback following consultation.

8.6 The opinions and views of the parents of children at the home are ascertained on a regular and frequent basis unless inappropriate, including views on the following:
- children's care at the home and the operation of the home
- the adequacy of staff looking after children at any given time
- the adequacy of space and furnishings in children's bedrooms
- the privacy of washing facilities, facilities for contacting significant people in the children's lives and sense of personal space.

8.7 Where consultation with and involvement of a child's family is inappropriate, (where it is not in the interests of the child) staff explain to children why this is so, and consult with significant others or an independent visitor, as appropriate.

8.8 Suitable means are provided, frequently, for any child with communication and/or learning difficulties to make their wishes and feelings known regarding their care and treatment in the home. This includes availability of different adults who understand how the child communicates.

8.9 The way the home functions enhances every child's independence and opportunity to make everyday choices.

8.10 Staff regularly and frequently seek the views of the relevant contact officers in children's placing authorities on the care of the children concerned, and the overall operation of the home.

8.11 The views of children, parents and placing authorities are taken into account in the development of and any necessary change in the operation of the home.

[Children's Homes Regulations 11, 15, 34, Children Act 1989, Sections 22, 61, 64.]

Privacy and Confidentiality
Outcome
Children's privacy is respected and information is confidentially handled. ...

Behaviour Management
Outcome
Children assisted to develop acceptable behaviour through encouragement of acceptable behaviour and constructive staff response to inappropriate behaviour.

Standard 22

22.1 Staff respond positively to acceptable behaviour, and where the behaviour of children is regarded as unacceptable by staff, it is responded to by constructive, acceptable and known disciplinary measures approved by the registered person.

22.2 The registered person has a clear written policy, procedures and guidance for staff based on a code of conduct setting out the control, disciplinary and restraint measures permitted and emphasising the need to reinforce positive messages to children for the achievement of acceptable behaviour.

22.3 Measures of control and disciplinary measures are based on establishing positive relationships with children which are designed to help the child. Such measures are fair and consistently applied. They also encourage reparation and restitution and reduce the likelihood of negative behaviour becoming the focus of attention and subsequent disruption to the placement.

22.4 The consequences of unacceptable behaviour are clear to staff and children and any measures applied are relevant to the incident, reasonable and carried out as contemporaneously as possible.

22.5 Any measures taken to respond to unacceptable behaviour are appropriate to the age, understanding and individual needs of the child, for example taking into account that unacceptable or challenging behaviour may be the result of illness, bullying, certain disabilities such as autism, or communication difficulties.

22.6 Sanctions and physical restraint are not excessive or unreasonable.

22.7 Physical restraint is only used to prevent likely injury to the child concerned or to others, or likely serious damage to property. Restraint is not used as a punishment, as a means to enforce compliance with instructions, or in response to challenging behaviour which does not give rise to reasonable expectation of injury to someone or serious damage to property. (For schools which are children's homes, this does not prevent the use of restraint in circumstances permitted by s. 550A of the Education Act 1996.)

22.8   The registered person's policy on the use and techniques of physical restraint and other forms of physical intervention, and the circumstances in which they may be used, is consistent with any relevant government guidance on approved methods of restraint and physical intervention. All staff of the home are aware of, trained in, and follow in practice the registered person's policy. Training covers reducing or avoiding the need to use physical restraint. All staff have signed a copy of the policy and evidence of this is retained on their personnel file.

22.9   A record of the use of restraint on a child by an adult is kept in a separate dedicated bound and numbered book, and includes the name of the child, the date, time and location, details of the behaviour requiring use of restraint, the nature of the restraint used, the duration of the restraint, the name of the staff member(s) using restraint, the name(s) of any other staff, children or other people present, the effectiveness and any consequences of the restraint, any injuries caused to or reported by the child or any other person, and the signature of a person authorised by the registered person to make the record.

22.10 A similar and separate record of any sanctions will also be kept in the same way.

22.11 The registered person will regularly monitor the record books to monitor compliance with the home's policy, procedure and guidance and to identify any patterns in incidents leading to disciplinary or restraint action becoming necessary. The monitoring will also address the implications for the care of individual uses of sanctions or use of restraint, together with any subsequent action taken, and signs against each entry to confirm the monitoring has taken place.

22.12 Measures of control, discipline and restraint used by the home are made clear to the placing authority, child, parent/s or carers before or, in an emergency placement, at the time the child is to move into the home.

22.13 Children are encouraged to develop a proper awareness of their rights and responsibilities. Staff and children alike are clear that each individual has rights and responsibilities in relation to those who live in the home, those who work there and people in the community. Where there has been physical intervention, the child will have the right to be examined by a registered nurse or medical practitioner within 24 hours.

22.14 All children are given an opportunity to discuss incidents and express their views either individually or in a regular forum or house meeting where unsafe behaviour can be discussed by children and adults. When disciplinary measures or restraint are used, children are encouraged to write or have their views recorded and sign their names against them if possible in the records kept by the home.

22.15 Unless the registered person can demonstrate that this is not appropriate, the home has procedures and guidance on police involvement in the home, which have been agreed with the local police and which staff are knowledgeable and clear about.

22.16 Staff meetings address issues of control and agree practicable and acceptable means of responding to behaviour and control problems of both the current group of children and of individual children in the light of their histories, any current problems and placement plan.

[Children's Homes Regulation 17.]

Questions

(i) *The Review of Child Care Law* (1985), para. 7.16 recommended against 'allowing legal powers over a child to be settled by informal agreement in individual cases. Great care would need to be taken to ensure that the parent was fully aware of the consequences of such an agreement and was in no way overawed or pressurised (however unwittingly) by the person obtaining consent.' What is the legal effect of the agreed arrangements under these standards?

(ii) What is the position of a parent who wishes herself to meet one of the parental responsibilities delegated in the agreement (see p. 497, above)?

(iii) What is a parent to do if (a) the agreed arrangements for contact are not kept, or (b) she wishes to make some different arrangements?

(iv) Do you think that the parent will see herself as being in partnership with the local authority (or voluntary organisation) to look after her child?

(v) What is meant by 'significant other' in *Standard 8.6* above? What if a 13-year-old girl in a local council children's home has a boyfriend (a) to whom the local council objects but the parents do not, or (b) to whom the parents object but the local council does not?

Before the Children Act 1989 abolished the concept of 'voluntary care', the research evidence painted a depressing picture (eg Rowe and Lambert (1973), DHSS (1985)). Once admitted to care, children frequently lost contact with their families, and there was a lack of planning to meet their long-term needs. We deal with these questions in the next chapter, but some of the concerns are addressed in s. 26, which requires regular reviews of why and how children are being looked after and a formal complaints mechanism:

26.—(3) Every local authority shall establish a procedure for considering any representations (including any complaint) made to them by—
- (a) any child who is being looked after by them or who is not being looked after by them but is in need;
- (b) a parent of his;
- (c) any person who is not a parent of his but who has parental responsibility for him;
- (d) any local authority foster parent;
- (e) such other person as the authority consider has a sufficient interest in the child's welfare to warrant his representations being considered by them,

about the discharge by the authority of any of their functions under this Part in relation to the child.

(4) The procedure shall ensure that at least one person who is not a member or officer of the authority takes part in—
- (a) the considerations; and
- (b) any discussions which are held by the authority about the action (if any) to be taken in relation to the child in the light of the consideration.

...

(7) Where any representation has been considered under the procedure established by a local authority under this section, the authority shall—
- (a) have due regard to the findings of those considering the representation; and
- (b) take such steps as are reasonably practicable to notify (in writing)—
  - (i) the person making the representation;
  - (ii) the child (if the authority consider that he has sufficient understanding); and
  - (iii) such other persons (if any) as appear to the authority to be likely to be affected, of the authority's decision in the matter and their reasons for taking that decision and of any action which they have taken, or propose to take.

(8) Every local authority shall give such publicity to their procedure for considering representations under this section as they consider appropriate.

The Children's Homes Regulations 2001, reg. 24 sets out detailed provisions relating to complaint procedures:

Complaints and representations

24.—(1) Subject to paragraph (8), the registered person shall establish a written procedure for considering complaints made by or on behalf of children accommodated in the home.

(2) The procedure shall, in particular, provide—
- (a) for an opportunity for informal resolution of the complaint at an early stage;
- (b) that no person who is the subject of a complaint takes any part in its consideration other than, if the registered person considers it appropriate, at the informal resolution stage only;
- (c) for dealing with complaints about the registered person;
- (d) for complaints to be made by a person acting on behalf of a child;
- (e) for arrangements for the procedure to be made known to—
  - (i) children accommodated in the home;
  - (ii) their parents;
  - (iii) placing authorities; and
  - (iv) persons working in the home.

(3) A copy of the procedure shall be supplied on request to any of the persons mentioned in paragraph (2)(e).

(4) The copy of the procedure supplied under paragraph (3) shall include—

(a)   the name, address and telephone number of the Commission; and

(b)   details of the procedure (if any) which has been notified to the registered person by the Commission for the making of complaints to it relating to children's homes.

(5) The registered person shall ensure that a written record is made of any complaint, the action taken in response, and the outcome of the investigation.

(6) The registered person shall ensure that—

(a)   children accommodated in the home are enabled to make a complaint or representation; and

(b)   no child is subject to any reprisal for making a complaint or representation.

(7)   The registered person shall supply to the Commission at its request a statement containing a summary of any complaints made during the preceding twelve months and the action that was taken.

(8)   This regulation (apart from paragraph (6)) does not apply to any matter to which the Representations Procedure (Children) Regulations 1991 (a) applies.

The procedures are developed further by *Standard 16* of the 'National Minimum Standards':

3 Complaints and Protection

Complaints and Representation

Outcome

Any complaint will be addressed without delay and the complainant is kept informed of progress.

Standard 16

16.1 Children know how and feel able to complain if they are unhappy with any aspect of living in the home. Any complaint is addressed seriously and without delay, and a complaint will be fully responded to within a maximum of 28 days, and children are kept informed of the progress.

16.2 Children, and where appropriate their families, significant others and independent visitors, are provided with information on how to complain, including how they can secure access to an advocate. Where necessary, this access is to an advocate who is suitably skilled (eg in signing or in speaking the complainant's preferred language).

16.3 The home's complaints procedure:

- enables children, staff, family members and others involved with children of the home outside the home, to make both minor and major complaints
- precludes any person who is the subject of a formal complaint from taking any responsibility for the consideration of or response to that complaint
- expressly forbids any reprisals against children or others making a complaint
- includes provisions for both informal attempts, such as negotiation, arbitration and mediation, at resolving the complaint and for the child and any complainant to have the matter pursued further if not satisfied with the proposed informal resolution
- provides appropriately for the handling of complaints against the manager of the home
- requires a written record to be made and kept of the person making the complaint, date of the complaint, nature of the complaint, action taken and outcome of the complaint
- does not restrict the issues they may complain about
- provides for relevant issues to be referred promptly to other procedures, including the local social services authority where child protection issues are involved
- provides appropriately for the handling of any complaint made against the registered person of the home
- is accessible to disabled children in a suitable form
- enables people other than the child to make complaints on behalf of the child, provided the child consents to this
- provides for complainants to be kept informed about the progress of their complaints and to be provided with details of the outcome, in an accessible format, at the earliest opportunity.

16.4 There is a procedure for handling external complaints, eg those from local shopkeepers, neighbours, the police, etc.

16.5 The registered person has provided the home with a written policy and procedural guidelines on considering and responding to representations and complaints in accordance with legal requirements and relevant government guidance. The policy clearly includes the right and the means for all children placed by an authority to access the complaints procedure of their placing authority, the right of children, parents, staff, others working in the home, and placing authorities to make complaints to the National Care Standards Commission, and details of how they may contact the Commission. The policy is provided in suitable summary or format(s) to children at the home, their parents and placing authorities, and to all staff and others working at the home (any of whom are provided with a copy of the full procedure on request).

16.6 All staff receive training in the complaints procedures covering the following areas:
- what constitutes a complaint
- what the procedure is for dealing with an informal complaint in the home and how this is recorded
- to whom a complaint is made outside the home
- the procedure to be followed should a complaint not be resolved promptly by informal means, including who should be notified and the keeping of record
- how the child can be assisted in making a complaint, including situations where the child has a communication impairment.

16.7 The registered person of the home regularly reviews the records of complaints by children or concerning the welfare of children, to check satisfactory operation of the complaints procedure, and to identify both patterns of complaint and action taken on individual complaints. The registered person takes any appropriate action from such a review in relation to the home's policies and practices, as well as taking any necessary further follow up action in relation to individual cases.

[Children's Homes Regulations 24 and 27.]

Questions

(i) You are a child aged 15 being looked after by Blankshire County Council in a small residential home. You like this because it is near to your school and friends. Visits to or from your family are easy. Blankshire then decides to privatise its provision of residential care and to close the home. You are likely to be sent to a similar home 50 miles away. What can you do?

(ii) Your mother is a disabled widow who found it impossible to look after you as well as your two sisters because your mild mental handicap has made your adolescence difficult for both of you. The relationship between you is still very close. What can she do?

(iii) Your mother's sister would have you to live with her, provided that she can have some financial and social work support. You have mixed feelings about this, but would prefer it to moving away. What can she do?

(iv) Your 16-year-old sister thinks you have a lovely life in the home and would like to join you. What can she do?

(v) Your 21-year-old boyfriend would like to visit you in the home, but the home's rules prohibit such visits. What can he do?

The operation of many of the provisions considered in this section are illustrated in the following case:

Re T (accommodation by local authority)
[1995] 1 FCR 517, [1995] 1 FLR 159, High Court, Queen's Bench Division

T, aged 17, had 'escaped' from an inadequate background, and found a home with Mr and Mrs B. It was agreed that she should remain living with them. Initially the local authority paid £25 per week to support this arrangement, and later this was replaced by £33 per week, paid by the Department of Social

Security. If T was accommodated by the local authority and placed with Mr and Mrs B, they would receive a fostering allowance of £79 a week. The local authority refused to accommodate her, and T applied for judicial review.

Johnson J: ... T's wish to be accommodated would, if successful, no doubt lead to payment of the fostering allowance and (as I think, every bit as importantly) would lead to the provision of the local authority's support after she becomes 18 and until she is 21.

The local authority decided, in considering s.20(3), that T's welfare would not be likely to be seriously prejudiced if they did not provide her with accommodation. That decision was made on 21 July 1992, and thereafter a complaints procedure was put in motion.

I think it needs to be said, in fairness to this local authority, that they were not seeking to escape their obligation to T for any blameworthy reason; simply that they had to allocate their resources as they thought best. The fact is that, throughout this episode of T's life, she has been supported by a social worker who has given her commitment to her to a degree that is deserving of the very highest praise.

As to the complaints procedure, that resulted in a meeting of the complaints review panel of the local authority which took place on 15 January 1993. It is described as having been a 'searching and vigorous inquiry'. It upheld T's complaint. The matter of her application under s. 20(3), therefore, came to be considered once again by the local authority's director of social services. It is usually the case that this director of social services follows the recommendations of such review panels but, on this occasion, he did not. It is plain to me that he considered the matter carefully and conscientiously. In the exercise of the discretion vested in the local authority, he concluded that T's welfare would not be likely to be seriously prejudiced if the local authority did not provide her with accommodation. That decision is attacked now on T's behalf.

I direct myself according to the dictum of Lord Brightman in *R v Hillingdon London Borough Council, ex p Puhlhofer* [1986] AC 484. In matters such as this, it is the local authority, not the court, which is to judge the facts. It is not for the court to monitor the actions of local authorities, save in exceptional cases where, by way of example, there has been a mistake as to the applicable law or there has been unreasonableness in the *Wednesbury* sense; in the words of Lord Brightman, 'unreasonableness verging on an absurdity'.

Under s. 20(6), before providing accommodation under s. 20, the local authority shall give due consideration to the wishes of the child in T's situation. Those wishes had been made known to the local authority, were clearly known to the director of social services and, in my judgment, he clearly took them into consideration. However, it is plain from the letters which were written on his behalf at the time that a factor that weighed with him very considerably was the existence of the local authority's duties under s. 17 of the Children Act 1989. That duty is expressed to be a general duty to safeguard and promote the welfare of children within the area of the local authority and to promote the upbringing of such children by their families. Unusually, for the purpose of this statute, 'family' has an exceptionally wide meaning and includes any person with whom a child has been living; here, Mr and Mrs B.

This local authority had been exercising its duty and its powers under s. 17. It had allocated social work support, and it had been making discretionary financial payments, albeit not of the amount desired by T, and certainly not with the regularity that they might have been. The powers under s. 17 can, I think, fairly be described as being the provision of support on an ad hoc emergency basis. They are none the less valuable for that. However, in reaching his decision, the director of social services was satisfied that the past provision of support under s. 17 made it unlikely that T's welfare would be seriously prejudiced if she was not provided with accommodation. In my judgment, the director was here in error.

As in other provisions of the Children Act 1989, the focus of attention is, or should be, upon the likelihood of significant harm (s. 31) or here, serious prejudice; but in the future. Under s. 31, the court, and under s. 20(3), the local authority, must put its mind to the future and seek to form a judgment about the future. ...

... As at present advised, it seems to me that, in exercising its discretion under s. 20(3), the local authority should look at all the circumstances of the case, and for my part I would not think it right that anything should be excluded: in particular, the powers and the duties under s. 17 should not be excluded. However, because those powers and duties are discretionary in nature, it does not seem to me that they can amount to factors to which much weight should be attributed for the purpose of s. 20(3).

... I do accept that, in a practical situation, it will usually be very difficult for a local authority to decline an application under s. 20(3) on the basis of the possibility (because it can be no more) of the provision of support under s. 17. Accordingly, I grant the relief asked.

It is to be noted, in passing, that if T had not had the advantage of living with Mr and Mrs B, then it might well have become necessary for the local authority to obtain a care order, so that under s. 22 she would have become a child being looked after by the local authority, and so would have become a qualifying person under s. 24 and entitled to the ongoing relief there provided.

Questions

(i) Do you agree that s. 17 is concerned only with 'ad hoc emergency' support?

(ii) In *R (W) v Lambeth LBC* [2002] EWCA Civ 613, [2002] 2 All ER 901, the Court of Appeal decided that in cases where a family with dependent children was not entitled to help from the local housing authority, s. 17 of the 1989 Act gave the local social services authority a power to assist the family with the provision of accommodation, but that the exercise of that power was a matter of discretion for the authority, and the latter could, if it saw fit, reserve it to extreme cases. Do you think that *T* is an extreme case?

(iii) In another Lambeth case, *A v Lambeth BC* [2001] EWCA Civ 1624, [2001] 3 FCR 673, another division of the Court of Appeal was concerned with the question whether s. 17 of the 1989 Act might provide a route to meet the need identified in the assessment whereby a social services authority might provide accommodation for the family of a child in need. The appellant in this case had three children, two of whom were autistic and required constant supervision. Her own health had started to deteriorate. The court rejected the appellant's contention that an assessment under s. 17 gave rise to an enforceable *duty* and by a majority rejected also the proposition that s. 17 *empowered* the authority to provide accommodation in these circumstances. Which of the two Lambeth cases do you think is truer to the principles of the Children Act 1989?

(iv) Can T's parents demand that she is returned to them? What if she had been 15 years old?

(v) Suppose that you are 12, and have been accommodated under s. 20 for several years. Blankshire Social Services thinks that returning you to your family at this crucial stage in your education and development will not be for the best. If your mother decides to take you away from them, what can Blankshire do? What can your foster parents do?

This last question involves the use of compulsion against parents, which is dealt with below (p. 717). Remember, however, that compulsion is also used against the children themselves. *The Pindown Experience and the Protection of Children: The Report of the Staffordshire Child Care Inquiry 1990* (1991) examined the harsh and restrictive regime ('Pindown') to which some children were subjected. This is Susan's story:

11.17 Susan, who was born in 1976, was put into Pindown when she was 9 years old.

11.18 At the beginning of 1986 Susan, her half-sister aged 13, and her mother were living with the maternal grandfather. Her half-sister is the child of her mother's former marriage. Susan's father was one of her mother's subsequent boyfriends.

11.19 Over a period of about a month, in early 1986, the mother contacted Staffordshire social services on a number of occasions requesting help with coping with Susan's behaviour. Susan was said to be mixing with older girls and smoking, stealing and upsetting her grandfather who did not want her to remain in his home.

11.20 Susan was then received into care and placed at 245 Hartshill Road.

11.21 She went straight into Pindown. The first entry in the log book was as follows: '(Susan) admitted – *very basic programme be very nasty to her*' (emphasis added).

11.22 Susan was required to wear pyjamas and kept in a sparsely furnished room. She was not allowed contact with other children or non-Pindown staff and was not permitted to attend school. She was required to knock on the door before going to the toilet. She remained in Pindown for a week and then returned home. Subsequently five 'family reviews' were held at The Birches at about weekly intervals before social services contact with the family ceased and the case was closed.

11.23 Immediately after Susan's admission to Pindown an entry in the log book at 245 Hartshill Road recorded a residential worker's conversation with her headmaster: he was concerned that she was in care because she was no trouble at all in school being a good attender, well-behaved, and a hard worker. She was also in his view very bright.

11.24 Further entries in the log book during her week in Pindown included:
- 'wants to go to the toilet a lot, soon put a stop to that. Had harsh words twice. Once for calling through the bedroom wall (to another child in Pindown).'
- 'will try anything to get out of her room, after several telling offs [sic] she stopped trying.'
- 'she thinks I'm room service, hasn't anyone told her its not an hotel.'
- 'the little knocker has not knocked so much tonight, when I go in I usually look for a tip as I feel like a waiter.'

11.25 On the evening of Susan's third day in Pindown a 'review' was held. Neither the log book nor the social services file on Susan records who was present. 'Susan's problems' were 'highlighted'. It was noted that the grandfather would not allow her back and her mother was prepared to move out of his home. It was 'agreed that [Susan] remain in care'. It was recorded in the log book that 'mother saw her 2 mins. Cried a little. Then later cried wanting to go home. Was her mother still here. Explained review system. Spoke to her about contract and may well come back if she breaks the rules. Bath, bed. Toilet a lot still. First sign of hope for her, maybe! ! !'

11.26 Susan is twice recorded in the log book as 'working hard'. What she was doing in the Pindown room is not specified.

11.27 A further 'review' was held after Susan had been in Pindown for 7 days. It was agreed that she should 'return home' on various conditions, one of which was that she should write a letter of apology to her grandfather.

11.28 Susan returned to the home of her grandfather. Soon afterwards she and her mother and half-sister were re-housed.

11.29 Just over a year later, the mother again brought Susan, then aged 10, to the social services office. She said that she had been having problems with Susan's behaviour for some considerable time. She would not do what she was told, called her mother unpleasant names and embarrassed her in public. The mother said that she had eventually lost her temper and attempted 'to strangle' Susan. She could not look at Susan without wanting to attack her and Susan was unrepentant about her behaviour. There were also problems with the mother's boyfriend who was living in their home and about whom Susan complained.

11.30 Susan was again received into care and placed into Pindown. The entry in the log book at 245 Hartshill Road records that '[Susan] admitted to pindown after family meeting. ... she is an extremely naughty and manipulative little girl: so much so that she has driven her mother to the point of violence. *Basic Pindown – plenty of schoolwork.*' Later on the day of admission to Pindown it is recorded that 'if she knocked on the door once, she knocked ten thousand times. Other than that *no* problems, she did *not* eat much tea, had a bath at 6.30 tucked up in bed 7 p.m.'

11.31 Three days later the following entry was made in the log book: '[Susan] reviewed this afternoon. She fully expected to go home. When she realised that this wasn't going to happen she became very upset. Cried off and on until 8.30 – at times becoming hysterical. She will go to school on Monday; she understands that this is a privilege and is the only one she will be given for some time to come.'

11.32 After ten days of Pindown it was noted by the child's social worker in the social services file that 'there are no complaints about [Susan's] behaviour at Hartshill Road but she is in no position to misbehave as she is restricted'.

11.33 Subsequently the mother recognised that 'problems can only be resolved at home' and Susan spent some of her time at home and some in Pindown at 245 Hartshill Road. It would seem that she actually spend some 20 days in Pindown before being transferred to The Birches.

11.34 After spending about 3 months at The Birches during which time she spent regular weekends at home, Susan was moved to another children's home. She eventually went home at the beginning of 1988, some six months after being received into care for the second time. More recently further problems occurred and Susan was placed in a foster home.

11.35 Susan at 9 years of age was one of the youngest children placed in Pindown. During her two spells in care in 1986 and 1987 she spent at least 27 days in the unit.

Questions

(i) Why should it be regarded as a privilege to be allowed to go to school?

(ii) Under s. 36 of the Education Act 1944, 'It shall be the duty of the parent of every child of compulsory school age to cause him to receive efficient full-time education suitable to his age, ability and aptitude and to any special educational needs he may have, either by regular attendance at school or otherwise'; under s. 114(1) (as amended by the Children Act 1989), 'parent' includes 'any person (a) who is not a parent of his but has parental responsibility for him, or (b) who has care of him' but for this purpose only includes such a person if he is an individual: should local authorities be under the same legal obligation as others to educate the children they are looking after properly?

There are limits on the circumstances in which children may be placed in 'secure accommodation', now contained in the Children Act 1989 (see p. 473, above for s. 25(3)(4)):

25.—(1) Subject to the following provisions of this section, a child who is being looked after by a local authority may not be placed, and, if placed, may not be kept, in accommodation provided for the purpose of restricting liberty ('secure accommodation') unless it appears—

    (a) that—

        (i) he has a history of absconding and is likely to abscond from any other description of accommodation; and

        (ii) if he absconds, he is likely to suffer significant harm; or

    (b) that if he is kept in any other description of accommodation he is likely to injure himself or other persons.

(2) The Secretary of State may by regulations—

    (a) specify a maximum period—

        (i) beyond which a child may not be kept in secure accommodation without the authority of the court; and

        (ii) for which the court may authorise a child to be kept in secure accommodation;

    (b) empower the court from time to time to authorise a child to be kept in secure accommodation for such further period as the regulations may specify; and

    (c) provide that applications to the court under this section shall be made only by local authorities.

Questions

(i) Why is this not restricted to 'children in care'?

(ii) Should the welfare of the child be the paramount consideration when a court is asked to authorise the use of secure accommodation? (See *Re M (secure accommodation order)* [1995] Fam 108, [1995] 3 All ER 407, [1995] 2 WLR 302, [1995] 1 FLR 418, CA); recall what Butler-Sloss P said in *Re K (a child) (secure accommodation order: right to liberty)* [2001] Fam 377, [2001] 2 All ER 719, CA (see Chapter 10, p. 474, above) that a secure accommodation order is a deprivation of liberty).

(iii) What legal action (if any) might be available to Susan and others like her? (See above, Chapter 10.)

(iv) Section 51 of the Act allows the Secretary of State to exempt from criminal liability for harbouring or assisting runaways specified voluntary organisations and others who provide refuges for children 'at risk': is this a better solution?

(v) Why should we tolerate a public care system from which children want to run away?

13.4 Child protection inquiries

Section 47 of the Children Act 1989 imposes extensive obligations upon local authorities to investigate cases of suspected child abuse and take action where necessary and upon other agencies to assist them. The reasons appear in the White Paper, *The Law on Child Care and Family Services* (1987):

42. Under existing legislation the local authority have a duty to investigate cases where information is received which suggests that there are grounds for care proceedings. The Review proposed that this should be replaced by a more active duty to investigate in any case where it is suspected that the child is suffering harm or is likely to do so. The Government endorse that proposal and accept that the enquiries made should be such as are necessary to enable the local authority to decide what action, if any, to take.

43. The Jasmine Beckford Report declared that there were powerful reasons why the duty on local authorities or health authorities to co-operate under section 22 of the NHS Act 1977 should in the context of child abuse be made more specific, to include the duty to consult and the duty to assist by advice and the supply of information so as to help in the management of such cases. Such a duty would, it was argued, operate as a positive and practical step to promote multidisciplinary working in this area, which is important not only at the stage of identification of abuse but also in subsequent follow-up action. The Government accept this view, and therefore intend to make legal provision for co-operation between statutory and voluntary agencies in the investigation of harm and protection of children at risk.

One of the startling things about almost all of the cases on which there have been official inquiries (see DHSS, 1982; DH, 1991) is that the family was well known to the social services and other agencies. A recent tragic event is the death of Victoria Climbie. This 8-year-old girl died following months of neglect, physical abuse and alleged sexual abuse. An inquiry was announced by the Government in January 2001, chaired by Lord Laming. Victoria had contact with a number of different statutory agencies, including housing, police, social services and the NHS in several London Boroughs.

Co-operation between health, education and social services, and the police, is seen as the key to effective protection by the Department of Health in *Working Together to Safeguard Children* (1999). It defines child abuse thus:

2.3 Somebody may abuse or neglect a child by inflicting harm, or by failing to act to prevent harm. Children may be abused in a family or in an institutional or community setting; by those known to them or, more rarely, by a stranger.

Physical abuse

2.4 Physical abuse may involve hitting, shaking, throwing, poisoning, burning or scalding, drowning, suffocating, or otherwise causing physical harm to a child. Physical harm may also be caused when a parent or carer feigns the symptoms of, or deliberately causes ill health to a child whom they are looking after. This situation is commonly described using terms such as fictitious illness by proxy or Munchausen syndrome by proxy.

Emotional abuse

2.5 Emotional abuse is the persistent emotional ill-treatment of a child such as to cause severe and persistent adverse effects on the child's emotional development. It may involve conveying to children that they are worthless or unloved, inadequate, or valued only insofar as they meet the needs of another person. It may feature age or developmentally inappropriate expectations being imposed on children. It may involve causing children frequently to feel frightened or in danger, or the exploitation or corruption of children. Some level of emotional abuse is involved in all types of ill-treatment of a child, though it may occur alone.

Sexual Abuse

2.6 Sexual abuse involves forcing or enticing a child or young person to take part in sexual activities, whether or not the child is aware of what is happening. The activities may involve physical contact, including penetrative (e.g. rape or buggery) or non-penetrative acts. They may include non-contact activities, such as involving children in looking at, or in the production of, pornographic material or watching sexual activities, or encouraging children to behave in sexually inappropriate ways.

Neglect

2.7 Neglect is the persistent failure to meet a child's basic physical and/or psychological needs, likely to result in the serious impairment of the child's health or development. It may involve a parent or carer failing to provide adequate food, shelter and clothing, failing to protect a child from physical harm or danger, or the failure to ensure access to appropriate medical care or treatment. It may also include neglect of, or unresponsiveness to, a child's basic emotional needs.

The Department of Health's *Child Protection – Messages from Research* (1995) outlines some of the difficulties involved in defining what is 'abusive':

A look at changes over the last century would suggest that the threshold beyond which child abuse is considered to occur is gradually being lowered. This is happening for a variety of reasons, including an emphasis on the rights of children as individuals, ease of disclosures, the influence of feminist social theories about victimisation and public expectation that the state should intervene in the privacy of family life. Society continually reconstructs definitions of maltreatment which sanction intervention; in 1871 the concern was abuse by adoptive parents; in 1885 it was teenage prostitution; in 1923 incest; then, later, neglect, physical abuse, sexual and emotional abuse. The state remains selective in its concerns and there is a difference between behaviour known to be harmful to children and behaviour which attracts the attention of child protection practitioners. For example, professionals' interest in school bullying is perhaps not as great as parents and children would wish it to be and domestic violence is only just beginning to achieve salience as a cause of concern. Jane Gibbons helpfully summarises the situation when she says that 'as a phenomenon, child maltreatment is more like pornography than whooping cough. It is a socially constructed phenomenon which reflects values and opinions of a particular culture at a particular time'.

Questions

(i) Can you think of any cultures in which it would not be considered abusive to deliberately inflict injury upon a child, or for an adult to have sexual intercourse with a child?

(ii) Is corporal punishment of a child abusive, or is 'moderate chastisement' an aspect of parental responsibility?

(iii) Would you expect there to be widespread agreement about what is emotional abuse or neglect?

Working Together to Safeguard Children (1999) describes the process of referral:

5.6 If somebody believes that a child may be suffering, or may be at risk of suffering significant harm, then s/he should always refer his or her concerns to the local authority social services department. In addition to the social services department, the police and the NSPCC have powers to intervene in these circumstances. Sometimes concerns will arise within the social services department itself, as new information/comes to light about a child and family with whom the service is already in contact. While professionals should seek, in general, to discuss any concerns with the family and, where possible, seek their agreement to making referrals to social services, **this should only be done where such discussion and agreement-seeking will not place a child at increased risk of significant harm.**

5.7 When a parent, professional, or another person contacts a social services department with concerns about a child's welfare, it is the responsibility of the social services department to clarify with the referrer (including self-referrals from families): the nature of concerns; how and why they have arisen; and what appear to be the needs of the child and family. This process should always identify clearly whether there are concerns about abuse or neglect, what is their foundation, and whether the child/ren may need urgent action to make them safe from harm.

For health professionals, this overrides the normal rules of confidentiality. The General Medical Council has revised its guidance for the medical profession several times. Advice appears in *Child Protection – Medical Responsibilities* (1994):

4.1 ... The [General Medical] Council's current advice, issued in May 1993, is that 'where a doctor believes that a patient may be the victim of abuse or neglect the patient's interests are paramount and will usually require a doctor to disclose information to an appropriate, responsible person or officer of a statutory agency'. This advice will guide a doctor's decisions on whether to disclose confidential information relating to abuse and neglect, both to medical colleagues and staff of the statutory agencies. The statutory agencies are social services, NSPCC and the police.
...
4.5 Distinction needs to be made between disclosing information which relates directly to a child and disclosing information which relates to a third party but which is directly relevant to child protection issues.
4.6 A doctor may be in possession of information relating to a third party and which is of direct relevance to child protection issues e.g. violent behaviour, sexual arousal to children, or information about a known or alleged perpetrator who may pose a continuing risk to children. It is essential that doctors are aware of risk factors and weigh this information very carefully. Disclosure of such information will usually be justified in relation to child protection.

Questions

(i)   Despite what the guidance says, health professionals are under no legally enforceable duty to report suspicions of child abuse: should they be? What about teachers? What about other people?
(ii) A study of 40 serious case reviews, half of them conducted before and half after the introduction of the new guidance in *Working Together to Safeguard Children* (1999), found that professionals were being helped to focus on the issues, but that the wide variation of characteristics and circumstances of the children meant that findings in one review were of little help in predicting child abuse (R. Sinclair and R. Bullock, *Learning from past experience: a review of serious case reviews* (2002)). So what is the point of all these reviews?

D v National Society for Prevention of Cruelty to Children
[1978] AC 171, [1977] 1 All ER 589, [1977] 2 WLR 201, 121 Sol Jo 119, 76 LGR 5, House of Lords

Lord Diplock: ... The uncontradicted evidence of the director of the NSPCC is that the work of the society is dependent upon its receiving prompt information of suspected child abuse and that, as might be expected, the principal sources of such information are neighbours of the child's family or doctors, school-teachers, health visitors and the like who will continue to be neighbours or to maintain the same relationship with the suspected person after the matter has been investigated and dealt with by the NSPCC. The evidence of the director is that without an effective promise of confidentiality neighbours and others would be very hesitant to pass on to the society information about suspected child abuse. There is an understandable reluctance to 'get involved' in something that is likely to arouse the resentment of the person whose suspected neglect or ill-treatment of a child has been reported. ...
    The fact that information has been communicated by one person to another in confidence, however, is not of itself a sufficient ground from protecting from disclosure in a court of law the nature of the information or the identity of the informant if either of these matters would assist the court to ascertain facts which are relevant to an issue on which it is adjudicating. ... The

private promise of confidentiality must yield to the general public interest that in the administration of justice truth will out, unless by reason of the character of the information or the relationship of the recipient ... to the informant, a more important public interest is served by protecting the information or the identity of the informant from disclosure in a court of law. The public interest which the NSPCC relies on as obliging it to withhold from the respondent and from the court itself material that could disclose the identity of the society's informant is analagous to the public interest that is protected by the well-established rule of law that the identity of police informers may not be disclosed in a civil action, whether by the process of discovery or by oral evidence at the trial (*Marks v Beyfus* (1890) 25 QBD 494; 59 LJQB 479) ... in *Rogers v Home Secretary* [1973] AC 388, [1972] 2 All ER 1057 this House did not hesitate to extend to persons from whom the Gaming Board received information for the purposes of the exercise of their statutory functions, under the Gaming Act 1968, immunity from disclosure of their identity analogous to that which the law had previously accorded to police informers. Your Lordships' sense of values might well be open to reproach if this House were to treat the confidentiality of information given to those who are authorised by statute to institute proceedings for the protection of neglected or ill-treated children as entitled to less favourable treatment in a court of law than information given to the Gaming Board so that gaming may be kept clean.

...

Question

Should busy-bodies be encouraged or discouraged?

Child-Protection – Messages from Research (1995) emphasises that a relatively small proportion of referrals will lead to more formal stages of the child protection process:

It is helpful to view the children and families caught up in the child protection process in the context of all vulnerable children. Although the evidence is not absolutely conclusive, it has been estimated by Smith and colleagues [1996] that, each year, 350,000 children will be in an environment of low warmth and high criticism. These children are 'in need' to the extent that their health and development will be significantly impaired if their families do not receive some help. Many of these children will be supported through the routine work of health visitors and other preventative strategies. We do not know how many, but a proportion of these children will receive help via Section 17 of the Children Act, 1989 including some who are accommodated under voluntary arrangements.

Many, however, will be subject to Section 47 enquiries to establish whether the local authority needs to take action to safeguard the child, what many currently think of as the start of the child protection process. We can interpret the work of Gibbons and colleagues [1995] to suggest that about 160,000 such enquiries take place in England each year, including 25,000 where suspicions of maltreatment or neglect are unsubstantiated.

Because the decision to investigate abuse is influenced by social and administrative factors, the family characteristics of the 160,000 children dealt with under child protection procedures are not typical of families and children generally; nor are they typical of all families in which children are maltreated. Gibbons and colleagues [1995] found that over a third (36%) were headed by a lone parent and in only 30% of cases were both natural parents resident. Nearly three fifths (57%) lacked a wage earner and over half (54%) were dependent on income support. Domestic violence (27%) and mental illness (13%) within the family also featured prominently and, in Thoburn and colleagues' study [1995], nearly a quarter (23%) had suffered an accident or serious ill health during the previous year. One in seven parents under suspicion were known to have been abused themselves as children. Most (65%) children had previously been known to social services and a previous investigation had been undertaken in almost half (45%) of the 1,888 cases Gibbons and colleagues [1995] scrutinised. So, it is the most vulnerable in our society who are most likely to become the object of a Section 47 enquiry. What should they expect from the child protection process?

...

First enquiry
Having described the characteristics of families subject to an abuse enquiry, what is it that triggers the interest of professionals? Cleaver and Freeman [1995] found that abuse came to

official attention in one of three ways. Most commonly, someone, usually the child or another member of the family, disclosed their concerns to a professional; just over half (51%) of enquiries began in this way. In about two-fifths (39%) of cases, professionals already working with the family identified child abuse. In the remaining 10% of all enquiries, abuse was suggested during an unrelated event, such as an arrest or home visit.

Family visit

Over a decade ago, Dingwall [Dingwall et al, 1983] stated that the most important step in a child abuse investigation occurs when an allegation becomes public property. This finding remains true. When the allegation becomes public, family members usually learn that they are under suspicion. Whatever else happens in the days, weeks, months and years following, the impact at this moment of realisation can be devastating. The Dartington [Cleaver and Freeman, 1995] and Oxford [Sharland et al, 1996] teams talked at length to parents in these early stages. The following quotation, from a mother who learned from a social worker that her son's teacher suspected sexual abuse, was typical:

> 'When I got the letter I was very shocked. I said "Ah-ah ... what's happening with the social worker! What have I done? Are they coming to take my child away?" I was scared. I hoped what happened to the Orkneys isn't going to happen to me now. I was just – "Oh, God, if anyone rings this bell, I hope – Oh God, it's not them!" Anyone who rings the bell, I look out of the window first – don't open the door and I say "Who is this?" From what I've heard from the telly, you know, I was very, very scared. And I phoned the social worker up. She wasn't in there! And I left a message. But I didn't get a reply from her.'

... [T]iny minorities of parents lose their children at the point of the first enquiry, but it is this wrench, more than anything else, that parents fear. Unease, which lingers as the case conference approaches hinders parental participation.

Conference and registration

Only a quarter of referrals led to a meeting of professionals. Several weeks can elapse between the first enquiry and the meeting: Gibbons and colleagues [1995] found the interval was 34 days on average, longer than the eight days recommended in guidance. The primary function of such conferences is to assess risk and decide how best to protect the child, but Farmer and Owen [1995] discovered several others: the conference acted as a gateway to resources; it ensured that vulnerable children were subject to regular monitoring and review; more important, it provided a context in which sensitive information could be shared.

The purpose of the child protection conferences is explained in *Working Together to Safeguard Children* (1999). It considers first of all the Initial Child Protection Conference.

5.53 The initial child protection conference brings together family members, the child where appropriate, and those professionals most involved with the child and family, following s. 47 enquiries. Its purpose is:
- to bring together and analyse in an inter-agency setting the information which has been obtained about the child's health, development and functioning, and the parents' or carers' capacity to ensure the child's safety and promote the child's health and development;
- to make judgments about the likelihood of a child suffering significant harm in future; *and*
- to decide what future action is needed to safeguard the child and promote his or her welfare, how that action will be taken forward, and with what intended outcomes.

Timing

5.54 The timing of an initial child protection conference will depend on the urgency of the case and on the time needed to obtain relevant information about the child and family. If the conference is to reach well-informed decisions based on evidence, it should take place following adequate preparation and assessment. At the same time, cases where children are at risk of significant harm should not be allowed to drift. Consequently, all initial child protection conferences should take place within 15 working days of the strategy discussion.

Attendance

5.55 Those attending conferences should be there because they have a significant contribution to make, arising from professional expertise, knowledge of the child or family or both. There should be sufficient information and expertise available – through personal representation and written reports – to enable the conference to make an informed decision about what action is needed to safeguard the child and promote his or her welfare, and to make realistic and workable proposals for taking that action forwarded. At the same time, a conference which is larger than it needs to be can inhibit the discussion and intimidate the child and family members. Those who have a relevant contribution to make may include:

- family members (including the wider family);
- social services staff who have undertaken an assessment of the child and family;
- foster carers (current or former);
- professionals involved with the child (e.g. health visitors, midwife, school nurse, *guardian ad litem*, paediatricians, education staff, early years staff, the GP);
- professionals involved with the parents (e.g. family support services, adult mental health services, probation, the GP);
- those involved in enquiries (e.g. the police);
- local authority legal services (child care);
- NSPCC or other involved voluntary organisations;
- a representative of the armed services, in cases where there is a Service connection. ...

Involving the Child and Family Members

5.57 Before a conference is held, the purpose of a conference, who will attend, and the way in which it will operate, should always be explained to a child of sufficient age and understanding, and to the parents and involved family members. The parents should normally be invited to attend the conference and helped fully to participate. Social services should give parents information about local advice and advocacy agencies, and explain that they may bring an advocate, friend or supporter. The child, subject to consideration about age and understanding, should be given the opportunity to attend if s/he wishes, an to bring an advocate, friend or supporter. Where the child's attendance is neither desired by him/her nor appropriate, the social services professional who is working most closely with the child should ascertain what his/her wishes and feelings are, and make these known to the conference.

5.58 The involvement of family members should be planned carefully. It may not always be possible to involve all family members at all times in the conference, for example, if one parent is the alleged abuser or if there is a high level of conflict between family members. Adults and any children who wish to make representations to the conference may not wish to speak in front of one another. Exceptionally, it may be necessary to exclude one or more family members from a conference, in whole or in part. The conference is primarily about the child, and while the presence of the family is normally welcome, those professionals attending must be able to share information in a safe and non-threatening environment. Professionals may themselves have concerns about violence or intimidation, which should be communicated in advance to the conference chair. ACPC procedures should set out criteria for excluding a parent or carer, including the evidence required. A strong risk of violence or intimidation by a family member at or subsequent to the conference, towards a child or anybody else, might be one reason for exclusion. The possibility that a parent/carer may be prosecuted for an offence against a child is not in itself a reason for exclusion although in these circumstances the chair should take advice from the police about any implications arising from an alleged perpetrator's attendance. If criminal proceedings have been instigated, the view of the Crown Prosecution Service should be taken into account. The decision to exclude a parent or carer from the child protection conference rests with the chair of the conference, acting within ACPC procedures. If the parents are excluded, or are unable or unwilling to attend a child protection conference, they should be enabled to communicate their views to the conference by another means. ...

Information for the Conference

5.61 Social services should provide to the conference a written report which summarises and analyses the information obtained in the course of the initial assessment and s. 47 enquiries, guided by the framework set out in the *Framework for the Assessment of Children in Need and their Families*. It is, of course, unlikely that a core assessment will have been completed in time for the conference, given the 35 working day period that such assessments are expected to require. The report should include:

- a chronology of significant events and agency and professional contact with the child and family;
- information on the child's current and past state of health and development;
- information on the capacity of the parents and other family members to ensure the child's safety from harm, and to promote the child's health and development;
- the expressed views, wishes and feelings of the child, parents, and other family members; *and*
- analysis of the implications of the information obtained for the child's future safety, health and development.

Parents and children, where relevant, should be provided with a copy of this report in advance of the conference which should be explained and discussed in advance of the conference itself in the preferred language(s) of the family.

5.62 Other professionals attending the conference should bring with them details of their involvement with the child and family, and information concerning their knowledge of the child's health and development, and the capacity of the parents to safeguard the child and promote the child's health and development. It is good practice for contributors to provide in advance a written report to the conference which should be helped in advance to think about what they want to convey to the conference and how best to get their points across on the day. Some may find it helpful to provide their own written report, which they may be assisted to prepare by their adviser/advocate.

5.63 All those providing information should take care to distinguish between fact, observation, allegation and opinion.

Apart from the services to be provided and the possibility of legal proceedings, case conferences discuss whether children should be placed on the child protection register:

Action and Decisions for the Conference

5.64 The conference should consider the following question when determining whether to register a child:
- **Is the child at continuing risk of significant harm?**

The test should be that either:
- the child can be shown to have suffered ill-treatment or impairment of health or development as a result of physical, emotional, or sexual abuse or neglect, and professional judgment is that further ill-treatment or impairment are likely; *or*
- professional judgment, substantiated by the findings of enquiries in this individual case or by research evidence, is that the child is likely to suffer ill-treatment or the impairment of health or development as a result of physical, emotional, or sexual abuse or neglect.

If the child is at continuing risk of significant harm, it will therefore be the case that safeguarding the child requires inter-agency help and intervention delivered through a formal child protection plan. It is also the role of the initial child protection conference to formulate the outline child protection plan, in as much detail as is possible.

5.65 Conference participants should base their judgments on all the available evidence obtained through existing records, the initial assessment and the full s. 47 enquiries. The method of reaching a decision within the conference on whether the test for registration is satisfied, should be set out in the relevant ACPC protocol. The decision-making process should be based on the views of all agencies represented at the conference, and also take into account any written contributions that have been made.

5.66 If a decision is taken that the child is at continuing risk of significant harm and hence in need of a child protection plan and registration, the chair should determine under which category of abuse the child's name should be registered. The category used in registration (i.e. physical, emotional, sexual abuse or neglect) will indicate to those consulting the register the primary presenting concerns at the time of registration.

5.67 A child's name may not be placed on the register, but he or she may nonetheless be in need of help to promote his or her health or development. In these circumstances, the conference should ensure that arrangements are in place to consider with the family what further help and support might be offered. Subject to the family's views and consent, it may be appropriate to continue with a core assessment of the child's needs to help determine what support might best help promote the child's health and development. Where the child's needs are complex, inter-agency working will continue to be important.

5.68 Where a child's name is placed on the register, the act of registration itself confers no protection on a child, and should always be accompanied by a child protection plan. It is the responsibility of the conference to consider and make recommendations on how agencies, professionals and the family should work together to ensure that the child will be safeguarded from harm in the future. This should enable both professionals and the family to understand exactly what is expected of them and what they can expect of others. Specific tasks include the following:
- appointing a key worker;
- identifying the membership of a core group of professionals and family members who will develop and implement the chid protection plan as a detailed working tool;
- establishing how children, parents (including all those with parental responsibility) and wider family members should be involved in the planning and implementation process, and the support, advice and advocacy available to them;
- establishing timescales for meetings of the core group, production of a child protection plan, and for child protection review meetings;
- identifying in outline what further core and specialist assessments of the child and family are required to make sound judgments on how best to safeguard the child and promote his or her welfare;
- outlining the child protection plan, especially, identifying what needs to change in order to safeguard the child;
- considering the need for a contingency plan if circumstances change quickly; *and*
- clarifying the different purpose and remit of the initial conference, the core group, and the child protection review conference.

5.69 The outline child protection plan should:
- identify risks of significant harm to the child and ways in which the child can be protected through an inter-agency plan based on assessment findings;
- establish short-term and longer-term aims and objectives that are clearly linked to reducing the risk of harm to the child and promoting the child's welfare;
- be clear about who will have responsibility for what actions – including actions by family members – within what specified timescales; *and*
- outline ways of monitoring and evaluating progress against the plan.

5.70 The conference should agree a date for the first child protection review conference, and under what circumstances it might be necessary to convene the conference before that date.

Working Together to Safeguard Children (1999) sets out the framework for review conferences and for de-registration:

The Child Protection Review Conference
Timescale

5.90 The first child protection review conference should be held within three months of the initial child protection conference, and further reviews should be held at intervals of not more than six months for as long as the child's name remains on the child protection register. This is to ensure that momentum is maintained in the process of safeguarding the registered child. Attendees should include those most involved with the child and family in the same way as at an initial child protection conference, and the ACPC protocols for establishing a quorum should apply.

Purpose

5.91 The purpose of the child protection review is to review the safety, health and development of the child against intended outcomes set out in the child protection plan; to ensure that the child continues adequately to be safeguarded; and to consider whether the child protection plan should continue in place or should be changed. The review requires as much preparation, commitment and management as the initial child protection conference. Every review should consider explicitly whether the child continues to be at risk of significant harm, and hence continues to need safeguarding through adherence to a formal child protection plan. If not, then the child's name may be removed from the child protection register. The same ACPC decision-making procedure should be used to reach a judgment on de-registration as is used at the initial child protection conference in respect of registration. As with initial child protection conferences, the relevant ACPC protocol should specify a required quorum for attendance at review conferences.

5.92 The core group has a collective responsibility to produce reports for the child protection review which together provide an overview of work undertaken by family members and professionals, and evaluate the impact on the child's welfare against the objectives set out in the child protection plan.

De-Registration

5.93 A child's name may be removed from the register if:
- it is judged that the child is no longer at continuing risk of significant harm requiring safeguarding by means of a child protection plan (e.g. the risk of harm has been reduced by action taken through the child protection plan; the child and family's circumstances have changed; or re-assessment of the child and family indicates that a child protection plan is not necessary). Under these circumstances, only a child protection review conference can decide that registration is no longer necessary;
- the child and family have moved permanently to another local authority area. In such cases, the receiving local authority should convene a child protection conference within 15 working days of being notified of the move, only after which event may de-registration take place in respect of the original local authority's child protection register;
- the child has reached 18 years of age, has died or has permanently left the UK.

5.94 When a child's name is removed from the register, notification should be sent, as minimum, to all those agencies representatives who were invited to attend the initial child protection conference which led to the registration.

5.95 A child whose name is removed from the register may still require additional support and services and de-registration should never lead to the automatic withdrawal of help. The key worker should discuss with the parents and the child what services might be wanted and needed, based upon the re-assessment of the child and family.

Some parents find all this rather unfair and heavy-handed. As 'Mrs Jones', the mother who burned her child (p. 660, above), says:

You know, once you get the authorities in you never get them out. They look at everything you do. Never a week goes past without there's somebody in our flat checking up. They think you'll think it's just a social visit-but it's not, you know what they're looking for. Once you're on their books! They keep having case conferences about our family, I think it's appalling: it's wrong! They call them without you knowing, they hold them behind your back and so many outsiders go to them. People you've never met before know you. You go in and there's a new doctor, and when you give your name they say, Oh, hello Mrs Jones! – just like that – and you know they know all about you. I mind it, I really do mind it. All sorts of people who've got no reason to know about me get told all the details – they sit in on conferences about me, that I know nothing about, and I'm not told about them. I don't think it's right. I feel I've no privacy left at all.

There would appear to have been a marked decrease in recent years in the number of children whose names are on the child protection registers. Between the year ending 31 March 2000 and the year ending 31 March 2001, the number fell from 30,300 to 26,800. To some extent this decrease is as a result of the change in the criterion for registration from a backwards look at the evidence that triggered the child protection enquiry to a prospective assessment of the likelihood of continuing risk of significant harm. That change has been brought about as a result of the implementation of the guidance that we have already quoted, *Working Together to Safeguard Children* (1999).

Questions

(i)   At 31 March 2001, there were more boys on the register than girls. This is a reversal of the position a decade ago. Can you think of any reason for this?

(ii) 14% of the children registered during 2000/01 had previously been registered. What does this tell us?

R v Harrow London Borough Council, ex p D

[1990] Fam 133, [1990] 3 All ER 12, [1989] 3 WLR 1239, [1989] FCR 729,
[1990] 1 FLR 79, Court of Appeal

Following divorce proceedings, the mother was granted custody of three children,
with fortnightly access to the father and a supervision order to the local authority.
Access to the two elder children had been a cause of continuing litigation between
the parents and there was a dispute over the paternity of the youngest child. In
May 1986, following the father's allegations that the children were victims of
physical abuse by the mother, the eldest child was examined by a paediatrician,
who found serious bruising and formed the view that the injuries were non-
accidental. The child accused the mother of inflicting the injuries. A place of
safety order was obtained and the two elder children were detained overnight in
hospital and were examined by a consultant paediatrician the following day. The
youngest child was never removed from home. The paediatrician found injuries
to the eldest child, which were incompatible with the mother's account. In June
1986 a case conference was convened, attended by the two paediatricians and the
headmistress of the children's school. The mother's request to attend was refused
but she was allowed to and did make written representations. As a result of the
conference, the names of the children and the mother were placed on the 'at risk'
register. The two children were then returned home. The mother applied for
judicial review of the local authority's decision, on the basis that the conclusion
of the case conference and the subsequent placing of the mother's and children's
names on the register were unfair and unreasonable and contrary to natural
justice. The judge dismissed the application and the mother appealed. The local
authority contended, inter alia, that judicial review did not lie in respect of a
decision to place a name on the register.

Butler-Sloss LJ: ... Before the judge it was argued that the mother should have been permitted
to attend the case conference and to have been heard. That suggestion is not pursued before this
court. Rather, it is urged upon us that the lowest degree of fairness to the mother, the opportunity
to know about and to be allowed to meet the material allegations made against her, was not
afforded to her. It is said that the decision was unfair, and the decision-making process was
defective on *Wednesbury* principles.

[Counsel], for the appellant mother, made a number of points. The effect of entry on the
register, even if the names of the children are subsequently removed, is to leave a stigma on the
character of the mother. He asserts that the inclusion of the name of the mother in the register
was the equivalent of a 'finding of guilt', that she had physically abused J. The record of J reads:

'3. Nature of injury and by whom inflicted, whether child abuse has been substantiated:
bruise on back and forehead, graze on side of nose, near eye (black eye), inflicted by mother.
Child abuse substantiated.'

That finding had to be on the basis of suitable evidence which she was entitled to know about
and to have an opportunity to answer. He accepts that not all the minutiae require to be
disclosed, but asserts that relevant and important matters were taken into account without
prior disclosure.

The case conference was given background information about the family, which included
the information that the child J had previously been on the register shortly after birth in 1979
for about 2 years. The mother says that she was unaware of that fact, and the accuracy of that
statement was not explored. There were other matters relating to why J did not attend swimming
lessons, why the children did not drink milk at school, the failure of the mother to take the
youngest for medical check-ups, the explanation for an earlier accident to D and the failure of
the social workers to ask the mother for an explanation of the injuries to J.

In the context of these facts, the earlier registration was of peripheral relevance.

What was critical was whether the mother was responsible for J's injuries. What the mother
required was an opportunity of giving her account as to how these injuries could have occurred,
and this was given to her by the consultant paediatrician. She took advantage of the opportunity
to give her account, both orally and in written representations.

The child J was clearly on the register as a result of the findings and conclusions of the consultant paediatrician, together with the allegations of the child J and the unsatisfactory explanations of the mother. The failure of a social worker to elicit an explanation from the mother was not only understandable but, in my view, probably wise. In allegations of physical injury, the most appropriate person to be given the account of the parent is likely to be the paediatrician who is often specially qualified to assess its probability in the light of the type, place, severity and other aspects of the injuries which have occurred.

Although the mother's request to attend, be represented and speak at the case conference was refused, [counsel for the mother] does not submit that the case conference erred in that respect. She was permitted to make written representations, both from herself and a friend. The representations were placed before the case conference. The decision to place the name of J on the register cannot, in my view, be faulted. [Counsel for the mother] accepts that if J's name was properly there, the inclusion of the other children was reasonable since they would be at risk.

I am satisfied that the procedure and the result did not in any way offend the *Wednesbury* principles. The conclusion of the judge was that the appellant failed ' ... to show that the decision was in any way unfair, unreasonable, or contrary to natural justice' (see [1989] 2 FLR 51, at p.55F).

I agree with him.

That would be sufficient to dispose of this matter, but it has been contended by the respondent council that judicial review does not lie in respect of a decision to place a name upon the child abuse register. [Counsel for the Local Authority] also submits that the decision of Waite J to grant judicial review of such a decision in *R v Norfolk County Council, ex p X* [1989] 2 FLR 120 was wrong. The facts in the Norfolk case were very different, of a plumber working in a house where a teenage girl made allegations of sexual abuse by him. She had twice previously been the victim of sexual abuse, and a few days later made similar allegations against another man. The plumber's name was entered in the child abuse register as an abuser, after a case conference. His employers were informed and suspended him, pending an internal inquiry. The first knowledge the plumber had of the allegations was the letter informing him of the decision to place his name on the register. He was not told that his employers had been informed. Although the contents of the register are confidential, a significant number of people inevitably have to be aware of the information contained in it. As the Norfolk case demonstrates, the effect upon outsiders may be dramatic. If the decision to register can be shown to be utterly unreasonable, in principle I cannot see why an application to review the decision cannot lie. In coming to its decision, the local authority is exercising a most important public function which can have serious consequences for the child and the alleged abuser. I respectfully agree with the decision of Waite J.

It would also seem that recourse to judicial review is likely to be, and undoubtedly ought to be rare. Local authorities have laid on them by Parliament the specific duty of protection of children in their area. The case conference has a duty to make an assessment as to abuse and the abuser, if sufficient information is available. Of its nature, the mechanism of the case conference leading to the decision to place names on the register, and the decision-making process, is unstructured and informal.

It is accepted by [Counsel for the mother] that it is not a judicial process. It is part of a protection package for a child believed to have been the victim of abuse.

In balancing adequate protection to the child and fairness to an adult, the interest of an adult may have to be placed second to the needs of the child. All concerned in this difficult and delicate area should be allowed to perform their task without looking over their shoulder all the time for the possible intervention of the court.

Appeal dismissed.

Questions

(i) Do you agree that it was 'probably wise' of the social worker not to 'elicit an explanation' from the mother?

(ii) What are the objections to parental attendance at case conferences? What are the advantages?

(iii) What are the objections to a more structured and formal procedure at case conferences? What are the advantages (a) to the child, (b) to the parents or carers, or (c) to third parties?

The Protection of Children Act 1999 requires child care organisations to refer the names of individuals considered unsuitable to work with children to the Department of Health and/or to the Department of Education and Skills.

Questions

(i) Suppose that a local authority is convinced that a man, trained as a teacher, has sexually abused a child he has taught in the past, but there has never been a successful prosecution. Suppose also that the Department of Education and Skills place his name on the list of those considered as unsuitable to work with children on the grounds of misconduct (Protection of Children Act 1999 amending the Education Reform Act 1988). If he moves into a household with a single mother and two small children, should the local authority warn her that he has been placed on a list of those unsuitable to work with children?
(ii) What can the man above do to have his name removed from the list? (See *C v Secretary of State for Health* [2002] Fam Law 515 (Protection of Children Act Tribunal) upheld by Scott Baker J *Secretary of State for Health v C* [2002] EWHC 1381.)

An important part of the investigation, particularly when sexual abuse is suspected is to 'interview' the child. Any interview which does not follow the guidance given in the report of the *Inquiry into Child Abuse in Cleveland 1987* (1988) will certainly attract judicial criticism and will probably lose the case (see *Re E* [1990] FCR 793, [1991] 1 FLR 420):

Introduction
12.1 An essential part of the investigation of an allegation or a complaint of sexual abuse will be an interview with the child if he or she is old enough to say what did nor did not happen to them. The child telling of abuse was often referred to as 'in disclosure' and assisting the child to talk of it as 'disclosure work'. The use and potential abuse of 'disclosure work' was the subject of a considerable amount of evidence to the Inquiry. Dr David Jones defined 'disclosure' as: 'a clinically useful concept to describe the process by which a child who has been sexually abused within the family gradually comes to inform the outside world of his/her plight'. He defined 'disclosure work' as: the 'process by which professionals attempt to encourage or hasten the natural process of disclosure by a sexually abused child'.

When the child speaks of abuse
12.2 The young child may speak innocently of behaviour which an adult recognises as abuse; an older child may wish to unburden and tell of abuse to anyone they may trust and that may occur informally to, for instance, a parent, school teacher, paediatrician on a medical examination or foster mother. Dr Zeitlin told us that: 'There is evidence that material produced spontaneously without prompting is undoubtedly the most reliable form of statements that children make, and often these have been made before disclosure interviews to various people.' However as a step in the inter-disciplinary investigation of sexual abuse there needs to be the formal process of interviewing the child.
12.3 During the Inquiry the question as to whether any child involved was or was not telling the truth was not an issue. The problems related to the interpretation by professionals of the comments of children who were not making clear allegations against their parents. Nevertheless, the question of whether or not to believe the child where there is concern about sexual abuse is important and evidence was given to the Inquiry about it.
12.4 What should an adult do when a child speaks of abuse? According to Dr Bentovim, until a few years ago, it was the practice for professionals to disbelieve the child. He said: 'If a child described a sexual experience, you first of all disbelieved and it had to be proven to you, rather than you first of all taking it seriously and saying he is entitled to belief and then obviously investigating it properly and thoroughly.'

12.5 In the [draft] DHSS paper 'Child Abuse – Working Together' (April 1986) it is stated: 'A child's statement that he or she is being abused should be accepted as true until proved otherwise. Children seldom lie about sexual abuse.' ...

Professor Kolvin said that the Royal College of Psychiatrists was not happy with the statement of the DHSS document: 'They felt that a statement by the child that sexual abuse has occurred should be taken seriously, but you are pre-judging the issue if you say that you believe it; in other words that you believe the child entirely.' He went on to say: 'Always listen to the child and always take what they say seriously.' ...

The interview with the child

12.10 When the possibility of sexual abuse is raised the formal interview with a child of sufficient age and understanding is a necessary step in the investigation. Different types of interview must be distinguished and the purposes for which the interview is being held must be clear.

12.11 In Cleveland there was confusion as to whether some interviews were being conducted to ascertain the facts or for therapeutic purposes or a mixture of both. It must also be clear whether it is intended to 'facilitate' or assist the child to speak and if so in what way and using which aids.

...

Disclosure work

12.18 The problem arises when there is reason to believe there may be abuse and the child may need help to tell, or where the assessment to that date is inconclusive and then a somewhat different type of interview may take place. This is a second or so-called facilitative stage which needs further consideration. The interviewer at this time may be trying a more indirect approach, with the use of hypothetical or leading questions, or taking cue from the child's play or drawings. According to Dr Bentovim, it should be used sparingly by experts, who may include suitably trained social workers. ...

12.19 There is a danger, which should be recognised and avoided from the experience in Cleveland, that this facilitative second stage may be seen as a routine part of the general interview, instead of a useful tool to be used sparingly by experts in special cases. In the first stage the child tells the interviewer. The second stage is a process whereby the professional attempts to encourage the child who may be reluctant to tell the story.

...

Disagreement between the professionals

12.27 The main area of disagreement between the child psychiatrists from whom the Inquiry received contributions, is as to the desirability of and limits upon the facilitative second stage.

12.28 On the one hand, in Dr Bentovim's opinion the use of leading, alternative, hypothetical questions should be available 'but it is very important that whoever uses such techniques should be very aware of what the consequences are in terms of the fact that the interviewer immediately has problems in terms of its probability, in terms of evidential value and there is always a balance between those factors. ... My reading of the research is that a free statement, a spontaneous statement made by a child is going to be the most acute.'

12.29 The experience of his team was that children were usually highly relieved by the interview

On the other hand Professor Kolvin said: 'I am uneasy with the concept of disclosure, which really goes hell-bent for trying to get some idea of 'yes' or 'no' on the basis of almost a coercive interview with the child and also does not take into consideration the possibility that perhaps nothing has happened or that perhaps we will not know.'

...

Agreement of the professionals

12.34 All those who provided evidence to the Inquiry were agreed on the following points to be observed in conducting all interviews. We endorse their views:

1. The undesirability of calling them 'disclosure' interviews, which precluded the notion that sexual abuse might not have occurred.

2. All interviews should be undertaken only by those with some training, experience and aptitude for talking with children.

3. The need to approach each interview with an open mind.

4. The style of the interview should be open-ended questions to support and encourage the child in free recall.

5. There should be where possible only one and not more than two interviews for the purpose of evaluation, and the interview should not be too long.

6. The interview should go at the pace of the child and not of the adult.

7. The setting for the interview must be suitable and sympathetic.

8. It must be accepted that at the end of the interview the child may have given no information to support the suspicion of sexual abuse and position will remain unclear.

9. There must be careful recording of the interview and what the child says, whether or not there is a video recording.

10. It must be recognised that the use of facilitative techniques may create difficulties in subsequent court proceedings.

11. The great importance of adequate training for all those engaged in this work.

12. In certain circumstances it may be appropriate to use the special skills of a 'facilitated' interview. That type of interview should be treated as a second stage. The interviewer must be conscious of the limitations and strengths of the techniques employed. In such cases the interview should only be conducted by those with special skills and specific training.

Parents at interviews

12.35 The professionals who gave evidence to the Inquiry were unanimous about the unsuitability of having a parent present at an interview held because of the suspicion of sexual abuse. Dr Bentovim said the presence of parents made the interview very difficult, but the presence of a person familiar to the child, such as teacher or social worker, may be helpful to the child. However he/she must not take part in the interview.

...

Disclosure work in Cleveland

12.40 In Cleveland before 1987 sexual abuse had been identified by complaint from the child or from an adult. The need to interview children believed to be sexually abused but reluctant to disclose such abuse was not widely recognised and there was a lack of expertise in the Cleveland area (and almost certainly in many other areas) in this specialised field. A number of social workers had attended conferences and work shops on the subject, some of them at Great Ormond Street.

12.41 During 1987 there appears to have been an immediate response to a suspicion of child sexual abuse that somebody should do disclosure work with the child. It is not clear whether this was intended to listen to the child's account or to use specialised techniques learnt at workshops attended by some professionals.

12.42 There can however be no doubt that there were interviews carried out in Cleveland during 1987 which fall into the type of interviews criticised in the Family Law Reports. It was apparent that various feelings came together at the time of interviewing some at least of these children – anxiety, the need for a solution, beliefs about 'denial' and the therapeutic benefits for children of talking about abuse, the perceived need to believe the child and some learnt information about techniques of interviewing. These included matching the pressure on the child not to tell with pressure by the interviewer on the child at the interview. There was in many instances a presumption that abuse had occurred and the child was either not disclosing or denying that abuse. There was insufficient expertise, over-enthusiasm, and those conducting the interviews seemed unaware of the extent of pressure, even coercion, in their approach. There were dangers, which became apparent in some cases, of misinterpretation of the content of the interview. Some interviews we saw would not be likely to be acceptable in any court as evidence of sexual abuse. The Official Solicitor refers to an aspect of this – the dangers with such interviews of costly and protracted litigation. There is also a danger with a great deal of written material available on how to conduct an interview, of the inexperienced interviewer going through each of a number of stages with each child interviewed, rather than considering the best way to interview a particular child.

13.5 Assessment and protection orders

Before the Children Act 1989, research showed that a high proportion of compulsory admissions to care began with a 'place of safety' order, which could be obtained without notice and last for up to 28 days with no right of appeal (Packman, 1986; Dartington, 1986). The *Cleveland Report* (1988) described something remarkably like abuse:

Place of safety orders

10.6 The initial route to the Juvenile Court was by way of place of safety orders. Between 1st January and 31st July 1987, 276 place of safety orders were applied for by social workers under the powers granted in s.28 of the Children and Young Persons Act 1969. ... All but one application appears to have been made ex parte, that is to say without the parent present, and none appears to have been refused. ...

10.7 The Social Services Department operated a highly interventionist policy in the use of place of safety orders. The effect of their general approach to the use of these orders was accentuated by the memorandum of the 29th May issued by Mr Bishop, directing social workers to apply for them on receiving a diagnosis of child sexual abuse from a paediatrician. Further a trend away from applications for the maximum 28 days to periods not exceeding 7 days as advocated in their manual was not maintained in 1987 and was specifically reversed in early June. ...

10.8 Before the crisis period of May/June and before the 29th May memorandum a number of place of safety orders in cases of diagnosis of sexual abuse were applied for and granted for 28 days. The reason for the longer order was not so much the need to protect the child as the need perceived by social workers to have sufficient time to engage in 'disclosure work' with the child.

10.9 Of the 276 orders 227 were applied for out of hours by the Emergency Duty Team. The majority of the orders were likely to have been granted during the day. We learnt however that of those 227, 174 were heard by a single magistrate at home, during the hours of court sittings, despite a clear understanding between the Clerk to the Justices and the Social Services Department that social workers would make these applications in the first instance to the full court. ...

Interim care orders

10.10 During early June the numbers of interim care orders applied for dramatically increased. On Monday 8th June there were 45 applications for interim care orders waiting to be heard. This increase in the workload led the Clerk to the Justices, Mr Cooke, to talk to one of the Court Liaison Officers, Mr Morris to discuss the implications for resources and to ask for a meeting with the Director of Social Services. In the evidence to the Inquiry there was some difference of recollection as to what was said between Mr Cooke and Mr Morris. Mr Morris went away with the impression that Mr Cooke was suggesting that Social Services should apply for 28 day orders to ease the strain on the courts, and he then advised the Emergency Duty Team to apply for 28 day orders. ...

Level of concern

10.13 Mr Davies said that there were three matters of special concern to magistrates receiving the applications.

1. The effect on the courts of applications which were increasing in volume and complexity. There was great concern about the backlog of cases and the delay to the regular work of the courts.

2. Prior to 1987 it was not the practice of the Social Services Department to refuse access to parents on the obtaining of a place of safety order and this approach was known to the Bench. Mr Morris told us that in the past access was almost invariably granted and denial was a marked change of policy. The requirement of separation of child from parents during 'disclosure work', which might take weeks or months was a new development. Mr Davies said that the denial of access on a place of safety order or on an interim care order was recognised by the magistrates as a most serious deprivation for parents and children and knowledge that it was now a common practice was a matter of deep concern. The reason for denying access in particular circumstances was known to the magistrates but there was unease that access might be denied too readily.

3. The conflict of medical evidence was also of great concern. Mr Davies told us that: 'It was the first time in my experience that Teesside magistrates had been invited to assess the quality of conflicting medical evidence provided by experts in child abuse.' Mr Cooke said that his magistrates were not used to dealing with that sort of thing. ...

Questions

(i) Look back at the account of child sexual abuse on p. 672, above. What level of concern do you think might justify removing a child and keeping him away from his parents for weeks in order to undertake disclosure work?

(ii) Look back to the discussion of *ex parte* orders in domestic violence cases on p. 430. Why do you think that well-meaning social workers prefer to remove the child before telling the parents that they are bringing proceedings?

Working Together (1991), an earlier version of *Working Together to Safeguard Children* (1999), encourages a different approach to removing children from home:

3.8 The removal of children from their home gives rise to public and professional concern, causes great distress if not handled sensitively, and can be damaging both for the child and for the rest of the family. Therefore, except when a child is in acute physical danger it is essential that the timing of the removal of children from their homes should be agreed following consultation with all appropriate professionals. They should weigh up the likely immediate and long term effects of removing the child against the possibility of harm if they leave the child at home, and balance this with the need to secure evidence of criminal offences and, in some cases, to arrest the suspects. In many cases there will be no need to remove a child and simultaneously arrest a suspect living in the same home. In other cases, however, particularly those involving several children and adults in different households, it may be important to prevent suspects from communicating with each other or destroying evidence. In those cases it may be necessary for co-ordinated police action, distressing though this may be, at a time of day when the whole family is at home. In other cases, although early morning police action might secure better forensic evidence, such action may not be crucial to the overall welfare of the child(ren) and should not therefore be part of the plan for investigation. In all cases, the long term protection of and well-being of the child will be the overriding concern; the likelihood of securing the child's well-being through the courts will be an important consideration.

As for the law, the Cleveland Report supported the proposals, made in the *Review of Child Care Law* (1985) and the White Paper (1987), to replace place of safety orders with a new 'emergency protection order'. The changes are explained by the Department of Health in *Court Orders* (1991), volume 1 of its *Guidance and Regulations on the Children Act 1989*:

4.28 Emergency protection orders replace the much-criticised place of safety orders which could be obtained under a number of provisions in previous legislation. The purpose of the new order, as its name suggests, is to enable the child in a genuine emergency to be removed from where he is or be kept where he is, if and only if this is what is necessary to provide immediate short-term protection. Nearly every aspect of the new provisions, including the grounds for the order, its effect, opportunities for challenging it and duration are different.
4.29 The essential features of the new provisions are:
   (a) the court has to be satisfied that the child is likely to suffer significant harm or cannot be seen in circumstances where the child might be suffering significant harm;
   (b) duration is limited to eight days with a possible extension of seven days;
   (c) certain persons may apply to discharge the order (to be heard after 72 hours);
   (d) the person obtaining the order has limited parental responsibility;
   (e) the court may make directions as to contact with the child and/or medical or psychiatric examination or assessment;
   (f) there is provision for a single justice to make an emergency protection order;
   (g) applications may be made in the absence of any other interested parties (ie ex parte), and may, with the leave of the clerk of the court, be made orally;
   (h) the application must name the child, and where it does not, must describe him as clearly as possible.
4.30 These key provisions have been limited to what is necessary to protect the child, but it remains an extremely serious step. It must not be regarded – as sometimes was the case with place of safety orders – as a routine response to allegations of child abuse or as a routine first step to initiating care proceedings. The new grounds require some evidence that the situation is sufficiently serious to justify such severe powers of intervention being made available.
   Nevertheless decisive action to protect the child is essential once it appears that the circumstances fall within one of the grounds in section 44(1). Under section 47(6) the authority must apply for an emergency protection order or another of the orders specified if they are refused access to the child or denied information about his whereabouts while carrying out enquiries, unless they are satisfied that the child's welfare can be satisfactorily safeguarded without their taking such action. ...

The grounds for an order are these:

44.—(1) Where any person ('the applicant') applies to the court for an order to be made under this section with respect to a child, the court may make the order if, but only if it is satisfied that—

   (a)   there is reasonable cause to believe that the child is likely to suffer significant harm if—
        (i)   he is not removed to accommodation provided by or on behalf of the applicant; or
        (ii)   he does not remain in the place in which he is then being accommodated;
   (b)   in the case of an application made by a local authority—
        (i)   the enquiries are being made with respect to the child under section 47(1)(b); and
        (ii)   those enquiries are being frustrated by access to the child being unreasonably refused to a person authorised to seek access and that the applicant has a reasonable cause to believe that access to the child is required as a matter of urgency; or
   (c)   in the case of an application made by an authorised person—
        (i)   the applicant has reasonable cause to suspect that a child is suffering, or is likely to suffer, significant harm;
        (ii)   the applicant is making enquiries with respect to the child's welfare; and
        (iii)   those enquiries are being frustrated by access to the child being unreasonably refused to a person authorised to seek access and the applicant has reasonable cause to believe that access to the child is required as a matter of urgency.

As the Department of Health *Guidance* observes:

4.44 As with all orders under the Act, even where the above conditions apply the court will not automatically make an emergency protection order. It must still consider the welfare principle and the presumption of no order [see pp. 589 and 616, above]. In most cases it is unlikely that the parents will be present at the hearing. With only one side of the case before it the court will want to examine very carefully the information it is given, especially where the basis of the application is likelihood of future harm or inability to see the child. It may be that the initial order will be made for a very short time such as the next available hearing date so that an extension to the order will be on notice to parents and others.

Section 44(1)(b) (local authorities) and (c) (authorised persons, see p. 719, below) seek to provide for children like Kimberley Carlile (see Greenwich, 1987), where the social worker was refused access but did not feel that he had sufficient cause to seek a place of safety order under s. 28 of the Children and Young Persons Act 1969 or a warrant under s. 40 of the Children and Young Persons Act 1933 (also repealed).

A local authority may begin legal proceedings because of some crisis, requiring immediate action to protect the child. Other cases may be brought because of a refusal by the parents to 'work in partnership' with the local authority in meeting the child's needs. The *Review of Child Care Law* (1985), White Paper (1987), and *Cleveland Report* (1988) did not adopt the idea of a 'lesser' order requiring the parents to co-operate with a multi-disciplinary assessment of the child, but this found its way into the Children Act 1989 during its passage through Parliament. Its purpose is explained in the Departmental of Health *Guidance* as follows:

4.6 The child assessment order, established by section 43, had no parallel in previous legislation. It deals with the single issue of enabling an assessment of the child to be made where significant harm is suspected but the child is not thought to be at immediate risk (requiring his removal, or keeping him in hospital), the local authority or authorised person considers that an assessment is required, and the parents or other persons responsible for him have refused to co-operate. Its purpose is to allow the local authority or authorised person to ascertain enough about the state of the child's health or development or the way in which he has been treated to decide what further action, if any, is required. It is less interventionist than the emergency protection order, interim care order and interim supervision order and should not be used where the circumstances of the case suggest that one of these orders would be more appropriate. ...

4.9 A child assessment order will usually be most appropriate where the harm to the child is long-term and cumulative rather than sudden and severe. The circumstances may be nagging concern about a child who appears to be failing to thrive; or the parents are ignorant of or unwilling to face up to possible harm to their child because of the state of his health or development; or it appears that the child may be subject to wilful neglect or abuse but not to such an extent as to place him at serious immediate risk. Sexual abuse, which covers a wide range of behaviour, can fall in this category. The harm to the child can be long-term rather than immediate and it does not necessarily require emergency action. However, emergency action should not be avoided where disclosure of the abuse is itself likely to put the child at immediate risk of significant harm and/or where there is an urgent need to gather particular forensic evidence which would not otherwise be forthcoming in relation to the likelihood of significant harm.

4.12 The court can allow up to 7 days for the assessment. The order must specify the date which the assessment is to begin. The applicant should make the necessary arrangements in advance of the application, so that it would usually be possible to complete within such a period an initial multidisciplinary assessment of the child's medical, intellectual, emotional, social and behavioural needs.

4.15 Section 43(9) provides for keeping the child away from home for the purposes of the assessment. This is intended to be a reserve provision, and if used the number of overnight stays should be kept as low as possible. The assessment should be conducted with as little trauma for the child and parents as possible. It is important that the child assessment order is not regarded as a variant of the emergency protection order with its removal power: The purposes of the two orders are quite different. The child may only be kept away from home in the circumstances specified, namely:

  (a) the court is satisfied that it is necessary for the purposes of the assessment;
  (b) it is done in accordance with directions specified in the order; and it is limited to such period or periods (which need not be the full period of the order) specified in the order.

Questions

(i) There has been a decrease in the numbers of emergency protection orders in recent years. The number was 2,232 made in 2000 and 2,127 made in 2001. Why do you think this is so?

(ii) Are you convinced by the arguments in the Department of Health *Guidance* of the need for a child assessment order?

(iii) Why is it thought less drastic than an emergency protection order?

(iv) What sort of assessment could usefully be undertaken during the period of a child assessment order?

(v) What should the local authority do if the parents refuse to co-operate with an assessment which will take longer?

Despite the provision of s. 1(2) of the Children Act 1989 (see p. 619, above), care proceedings can be a very lengthy process. According to the Lord Chancellor's Department in *Scoping Study on Delay in Children Act Cases* (2002), when the Children Act 1989 was implemented it was anticipated that it would take an average of 12 weeks for care cases to be resolved. This has rarely been realised in practice. By 1996, care cases were in fact taking 46.1 weeks from the time they started to the time of a final decision. By the end of 2000, this figure had risen again to an average of 50.3 weeks. It reduced slightly in 2001 to 47.1 weeks, but it is still almost a year of a child's life and four times as long as the original projection. In a Report for the Lord Chancellor's Department published in 1996, Dame Margaret Booth identified the need for:

• adequate resourcing
• effective administration
• more effective procedures for the transfer of cases
• firm judicial case management
• more certain timetabling and listing of cases
• better partnership working

Questions

(i) Do you think that it is acceptable for child protection cases to take so long to be completed? Are there any advantages?
(ii) How can the child be protected during this period? (See Children Act 1989, s. 38.)

It may be better for the child to stay at home while the proceedings are decided, provided that he can be adequately protected. The Department of Health *Guidance* talks about removing the alleged abuser rather than the child:

4.31 Where the need for emergency action centres on alleged abuse of the child the local authority will always want to explore the possibility of providing services to and/or accommodation for the alleged abuser as an alternative to the removal of the child. This could be on a voluntary basis backed up by the provisions of schedule 2 paragraph 5 which gives authorities the discretion to provide assistance with finding alternative housing or assistance to the person who leaves the family home. Such practical assistance may be crucial in persuading the alleged abuser to co-operate in this way. Existing legislation makes no public law provision empowering a court to order an alleged abuser out of the family home. However, in certain circumstances private law remedies may be used to achieve the same effect, and the local authority should explore these where it is in the child's best interest to do so. The non-abusing parent may agree to apply [for an occupation order], forcing the alleged abuser out of the home. This may be particularly appropriate in sexual abuse cases where the non-abusing parent has no wish to protect or shield the alleged abuser and where immediate removal of the child is not always in the child's best interests.

Occupation orders under the Family Law Act 1996 are considered in Chapter 9, above, but the 1996 Act also amends the Children Act 1989, so that an 'exclusion requirement' may be added to an emergency protection order:

44A.—(1) Where—
    (a) on being satisfied as mentioned in section 44(1)(a), (b) or (c), the court makes an emergency protection order with respect to a child, and
    (b) the conditions mentioned in subsection (2) are satisfied,
the court may include an exclusion requirement in the emergency protection order.
    (2) The conditions are—
    (a) that there is reasonable cause to believe that, if a person ('the relevant person') is excluded from a dwelling-house in which the child lives, then—
        (i) in the case of an order made on the ground mentioned in section 44(1)(a), the child will not be likely to suffer significant harm, even though the child is not removed as mentioned in section 44(1)(a)(i) or does not remain as mentioned in section 44(1)(a)(ii), or
        (ii) in the case of an order made on the ground mentioned in paragraph (b) or (c) of section 44(1), the enquiries referred to in that paragraph will cease to be frustrated, and
    (b) that another person living in the dwelling-house (whether a parent of the child or some other person)—
        (i) is able and willing to give to the child the care which it would be reasonable to expect a parent to give him, and
        (ii) consents to the inclusion of the exclusion requirement.
    (3) For the purposes of this section an exclusion requirement is any one or more of the following—
    (a) a provision requiring the relevant person to leave a dwelling-house in which he is living with the child,
    (b) a provision prohibiting the relevant person from entering a dwelling-house in which the child lives, and
    (c) a provision excluding the relevant person from a defined area in which a dwelling-house in which the child lives is situated.
    (4) The court may provide that the exclusion requirement is to have effect for a shorter period than the other provisions of the order.
    (5) Where the court makes an emergency protection order containing an exclusion requirement, the court may attach a power of arrest to the exclusion requirement.

(6) Where the court attaches a power of arrest to an exclusion requirement of an emergency protection order, it may provide that the power of arrest is to have effect for a shorter period than the exclusion requirement.

(7) Any period specified for the purposes of subsection (4) or (6) may be extended by the court (on one or more occasions) on an application to vary or discharge the emergency protection order.

(8) Where a power of arrest is attached to an exclusion requirement of an emergency protection order by virtue of subsection (5), a constable may arrest without warrant any person whom he has reasonable cause to believe to be in breach of the requirement.

(9) Sections 47(7), (11) and (12) and 48 of, and Schedule 5 to, the Family Law Act 1996 shall have effect in relation to a person arrested under subsection (8) of this section as they have effect in relation to a person arrested under section 47(6) of that Act.

(10) If, while an emergency protection order containing an exclusion requirement is in force, the applicant has removed the child from the dwelling-house from which the relevant person is excluded to other accommodation for a continuous period of more than 24 hours, the order shall cease to have effect in so far as it imposes the exclusion requirement.

An exclusion requirement can also be attached to an interim care order under s. 38A, which may be renewed as many times as necessary up to the final hearing of the local authority's application.

Questions

(i) Can you think of any reasons why the person mentioned in sub-s. (2)(b) would not apply for an occupation order under the Family Law Act 1996?
(ii) Why is it necessary for the local authority to have an emergency protection order, or interim care order, as well as the exclusion requirement?
(iii) Should local authorities be able to apply for an order excluding someone from the child's home indefinitely?

Under s. 46, where a police officer has reasonable cause to believe that a child would otherwise be likely to suffer significant harm, he may take the child into police protection for up to 72 hours.

Question

Why should such a power be thought necessary?

13.6 The threshold test

Care proceedings no longer cover both the villains and victims: they are designed solely for cases where the parental shortcomings are such that the local authority should assume parental responsibility for the child. The *Review of Child Care Law* (1985) recommended that the criteria for care and supervision orders should focus upon the condition of the child, the shortcomings of the home and the comparative advantages of local authority intervention:

15.12 In our view the primary justification for the state to initiate proceedings seeking compulsory powers is actual or likely harm to the child. ...
...

15.14 We consider that newly drafted grounds should make it clear that 'harm' consists of a deficit in or detriment to the standard of health, development and well-being which can reasonably be expected for the particular child. By 'development' we mean not only his physical progress but also his intellectual, emotional and social or behavioural development, so that it is clear that a child who is failing to learn to control his anti-social behaviour as others do is included. We refer to the standard expected for the particular child because some children have characteristics or handicaps which mean that they cannot be expected to be as healthy or well-developed as others, but equally it must be clear that if the child needs special care or attention (perhaps, for example, because he is unusually difficult to control) then this is to be expected for him. However, the standard should only be that which is reasonable to expect, rather than the best that could possibly be achieved, for each particular child. To apply the 'best' standard would be to introduce by other means the risk that a child could be removed from home simply because some other arrangements could cater better for his needs than care by his parents.

15.15 We consider that, having set an acceptable standard of upbringing for the child, it should be necessary to show some substantial deficit in that standard. Minor short-comings in the health care provided or minor deficits in physical, psychological or social development should not give rise to compulsory intervention unless they are having, or are likely to have, serious and lasting effects upon the child. The courts are used to assessing degrees of harm, for example in the context of prosecution for assaults, and we consider that they could also do so here.

15.16 The inclusion of 'well-being' in the standard to be expected is intended to cover those deficits which cannot necessarily be described in terms of health or development but which may equally amount to 'harm' to a child. Principal amongst these is ill-treatment. A child who has suffered non-accidental injury may not have suffered any lasting impairment in his health and the resulting emotional damage may be difficult to prove. The same may be said of older children who suffer sexual abuse. We consider that the concept of substantial detriment to their well-being will cover such cases and adequately distinguish between cases of real harm to the child and cases of acceptable variation in parenting standards.

...

15.18 In our view, a requirement that the harm be 'likely' will place a burden of proof upon local authorities which will be sufficiently difficult for them to discharge, especially in relation to mental or emotional harm, and this will prevent unwarranted intervention. A substantial or serious likelihood would be much more difficult to assess than substantial or serious harm and is not recommended. We have also considered whether anticipatory harm should be restricted by reference to specific circumstances from which risk could be inferred. ... However, a list would inevitably leave gaps unless the categories of risk were themselves very broadly expressed. Such broad expression would defeat the purpose of having express reasons for apprehended harm. In any event, it would perpetuate the arbitrariness and unfairness complained of by the Select Committee, would be complex and unwieldy, and would amount to a consolidation of the existing conditions rather than a genuine simplification in the law. ...

15.20 As regards more specific free-standing conditions, ... we do not consider them desirable. Their operation can be arbitrary or unfair and we doubt the traditional claim that specific preconditions of that sort operate to protect parents and children against unwarranted interference by the state. Rather we consider that such specific preconditions in practice may have the opposite effect and operate as magnets for drawing children within the sphere of compulsory care. ... Overall, there is a danger that very specific preconditions lead to a generalised view that once the conditions are satisfied an order follows unless there is some special reason for refusing one. What is more, the section 3 grounds, by focusing on parental unfitness, may have a stigmatising effect which may itself provoke unnecessary conflict and be detrimental to all concerned by unnecessarily prolonging proceedings and adding to their traumatic effects. We therefore, recommend that the sole primary ground should be actual or likely harm. ...

15.23 In our view the ground should also require that the source of the harm is the absence of a reasonable degree of parental care. Put another way, the court should be expressly required to find that the care available to the child is not merely wanting, but falls below an objectively acceptable level or that he is beyond parental control so that he cannot benefit from the care on offer. At present, the use of words such as 'prevented or neglected' or 'avoidably impaired', together with the care or control test in section 1(2), carry with them the flavour of lack of parental care. They fail, however, to express it clearly and more importantly give no indication of how great that failure must be. ...

15.24 We also consider that the grounds should in future make a clear reference to the likely effectiveness of an order. At present in section 1(2) there is the requirement that the child's need for care or control is unlikely to be met unless the court makes an order. Our impression is that the test is often satisfied by proof that his needs will not be met outside care, rather than by positive proof that a care order or supervision order will result in his needs being met or at least better catered for, and further that intervention will not do more overall harm than good. In our view the matter should be put beyond doubt. We consider that this might be achieved best by linking the idea of effectiveness with the child's best interests, that being the ultimate purpose of an order and in our view itself a matter which needs to be drawn expressly to the court's attention. Accordingly, we think there is a strong case in future for requiring the court to be satisfied before it makes an order that it is the most effective means available to it (including refusing an order) of safeguarding and promoting the child's welfare.

The Children Act 1989 provides as follows:

31.—(1) On the application of any local authority or authorised person, the court may make an order—
- (a) placing the child with respect to whom the application is made in the care of a designated local authority; or
- (b) putting him under the supervision of a designated local authority or of a probation officer.

(2) A court may only make a care order or supervision order if it is satisfied—
- (a) that the child concerned is suffering, or is likely to suffer, significant harm; and
- (b) that the harm, or likelihood of harm, is attributable to—
  - (i)   the care given to the child, or likely to be given to him if the order were not made, not being what it would be reasonable to expect a parent to give to him; or
  - (ii) the child's being beyond parental control.

(3) No care order or supervision order may be made with respect to a child who has reached the age of seventeen (or sixteen, in the case of a child who is married).

(4) An application under this section may be made on its own or in any other family proceedings.

(5) The court may—
- (a) on an application for a care order, make a supervision order;
- (b) on an application for a supervision order, make a care order.

(6) Where an authorised person proposes to make an application under this section he shall—
- (a) if it is reasonably practicable to do so; and
- (b) before making the application, consult the local authority appearing to him to be the authority in whose area the child concerned is ordinarily resident.

(7) An application made by an authorised person shall not be entertained by the court if, at the time when it is made, the child concerned is—
- (a) the subject of an earlier application for a care order, or supervision order, which has not been disposed of; or
- (b) subject to—
  - (i)   a care order or supervision order;
  - (ii) an order under section 7(7)(b) of the Children and Young Persons Act 1969; or
  - (iii) a supervision requirement within the meaning of the Social Work (Scotland) Act 1968.

(8) The local authority designated in a care order must be—
- (a) the authority within whose area the child is ordinarily resident; or
- (b) where the child does not reside in the area of a local authority, the authority within whose area any circumstances arose in consequence of which the order is being made.

(9) In this section—
'authorised person' means—
- (a) the National Society for the Prevention of Cruelty to Children and any of its officers; and
- (b) any person authorised by order by the Secretary of State to bring proceedings under this section and any officer of a body which is so authorised;

'harm' means ill-treatment or the impairment of health or development;
'development' means physical, intellectual, emotional, social or behavioural development;
'health' means physical or mental health; and
'ill-treatment' includes sexual abuse and forms of ill-treatment which are not physical.

(10) Where the question of whether harm suffered by the child is significant turns on the child's health or development, his health or development shall be compared with that which could reasonably be expected of a similar child.

(11) In this Act—
'a care order' means (subject to section 105(1)) an order under subsection (1)(a) and (except where express provision to the contrary is made) includes an interim care order made under section 38; and
'a supervision order' means an order under subsection (1)(b) and (except where express provision to the contrary is made) includes an interim supervision order made under section 38.

Questions

(i)   Does the idea of a 'similar' child in s. 31(10) mean a child (a) with similar physical or psychological characteristics, or (b) of a similar racial, ethnic or religious background?

(ii)   Section 31(9) is amended by the Adoption and Children Bill 2002 to extend the definition of 'harm' to include 'for example, impairment suffered from seeing or hearing the ill-treatment of another'. Do you think this will have any impact (a) in private law cases and (b) in public law cases?

The use of the present tense in the first limb of s. 31(2)(a) – 'is suffering' – has caused some difficulty:

Re M (a minor) (care order: threshold conditions)
[1994] 2AC 424, [1994] 3 All ER 298, [1994] 3 WLR 558, [1994] 2 FLR 577,
House of Lords

When the child, G, was 4 months old, his mother was murdered by his father. He went to live with foster parents, and his older siblings and half-siblings were looked after by the mother's cousin, Mrs W. The father was sentenced to life imprisonment, with a recommendation that he be deported on release. At first Mrs W did not feel able to care for G, and the local authority applied for a care order. Later Mrs W decided to seek a residence order for G, and the local authority supported this application. However, the child's guardian ad litem, and the child's father, argued that G should be adopted. Bracewell J decided that the s. 31 threshold test was satisfied because of the harm that the child had suffered when he was deprived of the love and care of his mother. A care order was made. The Court of Appeal allowing Mrs W's appeal, held that a court must decide whether the child is suffering or is likely to suffer significant harm at the time of the hearing. Since G was being adequately cared for by foster parents at the time of the final hearing, it was not possible to say that he was suffering harm. The father appealed to the House of Lords.

Lord Mackay LC: ... In my opinion the opening words of s. 31 link the making of an order by the court very closely with the application to the court by a local authority or authorised person. Section 31(2) then goes on to specify the conditions which are necessary to be satisfied before the court can make a care order or supervision order, but it is plain from this and the statute as a whole that even if these conditions are satisfied the court is not bound to make an order but must go through the full procedure particularly set out in s.1 of the statute. It is also clear that Parliament expected these cases to proceed with reasonable expedition and in particular I refer to s. 32 in which the hearing by the court is not regarded only as taking place at the time when the applications are disposed of. Indeed, I think there is much to be said for the view that the hearing that Parliament contemplated was one which extended from the time the jurisdiction of the court is first invoked until the case is disposed of and that was required to be done in the light of the general principle that any delay in determining the question is likely to prejudice the welfare of the child. There is nothing in s. 31(2) which in my opinion requires that the conditions to be satisfied are disassociated from the time of the making of the application by the local authority. I would conclude that the natural construction of the conditions in s. 31(2) is that where, at the time the application is to be disposed of, there are in place arrangements for the protection of the child by the local authority on an interim basis which protection has been continuously in place for some time, the relevant date with respect to which the court must be satisfied is the date at which the local authority initiated the procedure for protection under the Act from which these arrangements followed. If after a local authority had initiated protective arrangements the need for these had terminated, because the child's welfare had been satisfactorily provided for otherwise, in any subsequent proceedings it would not be possible to found jurisdiction on the situation at the time of initiation of these arrangements. It is permissible only to look back from the date of disposal to the date of initiation of protection as a result of which local authority arrangements had been continuously in place thereafter to the date of disposal. It has to be borne in mind that this in no way precludes the court from taking account at the date of the hearing of all relevant circumstances. The conditions in sub-s. (2) are in the nature of conditions conferring jurisdiction upon the court to consider whether or not a care order or supervision order should be made. Conditions of that kind would in my view normally have to be satisfied at the date on which the order was first applied for. It would in my opinion be odd if the jurisdiction of the court to make an order depended on how long the court took before it finally disposed of the case. ...

... It is true that an important change has been made in the statutory provisions in respect that it is now permissible under the second branch of s. 31(2)(a) to look to the future even if no harm has already occurred in the past. This is an important difference from the previous legislation but in my opinion to read the present legislation as the Court of Appeal has done is substantially to deprive the first branch of s. 31(2)(a) of effect, as in the argument before your Lordships became very apparent. It is also clear that while Parliament added the new provisions looking to the future without any necessary connection with harm already suffered, it wished to retain the first branch in respect of harm which the child is suffering. In my opinion the provisions of s. 31(2) must be considered before the question of any competing order under the provisions of Pt II of the Act are decided upon. The scheme of s. 1(3) and (4) and in particular s. 1(3)(g) appears to me to require that the court decide whether or not it has power available to it to make a care order or a supervision order before it decides whether or not to make an order at all and in particular whether or not to consider a s. 8 order. ... It remains to consider what should now be done in the present case. As I said, the information available to your Lordships at the hearing before your Lordships suggests that G's stay with Mrs W has been very satisfactory to date. In the light of the options available, and the provisions of s. 1 of the Children Act 1989, I am of opinion that the choice is between a residence order in favour of Mrs W or a care order as asked for by the appellant father. I am clearly of the view that it would be quite wrong at present to disturb the arrangements presently existing for G's residence and that whether or not a care order is made, the local authority would be perfectly right to continue the present arrangements for G making his home with Mrs W. However, we cannot foresee the future and the learned judge who heard all the evidence did foresee the possibility in the longer term of difficulties. Although I hope that no difficulties will materialise I think it best in the difficult circumstances of this child that your Lordships should restore the care order which will enable the local authority to monitor the progress of the child and also has features such as that provided for by s.33(3)(b) which might enable appropriate action to be readily taken if circumstances so required to determine the extent to which the father should meet his parental responsibility for G. ...

Questions

(i) If a local authority initially responds to a situation by providing services under s. 17, but later decides to seek a care order, can it argue that 'protective arrangements' have been continuously in place?

(ii) An 18-month-old boy has been accommodated by the local authority since birth. His mother was homeless and immature, but she has a decent home to offer. Can the local authority apply for a care order on the grounds that the child 'is suffering' significant harm, based on the facts at the date when accommodation was first provided? Alternatively, could they argue that the child would be likely to suffer significant harm if he was removed from the only parents he knows?

(iii) Can a local authority apply for a care order in order to acquire parental responsibility for an orphan who is currently accommodated under s. 20? (Cf *Birmingham City Council v D* [1994] 2 FCR 245, [1994] 2 FLR 502, which was decided before the decision of the House of Lords in *Re M* (above), and *Re SH (care order: orphan)* [1996] 1 FCR 1, [1995] 1 FLR 746.)

The House of Lords has also considered the second limb of s. 31(2)(a) – 'likelihood' of significant harm:

Re H (minors) (sexual abuse: standard of proof)
[1996] AC 563, [1996] 1 All ER 1, [1996] 2 WLR 8, [1996] 1 FCR 509, [1996]
1 FLR 80, House of Lords

The case concerned four girls (referred to as D1, D2, D3 and D4). When she
was 15, the eldest girl (D1) complained that she had been sexually abused by her
step-father, who was the father of D3 and D4. He was charged with rape, but
acquitted. D1 was no longer living in the household, but the local authority were
concerned that the younger children were at risk of abuse. They sought care orders
arguing that, although sexual abuse could not be proved to the standard required
for a criminal conviction, there was sufficient evidence to satisfy the civil standard
of proof in care proceedings. The judge dismissed the applications because he said
that he could not be sure 'to the requisite high standard of proof' that D1's allegations
were true. He said: 'This is far from saying that I am satisfied the child's complaints
are untrue. ... I am, at the least, more than a little suspicious that [her step-father]
has abused her as she says. If it were relevant, I would be prepared to hold that
there is a real possibility that her statement and her evidence are true.' By a majority,
the Court of Appeal dismissed the local authority's appeal, and an appeal to the
House of Lords was also dismissed by a majority of 3 to 2. Lord Nicholls gave the
leading speech, with which Lord Goff and Lord Mustill agreed.

Lord Nicholls: ...
'Likely' to suffer harm
I shall consider first the meaning of 'likely' in the expression 'likely to suffer significant harm' in
s. 31. ... In everyday usage one meaning of the word likely, perhaps its primary meaning, is
probable, in the sense of more likely than not. This is not its only meaning. If I am going walking
on Kinder Scout and ask whether it is likely to rain, I am using likely in a different sense. I am
inquiring whether there is a real risk of rain, a risk that ought not to be ignored. In which sense is
likely being used in this subsection? In s. 31(2) Parliament has stated the prerequisites which must
exist before the court has power to make a care order. These prerequisites mark the boundary line
drawn by Parliament between the differing interests. On one side are the interests of parents in
caring for their own child, a course which prima facie is also in the interests of the child. On the
other side there will be circumstances in which the interests of the child may dictate a need for his
care to be entrusted to others. In s. 31(2) Parliament has stated the minimum conditions which
must be present before the court can look more widely at all the circumstances and decide
whether the child's welfare requires that a local authority shall receive the child into their care and
have parental responsibility for him. The court must be satisfied that the child is already suffering
significant harm. Or the court must be satisfied that, looking ahead, although the child may not
yet be suffering such harm, he or she is likely to do so in the future. The court may make a care
order if, but only if it is satisfied in one or other of these respects. In this context Parliament cannot
have been using likely in the sense of more likely than not. If the word likely were given this
meaning, it would have the effect of leaving outside the scope of care and supervision orders cases
where the court is satisfied there is a real possibility of significant harm to the child in the future
but that possibility falls short of being more likely than not. Strictly, if this were the correct
reading of the Act, a care or supervision order would not be available even in a case where the risk
of significant harm is as likely as not. Nothing would suffice short of proof that the child will
probably suffer significant harm. The difficulty with this interpretation of s. 31(2)(a) is that it
would draw the boundary line at an altogether inapposite point. What is in issue is the prospect,
or risk, of the child suffering significant harm. When exposed to this risk a child may need
protection just as much when the risk is considered to be less than fifty-fifty as when the risk is of
a higher order. Conversely, so far as the parents are concerned, there is no particular magic in a
threshold test based on a probability of significant harm as distinct from a real possibility. It is
otherwise if there is no real possibility. It is eminently understandable that Parliament should
provide that where there is no real possibility of significant harm, parental responsibility should
remain solely with the parents. That makes sense as a threshold in the interests of the parents and
the child in a way that a higher threshold, based on probability, would not. In my view, therefore,
the context shows that in s. 31(2)(a) likely is being used in the sense of a real possibility, a
possibility that cannot sensibly be ignored having regard to the nature and gravity of the feared
harm in the particular case. By parity of reasoning, the expression likely to suffer significant harm

bears the same meaning elsewhere in the Act; for instance, in ss. 43, 44 and 46. Likely also bears a similar meaning, for a similar reason, in the requirement in s. 31(2)(b) that the harm or likelihood of harm must be attributable to the care given to the child or 'likely' to be given to him if the order were not made.

The burden of proof

The power of the court to make a care or supervision order only arises if the court is 'satisfied' that the criteria stated in s. 31(2) exist. The expression 'if the court is satisfied', here and elsewhere in the Act, envisages that the court must be judicially satisfied on proper material. ... The legal burden of establishing the existence of these conditions rests on the applicant for a care order. ...

The standard of proof

Where the matters in issue are facts the standard of proof required in non-criminal proceedings is the preponderance of probability, usually referred to as the balance of probability. This is the established general principle. There are exceptions such as contempt of court applications, but I can see no reason for thinking that family proceedings are, or should be, an exception. By family proceedings I mean proceedings so described in the 1989 Act, ss. 105 and 8(3). Despite their special features, family proceedings remain essentially a form of civil proceedings. Family proceedings often raise very serious issues, as do other forms of civil proceedings. The balance of probability standard means that a court is satisfied an event occurred if the court considers that, on the evidence, the occurrence of the event was more likely than not. When assessing the probabilities the court will have in mind as a factor, to whatever extent is appropriate in the particular case, that the more serious the allegation the less likely it is that the event occurred and, hence, the stronger should be the evidence before the court concludes that the allegation is established on the balance of probability. Fraud is usually less likely than negligence. Deliberate physical injury is usually less likely than accidental physical injury. A step-father is usually less likely to have repeatedly raped and had non-consensual oral sex with his under-age step-daughter than on some occasion to have lost his temper and slapped her. Built into the preponderance of probability standard is a serious degree of flexibility in respect of the seriousness of the allegation. Although the result is much the same, this does not mean that where a serious allegation is in issue the standard of proof required is higher. It means only that the inherent probability or improbability of an event is itself a matter to be taken into account when weighing the probabilities and deciding whether, on balance, the event occurred. The more improbable the event, the stronger must be the evidence that it did occur before, on the balance of probability, its occurrence will be established. Ungoed-Thomas J expressed this neatly in *Re Dellow's Will Trusts, Lloyd's Bank v Institute of Cancer Research* [1964] 1 WLR 451 at p. 455:

> 'The more serious the allegation the more cogent is the evidence required to overcome the unlikelihood of what is alleged and thus to prove it.'

...

The threshold conditions

There is no difficulty, in applying this standard to the threshold conditions. The first limb of s. 31(2)(a) predicates an existing state of affairs: that the child is suffering significant harm. The relevant time for this purpose is the date of the care order application or, if temporary protective arrangements have been continuously in place from an earlier date, the date when those arrangements were initiated. This was decided by your Lordships' House in *Re M (A Minor) (Care Order: Threshold Conditions)* [1994] 2 AC 424, [1994] 2 FLR 577. Whether at that time the child was suffering significant harm is an issue to be decided by the court on the basis of the facts admitted or proved before it. The balance of probability standard applies to proof of the facts. The same approach applies to the second limb of s. 31(2)(a). This is concerned with evaluating the risk of something happening in the future: aye or no, is there a real possibility that the child will suffer significant harm? Having heard and considered the evidence and decided any disputed questions of relevant fact upon the balance of probability, the court must reach a decision on how highly it evaluates the risk of significant harm befalling the child, always remembering upon whom the burden of proof rests.

...

A conclusion based on facts

The starting-point here is that courts act on evidence. They reach their decisions on the basis of the evidence before them. When considering whether an applicant for a care order has shown that the child is suffering harm or is likely to do so, a court will have regard to the undisputed evidence. The judge will attach to that evidence such weight, or importance, as he considers appropriate. Likewise with regard to disputed evidence which the judge accepts as reliable. None of that is controversial. But the rejection of a disputed allegation as not proved on the balance of probability leaves scope for the possibility that the non-proven allegation may be true after all. There remains room for the judge to have doubts and suspicions on this score. This is the area of controversy. In my view these unresolved judicial doubts and suspicions can no more form the basis of a conclusion that the second threshold condition in s.31(2)(a) has been established than they can form the basis of a conclusion that the first has been established. ...

Thus far I have concentrated on explaining that a court's conclusion that the threshold conditions are satisfied must have a factual base, and that an alleged but unproved fact, serious or trivial, is not a fact for this purpose. Nor is judicial suspicion, because that is no more than a judicial state of uncertainty about whether or not an event happened.

I must now put this into perspective by noting, and emphasising, the width of the range of facts which may be relevant when the court is considering the threshold conditions. The range of facts which may properly be taken into account is infinite. Facts include the history of members of the family, the state of relationships within a family, proposed changes within the membership of a family, parental attitudes, and omissions which might not reasonably have been expected, just as much as actual physical assaults. They include threats, and abnormal behaviour by a child, and unsatisfactory parental responses to complaints or allegations. And facts, which are minor or even trivial if considered in isolation, when taken together may suffice to satisfy the court of the likelihood of future harm. The court will attach to all the relevant facts the appropriate weight when coming to an overall conclusion on the crucial issue. I must emphasise a further point. I have indicated that unproved allegations of maltreatment cannot form the basis for a finding by the court that either limb of s. 31(2)(a) is established. It is, of course, open to a court to conclude there is a real possibility that the child will suffer harm in the future although harm in the past has not been established. There will be cases where, although the alleged maltreatment itself is not proved, the evidence does establish a combination of profoundly worrying features affecting the care of the child within the family. In such cases it would be open to a court in appropriate circumstances to find that, although not satisfied the child is yet suffering significant harm, on the basis of such facts as are proved there is a likelihood that he will do so in the future. That is not the present case. The three younger girls are not at risk unless D1 was abused by Mr R in the past. If she was not abused, there is no reason for thinking the others may be. This is not a case where Mr R has a history of abuse. Thus the one and only relevant fact is whether D1 was abused by Mr R as she says. The other surrounding facts, such as the fact that D1 made a complaint and the fact that her mother responded unsatisfactorily, lead nowhere relevant in this case if they do not lead to the conclusion that D1 was abused. To decide that the others are at risk because there is a possibility that D1 was abused would be to base the decision, not on fact, but on suspicion: the suspicion that D1 may have been abused. That would be to lower the threshold prescribed by Parliament.

Conclusion

I am very conscious of the difficulties confronting social workers and others in obtaining hard evidence, which will stand up when challenged in court, of the maltreatment meted out to children behind closed doors. Cruelty and physical abuse are notoriously difficult to prove. The task of social workers is usually anxious and often thankless. They are criticised for not having taken action in response to warning signs which are obvious enough when seen in the clear light of hindsight. Or they are criticised for making applications based on serious allegations which, in the event, are not established in court. Sometimes, whatever they do, they cannot do right. I am also conscious of the difficulties facing judges when there is conflicting testimony on serious allegations. On some occasions judges are left deeply anxious at the end of a case. There may be an understandable inclination to 'play safe' in the interests of the child. Sometimes judges wish to safeguard a child whom they fear may be at risk without at the same time having to fasten a label of very serious misconduct onto one of the parents. These are among the difficulties and considerations Parliament addressed in the Children Act when deciding how, to use the fashionable terminology, the balance should be struck between the various interests. As I read the Act Parliament decided that the threshold for a care order should be that the child is suffering significant harm, or there is a real possibility that he will do so. In the latter regard the threshold is comparatively low. Therein lies the protection for children. But, as I read the Act, Parliament also decided that proof of the relevant facts is needed if this threshold is to be surmounted. Before the s.1 welfare test and the welfare 'checklist' can be applied, the threshold has to be crossed. Therein lies the protection for parents. They are not to be at risk of having their child taken from them and removed into the care of the local authority on the basis only of suspicions, whether of the judge or of the local authority or anyone else. A conclusion that the child is suffering or is likely to suffer harm must be based on facts, not just suspicion.

Questions

(i) When the *Review of Child Care Law* (p. 717, above) recommended that harm must be 'likely', do you think that they intended to exclude only cases where there was 'no real risk' of harm?

(ii) Horrendous sexual abuse is, hopefully, less common than relatively trivial failures of parental care, but is a child who claims to have been repeatedly raped more likely to be lying than a child who claims to have been slapped once?

(iii) Lord Nicholls pointed out that the case was unusual because everything turned on one allegation. He said that there would be some cases where alleged maltreatment could not be proved, but other proven facts would demonstrate a likelihood of future harm. What sort of facts would demonstrate that someone is likely to harm a child, without demonstrating that he or she has already done so?

The two dissenting speeches focused on whether the evidence, although not enough to prove past abuse, might be sufficient to establish a likelihood of harm:

Lord Browne-Wilkinson: ... To be satisfied of the existence of a risk does not require proof of the occurrence of past historical events but proof of facts which are relevant to the making of a prognosis. ... So in the present case, the major issue was whether D1 had been sexually abused (the macro fact). In the course of the hearing before the judge a number of other facts (the micro facts) were established to the judge's satisfaction by the evidence. The judge in his careful judgment summarised these micro facts: that D1 had been consistent in her story from the time of her first complaint; that her statement was full and detailed showing 'a classic unfolding revelation of progressively worse abuse'; that there were opportunities for such abuse by Mr R and that he had been lying in denying that he had ever been alone either with D1 or with any of the other children; that D2 had made statements which indicated that she had witnessed 'inappropriate' behaviour between Mr R and D1; that the mother (contrary to her evidence) also suspected that something had been going on between Mr R and D1 and had sought to dissuade D2 from saying anything to the social workers.
...

[The judge's] conclusion that there was a real possibility that the evidence of D1 was true was a finding based on evidence and the micro facts that he had found. It was not a mere suspicion as to the risk that Mr R was an abuser: it was a finding of risk based on facts. My Lords, I am anxious that the decision of the House in this case may establish the law in an unworkable form to the detriment of many children at risk. Child abuse, particularly sex abuse, is notoriously difficult to prove in a court of law. The relevant facts are extremely sensitive and emotive. They are often known only to the child and to the alleged abuser. If legal proof of actual abuse is a prerequisite to a finding that a child is at risk of abuse, the court will be powerless to intervene to protect children in relation to whom there are the gravest suspicions of actual abuse but the necessary evidence legally to prove such abuse is lacking. Take the present case. Say that the proceedings had related to D1, the complainant, herself. After a long hearing a judge has reached the conclusion on evidence that there is a 'real possibility' that her evidence is true, ie that she has in fact been gravely abused. Can Parliament really have intended that neither the court nor anyone else should have jurisdiction to intervene so as to protect D1 from any abuse which she may well have been enduring? I venture to think not. My Lords, for those reasons and those given by my noble and learned friend Lord Lloyd of Berwick I would allow the appeal.

Lord Lloyd: ... The case has been fought on the basis that the sole cause for concern is the allegations of sexual abuse made by [D1]. It may be that in that respect the case is unusual, and that in many, if not most cases, a local authority applying for a care order will rely on a number of contributing factors. It is only when the local authority relies, as here, on a single incident or series of incidents relating to the same child, that the problem arises in a stark form. If the court finds on the balance of probabilities that the incidents did not occur, how can it go on to hold that by reason of those incidents there is a real or substantial risk of significant harm in the future?
...

In the usual case, there will be a number of interlocking considerations, all of which will give rise to separate issues of fact, and on all of which, if the Court of Appeal be right, the court would have to make separate findings on the balance of probabilities before proceeding to the second stage. Suppose, for example, there are three or four matters for concern which have led the social services to the belief that a child is at risk, on each of which there is credible evidence, supported, it may be, by evidence from a child psychiatrist, but suppose the evidence is insufficient on any of them to justify a finding that the child has been abused. Is the court powerless to proceed to the second stage? This is not what Parliament has said, and I do not think it is what Parliament intended. Parliament has asked a simple question: Is the court satisfied that there is a serious risk of significant harm in the future? This question should be capable of being answered without too much over-analysis. In an unusual case such as the present, which has been fought on the basis of a single issue of past fact, it will no doubt make sense for the court to start by deciding whether that issue has been proved to its satisfaction, or not. But this is only the beginning. Even if the evidence falls short of proof of the fact in issue, the court must go on to evaluate the evidence on that issue, together with all the other evidence in the case, and ask itself the critical question as to future risk. ...

Questions

(i) Do you agree with Lord Browne-Wilkinson that the opinion of the majority has left the law in an unworkable state?
(ii) What would you advise a local authority to do, if they were very worried that a child was being sexually abused, but did not feel able to prove it?

In many cases, medical evidence will be required to establish whether the threshold test is met:

Re AB (child abuse: expert witness)
[1995] 1 FCR 280, [1995] 1 FLR 181, High Court, Family Division

A baby of 10 weeks was found to have multiple fractures and some brain damage. Several expert witnesses gave evidence that the injuries were non-accidental. However, the parents called an expert who gave evidence that the child's injuries were due to 'temporary brittle bone disease'. Wall J found that the injuries were non-accidental, and gave guidance on the role of expert witnesses in cases of alleged child abuse.

Wall J: ...
The duties of experts in children's cases
...
In my judgment it is of critical importance in discussing the role of the expert witness in children's cases to bear in mind throughout the respective functions of expert and judge. The expert forms an assessment and expresses his opinion within the particular area of his expertise. The judge decides particular issues in individual cases. It is therefore not for the judge to become involved in medical controversy except in the extremely rare case where such a controversy is itself an issue in the case and a judicial assessment of it becomes necessary for the proper resolution of the proceedings. ... The judge's task is difficult enough as it is in sensitive child cases. To have, in addition, to resolve a subtle and complex medical disagreement or to make assessments of the reliability of expert witnesses not only adds immeasurably to the judge's task but, given his fallibility and lack of medical training, may help to lead him to a false conclusion. It is partly for this reason that the current practice of the courts in children's cases is to require disclosure of all medical reports and to invite the experts to confer pre-trial. By these means the ambit of agreement and disagreement can be defined. ...
    ... there are sometimes cases in which there is a genuine disagreement on a scientific or medical issue, or where it is necessary for a party to advance a particular hypothesis to explain a given set of facts. Where that occurs, the judge will have to resolve the issue which is raised. Two points must be made. In my view, the expert who advances such a hypothesis owes a very heavy duty to explain to the court that what he is advancing is a hypothesis, that it is controversial (if it is) and to place before the court all the material which contradicts the hypothesis. Secondly, he must make all his material available to the other experts in the case. ...

There is also no doubt that unnecessary investigation of medical issues is very expensive and time-wasting. In the instant case, four specialists were called: they all came from different parts of the country. More than a day was spent hearing the medical evidence.

Dame Margaret Booth, in her study for the Lord Chancellor's Department on the operation of the Children Act (1996), identified four shortcomings in the use of experts:

- The pool of experts giving evidence was small leading to pressure on experts' time and hence delays in the completion of the reports.
- Instructions given to experts were often incomplete or vague and this lack of focus contributed to the delay. Experts said that requests could have been more focused on the principal issues, allowing for shorter reports, and that they would welcome guidance on the relative priority of the case, for example the age of the child.
- Matters which could have been settled earlier were first discussed at the door of the court. Experts were kept waiting around on the day and asked to set aside days for a hearing when they were only needed for a short time, if at all.
- There were perceived to be significant disincentives to do court work with delays at court, long waits for legal aid, low remuneration and arguments over payment, particularly where the case became more complex.

The Lord Chancellor's Department *Scoping Study* (2002) found that little had changed. The *Scoping Study* states that the decision as to whether expert evidence is to be allowed is for the judiciary as part of their case management role.

Question

Does the European Convention on Human Rights require: (i) that parents should always be able to obtain expert evidence to challenge a local authority's case; (ii) that parents should always be entitled to the assistance of a lawyer during court hearings? (See *P, C and S v UK* [2002] All ER (D) 239 (Jul).)

13.7 The choice of final order

If the s. 31 threshold criteria are established, the court must go on to apply the welfare test in the light of the 'checklist' (p. 589, above) and the 'non-intervention principle' (p. 616, above). Expert evidence may also be important at this stage, and the court will also consider the recommendations of the child's guardian ad litem (see s. 41). The principal options are: a care order, a supervision order, a s. 8 order, or no order at all.

In many cases, the choice will be between a care order or a supervision order. The effect of a care order is the same as the effect of a residence order in favour of a non-parent (p. 768, below), except for the following:

33.—(3) While a care order is in force with respect to a child, the local authority designated by the order shall—
  (a)   have parental responsibility for the child; and
  (b)   have the power (subject to the following provisions of this section) to determine the extent to which a parent or guardian of the child may meet his parental responsibility for him.
  (4) The authority may not exercise the power in subsection (3)(b) unless they are satisfied that it is necessary to do so in order to safeguard or promote the child's welfare.

(5) Nothing in subsection (3)(b) shall prevent a parent or guardian of the child who has care of him from doing what is reasonable in all the circumstances of the case for the purpose of safeguarding or promoting his welfare.

...

(9) The power in subsection (3)(b) is subject (in addition to being subject to the provisions of this section) to any right, duty, power, responsibility or authority which a parent or guardian of the child has in relation to the child and his property by virtue of any other enactment.

Before the Children Act 1989, supervision orders were not widely used in child abuse cases. The *Review of Child Care Law* (1985) suggested:

18.5 The Select Committee were concerned about the small number of cases in which supervision orders were made (in 1983 there were about 1,400 supervision orders made in care proceedings as compared with about 3,000 care orders). They suggested that the reason was the perceived ineffectiveness of supervision orders and that these might be used more widely if the supervisor were given greater powers not only over the child but over the parents as well. In particular supervision might be used instead of a care order where the local authority intended to place the child at home on trial if a care order was obtained.

Imposing requirements on parents
18.6 One way forward would be to enable the court to impose conditions on the parent or whoever has the actual custody of the child provided that the actual custodian has had an opportunity to be heard. ...
18.7 Whether the requirements under a supervision order are met may depend on the parent rather than the child, especially where the child is young. At present orders may be frustrated, for example simply by the parent refusing the supervisor access to the child. Refusal to allow a supervised child to be visited or medically examined is now automatically reasonable cause for suspicion so that a warrant to search for and remove the child may be obtained. Nevertheless, where the object of the supervision is in fact to impose requirements on the parents for the protection of the child we consider that the court should have express power to do so. ...
18.9 As to what requirements precisely the court should be able to impose on adults the following list has occurred to us:
  a.   to keep the supervisor informed of his address and that of the child;
  b.   to allow the supervisor access to the child in the home and to assess the child's welfare, needs and condition;
  c.   to allow the child to be medically examined;
  d.   to comply with the supervisor's direction to attend with the child at a specified place (such as a clinic or day centre) for the purpose of medical examination, medical or psychiatric treatment, or participation in specified activities;
  e.   to permit the child to receive medical or psychiatric treatment; and
  f.   to comply with the supervisor's directions on matters relating to the child's education. ...
18.15 The power to require the child to live with a named individual will in our view be largely overtaken by our recommendation that the court in care proceedings should have power to grant legal custody to another person for example a relative or friend and should therefore be abolished. This will have the advantage of clarifying the legal status of the other person and enabling him to combine both the powers and responsibilities of a parent. The order could be coupled with a supervision order if required.

The Children Act 1989 implemented these recommendations in s. 15 and Sch. 2, Parts I and II. However, supervision orders are still made much less often than care orders. Judicial statistics show that, during 2001, there were 5,984 care orders made, compared with 1,466 supervision orders (Department of Health, 2002). Some of the reasons why care orders are often preferred are shown by the next case:

Re D (a minor) (care or supervision order)
[1993] 2 FCR 88, [1993] 2 FLR 423, High Court, Family Division

While in the father's care, a child aged 4 had been injured, and a baby aged two months had died from a fractured skull and many other injuries. The father had been convicted of wilful cruelty, but acquitted of murder. The case concerned a baby, R, who was born after the father was released from prison. The local authority applied for a care or supervision order, and the judge found that the s. 31 threshold test was satisfied because there was a serious risk of violence from the father towards the child. The local authority argued that a care order would undermine the co-operation which they were receiving from the child's parents. The guardian ad litem argued that a care order was necessary to protect the child.

Ewbank J: ... At first sight it would appear that a supervision order should be made if the child is living with the parents, a care order if the child is not living with the parents. But the statute is more flexible than that. ... it is open under a care order for the child to live with the parents, as in this case.

A supervision order can only be made in the first instance for one year, as provided by Sch. 3, para. 6(1) to the Children Act. Paragraphs 6(3) and (4) allow an extension for a further 2 years. Schedule 3, paras 2, 3 and 4 provide for directions to be given on a supervision order. ... It is suggested that these paragraphs and the powers given to the supervising officer would enable the child's welfare to be monitored by regular medical examinations, by attendance at a children's centre, and directions as to where the child should live, and any other directions which seem appropriate.

If there is a breach of a supervision order the supervising officer, under s.35(1)(c), has to consider whether to apply to the court for a variation of the supervision order or the discharge of the order. There is no direct way of enforcing the directions made under a supervision order.
...

If a care order were made then, under s.33(3)(a), the local authority would have parental responsibility for R and they would have the power to limit the parental responsibility of the mother and father if they thought it was necessary under s.33(3)(b). Under reg. 9 of the Placement of Children with Parents Etc Regulations 1991 the local authority have to satisfy themselves of the welfare of a child who has been placed by them and might visit the child in any event at intervals of not more than 6 weeks during the first year of the placement and thereafter at intervals of not more than 3 months. The advantage of a care order as opposed to a supervision order, in the submission of the guardian ad litem, is that a care order is unlimited in time and can only be revoked by an application to the court and even when revoked the court can substitute a supervision order. That is under s.39 of the Children Act. The local authority feel that a care order is too strong an order to be made in the circumstances of this case. They feel that they are working well together with the parents and that a care order would undermine that. But in my judgment that approach misses the real point in the case. The point in the case is the protection of R. ...

... The life of this family is harmonious. The child is thriving and much loved by his mother and father. But the protection of the child, in my judgment, is the most important aspect of this case and the decisive point in coming to a decision whether there should be a supervision order or a care order is that, in my judgment, if there is to be a lifting of the safeguards surrounding this child that lifting ought to be done by the court on consideration of the evidence and the lifting of the safeguards ought not to be left to the responsibility of individuals. So, in my judgment, a care order should be made in this case, despite the views of the local authority. ...

In *Re C (Care Order or Supervision Order)* [2001] 2 FLR 466, the local authority, supported by the guardian, sought a care order on the basis that it was necessary because the mother was vulnerable and isolated, because she might again become involved with a violent partner, and because she had shown a serious lack of judgment in leaving the child with the father. The local authority agreed to a condition being attached to any care order that the authority would not seek to remove the child from the mother without a court order save in an emergency. The judge made a supervision order for one year, concluding that such an order was proportionate to the risks currently presented. He took the view that the risks for the future lay in the mother failing to maintain her present standards, underestimating the child's needs, proving incapable of meeting them, or allowing a violent man once more into her household. The judge felt that even bearing in mind the condition offered by the authority, it had not satisfied the court that a care order was warranted.

The balancing act that has to be achieved when deciding on a supervision order rather than a care order is set out by Hale LJ in the following case:

Re O (Supervision Order)
[2001] EWCA Civ 16, [2001] 1 FCR 289, [2001] 1 FLR 923, Court of Appeal

A mother had had four previous children taken into care following allegations of sexual abuse by the father. The mother had failed to protect the children and neglected them. The proceedings concerned a fifth child, aged 15 months at the time of the hearing in the Court of Appeal. A new partner had fathered him. The mother suffered from mental health difficulties. The local authority did not seek to remove the child but sought a care order. The trial judge concluded that the appropriate order was a supervision order rather than a care order, and the local authority appealed.

(24) A care order is very different from a supervision order. There are 3 main points. First, it gives the local authority power to remove the child without recourse even to a family proceedings court for an emergency protection order. The parents' only means of challenging that removal is by an application to discharge the care order, which usually takes some time to be heard, especially if, as in this case, it would have to be transferred to a higher court. Given the judge's findings as to the nature of risk, the slowness of any deterioration, the level of protection available from other sources including the father, it is very difficult to say that the local authority need to have this power. The care plan itself, as I have already indicated, does not suggest that they do.
(25) Secondly, it gives the local authority parental responsibility for the child coupled with the power to control the parents' exercise of that responsibility. Again, the care plan does not suggest that the local authority wish to exercise parental responsibility or control the parents' exercise of it ...
(26) The third difference is one of timing. Mr Forbes in particular has argued that it might be difficult to achieve a further order in three years' time, but of course that difficulty would only arise if by then the risk of harm had disappeared or almost disappeared, or the need for an order had disappeared or almost disappeared. If that were not the case, the local authority would have to investigate and take any action which was thought appropriate to protect the child.
(27) ... Each case is an exercise of discretion on its own particular facts and earlier case law may be of limited help in this context. In any event, it has to be considered in the light of the Human Rights Act 1998 and Art 8 of the European Convention for the Protection of Human Rights and Fundamental Freedoms 1950. As I said in the case of *Re C + B (Care Order: Future Harm)* [2001] 1 FLR 611, paras (33)–(34) at 620–621;
'I do note that under Art 8 of the Convention both the children and the parents have the right to respect for their family and private life. If the state is to interfere with that there are three requirements: first, that it be in accordance with the law; secondly, that it be for a legitimate aim (in this case the protection of the welfare and interest of the children); and thirdly, that it be "necessary in a democratic society".'
There is a long line of European Court of Human Rights jurisprudence on that third requirement, which emphasises that the intervention has to be proportionate to the legitimate aims.
(28) Proportionality, therefore, is the key. It will be the duty of everyone to ensure that, in those cases where a supervision order is proportionate as a response to the risk presented, a supervision order can be made to work, as indeed the framers of the Children Act 1989 always hoped that it would be made to work. The local authorities must deliver the services that are needed and must ensure that other agencies, including the health service, also play their part, and the parents must co-operate fully.

Questions

(i) Are you surprised that the local authority placed so much weight on the need to maintain the co-operation of the parents?
(ii) Could the court have made a care order against the wishes of the local authority, if the local authority had not originally applied for a care or supervision order? (See *Nottinghamshire County Council v P* [1994] Fam 18, [1993] 3 All ER 815, [1993] 3 WLR 637, [1993] 2 FLR 134, p. 733, below.)

However, supervision orders are sometimes appropriate, even when there are very serious concerns about children's safety:

Manchester City Council v B
[1996] 1 FLR 324, [1996] Fam Law 202, High Court, Family Division

A baby, Z, was admitted to hospital and was found to have brain haemorrhages. After neurosurgery, he eventually recovered. There was a conflict of expert evidence as to whether the injuries were non-accidental. The local authority applied for a care or supervision order. At the hearing the guardian ad litem and the local authority both proposed that the child should be rehabilitated with his parents under a supervision order.

Bracewell J: ... On the totality of all the evidence, I find to the appropriate standard of proof, and commensurate with the serious nature of these allegations, that these normally loving, caring parents, were driven beyond their endurance and tolerance by the difficulties presented by this child and by the frustration of lack of medical support and in their stress, behaved wholly out of character in one desperate incident of shaking, probably accompanied by projection of the child onto a cot or bed. It was a temporary phase. It is even understandable in the light of their youth and inexperience and the difficulty of this child and I am sure it was not done out of any malice or desire to hurt the child. I find it was some act of despair but, of course, it was life-threatening and, in consequence, represents significant harm and it was not the care which it would be reasonable to expect a parent to give within the meaning of s. 31.

In those circumstances, I am satisfied that the threshold criteria are established. Once that is established, the court has a menu of options governed by the welfare checklist and s. 1 which I apply.

It was a life-threatening injury, but it is agreed by all, and I accept, that the welfare of the child demands rehabilitation to these parents who, apart from this isolated lapse, have demonstrated a high standard of care and commitment.

The question arises whether protection of any order is needed and, if one is needed, which order is best for the welfare of the child. I am satisfied that some statutory protection is required to safeguard the child, so that the local authority can monitor the situation. I have considered very carefully if a supervision order would be adequate. The parents have expressed willingness to co-operate and have done so in the past. Of course, it has to be borne in mind that a supervision order does not have teeth, does not lay down a statutory level of intervention, does not give the local authority parental responsibility, does not allow for rapid intervention to remove the child without further order of the court.

The potential consequences to the child of any further incident are very serious indeed. However, although a care order is in no way inconsistent with rehabilitation nor partnership with the family, I have been extremely impressed with the very careful and helpful analysis of the guardian ad litem. I would like to thank him for the way in which he has approached this task and I have concluded, in all the circumstances, that a supervision order for one year to the local authority is the order which will protect and provide for Z's welfare.

Question

Would the parents regard a supervision order as having 'no teeth'?

Another possibility, introduced by the Children Act 1989, is for the court to make s. 8 orders (see p. 585, above). Local authorities are prohibited from applying for residence or contact orders by s. 9(2) of the Children Act 1989. However, they can invite the court to make an order of its own motion under s. 10(1)(b), or support an application by another person. If the parents have separated, a residence order in favour of one parent may be appropriate where the risk to the child comes from the other parent, or there may be a member of the extended family who is able to care for the child adequately. However, as in *Re M* (p. 720, above), a care order may still be appropriate in such cases.

Re K (care order or residence order)

[1996] 1 FCR 365, [1995] 1 FLR 675, High Court, Family Division

The local authority applied for care orders in relation to two children, aged 5 and 6. One of them had suffered an injury while in the care of their mother, who was schizophrenic. The children went to live with their grandparents under interim care orders. They were diagnosed as suffering from an incurable muscle-wasting disease which would confine them to wheelchairs by the age of 10. The local authority asked the court to make a supervision order and a residence order in favour of the grandparents. The grandparents' position was that a care order would give them greater support, and they did not want the responsibility of a residence order. The mother supported the making of a care order because that would require the local authority to promote contact between her and the children (s. 34, see p. 756, below). The local authority eventually withdrew its opposition to a care order.

Stuart-White J: ... First, I find it rather difficult to conceive of circumstances in which it would not be wrong in principle to oblige an individual who has not applied for and does not desire a residence order, with its concomitant parental responsibility, to accept such an order and such responsibility. I accept that the power to make such an order does exist under s. 10(1)(b) of the Act, but it seems to me that the cases in which it would be right to exercise that power in the circumstances which I have mentioned, must be wholly exceptional, and this is not a wholly exceptional case of that kind.

The second principle which seems to me to emerge is this: that if I do not exercise the power to impose a residence order and parental responsibility on individuals who do not want it, then the only persons with parental responsibility will be the mother and the father. It is not suggested, as I understand it, that there exist any practicable means of preventing their exercising that parental responsibility with potentially harmful and possibly disastrous effects on the children, save by the making of a public law order: see *Nottinghamshire County Council v P* [1993] 1 FLR 514, and the Court of Appeal decision in the same case at [1994] Fam 18, [1993] 2 FLR 134. Thus, in the absence of a residence order, it seems to me that the argument that there are no child protection concerns could not be and cannot be maintained.

The third point of principle is this: I accept that in ordinary circumstances the court should be slow indeed to make a care order to a local authority which has applied for it but ultimately decides that it does not want it. The court will plainly, it seems to me, only make such an order under what may be unusual circumstances. The power to do so of course not only exists, it is in a sense emphasised by the Family Proceedings Rules 1991 (SI 1991/1247), r. 4.5, which provides that any application may only be withdrawn with leave. ... If the court concludes that the threshold criteria are satisfied and the welfare of the child demands it, a conclusion of course which would only be reached after considering the matters set out in s. 1(3) of the Act, then in my judgment the court should not shrink from making such a care order, even if the local authority which has applied for it should change its mind. Similarly, where the application is for a supervision order, the court should not in like circumstances shrink from exercising its powers under s. 31(5)(b) of the Act to make a care order.

Thirdly, whereas it will often be unnecessary and inappropriate to make a care order within the context of a family placement, I am not prepared to go so far as to say that it is only in exceptional circumstances that such an order should be made in that context. There may very well be circumstances where the making of a care order is the only way to protect children placed with members of their extended families from significant harm.

Fourthly, whilst it would be wholly inappropriate to make a care order solely for the purpose of conferring a financial benefit on the carers, the fact that such a financial benefit if it accrues will materially contribute to the welfare of the child, is in my judgment a factor which can properly be regarded as relevant in the balancing exercise which in any case like this is demanded. There is a complex interrelation between the general duties owed by all local authorities to children in need in their areas and the specific duties owed to children in care, as set out in ss. 31, 22, 23 and 24 of the Act, and in the relevant regulations, including the Review of Children's Cases Regulations 1991 (SI 1991/895) and the Foster Placement (Children) Regulations 1991 (SI 1991/910), to the details of which I have helpfully had my attention drawn.
...

Now bearing in mind these general principles as I have endeavoured no doubt inadequately to enunciate them, and on the overwhelming weight of the evidence in this unusual and in many ways tragic case, I have no hesitation in holding that the welfare of these children demands that a care order be made. That will provide them with security and protection during their minorities. I am quite sure that the applicant local authority has shown both good sense and, as one would expect, a true concern for these children in making the concession that it has made. I therefore make care orders in each case.

With leave of the court, local authorities can apply for specific issue orders and prohibited steps orders under s. 8. However, these are limited by s. 9(5) of the 1989 Act, and their use in child protection cases has been restricted following the decision of the Court of Appeal in the following case:

Nottinghamshire County Council v P
[1994] Fam 18, [1993] 3 All ER 815, [1993] 3 WLR 637, [1994] 1 FCR 624, [1993] 2 FLR 134, Court of Appeal

The eldest of three sisters claimed that she had been sexually abused by her father, and that he was also abusing her younger sisters aged 16 and 13. Leave was granted for the local authority to apply for a prohibited steps order requiring the father not to live in the same household as the girls, and not to have contact with them. The local authority decided not to seek care or supervision orders, which it considered would be ineffective. Ward J at first instance decided that s. 9(5) prevented him from making the order requested. The local authority appealed.

Sir Stephen Brown P: ... Section 9(5) of the Act of 1989 provides:

> 'No court shall exercise its power to make a specific issue order or prohibited steps order – (a) with a view to achieving a result which could be achieved by making a residence or contact order; or (b) in any way which is denied to the High Court [by section 100(2)] in the exercise of its inherent jurisdiction with respect to children.'

In the view of this court the application for a prohibited steps order by this local authority was in reality being made with a view to achieving a result which could be achieved by making a residence or contact order. Section 9(2) specifically provides:

> 'No application may be made by a local authority for a residence order or contact order and no court shall make such an order in favour of a local authority.'

The court is satisfied that the local authority was indeed seeking to enter by the 'back door' as it were. It agrees with Ward J that he had no power to make a prohibited steps order in this case. Submissions were made to the effect that a contact order in any event necessarily implied a positive order and that an order which merely provided for 'no contact' could not be construed as a contact order. There are certain passages in editorial comment which seem to support that view. We do not share it. We agree with the judge that the sensible and appropriate construction of the term contact order includes a situation where a court is required to consider whether any contact should be provided for. An order that there shall be 'no contact' falls within the general concept of contact and common sense requires that it should be considered to fall within the definition of 'contact order' in section 8(1). We agree with the reasoning of Ward J and would therefore dismiss the appeal of the local authority against his refusal of its application for a prohibited steps order. A wider question arises as to policy. We consider that this court should make it clear that the route chosen by the local authority in this case was wholly inappropriate. In cases where children are found to be at risk of suffering significant harm within the meaning of section 31 of the Children Act 1989 a clear duty arises on the part of local authorities to take steps to protect them. In such circumstances a local authority is required to assume responsibility and to intervene in the family arrangements in order to protect the child. Part IV specifically provides them with wide powers and a wide discretion. As already pointed out the Act envisages that local authorities may place children with their parents even though they may have a care order under section 31. A supervision order may be viewed as being less draconian but it gives the local authority a wide discretion as to how to deal with children and with the family. A prohibited steps order would not afford the local authority any authority as to how it might deal with the children. There may be situations, for example where a child is accommodated by a local authority, where it would be appropriate to seek a prohibited steps order for some particular purpose. However, it could not in any circumstances be regarded as providing a substitute for an order under Part IV of the Act of 1989. Furthermore, it is very doubtful indeed whether a prohibited steps order could in any circumstances be used to 'oust' a father from a matrimonial home. Although counsel had prepared detailed submissions upon this aspect of the matter it has not been necessary to consider the point in order to resolve this appeal. It is a most regrettable feature of this case that the local authority having initially intervened under Part V of the Act of 1989 in order to obtain an emergency protection order did not then proceed to seek orders under section 31 in Part IV of the Act. This is even more regrettable after Judge Heald had directed the local authority to consider the position pursuant to a direction under section 37 of the Act. ...

... Since the fact of the risk of significant harm to the children has been established and not contradicted there remains upon the local authority the clear duty to take steps to safeguard the welfare of these children. It should not shrink from taking steps under Part IV of the Act. It appears from submissions made by all counsel in this court that the mother, the father and the children by their guardian ad litem would not resist the making of a supervision order in favour of the local authority pursuant to section 31 of the Act. That at least would afford a basis for the local authority to take some constructive steps in order to protect these children. This court is deeply concerned at the absence of any power to direct this authority to take steps to protect the children. In the former wardship jurisdiction it might well have been able to do so. The operation of the Children Act 1989 is entirely dependent upon the full co-operation of all those involved. This includes the courts, local authorities, social workers, and all who have to deal with children. Unfortunately, as appears from this case, if a local authority doggedly resists taking the steps which are appropriate to the case of children at risk of suffering significant harm it appears that the court is powerless. The authority may perhaps lay itself open to an application for judicial review but in a case such as this the question arises, at whose instance? The position is one which it is to be hoped will not recur and that lessons will be learnt from this unhappy catalogue of errors. For the reasons set out in this judgment, the court dismisses the appeal of the local authority and allows the appeals of the other appellants.

Questions

(i) Would a care or supervision order have adequately protected the children in this case?
(ii) Should a court be able to require a reluctant local authority to bring proceedings under s. 31?

The restrictions of the High Court's inherent (wardship) jurisdiction are contained in s. 100 of the Children Act 1989, which was one of the most controversial parts of the legislation:

Restrictions on use of wardship jurisdiction
100.—(1) Section 7 of the Family Law Reform Act 1969 (which gives the High Court power to place a ward of court in the care, or under the supervision, of a local authority) shall cease to have effect.

(2) No court shall exercise the High Court's inherent jurisdiction with respect to children—
(a)   so as to require a child to be placed in the care, or put under the supervision, of a local authority;
(b)   so as to require a child to be accommodated by or on behalf of a local authority;
(c)   so as to make a child who is the subject of a care order a ward of court; or
(d)   for the purpose of conferring on any local authority power to determine any question which has arisen, or which may arise, in connection with any aspect of parental responsibility for a child.

(3) No application for any exercise of the court's inherent jurisdiction with respect to children may be made by a local authority unless the authority have obtained the leave of the court.

(4) The court may only grant leave if it is satisfied that—
(a)   the result which the authority wish to achieve could not be achieved through the making of any order of a kind to which subsection (5) applies; and

(b) there is reasonable cause to believe that if the court's inherent jurisdiction is not exercised with respect to the child he is likely to suffer significant harm.

(5) This subsection applies to any order—

(a) made otherwise than in the exercise of the court's inherent jurisdiction; and

(b) which the local authority is entitled to apply for (assuming, in the case of any application which may only be made with leave, that leave is granted).

These provisions mean that local authorities can only invoke the inherent jurisdiction in order to achieve a result which cannot be achieved under another provision of the Children Act 1989, and only then if there is reasonable cause to believe that the child is otherwise likely to suffer significant harm. These provisions were considered in the following case:

Devon County Council v S

[1994] Fam 169, [1995] 1 All ER 243, [1994] 3 WLR 183, [1994] 1 FLR 355, High Court, Family Division

The local authority was concerned because the mother of several children was prepared to treat a man with three convictions for sexual offences as a member of the family. The children were successfully protected by prohibited steps orders, until *Nottinghamshire County Council v P* (p. 733, above). Following that decision, the local authority attempted to achieve a similar result by an application under the inherent jurisdiction. The District Judge refused leave, and the local authority appealed.

Thorpe J: ... It is common ground between counsel that the terms of section 100(4)(b), namely, that there is reasonable cause to believe that if the court's inherent jurisdiction is not exercised with respect to the child he is likely to suffer significant harm, were satisfied. ... To my mind it is simple and not erroneous to conclude that the county council intends to invite the court to exercise its inherent jurisdiction to protect children rather than to have protective powers conferred on itself [contrary to section 100(2)(d)]. In relation to section 100(4)(a), [Mr. Meredith] submitted that the result at which the prospective application aimed was not one that could be achieved by any other route. Whilst the county council might apply for a care order under section 31, that would result in a far wider invasion of the mother's parental responsibility, with the risk of destabilisation of the children's parental care and with some risk of local stigma. In short, it might do more harm than good. He distinguished *Nottingham County Council v P* [1994] Fam 18, where the resident father constituted the risk to the children. That situation was classically managed by a care order, which would not necessarily be used to separate the children from their mother. But it would be quite inappropriate to protect the children from an external risk. Equally, Mr. Meredith submitted, a supervision order did not achieve the same result. All that would do would be to direct the functions of the mother, functions which she was already performing satisfactorily without direction. It did not control the only individual who required control, namely, Y. ... I cannot see how injunctions preventing an external adult from contacting or communicating with children at any time or in any place could be equated with either a care order or a supervision order. I did wonder why the possibility of the local authority protecting children from a potential abuser by invoking the inherent jurisdiction had not been considered in *Nottingham County Council v P*. Mrs. Gifford, who appeared for the father in that case throughout, said that it had been considered by the local authority to protect the eldest child who had left home. However, when mooted her client had offered an undertaking so that the point had not been argued. In respect of the younger children the local authority had relied exclusively on the prohibited steps application. I therefore conclude that the decision which I have reached is not at odds with the principles established by the judgment of Sir Stephen Brown P in *Nottingham County Council v P*. Any member of the family, or any other with a sufficient standing, might apply to the court to exercise its inherent power to protect these children. Where no one else invokes that protection, it seems to me quite wrong that the local authority should be excluded from doing so by a restrictive construction of section 100 of the Children Act 1989. I therefore allow the appeal and grant the leave sought.

Questions

(i) Why was the local authority in this case not criticised for failing to seek a care or supervision order, as the local authority in the *Nottinghamshire* case (p. 733, above) had been?

(ii) Could a local authority use the inherent jurisdiction to order a father to leave his home because he is a risk to his children? (See *Re S (minors) (inherent jurisdiction: ouster)* [1994] 1 FLR 623, cf *Pearson v Franklin* [1994] 2 All ER 137, [1994] 1 WLR 370, [1994] 1 FLR 246, CA.)

(iii) The Family Law Act 1996 amends the Children Act 1989, so that an exclusion requirement may be attached to an emergency protection order or an interim care order under ss. 38A and 44A of the Children Act (see p. 716, above). Why do these provisions not allow the court to exclude an abuser from the child's home indefinitely?

Further difficulties arise following another decision of the Court of Appeal:

Re H (prohibited steps order)
[1995] 4 All ER 110, [1995] 1 WLR 667, [1995] 1 FLR 638, Court of Appeal

A man, Mr J, sexually abused one of the mother's children while living with the mother. The local authority was granted a care order on one child and supervision orders on the rest. The judge placed a condition on the supervision orders that there be no contact with Mr J, and also made a prohibited steps order against the mother to prevent contact between Mr J and the children. He refused to make a prohibited steps order against Mr J, who was not a party to the proceedings. The children's guardian ad litem appealed.

Butler-Sloss LJ: ... The prohibited steps order appears to me directly to contravene s.9(5) since to make a prohibited steps order against the mother would achieve the same result as a contact order requiring the mother not to allow contact with Mr J and could be enforced in the same way. Equally, the condition made as part of the supervision order does not appear to come with the provisions of Sch. 3, Parts I and II. ... [A condition of no contact] cannot be imposed as part of a supervision order.

In my view a prohibited steps order which requires Mr J not to have nor to seek contact with the children does not contravene s.9(5). If a 'no contact order' had been made in this case to the mother the order would be directed at the mother as the subject of the order and the obligation would be placed upon her to prevent any contact by the children with Mr J. There could not be a 'no contact order' which would direct Mr J not to have nor seek contact with the four children since he does not live with the children. A contact order directed at the mother would not achieve the required result. ... With the best will in the world this mother could not protect her children going to or from school or at school or at play, nor could the school or even the police in the absence of any injunctive order directed at Mr J.

... [In *Nottinghamshire County Council v P* (p. 733, above)] the local authority sought to rely upon a prohibited steps order by the local authority in preference to applying for an order under Part IV of the Act. The objections expressed in the judgment of the court, with which I respectfully agree, to the application in private proceedings for a prohibited steps order, do not arise on this appeal. ... In the present case the local authority has obtained s.31 orders and the mother and the guardian ad litem of the children seek the prohibited steps order to meet a situation which cannot be achieved by a contact order.

Question

In the light of this decision, do you think that Thorpe J was right to find that s. 100(4)(a) was satisfied in *Devon County Council v S* (p. 735, above)?

A major area of concern that has exercised all those working in the field has been the ability of the courts to control the exercise of the powers of the local authorities. In *Nottinghamshire County Council v P* (p. 733, above) the court was concerned about its inability to force a local authority to make an application for a care and supervision order. In other cases, the concern relates to the inability to supervise the local authority after a care order has been made:

Re S (Children: Care Plan), ReW (Children: Care Plan)
[2002] UKHL 10, [2002] 2 AC 291, [2002] 2 All ER 192, House of Lords

We have already referred to the decision of the Court of Appeal in these cases in Chapter 10 (see p. 466, above) and included extracts from the judgment of Hale LJ. In the Court of Appeal, the court had decided, in a case concerning Bedfordshire County Council, that a court should have a wider discretion to make an interim, rather than a final care order where the care plan was inchoate or there were uncertainties that were capable of resolution. The Court of Appeal had held in relation to the second matter, from Torbay District Council, that essential milestones in the care plan should be assessed and 'starred'. The Court of Appeal had decided further that any failure to achieve a starred milestone within a reasonable time of a prescribed date should reactivate the interdisciplinary process. In those circumstances the guardian or the local authority should have the right to apply to the court for further directions.

In the House of Lords, Lord Nicholls of Birkenhead described the two innovations fashioned by the Court of Appeal in the following way:

First the court enunciated guidelines intended to give trial judges a wider discretion to make an interim care order rather than a final order. The second innovation was more radical. It concerns the position after the court has made a final order. The Court of Appeal propounded a new procedure, by which at the trial the essential milestones of a care plan would be identified and elevated to a 'starred status'.

This is Lord Nicholls' view of the 'starred status' idea:

23. Two preliminary points can be made at the outset. First, a cardinal principle of the Children Act is that when the court makes a care order it becomes the duty of the local authority designated by the order to receive the child into its care while the order remains in force. So long as the care order is in force the authority has parental responsibility for the child. The authority also has power to decide the extent to which a parent of the child may meet his responsibility for him: section 33. An authority might, for instance, not permit parents to change the school of a child living at home. While a care order is in force the court's powers, under its inherent jurisdiction, are expressly excluded: section 100(2)(c) and (d). Further, the court may not make a contact order, a prohibited steps order or a specific issue order: section 9(1).

24. There are limited exceptions to this principle of non-intervention by the court in the authority's discharge of its parental responsibility for a child in its care under a care order. The court retains jurisdiction to decide disputes about contact with children in care: section 34. The court may discharge a care order, either on an application made for the purpose under section 39 or as a consequence of making a residence order (sections 9(1) and 91(1)). The High Court's judicial review jurisdiction also remains available.

25. These exceptions do not detract significantly from the basic principle. The Act delineated the boundary of responsibility with complete clarity. Where a care order is made the responsibility for the child's care is with the authority rather than the court. The court retains no supervisory role, monitoring the authority's discharge of its responsibilities. That was the intention of Parliament.

26. Consistently with this, in *Kent County Council v C* [1993] Fam 57 Ewbank J decided that the court has no power to add to a care order a direction to the authority that the child's guardian ad litem should be allowed to have a continuing involvement, with a view to his applying to the court in due course if thought appropriate. In *In re T (A Minor) (Care Order:*

Conditions) [1994] 2 FLR 423 the Court of Appeal rightly approved this decision and held that the court has no power to impose conditions in a care order. There the condition sought by the child's guardian was that the child should reside at home.

27. This cardinal principle of the Children Act represented a change in the law. Before the Children Act came into operation the court, in exercise of its wardship jurisdiction, retained power in limited circumstances to give directions to a local authority regarding children in its care. The limits of this jurisdiction were considered by your Lordships' House in *A v Liverpool City Council* [1982] AC 363 and *In re W (A Minor)(Wardship: Jurisdiction)* [1985] AC 791. The change brought about by the Children Act gave effect to a policy decision on the appropriate division of responsibilities between the courts and local authorities. This was one of the matters widely discussed at the time. A report made to ministers by an interdepartmental working party 'Review of Child Care Law' (September 1985) drew attention to some of the policy considerations. The particular strength of the courts lies in the resolution of disputes: its ability to hear all sides of a case, to decide issues of fact and law, and to make a firm decision on a particular issue at a particular time. But a court cannot have day to day responsibility for a child. The court cannot deliver the services which may best serve a child's needs. Unlike a local authority, a court does not have close, personal and continuing knowledge of the child. The court cannot respond with immediacy and informality to practical problems and changed circumstances as they arise. Supervision by the court would encourage 'drift' in decision making, a perennial problem in children cases. Nor does a court have the task of managing the financial and human resources available to a local authority for dealing with all children in need in its area. The authority must manage these resources in the best interests of all the children for whom it is responsible.

28. The Children Act, embodying what I have described as a cardinal principle, represents the assessment made by Parliament of the division of responsibility which would best promote the interests of children within the overall care system. The court operates as the gateway into care, and makes the necessary care order when the threshold conditions are satisfied and the court considers a care order would be in the best interests of the child. That is the responsibility of the court. Thereafter the court has no continuing role in relation to the care order. Then it is the responsibility of the local authority to decide how the child should be cared for.

29. My second preliminary point is this. The Children Act has now been in operation for ten years. Over the last six years there has been a steady increase in the number of children looked after by local authorities in England and Wales. At present there are 36,400 children accommodated under care orders, compared with 28,500 in 1995, an increase of 27 percent. In addition local authorities provide accommodation for nearly 20,000 children under section 20 orders (children in need of accommodation). A decade's experience in the operation of the Act, at a time of increasing demands on local authorities, has shown that there are occasions when, with the best will in the world, local authorities' discharge of their parental responsibilities has not been satisfactory. The system does not always work well. Shortages of money, of suitable trained staff and of suitable foster carers and prospective adopters for difficult children are among the reasons. There have been delays in placing children in accordance with their care plans, unsatisfactory breakdown rates and delays in finding substitute placements.

30. But the problems are more deep-seated than shortage of resources. In November 1997 the Government published Sir William Utting's review of safeguards for children living away from home. Mr Frank Dobson, then Secretary of State for Health, summarised his reaction to the report:

'It covers the lives of children whose home circumstances were so bad that those in authority, to use the jargon, took them into care. The report reveals that in far too many cases not enough care was taken. Elementary safeguards were not in place or not enforced. Many children were harmed rather than helped. The review reveals that these failings were not just the fault of individuals – though individuals were at fault. It reveals the failure of a whole system.'

31. In autumn 1998 the Government published its response to the children's safeguards review (Cm 4105) and launched its 'Quality Protects' programme, aimed at improving the public care system for children. Conferences have also been held, and many research studies undertaken, both private and public, on particular aspects of the problems. Some of the problems were discussed at the bi-annual President's Interdisciplinary Conference on family law 1997, attended by judges, child psychiatrists, social workers, social services personnel and other experts. The proceedings of the conference were subsequently published in book form, '*Divided Duties*' (1998). The sharpness of the divide between the court's powers before and after the making of a care order attracted criticism. The matters discussed included the need for a care plan to be open to review by the court in exceptional cases. One suggestion was that a court review could be triggered by failure to implement 'starred' key factors in the care plan

within specified time-scales. The guardian ad litem would be the appropriate person to intervene.

32. This was the source of the innovation which found expression in the judgments of the Court of Appeal in the present appeals. The House was informed by counsel that the starred milestones guidance given by the Court of Appeal was not canvassed in argument before the court. This guidance appeared for the first time in the judgments of the court.

33. The jurisprudential route by which the Court of Appeal found itself able to bring about this development was primarily by recourse to section 3 of the Human Rights Act. Hale LJ said, at paragraphs 79-80:

> 'Where elements of the care plan are so fundamental that there is a real risk of a breach of Convention rights if they are not fulfilled, and where there is some reason to fear that they may not be fulfilled, it must be justifiable *to read into the Children Act* a power in the court to require a report on progress. ... the court would require a report, either to the court or to CAFCASS ... who could then decide whether it was appropriate to return the case to court. ... [W]hen making a care order, the court is being asked to interfere in family life. If it perceives that the consequence of doing so will be to put at risk the Convention rights of either the parents or the child, the court *should be able* to impose this very limited requirement as a condition of its own interference.' (My emphasis.)

Section 3 of the Human Rights Act

34. The judgments in the Court of Appeal are a clear and forceful statement of the continuing existence of serious problems in this field. In the nature of things, courts are likely to see more of the cases which go wrong. But the view, widespread among family judges, is that all too often local authorities' discharge of their parental responsibilities falls short of an acceptable standard. A disturbing instance can be found in the recent case of *F v London Borough of Lambeth* (28 September 2001, unreported). Munby J said, in paragraph 38 of his judgment, that the 'blunt truth is that in this case the state has failed these parents and these boys'.

35. It is entirely understandable that the Court of Appeal should seek some means to alleviate these problems: some means by which the courts may assist children where care orders have been made but subsequently, for whatever reason, care plans have not been implemented as envisaged and, as a result, the welfare of the children is being prejudiced. This is entirely understandable. The courts, notably through their wardship jurisdiction, have long discharged an invaluable role in safeguarding the interests of children. But the question before the House is much more confined. The question is whether the courts have power to introduce into the working of the Children Act a range of rights and liabilities not sanctioned by Parliament.

36. On this I have to say at once, respectfully but emphatically, that I part company with the Court of Appeal. I am unable to agree that the court's introduction of a 'starring system' can be justified as a legitimate exercise in interpretation of the Children Act in accordance with section 3 of the Human Rights Act. Even if the Children Act is inconsistent with articles 6 or 8 of the Convention, which is a question I will consider later, section 3 does not in this case have the effect suggested by the Court of Appeal.

37. Section 3(1) provides:

> 'So far as it is possible to do so, primary legislation ... must be read and given effect in a way which is compatible with the Convention rights.'

This is a powerful tool whose use is obligatory. It is not an optional canon of construction. Nor is its use dependent on the existence of ambiguity. Further, the section applies retrospectively. So far as it is possible to do so, primary legislation 'must be read and given effect' to in a way which is compatible with Convention rights. This is forthright, uncompromising language.

38. But the reach of this tool is not unlimited. Section 3 is concerned with interpretation. This is apparent from the opening words of section 3(1): 'so far as it is possible to do so'. The side heading of the section is 'Interpretation of legislation'. Section 4 (power to make a declaration of incompatibility) and, indeed, section 3(2)(b) presuppose that not all provisions in primary legislation can be rendered Convention compliant by the application of section 3(1). The existence of this limit on the scope of section 3(1) has already been the subject of judicial confirmation, more than once: see, for instance, Lord Woolf CJ in *Poplar Housing and Regeneration Community Association Ltd v Donoghue* [2001] 3 WLR 183, 204, para 75 and Lord Hope of Craighead in *R v Lambert* [2001] 3 WLR 206, 233-235, paras 79-81.

39. In applying section 3 courts must be ever mindful of this outer limit. The Human Rights Act reserves the amendment of primary legislation to Parliament. By this means the Act seeks to preserve parliamentary sovereignty. The Act maintains the constitutional boundary. Interpretation of statutes is a matter for the courts; the enactment of statutes, and the amendment of statutes, are matters for Parliament.

Lord Nicholls went on state that the starring system is judicial innovation that passes 'well beyond the boundary of interpretation'. He could see no provision in the 1989 Act which lends itself to the interpretation that Parliament was conferring a supervisory function on the court after a care order had been made. He said that the Court of Appeal's approach constituted an amendment of the 1989 Act, not its interpretation. After considering the important issues of ss. 7 and 8 of the Human Rights Act 1998 and any possible incompatibility with Art. 8(2) and Art. 6 of the European Convention on Human Rights (which he rejected), he turned his attention to interim care orders:

Interim care orders

89. I turn to the other 'reversionary application' of the Children Act adumbrated by the Court of Appeal. This concerns the extended use of interim care orders. The source of the court's power to make a interim care order is section 38. The power exists when an application for a care order or a supervision order is adjourned (section 38(1)(a)) or the court has given a direction to a local authority under section 37 to undertake an investigation of a child's circumstances (section 38(1)(b)). Section 38 contains tight limits on the period for which an interim care order has effect: eight weeks initially, thereafter four weeks. The circumstances in which an interim care order ceases to have effect include also the disposal of the application for a care order or a supervision order, in both section 38(1)(a) and section 38(1)(b) cases.

90. From a reading of section 38 as a whole it is abundantly clear that the purpose of an interim care order, so far as presently material, is to enable the court to safeguard the welfare of a child until such time as the court is in a position to decide whether or not it is in the best interest of the child to make a care order. When that time arrives depends on the circumstances of the case and is a matter for the judgment of the trial judge. That is the general, guiding principle. The corollary to this principle is that an interim care order is not intended to be used as a means by which the court may continue to exercise a supervisory role over the local authority in cases where it is in the best interests of a child that a care order should be made.

91. An interim care order, thus, is a temporary 'holding' measure. Inevitably, time is needed before an application for a care order is ready for decision. Several parties are usually involved: parents, the child's guardian, the local authority, perhaps others. Evidence has to be prepared, parents and other people interviewed, investigations may be required, assessments made, and the local authority circular LAC(99)29. Although the Children Act itself makes no mention of a care plan, in practice this is a document of key importance. It enables the court and everyone else to know, and consider, the local authority's plans for the future of the child if a care order is made.

92. When a local authority formulates a care plan in connection with an application for a care order, there are bound to be uncertainties. Even the basic shape of the future life of the child may be far from clear. Over the last ten years problems have arisen about how far courts should go in attempting to resolve these uncertainties before making a care order and passing responsibility to the local authority. Once a final care order is made, the resolution of the uncertainties will be a matter for the authority, not the court.

93. In terms of legal principle one type of uncertainty is straightforward. This is the case where the uncertainty needs to be resolved before the court can decide whether it is in the best interests of the child to make a care order at all. In *C v Solihull Metropolitan Borough Council* [1993] 1 FLR 290 the court could not decide whether a care order was in the best interests of a child, there a 'battered baby', without knowing the result of a parental assessment. Ward J made an appropriate interim order. In such a case the court should finally dispose of the matter only when the material facts are as clearly known as can be hoped. Booth J adopted a similar approach, for a similar reason, in *Hounslow London Borough Council v A* [1993] 1 FLR 702.

94. More difficult, as a matter of legal principle, are cases where it is obvious that a care order is in the best interests of the child but the immediate way ahead thereafter is unsatisfactorily obscure. These cases exemplify a problem, or a 'tension', inherent in the scheme of the Children Act. What should the judge do when a care order is clearly in the best interests of the child but the judge does not approve of the care plan? This judicial dilemma was descried by Balcombe LJ in *In re S and D (Children: Powers of Court)* [1995] 2 FLR 456, 464, perhaps rather too bleakly, as the judge having to choose between 'the lesser of two evils'.

95. In this context there are sometimes uncertainties whose nature is such that they are suitable for immediate resolution, in whole or in part, by the court in the course of disposing of the care order application. The uncertainty may be of such a character that it can, and should, be resolved so far as possible before the court proceeds to make the care order. Then, a limited

period of 'planned and purposeful' delay can readily be justified as the sensible and practical way to deal with an existing problem.

96. An instance of this occurred in *In re C H (Care or Interim Care Order)* [1998] 1 FLR 402. In that case the mother had pleaded guilty to causing grievous bodily harm to the child. The judge was intensely worried by the sharp divergence of professional view on placement. The local authority cautiously favoured rehabilitation. The child's guardian ad litem believed adoption was the realistic way to promote the child's future welfare. The judge made the care order without hearing any expert evidence on the disputed issue. The local authority would itself obtain expert advice, and then reconsider the question of placement. The Court of Appeal (Kennedy and Thorpe LJJ) held that the fact that a care order was the inevitable outcome should not have deflected the judge from hearing expert evidence on this issue. Even if the issue could not be finally resolved before a care order was made, it was obviously sensible and desirable that, in the circumstances of the case, the local authority should have the benefit of the judge's observations on the point.

97. Frequently the case is on the other side of this somewhat imprecise line. Frequently the uncertainties involved in a care plan will have to be worked out after a care order has been made and while the plan is being implemented. This was so in the case which is the locus classicus on this subject: *In re J (Minors) (Care: Care Plan)* [1994] 1 FLR 253. There the care plan envisaged placing the children in short-term foster placements for up to a year. Then a final decision would be made on whether to place the children permanently away from the mother. Rehabilitation was not ruled out if the mother showed herself amenable to treatment. Wall J said, at page 265:

> 'there are cases (of which this is one) in which the action which requires to be taken in the interests of children necessarily involves steps into the unknown ... provided the court is satisfied that the local authority is alert to the difficulties which may arise in the execution of the care plan, the function of the court is not to seek to oversee the plan but to entrust its execution to the local authority.'

In that case the uncertain outcome of the treatment was a matter to be worked out after a care order was made, not before. The Court of Appeal decision in *In re L (Sexual Abuse: Standard of Proof)* [1996] 1 FLR 116 was another case of this type: see Butler-Sloss LJ, at page 125E-H. So also was the decision of the Court of Appeal in *In re R (Care Proceedings: Adjournment)* [1998] 2 FLR 390.

98. These are all instances of cases where important issues of uncertainty were known to exist before a care order was made. Quite apart from known uncertainties, an element of future uncertainty is necessarily inherent in the very nature of a care plan. The best laid plans 'gang aft a-gley'. These are matters for decisions by the local authority, if and when they arise. A local authority must always respond appropriately to changes, of varying degrees of predictability, which from time to time are bound to occur after a care order has been made and while the care plan is being implemented. No care plan can ever be regarded as set out in stone.

99. Despite all the inevitable uncertainties, when deciding whether to make a care order the court should normally have before it a care plan which is sufficiently firm and particularised for all concerned to have a reasonably clear picture of the likely way ahead for the child for the foreseeable future. The degree of firmness to be expected, as well as the amount of detail in the plan, will vary from case to case depending on how far the local authority can foresee what will be best for the child at that time. This is necessarily so. But making a care order is always a serious interference in the lives of the child and his parents. Although article 8 contains no explicit procedural requirements, the decision making process leading to a care order must be fair and such as to afford due respect to the interests safeguarded by article 8: see *TP and KM v United Kingdom* [2001] 2 FLR 549, 569, paragraph 72. If the parents and the child's guardian are to have a fair and adequate opportunity to make representations to the court on whether a care order should be made, the care plan must be appropriately specific.

100. Cases vary so widely that it is impossible to be more precise about the test to be applied by a court when deciding whether to continue interim relief rather than proceed to make a care order. It would be foolish to attempt to be more precise. One further general point may be noted. When postponing a decision on whether to make a care order a court will need to have in mind the general statutory principle that any delay in determining issues relating to a child's upbringing is likely to prejudice the child's welfare: section 1(2) of the Children Act.

101. In the Court of Appeal Thorpe LJ, at paragraph 29, expressed the view that in certain circumstances the judge at the trial should have a 'wider discretion' to make an interim care order: 'where the care plan seems inchoate or where the passage of a relatively brief period seems bound to see the fulfilment of some event or process vital to planning and deciding the future'. In an appropriate case, a judge must be free to defer making a care order until he is satisfied that the way ahead 'is no longer obscured by an uncertainty that is neither inevitable nor chronic'.

102. As I see it, the analysis I have set out above adheres faithfully to the scheme of the Children Act and conforms to the procedural requirements of article 8 of the Convention. At the same time it affords trial judges the degree of flexibility Thorpe LJ is rightly concerned they should have. Whether this represents a small shift in emphasis from the existing case law may be a moot point. What is more important is that, in the words of Wall J in *Re J*, the court must always maintain a proper balance between the need to satisfy itself about the appropriateness of the care plan and the avoidance of 'over-zealous investigation into matters which are properly within the administrative discretion of the local authority'. This balance is a matter for the good sense of the tribunal, assisted by the advocates appearing before it: see [1994] 1 FLR 253, 262.

Questions

(i)   Where does all of this leave dissatisfied parents (and children) when confronted by a local authority that is unwilling, or possibly unable, to implement its plan?

(ii) If there is 'drift' can you think of any existing mechanisms that can be prayed in aid? (Look at ss. 22 and 26 of the Children Act 1989 and ss. 7 and 8 of the Human Rights Act 1998.)

(iii) Would you be better off in Wales?

(iv) Why is it appropriate for a court to attach conditions to a s. 8 order but not a care order?

(v)   How can the court decide whether a care order is in a child's interests, if it cannot be sure whether the child will be rehabilitated with the parents, or placed in a children's home, with a succession of short-term foster-parents, or with a long-term substitute family?

We end this chapter with a quote from the speech of Lord Mackay of Clashfern in *Re S and Re W* where, at para. 112, he said: 'I would strongly urge the Government and Parliament give urgent attention to the problems...so that we do not continue failing some of our most vulnerable children.' So the story of Jasmine Beckford, with which we opened this chapter, is sadly not a story of another age. You may well ask, having read this chapter, what else can be done to prevent the new century from being marred by more tragedies of this kind.

Bibliography

13.1   Children in need

We quoted from:

Brent Council, *A Child in Trust – The Report of the Panel of Inquiry into the Circumstances surrounding the Death of Jasmine Beckford* (Chairman: L. Blom-Cooper QC) (1985) London, London Borough of Brent.

Department of Health, *Children in Need 2000 National Results*, executive summary (2002) London, Department of Health.

J. Packman, with J. Randall and N. Jacques, *Who Needs Care? Social-Work Decisions about Children* (1986) Oxford, Basil Blackwell, pp. 194–197.

Department of Health, *Bulletin 2001/26* (2001) London, Department of Health, table 4, fig. 4, table M.

Department of Health, *Children Act Report for 2001* (2002) Department of Health, p. 24.

J. Renvoize, *Children in Danger* (1974) London, Routledge and Kegan Paul; (1975) Harmondsworth, Penguin Books, pp. 20, 24.

Report of the Inquiry into Child Abuse in Cleveland 1987 (Chairman: The Hon. Mrs Justice Butler-Sloss D.B.E.) (Cm. 412) (1988) London, HMSO, p. 4.

13.2 Out of the Poor Law

We quoted from:

'Whose Children? Wards of State or Charity' Letter to *The Times*, 15 July 1944.

J.S. Heywood, *Children in Care: The Development of the Service for the Deprived Child* (3rd edn, 1978) London, Routledge and Kegan Paul, pp. 7–10, 92–93.

. *Report by Sir Walter Monckton, KCMC, KCVO, MC, KC, on the circumstances which led to the boarding-out of Denis and Terence O'Neill at Bank Farm, Minsterley, and the steps taken to supervise their welfare* (Cmd. 6636) (1945) London, HMSO, paras. 2, 3, and 54.

Report of the Care of Children Committee (Chairman: Miss M. Curtis) (Cmd. 6922) (1946) London, HMSO, paras. 138, 140, 144, 154, 171, 427, 441, 443, 447.

J.M. Eekelaar, R. Dingwall and T. Murray, 'Victims or Threats? Children in Care Proceedings' [1982] Journal of Social Welfare Law 67, pp. 71–78.

J. Packman, *The Child's Generation: Child Care Policy in Britain* (2nd edn, 1981) Oxford, Basil Blackwell, pp. 57–59, 156, 161.

Report of the Inquiry into Child Abuse in Cleveland 1987 (Chairman: The Hon. Mrs Justice Butler-Sloss D.B.E.) (Cm. 412) (1988) London, HMSO, pp. 4–9.

Department of Health, *Child Protection – Messages from Research* (1995) London, HMSO, pp. 15, 25–29, 32, 54–55.

Report of the Tribunal of Inquiry into the abuse of children in care in the former county council areas of Gwynedd and Clwyd since 1974 'Lost in Care' (Chairman: Sir Ronald Waterhouse), HC 201 (2000) London, The Stationery Office, pp. 844–851.

Additional reading

Department of Health, *Quality Protects*, Circular LAC (98)28 (1998).

J. Masson, 'From Curtis to Waterhouse: State Care and Child Protection in the UK 1945-2000' in S.N. Katz, J. Eekelaar and M. Maclean, *Cross Currents* (2000), Oxford, Oxford University Press, pp. 565–587.

W. Utting, *People Like Us* (2000) London, The Stationery Office.

13.3 Services for children and families

We quoted from:

DHSS, *Review of Child Care Law – Report to Ministers of an Interdepartmental Working Party* (1985) London, HMSO, para. 7.16.

DHSS and others, *The Law on Child Care and Family Services* (Cm. 62) (1987) London, HMSO, paras. 16–18.

Department of Health, *Working Together – A guide to arrangements for inter agency co-operation for the protection of children from abuse* (1991) London, HMSO, para. 1.4.

Department of Health, *Children's Homes National Minimum Standards* (2002) London, The Stationery Office, Standards 7, 8, 16, and 22.

J. Packman, *The Child's Generation: Child Care Policy in Britain* (2nd edn, 1981) Oxford, Basil Blackwell, p. 156.

The Pindown Experience and the Protection of Children: The Report of the Staffordshire Child Care Enquiry (Allan Levy QC and Barbara Kahan) (1991) London, HMSO, paras. 11.17–11.35.

Additional reading

Department of Health, *Modernising Social Services* (Cm. 4167) (1998).

H. Ward, *Looking after Children: Research into Practice* (1995) London, HMSO.

A. Levy (ed.), *Refocus on Child Abuse* (1994) London, Hawksmere.

13.4   Child protection inquiries

We quoted from:

Department of Health, *Working Together to Safeguard Children* (1999) London, The Stationery Office, paras 2.3–2.7; 5.6–5.7; 5.53-5.55; 5.57–5.58; 5.61–5.63; 5.64-5.70; 5.90–5.95.

DHSS and others, *The Law on Child Care and Family Services* (Cm. 62) (1987) London, HMSO, paras 42–43.

Department of Health, *Child Protection – Messages from Research* (1995) London, HMSO, pp. 15, 25–29, 32, 54–55.

Department of Health and others, *Child Protection – Medical Responsibilities* (1994) London, Department of Health, paras. 6.1, 4.5–4.6.

Report of the Inquiry into Child Abuse in Cleveland 1987 (Chairman: The Hon. Mrs Justice Butler-Sloss D.B.E.) (Cm. 412) (1988) London, HMSO, paras. 12.1–12.42.

Additional reading

R. Sinclair and R. Bullock, *Learning from past experience: a review of serious case reviews* (2000) London, Department of Health.

13.5   Assessment and protection orders

We quoted from:

Department of Health, *Guidance and Regulations on the Children Act 1989*, vol. 1, *Court Orders* (1991) London, HMSO, paras: 1.4, 3.8, 5.11.1–5.11.2, 5.14.7, 6.1, 6.3, 6.10, 6.13, 6.15, 6.18, 6.24–6.28, 6.36–6.40, 6.44, 6.52–6.54.

Department of Health, *Working Together – A guide to arrangements for inter agency co-operation for the protection of children from abuse* (1991) London, HMSO, para. 3.8.

Report of the Inquiry into Child Abuse in Cleveland 1987 (Chairman: The Hon. Mrs Justice Butler-Sloss D.B.E.) (Cm. 412) (1988) London, HMSO, paras. 10.6–10.13.

Additional reading

Dame Margaret Booth, Report on the Delays in Children Act proceedings (1996) London, Lord Chancellor's Department.
Lord Chancellor's Department, *Scoping Study on Delay in Children Act Cases* (2002) London, Lord Chancellor's Department.
Department of Health, *Framework for the Assessment of Children in Need and their Families* (2000) London, Department of Health.

13.6 The threshold test

We quoted from:

DHSS, *Review of Child Care Law – Report to Ministers of an Interdepartmental Working Party* (1985) London, HMSO, paras. 15.12, 15.14–15.16, 15.18, 15.20, 15.23, 15.24.

Additional reading

Dame Margaret Booth, *Report on the Delays in Children Act proceedings* (1996) London, Lord Chancellor's Department.
Sir William Utting, *People Like Us* (1997) London, The Stationery Office.

13.7 The choice of final order

We quoted from:

DHSS, Review of Child Care Law – Report to Ministers of an Interdepartmental Working Party (1985) London, HMSO, paras. 18.5–18.7, 18.9, 18.15.

Additional reading

Department of Health, *Children's Safeguards Review: Choosing with Care*, HSC 1998/212 (1998) London, Department of Health.
Department of Health, *Quality Protects*, (1998) Circular LAC (98) (28).
M. Thorpe and E. Cooke, *Divided Duties* (1998) Bristol, Family Law.
R. White 'Planning for Children in Care' in Stephen Cretney (ed.), *Family Law Essays for the new Millennium* (2000) Bristol, Family Law, pp. 143–148.

Chapter 14

The 'permanency' principle: who are my family?

14.1 The 'permanency' principle

14.2 The law on maintaining family links

14.3 Legal options for relatives and other carers

14.4 Adoption as a child care resource

14.5 Adoption: an open or shut case?

14.6 The cross-cultural dimension

Former foster child A: It was only recently I was told that my natural parents could have removed me at any time if they wanted to. Even now when I think of it I shudder. ... For me they would have been total strangers. Why remove me when I was so happy? I have met my natural mother recently and I see her from time to time. There is no bond between us. My 'mum' is my foster mum and my 'dad' is my foster dad. If I call my natural mother 'mum' when I meet her it is just for saving face. ...

Former foster child D: I must have been 7 when I went to live with my foster parents. They were the second family I went to. The first family went abroad after promising to take me with them. They didn't and it broke my heart at the time. ... The [foster parents] had two of their own and another foster child. Somehow I never felt I belonged there. We foster children did not fit in very well. I cannot say that I developed much attachment to them. My foster mother often threatened to send me back to the Corporation. Sometimes she would ring them but they would make her change her mind. I suppose I was difficult too, and I would hark back or argue. She would then smack me and send me to bed ... I could be nasty and so could my foster mother ... I left at 17 when our quarrels became worse, and I went to live in a hostel.

These telling quotations come from John Triseliotis's study, 'Growing Up in Foster Care and After' (1980). The foster parent's position is no easier, as this quotation from a more recent study by Gillian Schofield and others of *Growing Up in Foster Care* (2000) shows:

We've got a lot closer relationship, especially since we've known she's staying here permanently. Because I always held something back because I thought she was going. And I also didn't want Roxanne to get too close to me so that she had to go away to someone else because that would have been another break in her life. Not just for my own sake but for Roxanne's sake. I kept a little bit of distance with her. Now I know she's staying permanently we don't need to do that anymore because there's not going to be a move.

Whenever children have to be looked after away from home for any length of time, for whatever reasons, three questions arise. First, is the ultimate plan that

746

they should go back home eventually, as most children do, or is it that they should stay away permanently? Secondly, if they are to stay away, what should be the legal basis on which they do so – fostering, adoption or something in between? Thirdly, what in any event should be their links with their family of origin? We shall look first at the development of social work thinking and research on these issues, then at how these have affected the legal position of relatives and foster carers, and then at the controversies and dilemmas arising from the development of adoption as a child care resource.

14.1 The 'permanency' principle

The evolution of the 'permanency' principle in child care began with the problems experienced with foster care, summed up by Jean Packman in *The Child's Generation* (1981):

Originally, fostering had frequently been seen as an *alternative* to parental care, when the latter had proved inadequate. Before children's departments existed many children who were fostered lost all contact with their natural families and the fostering became a 'de facto' adoption ... The Children Act [1948], moving away from this position, stipulated that children must be rehabilitated with their own families, when this was consistent with their welfare, and ... the concept was increasingly applied. Though fostering was the favoured method of care, promising as it did a 'natural' upbringing and the warmth and intimate relationships that children need, it was now more often a short-term or impermanent arrangement, incorporating a far greater degree of sharing. If children were to be rehabilitated, they must be kept in close touch with their natural parents. ... What was expected of foster parents became at once more subtle and more difficult. They must confer on the child all the benefits of loving family care, but should not seek to replace the parents in his affections. Their compassion and acceptance must be extended from the child himself, to his parents as well – even where the latter seemed 'to blame' for some of his past deprivations. They should act toward him as a good parent, yet give him up when the department judged the time to be ripe.

If it was difficult for the foster carers, it was even more difficult for the children, as Jane Rowe and her colleagues point out in *Long-Term Foster Care* (1984):

Being a foster child is not easy. The study children have revealed something of the stresses of having to answer questions, of feeling different and of anxieties and unanswered questions about the past and the future. ... Our findings confirm those of Triseliotis (1983) and of Fanshel and Shinn (1978). Summing up the differences between young adults who had been adopted as older children and young adults who had been fostered, Triseliotis concluded:

'Compared to those who grew up in long-term fostering, adoptees in general appeared more confident and secure with fewer doubts about themselves and about their capacity to cope with life ... In spite of the strong psychological bonds between those fostered and their foster parents, the ambiguous nature of the arrangement seemed to have a qualitative impact on the former's sense of identity.'

A very similar conclusion is drawn by Fanshel and Shinn (1978) though they, too, are tentative. At the end of their massive five-year longitudinal study of 624 children, these authors support the view that children should be afforded permanency in their living arrangements if at all possible, though they hasten to add that they do not take this position on the basis of their data but because:

'We are not completely sure that continued tenure in foster care over extended periods is not in itself harmful to children ... We fear that in the inner recesses of his heart, a child who is not living with his own family or who is not adopted may come to think of himself as being less than first-rate, as an unwanted human being.'

... The inescapable conclusion of our findings is that many long-term foster children would be better off if they were adopted by their foster parents, not because being fostered is so bad but because it is not quite good enough. However, one must hasten to add that it would be a serious mistake to assume that *all* long-term foster children could or should be adopted. ...

Distinguishing which children should be adopted is not easy and cannot be done by any general rule about length of stay or even on the basis of parental contact, though both may be useful guides. In our study we had examples of children who were in touch with parents but who nevertheless wanted very much to be adopted. There were a few children who had no parental contact who, nevertheless felt a strong sense of natural family identity. For them, adoption would have seemed like an intrusion. ... there are also foster parents who do not want to adopt even though they have a strong bond to the child and are committed to providing a permanent home. A crucial issue is whether or not the child *feels* secure.

The development of thinking about 'permanency' is described by Judith Stone in *Making Positive Moves – Developing Short-term Fostering Services* (1995):

Rethinking policy

A number of worrying themes had emerged in the early part of the 1970s. George's study [1970] confirmed that high levels of foster placement breakdown continued. Rowe and Lambert, in *Children Who Wait* [1973] had highlighted the problem of 'drift' in care and the deficiency in planning for children, and showed that policies of prevention and rehabilitation were not working as people had hoped. An estimated 7,000 children were adrift in residential care needing substitute families. At the same time the tragedy of the death of Maria Colwell, abused and killed by her step-father on her return to the care of her birth mother after spending much of her early childhood in foster care, emphasised other personal costs that might be paid by some children as a consequence of policies that emphasised prevention or rehabilitation as the only goals in child care. The result was a rethink of policy which, occurring at the same time as the Houghton Committee, influenced the Children Act 1975, and paved the way for more assertive planning for children entering the care system.

In 1973 the first of two books by Goldstein, Freud and Solnit [*Beyond the Best Interests of the Child*, 1973; see p. 575, above] raised the issue of 'psychological parenting' and its relation to the whole concept of 'permanence'. By 'psychological parenting' was meant the permanent and exclusive relationship between a child and his or her 'parent' (irrespective of blood ties) which was seen as all important for the satisfactory emotional growth and development of a child.
...

Other studies stressed permanence as a developmental need and in consequence as a 'right'. Rowe and Lambert [1973] made apparent the harmful effects when separation resulted in limbo and drift:

> 'It is our conviction that no child can grow emotionally while in limbo, never really belonging to anyone except on a temporary and ill-defined or partial basis. He cannot invest except in a minimal way (just enough to survive) if tomorrow the relationship may be severed. ... To grow the child needs at least the promise of permanency in relationships and some continuity of environment.'

Later research produced equally worrying findings: children stayed in temporary foster care for long periods; children moved frequently between placements; the state of being a foster child was likely to destroy their relationships with their birth family; and children themselves found the temporary nature of their foster home a source of deep anxiety and concern.

The 1970s–1980s: permanency planning – the least detrimental alternative
...

'Permanency planning' was a new approach to the provision of care for children, which had been developed in the USA (where over half of all foster children had typically been in temporary care for two years or more) in response to problems similar to those being experienced in the UK. This had shaped the philosophy, goals and services of child welfare agencies, re-forming them to accept the primacy of the needs of children over the 'blood tie'.
...

The concept of permanency planning is built on a number of basic beliefs. It stresses the value of rearing children in a family setting, based on a belief in the primacy of the family in the child's growth and development, and in the continuing need of each human being to belong to a family and the significance of the family in 'human connectedness'. The primacy of the parent–child attachment is part of the rationale behind permanency planning, which also emphasises the importance of stability in living arrangements, and of continuity, stability and mutuality in parent–child relationships.

...

Permanency planning also implies the right of every child to be provided with a stable home, quickly and with as few moves or temporary situations as possible. Adcock and White [1980] expressed this belief very firmly: 'No child should be deprived of an opportunity to grow up either in his own family or in a new family which he can legally call his own, unless there is a very strong reason to justify this.'

...

Permanency planning – the response in the UK

The most novel aspect of these policies was the placement for adoption of children who had previously been considered unadoptable, principally older children and those with physical and mental disabilities, or emotional and behaviour difficulties [Thoburn, 1990]. ...

...When permanency policies became part of child care practice in the UK it was, according to Thoburn, 'the adoption aspects of permanence which were to the fore, at the expense of preventive and rehabilitative aspects'. Such policies, it was hoped, would minimise 'drift' in unplanned care and cut down the numbers of young people leaving care at 18 who were attached to neither their birth families nor to substitute families. It aimed to give them, according to Triseliotis [1983], 'a family for life, with its network of support systems not only for them but also for their future children'.

The 1975 Children Act made adoption a more likely alternative for some children in long-term care, and both fostering and adoption were seen as options in a range of substitute family placements. In the UK there had always been the possibility that children in long-term foster care could be adopted by their foster carers, but the 1975 Children Act strengthened the position of foster families considering adoption. As adoption was to be considered an available option for a greater number of children in care, the adoption of children whose parents did not request it, and who might actively oppose it, became a possibility. Such an extension of the ranks of 'adoptable' children was, and still is, highly controversial.

...

The unacceptable face of permanence

Since the mid 1970s permanence had been seen predominantly to refer to substitute family care. In the mid 1980s it was, however, acknowledged that the emphasis upon adoption had perhaps gone too far. The Report of the House of Commons Social Services Committee [1984] regretted this trend towards equating 'permanence' with adoption:

> 'There is at the moment considerable confusion over the significance of the search for permanence in a placement. It should not have become a synonym for adoption. Adoption is only one eventual outcome among many. It is however, the most permanent possible outcome for a child unable to live with his natural family.'

Permanence within the child's birth family did not seem to be as energetically pursued. ...

Rowe [1983] surveying foster care in the eighties, suggested that one of the benefits of planning for permanence was the urgency and emphasis it brought to providing services to birth parents which would enable them to resume care of their children before they had put down roots elsewhere and developed bonds with psychological parents. Agencies which worked hard to achieve permanence reported a significant increase in rehabilitation of children to their birth families.

However, there were serious doubts as to whether enough was being done in this regard. Rowe also reported that conspicuous by its absence in most discussion of foster care was any adequate consideration of work with natural parents. ...

In 1986, Thoburn et al [1986] voiced the concern that the move towards greater compulsion in child care in order to facilitate planning for permanence may have had the unforeseen consequence of a less appropriate and sensitive service to those who should go home. ...

In 1986 Millham et al [1986] demonstrated that the majority of children coming into care did in fact eventually return to their birth families or move into independent living situations. Of the 170 children under six years on admission to care in this Dartington study, only 24 were in long-term care two years later. This finding was an important reminder that agencies, in initiating policies for the small numbers who needed permanent family placement, must take care that these did not result in inappropriate and unhelpful services to the far greater numbers who would eventually return to their parents and needed to be helped to do so as quickly as possible. Millham and his colleagues confirmed in a later study [1993] that 90 per cent of children and adolescents who are taken away from their families into the care of a local authority eventually go home.

The simple dichotomy between the permanence of adoption and the permanence of a return home is called in question by the research which pointed to the importance of maintaining family links, described by the Department of Health in *Patterns and Outcomes in Child Care* (1991):

a) Contact and placement stability

By the mid 1980s there was cumulative research evidence from both the USA and Great Britain showing that the well-being of children being cared for by social agencies is enhanced if they maintain links with parents and other family members. Unfortunately, other research showed that all too often links were not being maintained. ...

Berridge and Cleaver [1987] found that frequent access to parents was associated with fewer fostering breakdowns. Thoburn and Rowe's adoption survey [1988] showed that when other variables were held constant, few placements broke down when family links were maintained, while Wedge and Mantle [1991] discovered that even among a group of children who were being placed in permanent substitute families, those whose links with their birth families had been maintained were protected against the adverse effects of long periods in care. They noted that 50% of children referred for permanent placement had some link with their birth family at that time. They tended to be older children who presumably could maintain links themselves. These researchers conclude: 'The increasing trend towards access of family members to children in care needs to be further developed and extended if placements in substitute families are to be as successful as possible and if children are to acquire and retain the self-identity which is a crucial component in healthy emotional development.'

The findings, insights and conclusions from the Dartington Research Unit's study 'Lost in Care' (Millham *et al*, 1986) are admirably summarised in their follow-up research 'Access Disputes in Child Care' (1989). They are sufficiently important to require quoting at some length:

'... Managing a crisis, finding a suitable placement, coping with the anxiety, grief and frequent hostility of parents and children make it difficult for social workers to give the maintenance of links between parents and absent children high priority. Contacts are left to emerge, consequent upon other social worker decisions.

As a result, withering links with home affect many children in care; from the outset, nearly three-quarters of children experience great difficulty in maintaining contact with their parents. The barriers that they face are of two kinds. The first are specific restrictions, which are placed by social workers on the access of individuals, usually family or other household members. Such difficulties affect one-third of the children on entry. The second barrier is created by non-specific restrictions, difficulties inherent in placements, such as hostility, distance and inaccessibility. These hindrances affect two-thirds of the children in the early days of care.

As time passes, child isolation increases and restrictions on parental access to children actually increase, often to help maintain placements in difficulty, although the disruptive potential of visiting parents is over-estimated. Restrictions on contact do not receive continual scrutiny by social workers and constraints on unwelcome family members are frequently allowed to linger long after the original reasons for discouraging visits have evaporated. ...

Other factors increase the child's isolation. Social workers' visits to parents, children and care givers decline over time. ... Thus, the bridge between absent child and his or her family weakens and the social worker fails to stress the significance of parent/child reciprocal contact. Unfortunately, parents need encouragement to maintain relationships with their absent children, particularly when haunted by a sense of failure and bereft of a useful role.

... As a result, a third of those who remain in care will have lost contact with mother or father, siblings or the wider family at the end of two years and will be likely to stay in care for the foreseeable future. In the majority of cases, there are no cogent social work reasons for contacts with the family to wither. ...

...

Although Wedge and Mantle speak of 'the increasing trend' toward access, other researchers point out the low base from which this trend is starting. Thoburn's intensive and extensive studies of 'permanent' placements both show that family links which children wished to maintain were not always preserved, and in their studies of fostering breakdown Berridge and Cleaver noted an 'anti-family ideology' in some instances and more general lack of encouragement of contact, which meant that family links were too often allowed to wither and die.

The use of relations as a placement resource has received little attention until the last few years and has sometimes been frowned on as likely to exacerbate family tensions. However, if children's parents are unable or unwilling to care for them, an obvious way to preserve close links is to turn to the wider family, and the high level of stability and satisfaction found in foster placements with relatives which was first emphasised in 'Long-Term Foster Care' (Rowe et al, 1984) has been strongly reinforced in recent studies. ...

In 'Foster Home Breakdown' Berridge and Cleaver report a remarkable success rate for fostering by relatives and in 'Child Care Now' Rowe et al [1989] report that relatives tend to foster older children with more complex problems and still achieve better results than unrelated foster carers. Despite this, local authorities vary greatly in their use of fostering by relatives and their willingness to provide financial support for people looking after relatives' children.

b) Sibling relationships merit closer attention

Research underlines and supports the requirement in the Children Act 1989 (s.23 (7)(*b*)) that siblings should be accommodated together whenever 'reasonably practicable and consistent with the child's welfare'. Psychologists such as Judy Dunn [1988] point out that siblings provide our longest lasting relationships and can be a powerful influence on personality and development.

However, this explicit attention to the question of siblings is relatively recent and there are few references to siblings in local authority policy documents or practice guides.

...

There is also confirmation from research that children who are away from home, like being with siblings, but separation is a common experience. ...

Rowe et al (1984) found that long-term foster children placed with a sibling were usually glad about this and mentioned the benefit of having someone to talk to about their family of origin, while Fisher et al [1986] learned that children and young people who had been separated sometimes thought that this was a punishment.

...

The pros and cons of keeping siblings together if their needs seem very different is inevitably a matter for anxious debate among practitioners and decision makers. Until recently, research provided little assistance, but some useful pointers are emerging from recent studies. Although the evidence is sometimes conflicting, the overall conclusion seems to be that being with a sibling usually has a helpful effect on stability.

(1) *Placement at home.* In the Farmer and Parker study [1991], returning 'home on trial' with a sibling was associated with successful outcomes.

(2) *Long-term foster placements.* Berridge and Cleaver reported more breakdowns when the child had siblings in care but was separated from all of them (50% breakdown) than when placed with *all* siblings in care (33% breakdown) or with *some* siblings (26% breakdown). However, these findings were not entirely supported by the outcomes data in 'Child Care Now'.

(3) *Adoption and 'permanent' foster placements.*

   (i) In a survey of the outcomes of over a thousand 'special needs' adoption placements Thoburn and Rowe found that sibling placements break down *less* often. Only 18% of placements with one or more siblings broke down compared with 24% of single child placements. (This difference is statistically significant and still found when other variables are held constant.)

   (ii) After studying 'permanent' placements of siblings placed together or separately, Wedge and Mantle concluded that the impact can work both ways. Multiple placements may put too much stress on the new parents, but a child's adverse reaction to separation from siblings can also cause disruption. When siblings are placed together, the younger one may be more in jeopardy because of problems in the older one(s), but conversely, being placed with a younger sibling may reduce the chance of an older child feeling rejected by the new family.

   (iii) Intensive study of a small number of adoption placements of 9–10 year old boys left Rushton et al [1989] equally uncertain about the wisdom of splitting or separating sibling groups. They noted more progress in children placed with one or more siblings but point out that those placed alone tended to have more serious problems to start with.

Amongst the conclusions drawn were:

(16) Agency policies and practice need to take seriously the now well established research finding that visiting is the key to discharge. Contact enhances the welfare of placed children and does not increase the risk of breakdown.

(17) Concepts of permanence should be broadened to include the possibility of continued family contact through open adoption or permanent fostering.

(18) Informal barriers to contact are widespread but may not be recognised. Agencies ought to examine not just their stated policies but the prevailing climate of opinion among their staff about birth parents and the maintenance of family contact. Staff may need more support and encouragement to do this work.

(19) Premature or routine termination of contact when permanent placements are planned can do children a serious disservice by precluding the possibility of continued contact of some sort.

(20) Relatives provide a placement resource which should always be considered. The stability of such placements – especially for long-term cases – makes it worth trying hard to seek out relatives and overcome obstacles.

(21) Relatives are also an important source of family contact. Visits by grandparents or aunts and uncles can often be encouraged even if visiting by parents cannot be permitted.

(22) More attention should be paid to the role of siblings and other children. The importance of child-to-child relationships has been insufficiently recognised. Changes in the child members of the family to which a child returns or the presence of 'own' children close in age to a foster child are both associated with negative outcome, whereas placement with siblings is generally beneficial and sibling ties are valued by children.

Ten years later, the message is the same but the practice has changed, as reported by the Department of Health in *The Children Act Now – Messages from Research* (2001), summarising the findings of a study by Hedy Cleaver, *Fostering Family Contact: A Study of Children, Parents and Foster Carers* (2000):

Key findings
- The amount of contact foster children have with their parents has increased considerably since the Children Act 1989.
- Home was the most popular meeting place for children and families.
- Carers were more likely to promote contact if they were trained, understood the purpose of contact, had a good relationship with the child and felt well supported.
- Indirect contact was also important to keep emotional links alive.
- Parental contact was positively associated with the child's behaviour and well-being when fostered and with reunification.

...

The role of foster carers

The principle of contact between children and their families was accepted by all foster carers. When parental contact ceased, this was usually the result of the parents' behaviour and wishes rather than because carers blocked or hindered contact. However, contact was rarely a trouble-free process. Three types of problems dominated the carers' perception of contact: parents who demanded too much of carers' time for their own needs; parents who played the child off against the carer; and erratic and unreliable visiting. The role carers played in contact arrangements varied, but a number of factors were associated with carers promoting contact: formal training, a shared understanding with social workers of the aim and duration of placement and purpose of contact, a good relationship with the child and being well supported themselves.

Outcomes

The survey of social work files showed that four years after admission 41% of the children were living at home or with relatives, a quarter were with their original carers, 5% were living independently, 12% had been adopted and 17% were living with new carers or in residential care. The factors associated with children's well-being and adjustment while fostered were strong parent/child attachment relationships and continued parental contact. These were also associated with the likelihood of reunification.

Many children in public care who are candidates for permanent placement have been removed from abusive or neglectful homes. The results of the study of *Development after Physical Abuse in Early Childhood* (1995) by Jane Gibbons and her colleagues are indeed surprising:

Discussion

The results showed that children placed on registers following physical abuse were highly likely to lose one or both natural parents in the nine to ten year follow-up period. This came about through official protective intervention to remove a child from an abusive home, but also from action by parents themselves. Mothers in particular often acted to dissolve a violent relationship and eject an abusive partner from the household. They were then about as likely to end up as lone parents in conditions of some poverty as to share their households with another man. Children who remained with their natural parents were severely materially disadvantaged in comparison with the children who were placed in substitute families.

The children in substitute families in this sample did show some advantages in physical development and verbal ability, related to the professional and managerial backgrounds of the new parents. But measures of behaviour problems at home and school failed to find any advantages for the separated group of children.

Particular advantages have been claimed for adoption as opposed to foster care. In the present study the two forms of placement had been used rather differently, with children being adopted earlier while those in foster care tended to have been removed later, after further failures of home care. Thus the foster children might be expected to have less chance of overcoming the problems resulting from early poor rearing. In fact, there was no consistent association between age at placement and children's outcomes. There was a consistent trend for the children in foster care to have fewer behaviour problems, as rated by parents and teachers, fewer problems with peers and less depression, while the adopted group tended to have higher problem scores than children who remained with natural parents. It should be noted that this result is out of line with the weight of evidence from other studies, suggesting more favourable outcomes for children in adoptive homes.

How might the negative findings be explained? First, the follow-up point, while nine to ten years on from placement on the child protection register, still marked a relatively early stage in children's lives – they were only 11 on average. There is time for further maturation and a very different picture might be revealed after another ten years. Second, there is some evidence that around the age of 11 there may be a 'dip' in adopted children's performance for reasons that are not clear (Maughan and Pickles, 1990). If this were so, then the adopted group might come out of the dip in a further few years. Thirdly, it is possible that the adopted children differed from the remainder in some characteristics that weighed heavily against good outcome and were not captured by the study's baseline measures. There could have been pre-existing differences between the groups that were not identified because of the limitations of records. Lastly, even though a high proportion of the original sample took part in the follow-up and no more children in substitute families were 'missed', it is possible that the missing cases in some way distorted the findings.

However, the most obvious difference between the adopted and fostered groups lay in their current experiences of family life. It seemed that adoptive parents were not always using particularly sensitive methods of child-rearing. They tended to be more punitive and to use more physical punishment and these parenting styles were associated with poor outcomes for children in the total sample. Adoptive parents also tended to have more personal problems and to be more depressed than foster carers. They were often faced with children showing difficult and disturbed behaviour but, unlike the foster carers, they rarely had professional support and advice and they felt more isolated. It is perhaps not surprising that some fell back on punitive methods.

The need for more consistent post-adoption services is being increasingly recognised (Howe, 1992; Rushton et al., 1993).

In considering these results, it is important to take into account the climate of opinion at the time most of the social work was carried out. Within social service departments there was a strong policy emphasis on planning for permanence, and this was usually interpreted to mean rapid replacement in adoptive homes if parents were assessed as inadequate carers. The majority of the adopted children in the study had been separated from natural parents who wanted to keep them by means of legal methods which are no longer available. Such a start may have influenced the subsequent course of the placement. Current adoption policy is also more aware of the need to take children's cultural backgrounds into account when planning placement, so that the very wide discrepancies in the present study would probably not be found in today's climate of professional opinion.

This chapter should not end without some recognition of the loving and patient approach of many substitute families to the damaged children in their care. ... The records of some children showed how improvements in behaviour and adaptation to school were slowly occurring, even though there were setbacks. However, it is important to recognise that the provision of a new family for a child who has suffered abuse is not of itself enough to improve that child's life chances. Placement creates some new problems – more changes of carer, need to adjust to changing parental demands and expectations, loss of important aspects of one's own identity. 'New' parents can rarely hope for quick returns for their love and care, and ultimate success may well depend on exceptional levels of altruism, child-rearing skills and confidence.

The risk of breakdown in permanent placements, and the relationship with continued contact, are shown in the graph and figure, together with a commentary on the choices available, from June Thoburn's account of the findings and conclusions of her survey of over 1,000 special needs placements made by voluntary agencies in Britain between 1980 and 1984 in Fratter, Rowe, Sapsford and Thoburn, *Permanent Family Placement – a decade of experience* (1991):

Age at placement and percentage of placements disrupting

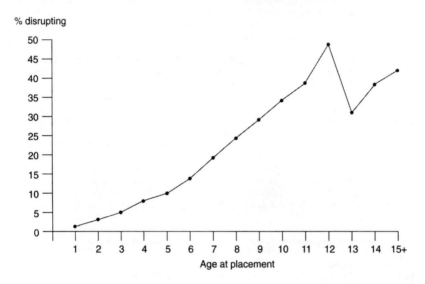

In view of the fact that the increased risk of breakdown is often given as a reason for placing for adoption rather than in foster care, and for terminating contact with birth parents, it is important to note that when age at placement was held constant, there was no significant difference in breakdown rates between adoption or permanent foster placement. Having continued contact with parents and other members of the birth family was a protective factor. However, it must be emphasised that all these placements were made with the intention that they would be permanent, and the social work service was based on maximising the sense of permanence of the new families.

This is a possible explanation for the lower breakdown rates for primary school-age children in this study compared with those in the study by Berridge and Cleaver [1987] of long-term foster placements (46 per cent broke down in the Berridge and Cleaver study, and 22 per cent in this study). However, there was no difference between breakdown rates of those placed at 11 or older in the two studies. It may be that, had it been possible to consider other outcome measures, the positive effects of foster placement intended to be permanent from the start, and the intensive work which goes with it both on the part of social workers and parents, would have been apparent even for the older group. There was some evidence from the qualitative study that even when placements broke down, the majority of the young people could describe positive benefits for themselves and were glad that their placement had happened.

...

How, then, should we advise those concerned with the placement of children in care to incorporate our results into their practice and decision-making? First, it is important to warn against a swing from overoptimism to overpessimism. Our finding that there is a greater risk of breakdown with children who are older at placement; who are described as institutionalised or as having behavioural or emotional problems; or who have a history of deprivation or abuse, should not lead to blanket rules. ...

Outcome by continued contact and age at placement

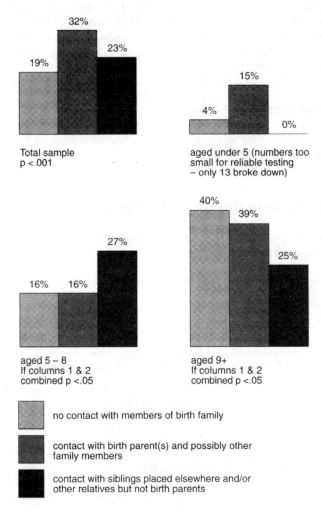

Total sample
p <.001

aged under 5 (numbers too small for reliable testing – only 13 broke down)

aged 5 – 8
If columns 1 & 2 combined p <.05

aged 9+
If columns 1 & 2 combined p <.05

no contact with members of birth family

contact with birth parent(s) and possibly other family members

contact with siblings placed elsewhere and/or other relatives but not birth parents

% = percentage disrupting

New knowledge about groups of children where the risk of breakdown is high should lead to a more careful consideration of alternatives. Other studies, using a wider range of outcome measures, have also shown that even those children whose placements do not break down continue to need post-placement support, and often adoption allowances. This new knowledge should lead to a more careful consideration of whether a similar level of financial and social work support could make a viable option of restoration to birth parents or other relatives, or a 'shared care' placement. Trent, in a small qualitative study, found that when the same methods of work were used to support restoration to the birth family, those placements had as good a chance of lasting as placements with new families. Our finding that children with a history of abuse or deprivation are a particularly high risk group should act as an antidote to the 'rescue fantasies' which it is so easy to engage in.

Questions

(i) What would your care plan be for the following children:

   (a) a family of four, ranging in age from 11 to three, removed from their parents because of father's drinking and mother's inability to cope alone, the two oldest having a strong sense of family identity and all still fond of their now-separated parents, but placed in two different foster homes because there was no foster home available for them all;

   (b) the new baby in that family, born after the parents' separation, removed because the mother's situation was unstable, and placed with a different foster mother?

(ii) How, if at all, would it affect your plans to know that the father's drinking problem was mainly due to the fear that he had inherited an incurable and severely disabling disease from his mother?

14.2 The law on maintaining family links

Among other things, Sch. 2 to the Children Act 1989 contains this duty towards all children who are looked after by local authorities:

15.—(1) Where a child is being looked after by a local authority, the authority shall, unless it is not reasonably practicable or consistent with his welfare, endeavour to promote contact between the child and—

   (*a*) his parents;

   (*b*) any person who is not a parent of his but who has parental responsibility for him; and

   (*c*) any relative, friend or other person connected with him.

(2) Where a child is being looked after by a local authority—

   (*a*) the authority shall take such steps as are reasonably practicable to secure that—

      (i) his parents; and

      (ii) any person who is not a parent of his but who has parental responsibility for him,

are kept informed of where he is being accommodated; and

   (*b*) every such person shall secure that the local authority are kept informed of his or her address.

If the child is in compulsory care, and so cannot simply go home, this duty is reinforced with the powers of the courts:

34.—(1) Where a child is in the care of a local authority, the authority shall (subject to the provisions of this section) allow the child reasonable contact with—

   (*a*) his parents;

   (*b*) any guardian of his;

   (*c*) where there was a residence order in force with respect to the child immediately before the care order was made, the person in whose favour the order was made; and

   (*d*) where, immediately before the care order was made, a person had care of the child by virtue of an order made in the exercise of the High Court's inherent jurisdiction with respect to children, that person.

(2) On an application made by the authority or the child, the court may make such order as it considers appropriate with respect to the contact which is to be allowed between the child and any named person.

(3) On an application made by—

   (*a*) any person mentioned in paragraphs (*a*) to (*d*) of subsection (1); or

   (*b*) any person who has obtained the leave of the court to make the application;

the court may make such order as it considers appropriate with respect to the contact which is to be allowed between the child and that person.

(4) On an application made by the authority or the child, the court may make an order authorising the authority to refuse to allow contact between the child and any person who is mentioned in paragraphs (*a*) to (*d*) of subsection (1) and named in the order.

(5) When making a care order with respect to a child, or in any family proceedings in connection with a child who is in the care of a local authority, the court may make an order under this section, even though no application for such an order has been made with respect to the child, if it considers that the order should be made.

(6) An authority may refuse to allow the contact that would otherwise be required by virtue of subsection (1) or an order under this section if—

(*a*) they are satisfied that it is necessary to do so in order to safeguard or promote the child's welfare; and

(*b*) the refusal—

(i) is decided upon as a matter of urgency; and

(ii) does not last for more than seven days.

(7) An order under this section may impose such conditions as the court considers appropriate.

(8) The Secretary of State may by regulations make provision as to—

(*a*) the steps to be taken by a local authority who have exercised their powers under subsection (6);

(*b*) the circumstances in which, and conditions subject to which, the terms of any order under this section may be departed from by agreement between the local authority and the person in relation to whom the order is made;

(*c*) notification by a local authority of any variation or suspension of arrangements made (otherwise than under an order under this section) with a view to affording any person contact with a child to whom this section applies.

(9) The court may vary or discharge any order made under this section on the application of the authority, the child concerned or the person named in the order.

(10) An order under this section may be made either at the same time as the care order itself or later.

(11) Before making a care order with respect to any child the court shall—

(*a*) consider the arrangements which the authority have made, or propose to make, for affording any person contact with a child to whom this section applies; and

(*b*) invite the parties to the proceedings to comment on those arrangements.

Section 34 cases tend to fall into two categories:

Re B (minors) (termination of contact: paramount consideration)
[1993] Fam 301, [1993] 3 All ER 524, Court of Appeal

Two little girls, now aged four and two and a half, had been removed from their mother because she left them unattended and placed with a short-term foster mother for some two years. The mother then had a baby boy, S, and was looking after him successfully with social work support. Contact with the girls was re-established and they visited her home twice a week. The local authority applied for an order under s. 34(4) of the Children Act 1989, authorising them to refuse contact so that the girls could be placed for adoption. The judge considered that it was not open to him to use the powers in s. 34 to challenge the local authority's plan. He made the order and the girls' guardian ad litem appealed.

Butler-Sloss LJ: ... The underlying reason for the continuing contact was the hope of the mother that it might lead to rehabilitation and the return of the girls to her. The contact already taking place was incompatible with placing the children with prospective adopters. The local authority accepted that they had never attempted to assess the mother's ability to care for the three children. Their view was, and is, that the mother has made significant strides in her ability to care for S, but to expect her to care for three children is too much and will probably lead to the breakdown of all three placements, including the placement for S. They were concerned about the length of time the girls had lived with the short-term foster mother and the delay in placing them permanently. They considered that the children would not miss the contact with their mother, which the judge found to be true since their primary carer remains the foster mother. But they accepted that the contact visits had been successful and enjoyable for the children. The local authority had identified particularly suitable potential adopters who were, like the children, of mixed race and who would not be willing to accept continuing contact with the mother.

[Apart from the duty and powers in section 34] there is another important difference [between the old law and the new] of which the judge was well aware and which had a marked effect upon his approach to this case. Before the implementation of the Children Act 1989 the powers of the magistrates' court to make care orders did not extend beyond the making of the order. Thereafter the local authority took over the care of the child and was not subject to judicial control or monitoring other than by the limited remedy of judicial review: see *A v Liverpool City Council* [1982] AC 363 and *In re W (A Minor) (Wardship: Jurisdiction)* [1985] AC 791. By contrast, when a child was committed to care by a judge exercising the wardship jurisdiction in the High Court, or a Matrimonial Causes Act 1973 care order in the High Court or the county court, the judge was able to make directions and require the case to return for further consideration by the court. This monitoring by the court of a child in care has been specifically excluded by the Act of 1989. ...

... If the local authority's plan to place for adoption is not capable of reconsideration, the judge was clearly right in his decision that contact was not possible in this case. The question arises as to the interplay between the plans of the local authority and the jurisdiction of the court and the proper exercise of its discretion under the wider range of orders available under the Act of 1989.

[Counsel] for the local authority submitted that the principle in *A v Liverpool City Council* [1982] AC 363 still inhibits the court from any interference with the adoption plans made for the two girls and the judge's approach was entirely correct. *A v Liverpool City Council* is still, in my respectful opinion, of the greatest relevance beyond the confines of child care law and the principle set out by Lord Wilberforce is equally applicable today, that the court has no reviewing power over the exercise of the local authority's discretionary decisions in carrying out their statutory role. ... I do not, however, believe that the important principle set out in *A v Liverpool City Council* [1982] AC 363 and *In re W* [1985] AC 791 applies to the intervention of the court in response to an application which is properly made, or fetters the exercise of the judicial discretion in an application, under the Children Act 1989.

...

My understanding of the Act of 1989 is that it aims to incorporate the best of the wardship jurisdiction within the statutory framework without any of the perceived disadvantages of judicial monitoring of administrative plans. It provides for the court a wide range of options and the possibility of its own motion to set in train a line of investigation not contemplated or asked for by the parties. Like wardship, however, these wide powers are to be sparingly used.

The present position of a child whose welfare is being considered under Part IV of the Act appears to me to be that he will not be placed in care unless a court has been satisfied that the threshold conditions in section 31 have been met and that it is better to make a care order than not to do so. After the care order is made, the court has no continuing role in the future welfare of the child. The local authority has parental responsibility for the child by section 33(3). However, issues relating to the child may come before the court, for instance on applications for contact or leave to refuse contact, to discharge the care order or by an application for a section 8 residence order. The making of a residence order discharges the care order: section 91(1). At the moment that an application comes before the court, at whichever tier, the court has a duty to apply section 1, which states that when a court determines any question with respect to the upbringing of a child, the child's welfare shall be the court's paramount consideration. The court has to have regard to the prejudicial effect of delay, to the checklist including the range of orders available to the court and whether to make an order. On a section 34 application, therefore, the court has a duty to consider and apply the welfare section.

Contact applications generally fall into two main categories: those which ask for contact as such, and those which are attempts to set aside the care order itself. In the first category there is no suggestion that the applicant wishes to take over the care of the child and the issue of contact often depends on whether contact would frustrate long-term plans for the child in a substitute home, such as adoption, where continuing contact may not be for the long-term welfare of the child. The presumption of contact, which has to be for the benefit of the child, has always to be balanced against the long-term welfare of the child and, particularly, where he will live in the future. Contact must not be allowed to destabilise or endanger the arrangements for the child and in many cases the plans for the child will be decisive of the contact application. There may also be cases where the parent is having satisfactory contact with the child and there are no long-term plans or those plans do not appear to the court to preclude some future contact. The proposals of the local authority, based on their appreciation of the best interests of the child, must command the greatest respect and consideration from the court, but Parliament has given to the court, and not to the local authority, the duty to decide on contact between the child and those named in section 34(1). Consequently, the court may have the task of requiring the local authority to justify their long-term plans to the extent only that those plans exclude contact between parent and child. In the second category, contact applications may be made by parents by way of another attempt to obtain the return of the children. In such a case the court is obviously entitled to take into account the failure to apply to discharge the care order, and in the majority of cases the court will have little difficulty in coming to the conclusion that the applicant cannot demonstrate that contact with a view to rehabilitation with the parent is a viable proposition at that stage, particularly if it had already been rejected at the earlier hearing when the child was placed in care. The task for the parents will be too great and the court would be entitled to assume that the plans of the local authority to terminate contact are for the welfare of the child and are not to be frustrated by inappropriate contact with a view to the remote possibility, at some future date, of rehabilitation.

But in all cases the welfare section has to be considered, and the local authority have the task of justifying the cessation of contact. There may also be unusual cases where either the local authority have not made effective plans or there has been considerable delay in implementing them and a parent, who has previously been found by a court unable or unwilling to care for the child so that a care order has been made, comes back upon the scene as a possible future primary carer. ...

I unhesitatingly reject the local authority argument. As I have already said, their plan has to be given the greatest possible consideration by the court and it is only in the unusual case that a parent will be able to convince the court, the onus being firmly on the parent, that there has been such a change of circumstances as to require further investigation and reconsideration of the local authority plan. If, however, a court were unable to intervene, it would make a nonsense of the paramountcy of the welfare of the child which is the bedrock of the Act, and would subordinate it to the administrative decision of the local authority in a situation where the court is seized of the contact issue. That cannot be right.

But I would emphasise that this is not an open door to courts reviewing the plans of local authorities. ...

This court, therefore, has to decide whether the mother should be assessed as the potential carer of all three children. There is a large question mark over the wisdom of straining the placement for S. by the possibility of putting all three children together in the care of a relatively untried mother. But the guardian ad litem and the social worker saw a real possibility that she might become an adequate mother for all three children. The decision requires consideration of the competing factors that on the one side there is the prospect that the mother may come up trumps and, if so, the enormous advantage for these three children to be brought up together by their own mother in preference to a substitute family, however suitable. On the other side there is the real danger that the problems would be too great, that the assessment would be disappointing and, most worrying of all, the danger that this attempt might imperil the relationship between the mother and S., who would be devastated by losing his mother at this stage. We must add to those factors the need to settle these children and the fragility of their present placement from which they will have to move in any event, and the question of delay is very important. However, I have come to the clear conclusion that the mother's potential must be investigated and not to do so would be unfair to the children and, if the prospective adoption application were to be made, might create a serious obstacle on the special facts of this case.

Appeal allowed.

Re E (a minor) (care order: contact)
[1994] 1 FCR 584, [1994] 1 FLR 146, Court of Appeal

The parents of two little boys, aged five and a half and nearly four at the date of the hearing had personality problems which made it difficult for them to look after the children. Over some 22 months before the hearing, the boys had been looked after first by family friends, then accommodated by the local authority, and then the subject of care proceedings. Everyone agreed that there should be a care order. But the local authority also applied for an order under s. 34(4) because the care plan was adoption. The judge adopted the approach that he could not order contact which was incompatible with the care plan unless this could be attacked as capricious or invalid in judicial review terms. He granted the application and the parents and guardian ad litem appealed.

Sir Stephen Brown P: ... Section 34 of the Children Act 1989 quite plainly begins with the provision that a local authority shall allow a child in care reasonable contact with, among others, his parents; there is therefore a presumption of contact: the onus is on the local authority to apply to the court for an order authorising it to refuse to allow contact; that is to say, to terminate contact. The emphasis is heavily placed on the presumption of continuing parental contact. ...

The submission made in this case therefore is that although the judge had before him evidence from the social worker in charge of the case, and evidence from the social worker in charge of adoption cases to the effect that in the relevant area, there was no real likelihood of the discovery or identification of proposed adopted parents who would countenance continuing contact after adoption; nevertheless, no specific investigation was made about the actual situation; ...

The case was strongly argued on behalf of the local authority that the care plan devised by the local authority was appropriate to these children; first of all because there was no prospect of actual rehabilitation with their parents; and secondly because the level and quality of contact between the children and the parents was of a relatively low quality. That matter took up a good deal of the hearing; ... The evidence of the guardian and Dr Williams ... was to the effect that although these children were in a particular category, if I may put it that way, they were not bonded in the full sense of the word with their parents; nevertheless, there was a benefit to the children of contact with their parents because the parents were in no way likely to undermine a permanent placement in another 'parent setting' whether it was an adoptive parent setting or a long-term foster setting and that in the light of a very strong likelihood in the view of the doctor, that an adoptive placement would either not be satisfactory or would break down, the constant presence of the parents in the lives of the children would have a stabilising effect. ... Dr Williams said that ideally, these children would prosper in a secure foster placement growing up knowing who their parents were and having regular access to them. ...

...I consider that in the light of very strong representation by the doctor and the guardian as to the particular value in this case of some continuing face-to-face contact, it was not sufficient for the local authority to dismiss the likelihood of obtaining suitable adopters prepared to entertain face-to-face contact upon the basis that there were none on the register at the time.

... The court has been very strongly pressed ... to give 'guidance' on s.34 of the Children Act 1989. I do not consider it appropriate to say more than that this court endorses the approach indicated by Butler-Sloss LJ in the case of *Re B* [p. 757, above] emphasising that contact must not be allowed to destabilise or endanger the arrangements for the child. However, since the court has a duty to consider contact between the child and the parents, it may require the local authority to justify its long-term plan where their plan excludes contact between the parents and the child.

Simon Brown LJ: ... even when the s.31 criteria are satisfied, contact may well be of singular importance to the long-term welfare of the child: first, in giving the child the security of knowing that his parents love him and are interested in his welfare; secondly, by avoiding any damaging sense of loss to the child in seeing himself abandoned by his parents; thirdly, by enabling the child to commit himself to the substitute family with the seal of approval of the natural parents; and, fourthly, by giving the child the necessary sense of family and personal identity. Contact, if maintained, is capable of reinforcing and increasing the chances of success of a permanent placement, whether on a long-term fostering basis or by adoption.

There is, I appreciate, an ongoing debate regarding the merits of open or closed adoption and it is not one that I propose to enter. But whatever be the arguments, there will undoubtedly be cases, and this I believe to be one, in which some continuing face-to-face contact is clearly desirable and which call, accordingly, at the very least for some positive efforts on the local authority's part to find, if at all possible, prospective open adopters; here, it seems to me, there have been none.

Even, therefore, were the appeal to be decided without reference to further evidence, I myself would have been inclined to allow it. For good measure, however, there is now before the court further evidence indicating at the very least this: that the admirable short-term foster-mother in whose care over the last 17 months these children have continued to thrive has indicated a wish to be considered, together with her husband, as a long-term foster-parent for these children, a placement which would allow continuing face-to-face contact.

For that reason too it seems to me highly desirable that this matter be considered afresh ... by a judge who will have the advantage of hearing from the local authority, both (a) what upon further investigation appears to be the up-to-date prospects of open adoption, and (b) their considered views upon the merits or otherwise of long-term fostering by the foster-parents.

Those advantages, in my judgment, clearly outweigh the disadvantages of delaying yet further a final decision upon the long-term placement of these children.
Order accordingly.

Question

Do you think that these appeals would have been allowed if the judges had not in each case applied the wrong approach in principle?

Taking children into public care is, of course, an interference with their own and their families' right to respect for their family life under Art. 8(1) of the European Convention on Human Rights. As such it must be justified under Art. 8(2) as proportionate to the legitimate aim of protecting the child (see p. 466, above). The approach of the European Court of Human Rights to the preservation of family links was recently summarised in the following case:

K and T v Finland
[2001] 2 FCR 673, [2001] 2 FLR 707, European Court of Human Rights, Grand Chamber

This was the first case in which the Court had held that taking a child into public care was a breach of Article 8. The Grand Chamber upheld the Court's decision in relation to a baby who had been removed from her mentally ill mother at birth when other less drastic ways of protecting her should have been explored. A care order over an older child whom the mother had placed in voluntary care was upheld. But the authorities had then taken insufficient steps to try to reunite the family. The Grand Chamber first explained the Court's approach:

3. 'Necessary in a democratic society'

154. In determining whether the impugned measures were 'necessary in a democratic society', the Court will consider whether, in the light of the case as a whole, the reasons adduced to justify these measures were relevant and sufficient for the purpose of art 8(2) of the Convention (see, inter alia, *Olsson v Sweden (no 1)* (1988) 11 EHRR 259 at 285 (para 68)).

In so doing, the Court will have regard to the fact that perceptions as to the appropriateness of intervention by public authorities in the care of children vary from one contracting state to another, depending on such factors as traditions relating to the role of the family and to state intervention in family affairs and the availability of resources for public measures in this particular area. However, consideration of what is in the best interests of the child is in every case of crucial importance. Moreover, it must be borne in mind that the national authorities have the benefit of direct contact with all the persons concerned (see *Olsson v Sweden (no 2)* (1992) 17 EHRR 134 at 181 (para 90)), often at the very stage when care measures are being envisaged or immediately after their implementation. It follows from these considerations that the Court's task is not to substitute itself for the domestic authorities in the exercise of their responsibilities for the regulation of the public care of children and the rights of parents whose children have been taken into care, but rather to review under the Convention the decisions taken by those authorities in the exercise of their power of appreciation (see, for instance, *Hokkanen v Finland* [1995] 2 FCR 320 at 330 (para 55); *Johanssen v Norway* (1996) 23 EHRR 33 at 67 (para 64)).

155. The margin of appreciation so to be accorded to the competent national authorities will vary in the light of the nature of the issues and the seriousness of the interests at stake, such as, on the one hand, the importance of protecting a child in a situation which is assessed to seriously threaten his or her health or development and, on the other hand, the aim to reunite the family as soon as circumstances permit. After a considerable period of time has passed since the child was originally taken into public care, the interest of a child not to have his or her de facto family situation changed again may override the interests of the parents to have their family reunited. The Court thus recognises that the authorities enjoy a wide margin of appreciation in assessing the necessity of taking a child into care. However, a stricter scrutiny is

called for in respect of any further limitations, such as restrictions placed by those authorities on parental rights of access, and of any legal safeguards designed to secure an effective protection of the right of parents and children to respect for their family life. Such further limitations entail the danger that the family relations between the parents and a young child are effectively curtailed (the above-mentioned *Johansen v Norway* (1996) 23 EHRR 33 at 67 (para 64)).

It is against this background that the Court will examine whether the measures constituting the interferences with the applicants' exercise of their right to family life could be regarded as 'necessary'.

Then it applied the underlying principles to the facts of this case:

178. The Grand Chamber, like the Chamber, would first recall the guiding principle whereby a care order should in principle be regarded as a temporary measure, to be discontinued as soon as circumstances permit, and that any measures implementing temporary care should be consistent with the ultimate aim of reuniting the natural parents and the child (see, in particular, the above-mentioned *Olsson v Sweden (no 1)* (1988) 11 EHRR 259 at 290 (para 81)). The positive duty to take measures to facilitate family reunification as soon as reasonably feasible will begin to weigh on the responsible authorities with progressively increasing force as from the commencement of the period of care, subject always to its being balanced against the duty to consider the best interests of the child.

179. As to the particular circumstances, the Court notes that some inquiries were carried out in order to ascertain whether the applicants would be able to bond with the children (see para 67 above). They did not, however, amount to a serious or sustained effort directed towards facilitating family reunification such as could reasonably be expected for the purposes of art 8(2)— especially since they constituted the sole effort on the authorities' part to that effect in the seven years during which the children have been in care. The minimum to be expected of the authorities is to examine the situation anew from time to time to see whether there has been any improvement in the family's situation. The possibilities of reunification will be progressively diminished and eventually destroyed if the biological parents and the children are not allowed to meet each other at all, or only so rarely that no natural bonding between them is likely to occur. The restrictions and prohibitions imposed on the applicants' access to their children, far from preparing a possible reunification of the family, rather contributed to hindering it. What is striking in the present case is the exceptionally firm negative attitude of the authorities.

Consequently, the Grand Chamber of the Court agrees with the Chamber that there has been a violation of art 8 of the Convention as a result of the authorities' failure to take sufficient steps directed towards a possible reunification of the applicants' family regardless of any evidence of positive improvement in the applicants' situation.

Questions

(i) Does this suggest to you that any change is needed in the approach of the English courts to this issue?

(ii) Does the research evidence tend to confirm or deny this approach?

Families are not only parents and siblings, but grandparents, uncles, aunts, cousins and many more. Before turning to them, however, we must look at the law governing applications or claims by all non-parents, whether or not they are related to the child.

14.3 Legal options for relatives and other carers

We have already seen how, in *J v C* [1970] AC 668, [1969] 1 All ER 788 (p. 444, above), the House of Lords decided that there was no presumption of law in favour of parents in private law disputes with non-parents. We have also seen how the Children Act 1989 deliberately endorses the paramountcy of the child's welfare. Even so, the courts have sometimes been more conservative in their utterances:

Re K (a minor) (wardship: adoption)
[1991] FCR 142, [1991] 1 FLR 57, Court of Appeal

The parents had two older children and, despite some social services involvement with the family, there was no question of removing them. The marriage was a stormy one, the father was addicted to gambling and had a criminal record, and the mother was receiving treatment for heroin addiction. The mother became unexpectedly pregnant with this child, N, during a particularly difficult time. A private arrangement was made to hand the child over to foster parents, as they thought permanently. This was done when the child was six weeks old but less than three months later the mother wanted her back. The foster parents made the child a ward of court and obtained interim care and control. When the child was seven and a half months old, the judge gave them care and control with a view to adoption and terminated the mother's access. Mother, father and local authority all appealed.

Butler-Sloss LJ: ... This is a very sad case in which the little girl was handed over by the mother at a time of great stress and financial difficulty within 6 weeks of the birth of the child to a much older couple who are childless and have for some years hoped to care for a child on a long-term basis. The mother and the father have repented of their decision to hand over N and wish to reintroduce her into the family with her elder brother and sister. She has, however, settled into a warm and loving family who are currently caring for her admirably and wish to continue to do so. If she moves there will be inevitable upheaval and upset for the child. If she goes back to her natural family there are question marks as to their suitability. There are also question marks as to the long-term suitability of the family with whom she is at present.

The core of counsel's submissions on behalf of the mother was that the judge correctly stated the law but did not apply it. The judge referred to ... the decision in *Re K (A Minor) (Custody)* [1990] 2 FLR 64, 67F in which Fox LJ stated:

'I come now to the law. In *Re KD (A Minor) (Access Principles)*, Lord Templemen said:

"The best person to bring up a child is the natural parent. It matters not whether the parent is wise or foolish, rich or poor, educated or illiterate, provided the child's moral and physical health are not endangered."

... The question was not where would R get the better home? The question was: was it demonstrated that the welfare of the child positively demanded the displacement of the parental right? The word "right" is not really accurate insofar as it might connote something in the nature of a property right (which it is not) but it will serve for present purposes. The "right", if there is one, is perhaps more that of the child.'

...

The difficulty in this case is that if the child had not been placed in such an unorthodox fashion with the plaintiffs and had been put into short-term care to help the mother it is most unlikely that efforts would not have been made to reintroduce the child back to her mother and brother and sister, unless there were exceptional circumstances which do not, in my view, arise in this case.

The mother must be shown to be entirely unsuitable before another family can be considered, otherwise we are in grave danger of slipping into social engineering. The question is not: would the child be better off with the plaintiffs? but: is the natural family so unsuitable that, as Fox LJ said, 'the welfare of the child positively demanded the displacement of the parental right'? I agree with Fox LJ that it is the right of the child rather than the parent and, borrowing from the philosophy of the Children Act 1989, I would rephrase it as the displacement of the parental responsibility. Once the judge found that this mother genuinely wanted her child back and was a mother who cared properly for the other two children, not to give her at least an opportunity to try to rehabilitate the family was to deprive the child of any chance of her own family. I recognise that the placement of the child back with the natural family poses considerable risks and requires careful consideration from the local authority concerned. But, backed as it is by all the professionals who gave evidence, it cannot be said to be wholly unreasonable. One attempt at rehabilitation with a young baby and a mother capable of loving her children would have been likely to have been attempted if this private arrangement had not been entered into ...

There is a second matter raised in the arguments of the local authorities. ... the position of the plaintiffs as permanent caretakers presents its own problems and would have done so even if the natural family had been entirely unsuitable. ...

Appeal allowed.

However, parents and non-parents do not have equal rights of access to the courts. The Children Act 1975 allowed non-parents to apply for 'custodianship' once they had looked after the child for some time. Even this was not implemented until 1985 and was little used. Emma Bullard and Ellen Malos summarised the results of their study of *Custodianship* (1990) thus:

9.31 The largest group of applicants were the grandparents applying for young children who had been living with them for all or most of their lives. The mothers themselves were likely either to have been in their teens at the time of their child's birth or to be in their early twenties and to be described as 'immature' either by their parents and the social workers or, among those we interviewed, to have that perception of themselves.

9.32 In the majority of such cases the reason for the application was the desire of the grandparents to safeguard the children's place with them, to be given a clear legal right to make the normal day-to-day decisions about their upbringing and to symbolise the child's place in the family.

9.33 In the cases involving relatives it appeared that the need for such an order arose most often in situations where there had been a substantial degree of agreement by the parents to the placement but also an element of uncertainty about its stability or about the formal powers of the carers to make day-to-day decisions about the children's care. ...

9.34 In some cases there had been a background of concern about the children's well-being while they were living with their parents and in a smaller number of cases the children had come into the grandparents' care from that of a local authority social services department following physical or sexual abuse.

9.35 There were also other circumstances in which relatives applied for custodianship but these were more common in the wider family than among grandparents. These included bereavement and marital breakdown and the most unusual case was one where custodianship was granted in adoption proceedings to an aunt who had taken over the care of the daughter of her brother and sister-in-law who were living in the same multi-generation family household.

9.37 The circumstances in which the children came into the care of the unrelated foster carers had features in common with those where relatives were caring for children following bereavement or marital breakdown or where the children had suffered or had been at risk of neglect or abuse. There were a small number of cases where children who had been in care before the application were suffering from severe health problems or disabilities.

They also looked into the reasons for *not* applying for custodianship:

9.39 ... Most of the responses received were from unrelated foster carers. 14% of the respondents had not heard of custodianship until receiving our letter and questionnaire. The great majority (90%) of non-users described it as an advantage that, under a custodianship order, the child in their care could not be moved to another placement by a social worker. Nevertheless they had not wanted to apply for custodianship, and gave a variety of reasons for their decision.

9.40 Apart from the people who had not heard of custodianship, there was a group who had heard of it but had found the available information confusing and inadequate. Some carers had decided that adoption was preferable, while others said simply that they could see no advantages to be gained by applying for custodianship. Financial considerations were mentioned by some carers who were caring for a child with special needs or who were dependent on state benefits. A number of respondents felt that they needed continued social work support for a variety of reasons such as making access arrangements, the child's special needs, or behaviour problems in adolescence.

The Law Commission discussed non-parent applicants in their Working Paper on *Custody* (1986):

5.37 The simplest way of removing the arbitrariness, gaps and inconsistencies in the present law is to allow non-parents the same rights to apply for custody as have parents. They already have the right to apply for care and control in wardship proceedings, so that no new principle is involved in extending the statutory procedures to them. Given the large numbers of children who have experienced divorce, after which in theory any person can intervene to seek custody (or indeed access), it might not be such a radical step in practice as it at first sight appears.

...

5.39 It may therefore be that a requirement of leave, which currently applies to most interventions in divorce suits, would be a sufficient deterrent against unwarranted applications and would allow the court to judge whether the applicant stood a reasonable prospect of success in the light of all the circumstances of the case.

Special considerations applied, however, to children in care:

5.41 As already seen, children in care are treated differently from others in both the matrimonial and wardship jurisdictions and the restrictions in custodianship have been devised partly with their special circumstances in mind. Most children are received into care under section 2 of the Child Care Act 1980 without any compulsory measures against them or their parents. ... Under the Review's recommendations, local authorities would only compulsorily acquire parental rights if they could show, not only that they could do better than the parents, but also that the child was suffering or was likely to suffer harm as a result of shortcomings in his home. It would therefore be surprising if local authority foster parents could acquire the parental right of custody more readily than could the authority.

5.42 The unqualified right in foster parents to apply for custody could also be seen as an unprecedented interference in the child care responsibilities of the local authority. As has recently been emphasised, both by the Review of Child Care Law and by the report of the inquiry team in the Jasmine Beckford case, it is important to strengthen rather than to undermine the responsibility of local authorities to make the best possible provision for each child in their care. If foster parents were able to challenge their placement decisions in the courts, there would clearly be even greater pressure to allow parents to do so.

5.46 ... The security and stability which might be gained from a custodianship order must be set against the difficulties which premature applications might cause in the making and realisation of the local authority's plans, particularly for children who have been compulsorily removed from inadequate homes. Current child care practice places great emphasis upon planning a secure and permanent home for children who might otherwise have to grow up in care. This may be achieved either through making strenuous efforts to solve the family's problems and reach a position where parents and child may be reunited or through finding an alternative family which can provide the sort of care which is best suited to the child's needs. Such plans may obviously take some time to formulate and put into effect.

The end result, in the Children Act 1989, is a modified 'open door'. We have already seen (p. 585, above) how s. 10(1) and (2) provide for the court to make any s. 8 order, either in any family proceedings or on free-standing application, and that applications can be made either by people entitled to do so or by anyone with the court's leave. The section continues:

10.—(5) The following persons are entitled to apply for a residence or contact order with respect to a child—

    (*a*) any party to a marriage (whether or not subsisting) in relation to whom the child is a child of the family;

    (*b*) any person with whom the child has lived for a period of at least three years;

    (*c*) any person who—

        (i)   in any case where a residence order is in force with respect to the child, has the consent of each of the persons in whose favour the order was made;

        (ii) in any case where the child is in the care of a local authority, has the consent of that authority; or

        (iii) in any other case, has the consent of each of those (if any) who have parental responsibility for the child.

    (6) A person who would not otherwise be entitled (under the previous provisions of this section) to apply for the variation or discharge of a section 8 order shall be entitled to do so if—

    (*a*) the order was made on his application; or

(b)   in the case of a contact order, he is named in the order.

(7) Any person who falls within a category of person prescribed by rules of court is entitled to apply for any such section 8 order as may be prescribed in relation to that category of person.

(8) Where the person applying for leave to make an application for a section 8 order is the child concerned, the court may only grant leave if it is satisfied that he has sufficient understanding to make the proposed application for the section 8 order.

(9) Where the person applying for leave to make an application for a section 8 order is not the child concerned, the court shall, in deciding whether or not to grant leave, have particular regard to—

(a)   the nature of the proposed application for the section 8 order;

(b)   the applicant's connection with the child;

(c)   any risk there might be of that proposed application disrupting the child's life to such an extent that he would be harmed by it; and

(d)   where the child is being looked after by a local authority—

   (i)   the authority's plans for the child's future; and

   (ii)   the wishes and feelings of the child's parents.

(10) The period of three years mentioned in subsection (5)(b) need not be continuous but must not have begun more than five years before, or ended more than three months before, the making of the application.

The criteria in s. 10(9) have also been applied to applications for leave to apply for contact to a child in care under s. 34(3)(b) (p. 756, above):

Re M (care: contact: grandmother's application for leave)
[1995] 2 FLR 86, [1995] Fam Law 540, Court of Appeal

Two boys, now aged twelve and a half and nine, had been in care since 1987, some seven and a half years, because of their mother's psychiatric illness. They still had contact with both their mother and their grandmother, even after they had been made wards of court and the court had endorsed the plan that they be placed for adoption, but the contact caused difficulties and was suspended in 1991. Shortly after that the older boy ran away to his grandmother and she returned him to care. The boys were not placed with prospective adopters until 1993. In 1994, the grandmother sought leave to apply for contact. The judge had no information on the children's views or those of the prospective adopter. He refused leave and the grandmother appealed.

Ward LJ: ... Section 34(3) gives the court a wide and unfettered discretion in dealing with such applications. This can be contrasted with s. 10(9) which deals with leave to apply for s.8 orders.

... If the court were faced with an application by a grandparent for leave to apply for a residence order, alternatively a contact order, it would be anomalous, in my judgment, were the court not to take into account for the exercise of the s. 34(3) discretion the criteria specifically laid out for consideration in s. 10(9). Those particular factors seem to me to be also apposite for s. 34(3). The court must, of course, have regard to all the circumstances of the case, for each case is different, but in my judgment the court should always have particular regard at least to the following:

(a)   *The nature of the contact which is being sought.* Contact to children in care varies infinitely from that which is frequent, to that which takes place two, three or four times a year to keep memory alive. It varies from contact which is face-to-face, to contact which is indirectly maintained through the exchange of letters, cards, photographs and gifts.

(b)   *The connection of the applicant to the child.* The more meaningful and important the connection is to the child, the greater is the weight to be given to this factor. Grandparents ought to have a special place in any child's affection worthy of being maintained by contact but it is easy to envisage family circumstances, very much like those before us in this case where, however loving the grandparent may be, life's wheel of misfortune has diminished the importance to the child of that blood tie and may, for example, have strengthened the claims for contact by former foster-parents who have forged close attachment to the child. The fact is that Parliament has refused to place grandparents in a special category or to accord them special treatment. Nevertheless, by virtue of Sch. 2, para. 15 [p. 756, above], contact between a child and his or her family will be assumed to be beneficial and the local authority will need to file evidence to justify why they have considered that it is not reasonably practicable or consistent with the child's welfare to promote that contact.

(c) *Disruption.* This seems to me to be the factor of crucial significance, a fortiori when the child is in care. The child will only have come into care if life had already been so thoroughly disrupted that such intervention was judged to be necessary. The need then for stability and security is usually vital. The breakdown of the foster placement may be so harmful that it should not be placed at risk. All that is obvious. It is, none the less, significant and appropriate that the risk of disruption which is primarily contemplated in s.10(9)(c) is the risk 'there might be of that *proposed application* [for a s.8 order] disrupting the child's life to such an extent that he would be *harmed* by it'. I add the emphasis to make two points. The harm envisaged is harm which, through s.105(1), is defined by s.31(9) to mean impairment of health or development as those words are there defined. A child's upset, unhappiness, confusion or anxiety, needs to be sufficiently severe before it can amount to an impairment of emotional, social or behavioural development. Secondly, the risk must arise from the proposed application. The very knowledge that litigation is pending can be sufficiently unsettling to be harmful; if leave is given, the process of investigating the merits of the application can be sufficiently disruptive if it involves the children in more interviews, psychiatric investigations and so forth. The stressfulness of litigation may impair the ability of those who have care of the child properly to discharge their responsibility to the child's detriment. Questions of that sort are the narrow focus of the court's attention in weighing this factor. That is not to say that the court shuts its eyes to what prospects of eventual success the application has, and if the making of a contact order would be so manifestly disruptive as to be totally inimical to the child's welfare, then such an obviously unsustainable claim will not be permitted to get off the starting-blocks. Except in the most obvious case, it is incumbent on the respondent to the application to produce some evidence to establish disruption.

(d) *The wishes of the parents and the local authority.* They are very material, though not determinative. That the parents' wishes are relevant is consistent with the whole underlying philosophy of the Act, a cornerstone of which is the protection of the integrity and independence of the family. When a care order is made, the local authority acquires parental responsibility. Their exercise of that responsibility commands equal protection from unwarranted interference. ...

I have attempted to identify the main factors which will be material for the court considering any application for leave. The list is not, however, intended to be exhaustive. I turn next to the question of what test the court must apply to decide whether or not to grant leave.

...

In my judgment the approach should be this:

(1) If the application is frivolous or vexatious or otherwise an abuse of the process of the court, of course it will fail.

(2) If the application for leave fails to disclose that there is any eventual real prospect of success, if those prospects of success are remote so that the application is obviously unsustainable, then it must also be dismissed: ...

(3) The applicant must satisfy the court that there is a serious issue to try and must present a good arguable case. 'A good arguable case' has acquired a distinct meaning: see the long line of authorities setting out this as the convenient approach for the grant of leave to commence proceedings and serve out of the jurisdiction under RSC Ord. 11. One should avoid unprofitable inquiry into what precisely these turns of phrase mean. Their sense is well enough known – is there a real issue which the applicant may reasonably ask the court to try and has he a case which is better than merely arguable yet not necessarily one which is shown to have a better-than-even chance, a fair chance, of success? One should avoid over-analysis of these 'tests' and one should approach the matter in the loosest way possible, looking at the matter in the round because only by such imprecision can one reinforce the importance of leaving the exercise of discretion unfettered. ...

It would be equally unwise to circumscribe rigidly the manner of the exercise of discretion. Each case is different and the weight to be given to the various factors will accordingly vary from case to case. The weight to be given to those factors is the very essence of the exercise of discretion.

Appeal allowed and case remitted to the High Court. Official Solicitor to act as guardian ad litem. Contact application to be heard on same day and immediately preceding adoption application.

However, in *Re P (a child) (residence: grandmother's application for leave)* [2002] EWCA Civ 846, the Court of Appeal warned against giving the prospects of success as described in *Re M* greater weight than the statutory checklist:

Thorpe LJ: ...
[8] In rejecting this application [by the grandmother for leave to seek a residence order in care proceedings] it seems to me from the terms of Judge Tyrer's judgment that he had greater regard to the three factors defined by this court in *Re M* than perhaps to the statutory criteria. It is to be remembered that all that was said in *Re M* was said prior to the arrival of Convention rights within domestic legislation. This was a very closely related family member who was seeking to present her case as primary carer at a final hearing. I do not myself see how she could feel that her Article 6 rights had been fully observed if the judge were only to say to her, 'your daughter's case is that you should be the primary carer and you can give evidence in support of your daughter's case'. He then went on to say, 'The prospects of you succeeding are too remote to satisfy the *Re M* test', which must inferentially have meant that he took the same view of her daughter's case. All that, of course, was said on a reading of the papers without having heard live evidence.

Question

How would you weight the comparative entitlements of grandparents (or other close relatives) who have a good relationship with the child but are not currently looking after him with those of his current local authority foster parents?

The Adoption and Children Bill, before Parliament in the 2001–02 session, in Sch. 3, para. 55(b), introduces a new s. 10(5A):

(5A) A local authority foster parent is entitled to apply for a residence order with respect to a child if the child has lived with him for a period of at least one year immediately preceding the application.

However, those local authority foster parents who do require leave have an additional hurdle to surmount:

9.—(3) A person who is, or was at any time within the last six months, a local authority foster parent of a child may not apply for leave to apply for a section 8 order with respect to the child unless—
   (*a*) he has the consent of the authority;
   (*b*) he is a relative of the child; or
   (*c*) the child has lived with him for at least three years preceding the application.
(4) The period of three years mentioned in subsection (3)(*c*) need not be continuous but must have begun not more than five years before the making of the application.

Under the Adoption and Children Bill, clause 110, the period in s. 9(3)(*c*) is reduced to one year and s. 9(4) is omitted. This is because, under clause 41(4), local authority foster parents will be able to apply to adopt after the child has had his home with them for one year. The changes to ss. 9 and 10 will mean that they may instead apply for a residence order. The effect of s. 10(1)(*b*) is that the court may make a residence order instead of an adoption order without anyone having applied for one. The consequences of non-parents' obtaining a residence order are as follows (cf the consequences between parents, p. 586, above):

12.—(2) Where the court makes a residence order in favour of any person who is not the parent or guardian of the child concerned that person shall have parental responsibility for the child while the residence order remains in force.

(3) Where a person has parental responsibility for a child as a result of subsection (2), he shall not have the right—

(*a*) to consent, or refuse to consent, to the making of an application with respect to the child under section 18 of the Adoption Act 1976;

(*b*) to agree, or refuse to agree, to the making of an adoption order, or an order under section 55 of the Act of 1976, with respect to the child; or

(*c*) to appoint a guardian for the child.

The Adoption and Children Bill, in clause 111, adds a further possibility:

111 Residence orders: extension to age of 18

(1) In section 12 of the 1989 Act (residence orders and parental responsibility), after subsection (4) there is inserted—

'(5) The power of a court to make a residence order in favour of any person who is not the parent or guardian of the child concerned includes power to direct, at the request of that person, that the order continue in force until the child reaches the age of eighteen (unless the order is brought to an end earlier); and any power to vary a residence order is exercisable accordingly.

(6) Where a residence order includes such a direction, an application to vary or discharge the order may only be made, if apart from this subsection the leave of the court is not required, with such leave.

Questions

(i) How many reasons can you think of why (a) the applicants, (b) the child, (c) the parents, or (d) the local authority might prefer (1) an adoption, (2) long-term fostering, or (3) a residence order?

(ii) Is there a need for something between a residence order and an adoption order?

The *Review of Adoption Law* (1992) still favoured residence orders over adoption for relatives and other long-term carers and looked for ways of making the former more attractive:

6.2 Where a child is living away from his parents and it is unlikely that he will be able to return home, he and his carers – be they relatives, foster-parents, or people with a residence order – may wish to enhance the security and stability of their relationship. Unless the child no longer feels part of his parents' family and would prefer to look on his present carers as his parents, his needs are more likely to be met by a residence order under the Children Act 1989 than by an adoption order. A residence order confers parental responsibility upon the child's carers without interfering with the child's identity and family relationships. Although it can be revoked, in practice a residence order will generally provide the necessary permanence for the family concerned, as once a child is settled the courts are reluctant to disturb the status quo and are most unlikely to discharge the order in favour of another party. Extra security may be gained by applying for a prohibited steps order restraining the parent from meeting aspects of parental responsibility without the permission of the court. The court may also prohibit any named person from applying for an order under the Act without the court's leave: this power could be used to prevent a parent disturbing the status quo by applying for a residence or contact order.

6.3 We are concerned that a number of adoption applications, particularly by relatives and step-parents, are made without giving proper consideration to the needs of the child and the effect of being cut off from his or her birth family. Adoption is too often regarded as the only way of securing permanence, in part no doubt because it is more familiar than other orders and because its long-term implications are not always fully understood. We therefore recommend that the court should have a duty when deciding whether or not to make a placement order or an adoption order to consider the alternative orders available under the 1989 Act or adoption legislation. ...

6.4 Responses to the review revealed a wide degree of concern that residence orders are not perceived as being likely to offer a sufficient sense of permanence for a child and his carers. It is hoped that in time residence orders will grow in familiarity and acceptance. One must nonetheless recognise the importance of the public perception of an order of this kind: some potential applicants may be deterred by the possible difficulty of explaining to other people what their relationship with the child is and by the relative attractiveness of an order which enables them to be regarded as the child's parents. It may therefore be beneficial to enhance the attractiveness of residence orders in certain circumstances.

6.5 We propose that, where a court makes a residence order in favour of a person other than a parent or step-parent and considers that that person will be responsible for the child's upbringing until he grows up, the court should have a further power to appoint, where appropriate, that person as the child's inter vivos guardian. Such a guardian would have parental responsibility until the child reached the age of 18, even though the residence order would normally come to an end at the age of 16. The guardian would have all the rights, duties and powers of a guardian under section 5 of the Children Act 1989 except for the right to agree or withhold agreement to the adoption of the child and the power to change the child's surname except with leave of the court. The appointment could of course be ended in the usual way by the court. An inter vivos guardian would be able to appoint a person to be the child's guardian after his or her death. Any guardian so appointed would have the right to agree or refuse to agree to the adoption of the child.

The Government's White Paper, *Adoption – a new approach* (2000), although generally enthusiastic about adoption for children in care (see further p. 776, below), also favoured something along these lines:

Adoption

5.5 Adoption can offer children who are unable to return to their birth families a legally permanent new family, which they will belong to all their lives. Children say that this security, and a sense of 'belonging', is important to them (see Box). Adoption is therefore a key means of providing a permanent family for these children.

> What children have said about adoption
>
> 'In adoption you have a real mum and dad'
>
> 'You cannot be taken away'
>
> 'I can call them mum and dad'
>
> 'I felt like my life was starting again'

5.6 Some looked after children, especially if they have developed a strong attachment to their foster carers, may want to be adopted by them. Some foster carers want to adopt the children in their care. Where this is in the child's best interests, it should be encouraged, as, like permanence with wider family, it allows the children to keep important attachments.

5.7 The new Standards specify that where a foster carer wants to adopt the child in their care, and that adoption would be in the interests of the child, the foster carer's application to adopt should be viewed positively and processed in three months – faster than adoptive parents who are not currently foster carers.

'Special guardianship'

5.8 Adoption is not always appropriate for children who cannot return to their birth parents. Some older children do not wish to be legally separated from their birth families. Adoption may not be best for some children being cared for on a permanent basis by members of their wider birth family. Some minority ethnic communities have religious and cultural difficulties with adoption as it is set out in law. Unaccompanied asylum-seeking children may also need secure, permanent homes, but have strong attachments to their families abroad. All these children deserve the same chance as any other to enjoy the benefits of a legally secure, stable permanent placement that promotes a supportive, lifelong relationship with their carers, where the court decides that is in their best interests.

5.9 In order to meet the needs of these children where adoption is not appropriate, and to modernise the law so it reflects the religious and cultural diversity of our country today, the Government believes there is a case to develop a new legislative option to provide permanence short of the legal separation involved in adoption. This view was strongly supported by responses to the consultation on the PIU report.

5.10 The Government will legislate to create this new option, which could be called 'special guardianship'. It will be used only to provide permanence for those children for whom adoption is not appropriate, and where the court decides it is in the best interests of the child or young person. It will:

- give the carer clear responsibility for all aspects of caring for the child or young person, and for taking the decisions to do with their upbringing. The child or young person will no longer be looked after by the council;
- provide a firm foundation on which to build a lifelong permanent relationship between the carer and the child or young person;
- be legally secure;
- preserve the basic legal link between the child or young person and their birth family;
- be accompanied by proper access to a full range of support services including, where appropriate, financial support.

5.11 We will work with the key interest groups and stakeholders to develop the detail of our proposals to be included in the new legislation.

The Adoption and Children Bill provides for the new status of 'special guardianship'. A special guardian will be in the same position as a guardian after death: thus his consent, along with that of any parent with parental responsibility, will be required for the child to be adopted and he will be able to appoint a guardian to act after his own death. The remaining consequences are spelled out in clause 112 of the Bill, inserting new sections into the Children Act 1989, among them:

14C Special guardianship orders: effect

(1) The effect of a special guardianship order is that while the order remains in force—

(a) a special guardian appointed by the order has parental responsibility for the child in respect of whom it is made; and

(b) subject to any other order in force with respect to the child under this Act, a special guardian is entitled to exercise parental responsibility to the exclusion of any other person with parental responsibility for the child (apart from another special guardian).

(2) Subsection (1) does not affect—

(a) the operation of any enactment or rule of law which requires the consent of more than one person with parental responsibility in a matter affecting the child; or

(b) any rights which a parent of the child has in relation to the child's adoption or placement for adoption.

(3) While a special guardianship order is in force with respect to a child, no person may—

(a) cause the child to be known by a new surname; or

(b) remove him from the United Kingdom,

without either the written consent of every person who has parental responsibility for the child or the leave of the court.

(4) Subsection (3)(b) does not prevent the removal of a child, for a period of less than three months, by a special guardian of his.

(5) If the child with respect to whom a special guardianship order is in force dies, his special guardian must take reasonable steps to give notice of that fact to—

(a) each parent of the child with parental responsibility; and

(b) each guardian of the child;

but if the child has more than one special guardian, and one of them has taken such steps in relation to a particular parent or guardian, any other special guardian need not do so as respects that parent or guardian.

(6) ...

14D Special guardianship orders: variation and discharge

(1) The court may vary or discharge a special guardianship order on the application of—

(a) the special guardian (or any of them, if there are more than one);

(b) any parent or guardian of the child concerned;

(c) any individual in whose favour a residence order is in force with respect to the child;

(d) any individual not falling within any of paragraphs (1) to (c) who has, or immediately before the making of the special guardianship order had, parental responsibility for the child;

(e)   the child himself; or

(f)   a local authority designated in a care order with respect to the child.

(2) In any family proceedings in which a question arises with respect to the welfare of a child with respect to whom a special guardianship order is in force, the court may also vary or discharge the special guardianship order if it considers that the order should be varied or discharged, even though no application has been made under subsection (1).

(3) The following must obtain the leave of the court before making an application under subsection (1)—

(a)   the child;

(b)   any parent or guardian of his;

(c)   any step-parent of his who has acquired, and has not lost, parental responsibility for him by virtue of section 4A;

(d)   any individual falling within subsection (1)(d) who immediately before the making of the special guardianship order had, but no longer has, parental responsibility for him.

(4) Where the person applying for leave to make an application under subsection (1) is the child, the court may only grant leave if it is satisfied that he has sufficient understanding to make the proposed application under subsection (1).

(5) The court may not grant leave to a person falling within subsection (3)(b)(c) or (d) unless it is satisfied that there has been a significant change in circumstances since the making of the special guardianship order.

A further consequence is in Sch. 3, para. 55(c), inserting a new s. 10(7A):

(7A) If a special guardianship is in force with respect to a child, an application for a residence order may only be made with respect to him, if apart from this subsection the leave of the court is not required, with such leave.

Questions

(i) Do you think that special guardianship will be any more popular than custodianship with (a) grandparents who have looked after their grandchildren from infancy, or (b) local authority foster parents?

(ii) If you were either, would you be attracted or put off by (a) the requirement, in new s. 14A(7)–(11) to notify the local social services authority, which must then make a report to the court before any order can be made; or (b) the prospect of special guardianship support services (including financial support), under new s. 14F?

(iii) Do you think that the consent of special guardians should be required before the child can be adopted? Do you see why the *Review of Adoption Law* recommended that an inter vivos guardian could not give or withhold consent to an adoption but a guardian appointed by such a guardian could?

(iv) Do you agree with the Review team (para. 6.1) that 'it is also important that adoption is not seen as the only or best means of providing a child with a permanent home'?

On the other hand:

20.4 We do not wish to rule out the possibility of adoption by relatives. There may be circumstances, however few, where it is appropriate: for instance, where a child's parents are dead, or they are living in another country and are unlikely ever to be able to make parental decisions in respect of the child's upbringing, and the child would like to be able to look upon a relative as a parent. But, as with applications by step-parents, we feel that the legislative framework must provide adequate opportunity for applicants to explore other possibilities, particularly residence orders.

...

21.1 There does not appear to be any reason why a child's carers should not at some point be able to apply for adoption. It would not be in the interests of a child to deny him the opportunity of adoption where, with the passage of time and changes in circumstances, carers find themselves fulfilling the role of parent and a child has come to look upon the carers as parents, and their family as his.

21.2 We propose, in line by and large with the requirements under the Children Act relating to applications for residence orders, that a person with whom a child is living should be allowed to apply for an adoption order at any time with the agreement of those with parental responsibility including, where the child is in care, the care authority; and that, where the necessary agreement has not been given, a person should be allowed to apply if the child has lived with him for a cumulative period of three years (within the previous five years). The leave of the court may be obtained in other cases but a local authority foster parent needs the consent of the authority.

21.3 We suggest that these recommendations should apply equally to applications by non-relatives and relatives. We think it important that rules for applying for residence orders and adoption orders are similar to avoid the foster parents making one application where their real intention is to secure the other. ...

22.1 Once an application has been made, there is a need to investigate the relationship between the child and the applicants; to ascertain the wishes and feelings of the child, parents, relatives and any other relevant persons; and to give the applicants and child opportunities to discuss the application in the light of any other possible arrangements that could be made. It is proposed that, for these purposes, there should be a mandatory period of 12 months between the application and the making of an adoption order in all non-agency applications.

Question

Why do you think that the Bill allows local authority foster parents to apply to adopt or for a residence order after the child has lived with them for one year, whereas relatives and other informal carers still have to wait for three years? Why the turn-around since the Children Act 1989? (There may be clue on p. 777, below.)

14.4 Adoption as a child care resource

We have already looked at the traditional type of adoption in Chapter 11, at adoption by step-parents in Chapter 12, and at adoption by relatives and foster carers above. Now we must draw the threads together by looking at adoption as a child care resource and the implications of this for parents, foster carers and prospective adopters, and for children. The context is summarised in *Adoption Now – Messages from Research* (1999), a report prepared by Professor Roy Parker with the help of an advisory group and the support of the Department of Heath:

Setting the context
The last 25 years have seen a dramatic change in the character of adoption. Its most significant feature has been the sharp reduction, from the early 1970s onwards, in the number of babies of unmarried mothers being given up for adoption. There were several reasons for this.

First, there was the 'contraception revolution', accelerated by the increasing use of the 'pill' from the early 1960s. Then, in 1967, the Abortion Act extended the grounds upon which a legal abortion could be obtained. ...

Gradually, the stigma associated with illegitimacy diminished, a trend reflected in the Family Law Reform Act 1987. It had been this sense of stigma which had persuaded many unmarried mothers to give up their babies for adoption. ...

In addition to these changes the status of unmarried motherhood came to be absorbed into the rapidly growing number of 'lone mothers' which followed the relaxation of the grounds for divorce introduced in the Divorce Law Reform Act 1969. ...

Another factor which contributed to the reduction in the number of babies of unmarried mothers who were given up for adoption was the shift in attitudes to sexual morality and to the institution of marriage. ...

There were, finally, various changes in housing and social security policies, especially in the 1970s, that eased (although they by no means eliminated) some of the practical problems of bringing up a child single-handedly. ...

Thus, as a result of these converging trends, the character of unmarried motherhood underwent a radical transformation, starting in the 1960s. Over much the same period, however, changes were also occurring in the way in which the well-being of vulnerable children was being perceived.

First, there was a growing conviction, which has continued to be supported by experience and research, that children should not be separated from their parents and family if at all possible. This encouraged efforts to restore to their families children who had been separated from them, a principle codified in the Children Act 1948 but only gradually put into practice. This was followed somewhat later by the official encouragement of preventive work which was aimed at avoiding the need for such separation in the first place, a development that was given legal endorsement in the Children Act 1963 but which, again, took time to gather momentum.

To the extent that these two policies – of restoration and prevention – were successful, the circumstances of the children coming into and remaining in local authority care became more problematic than those of the children who had preceded them. Of course, neither policy was pursued with equal vigour in all areas; but their cumulative effect, certainly after 1978 with the downturn in the number of children in care, was to increase the proportion who were considered to have 'special needs'. These children tended to be older and to have had more chequered and damaging childhoods. Furthermore, the emphasis upon rehabilitation also meant that social workers were expected to persevere in their efforts to secure the safe return of children to their families, thereby delaying the point at which any other plan was made for their future if that became necessary.

However, the 1970s saw a growing concern that steps should be taken to ensure that children like these had a stable home, reliable relationships and committed and enduring care. In 1973 Rowe and Lambert published *Children Who Wait* which showed that many children were indeed languishing in care for want of effective planning. Some, it was argued, could have rejoined their families; others required a long-term alternative. At much the same time the notion of 'permanency planning' was arriving in Britain from the United States. This, in particular, was thought to advocate adoption as the best permanent solution for separated children who could not, within a reasonable time, be rehabilitated with their families.

These ideas found expression in the Children Act 1975 and then in the Adoption Act 1976. In essence this made it easier for children who were in the care of local authorities to be adopted where that was appropriate. It also required each local authority to ensure that an adoption service was provided in their area. However, the legislation was not implemented until 1988, although by then most authorities had such a service as it was then understood to be.

Nevertheless, there was no substantial increase in the *number* of adoptions from care until after 1988. A peak of 2700 was reached in 1992, falling back thereafter to 1900 in 1996, although rising again slightly to 2000 in 1998. This fall, it has been claimed, was attributable to the effect of the Children Act 1989 which was implemented in October, 1991. It was reported that local authorities then became more hesitant to recommend adoption, believing that the court would now only be prepared to grant an order if there was indisputable evidence that a child's rehabilitation with their family was impossible or unwise.

However, adoptions from care came to account for an increasingly large *proportion* of all adoptions: from just 7% in 1975 to around 40% during the 1990s with most of the others being adoptions by step-parents or relatives. The current picture is set out diagrammatically in the figure opposite [see p. 775].

Although there were fewer babies being relinquished for adoption, by the second half of the 1970s social services departments were being encouraged to consider adoption for more of the children in their care, more of whom were older and regarded as having special needs. The characteristics of the children who could be considered for adoption therefore had changed in a far-reaching fashion. Rather than children being 'available' for adoption, the emphasis shifted to finding families for those children who needed a permanent home. Adoption came to be acknowledged in official and professional circles primarily as a means of meeting the needs of certain children rather than as a solution to the problem of unmarried motherhood or to the needs of infertile couples.

For all these reasons it is plain that the institution of adoption has undergone profound changes, changes that have brought with them new challenges. Many more adoptions are now contested; the selection of adopters and their suitability for particular children with particular needs demands more exacting assessment; once adopted, more children continue to have some form of contact with their birth families; and the need for adoptive parents and their children to be offered support after the order has been granted places special demands upon social and other services. In the past it has been assumed that having adopted a baby or infant with the agreement of the birth parents, and with all contact having been discontinued and secrecy preserved, the adopters could be left to raise the child as they would a child born to them; that is, without any special services needing to be provided. Such an assumption is no longer tenable.

It was the emergence of issues like these, and the failure of the law to reflect them, which prompted the Adoption Law Review that was set in train in 1989. Three of the studies reviewed here were commissioned by the Department of Health with the intention that they should contribute to this reconsideration. Others, commissioned somewhat later, continued to reflect the need to understand better the nature and implications of the changing character of adoption, changes that were acknowledged in the proposals for reform set out in the 1993 white paper *Adoption: the Future* (Cm 2288) and in the subsequent draft bill published in 1996 but taken no further. Since then a circular, several reports prepared by the Social Services Inspectorate and the latest government initiative entitled *Quality Protects* have highlighted the need for adoption to be treated as an integral part of the child care system and for attention to be paid to the repercussions of its changing character. It is this new climate that makes it particularly important for the messages from the Department of Health's programme of adoption research to be widely spread.

The pattern of adoption in England and Wales, 1996–97

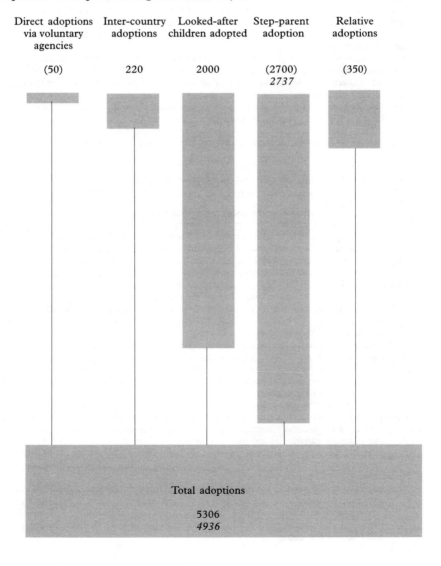

In 2000, the Government took up the challenge, as we see from *Adoption – a new approach*:

Children looked after by councils

2.1 Fifty-eight thousand children are now looked after at any one time by councils in England. Over the course of a year councils accept responsibility for over 90,000 children. These children are looked after by councils for a wide variety of reasons – some to provide family support through voluntary agreements with their parents, others are looked after under court orders. For many thousands of children every year the care system, through fostering, residential and respite care, provides the support and help they and their families need to sort out their problems and rebuild their family life. Many spend only a short time in the care of a council. Nearly 40% return home after less than eight weeks and more than half will have gone home within six months. Seventy per cent of all children who start being looked after return home within a year.

Children who stay in the care system

2.2 But there are many children who stay longer. Some of them never return home to their parents. Over 28,000 of the children looked after in the year to 31st March 1999 had been in care continuously for more than two years – about half of all those in care at any one time. Nearly 12,000 had been looked after for five years or more. By the time a child has been looked after for 18 months they have an 80% chance of remaining in care for four years or more (and probably right through until they leave the system at age 16–18).

2.3 For too many children the care system does not provide the chance for a long-term family life in which they can thrive:

- some 18% of looked after children experience three or more placements in the course of a year;
- an estimated 14% of children who are adopted have experienced six or more placements in their care history;
- only 46% of children looked after continuously for more than four years have spent at least the last two years in the same foster placement;

> What children say about stability
>
> 'If you're happy somewhere you should be able to stay.'
>
> 'Calling all foster parents. Get your act together. You and social workers move us about too much. DON'T.'
>
> '[moving is] scary, because you didn't know any people.'

2.4 Many of these children have led fractured and disrupted lives before coming into care. Many have mental heath problems and special educational needs. 67% of looked after children have an identifiable mental health problem. An estimated 30% of looked after children have statements of special educational need, compared with 2–3% of children generally. The results, when combined with the instability they can experience in care, are reflected in low opportunities while they are looked after and in poor chances for successful settled lives when they leave:

- 70% of young people leave care without having gained any GCSE or GNVQ qualifications;
- 25% of looked after children aged 14–16 do not attend school regularly and many have been excluded and have no regular educational placement;
- between 14% and 25% of young women leaving care are either pregnant or have a child, while in the general population only 3% of 20 year old women have a child;
- compared to the general population, those who have been looked after are 60 times more likely to be homeless;
- 39% of male prisoners under 21 have been looked after.

2.5 There are widespread concerns about whether the best use is being made of adoption to meet the needs of those looked after children requiring permanent homes with new families:

- there is wide variation in the use of adoption by councils, which cannot be explained solely by the characteristics of the children looked after by the council. In 1999–2000 the proportion of looked after children adopted during the year varied by council between 0.5% and 10.5%;
- inspections and surveys by the Social Services Inspectorate have identified concerns about the planning and management of council adoption services, and the way these services work with other services, including health and education;
- there is a widespread perception that the adoption process is prone to delay to the detriment of the child;

- there are concerns over the consistency, quality, clarity and speed of the process of applying to become an approved adopter.

2.6 This is why, in February 2000, the Prime Minister announced that he would personally lead a thorough review of adoption policy, to ensure that the best use was being made of adoption.

The view that adoption is primarily about looking after children is enshrined in s. 6 of the Adoption Act 1976:

Duty to promote welfare of child
6.—In reaching any decision relating to the adoption of a child a court or adoption agency shall have regard to all the circumstances, first consideration being given to the need to safeguard and promote the welfare of the child throughout his childhood; and shall so far as practicable ascertain the wishes and feelings of the child regarding the decision and give due consideration to them, having regard to his age and understanding.

The *Review of Adoption Law* (1992) made this comment:

7.2 The present welfare test requires courts and agencies to have regard to the child's welfare throughout his childhood. One of the special features of adoption is that it has a significant effect on a person's identity and family relationships not just during childhood but after the age of 18. It is known that some adopted people who have had no great difficulties during childhood coming to terms with the fact that they are adopted and have enjoyed a close relationship with their adoptive parents subsequently experience difficulties in the area of personal identity. We recommend that the legislative framework should underline the long-term significance of an adoption order and that the welfare test should refer not only to the welfare of the child throughout childhood but his welfare in adult life as well. We also recommend that one of the factors which the court must take into account in deciding whether to grant an order should be the likely effect on the child's adult life of any change in his legal status.

This is reflected in clause 1 of the Adoption and Children Bill:

Considerations applicable to the exercise of powers
1.—(1) This section applies whenever a court or adoption agency is coming to a decision relating to the adoption of a child.

(2) The paramount consideration of the court or adoption agency must be the child's welfare, throughout his life.

(3) The court or adoption agency must at all times bear in mind that any delay in coming to the decision is likely to prejudice the child's welfare.

(4) The court or adoption agency must have regard to the following matters (among others)—

  (*a*) the child's ascertainable wishes and feelings regarding the decision (considered in the light of the child's age and understanding),

  (*b*) the child's particular needs,

  (*c*) the likely effect on the child (throughout his life) of having ceased to be a member of the original family and become an adopted person,

  (*d*) the child's age, sex, background and any of the child's characteristics which the court or agency considers relevant,

  (*e*) any harm (within the meaning of the Children Act 1989) which the child has suffered or is at risk of suffering, and

  (*f*) the relationship which the child has with relatives, and with any other person in relation to whom the court or agency considers the question to be relevant, including—

  (i)   the likelihood of any such relationship continuing and the value to the child of its doing so,

  (ii) the ability and willingness of any of the child's relatives, or of any such person, to provide the child with a secure environment in which the child can develop, and otherwise to meet the child's needs,

  (iii) the wishes and feelings of any of the child's relatives, or of any such person, about the child.

(5) In placing the child for adoption, the adoption agency must give due consideration to the child's religious persuasion, racial origin and cultural and linguistic background.

(6) The court or adoption agency must always consider the whole range of powers available to it in the child's case (whether under this Act or the Children Act 1989); and the court must not make any order under this Act unless it considers that making the order would be better for the child than not doing so.

(7) In this section, "coming to a decision relating to the adoption of a child", in relation to a court, includes—

(*a*)   coming to a decision in any proceedings where the orders that might be made by the court include an adoption order (or the revocation of such an order), a placement order (or the revocation of such an order), or an order under section 25 (or the revocation of such an order),

(*b*)   coming to a decision about granting leave in respect of any action (other than the initiation of proceedings in any court) which may be taken by an adoption agency or individual under this Part,

but does not include coming to a decision about granting leave in any other circumstances.

(8) For the purposes of this section—

(*a*)   references to relationships are not confined to legal relationships,

(*b*)   references to a relative, in relation to a child, include the child's mother and father.

Another recommendation of the *Review of Adoption Law* (1992) was this:

7.1 ... We recommend that the welfare principle in adoption legislation should be brought into line with that in the Children Act in making the child's welfare the paramount consideration, but with the important exception that the child's welfare should *not* be the paramount consideration in determining whether to make an adoption order without the agreement of the child's parent. If the principle of the paramountcy of the child's welfare were to apply in this respect, the court would be able to override completely a parent's wishes, which we would consider unacceptable in relation to an order which irrevocably terminates a parent's legal relationship with a child.

This leads us to the vital subject of parental consent. The Tomlin Committee (p. 520, above) treated adoption as a consensual 'transaction' between birth and adoptive parents, in which the court's task was to ensure that their agreement did not prejudice the welfare of the child. The agreement of each parent with parental responsibility is still required, although it can be dispensed with on defined grounds. Over the years, the circumstances in which the court has been empowered to dispense with the parent's consent have expanded. The present list is in s. 16 of the Adoption Act 1976:

16.—(2) ... that the parent or guardian—

(*a*)   cannot be found or is incapable of giving agreement;

(*b*)   is withholding his agreement unreasonably;

(*c*)   has persistently failed without reasonable cause to discharge the parental duties in relation to the child;

(*d*)   has abandoned or neglected the child;

(*e*)   has persistently ill-treated the child;

(*f*)   has seriously ill-treated the child (subject to subsection (5)).

...

(5) Subsection (2)(*f*) does not apply unless (because of the ill-treatment or for other reasons) the rehabilitation of the child within the household of the parent or guardian is unlikely.

Question

Compare these grounds with the threshold for making a care order under s. 31 of the Children Act 1989 (see p. 719, above). Do these grounds appear to you to be wider or narrower? Do the differences seem, at least at first sight, to be justified by the different circumstances in which the procedures are used?

In practice, dispensing with parental consent to an adoption order arises in two quite different contexts: first, the parent who places her child for adoption and later changes her mind, and second, the parent who has never agreed to adoption.

Re W (an infant)
[1971] AC 682, [1971] 2 All ER 49, [1971] 2 WLR 1011, 115 Sol Jo 286, House of Lords

The mother was unmarried, in her early twenties. She was living in one room with her two little girls by an earlier relationship, now broken, when she found herself unintentionally pregnant again. She was a good mother to the girls but was doubtful of her ability to cope with a third child in that accommodation. Accordingly, she made arrangements before the birth for the child to be adopted. She was offered better accommodation just before the birth, but still had doubts and so did not alter the arrangement. The child went to the applicants as temporary foster parents when he was eight days old and had been there ever since. They began adoption proceedings when he was ten months old, and the mother signed the consent form a few days later. She withdrew that consent the day before the hearing was first due to take place. She was now well settled with her two daughters and a cousin in her new flat, but she had had no contact at all with the child, who was 16 months old when the county court judge came to decide the case. He decided that she was withholding her consent unreasonably and made the order. She appealed successfully to Court of Appeal, on the ground that her conduct had not been 'culpable' or 'blameworthy' ([1970] 2 QB 589, [1970] 3 All ER 990, CA) but a differently constituted Court of Appeal refused to follow this test in *Re B (CHO) (an infant)* [1971] 1 QB 437, [1970] 3 All ER 1008, CA. The applicants appealed to the House of Lords.

Lord Hailsham of St Marylebone LC: ... [Section 16(2)(*b*)] lays down a test of reasonableness. It does not lay down a test of culpability or self-indulgent indifference or of failure or probable failure of parental duty. ... It is not for the courts to embellish, alter, subtract from, or add to words which, for once at least, Parliament has employed without any ambiguity at all. I must add that if the test had involved me in a criticism of the respondent involving culpability or callous or self-indulgent indifference, I might well have come to the same conclusion on the facts as did Sachs and Cross LJJ. But since the test imposed on me by the Act is reasonableness and not culpability I have come to the opposite conclusion.

The question then remains as to how to apply the correct test. The test is whether at the time of the hearing the consent is being withheld unreasonably. As Lord Denning MR said in *Re L (an infant)* (1962) 106 Sol Jo 611:

> 'In considering the matter I quite agree that: (1) the question whether she is unreasonably withholding her consent is to be judged at the date of the hearing; and (2) the welfare of the child is not the sole consideration; and (3) the one question is whether she is unreasonably withholding her consent. But I must say that in considering whether she is reasonable or unreasonable we must take into account the welfare of the child. A reasonable mother surely gives great weight to what is better for the child. Her anguish of mind is quite understandable; but still it may be unreasonable for her to withhold consent. We must look and see whether it is reasonable or unreasonable according to what a reasonable woman in her place would do in all the circumstances of the case.'

This passage was quoted with approval by Davies LJ in *Re B (CHO) (an infant)*, by Lord Sorn in *A B and C B v X's Curator*, by Pearson LJ in *Re C* [1971] 1 QB 437, [1970] 3 All ER 1008, *Re C (L)* [1965] 2 QB 449, [1964] 3 All ER 483 and by Winn LJ in *Re B (CHO)*. In my view, it may now be considered authoritative. ...

From this it is clear that the test is reasonableness and not anything else. It is not culpability. It is not indifference. It is not failure to discharge parental duties. It is reasonableness, and reasonableness in the context of the totality of the circumstances. But, although welfare per se is not the test, the fact that a reasonable parent does pay regard to the welfare of his child must enter into the question of reasonableness as a relevant factor. It is relevant in all cases if and to the extent that a reasonable parent would take it into account. It is decisive in those cases where a reasonable parent must so regard it. ...

I only feel it necessary to add on this part of the case that I entirely agree with Russell LJ when he said in effect ([1970] 2QB 589, [1970] 3 All ER 990) that it does not follow from the fact that the test is reasonableness that any court is entitled simply to substitute its own view for that of the parent. In my opinion, it should be extremely careful to guard against this error. Two reasonable parents can perfectly reasonably come to opposite conclusions on the same set of facts without forfeiting their title to be regarded as reasonable. The question in any given case is whether a parental veto comes within the band of possible reasonable decisions and not whether it is right or mistaken. Not every reasonable exercise of judgment is right, and not every mistaken exercise of judgment is unreasonable. There is a band of decisions within which no court should seek to replace the individual's judgment with his own.
Appeal allowed.

Question

How many points of difference can you find between this case and *Re K (a minor) (wardship: adoption)* [1991] FCR 142, [1991] 1 FLR 57 (p. 763, above)? Are they enough to account for the difference in result?

Cases where the parent has never consented usually arise after a child has been taken into care and the local authority plans a permanent substitute home rather than rehabilitation. The court's approach is first to decide 'where does the child's future lie?' If it lies in a substitute home, the court must then decide whether a hypothetical reasonable parent would object.

Re D (a minor) (adoption: freeing order)
[1990] FCR 615, [1991] 1 FLR 48, Court of Appeal

The child was four and a half years old. The father played no part in her life, the mother's relationship with him having ended before the child's birth. Following unexplained injuries and evidence of emotional deprivation, a care order was made. The child was placed with short-term foster parents and visits with the mother were arranged. At about the same time the mother gave birth to a second child by another man. The relationship between the mother and that other man was unstable. The child returned home to the mother on trial with intense social work involvement. However, the child had a continuing loss of weight and suffered unexplained injuries. There was hostility by the mother towards the child. The child was again placed with foster parents. The local authority decided not to try further rehabilitation but to consider adoption. The mother was at first in favour of adoption but later changed her mind. By this time she was living with a different man. Contact between mother and the child continued, albeit infrequently, after the child was placed with prospective adopters. The local authority applied to free the child for adoption. The judge dismissed that application and the local authority appealed.

Butler-Sloss LJ: ... The judge said:

'I have been referred to a large number of authorities and there are two questions:

(1) Is adoption in the best interests of the child?

(2) Is the natural mother unreasonable in withholding her consent? . . .'

[A] criticism [of the judge's approach] relates to the first test, whether it is in the child's best interests that she should be adopted. Having set out very briefly some of the relevant facts and considered access to the mother and her present position in somewhat more detail the judge said:

> 'What I have to decide is not whether it is in K's interests in the near or foreseeable future or perhaps the long-term future that she should remain with the prospective adopters, but whether it is in K's interests, at this time and at this age, that her right of contact with her mother and with her half-sister should be terminated. Notwithstanding the present careful reports to the contrary, I find it difficult to hold that it is in her best interests that contact should cease. Access is taking place, she enjoys it and it is causing no ill-effects.'

[Counsel] has argued with considerable cogency that the judge never addressed the underlying question of the welfare of the child, nor did he analyse objectively the value of access to the child. That value in turn depended upon the quality of the relationship between the mother and the child. How strong was the bond between them? ... There was no evidence of any real bond between the mother and child, not surprisingly with the history of interrupted care throughout her short life, and some evidence of rejection by the mother during each of the two periods when K was returned to the mother's care. She had a period of one year between October 1985 and October 1986 with her mother, followed by a gap of 9 months away from her. She returned in July 1987 for 7 months and thereafter, in the subsequent 16 months had seen her mother, at most, five or six times. The evidence of the social worker was that she was indifferent to access. It was a time for her to play with toys. She was happy there and happy to say goodbye. The social worker also said that she did not believe that there was a meaningful relationship between the mother and the child and that she would not suffer from the cessation of access by her mother. None of that evidence was referred to by the judge. Further, although he referred to the reports, he did not refer specifically to the report of the child's guardian ad litem, who found a lack of sustained commitment by the mother to access over the year up to the hearing and gave careful reasons on behalf of the child why he recommended adoption.

The judge also failed to make a finding as to whether the child was likely to return to the mother in the foreseeable future. This was a matter of importance in applying both the first and second tests. The undisputed evidence before him was that the child would remain with the prospective adopters whatever the outcome of the application, even if they had to be redesignated long-term foster parents. The local authority had a full care order and unless the mother succeeded in revoking it, an application for which was not in prospect, the child would not be likely to return home. The purpose of access, therefore, had to be considered: was it to create a greater bond between them which might lead to a change of heart by the local authority; or was it to be contact access for a few times a year to keep alive the child's knowledge of her mother? ... Reasons for continuing the second type of access were given to the judge by junior counsel then appearing for the mother, as he informed us. But it is unclear which sort of access the judge had in mind and whether he believed that a return to the mother was feasible. If rehabilitation was not feasible, the realities of the situation of access as the child grew older and became more settled with long-term foster parents did not appear to have been considered by the judge.

For all these reasons we are satisfied that the judge failed to look beneath the surface and did not look at all the circumstances. He gave what he thought was the desirability of access continuing at this time predominant weight over all other factors. He did not give sufficient consideration to the child's long-term welfare throughout her childhood and did not correctly apply the test under s.6. In our judgment he erred in law in his approach to the first stage.

We now turn to the second stage. The test under s.16(2) as to whether a parent is withholding his or her agreement unreasonably is entirely different from that under s.6. ...

From *Re W (An Infant)* [p. 779, above] and subsequent speeches in the House of Lords and judgments of this court it is clear that reasonableness is to be judged by an objective and not a subjective test. Would a reasonable parent have refused consent? (per Lord Reid in *O'Connor v A and B* [1971] 1 WLR 1227, 1229). This involves considerations of how a parent in the actual circumstances of this mother, but (hypothetically) endowed with a mind and temperament capable of making reasonable decisions, would approach a complex question involving a judgment as to the present and the future and the probable impact upon the child (per Lord Reid in *Re D* [1977] AC 602, 625). There has become a greater emphasis upon the welfare of the child as one of the factors (but not the overriding one), and the chances of a successful reintroduction to or continuance of contact with the natural parent is a critical factor in assessing the reaction of that hypothetical reasonable parent (per Purchas LJ in *Re H: Re W (Adoption: Parental Agreement)* (1983) 4 FLR 614, 625). This test is to be applied at the time of the hearing and the court is not entitled simply to substitute its own view for that of the parent (*Re W (An Infant)* (above) at p. 667).

In his judgment, the judge said:

> 'Miss D looks forward to the eventual reunification of K and S with her and Mr B. Although Miss D has not really explained all of the past, on the evidence I have heard from

her I do not consider her aspiration eventually to have K back to be an unreasonable one. She has not said precisely how she expects this to come about. She is after all in the hands of the local authority, but I do not regard her aspiration as being unreasonable.'

Since the judge in considering the first test had never decided whether such an aspiration was objectively reasonable, the criticism of [counsel] that this was a subjective approach of the judge is, in our judgment, well-founded. The judge went on to say:

'Apart from eventual reunification there is access continuing and I do not see how I can say that she is being unreasonable to want it to continue as she thinks it is for the benefit of K and S. Especially when it is going on with no ill-effect to K.'

Again, since there was, as we have already set out under the first test, no finding as to the purpose or long-term benefit of access to K, [counsel's] criticism applies equally to this passage. ...

The question then arises as to whether this court should substitute its own discretion upon the facts before us or remit the application to the county court for a rehearsing and reassessment of the two tests. ... We are satisfied that in this case this court has sufficient information to enable it to consider the test of welfare and the objective assessment as to whether a hypothetical reasonable parent in the circumstances of this mother ought to have given her consent. On the first test we are entirely satisfied that there is no prospect whatever of this child returning to live with her mother. There is no evidence of a real relationship between the mother and the child. ... Further, the contact of K with her half-sister, S, has been infrequent and at their respective ages and in the circumstances it was not suggested by any one that any relationship at all has developed. We are satisfied that there is ample evidence upon which to answer the first test under s.6: the adoption would safeguard and promote the welfare of K throughout her childhood.

The second test of consent is more difficult and we keep well in mind the importance of 'the band of decisions within which no court should seek to replace the individual's judgment with its own'.

Looking at the hypothetical reasonable parent in the circumstances of this mother, we see that the factors in her favour are: she is the mother and the child lived with her for two main periods totalling about 18 months: she now has a settled home with a potential step-father and S has returned to live with her and is being cared for satisfactorily – if she were not, no doubt the local authority would have intervened; she desires to reunite the family; she is continuing to have access and the child on one level enjoys it and is having no ill-effects from it.

The contrary factors are: the efforts at rehabilitation have failed in the past, not only because the child was not well cared for and there was suspected non-accidental injury which may have been attributable to the then cohabitee, but also a failure of bonding, and hostility and rejection by the mother; K has not lived with her mother since 19 February 1988, there is no present evidence of any close or warm or effective relationship between them nor any foundation upon which to recreate it; there is no evidence of any relationship between the half-sisters; there is no real possibility of rehabilitation not only in the foreseeable future, but since children cannot wait for ever and will settle where they are, at any time thereafter – consequently the entirely natural aspirations of the mother to have K back and reunite the family are unrealistic; in the absence of eventual rehabilitation and without an adequate existing relationship, the continuance of access in the long term is not likely to be beneficial to the child in any real sense; contact a few times a year without any firm basis of a relationship between the mother and child for a child of 4 and a half years old would at best be entirely superficial and more for the adult than the child, and at worst, as the child settled with the present family and grew older, might be unsettling and upsetting. ...

In our judgment, a reasonable parent in the position of the mother would recognise the overwhelming force of the negative points and the unreasonableness of refusing to agree to the freeing for adoption. We, therefore, hold that the mother has unreasonably withheld her agreement under s. 16(2). We allow the appeal and accede to the application of the local authority to free K for adoption.
Appeal allowed.

Questions

(i) In a somewhat similar case, *Re L (a minor) (adoption: statutory criteria)* [1990] 1 FLR 305, Balcombe LJ stated: '[counsel for the mother] submitted that there was a presumption in the case of all children that access by the natural parent was desirable, and the onus ought to be on those who sought to stop access to prove it. It seems to me that that submission is ... misconceived'. But if this 'presumption' applies between separated parents (p. 598, above), why should it not apply between birth parents and prospective adopters?

(ii) If the court first concludes that adoption is in the best interests of the child, how can it then conclude that the mother is reasonable in objecting?

(iii) Why do you think that these cases were argued under 'unreasonable withholding' rather than one of the other grounds for dispensing with parental agreement?

(iv) Would a different type of order have been appropriate?

There are some cases where parents are reasonable in withholding agreement and an alternative may be more appropriate:

Re M (Adoption or Residence Order)
[1998] 1 FCR 165, [1998] 1 FLR 570, Court of Appeal

The child was placed with Dr and Mrs A when she was nearly nine, with an expectation that they would adopt her. When they applied to adopt her two years later, she said that she did not want to be adopted, having been saying that she wanted to return to her mother. Dr and Mrs A originally indicated that a residence order would be acceptable, but later became adamant that they were only prepared to keep the child under an adoption order. The mother withdrew her own application for a residence order and was prepared to agree to an order with a s. 91(14) restriction in favour of Dr and Mrs A, but withheld her agreement to an adoption. It was clear that it was best for the child to stay with them for the rest of her childhood. The judge dispensed with her agreement and made an adoption order. The mother appealed.

Ward LJ: . . .

Two distinct and separate questions have to be asked before deciding whether or not to make an adoption order, viz:

    (1) Should the child live with the applicants or with someone else,

    (2) Should the child live with that person(s) under the aegis of:

        (i) an adoption order; or

        (ii) a care order; or

        (iii) a residence order alone; or

        (iv) a residence order coupled with a s 91(14) restriction; or

        (v) no order at all?

...

In order to decide what form of order is appropriate, it is essential to have regard to the nature and effect of each order and the advantages and disadvantages each brings to the safeguarding and promotion of the welfare of the child throughout his childhood. The legal nature and effect of an adoption order is governed by s 39 of the Adoption Act 1976. It changes status. The child is treated in law as if she had been born a child of the marriage of the applicants. She ceases in law to be a child of her mother and the sister of her siblings. The old family link is destroyed and new family ties are created. The psychological effect is that the child loses one identity and gains another. Adoption is inconsistent with being a member of both old and new family at the same time. Long-term fostering does enable the child to have the best of both worlds by feeling she belongs to both families though she must reside with and will anyway usually choose to live with only one – the one who gives her the daily love and care.

The significant advantage of adoption is that it can promote much-needed security and stability, the younger the age of placement, the fuller the advantage. The disadvantage is that it is unlike any other decision made by adults during the child's minority because it is irrevocable. The child cannot at a later stage even in adulthood reverse the process. That is a salutary reminder of the seriousness of the decision. The advantage of the care/residence order is the converse – it can be adopted to meet changing needs, but therein lies its disadvantage – it does not provide absolute certainty and security. Section 91(14) of the Children Act 1989 minimises, if not eliminates, the uncertainty.

In weighing up these considerations, the court must have an eye to the realities of the child's situation, bearing in mind the torture of adolescence through which the child must live, finding and then asserting the independence of growing adulthood. When times are bad – and it would be surprising if there were not such times – it will be the emotional attachment forged between the adopters and the child, not that piece of paper entitled 'adoption order', which will prevent a disaffected child searching for a grass which will always seem so much greener in the pastures occupied by the old family, especially when there is extensive contact as is proposed in this case.
...

Nowhere in the judgment does the judge address the issue of whether or not a residence order, with or without the s 91(14) restriction, would have provided adequate security for the placement. The guardian broached 'the dreadful "RO" word' with some trepidation and if, as is certainly possible on a reading of the transcript, it was, as the judge said, 'agreed on all sides that [mother's] application for residence order must be dismissed and that as a fact M can only continue with the applicant's under an adoption order', that agreement was implicit, rather than explicit and it was made faute de mieux, any alternative having been dismissed by the judge as pie in the sky. In my judgment the judge was wrong to inhibit, as he clearly did, a full exploration of the important issue of whether or not the desired security could have been adequately achieved by other means and whether or not the threatened return of M would be implemented. ...

[On the issue of dispensing with the mother's agreement.] It was submitted that her refusal to consent was not unreasonable because the mother had taken into account and was entitled to take into account the facts that:

–   the local authority did not consider the adoption to be in the child's best interest;
–   the guardian had changed her mind, having originally been against adoption;
–   she was entitled to differ from the opinion of Dr B just as the guardian, (in particular) and the social workers did;
–   she believed her daughter did not wish to be adopted;
–   she knew the other children were against it;
–   the local authority saw some prospect of her offering M a home and M was telling her and the professionals in the case and even the applicants of her wish to live at home with her mother;
–   the adopters' refusal to keep M unless an adoption order were made indicated either they were not acting in M's best interests or they believed that the mother's home did not present serious risks for M; and,
–   the need for the child's links with her natural family to be maintained was shown by increased contact which would continue.

Those were legitimate matters for the mother to consider in arriving at her decisions. They affected the band of reasonableness of her choice. The judge overrode her decision because he regarded the child's welfare as decisively answering the question. He ought to have weighed those other matters in the scales and he did not do so or he certainly did not appear to have done so. In his judgment, he gave no reason why they were not valid factors for the mother to take into consideration. ...

Because it appears from his judgment that he carried into his decision that which he had expressed throughout the hearing, namely that there was really only one question in the case at all – welfare – I am satisfied that he erred in his approach to this question.

The appeal must be allowed accordingly.

Judge LJ agreed with Ward LJ, but Simon Brown LJ did not:

Simon Brown LJ: . . .

In the last analysis, however, this case seems to me to turn less upon any point of law than upon an evaluation of the answers to these basic questions:

(1)   How bad an option is rehabilitation with mother?
(2)   How much less bad an option is adoption by the applicants?
(3)   How much better an option than either is option 3?
(4)   If, despite the applicants' avowed intention to refuse to accept option 3, the court were nevertheless to make the relevant orders – ie a residence order in their favour coupled with a s 91(14) order – what chance is there that the applicants would, after all, accept this? (They could not, of course, be compelled to do so.)

(5) Is rehabilitation with mother so much worse an option than adoption that, even taking into account the possibility of the applicants accepting option 3 with such advantages as that is perceived to have over either of the other options, 'the advantages of adoption for the welfare of the child appear sufficiently strong to justify overriding the views and interests of the objecting parent' (to quote *Re C*, p. 787, below)?

In answering the all-important question (5) in the affirmative, as I would, I am really saying no more than that I find myself in full agreement with the views of the guardian as expressed to us through counsel, Mrs Barnett. If there is any risk that the applicants would not in the event accept the third option, that is not a risk which the guardian is prepared to take. Her views are not, we were told, finely balanced: rather she believes that M 'must' remain in the applicants' care. She believes that rehabilitation with mother here would be 'catastrophic', and submits that in those circumstances the hypothetical reasonable mother could not properly maintain her veto to adoption with that catastrophe the almost inevitable result.

Question

What do you think of parents who are prepared to send a child back if they cannot keep her under an adoption order? Would you have taken the risk that Ward and Judge LJJ did?

Re B (a child) (adoption order)
[2001] EWCA Civ 347, [2001] 2 FCR 89, [2001] 2 FLR 26, Court of Appeal

The child, now aged six, was accommodated at the mother's request when aged two and placed with his present foster mother soon afterwards. The mother was effectively out of the picture but the child remained in regular contact with his father and with two brothers who lived nearby. The local authority and foster mother favoured adoption with generous contact. The guardian ad litem and consultant child psychiatrist favoured a residence order with an order under s. 91(14) of the Children Act 1989, prohibiting applications by the father without leave of the court. The foster mother was not prepared to agree to this. The judge held that the father was withholding his agreement unreasonably and made an adoption order. The father appealed.

Thorpe LJ: . . .

[10] In relation to J the judge made it absolutely plain that he was not minded to impose a residence order upon Mrs F. He then went on to enumerate the pros and cons as he saw them of either continuing the status quo or, alternatively, making in its stead an adoption order in favour of Mrs F with a contact order to father. At the end of his analysis of the considerations for and against, he came to the conclusion that the balance fell in favour of an adoption order. He then went on to consider whether it was right to dispense with the father's consent. He had only to consider the father's objection since the mother who played very little part in the debate had indicated her readiness to consent to an adoption order in favour of Mrs F.

[11] In a short passage he reasoned that it was open to him to dispense with the father's consent and he concluded by making the adoption order. That of course he did in the face of reasonable opinions from both the guardian and Dr G that of the two options considered by the judge, the status quo would better promote J's welfare. However the course that he took had the support of the social worker in the case, Mrs B. ...

[17] ... the guardian's assessment is powerfully expressed in her written report. Having (at p 50) defined the reality in these terms, 'The reality is that J has two families and that this must form part of his integration', and having on the same page recorded J's strong attachment to his 'Dad', at p. 53 she distilled the case for the judge in this paragraph:

'This case questions the meaning of contemporary adoption. J lives in close proximity to his paternal family, has frequent contact with them and his brothers. He has a warm relationship with many of his paternal family and "idolises" his family. Mr B supports his placement. It cannot be feasible to say that Mr B is unreasonably withholding his consent to J's adoption.'

[18] It seems to me that that really defines the reality of the arrangements that had been achieved for this little boy by the date of the hearing in the county court. It amounted to a gap that was unbridgeable and the judge's endeavour to bridge it does not, in my opinion, stand up to analysis. His attempt is to be found at p. 7 of his judgment when he says:

'It has to be a long term view, because an adoption order is irrevocable and its effect considerable, since it is inconsistent with a child being a member of two families at the same time. However, it seems to me he can be a part of two families, but of course those parts would not be of equivalent status.'

[19] That endeavour seems to me to recognise but not to answer what was the root problem in this case. To make an adoption order was inconsistent with the reality that J was both a member of his foster mother's family and a member of his father's family.

[20] Secondly, I have grave doubts as to whether the judge sufficiently considered the father's right to family life. As Mr Horowitz has submitted, it does not seem that the judge considered whether the interference with the father's right to family life which would result from the making of an adoption order was necessary and proportionate in accordance with art. 8(2) of the Convention. It seems to me in this case that it is very hard indeed to demonstrate the necessary proportionality given the completely satisfactory arrangement that was open for judicial approval in the confirmation of the status quo for J, just as it had been confirmed for the older children of the family.

[21] Mr Horowitz's strongest ground, if I had to choose among the three, is perhaps his last. It does seem to me that the judicial licence to override the sustained objection of the natural parents would be stretched to quite unjustifiable limits if, in a case such as this where the adoption option was opposed to the extent it was within the professional counsel, the judge could set aside the father's objection. After all, there was perhaps nobody who knew more about this family and these children than Mrs L who had been consistently appointed to the responsibility of guardian ad litem time after time from the first initiated proceedings before even J was born. Nobody in the field of child and adolescent psychiatry has given such generous forensic service to family justice on the western circuit than Dr G, and the wisdom of his recommendations is widely recognised by all the specialist judges on that circuit. It seems to me that it would be extremely hard to label as unreasonable an opinion held by a father knowing that it was an opinion that he shared with such an experienced guardian and such an experienced forensic expert.

[22] For all those reasons I firmly believe that the order made by the judge below is plainly wrong and must be set aside and in its place an order in terms now to be considered in detail should be substituted.

Question

In *Re X (children) (adoption: confidentiality)* [2002] EWCA Civ 828, a large sibling group had stayed with the same foster parents since they were removed from home and the foster parents were now applying to adopt them. But the parents were led to believe that the children had been placed with new prospective adopters because the foster parents wanted to make a clean break from the past. One of the children was old enough to have a clear recollection of his birth family and wanted to remain in touch with them. The court allowed the prospective adopters to maintain their anonymity during the adoption proceedings. (a) Would you be able to decide whether or not the parents were unreasonably withholding their agreement in such circumstances? (b) Do you think that the parents can have a fair trial of their case?

The *Review of Adoption Law* (1992) said this about the grounds for dispensing with agreement:

12.4 Much of the difficulty surrounding this part of the law is associated with the ground used most often for dispensing with parental agreement – that the parent is withholding his agreement unreasonably. The court may dispense with parental agreement if it considers that a hypothetical reasonable parent would agree to the adoption. But it has not been clear how much weight a hypothetical reasonable parent would be expected to place upon the welfare of the child, particularly ... where a significant relationship has developed between the child and prospective adoptive parents. Even where (in freeing applications) the child has not yet been placed with prospective adoptive parents, there has been a tendency to decide that adoption is in a child's best interests and for this reason alone to dispense with parental agreement on the grounds that it is being unreasonably withheld. This has meant that the test has given paramount weight to the child's welfare, which we consider unsatisfactory when dealing with parental wishes and feelings in relation to so important a step as adoption. It is also unsatisfactory that the parent whose agreement is dispensed with on these grounds thereby acquires what may be perceived as the stigma of being an unreasonable parent.

12.5 Most of the other grounds for dispensing with agreement, although seldom used, are unsatisfactory in that they relate exclusively to shortcomings in parental care rather than to the needs of the child. Where there are faults or shortcomings in parental care, this should not imply that adoption is ipso facto a suitable option for a child. Nor in cases where it is decided that adoption is in a child's best interests should this imply that the parents are necessarily at fault. For instance, a mother whose eldest child has been in care for some years may have other children whom she has shown herself capable of looking after: although the child in care is not at risk of significant harm if he returns home, he may no longer consider himself part of that family and may want to make a fresh start with adoptive parents. Responses to the review largely favoured the removal of fault-based grounds for dispensing with agreement.

12.6 We therefore propose that, of the existing grounds in section 16(2) of the 1976 Act, only (*a*) ('the parent cannot be found or is incapable of giving agreement') should be retained. The remaining grounds should be replaced by a single test which should apply in all situations where a parent who is capable of giving agreement can be found and is withholding agreement. This test should:

    a.   address the question of the advantages of becoming part of a new family and having a new legal status (rather than the question of where the child should reside);

    b.   focus on the needs of the child rather than any parental shortcomings;

    c.   require the court to be satisfied that adoption is significantly better than other available options and that parental wishes should therefore be overridden.

It might be expressed in terms of the court being satisfied that the advantages to a child of becoming part of a new family and having a new legal status are so significantly greater than the advantages to the child of any alternative option as to justify overriding the wishes of a parent or guardian. The court should consider not just whether the child should go to live with, or continue to live with, the prospective adoptive parents but whether it is in the child's interests to sever his links with the birth family and become part of a new family. This should of course be considered carefully in any proposed adoption, but it is especially important where a child or a parent does not agree to adoption.

It is difficult to resist the thought that Lords Justices Steyn and Hoffmann may have had this in mind (although they do not say so) in their joint judgment in *Re C (A Minor) (Adoption: Parental Agreement: Contact)* [1993] [1993] 2 FLR 260 at 272:

... the judge had to decide that the mother was 'withholding her agreement unreasonably'. This question had to be answered according to an objective standard. In other words, it required the judge to assume that the mother was not, as she in fact was, a person of limited intelligence and inadequate grasp of the emotional and other needs of a lively little girl of 4. Instead she had to be assumed to be a woman with a full perception of her own deficiencies and an ability to evaluate dispassionately the evidence and opinions of the experts. She was also to be endowed with the intelligence and altruism needed to appreciate, if such were the case, that her child's welfare would be so much better served by adoption that her own maternal feelings should take second place.

Such a paragon does not of course exist: she shares with the 'reasonable man' the quality of being, as Lord Radcliffe once said, an 'anthropomorphic conception of justice'. The law conjures the imaginary parent into existence to give expression to what it considers that justice requires as between the welfare of the child as perceived by the judge on the one hand and the legitimate views and interests of the natural parents on the other.

... for those who feel some embarrassment at having to consult the views of so improbable a legal fiction, we venture to observe that precisely the same question may be raised in a demythologised form by the judge asking himself whether, having regard to the evidence and applying the current values of our society, the advantages of adoption for the welfare of the child appear sufficiently strong to justify overriding the views and interests of the objecting parent or parents. The reasonable parent is only a piece of machinery invented to provide the answer to this question.

Clause 51 of the Adoption and Children Bill, however, takes a different line:

Parental etc. consent

51.—(1) The court cannot dispense with the consent of any parent or guardian of a child to the child being placed for adoption or to the making of an adoption order in respect of the child unless the court is satisfied that—

    (*a*)   the parent or guardian cannot be found or is incapable of giving consent, or

    (*b*)   the welfare of the child requires the consent to be dispensed with.

Questions

(i) To what extent does this test, combined with clause 1(1), (2) and (7) (p. 777, above) differ from (a) the present law, or (b) the test recommended by the *Adoption Law Review*?

(ii) Would either have made a difference to the result in *Re B (a child) (adoption order)* (p. 785, above)?

(iii) If it would, do you think that this would be a good or a bad thing?

(iv) Do you think that the Bill test is compatible with either the child's or the birth family's right to respect for their family life, protected by Art. 8 of the European Convention on Human Rights (see p. 466, above)?

The *Report of the Departmental Committee on the Adoption of Children* (the Houghton Report) (1972) identified problems with the consent procedure:

168. ... There is considerable dissatisfaction with the timing and nature of the present consent procedure. Parental rights and obligations are not terminated at the time the parent signs the consent document. They continue until an adoption order is made some weeks or months later. The argument in favour of this system is that there is never a period when the child is not the legal responsibility of either natural or adoptive parents. But there is evidence that this procedure imposes unnecessary strain and confusion on the mother. Moreover, it may encourage indecisiveness on her part; and by maintaining her legal responsibility for the child until the adoption order is made, it may prevent her from facing the reality of her decision and planning her own future. This period of uncertainty can be considerably prolonged if there is a delay in the adoption arrangements.

169. The disadvantages for the adoptive parents are obvious. The welfare of the child is at risk while his future remains in doubt and there is a possibility that he may be moved. Even though this happens only in a small minority of cases, the knowledge that it is possible may give rise to anxiety on the part of all prospective adopters, who may hesitate to give total commitment to a child whom they may not be allowed to keep.

...

221. There is known to exist a sizeable number of children in the care of local authorities and voluntary societies for whom no permanent future can be arranged for a variety of reasons, for example, because the parents cannot bring themselves to make a plan, or do not want their child adopted but are unable to look after him themselves. Some of these children may have no contact with their parents and would benefit from adoption, but the parents will not agree to it. In other cases a parent may have her child received into care shortly after birth and then vacillate for months or even years over the question of adoption, thus depriving her child of the security of a settled family home life.

...

223. In some of these cases a court might well consider that there were statutory grounds for dispensing with the parents' consent because they had persistently failed to discharge the obligations of a parent, or were withholding consent unreasonably. Under the present law there is no way of testing this without first placing the child with prospective adopters and awaiting a court decision after at least three months care and possession by them. If the court then

decides that there are insufficient grounds for dispensing with the parents' consent the child must be returned to the agency. Moreover, unless the child is in the care of a local authority which has parental rights, or a care order has been made, the parents can frustrate the proceedings by removing the child before the court hearing. Agencies are therefore understandably reluctant to place these children for adoption.

The solution was a new procedure, currently contained in ss. 18–20 of the Adoption Act 1976, for freeing a child for adoption, either with consent or having dispensed with it, before the child was placed. Research into freeing for adoption in England and Wales (see Lowe, 1990) suggested that it had not lived up to expectations, mainly because of delays and differences in practice. The *Review of Adoption Law* (1992) voiced some more fundamental criticisms:

14.1 At present, the court fulfils a number of key functions in relation to adoptions which have been arranged by agencies. It scrutinises the report prepared by the agency to confirm that the agency has carried out the duties required of it. It ensures that the child, the parents and other people involved in the adoption are given the opportunity to put their views to the court and that their rights are protected. A court officer confirms that parental agreement has been freely given; where parental agreement is withheld, the court is responsible for deciding whether to dispense with that agreement. And the court confirms that adoption is in a child's interests before granting an adoption order.

14.2 Bearing in mind the new, permanent status that adoption confers on a child and the implications this has for the child, his birth family and the adoptive family, we consider that adoption should continue to be a judicial process with all the safeguards which this entails. However, we also consider that the court should become involved in the scrutiny of an adoption plan at a stage which is appropriate to the nature of the decisions which it is required to make – this is not always the case under the present adoption process. In all adoption applications and in some freeing applications, the court is given the opportunity to consider the issues only after the child had been living with the prospective adopters for some months and a relationship has developed between them. This may present the court with something approaching a fait accompli, such that it feels unable to do anything other than dispense with parental agreement, if it has been withheld, and grant an adoption order. This is clearly unsatisfactory. ...

Freeing for adoption

14.3 At present, it is possible for an agency to seek the court's judgment on the matter of parental agreement at an earlier date by applying for a freeing order before or at about the same time as the child is placed with prospective adopters. A freeing order transfers the parents' parental responsibility to the adoption agency, pending the making of an adoption order. This procedure was originally designed to enable parents to make an irrevocable decision to give up their child at an early stage in the adoption process. In practice, its more common use has been by care authorities seeking to have the question of parental agreement resolved before – or in the early stages of – an adoption placement, so that the parents cannot contest the later adoption application. But freeing is not mandatory, and some agencies place children who are in care with prospective adopters despite parental opposition and without applying for a freeing order, perhaps in part because the court is felt to be more likely to dispense with parental agreement after the child has lived with the prospective adopters for a time.

14.4 Freeing for adoption has attracted much criticism, mainly on account of the delays which are usually involved. We consider that the difficulties associated with freeing are not just procedural ones. Other problems include:

    a.   the court is expected to resolve the question of parental agreement without looking at a particular placement (or proposed placement): there is a danger that courts may contrast the readily apparent shortcomings in the care offered or likely to be offered in future by a child's parents with the care likely to be offered by hypothetically perfect adoptive parents;

    b.   where an order is made prior to the identification of prospective adoptive parents, there is a danger that the child may be left without a family: although the court is not allowed to dispense with parental agreement unless the child is already placed for adoption or the court is satisfied that it is likely that the child will be placed, this is no guarantee that a freed child will be found a suitable adoptive family, and in uncontested cases an order can be made regardless of the likelihood of placing the child;

    c.   a child may also be left without a family if the placement breaks down before an adoption order is made;

d.   although the agency may apply for a freeing order where the question of parental agreement ought to be resolved prior to placement, there is no requirement for the agency to do so, nor any guarantee that the hearing will take place before the placement has been made.

14.5 Freeing for adoption has been perceived to have some advantages. One reason why some agencies still find it helpful is that the application is by the agency, not the prospective adopters: this is felt to reduce the conflict between the birth family and adoptive family and lessen the risk that the child will later regard his adoptive parents as having 'taken him away' from the birth family. However, the distancing of the prospective adopters from the freeing process may not always work to the advantage of the child: it may in fact be that their closer involvement in the process at the stage when parental agreement is examined would encourage the different parties to discuss matters such as contact and share information about the child's background.

The Review's solution was that the child should not be placed with prospective adopters until the court had authorised that placement and in doing so had dealt with the question of parental agreement: thus the parents would not be faced with a *fait accompli* if the placement had already been made, or with a picture of the ideal placement which might be available. The system contained in the present Adoption and Children Bill, however, is very similar to that outlined in *Adoption – A Service for Children, Adoption Bill – A Consultative Document* (1996):

Placement with parental consent

4.4 Provisions continue to allow the placement of children for adoption with the consent of the parent or guardian. There are two forms of parental consent to a placement: consent to the child being placed with named prospective adopters, or general consent to the child being placed with any prospective adopters who may be chosen by the adoption agency. It is expected that most parents or guardians will give general consent.

4.5 Parental consent to a child being placed for adoption is not synonymous with their giving consent to an adoption order; these are two distinct stages, each requiring a separate consent to be given. However, consent to the making of a future adoption order can be given at the same time as consent to the child's placement or subsequently before the application to adopt is made. Consent of the mother to adoption may not be given until the child is at least six weeks old.

4.6 It is considered that before giving parental consent to placement or to the making of a future adoption order a parent or guardian should be counselled. It is also considered that the form of the agreement should be prescribed and should be witnessed. ...

4.7 A parent or guardian does not lose parental responsibility for the child until an adoption order is made, although the exercise of that responsibility is to be limited. Where a parent or guardian consents to placement, he will be required at the same time to agree to parental responsibility being given to prospective adopters while the child is placed with them (and in any case to the adoption agency). The prospective adopters will exercise parental responsibility subject to certain restraints.

Placement orders

4.8 Arrangements for placing a child for adoption introduce a new provision – placement orders. Where the parent or guardian does not consent to the placement for adoption and the adoption agency has considered all available options and is satisfied that adoption is in the child's best interests, the matter is to be put to the court at an early stage to enable the court to make realistic decisions about the child's future. The purpose of a placement order is to enable the court to be involved at an early stage in those cases where the agency considers that adoption is in the child's best interests but the parent or guardian is not prepared to give his consent to placement and while other available options for the child's future can also be considered.

4.9 A placement order authorises the adoption agency to place the child for adoption with suitable prospective adopters. An order will not restrict a placement to named prospective adopters even where they are known to the agency; this is to avoid the agency having to go back to court for a new placement order in the event of the first placement breaking down.

4.10 Once a placement order has been made, parental responsibility is given while the child is placed with prospective adopters, to them. Regulations will provide for the names of the prospective adopters to be notified to the court by the adoption agency. Where the child is removed from that placement and subsequently placed with another set of adopters, the court is to be notified of the change. Parental responsibility reverts to the agency when the child is removed and in due course is given to new prospective adopters.

Placement of children under a care order
4.11 A placement order will be required for a child who is the subject of a care order; once the placement order is made it is to have the effect of suspending the care order for the duration of the placement order. Where a local authority applies to the court for a care order most courts already require them to provide a care plan for the child. Where the recommendation in the care plan is that the child should be adopted, the authority must also apply for a placement order at the same time as they apply for a care order. Should the placement order be revoked, the care order will automatically revive. This means that where placement for adoption turns out not to be the best solution there is no obstacle to revoking the placement order because the child will remain protected.
4.12 Where the care plan did not originally contain a recommendation that the child be placed for adoption but is revised at a later stage to make such a recommendation, an application for a placement order must be made at this stage. This will usually be heard by the same court which made the care order.

Placement generally
4.13 Once a child is placed with prospective adopters whether with the parent's consent or under a placement order, he ceases to be a 'looked after' child under the Children Act. Where the local authority may place a child for adoption, the authority may provide accommodation for him at any time when he is not so placed and during that period he will be a 'looked after' child under that Act.

Removal provisions
4.14 Where placement is by consent, the parent may withdraw that consent and require the return of the child (subject to set procedures) at any time up to the time when an application to adopt is made. After that, leave of the court is required. Where a child is placed under a placement order, the parent will not be able to have the child back unless the placement order is revoked. An application to revoke the order by the parent may only be made where the child is not placed with prospective adopters, at least a year has elapsed since the order was made and the court gives leave, being satisfied that there has been a change in circumstances.

Questions

(i) The main change introduced during the passage of the Adoption and Children Bill is that, under clause 20(2), the court may not make a placement order unless (a) the child is already subject to a care order, (b) the court is satisfied that the conditions for making a care order in s. 31(2) of the Children Act 1989 (p. 719, above) are met, or (c) the child has no parent or guardian. Why do you think this change was made?
(ii) Clause 24 implements the recommendation that either consent to placement or a placement order gives parental responsibility to the agency, shared with the parents and with any prospective adopter once the child is placed but with the power to restrict their exercise of that responsibility. Is it acceptable for a state agency to acquire control over parental responsibility without a court order? Is this a return to the days of the old parental rights resolutions (see p. 666, above)?

14.5 Adoption: an open or shut case?

We saw in Chapter 11 how the Tomlin Committee had disapproved of secrecy in adoption, yet over the years since then the complete segregation of birth and adoptive families had become the norm. But there were exceptions, particularly for older children adopted by foster parents. In *Re B (MF) (an infant), Re D*

(SL) (an infant) [1972] 1 All ER 898, [1972] 1 WLR 102, Salmon LJ said this:

As a rule, it is highly undesirable that after an adoption order is made there should be any contact between the child or children and their natural parents. This is the view which has been taken, and rightly taken, by adoption societies and local authorities as it has been by the courts in dealing with questions of adoption. There is, however, no hard and fast rule that if there is an adoption it can only be on the terms that there should be a complete divorce of the children from their natural parents. ... Although the courts will pay great attention to the general principle to which I have referred, namely, that it is desirable in normal circumstances for there to be a complete break, each case has to be considered on its own particular facts.

The changing face of adoption, coupled with some of the research evidence discussed earlier, has contributed to a more flexible attitude. The court can now combine an adoption order with a contact order under s. 8 of the Children Act 1989, but is still reluctant to do so unless the adoptive parents agree:

Re C (a minor) (adoption: conditions)
[1989] AC 1, [1988] 1 All ER 705, [1988] 2 WLR 474, House of Lords

C was taken into care, together with her two older brothers, at a very early age. C became very attached to her brother M during the next seven years, spent mainly in children's homes, and remained in touch with him after her placement with the prospective adopters. C wanted to be adopted, but her mother withheld agreement in case adoption might weaken her relationship with M. The judge thought this should be preserved at all costs. Both the judge and the Court of Appeal refused to dispense with the mother's agreement, being doubtful of the power to make continued contact a condition of the adoption order. The prospective adopters appealed.

Lord Ackner: ... It seems to me essential that, in order to safeguard and promote the welfare of the child throughout his childhood, the court should retain the maximum flexibility given to it by the Act and that unnecessary fetters should not be placed on the exercise of the discretion entrusted to it by Parliament. The cases to which I have referred illustrate circumstances in which it was clearly in the best interests of the child to allow access to a member of the child's natural family. The cases rightly stress that in normal circumstances it is desirable that there should be a complete break, but that each case has to be considered on its own particular facts. No doubt the court will not, except in the most exceptional case, impose terms or conditions as to access to members of the child's natural family to which the adopting parents do not agree. To do so would be to create a potentially frictional situation which would be hardly likely to safeguard or promote the welfare of the child. Where no agreement is forthcoming the court will, with very rare exceptions, have to choose between making an adoption order without terms or conditions as to access, or to refuse to make such an order and seek to safeguard access through some other machinery, such as wardship. To do otherwise would be merely inviting future and almost immediate litigation.

The cases in the Court of Appeal have essentially been concerned with the question of whether provision can properly be made in an adoption order for access to a natural parent or parents. Although it is one of degree, a distinction can properly be drawn between access to natural parents on the one hand and other natural relatives on the other. Other relatives and, in particular, brothers and sisters have no parental rights which by the adoption order are being extinguished and then vested in the adopters. The Court of Appeal was, in my judgment, correct in paying no regard to the suggestions made by the judge that if C were told that M was no longer her brother, she would be bitterly and desperately hurt. Fresh evidence put before the Court of Appeal established that C, when interviewed a little over a year ago, had made it clear that she wanted to be adopted, that to her adoption meant that 'she would then know that no one could ever take her away from her mum and dad' (the appellants). She said she could not see how it would affect her relationship with M or how she felt for him and he for her. Even without this additional evidence, it seems to me that the judge's evaluation of C's reaction to learning that technically M was no longer her *legal* brother was quite unreal.

...

The order which the judge made sacrificed the benefits of adoption in order to provide for an event which might never eventuate, namely the failure of the adopters properly to co-operate in maintaining access between C and M. The fresh evidence put before the Court of Appeal established that there continued to be no obstacles put by the appellants in the way of such access and none were anticipated by M. Indeed, your Lordships have been informed, without objection, that the appellants took C to London twice last year so that she could visit M, and had invited M to come to see his sister in Norfolk. Contact had continued by phone and letter. Moreover, the judge failed to appreciate that, were it to become necessary to enforce access between C and M, to do so through the machinery of wardship was no easier and, indeed, might be more complex, then by seeking to enforce a term or condition of the adoption order. *Appeal allowed.*

Questions

(i) But what if the local authority had been unable to find prospective adopters who could recognise and respect the child's relationship with her brother?
(ii) Does the distinction drawn between birth parents and other relatives make sense?

A clinician's view of the advantages and disadvantages of post-adoption contact is given by child psychiatrist Dr Jonathan Dare in a paper presented at a Judicial Studies Board seminar (1995):

The advantages and disadvantages of open adoption and the merits of subsequent contact with the natural parents
It is axiomatic that children in adoptive placements should have a reasonable knowledge of their biological parents and origins. With the gradual increase in age of adoption children increasingly come for adoption with considerable direct knowledge, experience and profound feelings about their biological background. This can be both helpful and unhelpful in the process of their making use of adoptive placement.

In 'open adoption', this knowledge will be augmented and developed, which again can have beneficial as well as detrimental effects on the adoptive child.

The use of the phrase 'natural parents' involves a degree of ambiguity. In particular, its meaning 'in the normal course of events' suggests an attitude and idea which may not be appropriate in the context of a child being placed in an adoptive family. The phrase 'biological' is more neutral and perhaps more appropriate.

CONTACT WITH BIOLOGICAL PARENTS IN OPEN ADOPTION

Advantages	*Disadvantages*
Not cut off from biological roots.	Confusion – 'where do I belong?'
Helps establish adult persona.	How to make sense of two sets of parent(s).
Provides continuity. 'Best of both worlds', i.e. providing a good parenting experience without losing known background.	Undermine absolute security/stability which is the whole idea of adoption. If see biological parent(s) sufficiently to 'know emotionally', then this can make problems in child committing self to adoptive placement. If see very frequently, contact may become a 'ritual' of little benefit but may still undermine placement. Reduces ability of child to emotionally invest in adoptive placement.
Reduces feeling of guilt and low self-esteem always associated with removal from biological family and placement elsewhere. Enhances self worth through knowledge about self background.	Confusion to child as to whether they belong and have characteristics related to their adoptive or biological family.

Advantages	*Disadvantages*
Allows view of biological parents in the 'round' i.e. not as all positive or all negative – crucial to developing rounded self-image as child, adolescent and adult.	Confusion caused if gross disparity between attitudes of biological and adoptive family.
Biological parents can promote child to invest in adoptive family and reduce child's wish to return to biological family.	Contact with biological parent(s) almost inevitably leads child to feel that there is possibility of rehabilitation – again undermining investment in adoptive placement.
Help child to make more sense of reason for adoption.	Contact with apparently loving and caring biological parents may make adoptive placement completely inexplicable to child.
With biological parents supporting and promoting placement in adoption, child has clear view of where all important adults feel child should be.	Danger of being in middle of parental 'competition' between adoptive and biological parents. Biological parents may actively undermine child's commitment to adoptive placement.
Child seeing biological parents may facilitate adoptive parents' care of child.	Conflicts and uncertainties from adoptive parents' viewpoint. Perhaps undermining them in their ability to be 'all round' i.e. both setting firm limits and loving.

It must, however, be remembered that for the large majority of children (especially the older ones) being placed for adoption, these children are suffering from *chronic emotional damage and deprivation*. Thus their ability to make relationships and be able to cope with different sets of parents is almost de facto very significantly less than normal children. Such children have a much greater than normal need for absolute security and stability in order to facilitate them being able to invest emotionally in an adoptive family.

Similarly, the biological parents of such children are also likely to be adults with the type of parental characteristics which would make it difficult for them to facilitate and promote the placement of the child in an adoptive family. They will almost inevitably feel rivalrous and may unconsciously wish for the placement to fail in the adoptive placement in the same way that it failed with the child in their own care.

The researchers' views have become hotly debated. An enthusiastic promoter of post-adoption contact is Murray Ryburn in, for example, 'In whose best interests? – post-adoption contact with the birth family' (1998):

Extent of post-adoption contact today

Despite growing adversarialism in adoption, since the beginning of the 1990s there has been a significant trend in practice to more post-adoption contact, although the extent of this at a national level cannot, with any precision, be established. This trend began in the 1980s, and was helped by the voice of consumer and advocacy groups. In particular, the movement to greater openness received an impetus from the Children Act 1989 with its research-based emphasis on the importance of contact for 'looked after' children.

Although the national picture on contact is not completely clear, we can glean a fair amount from two recent studies, one a Social Services Inspectorate (SSI) report which set out to establish the extent of post-adoption contact in the North of England, the other a study which sought to establish the level of post-adoption contact where adoption had been opposed to the point of the final hearing. In the SSI study, researchers approached 51 agencies, 37 social services departments and 14 voluntary adoption agencies, and received responses, although not to each question, from a total of 44. In the year commencing April 1993 30 agencies identified 371 children placed during that year for adoption. In 14 per cent of cases there was continuing direct contact between the parties, in 41 per cent of cases there was indirect contact, in 13 per cent of cases there was both direct and indirect contact, and in only 31 per cent of cases was there either no contact or no knowledge of this contact. ...

In my own survey involving 74 placements, all made after contested final hearings in 42 per cent of cases, there was some form of post-adoption contact. Usually this was indirect, and often, but not always, involved the services of an agency as a mailbox. Typically, it involved the exchange of letters and photographs and the giving of presents at birthdays and Christmas. In 14 per cent of cases contact was direct, ranging from infrequent to very regular contact, including, in addition to meetings, a good deal of telephone contact. ...

What are the broad findings?
The research is clear that there can be advantages to all parties as a result of the maintenance of post-adoption contact. It indicates that, in general, if there is freedom for parties to set their own levels, contact tends to move from limited and indirect contact to more open contact, and to change, sometimes significantly, over time. It further indicates that greater advantages can accrue from more open forms of contact. A recent public attitudes survey on open adoption found that of a random sample of 136 adults, 66 per cent supported the practice of post-adoption contact, whilst 74 per cent believed that adoptees would want to search for birth parents, with most other responses in the 'do not know' category. Further, 90 per cent of the sample supported the idea of adoptive parents initiating contact for their children if their children wanted it. As the first public opinion survey on adoption in this country the results are particularly interesting, both as a common sense view and because they would appear to confirm a trend away from any climate of secrecy. ...

Advantages of contact for children
The research studies suggest that with indirect contact children's information needs begin to be met, but that with direct contact their questions are more likely to be met at a level that is satisfying. One of the key advantages of any contact is that facts can more readily replace difficult aspects of their past lives – aspects that might otherwise be a source of difficulty for them. Thus in the study on contact following contested adoption an adopter indicated how important it was for her daughter to have contact, including direct contact, with her mother, who suffered a mental illness. This contact had helped her to locate this illness realistically in contact, and otherwise, her adopters believed, it might have remained as a continuing source of worry and anxiety, especially in relation to her fears of inheriting it herself.

Children also appear to gain a sense of reassurance as a consequence of contact, particularly direct contact, with their birth relatives. In particular, it gives them a clear message that the placement is supported by their original family since otherwise they would not be visiting, and it is a visible symbol that their adoptive parents feel positively about their original family or contact would not be permitted. The largest survey of adoption and permanent foster care placements ever undertaken in the UK, involving 1165 placements, also found that birth family contact was the single factor which could be identified as enhancing the stability of placements. Finally, contact, in particular direct contact, appears to strengthen children's sense of attachment to their adoptive parents. Thus Dominick in her study of 156 adopters found that only two believed that contact diminished the strength of attachment between them and their child, three-quarters believed that contact enhanced feelings of attachment, and the remainder felt that the influence was neutral.

This was in response to a more cautious review by D. Quinton, A. Rushton, C. Dance and D. Mayes, 'Contact between children placed away from home and their birth parents: research issues and evidence' (1997). Their conclusions are summarised in 'Contact with birth parents in adoption – a response to Ryburn' (1998):

Conclusions from our review
In our review we dealt separately with the evidence on adoptions made in infancy and adoptions made later in childhood because of the different psychological implications of placement at different ages as well as the different family experiences of early and late placed children. Our conclusions can be summarised quite briefly.

Adoptions made in infancy
Research on infant adoptions could safely be taken to show: that continuing information about their children is important to many birth mothers; that direct contact can be acceptable to all parties in some cases; and that some birth and adoptive parents see this as bringing benefits. Our caveats were first that the majority of studies were of small self-selected samples or samples with

high refusal rates (which made them self-selected as well), and secondly, that no studies had yet compared the outcomes of adoption with contact to adoption without it. For this reason we observed that it was not possible to conclude that infant adoptions with contact are either superior or inferior to those without, nor what proportion of placements have difficulties directly related to openness. Finally, we pointed out that existing research concerned adoptive parents' reactions to openness when the children were still in early or mid-childhood and that it could not be assumed that the story would be the same as the children passed through adolescence.

As Ryburn pointed out we did not deal with some recent papers from the study by Grotevant and his colleagues that do contain the appropriate comparisons and throw further light on these issues. We review these below to see whether they alter our conclusions.

Adoption of older children

With respect to the permanent placement of older children we first pointed out that the arguments put forward in favour of contact had much in common with earlier arguments against it, but in neither case had these arguments been systematically tested against each other in research. However, we concluded that research had shown that open adoption with contact can work amicably and that there was no evidence that contact made placements less stable and some evidence that it made them more so. At the time we were writing no studies of infant or later adoptions had systematic data on the intellectual or psychosocial development of the children in closed and open adoptions, despite the fact that benefits are sometimes claimed in these areas.

Our overall summary located the current state of knowledge on contact in a stage model of research that begins with the identification of an issue, proceeds through small-scale practitioner studies, is followed by larger scale, sometimes epidemiological, research and finally leads to the testing of specific hypotheses. As far as studies of adoption were concerned we observed that these were still predominantly in the second stage with some third-stage investigations but none in which specific hypotheses had been tested using representative samples and comparative designs. We outlined testable hypotheses that could be derived from beliefs about the advantages of contact and concluded:

> 'In our present state of knowledge it is seriously misleading to think that what we know about contact is at a level of sophistication to allow us to make confident assertions about the benefits to be gained from it, *regardless of family circumstances and relationships* (italics added). At least in the case of permanent placements the social experiment that is currently underway needs to be recognised as an experiment, not as an example of the development of evidence-based practice. It is important that the effects of this experiment are properly evaluated.'

Methodological issues

These summary conclusions were arrived at following a discussion of the methodological problems that were common in much of the research in this field. ... We discussed four problems: the adequacy of sampling; the measurement of contact; failure to account for individual adjustment as a predictor; and analytic weaknesses. We presented tables summarising the studies we reviewed so that the reader could see whether these problems applied to them or not. ...

Re-examination of missing studies

It is now necessary to deal in a little more detail with the recent data from the major investigation that we did not review: the comparative study of the correlates of openness in infant adoptions by Grotevant and his colleague. ... We now review this and two subsequent papers to see whether this research alters our conclusions. This study is important because it included planned comparisons of children with and without contact. One hundred and ninety families who adopted children prior to one year-of-age were studied; the children were aged between four and 12 at the time of the research. They had been relinquished by their birth parents primarily because the mothers were young and poor rather than because of major mental health or parenting problems. The adoptions were not transracial, inter-country or 'special needs'. The sample was stratified according to the degree of openness and the study is exceptional in having data from a very high proportion of birth parents as well as adopted children. The research is methodologically sophisticated and the data are well analysed but, by definition, it cannot be used to draw conclusions about the effects of contact on children adopted later in life and/or following marked maltreatment.

Two major analyses have been presented. The first examined the associations between the level of openness in the adoptions and a number of issues. These included: the adoptive parents' communication with the child about adoption; their empathy with the need for connection with the past; empathy with the birth parents over their decision; recognition of the special nature of adoptive parenting; acknowledgment of the child's need for information; satisfaction with control over birth parent involvement; fear of reclaiming; perception of the strength of their relationship with the child; entitlement to act as a 'full' parent; and the coherence of their account of adoption.

The authors concluded first that what stood out was the similarity across the levels of openness on these measures, with the majority of ratings on all dimensions falling within a 'moderate range' for all levels of openness. Most parents felt secure in their roles and were not worried about permanence, regardless of whether the adoptions were confidential or fully disclosed. It was notable that parents in fully disclosed adoptions felt as much in control of birth parents' involvement as those in confidential ones and also that they showed a higher degree of empathy about adoption and talked more to the children about it; however, it was not possible to tell whether this was a consequence of prior parental characteristics or an effect of openness itself.

We agree with the authors' conclusion that 'the results of this study are not compatible with the hypothesis that openness necessarily produces undesirable outcomes for adoptive families'. In addition we would agree with their observation that the design makes it impossible to make causal statements about the effects of different levels of openness. Their conclusions are a model of appropriate caution. It is striking that Ryburn omits to mention their remarks on what the research can and cannot say about the associations between family patterns and the level of openness.

A second paper examined differences in the children's views depending on the level of openness. The interview with them revealed interesting but predominantly subtle effects. The level of openness was not related to the children's satisfaction with openness, to their understanding of adoption, to their self-worth, or to their curiosity about their birth parents, although most were curious, and girls more curious than boys. Parental withholding of information did not make children more curious but there was reasonable speculation that withholding would create more problems as adolescent identity issues arose.

There were two further interesting findings. Although the level of curiosity about birth parents did not differ according to the level of openness, the more curious children were about their origins the lower their self-worth, especially boys. Curiosity was negatively related to the level of satisfaction with their circumstances, except for the children in fully disclosed adoptions. This suggests a complex of responses that linked unhappiness with their situation, for whatever reasons, to their feelings of self-worth and to greater curiosity about their origins. On the other hand, the study does not link this complex of feelings to the level of openness in a consistent way, nor is it possible to determine whether the feelings are primarily a consequence of the quality of family relationships rather than the information the children had, although there is some suggestion that the way information is handled was important.

The general conclusion from both papers is the same. The study provides no evidence that openness is harmful to these early adopted children, an important conclusion. Neither does it provide evidence for obvious benefits to psychosocial development in the years leading up to adolescence. A follow-up of all the children through the teenage years, where identity issues become central, would be illuminating.

Summary

In summary the studies we omitted from our review do not alter overall conclusions that continuing information about their children is important to many birth mothers; that direct contact can be acceptable to all parties in some cases; and that some birth and adoptive parents see this as bringing benefits.

Questions

(i) If you had to decide what to do in an individual case, which would you find more helpful: (a) the views of a clinician who had interviewed all concerned, or (b) the results of the research studies discussed?

(ii) How would you go about being 'open' with a child whose birth parent had seriously abused or neglected him?

(iii) Would you consider openness more or less important in trans-racial or trans-cultural placements?

One last aspect of the blurring of distinctions between fostering and adoption is the implementation in 1982 of the following recommendation of the *Houghton Report* (1972):

Should adoption be subsidised?

93. We suggested in our working paper that consideration should be given to the possibility of guardians and adopters being paid regular subsidies in appropriate cases, and we said that we would welcome views on this. While there was considerable support for allowances for guardians ..., many witnesses saw a clear distinction between adoption and guardianship and opposed the idea of any payments to adopters. Some took the view that payment would conflict with the principle that adoption should put the child in precisely the same position as a child born to the adopters. While some agreed with our suggestion that, if allowances were payable, more homes might be found for children with special needs, others said that it would be unfair to the parents of handicapped children if the adopters of these children could get an allowance which was not available to their natural parents. Some said that the law should not forbid agency payments to adopters but that there should be no national system of allowances.

94. We recognise the objection to singling out handicapped adopted children for special payments, and we do not advocate payments for adopters generally. However, we still think that there is a case for allowances in some circumstances, for example, where suitable adopters are available for a family of children who need to be kept together but, for financial reasons, adoption is not possible if an allowance cannot be paid. Although most witnesses were opposed to our suggestion, we should like to see a period of experiment during which evidence could be gathered. But at present even experiment is not possible, because it would contravene the law, and we recommend that the law should be amended so as to enable payments to be made by a few charitable bodies specially authorised by the Secretary of State for this purpose. There may be a number of difficulties, and we suggest pilot schemes which could be reviewed after, say, seven years, although the subsidy would have to be continued to those who had adopted on that basis for as long as they needed it.

Questions

(i) In *Re X* (p. 786, above), the local authority had gone to great lengths to protect the prospective adopters' anonymity, buying them a large house in the country and supporting them in other ways. Would you draw a distinction between one-off 'set up' costs of taking on, for example, a large sibling group and paying a long-term allowance, for example for children with special needs? Or do you find the whole idea of paying adopters to have children questionable? But what about other forms of support with, for example, looking after seriously abused children?

(ii) How much do you think prospective adopters should be told about their prospective children's past?

14.6 The cross-cultural dimension

We have seen in Chapter 13 (p. 663, above) that disproportionate numbers of children looked after by local authorities come from certain ethnic minorities. How, then, are local authorities to place them appropriately, when the resources available to them are unlikely to match all the children's needs? The issue is discussed in *Adoption Now – Messages from Research* (1999):

Ethnicity

Several important points concerning the linking of children from minority ethnic groups with adopters or foster carers emerged from the Thoburn team's study. Both the children and their new parents in 'same-race' placements believed that this policy should be followed if at all possible. Some of the children who had been placed trans-racially also argued strongly for a policy of ethnically matched placements, although most also acknowledged that they had learned much from their white parents. Children of mixed parentage appeared to feel less strongly about the issue. Of course, all these arrangements had been made in the early 1980s when the placement of black children with white families was more common. ...

Nonetheless, the Thoburn results provide a benchmark, as well as indicating some of the characteristics of trans-racial placements. First, they were more likely to have involved foster carers than adopters. Secondly, it was more common for younger children to be placed trans-racially. Thirdly, this was also the case for children of mixed parentage, 88% of whom had been placed with new parents who were white compared with 63% of those whose birth parents were both black. However, as Thoburn and her colleagues point out, the idea of 'ethnic matching' can suggest a closer similarity between the child and the new family than is in fact the case. For instance, although some of the children of direct African origin had been placed with black parents, in no instance were they both also from a direct African background. Children of south Asian parents were the most likely to have been placed with those of a similar background, perhaps because of religious considerations. The importance of such findings lies in what they suggest about the assumptions which lie behind decisions concerning the 'matching' of children and new parents. In this case the clearest of these was a greater willingness to placed mixed-parentage than black children with white families and the belief that colour was a more significant consideration than race, ethnicity or culture, except possibly with respect to religion.

Some of the complexities of 'ethnic matching' are also exposed in the Quinton and Rushton research, although only one in six of the children in that sample had minority ethnic backgrounds. Half of them were 'ethnically matched'; but it was the descriptions of those who were not which illustrated some of the dilemmas faced by social workers. All except one were of mixed parentage, and all of these were more than one generation removed from their minority ethnic origins. The one African-Caribbean child who was placed trans-racially was placed together with a white sibling. Furthermore, many of these children had been born to white mothers and had grown up in a predominantly white culture.

A third of the children in the Owen study were black or of mixed parentage. All had been placed with black adopters except one whom the white adopter had known beforehand through family connections. The research suggested that the priority attached to racial or cultural matching by the three voluntary agencies concerned seemed to favour the choice of a single parent in some cases because a single black woman was seen as preferable to a white couple (although not necessarily to a black couple) and because such applicants were seen as having a high level of acceptability within the black community.

Almost all the agencies that replied to the Lowe and Murch postal questionnaire explained that ethnic or cultural matching was the preferred option but some two-fifths said that various circumstances could lead to a departure from that policy. It was notable, however, that the voluntary agencies were more likely than the local authorities to pursue unwavering 'same-race' policies (52% of them compared with 24% of the statutory bodies). Where second or third best options had to be found preferences tended to follow an order of diminishing connection with minority ethnic status; for example, from families where one of the adopters was black to those where the couple were of mixed parentage; then on to families where one of the partners had a mixed background, and finally to a white family, but one living in a multi-cultural community.

This last option draws attention to the extent to which efforts are or are not made to place minority ethnic children in areas where they will have the opportunity to mix with others of a similar background, at school, in clubs or simply in the neighbourhood. The importance of this was stressed by the black children in the Owen study and by those in the Thoburn research. However, the extent to which such considerations affected the selection of a particular family for a child was not explored in any of the studies, nor was the question of whether this only became a serious consideration if an 'ideal' ethnic 'match' proved impossible to achieve.

Compare that with the following case:

Re N (a minor) (adoption)
[1990] FCR 241, [1990] 1 FLR 58, [1989] Fam Law 472, Family Division

The child, N, was born in 1984 of Nigerian parents who were not married. The mother placed her with white foster parents, the Ps, two weeks after birth and went to the USA. The father lived there but they did not live together. The father took an interest in the child and sought consistently to have care for her, but there were visa difficulties. In 1987, the foster parents applied to adopt and then to dispense with the mother's agreement. The father, with the mother's support, applied for care and control. He proposed a gradual transition, through a relative or bridging placement.

Bush J: ... The most important question to decide is where does N's future lie. We are all of us parents or potential parents and it is very difficult and sad for us to say that a child should be brought up by someone other than the natural parents. It should of course always be borne in mind that in English law N is a person in her own right and not just an appendage of her parents.
...

Not only does the court in this case have to cope with practical difficulties involved in a transfer of N from the Ps to the father in a foreign land where the father will have to work long hours, and Miss F too has to work long hours, but I have also been bombarded by a host of theories and opinions by experts who derive their being from the political approach to race relations in America in the 1960s and 1970s. The British Agencies for Fostering and Adoption forcefully expressed the view that black children should never be placed with white foster parents. That that part of the approach was politically inspired seems clear from reading the summary to a practice note, the date of which is not clear. Nevertheless, it is an approach which due to the zeal of its authors has persuaded most local authorities not to place black children with white foster parents. The summary note reads as follows:

'Over and above all these basic needs, children need to develop a positive identity, including a positive racial identity. This is of fundamental importance since ethnicity is a significant component of identity. Ideally such needs are met within the setting of the child's birth family. Historically black people have been victims of racism for centuries. This has manifested and continues to manifest itself in many forms. Racism permeates all areas of British society and is perpetuated through a range of interests and influences, including the media, education and social service policies and practices. Negative and stereotypical images and actions can have a major impact on black children through the internalisation of these images, resulting in self-hate and identity confusion. Black children therefore require the survival skills necessary to develop a positive racial identity. This will enable them to deal with the racism within our predominantly white society.'

As Dr B, an eminent and experienced child psychiatrist ... pointed out ... there seems little real evidence, save anecdotal, to suggest that black-white fosterings are harmful. Indeed, Dr B says that her experience ... indicates to the contrary namely, that the placement of black children with white foster parents works just as well as black foster children with black foster parents, and the real problem, of course, is that black foster parents are in short supply in this country.
...

In my view – and I have no wish to enter into what is clearly a political field – the emphasis on colour rather than cultural upbringing can be mischievous and highly dangerous when you are dealing in practical terms with the welfare of children. Also, the fact remains that this child has been placed with white foster parents and they have been the only real family she has ever known. I do not for one moment think that the father subscribes to this dogma. He does not have to be condescended to because he is black; he has made his way and his children will make their own way in the world because of intelligence and flair. To suggest that he and his children need special help because they are black is, in human terms an insult to them and their abilities. Yet it is to this principle that a whole social work philosophy has been dedicated. I do not need persuading that if at all possible the parents being suitable, a child should be brought up by its natural parents. Nor do I need persuading that experience tells us that particularly during teenage years there is a desire in children who have not been brought up by their natural parents, or who have not been having a regular access to them, to seek them out and that, if the whole of their placement has not been handled responsibly and delicately throughout their childhood, and sometimes even then, there may be psychological problems. There are of course serious psychological problems likely to arise when an effort is made to part a 4 and a half-year-old child from the only carers she has ever known. ...
...

There is, of course, a very important question which relates not so much to colour as to national origins. The father and mother are Nigerian. The father is under some pressure from his father, who will be disgraced if it appears that even an illegitimate child has been abandoned. The father is a Roman Catholic, and I accept that he has a genuine desire to bring up his own child. An older illegitimate child of his, a boy, lives with a different mother in Nigeria and visits his father at regular intervals.

The evidence of Mrs B, a consultant social worker, as to Nigerian practice is of use. ... She said there is no concept of adoption in Nigerian society. It is the normal cultural pattern for children to be brought up by others, often for most of their minority, and to be aware of their birth parents. Adoption rather than fostering of a West African child has particular difficulties. Adoption is to transfer a child from one family into another permanently and although the adoptive parents strive to inform the child about its origins in adoption it is clear the child is as if it were born to the adopters. In fostering, even long-term carers and the child are aware this is another and different family from a true family. If the child is moved from a white foster home to Nigerian culture, with his foster parents not wanting the child to go, this can be devastating. Growing up with a set of values, a way of looking at family life, is constant in the same culture. However, to move from a British family with a closeness, autonomy and freedom to express what you want and to do what you want to a place where you cannot can be very distressing long-term. The damage of losing the people you trust at the same time as the trauma can be life-long. ...

... I am satisfied, as are the local authority and the guardian ad litem that N could not be moved without immense harm to her psychological development and her psychiatric health, both now and in the future. The later harm that may arise in her teens when she wished to seek out her cultural roots can best be dealt with by sympathetic understanding and education, upon which the Ps have already embarked, and it can also hopefully be met by the father continuing his interest and having access to N. It can only be helped if the father accepts the situation and enjoys access not on the basis of an expected rehabilitation but on the basis of a contact access designed to keep N in touch with her origins. If the father cannot accept this, then it may be that for N's security access would have to cease.

The Ps want adoption with an access order. The local authority and the guardian ad litem oppose adoption on the ground: (i) that the father has a useful and important part to play in the child's life in the future, particularly when she is nearing adulthood; (ii) that access to which the Ps are to some extent agreeable might very well be imperilled, the fact being that an adoption would result in the father and the whole of his family losing face. The father told me, and I have no reason to disbelieve, in the course of his argument that in his culture adoption is viewed as a restoration of slavery, which would be a deep and hurtful blow to him and his family. The question one has to ask oneself is whether the security that adoption would give to both the Ps and to N is offset by the fact that it clearly would not be in N's interests for her father to feel the shame and distress that in his culture an adoption order would bring. ...

I know all the arguments, I have heard them many times, about the security that an adoption could give and in the main I accept the arguments and have in the past acted upon them, but in the particular circumstances of this case I would not think it right to make an adoption order. Circumstances of course may change in the future. The guardian ad litem is most concerned, as we all are, that what has really become open warfare between the Ps and the father should cease. It is in the interests of N that it should so cease. I accept that the father is bitterly hurt and distressed and feels utterly betrayed by the Ps, and no doubt my decision has distressed him even more. However, the future of N throughout her childhood lies with the Ps and the father is intelligent enough and dedicated enough to his daughter to appreciate that changes of attitude on his part must come about. ...

Accordingly, the order that I make is that the wardship shall continue, that there be care and control to Mr and Mrs P, that there be reasonable access to the father to be agreed. In default of agreement it should be access once a week over a period of one year to begin with and that access to take place in England.

Questions

(i) How would you account for the different results reached in *Re N* and *Re M (Child's Upbringing)* [1996] 2 FCR 473 (p. 448, above), the case of the Zulu boy sent back to his parents in South Africa?

(ii) Would you have made an adoption order in *Re N?*

(iii) Does it surprise you to learn that Nigel Lowe and Mervyn Murch, in their study of *The plan for the child, Adoption or long-term fostering* (2002), found that, along with age and level of contact with the birth family, an ethnic minority background tended to militate against planning for adoption rather than long-term fostering?

(iv) Should white families be allowed to foster or adopt black children? What is 'black' for this purpose? Should black families be allowed to foster or adopt white children?

Bibliography

Introduction

We quoted from:

J. Triseliotis, 'Growing Up in Foster Care and After' in J. Triseliotis (ed.), *New Developments in Foster Care and Adoption* (1980) London, Routledge and Kegan Paul, pp. 138 and 148.

G. Schofield, M. Beek and K. Sargent with J. Thoburn, *Growing Up in Foster Care* (2000) London, BAAF, p. 291.

14.1   The 'permanency' principle

We quoted from:

H. Cleaver, 'Fostering Family Contact: A Study of Children, Parents and Foster Carers', in J. Aldgate and J. Statham, *The Children Act Now: Messages from Research,* prepared for the Department of Health (2001) London, The Stationery Office, pp. 178–181.

Department of Health, *Patterns and Outcomes in Child Care* (1991) London, HMSO, pp. 26–37.

J. Gibbons, B. Gallagher, C. Bell and D. Gordon, *Development after Physical Abuse in Early Childhood* (1995) London, HMSO, pp. 88–90.

J. Packman, *The Child's Generation: Child Care Policy in Britain* (2nd edn, 1981) Oxford, Basil Blackwell, pp. 137–138.

R. Rowe, H. Cain, M. Hundleby and A. Keane, *Long-Term Foster Care* (1984) London, Batsford and BAAF, pp. 225–226.

J. Stone, *Making Positive Moves – Developing Short-Term Fostering Services* (1995) London, BAAF, pp. 52–61.

J. Thoburn, 'Survey Findings and Conclusions,' in J. Fratter, J. Rowe, D. Sapsford and J. Thoburn, *Permanent Family Placement – a decade of experience* (1991) London, BAAF, pp. 37, 51–56.

Additional reading

M. Adcock and R. White, *Terminating Parental Contact* (1980) London, ABAFA (now BAAF).

R. Berridge and H. Cleaver, *Foster Home Breakdown* (1987) Oxford, Basil Blackwell.

Department of Health, *The Children Act Now – Messages from Research* (2001) London, The Stationery Office.

D. Fanshell and E.B. Shinn, *Children In Foster Care: A Longitudinal Study* (1978) New York, Columbia University Press.

E. Farmer and R. Parker, *Trials and Tribulations: Returning Children from Care to their Families* (1991) London, HMSO.

M. Fisher and others, *In and Out of Care: The Experiences of Children, Parents and Social Workers* (1986) London, Batsford.

V. George, *Foster Care: Theory and Practice* (1970) London, Routledge and Kegan Paul.

J. Goldstein, A. Freud and S. Solnit, *Beyond the Best Interests of the Child* (1973) London, Collier Macmillan.

D. Howe, 'Assessing adoptions in difficulty' (1992) 22 British Journal of Social Work 1.

B. Maugham and A. Pickles, 'Adopted and Illegitimate Children Growing Up,' in L.N. Robbins and M. Rutter, *Straight and Devious Pathways from Childhood to Adulthood* (1990) Cambridge, Cambridge University Press.

S. Millham, R. Bullock, K. Hosie and M. Haak, *Lost in Care – The problems of maintaining links between children in care and their families* (1986) Aldershot, Gower.

S. Millham, R. Bullock, K. Hosie and M. Haak, *Access Disputes in Child Care* (1989) Aldershot, Gower.

S. Millham, R. Bullock and M. Little, *Going Home* (1993) Dartmouth.

J. Rowe, *Fostering in the Eighties* (1983) London, BAAF.

J. Rowe and L. Lambert, *Children Who Wait* (1973) London, ABAFA (now BAAF).

J. Rowe, M. Hundleby and L. Garnett, *Child Care Now – a survey of placement patterns* (1989) London, BAAF.

A. Rushton, J. Treseder and D. Quinton, 'Sibling Groups in Permanent Placements' (1989) 13(4) Adoption and Fostering 5.

J. Thoburn, *Success and Failure in Permanent Family Placement* (1990), Avebury, Gower.

J. Thoburn, A. Murdoch and A. O'Brien, *Permanence in Child Care* (1986) Oxford, Basil Blackwell.

J. Thoburn and J. Rowe, 'Research: A Snapshot of Permanent Family Placement' (1988) 12(3) Adoption and Fostering 29.

J. Triseliotis, 'Identity and Security in Adoption and Long Term Fostering' (1983) 7(1) Adoption and Fostering 22.

P. Wedge and H. Mantle, *Sibling Groups and Social Work* (1991) Avebury, Gower.

14.3 Legal options for relatives and other carers

We quoted from:

E. Bullard and E. Malos, with R.A. Parker, *Custodianship – A report to the Department of Health on the Implementation of Part II of the Children Act 1975 in England and Wales from December 1985 to December 1988* (1990) Bristol, Department of Social Policy and Social Planning, University of Bristol, paras. 9.31–9.40.

Law Commission, Working Paper No. 96, *Review of Child Law – Custody* (1986) London, HMSO, paras. 5.37–5.46.

Review of Adoption Law, Report to Ministers of an Interdepartmental Working Group. A Consultation Document (1992) London, Department of Health and Welsh Office, paras 6.2–6.5.

White Paper, *Adoption – a new approach* (Cm. 5017) (2000) London, HMSO, paras. 5.5–5.11.

14.4   Adoption as a child care resource

We quoted from:

Department of Health and Welsh Office, *Adoption – A Service for Children, Adoption Bill – A Consultative Document* (1996) London, Department of Health and Welsh Office, paras 4.4–4.14.

R. Parker, for the Department of Health, Social Services Inspectorate, *Adoption Now – Messages from Research* (1999) Chichester, Wiley, pp. 1–6.

Report of the Departmental Committee on the Adoption of Children (Chairman: Sir William Houghton, later Judge F.A. Stockdale) (Cmnd. 5107) (1972), paras. 168–169, 221–223.

Review of Adoption Law, Report to Ministers of an Interdepartmental Working Group. A Consultation Document (1992) London, Department of Health and Welsh Office, paras. 7.1, 7.2, 12.4–12.6, 14.1–14.5, 20.4–22.1.

White Paper, *Adoption – a new approach* (Cm. 5017) (2000) London, HMSO, paras. 2.1–2.6.

Additional reading

E.J. Cooke, 'Dispensing with parental consent to adoption – a choice of welfare tests' (1997) 9 Child and Family Law Quarterly 259.

N. Lowe, 'Freeing for Adoption – the Experience of the 1980s' [1990] Journal of Social Welfare Law 220.

White Paper, *Adoption: The Future* (Cm. 2288) (1993) London, HMSO.

14.5   Adoption: an open or shut case?

We quoted from:

J. Dare, *The Advantages and Disadvantages of Open Adoption and the Merits of Subsequent Contact with Natural Parents* (1995) paper presented at Judicial Studies Board seminar.

D. Quinton, A. Rushton, C. Dance and D. Mayes, 'Contact with birth parents in adoption – a response to Ryburn' (1998) 10 Child and Family Law Quarterly 349, pp. 349–150, 355–357.

Report of the Departmental Committee on the Adoption of Children (Chairman: Sir William Houghton, later Judge F.A. Stockdale) (Cmnd. 5107) (1972), paras. 93–94.

M. Ryburn, 'In whose best interests? – post adoption contact with the birth family' (1998) 10 Child and Family Law Quarterly 536, pp. 56–61.

Additional reading

D. Quinton, A. Rushton, C. Dance and D. Mayes, 'Contact between children placed away from home and their birth parents: Research issues and evidence' (1997) 2:3 Clinical Child Psychology and Psychiatry 393.

D. Quinton and J. Selwyn, A. Rushton and C. Dance, 'Contact between children placed away from home and their birth parents: Ryburn's "Reanalysis" Analysed' (1999) 4:4 Clinical Child Psychology and Psychiatry 519.

H.D. Grotevant, R.G. McRoy, C. Elde and D.L. Fravel, 'Adoptive family system dynamics – variations by level of openness in the adoption' (1994) 33:2 Family Process 125.

14.6 The cross-cultural dimension

We quoted from:

R. Parker, for the Department of Health, Social Services Inspectorate, *Adoption Now – Messages from Research* (1999) Chichester, Wiley, pp. 42–44.

Additional reading

N. Lowe and M. Murch, *The plan for the child, Adoption or long-term fostering* (2002) London, BAAF.

M. Owen, 'Single-person adoption: For and Against' (1994) 8 Children and Society 151.

D. Quinton, A. Rushton, C. Dance and D. Mayes, *Joining New Families: A Study of Adoption and Fostering in Middle Childhood* (1998) Chichester, Wiley.

J. Thoburn, L. Norford and S. Rashid, *Permanent Family Placement for Children of Minority Ethnic Origin* (2000) London, Jessica Kingsley.

Index